Secrets & Scandals

SECRETS
&
SCANDALS

Reforming Rhode Island
1986–2006

H. Philip West Jr.

Rhode Island Publications Society
East Providence · 2014

For information write:
The Rhode Island Publications Society
1445 Wampanoag Trail, Suite 203
East Providence, RI 02195
tel: (401) 272-1776
fax: (401) 273-1791
http://ripublications.org

Printed in the United States of America
by Courier Westford

ISBN 978-0-9906293-0-6 (hard cover)
ISBN 978-0-9906293-1-3 (paperback)

Library of Congress Control Number: 2014947728

Cover design: Lars Grant-West and Cliff Garber
Interior design and production: Cliff Garber
Cartoons: Jim Bush

Typeset in Minion Pro with Myriad Pro

http://secretsandscandals.com

To Anne Grant

Contents

Author's Notes

It's easier to corrupt a small state.
If you have some dirty cops, some dirty politicians,
and a judge or two, you can corrupt the whole system.
Raymond L. S. Patriarca
New England Organized Crime Boss[1]

BETWEEN 1986 AND 2006 Rhode Island ran a gauntlet of scandals that exposed corruption, aroused public indignation, and moved thousands to march on the State House. Coalitions formed to fight for systemic changes. Under intense public pressure, lawmakers enacted significant reforms into law and approved ballot questions that allowed voters to repair defects in Rhode Island's Constitution.

Flawed government structures had spawned corruption in all three branches of Rhode Island state government. Since colonial times, the legislature had wielded vast executive powers that would have been unthinkable in most other states. Judges had established a limited independence but remained vulnerable. Supreme Court justices could never forget that on a single day in 1935 the General Assembly sacked the entire high court.

Throughout Rhode Island's history, the lack of constitutional checks and balances had enabled single party control. Republicans ruled during the nineteenth and early twentieth centuries; Democrats held sway from the 1930s into the twenty-first century. In their eras of unchecked control, both parties became corrupt. No amount of academic analysis could have persuaded Rhode Island's General Assembly to relinquish power. Throughout the state's constitutional history, outbursts had flared like fireworks in the night sky but never burned bright enough and long enough to lay the cornerstone of American government: separation of powers.

This book describes scandals that shook Rhode Island's culture of corruption and finally brought separation of powers in 2004. No single leader, no political party, no organization could have converted betrayals of public trust into historic reforms. But when citizen coalitions connected with dedicated public officials to address systemic government failures, change became possible.

Even the Rhode Island General Assembly's website now calls the years from 1986 to 2000 "The Era of Reform."[2] Rhode Island Historian Laureate Patrick

T. Conley describes "three momentous constitutional upheavals: the Dorr Rebellion of 1841–43, the Bloodless Revolution of 1934–35, and the crusade for Separation of Powers, waged from 1997 until victory in 2004."[3]

Chicago's Better Government Association (BGA)[4] has scored state laws that promote integrity, accountability, and government transparency three times. In 2002 and 2008, the BGA ranked Rhode Island second in the nation; in BGA's 2013 report, Rhode Island topped all the other states,[5] largely because of reforms that began with the Constitutional Convention of 1986.

When our family moved to Providence in 1988, I had no idea that Rhode Island had already entered a turbulent period of historic reform. Over the next eighteen years, like Forrest Gump, I wound up in crucial scenes whose depth I barely understood. I witnessed upheavals that transformed the state's government. My work with Common Cause Rhode Island put me in a position to help the reform effort.

Key themes in this narrative became part of an anti-corruption matrix that I developed for international visitors. Over more than a decade, the U.S. State Department sent foreign officials to learn from Rhode Island's struggle. Their programs had titles like "Anti-Corruption: Ethics, Accountability and Transparency in Government."[6] I later refined this matrix with graduate students at the University of Rhode Island. The specific problems and reform goals reflect our experience in Rhode Island, but its themes are universal. I hope they offer a blueprint for open and accountable government.

Rhode Island Anti-Corruption Matrix

THEME	PROBLEM	REFORM GOALS
Civil Rights and Voting Rights	Those in power often prevented political participation by immigrants, minorities, those who held contrary views.	Improve voter registration. Ban racial and other profiling that affects law enforcement, elections, and other government functions. Fund enforcement.
Right to Petition for Redress of Grievances	Citizens who sought justice often faced retaliation. Public employees or others who reported wrongdoing were punished rather than rewarded.	Protect citizen activists with anti-SLAPP suit laws and shield whistleblowers from retribution when they report wrongdoing, expose official mistakes, or embarrass powerful officials.

THEME	PROBLEM	REFORM GOALS
Separation of Powers	Government officials often abused the powers of their office. The General Assembly held unchecked government power for 340 years. Corrupt practices flourished.	Divide executive, legislative, and judicial power to create "turf interests" for each branch to stop the others from abusing the powers of their office or engaging in corrupt practices.
Legislative Power	Lawmakers held vast power but lacked staff for research and constituent services. They were among the lowest-paid legislators in the United States. Frustrated by voters' refusal to raise their pay, lawmakers created pensions that invited corruption.	Provide reasonable pay, health care, working conditions, independent research services, and modern communication tools. Enable lawmakers to see themselves as professionals. Provide staff, offices, and equipment for them to serve their constituents.
Executive Power	Governors had few constitutional powers and served only two-year terms. They had trouble recruiting professional staff and had to raise money constantly.	Establish four-year terms, with recall, for statewide general officers and provide reasonable compensation. Strengthen appointive power under separation of powers.
Judicial Power	Judges were chosen for their political connections rather than their qualifications. Some failed to render fair judgments.	Create an open process and high standards for judicial nomination and selection. Reduce opportunities for political interference.
Conflicts of Interest	Officials swore to protect the public interest, but many failed to recognize conflicts of interest. Many did costly favors for family, private business interests, lobbyists, or power brokers.	Outlaw common conflicts of interest and establish effective ways to investigate and prosecute conflicts. Provide clear advice to officials on conflicts, so they avoid using public office for private financial gain.
Financial Disclosure	Some part-time public officials who needed to earn a living preferred to conceal outside business dealings or financial connections that might affect their judgment in public actions.	Require officials to disclose their sources of income and remind them of their obligation to avoid conflicts related to their private businesses. Fine officials who fail to disclose, and ensure public access to financial disclosure forms.

THEME	PROBLEM	REFORM GOALS
Fiscal Oversight	Some officials who spent public money misrepresented the real costs in budgets, spending, or contracts. Fraud diverted resources and damaged trust.	Establish strict controls on purchasing and expenditures. Ensure independent, intelligible audits. Ensure complete transparency. Prosecute wrongdoing diligently.
Lobbyists	Lobbyists paid to push their clients' interests funded campaigns and entertained lavishly to influence decision-makers in the legislature and executive branch.	Require lobbyists to register and report their compensation, spending, and legislative activities. Make data about lobbyist compensation, expenditures and campaign contributions easily available to the press and public.
Campaign Finance	Money dominated public opinion about candidates and issues. Candidates who spent large amounts to win elections found themselves obligated to those who contributed to their campaigns.	Require disclosure of campaign contributions and expenditures. Provide public financing for candidates who limit their spending voluntarily.
Redistricting	Legislative leaders commonly gerrymandered districts to protect political allies and punish mavericks and reformers. Factional one-party rule stifled debate and public trust.	Establish clear standards and a public process for drawing legislative districts. Require an independent, nonpartisan redistricting commission.

Such themes rarely present themselves in neat grids and discrete categories; they emerge in the rush of events. Naming the themes and analyzing their dynamics lie in the discipline of political science; proposing and pushing solutions are the practice of reform.

Restoring public ethics and accountability in government is like renovating old houses. Run-down buildings require systemic repairs. To make a decrepit structure habitable workers must repair the roof, chimney, walls, windows, doors, wiring, plumbing, and heating system. Why install new plumbing but ignore a broken boiler? Why replace windows but fail to secure the doors?

Yet opportunities for comprehensive work on government systems come few and far between. During eighteen years with Common Cause, I saw only two chances to remake whole groups of laws at once. The first came in 1992, when Rhode Island lawmakers enacted comprehensive ethics and campaign finance reforms. They also placed a constitutional amendment establishing four-year terms on the statewide ballot. The second came in the 2005 and 2006 sessions, when the General Assembly passed scores of bills that restructured boards and commissions as required under the Separation of Powers Amendment approved by state voters in 2004.

More often, reform is a piecemeal process of patching and filling gaps rather than revising laws comprehensively.

The work never ends. In the real world, anti-corruption laws suffer damage almost before the ink dries. Hostile forces thwart their implementation. Poorly funded enforcement hollows them out, just as termites devour beams in historic houses. Contrary court decisions can inflict massive damage, just as hurricanes topple trees onto roofs. Even without direct assault, leakage and loopholes can weaken reforms and render them useless.

As long as I can remember, taking notes has been second nature to me. I relied on notebooks until 1993, when my first laptop allowed me to type wherever I went. My mother, a secretary and lively letter-writer, had encouraged me to take typing in high school. At the State House, my fingers flew over the keyboard while my eyes focused on dramas unfolding around me. Depending on what happened, I took broad summaries or near-verbatim accounts.

People reacted to my note taking in different ways. Community development groups made me their secretary. At the Rhode Island State House, some glared as I typed, as if I were a modern day Madame Defarge, knitting names in code that would mark victims for the guillotine.

This book depends on extensive notes I took at the State House, during coalition meetings, and after private conversations. I often recorded public hearings on audiocassettes or an iPod, and I relied on many Capitol Television videos. As noted in the acknowledgments, I interviewed forty-six protagonists in depth, and all but one consented to audio recordings. I reviewed specific issues or events with nearly fifty additional participants.

I also relied on official reports, House and Senate journals, Ethics Commission documents, and judicial decisions.

Even with all those materials, I could not have written this book without hundreds of newspaper stories, mostly from the *Providence Journal*, whose archives have enriched the narrative. Those who belittle "the press" often fail to appreciate the way good reporters recreate events. On countless nights I watched Kathy Gregg, Joe Baker, Jim Baron, and others take notes at hearings, then duck out around nine o'clock to pull stories from their spiral pads before an eleven o'clock deadline. The next morning, when I read their work in print, I felt awed by their success in tracing the drama, extracting the facts, and creating context for readers.

Reporters inspire me. Most try to describe events without bias. Outcomes matter to them, but they uphold the journalistic discipline of allowing protagonists and facts to speak for themselves. I hope this book honors that tradition.

Acknowledgments

I OWE THANKS to many public officials and private citizens who recorded interviews with me, typically between ninety minutes and three hours of valuable personal perspective and detail: Thomas Banchoff, Robert V. Bianchini, David N. Cicilline, Beverly and William Clay, William E. Colleran, Rae B. Condon, Robert Clark Corrente, James D'Ambra, James F. Davey, Elizabeth M. Dennigan, Edward D. DiPrete, David Duffy, Robert G. Flanders Jr., Charles J. Fogarty, Nicholas Gorham, John B. Harwood, Alan G. Hassenfeld, Martin F. Healey, Mark B. Heffner, Natalie C. Joslin, Robert D. Kilmarx, Richard E. Kirby, James R. Langevin, J. Michael Lenihan, James J. Malachowski, Robert P. Mattos, James P. McStay, James C. Miller, Richard W. Morsilli, James E. O'Neil, Antonio J. Pires, J. Richard Ratcliffe, Nancy C. Rhodes, Gary Sasse, Charles M. Silverman, Jeffrey J. Teitz, Robert A. Urciuoli, Arlene Violet, Sheldon Whitehouse, Kent A. Willever, Frank J. Williams, Myrth York, and Melvin L. Zurier. I relied on videotaped interviews by graduate students in my Ethics in Public Administration course at the University of Rhode Island with three officials: Francis A. Gaschen, Nancy J. Mayer, and Robert A. Weygand.

Others who shared insights on particular issues or parts of the narrative include Greta L. Abbott, Jane Kenny Austin, John D. Barr II, Irwin Becker, Judith Benedict, Carl T. Bogus, Herbert J. Brennan, Paul F. Caranci, Koren Carbuccia, Patrick T. Conley, Katherine D'Arezzo, Anthony DeSisto, Teresa Foley, Terrence M. Fracassa, Melissa Menard Goldberger, Jason M. Gramitt, Katherine Gregg, Andrew M. Hodgkin, Peter H. Hufstader, George N. Hunt, Robert Kando, Paul S. Kelly, Nancy W. Kirsch, Peter A. Lacouture, J. Stanley Lemons, Charlene Lima, Karen L. MacBeth, John Marion, Tory McCagg, Kevin J. McAllister, Richard M. McAuliffe Jr., Keven A. McKenna, Edwin R. Pacheco,

Alan G. Palazzo, Karen A. Pelczarski, Beth Perry, Gina M. Raimondo, Joshua Ravitz, Pablo Rodriguez, Solangel Rodriguez, John M. Roney, Lila M. Sapinsley, Daniel F. Schleifer, James A. Sheehan, Robert Sieczkiewicz, Daniel G. Siegel, Michael E. Smith, Mike Stanton, and Rita M. Williams. Several other individuals provided valuable insights but asked not to be listed here.

I owe a particular debt to state employees who have retrieved transcripts, court decisions, advisory opinions, reports, videos, photographs, and other materials that have enriched this narrative: Craig R. Berke, Kenneth Carlson, Steven Cross, Katherine D'Arezzo, Thomas Evans, Jason Gramitt, Derek M. Hayes, Martha Moore, Gwen Stern, Tracy Teixeira, and Steve Tymon.

Over many years I had enjoyed Jim Bush's cartoons in the *Providence Journal*, and I was delighted when he agreed to allow their use here.

Thanks also to Michael Delaney for access to the *Journal*'s photo archives and to Connie Grosch. I remain grateful to Frank Mullin for his *Providence Phoenix* photo of me which appears on the author bio page and in my online profiles.

Beyond the pages of this book, I need to thank scores of people in Common Cause whose wisdom and political vision kept the quest for reform on track. Hundreds more times than I mentioned in this narrative I relied on committees, the state governing board, and national staff for direction. Without the activism and financial support of the Common Cause community, none of this would have borne fruit.

Generous donors to Common Cause also encouraged me to write *Secrets and Scandals* and provided basic funding for its publication. When I could not find national publishers ready to undertake this project, I turned to Rhode Island supporters: Natalie Joslin, Leticia and John Carter, Warren and Joyce Galkin, Jocelin Hamblett, Alan Hassenfeld, Henry and Peggy Boyd Sharpe, Daniel Siegel, and John Hazen White Jr. Additional contributions came from Doree Goodman and Stanley and Martie Livingston. Without them this history might not have seen print.

I owe a particular debt of gratitude to Dr. Patrick T. Conley, Rhode Island's first historian laureate and president of the Rhode Island Publications Society. Although we had been on opposite sides of the separation of powers question, he acknowledged the campaign's success, and he agreed to publish *Secrets and Scandals*. He spotted mistakes of fact or historical context, corrected parts of this narrative, and offered wise counsel. His staff administered this project smoothly.

M. Charles Bakst, Paul F. Caranci, and John Marion each read portions of the text and offered valuable corrections.

Finally, this book depends on professional editors. Cynthia L. Shattuck suggested ways to fix the unwieldy structure of my first draft, and she became my primary editor. Carol Bragg proofed the entire book with great grace and skill under pressure.

Cliff Garber at Mutable Type designed and laid out the book with patient counsel to this novice author and co-designed the cover.

I end with special thanks to two family members who volunteered their services. Our son, illustrator Lars Grant-West, created the cover. Last and most important, Anne Grant led our family to Rhode Island in 1988, encouraged me to accept the job at Common Cause, stood by me through every struggle, listened to these stories as they happened, urged me to preserve the records, read drafts at every stage, and provided priceless critical corrections. Without her, this book would not exist.

1
DiPrete, RISDIC

1

Breaking Ground
1986–87

CONSTITUTIONAL CONVENTIONS can move mountains. The Philadelphia Convention of 1787 was called to strengthen the Articles of Confederation, but delegates went further and drafted the U.S. Constitution. On a smaller scale, Rhode Island's 1986 Constitutional Convention unleashed historic changes that would reverberate for decades.[1]

Preparations had already begun when two scandals shocked a state renowned for its indifference to corruption, souring voters both on Chief Justice Joseph A. Bevilacqua and on a powerful housing agency.

Bevilacqua had risen through the legislative ranks while serving as defense counsel for members of the New England Mob. The Providence Democrat became House majority leader in 1966 and won election as speaker of the House in 1969. Three years later he defended Raymond "Junior" Patriarca, son of the legendary New England crime boss Raymond L.S. Patriarca. In 1976, Bevilacqua's colleagues in the General Assembly elected him chief justice of the Rhode Island Supreme Court.

In 1985 the *Providence Journal* reported that Chief Justice Bevilacqua had continued his contacts with mobsters. State police surveillance confirmed his Mob connections, and even he acknowledged them. While a disciplinary panel moved with glacial slowness, the newspaper reported that Bevilacqua had met at least three times with women at the Alpine Motel, owned by organized crime figures, on Douglas Pike in Smithfield.[2]

The *Journal* also exposed corruption in the state's affordable housing agency, Rhode Island Housing and Mortgage Finance Corporation (RIHMFC), a quasi-public entity created in 1973 as a self-supporting corporation to finance, purchase, construct, and rehabilitate affordable housing.[3] Sons and daughters of favored politicians and business leaders landed cut-rate mortgages worth $2.9 million that were never logged into state computers. Moreover, RIHMFC's executive director, Ralph A. Pari, had used an agency credit card for airfare, posh hotel rooms, expensive meals, and limousines. At least one junket involved a trip to Florida with a staff member and her daughters. Investigators charged Pari with racketeering, embezzlement, larceny, and obstruction of justice.[4]

These scandals dominated news for weeks just before voters were to choose delegates for the constitutional convention that would recommend changes in the state's Constitution. Candidates ran in each of the state's one hundred representative districts, but were not listed by party affiliation. A total of 565 individuals gathered the requisite fifty signatures before the October 1 deadline.[5] Many promised voters that they would address government corruption.

Turnout was low for the off-year election in 1985, but a broad mix of candidates, ranging from political novices to seasoned statewide campaigners, were elected delegates. Among them were several former legislators, a brain surgeon, a radio talk show host, and the president of an international relief agency. Homemakers, firefighters, a bus driver, and a sculptor would share responsibility for reviewing the state's Constitution along with a dozen retirees and ten college students. James Langevin, a 21-year old quadriplegic from Rhode Island College, campaigned door-to-door in his motorized wheelchair and won.

These delegates had an extraordinary chance to reshape Rhode Island's Constitution, setting their own agenda with no topic off limits. Amendments recommended by the ConCon, as it was called, would bypass the General Assembly and go directly to the ballot. A 1973 convention had eased the process for amendments, which voters could now approve with a simple majority at a single election.[6] Proposals from the convention might shape state government for generations.

Politicians promptly suggested topics. Lt. Gov. Richard A. Licht, a Democrat, proposed campaign finance reforms that would provide matching public funds for candidates who agreed to limit their spending.[7] Then Republican Gov. Edward D. DiPrete hosted a reception for delegates. He urged them to present amendments that would strengthen the executive branch: four-year terms for statewide general officers and a line-item veto on the budget. DiPrete wanted the governor rather than the legislature to choose state Supreme Court justices. He also asked convention delegates to propose cutting the size of the General Assembly by half, creating an ethics code for all public officials and allowing citizens to create laws through voter initiative.[8]

The convention assembled on January 6, 1986 and elected former Rep. Keven A. McKenna as its chairperson. McKenna came with solid experience both in a U.S. Senate office and in Rhode Island posts: he had served as an assistant attorney general, state legislator, and Providence Municipal Court judge.[9] He in turn appointed a young lawyer named Anthony DeSisto to lead the committee on ethics.[10]

While the convention began drafting its rules, leaders in the House filed a bipartisan resolution to impeach Chief Justice Bevilacqua.[11] The impeachment inquiry, unprecedented in the state's history, cast a long shadow over both the 1986 legislative session and the convention. Investigators brought Richard "Moon" DiOrio, a Mob associate under federal witness protection, to Rhode Island in disguise. Hidden behind a screen from the audience and photographers, the mobster testified he had seen the chief justice meet twice with Raymond "Junior" Patriarca, who had succeeded his late father as the boss of organized crime in New England.[12]

On a more mundane level, an electrical contractor for the court system testified that his firm had done unpaid work at homes that belonged to the chief justice and one of the women who had met him at the Alpine Motel.[13] The motel's manager told of coded registration cards, adding that a man had warned her not to talk to anyone about the mystery guest.[14] Bevilacqua, like the mobsters he represented, did not have a checking account and did all of his personal business in cash.[15]

As impeachment pressure mounted, Bevilacqua finally resigned on May 28, 1986. House Judiciary Chairman Jeffrey J. Teitz, who presided over the impeachment hearings, read Bevilacqua's resignation letter into the record. The inquiry ended without the need for a vote.[16]

The chief justice's resignation reverberated through the constitutional convention, and the scandal emboldened those delegates who wanted a new process for selecting judges. Since the days when Rhode Island was one of thirteen British colonies clinging precariously to the Atlantic seaboard, all of the state senators and representatives had gathered "in Grand Committee" to fill each vacancy on the Supreme Court. In the 1970s there were twice as many representatives as senators, so speakers of the House easily dominated the selection process. Convention delegates remembered that former speaker Bevilacqua had orchestrated his own election as chief justice.

One week after his resignation, convention delegates voted unanimously to recommend a new process for selecting judges. The proposed constitutional amendment would create an eleven-member judicial nominating commission to select well-qualified candidates for each judicial vacancy. Lawmakers would still meet "in Grand Committee," but they would be required to elect each justice from the commission's lists. The proposed new judicial nominating commission would also have power to discipline errant judges or to recommend impeachment.[17]

Other proposals sparked fierce debate among delegates. Many saw voter initiative as a way around the legislature, which routinely stonewalled reform. In twenty-six other states, voters could sign petitions to place laws or constitutional amendments directly on the ballot. Rhode Island delegates battled over how many signatures to require and whether to limit the scope; the final resolution on voter initiative proposed to bar any that would affect state expenses, taxes, or collective bargaining.[18]

The convention's ethics committee remained all but invisible, shouldered off the front page by controversies over abortion and judicial impeachment. Its members recognized that only a strong ethics amendment could deter corruption and adopted a phrase from Hawaii's constitution: "Public officers and employees must exhibit the highest standards of ethical conduct."[19] Committee members who researched the matter thought Hawaii had erred by creating separate ethics commissions for various parts of state government. For this reason they proposed a single ethics panel with one set of rules to bind every government official in the state, whether elected, appointed, or hired as employees. They envisioned a beefed-up version of Rhode Island's ten-year-old Conflict of Interest Commission.

But who would write the new ethics code? Delegates knew they could not. Because language for the state's Constitution should spell out only broad principles, they must assign the task of writing detailed rules to others. At the same time Rae B. Condon, director of the Conflict of Interest Commission, reminded delegates that the current code of ethics was weak and warned that the General Assembly would welcome a chance to undermine it further.

After a lively discussion, Peter V. Lacouture, the ethics committee's attorney, suggested that the new commissioners be authorized in the Constitution to write the rules for public officials. In the words of delegate Roger Milette, having the commission draft the code would "take the fox away from the chickens." In minutes, Lacouture and DeSisto drafted a constitutional amendment in three parts. The first part offered their ideal of ethical service: "The people of Rhode Island believe that public officials and employees must adhere to the highest standards of ethical conduct, respect the public trust and the rights of all persons, avoid the appearance of impropriety, and not use their position for private gain or advantage."

The second section directed the General Assembly to establish an "independent non-partisan ethics commission." Once created in law, the new commission would "adopt a code of ethics, including provisions on conflict of interest, confidential information, use of position, contracts with government agencies, and financial disclosure." No one questioned what the verb "adopt" might mean. The delegates were determined that the legislature should not create a new code of ethics; only an independent and non-partisan ethics commission could write rules that the public would trust. These new rules would cover every government official in the state. The proposed constitutional amendment stated: "All elected and appointed officials and employees of state and local government, commissions, and agencies shall be subject to the code of ethics."

Finally, the amendment would empower the new ethics commission "to investigate violations of the code of ethics and impose penalties including removal from office of individuals who are not subject to impeachment."[20]

At that moment, delegates on the ethics committee seemed unaware that they were proposing a model that might prove controversial. By conferring both the authority to create the new code and the power to enforce it, they were proposing the strongest government ethics agency in the United States. Committee members refined their three-part text and read it again. Then they voted unanimously to send it to the full convention for a vote.

The committee also addressed the question of financing political campaigns. Their final resolution called on the General Assembly to set limits on campaign spending and to create a voluntary system of matching funds for statewide general officers.[21]

Other committees were wrapping up their resolutions and sending them to the convention floor. On June 26, the delegates gave final approval to a raft of constitutional questions for the November ballot. Question 14, the most contentious, proclaimed a "paramount right to life" and proposed a constitutional ban on public funding for abortions. Almost as controversial, Question 5 laid out a process for voter initiative that would allow citizens to gather signatures and place issues on the ballot without legislative approval.

Delegates also backed increasing terms for statewide executive officers and members of the General Assembly from two years to four, and they endorsed a pay raise for legislators, whose salaries were among the lowest in the country.[22] Other questions proposed to ease a lifetime ban on voting by felons, establish crime victims' rights, and guarantee public access to the shoreline.[23]

The ethics committee recommended three proposals that were consolidated under the rubric of ethics in government: a new standard of impeachment, an independent ethics commission, and a voluntary system of campaign financing that was modeled on the matching-funds program for presidential campaigns.[24] Despite their diverse content, these three proposals were bundled together as Question 6.

Weary delegates approved fourteen questions for the November 1986 statewide ballot and finally adjourned at 2:10 a.m.

The summer of 1986 slipped away with no visible campaigning except on the proposed abortion amendment. That issue quickly boiled over in the heavily Roman Catholic state. Mary Ann Sorrentino, the director of Planned Parenthood and a Roman Catholic, had lobbied against any amendment that might curtail or outlaw abortions. Her parish priest declared that she had "excommunicated herself" by her role in a clinic that performed abortions, and Bishop Louis E. Gelineau agreed. Gelineau later published an open letter encouraging voters to approve Question 14, titled "Paramount Right to Life/Abortion," and called outlawing abortions "the most fundamental civil rights issue of our time."[25]

The medical community quickly weighed in on Question 14. The medical staff at Roger Williams Hospital warned that the proposed amendment "could interfere with the ability of physicians, patients and families to make appropriate medical decisions in the care of some critically ill patients."[26]

Before the convention, Gov. DiPrete and U.S. Sen. John Chafee had warned delegates not to distract themselves with volatile social issues like abortion.[27] Now Question 14 filled front pages and drew media attention away from other proposed amendments.

To inform voters about all fourteen questions, leaders of the convention mounted a campaign that included billboards, bus shelter ads, regional forums, and voter information booklets. They sent two mailings to every household in the state. The first described the changes each proposed amendment would make in the constitution; the second gave the exact wording of each change.[28]

Peter V. Lacouture, counsel to the ethics committee, urged voters to support Question 6, Ethics in Government. In a *Providence Journal* opinion piece, he promised that the amendment would "establish a new standard of ethics for public officials and reduce or eliminate the abuses that have made Rhode Island notorious in the past."[29]

However, U.S. Senator John Chafee, a moderate Republican who had served six years as governor, dismissed the whole convention as overly influenced by legislative leaders even though his son Lincoln had been a delegate. He urged voters to reject all of the proposed amendments.[30] Gov. DiPrete also warned that the proposed new ethics commission would become a "fourth branch of government" and urged voters to reject the amendment.[31]

Finally, a week before the election, editorial writers at the *Providence Journal* took aim at both the proposed campaign finance reforms and the broad authority that would be conferred on the proposed new ethics panel. "This commission," the editors wrote, "will be empowered to act as legislator, prosecutor, jury, judge, and executioner." They argued Rhode Island should not put "such awesome power into the hands of an ethics commission which may not turn out to be quite so 'independent' and 'non-partisan' as this proposal anticipates."[32]

On November 4, 1986, state voters went to the polls in extraordinary numbers. In a nearly two to one landslide they re-elected the incumbent Edward DiPrete over Democrat Bruce G. Sundlun. And although Rhode Island was America's most Roman Catholic state, nearly two-thirds of the electorate rejected the anti-abortion amendment. Never before had the predominantly Roman Catholic descendants of Irish, Italian, Polish, Portuguese, and French Canadian immigrants rebelled so publicly against their bishop.

In a less dramatic revolt, voters ignored warnings from DiPrete, Chafee, the Bar Association, the American Civil Liberties Union, and the *Providence*

Journal that they should reject Question 6 on ethics and campaign reform. Behind curtains in antiquated voting machines, a surprising 53.3 percent pressed the lever for "Ethics in Government." Without exit polls no one could be sure what their votes meant, but voters made history by authorizing a panel of their peers to write and enforce ethics rules for all public officials. Many clearly agreed with the widely quoted comment of delegate Roger Milette that it was time to "take the fox away from the chickens."[33] The convention's innovative proposal to combat corruption became part of the Rhode Island Constitution.

Voters also trounced proposals they saw as sympathetic to legislators: a legislative pay raise, four-year terms for legislators as well as statewide executive officers, and a new judicial selection process that would allow lawmakers to continue choosing justices of the Supreme Court. The legislative pay raise would have been small, but it went down by a huge margin. Sixty-four per cent of the voters rejected the raise, a larger percentage than any other 'no' vote except the anti-abortion question. This overwhelming defeat delivered a stern rebuke to lawmakers. Their pay would remain $300 per year — an amount worth only a fraction of its value when it became part of the Constitution in 1900.

Voters rejected a voter initiative amendment that reform groups said had been gutted in the convention.

The electorate approved a gender-neutral rewriting of the entire state constitution and backed an amendment that required judges to allow crime victims to address the court before sentencing. They approved amendments that barred felons from running for office for three years after completing their sentence, and liberalized access to the voting booth by allowing convicts — who had previously needed an act of the legislature to vote again — to register and vote after completing their probation and parole. Few Rhode Islanders seemed aware that their newly revised constitution marked a watershed, but the delegates who had been elected under the shadow of the Bevilacqua and RIHMFC scandals had glimpsed a distant hope and set a course to reach it.

As many had feared, the General Assembly moved quickly to extract the teeth from the new ethics agency. During the 1987 legislative session, two competing bills proposed "an independent non-partisan ethics commission." One envisioned a watchdog that could bark and bite; the other provided a muzzle and leash.

Sara M. Quinn, a young lawyer at the Conflict of Interest Commission, drafted the tougher bill, which favored rebranding the existing body as the Rhode Island Ethics Commission. Her legislation ensured continuity, retained the nine current members, and allowed them to follow through with cases that were already under investigation.

Quinn departed from the old law in a significant way. Regardless of how notorious an official's behavior was, the Conflict of Interest Commission could not investigate without a sworn complaint from someone with first-hand knowledge. Quinn proposed to empower this new commission to investigate information it might receive in other ways — through leaks, tips, and newspaper stories — just as other law enforcement agencies could. She also proposed to raise the fines for wrongdoing from $10,000 to $25,000 per violation and empower the new panel to make violators forfeit three times the amount they gained from corrupt practices.

Sponsorship became a problem. Quinn offered her draft to House and Senate leaders of both parties, but none would touch it. She finally persuaded Sen. Victoria S. Lederberg, a Democrat from the East Side of Providence, to sponsor the bill,[34] but senate leaders responsible for assigning legislation to appropriate committees buried it. Instead of referring it to the Judiciary Committee, where such bills always went, they shipped it to the Joint Committee on Environment, where it sank into oblivion.

The second bill was more cautious. Rep. Jeffrey J. Teitz, a young Newport attorney who chaired the House Judiciary Committee, drafted what became a bipartisan leadership bill. Majority Whip Thomas A. Lamb and House Minority Leader Bradford Gorham became its co-sponsors.[35] Teitz proposed to replace the nine-member Conflict of Interest Commission with a fifteen-member ethics commission. Like its predecessor, the new panel would have to wait for a sworn complaint. To process an ethics complaint against any public official, the new commission would divide into two panels: a six-person investigative committee to decide whether there was probable cause to prosecute, and a nine-member adjudicative panel to hear the evidence in a trial-like hearing.

Teitz's bill, furthermore, kept the top fine at $10,000 and empowered the commission to make corrupt officials forfeit wrongful financial gains. Its list of "prohibited activities" was a detailed code of ethics — despite the convention's declaration that the code of ethics should be written by the new ethics commission.

Common Cause executive director Marilyn Hines testified before Teitz and his committee that the code incorporated in his bill seemed to say, "Let's not do anything to hurt a public official."[36]

Rae B. Condon, who had stepped down as director of the Conflict of Interest Commission, also blasted Teitz's bill. To many across Rhode Island, Condon epitomized the battle against corruption. In a *Providence Journal* essay, she wrote that Teitz's legislation "usurps the power granted the ethics commission by the people."[37] She also excoriated Teitz for "prescribing the internal structure of the commission, as well as the roles of its members and employees," a move she warned would cripple the new body.

Many lawmakers attacked Teitz's ethics bill as too stringent. On May 6, during public debate on the House floor, the bill's modest financial disclosure requirements drew fire from Rep. Joseph L. Casinelli, who chaired the House

Corporations Committee. He complained that the requirement to disclose outstanding debts would keep "quality people" from running for office. "I don't feel anxious about any loans," said Casinelli, who owned a drug store near the State House. "I feel it's my business, and it bothers me that we have to go to this length to satisfy somebody's prurient interest."[38] By a 90–3 vote, the representatives voted to delete a requirement that public officials report loans they owed to financial institutions regulated by the state or federal government.[39] The bill advanced to the senate, but this debate revealed the chasm between legislators and outside advocates of ethics reform.

During her testimony before the Senate Judiciary Committee, Marilyn Hines also argued that the bill's section on prohibited activities would violate the constitutional amendment.[40] She reminded senators that the voters had commanded the General Assembly to "establish an independent non-partisan" ethics commission that would then "adopt a code of ethics" for public officials.

Sen. Gregory J. Acciardo of Johnston, a Democrat on the committee, countered that the amendment could also be taken to mean that the General Assembly should pass the code and that the new commission could then simply adopt and enforce it.

"I've had it up to here with independent commissions," declared Sen. Ann H. Hanson, a Barrington Republican. "They create their own fiefdoms. Please don't get all wrapped up in a bunch of fifteen wonderful people who are going to solve all the problems of the world. Often they create the problems."

"The people passed this amendment," Hines insisted.

"Fine," shot back committee chair, John J. Bevilacqua, son of the former chief justice. "We're acting as we interpret that amendment."[41]

The full Senate passed Teitz's bill and sent it to Gov. DiPrete,[42] who signed it without fanfare. With DiPrete's signature the nine-member Conflict of Interest Commission was abolished and a shaky transition to the new fifteen-member Ethics Commission began.[43] Although the new law contained a section on transition, no one knew when new commissioners would be appointed, who they might be, or whether they could fulfill the high hopes many had for them.

As a disappointing finale, the Conflict of Interest Commission was forced to dismiss a complaint against Rep. Robert V. Bianchini of Cranston. While he wielded authority as vice chair of the powerful House Finance Committee, Bianchini routinely protected the interests of Rhode Island's homegrown credit unions. He earned his living as president of the Rhode Island Credit Union League, the industry's trade group. As a member of the House leadership, Bianchini could trade favors and twist arms beyond the dreams of any lobbyist.

Rhode Island knew the credit union insurance system, the Rhode Island Share and Deposit Indemnity Corporation, by its acronym: RISDIC. In the spring of 1986, while the Constitutional Convention was at work, Cumberland

Rep. Francis A. Gaschen, a Democrat, had proposed legislation that would require all Rhode Island credit unions to obtain federal credit union insurance.[44] The bill would have put RISDIC out of business and eliminated the need for Bianchini's employer, the Rhode Island Credit Union League. Gaschen's bill landed on the docket of the powerful House Finance Committee, where Bianchini served as vice chair.

Instead of admitting a conflict of interest and stepping aside, Bianchini arranged two sumptuous dinners for committee members with the head of RISDIC. Both men made a case for killing the bill requiring federal credit union insurance, and Bianchini dominated the hearing where Gaschen's legislation was scuttled.[45]

Robert Bergeron, the manager of the Woodlawn Credit Union, was furious. He had known for years that a number of Rhode Island's thrifts were overextended and underinsured. He believed that RISDIC was a sham, and depositors desperately needed safeguards that only federal credit union insurance could provide. After watching Bianchini use his influence to crush Gaschen's bill, Bergeron filed a complaint with the Conflict of Interest Commission. As required by law, commissioners investigated, heard testimony, and weighed the evidence behind closed doors. Throughout the proceedings, neither reporters nor the public knew Bianchini had been charged.

The prosecution failed on a technicality.[46] The Conflict of Interest law required five affirmative votes to find that a public official had violated the law. But of the nine commission members, one was an old friend of Bianchini's who had recused himself, and another had been appointed too late to hear the evidence. That left seven members to decide whether Bianchini had "knowingly and willfully" violated the requirement to disclose his business interest and recuse himself from further participation.

After hearing witnesses in a closed-door adjudicative hearing, four commissioners voted that Bianchini had violated the law while three — including the president of the Warwick Municipal Employees' Credit Union — voted that he had not. Without the five required votes, Bergeron's complaint against Bianchini was dropped.

Since the law required that complaints be kept confidential until the end, reporters had no advance word and were unprepared. When his acquittal became public Bianchini told them: "I never once believed I was in conflict. I certainly never intended to violate the spirit or the letter of the law." His dismissal landed on the front page of the *Providence Journal* for a single day in July 1987 and then vanished. Few readers would remember the story, and even fewer could have imagined what Bianchini's actions would eventually cost them.

But Robert Bergeron told reporters that the system had not worked. In fact, it had failed the public four times: when government leaders did nothing to protect the public from an unstable insurer called RISDIC, when Bianchini acted blatantly to kill Gaschen's bill, when legal strictures turned a majority vote of the Conflict of Interest Commission into dismissal, and when mandated confidentiality hid the wrongdoing from public view.

Three more years would pass before the credit union insurance system Bianchini had protected would fall like a house of cards. RISDIC's collapse would devastate Rhode Island.

2

Governor Pay-to-Play
1988–89

In June of 1988 my wife and I moved to an old two-family house on the South Side of Providence. A Connecticut lawyer we knew had warned against our move to Rhode Island, rattling off stories of scandals involving politicians and mobsters. I nodded politely, knowing little beyond the state's miniature size, famous beaches, historic homes, and picturesque lighthouses. My wife, Anne Grant, had already begun work in Providence as director of a center for battered women and their children. Our two sons were in college. At the age of forty-six, after twenty-odd years of serving as an activist pastor in New York City and Connecticut, I would try to make a living outside the church.

I began training as a copy editor at the *Providence Journal*, Rhode Island's only statewide paper. Each evening the newsroom thrummed with the subdued voices of reporters on phones, and I longed to join them. As keyboards clattered beneath their fingers, I struggled to learn computer systems and software: spotting typos, checking syntax, fixing punctuation, correcting to a style sheet, and writing headlines. But after two weeks my supervisor let me go — instead of fixing mistakes, I kept rewriting. I had majored in English but failed as a copy editor. Was I naïve to think I could find a secular job?

A few days later a notice came that our chimney's brickwork was a safety hazard and unless we made repairs, we would be fined. A neighbor suggested that an envelope to the building inspector could solve our problem, but instead I tried my hand at masonry. I lugged tools, new bricks, and mortar to a crawl space above our third floor, opened the hatch, and peered out. One mistake on our steep roof could launch me into a quick slide from chimney to gutter and a dizzying drop to the ground. I tethered myself to a beam inside and began to chisel away crumbling mortar and broken bricks.

During a break, I straddled the ridgeline. Less than two miles away, the State House dome gleamed in the afternoon sunshine. That morning's *Providence Journal* revealed that Gov. Edward DiPrete's family had scored a land deal: a DiPrete partnership had bought 8.8 acres of rocky ground and sold it the same day for four times the purchase price. In a few hours, they cleared almost two million dollars thanks to a zoning change that doubled the number of apartments allowed.[1] The denser development infuriated neighbors but turned an unfeasible project into gold.

From the peak of our roof, I wondered if DiPrete had left his office for the day. What did he think about the reporters who exposed him? Had someone tipped them off? Would he retaliate?

Closer than the State House I could see Federal Hill, home of the Patriarca crime family. A mobster named Vincent "Big Vinny" Teresa had testified before Congress that Raymond L.S. Patriarca controlled more than five thousand underworld operatives throughout New England, running his shadowy empire from a vending machine company on Atwells Avenue. Teresa, a protected federal witness, claimed the Mafia had turned Federal Hill into an armed camp, replete with spotters. He said Mob influence reached "the highest levels of politics, even in governors' mansions and the halls of Congress."[2]

Patriarca had demonstrated his political clout in the 1960s. When his son Raymond Junior did poorly in college entrance exams for the University of Rhode Island, Patriarca had a superior court judge write a recommendation and Junior was admitted. When Junior had trouble changing a course, Patriarca intervened with then-Gov. John A. Notte Jr. An FBI wiretap on the don's phone recorded a message that the governor was standing by and had the appropriate university official on the line — what course did Junior wish to take?[3]

At our kitchen table, I scoured classified ads, highlighting titles and brooding over job listings. In August, a tiny ad announced that Common Cause sought an executive director for its Rhode Island office.

Eighteen years earlier in Brooklyn, I had joined Common Cause after a full-page ad in the *New York Times* featured John Gardner, who had resigned from the cabinet of President Lyndon B. Johnson in protest over the relentless escalation of U.S. involvement in Vietnam. In an open letter, Gardner invited Americans to help him form "a citizens' lobby" to fight the power of wealthy special interests. He called the new organization "Common Cause." Now I visited our local library and found John Gardner's book about the organization. He wrote that citizens have a right to know what their government is doing, and they deserve a voice in its decisions. He also urged citizen-activists to avoid being co-opted by those in power, whether Republicans or Democrats. "If we are to be effective," Gardner wrote, "we must often do things that evoke resistance and anger from people involved in the political machinery. Sometimes they will accuse us of partisanship. Occasionally they may even believe it."[4] Those words, written before the Watergate and Iran-Contra scandals, struck me as more crucial than ever and much needed in Rhode Island.

I mailed my résumé. On my way to the interview, I envisioned a staff of two or three people with computers, a fax machine, and a photocopier. The reality was different: two tiny rooms at the top of an airless stairway. I waited my turn in a shabby hall. The current director, who was leaving the organization, told me to draft a press release on a tiny Macintosh computer. "Work from these talking points," he said. "Save it under your name. Here's the job description."

The job description revealed two humbling facts. The executive director had no staff and would earn $19,500 — a third less than I had made as a pastor — and a successful candidate must possess a thorough knowledge of the history and government of Rhode Island. I chuckled to myself, for I knew neither. I decided to enjoy the interview. As I drafted the press release, I relaxed.

Four days later I had the job and flew to Washington for a national Common Cause conference. I was eager to meet Archibald Cox, the former Watergate special prosecutor who now chaired Common Cause's national governing board.

A crowd packed an ornate room off the U.S. Senate chamber. No one knew me, but I recognized Cox from television and newspapers. In a bowtie and dark suit, he bent toward the microphone, reading an award in his distinctive New England inflection. Cox looked over half-frame reading glasses toward an elderly man in a wheelchair. The honoree had one leg partly amputated and gray hair slicked back from a broad forehead. I had never seen Mississippi Senator John Stennis in the flesh and could not fathom why he deserved to be honored.

While Cox lauded his work for congressional ethics and campaign finance reform, Stennis's depleted figure awakened my memory of a cold darkness at the Lincoln Memorial, where I had kept vigil since midnight with Catholic and Jewish seminarians in April 1964. Three of us had stood beneath Lincoln's bony hands, shielding our candles from the wind, pacing to keep warm, sometimes singing or praying awkwardly for passage of stalled civil rights legislation. As dawn spread its colors along the reflecting pool, beyond the Washington Monument, the Capitol dome glowed. Inside, John Stennis, Strom Thurmond of South Carolina, and others were reading segregationist screed into the Congressional Record. Our sense of justice was outraged. Would a handful of southern senators with their filibuster snuff out federal legislation to reverse generations of legally enforced racial oppression?

Applause snapped me back. Archibald Cox, a leader of the organization that had just hired me, was handing a framed award to the retired Mississippi senator. Cameras flashed, and all around me people were clapping. What kind of organization had I joined?

MY FIRST ASSIGNMENT at the dingy Common Cause office was to write an ethics complaint against Gov. DiPrete. A stack of newspapers, mostly the *Providence Journal*, lay on a small desk and Rae Condon stopped by to get me started. After running the state's Conflict of Interest Commission for ten years, she now served on the Common Cause state governing board. Her short sandy hair, owlish glasses, and strong chin personified authority without pretense. She suggested that I work my way through the pile of newspapers, clipping and organizing anything related to DiPrete. "Newspaper accounts roam all over God's creation," she said, "but they're full of details that reporters have dredged up." Then she slid pages photocopied from a law book across the table. "Sorry the office doesn't have a set of the General Laws, but most of what you'll need is on these pages." She guided me through a set of legal definitions and a list of prohibited activities.

My assignment was to create a set of declarative statements linking what the governor was reported to have done with activities that were prohibited by the Ethics Law. She showed me how to break each event down into separate facts that might be proven by the sworn testimony of witnesses or with documentary evidence. "Keep each item as concise as you can," she said, her inflection faintly Irish and plainly Rhode Island, "only one fact per statement."

"One more," Condon said and gave me another photocopy, her notes in a neat script trailing down the margin. "This ethics amendment came from the 1986 Constitutional Convention." She scanned words that were upside-down from where she sat and planted her finger. "Notice here. 'All elected and appointed officials shall be subject to the code of ethics. The ethics commission shall have authority to investigate violations of the code and to impose penalties, as provided by law.'"[5] She was not reading the inverted words; she knew them by heart.

No other statewide panel, Condon told me, had the authority both to adopt and enforce a code of ethics for all public officials. "By granting the commission authority to 'adopt a code of ethics,' the voters established the Rhode Island Ethics Commission as one of the strongest such panels in the country, at least theoretically."

I asked why she said *theoretically.*

The General Assembly was jealous of its prerogatives, she replied. Lawmakers had refused to believe that voters actually wanted an unelected commission to write rules that would carry the force of law. Nor would they relinquish authority over their behavior to an outside body, which is why the legislature had modified the old Conflict of Interest Law and passed it as the new code of ethics. The newly appointed Ethics Commission dutifully rubber-stamped it.

Condon added that the fundamental question of the commission's authority had never been tested in court — the ink was hardly dry on the page. She pointed to a note indicating that voters approved the amendment on November 4, 1986, less than two years earlier, so we were in uncharted legal territory.

"Would members of the new commission just turn their backs on what DiPrete has done?" I asked.

"They could," she said. "It's pretty frightening to pass judgment on the governor, particularly in a small state where everybody knows everybody." In the ten years she headed the old Conflict of Interest Commission, no one had filed a serious complaint against a governor. She added that the commission could drop our complaint into a black hole.

"How?"

She explained that the law enacted in 1987 required that complaints be kept confidential. There was no time limit for the investigation and no procedure for forcing the commission to act. "They could dismiss a complaint without telling anybody but the respondent," she said. "Meanwhile, any of us could be fined $10,000 if we talk about this."

I asked if we really wanted to proceed with a complaint.

"Absolutely! If Common Cause doesn't try to make the law work, this new Ethics Commission could become a joke."

She then outlined for me what would happen after we filed the complaint. First, there would be a preliminary vote authorizing a professional investigator to interview witnesses and collect documents. The investigator would present those materials to a six-person investigative committee, which was responsible for deciding whether credible evidence indicated that DiPrete had violated the law.

"That investigative panel then votes whether to go forward. In civil proceedings like this, that's called a 'finding of probable cause.' If this were a criminal case, that first step would be the indictment. Our goal," she said, with a smile, "is to give the commission no choice but to go forward with a full investigation."

She explained that if the investigating committee were to find probable cause, those allegations then went to an adjudicative committee that would actually try the case, as a court would do, only behind closed doors. Then, without reminding me that I was not a lawyer, Condon spelled out legal precepts I needed to know.

I said that writing a complaint would be tough without her, and she laughed. "It'll be tough *with* me, but there's no better way for you to learn the Ethics Law." She rose to leave and suggested we talk in a day or two. I immersed myself in Rhode Island's Ethics Law and clippings from the *Providence Journal*. Fortunately for my ability to concentrate, the phone hardly ever rang.

My research showed that DiPrete had won election as governor in 1984, promising to provide the best possible contractors for the state at the lowest price without any political involvement. As I studied the newspaper stories, he seemed to have done exactly the opposite. From one headline story to the next, financial advantages flowed to his family, friends, cronies, and campaign contributors. Those outside his circle, particularly taxpayers, got short-changed. I came back to the story I had read during the summer about DiPrete's land deal, which had quadrupled the value of a property in Cranston and paved the way for a family firm, DiPrete-Laurienzo, to buy the land for $470,000 and resell it the same day to a Texas developer for $2.4 million. As a shareholder in DiPrete-Laurienzo, the governor stood to gain around $300,000 on the transaction. The rest went to family members and to a friend who was clearly what the law defined as his "business associate."[6]

Once the story broke, DiPrete cut his ties with DiPrete-Laurienzo but could not make the facts go away.[7] Before the crucial zoning board vote, the governor had tantalized the board's chair, George DiMuro, with the offer of a prestigious state position, and two months after the sale, DiPrete quietly named him to head the Coastal Resources Management Council.

Equally shocking were reports that DiPrete had intervened on two projects where another family firm stood to gain. Texas developer Kenneth Lokey, who had bought the Cranston land, was reportedly shifting his focus from southern states to New England, where occupancy rates were high and residential properties would sell.[8] I wondered if Lokey had found the DiPretes or if they had found him. Had Lokey shrewdly bought some influence by paying the governor's family corporation such an inflated price right out in the open? No one suggested that it had been a bribe. Meanwhile Dennis DiPrete, the governor's son and head of another family firm, was working with Lokey on two other developments, Briar Hill and St. James Estates.

Providence Journal reporter Ken Mingis had written three stories about Lokey's tangles with the Department of Environmental Management (DEM). Officials had cited the Texas developer for bulldozing a wetland and clear-cutting undergrowth next to a marsh. Mingis reported that DiPrete's policy chief, Ronald DiOrio, had summoned two of the state's top environmental officials to his office at the State House.[9]

"I got called to the governor's office two or three times on this," the wetlands director told the reporter. "They wanted to know, 'Why is this being held up? Aren't you being nitpicky?' It was clear they wanted it back on track. They would say, 'Time is money.'"

On October 16, three weeks before voters would choose between DiPrete and his challenger, Bruce Sundlun, the *Providence Journal* ran another high-profile story on its front page. According to reporter Peter Lord, DiPrete had steered a state environmental contract to one of his largest campaign contributors, an engineer named Domenic Tutela who had contributed over $18,000 to DiPrete campaigns during the last four years. Those contributions appeared to give Tutela an inside track.[10] The DEM had received a federal grant of $100,000 to figure out why bacteria levels had soared at the state's largest freshwater public swimming area, Olney Pond in Lincoln Woods State Park. Eight firms filed bids to conduct the study.

A team of DEM specialists analyzed their proposals. A Massachusetts company, Lycott Environmental Research, had the most experience with polluted lakes and submitted the lowest bid, $73,294. The experts rated two other firms qualified, and both had filed bids below the $100,000 EPA maximum. Domenic Tutela, however, bid $178,000, and his firm was experienced in sewage treatment, not freshwater science, so by rights he should have been out of the running. But Frederick Lippitt, DiPrete's director of administration, named Tutela for the Olney Pond contract.

The reporter breaking this story had gotten hold of a memo to Lippitt from DEM director Robert Bendick. "I am concerned," he wrote, "that the EPA will seriously question the awarding of the contract to a firm which (1) presented a bid $78,000 higher than the grant amount and over $100,000 higher than the technical committee's first choice; (2) has no Clean Lakes Grant experience when other bidders have successfully completed dozens of such studies; (3) finished seventh out of eight firms in the technical committee's ratings . . . ." The DEM director's list of concerns went on.

Nothing changed, however, until someone leaked Bendick's memo to an EPA administrator in Boston. He contacted Lippitt, who phoned the governor at the 1988 Republican National Convention in New Orleans and asked DiPrete's permission to revoke the contract with Tutela. The governor agreed, and Lippitt announced that he had "reselected" Lycott Environmental Research, the firm originally judged both the most qualified and the lowest bidder. To me, Lippitt's call to New Orleans seemed to prove that DiPrete — not Lippitt — had picked Tutela. Why else would Lippitt have sought permission to pull the plug?

In the same article Peter Lord reported that Tutela had landed other controversial contracts. For example, in the spring of 1988, a quasi-public sewage treatment agency called the Narragansett Bay Commission had solicited bids to design a new way of coping with the mix of rainwater and raw sewage that gushed into Narragansett Bay from antiquated pipes during heavy storms. As with the Olney Pond study, a technical committee had judged other firms better qualified and less expensive than Tutela. One bid for $599,710 was far lower than Tutela's $753,034. The reviewers concluded that Tutela was "unable to deal with the specifics of this study." Yet Eric Jankel, the Bay Commission's executive director, said he had picked Tutela himself. "No one tried to promote this," he insisted. "Nobody called me from the governor's office about the selection."

Peter Lord's exposé supplied still more examples of Tutela contracts awarded during DiPrete's first term as governor. In what now seemed a familiar dance, DiPrete's director of transportation overruled a professional selection committee in order to award nine road and airport projects to Tutela and various partners. Consequently the Federal Highway Administration threatened to withhold federal funds, the transportation director resigned, and Atty. Gen. Arlene Violet, a Republican like DiPrete, launched an investigation. She found evidence of political favoritism but concluded that no laws had been broken.

It was hard to believe that there was no fire beneath all this smoke. The pattern seemed clear: administrators appointed by DiPrete overruled professional selection teams and awarded contracts to large campaign contributors. But how? Had he created a shell game that kept him at a deniable distance? Was proof hidden away somewhere that DiPrete had actually picked the contractors?

DiPrete had clearly flunked that test, but would a full-scale investigation show how he signaled his picks? Was there evidence that the governor or a "business associate" would "derive a direct monetary gain" by his official actions? Could we convince a majority of the Ethics Commission's members, all recently appointed by DiPrete, that he had committed "a knowing and willful violation" of the law?

On the next day's front page, DiPrete blasted the story of favoritism toward Tutela as "an outrageous distortion." He insisted that it contained "no allegations of any wrongdoing whatsoever directed at me or my office." DiPrete's chief of staff, Norman J. DeLuca, acknowledged the facts but added: "We believe the headline, the sense of perspective given the story and the priority attached to it completely misrepresented how the state purchasing system works."[11]

Yet after publishing a dozen front-page stories about corrupt practices of the governor's inner circle, the *Providence Journal* went on to defy logic by endorsing him for re-election. "We do not expect governors to be perfect," the editors wrote, "but we do hold public servants to reasonably high standards. And in these instances, at least, Gov. DiPrete has fallen short of those standards." I thought that would have settled it, but the editors continued, "As far as we can tell, the governor has fully and correctly acknowledged his mistakes. He has apologized for them, recognizing that the perception of wrongdoing is nearly as disturbing as wrongdoing itself."[12]

I was astonished at the chasm between the newsroom and editorial board. What amazed me even more was the fact that in the close election that followed, Rhode Island voters returned DiPrete to office. Out of 400,475 votes cast, DiPrete beat Democrat Bruce Sundlun by 6,625.[13]

These stories provided the background and the ammunition for my ethics complaint. As I worked, Rae Condon proved herself a patient tutor, reviewing draft after draft. What was taking me three months I knew she could have completed in three days. Furthermore, the national office of Common Cause was skittish about state ethics complaints. "You need to fax us what you've written," a senior staff member told me by phone. "Archie will review it." Archibald Cox invited everyone in the organization to call him "Archie," but he was still the precise and thorough Harvard law professor whose courage had brought down President

Richard Nixon. "It won't take him long," she assured me. "He'll make notes in the margin or add a memo. Without Archie's clearance, you don't file it."

My draft complaint came back from Washington by express mail. "This is generally acceptable," Cox wrote with a fountain pen. "I've marked several places where you might use somewhat less inflammatory verbs."

Then, on a bone-chilling December 27, the Common Cause Rhode Island board met to consider my draft complaint. The building's heat was turned off, and a dozen people in their coats huddled around folding tables. Rae Condon ran the meeting like a disciplinarian, reminding us that the law required strict confidentiality from anyone who filed a complaint against a public official. She passed out numbered copies and said she wanted them all back. For the next hour board members reviewed the complaint, one section at a time, asking questions as they went, as the weight I had been carrying for months settled on them, too.

Greta Abbott, probably the oldest member of the board, asked if DiPrete would receive a copy of the complaint with their signatures. "He will," said Condon. "The Ethics Commission must notify him within seventy-two hours."

Another asked if the governor could retaliate. "If you're in a position where he could," she replied, "you probably shouldn't sign."

No one suggested that Common Cause drop the complaint, however, and the board voted unanimously to go forward.

When Condon asked if they were ready to sign, several apologized and said that they could not. Finally, one at a time, seven members printed and signed their names: Greta L. Abbott, Albert L. Bensusan, Elizabeth M. Dennigan, M.L. Farrell Fletcher, Deborah G. Kohl, Edward J. Oliver, and Cathleen S. Speer. I did the same. Condon notarized our signatures and embossed each page with her seal. She collected the copies of the complaint and warned us again that the legal penalty for talking about it could be a $10,000 fine.

We were all shivering in the unheated room. The governor would soon have a copy of this complaint with our signatures on his desk. It would be the first ethics complaint filed in 1989 and the first ever against a sitting governor of Rhode Island.

Lawyers representing DiPrete quickly filed a motion to dismiss our charges. "The complaint," they wrote, "is simply a summary rehash of newspaper articles covered by the media. The complainants here have not made any allegation whatsoever based on personal knowledge that the Governor has knowingly and willfully violated the Rhode Island Code of Ethics."[14] The governor's motion to dismiss our complaint was signed by two lawyers: John J. Partridge and Normand G. Benoit. Both names were familiar; our small database showed both had donated generously to Common Cause, and a decade earlier, Partridge served as president of its board. I assumed that both were Republicans close to DiPrete, and wondered if our charges against him would end their financial support. A saying echoed in my mind that people in Common Cause recited often: "No permanent friends, no permanent enemies."

On a raw day in March Rae Condon phoned, asking if I wanted the good news first or the bad. "The good," I said.

She said the six-person investigating committee had rejected the DiPrete lawyers' motion to dismiss and ordered an investigation on four of our allegations. The bad news was that the panel had dismissed all charges that specified actions DiPrete took before June 25, 1987, the day he signed the law that established the Ethics Commission. DiPrete's attorneys had argued that the commission had no jurisdiction over events prior to his signature, and the investigating panel agreed.

I asked if we had any recourse, and she said she would file a motion to have the dismissal considered by the entire fifteen-member commission. It was doubtful that the full commission would reinstate, but those procedural matters were important nonetheless.

"So why did they contact you instead of the office?" I asked.

She laughed. "Because I'm your lawyer."

I hung up feeling even more thankful that she had come to Common Cause when she left the old Conflict of Interest Commission. Her father, Francis B. Condon, had served for thirty years on the Rhode Island Supreme Court, his last seven years as chief justice. She had absorbed his love for the law and his determination to practice it honorably. Her work on the conflict commission had made her iconic. I knew that without her, the complaint could never have come this far.

I woke up after midnight, wondering if I could make a living at Common Cause. None of my predecessors had stayed more than two years. But we had moved to Rhode Island and I had landed the job at Common Cause just as reporters were breaking stories of DiPrete's apparent pay-to-play. Could I have picked a better time to start? And what better teachers than Rae Condon and Archie Cox?

Like a grand jury, the Ethics Commission first probed our charges behind closed doors, but things were happening. An investigator called our office with preliminary questions. Then a lawyer named John Roney phoned to suggest that Rae Condon and I sit down with him at his office on Wickenden Street in the old Fox Point neighborhood of Providence. Condon said it was a good sign that the commission had hired Roney as an independent prosecutor to present the case, for she respected his integrity and tenacity.

Roney's office in an historic clapboard house had windows facing south toward Narragansett Bay. Sunlight reflecting from the hardwood floor brightened the quaint conference room where we settled into old wooden chairs. "I think you're aware," he began, "that the investigating committee dismissed those parts of your complaint that alleged wrongdoing before June 25, 1987."

Condon nodded. "We still believe the commission has jurisdiction. We were careful to charge the governor with things that constitute identical violations under the old and new laws. Under administrative law, the successor agency retains responsibility for the previous statute."

Roney understood, but reminded us that the commissioners were new. He thought they were being cautious so as not to overstep their authority.

"Be that as it may," Condon went on, "we intend to move that those charges be reinstated. Six members sitting as an investigating committee should not be making a policy decision for the entire commission about matters that predate their appointment."

Even with those items gone, Roney told us that four substantial matters remained to prosecute. First, DiPrete had awarded the Olney Pond environmental contract to Domenic Tutela after Tutela's company contributed $20,500 to his campaigns. Second, the governor got his campaign chair, James L. Taft Jr., hired to sue a contractor for abandoning work on the Jamestown Bridge. Third, DiPrete had appointed George DiMuro, who finessed the Cranston land deal, to head the Coastal Resources Management Council. And finally, the governor's policy chief had intervened with top environmental officials in order to speed up wetlands permits for St. James Estates.

I asked how DiPrete signaled his choices to those subordinates who eventually announced the contracts.

"We're working on that," Roney said. "I've interviewed a number of the primary decision-makers, and they've described what they call the Architects and Engineers Committee, which they usually call just the A&E committee." DiPrete had issued an executive order in 1985 that set up the selection process. The state purchasing agent and someone from the Department of Administration always participated; for each contract, they brought in specialists from the relevant departments. "It may sound legitimate," Roney concluded, "but in practice, it got pretty loosey-goosey."

Roney had interviewed Frederick Lippitt, DiPrete's director of administration, who all but acknowledged that the governor himself made the final selections. Lippitt said the A&E committee usually gave him a cover sheet that listed three or four qualified firms for each project. The firms would be listed in alphabetical order, with a box by each name. It did not give prices they had bid. For each project, the committee also prepared a second sheet that listed the Rhode Island state contracts those firms had gotten in the past five years and their dollar amounts.

Condon leaned back in her chair, smiling.

"These two forms," Roney continued, "went to Lippitt's desk, and it looks like Lippitt passed them on to DiPrete. I think the governor checked the box by his choice and sent the list back to Lippitt, who then announced the contract award."

Condon shook her head. "They're nothing if not clever," she mused. "And DiPrete admits this, too?"

"I haven't interviewed him yet," Roney said.

I asked about the link to campaign contributions.

"That may be harder to prove," Roney said. "I assume the governor knew from other sources who had been contributing large amounts, but that doesn't prove he picked them for that reason."

"That's not the point," Condon interjected. "As soon as he checks the name on a paper, he performs an official act to send financial benefit to a business associate."

Roney looked puzzled. He asked how she could equate campaign contributors with business associates.

"The definition of 'business associate,'" Condon answered, "carried over from the old law to the new. It is still 'a person joined together with another person to achieve a common financial objective.' They contribute generously and get state business."

"That may be a stretch," Roney said, "but it's worth a try."

The enforced confidentiality made the burden of our ethics complaint feel heavier with each passing day. But unknown to me and without public fanfare, the *Providence Journal*, the ACLU, and several community activists had filed suit in U.S. District Court to strike down the ethics gag rule. Their case involved a neighborhood activist who had filed an ethics complaint against the mayor of Warwick and talked about it on the radio. Federal Judge Raymond J. Pettine, who had a long record of knocking down restrictions on free speech, issued an injunction to stop the Ethics Commission from enforcing the confidentiality rule. From the bench, he called the section "a pretty broad statute that prevents people from discussing even matters that have already been disclosed."[15]

I phoned Rae Condon to ask if we could now speak publicly about our complaint against Gov. DiPrete.

"Until there's a final ruling," she said, "it wouldn't accomplish anything. I understand how eager you are to get this out in the open. But going public could play into their claim that Common Cause was politically motivated in filing against DiPrete." I knew she was right.

The Rhode Island Foundation occupied a historic farmhouse across from Providence's North Burial Ground. Doris Donovan, a program officer, led me into the conference room with a huge fireplace. She said the foundation might be interested in helping Common Cause engage the public in conversation about government ethics. "We need to steer clear of anything that smacks of partisan politics," she said, "and we couldn't participate in any personal attacks."

The project became a series of six half-hour public television shows on ethics in Rhode Island, produced by Common Cause in cooperation with the League of Women Voters and supported by the Rhode Island Foundation. It appeared on six Wednesday nights, from November 1 through December 13, 1989. Panelists included journalists, academics, clergy, and politicians who took questions from a live audience.

DiPrete arrived at the studio only moments before our program on open government was to go on air. As technicians mounted a microphone on his lapel, we shook hands. He smoothed his wave of thinning hair that cartoonists had caricatured mercilessly, portraying him as the Gerber Baby. He had large brown eyes and a round face. His tight-lipped smile always turned down at the ends.

The topic for that broadcast was the confidentiality of ethics complaints. Former Atty. Gen. Arlene Violet, also a Republican and a former Sister of Mercy, offered her opinion that if a complaint were dismissed, the Ethics Commission should have clearance under the law to acknowledge the dismissal and give the reasons.

"Governor," asked moderator Deborah Horne, a WPRI-TV news anchor, "do you think the Ethics Commission staff members should be able to talk about a complaint?"

DiPrete smiled confidently. "I would say that once the commission votes to dismiss the complaint as unfounded, it should be a matter of public record. I don't think anybody needs to be ashamed of saying that a commission consisting of very honorable people has found that they hadn't done anything wrong."[16]

Brown University historian William McLoughlin, a citizen plaintiff in the lawsuit seeking to overturn the ethics gag rule, stood up in the audience. "Governor, public officials are there because we elect them, and they should be responsible to us. If they are brought up on charges, they have a right to a public hearing, and we have a right to hear it. I wonder, Governor, would you support the public's right to hear the matter if a case is brought to a hearing?"

"I wouldn't have any problem," DiPrete replied, "as long as the facts on both sides are made known. I think the public is capable of making a decision as long as the facts are there." He maintained a perfect façade, with no hint that a complaint might be pending against him. He did not stay for refreshments.

3

Lobbying 101
1989

MY PREVIOUS EXPERIENCE with the New York and Connecticut legislatures never went beyond testifying on bills that others had targeted. Now in much deeper water, my job was to find the bills, analyze their content, prepare talking points, figure out hearing schedules, and notify witnesses when to appear. My first task was to recruit senators and representatives to sponsor Common Cause proposals in the 1989 legislative session.

Rae Condon had drafted several ethics bills that our board approved. For example, the 1987 Ethics Law barred both the press and the public from the Ethics Commission's trial-like adjudicative hearings unless "the respondent" opted for an open process. In order to change the wording, she struck through the word "closed" to signal its deletion and inserted the underlined word "open." The underlining showed new language: *The hearing shall be* ~~*closed*~~ *open to the public.* If enacted, her simple change of text would transform the prosecution of ethics complaints. We would argue that the public had a right to hear the evidence against government officials charged with wrongdoing. Bank robbers stood trial in open court. Why should public officials accused of corrupt behavior avoid public hearings?

A second Common Cause bill would prohibit officials from intimidating whistleblowers who leaked information about wrongdoing. It would also outlaw retaliation against witnesses or ordinary citizens involved in ethics complaints. Condon's text proposed a process that would allow anyone who felt targeted by an accused official to sue for damages and legal fees.[1] "Legal language is more complicated than ordinary speech," Condon told me, "but it's not mysterious. You'll learn how to write this stuff."

A third bill aimed to outlaw favoritism toward family members. The 1987 Ethics Law made it illegal for public officials to use their positions to create financial benefit for their spouses or dependent children, but nothing barred a governor from practices like fast-tracking wetlands permits to benefit an adult son working with a developer. Our complaint against DiPrete hinged on the fact that Dennis DiPrete was the governor's partner in several family businesses. Condon's draft expanded the circle of family members. Instead of barring an official from taking actions that would create financial benefit for merely a "spouse (if not estranged) or dependent child," we would add a list of family members related to the official as siblings, parents, grandparents, in-laws, children, or grandchildren.[2]

At Rhode Island's elegant State House, I introduced myself to lawmakers who had been sympathetic to previous Common Cause bills and explained our current drafts. Some clearly feared retaliation, but others seemed to relish sponsoring ethics bills. Rae Condon's name and reputation provided instant credibility with many senators and representatives.

I also tried to recruit sponsors for campaign finance legislation that Common Cause had been promoting for years. One bill aimed to ban cash contributions and would require contributors to list their businesses or employers; another sought to stop corporations and unions from contributing to candidates, just as federal law had done for nearly a century. Cash and corporate contributions were explicitly legal under Rhode Island law.

A third bill proposed to end the common practice of converting unspent campaign contributions for personal use. During one six-month period, for example, former Speaker of the House Matthew J. Smith had legally converted $14,100 in campaign cash for his private use.[3] The current law sent campaign gifts directly into office holders' pockets.

Another area in which we sought to pass legislation was Rhode Island's complicated and arcane voter registration law. I had a personal interest in this bill because, shortly after we moved to Rhode Island, I was barred from voting for the first time in my life. In August 1988 I registered with volunteers at a card table outside our neighborhood library. On primary day in September — in paint clothes and with speckled hands — I walked to a nearby polling place. Poll workers could not find my name. "It may just be because you're new," one said. "Maybe you should try over at the Mary Fogarty School."

I walked ten blocks to the school, where another worker said I was not on her roll. Half an hour later, I stood at an ancient linoleum-covered counter in Providence City Hall while the registrar scanned a master list and double-checked against our address. "Sorry," he said. "You're not registered."

"But I registered outside my local library," I said. "There were volunteers with clipboards."

"They make mistakes all the time. It's easy with seven different forms. One mistake in a signature, and . . . ."

"Why seven forms?"

He shrugged. "All I can do is register you now for the general election in November."

"I can't go back and vote in the primary?"

He shook his head, the counter chest-high between us. "I'm just following the law," he answered sympathetically. "There's really nothing I can do."

The sun set before I left City Hall. Was this intentional? A technical mistake? Whatever the cause, I felt humiliated and powerless. I wondered how many voters like me were also turned away and never returned.

That fall a call came to the Common Cause office from local activists who were organizing a new coalition — Vote Rhode Island — to open up voting procedures. "I know you're new," the caller said, "but we'd love to have you." The coalition met in a converted industrial building backed up against the Woonasquatucket River. At the first meeting I told the group about my failed attempt to vote in my new state. Everyone laughed.

Over several months of working with Vote Rhode Island, I learned the state's history of discrimination against landless immigrants. Outdated constraints lay embedded like layers of fossils in the state's laws and constitution. Ostensibly to protect against fraud, the law required voters to fill out seven separate forms. They had to swear — on penalty of perjury and a $500 fine — that everything was true. Each form had to be notarized, and officials had to crosscheck before they dispatched the documents to various state and local offices.

Vote Rhode Island drafted legislation to simplify and open up that process. In sync with other ongoing national voter registration reform efforts, we proposed a single registration form that new voters could complete at any state agency. Our push for one-form registration carried the hope of mail-in registration in future bills.

Coalition leaders had already asked freshman Rep. Patrick J. Kennedy to sponsor our bill. In 1988, while a junior at Providence College, the son of U.S. Senator Edward M. Kennedy of Massachusetts had defeated a five-term incumbent in the Democratic primary. He spent what the *Providence Journal* computed at $63 per vote in a race that shattered all previous records for spending in a General Assembly race.[4] With his abundant sweep of chestnut hair, a jutting chin, and quick smile, the young Kennedy evoked memories of his assassinated uncles and clearly relished the chance to sponsor legislation that embodied their ideals. In the face of scorn from machine Democrats, he clearly intended to prove his worth.

I asked Kennedy to introduce the Common Cause bill banning corporate and union contributions from Rhode Island campaigns. He agreed and managed to get a hearing before the House Judiciary Committee. "Corporate contributions have been illegal in federal campaigns for nearly a century," he testified earnestly. "I took lots of corporate contributions, but I hope no candidate in Rhode Island ever will again."

AFTER DIPRETE WON the November 1988 gubernatorial election, it took months of digging to uncover his campaign funding. Russell Garland, a *Providence Journal* reporter, sifted through hundreds of corporate lists to identify DiPrete's benefactors. He discovered that the governor had accepted piles of corporate checks from companies owned by a small circle of players.[5] Among them were developers J. Clark Donatelli and his cousin, A. Edmund Donatelli, who had been partners with Dennis DiPrete when they sold twenty-five acres of North Providence land to Texas developer Kenneth Lokey for St. James Estates and St. James Pointe Apartments. Garland reported that between July 1, 1988, and the November election, the Donatellis and their businesses, which included a state-regulated nursing home, gave $22,905 to DiPrete's campaign.

Another family of companies doing business with Dennis DiPrete also funneled money through various businesses to the governor's campaign. Nicholas E. Cambio and Vincent A. Cambio, two brothers who were also business associates of Dennis DiPrete's, gave individually to the governor's campaign, as did their partner Rodney A. Malafronte. The three also generated a stream of money through corporations whose names — Hope Hill Estates Inc., Universal Motors Inc., Quaker Lane Holdings Inc., 117 Inc., Bald Hill Investments Inc., and Continental Restaurants Inc. — offered no hint that these three men owned them all.

Garland also revealed that developer Richard P. Baccari contributed to DiPrete both as a private citizen and through a group of corporations he controlled — the Downing Corp., Capitol Hotel Corp., Ekim Co., Bald Hill Road Associates, Pilgrim Hill Road Ltd., and 1150 Reservoir Avenue Partners. When the journalist finally connected these corporate owners, he asked DiPrete about these streams of money into his campaign coffers. With artful evasiveness, the governor claimed not to know. He insisted that he had not called these developers for campaign funds. "I am not involved in the fund-raising operation," he said. "My guess is they gave it out of respect for Dennis. They like the kind of government that we've given the state for four years and they want to see it continue."[6]

In State House hallways and committee hearings I passed out copies of these news stories, trying to persuade legislative leaders to address these problems. But few seemed to care, and lobbying for Common Cause felt like a fool's errand.

Patrick Kennedy's proposed ban on corporate contributions to political campaigns died in the House Judiciary Committee, as did all of our ethics bills.

Kennedy's voter registration bill would have allowed citizens to register when they visited state agencies to pay taxes, renew drivers' licenses, or apply for unemployment.[7] It passed the House but stalled in the Senate.

DiPrete had vetoed a similar bill the year before. Steven P. Erickson, the governor's legislative director, told me the administration did not object to registering voters wherever people went for state services, but there were problems with unionized state workers. "It's not in their contract," Erickson said, "and the governor can't arbitrarily assign additional duties."

"Not even to register voters?"

Erickson smiled. "You think that's not a big deal? It takes training and time away from their primary duties. It would cost more and require additional personnel."

"So does the governor favor or oppose better voter registration?"

"He's not opposed, but we have to be practical."

Others in our Vote Rhode Island coalition got word that DiPrete would veto our bill unless we could get an agreement from Council 94 of the American Federation of State, County and Municipal Employees, which represented most state employees.

Weeks passed, and the legislative session was nearing its end when the governor's office phoned Pam Twiss, who chaired the Vote Rhode Island coalition. The caller said DiPrete might support a pilot program for voter registration at the Department of Business Regulation.

"Business Regulation?" Steven Brown guffawed. Brown led the Rhode Island affiliate of the American Civil Liberties Union (ACLU). All the coalition leaders around the large table thought that location was absurd, since few ordinary people ever went there. By contrast, a pilot program could work at the motor vehicles registry, where everyone had to go for drivers' licenses and auto registration. We sent that word to DiPrete.

On June 1, a group of about eighty, bearing petitions with thousands of signatures, marched on the State House. Signs demanded voter registration at all state agencies. The youthful Patrick Kennedy tramped up the cobblestone driveway with us, visibly buoyant even on a humid, gray day. We found the main entrance to the State House locked. Kennedy pounded on a massive oak door, and a capitol police officer appeared beyond its thick glass.

"We're going to the governor's office," Kennedy yelled. Demonstrators packed the space around him.

The officer shook his head and pointed to gold letters on the glass that said the building was open from 8:30 to 4:30. He pointed to his watch and spread his fingers and thumb to signal five o'clock.

"I'm a state representative," Kennedy shouted back. "The State House is never closed at this hour."

The officer mouthed through the thick glass that Kennedy could come in but not the rest of us.

"Let's just stay here," someone said. The crowd had already surrounded a black Lincoln Town Car with the governor's distinctive license plate: **1**. "If we can't take our petitions to the governor's office," one roared, "we can wait 'til he comes out. We can block his car right here."

Protesters had the luxury vehicle hemmed in. "Seven. . . One. . . Seven. . .

Eight," someone shouted the number of Kennedy's voter registration bill, "or we have to demonstrate!"

Instantly a rhythmic chant began: "Seven, one, seven, eight, or we have to demonstrate!" Shouts reverberated from cobblestones under foot and stone arches overhead. Hands beat out the rhythm on the governor's shiny black car.

"Seven, one, seven, eight! Or we have to demonstrate!"

A reporter appeared inside the building and scribbled in her notebook. Farther inside, DiPrete stopped on the marble steps with a trooper. They could see the governor's car blockaded by demonstrators in the stone portico.

"Seven, one, seven, eight! Or we have to demonstrate!" The compressed space made the protest sound even fiercer than it was.

Patrick Kennedy and Pam Twiss waved for quiet, and the crowd fell silent. "If the governor needs to leave," Twiss said, "we should let him go. All we ask is that he hear us briefly."

"Not too briefly," roared Joe Buchanan, a huge activist from South Providence.

"Not too briefly," Twiss agreed and slipped inside with Kennedy. Through the glass, we could see them arguing with DiPrete. Then they came back out.

"The governor's on his way to an event downtown," she said. "We're going to clear this space between the doors and his car. We'll explain briefly why this bill is important, and then he goes on his way. Okay?"

Everyone agreed, and a moment later DiPrete emerged with a trooper at his side. He seemed smaller than I remembered and had fear in his eyes.

Twiss and Kennedy outlined the bill. "We're agreeable to your suggestion of a pilot project," she said. "But we want it at the motor vehicles registry, where people go for drivers' licenses. Or we could live with the Department of Human Services."

"We want it where ordinary people go," Kennedy added. "Definitely not at the Department of Business Regulation."

"I won't promise you now," DiPrete said. "But we'll take your request under consideration."

"Take our petitions, too." Twiss handed him a bundle.

DiPrete waved for a staff person, who accepted an armload of petitions and carried them inside.

"When will you let us know?" Kennedy pressed.

"Next week," DiPrete answered. "Check with my office. Okay, Rep?"

Kennedy reached instinctively to shake DiPrete's hand, and then many surged forward to shake hands with the governor. As he and I shook hands, he glanced at my face without any hint of recognition. I had never before been this close to him.

"I'm late for a meeting downtown," DiPrete called out. Moments later, safe in his Lincoln, he fled.[8]

The House had passed Patrick Kennedy's legislation to provide voter registration in all state agencies that served the public, but the bill seemed all but dead in the Senate.

Then, to our surprise, the governor and senate leaders accepted our proposed compromise: a pilot program at the motor vehicle registry. Clerks would be trained as voter registrars. People who stood in lines would see prominent signs in several languages that they could register to vote. If it worked, all state agencies that offered services or benefits to the public would follow suit within three years.

Oiled by this compromise, Kennedy's bill passed the Senate and the House again. The governor's office scheduled a low-key signing ceremony at the Division of Motor Vehicles, an old brick structure across Smith Street from the State House. DiPrete and Kennedy each spoke idealistically about voting as the foundation of democracy. Neither mentioned Rhode Island's history of excluding voters.

The Royal Charter of 1663 allowed only landowners to vote. The Constitution of 1843 barred landless immigrants from voting even after they became U.S. citizens.[9] In 1870, Rhode Island became one of the last states to ratify the Fifteenth Amendment, which forbade state governments from denying the vote "on account of race, color, or previous condition of servitude." Some Yankee Republicans argued it would force Rhode Island to let Irish immigrants vote, since they were a separate race.[10]

Now Patrick Kennedy's bill lay on a table. Its top sheet was covered with marks from rubber stamps and scrawled signatures that marked each step of its travel through the House to the Senate. Amended and stamped several times, it had been carried back across the rotunda for a final vote in the House.[11] DiPrete added his signature, shook hands with Kennedy, and handed him the pen.

After the ceremony, I shook DiPrete's hand for the second time. "Nice to see you, Phil," he said, now aware who I was. He smiled, as if we were old friends.

"Thanks, Governor," I replied. "We appreciate your help in getting this done."

4

A Costly Election
1990

NINETEEN-NINETY WAS SHAPING UP as an expensive election year. Bruce G. Sundlun, a retired business mogul, had run twice against Gov. DiPrete and lost both times. In the campaign of 1986, Sundlun spent $1.39 million, much of it his own money. In 1988, when the governor was already weakened by scandal, Sundlun burned through nearly $2.39 million but fell short by a whisker-thin margin. He declared that his third try in 1990 would be the lucky one, but three other Democrats also prepared to challenge the vulnerable incumbent.

DiPrete kept raising vast amounts of money for his campaign, mostly from vendors who wanted state business. As well as being legal, corporate contributions were easy to disguise and even if he lost, DiPrete could convert any unused campaign funds for personal use. Through three elections, expenditures skyrocketed. In 1984, 1986, and 1988, DiPrete and his challengers had spent three times as much as his predecessor, J. Joseph Garrahy, and those who ran against him had paid out in four election cycles — 1976, 1978, 1980, and 1982.[1]

Because delegates to the 1986 Constitutional Convention recognized the strong tie between campaign costs and corruption, they had proposed campaign finance reform as part of their ballot question on ethics. Voters approved a constitutional amendment that directed the General Assembly to establish a system of voluntary public financing for candidates who agreed to limit their campaign spending.[2] In 1987 lawmakers passed legislation that DiPrete signed into law,[3] but in 1988, neither DiPrete nor Sundlun participated in the matching-funds program.

In January 1990, I wrote to five candidates rumored to be running for governor — DiPrete, Sundlun, former Lt. Gov. Richard A. Licht, Warwick Mayor Francis X. Flaherty, and Providence Mayor Joseph R. Paolino Jr. — urging them to enter the matching-funds program established under the 1987 Campaign Finance Law. Participants in the program were to submit an affidavit with their candidacy papers in June. By pledging to spend no more than $1.5 million, candidates who won their primaries could receive up to $750,000 in public matching funds. The law allowed candidates who faced primary opponents to spend an additional $500,000 and still take the full amount of matching funds for the general election in November.

Two Democrats — Richard Licht and Francis Flaherty — immediately promised to participate. Sundlun announced to the press that he would accept the voluntary spending limits and matching funds if all the other candidates would do the same. DiPrete's chief of staff, Arthur Markos, replied that the governor would put the matching funds into the budget he would submit to the General Assembly, adding that DiPrete was leaning toward participating in the program.

Joseph Paolino became the Democrats' wild card. He replied that he was concerned about the drag of public matching funds on the budget.[4] Paolino had immense personal wealth, and rumors flew that he would spend whatever it took to win the primary and the general election.

I wrote again, urging the candidates to accept the program's voluntary spending limits and to start negotiations. Licht suspended his campaign in March, and meetings finally began in May. Top campaign staff found their way to our tiny Common Cause office. No one asked if these two small rooms were all our organization had.

The governor's cousin, former Cranston Mayor James DiPrete, greeted me as if we were old friends. I assumed he knew of our complaint, but neither of us brought it up. Sundlun's campaign sent two lawyers, Flaherty's one. Thomas "Tad" Devine, a young lawyer who represented the Paolino campaign, whispered to me that he had helped run the presidential campaign of Michael Dukakis.

Metal folding chairs clanked into place around our collapsible tables, and the long-shot negotiations began with a round of position statements. Frank Cenerini, a chunky lawyer, spoke for the Flaherty campaign. "Mayor Flaherty is committed," he declared. "We hope all the other candidates will do this for the sake of the people."

Next Tad Devine held forth on Paolino's behalf. He spoke of three Democrats with different degrees of name recognition facing off in what could be a contentious primary. Meanwhile, the Republican incumbent would get a free ride until November.

"Not quite," grumbled Alan Gelfuso, a lawyer with the DiPrete campaign. "It's not a free ride to have three Democrats taking whacks at you. They're free to say anything they think you've ever done wrong, whether or not they have any facts to back their claims."

Their sparring always remained civil, and within an hour, the players agreed to meet again with position papers on campaign expenditures. All agreed on the need to rein in spending, but none seemed confident that the matching-funds program would work. They agreed not to characterize each other's positions or argue these issues in the press.

Three additional meetings produced no progress. Only Flaherty signed papers to accept the spending limits and draw down matching funds. The Sundlun and DiPrete strategists said their candidates would participate if all the others publicly pledged to do so. Tad Devine insisted that Paolino lacked name recognition and would have no way of catching up with the better-known front-runners.

After they left for the last time, I sat alone in our office, wondering if I could have done anything else to force the issue. These campaign insiders reminded me of professional football coaches, knowing each other's strengths and weaknesses. Still early in the game, they were following their playbooks, not looking for ways to improvise.

I drafted a release to tell the press that our effort to hold down campaign costs had failed. I expressed our concern that a financial arms race would push spending millions of dollars above the record five million dollars that DiPrete and Sundlun spent in 1988. "Everyone loses," I wrote, "when high public office is, in effect, auctioned off to the highest bidder."[5]

Candidates filed their required campaign finance reports with the Board of Elections on July 16. Four months before the election, Paolino had already spent $1.2 million, a threshold no campaign in the state's history had crossed until 1984. Tad Devine, his lawyer, insisted that Paolino had been forced to spend at record rates for broadcast and cable television.

Mayor Frank Flaherty, who had spent only $320,000, convened a press conference outside the Board of Elections to blast Paolino and Sundlun for spending "like drunken sailors" and for refusing to accept any reasonable limits. Over the noise of passing traffic, he sounded most angry that Paolino was accepting campaign contributions from workers in Providence city government. "When he ran for mayor of Providence," Flaherty shouted, "Joe Paolino stated he would not accept contributions from city employees and city vendors. Evidently it's okay to take money from these sources now that he's running for governor."[6]

The Democrats' three-way race toward the primary became a brawl. With polls that showed Paolino trailing Sundlun, Tad Devine launched a blitzkrieg of television ads. By the middle of August, Paolino's expenditures surged to $2.5 million, shattering all previous primary expenditure records and demolishing every statewide record apart from the $2.6 million DiPrete had spent by the end of his most recent battle against Sundlun.[7] By the September 11 primary, Paolino had burned through $3.2 million. When the votes were finally tallied the young Providence mayor ranked a distant third out of three, with only 27.4

percent of the vote. *Providence Journal* reporter Scott MacKay calculated that Paolino's losing effort cost him $69.45 for each vote.[8] Sundlun won the primary with 40.5 percent and pressed on to battle DiPrete for the third time.

DiPrete launched his fall campaign with a speech at the Old State House on Benefit Street. He told supporters it was time to limit the influence of personal wealth and special interests upon the electoral process. He blamed his Democratic opponents for ignoring voluntary spending limits that had been established in the 1987 Campaign Finance Law, not mentioning that he had also refused to comply.

The beleaguered incumbent then promised to ban all contributions from state vendors or contractors. If re-elected, he would lower individual contribution limits from $2,000 to $1,000 and prohibit campaign contributions from corporations and labor unions. Moreover, he would stop wealthy candidates from loaning money to their own campaigns and end the conversion of campaign funds for personal use. DiPrete told backers that as governor he would also double the time before government officials could return as lobbyists from one year to two. He listed other reforms that Common Cause had pushed without success and without his help throughout his tenure as governor.

Russell Garland, a *Providence Journal* reporter who covered the kick-off, showed DiPrete's list to Bruce Sundlun, who roared with laughter. "Is this man crazy?" the Democrat scoffed. "He's trying to run away from his record. This deathbed conversion serves only one useful purpose. It gives the voters of Rhode Island another chance to see the difference between what politicians say and what they do."[9]

DiPrete's righteous gambit prompted news reporters to remind readers of his record. The *Journal's* M. Charles Bakst obliged, recounting the story of DiPrete's founding a $1,000 Club in 1985; donors who reached that threshold got to dine with the governor every three months. Bakst also resurrected a 1986 story about DiPrete's campaign picking up the tab for a $9,000 family vacation in Las Vegas and a 1987 report of DiPrete's scuttling legislation that would have eased public access to records of campaign contributions and state contracts.[10]

DiPrete's eleventh-hour conversion came too late, however. On November 6, 1990, Sundlun routed him by a nearly 3 to 1 margin.[11]

When all the figures were tallied, spending in the 1990 gubernatorial race far surpassed all previous Rhode Island records. The $10.4 million spent in primary and general election campaigns doubled the previous record of $5.2 million that DiPrete and Sundlun had set only two years earlier.[12] In comparison with governors' races across the country, Rhode Island's gubernatorial spending — on a per capita calculation — ranked second only to Alaska's. Sundlun won a two-year term in a tiny state where his longest drive to meet voters might take forty-five minutes. By contrast, the same year Walter J. Hickel won a four-year term in sparsely populated Alaska, which had more than five hundred times Rhode Island's landmass and where candidates flew countless miles to towns accessible only from the air. Yet no one could explain why campaign costs in Rhode Island and Alaska should be comparable. Equally to the point, Sundlun spent over four million dollars to serve two years as governor of Rhode Island, while in neighboring Massachusetts William Weld spent less than that to win a four-year term, despite the fact that the Bay State had five times as many voters spread across three media markets, including Boston.

Sundlun reminded reporters that he had bankrolled his own campaign and owed nothing to special interests. He pledged to force state vendors and contractors to disclose their political donations, reiterating his campaign's central attack on DiPrete. He insisted that nobody would ever buy influence in return for a political contribution.

Money had fueled DiPrete's relentless political machine, a system in which vendors, architects, and engineers all understood that massive campaign contributions were the price of influence and power. For all the apparent wrongdoing catalogued in our ethics complaint, we had barely scratched the surface of DiPrete's pay-to-play corruption.

Ironically, while money flowed in torrents to political candidates, our branch of Common Cause was going broke, and I was going under. As I fell behind on basic tasks, checks vanished amid piles of papers. An elderly donor phoned to ask why we had not cashed his check.

I flipped through a dozen checks I needed to deposit but could not find his. I apologized and asked him to send another.

He agreed but asked if he should stop payment on the first check.

"I don't think you need to," I said. "I remember seeing it, and I'll probably find it again. I promise not to cash it."

He sent a second check, and I lost that one, too.

"Don't you want my money?" he asked on another call.

"We do," I pleaded. "We'd be lost without your support." Clearly, I could not both manage the office and lobby effectively at the State House.

On the twentieth anniversary of Common Cause, nineteen people attended our 1990 annual meeting in a lovely church hall on the East Side of Providence. There we honored Natalie Joslin, who had worked with other activists in 1970 to organize the Rhode Island office of Common Cause. Several days after the event Joslin appeared at our shabby office, where wastebaskets overflowed and the linoleum floor was gritty. "Looks like you need help," she said. "I could spend two days a week helping to build membership and financial support. I have a pretty good Rolodex."

Joslin had recently retired and sold an executive outplacement business she had built from scratch after a painful divorce. She seemed to know every CEO and CFO in Rhode Island. She set out to build membership and financial support for Common Cause, and her energy buoyed me. She organized phone banks to raise money. She loved to open the mail, often whooping with delight when a generous check arrived. Her cheerful telephone voice hid a steely determination to raise money for new computers, a photocopier, a second phone line, and a part-time secretary.

One day, with me in the leather passenger seat of her Jaguar, Joslin sped southbound on I-95 to introduce me to Henry and Peggy Sharpe. He was the retired president of Brown and Sharpe, once Rhode Island's world-famous maker of precision measuring instruments. "Hank's fixing johnny cakes," Joslin said, cheerfully. "They've been a Rhode Island tradition since colonial times."

She slowed on a narrow road through a forest of oak and pine. Her final turn took us down through the woods to a glass-walled house on a private pond. Canada geese splashed down noisily as we poured maple syrup onto tiny cornmeal pancakes. The Sharpes listened as Joslin explained her return to Common Cause. "We're really doing something about corruption," she said. "Back when the constitutional convention started the ball rolling, I was too busy with my business. But now I'm making time, and I hope you will, too."

Joslin began to outline the Common Cause agenda and asked me to fill in the details.

"I'm not asking you for money," she said.

"Yet," Henry Sharpe interjected dryly.

"Yet," she agreed. "We need your advice first. I'd like to invite you and a few other people for a conversation at the office over sandwiches and coffee."

Over the next several months, she formed what she called an advisory council. No one seemed bothered by our drab office or folding metal chairs. Each time the group met, I gave an update from the State House and answered questions.

The most outspoken member was Gus Hebb, president of American Steel and Aluminum. "I'd like to stop bidding jobs in Rhode Island," he declared bitterly. "With DiPrete as governor, they want money before they'll even look at your proposal. It's a shakedown, a goddamn racket. I can't imagine how I was stupid enough to vote for him the first time he ran. I don't believe there's a hell, but if it exists, I'd want to send him there."

I yearned to tell Gus Hebb that we had filed an ethics complaint against the governor two years earlier. DiPrete had run the state through an entire two-year term and had probably shaken down scores of business leaders. There was still no finding of probable cause, and I was sworn to silence under the possibility of a ten thousand dollar fine.

Only days before DiPrete lost the election, events slipped forever beyond his control. On November 1, state auditors reported to Atty. Gen. James E. O'Neil that the books of Heritage Loan and Investment Co., a Federal Hill bank that belonged to Joseph Mollicone Jr., lacked basic documentation for millions of dollars worth of loans. O'Neil, a former federal prosecutor, immediately called Mollicone to his office and confronted him about a shortfall that investigators thought might top thirteen million dollars. O'Neil launched a grand jury investigation but failed to order Mollicone's arrest.[13]

From the 1950s until the 1980s, Joe Mollicone's father had owned and operated a Federal Hill bank whose most prominent customer was Raymond L.S. Patriarca, the godfather of organized crime in New England. Patriarca managed his empire from the Coin-O-Matic Distributing Company, a short distance down Atwells Avenue. Mafia informant Vincent Teresa had testified that the elder Mollicone was in Patriarca's pocket and that he "coughed up ready cash" whenever necessary. Mob associates jokingly called the banker "Puppydog."[14]

After his father's death in 1986, Joe Mollicone Jr. took over the family bank, renaming it Heritage Loan and Investment Corp. Few believed that the younger Mollicone could cut his father's ties to Patriarca. Mollicone enjoyed a life of luxury and dabbled in businesses around Providence, particularly real estate. He reveled in the swirl of money, power, and politics. For example, in 1984, when Mayor Vincent A. "Buddy" Cianci Jr. went through a contentious divorce, Mollicone paid the mayor $345,000 for his elegant house on Blackstone Boulevard.[15] The banker always gave generously to high-profile politicians, regardless of their principles, parties, or rivalries. In 1990, he contributed to the campaigns of Edward DiPrete, Joseph Paolino, and Cianci. Top banking and business executives flew as Mollicone's guests on expensive trips. "I did very, very well this year," he would say. "I'd like to share my wealth, my good fortune, with my friends."[16] A year before auditors sounded the alarm on Heritage Loan and Investment, the state Department of Employment Security leased a loft building from Mollicone for one million dollars a year for ten years, roughly double what the agency had paid previously. Mollicone's partners in the lease included Rodney M. Brusini, Gov. DiPrete's trusted fundraiser, and Henry W. Fazzano, his latest chief of staff.[17]

On November 8, two days after the election, Joe Mollicone quietly vanished. Five days later, Atty. Gen. O'Neil announced with chagrin that Joseph Mollicone III had driven his father to Logan Airport for a flight to New Jersey.[18] From there, the fugitive banker's trail went cold.

As speculation spread about Mollicone's disappearance and the financial chaos at Heritage, those in the know drained their accounts. The bank's private insurer — the Rhode Island Share and Deposit Indemnity Corporation, known by its acronym, RISDIC — rushed in $6.6 million to cover withdrawals. On November 18, with millions missing and Mollicone gone, DiPrete ordered the bank to be closed. He announced that no more transactions would be allowed, acknowledging "the inconvenience and hardship this may cause for Heritage's depositors."[19]

As holiday lights went up on Federal Hill, few imagined that Joe Mollicone's embezzlement would suck all the reserves out of RISDIC and bring its collapse. DiPrete had known since 1985 that the state's private credit union insurance system was vulnerable, but he had done little to prevent the disaster now bearing down on ordinary citizens like a runaway train. No alarm sounded to warn that the worst financial scandal in Rhode Island's modern history had begun.

5

Collapse of Credit
1991

BRUCE SUNDLUN'S INAUGURATION and a new year fell together on January 1, 1991, one of the worst days in Rhode Island's history. I leaned into a stiff wind, crossing brittle frozen grass toward the inauguration on the south plaza of the State House. With temperatures well below freezing, the crowd's glove-muffled applause faded quickly.

Sundlun stood, triumphantly bareheaded, on white marble steps amid flags and dignitaries. At the age of seventy, he had finally toppled the scandal-tainted DiPrete. The campaign had touted Sundlun's decorations for flying bombers in World War II. When German anti-aircraft fire crippled his B-17, Sundlun and his crew parachuted into enemy territory, where he evaded capture for ninety-five harrowing days and nights. Sundlun, who was Jewish, often told audiences how a network of Catholic priests protected him and helped him escape to neutral Switzerland.[1]

The growling rumble of heavy propeller-driven planes sounded suddenly as a formation of four-engine olive drab military aircraft rose over College Hill and swooped toward the inauguration. They roared in low, their acrid diesel exhaust punctuated by artillery that thudded nearby and echoed sharply from the marble State House. Puffs of white smoke blasted upward and then dispersed in the wind.

In his inaugural address, Sundlun spoke of two storms that the people of Rhode Island must fly through with his new administration: a banking crisis that few understood and an unprecedented budget crisis. "On the approach," his voice boomed, "the storm cloud is ominous and dark. Once inside, it's a rough, difficult, tumultuous ride. But once you get to the other side, there is sunlight once again." He promised to restore the public confidence that DiPrete had shattered. "Nothing can withstand the weight of public cynicism," he roared. "Without the people's trust, our task will become an arduous, sullen struggle doomed to failure."[2]

Afterwards, in the warmth of the State House, word spread that Sundlun would hold a press conference. I squeezed into his formal office, where television lights blazed.

With cameras rolling, Sundlun signed two executive orders. In the first, he pledged high ethical standards of government and established an ethics task force to recommend systemic reforms. The new governor required companies and individuals who received more than $1,000 in state business to report their political contributions over $200.[3] In the second executive order, Sundlun closed forty-five credit unions, seven loan-investment companies, and three banks — the entire ensemble insured by the Rhode Island Share and Deposit Indemnity Corporation (RISDIC). Sundlun saw himself in the mold of Franklin D. Roosevelt, who had been inaugurated during a bank crisis in 1933. Roosevelt suspended banking nationwide, but euphemistically called his shutdown a "bank holiday."[4] Sundlun used the same term for his RISDIC closure. He said some of the insured institutions were healthy and could reopen quickly; others were shaky, but could be put on firmer footing and then reopened. But he said little about the rest — credit unions that were insolvent and must be liquidated.

News of the shutdown reverberated like a bomb blast. A third of all Rhode Islanders had their checking, savings, and mortgages in RISDIC-insured credit unions. The collapse plunged Rhode Island into its worst financial crisis since the Great Depression.

For years, the insurer had run reassuring television commercials featuring muscular hands that chiseled a slab of rock. Dust and stone chips flew, revealing the logo: an eagle holding a clutch of arrows above the letters RISDIC. An authoritative voice assured viewers that RISDIC's security was "carved in stone." Within hours, RISDIC's commercials became the butt of bitter jokes. Three years earlier, as Anne and I prepared for our move to Rhode Island, our realtor took us to the East Providence Credit Union for a mortgage. Anne asked him why the decal on the door said RISDIC and not FDIC.

"It's just how we do it in Rhode Island." At the time I had no job, and Anne's salary might not qualify us for a mortgage, so we went along with him. Now our accounts were frozen, too.

In the aftermath of RISDIC's collapse, furious depositors swarmed the State House. Thousands who had never before set foot inside their splendid capitol came tramping past silent Civil War cannons and faded battle flags, up the broad marble stairs. They waved protest signs and screamed their rage: "We want our money! We want our money!"

Each barrage of shouts echoed from the frescoed dome, two hundred feet above. Mobs of depositors surged past offices and committee rooms. Some kicked thick oak doors, making them bend inward and snap back against their jambs like gunshots. Volleys moved as battles shifted. Outside the House chamber, a huge ship's bell clanged incessantly until custodians removed its striker. Protesters spewed blame indiscriminately against any public officials they encountered and against government itself.

I found myself at the edge of one depositors' rally when word spread that two women standing nearby were state representatives. The mob pressed in around them.

Rep. Sandra J. Campbell, a newly elected Republican from rural Foster, stood her ground. "Listen," she shouted, "I was just elected. I had no part in making this mess." She made eye contact with a burly man in the front row and held his gaze. "I'm as mad about this as you are. I'm here to make it right." Her sheer courage kept them at bay and the surge eased. Jack Kayrouz, the leader of the newly organized Citizens for Depositors' Rights raised a chant through his bullhorn. Protesters shifted their attention back to Kayrouz.

Only days after this disaster hit, a confidential report surfaced. Written more than five years earlier, it predicted RISDIC's collapse with uncanny precision.[5] Arlene Violet, a former Sister of Mercy, had won election as the state's top prosecutor in 1984, the first woman in the United States to be elected state attorney general. In that role, she prosecuted the 1985 scandal involving top officials at Rhode Island's housing agency, RIHMFC. When she noticed irregularities in a routine report from RISDIC to the Department of Business Regulation, Violet appointed retired New York banking lawyer Robert Stitt as a $1-per-year assistant attorney general and set him loose to probe the insurer's practices. To back him up, she assigned a former banker, Charles O. Black.[6]

Stitt delivered his report to Violet on December 13, 1985, five years to the month before his nightmare scenario played out. He warned that many credit unions and loan companies were engaging in "all sorts of dangerous, indeed reckless management practices." He detailed seven hazards that ranged from "large, risky, improperly documented loans" that had produced "high delinquencies and substantial losses" to "unorthodox accounting/management practices" that attempted "to give an appearance of solvency to their balance sheets." One section of Stitt's report described "Unduly Concentrated Loans to Officers, Directors and other 'Insiders.'" The next described "Microscopic Reserves." Audits of RISDIC had been irregular and superficial; worse still, officers at several credit unions had intimidated state bank examiners. One employee at the Greater Providence Deposit Corporation was suspected of letting air out of bank examiners' tires, and also brandished an M-16 rifle in the room where auditors were working. Three institutions — including the East Providence Credit Union where Anne and I had gotten our mortgage and opened our accounts — were in serious financial condition, so that a run on any of the three "would exhaust RISDIC's available resources" and would probably bring down the entire system.[7]

"The Stitt Report," as it was quickly called, noted that state-chartered credit union insurers had failed recently in Nebraska, Ohio, and Maryland. RISDIC "would perform no better." Stitt concluded: "To allow $1 billion in deposits of some 300,000 persons to be held by financial institutions with no federal insurance is archaic and dangerous."

Atty. Gen. Violet had understood that Stitt's dire warning could trigger a run on credit unions and bring the system crashing down. She delivered a confidential copy to DiPrete, who ordered a follow-up analysis by one of his lawyers. Normand G. Benoit validated Stitt's description of a disaster waiting to happen: RISDIC-insured institutions would fail as their counterparts had in Maryland and Ohio.[8]

Violet also gave copies to Rhode Island's Board of Bank Incorporation, a regulatory body where she served with the general treasurer, director of business regulation, one state representative, and one state senator.[9] All received both Stitt's original report and Benoit's confirmation, yet the board took no action. As for DiPrete, he fired off a three-sentence memo to his director of administration, Fred Lippitt, acknowledging the "extremely serious potential" of these revelations, but apparently did nothing further.[10]

Stitt's report had remained secret for five years, and most Rhode Islanders had never heard of him before his dire warning landed on front pages and television news on January 4, 1991, shortly after Sundlun's inauguration. The *Providence Journal* printed what became known as "the Stitt Report" in its entirety. Stitt's unheeded warning hit me with a jolt of adrenalin. How could officials have known this for five years and ignored it? Why were ordinary people left vulnerable and unprotected?

On the *Providence Journal's* editorial page, Brian Dickinson wrote that he had called a national rating service in Wisconsin. "We've been flagging RISDIC for two years," an expert told him. Several Rhode Island credit unions were ominously overextended. Dickinson connected other dots and backtracked to a meeting of the House Finance Committee in 1986, which had rebuffed Violet and dodged the question of RISDIC's peril.[11] His column rang a bell for me. Hadn't there been a case before the old Conflict of Interest Commission? Deep in files transferred to the Ethics Commission, I found proof that Arlene Violet and Bob Stitt were not the only ones who agonized over the risks that RISDIC posed.

J. Robert Bergeron had been president of the Woodlawn Credit Union. In that role, he sat on the RISDIC board. He read what he believed were improper audits and raised hard questions, but other officers scorned his warnings. Bergeron gave up on RISDIC and persuaded the Woodlawn board to switch its insurance to the National Credit Union Administration. With his credit protected Bergeron might have dropped the issue, but instead, he reached out to Rep. Francis A. Gaschen, a Democrat from Cumberland. He asked Gaschen whether legislation could require all Rhode Island credit unions to do what Woodlawn had done: obtain federal credit union insurance. He believed some RISDIC institutions would qualify for federal insurance, while others that were overextended or weakened by risky loans might have to close.

Gaschen was not a banker and knew nothing about the attorney general's investigation, but he had heard worrying stories from RISDIC depositors in his district. He drafted legislation that would require all Rhode Island credit unions to get federal deposit insurance, a move he knew would end RISDIC's role as insurer. A copy of Gaschen's bill went to Sen. John R. D'Amico, a Cranston Republican, who introduced an identical version in the Senate.[12]

It was clear that RISDIC's allies in the General Assembly had a lot to lose if Gaschen's bill became law. Rep. Robert V. Bianchini of Cranston was president of the Rhode Island Credit Union League, RISDIC's trade association; thus his livelihood depended on the in-state self-insurance system. Because Bianchini also served as vice chair of the powerful House Finance Committee, under the Conflict of Interest Law then in effect, he should have disclosed his conflict of interest and recused himself from further action on Gaschen's bill.

Instead, three days before the hearing on the Gaschen bill, Bianchini hosted a dinner for his fellow committee members at the posh Aurora Club on Federal Hill. He and RISDIC president Peter A. Nevola pitched their case against federal insurance. Bianchini gambled the entire RISDIC system on a bet that its most reckless and overextended institutions would not fail.

Violet spoke to leaders of the committee and offered to present Stitt's report in a confidential executive session, subject only to the condition that Bianchini not be present.[13] They refused.

Despite his blatant conflict of interest, Bianchini had presided over part of the committee's five-hour hearing on May 12, 1986. Prepped with talking points from their Aurora Club dinner, RISDIC's backers hung tough. They cross-examined Gaschen as if he were a hostile witness and swatted away the warnings from within the credit union movement. During that tumultuous hearing, Robert Stitt met Frank Gaschen for the first time and handed him a copy of his report, which Violet kept confidential for fear of triggering a run on credit unions.[14]

RISDIC's obstruction crushed the federal deposit insurance bills in both the House and Senate. As I tried to piece these fragments together, the wrongs of 1986 came alive. The governor had been so busy running his pay-to-play scheme and amassing campaign contributions that he ignored clear warnings of the coming collapse. To protect Bianchini, the Finance Committee ganged up on Gaschen and trashed his bill. Just as Bob Stitt had feared, RISDIC's powerful allies at the State House won. With the help of generous campaign contributions, well-connected lobbyists, and inside players like Bianchini, RISDIC stayed in business. Gov. DiPrete and the General Assembly failed to protect the public.

But Robert Bergeron refused to let go. He spelled out the details of Bianchini's behavior in a complaint to the Conflict of Interest Commission, and his allegations led to a full hearing behind closed doors. Five votes were required to convict, but only four voted that Bianchini had "knowingly and willfully violated" the law. One of the votes to exonerate him was cast by Michael A. Morry, the president of the Warwick Municipal Employees Credit Union, which relied on RISDIC insurance.[15] Thus it seemed painfully clear that Morry had his own blatant conflict of interest on the very panel that was supposed to protect the public. Only a few days after Morry voted to clear Bianchini, DiPrete signed the law that put the Conflict of Interest Commission out of business and created the Rhode Island Ethics Commission. On the recommendation of House leaders, DiPrete named Michael Morry to the new panel.[16]

No amount of hindsight could undo that history: Bianchini was protected by the Constitution from being charged a second time for the same conflict of interest. Yet with our complaint pending against DiPrete and more complaints likely against key RISDIC players, it seemed absurd that Morry should be in a position to acquit his cronies in the future. Common Cause demanded that Morry resign, but he refused, and his fellow commissioners did nothing, while the media paid little attention.[17] Our concerns about one credit union executive vanished like a paper airplane swept up in a hurricane.

Within days of RISDIC's collapse, Bianchini became the villain. Angry depositors chanted his name as a curse. Protesters taunted him at the State House. On January 7, the beleaguered official resigned from his two powerful posts in the House leadership: deputy house majority whip and vice chair of the House Finance Committee. In a letter to House Speaker Joseph DeAngelis, he acknowledged his lead role in killing Gaschen's 1986 legislation. "I am saying openly and honestly today that I was mistaken."[18]

A few days later, I stepped out of a rotunda full of protesting depositors and into the relative quiet of a gallery that overlooked the House chamber. A steep stairway gave access to benches on either side. In the red-carpeted aisles below, representatives were chatting or collecting signatures on bills while they waited for the afternoon session to start. I took my usual seat in the gallery's front row and opened a folder of bills.

"Which one's Bianchini?" A man in a pale polyester suit had entered after me. His hair was white and neatly trimmed. I glanced at representatives on the floor. Bianchini was nowhere in sight, and I told him that.

"I've got a gun," he said softly, his right hand deep in a pocket. "I'm going to kill that son-of-a-bitch."

"That wouldn't solve anything," I said, trying to look calm despite a rush of adrenalin. Even with rage smoldering and flaring up everywhere across Rhode Island, the State House still had no metal detectors. Three entrances stood wide open and unguarded, with no checks of bags or briefcases. Anyone could walk in or out. Chaos reigned in the corridors. The House chamber lay vulnerable below us. No capitol police were in sight.

"Do you see him?" the man demanded. "Bianchini?"

With his neatly trimmed mustache and goatee, Bianchini would have been instantly recognizable. "I don't see him," I said truthfully. "Let's go outside and talk about this."

The man ignored my offer, his eyes searching the throng of people below. I thought of Puerto Rican nationalists firing on Congress from a gallery half a century before and wondered about this grandfatherly man. Would he recognize Bianchini if he entered the chamber? Did he really have a pistol? Would he try such a long shot?

The whole thing seemed wildly improbable. I hesitated, moved away from the white-haired man, and tried to fade from his presence. I climbed the gallery's carpeted stairs and escaped into the rotunda. I searched for a police officer but could not find one. Racing to the Speaker's office, I told a receptionist and asked her to call police to the gallery. Back in the gallery, I opened the door and looked inside, but the space was empty. The white-haired man had vanished. I bolted back out to the rotunda and scanned the long hallways without seeing him or police. An elevator beeped its arrival at the third floor, and a clutch of angry depositors spilled out. There were no officers among them. I hurried back to the Speaker's office just as DeAngelis came out with his entourage. I said it was an emergency and pushed through to tell him about the threat. Distracted, he thanked me and strode down the back stairs. His retinue of representatives and staff followed.

At the top of the stairs, I felt foolish. I stepped into the west gallery above the rostrum and looked across at the opposite gallery. A dozen or more protesters occupied the front row. On the House floor below, Bob Bianchini was nowhere in sight.

The public's hostility to RISDIC grew by the day. A week after the collapse, hundreds of us who had funds frozen in the East Providence Credit Union filled the seats and stood in the aisles of a school auditorium. The credit union's officers sat on the stage behind a table. Anthony Aragona, the thrift's president, rose with a microphone in hand but was hooted down.

"My business is going under," shouted one woman near me. "I want to know how many of you people took money out before they closed the bank."

Aragona shouted through the public address system that none had withdrawn funds and that his account was frozen along with hers. Meanwhile Sen. John F. Correia, a vice president of the East Providence institution, translated parts of the meeting into Portuguese. Correia tried in vain to convince the audience that he had not known that East Providence, or RISDIC, as a whole, faced grave financial peril.[19] But time would reveal what Correia tried to hide; within days other senators tipped off reporters that Correia had helped bury D'Amico's 1986 Senate bill requiring Rhode Island credit unions to get federal insurance.[20] He knew that the East Providence Credit Union could not qualify for insurance from the National Credit Union Administration.[21]

As the crisis mounted, Gov. Sundlun asked the president of Brown University, Vartan Gregorian, to form a panel and find out why the RISDIC system for protecting deposits had not worked. In answer to reporters' questions, he admitted that Gregorian's panel would have little money and no subpoena powers. The new governor had come into office with a mandate to clean up cronyism, but in the maelstrom, he seemed unable to focus on prosecuting those responsible for this disaster.

Atty. Gen. James O'Neil asked Sundlun for extra funds to hire investigators with expertise in white-collar financial crimes, but the governor refused, growling, "It's more important to get the money into the hands of the depositors than to find out who may have been at fault."[22] O'Neil offered instead to find volunteers to run an investigation. Bank examiners and state troopers were already poring through boxes of files from Heritage Loan and Investment. Meanwhile, other lawmakers proposed separate investigations. Senate Majority Leader John J. Bevilacqua appointed a committee of seven senators to study the causes of the crisis and suggest new banking laws. House leaders announced that the House Judiciary Committee would conduct its own probe. Its chair, Jeffrey J. Teitz, had led the impeachment investigation against Bevilacqua's late father, the former chief justice, for associating with mobsters.

RISDIC investigations multiplied like school closings in a blizzard. After two weeks it was hard to tell whose tracks might be lost in a snowy crime field trampled by many searchers. What would happen if legislative investigators were to grant immunity to key witnesses? It seemed clear that only an independent special prosecutor from outside Rhode Island could follow the money, as Archibald Cox had done with Watergate.

The newly elected Sundlun had no responsibility for the credit unions' collapse, but RISDIC was fast becoming his crisis. Days slipped away, and crucial decisions were skidding out of control. On behalf of Common Cause I wrote him that it was time for an independent prosecutor, which would help to avoid any appearance of a cover-up. The letter encouraged Sundlun to insist that legislative leaders halt their separate investigations, since otherwise key evidence might be lost: "Uncoordinated, compartmentalized investigations will inevitably have the effect of disbursing, losing or destroying information." Finally, I urged Sundlun to protect all RISDIC-related files from tampering, particularly documents scattered around various credit unions.[23]

On January 11, I hand-delivered the letter to Sundlun's office and then walked around the building, leaving copies for General Assembly leaders. Finally, I dropped off copies for reporters in their cramped basement offices.

A few days later, after an evening hearing of the House Judiciary Committee, Chairman Jeff Teitz drew me into his office. Teitz towered over me, looking down through thick glasses. "I wanted you to know," he began, "that I've been talking with our leadership in the House and with the governor. We've agreed on a single RISDIC investigation, as you requested." He described to me the commission that he would lead and whose members would be appointed by the governor, attorney general, and legislative leaders. "We will have the power to subpoena documents and witnesses, and I assure you that we will be extremely cautious in granting immunity."

"I don't mean to question your judgment," I said respectfully, "but we asked for an independent prosecutor from outside Rhode Island."

"I was just getting to that," Teitz said, not taking offense. "We've spoken with a number of people, but I'm leaning toward two respected prosecutors whose names I'm sure you'll recognize. Both are from out of state, and both have extensive experience with white-collar crime. We're nearing a final agreement that I think will please you."

Almost as if it had been planned, his phone rang. He thanked the caller for getting back to him. I rose to excuse myself, but he gestured for me to stay. The call was brief, confirming arrangements for a flight from Washington. Teitz hung up, wrote himself a note, and looked across his desk at me. "You may have guessed who that was, and I trust you to keep this confidential until we finalize the details and make an official announcement. That was John Nields, who was lead prosecutor in the Iran-Contra investigation."

The second outside prosecutor would be Alan I. Baron, who had led the investigation of a federal judge impeached in 1988 by the U.S. House of Representatives, found guilty by the U.S. Senate, and removed from the bench.

A few days later, Atty. Gen. Jim O'Neil called our office to let me know the governor would soon announce a RISDIC probe that would involve two out-of-state special prosecutors and a single investigating commission. "I have one appointment on the panel," he said, "and I'd be open to any suggestions from Common Cause."

I suggested Rae Condon. "She's an excellent lawyer who ran the Conflict of Interest Commission for ten years."

"I haven't met her," O'Neil said. "Is she related to former Chief Justice Francis Condon?"

"His daughter," I said and gave him her phone number.

As weeks passed, several credit unions got insurance from the National Credit Union Administration. While they reopened, most remained locked tight.

Impatient depositors turned their rage against Sundlun and his staff. No one seemed immune. After one late hearing, I went to ask Sheldon Whitehouse, Sundlun's young executive counsel, about an ethics bill. The receptionist had left, and I found Whitehouse alone in his office looking shell-shocked, sunk back in his chair.

"Sorry," he said. "Too many hours burning the candle at both ends."

I could feel his isolation. "Do you think that they can't tell who's responsible for the mess and who's stuck with cleaning it up?"

"I think they know by now who's who," the young lawyer said.

"But they're venting at you?"

"The word's around that we made it worse by declaring a bank holiday."

"Did you have a choice?"

"I don't think we did." In the dim light, Whitehouse looked utterly bereft. "I got here this morning at six-thirty and there was already a little old lady waiting at the sub-basement entrance. She looked sweet and grandmotherly, like the muffin lady. She squinted at me as if she recognized me. 'Are you Sheldon Whitehouse?' she asked.

"'Yes,' I told her. 'Why do you ask?'

"'You mother-fucker,' she hissed at me. 'I hope you burn in hell and that your children die of cancer.'" Whitehouse shook his head sadly. "It's like they've all flipped out on something. They can't hear a word about where we are or where we're going."

I suggested that he go home and have dinner with his wife and children.

"The kids are probably in bed already," he said. "We just got a big new TV for Christmas, and Molly saw me on it. She thinks I've gone somewhere far away. She keeps asking Sandra when I'm coming home."

"Right now," I said. "And I'm walking you to your car."

"And hope the muffin lady's gone by now?"

"And hope she feels some remorse."

"Don't hold your breath waiting."

We walked out to the parking lot. His was one of the last cars left.

On Valentine's Day, Rhode Island's new governor convened a press conference in the ornate State Room to announce the creation of a single RISDIC Investigating Commission. The white-haired governor burst from a doorway to his office and marched to the lectern, with aides in tow. Those who were to serve on the new commission filed in after him and took seats in rows of chairs slanted toward the lectern. Sundlun stood in front of the carved white marble fireplace, under the full-length portrait of George Washington.

Sundlun spoke with gruff authority. "I'm about to sign an executive order that will establish a select panel to probe the risks taken by RISDIC and its member institutions. Our investigation will search out failures of government, particularly insider influence." The entire crisis, he told us, was caused by "irresponsibility, naked greed, and a casual standard of political ethics." Then he introduced Jeff Teitz to lead the investigation: "I have complete confidence in his integrity, his intellect, and his independence."

Sundlun next presented his four appointees: retired Superior Court Judge William M. Mackenzie, District Court Judge Alton W. Wiley, Supreme Court Disciplinary Counsel Mary Lisi, and North Kingstown Police Chief John J. Leyden. He also introduced four panelists selected by other state leaders: Common Cause vice president Rae B. Condon, chosen by the attorney general; Rep. Francis A. Gaschen, by the House majority leader; Sen. John F. McBurney, by the Senate majority leader, and Rep. David W. Dumas, by the House and Senate minority leaders.

By naming Gaschen, House leaders seemed to show that they understood how wrong their predecessors had been only five years earlier when the House Finance Committee scorned him and his bill to require federal credit union insurance. For his part, Sundlun clearly relished presenting Nields and Baron as co-counsels. He outlined their accomplishments in a list of high-profile federal cases. "As a former federal prosecutor," he proclaimed, "I have an absolute intolerance for corruption. If there have been insider deals, they will be exposed. If we find civil liability, we will sue. And if we find evidence of crime, Mr. Baron and Mr. Nields will recommend indictments. Starting today, the people's demand for justice will be served."

Teitz rose to speak. He dwarfed Sundlun at the podium and had to bend down over the bank of microphones. He promised gavel-to-gavel cable television coverage. "We will ask all the tough questions," he assured the crowd, "and we will follow the evidence wherever it leads."[24]

Since January, Brown University President Vartan Gregorian and his faculty team had been poring over documents and interviewing RISDIC players. On a rainy Thursday in March, Gregorian delivered a 186-page report whose title played off RISDIC's television commercials showing muscular hands sculpting a fierce eagle into granite while an authoritative voice promised security "carved in stone." The cover displayed RISDIC's familiar logo with the ironic title, *Carved in Sand*.[25] This illusion of strength and invincibility, Gregorian said, "remained intact until RISDIC actually had to fulfill its function as an insurer for a major loss."[26]

The report singled out strong ties between lawmakers and the boards of RISDIC and its member institutions. Gregorian called the relationship "incestuous," and his report noted: "Bills endorsed by RISDIC were received with favor; those opposed by RISDIC were not."[27] Gregorian criticized Arlene Violet for failing to press legislative leaders over Stitt's report and faulted Atty. Gen. James E. O'Neil, who defeated Violet less than a year after she received the Stitt Report.

Gregorian noted that during four years as attorney general, O'Neil had paid little attention to RISDIC. The report also blamed DiPrete and his Department of Business Regulation, which was responsible for bank examinations, for failing to communicate what they knew or do anything to head off the disaster.

Only days after banner headlines about *Carved in Sand*, Ira Chinoy reported in the *Providence Journal* that during six years as governor DiPrete had taken "a steady stream of contributions" not only from RISDIC itself but also from its insured institutions and from their officers.[28] Several top players belonged to DiPrete's $1,000 dinner club, giving them regular access. The reporter also identified $8,900 that Mollicone, the fugitive owner of Heritage Loan and Investment, had funneled into DiPrete's campaigns. At least $29,000 had come from other officers of two troubled RISDIC institutions: Heritage Loan and the Greater Providence Deposit Corporation. Meanwhile it came to light that Duffy & Shanley, the public relations firm that created RISDIC's "carved in stone" commercials, had given $16,400 to DiPrete, who insisted that the connection was only "coincidental."

"I don't care how much they gave or didn't give," DiPrete said. "It didn't do them any good." But Frank Gaschen had told me that DiPrete had done nothing to support his 1986 bill to require federal credit union insurance. If RISDIC'S contributions "didn't do them any good," why had DiPrete apparently not lifted a finger during the next four years to prevent RISDIC's collapse?

After her narrow 1986 loss to James O'Neil, Arlene Violet parlayed her legal training and gift of gab into a daily talk show on WHJJ-AM. Rapid-fire, she spoke with authority. Detractors had lampooned her as "Attila the Nun," but in the wake of RISDIC's collapse and Stitt's report, callers treated her like a modern Joan of Arc.

Several times, she brought Bob Stitt to her cramped studio at WHJJ. On April 17, he arrived with a briefcase full of papers and went live with Violet after the 5 o'clock news. They were talking with Lou from North Providence when Stitt fell silent. He rubbed his eyes, then slumped over the counter on top of his documents.

Violet signaled for a break, rushed to him, wrapped her arms around him. "Stay with me," she urged. "Come on, Bob, breathe!"

She shouted to call 911. Doctors at Rhode Island Hospital pronounced him dead of a heart attack.[29]

The inconvenience Anne and I experienced from RISDIC's collapse never compared with the anguish of thousands who were locked out of their retirement funds. Our checking and savings accounts were frozen with our mortgage in the East Providence Credit Union, but our paychecks were drawn on commercial banks, and we opened new accounts at a federally-insured bank.

Just after Memorial Day, a rumor spread that the governor would announce a rescue plan for the East Providence Credit Union. I slipped into the State Room behind a crowd of reporters and dozens of people eager with anticipation. Members of Sundlun's staff emerged from a door to his office, followed by legislative leaders from both the House and Senate. Sundlun strode in with four men I did not know and positioned himself at a lectern full of microphones. "Without a lot of preliminaries," he declared in drill sergeant mode, "we have a deal to reopen the East Providence Credit Union. We couldn't have pulled this off without the cooperation of the people I'm about to introduce."

The four were investors from Boston who had put together thirteen million dollars from private sources to take over the credit union's modern building, properties, and portfolios. They would form a community bank under a complex agreement that Sundlun outlined. The deal would need approval by federal bank regulators and the Superior Court, as well as to be ratified by a newly formed Depositors' Economic Protection Corporation (DEPCO) that had custody over insolvent credit unions and banks. As the white-haired governor spoke, people sighed and relaxed. A woman in front of me wept silently.

"This is a good deal," Sundlun rumbled. "It's good for the depositors and good for the state."[30]

A few days later, DEPCO began making payouts to depositors at other RISDIC institutions that would never reopen. Newspapers printed the rules and conditions of repayment. The computations were complicated, but money finally began trickling back to depositors.[31] A few grumbled that they were required to sign waivers absolving the state of further liability before they got their funds; others complained that they had more on deposit than DEPCO would repay. Thousands were in the dark about their accounts, worth an estimated $1.16 billion, still frozen in credit unions that would probably never reopen. Meanwhile critics railed about the higher taxes needed to cover the bailout of RISDIC institutions that had been underinsured and poorly regulated.

Bruce Sundlun never projected sympathy well, and his repertoire did not include charm. Instead he came across as self-assured to the edge of arrogance. No sooner had the burdens of office landed on him than he became the target of taunts and jeers nearly every time he ventured into a public hallway at the State House. Nor did Sundlun seek sympathy. He had turned seventy-one during his first month in office but seized the RISDIC disaster like someone half his age. Lights burned in his corner office long after the rest of the State House had gone dark. Gruff and abrasive, he seemed to harbor no doubts about himself or his mission. Like Roosevelt taking office in the depths of the Depression, Sundlun seemed sure his grit and gumption would triumph.

Early in the crisis, he bulldozed the General Assembly into creating what he called a Depositors Economic Protection Corporation (DEPCO), which few understood.[32] Sundlun exposed himself to blame by chairing DEPCO's board as it seized the assets of credit unions that would never reopen. Depositors whose accounts were still frozen quickly forgot the insider loans and risky practices that had brought the system down as their rallies turned venomous against DEPCO and its creator, Bruce Sundlun.[33]

As weeks stretched into months, Sundlun increasingly became the target of caricature and blame, even though RISDIC had declared itself insolvent before he took the oath of office. After June, when Rhode Island's part-time legislature adjourned and stopped coming to the State House each day, Sundlun became the depositors' primary target.

"I made a mistake," Sundlun told a *Providence Journal* reporter. "I spent too much time encouraging these depositors groups to come up with these plans. We should have moved quicker and said, 'The hell with you.'"

The bitter depositors returned his taunts on talk radio, picketed his house, burned a T-shirt from his campaign, and dumped its ashes on his doorstep. Their placards turned DEPCO into DEATHCO. Images of Sundlun with tiny mustaches like Hitler's were a graphic insult to the state's second Jewish governor. Sundlun admitted his annoyance but told reporters: "It doesn't arouse a feeling in me where I want to strike back at the people who are doing it and hurt them. I've been Jewish all my life, so I've heard that stuff since I was in the schoolyard."[34]

Others attempting to solve the crisis inadvertently fueled the protesters' rage. DEPCO mailed invitations for cocktails and dinner to its staff and the surviving workers at Rhode Island Central Credit Union, whose building the new agency occupied. But a copy of the invitation fell into the hands of Jack Kayrouz, the head of Citizens for Depositors' Rights, and he reviled the party as proof DEPCO was immune to the suffering of the depositors, taxpayers, and the elderly. On a sultry summer night, Kayrouz rallied a crowd of about 250 protestors at DEPCO headquarters in Warwick. Most were elderly; many were veterans wearing American flag pins on their jackets or caps. Yet the crowd crossed the threshold of civil restraint, spilling onto Jefferson Boulevard, a four-lane highway. Cars and trucks screeched to a halt. Horns blared.[35]

"What do we want?" Kayrouz shouted.

"Our money," the crowd roared.

"When do we want it?"

"Now!"

Most in the march had never engaged in civil disobedience, but they surged along Jefferson Boulevard and onto a nearby access road to Interstate 95. "We want our money," they chanted as they tramped along. "We want our money!"

Police cars with sirens and flashing lights converged from all directions. There was no violence, but seven depositors were arrested, five of them over the age of sixty.

Depositors also began picketing Sundlun events. Hundreds protested outside Rhodes-on-the-Pawtuxet, where Sundlun and his political allies were scheduled to hold a black-tie reception for Ron Brown, chair of the Democratic National Committee. A quarter-mile driveway stretched from Broad Street to the hall, and depositors caught Sundlun in his Lincoln with Rhode Island license plate number one. They surrounded the car, pounded on its hood and roof, and splattered its windows with spit.

Sundlun shouted for his driver to stop. Through sheer determination he forced a car door open and stepped out into the hostile crowd. Aides and state troopers ringed the 71-year-old governor as he strode through the throng toward the hall.

Depositors spit at him. "Choke!" yelled one, waving a dollar bill.

"Choke," the crowd shouted. "Choke! Choke!"

6

Dashed Hopes

1991

NEAR THE COMMON CAUSE OFFICE on Smith Street were two Chinese restaurants. Mandarin Garden was plain, quick, and cheap. Little Chopsticks charged more but offered the choice between a glassed-in patio facing the street and secluded booths inside. I met Michael Smith at Chopsticks in a booth at the back. He said he had wondered whether I would agree to meet anyone from the DiPrete administration.

I laughed. "You took me by surprise. Not many DiPrete people call me."

Like his mentor, Smith had deep brown eyes and a broad face. He could have passed for a younger cousin or a nephew. He said most of his former colleagues felt that DiPrete had done nothing worse than previous Rhode Island governors: "They would argue that the rules have changed, that this governor was being held to a higher standard."

"What would they think if they knew you were having lunch with me?"

He chuckled. "They might say I always was an outlier."

Michael Smith had served as DiPrete's policy director and speechwriter. "I believe in campaign finance reform," he said. "I didn't get the issue onto his agenda until the very end. I sometimes drafted speeches calling for campaign reforms, but he struck those parts."

"When did you become aware that DiPrete was steering contracts to campaign contributors?"

"Only when the stories broke in the newspaper," he said. "Even then, I had found it hard to believe. However they pulled it off, they kept it close. I'm one of those Republicans who agree with Teddy Roosevelt that if political contributions are in any way extorted, 'then the giving and receiving becomes not only improper but criminal.'"

"Don't you mean Franklin Roosevelt?"

"I mean Teddy," he said. "In his 1905 State of the Union address, he urged Congress to outlaw corporate contributions. He wanted both Congress and state legislatures to prohibit the use of stockholders' money for political purposes."

I admitted I had never heard that.

"You're not alone. It's rarely taught in schools." He munched his chicken and cashews. "Theodore Roosevelt also called for full reporting of contributions, both to candidates and to political parties. He told Congress the result would be 'wholesome.'"

Smith had kept an eye on the campaign finance reforms Common Cause had pushed without success over several years, and he had urged the governor to participate in the matching-funds program. "The blow-out of spending," he said, "shows how badly Rhode Island needs campaign finance reform."

I mentioned that Rep. Jeffrey Teitz was developing a comprehensive campaign finance bill, interweaving his own ideas with separate bills Common Cause had developed. Teitz aimed to improve the reporting of campaign contributions, end the laundering of contributions through political parties, ban all corporate contributions, and outlaw the personal use of campaign contributions.[1]

"All excellent and much needed," Smith said. "That's part of why I wanted to serve in government. I wish we could have passed campaign finance reforms when I was in the governor's office. Now that the DiPrete administration is history, I'd like to help Common Cause. Call it contrition or penance, I'm ready to help."

From its inception Common Cause had declared itself a "citizens' lobby," constantly pushing for laws and court decisions that would make government more open and accountable. In hopes of drawing attention to our 1991 legislation, that February we scheduled a press conference in Room 313, the mahogany-paneled hearing room used by the Senate Judiciary Committee. Sponsors of our bills sat in a row of senators' seats.

Cathy Speer, our board president, opened the event by announcing that Common Cause had filed an ethics complaint against then-Gov. DiPrete more than two years earlier, but the Ethics Commission had yet to move forward with a full investigation. One of our bills, Speer said, would require the commission to complete its preliminary investigation of a complaint within six months. If commissioners missed that deadline, they would have to dismiss the complaint and explain why.[2] The gag rule, which threatened a $10,000 fine, remained on the books but could not be enforced after Judge Raymond Pettine's 1989 ruling that it was unconstitutional.[3]

I watched for reactions as she broke the news. If any in the hearing room were shocked, they hid it.

Speer segued to other reforms: lifting the secrecy of ethics complaints and removing hefty fines for complainants who might speak to the press. Although

Judge Pettine had enjoined the commission not to enforce the gag rule, it re-mained in the law. Her deep alto timbre communicated more sorrow than indignation. "When the Ethics Commission finally begins an adjudicative hear-ing on our complaint — if it ever does — that will happen behind closed doors, because that's what the law still requires. We think it's time for the public to hear the witnesses and see the evidence in open session."[4]

Legislative sponsors took turns describing the bills they were introducing on behalf of Common Cause.

Rep. Frank Gaschen outlined four. "As Cathy mentioned," he began in a reedy voice, "one would require the speedier finding of probable cause. There's no rea-son for the commission's preliminary investigation to take two years." He never mentioned his 1986 effort to require that Rhode Island credit unions get federal insurance. Thin and with prematurely graying hair, he now seemed prescient, even heroic, as he described his bills. "I wish these had become law last year. I hope they'll fare better amid the RISDIC scandal than they did before it."

Seven other sponsors at microphones took turns explaining their bills. Myrth York, a lawyer and first-year senator from the East Side of Providence, described how lawmakers traded their duty to the public for permanent state jobs. "My revolving door bill would make it illegal for any member of the General Assem-bly to seek or accept any state employment while they serve in the Senate or House and for one year after they leave office. In simple terms, it would stop the revolving door from elective office to a judgeship with a high salary and life tenure."[5]

York was new to the Senate and understood that her bill would enrage leg-islative leaders. A reporter asked if she had any trepidation about filing contro-versial legislation that would probably never pass.

"Why should I be afraid?" she asked. "The voters sent me here to challenge a dysfunctional status quo. And I believe that — sooner or later — this will become law in Rhode Island. I believe we will abolish the revolving door. If we don't start now, when will we start?"

Most of our sponsors had filed similar Common Cause bills in previous years and were ready to try again.

After the event, Scott MacKay, a reporter for the *Providence Journal*, ap-proached me. "So why didn't you go public with this complaint against DiPrete before now?" he asked.

"Some of us would have liked to," I told him, "but we're nonpartisan. We never endorse candidates, and our board didn't want to be seen as politicizing our complaint against DiPrete."[6]

As winter melted into spring Rep. Bob Bianchini seemed ever more isolated. After years at the epicenter of political power, he had become a pariah. He walked alone from committee hearings and sat alone at his desk on the House floor before the gavel came down. Whatever they felt about his responsibility for RISDIC, other lawmakers and lobbyists kept their distance, at least in public.

Bianchini bumped into me in a doorway. "I'd like to have breakfast with you," he said, as if he were expecting me. I knew him only superficially; we had met several times and shaken hands after a hearing. I brushed him off, and a few weeks later, I put him off again. The third time, he caught up with me in the dimly lit hallway outside the House Finance Committee's basement hearing room. "So can we get together?" he asked again. "I'd like you to hear my perspective."

We finally met on a May morning for coffee and bagels at a secluded shop he suggested in Richmond Square. I wondered if his hair had grayed in the course of the spring or if I had never noticed before. His goatee was perfectly trimmed.

"I appreciate your coming," he said. "I wanted you to hear my side of this." He had a folder full of photographs and news clippings that went back to the 1960s. In one glossy print, he stood in the doorway of a storefront credit union with several other men. Their hair and sideburns were full, their expressions confident. He described them and their movement. "We were frustrated with the commercial banks and red-lining," Bianchini said, referring to the reluctance of traditional lenders to invest in inner-city properties. "We knew there had to be some way of getting money into the hands of blue-collar people who hadn't inherited. We knew that given half a chance, most of them would pay it back."

Bianchini and I were about the same age and, if I could believe him, we had shared the same idealism a quarter of a century before. He had set out in practical ways to build the institutions that would help the poor and working class to earn their own way.

"So where did it go wrong?" I asked.

His brow furrowed. "I've asked myself that, and I'm not sure. We thought we were creating a system that was unique and specific to Rhode Island. We built a deposit insurance system that worked really well for years. We intended to protect the little guy. And in the end, I don't think people will lose their money."

I asked why RISDIC kept running TV ads that showed its seal chiseled out of granite, emphasizing its enduring stability.

"That wasn't false," he said. "We never deceived anybody. Our insurance protected all of the individual institutions. Even Joe Mollicone's abuses could have been covered."

At some point, however, Bob Bianchini had started shaping laws to gain an advantage for RISDIC. Was he a noble character who started with good intentions? Had he blinded himself to the risks RISDIC posed? And I was even more perplexed over the larger question: how had Rhode Island's government allowed so many conflicts of interest to flourish for so long and do such great damage?

I later learned that Bianchini had represented the House speaker on Rhode

Island's Unclassified Pay Plan Board, which set salaries for bank regulators. No wonder they failed to blow the whistle on RISDIC.

Amid the never-ending cascade of revelations about the RISDIC debacle, one tenacious reporter caused a spectacular splash by holding Rhode Island's new governor to a campaign promise. During a candidate forum the previous fall, the *Providence Journal's* Katherine Gregg asked Sundlun about opening up the state's sealed pension records.

He replied unequivocally: "Public pensions are publicly funded for public employees with taxpayers' dollars. Clearly, they should be public records."[7]

In January of 1991, when nearly everyone was absorbed in the RISDIC collapse, Gregg reminded the new governor of his campaign pledge and Sundlun launched his push to open the records. He directed his staff to unseal the pension records of current or former government officials who had used special pension bills to purchase pension credits at less than full actuarial cost.

The Rhode Island Federation of Teachers, whose union leaders had gamed the system, sent their lawyers racing to Superior Court for an injunction to stop Sundlun's disclosure. Superior Court Judge Robert D. Krause issued a temporary restraining order and scheduled a hearing on the merits of the case. General Treasurer Anthony Solomon, who chaired the State Retirement Board, sided with the unions and blocked the release of pension-related documents.

One January day early in this legal drama, Gregg and her colleague Bruce Landis took a fateful walk from the *Providence Journal* headquarters across Fountain Street to the office where the State Retirement Board had just moved and was still getting settled. Amid the chaos Gregg and Landis confronted Solomon's press secretary, Frank Prosnitz, who gave his reasons why the records would remain sealed despite the governor's order. While they were arguing, Gregg noticed a thick computer printout in a green wastebasket by Prosnitz's desk. Instinctively, she reached down and pulled it out. "What's this?" she exclaimed, clutching it tightly. In her possession was a list of sixteen thousand pension checks issued that month.[8]

The press secretary, a former reporter, protested but did not try to wrestle the discarded document away from her. Along with him, the two reporters struck out all Social Security numbers; they then carried their trove of data back to the newsroom. For years, Gregg had been reporting on special pension bills that routinely passed in the last hours of each legislative session, teasing out vital details from arcane legislative language. Now she could attach names and precise amounts from the discarded printout.

While the union, Sundlun, and the *Providence Journal* honed their legal arguments, Gregg wrote about the ugly underside of what she called "a pension system gone awry." The newspaper published her series, "Set for Life — Special Deals," as a barrage of twelve blockbuster stories that ran in swift succession from March 31 to April 3, far too quickly for those whose cover she blew to sue the paper. She listed insiders who had bought pension credits at fire sale prices. Most had relied on special bills that allowed them credits for years on the payrolls of unions, private companies, and even governments in other states.[9]

Former Sen. William O'Neill admitted to Gregg that some special pension bills were legitimate but others were "kind of pukey." He added: "They get passed when everyone is tired, half asleep, drinking Diet Coke at 3 a.m. That's how it happens." Moreover, "every year it seems to get worse and worse. Even the good people begin to think this is the way it works. There's nothing wrong with it. The fund is capable of handling it."

Favored insiders had received legal permission to buy pension credits at a small fraction of what ordinary state workers had to pay. One University of Rhode Island professor bought credits for six years at an Ohio school, paying only $2,020 for benefits that would have cost $72,521 if he had paid the real actuarial cost. Another bill had allowed Richard Blaine, a retired House Minority Leader who now sat on the Ethics Commission, to buy credit for two years on the Scituate zoning board. Those credits made him eligible for a lifelong legislative pension of just over $12,000 per year, which grew with a cost-of-living escalator.

Gregg noted that these special pension bills hit their peak in 1987, when 834 workers paid just under $2.2 million for pension credits that would cost taxpayers $39.9 million through the year 2016. For example, a University of Rhode Island baseball player from the 1950s who went on to a career in state government enriched his retirement with the help of a special bill that allowed him to buy pension credits for part-time work at the college gym. His special deal added $1,399 a year to the $30,780 pension he earned during his professional career. "I found out that other guys had done it," the former athlete told Gregg. "Those jobs we had at URI, they were state time."[10]

Gregg also reported that Donald McKiernan, the Senate's fiscal advisor and an expert on state pensions, had retired at age 50 with three pensions: one for $48,609 and two totaling over $62,000 that would kick in when he turned fifty-five. McKiernan was a former teacher, Providence City Councilman, and city treasurer in Warwick and Providence. By paying $678.70 for 18 months of credit, McKiernan boosted his pension by $2,691 per year for life. "They didn't do that just for me, believe me," McKiernan told Gregg. "I wasn't the only one who bought that time."[11]

Gregg's "Set for Life" series reminded readers already furious over RISDIC how costly corruption could be. She pointed out a $1.1 billion discrepancy between the funding stream and the soaring obligations to retirees.[12]

Lawmakers scrambled to file legislation that would open pension records for public review. Bills filed by Rep. Jeff Teitz in the House and Sen. John Bevilacqua in the Senate proposed to open state pension records, including the purchase of retirement credits.[13] Language in the bills ensured public access to employees' salaries, fringe benefits, overtime, and job descriptions. Even as I testified in support of these bills, however, I found it hard to believe they would ever pass. One reporter's investigative stories had removed the cover of a cesspool that many had thought would never see the light of day, but would her disclosures end Rhode Island government's culture of deep-rooted secrecy?

On April 24, 1991, Judge Robert D. Krause issued a landmark ruling on the teachers' union suit that had aimed to keep pension records confidential. Krause flatly rejected the union's claim that the Access to Public Records Law created a "substantive right of privacy" or that the plaintiffs could use the law to deny access to records of wrongdoing. In what seemed a trumpet call for change, the judge wrote that the recipients of such uncommon benefits had no privacy interest "which would in any manner outweigh the citizenry's predominant interest in knowing how its public fisc is being administered, and whether it is being administered in evenhanded fashion." Then he added, "If ever a court were justified in reading a statute, not narrowly as through a keyhole, but in the broad light of its intended purpose, it is here."[14]

Pawtucket Mayor Brian J. Sarault always struck me as a man made for politics. Throughout the spring of 1991, he appeared often at the State House. Among lobbyists and lawmakers in a crowded hallway, he stood out — taller than most, broad across the shoulders, handsomely telegenic, impeccably dressed. His booming baritone rose above the din. Sarault sought passage of legislation to allow off-track betting parlors. Narragansett Park, Pawtucket's once-glorious track where Seabiscuit, Whirlaway, and War Admiral had galloped long ago, had fallen on hard times and closed in 1978, and Sarault needed new gambling revenues. He promised the state a share of any OTB take from television simulcasts of races in other venues. On June 3, he announced to a crowd of cheering supporters that he would run for a third term as mayor of Pawtucket, fighting for reform under the motto "Progress, not politics."[15]

Nine days later FBI agents arrested Sarault in his office on charges of extortion. Rep. Robert A. Weygand of East Providence made his living as a landscape architect. As the story emerged, the mayor had called Weygand to his office at Pawtucket City Hall and offered a deal. Weygand would bill an extra $5,000 on a contract for Slater Park, kick back $3,000 in cash to Sarault, and keep $2,000.

Weygand hid his shock, told Sarault he would be in touch, and left.[16] As he drove from Sarault's office, Weygand dictated the details into a microcassette recorder before they faded from memory. He told his wife, then went to his friend and mentor, Sen. James P. McStay of East Providence. They contacted the state police and then the FBI, whose agents prepared to snare Sarault.

Trembling, Weygand returned to Pawtucket City Hall with an envelope full of marked bills. He wore a pager that concealed a tiny transmitter; a recorder was taped inside his thigh. FBI agents warned that Sarault might casually stroke his back to check for a wire. From a van outside agents listened to the conversation and heard Weygand pass the envelope. As Sarault walked the young architect toward the door, he threw an arm across Weygand's shoulder and ran it down his spine.[17]

Weygand escaped down the broad stairs, just as two FBI agents strode up to the mayor's office. They found Weygand's envelope in a wastebasket and the cash in Sarault's pocket. They arrested the mayor and drove him to the massive gray federal courthouse in Providence for arraignment on three felony charges.[18]

Sarault's lawyer denounced the charges as nothing more than allegations, but the mayor's arrest shocked Rhode Island, reinforcing the public's sense of widespread corruption. Five months later, Sarault would admit to racketeering in fifteen extortion schemes. His kickback routine had corrupted a half-dozen city departments. Pawtucket's suave mayor would eventually plead guilty, go to federal prison for five years, and be required to pay $80,829 in restitution.[19]

But his plea and punishment lay months in the future as the General Assembly lumbered slowly toward adjournment in June 1991. Despite the ongoing RISDIC scandal and Sarault's arrest, only a handful of anti-corruption bills seemed to have any chance of passage. Meanwhile Katherine Gregg's "Set for Life" exposé had led to court decisions on pension records. Superior Court Judge Robert D. Krause had ruled in April that public employee unions lacked standing to block Sundlun's move to open the pension records, and in May the Rhode Island Supreme Court declared in a three-paragraph order that the unions had no standing to challenge Sundlun's order.[20] On May 28, Sundlun ordered more than 49,000 pension records opened to the public, the first such disclosure since the retirement system was created in 1936.[21]

With disclosure virtually inevitable, General Assembly leaders knew they must pass something, but what? Competing versions of an open records bill had been inching forward all spring. Senate Majority Leader John Bevilacqua had sponsored legislation that was encumbered by a provision requiring a costly notice by certified mail to anyone whose records were requested. House Judiciary Chairman Jeff Teitz had filed a bill that preserved the confidentiality of most current pensions and would have released data only for future retirements.[22] In the final hours, both chambers passed a compromise bill that preserved the confidentiality of medical records, student records, and individual job evaluations, but it allowed public access to the names, salaries, fringe and pension benefits, and similar data.[23] Hundreds of supposedly respectable public servants had been padding pensions for themselves and their cronies. Almost single-handedly, Katherine Gregg forced a change in the state's Access to Public Records Law.

The question remained whether the General Assembly would finally pass other needed reforms.

To my surprise, our legislation to establish a time limit for Ethics Commission investigations began moving. Under the bill, the filing of a complaint would start a stopwatch for an initial inquiry: would these allegations constitute a violation of the ethics law? Under our legislation, the commission would have to decide on probable cause or dismiss the complaint within 300 days.[24] Our bill took flight in the last hours of the session, on its way to becoming law, but all the rest seemed stuck.

Amid everything else he was doing, Rep. Jeff Teitz had woven together a comprehensive campaign finance reform bill from his own ideas and a half dozen separate bills that Common Cause had developed over several years. His legislation aimed to improve the reporting of campaign contributions, end the laundering of contributions through political parties, ban all corporate contributions, and outlaw the personal use of campaign contributions.[25] He explained the details to members of his House Judiciary Committee, and they passed his bill on May 30, 1991.[26] To my delight, Gov. Sundlun declared his support, and the entire House passed it a few days later, as lobbyists speculated about when the session would finally end.

Senate Judiciary Chairman Thomas A. Lynch listened to my plea for a hearing and vote on Teitz's bill. Lynch was tall, had chiseled features, and watched me with expressive eyes. "I'll look at it," he said agreeably, "but it's late in the session, and I'm not making any promises."

"Anything to do with the sponsor?" I asked.

We both knew that Senate Majority Leader John Bevilacqua resented Teitz for leading the 1986 impeachment inquiry against his father, Chief Justice Joseph A. Bevilacqua, who had resigned under a cloud and died a few years later. "Don't go there," Lynch warned. "I've cleared your ethics bills for hearing. More than that I can't promise."

Good to his word, Lynch led the Senate Judiciary as it approved two ethics reforms drafted by Rae Condon. Lynch had sponsored one for the speedier finding of probable cause.[27] He reminded his committee that Common Cause had filed an ethics complaint against former Gov. DiPrete. "Twenty-nine months without a simple finding of probable cause," Lynch declared, "is too long. My bill requires them to reach probable cause in a year. If they can't do that, let them dismiss it and explain to the public."

With Lynch's push, the Senate Judiciary Committee seemed on a roll. They approved his bill and two more Common Cause bills in quick succession. One would establish a stringent new standard for public officials who had routinely represented private clients before their own boards. It prohibited self-representation except in cases of hardship, and only then after consultation with the Ethics Commission.[28] A second, filed by freshman Sen. Walter Gray, dramatically expanded the ban on nepotism.[29] Lynch's committee also recommended a bill by Jeff Teitz that would require state vendors to file reports on their campaign contributions to state general officers.[30]

Sitting among lobbyists under a colonial portrait in the committee's wood-paneled hearing room, I wanted to cheer.

Despite the scandals of RISDIC and public knowledge of insiders' pension padding, most of our bills simply died. Our revolving door bill aimed to stop members of the General Assembly from seeking or accepting state employment during their time in office. I could not get a vote in either judiciary committee.[31]

On what would clearly be the last night of the session, Sen. J. Michael Lenihan asked me if Common Cause would favor a parliamentary maneuver that might win passage of Teitz's Comprehensive Campaign Finance Reform. Lenihan had played on Brown University's football team, and he offered a gridiron choice. "It's beyond hopeless," he said. "Either we try a Hail Mary, or we come back next year and start over."

"Hail Mary?" I asked. I knew what that meant in football but not in the State House.

"Lynch will bring the State Vendors' Disclosure bill to the floor," Lenihan said. "We could prepare a floor amendment that would incorporate the entire Comprehensive Campaign Finance Reform bill."

"Won't one of the lawyers downstairs tip Bevilacqua and give him time to rally his troops?"

Lenihan smiled mischievously. "We can draft the amendment and make copies ourselves. We think Bevilacqua's people have Teitz's state vendors' disclosure bill tagged for a trade against one of their bills being held hostage in the House. It may be one of the last bills considered, probably after one o'clock in the morning. By then, some of Bevilacqua's troops may have gone home or be off the floor."

Midnight passed, then one o'clock and two. With Lt. Gov. Roger N. Begin presiding, the Senate dragged through its calendar. Most bills passed by routine majorities with little debate. After each final vote, senators dumped the mostly unread papers between their desks. Finally, Lynch presented Teitz's House bill on political contributions by state vendors.[32] From the majority leader's seat on the center aisle, John Bevilacqua moved passage. A second came automatically from the majority whip.

In the instant before the lieutenant governor could call for a vote, David Carlin, the former Senate majority leader, rose. "Mr. President, I have an amendment."

Several senators shouted, "Second!"

Senate pages with glazed eyes began distributing copies of the amendment along the curved rows of desks.

I took a hasty head count. More than a dozen of the fifty seats were empty. Bevilacqua might lack the votes to block Carlin's amendment. The stunt seemed to be working.

Carlin explained the amendment. A sociology professor, he was a Don Quix-ote figure, full of idealism and whimsy. He had served briefly as Senate majority leader before Bevilacqua's *realpolitik* toppled him. Carlin was a conservative Catholic and Teitz was Jewish, but their Newport districts overlapped, and they often backed each other. Carlin spoke passionately about why it was crucial to fix Rhode Island's broken campaign finance system without delay.

"Mr. President," Lynch interrupted, waving the copy he had just received, "I move to table this amendment. This is a large and complicated piece of legisla-tion. It looks superficially like a bill that came over from the House very recently, but the Judiciary Committee hasn't had time for a hearing on it, and I'm not even sure what this is."

"I second that," Bevilacqua roared from his seat.

"Mr. President," Carlin shouted, "this is identical to the Campaign Finance Reform bill that the House passed and that has been amply described in the newspapers."

From the rostrum, Begin declared that a motion to table was not debatable. He pounded the gavel. "Clerk will unlock the machine. Please cast your votes. To table: press green. To continue with the matter before us, vote red."

Everyone was exhausted, but green and red lights blinked on the electronic board beside the columns of senators' names. Sixteen were green to table, but twenty-one shone red. Lynch's motion failed. The seats of key Bevilacqua backers were empty. Debate would continue. For an instant, I believed we had won.

"On Sen. Carlin's motion to amend." The lieutenant governor paused. "Are you ready to vote? Vote green to amend. Vote red to defeat the Carlin amendment."

Red and green lights flickered on, the tally computed instantly above the bill number. Green lights were 24, only 17 red.

Teitz's massive reform was poised to go. The Senate would cast a final vote. Then the amended bill, now slightly different from what had passed the House, would be hand-carried back across the rotunda for final passage.

Lynch was on his feet. "Mr. President, I move passage of the amended bill."

Seconds boomed all around the domed chamber.

In a momentary pause, I heard voices in the rotunda. I looked across into the House. Members were shaking hands in the aisle. Many were heading for the elevator or streaming down the broad marble stairway. The House had just adjourned.

"Wait!" I wanted to shout. "Come back! You need to vote on campaign fi-nance reform!"

"Moved by Sen. Lynch and seconded by Sen. Marciano," the lieutenant gov-ernor called. "Please cast your votes. Yeas, green. Nays, red."

Green lights flooded the tote board, and Begin banged the gavel. Teitz's Campaign Finance bill had passed an instant too late.

I raced into the rotunda and around to the House door with a heavy sense that the House could not be called back. The House and Senate had approved slightly different versions. Neither had passed both chambers, and neither would become law. Had we been tricked?

7

New Beginnings

1991

AFTER THE RISDIC DISASTER and a bitter 1991 legislative session, fragile signs of change began to sprout. Three shoots emerged, each independent of the others, promising yet vulnerable.

The first revealed key RISDIC players. During the tumultuous session, Rep. Jeffrey J. Teitz and his special investigators, Alan I. Baron and John W. Nields Jr., had subpoenaed testimony and deposed insiders behind closed doors in the new administration building, across Smith Street from the State House. Shielded by their lawyers, brushing past reporters into the guarded room, most spent an hour or more testifying. Others emerged only moments after they entered, a clear sign they had invoked their Fifth Amendment right to remain silent.[1] Details remained under wraps.

In July, sunlight burned through the fog of secrecy as the RISDIC Investigating Commission announced televised public hearings. Cable TV subscribers could watch from their living rooms.

I went to the State House, crossing the lawn toward basement doors, my usual shortcut. For the first time I could remember, I found those doors locked. I walked around the broad marble pedestal and up a flight of stairs to the main entrance. Inside, there were still no security scanners, but yellow police tapes and police officers blocked my way. I smiled and said I was going to the RISDIC hearing in Room 35.

"That's closed to the public," an officer told me. He directed me upstairs to a room where depositors occupied seats near a large TV monitor that glowed blue. Through six months of bitter threats, I had seen frightening lapses of security at the State House. Now, the tight police presence was comforting but inconvenient.[2]

The blue screen flickered to life. After preliminaries, Special Counsel Alan Baron opened the hearing by reading from minutes of the RISDIC board's meeting on December 10, 1990. Eerily, the insurer's president, Peter A. Nevola, warned that if word of RISDIC's plight got out there would be "one hell of a crisis in this state." Nevola urged board members to keep putting out the word that RISDIC could fulfill its responsibilities. Baron hammered Nevola's duplicity: "I submit that this statement crystallizes what being an insider is all about. To know what the real facts are, to refrain from disclosing those facts to the public, indeed, to lull the public into a false sense that all is well."

The first witness was Sen. John F. Correia, the president *pro tem* of the state Senate. He had been a vice president at the East Providence Credit Union when RISDIC crashed. With white hair above an unlined face, Correia looked like a successful banker in his tailored suit, starched shirt, and finely patterned tie. On screen, he was suave and did not seem at all nervous. Records from his failed credit union showed that in the days after Nevola's dire warning, Correia began making trips to its gleaming modern headquarters. He arrived unobtrusively, went to different tellers, and quietly withdrew money from his business and personal accounts, $210,000 in all. To cash out certificates of deposit prematurely, he paid early withdrawal penalties of $750. He opened accounts at a commercial bank insured by the FDIC.

"Senator," Baron asked Correia, "I want to ask about the $150,000 that you moved from East Providence to Shawmut Bank on December 28. How do you reconcile the transfers of the monies that we have been talking about with your statement on January 6, when you denied taking your money out?"

Baron had used the term "withdrawal," and Correia quibbled. He said he was not as sophisticated as Baron. "What I was doing was transactions, not withdrawing money."[3]

"You didn't regard that taking out, that transferring of money as a withdrawal from the institution?"

"No," the senator replied.

"Why is that not a withdrawal from the institution? I'm not sure I can follow."

Correia frowned. "Because the way I look at it, it's transactions that I made. Transactions, not withdrawals. Withdrawing to me is going to the bank and they give me the money and I put it in my pocket and go home."[4]

Viewers around me watching the public monitor guffawed at the senator's attempt to twist words. Several cursed him.

Still on the screen, Correia defended his actions. "At all times, my actions were motivated by my duties as a director," he said. "Any suggestion to the contrary is wrong."

Other stories were similar. RISDIC's long-time attorney, V. James Santaniello, had pulled $120,000 out of RISDIC institutions during the two weeks before they closed. During his time under the television lights, Santaniello testified: "My intent was never to gain an advantage over other depositors."[5] Records showed that John R. Lanfredi, the treasurer of RISDIC and president of the Rhode Island Central Credit Union, had also pulled more than $300,000 from his credit union. To cash out certificates of deposit, Lanfredi paid $11,700 in early withdrawal penalties.

Lanfredi approached the witness table with his lawyer. During the closed-door depositions he had invoked the Fifth Amendment. Now he was on television. Special Counsel John W. Nields quickly asked a double question: Had Lanfredi withdrawn $284,000 from Rhode Island Central on December 21, 1991? And if so, why?

"On advice of counsel," Lanfredi answered blandly, "I respectfully exercise my rights against self-incrimination on both the Rhode Island and U.S. constitutions and decline to answer the question."[6]

Not content to let it go, commission member Rep. Frank Gaschen, whose 1986 bill would have required federal credit union insurance, asked Lanfredi whether any of that money was now going to pay his lawyer. Lanfredi again claimed his constitutional right not to incriminate himself. One reporter noted that nearly every time Lanfredi invoked the Fifth Amendment, his tongue darted nervously. His television debut lasted less than five minutes but left an indelible impression.[7]

After airtight security for the first session, authorities eased up on a steamy July night when the primary witness would be Rep. Robert V. Bianchini. Capitol police shuffled spectators through metal detectors and directed us to Room 35, a bare-brick basement hearing room equipped as a studio. As I came from the sultry night, air-conditioning made me catch my breath. Hostile depositors quickly filled ranks of black chairs between bared brick walls. The nine-member RISDIC Investigating Commission filed in from a back hallway and took seats in front of a blue drape.

When Rep. Robert V. Bianchini entered the room where he had often presided, depositors booed him. The wan look that had marked him through the spring had given way to a summer tan. Documents showed that Bianchini, as president of the Rhode Island Credit Union League (RICUL), had pumped $20 million into Rhode Island Central Credit Union as it tried to satisfy worried depositors demanding their money. In the witness chair he faced the commission; the audience behind him saw his face on wall-mounted monitors.

Special counsel John Nields reminded Bianchini that Rhode Island Central had run out of cash in December 1991. Had RICUL loaned the credit union money?

"They had a liquidity problem," Bianchini answered, calmly. "They were accessing their line of credit."

"In effect, you were lending them money?"

"That's correct." Bianchini's eyes were large and limpid.

"Significant amounts?" Nields asked. "In the millions?"

Bianchini assented, as if that were obvious.

Nields asked Bianchini whether he had had any doubts about whether RISDIC would be able to keep functioning as a viable insurer.

"I did. Yes, sir."

Nields pressed Bianchini about whether he had known that examiners from the National Credit Union Administration were checking the books at Rhode Island Central. Bianchini said he had thought the national examiners were examining all of the RISDIC-insured institutions. "Are you saying that in your job at RICUL you made absolutely no effort to find out how their examination was coming? What the results were?"

"The National Credit Union Administration didn't share that information," Bianchini said, "and wouldn't share it until the first week in January."

"That's not quite my question. Did you make any efforts whatsoever to find out from Rhode Island Central how the NCUA exam had gone?"

"I do not recall doing that." Bianchini added that his duty was to protect RICUL's interest with enough collateral, which he had done.

"Are you saying that as you continued to loan increasing amounts of money to Rhode Island Central during this period of time that it didn't matter to you at all how the NCUA exam had gone?"

"It mattered, as it did to every other credit union in the state."

"Did you make inquiries?" Nields asked.

"About that specific exam? No, we didn't."[8]

Bianchini had doled out millions to shore up the tottering giant. He stuck to his story: he had believed in December that the loan would help and that the state would never let RISDIC fail.

Then Nields switched to the subject of loans. Records showed that while Bianchini was pumping RICUL money into Rhode Island Central, he had borrowed $85,000 from the same institution and deposited it in his mother's checking account in a federally-insured bank.[9]

For nearly four hours, Bianchini sparred with Nields over the facts and how to interpret them. Under pressure, he held his own. The fact that he came without a lawyer and testified with passion made for gripping theater. Bianchini seemed confident that he had done no wrong.

I left the State House deeply perplexed about Bob Bianchini's story. Though he had a blatant conflict of interest, he led the way in killing Gaschen's 1986 bill to require federal credit union insurance. The ethics complaint against him had fallen one short of the five votes necessary to find a violation. Would a violation and fine in 1987 have changed his course? Had he done anything to fix the system he had helped create? Had he thought he would never have to pay off the $85,000 he borrowed from Central? How true was the story he told me over breakfast? Finally, why had he not hidden behind the Fifth Amendment, as several others had? For all the grievous mistakes he had made, Bianchini seemed certain that a different kind of intervention by Sundlun might have averted RISDIC's collapse.[10] How could he sound so sure of himself?

RISDIC's president, Peter A. Nevola, was far less transparent under the television lights. He had apparently told his wife and mother-in-law about RISDIC's likely failure. Records showed that in the days before the collapse they emptied their accounts and moved their money to FDIC-insured banks. During what turned out to be the last meeting of the RISDIC board, Peter Nevola had suffered severe chest pains. Other board members wanted to call an ambulance, but Nevola refused. He gulped medicine prescribed for his heart condition and returned to his seat at the head of the RISDIC table. Afterwards, he drove to the Providence Teachers' Credit Union and withdrew $50,416 to pay off a loan. He then asked for $13,000 in cash from another account. When told he had to complete an IRS form for cash withdrawals over $3,000, Nevola took $2,900 in cash and a $10,000 check.[11]

Under oath and on television before the RISDIC Commission, Nevola, his wife, and his mother-in-law refused to answer and claimed their constitutional right not to incriminate themselves twenty-seven times. Rep. David Dumas, a Republican member of the panel, spoke later with reporter Mike Stanton. "I should think they would know better," Dumas said. "Once you start a paper trail, you can't undo it. If you start to fudge it, the fudge appears."

Seven months after the collapse, there was plenty of fudge. No one knew whether DEPCO could "make whole" thousands of depositors who still found themselves frozen out of an estimated $1.16 billion in thirteen RISDIC institutions that would never reopen.[12] The public's bitterness swelled against the cast of RISDIC insiders who had cashed out before their system crashed.

Another hope sprouted in July 1991. I was not expecting much when I went to meet the new executive minister of the Rhode Island State Council of Churches, an interfaith alliance that represented broad swaths of Protestant and Orthodox congregations. In the three years since Anne and I had settled in Rhode Island, the council's pronouncements had struck me as predictably bland.

The new head of the ecumenical group greeted me with a soft West Virginia lilt in his voice. "I'm Jim Miller," he said. "Believe it or not, you're my very first appointment."

Miller was an American Baptist, the branch of Baptists that trace their lineage to Roger Williams and regard the First Baptist Church in America in Providence as their founding congregation. He had served a large congregation in Rochester, New York, where executives from Kodak and Xerox sat on the church board and supported ministries with street people.

A stack of newspapers lay on his desk. He had visited Rhode Island at intervals during the spring and had been reading about the RISDIC scandal in the *Providence Journal.* "What gets me in the gut," Miller said, "is how deeply people feel betrayed. They blame everyone in public office, but they seem to be scapegoating Bruce Sundlun for declaring his 'bank holiday.'" He tamped his pipe but did not light it. "I give this governor credit for making the best of a terrible mess."

I told him that, for all the rage people were expressing over RISDIC, little had actually changed at the General Assembly.

"Were the churches any help?" he asked.

"No. But things happened so fast. We never really asked for their support."

Miller smiled. "Is it worth trying to build a coalition that could put real pressure on the General Assembly next spring? The preacher in me senses that we need some old-fashioned repentance. Elected officials need to repent for what they've done wrong and for what they've let their cronies do. And people outside the State House need to repent for tolerating so much corruption for so long. If you'll permit me a West Virginia turn of phrase: Unless everyone repents for running the state into a ditch, we'll never drag it up onto the road again."

A few weeks later, the setting August sun cast a bright glow above the suburban office park headquarters of the Northern Rhode Island Chamber of Commerce. When I found the right room, Jim Miller was already there, seated alone at a polished conference table. As organizational leaders straggled in, he moved among them, shaking hands and connecting one by one. Herbert Hansen, who headed the Northern Rhode Island Chamber, welcomed us. He suggested that we introduce ourselves around the table and share what we hoped a coalition might accomplish.

Jim Hagan led the Greater Providence Chamber of Commerce. He explained why their priority was four-year terms for governors. Rhode Island had one of the weakest governorships in the country — only two other states still elected statewide officials for two-year terms. "That hurts us," Hagan said. "I served in the General Assembly, and I've worked with governors — both Republicans and Democrats — Chafee, Licht, Noel, Garrahy, DiPrete, and now Sundlun."

"So," came a question, "how old does that make you?"

"Old enough," Hagan quipped, "to know that this is about more than personalities. Every governor had strengths and weaknesses. Some were better executives than others. But from inauguration day on, every single one of them had to start thinking about running for re-election the next year. A two-year term meant no long-term initiatives, little chance to engage the legislature over big issues. Four-year terms would change Rhode Island."

John Gregory introduced himself as Hagan's associate. He had the build of a wrestler but spoke softly, adding to what Hagan had said. "No executive can hire quality subordinates if he can only promise two years. Who would relocate here?"

Gary Sasse was director of the Rhode Island Public Expenditure Council (RIPEC), a business-backed think tank. He suggested that RISDIC gave us a brief window of opportunity to make dramatic improvements in government structure. He said RIPEC wanted both a stronger executive and a more accountable legislature. "We'd like to see four-year terms and significant ethics reforms," he said. "Nothing will matter unless we can restore trust in elected officials."

"I'm new to Rhode Island," said Jim Miller, almost exaggerating his Appalachian twang. "Our denominational leaders tell me their people are sick of the insider dealing that brought us RISDIC. They may not know exactly what new laws will stop the dirty dealing, but they want to push back against corruption in high places."

Next Curt Spalding introduced himself as director of Save the Bay, the state's largest environmental organization. In his late thirties, Spalding was the youngest person at the table. Unlike those in summer suits, he wore a faded knit pullover. "We agree about four-year terms for governor," he said. "No matter who gets elected, there's always political pressure to relax environmental rules for insiders. Just like with lax supervision of credit unions, when you have weak enforcement of environmental rules it's only a matter of time before catastrophe strikes."

Suzette Gephard was president of the League of Women Voters. She said her members were disturbed that the General Assembly went home without addressing the root causes of RISDIC. "Ethics and campaign finance reforms are high priorities for us," she said. "I would like both in a platform that we could report back to our members."

"Same for us," said John Gregory. He described an all-day retreat the chambers would have in September. "They'll insist on seeing a specific platform."

I wondered if the diverse organizations that these leaders represented could agree on a platform. I outlined legislative proposals that Common Cause had promoted over the years without success, hoping that they might embrace parts of our agenda. Over the course of several summer evening meetings, a consensus formed around a three-part platform: stronger ethics laws, effective campaign finance reforms, and a constitutional amendment establishing four-year terms for statewide general officers. We began thinking in terms of a three-legged stool that could provide firm seating even on rough ground.

Our embryonic coalition still had no name, and we struggled over who would lead it. Everyone liked Jim Miller, but he was new to Rhode Island, and no one thought a Baptist preacher could lead the charge in the most heavily Catholic state. Business interests were clearly not ready for Common Cause to lead, and grassroots groups seemed skittish about lining up behind the chambers of commerce.

After an August meeting that made progress on a platform but not on the question of leadership, Marcel Valois, director of the Blackstone Valley

Development Foundation, drew several of us into his office. "I know who could make this go," Valois said. "Why don't you talk with Alan Hassenfeld?"

Hassenfeld was the president and CEO of the Hasbro toy company, which had its world headquarters in Pawtucket and was one of Rhode Island's largest employers. I had never met him and asked if he cared about ethics reform.

"Very much," Valois replied. "At a recent luncheon, Alan lamented the sorry state of Rhode Island. He hinted — pretty directly — that Hasbro might move out of state. That got everyone's attention."

Alan Hassenfeld was the grandson of Henry Hassenfeld, an immigrant from Poland, who started a small business in 1923 with his brothers, Hilal and Herman. The three Hassenfeld brothers bought remnants from clothing factories and used the fabric to cover children's pencil boxes. First incorporated as Hassenfeld Brothers, they sold school supplies and toys from a shop on Broad Street in Providence. Over the next sixty years, the brothers and their descendants created a worldwide business. They condensed "Hassenfeld Brothers" into a single word and named their organization "Hasbro."

I met Alan Hassenfeld for the first time in Pawtucket when several of us from the fledgling coalition went to his office at Hasbro headquarters. Mr. Potato Head waved across the room while G.I. Joe figures scrambled along a windowsill. Bright blocks filled several bookshelves. A table held specialty versions of Monopoly.

"I'm embarrassed to be from Rhode Island," Hassenfeld confessed. "When I'm in New York or Los Angeles or London, people ask why our little state has such terrible corruption. They can't believe we keep our company here." With unruly hair, an engaging grin, sleeves rolled up, and rubber bands around his wrists, Alan Hassenfeld shattered my stereotype of a corporate mogul.

"When I talked to people from the legislature," he went on, "one senator actually told me that people will eventually see that they've done a pretty good job of running Rhode Island. I wanted to start screaming: 'If you've done a pretty good job, why is our state in such a god-awful mess? Are you really that blind?'"

Hassenfeld agreed to lead the coalition, which still had no final platform and no name, and asked me to serve as his vice chair. He invited the nascent coalition to Hasbro for coffee and chocolate chip cookies around his boardroom table. For all the seriousness of what we were doing, he remained impishly playful, with a gift for affirming people and making them laugh. "I want Jim Miller to be our spiritual adviser," he said wryly. "We need to bring in the Catholic Church, and if anybody can win over Bishop Gelineau, it will be Jim."

As we zeroed in on the question of a name for the coalition, David Duffy, a well-known advertising executive, arrived one afternoon with foam core boards wrapped in brown paper. "If Alan will forgive me," Duffy said, "we've toyed with a few concepts." He waited out the groans. "We think the logo has to be simple enough to fit on a button or a bumper sticker." He held up a board that held the sketch of a round political pin. At the top was a bold, blue RI, printed backwards. Below it, in smaller black letters, was a slogan: *Let's turn it around.*

Several people said it was clever, but no one seemed enthused. Next, Duffy unwrapped another with bold letters: *New Hope Rhode Island.* It echoed the state's one-word motto, "Hope," but the slogan rang no bells. Duffy patiently took several questions and comments, smiling.

"Okay," he said. "Let's try this." His next board showed a white button with three words in bold block capitals: **MAKE IT RIGHT**. The letters were black, except for the RI in RIGHT. Those two letters, the state's initials, were in bold blue.

I heard relief around the table. This would work.

"I like the 'RI' in blue," said Suzette Gephard. "It's vivid, even fearless." Others agreed.

Duffy asked us to look at one more idea. Without a word, he slid the last board out of its brown paper wrapper and held it up. It had two words. In a white field at the top, a bold RIGHT with RI in bright blue rested above a black field that held an equally bold NOW! in white.

Several people said aloud: "Right now!"

Duffy smiled modestly. "Our aim is to make Rhode Island right, right now. It works for buttons and bumper stickers. It's easy to read and already in people's heads. When you watch the weather on TV, every forecaster every night on every channel gives an update under the banner 'Right Now.'"

Jim Miller convened a breakfast for top leaders of Rhode Island's religious communities at the Brown Faculty Club. During the four months he had been in the state, Miller had connected with a diverse group ranging from Congregationalists and Unitarians, who could have passed for college faculty in their tweed jackets, to Dominican priests. There he introduced me to the Roman Catholic Bishop, Louis E. Gelineau. Under Gelineau's leadership the diocese had wisely warned parishes to put their funds in financial institutions insured by the FDIC, not RISDIC. Gelineau had also instructed priests not to put more than $100,000, the maximum insured by FDIC, in any one bank.[13]

As I shook his hand, Gelineau asked without any preliminaries: "Does

Common Cause support abortion?" Startled, I said we did not. I added that our state board was not allowed to take positions outside specific government reforms.

"Good," said the bishop, smiling beneficently.

After breakfast in the faculty club's Victorian parlor, I handed out a summary of the RIght Now! Coalition's three-part platform. I explained our proposals and answered questions. I closed by suggesting that Rhode Island had all the symptoms of a dysfunctional family that finally hits bottom. "Each of you," I said, "has dealt with families that struggled with alcohol or drugs for years before they named their problem and undertook a program for recovery. That's where we are as a state. Corruption in government has brought financial ruin, shamed us, and made us the butt of jokes across the country."

I said the RIght Now! Coalition needed their support for an intervention. They and their congregations could convince government leaders to accept the program. "We are not attacking anyone," I said, "but we demand that political leaders renounce corrupt practices and outlaw them."

Jim Miller closed the gathering by reminding the interfaith leaders that all of their faith traditions stressed repentance. He said that the Rhode Island Council of Churches would coordinate an interfaith rally at the State House on the first Sunday in January. "We want to call the entire state to repentance," he said. "We want government leaders to repent for the corruption that's gone on too long," he said. "We want the people to repent for allowing the very behaviors that have laid us low."

Miller promised that the rally would move beyond bitterness toward hope. He said their leadership could launch historic change.

"Amen," someone called out. "Amen!" Many affirmed. "Amen and amen!"

George N. Hunt, bishop of the Episcopal Church in Rhode Island, did not wait until January. At his diocesan convocation in November, Hunt challenged every congregation under his authority to work for reform. Lambasting a degree of corruption that "boggles the mind," he told delegates it would take his whole address just to list the abuses of elected officials, which he called "a litany of malfeasance which seems to go on and to be unending."[14] The bishop called on everyone present to reject the notion that corruption was so widespread and deeply rooted in the state it could never be eliminated. He urged them instead to get personally involved in "turning this ship of state around."

The third hopeful sign of progress lay in the Ethics Task Force that Gov. Sundlun had appointed. Dr. William T. O'Hara, the retired president of Bryant University, led the panel that included business and union leaders, academics, a rabbi, and several attorneys. Sara Quinn, a lawyer who had worked under Rae Condon at the Conflict of Interest Commission, became its resident expert.[15]

In September 1991, the task force invited public testimony. House Speaker

Joseph DeAngelis used the forum to present his proposals for the 1992 legislative session. I had watched him preside over countless debates, always civil and
restrained, but I had never heard him testify. DeAngelis spoke without notes,
beginning with the need to restore confidence in state government. He outlined
Rep. Jeff Teitz's Comprehensive Campaign Finance legislation, which he said
had passed the House but stalled in the Senate. His support for Teitz's legislation
came as no surprise. The shock came when he endorsed a litany of ethics bills
that had died year after year in the House Judiciary Committee or on the House
floor.[16] DeAngelis called for broader prohibitions against nepotism, ending the
confidentiality of ethics complaints, better reporting of campaign contributions,
and a ban on the personal use of campaign contributions.

DeAngelis never mentioned that these were Common Cause bills, but they
were. If enacted, they would change the state's political culture. I wondered how
hard he would push. If he tried herding his ninety-nine fellow representatives
down this path, would they go or scatter?

On a warm, hazy October Monday, the task force issued a seventy-page final
report. In its presentation letter, O'Hara wrote: "The cynicism, suspicion and
mistrust of the people of Rhode Island related to their state government offers
no other alternative but bold and comprehensive action."

The report, drafted by Sara Quinn, laid out seventy-eight specific recommendations for changes in the state's Constitution and laws. A front-page story in
the *Providence Journal* reprinted blocks of her searing text: "In some quarters of
Rhode Island State government a sub-culture has developed, dependent solely
on the largesse bestowed by that same state government. The commerce of this
sub-culture has been conducted until recently with a currency of favors, jobs,
state contracts, campaign contributions . . . ." Sundlun seemed buoyed by the
thick report. He promised to push hard for "four-year terms for general officers,
for tougher campaign finance laws, for term limits, for pension reform, for an
end to the political revolving door between elected officers and lucrative state
jobs, for a much more open and effective ethics commission, for judicial and
legal reforms and, most particularly, for ethics education."[17]

In a political commentary, *Providence Journal* reporter Brian C. Jones reminded readers that only a few days earlier "every story on the front page — every
local story — had to do with corruption. Or the suspicion, the investigation,
the attempted resolution of corruption." He listed the stories and concluded:
"Rhode Island's system of government is broken. Until it's fixed — and fixed big
and fixed good — nothing else matters."[18]

8

Hope for Ethics
1991

ALTHOUGH WELL HIDDEN from public view, the Common Cause complaint against Edward DiPrete was inching forward. In June 1991, more than two years after we filed with the Ethics Commission, an investigating subcommittee finally seemed ready to decide whether there was probable cause to believe that DiPrete had violated the law while governor of the state. Officially, I represented "the complainant," and Rae Condon was our attorney. We could observe the closed-door hearing but not speak.

We passed through a scrum of reporters who knew from public notice of the "executive session" that commissioners would consider Complaint 89-1 against DiPrete. While the press kept vigil outside, Condon and I took seats in the white-walled hearing room. Moments later DiPrete and his lawyers burst through the hubbub of media questions and into the room. Unlike times we met in public settings during his last two years as governor, DiPrete now glared through me as if I were a hostile apparition.

The former governor had appointed the entire commission, with Michael A. Morry as chair of the investigative panel. Morry had been president of a Warwick credit union when he voted to exonerate Bob Bianchini. He had ignored our demand that he resign. He and four other commissioners took their seats.

Morry called the meeting to order and explained that the law required this to be an executive session. Without explaining why, he said one commissioner, William H. Rizzini, had been excused and Paul L. Gaines, although present, had recused himself. Only four remained. Michael Morry, Richard A. Blaine, Peter J. Davis, and Roger R. Hall would decide whether our complaint against DiPrete could proceed. Everything rested on these four.

John M. Roney, the lawyer hired to prosecute our complaint, presented his findings from a thick memo that had been mailed to these commissioners. He reminded them that they had already voted to dismiss charges that cited actions taken by DiPrete before June 25, 1987, the day DiPrete signed legislation that created the Ethics Commission.[1]

Roney — with thinning hair, wire-rimmed glasses, a neatly trimmed beard, and bow tie — explained that he would present the case in four distinct parts. He argued first that DiPrete had wrongly steered the contract for studying pollution in Olney Pond at Lincoln Woods State Park to Tutela Engineering Associates, which had contributed $20,500 to Friends of DiPrete.[2] The governor had issued executive orders that called for state agencies to negotiate contracts "on the basis of demonstrated competence and qualification for the type of services required," but that process was a sham. The director of administration, who was officially responsible for final selections, had clandestinely forwarded lists to the governor. Under a secret protocol, DiPrete routinely penciled checkmarks by his choices and returned the lists for contract awards. Roney added that DiPrete had covered his tracks well, so that even trusted members of the governor's staff never knew that DiPrete was deciding which firms would get state contracts.[3]

Members of the investigating committee asked perfunctory questions. DiPrete had interviewed each of them separately before he put them on the Ethics Commission, and the gravity of charging someone who had been governor for six years seemed to weigh heavily on them.

Roney went on to describe DiPrete's relationship with James L. Taft Jr., a lawyer and former mayor of Cranston who had chaired the governor's fundraising committee. Taft was also DiPrete's partner in the development company that had benefited from the Cranston land deal back in 1987.[4] Taft had also won a lucrative state contract to sue the contractor who had abandoned work on the new Jamestown Bridge, where unfinished concrete columns still jutted up from the water.

Seated behind their long table, the four commissioners listened impassively as Roney turned to the Cranston land deal. Documents and interviews added detail to our charges. Before the Cranston zoning board granted a variance that doubled the number of apartments, DiPrete had met with the chair, George DiMuro, and offered him a plum post as head of the Coastal Resources Management Council. After the crucial vote, DiPrete's family firm walked away with a $2 million windfall, and the governor quietly appointed DiMuro.

Finally, Roney told of the pressure brought to bear on top environmental officials to expedite certain wetlands permits where the governor's son Dennis was the project engineer. DiPrete's director of policy, Ronald L. DiOrio, had called the governor's environmental director and wetlands chief to a meeting at his State House office. DiOrio had demanded to know why the permits were taking so long. Dennis DiPrete sat at the table across from the environmental regulators, but both DiPretes had denied any collusion.[5]

DiPrete's attorney, Joseph A. Kelly, rose for rebuttal. He repeated the gist of motions filed earlier in the process and claimed that the Common Cause complaint was politically motivated, based on hearsay, and not grounded in fact. He urged the investigating committee to dismiss all the charges. Kelly then stunned everyone by announcing that DiPrete would speak in his own behalf.

The former governor greeted the commissioners as if they were old friends. He spoke gently and calmly, as if not to dignify the accusations. "This investigation has dragged on for more than two years," he said. "These charges are purely political. They are groundless." He came across as gracious, unperturbed by the annoyance of this hearing. Had I not known so many details about the case, I might have believed in his innocence.

"I have a right to get on with my life," DiPrete said. "I'm under consideration for a position in the Bush Administration. It would require confirmation by the U.S. Senate, but I'm stuck here on hold until you remove this cloud. I respectfully ask you to do that."

This was news. During DiPrete's last term as governor, President George H.W. Bush had flown to Rhode Island on Air Force One for a big ticket fundraiser at DiPrete's home in Cranston.

None of the commissioners showed any reaction. Morry announced that the investigative panel would deliberate with its lawyer and everyone else had to leave. During the closed-door deliberation, the parties, lawyers, stenographer, and reporters shared a tiny reception area. Rae Condon and I stood at an awkward distance from DiPrete and his lawyer as reporters milled around, made small talk, and probed for tidbits. Half an hour ticked away. The receptionist fielded calls. A secretary came out to greet Rae Condon.

Finally, the hearing room door opened, and Gary Yesser, the commission's counsel, waved the participants inside while again shutting the press out.

The stenographer adjusted her equipment, and Morry gaveled the committee back onto the record. Richard Blaine, a member of the committee read carefully from what was clearly a boilerplate motion. The committee, it read, was "satisfied that probable cause exists" that DiPrete had committed "a serious, knowing, and willful violation of the Rhode Island Ethics Law." The motion was to refer the case to the adjudicative panel. At issue were facts related to the Tutela/Olney Pond charges.

Without pausing for a vote or looking up, Blaine turned to the financial ties between DiPrete and James Taft. They were business partners in both Atwood Associates Realty Trust and DiPrete-Laurienzo Construction. A state contract to litigate over the Jamestown Bridge had been awarded to a joint venture that involved James L. Taft and Joseph A. Kelly.

"On the basis of the above facts," Blaine continued with the longest single motion I had ever heard, "and by virtue of his actions, and for failing to prepare and deliver a statement of conflict of interest to the commission," there was probable cause that DiPrete had violated specific enumerated sections of the Code of Ethics.

"Second," said Commissioner Peter J. Davis, a former principal of Classical High School in Providence.

One by one, each voted "Aye."

With a bang of his gavel, Morry adjourned the meeting.

"That's it?" I whispered to Rae Condon. "What about the Cranston land deal and St. James Estates?"

"They're obviously gone," she whispered. "I'm sorry."

That came like a slap in the face. How could they simply drop those charges? Why not conduct a complete investigation?

Condon said they were not required to explain.

"Just like that?" I asked her. "Those parts vanish?"

She nodded.

Commissioners were on their feet. It was over. Several members who had served on the old Conflict of Interest Commission greeted Condon and exchanged small talk with her.

I wanted to stand up and shout. Evidence showed clearly that the Cranston zoning change had swept a $2 million windfall to DiPrete-Laurienzo Construction, and DiPrete then named the zoning board chair to a plum post. How could they brush it aside? Or the fact that the governor's son and policy chief had put immense pressure on the wetlands permitting process? Was that not worthy of a full hearing on the evidence?

DiPrete and his entourage left swiftly through a side door.

Anger has always been a problem for me, and now I could feel a rush of adrenalin. Air in the room became heavy. Reporters wanted to know what happened. I shook my head, forcing a smile, trying not to speak.

The next day, Russell Garland phoned from the *Providence Journal*. He said DiPrete had convened a press conference to announce that he had "been cleared" of nine allegations in a complaint filed by Common Cause.

"You were at the hearing," Garland said. "Did they clear him on nine?"

"He wasn't 'cleared.'" In an instant I decided that if DiPrete convened a press conference, I was free to comment on the charges that had been dropped. I explained that this investigating committee had ruled two years earlier that the Ethics Commission had no jurisdiction over events that occurred before it was established by law. "They decided they didn't have jurisdiction. We thought they did, since his actions constituted violations under both the old Conflict of Interest Law and under the 1987 Ethics Law. He got off on a legal technicality, but that's far from saying he's 'been cleared.'"[6]

I summarized the four parts of our original complaint that John Roney had presented. "I wish the investigating committee had explained why they dropped our charges related to the Cranston land deal and St. James Estates. We thought they had ample reason for a full hearing on the evidence." Furthermore, I added, our bill to require open adjudicative hearings had died in the legislature. "But the current law provides for an open hearing if the public official waives his right to a confidential one." I added that I thought DiPrete had waived confidentiality by convening his press conference. "By rights, the adjudicative hearings should now be open to the press and public."[7]

Other reporters called and went through the same details. I wished this story had broken before the General Assembly adjourned. Our legislation to open adjudicative hearings had died without a vote.[8]

On June 13, 1991, thirteen members of the Ethics Commission took seats behind their nameplates around tables arranged like three sides of a square. The RISDIC disaster, the news of corrupt pensions, and the bribery charges against the mayor of Pawtucket, Brian Sarault, had touched them all. Commissioner Mel Topf said the time had come for the Ethics Commission to adopt specific ethics rules for public officials.[9] Topf was thin and boyish in horn-rimmed glasses. He taught writing at Roger Williams University and often voiced impolitic truths, the wide-eyed innocent who piped up that the emperor had no clothes. Topf reminded his fellow commissioners that the General Assembly had gone home without reining in nepotism[10] or the persistent practice of trading key votes for permanent state jobs, particularly judgeships. Concluding that the legislature would never rein itself in, he urged the commission to follow its constitutional mandate and start "adopting" a code of ethics.

Two weeks later, the commission's jovial executive director, Mark Eckstein, distributed a memo that summarized ethics legislation which the commission had supported.[11] He focused on the two Common Cause bills Topf had mentioned: nepotism and the revolving door. The first would dramatically enlarge the circle of family members officials were forbidden to favor with official acts.[12] The second aimed to bar lawmakers from seeking or accepting state jobs while they served in the General Assembly and for a year after they left office.[13] Both bills landed in overflowing legislative wastebaskets.

Gary Yesser, the commission's suave legal counsel, provided a memo on constitutional issues.[14] He described the 1986 constitutional amendment that created the Ethics Commission and directed it to "adopt a code of ethics," including provisions on conflicts of interest. Older sections of the Rhode Island Constitution authorized the General Assembly to "pass all laws necessary to carry this Constitution into effect" and declared that the "legislative power" was vested in the state Senate and House of Representatives.[15] Ultimately, Yesser said, the Rhode Island Supreme Court would need to resolve that contradiction.

He then reminded the commissioners that they had maneuvered between those sections in 1987 when they voted "to adopt" the code of ethics that the General Assembly had already enacted into law, and suggested that they ask Gov. Sundlun to seek an advisory opinion from the Supreme Court. One way to force the question might be to approve an ethics rule that would "significantly modify" current law. They could avoid a constitutional crisis by making the new rule take effect at some future date. The Supreme Court would then have time to decide whether the commission had acted within its constitutional authority.[16]

Mel Topf came back in July with a memo in which he analyzed the records of the 1986 Constitutional Convention. The convention's ethics committee, he wrote, had proposed "an independent non-partisan ethics commission" that would be responsible for adopting the ethics rules. He noted that the entire convention had voted specifically that the ethics commission should write the code of ethics. That proposal went onto the 1986 statewide ballot as the "Ethics in Government" amendment to the state's Constitution, and voters approved.

"In spite of all this," Topf wrote, "the General Assembly included a code of ethics in the 1987 legislation that established the Ethics Commission." By imposing its own code, the legislature violated the state's Constitution. Rail-thin and professorial, Topf told his colleagues that the word "law" encompassed more than books of statutes; decisions of the Supreme Court carried the full force of law, as did rules adopted by administrative agencies and executive orders issued by presidents or governors. For all those reasons, he argued, the Ethics Commission should adopt specific provisions that would significantly modify the present Code of Ethics. "We must act as if we had the authority we clearly do have," he wrote, "and if anyone wishes to challenge us, he or she may do so in Superior Court."

Topf concluded that the commission's constitutional mandate was "so clear, so strong, and so integral to our purpose" that failure to act made them guilty of misfeasance for neglecting their mandate. "We do not need the Supreme Court to advise us to do our duty. We do not need the Governor to ask the Supreme Court to advise us to do our duty. We need simply to do it."[17]

On a dry August afternoon when Rhode Islanders jammed roads to the beaches, the commission prepared to act. Fourteen of the fifteen commissioners took their seats, most in jackets and ties. The question of adopting specific ethics rules for public officials topped their agenda.

Topf reminded his colleagues that no one was proposing that they scrap the code approved four years earlier by the General Assembly. Rather than trying to write an entirely new code of ethics, he suggested that they approve two rules they believed were sound but which the legislature had rejected.

Commissioner Richard McAllister warned against any effort to exercise what he called "the legislature's lawful authority." For nine years, McAllister had represented Cranston in the state Senate but left for a job at a nonprofit agency that received nearly all its funding from the state.[18] Here was a common pattern: Rhode Island lawmakers who did their leaders' bidding often got state-funded jobs. On this occasion he clearly sensed that the vote would go against him. He said the commission would make a mistake and risk its credibility by grasping for legislative powers. He warned that such a move would cause only turmoil.

Commissioner Michael Morry moved to nip Topf's proposal in the bud. House leaders had nominated him, and I assumed that he stayed in touch with them. Now he argued against trying to amend the Code of Ethics: "This is a mistake. I believe you genuinely want to produce a stronger code, but I think you'll get a weaker commission, and it will be open to lawsuits that we can't win." As he spoke, I wondered if others around the table saw McAllister and Morry as doing the legislature's bidding.

Several other commissioners wondered aloud why the General Assembly seemed so tolerant of wrongdoing in its midst and why RISDIC's collapse had produced so little legislative change. They seemed to be girding their loins for the struggle ahead.

Commissioner William Rizzini, the former president of Roger Williams University, offered a resolution: "The Commission has the right, and intends to, change provisions of the Code of Ethics without legislative approval."[19] With portly gravitas, Rizzini revealed no fear of retaliation. Without mentioning the nepotism or revolving door proposals, he backed Topf, arguing that the state's Constitution was clear.

The ayes carried easily, a vote of 11–3, and the commissioners agreed to notify Gov. Sundlun of their decision. Their vote marked a watershed, the first step in a rule-making process that would take months. When reporters called, I said Common Cause had encouraged commissioners to adopt the nepotism and revolving door proposals. "They should be in position to adopt tougher provisions in areas where the legislature has refused to act," I said. "This embodies the will of the people that there be a strong code of ethics."[20]

Within days, however, legislative leaders fired a heavy cannon across the commission's bow. In a three-page letter emblazoned with their florid signatures, House Speaker Joseph DeAngelis and Senate Majority Leader John J. Bevilacqua denounced the commission's plan. House Majority Leader Thomas A. Lamb also signed, his inscription tighter and lighter than those of his younger superiors. "As we are sure your own attorneys will advise you," the leaders wrote, "the legislative power of the State of Rhode Island is — and always has been — vested exclusively in the State's democratically-elected General Assembly."[21] They scoffed at the commission's claim that the 1986 Ethics in Government Amendment had conferred upon the Ethics Commission "concurrent legislative authority over matters relating to governmental ethics." DeAngelis and Bevilacqua also threatened that this move would bring "unnecessary and expensive litigation." By invoking the specter of costly lawsuits, the two men served notice of their chokehold on the commission's budget. Not only did they control the purse strings, they could write their own check for top-flight lawyers. The letter closed with an invitation to meet.

The commissioners instructed their attorney and executive director to talk with legislative leaders and with the governor. On September 23 lawyers from the Senate, House, and Ethics Commission slipped secretly into the governor's office. The only outsider invited was Peter Lacouture, who had served in 1986 as counsel to the constitutional convention's ethics committee.

Sheldon Whitehouse, Sundlun's policy director, opened the meeting by stating his hope that all parties could agree on the commission's constitutional authority to strengthen the state's Code of Ethics. At that, the General Assembly's lawyers erupted. A bearded, bearish Edward Fogarty, legal counsel to House Speaker Joe DeAngelis, rehashed the points already made in the leaders' letter.

Lacouture circulated minutes from crucial meetings of the constitutional convention's ethics committee. He parsed the text he had drafted five years earlier, showing how the committee had reached consensus that the Ethics Commission — not the General Assembly — should make ethics rules for public officials. He reminded the roomful of lawyers that voters had approved this language as a constitutional amendment.

Both Fogarty and the Senate's top lawyer, Thomas DeSimone, denounced the ethics amendment as contradicting centuries of legislative control. Though the two were outnumbered in the meeting, they gave no ground. They represented the most powerful politicians in Rhode Island.

Afterwards, Gary Yesser described the donnybrook in a confidential memo to the Ethics Commission. He predicted that the General Assembly would fight for its exclusive authority over ethics rules. Yesser added his own view that the Ethics Commission had both a constitutional right and an obligation to adopt a code of ethics for public officials and employees.[22]

Although his memo remained under seal, Yesser rehearsed part of what had happened during a public session on October 3. He revealed enough to let everyone in on the fiery closed-door debate. Meanwhile, in what would prove a crucial personnel change, former Sen. McAllister's term ended, and Gov. Sundlun appointed Richard W. Morsilli in his place.[23]

With the sober fortitude of people who know their duty but do not relish it, the commissioners approved a series of motions required by the state's Administrative Procedures Act, normally cited by its initials "the APA." The commission had to approve draft regulations, advertise them, and invite comments at a public hearing. As they began voting, one proposed regulation at a time, no one spoke what everyone knew: the act of approving these rules would spark a constitutional confrontation.

The first would remove the confidentiality of ethics complaints and open the commission's adjudicative hearings to the public.[24] Twelve commissioners, including Morsilli, heard their names called and answered, "Yes." Roger Hall abstained but did not explain why, and Michael Morry voted "No."

The second proposed new regulation would expand the list of family members an official could not favor from "spouse or dependent child" to "any of the following relatives . . . whether by blood, marriage, or adoption: parents, grandparents, adult children, siblings, grandchildren, uncles, aunts, nieces and nephews."[25] Again, twelve voted yes, Hall abstained, and Morry voted no.

The third would bar officials who were members of town councils, zoning boards, or quasi-public bodies —whether they were elected or appointed — from accepting salaried positions from the body in which they served for as long as they served and for one year after they left that position.[26] Again the votes held.

The final draft rule took direct aim at the General Assembly. Almost word for word, it was the Common Cause revolving door bill to stop legislators from seeking or accepting state jobs for one full year after they left their seats as senators or representatives. Without fanfare or speeches, the commissioners again voted 12–1, with one abstention.[27]

With this series of quiet votes on a gray October afternoon, the commissioners moved across a divide that no ordinary Rhode Islander had crossed since the Dorr Rebellion, a century and a half before. They declared that they would fulfill their constitutional duty to make rules for all public officials, including elected legislators. Without shouts or muskets, they assaulted the sturdy bulwark from which the General Assembly had resolutely repulsed all challenges for more than three hundred years.

The news ricocheted around the state. A *Providence Journal* headline declared: "Tougher rules on ethics kindle political fire storm." Reporter Scott MacKay wrote that the most controversial part of the proposed new code would ban legislators from "full-time state employment while serving or within a year of leaving the assembly, unless exempted by the commission."[28]

Senate Majority Leader John Bevilacqua blasted the vote: "I'm not going to take a whole class of people and say you can't compete for a state job." Bevilacqua rattled off a list of top judges who had advanced directly from the legislature to the bench. "They're good judges," he insisted. "You can't just put a label on these people and say they're not good because they've been members of the General Assembly." More ominously, Bruce Sundlun growled to MacKay that he thought the Ethics Commission had gone too far in trying to ban lawmakers from judgeships for a year after they left office. The governor portrayed himself as the prime mover in ethics: "Everybody has gotten onto my ethics train," he said, "but I still think I'm driving the engine."

On November 4, Sundlun formally asked the Rhode Island Supreme Court to decide whether the Ethics Commission or the General Assembly had authority to approve ethics rules for public officials.[29] Two days later, at the State House shortly before sunset, the Ethics Commission began its final required public hearing and public votes on the proposed new rules. The commission's chairperson, William Rizzini, invited witnesses to sign in on half-sheets of paper, which a clerk collected and passed to him. Rizzini outlined the proposed new regulations and invited public comment.[30]

Sen. Walter Gray of North Kingstown spoke first. With a twinkle, Gray announced that he had won election only a year earlier. "I've only been a senator since January first, so you can't blame everything on me yet." Gray said he had sponsored the Common Cause nepotism proposal that was now before the Ethics Commission. Gray told how the Senate Judiciary Committee pared down the list of family whom public officials could not favor. The Senate had passed his bill on May 2, but the House, which had passed similar legislation the previous year, rejected its equivalent on May 29.

Gray declared that the Ethics Commission had the right and responsibility to enact nepotism rules. He warned that legislative leaders would "so emasculate the reforms that they will be unrecognizable when they finally come to a vote — if they progress that far." He described the practice of advancing favored bills in return for loyal votes that often harmed the public interest. "It's obvious that we're in a war," Gray said, "and it's not the time for timid people or timid actions. It's a time for courage."

My message dovetailed with Gray's. I listed ethics bills introduced year after year but never enacted. Even after RISDIC had left citizens feeling betrayed, lawmakers protected loopholes for family favoritism. Neither chamber would close the revolving door that carried many into judgeships and other permanent state jobs. I urged commissioners to outlaw these abuses. "The people authorized you, as members of the Ethics Commission — in an orderly process — to prevent such scandals. You now have that opportunity."

Rae Condon passed out copies of her legal memo on the problem of nepotism, which she had presented to the commission three months earlier. "We're happy this day has come," she said. "We encourage you in your constitutional mandate to adopt the code of ethics." Then, without mentioning that she had drafted most of the proposals, Condon explained them briefly. "We urge you to fight vigorously for your right — as given by the Constitution — to set standards of conduct for public officials and to establish what acts are prohibited."

Rep. Bruce Long, a Republican from Middletown, testified that the General Assembly had proven itself unwilling to restrict its members' behavior. Both representatives and senators, he said, would campaign on claims that "they passed several ethics bills proposed by Common Cause," even though each chamber routinely killed bills the other had passed. As a result, Long said, "there is no fruit born."

Paul Boghossian walked to the microphone. His grandfather had escaped the Armenian genocide and founded the textile company that he now ran. A slender man in his thirties with curly black hair, he introduced himself as the employer of 165 people in Coventry. He told the commission that businesses were leaving Rhode Island because "the sleaze factor" was driving jobs out to other states and countries. Urging tougher ethics rules for lawmakers, judges, lawyers, and independent contractors, Boghossian insisted that the commission had both the right and the responsibility to go forward. Yet for all that was wrong, he harbored the hope that these strong rules could address chronic problems. "Look at the mess we're in because of halfway measures in the past," he testified. "We cannot settle for halfway measures."

Alan Flink introduced himself as a partner at Edwards & Angell, one of the state's most prestigious law firms. Flink said that although he was president of the Rhode Island Bar Association, he was not speaking in any representative capacity, although he hoped most lawyers would affirm what he was about to say. "This commission," he declared in a rumbling baritone, "has been assigned the difficult task of acting as the conscience of the community. You are performing the public's business as no other body." Flink affirmed the proposed rule for an open complaint process. The American Bar Association, he said, had urged that all complaints against lawyers be made public from their inception. "There is no room for closed hearings on alleged public misconduct. When we open up the process, we all become more accountable to the public we serve. If we seek the public's trust and confidence, we should be prepared to do no less."

Flink also endorsed the revolving door rule with a new twist. He noted that there were roughly four thousand lawyers in the state: "On their behalf, I strongly object to the fact that the vast majority of those lawyers have been excluded from consideration for judicial appointments." An informal analysis of the state courts showed that three-quarters of the judges were former legislators or had been directly involved in political activity. He also thundered against Senate Majority Leader Bevilacqua's claim that the revolving door rule would treat legislators as second-class citizens: "To the contrary, it would appear that most of us who have been effectively excluded from the process have a more legitimate right to make that claim." Flink struck me as a lion, deep-throated and fierce. "By creating a one-year waiting period, your proposals will assist in creating an appropriate separation between state political service and public employment. In the process, you will assist in allowing judges to be chosen on the basis of merit."

He gathered his notes and drew a deep breath. "The message from the state's ethical conscience should be clear and unambiguous: 'If you serve in the legislature, concentrate on your legislative duties. Your office is not to be used as a springboard to other public employment.'"

A dozen other witnesses spoke, including Operation Clean Sweep leader Charles Silverman. With minor variations, most supported the commission's proposed new rules.

The only disagreement came from the ACLU. Associate Director Andrea Geiger criticized the one-year revolving door prohibition: "We realize there have been some terrible abuses in the hiring system, where favoritism has clearly been used to advance legislators to high-paying state jobs." Still, she insisted that the proposed rule was "an inappropriate and overbroad way of dealing with the problem it seeks to correct." She added that the most controversial jobs had been created for specific legislators, or had been filled without an open and public hiring process. "Sweeping with so broad a brush as this rule does," she reasoned, "penalizes individuals solely for serving as elected officials, not for any misconduct on their part."

Commissioner Mel Topf asked Geiger what she thought of the one-year revolving door cooling-off periods that existed in other states.

Geiger hesitated. "I can bring that question to the director, and he would be happy to answer your question in writing."

Topf mentioned a one-year prohibition established by the town council in Middletown. "Has the ACLU taken a stand on that?"

Geiger said she could not answer.

Sara Quinn began her testimony by refuting the ACLU position. "The revolving door philosophy," she said, simply recognized that "the very position that an individual holds while in public office should not become an opportunity for personal benefit."

Quinn had learned her craft under Rae Condon at the old Conflict of Interest Commission. She ridiculed the wink-and-nod corruption that could not be prosecuted under deliberately vague ethics laws. More recently, she had served on Sundlun's Ethics Task Force, which she said had heard the "despair and cynicism" that spread because many thought Rhode Island could never change. She affirmed the commission's efforts to restore public confidence by tightening the rules. "The change has already occurred," she testified. "You are that change. When the people of Rhode Island voted in 1986 to amend the Constitution, they changed the way we must govern ourselves ethically in Rhode Island." Quinn reminded commissioners that convention delegates had just come through the RIHMFC mortgage scandal, and the state's chief justice was under investigation while they met. Bevilacqua's continuing associations with organized crime figures drove him out of office. It was this sense of endemic corruption that had given rise to the 1986 Ethics in Government Amendment, which mandated a strong ethics commission.

She added that voters in 1986 had understood the power they were vesting in the Ethics Commission. "I am convinced that the citizens fully intended to create an autonomous, nonpartisan commission which would act as the conscience of government to compel a higher standard of public service in this state."

The moral force of her message rang through the room. "The people of this state chose you as their guide — not the legislature, not the supreme court, not the governor, not Common Cause, not the Governor's Ethics Task Force — but you. You possess the moral consensus of the community. You have the expertise necessary to develop a code of ethics by which all government officials and employees must abide."

Quinn challenged the commissioners to fulfill their destiny. "The call to leadership beckons," she said. "You have been chosen to bear this standard."

Fully aware of what they were doing, commissioners crossed the Rubicon.

9

Olney Pond

1991

Nearly three years after Common Cause board members and I signed our complaint, the hidden trial of Edward DiPrete finally began. What had started with newspaper clippings and a copy of the Ethics Law came, at last, to oaths and evidence.[1]

On an overcast October afternoon, Rae Condon and I needed to make a decision. We leaned on a balcony railing in the two-story glass entrance to the Rhode Island Ethics Commission's headquarters and spoke quietly. Eleven months earlier, only days before he lost to Bruce Sundlun, DiPrete had appointed Ernest G. Ashton to the panel that would now weigh evidence against him. Ashton had been DiPrete's friend for thirty years. He did business with DiPrete Insurance and contributed to many DiPrete campaigns.

I asked Condon if we should try to disqualify Ashton.

"We could," she said, "but I'm not sure we should." Three commissioners on the nine-member adjudicative panel had already recused themselves, leaving only six to hear the case. The law required five affirmative votes to find a violation; it had no provision for alternates, as there would be in a jury trial. The commission's first chair, John J. Tuohy, had been fatally struck by a car in a crosswalk.[2] Condon's math was simple: if we disqualified Ashton, only five members would remain. The hearings might take six or eight weeks. If accident, illness, or death incapacitated one, the entire complaint might founder under the five-vote requirement. We had no choice but to let Ashton sit.

By law, the hearing would be secret. Condon and I took seats inside the hearing room moments before the ex-governor swept in with a pair of lawyers. As he had at the probable-cause hearing, DiPrete glared through me. He sat down a few empty chairs away.

John Roney, the lawyer hired to prosecute our complaint, backed in through a door, his arms loaded with loose-leaf binders of evidentiary documents. Nameplates for the six commissioners who would hear our complaint marked their places at a table. The six, including Ernest Ashton, entered from the commission's administrative office. Francis P. Pellegrino, a retired high school principal from Westerly, would chair the panel. He tapped his gavel.

Pellegrino called on Richard Ratcliffe, an assistant attorney general. Thin, in his mid-thirties, with a bald forehead above wire-rimmed glasses, Ratcliffe spoke with monkish humility and asked to postpone the Tutela/Olney Pond case. "Several of the witnesses that you're expecting to hear from have testified before a statewide grand jury," Ratcliffe explained. "These hearings could compromise the grand jury proceedings."[3]

I relished news that a grand jury was weighing criminal charges. An awareness of an unseen criminal investigation might make these commissioners receptive to our ethics charges, which I believed were only the tip of a vast iceberg.

Pellegrino asked both lawyers about Ratcliffe's motion to delay the hearing. From the prosecution table John Roney opposed delay because he had a witness waiting outside. Joseph A. Kelly, DiPrete's defense lawyer, agreed. He cited many months of getting to this point, adding indignantly that DiPrete had been waiting two years to clear his name and get on with his life.

From his seat at the center of the table, Pellegrino asked if there were other questions before the panel cleared the room to deliberate.

Rae Condon rose. She reminded the commissioners that the investigating committee had dismissed other charges — not for lack of evidence, but because they involved actions the governor had taken before he signed the Ethics Commission into existence on June 25, 1987. Condon moved to reinstate those charges. She argued that six members of a fifteen-member commission had "gratuitously granted a general amnesty" for actions that were illegal under both the law DiPrete signed and the previous Conflict of Interest Law.[4]

After deliberations, the six-member panel rejected the motion to delay the Tutela portion of the complaint, but it also tabled our motion to reinstate the charges previously dismissed.

Condon addressed the question of Ernest Ashton's participation. She reminded the commissioners that "a very stringent statute" created a predicament: if death, incompetence, or sickness were to leave fewer than five, the case could never be resolved. For that reason, she said, Common Cause would not object to Ashton's participation.

From his seat at the center of the table, Pellegrino thanked her.

Commissioner Roger M. Freeman, a Republican and a retired insurance executive, raised his hand and spoke: "I'd just like to get this on the record that every one of us on this Ethics Commission who was appointed prior to January 1, 1991, was appointed by former Gov. DiPrete." DiPrete had personally interviewed and named five of six panelists who would weigh the evidence against him.

As prosecutor, Roney led off, promising that witnesses would explain how the governor had secretly picked Domenic Tutela, a $20,000 campaign contributor, for a state environmental project at Olney Pond in Lincoln Woods State Park.

Then Kelly rose for the defense. Tall and gaunt, with head completely shaved, he commanded attention. "The first thing you're going to learn," the lawyer said, "is that Mr. Tutela did not receive the so-called Olney Pond contract. You're also going to learn that Mr. Tutela was never advised that he had been selected to receive the so-called Olney Pond contract."

Before DiPrete took office, Kelly said, many state contracts went "to particular firms and to a very few particular firms." To spread the work around, the governor established an Architectural and Engineering Services Selection Committee to screen qualified contractors. That committee, he added, had put Tutela on a short list for the Olney Pond contract.

Kelly made light of the fact that a list went to the governor: "As was his hands-on procedure, the governor might make a recommendation, not a selection. He really couldn't make a selection. He didn't know the contract price." When Kelly explained it that way, the process sounded credible. He said Tutela would testify that he had never contacted DiPrete about the Olney Pond job.

John Roney called Judith Benedict as his first witness. She described her duties as chief of planning and development at the Department of Environmental Management (DEM) and cited problems with water quality in Olney Pond. Scientists under her supervision used criteria established by the U.S. Environmental Protection Agency (EPA) to evaluate proposals for finding the source of pollution. Lycott Environmental Resources and IEP Inc. had ranked highest on qualifications and filed the lowest bids. Benedict testified that their prices fell below the $100,000 grant expected from EPA, and none of the other firms "were found to be acceptable."[5] Benedict said she had put all this in writing and sent the complete file to State Purchasing Agent Dennis Lynch of the Architects and Engineers Selection Committee, known as "the A&E committee."

Significantly, Benedict had sat in for DEM director Bob Bendick at the A&E committee on April 8, 1988. It was her first A&E meeting, and the process baffled her. She met the three other participants for the first time that morning, presented her department's review, and explained why only two firms were acceptable. She was flummoxed when they insisted on sending a "short list" of at least three firms to the director of administration.[6]

"What happened after you made your recommendation?" Roney asked.

"Someone suggested that Tutela's name be added, and there may have been another firm as well."

Roney let her comment sink in. "Do you recall who suggested that Tutela's name be added to the list?"

"I don't," Benedict said. Roney asked her to look at the binder of evidence and examine minutes that noted the committee had agreed unanimously to Tutela and a fourth firm. "Do you recall whether a vote was taken?"

"I don't remember," Benedict said softly.

"Did you vote to include Tutela on the list?"

"I don't recall, but I've since been told that I did."

Roney asked why she agreed to include Tutela on the list.

"My memo to Mr. Lynch clearly stated that we thought there were only two qualified applicants, so it didn't seem important to me if there were other names added."

Roney directed her to review a document in the binder addressed to Frederick Lippitt, DiPrete's director of administration. A&E committee chair Dennis Lynch had signed the memo that recommended four firms for the Olney Pond Project, giving no hint that the professionals at DEM strongly preferred Lycott and IEP or found the other firms, including Tutela, unacceptable. Nor did Lynch note that only bids from Lycott and IEP fell within the $100,000 EPA grant.

The binder also held Lippitt's response to Lynch, announcing that he had "selected" Tutela for the Olney Pond project.[7] Roney asked Benedict and the commissioners to review these documents.

"When you learned that the Tutela firm had been selected," Roney asked her, "what did you do?" Benedict replied that she told DEM Director Robert Bendick what happened, and she drafted a memo Benedict could send to Lippitt, DiPrete's director of administration.

Roney directed her to review her memo in the binder. She had written that Tutela's $178,000 bid was "substantially higher than the EPA Clean Lakes grant of $100,000," that Lycott Environmental Research and IEP each had the required experience, and that their bids of $73,294 and $88,920 fell within the budget of the grant. Benedict's memo informed Lippitt that Lycott had scored 91.5 on the federal criteria, while IEP got 91.8. By contrast, Tutela ranked seventh of eight with a score of 67.5.

Her memo was moderate in tone, but its substance exploded off the page. "Tutela Engineering, although experienced in the field of wastewater management, has not performed any Clean Lakes grant studies." For all those reasons, DEM found it necessary to "request that you reconsider the awarding of the contract."[8] Benedict testified that Bendick initialed her memo and fired it off to Lippitt.

In cross-examination, Kelly tried to have Benedict state that, contrary to what she had said, all of the bidders were qualified and the only problem was cost. She stood her ground: her professional review committee at DEM had found only two qualified.

Unlike jurors at a criminal trial, members of the Ethics Commission were allowed to ask questions. Richard W. Morsilli, the only panelist appointed by Gov. Sundlun, spoke softly: "What really gets me confused is that when the list is finally submitted, all the names are in alphabetical order. Alphabetical means everyone is equal and as qualified as the next. Almost like someone was trying to hide something."

Benedict told him that was how the A&E committee operated.

State Purchasing Director Dennis M. Lynch, a former mayor of Pawtucket, followed Benedict in the witness chair. As at any trial, he had not heard the prior testimony. Under Roney's questions he acknowledged chairing the A&E committee on April 8 and sending the Olney Pond short list to Lippitt. Then Roney directed him to the agenda, which noted that DEM director Robert Bendick had been scheduled to represent his agency but Judith Benedict had attended in his place. He asked Lynch if Benedict had participated in any previous A&E committee meetings.

"I'm not sure she had," Lynch answered. "I think very highly of Judith, and I think she's a true professional, but in answer to your question, I think the process was unfamiliar to her at that time." He affirmed that Benedict had presented DEM's position. "Their in-house study had concluded that two firms were qualified, one in particular that they felt strongly about."

"Who recommended that the Tutela firm be added?"

Lynch said he did not know. Nor could he recall who proposed to add the fourth company to the short list. The afternoon had vanished, and the panel adjourned.

The next hearing took place on October 31. At that hearing Kelly asked Lynch if it was his job to submit the names of qualified people for state contracts. Lynch said it was.

"And I take it that all of those people were therefore qualified?"

"Yes, sir," Lynch answered.

Kelly did not ask how the committee had certified Tutela after the DEM review team had found this firm unqualified. Instead, he inquired about political influence. Had DiPrete or anyone on his behalf said to put any firm on a short list?

"No, sir," said Lynch.

When time came for questions from the adjudicative panel, Chairman Frank Pellegrino wondered how Lynch's committee had washed away the DEM reviewers' ranking and put Tutela on the short list.

Lynch answered evasively: "My testimony was that I can't recall who recommended Tutela."[9]

"Do you have minutes of those meetings?"

"Yes, sir. The minutes do not show."

"Do you have a tape of the meeting?"

"No, sir."

In his turn, Richard Morsilli pushed Lynch for more. He asked why the A&E committee ignored the recommendation of the environmental experts.

"They made two recommendations," said Lynch. "Those two names were forwarded to the person making the selection."

Morsilli frowned. "Mr. Lynch. I would love to know how Tutela's name . . ." He stopped, puzzled. "I mean, someone must have said favorable things about Tutela for that name to get on the list."

"That's right, and I can't recall, but that's exactly how the committee works. The record also shows that DEM did not oppose any of those four names going to the director."

Beneath curly dark hair, Morsilli's brow furrowed, and the newest commissioner asked more questions, but Lynch gave no more. For nearly an hour, he defended the A&E process without explaining how or why Tutela landed on the list. I caught myself tuning out. Although Dennis Lynch was responsible for all state purchasing, he had presided over a bumbling and poorly documented process.

I was surprised when Judith Benedict was called back to the witness chair. She explained the EPA requirements again, adding the fact that three members of the DEM review committee had doctorates in their scientific specialties. She insisted that she had told the A&E that Tutela was not qualified to analyze fresh water lakes, and that neither she nor Lynch had suggested Tutela. She barely remembered the two other men she met for the first time that day, but thought that one of them had named Tutela.

Pellegrino asked if the A&E committee had voted separately on the proposals.

"No," Benedict said decisively.

"In other words, there was a single vote for the four companies?"

"Yes."

"And it was unanimous?"

"Yes," she admitted with an air of defeat. Benedict had found herself in a Kafkaesque predicament. She had failed to object when a stranger proposed Tutela for the short list. Later, when she learned that Tutela had been selected, she drafted a memo that exposed the sham.

Her testimony ended the afternoon, and I followed her out into the glassed-in landing. I said her decision to blow the whistle had exposed the scam.

"I had no choice," she said modestly. "I had to live with myself."

I drove home on I-95, wondering if a sloppy system and vague minutes would forever hide DiPrete's hand. The prosecution would have to show by "a preponderance of the evidence" that the governor had steered the Olney Pond contract to Tutela. This standard of proof, widely used in civil litigation, is only slightly less stringent than the criminal standard of proof "beyond a reasonable doubt."

On both sides of my exit ramp, curving rows of maples still full of autumn colors flared in final brilliance. The names of Judith Benedict and Bob Bendick, her boss at DEM, played in my mind. During my years as a pastor, I had dismissed worshipers hundreds of times with a benediction. That word, derived from the Latin, meant to "bless" or to "speak well." It struck me that Judith Benedict had spoken well in the deepest sense, and Bob Bendick had done the same when he backed her up. Both denounced the sham. Benedict and Bendick had blessed Rhode Island.

Gilbert R. Parrillo was the "public member" DiPrete appointed to uphold — at least theoretically — the public interest on the A&E committee. Parrillo testified that he could not recall who suggested putting Tutela on the short list.

In answer to questions from John Roney, Parrillo said he had known Edward DiPrete more than twenty-five years and had helped with DiPrete's campaigns for mayor of Cranston as well as for governor. For thirty-seven years he had worked for the City of Cranston. "I started out as a truck driver in the Highway Department, and I'm presently an architectural technician in the Department of Public Works." He had served on the A&E committee since its inception and received $25 per meeting. When bids came in, Parrillo testified blandly, "we would try and short-list them down to no less than three names."

In response to Roney's questions, Parrillo recalled Judith Benedict but could only vaguely remember the meeting that picked firms for the Olney Pond contract. Roney asked if he remembered who suggested Tutela.

"No, sir," Parrillo said, "I do not."

"Did you suggest the name Tutela Engineering Associates for this project?"

"I don't recall if I did or not, sir."

Roney asked if he knew Tutela.

"Yes, I know Domenic Tutela. I met him when he did some work for the City of Cranston."

Roney asked Parrillo if he recalled the reason Domenic Tutela was added to the short list.

"As I recall, we selected his name because he was a mechanical engineer. He falls within that field. We just kept his name on the list, if memory serves me right."

"Do you recall anyone on the committee speaking in favor of Domenic Tutela for addition to this list?"

"I don't recall, sir." Parrillo kept reprising that line. He could not recall who suggested putting Tutela Associates on the short list. "Memory doesn't serve me," he added politely.

Commissioner John O'Brien was in his seventies and had retired as director of the IRS office in Rhode Island. He asked Gilbert Parrillo again if he had worked for DiPrete's campaigns.

"Yes, sir. I did."

"What position did you have in the campaign?"

"I used to hang signs."

"Hang signs?" O'Brien sounded incredulous.

"Yes," said Gilbert Parrillo.

Finally, the adjudicative panel's chairperson, Frank Pellegrino, asked Parrillo how the A&E committee added or eliminated names from the list.

Parrillo said the A&E studied the proposals and reviewed the bidders' experience.

"How long would it take to do that?"

"Anywhere from five to six minutes. It would be a brief summary of their work."

No one could calculate how much time the Ethics Commission was spending to discern what happened at one brief committee meeting on April 8, 1988. Every minute of that meeting was now costing state taxpayers thousands of dollars for investigators, lawyers, and stenographers, not to mention judges to hear the appeals that were sure to follow. Corruption might have enriched DiPrete and his cronies, but giving him due process of law would cost immeasurably more.

I had never seen Domenic V. Tutela before the stenographer swore him in. Was he painfully shy or extremely reluctant?

As John Roney posed groundwork questions, Tutela relaxed slightly. He had met DiPrete during the early 1980s while vice president of a Rhode Island company that did work for the City of Cranston. DiPrete was then mayor of Rhode Island's third largest city. In 1982, Tutela founded his own company, Tutela Engineering Associates, headquartered north of Boston. He also opened an office in Providence.

Without warning, Roney had Tutela look in the binder at lists of contributors to DiPrete's 1984 campaign for governor. Tutela had started contributing to Friends of DiPrete under his own name: $100 in June 1984, $1,000 in August, and $100 in September, all before the election that made DiPrete governor.

After DiPrete won the election, Tutela multiplied his contributions: $1,000 between the November 1984 election and DiPrete's inauguration in January 1985, then $2,600 in January and $1,500 in June. These checks and subsequent ones were drawn on Tutela's corporate account. Roney asked if his math was correct that during 1985, a non-election year, Tutela Engineering Associates contributed a total of $5,900.

Tutela hesitated but had to agree.

Roney asked if Tutela could recall being awarded any contracts by the DiPrete Administration.

"I object," Joe Kelly interjected. "I think we're trying one case here, the Olney

Pond case. Are we going to now litigate any other contracts? We're going to be far afield. I object."

After a skirmish, Roney cited a 1985 contract with the Department of Transportation. "Do you recall that the federal government objected and that the contract was canceled?"

Kelly objected boisterously, but Tutela answered, "No, I do not. I don't recall this at all."

Roney directed his witness to the binder and asked him to read a *Providence Journal* story: the Federal Highway Administration had threatened to block funding for nine projects awarded to Tutela.[10] The story said Transportation Department Director Joseph Pezza had overruled his own selection committee and picked Tutela anyway.

In the face of objections from Joe Kelly, Chairman Frank Pellegrino sent Tutela out and asked the defense lawyer why he kept objecting.

Kelly insisted that allegations involving the highway projects had been adjudicated and dismissed. "If a person is acquitted of a crime and is now charged with another crime," he demanded, "can you use the acquittal of that crime to impeach him or to attack his credibility on another crime?"

Commissioner Roger M. Freeman raised a hand. In his late sixties, Freeman had retired from a career in insurance. He wanted to correct what Kelly had just said: that the commission had previously adjudicated these matters. "They never reached our adjudicative panel," Freeman said softly. "They were dismissed prior to reaching the full commission."

"I understand that," Kelly said with a smile. "Those matters were dismissed. That's an exoneration."

Freeman shook his head. "I'm not legally trained. . . ."

"I am legally trained," said Gary Yesser, the commission's counsel. "Mr. Kelly, I think you said adjudication was exoneration. In fact, the record ought to clearly indicate those matters were dismissed because of the chronology. The events occurred before this commission was formed. That's hardly exoneration on the merits."

They brought Tutela back, and Roney asked him if he had testified in 1987 as an expert witness before the Cranston zoning board in support of DiPrete-Laurienzo.

Kelly objected again. "How does that materially bear upon this case?"

Without waiting, Tutela answered: "I did."

"And you're aware," Roney asked, "that the zoning board approved the petition of DiPrete-Laurienzo for a zoning change. Isn't that correct?"

"Yes," Tutela replied.

"And as a result of that petition, they were allowed to build substantially more apartments than had been previously allowed?"

Kelly objected again.

"I can't address that," Tutela replied without waiting. "I don't know anything about it."

Roney had scored points. Domenic Tutela had multiplied his contributions after DiPrete was elected governor, giving heavily from his corporate account. His testimony had helped DiPrete-Laurienzo win an extraordinary zoning change that netted $2 million in a single day. Long before the Olney Pond project, Tutela had established himself as a stalwart supporter of Edward DiPrete. Roney pressed his advantage. "And your last contribution was August 4, 1988?"

"That's right," Tutela said.

Roney asked the businessman why he stopped contributing to DiPrete. Tutela said ruefully that the publicity around DiPrete's dealings, especially the insinuations that campaign contributions got him state work, had hurt his reputation. "I felt it was a negative thing, so I stopped contributing."

Roney nodded sympathetically. "And your last contribution to the governor's campaign was in August of 1988. Is that correct?"

"To the best of my recollection," Tutela agreed.

"And you made no further contributions for the governor's election campaign in 1990?"

"That's right," the engineer said.

Joe Kelly asked a few desultory questions. Nothing he did could erase the portrait John Roney helped Tutela paint of himself as a sycophant currying favor with DiPrete.

On the Tuesday before Thanksgiving, Frederick Lippitt finally took his turn as a witness.[11] Descended from a prominent Rhode Island Republican family, Lippitt was a nephew and grandson of governors and the son of a U.S. Senator. He had stood among the dignitaries who welcomed President Gerald R. Ford to Rhode Island in 1975. Minority leader in the Rhode Island House, Lippitt had also run for mayor of Providence and lost twice to Vincent "Buddy" Cianci. He had always struck me as thoroughly decent.

After the stenographer swore him in, Roney quizzed him about conversations with DiPrete before his appointment as director of administration in 1985. "Do you recall having a discussion regarding the selection of architects and engineers for state contracts?"

"Yes," said Lippitt. "The governor wanted a list of at least three names for each contract. He wanted to have a say and actually tell me which ones he wanted. That's the way we operated."

Roney nodded. "Did the governor tell you that he wanted to make the selections of the A&E committee?"

Kelly objected. "That's not his testimony. His testimony was that the governor wanted to 'have some say.' It's a leading question, a suggestive question, and it doesn't correctly paraphrase the witness's testimony."

Roney drew a breath and turned back to Lippitt. "Mr. Lippitt, did the governor use the words 'have a say in the selection process'?"

"I think it was clear what the governor wanted," Lippitt replied. "Among three qualified people, he wanted to pick the person. That was my understanding of our conversation."

Kelly leaped to his feet again, demanding that Lippitt's answer be stricken from the record. "That's speculation. He's saying what's in his mind. He's supposed to testify what he knows through his five senses."

"Mr. Lippitt," said Gary Yesser, the commission's counsel, "why don't you tell the panel what the governor said to you that led you to the belief that you just reiterated a moment ago?"

"What the governor said was that he wanted to be sure that qualified people got the contracts, that at least three names were to be given to him, and that he would like to pick the one — assuming the person was qualified — to get the job."

"Do you recall," Roney asked, "whether or not the governor ever put this request to you in writing?"

"No," replied Fred Lippitt. "I don't think he did. There was never any further discussion of it."

"And after your conversations that you've related to us, you took the job?"

"Yes." If Lippitt felt embarrassed or ashamed, he hid it well. I glanced at DiPrete but saw no emotion.

Under Roney's carefully segmented questions, Lippitt told how he received short lists from the A&E committee. His assistant routinely prepared a package that went to DiPrete: names in alphabetical order and a separate page that showed how much state work each firm had received. "As long as I was there, this was the format."

"Was that procedure embodied in any regulation or rule?"

"No," Lippitt replied. "I don't think so."

Roney asked Lippitt to review the evidence book, which held executive orders DiPrete signed in 1985 and 1986.[12] The first ran three pages, single-spaced. The second stretched to a fourth page. Both contained sections about the process for selecting firms that were professionally and technically qualified. Both specified that the director of administration would select the highest qualified firm. "Is that correct?" he asked.

"Yes," Lippitt replied.

"The executive order does not say anything about sending the names to the governor. Is that correct?"

"That's correct." Lippitt sat ramrod straight.

"Do you recall mentioning to anyone that there was a step in this process that wasn't contained in this document?"

"No."

Roney had Lippitt look at another tab in the binder, a cover page that listed vendor information. To the left of the firm's name was a box. "Do you recall getting these forms back from the governor on a regular basis?"

"Yes," Lippitt said.

"Would you get these forms back from the governor with some indication of his preference or choice?"

Kelly objected. "'Choice' could very well be a recommendation, so I object."

Yesser asked gently: "Mr. Lippitt, would there be any marks?"

"Yes."

"What would be the nature of those marks?"

Kelly objected to the repetition. "It was a check mark," he said.

"That's right," Lippitt agreed. "It would be a check mark."

After further skirmishing, Roney tried again. Had Lippitt and DiPrete used this procedure "a number of times?"

"Relatively frequently," Lippitt said. "I mean in three years a substantial number of things that went through."

"Fair to say a number? Thirty or forty contracts?"

"I would think at least that," Lippitt agreed.

Roney circled back: "So the choice of Tutela Engineering was made by the governor. Is that correct?"

Kelly objected again but was overruled.

Lippitt said he could not remember preparing the Olney Pond list. "I can't say to you three years later I remember that specific one, but I'm sure that's what happened because that was a regular procedure."

His large horn-rimmed glasses gave Lippitt an owlish look. Under cross-examination, he had bared DiPrete's secret protocol, shuffling lists that no outsider could have seen. Lippitt had abetted this routine deception but saw nothing wrong.

Roney pounced. "So the choice of Tutela Engineering was made by the governor. Is that correct?"

Kelly objected. "That's the issue to be decided by this board."

Pellegrino overruled him. "Mr. Lippitt, please respond."

"Yes," said Lippitt without visible embarrassment. "I should perhaps add that Tutela never got the contract."

Without celebrating, Roney directed Lippitt to Judith Benedict's memo that spelled out the reasons Tutela was unacceptable for Olney Pond. DEM director Robert Bendick had initialed her memo and sent it to Lippitt.

Lippitt acknowledged receiving the memo but said he had lost it, a mistake that prevented the water quality study from going forward that summer. He said DEM had started calling him. "Unfortunately, I'm not noted for a very clean desk. One way or another, this memorandum disappeared. I couldn't find it so they sent another copy to me in August."

Finally, four months after the original Tutela choice, Fred Lippitt had grappled with the need to rescind it. "I think I talked with Mr. Bendick or someone in his department," he said straightforwardly. "I felt we ought to look again at who should get that contract."

No one guffawed, and Lippitt plunged ahead. "The governor was away. I don't remember whether he was in the Governor's Conference or Republican National Convention. I reached his chief of staff, who was with him. He talked to the governor and called back. He said the governor agreed we should review it, and so then he said . . . "

"Well, I object," Kelly shouted. "This is double hearsay."

Yesser asked Lippitt if he had finished his answer.

"I got interrupted," Lippitt said, as if miffed that Kelly impugned his recitation. "The governor agreed that we were having a problem with this and that it would be appropriate to select one of the others." Lippitt said he then felt free to choose Lycott Environmental Research for Olney Pond. "Frankly, it was perfectly clear to me that this was the way the government should operate."

Roney finished his cross-examination. He had forced Lippitt to reveal vital secrets.

Joe Kelly rose and took off his jacket. He hung it neatly over the back of his chair.

"Mr. Kelly," said the chairperson, Frank Pellegrino, "it seems like you're ready to question this witness."

Kelly forced a laugh. He turned to Lippitt. "You said the press was inquiring about the Tutela matter. Is that correct?"

"Yes."

"And you also said, if I heard you correctly, 'I don't know why they were making an issue of that.' "

Lippitt seemed relieved. "I've always had trouble with wanting to make an issue of this because Tutela never got the contract."

"Tutela never got the contract?" Kelly sounded shocked.

"That's correct," said Lippitt. "I frankly thought it was a very political thing. We were in the middle of a political campaign. These make wonderful things during campaign time."

Kelly kept it brief and cordial with Lippitt. "It was your understanding that DEM approved Tutela as qualified?"

"The record shows they did," Lippitt said, apparently unaware of Judith Benedict's predicament in the A&E committee.

Under Kelly's questions, Lippitt affirmed that DiPrete had acted in keeping with his stated intention to hire Rhode Island firms whenever possible. Lycott and IEP were Massachusetts companies, he said, while Tutela was the only in-state outfit on the short list. He seemed oblivious to the fact that Tutela's primary office was in Wilmington, north of Boston.

Lippitt came across as reasonable and sincere but emotionally detached. He answered Kelly with disarming candor but then offered a tidbit that Kelly could not block, object to, or strike from the transcript. "Since the governor had made the original selection," Lippitt said, "I thought it could not be changed without checking with him, telling him what the problem was."

Lippitt's call to DiPrete at the Republican National Convention was the essential final link in a chain of proof.

Joe Kelly never flinched. "And you selected Lycott then?"

"That's right," Lippitt said agreeably.

"And you also said, if I noted it correctly, 'It's perfectly clear to me that that's the way government should operate.'"

"That's right. The wrong person didn't get the contract."

Ernest Ashton, DiPrete's friend for thirty years, had sat silently through hearing after hearing. His expression gave no clue about his feelings. Finally, he raised a hand to be recognized. "Mr. Lippitt," Ashton said politely, "I have one question. You were asked, I believe, did you always follow the governor's recommendation when the names came back to you? You answered: 'Most of the time with one or two exceptions.' Is that right?"

Lippitt described the River Walk project in downtown Providence. "Bill Warner designed it, and he wasn't selected for it." Lippitt said he challenged the governor's choice of another firm.

"And the governor's reaction to that?"

"He said, 'You have a point.' And he took Warner."

I wondered if someone on the DiPrete side had fed those questions to Ashton. The exchange lessened the impression that Lippitt always took DiPrete's check marks as contract orders.

On December 4, Mathies J. Santos followed Fred Lippitt in the witness chair.[13] Santos had been Lippitt's executive assistant and was the fourth member of the A&E Committee that short-listed Tutela. I had often seen Santos at the State House in an Air Force uniform resplendent with ribbons, combining an officer's bearing with a ready smile. He came before the adjudicative panel in a business suit.

After preliminaries, John Roney asked him if he recalled the discussion that put Tutela on the list.

Santos said he could not remember it.

Roney persisted: "Did you recommend Tutela Engineering Associates for inclusion on the short list?"

"I don't know," said Santos. "I don't specifically recall recommending Tutela."

"Do you recall recommending any of the four firms' inclusion on the short list?"

"No."

Roney pointed Santos to minutes that suggested that the A&E meeting began at 10:00 a.m. and ended at 10:45. "So you were able to review and conclude the discussion on four projects within forty-five minutes?"

"That's what the minutes say."

Roney directed Santos to a series of documents: the short list of projects and a cover sheet that would have gone to the governor.

Santos agreed that he had prepared the cover sheet, which included bare basics of the proposed project. To the left of each firm on the short list was an empty box. Roney asked if the lists routinely had little boxes next to the names of vendors.

"Correct," said Santos, clearly on guard. He explained that the list with boxes and the sheet that summarized prior contracts went together in an envelope to the governor's office.

"And how would it be sent?" Roney asked.

"Someone would drop it off up there. If I were going that way, I'd drop it off."

"How did you know to send this to the governor's office?"

"To get his feedback," Santos answered, seeming not to notice how much he had just given away.

"Was there any notation on those documents?"

"There would be an indication for selection."

Kelly objected and moved to strike. "If there's a check mark or a dot, that may not be an indication of selection. It could easily be a recommendation. It's not fair to this witness to have him say that a check mark means selection or choice or acknowledgment."

Gary Yesser, the commission's lawyer, reminded Kelly that he could clarify the meaning of a mark during his cross-examination.

"A check mark," Santos said without being asked. "There was a check mark."

Kelly objected. Every exchange sparked a sparring match between him and Roney. The legal nuances vanished, but an impression of lists secretly shuffled back and forth remained.

Roney focused on Santos: "The cover sheet and short list that went to the governor, how would that be returned to you?"

"Usually in the mail from the governor's office."

"And having received that from the governor's office, you would simply prepare the letter you've identified. Is that correct?"

"Correct."

"And this letter was prepared for Mr. Lippitt's signature?"

"Yes, it was."

The point was unmistakable. DiPrete's check mark with no further input from Lippitt prompted Santos to prepare the selection letter. Lippitt then signed the document, as if the choice were his own, another telling detail.

In their turn, commissioners quizzed Santos. Roger Freeman directed him to the DEM technical committee's original memo to Judith Benedict. One conclusion stood alone as a paragraph. Freeman read it aloud: " 'None of the other firms that submitted proposals were found acceptable to the committee.' " He paused and focused on Santos. "Was that given to you prior to the April 8 meeting?"[14]

"No," said Santos. "To the best of my recollection, it wasn't handed out as part of our package."

In his turn, John O'Brien asked Santos whether anyone on the A&E committee, except Judith Benedict, had qualifications to select a firm for the Olney Pond Project.

Kelly objected that O'Brien was wrongly impugning the A&E members' qualifications.

"Well, I'll rephrase it," O'Brien answered. "Did anyone on the A&E committee have knowledge of the type of work that was to be accomplished except DEM?"

"I think," said Santos, "Mr. Parrillo had some background or had dealt with those types of firms before."

O'Brien asked if Santos thought that — other than Benedict — Parrillo was the most qualified on the A&E committee to rate the applicants.

"Off the top," said Santos, "I'd say yes."

O'Brien smiled. Santos had not heard Gilbert Parrillo testify that the DiPrete campaigns assigned him to hang signs, nor that the City of Cranston had promoted him from truck driver to an "architectural technician."

"Who made the final selection saying Tutela gets the job?" O'Brien asked. "Who made the selection?"

"The governor," Santos said meekly.

"The governor did?" O'Brien sounded shocked.

"On the documentation there was a check mark indicating Tutela," Santos said, then pulled back: "Tutela, as you're aware, did not get the job."

"I know that," said O'Brien. "I'm talking about how he was selected to get the job."

Kelly kept objecting. After another legal volley, O'Brien tried a backhand. "You don't know who made the check in the governor's office, do you?"

"I assume the governor," said Santos.

"When you sent that form up, who did you address it to?"

"To the governor."

O'Brien nodded. "To the governor personally?"

"Correct," said Santos.

O'Brien said he was finished. The wily former IRS director had elicited damning facts.

Pellegrino, the chairperson, posed a follow-up question to Santos. "When Tutela was 'selected' or 'recommended' on the list that came back from the governor's office, you directly prepared the letter?"

"Yes," said Matt Santos, reinforcing the point that Lippitt signed the letters but did not select the contractors.

"You prepared the letter for Mr. Lippitt's signature?"

"Yes."

Pellegrino saw Ernest Ashton's hand go up, and signaled permission to speak.

"Mr. Santos," Ashton began, "did you say that you were influenced prior to A&E meetings by someone to make a choice of vendors? Did you say that?"

Kelly objected but was overruled.

Unperturbed, Ashton asked again, "Were you influenced?"

"My sense," said Santos, "was that the firms were qualified. If they could get on the short list, I would get them on the short list."

"Did anyone suggest to you that Tutela's name be placed on the short list?"

"Not to the best of my recollection."

"You were never influenced in any way to put a particular vendor's name on the A&E short list prior to a meeting?"

"This meeting?" Santos asked. "Are we talking about the Tutela meeting?"

"You already answered that," said Ashton. "You said you were not influenced. Were you influenced in any other situations?"

Kelly objected for the record.

"I think I went to some meetings that a firm. . . ." Santos floundered. "If it were possible to get a firm on the list, I would get them on the list."

Kelly shouted to strike that, but Santos pushed on: "Assuming that the firm is qualified."

"But never in the case of Tutela?" Ashton asked.

"Not to the best of my recollection."

Ashton sounded sympathetic. "That's what we're talking about today. You sent it to the governor to get his feedback. That was your testimony?"

"Right," said Santos. "I took it to be his recommendation when it came back with the check mark. I would write up the letter in that fashion."

Before his grilling was over, Santos admitted that he sometimes brought the names of firms to the A&E meeting and that those names routinely made the short list. The stark truth settled in. One witness after another claimed not to remember crucial details, and minutes of the A&E committee were worthless.

Mathies Santos returned another afternoon for further testimony. Just before he was to be ushered in, Joe Kelly stunned the room by suggesting that commissioner Cheryl Fisher-Allen be disqualified.[15]

Before Santos's first testimony, Fisher-Allen had informed the panel that she knew Santos but had not seen him in years. She had said their relationship would not affect her objectivity.

Now Kelly said she had not recused. "Nor did I ask her to be excused," he said. His ploy was clever but risky. If Fisher-Allen were to leave, only five commissioners would remain, and Kelly's chances of having DiPrete exonerated would soar. But if she stayed, Kelly's move might antagonize her and her fellow commissioners. She and Santos were both part of an emerging black middle class in Providence, and the only people of color in these hearings.

Kelly insisted that questions asked of Santos had put Fisher-Allen in an unfair position. "That never should have happened," he declared, "except by inquiry into irrelevant matters. She may now have to judge the credibility of someone who is a friend or a social acquaintance and that just should not be." He suggested, he said "respectfully," that she be excused.

John Roney pounced on Kelly's suggestion, reminding the panel that Fisher-Allen had already said her acquaintance with Santos would have no bearing on her ability to judge the matter fairly. He noted that Santos was testifying under oath and that his credibility was no more an issue than it had been from the start.

The six commissioners prepared to deliberate on Kelly's challenge with their counsel, Gary Yesser. Everyone else stepped out into the bland reception area. DiPrete's forces staked out one corner, whispering among themselves. Rae Condon and I stood near the doorway. John Roney found a neutral spot and studied his notes. The stenographer thumbed through a magazine.

When the session reconvened, Cheryl Fisher-Allen asked to make a statement on the record. A fourth-grade teacher, she had won several awards for excellence. Now, in a deep contralto, she enunciated every word. "Before Mr. Santos was sworn in as a witness, I asked that the record show that I knew him personally. We grew up in the same neighborhood, and our families knew each other quite well."

She directed her full force at Kelly. "I was closer to his sister than I was to Mr. Santos. I have not seen him more than twice in the last ten years, and that was only on a professional basis." She described brief contacts at an educational forum and a foundation reception. "I have not seen Mr. Santos or talked to him since, so I still do not feel that I should recuse myself. I think I can be very objective with his testimony and that of other witnesses."

Like a schoolboy caught out in mischief, Kelly said blandly that he had spoken only for the record and that he had not actually made a motion to disqualify her.

The tension dissipated, and Santos returned to the witness chair for a few further questions from Roney, Kelly, and John O'Brien. Nothing of substance emerged. Santos's answers seemed to have little consequence for either side, and as Santos left, I wondered why they bothered to bring him back. Perhaps Roney had recalled him as a ruse, luring Kelly to challenge Fisher-Allen. I sensed that Joe Kelly had made a strategic blunder.

Finally, Dennis L. DiPrete entered the hearing room, taller than his father but with the same large brown eyes. He seemed naked without his mirrored, wrap-around sunglasses. Under the shadow of grand jury proceedings, he brought his own lawyer, Mark Freel, who sat beside him. The younger DiPrete gave his name and swore to tell the truth.

Under Kelly's questions, Dennis DiPrete acknowledged a social relationship with Santos. Of the governor's entire staff, only two besides Santos had been invited to the younger DiPrete's recent wedding. Kelly established an explanation for the fact that Dennis DiPrete and Matt Santos spoke often on the phone and met frequently. His questions enabled the governor's son to say Santos had asked advice from him because he wanted to do a good job.

"You never delivered any of that information to your father?" Kelly asked.

"That's right," Dennis DiPrete said.

In cross-examination, Roney asked him: "Did you ever tell your father that Matt Santos was regularly asking for your advice on architects and engineers?"

"No."

"So, your father was the governor of Rhode Island at the time, and someone you've referred to as a member of his staff was regularly asking you for advice as to his job and you never mentioned it to your father?"

"No," said Dennis DiPrete. "I never told my father about it."

Roney nodded and took a step backward. "Do I understand you to be testifying that Mr. Santos would ask you your opinion about various architects and engineers who had made proposals for state contracts?"

"Matt and I would talk about many things. Quite a few were issues that we dealt with during the campaigns. I remember talking to him in the context that he was going to be part of selecting architects and engineers. It really wasn't his field of specialty. He knew me to be a friend with no hidden agenda."

Roney let Dennis DiPrete ramble, and he kept explaining. "Sometimes when he asked me, I wouldn't know any of them. Sometimes I would know them by reputation. Sometimes I might know some of them personally."

Roney asked if these conversations occurred in Santos's office.

"Usually, or else I may have gone out to lunch with him."

"Would he call you and ask you to come down specifically for this purpose?"

"Yes, several times he did. I remember specifically a few times Matt saying that he had to go to a meeting later on that morning, and would I have time to come down and meet with him?"

"And would Mr. Santos have a list in front of him when he was going over these?"

"Ordinarily, yes." The younger DiPrete's tone was matter-of-fact, but it strained credulity that his father did not know.

Several commissioners asked about the documents. Had he read them? Had he taken any with him from these meetings?

Dennis DiPrete's lawyer objected, citing huge numbers of documents being produced in response to grand jury subpoenas. He directed the former governor's son not to answer.

Roney asked Dennis DiPrete if he had worked with Domenic Tutela on the 1988 zoning change in Cranston.

Kelly shouted his objection. "Now we're going to try the Cranston land case? You know, it's okay for Common Cause to be present here, but I didn't get this nose from not knowing where I'm running as a lawyer. I certainly know these questions are coming from Common Cause. They've got a motion here to re-open the Cranston land case, and we take a recess, and all of a sudden start asking questions on it? Not fair."

Rae Condon rose. "Objection to that statement!"

"I object," roared Kelly.

Condon moved to strike Kelly's remark from the record. "Mr. Chairman, Common Cause has abided by the rules of this commission and has not provided any particular questions at recess to counsel for the commission. And we still hope to be heard on our pending motions."

"That's typical of the attitude!" Kelly swelled with indignation.

Condon demanded that his remark be struck from the record.

"Enough!" Pellegrino pounded his gavel, and the room fell silent.

After that uproar, John O'Brien asked a series of gentle questions that established Dennis DiPrete's closeness to his father and frequent meetings with Matt Santos before A&E meetings. Dennis DiPrete acknowledged that he often combined those sessions with stops to see his father.

O'Brien looked puzzled. "And you never discussed your meeting with Mr. Santos at any time with your father, the governor?"

"I never discussed the A&E issues with him. I didn't think it was that big of a deal."

O'Brien scowled. "I'm trying to understand what your thinking was. Don't you see how embarrassing it would be to your father if it came out that you were in the office on the day of an A&E meeting, and you talked to Mr. Santos? And these contractors were talked about? He may have made some notes, and some clerk got hold of them? Didn't you have your father's welfare in mind?"

Kelly objected. "How does that impinge on his father's welfare?"

O'Brien raised his eyebrows and said he had no more questions.

The commission's attorney, Gary Yesser, asked Dennis DiPrete whether he had given Santos information about vendors before January of 1989.

Dennis DiPrete said he was absolutely certain he had not.

"So for the year 1988, even on an informal basis, you didn't have any input to Mr. Santos regarding a prospective A&E vendor?"

"I'm absolutely certain. He never asked, and I never offered."

Yesser stroked his stylish chin whiskers. "Did you have any input with anyone in your father's office or your father regarding the awarding of A&E contracts prior to January 1, 1989?"

"No."

"You're quite certain of that?"

"I'm certain," said Dennis DiPrete.

"Your father would never ask you: 'Gee whiz, I've got a list of five. What do you think, Dennis?'"

"I don't recall my father ever referring to a list having to do with selections." The longer it went on, the odder it sounded. Could anyone believe Dennis DiPrete was telling the truth?

Finally, the stenographer swore in former Gov. Edward DiPrete. He might have claimed his Fifth Amendment right not to incriminate himself but raised his right hand and swore to tell the truth. Week after week, he had listened to the witnesses. Prosecutor John Roney walked him through two executive orders he had issued, and DiPrete affirmed that minor revisions from the first executive order to the second had not altered the actual selection process.

Roney asked if either document mentioned the fact that the governor would have input on the selections.

"It's not specifically spelled out," DiPrete said. "No."

Roney pointed DiPrete to a *Providence Journal* story where his chief of staff, Norman DeLuca, had declared that there was no favoritism by the governor for any firm. "We are not involved in the selection process," DeLuca had told the reporter.[16]

As if to buy time, DiPrete read the paragraph aloud, ending with a tepid denial that the governor's office had "been involved in" choosing contractors.

"That wasn't exactly the case, was it?" Roney asked. "You were involved in the selection process, isn't that correct?"

Kelly objected loudly but was overruled.

DiPrete calibrated his answer, equivocating but not sounding defensive. "Of course the statement refers to Norman DeLuca, my chief of staff. He is saying that we are not involved in the selection process and, to the extent of the meaning of the word 'selection,' that's correct, As far as having a say in the recommendation to the director of administration? Yes, I did have input."

"And you were certainly part of the selection process. Isn't that correct?"

Kelly objected again and was overruled again.

"Not of the selection process," DiPrete answered coolly.

Roney would not let him escape. "You had a role in the process pursuant to which the final selection for these contracts was made. Isn't that correct?"

"I had a role which was restricted to a recommendation to an expression of opinion to the director of administration, who was free to accept or reject it."

Another volley of objections rattled around the room.

DiPrete replied, "I was part of the process — in the sense of when a certain number of firms were deemed to have been qualified, the director of administration sent that list to me with only the names of the firms and the backup sheet on two or three as may be required with the amount of state business they had had since January 1, 1985. I tried to express an informed opinion when I could."

Roney absorbed DiPrete's run-on sentence. "So Mr. DeLuca's statement — to the extent it refers to the governor's office as not being involved in the selection process — is incorrect, is it not?"

After another objection from Kelly, Roney tried again. "Did you ever, after reading this article, speak with Mr. DeLuca and say: 'I have a role in this process'?"

DiPrete smiled, the corners of his mouth still characteristically turned down. "I don't recall if I did or not. That was in the fall of 1988. It was a chaotic time of the year, I'm sure you'll agree. I may have said something to him. I may not have. I honestly don't recall."

"Did you instruct Mr. DeLuca to issue any statement to the press about your role in this matter?"

"No, I don't believe I did."

Joe Kelly took his turn asking questions. DiPrete explained that he had issued the executive orders to establish a fair process for applicants. In response to the question whether he had made the final decision on architectural and engineering jobs, he answered unequivocally that he had not.

"Did you recommend Domenic Tutela because he gave you campaign contributions?"

"Absolutely not," said DiPrete.

"When you made your recommendations, did you on occasions recommend people who hadn't given contributions to your campaigns?"

"Sure did," said DiPrete. "Yes."

Kelly looked genuinely puzzled. "If a person makes a political contribution, are they automatically barred from bidding state jobs?"

"No," the former governor said. "They're not."

"Is there anything in the law or the executive order that says people who make contributions can't bid the jobs?"

"No, not at all."

"Is there anything in that regulation that says those people are not qualified because they gave campaign contributions?"

"No," said DiPrete.

"You testified that Mr. Tutela did get some state contracts, correct?"

"That is correct."

"Mr. Tutela did not get this particular Olney Pond project, did he?"

"No, he didn't get it."

"And when you heard that Mr. Bendick of DEM wanted someone else your remark was: 'Fine, he can have who he wants'?"

"That's correct," said Edward DiPrete.

Kelly led him through the differences between the words "recommendation" and "selection."

DiPrete insisted that he did nothing more than express an opinion to Lippitt, who made the selection.

In his turn to ask questions, John O'Brien went back to parsing the executive orders. "Lippitt looks like the person that was going to select, but he had to send it up to you for a recommendation. You had set up a procedure that contravenes these two executive orders. Do you think the way this is worded gives the impression that you're out of it? What do you think?"

DiPrete maintained eye contact with O'Brien and answered patiently: "It clearly spells out the procedures, but the governor is not out of anything. If something blows, even though there's no executive order that says the governor should be involved in the loop, the chief executive is there, Mr. O'Brien."

O'Brien scowled. "The executive order has nothing to do with what you're talking about. It's not even covered in the executive order. What you're doing is circumventing the executive order."

DiPrete stared back at him. "I respectfully disagree, sir."

"That's okay," said O'Brien, his views clear.

At the end of questions about Olney Pond, DiPrete insisted that during eight years as mayor of Cranston, he had worked with Tutela and knew he was qualified. He rejected every suggestion that DEM's team of scientists had any better basis for judgment.

After the hearing ended, Richard Morsilli left the room last and we shook hands. I risked a question about a brass plaque I had noticed not far from our home. The tennis courts in Roger Williams Park had been renamed for a young player killed by a drunk driver. "Commissioner," I asked, "may I ask if you're related to Todd Morsilli?"

"He was my son," Morsilli said softly, his mournful eyes now focused on me. "Something happens when you lose your child. You absolutely cannot undo what's happened. You either turn inward and start dying, or you open up and commit what's left of your life to those positive things you can still do."

Jamestown Bridge
1991

IN 1987 contractors had quit work on a soaring new bridge between Jamestown and North Kingstown. Unfinished concrete pillars jutted up from the mile-wide channel. At their tops, tangles of rebar rusted in the salty air. The project fell three years behind schedule and ran $50 million over budget. The construction firms blamed the Rhode Island Department of Transportation (DOT) for faulty data and mismanagement. The DiPrete administration prepared for a legal battle.[1]

In January 1989, Common Cause charged Gov. Edward DiPrete with conflicts of interest in the hiring of James L. Taft Jr. — the governor's mentor, friend, lawyer, business partner, and campaign finance chair — to represent DOT in court. Taft had preceded DiPrete as mayor of Cranston and now led a prosperous law firm, Taft & McSally. The question for the panel hearing the case was whether DiPrete had improperly steered the litigation contract to Taft.

The case oozed with irony, since Taft had won the controversial contract in a joint venture with DiPrete's primary defense lawyer, Joseph A. Kelly. Kelly was not present for Taft's testimony, and two of his law partners, Keith B. Kyle and John R. Mahoney, sat beside the former governor. Kyle told the panel that Kelly was on vacation.

Under questioning from John Roney, Taft acknowledged that he and DiPrete were partners in Atwood Associates Realty Trust, the corporation that bought and sold property on Atwood Avenue in the notorious Cranston land deal. Roney directed Taft to a document in the binder of documents, and Taft quickly agreed that Atwood Associates purchased that property, did the permitting on it, and sold it to Kenneth Lokey.[2]

From the defense table John Mahoney objected that there had been no finding of probable cause in connection with the Cranston land deal. "Whether it was sold for ten cents or ten million dollars is of no significance here," he declared. "With all due respect, it's inflammatory. It's prejudicial."

Roney smiled and turned to address the chairperson, Frank Pellegrino. "Shortly after the zoning matter that Mr. Taft has testified to, the chairman of the Cranston zoning board, George DiMuro, was appointed chairman of the Coastal Resources Management Council by the governor." Roney also noted that DiPrete had been fully aware that he had a business relationship with Taft at the time Taft and Kelly got the Jamestown Bridge contract.

Abruptly, Roney sat down without asking Taft about the Jamestown Bridge lawsuit.

DiPrete's counsel, Mahoney, seemed befuddled. He had no questions for Taft.

I felt like clapping for John Roney. He knew Taft and DiPrete's lawyers had come expecting to deal with the Jamestown Bridge contract. Under his questions, Taft had admitted in unmistakable terms that he and DiPrete had made a killing together on the Cranston zoning case and land sale. Roney had also locked down the fact that DiPrete and Taft were unarguably "joined together to achieve a common financial objective." Under the state ethics law they were unmistakably "business associates."

Commissioner John O'Brien, the retired IRS district director, asked Taft nonchalantly what his thoughts were when he bid on the Jamestown Bridge contract.

"To present the best proposal possible," Taft said. "To convince the Department of Transportation that we could do the best job at the best price and to obtain the contract."

O'Brien's eyebrows lifted. "You never had any apprehension about public perception because of your friendship with the governor?"

Taft chuckled. "I think if everyone who was to do business with the State of Rhode Island had an apprehension about a friendship or acquaintance with the governor, there wouldn't be many doing business with the state."

O'Brien asked Taft who might have recommended him to the governor.

"I didn't need any recommendations. I've known him since I was a boy. I worked for his father in the apple orchard up in Scituate on Saturday mornings."

Commissioner Richard Morsilli followed. "Mr. Taft, I know you've had a long relationship with the governor. Why wouldn't you have thought to mention to the governor that he should seek an advisory opinion from the Ethics Commission?"

Mahoney objected. "We're asking the witness why there wasn't an advisory opinion concerning a presumable conflict which has not been established on this record. We're presupposing facts that are not in evidence, to the detriment of my client."

Chairman Frank Pellegrino explained that advisory opinions were to help officials decide whether they had a conflict. He denied the objection, and Mahoney backed off.

Taft answered that he did not know why the governor had not sought an advisory opinion.

Persisting, Morsilli asked Taft why — as DiPrete's friend and a former public official — he had not suggested to the governor that he seek an advisory opinion.

"I was looking at this as a piece of business," said Taft. "It's a lot easier to look at it four-and-a-half or five years later and say something went wrong. Technical violation, whatever it is. And I don't think the governor did anything wrong. I know he didn't." Taft added that nothing even faintly suggested that DiPrete had intervened on his behalf to get the contract for legal work.

Finally, DiPrete crossed to the witness chair, and he swore to tell the truth. Roney probed the decision to seek outside legal counsel.

"I approved the concept," DiPrete said cheerfully. "At the point I was advised they would have to go to outside counsel, I said: 'If that's what you have to do, I agree. Do it.'"

After that relatively smooth start, the hearing erupted.

In answer to a question from Roney, DiPrete flatly denied that he had recommended Taft's firm to DOT Director Matthew J. Gill Jr., whom he had appointed in 1986.[3]

Roney seemed startled. With elaborate care, he asked again: "You don't deny, Governor, that you gave Matt Gill the name of the firm Taft & McSally for consideration?"

"No," said DiPrete. "I did not give him any specific name for consideration."

Carefully, Roney posed a follow-up: "You recall, Governor, a meeting in your office on December 24, 1990, where I was present. Is that correct?"

"I recall a meeting in my office. If it's December 24, so be it. I do remember. Yes."

Roney focused and then spoke: "Lynette Labinger, a lawyer from Rhode Island, was present?"

"Yes. She was there."

"And you had three lawyers present. Isn't that correct? Joseph Kelly was present?"

DiPrete seemed wary. "I believe he was."

Roney reminded DiPrete that the lawyers had come to the governor's office at his request. The Christmas Eve meeting, a week before DiPrete would leave office, was to review the pending ethics complaint.

DiPrete agreed.

"And you were aware that one of the allegations concerned the hiring of counsel for the Jamestown Bridge. Is that right?"

"I was aware that was one of the allegations."

"And do you recall stating in that meeting that . . ."

"I object," Mahoney shouted, suddenly on his feet. "I mean he's acting as a prosecutor and witness at the same time. I have to interrupt this question." Mahoney sparred with commission counsel Gary Yesser.

John Roney asked to speak. He ignored Mahoney and spoke directly to the adjudicative panel. "The governor has just made a statement to you, which I believe we will be able to show is at variance with what he said earlier. It's a classic prior inconsistent statement. He made the statement before a number of people, including Lynette Labinger, a lawyer." Roney paused. "I had no idea that the governor would deny facts that he stated as facts at that meeting. He has done so. If he continues doing so, we'll put on a witness that will say he stated these facts at a different time under different circumstances."

DiPrete looked bewildered.

Roney told the commissioners that it would be their responsibility to judge the credibility of witnesses. It would be for them to decide whether the former governor had changed his story from what he said in his office on December 24, 1990.

Pellegrino allowed Roney to ask his prior question again.

"Governor," Roney said respectfully, "do you recall stating at that meeting that you had written to Matthew Gill, stating the need for the appointment of outside counsel and recommending Taft & McSally?"

"I'm glad to clarify this," DiPrete answered. "I understood your question a few moments ago to be did I, in fact, recommend Taft & McSally to Matthew Gill. Is that substantially what your question was?"

Without an answer from Roney, DiPrete answered the question. "I said, 'No, I did not recommend any specific attorney.' I thought I had sent a written letter recommending different attorneys to be considered. I thought a written communication had gone over. Maybe it could have contained names. In fact, no letter evidently was ever sent. My office didn't have a copy of it. Legal counsel didn't have a copy of any such letter. Nor did the Department of Transportation have a copy of any such letter."

Whatever DiPrete actually said on Christmas Eve, barely a week before he left office, had obviously shocked his lawyers. They had scoured three sets of files for the letter he mentioned.

"I was confused in answering you on the 24th," DiPrete said. "My recollection is that I sent a handwritten note back on his memo to me, literally with a Flair pen, as was my practice on short replies of this nature. The gist of it was: 'While I have no specific objection to any of the above firms, aren't there any qualified law firms in the State of Rhode Island that you could consider?'"

DiPrete seemed to have regained his footing. He sounded plausible, down to the Flair pen. "It's been state practice — and I think it's a good policy — if there are qualified vendors in the state. We're not giving up either in terms of competitiveness or quality."

Roney spoke carefully. "Governor, at that same meeting on December 24, with your counsel present, do you recall stating to us that you had recommended Taft & McSally because you knew them and knew they had handled nine major public works matters for the City of Cranston, and had the wherewithal to handle the case, or knew how to get it?"

"I don't recall saying that, because — quite frankly — I don't."

Roney spoke with deliberate care. "Do you recall saying later in that same meeting, after we requested a copy of your letter to Matt Gill, that perhaps you had made the recommendation in a meeting with Mr. Gill?"

Cautiously, DiPrete said he thought Roney had mentioned a verbal, rather than written, recommendation to Gill.

Roney absorbed what sounded like a deliberately garbled answer. "Just so we are clear on the record, Governor, you agree that you stated to us that you had written to Matt Gill recommending Taft & McSally?"

Mahoney objected, and Roney tried again. "Governor, do you deny that you stated at the meeting we have described on December 24 that you had written to Matt Gill stating the need for the appointment of outside counsel and that you had given him the name of Taft & McSally?"

"I may have said that, but subsequent investigation indicated that I was incorrect. And I think we subsequently notified you to that effect," he rambled on.

Roney persisted. "Do you deny stating to us at that meeting that you had recommended Taft & McSally because you knew them and they had handled major public works in the City of Cranston?"

"I don't recall saying that, but I've known Taft as an individual and that the law firm of Taft & McSally was believed to be a good one."

"Do you deny stating at that meeting that Gill took over the process and that you never spoke to him about the selection again?"

DiPrete looked Roney in the eye. "I never spoke to him about the selection. Period. He kept me abreast, as I mentioned a moment ago. I had no input into the process."

"Do you deny that you gave him the name of Taft & McSally?"

"Absolutely."

Roney drew a deep breath and stepped backward. "Mr. Chairman, we will be adding another witness to this matter, who was a participant in this meeting."

A week later, John Roney called as his first witness attorney Lynette Labinger, his law partner. Defense counsel John Mahoney objected to her and to the next witness Roney had listed: Deming Sherman, a lawyer who had bid on the Jamestown Bridge litigation contract. Commission chairman Frank Pellegrino listened to Mahoney, consulted in whispers with Gary Yesser, and announced that the panel would hear testimony from both Lynette Labinger and Deming Sherman.[4]

Labinger told of practicing law in Rhode Island for twenty-five years. She had assisted Roney at the Christmas Eve meeting by taking detailed notes. In response to his question, she skimmed her notes and outlined the conversation. DiPrete had said that neither legal staff at the DOT nor the attorney general could handle the Jamestown Bridge matter. With her index finger in the margin, she read verbatim: "The governor stated that he felt he would be remiss if he did not take action. He wrote to the department director, Gill, stating that outside counsel was needed, and he suggested the firm of Taft & McSally."

Labinger quoted DiPrete as saying the DOT solicited bids and ultimately hired Taft & McSally, but he had "no part in the selection process."

Roney nodded. "Did the governor state why he had recommended Taft & McSally for the Jamestown Bridge litigation?"

Labinger skimmed to another point in her notes and read again: "He was asked the basis for his recommendation of Taft & McSally. The governor stated that he knew Taft & McSally. They had handled major public works matters for the City of Cranston. He believed they had the wherewithal to perform the legal duties or knew how to get them."

In answer to another question, Labinger quoted DiPrete's assumption that Gill's letter and his written response were at the Department of Transportation.

Roney asked if the letter to Mr. Gill came up again during that meeting.

"Yes." She found a section in her notes. "Towards the end of the meeting when we were talking about collecting documents, Gov. DiPrete stated that maybe there was no letter, that he could have made the statement at a meeting with Mr. Gill."

"Did the governor in any way retract or revoke his statement that he had recommended Taft & McSally for the Jamestown Bridge litigation?"

Labinger looked up from her notes. "No, he did not."

In his turn, Commissioner John O'Brien asked Labinger whether she had done other interviews with Roney.

"We've done client interviews jointly in the office. Sure."

"Do you usually take notes?"

Labinger smiled. "Yes, I'm a compulsive note-taker. In fact, I used to give away my notes during law school to people. We had 'open note' exams, and other people would borrow my notes."

Labinger was excused. Her testimony seemed unassailable. Had DiPrete's lawyers not recorded the session or made verbatim notes? What had they said to DiPrete after that meeting? Had they prepped him to claim he had never recommended Taft? Had he now committed perjury?

Deming Sherman was the managing partner at Edwards & Angell, a prestigious Providence firm. Roney led him through preliminaries. Sherman testified that Veronica Ridolfi, the chief legal counsel at the DOT, had invited proposals to handle the Jamestown Bridge lawsuit. Sherman described his proposal and pointed in the evidence book to Ridolfi's date-stamp on his cover letter: September 11, 1987. "My recollection is that was a Friday," he said. "And sometime that day — possibly even before our document was delivered — I learned that the legal representation was going to be awarded to Taft & McSally."

Under Mahoney's cross-examination, Sherman described a phone call with Ridolfi. "I told her that I was extremely upset. Not because we had lost the contract, but that the decision had apparently been made before our proposal had even been considered. I told her she had wasted my time and that she need not ask for any proposals from me again."

Sherman's outrage electrified the hearing. Four years after the event, his resentment still smoldered. Commissioner John O'Brien asked whether he would have had the same reaction if he were turned down for another state job.

"No," said Sherman. "I was upset with the process. My concern was with the fact that I had been asked to submit a proposal, which — as far as I knew — wasn't even considered. The whole thing was a charade. That's what I was upset about."

Richard Morsilli signaled for a question. "Mr. Sherman, were you aware that Mr. Taft was a close friend of the governor's?"

"Yes, sir."

"That was common knowledge?"

"Yes, sir." Sherman glared at DiPrete, who sat at the defense table only a few feet away. While not speaking directly to the former governor, Sherman radiated contempt.

In his turn to ask questions, Mahoney pressed Sherman. Had he not testified already that Veronica Ridolfi told him her department had made the decision to hire Taft?

"She indicated the decision wasn't hers. I interpreted what she said to mean that the decision was made by someone she reported to. It's my interpretation that the decision was made by the governor."

Ridolfi had testified on November 7 that she and the lawyers on her staff had developed a list of six firms capable of handling a lawsuit as large and complex as Jamestown Bridge would be. She had phoned principals in these firms, including Deming Sherman at Edwards & Angell, then followed up with written requests.[5] She had testified with restraint, not blaming others but forceful in defending what she had done.

At the heart of Ridolfi's testimony was the fact that on the day after the invitation letters went out, DOT Director Matthew Gill directed her to add Taft & McSally to the list. She said she warned Gill of an uproar if the contract went to Taft, since everyone knew of his close ties to DiPrete. But Gill insisted, and she obeyed. Her letter to Taft went out five days after the first batch. Gill had testified before the ethics panel that he had chosen the Taft-Kelly proposal and admitted that he chose Taft-Kelly without interviewing any other firms. Fred Lippitt signed off on the contract, and State Purchasing Agent Dennis Lynch negotiated the details. As the Jamestown Bridge lawsuit went forward, Taft & McSally received $258,125.60, while $465,282.19 went to Carroll, Kelly & Murphy.[6]

In his closing argument on the Jamestown Bridge portion of the case, John Roney rehearsed the irreconcilable differences between the testimony of Veronica Ridolfi and Matthew Gill. He emphasized contradictions between DiPrete's testimony and the handwritten notes taken by Lynette Labinger on December 24, 1990. In the face of conflicting evidence, he challenged the commissioners to decide which version of those events was credible. Roney ended his summation of the Jamestown Bridge charges by pointing to the larger damage that occurs when "honest bidders like Deming Sherman become cynical and drop out."

Snow blew from impenetrable clouds on December 17, one of the year's shortest days, and night seemed to be falling at mid-afternoon. Commissioners, lawyers, DiPrete, and two of us from Common Cause settled in the Ethics Commission's hearing room. Beyond narrow windows the world looked gray. We were waiting to hear final arguments on the Olney Pond portion of the complaint, which had been running concurrently with the Jamestown Bridge adjudication.

After preliminaries,[7] Joseph Kelly launched his closing argument on the Tutela/Olney Pond case. He argued that the Department of Environmental Management had been at fault when its director, Bob Bendick, sent Judith Benedict as his designee to the A&E meeting. Kelly described Benedict as "a very knowledgeable person, but a novice on this question." He then went on to blame Benedict because she considered only two firms acceptable but voted for all four on the short list. "If Judith Benedict had voted as she should have voted, we wouldn't even be here. If Bob Bendick had gone to the meeting, the meeting he should have gone to, we wouldn't have been here."

Next he blamed Roney for not calling the secretary, Irene O'Donnell, as a witness, since she had written and signed the A&E committee minutes. "Who would know better than her as to the votes and how they were cast? She's the recording secretary. Did they call her? Absolutely not."

I had never thought of that. I assumed that O'Donnell would have long forgotten the details of a meeting where she only took notes. But Kelly had a point. He argued that the burden of proof lay with the prosecution: "They must satisfy you on every facet of this case before you can make any adjudication against this respondent." He reminded the commissioners that they had wanted more information than they had received.

After that he homed in on the list that went to the governor without prices or a description of the Olney Pond project. "If the governor made a selection from the short list without knowing the bids, he wouldn't be a very smart governor. If the governor made a selection that was binding, it would be ludicrous. The governor makes a *recommendation*."

Kelly made it sound self-evident that there could be no final selection until the purchasing officer negotiated a price with the contractor. "So the governor does not make the selection. The governor makes a recommendation, and there isn't anything wrong with the governor making a recommendation. As the captain of the ship, he should have input as to what goes on in the state. It's amazing to think anyone would feel he shouldn't have input into who is going to get jobs and protect Rhode Island engineers and architects."

He reminded commissioners that Tutela never got the job. "Bendick said, 'I don't want Tutela,' and what happened? On the very next day Tutela was out." He pointed to the evidence book. "In that very book, there is a notation under the date of May 4 — the day after the Bendick memorandum — saying 'Hold up on Tutela.'"

"What did Mr. Lippitt say?" Kelly asked rhetorically. "He said: 'I don't know why you're bringing this case. This is the case that you shouldn't bring.' This is a case of government the way it's supposed to go. The people with the hands-on expertise didn't want Tutela. They didn't get Tutela. They got who they wanted. What does the little old lady say in the Wendy's ads? 'Where's the beef?'"

Kelly circled back to the fact that Tutela never got notice of his selection. "Tutela had no idea that his name had been bandied around."

He then flagged the newspaper story. "I suppose they were trying to make some heat within the political arena, and it did make some heat. It made heat for Tutela. What did Tutela say? 'After that, I'm not going to make any more contributions.'" Kelly paused. "And the telling tale is this: Even though he didn't make any contributions, he got further work. The main point of his testimony is that he never sought and never got any edge by reason of any association with Gov. DiPrete."

Kelly then turned to testimony that Lippitt's assistant, Mathies Santos, had discussed contractors with Dennis DiPrete. "What's wrong with that?" he demanded. "What's wrong with someone in state government seeking advice from people who have expertise? There isn't anything wrong with it. That's done day in and day out in government. I call tax lawyers for information. Tax lawyers call me. Many people call me to find out what the expertise of a witness is.

"Furthermore, where is the link between that conversation and Gov. DiPrete? Mr. Santos, because he was pressed, said: 'Well, I assume he may have talked with his father.'

"No good! No good! That's assumption. That's speculation. That's not evidence. The evidence is what Dennis DiPrete gave you: 'I never discussed this Tutela matter with my father. I never took any lists. My sole purpose was to advise my friend, Mr. Santos.' That's it. There isn't anything wrong with it. That's how the record stands.

"Dennis DiPrete says: 'I never discussed this with my father.' Gov. DiPrete says: 'I never discussed this with Dennis.' That's it: direct, uncontradicted evidence. It's worthy of belief. That's the rule of law."

With infectious sincerity, Kelly neared his conclusion. "Gov. DiPrete said: 'I did nothing to favor Tutela in this contract or in any other contract.' Tutela said: 'I never approached Gov. DiPrete. I never got any favor by reason of anything that I did or didn't do for Gov. DiPrete.' That is the strict unequivocal direct testimony that must be believed. There is no foundation for the charges that have been laid here."

Kelly closed with his "Where's the beef?" question. "There is no beef here," he insisted and urged them to dismiss the complaint.

John Roney began his closing statement in a wistful tone. "You've seen a small part of how government worked, the hiring of architects and engineers during the respondent's administration. Gov. DiPrete created and controlled and manipulated a secret, superficial, and ultimately corrupt process designed to permit him to clandestinely select who got state contracts while telling the public that he had created a publicly accountable system."

Next Roney walked commissioners through the A&E process that was supposed to produce a short list of qualified firms. He reminded them that the executive order handed decision-making off to Fred Lippitt, who was to select the highest qualified applicant and have a contract negotiated. "Sounds good on paper," Roney said, "but we saw what the system really was. We saw the A&E committee: superficial, cynical, manipulated, cursory, an example of how government ought not to work."

Roney checked his notes and went on. "The A&E committee here is important — if for nothing else — to show you how little it meant and how easy it was for Tutela to get on that list. Dennis Lynch told you all you really need to know about the A&E committee. He told you that if anyone felt strongly enough, they put the name on the list."

Sadness seemed to fill the room as winter darkness settled outside.

"Why Tutela?" Roney asked. "You have interviewed every member of the A&E committee. Mr. Lynch and Ms. Benedict say they didn't make the selection. Mr. Parrillo can't recall whether he did or not. Mr. Santos can't recall whether he made the selection or not."

Roney said he had wanted commissioners to see the A&E committee, so they would understand that getting on the short list did not necessarily mean excellent qualifications. The process had been easy to manipulate, so that any member for any purpose could get any contractor on the short list.

"Poor Judith Benedict," he added. "You were kind of tough on Ms. Benedict.

You asked her again and again: how did this happen? Judith Benedict got snookered. She believed the executive order. She believed there was another deliberative process."

Roney's tone became indignant. "So what happened? We have the truly amazing tale that a sitting governor secretly demands the right to make A&E selections as a precondition to selecting Mr. Lippitt. So important that he talked to him before hiring him and told him: 'I want to make the selections.'

"Fred Lippitt told you it was one of the conditions under which he accepted the job, and he showed you several times that the only way he ever made a different selection was if he went back to the governor and got his permission. He didn't just select Warner for Water Place. He went back and got the governor's permission. That's exactly what he did with Tutela. Afraid they were going to lose the federal grant, with Bob Bendick raising objections, he went back to the governor and said: 'Governor, can I change this?' He made no move without obtaining the governor's permission.

"You might have reservations about Fred Lippitt, and you might find his abdication of his responsibility — his willingness to accept a job under these conditions — was sad and shocking.

"But I don't think you'll find that Fred Lippitt is a liar. He told you what the process really was. The governor's choice was the final selection. There was no deliberative step. That final, crucial step so trumpeted in the executive order — that the director was going to interview people, the director was going to look at the proposals, the director was going to consider the project — none of that happened.

"The short list went up to the governor. The governor made his check mark, and the contract went down for negotiation on the price."

Roney took umbrage at the deception. Tutela would have gotten the contract if DEM had not pressed its objection with Lippitt. "If federal funds had not been involved, Bob Bendick couldn't write to Lippitt: 'We're going to lose federal funds if you do this.' So you're at the point where the governor is faced with making a choice using the system he created."

Roney laid out the stark choice between Tutela, who had contributed more than $20,000 to DiPrete's campaigns over the previous four years, and Lycott, the firm that DEM scientists believed would pass federal muster.

In closing, Roney turned to the law that prohibited all public officials in the state from any transaction "in substantial conflict with the proper discharge of his or her duties."

"The governor knew that Tutela had been contributing to his campaigns. He had every reason to believe and expect that this contract would continue that symbiotic relationship. The governor knew he had a conflict. He knew what he was doing was wrong, and that's why the whole process was so secretive. That's why it wasn't in the executive order."

Roney then pointed commissioners to another section of the law, which required DiPrete or any public official who faced a conflict of interest to file a statement of the conflict with the Ethics Commission, refrain from taking action, and assign the decision to a disinterested third party.[9] "The governor should have come to you. He should have filed a statement. He should not have been in this selection process, and he should have left the decision where it belonged, with Mr. Lippitt. It would have been so easy."

Still another section of the law barred public officials from using their powers of office to obtain financial gain not provided by law or from accepting any political contribution "based on any understanding" that their official actions or judgment would be influenced.[10]

He reminded commissioners that DiPrete's two executive orders never mentioned that the governor would play a central part in choosing architects and engineers. "The duplicity of the selection process was a condition of employment. It was never embodied in any memorandum or regulation. It was never mentioned in an otherwise extensive executive order signed with the knowledge that it was dramatically incomplete at best and fraudulent at worst."

Roney added that the process was "so clandestine that the chief of staff felt called upon to deny its existence to the press, so secret that Lippitt did not reveal it until after he left office, so secret that Lippitt dissembled, denying any mention of the governor's role."

He continued to demolish DiPrete's defenses: "How could he choose Tutela over Lycott? He told you he didn't even know Lycott. If he wanted to make a qualitative decision, he would have asked for more information. Yet, time and time and time again, he got only the prior contracts and names of the firms."

Roney reminded commissioners of the standard form that went to the governor's office. "This went up into his office — from Mr. Lippitt's testimony — thirty or forty times! It contains no information about Rhode Island connections, only the name of the firm!"

He asked how a governor who held the single most important job in the state could take time out to check a list. He asked why the transfer of lists had been left out of two executive orders. "Why is this power so important to him that he asked for it as a precondition to appointing Fred Lippitt as director?"

Roney paused dramatically from the rush of rapid-fire questions. "Because the power to control state contracts is the power to reward."

Then he asked softly, "Do you believe that Dennis DiPrete would have become regularly involved in helping to select A&E contracts without telling his father?" He reminded the commissioners of Mathies Santos's testimony that after the *Providence Journal* exposé, he stopped sending the short lists to the governor's office and gave them to his son instead. "Dennis DiPrete had become the courier. And this is important only because it shows there was no legitimate governmental purpose for this secret selection process."

Finally, Roney traced the arc of Tutela's contributions during DiPrete's first four years as governor. "Look at the fact that he stopped after he was denied a contract and informed that he wasn't qualified. His reasons for stopping are simply not credible. Tutela told you his contributions were hurting the candidate, which is ludicrous. The real reason is that he didn't get the contract."

Roney then asked if campaign contributions influenced the decision to give the Olney Pond contract to Tutela. "What distinguished Tutela from the others? Tutela had contributed $20,000."

In an instant, Roney pivoted back to DiPrete's claim that he had not steered the Jamestown Bridge contract to James Taft.

"Just a moment!" Joe Kelly sprang to his feet, interrupting Roney's summation. "I object to the infusion of the Jamestown Bridge into this hearing. I understood that the Jamestown Bridge has already been tried and argued. That's a closed case, and I point out that counsel for the Jamestown Bridge isn't here."

Roney paused, looking puzzled. "This matter was bifurcated at Mr. Kelly's request. I certainly have the right in my closing to expose the contradictions between what the governor stated in his testimony in the Jamestown Bridge matter and what he said here."

Pellegrino told Roney he could continue.

"In Jamestown Bridge," Roney said, "the governor's defense was that he didn't make a recommendation. He simply told the director to pick a local firm and stayed out of the decision for what turned out to be a three-quarters of a million dollar contract." Roney stressed the contrast between DiPrete's insistence that he needed to be a "hands-on manager" for small contracts and his claim to have stayed out of the Jamestown Bridge selection.

Kelly objected, but Roney kept going. He described the corrosive effect of the process on workers and administrators like Fred Lippitt, who have to go along with a corrupt process: "Honest, conscientious, and qualified contractors cannot be expected to bid in a process that's rigged to favor the political contributor. I ask you to find a violation. Send a message to elected officials that when they're faced with decisions that will benefit political contributors, they must step aside or face the consequences of violating the Code of Ethics." He ended by calling the commissioners to judge "on behalf of an exasperated and angry public."

The arguments were over. Frank Pellegrino thanked all the participants and closed the hearing. He said the commissioners would take a short break and then deliberate.

Rae Condon had to leave, but I waited to thank John Roney for his blistering summation. I asked what he thought they would decide.

Roney slid his scrawled notes into his briefcase. He replayed the proceedings the way a shortstop might rerun his mental video of a double play. He thought DiPrete and his lawyers made several serious mistakes. One mistake came on

Christmas Eve the year before, when DiPrete acknowledged that he had recommended Taft for the Jamestown Bridge litigation. "The fact that DiPrete thought he had sent a letter to Gill, when he actually made the recommendation verbally, only strengthened our case. And they had no way to impugn Lynette's notes."

I asked about other mistakes.

"I think they underestimated how it would play to have Joe Kelly represent the governor on the Olney Pond portion but then remove himself from Jamestown Bridge because he did the joint venture with Taft."

"Wouldn't it have been worse if Kelly had tried to defend his firm's work with Taft & McSally on Jamestown Bridge contract?"

"Absolutely," Roney agreed. "But they wound up working with two teams of lawyers and failed to harmonize the governor's actions. Once it became clear that they would have to defend Jamestown Bridge, DiPrete should have chosen a single lawyer to handle both parts. John Mahoney had made his closing argument in November and never even showed up after that."

I told Roney I thought he had caught Joe Kelly flat-footed when he tied the two cases together.

Roney smiled. "He had no real grounds to object. We never agreed not to mention Jamestown Bridge again."

"So will the commissioners find DiPrete in violation?"

"I couldn't tell with Ashton," Roney said, "but I think all the others were with us at the end."

By the time I stepped out into the winter darkness DiPrete and his lawyers were gone. Fresh snow covered cars in the tiny parking lot behind the Ethics Commission's office. I drove north on I-95 without turning on the radio. Whatever the outcome, this complaint against a sitting governor had shaped my first three years in Rhode Island. Like John Roney, I thought we would prevail.

Three days later, on December 20, the written decision came by fax. The six panelists had ruled unanimously that DiPrete had violated the law in both the Tutela/Olney Pond and the Taft/Jamestown Bridge portions of the case.[11] All six had agreed on "findings of fact," a list that ran eight single-spaced pages. Their findings followed our complaint and Roney's prosecution, each fact articulated in a precise legal statement. Their conclusions filled four dense paragraphs. The first found DiPrete "in substantial conflict with the proper discharge of his duties" in the Tutela selection. It cited "the improper solicitation or acceptance of a political contribution." Then followed DiPrete's failure "to prepare or file a written statement of conflict of interest."

The Taft/Jamestown Bridge findings followed the same format but without the reference to campaign contributions. Under a heading called "civil penalties," the commission ordered DiPrete to pay a total of $30,000 in fines: $10,000 each for his actions in the Tutela and Taft sections of the complaint, and $5,000 each for his failures to notify the Ethics Commission and recuse himself from those conflict situations.

The last line of the document lay there in ordinary type, without any box or boldface or underlining: "The Vote on the above Decision and Order as to Findings of Fact, Conclusions of Law and Civil Monetary Penalties was unanimous."

I felt like cheering. Even Ernie Ashton had recognized DiPrete's wrongdoing. Russ Garland phoned from the *Providence Journal.* "You must be happy," he said.

A brief story made the front page of the paper's evening edition on December 20, and a fuller account dominated the front page of the edition I read over breakfast the next morning. DiPrete told the reporters that he was "really disappointed" with the decision and would file an appeal in Superior Court. Then, a few days after Christmas, the *Providence Journal* ran an editorial entitled "The $30,000 message," which skewered DiPrete: "The public was told the most qualified contractors would get the job while, in fact, the chief criterion was closeness to the governor." In 1988, the paper had printed front-page stories about DiPrete's wrongdoing, but its editorial board endorsed him for re-election. Now, three years later, an editorial declared the hope that "a stiff price tag should help to concentrate some officials' minds in the future."[12]

On New Year's Eve 1991, only days after the Ethics Commission's unanimous decision against DiPrete, Gov. Bruce Sundlun announced that he had fired Taft's firm from the ongoing Jamestown Bridge litigation.[13] Ironically, the case had been restarted the previous summer when the presiding Superior Court Judge Antonio S. Almeida was arrested for taking bribes from lawyers. After the costs of restarting the trial and then replacing the legal team chosen by a corrupt governor, the legal costs soared higher than the graceful span that would eventually cross the deep western channel of Narragansett Bay.[14]

The year 1991 finally came to its end but questions remained. Would DiPrete's appeal get him off the hook? And would public indignation over systemic corruption dissipate or produce lasting reform?

RIght Now!

1991–92

On December 11, 1991, precisely at 10:30, church bells pealed across Providence. The clanging rang from all directions: from belfries of the First Baptist Church in America and the Cathedral of St. John, from Gloria Dei Lutheran and the Armenian Church of Saints Sahag and Mesrob. Thick State House walls seemed powerless to block their reverberation, a palpable clangor that evoked history.

Television lights flooded the House lounge. Behind a podium studded with microphones hung a white banner with the RIght Now! logo. Deep crimson walls held the oversized portraits of former House speakers in gilded frames. Each in his turn had been arguably the most powerful politician in Rhode Island, often going on to lucrative state jobs. Those who gazed down at the crowd of legislators, reporters, and coalition leaders, would have been flabbergasted by the twenty-eight point platform that the RIght Now! Coalition was about to unveil.[1]

Alan Hassenfeld stepped to the bank of microphones, framed by the RIght Now! logo behind him. "Let the bells ring for a new dawn" he began, his public voice rich with the cheerful intimacy of a conversation among friends. "My business is toys, but we're here today — half way between the first day of Hanukkah and Christmas — to give Rhode Islanders a different kind of holiday gift. Today, we announce the formation of what we think is the broadest coalition in the history of Rhode Island."

He called reporters' attention to a handout that listed the groups whose leaders comprised the steering committee.[2] "We call this coalition 'RIght Now!' Our goal, very simply, is to make Rhode Island right again and do it right now."[3]

Hassenfeld said there was no need to revisit the bank closings, fiscal crises, and political scandals that had made Rhode Islanders despondent. It was obvious, he said, that RIght Now! could not turn back the clock. Instead, our goal was to make Rhode Island right for the future. "We cannot wait any longer. We must enact lock-tight reform measures that will serve as a model for every other state in America." Then he announced that our organization would work toward three goals: tougher ethics laws, effective campaign finance reforms, and a constitutional amendment to establish four-year terms, with recall and a two-term limit, for the five statewide general officers.

Outlining our platform, I highlighted twenty-eight specific reforms. We welcomed bills already announced by Gov. Sundlun and leaders of the General Assembly, but added that we wanted substantially more than we had seen so far. "It's not enough to close a few loopholes. We have to make a tight seal. When we're trying to keep hot air in our house and cold air out, it doesn't make any sense to weather-strip the doors if we leave the windows open."

I added that RIght Now! was determined to stop senators and representatives from trading their votes for state jobs when they left the legislature. A *Providence Sunday Journal* story had identified forty-nine legislators who, during the last ten years, had moved directly from their seats in the General Assembly to judgeships or other permanent, well-paid state jobs.[4] "We're not saying never," I said, "only for one year. But make no mistake, we are passionate about this."

Streamlining the Ethics Commission and opening up its adjudicative hearings was another goal. I wanted to add that the day before I had heard former Gov. DiPrete and his son testify, but the law kept their testimony secret. My list ended with our proposal for four-year terms for the governor and other statewide general officers. "No matter who wins, we're putting that person in charge of a $2 billion-a-year corporation. With two-year terms, we're saying: 'Recruit great staff and produce flashy results in a hurry, because your next campaign starts in earnest only twelve months from now. And by the way, you'd better start raising $40,000 a week so you can get re-elected in two years.'"

News outlets loved the story. Cartoonists showed Hasbro's G.I. Joe storming the State House. Editorials welcomed the effort, although several columnists wondered whether this unlikely coalition could hold together through the inevitable battles ahead.

Even as the klieg lights cooled, RIght Now! faced both internal stress and outside attack. Without consulting the steering committee, Alan Hassenfeld announced a moratorium on campaign contributions. He pledged to *Providence Journal* reporter G. Wayne Miller that he would not give to political campaigns or parties until meaningful reform was enacted. "I will call upon my colleagues at Hasbro to do the same, and I will implore all the people to tighten their belts and stop feeding the machine."[5] Once he went out on that limb, how could his moratorium not also become the coalition's policy?

I stood in awe of Alan Hassenfeld. I wished we had discussed his idea for a moratorium before he declared it, but how could I criticize his bold move? A freeze in contributions made little difference for me, since national Common Cause barred staff from endorsing candidates or making campaign contributions, but I still feared its effect. A moratorium that dried up campaign contributions would hurt challengers while money flowed as usual from professional lobbyists to legislative leaders and their loyalists.

At our next steering committee meeting, I timidly raised my concern. If the moratorium dragged on for months, it could have unintended consequences.

"I hear you," Hassenfeld said graciously, "but I think we have to send a strong message to everybody in that building that we can't continue with business as usual. They simply must pass campaign finance reform with teeth." He did not sound angry or bitter. "The real litmus test is: 'Are you willing to sign on to the moratorium?'"

I nodded and said no more.[6]

Throughout the fall, those of us who were organizing the coalition had reached in every way we could to two major powers: the Roman Catholic Diocese and organized labor. Only days after we unveiled the coalition with pealing church bells, Bishop Louis E. Gelineau announced that he supported RIght Now!'s goals.

Gary Sasse and I had presented the RIght Now! platform to the AFL-CIO Executive Council at their headquarters, only a block from the State House. We left with a sense that the unions would not support our proposals. On the sidewalk afterward, Sasse said it was still important that we had reached out to labor. "Most of them will protect the legislative status quo," he said, "but they'll be less vehement after our visit. If we can keep them out of the fight, that helps us."

Since 1935, when Democrats broke the Yankee Republican stranglehold on Rhode Island's government, unions had become a dominant force. Lobbyists for teachers, social workers, firefighters, police, correctional officers, and other public employees constituted the most disciplined and professional force at the State House. Unions for teamsters, electricians, machinists, pipefitters, and longshoremen had lost membership when traditional industries fled the state, but their solidarity endured.

As Sasse predicted, AFL-CIO President Edward McElroy announced that labor would not join the RIght Now! Coalition on the grounds that some of its proposals were "antidemocratic." Promoting them would lead to an unnecessary "bashing" of lawmakers. "We'll do our own thing in choosing those issues we choose to support and opposing those we feel are not wise policy," McElroy said.[7]

George Nee, the AFL-CIO secretary-treasurer, spoke of labor's objection to strengthening the governor's position with a four-year term while leaving lawmakers with two-year terms. "It's important that we don't get caught up in such a bandwagon of reform that we start upsetting the balance between branches of government," Nee told the *Providence Business News*. "We shouldn't harm these institutions in our quest to get rid of every injustice."[8]

While organized labor found RIght Now! too disruptive of the General Assembly's dominant role in state government, an array of militant depositor and reform groups declared our new coalition not radical enough. Since RISDIC's collapse, protesters had sorted themselves around differences over substance, tactics, and leadership. Besides Citizens for Depositors' Rights, other new groups had coalesced: the Government Accountability Project, the Rhode Island Taxpayers Association, Reform 92, and Operation Clean Sweep.

Maurice "Mo" Guernon of Operation Clean Sweep told the *Providence Journal* he had considered joining existing reform groups but none had the "sweeping" approach needed. "With the current crew in the state legislature," Guernon said, "you're not likely to get any fundamental reform that has teeth in it." On talk radio and in public statements, Guernon declared it time for ordinary citizens "to strip corrupt politicians of their special privileges." Press releases warned that Operation Clean Sweep would "target corrupt public officials for removal." Like Jack Kayrouz of Citizens for Depositors' Rights, Guernon laced his comments with sarcasm.[9]

As we organized the RIght Now! Coalition, I asked the steering committee if we could draw these grassroots groups in,[10] but business leaders cringed. "You can't deal with those people," said Jim Hagan, who led the Greater Providence Chamber of Commerce. "They tar everybody with the same brush. Even their name says they think they can sweep corrupt politicians out — as if they can tell by just looking who's crooked and who's not."

From the head of the table, Hassenfeld asked for candid comments. "Here's the question," he said. "Would they moderate their position at all? Could we bring them in?"

"What bugs me about Mo Guernon and his crowd," said Jim Miller in his turn, "is that they constantly condemn public officials across the board. A lot of politicians have feathered their own nests, but no one will simply sweep them all away. Until the election next November, we have to work with the current senators and reps. We have a brief window to persuade the General Assembly to act. I'm all for being firm, but punching them in the gut will only make them resist our bills.

"I believe our message has to be that all of us — elected officials and ordinary citizens alike — need to repent for tolerating such corruption. Once we repent for letting corruption fester so long, then we can demand that legislators also repent and fix the political system."

Norman Orodenker spoke for the Jewish Federation. "I'm obviously not a Baptist," he said, "but I agree wholeheartedly with Jim. These 'clean sweep' people may mean well, or they may not mean well. Frankly, I have no way of knowing, but I don't believe that bringing them to this table will moderate their behavior. It may even embolden them."

Gary Sasse agreed. "A crisis like this attracts people who enjoy the politics of personal attack. I don't think they'll temper their militancy for the sake of passing genuine reforms. I'm not even sure they want reforms to pass, since that would undercut their case for sweeping all the incumbents out.

"In answer to Alan's question," Sasse said, "I agree with Jim and Norman that we would make a mistake by inviting Operation Clean Sweep into this coalition. Partners in a coalition don't need to agree on every point, but they've got to be pragmatic and respect differences, which I don't see." He paused, as if to reflect. "I also need to say that if Operation Clean Sweep joins this coalition, my board would probably pull RIPEC out."

Hassenfeld had said nothing while he listened to opinions around the table. He asked if anyone wanted to say more. He waited for the silence to work and then spoke. "Sounds like we're in agreement. We may wish there were a way to invite Operation Clean Sweep onto this steering committee, but we can't handle their belligerence. We can't expect a leopard to change its spots."

He scanned the table again. "And, hey, we're no less committed than they are to making serious change in this messed-up state that we love. We're simply admitting that you can't achieve real reform through personal *ad hominem* attacks. So we reaffirm our position that we will fight to the death on principle, but we will never attack people."

Weather forecasts predicted heavy rain for the first Sunday of 1992, and a cold drizzle fell from leaden skies. Thousands were expected for an interfaith rally on the broad plaza below the State House. The decision whether to move into a nearby auditorium rested on Jim Miller, who decided to risk the rain. Throngs gathered in cathedrals, churches, and synagogues of their choosing. Those not affiliated with any religious institutions could use a specified parking lot where parking would be free.

Processions stepped off with banners aloft. From Saints Sahag and Mesrob Armenian Cathedral bearded priests in black robes carried ancient icons across a bridge over I-95 to the beat of drums and the clanging of church bells. They met and mingled with the Lutherans who had gathered at Gloria Dei Church on nearby Hayes Street. Marchers tramped up Smith Hill from the Episcopal Cathedral of St. John, across from the Roger Williams National Memorial, while Roman Catholics from the Cathedral of Saints Peter and Paul on Weybosset Hill wound their way through downtown Providence, merging with streams of Protestants from Beneficent Congregational and Mathewson Street United Methodist churches. Unitarians came from several directions. Processions flowed together up Francis Street, over the Woonasquatucket River, and toward the

State House. American Baptists, who had gathered at the First Baptist Church in America, crossed a bridge over the Moshassuck River near the spot where Roger Williams had founded Providence and their congregation more than three and a half centuries earlier.

A year earlier, low-flying military planes and artillery rounds had punctuated Bruce Sundlun's inauguration. The new governor interrupted festivities by announcing the collapse of RISDIC. Since then, bitter protesters had come by the thousands, shouting for their money, but now church bells pealed across the city, a wild clanging cacophony of high chimes and deep gongs.

Streams of marchers flooded onto the State House grounds from all directions with triumphant music of fifes and drums, trumpets and bagpipes. They mingled on brick walkways under bare winter trees. A cheerful multitude filled the broad south plaza and overflowed onto wide swaths of soggy grass. Waves of people flowed up broad staircases and crowded the white marble terraces. A man and woman appeared on horseback representing Roger Williams and Anne Hutchinson, exiles from the Massachusetts Bay Colony. As if turning a new page, this vast ecumenical throng seemed to have left bitterness behind. As their numbers swelled, the sky cleared, and sunshine bathed the scene.

I watched Jim Miller, in a black preaching robe, make his way to a pulpit that held a single microphone. Nearby, an Orthodox icon portrayed a dark-skinned Jesus with gold halo. Behind Miller, the bold RIght Now! banner fluttered. Farther back, white marble pillars rose to a broad lintel engraved with words from the Royal Charter: "To hold forth a lively experiment that a most civil state may stand and best be maintained with full liberty in religious concernment."

Miller welcomed the throng and thanked them for risking rain. He promised a gathering different from any ever held on this historic ground. "Our theme today," he said, "is repentance. We want those who work in this building to repent of decisions made in this splendid structure, and we must repent of our indifference. We must repent for allowing so much that was wrong to go on for so long."

Rabbi Wayne Franklin from Temple Emanu-El stepped forward in a white prayer shawl. He explained the ancient blowing of a ram's horn for repentance at Rosh Hashanah and Yom Kippur. Then he lifted a shofar of polished onyx and gray to his lips. He blew, but no sound came. He put his lips to the horn and blew again but only sputtered. The rabbi drew a deep breath and blew again. This time, an eerie wail rose through and over the crowd, its pitch soaring like nothing heard in this space before. Then a cantor sang Psalm 15 on speaking truth from the heart, doing no harm to the neighbor, keeping oaths amid pain, and not accepting bribes against the innocent.

Bishop Louis E. Gelineau stepped to the podium in a simple black cassock and red cap. He spoke from a pastoral letter he had published in the diocesan newspaper a few days earlier, lamenting those who took advantage of their positions to commit crimes: "Were not some of them raised in good Catholic homes? Do they not see a relationship between their faith and their moral duties?" In a solemn liturgical voice, Gelineau called for "a renewed sense of public morality." He told the crowd, "In the end, we shall each stand before God to be judged. I pray that when your moment and mine comes to give an accounting, we shall not be found wanting."[11]

Rabbi David B. Rosen, president of the Rhode Island Board of Rabbis, picked up the same themes. "We are not here to condemn state government as a whole," he told the crowd, "for we know there are thousands of hardworking, dedicated and honest men and women in every branch of government who deserve our admiration and respect. But we cry out for repentance."

Miller had made the event truly catholic and inclusive. Rev. Dietra C. Bell, from the Allen African Methodist Episcopal Church in the neglected West End of Providence, asked God to soften the hearts of public officials. Then she sang with power that set hands clapping and bodies swaying. The chief Narragansett medicine man, Lloyd Wilcox, called out in a booming baritone, "Brothers and sisters, we gather in the presence of the great spirit." With a beaded headband across his brow, he embodied the state's paradoxical history of respect and cruelty toward its indigenous people. His voice reverberated across the city: "Broken promises, broken treaties, broken hearts, and broken bodies are echoed in this present time due to the abuse of leadership in government for selfish gain. Once again, trust between brothers and sisters is shattered and denied, and human dignity violated.[12]

"Great Spirit, renew our trust!" Wilcox called and waited, then called again: "Great Spirit, renew our trust!"

This time, the crowd shouted back: "Great Spirit, renew our trust!"

He boomed again: "Great Spirit, renew our trust!"

Thousands responded: "Great Spirit, renew our trust!"

As if voices were not enough, Miller invited the crowd to climb the broad white marble stairs and march around the State House. The crowd surged upward behind rabbis blowing shofars. Once on the pedestal, they joined hands, forming a ring around the entire building. With church bells clanging from all directions, the line of marchers clasped hands to form a second circle around the iconic structure, and then a third. People cheered, and many danced.

I watched the rally on television news that night, flipping from channel to channel. Reporters expressed surprise — they had not heard a word of personal attack from the speakers or the crowd. The weather report showed a satellite photo of rain clouds swirling over southern New England. In time-lapse images, a clear eye of the storm opened up over Westerly and tracked northeast across Providence. As in ancient times, many took that patch of clear sky as a sign of God's favor or, as Roger Williams might have said, of divine and merciful providence.

From the start of the 1992 legislative session, RIght Now! proved powerful and provocative. Publicity from newscasts and newspaper stories lent heft to our lobbying efforts. Volunteers arrived at the State House and cleaned out the stocks of RIght Now! buttons that I brought in my briefcase. They pinned the badges on proudly and went to find their senators and representatives. A few legislators asked for buttons and wore them for a day or two below legislative lapel pins, while others merely peered at the one on my jacket. "Would you like one?" I would ask as we shook hands.

"Not today," some would say but then assure me they would give our bills every consideration.

Increased visibility also made RIght Now! a target. Near the end of January, the Rhode Island Black Caucus of State Legislators convened a press conference to demand that we add their issues to the RIght Now! platform. With the caucus were leaders of the NAACP, several smaller civil rights groups, and the president of the largely African-American Ministers' Alliance of Rhode Island. Rep. Joseph E. Newsome, who represented the district where Anne and I lived on the South Side of Providence, declared that the debate must be broadened beyond "the Common Cause agenda. That agenda is very narrow." Newsome insisted that any reform must also help children in poverty, increase funds for education, and make corporations socially responsible.[13]

Newsome's words stung. He and I had worked locally together to end *apartheid* in South Africa and to help refugees from Liberia's civil war. We had been allies in streamlining voter registration, which increased voting in our neighborhood. He knew that the executive director of the Urban League, B. Jae Clanton, served on the RIght Now! steering committee. I began to sense that the real target of this press conference was Thomas J. Skala, the president of Fleet National Bank. Newsome insisted that banks needed to commit more to low-income neighborhoods, calling it "obscene and unethical" for corporate leaders with huge salaries and bonuses to lay off workers in poor neighborhoods.

Rep. Harold M. Metts, who chaired the Black Caucus, also weighed in. "Ethics reform, to be truly meaningful, needs to be all-inclusive," he declared. While he spoke, I noticed Jim Miller's name on the list of speakers on the list. The unprecedented racial inclusiveness of the January rally for ethics reform had been Miller's doing.

"I'm honored to speak here today," Miller began gently. "There's no question that the concerns of our youngest and poorest and weakest must truly be our own. We must be attentive to all who bear the legacy of America's deep original sin. We must all redress the wrongs and injustices perpetrated against persons of color. I want you to know that the Council of Churches is fully committed to addressing these concerns."

Miller turned a page in a tiny notebook. "But I need to say that — as important as these issues are — RIght Now! cannot suddenly add them to its agenda.

There are narrower anti-corruption issues that it must deal with first if we hope to get Rhode Island back on its feet. I hope this caucus in its wisdom will recognize that political reality."

Miller was a newcomer in Rhode Island and the only Caucasian invited to speak, so he took a great risk in challenging the Black Caucus's demand. He spoke carefully but firmly. "To push all these things in 1992 will mean that none will get done. With RISDIC's collapse, our urban centers have suffered as much or more than any other parts of the state. Our inner-city neighbors will not trust state government until it is cleansed of corruption that bleeds the poor."

I understood the anger behind this press event. Year after year, I had testified before the House Judiciary Committee on Common Cause legislation to widen the circle of those who could not benefit directly from family members who held public office.[14] In prior years Metts had listened to testimony about the harm nepotism inflicted, and once, as I left the hearing room, he followed me into the hallway. "I'm against your so-called nepotism bill," he declared. "I don't agree with your supposedly righteous reasons. Do you want to know why?"

With lobbyists and other representatives around, I wanted a space for a private conversation, but he clearly meant to make his point in public.

"Do you want to know why?" Metts demanded. "I'll tell you why. When the Yankees were in power, they got jobs for their relatives, and that was okay. When the Irish got power and doled out jobs for their kinfolk, nobody raised a ruckus. When the Italians came along, they took their turn. Where was Common Cause in those days to say that doing for their kin was wrong?" His voice grew louder. "So, what happens now that our community finally gets a few seats in the General Assembly? What happens when we finally get a foot in the door? All of a sudden you push to say no more nepotism. You say that's good ethics. I say it's not fair."

As he turned and stalked back into the hearing room, his anger made complete sense to me. From his perspective, we were trying to outlaw family patronage just when African Americans could finally dispense a few government jobs.

On a rainy March day, the Episcopal Bishop of Rhode Island, George N. Hunt, faced a different attack. He signed a list of more than fifty witnesses and waited his turn to testify before the Senate Judiciary Committee. Dressed in a black suit, purple shirt, white clerical collar, and a RIght Now! button, he stepped to the witness box.

"In recent weeks," Hunt began in his resonant baritone, "I have had a number of occasions to be reminded by members of the General Assembly that we who represent the larger religious community have little or no expertise in the writing of legislation or in the processes of government. This is certainly true. However, please permit me to claim a modest expertise in the matter of ethics and morality and honesty and integrity in human affairs." Calm and unhurried, Hunt declared support for the ethics bills listed on the committee's agenda: legislation to streamline the Ethics Commission, trim its size, and open its adjudicative hearings to the public. He explained the concepts and illustrated the need for each bill. At the end of his prepared statement Hunt urged passage of bills that would close the revolving door and outlaw nepotism.[15]

From his nearby perch behind the polished mahogany façade, Sen. Gregory J. Acciardo of Johnston challenged the bishop about the larger circle of relatives that our bill would place out of bounds for favored treatment. "How can you draw those lines?" Acciardo asked. "I read through this list, and it gets down to pretty fine detail. It says no official action to help a 'nephew, niece, grandfather, grandmother, grandson, granddaughter, father-in-law, mother-in-law, brother-in-law, sister-in-law, son-in-law, daughter-in-law, stepfather, stepmother, stepson, stepdaughter, stepbrother, stepsister, half-brother or half-sister.'" Acciardo made the whole task sound exhausting. "Have you thought about all those relatives you'd have to keep track of?"

The bishop smiled. "I grant you, Senator, it's an exhaustive list, but we both know that legal language must be precise to be enforceable."

Acciardo teased: "Do we really have to go from 'spouse and dependent child' to this humongous list?"

"It's a reasonable list, Senator," Hunt replied. "I hope putting those family members off limits for favors will restore public trust that you're here to do the people's business and not your own."

Acciardo drew back momentarily. "What about my nephew's wife?" He chuckled. "I mean, shouldn't she be included, too? When you come right down to it, isn't everybody related?"

"Senator, there's room for negotiation on the details."

"So you agree we could leave nephews, nieces, and their spouses off the list?"

"Senator, that's not for me to negotiate with you here. The point is that those in authority should never be in a position to hire or supervise their own relatives."

"Never? Are families so evil?" He struck a pose of astonishment.

"If you'll permit me a personal example," the bishop replied. "My son was recently ordained a priest." He gazed at Acciardo, who had begun whispering to the senator seated beside him.

Hunt stopped speaking until Acciardo again made eye contact. Then he continued, "My son phoned recently to ask whether there were any churches open in Rhode Island. The first thing that came to my mind was what a joy it would be to have him and his wife and our grandchildren close by, and I told him that."

The bishop paused again. Everyone in the hearing room was riveted. "But I explained to him that no matter how fair I tried to be, people would inevitably wonder how I could supervise my son's work without favoritism. I told my son that I loved him and his wife and their children, but that to avoid any appearance of impropriety, I had to ask them to look elsewhere."

While lawmakers resisted making ethics and campaign finance laws more stringent, RIght Now! began taking fire from a new coalition that called itself the Public Interest Alliance. The new group included Operation Clean Sweep, the Government Accountability Project, the Coalition for Consumer Justice, and the Rhode Island Taxpayers Association. None of these groups had promoted ethics or campaign finance legislation in previous years, but they lambasted the RIght Now! proposals as too soft. Where RIght Now! called for a one-year hiatus between service in the General Assembly and state jobs, including judgeships, the Alliance called for a two-year ban. Where RIght Now! proposed reducing the top individual contribution to any candidate from $2,000 to $1,000, the Alliance demanded that political donations be capped at one hundred dollars. At an early February press conference, leaders of the new coalition blasted our efforts at reform as "a total capitulation to and appeasement of the leadership of the House and its speaker, Joseph DeAngelis." Nancy St. Lawrence, chairperson of the Coalition for Consumer Justice, completely dismissed the RIght Now! platform: "What they wanted was just so weak, we didn't want to pursue it."[16]

I told reporters of my deep personal sorrow that we had not been able to bring all of those who wanted reform into the same tent. I tried to put a positive face on an increasingly divisive situation, reminding them that we had earnest people "working together or on parallel tracks toward similar goals of reform." But I did not say how much I feared that these differences over details might play into the hands of lawmakers who wanted no reform at all.

In February, word leaked that a key player in the RIght Now! Coalition had undercut Alan Hassenfeld's moratorium on campaign contributions. Scott MacKay reported that the Greater Providence Chamber of Commerce was quietly soliciting large contributions for pro-business legislative candidates. Paul J. Choquette Jr., the CEO of Gilbane Building Co. and head of the Chamber's political action committee, had mailed a letter to chamber members asking for contributions of up to $1,000 to elect senators and representatives who would be "responsive to the needs of the business community."[17]

Choquette claimed to see no conflict between building the pro-business war chest and supporting campaign reform, since the money would all be collected before our proposed new law could be enacted. Jim Hagan, executive of the Greater Providence Chamber, insisted that the business leaders were "operating within the parameters of the existing law." It looked hypocritical or worse — a major group in the coalition was collecting corporate cash that would be banned under the proposed new campaign finance law it claimed to support. George

Nee, the head of the state AFL-CIO, told MacKay: "It looks like an effort to raise as much money as they can before the law takes effect."

When Scott MacKay called me for a comment, I answered evasively. "I don't know," I said lamely. "You could probably argue it both ways." He used my comment to end his story. Reading it the next morning over breakfast, I felt chagrined. How had I so badly underestimated the forces — both internal and external — that seemed to be tearing RIght Now! apart?

12

Struggles

1992

On March 4, 1992, an overflow crowd filled every seat in the majestic wood-columned Rhode Island Supreme Court chamber. As the deep green velvet curtain swooshed open, the five justices took their seats to hear oral arguments on the authority of the state Ethics Commission.

Gov. Bruce Sundlun's executive counsel, Judith C. Savage, argued that allowing the Ethics Commission to write and enforce a code of ethics for elected officials would create an unconstitutional fourth branch of government. "The dangers," Savage warned, "cannot be overstated."[1] She asserted that Rhode Island voters did not mean to endow the proposed new commission with vast power to write ethics laws. Her argument marked a 180-degree turn from what the governor's policy chief, Sheldon Whitehouse, had declared only six months earlier. There had been no public announcement, but I assumed that threats from General Assembly leaders had backed Sundlun away from supporting the commission's power to adopt ethics rules.

Next Edward M. Fogarty lumbered toward the central podium to argue on behalf of House leaders. He asked what would prevent the commission from writing rules for campaign finance under the guise of ethics. "I submit that is terrifying," Fogarty told the five black-robed justices, "absolutely terrifying."

Commission attorney Gary Yesser began his rebuttal with a wry smile: "In one of my arguments today, I hope to convince Mr. Fogarty that the sky is not falling." Yesser pointed out that the General Assembly controlled the commission's budget and nominated individuals who were then appointed by the governor. He added that any ruling of the Ethics Commission could be appealed to Superior Court.

Several months earlier, Frederick "Rick" Cass, a lawyer on the Common

Cause state board, had told me that a top appellate lawyer had expressed interest in arguing our case *pro bono*. That came as welcome news, since our organization had little money and no budget for litigation. Cass took me to meet Lauren E. Jones at his office near the courthouse. Together, Jones and Cass wrote a brief that layered simple arguments into a cogent whole.

Lauren Jones stepped to the podium. Though the hair on top of his head had thinned, the rest was tied back in a ponytail that made him look like an aging rock star. "May it please the Court," Jones began, as each lawyer before him had. He urged the Supreme Court to take the 1986 Ethics Amendment at face value. He said that the people, "engaging in the most solemn of functions the people have, voted to amend the Rhode Island Constitution." They voted to create a new constitutional entity, and "they infused this Ethics Commission with the power to 'adopt a code of ethics.'"[2]

"This court," Jones told the justices, "has ruled consistently that the words of the Constitution, as adopted by the people, must be given their usual and accepted meaning. It is not up to the legislature or the courts to question the wisdom, convenience, or effectiveness of a constitutional provision."

Jones read out dictionary definitions for "independent" and "nonpartisan," words that lay at the amendment's core. "No other entity in the government constellation is expected to be either independent or nonpartisan." He argued that by adding these words to the Constitution in 1986, the people had set the Ethics Commission apart from normal political struggles and influences. He suggested that if the high court wished to go further and consider the intent behind the words, transcripts of the 1986 Constitutional Convention were equally emphatic.

Further, Jones argued, delegates knew precisely what they were doing when they placed the amendment on the ballot. Under the rules of the convention, they were required to approve the same text in two separate votes. On June 4, 1986, they supported the "independent and nonpartisan" language, 71–2. Three weeks later they reaffirmed that text by a vote of 92–2.

Jones concluded that the people of Rhode Island had given the Ethics Commission, rather than the General Assembly, three extraordinary powers: to adopt the Code of Ethics, to investigate violations of the code, and to impose penalties which would be provided by law. None of this had happened in a vacuum, he added. "The perception of the state's ethics at the time of the constitutional convention in 1986 was low. The concern was that without an independent ethics commission, the sharp teeth in any code of ethics could be removed by those who feared being bitten." Finally, the General Assembly was not being stripped of its power to write laws involving ethics. The legislature remained free to enact any provision that was "not contradictory or inconsistent" with the code that had been adopted by the constitutionally-established Ethics Commission.

Rae Condon had filed her own brief and approached the lectern last. The five justices knew that her father had served thirty years on the state's highest court, his last seven as chief justice. "May it please the Court," she began in the magnificent courtroom she had first visited as a child. "The governor and the speaker of the House want you to believe that the voters did not understand what they were doing when they directed the Ethics Commission to adopt a code of ethics for all public officials. Besides being false, that assertion is elitist and not the least democratic."[3]

Condon focused on the reasons why the 1986 Constitutional Convention's ethics committee had proposed that the new Ethics Commission, rather than the General Assembly, must adopt a code of ethics. She reminded the justices behind their long wooden dais that both the text of the 1986 Ethics Amendment and the question presented to voters had been plain: "Shall an ethics commission be established with the authority to adopt a code of ethics and to discipline or remove public officials and employees found in violation of that code?"[4] She said it strained credulity to believe that voters who approved the constitutional amendment "were confused, uninformed, and misled." In addition to newspaper stories, she argued, each household had received two detailed mailings about the amendments on the ballot.[5]

Condon ended with a legal flourish, quoting the high court's ruling from another pivotal time, just after the Bloodless Revolution of 1935 when Democrats became the majority party. "'This court is the agent of the people in the administration of justice in this state. It would be recreant to the great trust reposed in it if it did not guard every agency by which justice is administered.'"[6] She did not need to tell them that her father, the legendary Chief Justice Francis Bernard Condon, had penned those words.

A week later Rep. Jeff Teitz convened a fresh round of RISDIC hearings on live television, helped by his special prosecutors, John Nields and Alan Baron, now nicknamed "the Baltimore Bullets" after the basketball team. With ample police protection, Teitz again opened the basement hearing room to the public. I found a seat near the front. Reporters from the *Providence Journal* arrived with new laptop computers. RISDIC Commission members, Rae Condon among the nine, filed in from backstage, marching past a blue drape to their chairs.

Ever since Joe Mollicone had vanished with $13 million from his Mob-connected bank on Federal Hill, people had been asking about organized crime. What role had Patriarca's associates played in RISDIC's collapse? Investigators tracking defunct loans quickly recognized a pattern. Ten groups with links to mobsters had borrowed nearly $175 million from RISDIC institutions. Contrary to the credit unions' stated purpose of providing small loans to homeowners and Rhode Island businesses shut out by commercial banks, developers had received loans whose totals ranged from $9.2 million to $48.8 million. Many of their projects were located not in Rhode Island but in New York, Ohio, and Florida. Investigators estimated that $115 million would never be recovered.[7]

Robert Stitt had raised the question of money laundering in his 1985 report, and the *Providence Journal* had reported that deposits in the three largest credit unions — Central, Davisville, and Marquette — had swelled from $364 million to $741 million during RISDIC's last four years. The *Journal*'s Peter Phipps speculated that Mob figures might have used RISDIC institutions to launder cash from their drug and gambling operations, noting that "the virtually unregulated RISDIC institutions look like a perfect place to wash the traces of illegal activity from the Mob's money."[8]

Howard F. Rosenstein, a financial investigator who worked with Nields and Baron, had been following the money. He told Teitz's panel that Greater Providence Deposit & Trust had lent $700,000 to a pair of Mob-connected brothers, Robert and Donald Barbato. The Barbato brothers had repaid only $45,000 during the next five years. They had also borrowed heavily from Rhode Island Central, flipping properties and leaving the institution in the hole for $4.8 million while they pocketed more than $2 million from a condominium project they named Wildflower Commons. Rosenstein suggested that part of the Barbatos' take had gone for $60,000 luxury skyboxes at Fenway Park and $194,461.86 for a Rolls Royce convertible.[9]

Defense lawyer Joseph A. Bevilacqua Jr., brother of Senate Majority Leader John J. Bevilacqua, had tried in vain to quash the commission's subpoena of Donald Barbato, and he marched ahead of Barbato to the witness table. Under the television lights, Bevilacqua glared at Teitz and accused him of using the hearing "as a convenient tool for publicity for self-serving purposes."

The showdown could not have been more personal. Teitz had led the impeachment investigation against the lawyer's late father and namesake, then-Chief Justice Joseph A. Bevilacqua, and the Barbatos' Mob connections played prominently in the impeachment. State police surveillance placed the chief justice in Robert Barbato's home at least seventeen times in one year. Barbato had coordinated the chief justice's trysts at a Mob-owned motel. State police had also staked out Montecello's, a North Providence clothing store owned by the Barbato brothers, where Patriarca crime family associates often met. When Raymond "Junior" Patriarca was arrested in 1990 on federal racketeering charges, Donald Barbato pledged $2.7 million, including Montecello's, to bail him out.[10]

Now Joseph A. Bevilacqua Jr. sat beside Donald Barbato at the witness table, glaring at Rep. Jeffrey Teitz. Bevilacqua declared that he had informed the commission that his clients would cite their rights against self-incrimination. "I can only view their compelled attendance before your commission as outright harassment," he said, "a deliberate attempt on your behalf to create a circus atmosphere to have my clients viewed by the TV audience as individuals who have broken the law." He denounced what he called the commission's "abuse of its subpoena authority." He warned of "a hit-and-run effect upon their constitutional rights."[11]

Teitz listened stoically and kept silent.

At Teitz's side, John Nields began questioning Donald Barbato: "Mr. Barbato, do you have a brother named Robert Barbato?"

Barbato glanced at Bevilacqua and began reading from a paper: "Upon the advice of counsel, I refuse to be compelled to be a witness against myself, and I invoke all my rights onto the Fourth, Fifth and Sixth Amendments of the United States Constitution." He drew a breath, and went on to the Rhode Island Constitution and sections of state and federal laws.

After Donald Barbato's second boilerplate refusal to answer, Bevilacqua suggested saving time by having him answer "same response."

Teitz agreed.

Neilds asked Barbato basic questions about millions that he and his brother owed to Rhode Island Central Credit Union. "Same response," Barbato replied. Again and again, he recited the answer. Soon, spectators around me in the audience began parroting it with him.

Robert Barbato followed the same script, repeating the mantra fifteen times in a litany that quickly became tedious. The Barbato brothers and corporations they controlled had parlayed fake loans into real fortunes. They had left RISDIC credit unions holding bags full of properties worth far less than their face value. When state examiners checked Wildflower Commons to see if it could be sold to cover the Barbatos' default, they discovered that only thirty of the one hundred condos had been completed.[12]

Oversized men in expensive suits, Donald and Robert Barbato sauntered out of the room looking triumphant. They had pulled off a classic scam and almost dared the RISDIC Commission to recommend criminal prosecution.

Nor were the Barbatos exceptional. Another pair of brothers, Nicholas and Vincent Cambio, turned up among the largest borrowers from five closed credit unions. *Providence Journal* reporter Ira Chinoy calculated their take at $19 million.[13] On April Fools' Day 1992, the Cambio brothers and their partner, Rodney A. Malafronte, followed the Barbato brothers to the witness table and also claimed their constitutional right not to incriminate themselves. To many in the audience, they seemed to be thumbing their noses at the rule of law.

RISDIC investigators had followed the money Nicholas Cambio pocketed from one subterfuge in 1988. With no money down, he borrowed $975,000 from the Davisville Credit Union to buy a closed Warwick restaurant called the Quaker Pub. No one at the credit union bothered to get an appraisal or find out that the eatery was advertised for sale at $650,000. From that venture Cambio cleared $325,000, which he processed through a bevy of corporations he controlled to produce nine separate corporate checks to the campaign of Gov. Edward DiPrete. An infusion of Cambio checks worth $17,800 arrived just in time to help the scandal-tainted DiPrete eke out a narrow win in the 1988 election.[14] The governor had taken mountains of RISDIC money while he ignored warnings that the state credit union system was a disaster waiting to happen. Teitz, who had drafted Rhode Island's 1988 Campaign Finance Law, argued that the Cambios' huge contributions defied the legal limit of $2,000 from any single entity.[15]

Investigators had also tracked funds Nicholas Cambio had borrowed from Marquette Credit Union to futures trading on risky stocks and commodities. Howard Rosenstein, the forensic auditor, told the RISDIC panel that between 1987 and 1990, Cambio had lost $7.4 million — all borrowed. "Basically," he testified, "it's like going to Atlantic City or Las Vegas. A significant portion of those losses got funded by RISDIC institutions." In May of 1992, federal agents arrested the Cambio brothers and Rodney Malafronte, charging all three with wire fraud and conspiracy.[16]

Despite the deluge of information about how vulnerable RISDIC-insured institutions had been to Mob associates, Teitz's practice of forcing thugs in expensive suits to assert their rights against self-incrimination sparked controversy. Rae Condon told me it was unfair to force even reprehensible characters like the Barbatos and the Cambios to keep reciting their rights. "What earthly good does it do to parade them in public?" she asked. I pointed to the need for ordinary citizens to see the faces and schemes of those who had systematically looted the credit unions: "People would tune out after a while if the only show was Howard Rosenstein connecting the dots."

"So you're saying I have to sit up there like a sphinx and be party to this spectacle? To entertain people in their living rooms?"

There was no point in trying to answer. I believed Teitz was on the right track, but Condon would not be swayed by my arguments about the public's right to see what had been going on with RISDIC-insured funds.

As Gov. Sundlun and legislative leaders inched toward compromise on the RIght Now! bills, word spread that I was negotiating the details. When I left State House offices, I never knew whether reporters would be waiting in the hall. Mo Guernon, head of Operation Clean Sweep, blasted me for "back-room meetings" and branded me "the Judas Iscariot of the reform movement."

Passover and Easter fell late in 1992, and the airwaves crackled with talk of betrayal. For months, Sen. Bill Irons had been pushing RIght Now! to denounce Senate Majority Leader John Bevilacqua. Irons made the struggle personal, insisting that no reforms would matter as long as Bevilacqua ran the Senate. In private conversations I told him that RIght Now! was committed to changing the political system and would not join in personal attacks.

Our strategy of negotiating gained credibility when the Senate approved Jeff Teitz's Comprehensive Campaign Finance Reform package. Ironies multiplied when Irons and his faction of senators declared their opposition to key provisions as not stringent enough, even though on the last night of the 1991 legislative session they had battled for the very legislation that they now dismissed. The final vote was 37 to 13 for passage, with most of the Irons faction voting against the bill.[17]

On April 16, the day before Good Friday, I was on a WHJJ radio talk show hosted by Steve Kass, when Irons phoned in. As he had been doing for weeks, Irons slammed our negotiations with legislative leaders: "You have to ask how we are ever going to make any progress when the people who are supposed to be your friends are cutting deals behind closed doors," he declared. "Phil West lost that battle when he agreed to negotiate. That was the end."

I wanted to interject that the steering committee had decided to negotiate, but Irons was already declaring that I was "a phony's phony." He added: "I'm trying to fight the good fight, but I'm getting my legs cut off by people who are supposed to be the good guys." In an emotional crescendo, Irons announced he would not seek re-election. In calmer comments after the on-air exchange, Irons told a *Providence Journal* reporter that he had been thinking about leaving public life for several months. His angry announcement prompted calls from friends and allies, asking him to reconsider.[18]

As the General Assembly started its spring break, Alan Hassenfeld quietly invited Irons and his Senate faction to Hasbro for breakfast. On a glorious late April morning, seven senators arrived for breakfast in a glassed-in garden room at Hasbro headquarters. Most were meeting the famed toymaker for the first time. After coffee, cut fruit, bagels, and scrambled eggs, Hassenfeld charmed them, his hair tousled, and his sleeves rolled up. "I wanted to hear your concerns," he said. "I think all of us love Rhode Island. All of us understand the need to pass systemic reforms. I know we have different roles, but I'd like to hear your concerns and — hopefully — have us all pulling in the same direction."

Irons rose at his place. The shortest person in the glassy garden room, he wore a double-breasted blazer, pressed white shirt, and muted tie. "Alan," he began in a moderate tone, "I have the greatest respect for you, and I have no quarrel with what you've said. But I think you need to comprehend the nature of John Bevilacqua and his cohorts. I don't know if you've met them."

"I haven't," said Hassenfeld, agreeably. "I know you've been dealing with them for years."

"We have, and they've been utterly disingenuous. They have nothing but contempt for systemic reform." Irons argued that Bevilacqua and his backers were corrupt to the core. "That being the case, it's utterly demeaning for you to negotiate with them. In the end, they'll give you less than half a loaf."

Hassenfeld tamped his pipe but did not light it. "It's obvious what you've been up against," he said, "but we hope you understand that the RIght Now! Coalition has a role that's different from yours. From the start, we've demanded specific changes in the law and Constitution, and we've also made it a matter of principle never to attack people."

"With all due respect," Irons interrupted. "You don't have to negotiate with them behind closed doors."

"Our steering committee thinks negotiation is necessary," Hassenfeld insisted. "We need to know where there may or may not be room for compromise. We're fully aware that the various players may have different bottom lines that they're not willing to announce to the world."

"Respectfully, Alan," Irons replied. "I know you're sincere, but your enemies — and believe me, they are your enemies — are not sincere. They intend to string you along, and in the end, they'll give you nothing."

Hassenfeld rose, his hands poised as if holding an invisible basketball. "As of right now, the ball's still in play, and we intend to win. We intend to play hard until the final buzzer." The toymaker brightened. "And, hey, we're not relying on their kindness or good intentions. If anybody tries to run out the clock and block reform, I assure you we will let the voters know who did it. Right now," he said, smiling at his play on words, "we're glad you came this morning. We're eager to work with you, and we hope you'll recognize that our methods may not always be the same as yours."

Irons clearly wanted the last word. "We hear you, but we still think you're making a mistake to negotiate. That said, we're with you in wanting systemic reforms. We carried the ball before RIght Now! got started, and we'll be in the game after your coalition packs it in. I just hope you don't let genuine reform slip away."

There was no point in arguing. Breakfast ended with smiles and handshaking all around. After the senators left, I asked Hassenfeld what I could have done differently.

"Movements get divisive." He lit his pipe and drew on it. "Irons knows they can't win without us. At the end of the day, everyone will want to own these reforms. Keep in mind what President Kennedy said: 'Victory has a thousand fathers, but defeat is an orphan.'"

By the last days of April, as pale green softened a thousand trees on College Hill, a sense of inevitability spread at the State House. Jeff Teitz's campaign finance bill had come back from the Senate with only minor amendments and landed on the House calendar for final passage. After years of work on its elements and countless legislative setbacks, final passage suddenly seemed possible.

Operation Clean Sweep blasted the legislation and demanded tougher language. Graying volunteers stood at all three entrances to the House chamber, handing out lists of amendments that they said would constitute genuine reform.

As debate began, Teitz rose from his seat, microphone in hand, towering above everyone else in the chamber. "Today is truly an historic day," he announced with obvious pleasure. He began to guide his colleagues through the bill, announcing that this legislation would — for the first time in Rhode Island's history — ban corporate contributions to political campaigns. He reminded his colleagues and the reporters, who filled a long desk below the rostrum, that money from prime players in the RISDIC scandal had traditionally flowed through multiple corporations to candidates for governor.

Without mentioning former House Speaker Matthew Smith by name, Teitz noted that his bill would outlaw the widespread practice of converting leftover campaign funds for personal use. Smith had drawn more than nine thousand dollars from his campaign account to pay his sons' college tuition payments. Gov. Ed DiPrete had tapped his war chest to take family members on a Las Vegas vacation.

Teitz outlined how his bill would allow a former office-holder to donate unused campaign funds to other candidates, political parties, political action committees, charities, or the state. Or, he added with a smile, ex-officials could maintain their accounts for subsequent campaigns or return unused money to the donors. Ever professorial, Teitz also explained how one section of the new law would cut in half the amounts an individual or political action committee could contribute to any candidate. "Equally important," he added, "it would establish sweeping new disclosure requirements that would allow the public to see the names and businesses of all contributors over $100."

He turned to the matching-funds program that would make it possible for candidates who lacked personal wealth to run for statewide office. Enacted four years earlier, the new system had not worked in the 1990 gubernatorial contest, which shattered all previous spending records. He explained that if a wealthy candidate were to spend more than $1.5 million from his own pocket, public matching funds would become available for any challenger who played by the rules. "No system is perfect," Teitz said, "but these provisions surely level the playing field."

To emphasize the importance of this debate, Alan Hassenfeld and I watched from chairs at the side of the House chamber.

Rep. Ray Rickman offered what seemed to be a noncontroversial amendment to require the Board of Elections to notify citizens each year that campaign finance reports were available for public inspection. I winced at that. Any change would send the bill back to the Senate and delay its implementation for an entire election cycle. The legislation might even drop through the cracks, as Teitz's bill had done the year before.

Rickman, an implacable foe of DeAngelis and Teitz, turned some of his anger against Hassenfeld and me. "I'm going to vote against this bill because my conscience tells me to," he said, "because I'm not afraid of the rich and powerful, and because I'm not afraid of anyone right now." He was running for secretary of state, and his militant stand won support from Operation Clean Sweep and the Public Interest Alliance.

Teitz moved to table Rickman's amendment. When Speaker Joe DeAngelis called for the vote, 51 green lights to table prevailed over 38 red lights to continue debate.[19]

Other amendments followed: to cut the top contribution anyone could make to a candidate in half, to delete a provision that would allow individuals to give up to $10,000 to political parties for "party building activities," and to drop the threshold for reporting political contributions from $100 to $25. Pages distributed copies of each amendment to the representatives, who debated and then voted to table one after another.

As the final vote neared, House Minority Leader David Dumas rose at his desk. "I'm so used to creeping in this area that when I get a chance to leap, I'm going to take it," he said, urging the House to approve.

When DeAngelis called for the final vote, 94 voted to pass Teitz's bill, and only five voted against it.[20]

With reporters trailing, Alan Hassenfeld and I made our way through the House lounge, where we had announced the RIght Now! Coalition five months earlier. As we left the building, bright spring sunshine filled the plaza. I asked if he was ready to call off the moratorium on campaign contributions.

"As soon as Bruce signs the bill," he laughed. "I told you it wouldn't last forever." He asked me to draft a press release to fax out after the signing. "Make it dramatic! This is a huge victory."

The next day, in a State Room suffused with sunshine that made the white marble glow, Bruce Sundlun prepared to sign Teitz's bill into law. "Today marks an important milestone in the journey toward a more ethical government in Rhode Island," Sundlun intoned in his Pattonesque growl, standing beneath the portrait of George Washington. "It's a good start, and other reforms will follow."

Political leaders filled rows of chairs angled toward his podium. Near the windows, a modest table held the bill that awaited Sundlun's signature.

House Speaker Joe DeAngelis injected a note of humor, directing his comments toward the governor. "I'm keeping a promise today," he said. "When the session started, I promised that we would have this legislation on your desk no later than the beginning of February. I'm aware that we missed that date, but we have the bill. In legislative time, this is timely!"[21]

Then Jeff Teitz leaned into the microphone. "This moves us into the ranks of states with the strongest regulation of campaign finance. For those who are repulsed by the ever-increasing costs of campaigns, this is progress. For those of us who want issues to shape campaigns, this is real progress."

After the speeches, Sundlun moved to a chair by the small table. Among a dozen legislators, Alan Hassenfeld and I stood behind him. He scrawled his name on the coversheet of the bill and handed the pen to me. It felt surreal to be shaking his hand, thanking him.

Hassenfeld told reporters that RIght Now's moratorium on campaign contributions had ended. I faxed a press release declaring that enactment of Comprehensive Campaign Finance Reform sent a clear message to any who might seek unfair advantage: "Rhode Island State Government is not for sale, not for rent, not for hire."[22]

I had known from the start that our toughest struggle would be over what we called "the revolving door." Common Cause board member Bill Colleran, an engineer who had computed trajectories for Apollo flights to and from the moon, turned his expertise to tracking the paths General Assembly members had taken to judgeships. He found that of fifty-four judges appointed during the last twenty years, twenty-five went directly from the State House to the bench. Fifteen had been lawmakers, and ten others were legislative staff lawyers. By contrast, although thousands of attorneys practiced in the state, Colleran found only twenty-six without these political connections who had become judges during the same time.

For example, I knew two House Judiciary Committee members who had recently become judges: Rep. Gilbert V. Indeglia advanced to the District Court bench in 1989, and Rep. Paul A. Suttell got a Family Court judgeship in 1990.[23] I also knew of two spectacular leaps from the House to the Supreme Court. Speaker Joseph A. Bevilacqua orchestrated his elevation to chief justice in 1976, while House Judiciary Chairman Thomas F. Fay became a Family Court judge in 1978 and chief justice in 1986.

Another judicial appointment had "political payoff" written all over it. Over several months in 1988 and 1989, factions of Democrats had battled for control of the Senate. A slim majority had elected Sen. David R. Carlin Jr. as Senate majority leader, but Sen. John J. Bevilacqua gained *de facto* control by aligning with Senate Republicans, whose minority leader was Robert D. Goldberg.[24] Carlin bitterly accused Goldberg and Gov. DiPrete of forging an "unholy alliance" with Bevilacqua to avert a legislative investigation of the contractor defaults on the unfinished Jamestown Bridge.[25]

Whatever lay behind the bipartisan partnership, Bevilacqua gave plum posts to Carlin allies who had switched sides, and the next available appointment on the Superior Court went to Maureen McKenna Goldberg, the wife and law partner of Senate Minority Leader Bob Goldberg.[26] Few doubted that Bevilacqua had engineered her appointment. While governors publicly appointed judges, the Senate routinely confirmed them. I often heard that the governor, Senate majority leader, and speaker of the House followed an unwritten protocol: they took turns choosing jurists.

Bevilacqua took the revolving door bill as a personal affront and tried to stand the problem on its head. Though he agreed that many political players had moved up to judgeships, he insisted that those chosen were good judges. "You can't just put a label on these people and say they're not good because they've been members of the General Assembly."[27]

John Bevilacqua's obdurate opposition to our revolving door bill had buried it without a vote in 1991, and he had railed against the Ethics Commission's vote to adopt the same ban. Throughout the spring of 1992, he bristled whenever I raised the subject. "You should wise up," he once thundered at me. "What don't you understand about the meaning of 'No'?"

Bruce Sundlun seemed equally adamant. One afternoon, as I trailed him down the broad rotunda stairway, he roared over his shoulder: "I haven't made a single goddamn revolving door appointment, but if the best person happens to be a legislator . . . ." He let it hang ominously. "I'm a lawyer. I can pick good judges, and I'll be damned if I'll let you or Alan Hassenfeld stand in my way."

The RIght Now! steering committee had wrestled with this resistance and settled reluctantly on a compromise that would exempt judgeships. That concession appeared to be the price for passing the rest of our ethics package, including strong anti-nepotism rules and a streamlined Ethics Commission with open adjudicative hearings. No one liked the trade, but as Hassenfeld asked around the table, most thought we had no choice.

Our compromise on the revolving door left no one happy. On a misty spring night RIght Now! supporters arriving for an ecumenical rally had to cross through a half-dozen pickets from Operation Clean Sweep and its allies, who handed out leaflets and chanted that we were not tough enough on corrupt politicians. Inside the Bishop McVinney Auditorium, part of the Roman Catholic Diocese of Providence headquarters, attendees barely filled the banked seats. The enthusiasm that had galvanized many thousands in January had dissipated.

Episcopal Bishop George Hunt told the audience he was not a member of the steering committee, nor was he about to question our revolving door compromise, but asked, "Why does the Assembly need us to prod them to do what is ethical and right? The very fact that such a prod is needed is eloquent testimony to the need for such reforms." On the brightly lit stage, Alan Hassenfeld embraced Bishop Hunt and then spoke with the gentle intimacy I had come to feel was second nature to him. "More than anything else in this state, we need change, and we need change very, very quickly because too many people are fed up." Without explaining the vicissitudes of our negotiations or the reasons for compromise, he stayed upbeat. "Ninety-five percent of what RIght Now! has sought is coming up for a vote," he said. "Sooner or later, reform will be ours."[28]

I HAD NO ADVANCE NOTICE that Operation Clean Sweep would issue a legislative report card, but early in June people with signs clustered on the landing where broad marble stairways down from the House and Senate meet beneath the dome. A huge bronze Rhode Island seal marked the epicenter. At a microphone Mo Guernon was describing the results to reporters, his voice muffled in the hubbub of passing lobbyists and lawmakers. I moved closer to listen and took a packet from a volunteer. Guernon said their scorecard brought a "day of reckoning" for legislators.[29]

The Clean Sweep scorecard used what it called an IQ, which stood for "Incumbent Quotient." From a base of 100, the scorers added one point for each vote they considered pro-reform and subtracted one for each anti-reform vote. On their list Rep. Jeff Teitz had the worst score in the House, an IQ of 69, while Speaker Joe DeAngelis had a 71. Representatives who had voted to table the more radical amendments to Teitz's campaign finance bill did poorly, while those who one-upped the RIght Now! proposals were rated "genius." In the Senate, the same pattern held. Bill Irons scored 114 for backing the most radical cuts in campaign contribution limits and reporting thresholds.

Neither Guernon nor his followers had worked on these issues in previous legislative sessions, and their efforts in 1992 consisted of issuing demands that were twice as tough as RIght Now's. They mocked the work Teitz had done on campaign finance reform. In their scorecard, he became a reactionary bent on preserving the corrupt status quo.

"What do you make of these scores?" Reporter Wayne Miller found me behind a pillar that held up the dome.

I shrugged. "I'm not saying they're totally wrong," I said, "but it's not as simple as they suggest. Their bottom line turns Jeff Teitz into a bad guy who 'needs a career change.' In that sense, their study misrepresents the legislative process to the public."

I sensed Mo Guernon and his group had acted impulsively, but I had no idea why they fired this salvo before the session ended. They caricatured the central characters before the final votes. Guernon's scorecard would confuse people who got their news on television.

Later in his office, Jeff Teitz seemed unperturbed. "When they produce such an extreme document," he said, "they make themselves absurd. You know and I know we've put forth genuine reform. In time, members of the public will recognize that, and I will gladly stand on my record."

Through the four years I had known him, I often marveled that Jeff Teitz could recall details from countless bills, as if he stowed them in mental pigeonholes with the latest versions on top. He worked through complex questions, seeming to embody a unique blend of realism, pragmatism, and unflappable civility. Through thick glasses he communicated a sense that he genuinely cared about relationships and wanted to resolve disagreements.

I rose to leave his office and asked if he could clue me in on the constitutional amendment for four-year terms.

"You know," he said quietly, "there's a strong feeling that we should have four-year terms for the General Assembly as well as the governor and other general officers."

"And you know that voters already said no to that," I said, trying not to sound argumentative.

On his feet, Teitz towered above me. "Candidly, I can tell you that a four-year term for the governor and other general officers is not popular on the third floor. Nobody really thinks we should shift power toward the executive. And frankly, even if we agree to put your question on the ballot, I don't think you'll prevail."

"Our point," I replied, "is that voters should decide the constitutional question. It would be fine for you to put up a separate question on four-year terms for legislators. The steering committee thinks it's crucial that you let the people vote separately on four-year terms for the governor and legislature."

"You've made that abundantly clear," he said.

13

RISDIC TV
1992

THE RISDIC INVESTIGATING COMMISSION launched its final hearings in May 1992, just as the General Assembly lurched toward adjournment. Commission Chairman Jeffrey Teitz told reporters that investigators would now ask why government had failed to detect RISDIC's flaws in time to address them "without such catastrophic consequences."[1] As I struggled to balance lobbying against watching the proceedings unfold, I could barely imagine how Teitz managed his time.

Former Atty. Gen. Arlene Violet finally took her turn in June, testifying that RISDIC crushed legislation that would have mandated federal credit union insurance. With owlish glasses and close-cropped hair, the woman often called "Attila the Nun" radiated moral authority. A resonant voice and gift of gab had made her a talk-radio celebrity, and Violet reveled in her vindication. On June 3, 1992, in a dramatic opening statement, she blamed political insiders she derisively called "The Network," comparing their power to the Mafia's. "Except for one thing," she said. "They make what they do legal. They've raped and plundered the people of this state."

She reminded Teitz's panel that she had testified six years earlier in this very room before the House Finance Committee and its vice chair, Rep. Bob Bianchini. Violet had feared then that rumors of RISDIC's peril would start a calamitous run on the credit unions. She said that exercise had been futile, because House Speaker "Matty Smith had already given the word that the bill was six feet under." She had also urged then-Gov. DiPrete to enter the fray, but even after DiPrete's trusted attorney, Normand Benoit, confirmed the dire warnings in Robert Stitt's report, DiPrete never made RISDIC a priority. Violet also charged that former state treasurer Roger Begin had pumped $30 million of taxpayer funds into the Rhode Island Credit Union League to prop up the insurance system.

Next she went after Teitz himself. "Do you ever intend to come to this side of the microphone?" she demanded.

"This is not a radio talk show," he shot back. "This is a legal proceeding, and we expect you — as all witnesses — to conform with the rules of the proceeding."

"Are you refusing to answer the question, sir?" Violet demanded.

Teitz rebuffed her with silence. During a break, he expressed his exasperation to reporter Mike Stanton: "What you're seeing is classic Arlene Violet: rhetoric without regard for facts."

Alan Baron quizzed Violet on why she had not gone privately to House Speaker Matthew Smith. "Why did you not say to him, 'You may not like me, and I don't like you, but there is something here that's bigger than both of us'? You've got to read this report. You've got to pay attention to it. You've got to help us get this legislation through.' Why did you not do that?"

"For heaven's sake!" Violet shot back. "In 1985 the leadership in the General Assembly had supported RISDIC through thick and thin. They had malnourished the Department of Business Regulation. They knew how to read. They heard what I was saying. They saw what was happening in banking. How naïve to think Mr. Smith had any intention of doing anything. He's one of the boys."

"Miss Violet," Baron persisted, "what did you have to lose by giving it a shot? He was the one guy who could have pushed this legislation through if you won him over."

"You need to stay here longer, Mr. Baron," she scolded. She told how Auditor General Anthony Piccirilli had raised concerns over RISDIC in 1979 but had been "chastised in the press" by Thomas J. Calderone, Gov. J. Joseph Garrahy's director of business regulation, who later became a judge. She reminded Baron that DiPrete's top regulator had followed the same career path. "Mark Pfeiffer was head of business regulation. He does nothing. He becomes a judge. Mr. Teitz might become a judge. I don't know. But nobody does anything. Legislators told me: 'Read my lips. No.'"

John Nields, Baron's co-counsel, took a turn. "Why didn't you leap at the chance of going behind closed doors at an executive session or at a private meeting and sticking those facts right in their face: 'You have three big RISDIC-insured institutions that are insolvent. You have got a real problem right now.'"

Violet reminded Nields that members of the House Finance Committee had met privately twice with RISDIC leaders over dinner at the Aurora Club. She insisted that they knew RISDIC's problems and that they had the Stitt Report. "You're missing the whole point here," she remonstrated. "What went wrong with government? The network I've been talking about. This was their power base. They wanted these institutions. There's no way they wanted the federal government poking its nose into their loaning practices, the passage of information around to developers, the types of campaign contributions they were making to members of the General Assembly, the kinds of jobs that people in that General Assembly got promoted to. That's what RISDIC is about. The rest of it is show. It is a play, sir."[2]

On June 8, 1992, Rep. Robert Bianchini took his turn under the hot lights as the panel took aim at his conflicts of interest. While director of the Rhode Island Credit Union League (RICUL), he had hosted two dinners at the Aurora Club for his colleagues on the House Finance Committee. RISDIC President Peter Nevola had used the gatherings to argue against legislation that would require federal insurance of credit unions. Bianchini later sent his tab to Nevola.

Bianchini even chaired part of the Finance Committee's crucial meeting on May 12, 1986. Now, six years later, the RISDIC panel, spectators, and television audience watched a videotape of Bianchini grilling Rep. Frank Gaschen for having sponsored the bill to require federal insurance. Now their roles were reversed: Gaschen sat on the investigating commission and Bianchini came under attack in the witness chair.[3]

The blotchy video showed Bianchini badgering Robert Stitt—now revered for his 1985 warning of RISDIC's collapse, his nobility burnished by his sudden death on live radio with Arlene Violet. Monitors mounted around the room showed Bianchini bullying Stitt as if in a TV courtroom drama.

"I would certainly suggest to you that I was overly aggressive," Bianchini acknowledged, "and I'll tell you why. I was angry." He said he had believed Gaschen's legislation impugned the credit union system. He accused special counsel Alan Baron of taking the video clips out of context. "I would certainly suggest to you that I was overly aggressive and I'll tell you why! I was angry!" He thought Gaschen's legislation was designed to discredit the credit union system.

Baron asked why he treated Stitt as if he knew nothing about banking practices.

"I was overly aggressive and I should not have been," Bianchini said. "Just similar to what you are doing to me, by the way."[4]

John Nields took over. He asked Bianchini about the conflict between his separate roles as RICUL executive and state representative. "How do you ignore that industry position when you turn to do your job as a legislator?"

With a straight face, Bianchini answered: "I had very little occasion to ever have a conflict in that regard." He said his constituents were members of credit unions, and he was protecting them when he shielded credit unions from attack. He explained that he often left the House floor when bills favored by RISDIC came up for a vote. "No matter what the industry position was, I would not participate in the vote."

"Now wait," Nields interrupted. "You're saying that on those bills where the government affairs committee had developed a position, you would generally not participate in the legislative process?"

"That's right," Bianchini said. "I would leave the floor of the House if those bills came up on the calendar."

"Then why did you participate so actively on the federal deposit insurance law?"

Bianchini said again that he had been angry. "I was absolutely convinced that the reason that Rep. Gaschen introduced the legislation had nothing to do with the real issue at hand. It had more to do with the people he was close to." He named several, including Robert Bergeron, the head of a credit union that had already switched to federal insurance. "I was angry and aggressive," Bianchini repeated, "and I shouldn't have been."

Commission member Mary Lisi asked Bianchini if he felt compromised when he called committee members together on legislation they would be hearing.

"No. I did not."

Lisi asked if he had thought about seeking an advisory opinion under the state's conflict of interest rules.

He answered calmly that he had always understood the law to mean that unless monetary gain was involved, there was no conflict.

Her eyebrows rose. "So unless you're going to make some money on something, it's not a conflict?"

Bianchini garbled his answer: "Unless you were going to, you personally, were going to benefit. . . ." His sentence fell away.

A former member of RISDIC's board, who had originally charged him with a conflict of interest for quashing the Gaschen bill, now sat in the audience, unheralded and unrecognized by most. Robert G. Bergeron, president of the Woodlawn Credit Union, knew RISDIC from the inside. He had watched RISDIC credit unions abuse their power, take excessive risks, and mislead their depositors. Concerned that any large claim on RISDIC might topple the entire system, Bergeron had led Woodlawn to obtain federal insurance and quit RISDIC. He knew vast numbers of depositors remained at risk in RISDIC-insured credit unions, and he contacted Gaschen, and they drafted the 1986 legislation requiring federal insurance. Neither knew that investigators working for the attorney general had reached similar conclusions.

Gaschen's bill had provoked the ire of many RISDIC players. Former colleagues cursed Bergeron and mobilized against the legislation, treating Bergeron and Gaschen as enemies. When Gaschen's bill was defeated, Bergeron was livid over Bianchini's role and filed a complaint against Bianchini — the last complaint adjudicated by the old Conflict of Interest Commission before it went out of business.[5]

Back in the same hearing room six years later, the two protagonists never

acknowledged each other. Bergeron later told a reporter that he had come because Bianchini was lying.[6]

Several nights after Bianchini's testimony, Rep. Francis A. Gaschen strode
from his seat on the RISDIC Investigating Commission to the center table and
became a witness. I had gotten to know him as a young lawyer who served on
the House Judiciary Committee and eagerly sponsored ethics bills for Common
Cause. Gaschen was thin and soft-spoken, but fearless. In dozens of conversations since RISDIC's collapse, he had only hinted about what happened when
he filed his now famous 1986 bill to require federal credit union insurance for
RISDIC-insured institutions.

Gaschen testified that constituents from his Cumberland district had asked
him if their credit unions were safe. He explained to his fellow commissioners that the hostility against him had built steadily from the moment he first
filed the federal credit union insurance bill. Colleagues had warned him that
he faced an uphill battle, while Bianchini and the RISDIC lobby treated him as
an enemy. Gaschen testified that he had asked House Speaker Matthew Smith
to mediate between him and Bianchini, but Smith refused. Then the House
Finance Committee pounced.

Six years after the event, Gaschen's emotions remained raw. "In thirteen
years' experience in the House," he testified, "I've never seen anyone grilled as
toughly as I was."[7]

Nor had Gaschen's punishment ended when they buried his bill. Retribution
followed. He testified that law clients were pressured to dump him. He never
knew how many real estate closings he forfeited, but two homebuyers had told
him that officers at the East Providence Credit Union warned against using him
as their attorney. "One was told he could use any attorney in the state but me,"
Gaschen said. When the buyer asked why, he was told: "that RISDIC thing."

In mid-June, former House Speaker Matthew J. Smith finally testified before
the RISDIC panel. Smith had spun through the revolving door from speaker
to administrator of the state court system. I had seen him return triumphantly
to the State House, always surrounded in the hallway by a retinue of lobbyists
and legislators. I recognized his charisma and heard legends of his power. Now,
though called as a witness, he cheerfully greeted members of the RISDIC panel
by their first names.[8]

Two former House Finance Committee members had testified that Smith
spurned Arlene Violet's offer to share the Stitt Report in a confidential session.
Both quoted the speaker as refusing her offer and protecting Bianchini with the
unforgettable phrase: "We don't want to embarrass Bobby."

Smith flatly denied that he had said any such thing. He also rebuffed prior
testimony that he had the power to "give the nod" on any particular bill, and he
bristled at charges that he had done anything to kill Gaschen's bill.

Alan Baron asked if he could have saved the legislation. More tentatively, the former speaker answered, "I think that if information was supplied to us, we would have acted decisively."[9]

Whatever happened in a closed-door meeting six years earlier, it all came down to vague memories of private conversations and highly public spin. This was not a court of law, and the RISDIC commissioners were not jurors. Whatever the viewers' verdict, Matty Smith would not pay a fine or go to jail.

In his turn as a witness Senate Majority Leader John J. Bevilacqua radiated resentment, but his testimony pulled several facts into sharp focus. Records from the now-defunct Greater Providence Deposit Corporation showed that his mother, widow of the disgraced late chief justice, had cashed out certificates of deposit worth $176,088 on December 21, 1990, only hours after her powerful son learned of RISDIC's looming collapse. Like others who rushed their funds to federally-insured banks, Josephine Bevilacqua paid a hefty penalty for her early withdrawal. On that same day Bevilacqua's top aide, former Cranston Rep. Anthony DeLuca, cashed out a passbook account worth $115,000 from the Rhode Island Central Credit Union.

In answer to questions from Alan Baron, the Senate's powerful leader testified that he had attended a meeting with House Speaker Joseph DeAngelis and Gov.-elect Bruce Sundlun at Sundlun's transition office. Bevilacqua said he was unsure of the date. He insisted that he had received only vague information about the looming crisis. "I was never informed of any RISDIC-insured institution being in jeopardy," Bevilacqua told the panel. "I was never privy to this information."[10]

Baron tried to refresh his memory, noting that other witnesses put the meeting on December 20 and described "a much more dire situation," including the likelihood that several institutions would have to close and have their assets sold off. "Do you recall being present at a meeting on or about that date in which the issue was discussed concerning the status of the RISDIC-insured institutions?"

"That's the first I've heard of that meeting," Bevilacqua insisted.

Bevilacqua might have forgotten exactly when and how he learned about RISDIC's impending crash, but several witnesses put him at the crisis meeting with Sundlun and DeAngelis on December 20, and records from two RISDIC institutions showed the massive withdrawals by his mother and chief of staff on December 21. How was that possible unless Bevilacqua learned on the 20th and confided separately in two people he trusted?

Bevilacqua finished testifying and stalked out without waiting to see what his counterpart, House Speaker Joseph DeAngelis, would say. DeAngelis had not been present for Bevilacqua's testimony. He claimed that he and Bevilaqua had learned together at the December 20 meeting with Sundlun and his staff that several RISDIC institutions would fail. Baron asked DeAngelis if that news came as a shock to him and Bevilacqua. "To me," the speaker answered, "no. The rumors of that issue were around the State House and on the street for days before that. We had Heritage, which had gone down. Jefferson had gone down."

Baron asked whether they had suggested shutting down the thrifts. "Did you and Sen. Bevilacqua discuss that issue with the governor at this meeting?"

"I'm not sure if we did at that meeting," DeAngelis answered. He said he and Bevilacqua had told Sundlun that closing the credit unions would harm the economy and many depositors.

Baron seemed to relish finally getting a straight story. "Subsequent to this meeting of the 20th, did you and Sen. Bevilacqua take any steps to solve or ameliorate the situation?"

"We met a lot," DeAngelis said, "and we did a lot of hand-wringing, I guess. Candidly speaking, the General Assembly was not equipped to deal with that kind of issue. I know that Sen. Bevilacqua and I visited with the presidents of two of the major banks in Rhode Island to find out what help they could be."

Though resentful depositors had branded DeAngelis "the Prince of Darkness," I sensed that he believed in government and tried to make it work. He was arguably the most powerful politician in Rhode Island, but nothing he could do would repair the damage of RISDIC's collapse.

Only days before former Gov. Edward DiPrete would take his turn as a witness before the RISDIC panel, three *Providence Journal* reporters produced a stunning story: in 1985 and 1986 DiPrete had received no fewer than five explicit warnings that RISDIC was overextended and at risk of collapse. In their coverage, reporters Mike Stanton, Ira Chinoy, and Christopher Rowland cited the Stitt Report, Norman Benoit's confirming memo, and three additional red flags that DiPrete ignored. In April 1985 DiPrete's friend and confidant, lawyer John J. Partridge, delivered a twenty-three page confidential report about how private deposit insurance had failed in Ohio and Maryland, plunging those states into crisis. Later, DiPrete's director of business regulation, Clifton Moore, sent the governor a private summary of concerns the Federal Reserve Bank had raised with him: federal officials concluded that RISDIC-insured institutions were at risk and should apply for federal insurance. Moore begged DiPrete for additional bank examiners to ride herd on RISDIC. He told the *Providence Journal* that he had been kept out of the loop on RISDIC and that Stitt's report had remained "a deep, dark secret." DiPrete did nothing, and Moore quit.[11]

Finally, on March 21, 1986, Frank E. Morris, the president of the Federal Reserve Bank of Boston, drove to the State House with two of his top staff to warn the governor. "We had been following the situation in Rhode Island for some time," said Thomas E. Cimeno, the Fed's senior vice president of bank supervision. "We were concerned about the financial stability of RISDIC, and that it threatened the financial stability of the state." The federal officials urged DiPrete to back legislation requiring federal credit union insurance.

Instead of action from the governor's office, they got an angry phone call from RISDIC President Peter A. Nevola. Nevola complained that they were interfering. Now, six years later, Cimeno testified that, after Nevola's call, "we went from having marginal cooperation to zero cooperation" from RISDIC.[12]

News that DiPrete had shrugged off five explicit warnings from credible sources became a hot topic among lobbyists and lawmakers in the marble corridors. Callers to talk radio programs railed against the former governor, but few made the connection to large amounts of campaign cash DiPrete had taken from RISDIC-insured credit unions and their officers. In his desperate dash toward the 1988 election, DiPrete extracted $2.6 million from architects, engineers, developers, and RISDIC operators.[13] Corporate donors easily skirted the weak Campaign Finance Law then on the books. The Olney Pond contract that DiPrete had steered to Domenic Tutela was only the tip of the iceberg. Unseen below the surface and far more dangerous were his financial obligation to RISDIC and his failure to address the looming catastrophe.

On June 18, in a red paisley tie and gray suit, DiPrete raised his hand and swore to tell the truth. In a ferocious opening statement, he lashed out at the *Providence Journal*, the General Assembly, and his successor, Bruce Sundlun, whom he blamed for wrongly closing down all forty-five credit unions. DiPrete insisted that he had done all he could to avert the RISDIC disaster.

Special Counsel John W. Nields picked at that claim. "Did there come a time during the budget negotiations when you sat down with anybody from the leadership, and said 'This has got to happen and you're going to avoid it over my dead body' or words to that effect?"[14]

DiPrete hedged. "If I say, look, this is something that is a priority for the administration, we have people write them letters, go see them, testify at a hearing. The attorney general is there, special counsel. If they don't get the message on that, I think they either don't want to hear the message or they had made up their minds. And come hell or high water, they were not going to pass federal mandatory insurance, as Rep. Gaschen knows."

At his seat on the dais, Gaschen nodded.

Nields asked DiPrete, "How important was this issue to you?"

"Very important," the former governor replied.

Nields then asked if moving RISDIC-insured institutions into federal credit union insurance was the governor's most important issue that year. Did it rank among the top three or top ten?

"Top three," DiPrete supposed. "It was in the top handful. Yes, out of hundreds of bills in the session."

"Why do you think you lost?"

"Because the key leadership in the General Assembly was tightly aligned with credit union and RISDIC interests." DiPrete added that he thought the legislation never had a chance.

Nields asked about RISDIC's backers.

"I know they relied on Bob Bianchini very heavily for advice on financial matters, specifically credit unions."

"And do you know what Mr. Bianchini's position was outside of the legislature? Was he head of the Rhode Island Credit Union League?"

"Yes," DiPrete agreed emphatically, "Yes."

"And are you saying, in effect, that if Bob Bianchini was against this bill, that there was no way that the governor's office could get it passed?"

"You got it."

Nields continued to press DiPrete: "Did you or anybody acting for you ever show the Stitt Report to members of the legislature?"

DiPrete equivocated. "If they didn't see the actual report, I'm sure the key information was discussed. They knew it existed." DiPrete said he thought that the Stitt Report had been reported in the press. "It was no secret that there was a report by Stitt given to the governor by Violet. We identified that as a priority. We spoke about, wrote about, sent letters to people. Sent Norm Benoit. . . ."

Nields interrupted: "What's the answer to the question of whether you ever showed the Stitt Report to members of the General Assembly?"

"Did we show it to all of them? No."

"Did you show the report to anybody?"

"To my knowledge people in the Assembly have seen the Stitt Report."

Nields honed in. "My question was, did you or anybody from your administration ever show it to anybody from the General Assembly? It's a very simple question."

"Excuse me, please," DiPrete countered. "I can't tell you if I showed them the verbatim report word for word, cover to cover. There is no question in my mind key people in the Assembly knew the context of that report."

Nields asked if he had told them that Federal Reserve officials had come to his office and raised concerns.

"Probably not," DiPrete said.

"Why did you not call up the leaders and ask for a meeting specifically on this subject? Why didn't you sit down with them and say, 'Look, guys, we have got a serious problem that has just got to be addressed. Let me show you the information in the report about the specific institutions that are either insolvent or close to being insolvent. We've got to put party differences and biases aside and get this done.' Why didn't that happen?"

DiPrete replied with an evasive double negative: he was "not sure such a meeting didn't happen." He added that it would not have mattered. "If they didn't know where I stood, I wouldn't have known how else to communicate an idea. There is no question they knew where we positioned that bill. There is no question in my mind."

The former governor's time as a witness stretched to more than five hours. He continued to insist that even as he prepared to leave office at the end of 1990, there was no need to close the RISDIC-insured credit unions.

Next Alan Baron took over the questioning. He asked about land deals that brought windfall gains to DiPrete family businesses. "Who's supplying the money?" he asked rhetorically and then answered: "Another RISDIC institution."

Baron tied lucrative DiPrete family land deals to Nicholas E. Cambio, a developer who borrowed vast sums from RISDIC institutions and bought land from Dennis DiPrete at inflated prices. Cambio funneled money through nine corporate shells into DiPrete's campaigns. Financial shell games that enriched both the Cambios and the DiPretes had begun in the mid-1980s, swindles that sapped the assets of the Rhode Island Central and Marquette credit unions. Nicholas Cambio would later be charged with fraud, but Dennis DiPrete cleared profits above $700,000 on deals related to Briar Hill Estates.[15] Some key transactions had occurred in the spring of 1986 while Gaschen's bill was under attack. If the lending institutions had been forced to apply for federal credit union insurance, these deals would have stopped.

Seeing Briar Hill on the lists of flipped properties gave me grim satisfaction. I had written it up in the Common Cause complaint, but those charges had been dismissed because the events occurred before DiPrete signed the ethics law in 1987. Now RISDIC investigators had followed money from looted credit unions through Mob-connected developers to DiPrete's campaign and family. As intricate and mind numbing as the financial patterns were, I was glad to have these witnesses appear on television.

But questions remained. Would viewers recognize this as an organized criminal enterprise? Would they pressure their senators and reps to enact the RIght Now! package of campaign finance and ethics reforms? I could only hope.

14

Triumphs
1992

REPORTER WAYNE MILLER phoned our office on the morning of June 10, 1992, to ask what I thought of the decision.

"What decision?"

"I understand that the Rhode Island Supreme Court just issued an advisory opinion on the Ethics Commission."

I promised to call him back and raced to the court complex. On the seventh floor, a clerk handed me the advisory opinion. The justices were unanimous. I scanned for key phrases: "The years preceding the 1986 constitutional convention were marked by scandal and corruption in both state and local government. Indeed, widespread breaches of trust, cronyism, impropriety, and other violations of ethical standards decimated the public's trust in government." They wrote that scandals had prompted the amendment, and concluded that voters who approved the amendment intended to bestow "the power to legislate substantive ethics laws upon an independent nonpartisan ethics commission subject only to judicial review."[1]

I stepped into the ornate brass elevator and rode down alone, leafing hungrily through pages. In a coffee shop on South Main Street, I started making notes in the margins. Much of the document reprised proceedings of the 1986 Constitutional Convention, the year Chief Justice Joe Bevilacqua had resigned in disgrace. The justices flagged a comment from delegate Ken Phillips, who had proposed that the Conflict of Interest Commission or its successor agency should "draft, promulgate, and implement" the code of ethics. They also quoted Roger Milette's remark about getting "the fox away from the chickens. . . . If we are all concerned about the state legislature doing it or doing it right, let's take it away from them. Let's give it to another body."

I sipped coffee to keep from cheering.

The justices quoted section after section of Lauren Jones's brief. They noted that information booklets had made clear to voters that passage would confer "substantive legislative power regarding ethics" on the proposed new Ethics Commission. This new constitutional language, the justices wrote, now limited the General Assembly's otherwise unbounded legislative power. "This is not to say, however, that the General Assembly is prohibited from enacting ethics laws altogether; rather, the General Assembly could pass such laws only if they were not inconsistent with, or contradictory to, the code of ethics adopted by the commission."

That struck me as a crucial concept. The justices seemed to be saying that if the Ethics Commission barred lawmakers from revolving door jobs for one year, the General Assembly could not cut the cooling-off time to six months.

The justices also flatly rejected arguments that the Ethics Commission was an unelected and unaccountable fourth branch of government. They wrote that voters had "transferred a portion of legislative power from one representative body to another." They added: "The representative character of the government still remains. The people have simply vested in the commission a limited share of legislative power to make law in the area of ethics."

The high court's only caveat came in a final declaration that no one should construe this opinion as approving all of the Ethics Commission's decisions and orders. The justices wrote that they would weigh the constitutionality of new rules on a case-by-case basis. Parties who felt aggrieved by a particular prohibition would be free to challenge it in court.

As I stepped out of the coffee shop into bright sunshine, I felt like pumping my fist in the air. Drivers jostled their way northward on South Main Street oblivious to the historic words on these photocopied pages. Back at the Common Cause office, I phoned the reporters who had called for comments, telling them this decision marked a watershed in Rhode Island's history that would go a long way toward establishing the Ethics Commission's power. Gary Yesser, the commission's unflappable attorney, told reporters that the high court's unanimous opinion was "a victory for the commission and for the people." He added that the opinion strengthened the commission as "a truly independent body, exclusively given the responsibility to set and enforce conduct by elected and appointed officials."[2]

The notion that the General Assembly must not undercut ethics rules passed by the Ethics Commission seemed more than legislative leaders could stomach. House Speaker Joe DeAngelis told the *Providence Journal*, "I don't really believe we have been given any specific guidance." Regardless of what they said, however, legislative leaders had to grasp a new political fact: any ambiguities in the Supreme Court's advisory would not be resolved before Election Day, now less than five months away. The Ethics Commission's rules against nepotism and revolving door jobs now carried the force of law. To protect themselves, rank-and-file lawmakers would need to tell voters that they had also addressed these problems.

Ever cordial, Jeff Teitz drew me into his office to review a revolving door bill he was drafting. Written in longhand on a yellow pad, its text made clear that House leaders had decided to go beyond our legislation and the Ethics Commission's ban on revolving door jobs for lawmakers. His new bill also proposed to bar members of the governor's staff and other political players from advancing to judgeships or other permanent state jobs. He looked up from his text. "I'm not wild about your revolving door prohibition," he said. "But if it's inevitable, then we may as well include executive branch officials who may seek to take advantage of their inside positions. You might say that 'What's fair for the goose is fair for the gander.'"

Long before I knew Frank Gaschen had sponsored legislation that might have prevented the RISDIC collapse, I appreciated his conscientious work on Teitz's House Judiciary Committee. Over several years he had sponsored Common Cause proposals that others refused to touch. Gaschen made bills his own by mastering their substance. He had worked on our bill to streamline the Ethics Commission and open its adjudicative hearings to the public, but with the legislative session almost gone, it still languished in the House Judiciary Committee.[3]

On the last Friday afternoon in June, Teitz's secretary phoned to ask me to meet "the Chairman" in his office. When I arrived, he handed me a draft of a bill. "I'm posting this for a vote on Tuesday," he said. This was not the RIght Now! bill that Gaschen had filed for Common Cause, but one that had just been introduced by House Majority Leader Tom Lamb and was already marked "Substitute A/7," which showed that it had already gone through a half dozen drafts before House leaders agreed among themselves.[4]

"Why not Frank Gaschen's bill?" I asked.

"Not a helpful question," Teitz answered. "But I think you'll find most of what you want in this draft."

I left his office annoyed. Gaschen had shown heroic courage, but House leaders were refusing to credit him for revamping the Ethics Commission. If they passed anything, it would be some version of Lamb's bill.

Tom Lamb owned several car dealerships. With a grandfatherly smile, he enjoyed negotiating agreements. In 1987, as House majority whip under Speaker Matty Smith, Lamb had sponsored legislation that created Rhode Island's new Ethics Commission and Code of Ethics. Now, as majority leader, he was the logical sponsor for a leadership bill to improve the commission.

Back at our dingy office, I phoned Rae Condon and faxed her a copy of the bill, then made calls to schedule a meeting of the RIght Now! steering committee. I laid the two bills side by side and began comparing sections. The more I read, the worse Lamb's bill looked.

Condon phoned back with her concerns and a stream of insights about the state's history and legal tradition. From her ten years as director of the state's Conflict of Interest Commission, she knew all the permutations of prosecuting public officials. As she rattled off procedures and cases, I took notes in the margins of Lamb's bill. She remained deeply skeptical about whether House leaders, including Teitz, would allow any functional changes in the way ethics complaints could be prosecuted. "This may be better than nothing," she mused, "but not by much. God bless you, if you can persuade Jeffrey Teitz to accept these changes!"

I spent much of the weekend comparing Lamb's legislation with Gaschen's. The majority leader's bill would continue troubling features of the current law: a cumbersome two-step hearing process and the micromanagement of commission procedures. Worst of all, its rigid quorum requirements would make findings of violation against top political players difficult or impossible. Our goal from the beginning had been to reduce the size of the Ethics Commission and open up the complaint process. The three-year saga of our complaint against Ed DiPrete had taught us many lessons. For example, the 1987 Ethics Law allowed lawyers for the accused to contest each piece of evidence twice, both times in secret: first before a six-person investigative committee, and then with the nine-member adjudicative panel. In effect, the law required our complaint against DiPrete to be tried twice, and Lamb's bill would perpetuate that process.

"Dear Jeff," I wrote to Teitz. "The Ethics Commission draft you handed me on Friday afternoon is flatly unacceptable. It retains the worst features of the 1987 statute. If enacted, it would only perpetuate fundamental procedural problems which have hamstrung the commission."[5] My reply ran three pages. On Monday morning, I hand-delivered it to Teitz's secretary at the State House and within an hour he called me. "There's no need for alarm, " he reassured me. "I needed to come up from Newport this afternoon anyway. Why don't we meet at my office and go over your concerns with this legislation?"

Blinding sunlight filled the State House plaza. I found Teitz at his massive desk, silhouetted against a multi-paned window more than twice his height. I knew he had drafted the intricate legal procedures that had forced the fifteen-member Ethics Commission to conduct what amounted to two successive secret trials of former Gov. DiPrete. Lamb's bill would keep the duplicate process.

"You haven't been through this," I told him. "I have."

After nearly two hours of what felt like arm-wrestling with a giant, I had a sense of which elements in the Lamb bill simply reflected Teitz's pride of authorship and which were nonnegotiable positions of the House leadership. Each of us backed off on minor details in the text. To my amazement, he went along with the major point: downsizing the Ethics Commission from fifteen members to nine and streamlining its procedures. As with a grand jury, the preliminary investigation would occur behind closed doors, but the trial-like adjudicative hearing would be open to the press and public. The new legislation would raise the maximum fine the commission could levy from $10,000 to $25,000 for each violation.

He rose and reached to shake my hand across a corner of his desk. "I always believed we could reach an agreement," he said with a smile.

Each of us would have to clear this version with higher authorities. He would carry his notes up to the speaker's office while I took my understanding of these changes to Rae Condon and the RIght Now! steering committee.

The next afternoon his clerk passed out thick drafts of Lamb's bill, still warm from the photocopier. It was now marked "92-H 9002 Substitute A/12." I scanned this twelfth version, checking points of contention, and found Teitz had been true to his word. From the captain's chair at the head of the long oak table, Teitz walked his committee through the new draft. "This legislation," he said, "streamlines the Ethics Commission from fifteen members to nine. It deletes the requirement that there be two sets of hearings on the evidence."

His exposition took ten minutes. I sat with my back to a tall window open to a bright summer sky and double-checked each section. All the changes appeared exactly as we had agreed.

"Finally," Teitz told his committee, "we have increased the maximum fine the commission can impose for ethics violations from $10,000 to $25,000 per violation, a significant increase but a reasonable one."

He called me as the first witness, and I moved quickly to a chair at the far end of the long oak table. Predictably, this close to ending the legislative session, representatives filled every chair along both sides of the table, their loose-leaf binders overstuffed with hundreds of bills. Halfway between Teitz, at the head of the table, and me at its foot, sat Frank Gaschen. His RISDIC testimony had raised his public profile and briefly made him a hero. I assumed that some of the representatives in old oak chairs around this table had badgered him on RISDIC's behalf, but if he harbored any resentment, no trace showed in his eyes.

I introduced myself as testifying both on behalf of Common Cause and the RIght Now! Coalition, and went on to reinforce the points Teitz had already made. Lamb's bill was the one slated for passage. Following me, Sara Quinn testified that the revised bill still fell far short: "You're just compounding the problem." She suggested that this bill might actually be intended to discourage complaints. Then Rep. Mary E. Levesque, a lawyer from Jamestown, cut her off. "How can you infer motive?" she demanded. "To suggest that we're doing this for some horrible reason really is not fair."[6]

Without taking umbrage, Teitz compared the bill's new receptiveness to complaints against public officials with procedures for investigating medical professionals. "I don't think what we're doing here is treating public officials more favorably," he said.

I felt for Teitz. He had to walk a line between many lawmakers who hated the Ethics Commission and keen-eyed critics, like Quinn, who demanded perfection. This was not perfect but would achieve most of our goals. Teitz had nudged House leaders toward a compromise that would streamline the Ethics Commission and open its proceedings to the public as never before. This bill would address many problems the Common Cause complaint against Ed DiPrete had revealed.

The Judiciary Committee voted unanimously to send Lamb's bill, 9002 SubA/12 to the House floor.

Teitz drew me into his office and handed me a revision of our revolving door bill. Instead of fitting on half a page, as Rae Condon's original text had, this version filled three legal sheets. It retained the original bill number and still listed Rep. Nancy Benoit as sponsor, but everything else had mushroomed.[7]

"You and I both admire Nancy," Teitz said. "But there's no consensus within the House leadership to enact a law so narrowly focused on legislators. It seems unreasonable to bar members of the legislature from judgeships and other lucrative jobs while you leave the door open for a governor to insert his favored staff into those same positions. You and I both know that happens all the time."

This was a seismic shift. Instead of resisting Rae Condon's original revolving door draft, Teitz was now proposing to expand its reach; his new draft barred both state elected officials and senior State House staff. Based on a U.S. Supreme Court decision, he targeted top staff in "senior policy-making, discretionary, or confidential positions," whether in the executive branch or the legislature. "The point," he said, "is to make sure a governor can't buy the silence of his legal counsel by appointing him or her to the judiciary."

I assured him that he would have no quarrel from our side if he chose to close the revolving door on both legislators and staff members. I slid a copy of Bill Colleran's revolving door chart across Teitz's desk. It showed that during the six years DiPrete served as governor, five of his top staff had become judges.

Teitz smiled. He directed me further down the page. "On the other hand, I'm sure you'll also agree that it would be acceptable for a governor to appoint a member of the legislature to what we've called a 'senior policy-making, discretionary, or confidential position.'"

I asked for an example.

He smiled. "Suppose Bruce Sundlun wanted a new director for the Department of Health. And suppose, hypothetically, that he recognized the expertise Nancy Benoit has developed during her years in the House. Under the bill she introduced at your request she would be excluded — in spite of her obvious abilities and that expertise — from seeking or accepting that employment."

I asked if his point was that such a position would last only as long as the governor's term of office.

"Precisely," he agreed with a smile. "As a department director, she would serve at the governor's pleasure. A subsequent governor might keep her in office, but no one could rationally argue that her appointment constituted a permanent state job."

Finally, Teitz proposed an exception that would allow legislators or senior staff members to seek election to other constitutional offices. "Technically," he explained, "your narrow ban on employment might preclude me from running for attorney general."

I knew from previous conversations that Teitz longed to become the state's top prosecutor. During twenty years in the General Assembly he had gained vast expertise, but his private law practice had languished. He had never built up the financial resources needed for a statewide race. Now he thought our proposed ban on lawmakers' seeking or accepting state employment not held at the time of their election might be interpreted to bar him from campaigning for attorney general.

"I think you agree," he continued, "that election to a constitutional office is an entirely reasonable exemption. The notion of getting a job through election is categorically different from a revolving door appointment."

I did agree. From the beginning, our goal had been to stop the backroom deals that allowed legislative leaders or governors to reward their loyalists with permanent state jobs. His proposal required the legislator or staff member to campaign for election.

As I slid documents into my briefcase, I asked how ready House leaders were to pass other items in the RIght Now! platform that still seemed stuck in his committee.

Teitz smiled. "I think you have every reason to be optimistic. While I'm not as sanguine as you are about the Supreme Court's recent ruling on the powers of the Ethics Commission, there's no question that it has shifted the political calculus."

Other factors shifted the calculus in wild ways.

On June 18, like a mischievous boy one-tenth his age, Bruce Sundlun up-ended the game board. He nominated four judges, including his executive counsel, Judith Colenback Savage. Had Teitz's latest draft passed, her seeking or accepting the judgeship would have constituted a revolving door violation. I knew Savage as the ambitious lawyer who argued for Sundlun against the Ethics Commission's authority to adopt a code of ethics. Only thirty-four, she would vault over the state's three lower courts and begin her judicial career in Superior Court, the state's penultimate tribunal. Sundlun thrust her ahead of three seasoned men he nominated for the more pedestrian District Court.[8]

The Senate also went wild in those final days of June. Factional intrigues that had roiled Senate proceedings for many months suddenly surged out of control. After the Supreme Court's June 10 advisory opinion on the authority of the Ethics Commission the hallways hummed with rumors. The high court's advisory undercut Majority Leader John Bevilacqua, who often ranted against the commission, its rule-making powers, and its revolving door rule. Only five days after the high court's advisory, Bevilacqua had embarrassed himself in testimony before the RISDIC investigating panel. He could not shake off the fact that only a day after he learned of RISDIC's peril, his mother and his top adviser had cashed out their credit union accounts. As if to rub salt in that wound, Jeffrey Teitz — who had led the 1986 impeachment investigation against the son's late father — now sat in judgment on his actions.

Like a volcano that makes the earth quake before it erupts, members of the Bevilacqua faction began dropping hints. When I asked Judiciary Committee member David Sholes about the revolving door bill, he answered with a cryptic comment: "If we were going to pass a revolving door bill, it might as well include municipal office holders and candidates for state office, don't you think? If you want reform," he added coyly, "you might as well go all the way!"

Sholes's uncharacteristically precise answer startled me. During the next hour, I managed to speak with Sen. Tom Lynch, who chaired the Judiciary Committee, and with Bevilacqua himself. Almost verbatim, each mentioned "going all the way" by closing the revolving door for "municipal officials and state candidates." That formula gave me a glimpse of their battle plan. Instead of burying the revolving door in committee, they had decided to pack it with amendments and send it back to the House. Senators loyal to Bevilacqua would claim the mantle of radical reform and stuff the bill until people choked on it.

Members of the Senate Judiciary Committee sauntered into the mahogany-paneled Room 313 and took their seats. Then Lynch arrived and his clerk distributed Benoit's revolving door bill — now in the Senate's substitute version. As I skimmed a copy, it became clear that Bevilacqua loyalists were orchestrating a radical reversal. This version would still bar members of the General Assembly and top staff members from almost all permanent state jobs, including judgeships, for one year after they left office. But it would also lock the revolving door often used to reward candidates for statewide office with judgeships, and seal off the ways that local officials landed permanent municipal jobs.[9]

Lynch described the tougher revolving door restrictions now embodied in the bill, and his committee instantly recommended passage to the entire Senate. This version seemed supremely clever and cynical. Senate leaders meant to choke the process. Rather than let their move pass in silence, I told reporters this was a ploy: "What we have now is a bill that's prepared to self-destruct."[10]

On the Senate floor two days later, the faction led by former Majority Leader David Carlin attacked with the most personal sarcasm I had ever heard in the

Senate chamber. "Sometimes motives are so conspicuous they poke you right in the eye," Carlin declared, heaping scorn on Bevilacqua and Lynch. "Senator Lynch finally has religion? That is baloney. It's a crock! The only thing Senator Lynch has done before the day before yesterday was serve as an obstruction to revolving door."[11]

Senator Bill Irons followed, shouting that the latest iteration was "a smoke screen, a falsehood." He warned that Lynch's new version could not pass the House and would never reach the governor's desk.

I watched in amazement. Only days earlier, Bevilacqua's troops had done all they could to kill any ban on revolving door jobs, while the Carlin forces had demanded the toughest restrictions imaginable. Now their positions had completely flipped. Amid accusations of hypocrisy and obstructionism, Bevilacqua's Democrats all voted to pass the more radical bill and send it back to the House, while Carlin's faction and a handful of Republicans voted no. The bill passed by a vote of 25–23.

Carlin's forces had lost the vote, but their arguments had made the complicated legislative process intelligible. The victorious Bevilacqua team saw that they might bear the blame if the revolving door bill did not become law.

One day later, to prove his sincerity, Lynch marched into his committee room and handed four separate revolving door bills to the clerk. While they were being distributed, Lynch took his tall center chair with gleaming dark wood behind him. "Anyone who wants to vote on these bills," he announced, "can vote 100 percent for revolving door, 75 percent for revolving door, 50 percent for revolving door, 25 percent, or against revolving door."[12]

That was true. His bills addressed nearly every conceivable revolving door option. Bevilacqua's leadership team had clearly decided they must undercut the charge that they had scuttled reform by passing a bill they knew the House would kill, so they would send the House an entire menu of revolving door options. With the Bevilacqua and Carlin factions now vying to prove their purity, Lynch's Judiciary Committee approved all four bills in a series of unanimous votes. All four bills went to the full Senate. On the Senate floor, Lynch moved each bill, and Irons offered each seconding speech. All four passed unanimously, and a Senate page marched them across to the House of Representatives.[13]

I had not been privy to conversations in the Bevilacqua camp but marveled at the mercurial transformation. I smelled fear and sweat in the Senate chamber. The surge of victory felt better than the shock of failure only one year earlier when our Hail Mary maneuver had won Senate passage of Teitz's Campaign Finance Law moments too late for final passage in the House.

Then news leaked that a screening panel Sundlun had appointed to winnow judicial candidates had given the governor a list of ten judicial candidates that did not include Judy Savage. Sundlun growled to the reporter who broke the story that his handpicked panel was wrong: "They chose not to consider everybody. I thought they owed it to the people who had expressed an interest to interview them."[14]

Throughout the legislative session, Sundlun had scorned the revolving door bill as intruding on his authority to appoint. Now that he had sent four names to the Senate, he threatened to veto any revolving door bill that interfered with their confirmation.

Jeff Teitz handed me the text of an amendment that Sundlun had sent him. He said Sundlun had demanded that this revolving door exemption be included in the final bill. Only a few lines long, it declared unequivocally that any judicial nominee appointed before the bill became law would be exempt. Without that line, Sundlun would veto the bill. I assumed that Savage had drafted it for him. I asked Teitz if we had any choice.

"That depends on whether you think he's bluffing."

"I don't think he's bluffing."

"Neither do I," said Teitz. "The practical question is whether getting your bill enacted is worth letting him make two final revolving door appointments."

The House and Senate chambers had no air-conditioning, and the humidity soared during debates that stretched late into the first two nights of July. Jackets and ties came off. Fans did little good. The acrid vapor made lawmakers petulant and prompted an almost uncontrollable urge to escape.

For all the newsprint and ink lavished upon the RIght Now! proposals, only Jeff Teitz's Comprehensive Campaign Finance had become law. Other bills seemed either beached or swept away in riptides. The inspiring January rally that ringed the State House with chanting activists had faded from memory.

On July 3 members of our steering committee made their way into Hasbro's headquarters in Pawtucket. The air-conditioned boardroom smelled of fresh coffee. Trays of gourmet chocolate-chip and oatmeal-raisin cookies lay on a snack table. Alan Hassenfeld set a sympathetic tone. "We may not end all uncertainty today, but I'd like to hear what you want to do about the latest revolving door developments. I know some of us are suspicious that they'll adjourn the session with our bills left becalmed, like sailboats on a sultry day."

Business leaders around the blond wood table said they were more troubled over our failure to get four-year terms for the governor onto the November ballot. That constitutional issue had been their primary goal during our entire year together.

I reminded them that in spite of negative remarks John Bevilacqua had made about four-year terms, both the Senate and House had passed ballot questions. "Once they've done that," I said, "they're almost certain to finish the job."

"There's many a slip 'twixt the cup and the lip," said Jim Hagan, the Greater Providence Chamber of Commerce executive. He had served in the Senate and knew the drill. "The word I'm getting," he said, "is that each side might pass versions that would differ by only a word but would not be identical."

"Are there any differences between the House and Senate versions?" Hassenfeld directed his question toward me.

"None that I know of," I said, with a sudden sweat. Weeks had passed since I checked the House and Senate resolutions side by side, word for word. "Both versions accomplish what we want."

Hagan pursed his lips. "The only thing that counts is when exactly the same resolution passes both chambers."

Our proposed amendment ran more than five hundred words. Besides changing the length of terms for the governor and the other four statewide executive officials, we had sweetened the mix by allowing voters to recall any general officer charged with a felony, convicted of a misdemeanor, or against whom the Ethics Commission found probable cause for a full investigation. We had also proposed that a blue ribbon commission be appointed to study the General Assembly, which was one of the largest in the United States and among the lowest paid.

Gary Sasse, director of the Rhode Island Public Expenditure Council (RIPEC), said he had been talking with leaders in both the House and Senate about the proposal. "They recognize what's wrong with the status quo," Sasse said. "I'm not sure how serious they are about making changes, but I think they're ready to appoint a panel that would do the work and report back."

"And if that happens," Hassenfeld asked, "would they appoint you to chair the study?"

"You never can tell," Sasse said with a self-effacing smile. He knew legislative process as well as anyone in the state. Most people in or out of state government saw him as an honest broker.

I gave a status report on our bills. Most had passed the House or the Senate but not both. I explained the plethora of revolving door bills and Sundlun's threat to veto any version that failed to exempt the judicial nominees he had already sent for Senate confirmation. We quickly reached consensus — Sundlun would not back down and we had no choice but to accept his one-time judicial exemption to the revolving door legislation.

"I can live with that," Jim Miller said, "but a lot of people across the interfaith community are really bewildered by all this gamesmanship they see. They don't trust the last-minute wheeling and dealing over what should be clear principles."

"Would they rally one more time?" Hassenfeld asked.

Miller replied that he could get the word out but it would be hard to organize much over a July 4th weekend.

"Would they make announcements in churches and synagogues?"

"Many would."

Hassenfeld asked Hagan if he could rally the chambers of commerce.

"I'd try," came the reply, "but I have no idea who checks their fax machines on the Fourth of July."

"You don't have their home numbers?"

Hagan flinched at the thought.

"Hey, Jim," Hassenfeld chided gently, "we've come so far. If you'll fax me ten names, I'll phone them myself. And I'll ask those ten to call ten. If everyone around this table contacts ten people, and the Council of Churches gets word out to its congregations, we can rally one more time."

And so, over a gray and drizzly Fourth of July weekend, the steering committee called out the troops for one final State House event. We would signal the General Assembly that people were still watching. As a result, when senators and representatives returned on July 7, many stepped out of the elevators into a swarm of protesters who crowded the rotunda, central stairways, and balconies. Most lawmakers and lobbyists dodged the crowd by climbing zigzag stairways at the far ends of each floor.

In the rotunda Alan Hassenfeld addressed the crowd, his tone at once sad and fierce. "I am angry and disillusioned," he said. "I don't believe that our lawmakers understand that the will of the people must be served. We have written thousands of letters. We have made thousands of telephone calls. We have held numerous news conferences. And this time, we are angry. As the General Assembly enters its final hours, it is time for action. The people have clearly spoken. Yet, to this date, they have been ignored. This is wrong."[15]

The following afternoon, members of the House Judiciary Committee listened to Jeff Teitz's explanation of the latest revolving door legislation. After countless meetings with Teitz and hearings in the judiciary committees at both ends of the building, it felt like déjà vu for the tenth time. During three intense weeks since the Supreme Court affirmed the Ethics Commission's authority to adopt a code of ethics, the revolving door bill had caromed back and forth, improbably gaining energy with each bounce.

Teitz explained that they had before them a Substitute B version of Rep. Nancy Benoit's bill, which they had approved weeks earlier. "As you may remember, the Senate closed off access to a number of positions, including judgeships, that were allowed in our earlier version."

Though his committee was weary, Teitz parsed an exemption that would allow staff members who had served five years in state service before moving into a senior position to move back. He then explained a section that would authorize the Ethics Commission to grant exemptions to the revolving door law if that would not "create an appearance of impropriety."[16] Then, asking for a motion to delete the Senate's most recent move to make municipal officials and statewide candidates subject to the revolving door, Teitz explained why that represented an unreasonable expansion of the original bill.

Exhausted, the committee voted to delete.

"The final section," Teitz said, "addresses the governor's request to exempt his four recent judicial nominations. I believe the RIght Now! steering committee has not taken a position on this but will not actively oppose it." Through thick glasses, he looked my way, and I nodded in affirmation.

Frank Gaschen signaled Teitz. "Mr. Chairman, do you have any word from the Senate that they'll go along with this?"

Teitz said he did not, but he hoped they would be satisfied. "This version prohibits legislators and senior staff members from permanent state jobs, including judgeships. It accomplishes more than anyone thought possible when we passed an earlier version in this committee a few weeks ago."

Rep. Charles T. Knowles, a burly Democrat from Narragansett, announced that he would vote for the much-amended measure, but he poked fun at the process, teasing, "One can only begin to imagine what the Ten Commandments would have looked like had the Rhode Island General Assembly been on Mount Sinai with Moses."

The next day on the House floor, representatives offered amendments that would have blasted loopholes in the bill and others that would have excluded Sundlun's recent nominees to revolving door judgeships. Teitz fended them all off, warning that further changes would kill the bill. After fractious debate, representatives punched their green and red buttons an hour before midnight on July 9. By a vote of 82–4, they approved this latest iteration of the revolving door bill.[17]

They also approved Majority Leader Tom Lamb's revised bill to streamline Rhode Island's Ethics Commission and reduce its size from fifteen to nine members.[18]

On a rainy day with temperatures near ninety, the 1992 General Assembly began what everyone expected to be its final day. Amid distant thunder and rumblings that Sundlun's judicial nominees might escape the new law but be scuttled in confirmation hearings, senators began slogging through hundreds of bills on their final calendar.

Ten months earlier, John Bevilacqua had railed against the Ethics Commission's move to promulgate rules for public officials and publicly blasted the original revolving door rule. Only last March his Judiciary Committee had pummeled Bishop George Hunt during his testimony in support of ethics bills. But now Bevilacqua's faction had executed a 180-degree pirouette in unison — from scorning a revolving door ban to demanding the toughest one imaginable, from mocking an anti-nepotism bill to claiming it as their own.

While senators droned through their calendar, I had hours to ponder the change. During the past month John Bevilacqua had squirmed under television lights, trying to explain away his ethical lapses regarding RISDIC. Meanwhile, the Rhode Island Supreme Court had unanimously affirmed the Ethics

Commission's authority to adopt specific ethics rules for public officials. Scores of insurgents had filed candidacy papers to challenge his troops in the September primary, now barely two months away.

Beneath those motivators I sensed a deeper spur to action. The very vehemence of Bevilacqua's protest made me believe Sundlun had picked these four judges without consulting him. Had the proud Senate leader pushed to name one or two judges among the four and been spurned? Without an electronic bug in the majority leader's office I had no way of knowing.

During a break for committee meetings, the Senate Judiciary Committee voted unanimously to recommend the House-passed revolving door bill to the full Senate. Final passage seemed to be a foregone conclusion.

My sense of duty compelled me to watch the Senate's final debate on our legislation to streamline the Ethics Commission and open its adjudicative hearings to the public. Charlie Silverman came into the Senate chamber, and I waved him to an empty seat next to mine. Short, bald, and immaculately dressed, Silverman was a key player for Operation Clean Sweep and the Public Interest Alliance. Unlike firebrands who seemed to relish bashing politicians and reformers alike, and the RIght Now! Coalition, Silverman focused on the issues. Throughout the spring I had seen how hard he worked for reform. He was quietly pragmatic about legislation and those who struggled to produce it.

"Did you ever think you'd see this day?" he murmured.

I shook my head and whispered my amazement at the change we were witnessing.

"Maybe it hasn't been so bad for us to play bad cop while you play good cop," he mused. "I would never have guessed that John Bevilacqua and Tom Lynch would become champions of a tougher revolving door bill."

When the revolving door bill finally came up, there was little debate and even less grandstanding. After being bent, bashed, twisted, and bounced, it came out better than I could have dreamed. It had become more comprehensive and better prepared to withstand legal challenge. The final Senate vote was 42–4, with four senators absent.

David Carlin had announced his candidacy for Congress from the 1st District, which stretched from Newport up the East Bay to Woonsocket and Burrillville. While he faced two primary opponents, these State House battles were over for him. Win or lose in the primary and general election, Carlin would leave the state Senate. His loyalists were already coalescing around Senators Bill Irons and Paul Kelly to carry on the battle against Bevilacqua.

In the final grueling hours, the other bills on our RIght Now! list won final passage: a ban on nepotism, bills to streamline the Ethics Commission and open its adjudicative hearings to the public, and the proposed constitutional amendment that would let voters decide on four-year terms for statewide general officers. Completely beneath the radar, legislators also passed a resolution that authorized DeAngelis and Bevilacqua to appoint a commission to study the operations of the General Assembly and recommend a blueprint for the twenty-first century. Gary Sasse had talked about this, but I wondered how he pulled it off. The legislative marathon finally ended well after dawn the next day, deeper into July than any session since 1971.[19] A final gavel at 6:59 a.m. sent senators on their way without confirming Sundlun's four judicial nominees.

The governor announced a celebratory bill signing in the magnificent State Room adjoining his office. I arrived early and found the bills he would sign arrayed on a table by the podium. Rectangular red stamps marked each bill's travel from committees to floor calendars and then to committees and floor calendars in the opposite chamber. Over the months, I had piled up photocopies and scribbled in their margins, but now the actual bills lay within reach, and I touched each one.

After Sundlun's bluster against the revolving door legislation, I half expected him to let it become law without his signature, but it lay on the antique table with the others. With Jeff Teitz's comprehensive campaign finance bill, which had become law in April, these neatly folded documents spanned the entire RIght Now! agenda: open adjudicative hearings on ethics complaints, a streamlined Ethics Commission empowered to impose a $25,000 fine for each violation, a broader ban against nepotism, and a durable law to end revolving door appointments.[20] Also on the table lay the joint resolution that would place our constitutional amendment for four-year terms before the voters. Since the people — rather than the governor — needed to ratify the proposal, there was no legal need for Sundlun to autograph it.

Sundlun marched into the room, buoyantly triumphant after his trip to New York for the Democrats' 1992 nominating convention. He seemed to exult in having closure after the contentious struggles that marred his first two years in office.

Speeches brimmed over with mutual admiration. "This has been an extremely positive session," Jeff Teitz told the crowd. He had crafted legal language and brokered political compromises that lay behind every document on the table. He predicted that these bills would "mark a rebirth in public confidence."

In his turn toymaker Alan Hassenfeld radiated the playful energy that I had come to love. "We proved to all the naysayers in this state that the people of Rhode Island can make a difference and can stick together."

Sundlun signed the bills into law, applause filled the room, formality dissolved, people shook hands, and some hugged.[21]

Throughout the ceremony, a breeze blew through tall southerly windows. As people scattered, I stepped out onto the balcony above the plaza where Sundlun had been inaugurated nineteen months earlier. The broad marble stairs below gleamed white in the sunshine, empty now of flags and dignitaries. Gone also were the crowds of depositors who had assembled there to vent their rage. Instead, the scent of fresh-cut grass wafted up as a groundskeeper drove his ganged mowers. Trees that had been bare when marchers arrived in January for the interfaith rally now shaded the three parallel brick walkways. The icons and banners had vanished. The rattle of drums and blare of trumpets had long since faded away, but the seven months since a shofar wailed for repentance had been the most momentous of my life.

15

Keeping Score
1992

POLITICS HAS ALWAYS BEEN a game of smoke and mirrors. The RISDIC scandal and political machinations of two General Assembly sessions that followed had left many Rhode Islanders confused. Which legislative factions could they trust? Were the reform groups any better?

Our midsummer challenge was to pick through the legislative detritus and create a scorecard that would show voters how their senators and representatives actually performed. Bill Colleran, our resident rocket scientist, came to help. In the final hours of the 1992 legislative session, nearly every member of the General Assembly had voted for the bountiful crop of reforms that were now law.

"So were they holding their noses?" Colleran asked.

"Not visibly," I said, "but if they'd had secret ballots, I think we'd have lost."

On the table before us lay piles of House and Senate journals, daily records that contained every legislative vote cast during the two-year term.

"So all we need to do," Colleran observed wryly, "is reduce words to numbers." An engineer by training, he had calculated orbits and trajectories for NASA and believed that anything worth thinking about could be presented in digital form. His wife Julie, a high school English teacher, was equally committed to the project. "You know these senators and reps," she said. "You know the bills and amendments they voted on. All you need to do is tell us which votes really mattered."

That was easier said than done. Legislative leaders relied on killing bills in committee to protect their troops from having to cast awkward votes, so we had no way to score the death of legislation that died without a vote.

The Collerans constructed spreadsheets to tally House and Senate votes, with legislators' names filling the left-hand columns. We would list key votes at the top of vertical columns, marking each with the bill number and page in a House or Senate journal for that date. For each vote, we would use three columns: one for votes we considered pro-reform, a second for votes we took as anti-reform, and a third for absences. "Everybody gets a '1' in one of those three columns," Colleran said. "By adding the columns vertically, we check our totals against the journals."

To compute the grades for each senator or representative, we would tally the horizontal rows of votes. We would compute votes on campaign finance, ethics, and four-year terms that RIght Now! had promoted; we would also tabulate votes on redistricting, lobbyist disclosure, and judicial selection that Common Cause had pushed without RIght Now! support.

"It's a lot of data entry," Colleran said, "but it's ultimately foolproof. If somebody challenges your numbers," he quipped mischievously, "you unroll your spreadsheet and show how he voted on any particular bill. You'll even have reference to a specific page in the House or Senate journal."

I nodded. My first task would be to pick votes that tracked each bill's travel through the House and Senate. We would count bills both from 1991, when few bills passed, and from 1992, when many became law.

"Here's the deal," Colleran said. "You give us the identifying information for each vote. I'll create the formulas. Julie and I will enter the data and double-check for accuracy."

I immersed myself in the journals and made notes. A week later, the Common Cause executive committee reviewed my list. I suggested that — except for Jeff Teitz's campaign finance bill, which wove together many previous bills — we count votes for only one amendment and final passage of each bill each year in each chamber. The executive committee agreed on thirty-two votes in the Senate and thirty-three in the House of Representatives.

Bill Colleran explained how important it was to agree on all the votes before he and Julie started entering data. "We need to make clear to friend and foe alike that we're not skewing numbers to hurt or help particular legislators."

As their data accumulated, patterns formed before my eyes. Some senators did well in 1991 but plummeted in 1992. All were supporters of former Majority Leader David Carlin, who scored 91.7 percent in 1991 but only 66.7 percent in 1992. Bill Irons scored 100 percent the first year but dropped to 73.7 percent the second. John Bevilacqua, by contrast, scored 53.8 percent in 1991 and went up to 68.4 percent in 1992. Tom Lynch improved from 53.8 percent to 73.7 percent. Even Gregory J. Acciardo, who had taunted Bishop Hunt about nepotism, rose from 46.2 percent to 77.8 percent in 1992.

On the House side, Jeff Teitz raised his score from 80.0 percent in 1991 to 91.7 percent in 1992.

Colleran followed my finger on the screen. "That's a big difference from Clean

Sweep putting Teitz at the bottom of their scorecard," he mused. "Look at my rep." He pointed at Rep. Mark Heffner from Barrington. "He drops from 83.3 percent in '91 to 59.5 percent in '92."

A quick look showed that Heffner supported Teitz's comprehensive campaign finance bill in 1991 but voted — only a year later — for radical amendments that might have doomed the same bill. Teitz's bill cut the top allowable contribution to each candidate from $2,000 to $1,000 a year, but Heffner supported a 1992 Clean Sweep amendment that would have slashed the allowable individual contribution in half again, to $500.[1] Reducing contribution limits so drastically would have put challengers at an overwhelming disadvantage.

"You warned them, didn't you?"

"We did," I said. "With memos to each representative. And I spoke to many myself."

"Did they really believe those amendments would improve campaigns?"

"Some probably did. We warned them that adding new amendments and sending Teitz's bill to the Senate a second time would have prevented its use for the 1992 elections. And might have killed it entirely."

Colleran stroked his mustache. "I don't see how we can overlook those realities. Giving them a pass on those votes might make some look better, but it would be dishonest. Maybe," he mused, "you just post their grades and let them explain to their constituents. We could also mark them on a curve."

He quickly produced a formula that filled an additional column beside the names of all 150 members of the General Assembly. "This formula is exactly the same for everyone," he said. "No special breaks or penalties." With a click, he turned the formulas into percentages. Every score rose. Colleran's final percentages lifted the Senate average to 75.4 percent, the House to 76.5 percent. "You might say these numbers reflect their real commitments," he said. "For different reasons, many barely passed."

I spot checked the final percentages his curve formula produced against several I believed were committed to reform. Jim Langevin of Warwick came out on top with a score of 92.1 percent. Jeff Teitz came close behind with 89.9 percent, and Frank Gaschen had 89.2 percent. On the curve, Mark Heffner's score rose to 81.4 percent.

I asked Colleran again if he used the same formula for all of them.

"Exactly the same delta factor from top to bottom. We're counting every vote you described, and we're giving everybody a mathematically consistent benefit of a doubt. That's how you mark on a curve."

I knew he was right but asked how these relatively low grades meshed with the fact that legislators had eventually enacted virtually the entire RIght Now! platform.

"We used data from two years," he observed. "In 1991, even after RISDIC, they passed almost nothing you proposed. Isn't that right?"

I nodded. In fact, over three or four years many of the same legislators had buried these proposals in committee.

"Do you think these figures are lying?"

I knew they were not. We decided to publish our legislative scorecard with an opinion piece to help voters sort through this welter of information. I explained that no scorecard could discern legislators' motives — we could not judge the difference between a sincere vote for a radical amendment and mere grandstanding.[2] Beside lawmakers' names we included columns showing an individual's support in 1991 and 1992. A third column, "two-year weighted support," curved all scores upward. I wrote that our organization never endorsed or opposed candidates for public office, and urged voters to use our legislative scorecard and those of other groups with great care.

We bundled lists of senators and representatives by regions of the state with comments on specific votes they had cast. We faxed press releases with legislative scores to newspapers, television, and radio stations.

As we hoped, newspapers listed senators and representatives in their regions in our ranked order of their support.[3] Reporters picked up key differences between the Common Cause rankings and a second report card from Operation Clean Sweep. The *Providence Journal* noted "a distinct split in the reform movement," suggested by the fact that "Rep. Jeffrey J. Teitz, D-Newport, finished last in Clean Sweep's rankings of the House. But in Common Cause's rankings, Teitz was fifth from the top."[4]

A *Journal* editorial on "the ratings game" urged readers against any "automatic acceptance" of candidates based on scorecards. Although the editors urged readers to learn about the groups that issued scorecards, they affirmed Common Cause's values "and strongly supported the landmark ethics reform agenda it successfully advocated in the General Assembly this year."[5]

Several lawmakers or members of their families phoned our office to grouse about the scorecard, and others complained in person. One crisp fall evening I drove to the King Philip Inn in Bristol to address the Bristol County Chamber of Commerce at its annual meeting. I had forgotten that Sen. Richard M. Alegria, a member of the Bevilacqua faction, owned the hotel. Even after we curved the grades, Alegria ranked at the bottom of the Senate.

While chamber members were enjoying cocktails, I went through the dining room and left copies of our scorecard on each table. As I walked back to the reception, I ran into the hulking Alegria as he proffered his election materials to dinner guests. His powerful grip almost crushed my hand. He pulled me close and growled in a voice barely above a whisper, "So you think I'm a bad person."

"No, Senator," I forced a smile. "I don't think you're a bad person, but we disagree with a lot of your votes." I took his flyer and escaped into the convivial crowd. Later, I read Alegria's campaign flyer. In a bulleted list of accomplishments he claimed to have been a leading advocate for ethics reform.

With their deep suspicion of government, Rhode Island voters had nixed four-year terms three times since the 1973 Constitutional Convention first recommended that change. The most recent came in 1986, when a proposed amendment would have granted quadrennial terms to both legislators and general officers. Fifty-nine percent of voters rejected the amendment. Our 1992 version, Question One on the November ballot, would establish longer terms only for statewide general officers and would add a recall provision. Would these differences change the outcome?

The opposition to Question One was fragmented. Organized labor seemed to believe it could defeat four-year terms without spending much money. The state AFL-CIO Executive Council launched a wave of mailings that urged roughly eighty thousand current and retired union members to vote no. The ACLU, Government Accountability Project, and Reform '92 all came out against Question One, but they had no money for TV or radio commercials.

One opponent enjoyed unlimited airtime. Moe Lauzier, a Libertarian talk show host on WHJJ-AM, dominated the afternoon commute. "How dumb are these do-gooders?" he inveighed. "Not only should those ninnies not get four-year terms! We should roll them all back to one-year terms!"

I turned into one of Hasbro's parking lots for a meeting of the RIght Now! steering committee. Of a dozen major manufacturers that once provided steady blue-collar jobs for generations of workers, only the Hassenfeld brothers' toy company still operated its worldwide business from Rhode Island. At the security desk, I signed in and clipped a visitor's badge on my lapel. Departments along a wide corridor to the conference room overflowed with bright color. The scent of freshly brewed coffee met me before I stepped through sleek modern doors.

Our agenda for the afternoon was the campaign for four-year terms. Seated beside Alan Hassenfeld at Hasbro's board table, David Duffy passed out packets. "I have some polling data from the Becker Institute," Duffy said. Each page of the stapled document held a single question with responses graphed in wide, boldly colored bars. "The bad news, " Duffy said, "is that we're losing. The good news is that as people get more information — like the fact that they could recall a governor — the more likely they are to vote yes on Question One."

"It's a tough sell," said B. Jae Clanton, executive director of the Urban League. "You know that when white America gets a cold, the black community catches pneumonia. RISDIC caused deep wounds that haven't even begun to heal. Whether people will even vote is an open question."

Hassenfeld asked if people served by the Urban League were talking about four-year terms.

"None that I've heard," Clanton said. "They wonder what's the use."

Jim Miller said many pastors understood the need for sound governance. "They may not have thought much about four-year terms for governor, but they know it often takes several years for a new preacher to learn the ropes. They get giving the governor four years to deliver."

I passed out flyers that would be distributed in church bulletins on Sundays before the election. The Girl Scouts, Clean Water Action, the Sierra Club, the League of Women Voters, and Common Cause had begun distributing several hundred thousand of these in neighborhoods.

Thomas J. Skala, the president of Fleet Bank, studied the flyer and nodded his approval. Skala and his company had been absorbing institutions formerly insured by RISDIC. "Fleet couldn't take a partisan position," he said, "but I would distribute a well-designed informational piece on four-year terms."

Dave Duffy — whose firm had created both RISDIC's "carved in stone" commercial and the RIght Now! logo — offered to prepare a version of our brochure in plain vanilla language for bank customers and employees. "Four-year terms is about as nonpartisan as you can get," Duffy said. "Constitutional reform doesn't help any one politician or party."

Alan Hassenfeld suggested that employers in the various chambers of commerce stuff information pieces into pay envelopes. "Between all of our chambers," he said, "we could achieve fairly wide distribution."

The smell of printer's ink permeated the Common Cause office. Boxes of flyers were stacked high between windows and near the door. Our mission was to convince voters that the proposed Four-Year Terms Amendment would create a more professional executive branch under less constant pressure to raise money for the next election. Business leaders donated funds to pay three organizers who would disseminate flyers and train grassroots groups to promote four-year terms. Suzette Gephard, the former League of Women Voters president, had run for Congress but lost in the primary to David Carlin. Bob Cox had worked with the Rhode Island Council of Churches, while David Leach knew the inner workings of the Jewish Federation and its member groups. All three hit the ground running. Beyond distributing flyers, they organized local groups to distribute leaflets at art fairs, fall festivals, farmers' markets, and outside supermarkets.

During the fall of 1992, I crisscrossed Rhode Island, seeking support from the editors and publishers of the state's five daily newspapers and the half-dozen small-town weeklies. My road atlas fell apart as I navigated back roads to out-of-the-way hamlets for meetings of chambers of commerce, church groups, art clubs, and societies named for Narragansett chiefs. I enjoyed the energy of the crowds as I preached the gospel of political reform and thanked audiences for participating in RIght Now! rallies and trekking to the State House during the session. I reminded them that the Rhode Island Supreme Court had helped the cause of reform with its unanimous June 10 ruling that the Ethics Commission had power to write and enforce ethics rules for all public officials. Televised

RISDIC hearings had added pressure for landmark campaign finance and ethics laws, but it was their calls, I told them, that had gotten this done. "Senators and reps kept telling me their constituents were after them wherever they went."

We still had unfinished business, I said. RIght Now! saw reform as a three-legged stool. Two legs — campaign finance reforms and the new ethics laws — were in place, but to make it sturdy we needed the third leg in the form of four-year terms for the governor and other statewide officers. Furthermore, we could learn from the experiences of other states. During the last forty years, twenty-eight states had amended their constitutions to establish four-year terms for their governors. No state that established four-year terms had reverted to two year-terms. Only three states still clung to two-year terms: Vermont, New Hampshire, and Rhode Island.

I asked whether Rhode Island could afford to keep its governors on a fund-raising treadmill. Bruce Sundlun had poured out $4.1 million of his own money to beat Ed DiPrete for a two-year term. By contrast in neighboring Massachusetts, also in 1990, William Weld spent only $3.8 million to win a four-year term. Weld had faced the challenge of reaching five times as many voters in three costly media markets, including Boston. On a per capita basis, Rhode Island's 1990 gubernatorial campaign was the second most expensive in the entire country, second only to Alaska's, where candidates faced high media costs and had to campaign in planes across vast distances.

Listeners often asked when the first four-year election would take place. "In 1994," I replied, "midway between presidential elections. We hope that will concentrate more attention on state races."

When people asked about the two-term limit, I said RIght Now! had followed the federal model that limits American presidents to two four-year terms. Eight years and out would prevent anyone from becoming governor for life.

In answer to questions about how a governor or other general officer could be recalled, I explained that we did not want recall simply because a governor took an unpopular stand. Launching a recall would require some credible indication of wrongdoing: an arrest for a felony, conviction of a misdemeanor, or a finding of probable cause by the Ethics Commission.[6]

"STRICTLY PRIVATE," warned the sign on the wire gate at the edge of a North Kingstown forest: "Hebb Waterfowl Trust." Gus Hebb had become a mainstay at Common Cause. His white-hot rage against corrupt officials rarely cooled. The wealthy industrialist had rejoiced when the Ethics Commission fined former Gov. Edward DiPrete $30,000; he reveled when the business community rallied under the RIght Now! banner.

Hebb had phoned to invite me. He swung the gate open and waved me onto a dirt road that led through a stand of towering pines. As he strode ahead of me, a long-legged bird marched possessively at his shoulder. A moment later, he introduced us. "This is Gertrude. She's a sandhill crane. She imprinted on me when she hatched, and she thinks I'm her mother."

Gertrude stood as high as my shoulder and eyed me over a sharp beak, unperturbed by the cloud of cigar smoke that Hebb said would protect us from gnats. Few would guess that this rustic figure with his stogie, unlaced work shoes, and broad-brimmed hat was the president of a company that fabricated steel and aluminum for major construction projects.

As he showed me around, rare ducks waddled away. A sturdy steel structure stood incongruously in the woods. Gertrude and I followed him into shadows beneath its black framework, where we climbed a steel stairway into bright sunshine and gazed out on a series of interconnected observation decks.

"I call it 'Treetops,'" Hebb said. "I've been building it for twenty years with leftovers of buildings and bridges. You could put three hundred elephants up here, and it wouldn't budge."

Trees rose through openings and around the edges. Below the railing, a herd of diminutive deer with great racks of antlers galloped toward a pond. Even the adults sported fawnlike spots. "They're fallow deer," he said. "Probably evolved in what's now Iran and spread to Europe. Aren't they gorgeous?"

Miniature deer with pronghorns and black facial markings paused below us and peered up, as if expecting to be fed. Hebb told me they were 'muntjacs.' "That means 'barking deer,'" he said. "People are starting to keep them as pets, but they belong in herds and this is the only herd in New England."

Hebb led me across the platform and pointed at the most regal birds I had ever seen. "Those are East African crowned cranes," he said with obvious pride. Gold bristles framed their heads like haloes; their faces were stark black and white panels with brilliant red accents. "We made them comfortable enough to mate here. When we go down, I'll show you their chicks."

From another spot at the rail he pointed to his most endangered bird. "It's called a 'nene,'" he said. "They're related to Canada geese, but they evolved and flourished on the Hawaiian Islands before sailing ships arrived with rats and cats and pigs." He said nenes had plummeted to the edge of extinction.

I had never seen this tender, protective side of Gus Hebb. "I've been building my wildfowl refuge to protect and propagate these endangered species," he explained. "I designed these treetop platforms to let people view my rare birds without disturbing them."

He relit his cigar and inhaled. "In all these years, I've never brought people in. Never felt we had the occasion." He blew a cloud of smoke. "Now I do. I'd like to host a celebration up here in the treetops."

I sensed where he was going but waited for him to finish.

"What you and Alan Hassenfeld have done for this state is just beyond belief. I never thought I would see it in my lifetime."

I thanked him and said we were not finished.

"Never will be," he agreed. "But what an amazing start." He offered to host a celebration, an October Sunday brunch with boxed lunches and champagne.

Gertrude and I hung on his every word. "That's wonderful," I said. "I'll find out Alan's schedule."

Natalie Joslin mobilized our board and advisory council to plan the biggest party of her life. She formed a working committee and an honorary committee to promote what everyone quickly began calling "the Hebb Event." The *Providence Sunday Journal* ran a color spread, headlined "Wild Kingdom," with a photo of Gus Hebb holding Gertrude.[7] Reporter Paul Edward Parker wrote that Hebb had spent more than a million dollars building his wildlife refuge, which he preserved while surrounding farms were being carved into housing developments. "I could've been a rich man," Hebb told the reporter, "but I've spent all my money on this sanctuary. You have to really devote your life to something like this, accept the losses, plan to die broke."

Only a handful of researchers had ever been inside, but now it would be open for a single day to Common Cause members for $30 each.

From phone calls and the flurry of replies that arrived each morning, it was hard to tell whether crowds were coming because this would be the first public look at Hebb's fabled wildfowl sanctuary or because there had been a surge of converts to the cause of reform. "Bring them all in," said Natalie Joslin. "They all become members of Common Cause."

Fall colors neared their peak on a crystalline October Sunday when volunteers lugged cases of wine up the stairs to Gus Hebb's interconnected treetop platforms. Caterers positioned gourmet boxed lunches on long tables. Hundreds of cars threaded their way into a fresh-mown field, where students directed them to park in tight rows. Political candidates who had not made reservations appeared, paid admission, and worked the crowd.

Gus Hebb alternated between anxiety that the hoard of people might unnerve his animals and exuberance as he welcomed more than twelve hundred visitors to his sanctuary. An extrovert and showman, he radiated charm. Since my first visit, he had rigged an elevator for any who could not manage the stairs to his treetop platform. His lift groaned like an industrial hoist but did its job.

His African crowned crane chicks and their regal parents wowed the crowd. Bird-watchers with cameras peered into cages and craned their necks. The Treetops felt solid underfoot even with a thousand people filling its platforms and walkways from railing to railing. Maples at their autumn best seemed to dance in the sun. From a podium with brilliant color at his back, Gus Hebb welcomed the crowd. "I wanted to open this place as a way of thanking Common Cause for being up there at the State House every day, fighting for us," he said. He urged everyone present to join the battle against corrupt government.

Alan Hassenfeld picked up on that theme, reminding people it had been barely more than ten months since we unveiled the RIght Now! Coalition with pealing church bells. "Our goal from the beginning has been to make Rhode Island what it should be — a place of hope, a place of equality, a place of freedom — rather than what it had become — a place of despair, a place of inequality and special interests, a den of corruption, almost a prison."[8]

Applause swept the crowd.

Hassenfeld turned toward the future, a final seventeen days before the election when Rhode Islanders would vote on Question One. In a familiar flourish, he asked each person present to talk with others about four-year terms. "In the toy business," he said, "it all comes down to retail sales. If each of you takes a bunch of flyers with you today, and you reach out to ten friends or family members who may be skeptical, we will win this mother of all referendums."

Never one to take himself too seriously, Hassenfeld ended by turning a phrase of Robert Frost: "I have miles to go before I sleep. I have promises to keep, so no more will Rhode Island weep." He winked and laughed.

The crowd laughed with him and washed the woods with warm applause.

During the election's home stretch, David Duffy's firm produced three television commercials for four-year terms. The first started with a cuckoo clock whose hands spun forward over the sound of an accordion playing a frumpy waltz. A door on the right side popped open, and a mechanical puppet wearing a straw hat ran out, revealing campaign signs, confetti, and bunting. An amused voice-over said, "Two-year terms force the governor to spend as much time running for office as running the state."

Another door sprang open and a puppet circled out, sitting at a desk with American and Rhode Island flags behind him. The clock chimed, and a yellow cuckoo popped out above them, crying, "Cuckoo! Cuckoo!" While the bird swung frenetically back and forth between the campaigner and the working governor, the announcer urged viewers to vote "Yes" on Referendum #1. "It gives the governor four years to do the job right. Two years is for the birds!"

In the second commercial, the same friendly voice announced that Question One would "give the governor four years to do the job right." The camera zoomed in on the denim pant-legs and heavy work boots of a man hop-stepping to kick. "And here's the kicker," the voice-over continued, "It gives you the power to exercise this option." A close-up showed the face of a politician turning in fright as the booted foot shot past the camera and landed hard. The ad ended with a bold sign and voice: "VOTE YES ON #1. Four years. Time for a Change."

In two wacky fifteen-second spots, Duffy and his team had captured the essence of complex arguments. The third featured a merry-go-round whirling brightly at twilight, and appealed to parents' hope for their children in Rhode Island. The announcer asked if we could again make the state a joy for our children.

Alan Hassenfeld had put up $50,000 for production, companies would pay TV stations, and Duffy would book broadcast times. I began to believe we could overcome the cynicism.

But the bitter aftertaste of corruption remained. One chilly October night, I finished speaking at the Sockanosset Cross Road Library in Cranston. As I walked toward my car, a man who had been in the audience crushed his cigarette and shook my hand. His calloused grip felt far stronger than mine. He did not offer his name. "Things happen here that you'll never change," he said. He told of inspecting road construction for the Department of Transportation. He glanced into the darkness and spoke warily: "This buddy of DiPrete's used to short us on paving contracts."

"Shorted?" I asked. "How?"

He rubbed his thumb and index finger together, as if separating bills. "Specs might call for five inches of concrete, but they'd fill the bed a little higher and pour a half inch less. The finished road would look the same but might not last as long."

"Which contractor?" I asked.

He shook his head, refusing to name names, and lit another cigarette.

"Did you report this?"

"I told my supervisor, and he looked the other way. So I went up the chain and reported both the contractor and my supervisor. And do you know what happened?"

I shook my head.

"Exactly nothing. Except I got transferred off that job."

"We have a whistleblower law," I said.

He shrugged. "And how many guards will you give me?"

16

A Pivotal Election

1992

REP. ROBERT A. WEYGAND'S COURAGE in wearing a hidden microphone for the FBI sent Pawtucket Mayor Brian Sarault to federal prison, and when the story broke in June 1991, Weygand became a Rhode Island hero who admitted his fears at a news conference. "I've never done it before. I don't know how I went through with it."[1] Afterward rumors around the State House oozed suspicion: federal agents must have trapped Weygand and forced him to deliver Sarault. For months after the scandal broke, Weygand's role as a witness kept him from setting the record straight. He and his family lived under a cloud, isolated and in danger.

After Sarault pleaded guilty and went to prison the FBI, U.S. attorney, and State Police lauded Weygand at a State House ceremony. At forty-four he was a telegenic, conservative, Irish-Catholic Democrat, with a picture-perfect marriage to his childhood sweetheart and three outstanding children. Weygand had played no role in RISDIC, and from the moment he announced his candidacy for lieutenant governor he became the odds-on favorite. Rather than tangle with Weygand in a Democratic primary, the incumbent, Roger N. Begin, announced that he would not run for re-election.[2]

Under the Rhode Island Constitution, the lieutenant governor has no duties beyond presiding in the state Senate and standing ready in case the governor dies. In typical election years, candidates for lieutenant governor were left in the shadows, but Weygand stayed in the spotlight. Criticism never seemed to faze him. It made little difference when the state's largest teacher's union broke ranks with Democrats to endorse an independent in the three-way race.[3]

Most candidates for public office spent the fall of 1992 demonstrating their diligence against corruption or stepping warily over RISDIC tripwires. Atty.

Gen. James E. O'Neil, a Democrat, struggled to deflect charges from Republican Jeffrey B. Pine, a prosecutor from his own office, that he had done too little to stop RISDIC. Pine accused O'Neil of giving a pass to friends at Jefferson Loan and Investment, which later failed.[4]

O'Neil had ousted Atty. Gen. Arlene Violet in 1986. For nearly two years after RISDIC's collapse, O'Neil and Violet blamed each other for failing to prevent the catastrophe. Other Republicans, including Nancy J. Mayer, the former chief legal counsel for the Department of Business Regulation, a candidate for general treasurer, also attacked O'Neil.

Mayer was rich, brilliant, and peppery. The craggy attorney general towered a foot above her, but she knew his weaknesses. She had testified before the RISDIC commission that O'Neil had ignored wrongdoing at Jefferson, which belonged to his close friends of thirty years. She insisted that she had tried to persuade O'Neil to investigate the troubled thrift, but nothing happened. Without actually running for the office O'Neil held, she campaigned hard against him.[5]

Pine, O'Neil's former assistant and current challenger, proved equally aggressive. He accused O'Neil of making what he called "patently contradictory statements" about when and how he learned of the Stitt Report. One of his attack ads showed O'Neil on a news program in January of 1991, announcing that he had reviewed the Stitt Report in 1987, "when we first arrived in office." In another video clip he came across as evasive: "That document was not read by me or presented to me. That document was located . . . sometime after the credit union crisis erupted." Pine pounded on his former boss: "The question now has to be, 'Mr. O'Neil, when were you telling the truth?' "[6]

Although these and other attack ads filled TV screens, the furor over RISDIC was fading. Mo Guernon had left Operation Clean Sweep, and moderate leaders began to emerge. Charlie Silverman now led a group of volunteers that included Beverly and Bill Clay, retired teachers who struck me as decent, diligent, and unpretentious. With little money and less hierarchy, they devoted themselves to the quest for honest government. It became possible to close rifts in the reform community and to begin working toward goals we all shared.

During the fall of 1992, six organizations began a quiet campaign to hold the General Assembly more accountable. Operation Clean Sweep brought four other groups to the table: the Government Accountability Project (GAP), Reform '92, US-PAC, and the Rhode Island Taxpayers' Association.[7] Most of these groups had been members of the Public Interest Alliance that attacked RIght Now! and pushed for draconian ethics and campaign finance rules. But in spite of our disagreements through the spring, we began a series of meetings at GAP's office in a triple-decker near the State House. Without ground rules, we began hammering out goals all could support.

We knew that clerks for various legislative committees typed their data into computer terminals that linked to the General Assembly's mainframe. Committee agendas appeared as bright green text on dark screens, then as printouts that were posted outside the hearing room. The clerks could locate any bill and generate tracking reports. Their knowledge served the legislative leaders who controlled the committees, while rank-and-file legislators and members of the public knew the information existed but were not allowed to touch the terminals. This meant that committee leaders got the latest versions of bills printed instantly; the public waited days before printouts became available in a musty basement bill room.

Everyone around the table at GAP's office agreed we should push for public terminals with access to this digital treasure trove. We would argue that taxpayers had paid to produce this data, and everyone — whether lawmaker, journalist, lobbyist, or citizen — should be able to search for bills and committee schedules in real time. No one should have to drive to the State House each day and dash from room to room to learn which bills were posted for committee hearings, so we would push for terminals at the State House library and in public libraries around the state.

"While we're at it," suggested Beverly Clay, "we should also ask for timely printouts of bills and amendments. It drives me crazy to watch from the gallery when they pass out an amendment. Legislators and reporters on the floor get copies, but I can't read what's being debated."

Our fledgling coalition also decided to press for a more public process in awarding legislative grants. Campaign brochures often showed representatives and senators presenting enlarged checks to sports teams, neighborhood groups, and other causes. It was a mystery how these grants were awarded in amounts that ranged from a few thousand dollars to megabucks. House and Senate leaders used such grants to exert immense pressure on incumbents seeking re-election, but so far GAP's efforts to get the data about these grants always hit a stone wall.

In place of legislative grants, our coalition proposed an open process with clear criteria and public votes. "Fat chance," Charlie Silverman snorted with his characteristic smile. "The leadership will never go along with that."

These meetings at GAP encouraged me. Whatever our differences had been, these were honest people who felt betrayed by their government. Rage over RISDIC had drawn them into the public arena, and they were staying involved. As I walked back from GAP to the Common Cause office, I wished we could have drawn these activists into our ranks, yet I knew the time when all could have coalesced into a single organization had long passed. Like planets revolving around the sun, we would forever circle the State House in separate orbits. At least we were orbiting in the same direction, and beginning to work toward mutual respect and consensus.

In an August questionnaire, "Opening the Legislative Process," we spelled out five top priority reforms. We asked every candidate across Rhode Island to indicate support for or opposition to each proposal. Bunches of questionnaires landed on my desk from challengers, but fewer from incumbents. Many liked the idea of public access to computer terminals to see bill texts and schedules; most wanted to reform the legislative grants process. Solid majorities supported rules requiring fiscal notes with all bills that carried financial obligation, while respondents split over ideas for reducing the huge number of bills introduced.[8]

The *Providence Journal* had covered the debate over four-year terms extensively. Its editors had been urging readers to vote "yes" on Ballot Question One, but they outdid themselves on the Sunday before Election Day. An editorial supporting four-year terms filled an entire column on the paper's front page, reiterating the RIght Now! case. Without mentioning DiPrete's disgrace, the editors decried the distraction of nonstop fundraising, which, they wrote, "our state just cannot afford."[9]

The *Providence Sunday Journal* had a circulation close to 250,000, and most households had several readers. With one timely and highly visible run, this single editorial might reach more people than all of our flyers combined. Even with our television commercials and newspaper endorsements across Rhode Island, however, I was not sure that voters would finally approve the longer terms that they had previously rejected three times.

That Sunday night, with the election two days away, our coalition of grassroots reform groups gathered with flashlights for a rally outside the darkened State House. John Hazen White Sr., who had promoted reform with full-page ads in the *Providence Journal,* had rented a truck with four high-powered spotlights that sent beams into the clouds. At one point, White asked the crowd to turn their lights off. He led a countdown that ended with noisemakers and all the lights shining on the white marble façade, against darkened windows, and toward the looming dome. Each of us who spoke emphasized one self-evident theme: citizens must keep shining light on government.[10]

Nearly an inch of rain fell on Election Day, but the pull of a three-way presidential election boosted turnout. Alan Hassenfeld hosted a seafood dinner at the Lobster Pot in Bristol for the RIght Now! steering committee. After dinner, we drove over surprisingly empty roads to Providence for stops that Dave Duffy recommended — first to the Biltmore for the Democrats' victory party and then to the Mariott for the Republicans' celebration. "You're not endorsing either party," Duffy told me in the car, "but you need to show your face. I'm almost sure we've won four-year terms. Reporters will want comments from you and Alan."

The polls closed at 9:00 across Rhode Island, and returns started appearing almost immediately on large TV monitors in the Biltmore's ballroom. Sundlun and Weygand were winning handily. The battle between O'Neil and Pine for attorney general was too close to call. Question One, for four-year terms, jumped off to a comfortable lead that held as precincts reported.

"So what do you think?" asked Brian Jones, a reporter for the *Providence Journal*. He planted himself between Hassenfeld and me.

"It's a real beginning," Hassenfeld beamed. "Now people can plan for the future, and we can do the right thing for the state. Then it will be up to all of us to make sure that real solid, good candidates run."[11]

I reminded the reporter that voters had rejected four-year terms in 1973, in 1982, and in 1986. "The most recent question coupled executive and legislative four-year terms. Nearly sixty percent of voters said 'no.'"

"So what does it mean that you seem to be winning by almost that same percentage?"

I said RISDIC had produced a toxic negativity that heaped blame indiscriminately on politicians. The RIght Now! Coalition had aimed to fix a dysfunctional system. "If these numbers hold up," I said, "I think this vote is a victory over cynicism and suspicion."

After months of uncertainty, our constitutional amendment establishing four-year terms for the five statewide general offices cruised to a comfortable 60.2 percent victory.[12]

In statewide races, Bruce Sundlun crushed Elizabeth A. Leonard, a lackluster Republican challenger, and several independents.[13] Bob Weygand overwhelmed his Republican and independent opponents with an astonishing two-thirds of the votes cast.[14] Ethical issues had contributed to Weygand's victory and those of the other three general officers. In the race for general treasurer, Republican Nancy J. Mayer convinced voters that brokerage firms that relied on state investments were financing the campaign of Democrat Marlene Marcello McKenna. Mayer trounced McKenna with 58 percent of the vote.[15]

After a bruising battle for attorney general, the Republican challenger Jeffrey B. Pine ousted his former boss James E. O'Neil by a narrow margin, largely over questions about O'Neil's failure to follow up on the Stitt Report or to investigate his friends' credit union. The final count relied on mail ballots and took several days.[16] In the race for secretary of state, Republican Barbara M. Leonard charged that incumbent Democrat Kathleen S. Connell had steered a no-bid printing contract to a company that donated $15,000 to her campaign. Except in emergencies, Leonard promised, she would award contracts only through competitive bidding.[17] Although Connell had led all Democrats in previous statewide races, Leonard captured the third general office for Republicans.

The 1992 election brought a sea change in the Rhode Island General Assembly. As polling places phoned in their results, the tallies showed that newly elected representatives and senators would occupy 55 of 150 seats, more than double the normal rate of turnover. On the morning after the election it also became clear that Senate Majority Leader John Bevilacqua had been ousted. Four of his allies had not run for re-election,[18] and GOP challengers knocked off four other Bevilacqua loyalists.[19] While I was careful never to take sides, I reveled privately in the results from Bristol, where Richard M. Alegria — owner of the King Philip Inn, Bevilacqua confidant, and the lowest ranking senator on our scorecard — lost decisively to his Republican challenger, Mary A. Parella, who captured 53.7 percent of the vote.[20] In her campaign, Parella had hammered Alegria's low standing in scorecards of both Operation Clean Sweep and Common Cause,[21] and she pounded his political machinations for construction of his King Philip Hotel. In victory, she cited Alegria's ties to Bevilacqua and a perception that he had used his political power for his personal gain. "People felt he needed to be defeated, that he had become too powerful. I provided an opportunity for people to do that."[22]

Bevilacqua dodged reporters, but his loyal Judiciary Committee chairperson, Sen. Tom Lynch, announced that the majority leader would not fight to keep his post.[23] Nor could the former majority leader, David Carlin, return. He had run a quixotic campaign against incumbent Republican Congressman Ronald K. Machtley in the 1st District but garnered less than a quarter of the votes cast.[24]

Senate Democrats caucused behind closed doors and elected Sen. Paul S. Kelly of Smithfield as their leader. Kelly promised that Senate committee meetings would start on time and would take timely votes on legislation. "A senator shouldn't have to sell his soul to get his or her bill heard," Kelly announced. I liked Paul Kelly, who showed neither anger nor arrogance. He stood taller than most other members of the Senate. Abundant silver hair framed blue eyes and a cheery smile. He wore ties emblazoned with Peanuts cartoon figures and had the gift of concentrating completely on every conversation.

The battle to succeed House Speaker Joe DeAngelis would stretch into January. DeAngelis had thrown in the towel five months earlier, when he chose not to file candidacy papers. In the bitter aftermath of RISDIC, 26 of 100 representatives had abandoned their seats. Other incumbents had lost, either to reformist Democrats in the September primaries or to Republicans in November.

The struggle to become speaker — arguably the most powerful political office in Rhode Island — boiled down to a battle between Warwick Representative Russell Bramley, who inherited DeAngelis's mantle, and Pawtucket Representative John Harwood, a muscular Ivy League hockey player who often joked that he had been "in Siberia" since he lost to DeAngelis four years earlier. As Rhode Island recovered from the RISDIC scandal, would either man support further reforms?

Loose Ends
1992–93

WITHIN DAYS OF BRUCE SUNDLUN'S RE-ELECTION, I discovered that the former bomber pilot had outmaneuvered both the Senate and the reform community. Four months earlier, the crusty governor signed the revolving door bill into law.[1]

As legislators and lobbyists scattered for the summer and the marble hallways settled into stillness, Sundlun had quietly withdrawn his four judicial nominees and reappointed them as recess appointments. For three nominees the governor's move presented no problem, but the fourth was his executive counsel, Judith C. Savage. Her appointment flew in the face of the newly enacted Revolving Door Law, but those of us who should have noticed his move missed it entirely.

Two days after the 1992 election, I heard what Sundlun had done and raced to the State House. Brian Gallogly, one of Sundlun's senior staff, tried to duck my questions but finally insisted Savage's appointment was perfectly legal and had been duly reported in the *Providence Journal*.[2]

"When?" I demanded.

"In July, when he made the appointment. You can look it up."

Chagrinned, I rushed back to the Common Cause office, where our ethics committee had begun its monthly meeting, and told them about Savage. All were shocked, and no one remembered the newspaper story. We were talking about how Sundlun's move would have cost him votes when the phone rang, and I picked up.

"Philip," Bruce Sundlun roared at the sound of my voice. "Brian Gallogly says you just went ballistic about my judges."

I excused myself, went into my office, and closed the door. "I'm flying out in the morning for my vacation home in Jamaica," Sundlun yelled. "I want you to cool down and keep this quiet until I get back."

"Respectfully, Governor," I stammered, "I've already told people at a meeting here."

"How soon can you be in my office?" he demanded.

An hour later, Rae Condon and I met Sundlun in a tiny conference room beside his formal office. Indignant from the start, he asserted his legal right to proceed with the judicial nominations. He emphasized that he withdrew the four as legislative session appointments and then signed recess appointments instead. "They're perfectly legal," he declared triumphantly. "They were true interim appointments. The General Assembly was not in session. They're valid until January."

"Governor," Condon said respectfully, "we acknowledge that technicality. But you must have had a reason to make important judicial appointments in July and then keep them quiet all these months."

"I didn't keep them quiet," Sundlun growled. "There was a story in the *Providence Journal*."

Condon met his glare with a steely smile. "These judicial appointments were so stealthy that no one seems to know about them."

"Don't blame me if you don't read the goddamn paper. Besides, you know about them now. That's why you're here."

Condon did not flinch. "Don't you think people will conclude that you played fast and loose with the principle? They might even question your veracity."

Sundlun scowled at her. "You know what I'm going to do? I'll take your fucking Revolving Door Law, and I'll challenge its constitutionality before the Rhode Island Supreme Court."

Condon held his gaze. "Certainly, Governor, that's your prerogative. But you campaigned as 'the ethics governor,' and you signed the Revolving Door Law."

Sundlun held off several months on his threat to challenge the law he had signed. In January, he presented the four nominations as normal legislative session appointments. At Judith Savage's confirmation hearing, I testified that her appointment violated the Revolving Door Law enacted only six months earlier. Yet whatever members of the Judiciary Committee may have thought, they voted to confirm all four of Sundlun's judges. Reporter Russell Garland observed: "The journey of this quartet of nominees has been one of the strangest in Rhode Island history."[3]

Despite Sundlun's triumph, he chafed against restrictions on his ability to appoint. He formally asked the state Supreme Court to advise him whether two rules were constitutional — both the Ethics Commission's narrow 1991 revolving door ban on legislators moving into state jobs and the General Assembly's broader 1992 revolving door statute. When a reporter asked for my opinion, I vented my frustration. "Why did he sign that bill if he thought it was unconstitutional? He could have vetoed it. I think the obvious reason he didn't was because it was a hot issue when he was facing a primary challenge and a general election."[4]

On December 8, 1992, less than two years after the RISDIC tsunami surged through Rhode Island, Jeffrey Teitz convened a press conference to release his investigating panel's final report. Volume one laid out the irresponsible lending practices of institutions insured by RISDIC, while volume two bore a title that said everything: "The Failure of Governmental Oversight."

"There are no heroes here," RISDIC special investigator Alan Baron told a small crowd. "Everybody was justifiably dealt a share of the blame."[5]

I thumbed through copies of the bound documents that ran hundreds of pages. My eyes went first to a summary chart that listed RISDIC officers and borrowers. Some were being referred for criminal prosecution; others could be sued for financial recovery. The investigators recommended indicting Robert and Donald Barbato, the Mob-connected developers who had drained more than $2 million from the Rhode Island Central Credit Union, but to my astonishment they did not suggest any public officials for criminal prosecution.

The report noted that Arlene Violet was the first to recognize the risk and summarized her warnings to DiPrete and others who failed to act: "The Governor and his staff appear to have viewed the Attorney General's report more as a political hot potato than as an expert analysis of the viability of RISDIC and its insured institutions."[6]

Democrat Jim O'Neil, who had ousted Violet in the 1986 election, claimed not to have read Robert Stitt's report until the crisis at Heritage Loan and Investment set the final collapse in motion. Other sections blamed General Assembly leaders for their part in the crisis and found House leaders culpable of allowing Bob Bianchini to dominate General Assembly decisions that might have reined in RISDIC: "The evidence suggests that Bianchini was given a virtual veto over legislation affecting credit unions and certain other financial institutions."[7] Bianchini always claimed he had been scapegoated for RISDIC's wrongs, but now the independent investigating panel led by his colleague, Jeffrey Teitz, portrayed him as a ringleader. Finally, the investigators reserved their harshest criticism for Edward DiPrete, who had served as governor during the six crucial years when his efforts might have averted the cataclysm.

The commission ended its monumental effort with seven major recommendations that commissioners hoped would "strengthen Rhode Island's regulatory capability."[8] It laid out practical steps to make the Department of Business Regulation more professional, proposed a financial crimes unit within the attorney general's office along with new state laws to combat fraud at financial institutions, and urged tighter restrictions on the financial activities of the five statewide general officers.

It also proposed two future studies: one to examine the fiscal soundness of the state's insurance industry, including the system for insurance regulation, and a second to focus on the General Assembly, particularly the question of whether a full-time professional legislature might better serve the state. In fact, that legislative study had already begun. One final act of the 1992 General Assembly had established a blue ribbon panel to study the legislature's structure and operations. Departing House Speaker Joe DeAngelis and Senate Majority Leader John Bevilacqua had appointed sixteen commissioners. The group included academics, retiring legislators, business executives, a labor leader, a hospital CEO, and me.[9] Our mission was to produce a "Blueprint for the General Assembly in the 21st Century." Retiring House Minority Leader David W. Dumas, who served on this commission, told the *Providence Journal* "that we really have come to a crossroads about whether or not you can continue with the sort of mob-scene citizen legislature that we now have, or whether we need to go to a smaller and much more professional body."[10]

So despite what I saw as the RISDIC panel's failure to refer any public officials for criminal prosecution, few could accuse Teitz and his investigation of whitewashing the General Assembly's abysmal performance and culpability for the disaster.

Commissioner Mary Rogers, a former state prosecutor, told reporters that the public would never have heard the RISDIC story in a "cohesive fashion" without the televised hearings. She suggested that people could not have grasped "how much the good old boys were helping each other out, how the credit union directors were acquiescing to such a tremendous volume of money being shipped out so carelessly, if not for seeing the hearings on TV."[11] On the other hand, Rae Condon disagreed, writing in an op-ed that she saw the televised hearings as "the dark side" of an otherwise worthy investigation. She lamented that witnesses subpoenaed to testify on camera faced a severe disadvantage. They could claim the Fifth Amendment, but their lawyers "could not question them, could not produce witnesses to corroborate their testimony, and could not cross-examine other witnesses presented by the commission." Condon added that "allegations, accusations, or insinuations of criminal conduct against specific individuals by government agents are not proper subjects for televised hearings or public reports. They are matters for prosecutors."[12]

Could both women be right? Certainly witnesses had been shamed, but some had escaped with bags full of other people's money and would never face formal prosecution. The General Assembly had coddled RISDIC at Bob Bianchini's behest and stacked state laws in its favor. Lawmakers had kept ethics laws so loose that Bianchini had escaped Robert Bergeron's 1986 complaint on a technicality. I sensed that Bianchini's faith in the credit union model and in RISDIC's self-insurance had blinded him to its self-serving institutional culture, while his pique at Arlene Violet and Robert Stitt prevented him from doing what he could have done to avert the looming disaster.

As for DiPrete, he had given five hours of videotaped testimony before the commission and had not pled the Fifth Amendment, but his words might yet come back to haunt him. I believed he had mastered pay-to-play while serving as mayor of Cranston and brought it with him to the governor's office. A year had passed since the Ethics Commission fined him $30,000. A Superior Court judge had upheld the commission's decision, but his lawyers appealed to the Rhode Island Supreme Court. A grand jury was deposing witnesses and weighing evidence against him. Was it remotely possible that DiPrete was telling the truth? Or had he learned to lie without a flicker of doubt disrupting his placid façade?[13]

In August 1992, the Ethics Commission had been reduced from fifteen members to nine, all appointed by Gov. Bruce Sundlun. Five came from lists presented by General Assembly leaders, and four were his alone. I had waited in suspense for their names. Sundlun made no secret of his frustration with the Supreme Court's unanimous June 10 ruling that the commission held constitutional authority to write ethics rules for all public officials, and I feared he would appoint his political allies to soften the nepotism and revolving door rules.[14]

Reading the list let me relax, since four of them were stalwarts of ethics reform. Richard Morsilli, who had pushed resolutely to strengthen the nepotism rule and to ban revolving door jobs for members of the General Assembly, would chair the panel. I had never spoken with him outside the commission's headquarters, but I sensed a moral courage that grew from grief after a drunk driver killed his son. Another, Mel Topf, once served on the Common Cause board. In 1991, Topf wrote the compelling memo that launched the old commission toward claiming its constitutional authority to adopt ethics rules.[15]

Two courageous retirees from the old commission also appeared on Sundlun's list. Frank Pellegrino, a retired high school principal from Westerly, had chaired the adjudicative panel that ruled against DiPrete and fined him $30,000. John O'Brien, former director of the Providence IRS office, would also be back. Furthermore, two of Sundlun's new ethics appointees had served on the RISDIC Investigating Commission. Stephen R. Famiglietti, a criminal defense lawyer, had often asked probing questions, and Jean E. Hicks, the commission's only person of color, had founded and built New Visions, a respected social service agency in Newport's troubled North End.[16]

About the three other new appointees that Sundlun had chosen—William T. Nero, Dr. Richard A. Reuter, and Amanda H. Clark—I knew virtually nothing.

From day one, Morsilli signaled that the commission would be "proactive" in educating public officials and vigilant in enforcing the law. As manager of the Smith Barney Harris Upham brokerage in Providence, he understood the need for accurate financial data, and he was troubled that nearly a third of all public officials in Rhode Island routinely failed to file annual financial disclosure forms that were required by law.

When Mark Eckstein, the commission's affable executive director since 1987, announced that he would move on, Morsilli made little effort to have him stay. Instead he appointed a search committee with Amanda Clark as its chairperson and the new panel cast a wide net. After the committee's top choice for the job fell through, Clark phoned to ask what I thought of Sara Quinn as a candidate for executive director.

I had a high regard for Quinn, who had served with Rae Condon at the old Conflict of Interest Commission and followed her as executive director for the final year. I described Quinn's 1987 bill to establish the Ethics Commission, which the General Assembly had buried, enacting a poor substitute. I said Quinn had been a leader in the Ethics Task Force that Gov. Sundlun had appointed to recommend changes in the ethics law. "Sara drafted the bulk of their final report," I said. "That work vindicated her after the Ethics Commission passed up its chance to hire her as executive director in 1987."

"So you think she's qualified?"

"Absolutely."

"Some people say she's pretty zealous," Clark said cautiously. "What do you think?"

I said Quinn saw things in black and white more than in shades of gray. "I believe she's utterly committed to combating corruption. Sadly, that makes her stand out in Rhode Island."

"But is she too zealous?"

I said "zealous" should not be a dirty word.

The conversation seemed to be over, but Clark changed the subject. "Before we get off," she said. "Your name has been suggested."

I felt stunned, humbled, and elated all at once, but I reminded her that I was not a lawyer.

"The job description says 'law degree or professional equivalent.' Our goal is to get the best director we can. Would you be interested?"

I said I had never even thought of applying. Within minutes of Clark's call, Richard Morsilli phoned, urging me to submit a résumé. Their back-to-back calls floored me, but the thought of running Rhode Island's Ethics Commission appealed to me. Tepid public relations had often left the panel looking indecisive, and my work over four years had taught me volumes. From utter ignorance of ethics laws and the state's fabled culture of corruption, I had learned the legal framework and procedures. The position paid more than triple what I was making at Common Cause. I said I would consider it.

Morsilli said I would need to decide over the weekend. "The personnel committee meets on Monday at three o'clock."

It was Friday, one week before Christmas. In five days, Anne and I would drive to Florida, where her mother had recently died. Over supper, Anne raised some procedural questions that gave me pause. For instance, I had no idea whether the commission had actually voted to reopen the search process. I thought the job required a "law degree or equivalent," but in the flurry of events I had never gotten a copy of the job description. I asked her if I should let it go.

"You didn't seek this," she mused. "And you're not a lawyer. But you're more than qualified to manage an agency whose mission is ethics."

Beyond college, I had a master's degree: three years of full-time graduate study at Union Theological Seminary and one year at Cambridge University in England. During the 1970s in New York, I had managed a staff of thirty-eight and a budget greater than that of the Ethics Commission. Through four years in Rhode Island, I had worked with the commission and helped to rebuild it. I had been through the complaint process and had won grudging respect at the State House. Skilled attorneys would always be necessary for legal research and litigation, but I believed that strategic vision and political savvy might matter as much as a law degree.

On Monday morning, I drove to the commission's office to deliver my résumé and cover letter. A call came for an interview with the personnel committee that day. The full commission would meet the following afternoon. Few opportunities in my life had ever moved that fast.

Light snow fell as I drove south on I-95 for an interview with the full commission. One year ago the adjudicative panel issued its unanimous decision that the former governor had violated the code and must pay a $30,000 fine, and now three members of the panel that judged DiPrete — Richard Morsilli, John O'Brien, and Frank Pellegrino — were interviewing me as members of the renewed commission.[17] This time I came before them not as complainant but as a potential employee. I had often represented Common Cause in suggesting new initiatives and policies. Now the question hung in the air whether I would implement plans on their behalf.

I suggested that one crucial responsibility of the new executive director would be to file complaints against public officials, initially in cases related to the RISDIC scandal. I added that the RISDIC Commission had not referred any public officials for prosecution but that thousands of pages of transcripts contained chargeable conflicts of interest. I said I hoped the Ethics Commission would review those documents and use its power to file complaints.[18]

Beyond initiating RISDIC-related complaints, I said I hoped the commission would guide citizens in filing complaints. I told how Rae Condon had mentored me in drafting the Common Cause complaint against Edward DiPrete. No matter who became director, I said, it was time to develop a citizen's complaint kit with user-friendly forms, clear instructions, and sample complaints.

I drove back to the Common Cause office for our December board meeting. Over the weekend, I had called several members of our executive committee to let them know about my being considered for the top slot at the Ethics Commission. The board worked through a long agenda in preparation for the 1993 legislative session. Finally, under "new business," I related the rush of events since the Friday morning phone calls. Around the table, faces sagged.

"They probably pay a lot more than we do," said Cathy Speer, the president.

"Substantially more," I said, "but that's not why I would do this."

I had not asked their permission, and the board had not affirmed my decision to apply. People lingered longer than usual after the meeting, but no one seemed shocked and most wished me good luck. Robert Spink Davis, a lawyer who had recently retired from Edwards & Angell, a major downtown firm, drew me aside. "I've never thought there was magic in a law degree," he said gently, "but this is one position that could be particularly difficult without one. I hope you'll think carefully before you go forward."

The next morning, before Anne and I set out for Florida, we read a *Providence Journal* story whose lead described me as "a finalist" for the Ethics Commission post and as "a champion of ethics reform." Reporter Thomas Frank noted that my application went in after the original deadline and that the commission had then postponed its decision. He mentioned that I was the only non-lawyer among four finalists but that I had been "behind many reforms that swept through state government this year," including those that downsized the commission, opened its adjudicative hearings, and raised maximum penalties from $10,000 to $25,000 per violation.[19]

Frank also profiled Sara M. Quinn as a lawyer for the Conflict of Interest Commission and then as its director for about a year before the Ethics Commission took its place. Frank noted that Quinn had "taken shots from legislators, who called her 'overzealous.'" His story barely mentioned two other finalists, however. One had worked for Attorney General Jim O'Neil but was being dismissed by Jeff Pine; the other had been the director of the New York State Commission on Local Government Ethics, which was going out of existence.

During our long drive down the East Coast, Anne and I discussed this surprise opportunity at the Ethics Commission. Like astronauts on the far side of the moon, we had no contact with events in Rhode Island. In Florida, we comforted her father and were unaware that controversy had erupted in Rhode Island over my application. The commission voted to extend its deadline and advertise again. As it turned out, two of the commissioners disagreed. "Something's wrong here," declared John O'Brien, the vice chair. He told the *Providence Journal* he had not been consulted about the new ad. "It all seems directed toward acquiring Mr. West as the director."[20] Commissioner Mel Topf also objected: "The change broadens the language so that it would allow candidates like Phil West to apply."

Louis A. Scudieri, an unsuccessful candidate for lieutenant governor, filed an ethics complaint against Richard Morsilli for "clearly earmarking the position" to benefit me and for subverting the selection process. "If we're going to have an Ethics Commission," Scudieri told the newspaper, "everything they do must be ethical. Otherwise we're pretty much lost."

Morsilli reacted defensively. He told reporters he felt the director did not need a law degree "as long as the person under him has a law degree."

Jim Baron, a reporter for the *Pawtucket Times*, reached me by phone while I visited my mother, who lived near Anne's father in Florida. "Word is that they deep-sixed the law degree requirement for your benefit," he said. "What's your take on that?"

"I thought the 'or professional equivalent' was in from the beginning," I told him. "Frankly, I hadn't even considered applying." I added that I had been backing Sara Quinn for the position when the question came up.

For much of our drive north Anne and I circled through the questions sparked by my application. On a quiet New Year's Day in Providence, I scanned the newspapers that had piled up while we were away. It seemed that instead of helping the commission, I had become a lightning rod and caused embarrassment for Richard Morsilli.

I drafted a statement that rehearsed what happened and laid out my qualifications. I faxed it to media outlets. Most troubling, I wrote, was that Morsilli had become the target of an ethics complaint. The *Providence Sunday Journal* covered my rebuttal, ending with the commission's new deadline for applications and its revised plans for choosing a director. Only days into the New Year, my chance to lead the Ethics Commission had turned sour, and events were taking a toll on people I trusted.[21]

The Common Cause executive committee met on an unseasonably warm and rainy January afternoon. Natalie Joslin, who had achieved spectacular successes in recruiting new members and raising money, arrived first. Only moments later, our state president, Cathy Speer, shook out her umbrella. I had not seen either of them since the board meeting when I announced my application. Both were somber. Neither chided me, but the strain was palpable.

"I know you believe in the Ethics Commission," Joslin said. "You've worked to make it effective, but the dynamics around your application are hurting its credibility and yours." She spoke from a well of experience with the executive placement business she had built. "I don't want to be selfish or hold you back from what you want to do," she added, "but I can see that this is harming you, and I know it's hurting Common Cause. Without public trust, we're nothing."

Mike Smith, who had worked in DiPrete's office, arrived. He asked for a word in private before the meeting. "I know you've been in Florida with your family," he said, "and far be it from me to tell you what to do. But I need to tell you confidentially that I'm hearing from people who respect and trust you that they're disillusioned. I don't think your rebuttal is turning the tide."

During my years in the church, I often explained the concept of sin with an archery metaphor. The primary Greek verb for sin is *hamartano*, meaning "to miss the mark." Sin is not always deliberate wrongdoing. It can also occur when we aim for a worthy goal but instead cause unintended harm. I sensed now that I had sent my arrow sailing beyond the target and missed the mark.

Spink Davis, a grandfatherly lawyer new to our board, lingered after the others left and asked for a private conversation. He followed me into my cluttered office and settled into my couch between a credenza piled with papers and a box of folders waiting to be filed.

"I know this ethics application has been gnawing at you," he began gently. "You never meant to put Richard Morsilli into an embarrassing predicament. Nor did he mean to draw you off base."

I nodded, listening.

"There's a facet of this that you may not have considered. The administrative part of this job could become a tar pit for you. Any clerical slips or scheduling errors, and lawyers on the other side will tear you apart."

With my heart sinking, I asked him to explain.

"You helped pass the law that requires a prompt finding of probable cause. Complaints have to move like clockwork, with systematic notice to counsel and all the rest." He smiled. "You have numerous strengths, but timely attention to administrative detail is not among them."

We both laughed. Like the seasoned lawyer he was, Davis seemed under no pressure to change my mind, but he rightly saw my central flaw. Without judging or threatening, he warned that my chaotic managerial style would eventually scuttle any leadership I could provide at the commission. "Be of good cheer," he said kindly and pulled himself up. "I know you'll make the right choice."

His departure left a vast silence. I needed to leave for the State House but I had to think this through. I settled at my computer and began drafting a letter to the Ethics Commission. Words appeared on my screen as if by automatic writing: "I hereby withdraw my name from consideration as possible executive director. I feel particular sorrow that two well-intentioned phone calls, which prompted my application, may have also spawned a cloud of misperceptions. I withdraw because I doubt that this cloud can be dispelled while my résumé remains on the table."[22]

Withdrawing lifted a burden I had felt but not understood. Reporters who called about my decision expressed surprise. I explained to Thomas Frank that the whole thing had happened innocently, but once the controversy began, no amount of public relations could make it right. I said the clumsy process provided a kind of weird proof that this was not a secret scheme. "If there had been an effort at collusion," I said, "nobody would have done it this chaotic way." I added that plenty of people were looking to undermine the commission's credibility. I did not want to hand them more ammunition.[23]

In the end, no one suffered lasting harm. The complaint Lou Scudieri filed against Richard Morsilli failed to allege any specific violation of the law, and many people seemed grateful that I had stepped away.[24]

Reporter Brian Jones ended a *Providence Journal* piece on my withdrawal by describing "the difference between the good guys and the bad guys." Jones wrote that he had asked what changed my mind. "West said he'd been meeting with Common Cause's high command last Monday, and the session seemed like a wake. In the timbre of voices, the look on faces, even the skin tone of his colleagues, he felt the controversy's effect."

Jones wrote: "This is the difference, of course, between the good and the bad guys. The good guys listen, they care when people are hurt. They are able to look past their own bruised feelings, their own interests, and finally to do what's right.

"The bad guys have to be rooted out by people, like those who serve on ethics commissions, looking at the details, measuring public conduct against public rules. The irony is that Phil West would have been just the kind of guy to do that."[25]

I wanted to believe that was true, but I also knew that a desire for self-justification lay just beneath what people saw as my reformist reputation. Maybe I could be as receptive as Bob Bianchini or Ed DiPrete to opportunities that would harm the very institutions I wanted to build. In reflecting later on all that had happened, I found myself particularly thankful for those whose questions had given me pause. Throughout our marriage, Anne had often pushed back when I rushed impetuously ahead. On our Florida trip, she had raised questions about administrative intricacies at the Ethics Commission, but I kept my foot on the gas.

Within Common Cause, Natalie Joslin, Cathy Speer, and Mike Smith had all tried to help me focus on the damage my rash application might inflict on the commission's moral authority, not to mention the toll it was taking on our organization's credibility. Spink Davis, ever the patient attorney, had tried on two separate occasions to warn that my loose administrative style might work at Common Cause but would fail at the Ethics Commission. Even Mel Topf and John O'Brien, the commissioners who publicly challenged my candidacy, had not launched personal attacks. As much as their comments stung, they had tried to say that job requirements and application deadlines existed to protect the commission from chaos.

It made me wonder if Bob Bianchini and Ed DiPrete ever had equally supportive critics within their circles. Could anyone have convinced them to change course? Over coffee I asked Mike Smith, now vice president of the Common Cause board. He had grown up in Cranston and had worked for Ed DiPrete, developing policy and writing speeches. I asked him whether people on the governor's staff understood the pay-to-play that DiPrete had run for years.

"Some may have been suspicious," Smith said, "but I wasn't. I look back and wonder now how I could have missed it. I can't explain."

I asked if, in retrospect, he saw other clues.

"One thing that should have clued me in was what the governor resisted saying in public." Smith closed his eyes to dredge up memories. "I would write policy memos or speeches about the dangers of political influence that went with large campaign contributions. My drafts would come back with those portions crossed-off."

I asked if the outcome for DiPrete might have been different if he had changed course in the late 1980s.

"Probably," Smith said. "He could have announced that he would no longer do things in the old Rhode Island way. People in power who really change course can regain public trust. Even after all the headlines in the summer and fall of 1988, he won the election."

"But he didn't change course? He went deeper?"

Smith raised his eyebrows. "I didn't see it then, but it looks that way."

"When did you know it was too late?" I asked.

"Probably a year before the 1990 election. He couldn't see the loss coming. He thought he could beat Sundlun a third time. By September of 1990, when he finally promised to make campaign finance reform a priority, it was too late. By then, nobody believed him."

18

When Prosecutors Fail

1992–98

THE LEGAL CASE against Edward DiPrete tested Rhode Island's justice system. By the end of 1991, when the Ethics Commission fined the former governor $30,000, a grand jury was preparing criminal indictments. Few could have imagined the bizarre turns this case would take; only a mystery writer could have plotted the blunders and blind alleys that lay ahead. It turned out that the attempts to try DiPrete would put Rhode Island's attorney general and Supreme Court on trial as well.

In August 1992, Superior Court Judge Paul P. Pederzani Jr. upheld the Ethics Commission's finding that Edward DiPrete and James Taft were "business associates" under the law and that DiPrete had intervened on the Jamestown Bridge contract. He also ruled that DiPrete had selected Tutela for the Olney Pond contract and that the governor had "reason to believe or expect" monetary gain in the form of Tutela's large campaign contributions. "The absence of any formal understanding, written or oral, is hardly surprising," Pederzani wrote, adding that politicians know enough "not to corroborate the fact that an agreement existed." The judge concluded that the Ethics Commission's ruling "was supported by competent, reliable, and probative evidence."[1] Predictably, DiPrete rejected this as "unfair" and "erroneous," and appealed to the Supreme Court, insisting again that he had done nothing wrong.[2]

Over a year later, on October 7, 1993, Joseph Kelly stepped to the central podium of the Rhode Island Supreme Court. "May it please the Court," he said respectfully, then launched a blistering attack on the Ethics Commission. "There's a misconception down there that any action by anybody is a violation of the statute. I would have stood a better chance if I had faced a herd of stampeding pachyderms."[3]

"The fact-finders," Kelly groused, "left their table in order to greet and shake hands with the attorney for Common Cause, who was prosecuting this case."

I wanted to stand up and protest that Kelly was lying to the court. He knew that Rae Condon had not prosecuted the case, and he misrepresented her brief exchange with members of the former Conflict of Interest Commission — where she had served for ten years as executive director — as if it were proof of bias. Furthermore, DiPrete had appointed all but one member of the adjudicative panel that weighed the evidence. Even Ernest Ashton, DiPrete's long-time confidant and final appointment, had joined in the unanimous ruling against him.

Kelly argued, "The statute contemplates a *quid pro quo* or an explicit understanding, and there is not a scintilla of evidence that Tutela knew he was going to get anything or that DiPrete did anything for him." Outside, after the oral arguments, DiPrete repeated his mantra to reporters: "I don't think I've done anything wrong, or we wouldn't even be here arguing this."

The Supreme Court issued its ruling on January 11, 1994, five years after I had delivered our complaint to the Ethics Commission. I stood outside the court clerk's office, decision in hand, flipping pages. Justice Florence Murray had written for the unanimous court. The justices agreed that "whether by recommending or selecting," DiPrete had delivered the Olney Pond contract to Tutela. The governor had violated his own executive order and failed to step away from a potential conflict of interest, and DiPrete had received $20,500 worth of campaign contributions from Tutela.

But then the justices tacked away. "We believe the commission and the trial justice erred by adducing that an agreement did exist between DiPrete and Tutela." They insisted on a specific deal. "We believe that there must be some evidence to suggest that some form of a *quid pro quo* existed between the contributor and the official regarding the inspiration behind the donation." Their conclusion was absolute: "We find no such understanding or agreement in any evidence of record."[4] Thus in a few paragraphs the justices tossed out half the meager remains of our original complaint. They wiped out the finding that DiPrete had steered the Olney Pond contract to Domenic Tutela, along with $15,000 in fines.

On the Jamestown Bridge case, they agreed that DiPrete had maneuvered the contract for litigation to James Taft and that Taft was the governor's business associate, as charged. They left only $15,000 for DiPrete still to pay for steering the Jamestown Bridge litigation to James Taft.

My heart sank.

"So what do you think?" asked *Providence Journal* reporter Tom Frank. He had been waiting near the antique bronze elevators until I finished reading. I reminded him that all five members of the Supreme Court had served in the General Assembly. "They know that candidates and contributors are sophisticated enough not to cut specific deals in the course of a campaign. The kind of payback a contributor wants may not even be visible on the horizon — much less already on the table — when the contribution goes in."[5]

Eleven weeks later, on a rainy winter Tuesday, Atty. Gen. Jeffrey Pine unsealed criminal indictments against Edward and Dennis DiPrete. Although a Republican like DiPrete, Pine declared that the governor and his son had "solicited and accepted bribes in excess of $294,000 from state vendors, namely architects, engineers and developers, in exchange for contracts." The first count charged that during and possibly before his terms as governor DiPrete had conspired to conduct a criminal enterprise, as defined under the state's RICO (Racketeer Influenced and Corrupt Organizations) Law. The corrupt organization was described as a group that raised "campaign contributions for the Friends of DiPrete, and other money for the benefit of Edward D. DiPrete and that of Dennis DiPrete."[6] A second count cited the DiPretes and three Cranston men — Rodney M. Brusini, Frank N. Zaino and Michael Piccoli — for conducting and participating in the RICO organization.

Then followed twenty charges that named specific architects, engineers, contractors, and developers. Ten counts alleged that Edward DiPrete — either alone or with Dennis — had extorted bribes. Ten further counts cited the DiPretes for agreeing to accept or actually accepting bribes in exchange for state contracts. Those who gave bribes were named but were what the indictment artfully called "unindicted co-conspirators." I assumed that most had been promised immunity in exchange for agreeing to testify against the DiPretes. Their projects ranged from a modernist addition to the library at the University of Rhode Island to leases for state offices, mostly in converted mill buildings scattered across downtown Providence. From the lists, it looked like state agencies were paying exorbitant rents and the developers had kicked cash back to the governor.

I recognized some of the names. Joe Mollicone, whose $13 million embezzlement had triggered the RISDIC collapse, had apparently made a $12,000 payoff to the DiPretes. In return, the state's troubled housing finance corporation, RIHMFC, signed a lease for far more than market rent and moved its offices into a building Mollicone co-owned with developer Joseph M. Cerilli. Architects had also paid to play. David Presbrey, noted for his historic restorations, was alleged to have paid $32,850 in campaign contributions between March of 1988 and September of 1990 in return for state contracts.

Two final charges almost burned off the page. Counts 23 and 24 named Edward and Dennis DiPrete, declaring that each had committed perjury before the Ethics Commission on December 10, 1991. That was the day they had bobbed and weaved through testimony that the governor had recommended but not chosen Tutela for the Olney Pond contract.

These perjury indictments brought me a rush of satisfaction. The Supreme Court had vacated that portion of our complaint, but Pine and his prosecutors would now try to prove that both DiPretes had perjured themselves. Charges of extortion and bribery seemed to vindicate our complaint that Tutela's $20,500 in campaign contributions paid for the Olney Pond contract. The Supreme Court had dismissed our charge for lack of a *quid pro quo,* but Pine would present evidence that cash for contracts was DiPrete's *modus operandi.*

In the face of overwhelming indictments, both Edward and Dennis DiPrete again declared their innocence. "I'm really as shocked as anyone at the allegations that came down today," Ed DiPrete said at a press conference outside Joe Kelly's office. "These allegations are completely untrue. In the end, I have no doubt as to the fact that we will be vindicated." Standing with DiPrete and Kelly during the press conference was Richard Egbert, a Boston lawyer who specialized in defending mobsters and politicians. Egbert ridiculed the indictments as based on the word of people who had "sold their souls in order to testify." Predicting acquittal for both father and son, he echoed the refrain of DiPrete's defenders since the beginning that the charges had been "brought for political purposes, with witnesses who have no right being in our system of criminal justice." Dennis DiPrete faxed a press release asserting that he and his father looked forward to "refuting those charges and clearing our names."[7]

I had first met J. Richard Ratcliffe in the fall of 1991, when he asked the Ethics Commission to delay the adjudicative hearings on the Tutela/Olney Pond case. I had no idea that the thin, balding man in his mid-thirties had already been working nearly a year to unravel snarled strands of evidence involving figures high in the DiPrete administration.[8] Ratcliffe and investigators working with him had dug their way into the heart of DiPrete's corruption from an unlikely angle, an entirely separate probe of Joseph Molliconc Jr., the flamboyant banker who precipitated RISDIC's collapse. Ratcliffe had already proved himself a master of forensic detail, and he had help from a state police lieutenant with twenty years of experience investigating white-collar crimes, Robert P. Mattos. Tall and taciturn, Mattos had a reputation for stunning witnesses with quick and deadly questions. Other detectives nicknamed him "the Cobra."

Before the 1990 election, Atty. Gen. James E. O'Neil had assigned Ratcliffe to investigate a bank examiner's report that Mollicone's family bank was short $13 million, but Ratcliffe and Mattos had barely begun their investigation when Mollicone vanished. Many knew that Joe Mollicone, like his father before him, had provided banking services for the Patriarca crime family. Rumors flew that the Mob had hidden Mollicone to protect its secrets or that mobsters had buried the fugitive banker in cement. Some speculated that Mollicone had fled because he feared the Mafia more than the prosecutors.

While the drama of Mollicone's embezzlement and disappearance continued, and the newly-elected Gov. Bruce Sundlun closed insolvent credit unions and savings-and-loans in January of 1991, Ratcliffe and Mattos continued their investigation behind closed doors. Meticulously they traced leads from Joe

Mollicone's financial tangles into the heart of DiPrete's corrupt administration. Their vital clue was a stub in Mollicone's checkbook that noted payment of $875 to Anjoorian Carpets for "Renza's rug." John S. Renza headed DiPrete's Department of Employment Security, which had leased office space in a building that Mollicone co-owned with businessman Henry W. Fazzano, a wealthy businessman who served as DiPrete's last chief of staff. Under pressure of a grand jury investigation, John Renza admitted that he had received the rug and other gifts from the building's owners: Joe Mollicone, Henry Fazzano, and Rodney Brusini, DiPrete's long-time friend and fundraiser. DiPrete insiders got $350,000 for unauthorized renovations and $10 million for a ten-year lease.[9]

Ratcliffe and Mattos targeted individuals who participated in pay-to-play contracts, but the criminal case against Ed DiPrete was vastly more complicated than the complaint Common Cause had filed with the Ethics Commission in 1989.[10] Over two painstaking years, the investigators saw how DiPrete insulated himself from the tawdry deals done in his name. Meticulously, Ratcliffe and Mattos wrapped up otherwise reputable architects, engineers, developers, and builders who had paid the legal limit in campaign contributions and switched to envelopes full of cash. O'Neil and his lead investigators granted immunity to several in exchange for testimony.

On January 13, 1993, Richard Ratcliffe sent the newly inaugurated Atty. Gen. Pine a twenty-seven-page memo that laid out what a *Providence Journal* special report would later call the "interlocking intrigues, stories of payoffs, deceptions, confessions, denials — corruption on a grand scale." Only a year younger than his new boss, Ratcliffe had spent years on the case and knew its details intimately. But then Pine brought back a disgraced former prosecutor named Michael F. Burns, who had been forced to resign abruptly in 1989 when a Mob informant in his custody died mysteriously while driving alone to go skydiving in Connecticut. In the dead mobster's parachute bag, detectives found nineteen packets of cocaine.[11]

No one outside Pine's office and the State Police Financial Crimes Unit understood the intricate case Richard Ratcliffe had been assembling against the DiPretes, so few noticed when Pine put Burns in charge of the Special Prosecutions Unit and its most crucial case. Pine also appointed Joseph L. DeCaporale Jr. to the prosecution team, seemingly unaware that the Supreme Court had reprimanded him for professional misconduct. DeCaporale had faced two separate hearings before the court's disciplinary panel for mishandling clients' funds. His record was also littered with a divorce, professional failure, and two bankruptcies. Finally, the new attorney general promoted Burns to head the Criminal Division and appointed DeCaporale to run the Special Prosecutions Unit. In a word, Pine handed the most complex and crucial prosecution in Rhode Island's history to two deeply flawed lawyers.

After building his case against Edward and Dennis DiPrete for nearly five years, Richard Ratcliffe found himself shouldered aside. He tried to balance his sense of obligation as a prosecutor with his concerns about these flawed supervisors who would now control his every move. Without public announcement, he quietly resigned.

These tensions lay beneath the surface when Pine unsealed the grand jury indictments against Edward and Dennis DiPrete on March 29, 1994. Evidence compiled by Ratcliffe and Mattos suggested that DiPrete's surrogates had routinely extorted anyone who wanted state business to contribute the maximum amounts allowed by law to the governor's campaign war chest. Once donors reached their legal contribution limits, DiPrete surrogates pushed to have contractors' family members and employees make "straw" contributions. Such "straws" were illegal but hard to prove, since reimbursements could be disguised as legitimate business expenses. Lies spread like crabgrass, as employers gave "bonuses" that employees then passed on to Friends of DiPrete.[12]

Straw contributions had fueled the RISDIC conflagration. The insurer reimbursed its president, Peter A. Nevola, for roughly $35,000 worth of straw contributions and DiPrete ignored multiple warnings. During those years, Nevola alone contributed $5,875 to Friends of DiPrete, and RISDIC corporations, officers, and straws gave many times that amount.[13] An investigation by U.S. Attorney Lincoln C. Almond revealed that between 1988 and 1990, Marquette Credit Union also secretly reimbursed its employees nearly $25,000 for straw contributions to top elected officials. Marquette was dangerously leveraged and top-heavy with risky loans. By the time Joe Mollicone's embezzlement from Heritage drained RISDIC's reserves, Marquette was also insolvent. After proudly serving generations of French Canadian immigrants in Woonsocket, Marquette collapsed and never reopened.

Ratcliffe and Mattos had discovered that straw contributions did not satisfy the DiPrete machine. When architect David A. Presbrey learned that he might be indicted, for example, he confessed to the grand jury that he had been moved up from straw contributions to envelopes full of $100 bills that he avoided touching. "You've got to remember," Presbrey testified, "they never said to me, 'Give me ten thousand dollars, and I'll give you this contract.'" But he learned the formula: pay in advance five percent of the project fee. The price of entry for a $200,000 contract would be $10,000. Presbrey's payments totaled $27,500 during DiPrete's final two-year term, and he received plenty of state architectural work. Presbrey testified before the grand jury that he thought Dennis DiPrete and his father were using the Architecture & Engineering Committee to sanitize their decisions.[14] Ironically, Presbrey and others had spilled their stories to the grand jury in November 1991, only days before the former governor and his son swore before the ethics panel that they were innocent of all wrongdoing.

Presbrey's testimony remained under seal in January 1994, when the Supreme Court dismissed the Tutela/Olney Pond portion of the Common Cause complaint, but the felony indictments unsealed two months later revealed wide-spread and systematic extortion.

Pine made a cataclysmic mistake when he assigned Burns and DeCaporale to run the case that Ratcliffe and Mattos had developed. Neither was as de-tail-oriented as Ratcliffe, yet they became responsible for discovery, the legal process of disclosing evidence that might assist the DiPretes' defense. Under their supervision, prosecutors turned over six hundred cartons of documents and two hundred volumes of grand jury transcripts to lawyers for the former governor.

But battles over these documents exposed Pine's new prosecutors to pub-lic ridicule. In a hearing before Superior Court Judge Dominic F. Cresto on August 24, 1995, DiPrete's lawyers demanded any further exculpatory evidence, particularly plea agreements prosecutors might have made with the bevy of witnesses named as participants in the DiPretes' alleged pay-to-play schemes. DeCaporale, head of the Special Prosecutions Unit, invited DiPrete's lawyers to go through "everything" for themselves. In one phone call DeCaporale said there were five or six boxes of documents left. When he hung up, a staff mem-ber corrected him — there were around thirty. The DiPretes' lawyers promptly charged the attorney general's office with prosecutorial misconduct for with-holding evidence.

The battle raged. In October 1996, a newly assigned assistant attorney gen-eral, Bruce Astrachan, faced withering cross-examination about what promises might have been made to witnesses against DiPrete. Defense lawyer Richard Egbert had just received a memo dated four years earlier that showed that prosecutors had intended to charge DiPrete confidant Rodney Brusini with perjury. He demanded that Astrachan explain. Feebly, Astrachan replied that the document had been prepared before his involvement in this case or even his association with the attorney general's office.

"So was the Constitution," Egbert fired back.[15]

Astrachan gamely said that he had relied on the word of his superiors, Burns and DeCaporale. The more he spoke, the worse it sounded.

Judge Cresto listened to days of back-and-forth about the state's failure to turn over evidence. The DiPretes' lawyers charged that prosecutors were still withholding exculpatory evidence and demanded that the case be dismissed.

Then Pine's team found twenty audiotapes of grand jury testimony that they had overlooked. Even with credible witnesses and mountains of documents, prosecutors were flailing. They denied that they had intentionally held anything back.

Cresto was perturbed. "The allegations being made are most distasteful to me," he declared. "They should be distasteful to anybody involved in the criminal justice system and anybody in the legal profession."

Under oath and close questioning, chief prosecutor Michael Burns admitted that he had just read Ratcliffe's 1993 memo to Pine describing developments since the case began. Then, when it seemed nothing worse could happen, a woman who worked in the State Police Financial Crimes Unit discovered eleven spiral notebooks of interviews in a drawer. A state police investigation never determined whether the notebooks had been there all along or how they got there.[16]

In February of 1997 Pine replaced the entire DiPrete prosecution team, but the damage had been done. On March 11 Judge Cresto dismissed the case against Edward and Dennis DiPrete. "The manner and magnitude of the prosecutorial misconduct found by the court to exist in this case," Cresto wrote in a thirty-eight-page decision, "has not only resulted in substantial prejudice to the defendants, but has the effect of eroding confidence in the criminal justice system."

To ordinary people watching the news on television or reading their morning paper, this dismissal made no sense. As far as most could tell, their former governor was corrupt, their prosecutors were incompetent, and a judge had used a technicality to make the case go away.

Atty. Gen. Jeffrey Pine appealed to the Rhode Island Supreme Court, and the high court heard oral arguments on November 12, 1997. Prosecutor Michael Burns, who had been promoted to supervising prosecutor in the DiPrete case, sat in that majestic forum and heard his errors dissected. Ten days later, Burns walked into snowy woods near his home. The next day, state police followed the trail of his solitary footprints in fresh snow to his body with a single gunshot wound in the head.[17]

William Devereaux, a lawyer who had worked with Burns in organized crime prosecutions, told reporters it was a mistake for Burns to have been saddled with responsibility for overseeing both the DiPrete prosecution and the Criminal Division. "He felt like a good pitcher who had been shelled in the early innings," Devereaux said. "He couldn't say no to challenges like that."

On January 9, 1998, nine years after Common Cause filed its ethics complaint against Gov. DiPrete, a sharply divided Rhode Island Supreme Court issued an order reinstating criminal charges against Edward and Dennis DiPrete. Two retired justices, Florence K. Murray and Donald F. Shea, had come out of retirement to hear the case. Both joined with Chief Justice Joseph R. Weisberger in a majority opinion that ordered the case to go forward. The full decision, issued on May 1, revealed the depth of the justices' dismay.[18]

Weisberger wrote for the majority that Superior Court Judge Dominic F. Cresto had taken "a drastic step" that could "increase to an intolerable degree interference with the public interest in having the guilty brought to book." Weisberger, Murray, and Shea held that the DiPretes had not been "irreparably prejudiced" by mistakes of the prosecutors. The case, Weisberger wrote, was one of discovery delayed, not discovery denied.

But two other sitting justices, John P. Bourcier and Victoria S. Lederberg, backed Cresto's dismissal. They declared the prosecutors' misconduct so egregious that a fair trial would be impossible: "The prosecution apparently immunized witnesses, entered into nonprosecution agreements, took other active steps to sanitize state witnesses, and then deliberately withheld this information from the defendants." Bourcier wrote separately that the prosecutors had used "deceit and trickery" to deny the DiPretes their right to a speedy trial, adding that the misconduct had been "flagrant and intentional."[19]

The majority ordered the case to trial. "We must bear in mind that when a grand jury returns an indictment," Chief Justice Weisberger wrote, "the people of the State of Rhode Island are entitled to have the issues of fact and the issues of guilt or innocence tried on their merits. The punishment of an errant prosecutor by the dismissal of charges is, in effect, a punishment imposed upon the people of this state."

Judge Cresto removed himself from the controversial case, and Atty. Gen. Jeffrey Pine then announced that he would not run for re-election. Pine insisted that his decision had nothing to do with the bungled DiPrete prosecutions, but he refused interviews with *Providence Journal* reporters who were compiling a massive summary of the case. Pine accused them of "reportorial misconduct."[20]

Their special report appeared on two successive Sundays in August 1998. At 53,500 words, it could have been a paperback book whose title — *Rhode Island on Trial: The Story of the Case against Edward DiPrete* — understated its drama. A prologue noted that much rode on the trial, finally to begin on January 4, 1999: "The stakes are high. This case has grown to involve more than just the DiPretes' innocence or guilt. Rhode Island itself is on trial — its political culture, its way of government, its system of justice. The story of the *State* v. *DiPrete* stands as a morality play, depicting power, greed, and infidelity in a place where the motto is *Hope*."[21]

On December 11, 1998, seven years and one day after he testified to his innocence before the Ethics Commission, Edward DiPrete stood before Superior Court Judge Francis J. Darigan in a courtroom of wooden walls and pillars. The former governor declared himself guilty of eighteen felonies. Jeffrey Pine, now a lame-duck attorney general, personally read a lengthy plea agreement that summarized the eighteen felonies.

Darigan peered down from the bench. "To those charges, how do you plead, Mr. DiPrete?"

"Guilty, your honor."

The former governor then apologized "for the trauma, the pain and the suffering that I have caused to my entire family. And to the people of the state," DiPrete added. "I'm deeply sorry."[22]

But in his prepared statement, DiPrete rationalized. He insisted that he was taking the plea agreement to spare his son time in prison and to save his family from the agony of a trial. He added that he regretted "mistakes of judgment" in connection with his war chest. "The pressures of raising money for campaign spending obviously clouded my perspective." Nor could he resist a final word of self-justification: "At no time did I ever select or recommend for selection any firm which I did not believe to be eminently qualified to perform the best possible services to the citizens of this state."[23]

Darigan read from his prepared statement that the guilty pleas brought closure "to a particularly sad and sordid chapter of Rhode Island history." He added that the scandal had "consumed public interest and attention for too many years." Then he looked down from the bench at DiPrete. "You have betrayed the public trust bestowed on you," he said, "and that is most reprehensible and contemptible."[24]

Under the plea agreement, Edward DiPrete became the first governor in the state's history to be sentenced to time in prison: one year that allowed work-release. If the case had gone to trial and DiPrete had been convicted on all counts, he could have been sentenced to 395 years in prison. His son, Dennis DiPrete, confessed guilt for a misdemeanor: illegally accepting a $1,000 straw contribution. He would be required to pay a $1,000 fine but would not be sentenced to time in prison.[25]

Now retired, former State Police Lt. Robert "the Cobra" Mattos, who had played a key role in tracking the massive fraud, told reporters he was disappointed the case had not gone to trial, where the evidence would have been laid out, day after day, for all to see. Without watching the trial, Mattos said, the people of Rhode Island would not comprehend "how the corruption worked." He said, "The governor's house was for sale. You could walk into the State House, and everything was up for grabs."

But Richard Ratcliffe, who had led the criminal investigation until Pine shoved him aside, told reporters he was glad the case had finally come to its end. "Everybody always asks me, 'Is he guilty?' Now, he is." Then he added that the guilty plea was finally good for Rhode Island. "If the governor goes to jail, it shows that the system worked. Nobody's above the law."[26]

2
Judges and Lawmakers

19

Paying the Piper
1992–93

"We've got our shot," Gary Sasse told me with a wry smile. "How often do legislative leaders invite you to redesign their bailiwick?" He had nurtured the vision for an independent blue ribbon commission to create "a blueprint for the General Assembly in the 21st Century." The legislation passed easily. During the summer of 1992, as a final concession to the RIght Now! Coalition, Speaker Joe DeAngelis and Senate Majority Leader John Bevilacqua appointed a sixteen-member panel, with Sasse as chair.[1]

Before coming to Rhode Island, Sasse had served on the senior staff of Tennessee Gov. Winfield Dunn. Lean, lanky, modest, and around fifty, he had played college football for Florida State and flew to Tallahassee several times each fall to cheer the Seminoles. Years of reading gridiron defenses had prepared him to see pathways through political minefields.

He brought the commission together for an overnight retreat within walking distance of Quonochontaug Pond, a stretch of salt water behind the dunes on Rhode Island's southern coast.[2] Without lobbyist badges or legislative lapel pins, we settled into lawn chairs and met as peers. "This is casual, " Sasse told the opening session, "but we have real work to do. We need to reach consensus on reforms that will improve future operations of the General Assembly."

A national expert, William T. Pound from the National Conference of State Legislatures (NCSL), had come to guide us. "You couldn't undertake this study at a more opportune time," he began. "Over the last decade or so, we've watched decision-making shift from Washington to state capitals, which raises questions of legislative expertise and capacity." Pound had an easy smile, white mustache, and round face. He did not mention the RISDIC disaster that had revealed ignorance, gullibility, and many conflicts of interest in the General Assembly.

Long before the colors red and blue automatically identified Republicans and Democrats, Pound's organization had begun using those colors to describe characteristics of state legislative bodies. "Blue legislatures" were part-time operations, typically with small staffs and low pay, where legislators needed outside work. By contrast, "red legislatures" functioned like Congress, with full-time lawmakers and professional staff to do research, draft legislation, and manage constituent services. Between these extremes Pound identified hybrids, which he called "white legislatures." In those bodies, he explained, lawmakers spent most of their time representing their constituents but received modest pay. Further gradations included "light red" and "light blue." A chart listed states in each category. Rhode Island's General Assembly fell between "blue" and "light blue," since most lawmakers had no staff and ranked near the bottom in legislative compensation.[3]

Rep. David Dumas, who was retiring from his post as House minority leader, said the abysmal pay forced him to step down. Since 1900 Rhode Island's Constitution had specified legislative pay as five dollars a day up to a maximum of sixty days: a total of $300 per year. Three times in the last twenty years pay raise amendments had gone before the voters, who spurned them every time. In 1986, more than 64 per cent of state voters rejected higher salaries.[4] After that rebuff, lawmakers thumbed their noses and doubled their pensions. Then scores of General Assembly members secretly secured special pension bills that allowed them to buy pension credits for military service or years served on local boards.

"Pension shenanigans have poisoned the body politic," Dumas said as we lounged on Adirondack chairs. "But lots of luck in convincing voters to pay more. People in my district know I run a solo law practice. They know I'm at the State House three or four afternoons a week for six months every spring. They know I can't afford to continue. But if you think they'll approve a legislative pay raise, I'll give you a deal on the Brooklyn Bridge." Dumas shook his head. "Legislative pay is an utterly intractable conundrum."

I knew he was right. When I first went to the State House, the sheer size of the General Assembly shocked me. How could a state just over a million people afford 150 state legislators? Rhode Island and nine other states averaged fewer than 10,000 people for each lawmaker, but all the others were rural and sparsely populated.[5] By contrast, Rhode Island ranked second only to New Jersey in population density, and New Jersey had nearly ten times as many constituents per legislator.[6] Since 1987 Common Cause had favored downsizing Rhode Island's senate from 50 to 25 seats and shrinking the House from 100 to 50 representatives. Even after those reductions, Rhode Island legislators would still represent fewer people than their counterparts in any other urbanized state.[7]

James Madison, the political theorist widely regarded as the architect of the U.S. Constitution, had warned against the assumption that large legislatures were more representative than small ones. "After securing a sufficient number for the purposes of safety, local information, and of diffusive sympathy with the whole society," Madison wrote, any further increase in numbers would counteract effective representation.[8]

After our initial retreat, the group met at the State House every two or three weeks through the fall. Sessions were always posted under requirements of Rhode Island's Open Meetings Law, but reporters rarely came, and only a handful of citizens showed interest. Gary Sasse held back his own expertise and drew others out, remaining patient even when comments came with an edge. He often defused arguments by asking how an idea translated into a better legislative system. "Remember," he said once, "we're trying to build a train that stays on the tracks no matter who's at the throttle."

John Bevilacqua had appointed Ray Dettore, a lawyer who worked for the City of Providence. Legally blind, Dettore held a complex chart on legislative pay only inches from his thick glasses and extracted its essence: "This confirms that Rhode Island's legislative pay is among the lowest in the country, only above New Hampshire's." With wide, half-seeing eyes, Dettore panned around the table. "How many of us would enter a profession where there hasn't been a pay raise in ninety years? Should we be surprised when some senators or reps compensate themselves in dubious ways?"

"Five dollars a day was standard pay for railroad managers in 1900," said Patricia Houlihan of the AFL-CIO. "The problem is that voters have kept refusing to amend the Constitution to raise legislative pay. Even after ninety years of inflation."

Everyone agreed that the pay scale made no sense, but there was no consensus on what it should be. And no one knew how to market a pay raise to voters whose wounds from RISDIC were still raw.

I had much to learn about the constitutional powers of legislatures and the history of Rhode Island's General Assembly. Why did Rhode Island legislators introduce more bills than lawmakers in all but four other states? Why did legislative leaders tolerate the stampede of session-ending special pension bills? Before our move to Rhode Island I had testified before legislative committees in New York and Connecticut, but never watched the intricacies of what many called "legislative sausage-making." I knew virtually nothing about how legislatures functioned farther west and south.

Inflation had driven the Consumer Price Index up 234 percent in the last twenty years, but Rhode Island had not raised legislative wages since the State House was built in 1900. Only a constitutional amendment approved by voters could lift the General Assembly's pay, and voters had rejected higher compensation in 1962, 1973, 1980, and 1986.[9] Sixty-four percent of the electorate had crushed a pay raise proposed by the 1986 Constitutional Convention.[10]

Lawmakers found ways around voters' resistance. In 1947 the General

Assembly created a legislative pension system; after the proposed 1986 pay raise was defeated, bills appeared to double the size of legislative pensions. One sponsor, Federal Hill Sen. John Orabona, spoke candidly to reporter M. Charles Bakst: "If the voters feel legislators do not merit a pay increase, then you have to have some other type of compensation. It's fair, and it's just." Bakst reported that despite the likely public backlash, the pension-doubling legislation "leaped off the starting block" on the next-to-last day of the 1987 General Assembly session. It passed among hundreds of bills on the final night.[11]

Beyond infuriating the voters, the doubling of legislative pensions created a sense of entitlement as lawmakers channeled a flood of special pensions to themselves and their cronies. Pension abuses in 1987 left an indelible high-water mark. One of the most egregious bills allowed a bevy of union officials to buy into the state pension system at bargain basement prices.[12]

Steve Kass, a WHJJ-AM radio talk show host, had served as a delegate to the 1986 Constitutional Convention. He supported a General Assembly pay raise but took offense. "This kind of activity is why people won't give them a pay raise," he told listeners. "They took the back door."[13] Kass soon filed suit to block the newly doubled pensions, and angry listeners mailed enough checks to fund the lawsuit, but he remained skeptical about the judicial process. "Let's face it," Kass asked listeners, "where does the judiciary come from? The legislature, and that's a concern. Can we get a fair hearing?"[14] More than he knew, Kass had reason to be suspicious. His case, *Kass* v. *Retirement Board*, landed on the calendar of Superior Court Judge Antonio S. Almeida.

Kass's attorney, George Vetter, argued that although legislative pay was low, lawmakers had violated the Constitution's compensation clause when they boosted their pensions.[15] Vetter zeroed in on the actuarial discrepancy between $90 per year that lawmakers would pay in and the generous pensions — $600 per legislative year, up to a maximum of $12,000 after twenty years — that taxpayers like Steve Kass would have to fund. "If the people wanted to have the General Assembly set their own salary," Vetter insisted, "they would have said so."[16]

Plaintiffs who supported doubling the pensions included the General Assembly, the State Retirement Board, and General Treasurer Roger N. Begin, a former state representative from Woonsocket. Attorney John Dolan argued that pensions were mere fringe benefits and that the Constitution did not forbid the legislature to grant or raise them.

Kass's suspicion of the judiciary proved prescient. Judge Almeida ruled that doubling legislative pensions did not violate the Constitution, and the Supreme Court, comprised entirely of former legislators, agreed. In a unanimous opinion, Joseph R. Weisberger wrote that retired senators and representatives had been receiving legislative pensions since 1947. He added that the 1986 Constitutional Convention could have proposed to end or restrict those pensions but it did not. "Had those delegates desired to prohibit statutory pension benefits to state legislators," Weisberger wrote for the high court, "they would have done so explicitly."[17]

Beyond the fact that the Supreme Court had ruled in favor of doubling legislative pensions, the judge upheld in *Kass* v. *Retirement Board* achieved his own notoriety barely a year and a half later. In July 1991, Judge Almeida was arrested only moments after he pocketed an envelope stuffed with $1,500 in marked bills, and he eventually pled guilty to accepting $45,100 in bribes.[18] A colleague on the Superior Court fined him $50,000 and sentenced him to six years in prison. The Retirement Board sued to revoke Almeida's $97,904-per-year judicial pension and ultimately succeeded.

Could our Blue Ribbon Commission ever resolve this bitter legacy of blame? Even if we could diagnose chronic dysfunction and propose solutions, could we persuade mutually resentful audiences — 150 members of the General Assembly and hundreds of thousands of state voters? In an effort to try, we issued an open invitation for witnesses to testify — in person or in writing — at a series of televised hearings from January to March of 1993, with specific topics scheduled for each Monday evening. The *Providence Journal* quickly weighed in with an editorial. "The General Assembly," the editors wrote, "is a part-time, underpaid, overworked, intensely politicized aggregation of amateurs, imprisoned by a process that tends to hinder excellence and independence and reward self-promotion — and, from time to time, out-and-out corruption."[19]

The editors added that the legislature could not fulfill its duty "when it is mired in inefficiency; when some of its members indulge in glaring conflicts of interest; when some of its committee chairmen brandish autocratic power; and when the institution is so large as to be sluggish and unwieldy." The editors urged Rhode Islanders to attend the hearings and speak up "for the legislature they want."

Room 35 in the State House basement was equipped for television. Its walls had been stripped to century-old bare bricks, and a blue drape hung behind the boxy dais. I had watched witnesses testify before the RISDIC Investigating Commission and House Finance Committee, but I had never sat in one of the high-backed black chairs behind the dais.

From the center seat, Gary Sasse summarized our commission's work over six months. He introduced members of the panel and invited witnesses to share their ideas about structural steps for improving the General Assembly. Should Rhode Island switch to a unicameral legislature, as Nebraska had done? Should we go to a full-time legislature? Reduce the number of legislators? Set term limits?[20]

Former Lt. Gov. Richard A. Licht declared unequivocally that a General Assembly of 150 was far too large for a state of only a million people. He suggested cutting the House from 100 to 50 representatives and the Senate from 50 to 24. Downsizing the legislature, Licht said, would make lawmakers more visible in their districts, and might persuade voters to consider a pay raise that was long overdue.

Next to testify was Lt. Gov. Robert Weygand, who had helped put Brian Sarault in prison two years earlier. "As we move into the twenty-first century," Weygand testified, "the question is whether we'll continue with an amateur legislature or create a body that can deal head-on with the complex issues that face our state." He urged reducing the number of legislators. "Last year, we had over four thousand bills introduced, and that was fewer than the year before. When I chaired the House Corporations Committee, I had to read thousands of bills. I tried to be responsible, but there was no way I could stay on top of them all." He urged stronger professional staff to help lawmakers with research and constituent services, as well as improved equipment and computer access for every legislator.

Although the question of legislative pay no longer affected him, Weygand continued, the state must deal with it. Even increasing from $5 to $100 per day might not solve the problem. "There's huge stress and pressure in having to leave your regular place of business after lunch three days a week all through the spring. For my work as a landscape architect, that was the busiest time of year." Although he was not sure how to persuade the public of this, "it's basic in any business to pay your employees fairly. When you don't, you invite precisely the kind of problems we've seen in recent years. Either you are going to make the leap to reasonable salary or strip responsibilities and go back."

Former Senate Minority Leader Lila M. Sapinsley was a moderate Republican with elegance and gravitas who had lost a race for lieutenant governor and now volunteered with several nonprofits, including Common Cause. She proposed higher legislative salaries and an end to legislative pensions, adding that nobody should get a pension for part-time work. Sapinsley expressed particular concern about expensive dinners that lobbyists routinely provided: "Until people in the General Assembly recognize a conflict of interest and steer clear, all the rest will be merely cosmetic."

Week after week witnesses testified. Some had served as statewide officers or legislators, others worked in government agencies, one taught political science, and a few were citizen activists. One evening in March, both Joe DeAngelis and former Senate Majority Leader Jack Revens spoke.

DeAngelis, with his neatly trimmed mustache, remained one of the most successful lawyers in the state. No longer speaker of the House, he seemed diminished as he sat before the commission, since decades of ethical conflicts of interest and lax legislative oversight had come crashing down on his watch. Nothing would change his responsibility for that. Defensively, he recited the reforms approved since RISDIC. "We enacted DEPCO in thirty-six days," he said. "We reformed pensions and restructured state purchasing." He ended by saying plaintively that he and other leaders had "done a lousy job of promoting ourselves."

Jack Revens had risen to the top spot in the Senate after his old-school predecessor, Rocco Quattrocchi, botched the redrawing of Senate districts in 1982. Taxpayers paid for the protracted state and federal litigation, while the courts blocked the 1982 elections for the entire Senate and forced a redrawing and costly special election in June 1983.[21] Voters expressed their disgust by electing fourteen new Republicans, a record number since the Bloodless Revolution of 1935 ensured a permanent Democratic majority. Senate Democrats dumped Quattrocchi and elected Jack Revens majority leader at thirty-six. He had already spent half his life in politics.[22]

I had come to respect Revens for his intelligence and clarity. A tragic accident had seared his character. While a student at Providence College, he struck and killed a pedestrian one night on Boston Neck Road; although no charges were filed, Revens never forgot. "You know," he told a reporter, "you wish you could find some way to change it. You rethink it and rethink it and rethink it. Was there anything you could have done differently?"

He testified with cool detachment. "It's difficult for the legislature ever to look good," he said. Thin, tall, and balding, he spoke with wry self-confidence, as if he had no need to persuade. "I have legislation pending to reduce the size of the Senate by half. You can imagine how popular that makes me with my colleagues, but it's necessary and the right thing. We have far more senators than we need, and with so many, it makes questions of a pay raise all the more complicated."

Revens scanned the dais. "If we were asking in the abstract what size the General Assembly should be, no rational person would say a hundred reps and fifty senators." He said the legislature's size distracted from the central issue: legislative pay. "Pay should reflect fairly what work the public expects the legislature to do. A real problem in Rhode Island is that all state officials are significantly underpaid. The attorney general makes only half the salary of the U.S. attorney or a lawyer who's made partner in a downtown firm. I know it's not easy to get the public to pay, but our pay should be in the ten-to-fifteen-thousand-dollar range. To quote an old cliché, 'You get what you pay for.'"

He urged us to preserve what he called "a citizen legislature." With his characteristic detachment, Revens saw no reason for a full-time professional legislature. "You don't need full-time legislators if you improve the quality of staff to analyze complex issues." He spoke laconically, moving through the matrix of legislative functions, schedules, and structures like a plumber tracing pipes through the basement of an old house, explaining what each did and how they connected.

BEYOND THIS OPPORTUNITY for public testimony, our commission also surveyed current and former legislators, of whom 175 returned questionnaires. Nearly all said they felt overworked, undervalued, and underpaid. Their feedback showed a surprising amount of agreement, including the need for access to reliable legislative information. They wanted computer access for everyone, including the public, to bills and legislative data, and asked for more staff to help sort through torrents of data. "It's like trying to drink from a fire hose," one wrote. Many requested fiscal impact statements and professional analysis of major bills before their transfer from committees to the floor.[23]

Among former lawmakers who took time to respond, nearly four out of five agreed that the General Assembly should continue as a "part-time citizens' legislature" rather than become a full-time professional body. Almost all of them favored a dramatic increase in pay, and 59 percent wanted to keep legislative pensions based on years of service. Nearly 84 percent thought it would be wise to downsize the House by 25 percent and to cut the Senate by half. Most also favored four-year terms for senators; 89 percent called for shared office space, phones, voice mail, and secretarial support.

By contrast, there was no agreement on term limits for legislators, which had become popular in other parts of the country. In 1990 and 1992, voters in a dozen states had established term limits, typically six or eight years for senators and representatives.[24] Most former Rhode Island lawmakers did not like that idea.

With mounds of testimony, completed surveys, and research data from other states, the Blue Ribbon Commission spent four months drafting a preliminary report. The work reminded me of boiling down maple syrup in the Catskill mountain valley where I grew up: lugging buckets of clear sap to an oblong tub over a stone fire pit, pouring into the steam, stoking the fire, then climbing through snowy woods for more. Gradually, the clear liquid turned amber. Our panel's final product might not be sweet, but it would be genuine.

We would propose current compensation of $10,000 per year with full family health insurance — costs that roughly equaled the pensions that would be eliminated. The official position of the Common Cause state governing board was for a salary equivalent to 125 percent of Rhode Island's average wage, approximately $8,352, with no health insurance. I urged the board to accept the commission's slightly higher amounts, and they agreed. And to avoid future battles over raises, we would put a cost-of-living escalator in the proposed constitutional amendment.[25]

Along with a grand bargain over pensions and pay, most of us were ready to recommend downsizing the General Assembly by one third, from 150 to 100 members. All but one member of the panel affirmed Sen. Jack Revens's legislation to cut the House from 100 to 75 representatives, the Senate from 50 to 25 senators.

"I like Jack Revens, but downsizing makes no sense." The AFL-CIO's Patricia

Houlihan was adamant. "There would be a terrible blood-letting to see which twenty-five senators survive. It's wrong to chop away at the General Assembly, especially if we're not proposing four-year legislative terms."

I reminded her that Revens had proposed four-year terms in exchange for a smaller state senate.

Houlihan glared. "Labor's position last year was to create four-year terms both for general officers and the General Assembly, but your reform groups never took it seriously."

Sasse tried to mollify her. "Downsizing wouldn't take place until after the next census, and that would be eight years after passage of the amendment. If past experience is any guide, many current members of the General Assembly may move on in that time."

"That's fantasy," she shot back. "Window-dressing. Rhode Island voters have a closer connection to their senators and reps than you see in other states. In all the research we've done, in all the conversations we've had, I have yet to see a shred of evidence that closeness is bad for democracy."

I reminded her of the RISDIC scandal and pointed out that Rhode Island legislators would still represent fewer constituents than their colleagues in forty other states.

"You've said all that before," Houlihan said, "and I'm sure you'll say it all again. But you haven't convinced me, and I don't think you'll convince many in the Senate. It's obvious that if you double the number of people in their districts from twenty to forty thousand, they won't have anything like the intimate relationship that people enjoy now. It simply won't be the same, and it doesn't matter whether you downsize next year or in 2002."

She would not budge. "I want AFL-CIO's opposition to downsizing noted in our final report."

"You got it," Sasse agreed.

Item by item, most members of the commission supported a preliminary report we would release for discussion. At its core were two compromises: first, an end to legislative pensions for all lawmakers elected after passage of a constitutional amendment that would raise compensation to $10,000 per year, adjusted to follow the federal Consumer Price Index; second, downsizing the House from 100 to 75 representatives and the Senate from 50 to 25 senators. Senators would get four-year terms, while representatives would continue with two. The downsizing would occur in eight years, when data collected in the 2000 federal census would guide the drawing of larger districts.

These historic changes could occur only if the General Assembly placed a constitutional amendment on the statewide ballot and voters approved. A less controversial constitutional amendment would end the roles of the lieutenant governor and secretary of state as presiding officer and secretary of the Senate. In their place, senators would elect their own officers.

We would also propose improvements that the General Assembly could provide for its rank-and-file members: staff to help with research and constituent services, office space in or near the State House, voice mail, laptop computers, and a computer database of legislative information. We would urge that the legislative database be accessible to the public from computer terminals at the State House and in public libraries. "Above all," we wrote, "the General Assembly should conduct itself in accord with the highest ethical standards." No one was certain how to make that happen, but we urged ethics training to ensure that lawmakers would never be ignorant of the law.

Meanwhile the situation in the legislature had shifted since Joe DeAngelis and John Bevilacqua first appointed the commission in July of 1992. DeAngelis had stepped down voluntarily, and the November elections had swept Bevilacqua from power. Now new leaders — House Speaker John B. Harwood and Senate Majority Leader Paul S. Kelly — controlled the General Assembly. Neither had been involved in designing our commission or appointing its members, although Gary Sasse had kept them informed and provided advance copies of our draft report. Two years and two days after the RIght Now! roll-out with pealing bells, we released the final seventy-page report at a press conference in December.[26]

Paul Kelly attended. Cheery and positive, he accepted his copy and said he favored the idea of keeping the General Assembly as "a citizen legislature." Afterward, he told reporter Russell Garland that he liked the idea of four-year terms for senators, but preferred to decrease the size of the Senate and House by equal percentages. John Harwood ignored the event. He later told reporter Russ Garland that while he could affirm four-year terms, additional staff, and office space — the question of downsizing "must be looked at carefully."[27]

It was clear that both Kelly and Harwood were consolidating their power. Would our recommendations gather dust on a shelf, as commission reports traditionally did? Were we fools to think we could move these proposals through the General Assembly and onto the 1994 ballot? Even if we did, would voters approve?

20

Under New Management
1993

IN SPORTS AND POLITICS, John Harwood always played to win. Physically and mentally, he took his teams to new heights. In 1970, he had won the *Providence Journal*'s designation as state "Honor Roll Boy of the Year" for leading the Mount Saint Charles Academy "Mounties" to the state hockey championship and serving three years as class president. Muscular and handsome, he went on to star in varsity hockey and baseball at the University of Pennsylvania, winning All-Ivy League honors in both sports. Instead of pursuing a career as a professional athlete, however, he earned graduate degrees in business administration and law. Long after his glory days on ice rinks and manicured ball fields, Harwood still played hardball. Only now his hits ricocheted through marble corridors at the State House.

In 1980, Harwood won a Pawtucket seat in the House of Representatives. He quickly learned the ropes, became a deputy majority leader, and set his sights on what many considered the most powerful political position in Rhode Island: speaker of the House. Late in 1987, rumors flew that Speaker Matthew J. Smith would take a lucrative job as the top state court administrator and pass his gavel to Joseph DeAngelis, his loyal majority leader. Harwood challenged DeAngelis, campaigning on promises to shift power from leadership to rank-and-file representatives. Harwood defied the odds, insisting that his team could beat DeAngelis, but DeAngelis crushed him by a three-to-one margin in the Democrats' caucus and easily prevailed in the full House, where nineteen Republicans cast symbolic votes for minority leader Bradford Gorham.[1]

On the last night of the 1992 legislative session, I bumped into Harwood and his alter ego, George Caruolo, a brilliant but gruff representative from East Providence. As the three of us waited outside John Bevilacqua's office, I sensed buoyant energy in Harwood and Caruolo. "Everyone else in the building is exhausted," I said, "but you look like you're raring to go."

Harwood smiled broadly. "A year from now," he told me with unabashed self-confidence, "we'll be running the House."

Caruolo feigned shock, then smiled broadly.

Five months later, that goal lay within their reach. In the November election, a record twenty-six new representatives won seats. No one knew whether the Democrats would line up behind Harwood or Warwick Rep. Russell Bramley, who was heir apparent to the departing DeAngelis. Nancy L. Benoit, prime sponsor of what had become the Revolving Door Law, stood with Bramley and sought her colleagues' support to become the House majority leader.

A week after the 1992 election, Bramley summoned the eighty-five House Democrats to a caucus at the State House. Harwood countered by inviting them to gather at the same hour in East Providence. Forty-three went to Bramley's caucus and forty-two to Harwood's. The Bramley faction elected Nancy Benoit as the first female majority leader in Rhode Island's history; the Harwood Democrats chose Caruolo. Bramley's razor-thin majority created a rare chance for Republicans to decide who would become the state's most powerful politician.[2] As the Bramley and Harwood factions lured defectors away, Benoit claimed the mantle of reform. She moved into the majority leader's suite, mounted photos on the walls, and hosted a welcome party. The next day three Bramley backers absconded to Harwood's camp.[3]

The *Providence Journal* plunged into the melee with an editorial that reminded readers how Harwood had pushed legislation that enriched his law firm. Years earlier, a motorcyclist tried to outrun a police cruiser but crashed and died. On behalf of the dead man's mother and his estate, Harwood accused the cops who chased him of negligence and sued the town. With that case pending in court, Harwood filed a bill to raise the limit on tort recovery from a municipality fifty-fold, from $100,000 to five million dollars. The *Journal's* editorial noted that Harwood's bill had passed the General Assembly but was vetoed by Gov. DiPrete. The editors concluded: "Now the question becomes whether Mr. Harwood's actions in this case reflect the kind of values that House members should seek in the next speaker."[4]

Harwood had pushed other bills that enriched his clients and law practice. A 12-year-old had been working on a go-cart when he was sprayed by flaming gasoline. After six weeks in a hospital, the boy died, and Harwood sued his parents on behalf of their son's estate, charging that they had been negligent in exposing him to "explosive and deadly conditions." In his capacity as a state representative, Harwood filed legislation that allowed children to sue their parents. In effect, his bill allowed the dead child's estate to reach a settlement with the parents' insurance company. The grieving parents were found negligent but profited handsomely, as did their lawyer. The insurance company's lawyer blasted Harwood's legislation as "a bill put in to assist them in skinning Amica Insurance for $230,000."[5]

Providence Journal reporter Katherine Gregg delved into the legislative records of Harwood and Bramley. She wrote that both had engaged in "cozy, self-serving practices that pervaded the General Assembly for decades before the banking debacle and other recent scandals blew the lid off." But, as she noted, "Harwood, unlike Bramley, sponsored bills that benefitted his own clients. Harwood also championed some of the most controversial pension bills the Assembly considered in the past decade," including the bill that allowed union leaders to buy their way into the state pension system at bargain basement rates.[6]

The RISDIC Investigating Commission had already faulted Harwood's 1985 bill that enlarged the credit unions' mission from "promoting thrift to promoting economic development."[7] That move, among a series of incremental changes in state law, opened the floodgates for the thrifts to make risky commercial loans. Bramley brandished the ethics sword against Harwood, calling for the Ethics Commission to investigate whether his rival had violated conflict-of-interest laws to help his own clients. At a State House news conference, Bramley declared: "His actions fly in the face of the ethics laws, and his statement that his actions were proper then and are proper now demonstrate that Mr. Harwood just doesn't get it."[8]

But ethics charges based on past offenses counted for little in the hard-checking contest for speaker. Caruolo demanded that Bramley concede for the sake of Democratic unity.[9] With Democrats split, fifteen Republican votes could control the outcome. The minority caucus weighed Harwood's ethics against his promise to give them a veto over suspending House rules in the session. Minority Leader Wayne Salisbury told reporters that the practice of shelving the rules had often opened the door for questionable bills to pass.[10]

On January 5, 1993, Gov. Bruce Sundlun was inaugurated for his second term, which would also be Rhode Island's last two-year gubernatorial term. Harwood and Bramley marched side by side in the inaugural procession, followed by Caruolo and Benoit. An hour later representatives convened in their grandiose chamber, where Harwood won the speakership with 60 votes: 45 Democrats and 15 Republicans. He promised to rebuild trust and cooperation. Pundits noted that this was the first time in the state's modern political history that a faction of Democrats had aligned with Republicans to elect a speaker.[11]

George Caruolo ousted Nancy Benoit as majority leader. Harwood appointed Rep. Charles T. Knowles to the coveted post of Judiciary Committee chair, evicting Jeffrey Teitz from his office and from the powerful committee he had chaired for a decade. As a consolation prize, Harwood named Teitz to a newly created post — chief of policy — with no clear description or powers.[12]

"At least I'll have an office," Teitz told me with a smile. "I have no doubt that I'll find worthwhile things to do."

"But will you have any power to do them?" I asked.

"That remains to be seen," said Teitz.

Harwood had won the speakership on promises to ensure a more open leg-islative process, where representatives could expect hearings on their priority bills. "We're going to listen to ideas from everybody," he told reporter Scott MacKay.[13] Paul S. Kelly, the new Senate majority leader, also pledged an open legislative process. "A senator shouldn't have to sell his soul to get his or her bill heard," Kelly told reporters, explicitly rejecting the negotiations and deal making that had been standard under Bevilacqua's leadership.[14]

The Unclassified Pay Plan Board was an obscure vessel in the state's fleet. Often called "the pay board" or by its unpronounceable acronym, the UPPB controlled the salaries of top officials across state government, not to mention hundreds of low-salaried administrative workers. Early in 1993, a rogue wave swamped the ship.

Responsibility for salary scales had begun in the 1950s under a purely ex-ecutive office. In 1973, the General Assembly created the Unclassified Pay Plan Board, which included the director of administration, general treasurer, and budget officer, with chairs of the House and Senate Finance committees as non-voting members. In 1978, while he was speaker of the House, Matthew Smith rammed through a new law that transformed the UPPB: adding a top court administrator to the board, doubling the number of legislators, and letting them all vote.[15] Suddenly, with four of seven votes in the Unclassified Pay Plan Board, state legislative leaders controlled job creation and salaries for about 2,500 "unclassified" appointees at all levels of state government. With this new power over top executive and judicial salaries, they also gained leverage in negotiations with department directors, regulators, and judges.[16]

Matthew Smith had orchestrated these changes, appointed himself to the pay board, and arranged his election as its chairperson. In 1988 he moved from being speaker of the House to administrator of the state court system, and he continued to run the Unclassified Pay Plan Board until December 1992.[17] But his years at the helm ended abruptly when John Harwood and Paul Kelly gained control of their chambers. Each quickly named two new legislators to the UPPB. Harwood appointed Reps. Antonio Pires and Joseph DeLorenzo, while Kelly chose Sens. Charles Fogarty and Charles Walton. Rhode Island's new general treasurer, Nancy Mayer, who had campaigned against Smith's role in RISDIC, occupied a fifth seat. Once all-powerful, Smith found himself suddenly sur-rounded by political opponents who had long chafed under his rule.

The previous summer, when Matthew Smith's power seemed unassailable, he had presided over routine votes that quietly created twenty-two new unclassified jobs, awarded steep mid-year pay raises to thirty-seven favored employees, and slipped his son Andrew into a state job. A prime player in those transactions was

Leo Skenyon, who had managed Bruce Sundlun's 1986 campaign, later served on the governor's staff, and now ran the state's troubled traffic court, which got fourteen of the twenty-two new workers, including Matthew Smith's son. In contrast to 4.5 percent raises that would go to ordinary state workers, Skenyon got 24.5 percent, partly on his promise that service would improve; he seemed unaware that traffic court was speeding toward a crash.[18]

In December 1992, Matthew Smith presided over routine votes that confirmed the summer pay raises and new hires. The pay board also made Andrew Smith's temporary job permanent.

Under state law, actions of the Unclassified Pay Plan Board were merely advisory, since the governor could approve, modify, or reject its recommendations within thirty days. The General Assembly could also reject the UPPB's actions but had never done so.

Shortly after he became speaker, John Harwood demanded that Sundlun block the raises Smith had pushed through. "The actions of the Unclassified Pay Plan Board are not only unreasonable and illogical," the new speaker declared, "they are an affront to every decent citizen." Paul Kelly called the raises "unconscionable." Accordingly Sundlun vetoed the raises but let the new jobs stand.[19]

With his foes controlling the Unclassified Pay Plan Board, Matthew Smith's secret machinations began leaking into public view. Always tenacious in her questions, Kathy Gregg pushed Skenyon to explain the hiring of Andrew Smith. Skenyon admitted hiring the young man but claimed not to have known he was the son of the pay board's chairman, court administrator, and former speaker. "With a name like Smith," Skenyon told her, "it didn't dawn on me."[20]

The next secret revealed a favor Matty Smith had done for his old friend, State Auditor General Anthony Piccirilli. As administrator of the state court system, Smith ignored the fact that Piccirilli's son — also named Anthony Piccirilli — had drug problems and a recent criminal conviction for passing a bad check. He hired the younger Piccirilli and put him in charge of the court system's fund for victim restitution. An alert auditor soon discovered $4,200 missing from the restitution fund, but instead of firing the young Piccirilli and calling the police, Smith covered it up. Two cashiers' checks — an untraceable repayment totaling $4,224.50 — were mysteriously deposited in the restitution account.

When confronted by investigative reporters John Sullivan and Dean Starkman, Smith admitted that he had approved the replenishments. He explained that the young man had a substance abuse problem and that state personnel policy prevented his being arrested for the crime. "That was my interpretation of our drug policy," Smith told the reporters. Then, in a classic use of passive voice, he added: "The decision was made to get him some help first — to save an employee's life."[21]

Smith's cover-up resonated with the loyalty and compassion that undergirded his political success. Quiet favors were the coin of his realm. Once exposed, Smith claimed absolution under ordinary human decency. "Anyone who looks at this objectively," Smith told reporter Scott MacKay, "will understand the steps I took and exactly why I took them."[22]

While questions of restitution and cover-up sizzled, secret pension deals suddenly burst into headlines. Many problem bills had been enacted while Smith was speaker of the House. One allowed a state representative's widow to collect for three legislative sessions after her husband died; another let Smith's sister, Rose Reynolds, buy pension credits for a ten-year maternity leave from teaching; others permitted purchases of public pension credits for years of teaching at parochial schools. Katherine Gregg reported that over the previous two decades, 174 favored people had been allowed to invest $721,309 that would return almost four million dollars in pension benefits.[23]

No matter how outrageous and costly, those special pension bills had been legally enacted, and Smith could not be prosecuted for greasing their passage. Nor could he be punished for forming a real estate partnership with his close friend, Chief Justice Thomas F. Fay. With three other partners, Smith and Fay had constructed a lawyer-friendly office complex only a half-mile from property the state was pondering for a new regional courthouse. When questioned by a reporter, Smith insisted that the proposed courthouse was years from completion and would not have "any direct effect" on the offices he and Fay owned nearby.[24] Chief Justice Fay denied any conflict: "I didn't lose any constitutional rights to make an investment when I became a judge."[25]

Rhode Island's new attorney general, Jeffrey B. Pine, had no grounds to prosecute the special pensions or the well-situated office building, but he ordered the state police to investigate young Anthony Piccirilli's alleged theft and Smith's obvious cover-up. Pine made an extraordinary public announcement that he would convene a statewide grand jury, but skeptics wondered whether anything would come of his probe. Over the years, Smith had maneuvered deals involving conflicts of interest and favoritism that had cost taxpayers millions. Like escape artist Harry Houdini, he seemed to slip out of the most cleverly devised entanglements. He offered to resign but stayed on, apparently invincible.

Rhode Island was one of only three states, along with South Carolina and Virginia, where lawmakers still chose justices of the Supreme Court. The Royal Charter of 1663 granted the General Assembly vast powers, including the authority to name judges. For 330 years lawmakers had elevated every justice who sat on the state's Supreme Court. Under a process called "the Grand Committee," senators convened with representatives to elect each new justice. In 1935, victorious Democrats had used the Grand Committee process to sack the entire Supreme Court, electing five new justices who affirmed their political coup.

In September 1992, Supreme Court Justice Thomas F. Kelleher retired. As their predecessors had for three centuries, Joseph DeAngelis and John Bevilacqua summoned lawmakers to the State House to elect a new justice "in Grand Committee." But the RISDIC tsunami had swept away business as usual. In their separate chambers, lawmakers debated whether the momentous choice of a new justice should wait until after the November election. Senators split evenly over going into Grand Committee: eighteen in favor and an equal number opposed. Lt. Gov. Roger N. Begin, cast a tie-breaking vote to fill the vacancy, but it made no difference.[26] Across the rotunda, representatives in the House voted to adjourn, leaving the post unfilled. Then, in January 1993, the prospect of a second vacancy arose. Justice Joseph R. Weisberger, already seventy-three, announced that he would retire and take a less demanding position with the U.S. Circuit Court of Appeals.

These two looming vacancies galvanized an odd coalition. Despite differences in their memberships and missions, the Rhode Island Bar Association and Common Cause had been trying for years to wring politics out of judicial selection. Both organizations favored a process developed fifty years earlier in Missouri where, during the Great Depression, reformers had pioneered a process they called "merit selection of judges." Fed up with corrupt judicial elections, Missourians had proposed a nonpartisan judicial nominating commission to evaluate applicants for judgeships. The panel would select three highly qualified candidates for each vacancy and present these names to the governor, who was required to appoint from that list. In 1940, a coalition of reform groups mounted a petition drive to place a constitutional amendment on Missouri's statewide ballot. Voters amended the state's Constitution. Although lawmakers tried to rescind merit selection and restore judicial elections, an overwhelming majority of Missouri voters held their ground.[27]

During the next half-century, voters in thirty-four other states adopted variations of what became known as "the Missouri Plan." No state that adopted merit selection went back to its earlier process for picking judges.

Over several years, Rhode Island's Bar Association and Common Cause had each filed proposals for a similar way of selecting of Rhode Island judges. Few pieces of legislation were less welcome in the General Assembly. Legislative committees stonewalled merit selection bills, and newspapers gave them almost no ink. Without a voter initiative process, Rhode Islanders had no way to go around the General Assembly, as Missourians had done in 1940. However, the prospect that the Grand Committee would elect two new Supreme Court justices brought the Bar Association and Common Cause together to try again. The League of Women Voters and Operation Clean Sweep joined the effort.

The booming courtroom voice of attorney Alan Flink filled our drab Common Cause office. Flink had just finished his term as Bar Association president. "To tell the truth," he intoned, "most lawyers think promoting merit selection is a fool's errand, but respectfully I disagree. With enough pressure, the entire edifice of Grand Committee elections could keel over."

Charlie Silverman, now the leader of Operation Clean Sweep, agreed with the concept of merit selection but had his doubts. "John Harwood and Paul Kelly are consolidating control of their chambers. Won't they just cling to the Grand Committee?"

"They may try," Flink said, "but we should push back hard and demand that they fix the process."

Sponsors had already introduced bills drafted by the Bar Association and Common Cause.[28] Around the table, we studied them and highlighted our common ground. Both organizations wanted a judicial nominating commission that would be appointed by the governor. The Bar Association would nominate lawyers; legislative leaders would propose non-lawyers. No current officeholders or recent political candidates would be allowed on the panel.

Flink smiled mischievously. "The General Assembly leadership won't like having the Bar Association nominate commissioners."

"In all honesty," said Mary Alyce Gasbarro, now president of the state's League of Women Voters, "the League hasn't taken a position on whether the Bar Association should name people to the nominating commission. But we agree absolutely on keeping commissioners at arm's length from politics."

Unlike the closed-door confidentiality of Missouri's commission, all agreed that Rhode Island's judicial nominating process must be transparent and public. Any lawyer should be able to apply for any judgeship. The judicial nominating commission should interview candidates in public session. We all favored language from the American Judicature Society that the commission should present from three to five "highly qualified" candidates for each judicial vacancy.[29] The governor should receive the list, interview the candidates, and appoint one person. As in the federal system, the Senate should then confirm or reject that candidate.

Most important, we agreed the new process should require every judicial candidate in Rhode Island — from the Traffic Tribunal to the Supreme Court — to undergo merit selection.

"I love this idea," Charlie Silverman said, "but I'm a realist. I just don't see how we get it done."

Tom Banchoff, a math professor from Brown University, now chaired the Common Cause judicial reform committee. "We need to look for variables that could make this situation break our way," he said.

"What variables?" Silverman asked.

"I'm not sure," said Banchoff. "Think of the RISDIC scandal, the whole list of reforms enacted in 1992, and the fact that DeAngelis and Bevilacqua couldn't persuade their troops to fill the Kelleher vacancy. These seem like disparate events, but any of these could become catalysts for bigger changes. We may think that because things happened a certain way last week, we'll see similar results tomorrow. In reality, small variations in one variable may produce dramatically different results."

In March 1993, I watched from a gallery as the fifty state senators traipsed into the House chamber and filled seats along the walls. Roughly a hundred representatives settled themselves behind their hardwood desks in curved rows. A clerk read aloud the announcement of Grand Committee, then called the roll.

George Caruolo rose to his feet at his desk near the front. Tethered by a microphone cord, he moved to adopt rules for the Grand Committee. "Under the rules we're proposing," he said with a grin, "any member of the General Assembly is welcome to place any name in nomination. The rules allow ten-minute nominating speeches and two-minute seconding statements." He explained that all nominations would go to a joint meeting of the House and Senate judiciary committees. "Let's be clear," Caruolo continued, "these rules give everyone an opportunity to speak, but our aim is to keep the process positive and dignified. If you wish to praise or criticize any of the candidates, the proper forum will be in the joint hearing of the judiciary committees."

Caruolo batted away several proposed amendments and won approval of the Grand Committee rules in a droning roll call vote.

Nominating speeches began with Jack Revens endorsing Family Court Judge Raymond E. Shawcross, who had been counsel to the House leadership before he swung through the revolving door and onto the court. Harwood ally Antonio J. Pires nominated Superior Court Judge John P. Bourcier, whose moniker was "Maximum John" for the tough sentences he meted out.

After four years of being isolated and ignored by the House leadership under DeAngelis, Rep. Patrick J. Kennedy had come into his own with Harwood. On his feet with a microphone, he nominated a former senator, Victoria Santopietro Lederberg, clearly relishing the honor of naming her. The odds among lobbyists were that she was Harwood's pick.[30]

Rep. Paul Sherlock nominated Peter J. McGinn, a lobbyist for Fleet Bank, Brown University, Blue Cross Blue Shield, and Anheuser-Busch. McGinn had gone gray before his time and moved in wraithlike silence through crowds of lobbyists, seldom making small talk. Another Harwood ally, Vincent J. Mesolella Jr., the deputy House majority whip, rose to nominate Superior Court Judge Vincent A. Ragosta. A lobbyist at my shoulder in the gallery whispered that Ragosta was Mesolella's cousin. "Ragosta has no chance," the lobbyist whispered. "Vinny's just honoring him."

Two women lawmakers, Family Court Judge Pamela M. Mactaz and District Court Judge Patricia D. Moore, were nominated for the high court. The lobbyist beside me said confidently that neither was a real contender. Next Rep. Linda Kushner rose at her desk to nominate Lauren Jones. Less than a year had passed since Jones argued Common Cause's "friend of the court" brief before the Supreme Court. Jones loved legal ideas, wrote with elegant clarity, and seemed not to fear retaliation. I admired him, but doubted that legislators would elevate a lawyer whose arguments had clipped their authority to write ethics rules.

Other nominations followed, and the Grand Committee adjourned amid a hubbub of talk and handshaking in the aisles. In the hallway afterward, Rep. Frank Gaschen, slim and prematurely graying, vented to me in a whisper. "Can you believe they're pushing Lederberg? Can you imagine? They're going to ram her through despite her lack of credentials!"

"Why?"

Gaschen guffawed. "Because she shifted a few votes that made Harwood speaker. I wouldn't mind if she were even remotely qualified, but she's not." Gaschen reiterated his complaint to reporters.

Others recognized Lederberg's political clout but thought her unqualified. Superior Court Judge Thomas H. Needham called reporters to his courtroom. He affirmed her as a psychology professor at Rhode Island College and "one of our very distinguished educators." But, Needham groused, she had never tried a case, never practiced law, and never solicited clients. "If I were a candidate today," Needham declared, "I would be offended." Bruce Sundlun joined the chorus. "Vicki, whom I know personally and like, has no experience in the court system. That lack of experience is not fair to the litigants; it is not fair to the other members of the court." He declared that a seat on the Supreme Court was not "an academic position."[31]

Lederberg fired back, insisting to the *Providence Journal* that she was the "best qualified" of all the candidates. She acknowledged never trying a case before a judge or jury but had presided in Providence Municipal Court. "Judge Needham is responding to the fact that I am not a clone of the judges on the Supreme Court," Lederberg said. "I'm not one of the mold. I think that's an advantage. I'm a very independent-minded person. I make my own decisions. That has often gotten me into trouble."

Presiding Justice Joseph F. Rodgers Jr. of the Superior Court shocked many by firing a salvo. "She's never appeared before the Supreme, Superior, Family, District Court or Workers' Compensation Court," Rodgers announced in a thick Rhode Island accent. "It is preposterous to say that she is now qualified to sit on the Supreme Court." Rodgers also made light of her service with two other part-time judges on the Providence Municipal Court: "Each sits one out of every three weeks. They handle overtime parking, runaway dogs, public intoxication, and disorderly conduct cases."[32]

A phalanx of women mounted a press conference on the courthouse steps to protest these unprecedented attacks by male judges. At a joint hearing of the House and Senate judiciary committees, Patrick Kennedy voiced raw indignation toward Lederberg's critics: "I find it interesting that her detractors overlook that she was a state legislator. She was the original sponsor of our Open Meetings Law and our Conflict of Interest Law. Are they against her because she was an independent voice? Is it because she doesn't go along to get along? Is it because she is not a member of the old boy network?"

For three hours, a parade of influential witnesses defended Lederberg: the dean of the new law school at Roger Williams University, a former Providence police chief, the chief judge of the Providence Municipal Court, a retired *Providence Journal* editorial writer, and former Atty. Gen. Dennis J. Roberts II. One lone lawyer, Matthew Callaghan, urged the legislators to reject Lederberg's nomination. "I have some questions about someone who practices law part time," he said, adding that she was not even listed as an attorney "in the White Pages or Yellow Pages."

Finally, Victoria Lederberg spoke for herself. A petite woman with close-cropped hair, she greeted the combined judiciary committees like old friends. Without sounding defensive or haughty, she insisted quietly that she possessed the qualifications, judicial temperament, and demeanor to handle cases that come before the Supreme Court.

"I am very much in the camp of the reformers," she said, calmly reprising Kennedy's points about her role in passage of open government and ethics legislation. She noted that she had spent fourteen years in the General Assembly writing laws and was ready to interpret laws on the Supreme Court. "I'm someone who comes in from outside the system," she continued. "I know I'm nontraditional, but I think that's a great strength. I think that would be good for the system. And I know I can do the job."[33]

As the furor over Lederberg's nomination continued, the Rhode Island Bar Association also weighed in on Judge John Bourcier. Bruce Pollock, the group's president, reported a survey sent to four thousand lawyers and answered by six hundred. The query had asked attorneys to rate the candidates on criteria for judicial selection established by the American Judicature Society: impartiality, judicial temperament, industry, integrity, professional skills, and overall rating. Pollock announced that 95 percent of those who said they knew Bourcier rated him as "qualified" or "highly qualified." Through Pollock the Bar Association also rejected the charge of bias against a female candidate, noting that lawyers gave Family Court Judge Pamela M. Mactaz an overall rating of 87 percent and District Court Judge Patricia Moore 84 percent. Lederberg, he said, was second from the bottom, with an overall rating of 29 percent. He added that although the survey was not scientific, he believed it fairly reflected the opinions of Rhode Island attorneys. [34]

John Harwood never announced his pick for the Supreme Court vacancy, but it was rumored around the State House that he would vote for Lederberg. The hallways teemed with reasons for Harwood's apparent choice. Several representatives affirmed confidentially what Frank Gaschen had declared openly:

in the recent fight to become House speaker, Lederberg had swung crucial votes to Harwood.

On the day the Grand Committee assembled to vote, I was in Washington for a Common Cause conference. After dinner and an evening session, I found the phone in my hotel room blinking. Tom Banchoff, who chaired our judicial reform committee, had left a message. "No need to call back," he said. "I just thought you would want to know that the Grand Committee elected Victoria Lederberg to the Supreme Court this afternoon." All fifty senators and one hundred reps had been present. Lederberg won on the second ballot. "You won't be surprised," Banchoff added, "that Harwood and his leadership team all voted for her. I think this bizarre process reinforces our case for merit selection."

Editorial writers slammed the Grand Committee. "There's a better way," the *Providence Journal* declared. But the editors still preferred direct gubernatorial appointment to merit selection. Meanwhile the *Woonsocket Call* blasted the Grand Committee for producing a high court where all five members were former legislators, declaring flatly: "The system does not work, and won't as long as politicians are so heavily involved." The *Call* also described the Common Cause proposal for an independent commission and cited the support of all the state's reform groups.[35]

From the southern end of Rhode Island, the *Newport Daily News* opined, "It takes political connections to become a judge in Rhode Island." Its editors then scorned both the Grand Committee process and the judicial screening panel Sundlun had appointed, saying, "Decisions are made in back rooms as political rewards. For obvious reasons, we are skeptical."[36]

The *Providence Phoenix*, a free weekly, published a feature that explored the permutations of judicial selection. Reporter Steven Stycos contrasted the proposals put forward by Gov. Sundlun and Common Cause. Sundlun, who had called for a panel comprised entirely of lawyers, told Stycos he had made a mistake in putting two women who were not lawyers — Sister Claire Dugan and Urban League Executive Director B. Jae Clanton — on the panel that screened candidates for the lower courts. He objected that the women had relied on their knowledge of social issues rather than on trial experience and other legal qualifications.[37]

Dugan, a tiny white-haired nun, fired back that judges needed a social conscience. "I was there," she insisted, "to represent the poor, because they get the raw end of the justice system."

In the midst of touting his judicial appointments, Sundlun told Stycos that the Senate had blocked four of his judicial appointments because he refused to appoint any lawmakers to the bench. I asked Sheldon Whitehouse, Sundlun's policy director, about that. "The tradition," Whitehouse replied, "has been that the governor, speaker, and Senate majority leader took turns picking judges — one for you, one for me, one for him. Our screening committee violated that protocol by refusing to interview legislators."

Although many knew about that unspoken protocol, Whitehouse asked me not to name him as my source, at least for the time being. He continued: "The judicial system has always been Valhalla for lawmakers. You go there and play in Elysian Fields. When Bruce wouldn't go along — in fact, when he took all four of those appointments — Bevilacqua was mightily pissed."[38] In fact Bevilacqua had refused to confirm Sundlun's four judges, and Sundlun withdrew them, only to name them later as recess appointments. When Paul Kelly became majority leader, the Senate quietly confirmed them.

Whitehouse had also helped me understand why Sundlun rejected the central feature of our merit selection process. He did not want to be stuck with a short list of only three to five candidates for each vacancy. His quasi-official panel had taken a tough stand, and Sundlun wanted a committee that would only rank candidates as qualified, highly qualified, or not qualified. He demanded freedom to choose from a large pool of candidates.

On her radio talk show, Arlene Violet also dismissed Sundlun's call for a screening panel composed entirely of lawyers, but she redirected the discussion, arguing that Rhode Island should join the thirty-nine states that elected at least some of their judges.

Two weeks after Lederberg's election in Grand Committee, I bumped into House Majority Leader George Caruolo. I had asked several times for a meeting with him and Harwood to talk about judicial selection. "Nobody calls me back," I groused.

"Nothing personal," Caruolo said. "We've been busy. We haven't had a minute to focus on it."

"So when can we sit down with you and the speaker?"

"When you figure out how to fit the Grand Committee into your scheme. Otherwise we're not going to touch it."

"Sounds non-negotiable," I said.

Caruolo smiled broadly. "You got that right."

Petitioning Government
1993

"I'D LIKE YOUR SUPPORT for our SLAPP suit legislation," ACLU Director Steven Brown said on the phone early in 1993. "SLAPP is an acronym," he explained, "for Strategic Litigation Against Public Participation. It means that ordinary people get 'slapped' for exercising their First Amendment right to petition government for the redress of grievances." The bill to counter SLAPP-suits had died in the two previous legislative sessions. We agreed to talk that afternoon at the State House.

Steve Brown had led the ACLU's Rhode Island affiliate long before I came to Common Cause. Our organizations took opposite sides on some issues but worked together on others. We had pushed together to simplify voter registration but crossed swords over ethics and campaign finance reforms. Common Cause wanted disclosure by campaign donors, while the ACLU resisted any revelations that might invade givers' personal privacy. The ACLU had filed suit in U.S. District Court to overturn sections of the 1992 Comprehensive Campaign Finance Law, and Judge Raymond J. Pettine overturned several minor provisions.[1] Despite frequent public disputes, our differences never became personal.

In a file of newspaper clippings I found accounts of lawsuits filed by a former candidate for Congress. In 1990, Charles H. Gifford III had run for Congress in the 2nd District but lost the Democratic primary to Jack Reed, then a state senator. After RISDIC's collapse in 1991, state bank examiners reported that Gifford had received favored treatment from the Davisville Credit Union. He had borrowed $2.6 million — $600,000 more than the legal limit. He sued two North Kingstown women — Isabel Bergeron and Nancy Hsu Fleming — who blamed him publicly for contributing to the RISDIC crisis. Claiming that their remarks were "willful, wanton, and malicious," he sought punitive damages.

Gifford and two business partners[2] ran a fifteen-acre landfill that had prompted numerous complaints over strange odors that wafted through nearby neighborhoods. The North Kingstown *Standard-Times* published a story in which neighbors charged that samples of water from test wells around the dump had been "doctored." Gifford demanded a retraction, but when the paper refused, Gifford and his partners sued. They filed a second suit against Nancy Hsu Fleming, who had written to the state Department of Environmental Management (DEM) that toxic chemicals from what she called "their dump" were leaching into nearby wells.[3]

Providence Journal reporter Peter Lord described other Rhode Island cases that appeared to be SLAPP suits. In one instance an environmental group in Warwick had tried to block plans to bulldoze towering pine trees for development. Neighborhood leaders raised $20,000 for lawyers but lost in court. The project went forward, and the developer, Hugh A. Fisher, sued the local activists for $500,000, claiming the environmental group "never had a case." He called their tactics "legal sleaze" and "environmental terrorism." He insisted that the activists had cost him half a million dollars, and he wanted to be made whole.[4]

Other retaliatory lawsuits sprouted. In Narragansett, homeowners opposed the renewal of a liquor license at a nightclub renowned for rowdy parties. The club owner sued, claiming financial harm. In Burrillville, when an activist warned the town council against a proposed harness track, the promoter sued.[5]

Steve Brown and I met in a nook between soaring marble columns. He plopped a thick folder full of bills on the balustrade. With our backs to the throng of other lobbyists, he talked about how Nancy Hsu Fleming personified the need to counter SLAPP suits. "She got her facts right, and she petitioned DEM to protect the public from serious hazards. For doing her civic duty, she got slapped." He handed me a faxed letter from Fleming to DEM director Louise Durfee. It claimed that Gifford's dump contained construction debris and other hazardous waste, that toxic contaminants had seeped into monitoring wells, that the EPA was considering a Superfund designation, and that the owners had resisted DEM's efforts to regulate their activities.

Brown said California and Washington State had already enacted laws to blunt the use of SLAPP suits, and he hoped Rhode Island would do the same. He pointed to the section of the bill on legislative findings: "There has been a disturbing increase in lawsuits brought primarily to chill the valid exercise of constitutional rights of freedom of speech and petition for the redress of grievances."[6] The text specified that anyone sued while exercising the "right of petition or of free speech under the U.S. or Rhode Island constitutions in connection with a matter of public concern" could file a motion to have that suit summarily dismissed. A court could then delay the SLAPP suit or throw it out entirely.

"What we need to do," he said, "is shift the burden of proof from those who petition government to those who try to silence them. This bill would grant the petitioner who gets slapped what we call 'conditional immunity' against libel and slander suits. That means that a SLAPP suit can't stick if the petitioner has been trying in good faith to have government act in the public interest."

Although I had never met Nancy Hsu Fleming, a Common Cause recruiting poster came to mind, and I described it to Brown. People in work clothes glared at the camera. One word in bold type called them "troublemakers."

Brown laughed. "That's Nancy Hsu, all right."

I promised to take the issue to our board. After he left, I sorted through the bill's dry legal algebra as radiant sunshine spread across the fluted marble columns. Players became the "moving party" or the "responding party." All were entangled in what the bill called "claims, counterclaims, or cross-claims." Missing from the verbiage on paper was the adrenalin rush of waking up terrified in the dark of night. How could any ordinary person raise enough to pay lawyers for a protracted court battle?

Nancy Hsu Fleming became a perfect icon for the fight against SLAPP suits. She had been raised in Taiwan under brutal martial law that lingered after the death of President Chiang Kai-shek. At the Taipei American School she developed a flawless command of English. She went to college in San Francisco, where she met and married a Vietnam War veteran named Christopher Fleming. Like many immigrants who escape repressive regimes, she cherished the U.S. Constitution and was mystified when Americans took it lightly. "Gifford's lawsuit scared us," she told me over the phone. "But I went from scared to angry. That man was trying to take away my constitutional right to petition the government for the redress of grievances."

Unknown to me, Nancy Hsu and Christopher Fleming were already members of Common Cause. She arrived early for our board meeting, petite and graceful with a resonant voice. I helped her mount scientific maps imprinted with the EPA's logo on one wall.

With precise strokes, she oriented board members from where Dry Bridge Road crossed over the Amtrak main line. "Here's the dump," she explained, "and here's where families live. These dots show test wells that the EPA drilled. This shading marks what hydrologists call 'the plume,' the flow of underground water in the aquifer that feeds neighborhood wells." The EPA had documented excessive levels of lead, cadmium, and DEHP, a chemical used in the manufacture of plastics. "What troubled me," she said, "was a long history of citizen complaints about midnight dumping, chemical odors, and all the rest. But DEM did nothing. They didn't close the dump. They didn't even issue a citation."[7]

Fleming said she had written to the Department of Environmental Management: "Besides polluting our aquifer, I specified the kinds of solid wastes that were being dumped, including thousands of old railroad ties treated with creosote and mountains of construction debris. The EPA was in the process of designating the dump as a Superfund site. I reminded the DEM that Mr. Gifford and his partners had resisted every effort to regulate their operation."

Her contralto voice had the warm timbre of a bassoon. "Before DEM could even respond, I started getting letters from Mr. Gifford's lawyers. They charged that I was 'engendering unjustified concern about the safety of their operations' and that I was 'jeopardizing their license.' They demanded legal proof or a retraction. They threatened a lawsuit."

Her voice rose. "How could I retract the facts? If I had retracted, I would have been lying. Instead, I wrote back to Mr. Gifford's lawyers: 'The United States Constitution grants me the right to petition government. In this instance, I am petitioning state government to close and clean up your client's dump.'"

The SLAPP suit came quickly, charging that she had made "defamatory statements." Gifford's lawyers wrote: "Her conduct clearly has been designed to malign the plaintiffs and generate public opinion adverse to them and the facility." The suit demanded an award of compensatory and punitive damages, as well as court costs with interest.

Fleming paused to let her story sink in. "Can you imagine how it feels when people with political power and lots of money and teams of lawyers come after you? Chris and I thought we would have to mortgage our home to pay a lawyer. What a relief when the ACLU agreed to take our case."

After her presentation, Don Elbert, a lawyer who now chaired our ethics committee, described SLAPP suits as an unsavory fad among lawyers. "I'm not an expert," he said, "but it's clear that they're wreaking havoc across the country, suing activists who have done nothing more than raise concerns, as Nancy has tried to do."

He explained that most retaliatory lawsuits would fail if they went to trial, but they seldom did. "Unfortunately, many people without Nancy's courage simply give up the fight. When that happens, the SLAPP suit serves its purpose." Then Elbert walked our board through the bill's intricate language. "In a word, this bill sets up a legal procedure which allows the target of a SLAPP suit to go to Superior Court and seek its dismissal through a declaratory judgment."

As sensible as that seemed, the bill had run into a buzz saw of opposition in 1991 and 1992. "They buried it in each of the last two years," Elbert said. "Our committee recommends that Common Cause Rhode Island declare our support and help secure passage this year."

Elbert and his committee had done their homework. The board voted unanimously to go forward.[8]

CHARLIE SILVERMAN, now the leader of Operation Clean Sweep, phoned to seek support for voter initiative. He knew Common Cause had supported the concept, often called "Initiative and Referendum," in the mid-1980s. He hoped we would again.

"That was before my time," I said. During months that we had worked together on merit selection of judges, I had developed an abiding appreciation of this short, bald man who made his living as an illustrator, drawing exquisite shorebirds, sailboats, and lighthouses. He feared no one, and his reformist passion won grudging respect even from hardened politicians. I promised to do some research and call him back.

The right to petition government has deep roots in English common law. The First Amendment of the Constitution forbade Congress — and by extension any part of government — from interfering with religious practice, free speech, freedom of the press, the right of assembly, and the right to petition government for the redress of grievances.

I had heard of voter initiatives in other states but knew virtually nothing about the process itself. In our files, I found a printed report on initiative and referendum that Common Cause had produced for the 1986 Constitutional Convention.[9] Marilyn Hines and Mollie Gibbons described a process that allowed citizens to place questions directly on the ballot by collecting signatures rather than by lobbying state legislators. They wrote that one Swiss canton had allowed citizens to petition for laws since 1309, and nineteenth-century American progressives had adapted the process. During the 1890s, the Populist Party embraced voter initiative, and South Dakotans approved a constitutional amendment in 1898.[10] Over the next twenty years, eighteen additional states amended their constitutions to allow citizens to initiate laws or constitutional amendments.[11] Then, for forty years, no state approved the voter initiative process.

Alaska became a state in 1959 and included voter initiative in its constitution. Between 1968 and 1992, four other states — Wyoming, Illinois, Florida, and Mississippi — amended their constitutions to permit initiatives. Most of the states where voter initiative took root lay west of the Appalachian Mountains, while along the East Coast only Maine, Massachusetts, and Florida practiced what many called "direct democracy."

Common Cause had hoped Rhode Island would join the movement. As executive director in the mid-1980s, Marilyn Hines distributed copies of her report and lobbied delegates at the 1986 Constitutional Convention to place voter initiative on the ballot, but the issue proved divisive. The AFL-CIO and the business-backed Rhode Island Public Expenditure Council (RIPEC) both warned convention delegates about the way that financial interests had fueled initiatives in other states, such as California's Proposition 13 against increases in property taxes, enacted in 1978. Taxpayer groups, meanwhile, argued that only voter initiative could impose meaningful restrictions on burgeoning taxes in Rhode Island. Convention president Keven A. McKenna and others close to House Speaker Matthew Smith insisted that initiative petitions must not be allowed to alter the taxing or budgeting authority of the General Assembly.[12]

A spectrum of grassroots groups ranging from the ACLU to Ecology Action and the League of Women Voters had opposed any restrictions on issues that initiatives could address. Delegates narrowly backed a version that would forbid initiatives aimed at changing the state's tax system or restricting its budget.[13] Common Cause reluctantly supported what it saw as a flawed proposal.[14] By a narrow margin voters rejected the 1986 voter initiative question.

An entirely different issue gave me pause. Conservative Christian groups in Colorado had recently used voter initiative to write an anti-gay amendment into that state's constitution. Between 1977 and 1991, the cities of Aspen, Boulder, and Denver had passed ordinances that banned discrimination against gays and lesbians in education, housing, and employment. Anti-gay crusaders collected enough signatures, and 53 percent of state voters barred the state or any of its municipalities from protecting gay rights of any kind. A Colorado district court judge blocked enforcement on the ground that the amendment violated the Equal Protection Clause of the Fourteenth Amendment.[15] No one knew how the nation's highest court might rule if the case ever got that far.

I phoned Charlie Silverman to ask what he thought.

"We have no position on gay rights," he replied. "That's not our issue in any way."

I understood. "But your legislation doesn't protect against what happened in Colorado."

"Our bill is exactly what Common Cause supported in 1986."

"It is," I agreed. "But times have changed. What if anti-gay groups tried to use voter initiative against minorities in Rhode Island?"

"I couldn't support that," Silverman said.

"So would Operation Clean Sweep support modifying the text to prevent any Rhode Island initiative from attempting to roll back civil rights, as they did in Colorado?"

"That's not my decision alone," he said. "But it's worth considering."

I mentioned a second problem that the current legislation did not address. Several banks had challenged a Massachusetts law that barred them from spending to influence voters on ballot questions. In 1978, the U.S. Supreme Court ruled that corporations — like individual citizens — were entitled to express their views on state constitutional amendments. The decision, *First National Bank v. Bellotti*, allowed corporations to spend unlimited amounts on ballot questions.[16]

Judge Raymond J. Pettine had cited *Bellotti* in blocking part of our 1992 Comprehensive Campaign Finance Law that barred corporations from contributing to ballot campaigns.[17] I told Silverman that those related federal decisions could open the floodgates for unlimited corporate spending on Rhode Island ballot questions.

Silverman pondered this. "You mean there's no way to stop big corporations and unions from spending whatever they please?"

"For all practical purposes," I said, "these rulings made corporate spending legal and limits on spending unconstitutional." Before passage of the 1992 Campaign Finance Law, Alan Hassenfeld had spent $50,000 to produce three campaign commercials for four-year terms, and I knew that several banks and chambers of commerce had paid to broadcast the ads.

"And you got sixty percent of the vote," Silverman said. "Isn't it strange that a reform intended to counter corporate interests a century ago could now be overwhelmed by big money?"

The director of California Common Cause had told us that corporate interests were investing in initiative campaigns rather than traditional lobbying. I told Silverman about armies of paid signature-gatherers deployed to resemble grassroots groups.

"I've heard about that," Silverman agreed. "They call it 'Astroturf.'"

I suggested stringent financial disclosure rules for ballot questions. We would not stop moneyed interests from hiding behind phony front groups, but we might force them to disclose.

There was a third problem. Initiative propositions in California had become too long and complicated for voters to understand. In 1988 and 1990, a dozen propositions on California ballots had run more than five thousand words each.

"And not simple words," he agreed. "Complicated legal gibberish."

I described a California requirement that the attorney general provide a brief, nonpartisan summary. Even with that, I said, details often overwhelmed voters.

Ever the optimist, Silverman suggested that we develop a list of changes to the bill. "We want something that's going to work, and we want Common Cause on board again."

Over several weeks in the fall of 1993, we drafted specific wording to lessen opportunities for abuse and presented them to our boards. We added language to block any initiative that might undercut civil rights or liberties. Any individual or group that felt their rights were at risk would have automatic standing to ask a Superior Court judge to block the signature-gathering from going forward.[18] Those who gathered signatures, furthermore, must be registered Rhode Island voters and wear badges that gave their names. Solicitors' badges must include bold labels in block capitals indicating a VOLUNTEER CIRCULATOR or a PAID CIRCULATOR. To avoid the problem of lengthy and complex questions, we would require that the text of the initiative be no longer than 125 words.

Even with these changes, Common Cause board members were less support-ive of voter initiative than their predecessors had been in 1986. Greta Abbott, who chaired the government reform committee, summarized the organization's historic support and recent developments. "In states with voter initiative," she said, "citizens groups often have to spend enormous amounts fighting bad ini-tiatives rather than promoting positive changes."[19]

Mike Smith, now vice president of the board, said he thought voter initiative would again face concerted opposition from labor, business, and civil rights groups, not to mention legislators themselves. "There's virtually no chance that the General Assembly will agree to put voter initiative on the ballot," he said. "And frankly — with some of the abuses we've seen in other states — I'm not sure we should pour a lot of political capital into a fight we won't win. I suggest that if we support voter initiative, we should not make it a priority."

Our victories in 1992 had propelled board president Cathy Speer onto the Common Cause national governing board. "Almost every time I go to Wash-ington," she said, "people from other states talk about problems with voter initiatives. But in the next breath, they say it's a tool they'd never want to lose." Speer said she was of two minds about supporting voter initiative.

Without passion or disagreement, Common Cause Rhode Island reaffirmed its previous support for voter initiative and referendum — provided the amend-ment establishing the process included the specific prohibitions we had dis-cussed. No one in the room suggested that this vote might prove contentious or bring fierce struggles in years to come.

Nancy Hsu Fleming personified the campaign against SLAPP suits. Although English was her second language, she vividly evoked constitutional principles. She enjoyed reporters, and they warmed to her. Charles Gifford, by contrast, was aloof and hid behind his lawyers. He had money and power, but his behavior made him seem callous.

Women legislators also championed Fleming's cause. North Kingstown Rep. Suzanne M. Henseler and Providence Sen. Myrth York, both Democrats, spon-sored the anti-SLAPP legislation in their chambers. Henseler argued that law enforcement depended on citizen complaints: "The little guy with pertinent information stands no chance against large companies with the financial where-withal to threaten or pursue legal action."[20]

When Gifford's SLAPP suit advanced to Superior Court, Atty. Gen. Jeffrey Pine moved to have it dismissed. "The threat of such a lawsuit tends to inhibit public participation," Pine declared, "and thereby limits the flow of information from citizens to their elected officials."[21] His 25-page *amicus* brief added little to the legal discussion, but the weight of his office balanced the scales against Gifford's SLAPP suit.

Every new story summarized Fleming's case for readers who might have missed earlier accounts. "It's not me alone they're attacking," she told one reporter. "It's really a very basic right that we're all entitled to."[22] The House had passed SLAPP suit bills in both 1991 and 1992, but the Senate refrained. In 1993, with leadership changes in both chambers, the legislation passed easily in the Senate but nearly died in the House. John Harwood had resisted passage in previous years. One of Harwood's most enthusiastic supporters was Rep. Vincent J. Mesolella, a developer renowned for his hard-fisted tactics. Mesolella had railed against local groups that opposed his projects, claiming they engaged in emotional arguments and "failed to get their facts straight."[23]

Rep. Charles T. Knowles, a Narragansett lawyer who had supported earlier iterations of the anti- SLAPP bill, now chaired the House Judiciary Committee at Harwood's behest, and his position shifted. He seemed reluctant about the very legislation he had pushed in two prior legislative sessions. From his end of the committee's long oak table, he treated Nancy Hsu Fleming with elaborate courtesy but challenged my testimony. "What bothers me with all this gobble-dygook about these 'civil claims, counterclaims, or cross-claims against said party' based on a claimed 'right of petition or free speech' is just this: What if some disgruntled citizen is just engaging in character assassination? What if their real goal is just stalling a project to death?"

"Respectfully, Mr. Chairman," I replied. "That wasn't the case when these dump owners filed their SLAPP suit against Nancy Hsu Fleming. You've seen her maps. . . ."

"But suppose it was? Just suppose that — instead of being as pure as the driven snow — she just didn't like the owners of the landfill? Suppose she made herself a royal pain in the posterior for no purpose but to drive them out of business?"

I smiled down the long table at him. "We think a judge would read the law and say: 'Look, the preponderance of the evidence doesn't satisfy me that her petitioning is only a stall.'"

"But without criteria written into the law how can a judge predict the petitioner's motivation?" Knowles demanded.

The bill said nothing about motivation. I tried to respond that a judge would decide whether evidence supported Fleming's claim that she had petitioned a government agency to act purely on a matter of public concern.

"But help me understand here," Knowles countered. "What if her motive really is to delay the project and make it economically unfeasible? What judge can judge that? Have you provided any standard in the bill?"

I had to admit we had not.

"So would Common Cause be amenable to adding a standard here? What if we were to add that a petitioning party who engaged in 'a course of tortious conduct' might not get a declaratory judgment to dismiss?"

I was caught flat-footed. In a chair along the wall, Steve Brown sat stoically.

I said I could not agree to change the bill's text. I said only the sponsor, Rep. Suzanne Henseler, and the ACLU, which drafted the bill, could agree to such a change.

"But don't you think it makes sense to add an exception? What if your supposed SLAPP suit victim had engaged in a course of tortious conduct?"

I had only a vague idea what he was talking about. "At this point," I said, "I'd be reluctant."

"At this point?" Knowles demanded. "Then, when? We're nearly at the end of the session, and I'm not ready to recommend passage without some changes. You and Steve Brown stick around after this hearing."

After the committee adjourned, Brown and I watched from our seats while other lobbyists stroked Knowles's ego. Committee members made their way into his office for sandwiches and cans of soda. It was the ACLU's bill, and any decision on compromise language would be Brown's call.

Rather than inviting us into his office, Knowles convened us at his end of the committee table. "I didn't say we wouldn't pass this," he said slyly. "I just can't imagine it passing in this form."

"So what exactly would you change?" Steve Brown asked.

"What if we inserted a requirement," Knowles grinned, "that the SLAPPee, if you'll allow me to coin a word, not have engaged in 'a course of tortious conduct'?"

"Meaning exactly?" Brown asked.

"A course of tortious conduct," Knowles repeated his phrase. "If they're slamming the government agency with repetitive motions that keep hammering the unfortunate business owner as if he were a Simon Legree. . . ." He let it hang.

It was clear that Knowles would not move the very anti-SLAPP legislation he had supported in two prior years and which had finally passed the Senate. His price for passage would be additional language that those initiating SLAPP suits had not engaged in "a course of tortious conduct."

"Let us get back to you," Brown said. Afterwards in the empty hallway he said that clause would create a huge loophole in the bill.

"Would it be fatal?" I asked.

"In my mind, it would," he said. "But I'll call around to our committee and ask. They may say we should reject it outright. Or they may agree to pass the concept this year and — if there's a problem — fix it later."

The rotunda was empty as we descended the marble stairs. "My prediction," Brown said as we stepped out into the humid night, "is that if this passes the way Knowles wants, a judge will decide Nancy Hsu has engaged in 'tortious conduct,' and we'll wind up having to fight this one more time."

We crossed Smith Street and turned in opposite directions toward our cars. From a traffic light down by the Moshassuck River, cars accelerated around the Roger Williams Memorial and up Smith Hill. Since the early days of Rhode

Island's "lively experiment," idealistic people like Roger Williams and Steve Brown had struggled against those who scorned civil liberties. As sharply as Brown and I sometimes disagreed, I felt certain he would never betray principles we shared. But if Knowles's amendment weakened the anti-SLAPP bill, would we spend years waiting for a remedy to protect the likes of Nancy Hsu Fleming?

The 1993 General Assembly session stretched deep into July and became the second longest in Rhode Island's history. In spite of losing his post as chair of House Judiciary, Jeffrey Teitz had sponsored two significant reforms that became law. The first was a ballot question to let voters decide in 1994 on a constitutional amendment that would require any future casino to win voter approval both statewide and in the community where a gambling facility would be located.[24] The second, called "State Vendors' Disclosure," required any corporation that received state contracts worth $5,000 or more to report political contributions of $250 or more made by its officers and their family members to candidates for statewide general office.[25] The vendors' disclosure law was the only plank in the RIght Now! platform that had not passed in 1992. It would finally become law a year later.

Final passage of the anti-SLAPP legislation came on July 19 after the ACLU agreed to Knowles's "course of tortious conduct" clause.[26] Gov. Sundlun signed it into law. Court challenges began almost immediately and would continue for years.

22

Empire of Cronies
1993

On July 25, 1993, the *Providence Sunday Journal* landed on our porch with a thud. A banner headline burst from the front page: "THE MAKING OF AN EMPIRE: Chief judge, top clerk preside over network of high-priced patronage."

The exposé by Tracy Breton, Dean Starkman, and John Sullivan began with the steamy July day seven years earlier when Thomas F. Fay became chief justice of the Rhode Island Supreme Court. Speaker Matthew J. Smith had overseen the impeachment of Chief Justice Bevilacqua for his continuing Mob connections. After Bevilaqua resigned, Smith led the Grand Committee in electing Fay as chief justice and presided over the swearing in. Smith and Fay were friends, confidants, allies, and business partners. Eighteen months after Smith made Fay chief justice, Fay returned the favor by picking his mentor for the top administrative post in the state court system. At the same time Smith continued to run the Unclassified Pay Plan Board which bestowed a series of raises that made Fay — five years into the Fay-Smith judicial administration — the highest-paid state supreme court chief justice in the United States.[1]

The investigative team had scoured public records and tracked secret favors. They reported that Smith had become the fourth-highest-paid state court administrator in the nation, earning more than his counterpart in the far larger court system of neighboring Massachusetts and only $5,000 less than the top court administrator in California, a state with thirty times Rhode Island's population. "The Making of an Empire" showed how Smith and Fay turned the court system into a patronage mill. They awarded jobs with high salaries to "ex-politicians and their relatives," driving the judiciary's budget dramatically upward. During five years Fay served as chief, the Supreme Court's spending spiked more than 250 percent, from $5 million to more than $17 million per year.[2]

Rep. Anthony J. Carnevale Jr. had worked at Smith's behest to deliver Grand Committee votes for Fay. Though Carnevale was woefully unqualified for a judgeship, his old allies in the General Assembly quietly passed legislation establishing a new "general master" of the Superior Court. Though the duties were judicial, there was no need to negotiate for an appointment by the governor or confirmation by the Senate. The law empowered Chief Justice Fay to appoint, and he named Carnevale.

The investigative team reported that many others who had proved their loyalty to Smith and Fay landed lucrative jobs, and the General Assembly shoveled cash into the courts. The Supreme Court budget swelled an average 37 percent each year. From 1988 to 1993 its staff ballooned from 88 to 158.

The investigative team reminded readers that Smith — while he was speaker — had appointed both the chairperson of the House Finance Committee that set the court system's budget, Rep. Robert Tucker, and its vice chair, Rep. Robert V. Bianchini. The exposé noted that most court personnel fell under the jurisdiction of the Unclassified Pay Plan Board, which Smith chaired and where Bianchini served. The pay board's meetings were "held bimonthly at various locations at the call of the chairman. Its records were scattered, incomplete, and indecipherable." The article included a sidebar that listed new hires with their positions, salaries, and raises over two years. All had potent political connections. Of the fifteen people who had landed jobs, the reporters tracked several down and asked about how they applied. Former Rep. Louis M. Cioci said he had spoken twice with Fay. "I went to see the chief justice personally," he said. "I hand-delivered the résumé and talked to him about it."

The reporting team wrote, "Patronage has a corrosive logic all its own. Inherently unfair, it coddles incompetence and discourages achievement. One favor requires another, then another. Slowly, the organization is compromised and morale is poisoned. In a court system, it is doubly damaging."

The three reporters had asked to interview Chief Justice Fay but were told they must submit written questions, which he would answer in writing. When they asked if political influence had played any part in hiring fifteen individuals whom they named, Fay replied, "The policy of the courts is to hire the best qualified individuals. Prior experience in the public sector is not a liability or a preclusion to hiring."[3]

The reporters then asked if any individuals without personal or political connections to top administrators had been "recruited and/or hired" through Smith. Fay again answered that court procedures were "consistent with good hiring practices in the private sector . . . . They were not designed, however, to create a system of 'reverse discrimination,' wherein qualified candidates are automatically eliminated from consideration simply because they had previous public service experience or knew an individual in public service." In response to a question about pay levels, Fay noted that the Unclassified Pay Plan Board was responsible and that the court salaries "track the salaries of similar positions throughout state service." The written Q&A made dull reading but revealed Fay's defensiveness.

The patronage scandal engulfed Fay and Smith like a rogue wave. Before the pair could regain their footing, a second breaker tumbled them again. Reporters Starkman and Sullivan reported that the chief justice and the court administrator had been using bar exam fees as a secret slush fund that violated state laws. Chief Justice Bevilacqua had begun the fund when his court charged aspiring lawyers $50 to take the bar; Fay raised it to $200 and began generating $40,000 or more per year. Auditors swooped in, and newspaper photos showed checks emblazoned with Smith's serpentine signature.

Most expenditures from the fund seemed mundane: $275 for a bus to a Red Sox game at Fenway Park, $268 for beer and wine, and $4,900 for a public opinion poll. Others seemed personal, such as the tuxedo Fay rented to receive an honorary degree. When Smith filed a voucher for reimbursement as a court expense, the state purchasing agent refused it and Smith paid for the tux with a check labeled "R.I. Supreme Court Special Account." In 1990, Fay commissioned a full-length portrait of himself that was paid for with $11,500 from the special account, and in 1992, Smith wrote a check for $588 to an auto body shop to repair a dent in his car. The payments might have seemed trivial, but all were processed through illegal accounts. When auditors tallied the illegitimate disbursements over five years, the total swelled to $175,000.[4]

On August 11, after thirteen years as the dominant player in Rhode Island politics, the jaunty leprechaun everyone called "Matty" signed a letter of resignation and Smith walked out of public life. The next day, House Minority Leader Wayne L. Salisbury and Rep. Bruce J. Long charged that Smith had made "personal and private" use of state money. Long also filed a complaint against Chief Justice Fay with the Commission on Judicial Tenure and Discipline.

Two days later justices of the Supreme Court issued a report that blamed Smith for failing "to apply good accounting principles and appropriate guidelines" in his expenditures. In what looked like an effort to shield Fay, they added, "Neither the court nor the chief justice supervised routine management of the fund including deposits and expenditures from it." House Republican leaders renewed their attack on Fay, with Salisbury telling reporters the chief justice had disregarded the laws he was sworn to uphold. Long spoke of "impeachable offenses." Each news story prompted a flurry of political pronouncements as radio talk shows amplified the details, and the uproar spread to the farthest corners of Rhode Island.[5]

After refusing an interview with the *Providence Journal* reporters, Fay went to the WPRO-AM studio for an on-air interview with Mary Ann Sorrentino. As she plied him with questions submitted by listeners before the program, he blamed the media for unfair coverage and "misinformation," claiming that state auditors had known about the special account since 1990 but never investigated. "It is a lynching kind of atmosphere out there," the chief justice told Sorrentino. He insisted that he had never done a dishonest thing in his life and that he would "stay the course." In a later interview on WHJJ-AM, Fay insisted that problems with the account represented "sloppy management" rather than "criminality," adding that he considered his radio appearances a public apology.[6]

Despite Fay's efforts to deflect the blame, the Senate majority leader and twenty-two senators issued a public call for him to relinquish his administrative duties while the Commission on Judicial Tenure and Discipline investigated. "There's a cloud hanging over the court," Kelly told reporters, "And that cloud has got to be removed." Harwood was more blunt. He summoned reporters to a press conference in the House lounge. Flanked by Caruolo and Salisbury, both of whom had already called for Fay's impeachment, Harwood announced that he had written to the chief justice asking him to resign. "I feel that significant damage has been done to the reputation and credibility of the highest court of our state," Harwood read from his letter. "No person or group stands above the Supreme Court or the integrity of that body."[7]

A television reporter asked Harwood about a comment Fay's spokesperson had made to the effect that "no way in hell" would the chief justice resign. Rather than answer, Harwood stalked out of his own press conference.

Caruolo took over in a soothing tone. "This is a delicate position to be in, because we may be called upon to begin an impeachment process if things keep developing. It's very, very hard for us to ask for this. This may end up in House chambers."

The other shoe dropped when state auditors reported that expenditures of $32,000 from special court accounts were clearly improper, while others worth $138,000 lacked documentation. As the revelations piled up, Gov. Sundlun insisted to reporters that Fay deserved the same "due process" that any ordinary citizen would receive, and would face an extraordinary public hearing before the Commission on Judicial Tenure and Discipline.[8]

The final straw for Fay was a front-page investigative report by four *Providence Journal* reporters. Dan Barry, Ira Chinoy, Dean Starkman, and John Sullivan wrote that the chief justice had assigned lucrative arbitration work to five favored attorneys. One was a fishing buddy, another a political ally from years Smith was speaker. A third shared ownership of Fay's office building in Lincoln, where the fourth was a tenant. The fifth was a Fay protégé who rented space there for arbitration hearings.[9]

On August 25, a month to the day after the first headline story, Fay relinquished his judicial duties temporarily. The next day — gaunt, pale, and wearing a navy blue suit — the chief justice was arraigned on three misdemeanor ethics counts before a subordinate in judicial robes. Joseph A. Kelly, who had defended DiPrete before the Ethics Commission, now stood in District Court beside Fay and said his client was not guilty. Fay was led to a back room to be photographed and fingerprinted.[10]

As obvious as the facts seemed to be, the process for testing them in court or before the Commission on Judicial Tenure and Discipline could take months. As summer slipped away a collective impatience gained momentum. While rumors of impeachment spread, James R. Langevin circulated a letter among his fellow representatives, asking Fay to resign. A member of the House Judiciary Committee, which could initiate impeachment proceedings whenever it chose, Langevin steered his motorized wheelchair into the House lounge to speak with reporters as lawmakers crowded around him. Beneath the portraits of Bevilacqua, Smith, and DeAngelis, he announced that fifty-eight representatives had signed his letter. "This is a clear sign," he said, "that a majority of the members of the Rhode Island House have lost confidence in Judge Fay's ability to lead the court. If Judge Fay does not resign, there will be significant sentiment to move for impeachment." Langevin said resignation would avoid "a long, drawn-out impeachment process that could take four to six months," a time when he said the Supreme Court "would be paralyzed."[11]

Fay wrote back to Langevin pleading for time and for due process. He summarized what he called "sweeping reforms" during his six years as chief justice, acknowledging in the passive voice that "mistakes have been made, and there are problems that clearly must be addressed." But he clung to his office. "For me to resign," he wrote, "would short-circuit the very process through which the public's questions could be best answered."[12]

M. Charles Bakst, the *Providence Journal*'s acerbic government affairs editor and political columnist, surmised that Fay might be clinging to his office as a bargaining chip to avoid jail. Bakst noted that the magnitude of the Smith-Fay scandal lay, ironically, in its smallness. Expenditures from the Supreme Court's secret slush fund were trivial by comparison with DiPrete's Cranston Land Deal and RISDIC's complex financial machinations. "Here's a question," Bakst wrote, "Why does the nation's highest paid chief justice have to engage in business sidelines — in this case, a real estate partnership?"[13]

As August faded into September, the political season also turned. A resolution signed by a mere quarter of the representatives could begin impeachment proceedings, and nearly three-fifths had signed Langevin's letter over a weekend. The outcome became inevitable. In mid-September, a month after he had called for Fay to resign, Harwood formally initiated impeachment proceedings, citing the "cumulative effect" of revelations about Fay's use of court staff and offices on business related to the Lincoln office building.[14]

Fifty-two representatives signed an impeachment resolution alleging that Fay had engaged in conduct that had "brought his judicial office into serious disrepute, substantially impaired the integrity of the judiciary, undermined public confidence in the integrity of the judiciary, and has demeaned his judicial office." This move to impeach would be the first under an amendment that had been recommended by the 1986 Constitutional Convention and approved by state voters. The House Judiciary Committee would determine whether there was probable cause that the chief justice had committed "a felony or crime of moral turpitude, misfeasance or malfeasance in office or violation of the canons of judicial ethics." The resolution to start the process passed by a vote of 74–15, with 11 not voting.[15]

Meanwhile a Brown University poll showed that an overwhelming 76 percent of the public supported impeachment and 80 percent said Fay should resign.[16] Public disgust surged when the news broke that Fay had written on Supreme Court stationery to various traffic court judges to recommend leniency for traffic tickets issued to his brother-in-law, his law clerk, his secretary's husband, and two teenage children of a friend who was president of Women & Infants Hospital, where Fay was a trustee. In one case Fay had written: "He is a salesman who does much traveling, and it certainly would not be helpful to have one speeding ticket on his record." Fay often addressed administrators or judges by their first names but then signed: "Sincerely, Thomas F. Fay, Chief Justice."[17]

On October 8, Fay finally resigned. In a long letter to the governor, he wrote, "The events of recent days have convinced me that while I have been guilty of no intentional wrong-doing, my actions have, however well-intentioned, created an appearance of impropriety for which I alone must accept full responsibility." Fay professed "a heavy heart but clear conscience" and said he was resigning to avoid additional suffering for his family "and for the people of this state that I have served so faithfully over the last sixteen years."[18]

For the second time in seven years, a politically connected chief justice of the Supreme Court had been forced to resign under a cloud of pending impeachment. Network television and major newspapers covered the story as another Rhode Island howler. The *Washington Post* gave two samples of the state's "dark humor with an edge":

Q: *In Rhode Island, what do you call a man in a suit?*
A: *The defendant.*

Q: *How bad is the recession in Rhode Island?*
A: *So bad the Mob had to lay a couple of judges off the payroll.*

Meanwhile, far below the radar, our embryonic judicial reform coalition had been planning strategy. The controversial election of Victoria Lederberg in Grand Committee had left many shaking their heads. Now a second Supreme Court scandal in seven years offered a unique chance to change the system. No one knew yet whether Fay would resign, as Chief Justice Bevilacqua had.

Charlie Silverman stunned our August meeting with a simple question.

"What would happen if we could block the Grand Committee from filling that vacancy?"

He had our full attention. "The Constitution lays down requirements for the Grand Committee," he smiled. They can't do anything until they have a quorum — more than half of all the representatives and senators together. I'm not making this up. It's Article IV, Section 7."[19] After reading the section aloud, he suggested that we get pledges from more than half of the members in each chamber demanding merit selection and refusing to go into Grand Committee. "If we accomplish that," he said mischievously, "the Grand Committee can't fill the vacancy when Fay goes."

"Wow!" said Alan Flink, former president of the Bar Association. "That could work! Rank-and-file lawmakers could block the Grand Committee."

Silverman thought Harwood had the most to lose. "The speaker can bring incredible pressure to bear on individual legislators," he said, "but signed commitments from a majority in each chamber would protect them and give us leverage." Tom Banchoff suggested that we promise each potential signer that we would not go public with the idea of a moratorium until we had signed pledges from a majority.

With Silverman and Operation Clean Sweep taking the lead, our fledgling coalition divided up the list of lawmakers. We agreed to work quietly until we attained a critical mass.

At noon on a brilliant Thursday in August, RIght Now! returned as the public face of reform. Unlike our first announcement in December 1991, this time there were no pealing church bells, but leaders of churches and synagogues filled the State House rotunda along with citizen activists, lawyers, and business leaders. Charlie Silverman brough Operation Clean Sweep, the Government Accountability Project, United We Stand, and the Rhode Island Taxpayers Association. A new addition was the American Association of Retired Persons' State Legislative Committee, which had telephone links to more activists than most of the other groups combined.

As a phalanx of lawmakers gathered on the marble stairs behind the podium, Alan Hassenfeld proclaimed the return of RIght Now! He reminded everyone that we had gone into "hibernation" until needed again. He said that the Supreme Court scandal had been "an electric cattle prod" that shocked the coalition back into action. "So now," Hassenfeld declared with a wave across the crowd, "we're all needed — every one of us! We stayed the course last time, and we're going to be even more tenacious this time around."

He rehearsed what RIght Now! had accomplished in 1992, including new ethics laws, campaign finance reforms, and four-year terms for statewide general officers. "Now we're back," he announced, "to deal with this embarrassing mess in our courts — a scandal that springs from the archaic way that Rhode Island chooses judges."

In my turn at the microphone, I outlined the legislation that the Bar Association and Common Cause had been promoting for years without success. I renewed our demand that the General Assembly let voters end the Grand Committee's role in picking Supreme Court justices and establish an independent judicial nominating commission to pick qualified candidates for all judicial vacancies. "Until all of our state judges are chosen on the basis of merit rather than for their political connections," I said, "the citizens of Rhode Island will risk renewed embarrassment and outrage."[20]

Charlie Silverman quickly proved his worth. On September 13, he released signed pledges from twenty-six of the fifty state senators and fifty-three of the hundred representatives. In an interview with *Providence Journal* reporter Scott MacKay, Silverman spoke with restrained passion: "The citizens of Rhode Island have been electrified for the second time by the unethical behavior of a chief justice of the Supreme Court. Just seven years ago Judge Bevilacqua was forced to resign in disgrace, and now Judge Fay faces a similar fate. If we don't change the system we have we're doomed to have more of the same."[21]

I marveled at Silverman's chutzpah. With no title but head of Operation Clean Sweep's legislative committee, he had contacted scores of lawmakers. One by one, he persuaded them to risk retaliation for the stand he hoped they would take. Against all odds, he achieved a majority in each chamber.

Predictably, John Harwood defended the status quo. He told MacKay he had always thought the Grand Committee was "the most democratic process for choosing the justices." Harwood did not say that he would lose his pivotal role as judge-maker if the General Assembly "in Grand Committee" no longer elected justices to the Rhode Island Supreme Court. Although Paul Kelly had not signed Silverman's pledge, he split with Harwood precisely as we hoped. He appointed a nine-member Senate Select Committee to study methods of judicial selection and recommend changes in Rhode Island's process.[22]

Only seven weeks had passed since the *Providence Journal* launched its exposé of patronage at the top of Rhode Island's judicial system. Even through the summer doldrums, the scandal had galvanized public attention. The investigative reporters who exposed Matthew Smith's empire of secret patronage would win a Pulitzer Prize. Yet despite this apparent victory, a crucial question remained. Would the General Assembly's centuries-old tradition of picking Supreme Court justices endure?

23

Revolving Door
1993

ONLY DAYS AFTER HE WON RE-ELECTION in 1992, Gov. Bruce Sundlun warned Rae Condon and me that he would challenge the Revolving Door Law, which he had signed the previous summer. Neither the governor nor his advisers explained why he had signed the law he now sought to overturn. He also challenged the Ethics Commission's revolving door rule, which prohibited members of the General Assembly from seeking or accepting permanent state jobs — including judgeships — for one year after leaving office.[1]

On September 21, 1993, spectators rose as the Supreme Court's deep green velvet curtain swooshed open. Only four justices stepped forward to seats behind their long elevated desk: Acting Chief Justice Joseph R. Weisberger along with Justices Florence K. Murray, Donald F. Shea, and Victoria Lederberg. Chief Justice Thomas Fay had not yet resigned, but his chair remained empty.

Appellate lawyer William P. Robinson strode to the center podium on Sundlun's behalf and intoned the ancient judicial greeting: "May it please the Court." His wild white mane of hair standing out amid the dark wood columns and carved panels, Robinson attacked both revolving door rules as unconstitutional, arguing that barring legislators and senior government staff from permanent state jobs stigmatized "a whole class of people." He ignored the fact that the rules allowed public officials to accept top positions as long as the job would end when the governor left office. Robinson declared it "irrational to exclude from government service people whose only distinguishing characteristic is that they have been in government service."

Ethics Commission attorney Gary Yesser countered his arguments. The revolving door rules — both the commission's and the legislature's — freed the governor from the pressure to hire politically connected players who traditionally won such appointments as rewards for loyal service. "The message," Yesser told the court, was that people who sought public office must understand that there would be "no job at the end of the rainbow." So, far from narrowing the field of candidates a governor could consider, the revolving door had broadened the chief executive's choices beyond political insiders: "There are a million others he can go to."[2]

Lauren Jones took the podium for Common Cause and asked why Sundlun was challenging the constitutionality of a law he had signed only months earlier. "Where was his sensitivity to the Constitution then?" Jones asked. "The only thing I can see that intervened was an election." The brief Jones had written *pro bono* for Common Cause reminded the justices of their words only fifteen months earlier about rampant corruption in the mid-1980s that had given rise to the Ethics Commission and led to the revolving door rule.[3]

Jones skewered Sundlun's argument as self-contradictory. "The Governor asserts that the revolving door measures serve as a disincentive to 'people of talent and selfless vision' who might seek public office. That statement describes the problem in a nutshell. If the only reason that people accept public service is to better enable them to gain a state job, it demonstrates that there is a need to stop that practice."[4] He noted that the Ethics Commission and General Assembly had both approved revolving door rules to control widespread abuse, citing precedents to insist that it was "not the function of the court to substitute its judgment for that of legislators."

Less than two months later, the four justices ruled unanimously in support of both laws. With refreshing clarity, they wrote, "The revolving door legislation addresses the imbroglio of public officials who use their present positions and contacts as unfair bargaining tactics in gaining future employment with the state or a municipality."[5] The justices also tied the revolving door ban directly to language of the 1986 Ethics Amendment: "The legislative aim of the revolving door provisions is to ensure that public officials adhere to the highest standards of conduct, avoid the appearance of impropriety, and do not use their positions for private gain or advantage."[6]

Finally, the four justices stated that rules adopted by the commission and the law enacted by the legislature complemented one another and were thoroughly compatible. They added, "The General Assembly has properly enacted the statute under its concurrent jurisdiction in the ethics arena."[7]

Reading the opinion made me light-headed. Rhode Island's highest court was unequivocally affirming both the revolving door prohibition Common Cause had pushed for four years and the legislature's more comprehensive ban. The justices slammed and double-locked the door through which pliant insiders had — for generations — made their way into permanent state jobs. Lawmakers who held their noses when they voted for it would now have to live by its provisions.

With his challenge now decisively rejected, Sundlun said he would abide by the law. "The legality of the revolving door statute has been established," he announced. "Any doubts as to the constitutionality of the legislation have been resolved. I am satisfied with the result. The executive and legislative branches now know what the rules are and how they apply."[8]

Deep in the opinion lurked an issue I was only beginning to understand in its Rhode Island context: separation of powers. Sundlun's lawyers had argued that the revolving door rules improperly impinged on his executive authority to appoint government officials. In fact, the high court declared, Rhode Island's Constitution gave the governor only flimsy appointment.[9]

In his *amicus* brief for Common Cause, Lauren Jones contrasted the powers of appointment granted to Rhode Island governors and to American presidents. "The tradition established by Rhode Island's Royal Charter," Jones wrote, "which carried over into the Constitution of 1842, was not one in which the appointment power was an executive branch function as found in the U.S. Constitution. Virtually all governmental power was given to the legislative branch."[10]

The justices agreed that no Rhode Island governor had possessed appointing powers comparable to those of an American president. Their advisory opinion noted that the revolving door rules of the Ethics Commission and General Assembly had not seized "powers that are central or essential" to the governor. Neither had the ban on revolving door jobs disrupted his performance of any constitutional duties.

All my adult life I had assumed that state constitutions were scaled-down versions of the U.S. Constitution. I had finished high school, college, and graduate school without recognizing significant differences that now began to dawn on me. How had I remained so ignorant for so long? Would my ignorance ultimately undermine what we were trying to accomplish?

24

Electronic Access

1993–94

IN 1993, I RECEIVED one of ten Macintosh laptops in a nationwide Apple Computer contest.[1] In a row of ports along the computer's spine I recognized a telephone receptacle. I plugged in a phone cord but had no idea what to do next.

Michael C. Cerullo, a member of our board, laughed. "You can't just plug in and use it like a phone," he said. He searched through my software and punched in a series of numbers. This time, I heard a dial tone and what started like a ring but turned into a fax-like squawk. "You'll love this," he enthused. "You'll be able to connect with computer libraries and send electronic mail. The World Wide Web will change your life."

Cerullo had been helping to create the Ocean State Free-Net, a system that would allow computers to connect through ordinary phone lines. We hoped the Free-Net would open vast mines of government data to ordinary citizens. As part of this task he had pulled together what we called the telecommunications committee, people from universities and tech companies. Members shared an infectious excitement about getting government information. We knew that legislative leaders had instant access to computerized drafts of bills and committee schedules, and our goal was to open those data deposits to ordinary citizens.

Most mornings throughout legislative sessions I went to the State House, notebook in hand, to gather data from printouts: agendas posted late at night on bulletin boards outside the library and on the doors of committee rooms. I often met junior employees of law firms on the same quest. We searched for the printed bills heaped up on industrial shelving in a musty basement room, but those we found were often days or weeks out of date.

Since before the RISDIC collapse, leaders of various reform groups had made polite requests for public terminals at the State House where ordinary citizens could gain access to the electronic legislative data. General Assembly leaders always maintained that it could not be done. "Hackers would get into our mainframe," Jeff Teitz had told me. "They'd destroy the legislature's data, and we can't risk that."

Our committee intended to crack that nut. One afternoon in October 1993, Cerullo triumphantly described a new technology from Silicon Valley. "It's called a firewall," he announced. "They download data onto a firewall computer that's connected to a phone line. There's no link back into the mainframe. Anybody with a computer can dial in and download documents. Hackers can't get back into the original data." He had learned about a system installed only months earlier in the California legislature.

I stepped into another room and phoned California Common Cause. "That's right," said my counterpart in Sacramento. "We wrote the bill that made them put it all online. Would you like me to fax it?" Fifteen minutes later, we were drafting Rhode Island legislation based on the California model. Our bill would require the General Assembly to make all of its bills, committee calendars, House and Senate journals, and the state's General Laws accessible via telephone lines.

With shoulder-length hair, bow tie, and geeky glasses, Kevin Grau brought political savvy and technical expertise to the committee. "We'll need to keep reminding legislators that we're not asking for any new disclosures," he said. "They already publish all those data on paper. We're just asking for the same materials in electronic formats."[2]

"Which they already have on their mainframe," Cerullo added.

"What will it cost?" someone asked. "Do we know?"

"Only ballpark," Cerullo said. "The actual firewall computer would be way less than twenty thousand dollars. The real costs would be for a distributed network of PCs, storage units, and software. Installation and training would add more. There's no way to know how much more till they bring in a consultant to analyze what they already have."

Grau added that legislative leaders knew their old IBM mainframe was obsolete. "That they've kept it operational without a catastrophic crash is testimony to skilled staff, but everybody knows they're overdue for a new system."

I asked if the General Assembly could charge for the data.

"They might try," Cerullo said, "but we would stand on the principle that citizens have already paid for this information. Taxpayers paid to compile the legislative data and maintain it. It belongs to the people."

"And there's an analogy," Grau added. "They already provide television feeds of legislative sessions to cable subscribers without charge. Computer access only expands that paradigm to the release of digital data."

No one knew how soon any of this could be done, but we prepared a draft for the board and legislative sponsors.

During five years of lobbying at the State House I had learned vital lessons about sponsors. We needed legislators who would stake their reputations on challenging the *status quo*. Those who sponsored our bill for online access to legislative data would need to expose problems with the General Assembly's old mainframe and defend the costs of a new system.

I approached the chairs of the two finance committees, Sen. J. Michael Lenihan and Rep. Antonio J. Pires. As the House prepared the state budget, House Finance logged more hours under greater pressure than any other legislative committee. Tony Pires had large brown eyes and an earnest look. He engaged all kinds of witnesses with gracious respect. On a walk with him from his committee to the House chamber, I outlined our proposal and he asked me to schedule an appointment at his office on the third floor. The next day he waved me to a chair by his desk. "You're right that we need to retire our cranky old mainframe," he chuckled. "I've never actually seen the thing, but it's ancient. I don't know how you've learned so many of its secrets."

I told him members of our committee had done the research. "They tell me we're at the dawn of a whole new approach to interconnected computing," I said. "Most of it's above my pay grade."

"Mine, too," Pires laughed. "I can just about log onto my own PC. I got a modem but haven't figured out how to use it yet."

I said I was just learning. I pulled out my new Macintosh laptop. "Here's the port for a phone-line. The modem's built-in."

"And isn't your Blue Ribbon Commission recommending that we get laptops for each member of the House and Senate?"

"We are," I said, "but this legislation only deals with access to legislative data." I explained how a firewall computer had allowed California's legislature to release electronic data to its members and the public while protecting against hackers.

He liked the idea. "Our clerks already order bills and committee calendars printed every day. I assume you're saying we could dump those same data into a firewall computer."

I nodded. "People could retrieve the data from any computer connected to a phone line — whether in their homes, offices, or local libraries. It would save countless hours and deliver reliable data."

"And if we bought laptops for reps and senators, would we need to order them with special online capacity?"

"Built-in modems are becoming standard equipment," I said.

He reviewed our draft and said he would be glad to sponsor it. "I'll have to get a fiscal note on what the costs would be. In all candor, cost may not be the primary obstacle."

"You mean there's other resistance."

"I want to hope there's not," he shrugged. "I see this as a genuinely democratic technology. But we've both been around long enough to know that even the least controversial changes can take years."

A close ally of Senate Majority Leader Paul S. Kelly, Sen. J. Michael Lenihan of East Greenwich had become chair of the powerful Senate Finance Committee at the start of only his second term. He drew me from his committee room through a tall oak door into his office. As with the House Judiciary office, the ceiling looked higher than the room was wide. Lenihan needed no convincing to sponsor our online access bill. "We're committed to opening up the process in every way that's technologically feasible," he said. "I have no idea whether this firewall technology you describe is compatible with the Assembly's old mainframe, but I'll find out and get back to you."

On his desk lay a two-by-four with letters painted in broad green strokes: THE VOTER. Lenihan had carried it into the Senate chamber during the RISDIC crisis and lifted it high for all to read — a symbolic warning, as he told his colleagues. He brought it down on his desk with a whack that reverberated like a gunshot. With Bevilacqua's majority swept away in the 1992 election, Lenihan now bore the weight of leadership, and no one who sat across his desk could forget the message of his two-by-four.

No one quarreled with the need to get legislative data online. The Blue Ribbon Commission had recommended that legislators and members of the public be given access to the General Assembly's database.[3] In the 1994 legislative session Pires and Lenihan sponsored identical bills to ensure online access to the proceedings of the General Assembly.[4] Together they told reporters that online access to legislative data — bills, amended bills, committee agendas, calendars, journals, and the Rhode Island General Laws — was a top priority.

In committee hearings no one testified against his legislation, but Lenihan told me privately that the publisher of Rhode Island's emerald-green law books was determined to kill the bill unless his committee deleted the requirement that the General Laws become available electronically. The printed version was a significant source of income, since law firms across the state and libraries across the country purchased each biennial set for over $2,000.

As Pires adjourned a hearing of the House Finance Committee, he waved me to the dais. "The publisher's making the case," he said, one hand covering his microphone, "that electronic versions will undercut the printed versions of the General Laws. They say it won't be worth their while to publish."

"That's a huge carve-out," I said. "What can we do?"

Pires pursed his lips. "They're making their case directly to John Harwood and George Caruolo. I'm trying to persuade them. Maybe you should do the same."

The next afternoon, I waited in a red-carpeted House aisle while George

Caruolo dealt with representatives. The majority leader was visibly weary and irritated, but I had to talk with him or risk not getting another chance. Finally, I shook his hand and mentioned Pires's electronic public access bill.

"Jesus H. Christ," Caruolo roared. "Look how much you get if we move this bill — even without putting the General Laws online!" His jaw clenched. "If you think I'm going to make all this available for free to those bastards at Edwards & Angell, you are out of your fucking mind! They can pay."

His vehemence jolted me, but I forced a smile. "Of course they could pay, and maybe you could find a way to put a meter on legislative data. But you created it in electronic form at taxpayer expense. How can you provide it free for lawmakers and the public, but then turn on a meter for downtown law firms? And in technical terms, how would you do that?"

Caruolo scowled. "Have you talked with Kilmartin?" Michael Kilmartin was the executive director of the Office of Legislative Data Systems.

"Several times," I said. "He sees other states starting to put their legislative data online."

Kilmartin and his staff occupied a warren of tiny offices in the northwest corner of the State House basement. A raised floor left room for bundles of cables that connected PCs to mainframe terminals. Banks of bulky units occupied closets and entire rooms. Relentlessly cheerful, Kilmartin spoke candidly about technical problems but never revealed political secrets. His electronic lair operated under the aegis of the Joint Committee on Legislative Services, a powerful but little known administrative body called by its initials, JCLS. It was made up of five members: the speaker of the House, the majority and minority leaders of the House, and the majority and minority leaders of the Senate.

Our bill assigned responsibility for online disclosure to the JCLS. Kilmartin and I worked through the latest draft. "We still have a technical problem," he said. "We can't mount all the data as quickly as your legislation requires. I'd feel better if we could say we would make the information 'incrementally accessible,' as we install and configure new equipment."

I suggested that the text read "as quickly as possible."

"How about 'in a timely manner on a current basis'?" he countered. "I think we can get some items online for next year's session, but I wouldn't want a date certain in the law until we know."

We agreed to that wording. Farther down, we finalized new language that would make available the original bills, substitute versions, and final texts of every bill enacted. "I actually think that will help us in the future," Kilmartin said. "I can envision a time when we stop passing out reams of paper and let senators and reps read legislation on their laptops."

I asked if he had any insight on the resistance from West Publishing, which produced the green-bound editions of the Rhode Island General Laws.[5]

"I don't," Kilmartin said. "I understand they're afraid of losing sales. The truth is we can't possibly publish the legislative history that they present for each section. I really don't think we would undercut their market."

We marked up what would become Substitute A/3 of the legislation. Kilmartin agreed to review our revisions with Caruolo while I cleared them with Mike Lenihan, Tony Pires, and the Common Cause committee.

A few days later, I sat on a bench behind members of the Senate Finance Committee while Lenihan explained his bill to them. All were weary and eager for the session to end. Few seemed enthusiastic about anything, but their unanimous vote moved the bill to the Senate floor. Passage would benefit many, a win-win for all but the publishers of green law books.[6]

Support for online access came from unexpected voices. Rep. Eileen Naughton, a former librarian, told reporters that she had begun doing legislative research from her home computer. "If you know how to search, there's a huge amount of information available. But when I go to the State House, I go into the Dark Ages."[7]

Several years earlier I often welcomed help in getting legislative data, but never recognized the risk I was taking. My mistake became clear on a bright day as I walked toward the State House. A red Mitsubishi sports car slowed to a stop, and its window buzzed down. A young woman at the wheel called a cheery greeting.

I waved and said I remembered her face but not her name.

She reminded me, then added, "My uncle says hello."

"Oh? Who's your uncle?"

"John Bevilacqua."

I caught my breath. "How is he?"

"Fine," she said with a wide grin. We chatted briefly, and she drove away, her expensive red car disappearing in traffic.

I continued toward the State House, remembering an unusal call I had received from an alternative high school before the RISDIC crisis. A guidance counselor at School One said a student had asked about an internship with Common Cause. Melissa Menard had come for an interview, and I put her to work a few hours a week answering the phone, searching agendas at the State House, finding copies of legislation, and maintaining a database. Each week we met to discuss her work, and she asked good questions. She had never mentioned — and I never guessed — that her uncle was the powerful Senate majority leader. She never had our office key and would not have found much to report. Had she been sent as a spy? Was her uncle trying to get names of people who called Common Cause? Some impropriety to discredit me?[8]

The SubA/3 of Sen. Mike Lenihan's bill appeared on the Senate's calendar for June 30. Exhausted senators droned through until its number appeared on the electronic board. Lenihan rose, a copy in hand. He explained that senators and the public would soon find vast amounts of legislative data at their fingertips. His colleagues hit their green buttons, and the tote board registered 38–0. Moments later a motion of unanimous consent dispatched a load of bills across to the House.

The humidity was thick enough to be visible in the House chamber. I watched from the gallery as Tony Pires explained the bill and offered to answer any questions. As in the Senate, the board lit up with rows of green lights, 81–0.

From a coin phone in the basement, I called Mike Cerullo and Kevin Grau to congratulate them. I told Cerullo I could not remember one of our bills passing in its first year. "It's also our first to win unanimous passage in both chambers."

"Thank Jim Warren for creating the firewall," Cerullo replied. "Without that technology, you never know how long this would have taken."

25

Hard Choices
1993–94

CHARLIE SILVERMAN turned the *Providence Journal*'s exposé of Supreme Court patronage into political leverage. Almost single-handedly the Operation Clean Sweep leader had persuaded fifty-three representatives and twenty-six senators, a majority in each chamber, to sign pledges that they would not participate in the Grand Committee election of a new chief justice.[1] Each pledge card called for merit selection of all Rhode Island judges. No one knew whether legislators could have breached Silverman's bulwark and convened the Grand Committee because they never tried.

Weeks before Thomas Fay finally resigned, Paul Kelly had appointed a nine-member Senate commission to recommend a better way of choosing judges. The panel, headed by the chair of the Senate Judiciary Committee, Domenic A. DiSandro III, began pondering possible fixes. Late in October, Robert Weygand announced that he would propose legislation for both merit selection of judges and a process for reviewing judicial performance.[2]

Even Gov. Bruce Sundlun toyed with the idea of a judicial nominating commission. Throughout the 1992 and 1993 legislative sessions he had refused to discuss any plan that would "tie the governor's hands" with a list of candidates. But as the autumn rains of 1993 brought down the last leaves, Sundlun called Alan Flink and me to his office. He ranted at us, but seemed to be inching in our direction. Then on December 10, Sundlun stunned the state. During the taping of *10 News Conference*, the NBC-TV affiliate's Sunday political show, Sundlun announced that he would support "a Missouri Plan approach." Sundlun said he had held "fruitful negotiations" with the Bar Association, Common Cause, and the RIght Now! Coalition. A reporter phoned for my reaction to this breaking news. I confirmed that we had met with the governor and that his principles were now "almost entirely compatible" with ours.[3] That afternoon I told the RIght Now! steering committee that Sundlun had stolen our thunder. Alan Hassenfeld laughed. "Should we be surprised? He's running for re-election!"

On December 16, two years after our first RIght Now! press conference, we celebrated our coalition's return. In the State House rotunda, Hassenfeld lamented the fact that the people had again been "sold out by power, greed, and corruption"[4] and decried "the flagrant abuse and embarrassment that we, as Rhode Islanders, have been subjected to."

We unveiled two constitutional amendments for the November 1994 ballot. The first would establish a nonpartisan judicial nominating commission. For any judicial vacancy the commission was to present a list of three to five highly qualified candidates to the governor, who would then appoint one, subject to Senate confirmation. The second contained constitutional proposals of the Blue Ribbon Commission to end lawmakers' pensions, raise legislative pay, and reduce the size of the General Assembly.[5]

In February 1994, Providence Sen. Myrth York announced that she would challenge Bruce Sundlun for the Democratic gubernatorial nomination. Were she to win, York would become the state's first female governor and the first chief executive to serve a four-year term. Her quest renewed an old rivalry. Nine years earlier, she had battled Sundlun for a seat in the 1986 Constitutional Convention. She had promised proposals to reduce the size of the General Assembly, end legislative pensions, raise lawmakers' pay, and establish a four-year term for the state's governor.[6] Sundlun had won that contest and used the convention as a springboard for his unsuccessful 1986 campaign against DiPrete. He finally overwhelmed DiPrete in November 1990 — only to face the collapse of RISDIC on his inauguration day.

Though less visible, York had won election to the Senate in 1990 and also took her oath of office on that tumultuous New Year's Day. As a new senator, she had sponsored revolving door legislation that became law in 1992 and survived Sundlun's Supreme Court challenge in 1993. Paul Kelly, then the new majority leader, had appointed Sens. York and Maryellen Goodwin to head standing committees, the first women to hold such power in the state Senate.[7] York had sponsored Sundlun's 1993 legislation to enshrine his judicial screening committee in law, but as the 1994 session approached, she committed herself to the Missouri model of merit selection drafted by the Bar Association and Common Cause.[8]

She announced her gubernatorial campaign in the lobby of the Supreme Court, saying that she chose the venue to remind Rhode Islanders of the court scandal. "We will never move forward as a state," she said, "until our officials stop fixing tickets and start fixing problems." York promised systemic reforms:

merit selection of judges, the end of General Assembly pensions, and laws that would either make quasi-public agencies accountable or put them out of business. "I want to be the governor for every Rhode Islander who doesn't have a relative on the Supreme Court," she told supporters. "I want to be the governor for every Rhode Islander who doesn't own a credit union. I want to be the governor for every Rhode Islander who doesn't have a special pension."[9]

I admired Myrth York but stayed away from her announcement. Common Cause barred staff or board officers from endorsing candidates.

Sen. Jack Revens was tall. Whenever I spoke with him I tilted my head back to look him in the eye. We stood at handshake distance on the Senate chamber's deep green carpet. He had already redrafted his constitutional amendment for a smaller legislature to reflect the Blue Ribbon Commission's recommendations. He said the idea of downsizing the Senate by half scared his colleagues. "They know it wouldn't happen until the next redistricting," he said. "Eight years may seem like a long time off, but it's really not. And some would prefer to take a pay raise and keep their pensions."

"Will we get a fair hearing?"

Revens smiled. "Of course."

A day or two later, on the House chamber's red carpet, I knelt on one knee beside Jim Langevin's motorized wheelchair. Beside the lapel pin that marked him as a state representative, he wore a mustard seed encased in clear glass as a witness to his Catholic faith. Langevin and I had spoken several times about the proposed constitutional amendment he would introduce for our commission.[10] "It's no slam-dunk," he said softly. "People have read enough to get suspicious, but not enough to understand why it's right."

I asked what he thought Harwood and Caruolo were thinking. Langevin shook his head. "They haven't focused on it yet. I don't think the proposed structural changes bother them much. But you can be sure they'll resist merit selection of judges, which would take a real bite out of their power. They might just let legislative reform go onto the ballot, if only to show that they're reformers."

Neither of us laughed. Lobbyist conversations ebbed and flowed above our heads. Few noticed Langevin in his wheelchair and me on one knee, except to step around us.

"I need to mention something in strictest confidence," Langevin said quietly. "I may run for secretary of state. Just in case that makes you want to consider a different sponsor."

I shook my head. "I appreciate knowing that. Gary Sasse and I both want you as sponsor. You work hard on the bills you introduce, and your colleagues hold you in high regard."

Speaker John Harwood had made his way through a throng of lobbyists and ascended the podium. He banged his gavel. "All reps please take your seats. All guests please clear the aisles. The House will come to order."

Nebraska's single-chambered legislature got my attention during our study of lawmaking across the country. Too often I had watched reforms pass in one chamber of the General Assembly only to die in the other. I suggested to Gary Sasse that we propose the Nebraska model for Rhode Island.

"Sounds like a great idea," he said, "but you might soon miss the checks and balances of a bicameral legislature. Nebraska's been unicameral since 1937. You might ask why no other states have followed."

I saw his point in January. After a year in their new roles as speaker and Senate majority leader, John Harwood and Paul Kelly appeared together on the WPRI-TV Sunday program *Newsmakers*. In answer to a question, Harwood said the General Assembly should move quickly to install the acting chief justice, Joseph R. Weisberger, as chief.[11] He reprised his argument that the Grand Committee was the "most democratic process" for choosing judges. "You have 150 elected people who are making the decision."

Politely but firmly, Kelly said he would wait for the report of the bipartisan Senate judicial selection panel he had appointed. "The problem is not Justice Weisberger," Kelly insisted. "The problem is to resolve the integrity of the court system. We want to address the process."[12]

Rep. Nancy Benoit had sponsored the merit selection amendment for Common Cause in 1993 and filed a revised version in 1994.[13] "I'm filing with fifty-nine signatures," she said, handing her original to me. A scrawled list of names filled its cover, mostly Democrats but with all fifteen House Republicans. Her Woonsocket neighbor, Rep. Barbara Burlingame, had nearly as many names on the proposed merit selection law that covered details of creating the Judicial Nominating Commission (JNC).[14]

The evening before a press event where the RIght Now! sponsors were to present their bills, Caruolo phoned me. "You wanted to meet with us," he said gruffly. "I can see you for a few minutes at 1:30 tomorrow. Only you."

Instead of taking me into his office, he led me into Harwood's corner office. The speaker shook my hand. Caruolo and I took chairs across from his desk. "Here's the deal," Caruolo said without preliminaries. "You get your nominating commission, and we keep confirmation in joint session."

I asked how that was different from the Grand Committee.

"It's entirely different," Caruolo said. "The House comes in at the very end. And we're not giving that up."

"And if RIght Now! doesn't agree?"

Caruolo smiled. "We have lots of ways to peel away those reps who signed with Benoit. Or we can stall this to death and let time run out." His gaze shifted out a south window. Beyond unpaved parking lots on both sides of Francis Street lay downtown Providence, where the gleaming new Rhode Island Convention Center had just opened. Under broken clouds, its glassy turret gleamed in sunshine. "I assume you're aware, that one of your buddies on the steering committee has been up to some corrupt things down there."

"Who?" I demanded.

Caruolo smirked. "I don't have all the details yet, but we can get them."

"Who are you talking about?"

He hinted that a RIght Now! leader had played an unsavory part in the development of the mall where construction would soon begin. "At this point there's no firm proof," Caruolo chuckled, "but who knows what a little digging will turn up? It would certainly divert attention from your righteous cause."

Behind his massive desk, Harwood smiled but said nothing.

"Look," Caruolo resumed reasonably, "you can achieve a truly historic change and look good at the same time. Just don't blow your chance to get this right." He rose to signal that the meeting was over.

Escorting me out, he shook my hand. "We wanted you to be clear about our bottom line. Understand that if you repeat this conversation, I'll deny it. And keep in mind that the difference between you and me is that I have a witness." He released my hand and opened the door.

I stepped into the marble hallway as the door closed behind me. I pulled out my new laptop to write down Caruolo's words.

Half an hour later, the RIght Now! sponsors spoke to reporters in the rotunda. "Merit selection has a proven track record of success," Myrth York declared. "It will be simple to implement and easy to administer."[15] Our press packet showed that she was filing the constitutional amendment, while her East Side colleague, Sen. Rhoda Perry, would introduce what we hoped would become the enabling legislation for merit selection.[16]

That same day, Sen. DiSandro released the report of the nine-member Senate Select Commission he had led, co-sponsoring its legislation with Paul Kelly.[17] It drew from versions Common Cause and the Bar Association had sponsored in prior years. No one doubted that DiSandro's name would grace whatever might finally pass. Our sponsors — Myrth York and Rhoda Perry in the Senate, Nancy Benoit and Barbara Burlingame in the House — would be relegated to historical footnotes.

With a glut of proposals that bore the title "merit selection," we faced the challenge of explaining differences.[18] Frequently asked questions provided the framework for a four-page handout.[19]

Q: What's wrong with the way we pick judges?

A: Rhode Island retains two distinct but highly politicized mechanisms for selecting judges:

- *Rhode Island's Supreme Court justices are elected by all members of the House and Senate meeting "in Grand Committee." Only two other states — South Carolina and Virginia — follow this practice. For all the talk about how "democratic" this is, there is no more efficient way of handing the choice to the Speaker of the House. Joseph Bevilacqua moved directly from his post as Speaker to the Chief Justice's chair in the Supreme Court. Matthew Smith engineered the election of his friend and business partner Thomas Fay; then Fay chose Smith as Administrator of the Court.*

- *Lower court judges are appointed by the Governor in a process that has often deteriorated to deal-making. A top former executive branch official recently admitted that there has long been an informal protocol as governors and leaders of the General Assembly took turns in picking judges: 'Mine... yours... his.'*

Neither system works. Both must be replaced.

As the legislative session geared up, several op-ed writers and talk show hosts argued that Rhode Island should elect its judges, as many other states did, but no lawmakers introduced bills for judicial elections.

In the RIght Now! steering committee,[20] Alan Flink warned of the need to keep political hacks off the Judicial Nominating Commission. "Unless we can make the panel genuinely independent," he declared, "we'll accomplish nothing."

Our legislation would direct the governor to appoint an eleven-member commission: two lawyers and a law professor from lists provided by the Bar Association, other appointments from lists submitted by legislative leaders, and several public members independent of those lists.[21] We were determined to keep commissioners at arm's length from public officials and political parties.

Confirmation of Supreme Court justices became the key sticking point. The RIght Now! bill followed the federal system and other states in having the Senate confirm all judges.

"House leaders expect a voice in confirmation," said Fr. Robert Newbold, who represented the Roman Catholic Diocese of Providence. For the first time in several months, he sat with the steering committee. "The feedback I'm getting from House leaders is that they're not willing to give up the Grand Committee. Until now, as we all know, they've controlled Supreme Court appointments."

"Exactly the problem!" roared Alan Flink.

"I'm saying they feel strongly about this," Newbold shot back. In his black suit and priest's collar, he sat across the Hasbro board table from Flink. "This legislation — in its current form — requires the House to give up everything, while the Senate gets everything."

"This isn't about political formulas," Flink retorted. "We're talking about a merit selection model that has been tested over decades."

"That doesn't mean we can't adapt the model." Newbold did not back down. Usually he lobbied for the diocese; now he seemed to be lobbying RIght Now! on behalf of Harwood and Caruolo. "As you know, the House would accept a judicial nominating commission that presented candidates to the Grand Committee."

"That's entirely off the table," Flink thundered. "We brought RIght Now! out of hibernation to end the Grand Committee's role in picking Supreme Court justices. There's no way we can cave in on that issue."

Unruffled, Newbold insisted the House might settle for joint confirmation of Supreme Court justices. "They're willing to step back from the current situation, where they control the entire process. They'll never agree to a plan that cuts them out of Supreme Court appointments entirely."

At Flink's elbow, Norman Orodenker raised a hand. A dark beard framed his jaw and made him look like Abraham Lincoln. "I don't want to be disrespectful of the good Father, but I must mention that we had lengthy discussions about the Grand Committee, and we resolved that issue many months ago. Nothing I know of has changed in the interim."

Like Flink, Orodenker was a lawyer; unlike Flink, he rarely raised his voice. As if to prevent Flink from leaping over the table, he laid a hand on his shoulder and extended the other toward Newbold. His tone was soothing. "With all due respect, Father, this is not about horse-trading between the House and Senate. This is not about saving face for individuals in high office."

When Orodenker breathed, Newbold interrupted: "Do you believe the House has to give up everything while the Senate gets everything?"

Orodenker shook his head. "If I'm not mistaken, they've mentioned 'advice and consent of the two chambers in joint session.' No matter how you dress that up, that's the Grand Committee in another guise. I believe this steering committee has an obligation to the people. Otherwise, all this effort toward judicial reform will have gone for naught."

"You may get nothing in the end," Newbold said.

"If we go down in flames," Orodenker said softly, "so be it. But we cannot leave the Grand Committee with any role in selecting or confirming judges. It's my considered judgment that we need to stand firm on this issue."

At Newbold's side, Leo Cornelius motioned to Alan Hassenfeld for permission to speak. Recently retired as a United Way executive in California, Cornelius now led strategic planning for Rhode Island's statewide Catholic diocese. "I like to be reasonable," he said. "I understand that feelings here are strong. But I want to suggest that an anti-Grand Committee strategy is simply unrealistic."

Newbold and Cornelius were attending their first meeting in months, and Hassenfeld let them speak at length. Then, in his endearing way, he explained that he would put the question of compromising on the Grand Committee to the group. "Our practice is to have one person speak for each organization around the table. I encourage organizations to bring several people but vote only once."

He looked to Max Riter from the AARP State Legislative Committee to start.

"I don't think we can compromise at this time," Riter said "I'm not saying we won't later. But definitely not now."

Tom Banchoff spoke for Common Cause. "Our goal has been to squeeze politics — as much as possible — out of this process. Even without the Grand Committee, the governor will feel pressure to cut deals for judicial appointments. House leaders will have input at the front end when they give the governor names he must consider for the commission. The idea of allowing the House to veto a Supreme Court nominee would perpetuate the speaker's dominant role. Only three states in the entire country allow representatives any role in Supreme Court appointments."

"The Diocese of Providence votes for compromise," Newbold declared. "Joint confirmation of Supreme Court justices."

One after another around the table, members of the steering committee opposed any House role in confirming judges. Even chambers of commerce opposed accepting Caruolo's compromise so early in the process.

Hassenfeld summarized the obvious: except for Newbold's vote, there was a clear consensus not to accept House involvement.

"If I may?" Jim Miller, now a seasoned church executive, asked. "I'd like to ask where this leaves the diocese."

"Not sure," Newbold said. "Bishop Gelineau knows my concerns about throwing down a gauntlet. But he may not agree with what I've said here today. I'll report this to him and get back to Alan."

Dave Duffy, who had envisioned the RIght Now! name and logo, suggested that nobody mention this dispute outside the meeting. "Our position remains exactly what it's been since last August: merit selection for all Rhode Island judges, nothing less. No room for any semblance of the Grand Committee. We can say that without rubbing it in their face. We get the public to lobby their representatives. Let the people push House leaders. The speaker has far less control over this issue than he had before the court scandal broke."

He glanced around the oblong table. "Will House leaders come around? At this point in February, none of us can say. Will we need to compromise in April or May? We don't know that either. What we do know is that the organizations around this table can rally many thousands of constituents across the state. We've got two months to pressure individual members of the House — all of whom must run for re-election in November."

Jim Miller segued to mobilizing. The RI Council of Churches was preparing information for every church, synagogue, fellowship, and service group in their database. "We hope to generate a first wave of twenty or thirty thousand personal letters to members of the General Assembly." Miller promised thank-you notes to lawmakers who had signed pledges not to participate in the Grand Committee and "a little prodding" for those who had not. "We won't threaten," he said, "but they'll know we're watching."

The combined memberships of all the congregations in the council fell below the number of Catholics in the Diocese of Providence, and Miller had no authority over any clergy, yet he mobilized people through sheer moral force and tenacious outreach. He went on to describe training sessions for the interfaith community. Besides traditional Protestant denominations, Miller had drawn Orthodox congregations into the council and built alliances with the Board of Rabbis and the Unitarians. He also worked with Muslims, which was still innovative in the 1990s. Then he suggested bringing religious leaders to the State House for a lobbying day.

"Wow!" exclaimed Hassenfeld. "And I thought Jews were good organizers."

Because I had spent years in parish ministry, Miller arranged for me to preach in churches across Rhode Island. Drawing on the book of Exodus, I told an ancient story of judicial selection: when Moses confronted a restive Israelite camp in the desert below Mount Sinai. The never-ending task of resolving disputes left him exhausted, so Moses' wise father-in-law, Jethro, urged him to appoint judges with specific qualities. They should be "capable leaders who fear God," are utterly "trustworthy," and "hate dishonest gain." Such judges could resolve routine conflicts and bring the most difficult cases to Moses.[22]

I preached that although governments had changed dramatically over three thousand years, people still needed trustworthy judges who loved the law and "hated dishonest gain." I reminded congregations that forty-four Democrats and fifteen Republicans in the House had co-sponsored the RIght Now! legislation, and all the announced candidates for governor had declared their support. But we needed people of faith to help squeeze politics out of judicial selection.

Media stories kept rehearsing the recent scandal caused by former House Speaker and Supreme Court Administrator Matthew Smith's cover-up of embezzlement from court funds. Smith had run up parking fines worth more than $2,000 but wrote on Supreme Court stationery to get his tickets dismissed. He and Fay had run the court system with a sense of entitlement that no ordinary citizen enjoyed.[23]

As winter gave way to spring in 1994, widespread public bitterness still lingered like mounds of dirty snow. Smith and Fay were long gone, but their abuses of power left an ugly residue. Taxpayers felt themselves swept inexorably toward April 15, preparing their returns with a sense that their pockets had been picked. Reminders of special privilege piled up. General Treasurer Nancy J.

Mayer struggled to evict twenty-four union officials who had bought their way into the state pension system at flagrantly reduced prices when Matty Smith ran the House. One teacher's union executive had bought thirty years of state pension credits for a mere $28,352, and Mayer noted that if he had purchased an identical annuity from a private insurance company it would have cost him $788,929.[24] His state pension paid $61,430 per year, at taxpayer expense.

The General Assembly had repealed the 1987 law that allowed this abuse, but Superior Court Judge Antonio S. Almeida ruled that the union leaders were entitled to pensions they had bought in good faith.[25] Almeida had been arrested in 1991 for taking bribes, and he went to jail, but his ruling stood.

Finally, in 1994 and at Mayer's request, Senate Minority Leader Michael J. Flynn filed legislation to revoke the 1987 law and evict those union employees who had never worked for the state, returning their contributions with interest. Mayer and a posse of reformers testified in support of Flynn's bill. Senators approved it unanimously in March, but it seemed doomed in the House of Representatives.[26]

Meanwhile I had expected merit selection to sail through the Senate Judiciary Committee. I was wrong. Witnesses had trekked through heavy rain to testify in support of the RIght Now! legislation sponsored by Myrth York and Rhoda Perry.[27] I gave Domenic DiSandro's secretary a list of witnesses who were ready and wrote that others would sign in when they arrived. Just before the hearing, a clerk handed out copies of DiSandro's SubA, twenty-eight pages of dense legal language.[28] I skimmed it and made notes in the margins. In a sharp departure from what we had discussed, Senate leaders had clearly decided to exclude the Bar Association from the process of appointing lawyers or law professors to the Judicial Nominating Commission. DiSandro's substitute also dropped a crucial requirement for "racial and gender" diversity on the panel, although Perry's bill required that the nominating authorities and governor "endeavor to ensure that, to the fullest extent possible, the composition of the commission reflects the diversity of the state's population."

DiSandro was clearly planning to take testimony and a vote on his bill before he heard from our witnesses on the York and Perry versions. If we waited for the York and Perry legislation, the vote might be over. We caucused in the hallway and agreed that all would testify for essential principles of merit selection but not support DiSandro's new iteration. I urged the Judiciary Committee not to vote on any bill before they had heard testimony on all of the merit selection bills.

"Is there a motion?" DiSandro barked. In an instant, he had a motion for passage and a second. The vote sounded unanimous. His slam-dunk made no sense.

I never learned why Senate leaders, who had led on merit selection, rushed the process. Weeks earlier, Myrth York and I had met amicably with DiSandro about these bills. Was it because she had announced for governor, or did he mean to pay RIght Now! back for being too pushy? Was he afraid reporters would compare the two bills in detail?

After the hearing, I caught up with Paul Kelly in the hallway and reminded him that RIght Now! was concerned that too many state boards had no women or racial minorities among their membership, and that our legislation required the Judicial Nominating Commission to address this. I told him the bill just approved in the Judiciary Committee did not.

"I hear you," Kelly told me. "Let me see what we can do."

On a blustery day in March, the full Senate took up judicial selection. DiSandro proposed a floor amendment to restore the diversity requirement, and senators approved it without debate. They then passed both the enabling legislation and the constitutional amendment with unanimous votes.[29]

On the House side, Judiciary Chair Charles T. Knowles had filed a constitutional amendment that would create a judicial nominating commission without specifying that it be "independent and nonpartisan" or that judicial candidates be "highly qualified by merit."[30] Even worse, Knowles's proposed amendment allowed the governor to appoint justices of the Supreme Court, but it required their confirmation by the House and Senate "in joint session."

The struggle peaked when two leaders of the East Providence Clergy Association, Fr. Jude McGeough and Rev. Ray Bradley, convened a forum in the heart of George Caruolo's district. The clergy group invited the community's entire legislative delegation. In a large assembly hall at the Riverside Congregational Church, hundreds of people filled rows of folding chairs. Dozens more stood along the walls. Seats on a low stage were reserved with conspicuous name cards for each lawmaker.

The three East Providence senators — Bill Irons, Jim McStay, and Paul Tavares — took turns reflecting on the scandals that had brought down two chief justices in seven years. Each spoke proudly of pledging not to participate in the Grand Committee election of another Supreme Court justice. "That was the only leverage we had," Irons declared. "Everyone knew the House controlled the process from start to finish, and they weren't about to give it up."

McStay, who ran a nearby funeral home, was unfailingly polite. "I don't know why my good friend George Caruolo didn't make it here tonight," he said without sarcasm. "My sense is that those of you who have come tonight care about our judicial system and want real reform."

Applause erupted, and McStay paused until the cheers subsided.

"This is issue number one," he continued, "but it won't happen just because it's right. It'll only happen if all of you speak to George Caruolo. Those of you who live in his district have enormous power. He may not be here tonight, but you'll bump into him in the market or at a gas station. Tell him how many people were here. Tell him that you and your neighbors are fed up. Tell him you demand judicial reform. Better yet, phone him and leave a message on his machine. He needs to hear from you."

Fr. Jude McGeough bounded onto the low stage. Always warm and down-to-earth, he wore his authority lightly. "For those who don't know me," he said cheerfully, "I'm Father Jude from St. Margaret's in Rumford, which puts me outside Rep. Caruolo's district. But I spoke to him, and he told me he couldn't make it tonight. Do you agree with Senator McStay that we should let him know we missed his presence?"

"Yes!" came a shout, and the audience roared.

"What?" Father Jude cupped a hand to his ear.

A deafening shout came back.

When it ended, host pastor Ray Bradley and I shook hands with people as they filtered out onto the sidewalk. We handed them flyers and urged people to call Caruolo. Afterward, Bradley walked me to my car in the church's parking lot. Nearing retirement, he glowed with satisfaction. I told him that he and Fr. Jude made a formidable team.

"One thing before you leave," Bradley said. "I met with Caruolo on Ash Wednesday. He made it clear that they won't budge on the Grand Committee. That's part of why Father Jude and I thought it was so important to do this tonight. Caruolo needs to know that without some meaningful merit selection, a lot of people could turn against him in November."

"You think he worries about that?"

"I barely know the man," Bradley replied. "But a lot of people say that beyond being brilliant and having a photographic memory, he's genuinely decent."

A few days later, Caruolo saw me in the House chamber and waved me over to his desk. Representatives and lobbyists stood at a respectful distance while Caruolo drew me close.

"Listen carefully." He looked me in the eye. "You're about to hear my last and most generous offer." He proposed a compromise under which the Judicial Nominating Commission would present highly qualified nominees for each judicial vacancy, including the Supreme Court, to the governor. Nominees for the Supreme Court would undergo separate confirmations in both the Senate and the House of Representatives. "Confirmation is the historic vestige we keep," he insisted.

I asked about Bar Association recommendations for the Judicial Nominating Commission.

Caruolo shook his head. "Won't happen. Only nominees from elected officials. Of all people, you should recognize that the Bar Association is a special interest group."

"You name professionals to all kinds of commissions," I said.

"You just heard our final offer," Caruolo insisted. "The governor gets four appointments without lists. He can ask the bar if he likes, but that doesn't go into the statute. Nine members — just like your beloved Ethics Commission. Separate House and Senate confirmations. That's our bottom line."

I nodded, knowing better than to argue.

"Look," he pressed, "you've got ninety percent of what you asked for. We sacrifice Grand Committee election of Supreme Court justices. We even give up confirmation in joint session. But if you insist on Bar Association seats on the commission or on having only the Senate confirm — either one is a deal-breaker."

"I'll take it to the steering committee," I said.

"Do that," he muttered. "Take it while it's on the table."

We shook hands, and I ducked out into the rotunda to write down his terms. The entire exchange took less than a minute.

Around the board table at Hasbro, the RIght NOW! steering committee struggled over Caruolo's compromise. No one liked surrendering an official role for the bar.

With perfectly trimmed dark hair, Kelly Sheridan wore horn-rimmed glasses, a starched shirt, striped tie, and charcoal suit. A vice president of the Rhode Island Bar Association, he had merged its legislation with the Common Cause bill. "Most of you have never seen the House of Delegates," he said. "Forty-four delegates are elected by their peers. They represent diverse kinds of legal practice. Only seven come from big firms of fifty or more attorneys. Having the delegates present a list of potential commissioners to the governor would guarantee independent voices on the panel."

"For those of you who aren't lawyers," Norman Orodenker added, "there's a dichotomy to understand. Early in their careers, most lawyers choose between a political avenue in the legislature and the politics of the Bar Association. Most don't have time or inclination to do both, and some who take the legislative route try to paint the bar as elitist."

Sheridan nodded. "The insinuation of elitism is a smokescreen," he said. "In fact, members of the judicial nominating committee who came via the Bar Association would be independent, and they'd be vocal — which is exactly what some in the State House don't want."

Orodenker smiled. "That's a polite way of saying they fear that attorneys nominated by the Bar Association would be hard to control. The leadership fears having knowledgeable attorneys who could demolish the political hacks they might send up for judgeships. Once judges are on the bench, they're there for life unless they do something criminal. But we're pulling the process out of the closet for everyone to watch."

"So the question," Alan Hassenfeld interjected, "is whether Caruolo's refusal to grant the Bar Association a role on the commission is a deal-breaker for us. Is that right?"

Orodenker answered: "I'd love to specify a role for the bar in nominating members of the commission. That's the way to produce a truly independent and qualifications-driven commission. But if, in the grand scheme of things, the two pills we have to swallow are a panel chosen by elected officials and separate House and Senate confirmations, I think we've achieved a reasonable compromise. Particularly when you remember where we started."

"You're ready to throw in the towel?" Alan Flink demanded.

"No, " Orodenker replied. "I take Caruolo at his word when he tells us any more than that would be a deal-breaker. And I recognize that he's agreeing to a deal that's substantially on our terms, a deal that's historic. I don't think we can let the perfect become the enemy of the good."

That became the RIght Now! consensus.

On April 8 a standing-room only crowd filled the House Judiciary Committee's hearing room as Charles Knowles presented the revised legislation to his committee. "The eyes of the entire state of Rhode Island are upon us," he declared.

The only drama came when Rep. Harold Metts, head of the Black Caucus of State Legislators, announced he would vote against the bill. "I like the present system," Metts said. "There is no one in South Providence who is going to be on that commission. I can tell you that."

I challenged Mett's assumption and testified that several civil rights organizations were members of the RIght Now! Coalition. We wanted an explicit requirement that the membership of the commission fully reflect the racial diversity of the state.[31]

The committee voted to send the bill to the full House, where Knowles would offer floor amendments. When under pressure the General Assembly often passes complicated bills with an understanding that the committee chairperson will present a floor amendment to address technical problems. This practice avoids having to bring the committee back for a final vote. I stepped out of the State House into a brisk April breeze. The promise of passage rose like daffodils in spring.

Proposals to modernize the General Assembly also moved. Our sponsors, Rep. Jim Langevin and Sen. Jack Revens, worked overtime to get hearings and votes. Revens introduced two constitutional amendments. The first proposed to raise legislators' compensation from $300 to $10,000 per year and end legislative pensions, precisely the bargain recommended by the Blue Ribbon Commission.[32] The second would cut the Senate and the House of Representatives in half, with downsizing to occur in redistricting after the 2000 federal census.[33] "I believe we have far too much bureaucracy," Revens told his colleagues in floor debate. "I believe we have far too many people serving in this General Assembly."[34]

Senators approved both reforms by overwhelming margins and sent them to an uncertain fate in the House.[35] There Jim Langevin had packaged all of the constitutional provisions in a single bill, with Charlie Knowles as a co-sponsor.[36] The House Judiciary Committee recommended it for passage, but several representatives who normally avoided me now stopped to argue about downsizing and the end of legislative pensions. I pointed out that they could continue under the old pension system and salary scale. Only those elected after passage of the amendment would be required to take the new compensation without pension benefits.

A few times I pulled out my dog-eared paperback of *The Federalist Papers* and showed them James Madison's warning that large legislatures often undermined representation.

"Madison had nothing but contempt for Rhode Island," Rep. Mabel Anderson retorted. "You think you know so much, but you don't."

"What's your corsage for?" I asked her.

Beneath one of her quirky hats, she smiled in spite of herself. "For my birthday." The word among lobbyists was that this was her seventieth. "And don't think you can fool me by changing the subject!"

Week after week through April and May, Langevin's legislation lay in limbo. I asked him why it was not posted on the House calendar.

"They won't tell me," he confided. "I think they're having trouble corralling enough votes."

"Anything I can do?"

"Keep the letters and phone calls coming in," he said. "They expected pressure on judicial selection, but I think they're genuinely surprised that so many constituents care about modernizing the legislature."

Langevin's proposed constitutional amendment finally came up for debate in the House on June 2, the same afternoon Bruce Sundlun was to sign the Judicial Nominating Commission bill into law. For five weeks we had been lobbying representatives who now milled in the aisles below the House gallery where I sat. Many took our commission's *Blueprint for the 21st Century* as an insult, and I doubted that John Harwood and George Caruolo would risk political capital to put the amendment before state voters. Worse, the ballot question contained many moving parts: any difference between House and Senate versions would spell doom. No one knew whether this delicate deal could pass in both chambers.

The amendment increased Senate terms to four years while cutting the number of senators in half; the House would be downsized from 100 to 75 representatives who would continue with two-year terms. It would raise legislative compensation to $10,000 and keep up with inflation with periodic cost-of-living adjustments. The General Assembly would remain a part-time body, but lawmakers would receive the same health coverage as full-time state employees.

Legislators currently serving could choose to continue with the existing salary and pension benefits, but no one elected after November could get pension credits for service in the General Assembly.

Charlie Knowles rose to offer a floor amendment. While House pages distributed copies, he explained that his motion would delete parts of the text that granted four-year terms to members of the Senate.[37]

My heart sank. Knowles, a co-sponsor, was scuttling the deal.

With little debate, Harwood called for a vote. On the board, columns of green lights showed broad support for dumping Senate four-year terms. Green lights glowed by Harwood and Caruolo. Only a few red lights said no to Knowles. The final tally was 78–8. In an instant the Senate's reward for a dramatic downsizing had vanished. Were House leaders about to scuttle the entire package? Was this lopsided vote payback for our pushing so hard against the Grand Committee?

Shortly after five o'clock, a tap on my shoulder signaled that it was time for the governor to sign the Merit Selection Law. As I climbed toward the exit, I heard several representatives asking to vote section by section on Langevin's bill, always an ominous request.

Harwood and Caruolo slipped out of the House chamber, and I followed them into the State Room. While Sundlun trumpeted merit selection as a landmark accomplishment of the 1994 legislative session, I kept a straight face. Only a year earlier he had declared his opposition — now, in full campaign mode, he praised House and Senate leaders for negotiations that had resolved differences over judicial selection. He declared that the bill he would sign was proof that government could be responsive to the people.[38]

Myrth York was not present for the bill signing. She had dared to run against him, and I assumed Sundlun had warned Senate leaders he would never sign legislation she sponsored.

In his turn at the podium, Harwood returned the governor's compliments and cited this legislation as transcending the politics of the House, Senate, and political parties. "I think this shows the state of Rhode Island that good government bills like this will promote what all of us are looking for, and that is a better judicial system, a system where we in fact will have the highest caliber of judges in the land."

While Harwood spoke, Caruolo lifted a portable phone to his ear. It was as big as a brick with an antenna. When Harwood returned to his seat, Caruolo whispered to him, one hand hiding his lips. Swiftly, they ducked out, which probably meant trouble for Langevin's bill on the House floor.

I waited my turn to speak. I thanked Sundlun and legislative leaders for bringing us all to this day. "This is genuine merit selection by any standard extant anywhere in the United States," I said. "This will make it much harder for the old political trades to involve judgeships." Sundlun signed the legislation, but I had no time to savor the moment. I rushed back upstairs to the House gallery.

Caruolo was on his feet, reasoning with his colleagues. From his comments I surmised that representatives had deleted a section that would cut their number from 100 to 75 but passed the Senate downsizing from 50 to 25. Like a disappointed schoolmaster, Caruolo scolded gently: "I don't know if it's the air in here, but we have to keep in mind that this can only pass as a balanced package. It has to be even-handed for all parties."

He asked for a motion to reconsider and quickly got one. Clearly in a rebellious mood, 21 reps voted against reconsidering, but Caruolo prevailed. In a second vote, House members acquiesced — by a vote of 48–36 — to cutting their number from 100 to 75. The final vote in favor of Langevin's entire package, as now amended, was 61–11. Through a fog I heard Caruolo on the floor below recommending that the remainder of the House calendar be carried over to the next week. All the satisfaction I felt when Sundlun signed merit selection drained away.

The House rebellion reinforced our case for a smaller and more accountable legislature, but our package had come unglued. Once stamped by the clerk, Langevin's legislation was hand-carried through the massive oak doors at the back of the chamber and across to the Senate, where it would likely die.

"I don't want to burst your bubble," Paul Kelly told me later, "but this is a deal-breaker. Without four-year senate terms, senators won't agree to downsize."

"Do you see any room for compromise?"

Kelly shrugged. "Since the House has agreed to cutting their number to seventy-five, I would talk to people here about the same percentage. Understand I'm not promising. I'm not sure I can sell any downsizing without longer Senate terms."

Both chambers had passed legislation to downsize the General Assembly, end its corrupt pension system, and raise legislative pay for the first time in a century. Senators and representatives could tell their voters that they favored the concept, but unless both voted to put the same amendment on the ballot, nothing would change. The impasse reminded me of years past when the Senate and House approved different versions of our nepotism and revolving door bills.

I carried a checklist of bills that might still pass. Months earlier, I had testified in support of Nancy Mayer's legislation to evict teachers' union officers who had burrowed their way into the state pension system.[39] With scrupulous fairness, Mayer proposed to repay what the union officials had paid in, plus eight percent interest. "I am the eternal optimist," she told a reporter about her long-shot legislation. "I can't understand what argument anybody could muster to vote against this bill."[40]

The Senate passed her repeal in March, but union leaders argued before the

House Finance Committee that Mayer's bill amounted to a "retroactive repeal of a constitutional right." The ACLU also opposed Mayer's legislation, citing what it called "grave constitutional questions." But as the General Assembly raced toward adjournment, the House finally followed the Senate's lead, passing the repeal with an astonishing bipartisan vote of 76–7. Despite threats of another legal challenge, the bill went to the governor. After promising he would sign the repeal, Sundlun allowed it to become law without his signature. Pressure from constituents had convinced many General Assembly Democrats to back the Republican general treasurer's bill, but union lobbying had apparently persuaded Sundlun — now less than three months away from his primary showdown with Myrth York — not to sign what he might have claimed as a significant reform.[41]

Legislative sessions normally ended with lobbyists trying frantically to move stuck bills while armies of legislators fanned themselves and longed for the final gavel. Behind the scenes, House and Senate leaders wrangled over lists of bills. I never attended one of those exchanges, but I knew a staff member who had. I asked him about the "horse-trading."

"'Horse-trading?'" He guffawed. "It's hostage-taking."

Our search for compromise on downsizing the General Assembly, raising members' compensation, and ending legislative pensions seemed fruitless. Rumors flew among lobbyists that House and Senate leaders were at loggerheads about other bills and might simply adjourn.

Patience was running thin when Jack Revens waved me toward the rear door of the Senate and drew me into a windowless conference room. He said the best compromise we could get would cut the Senate to 38 and the House to 75. Both would stay with two-year terms. "It's not what I'd like," Revens said, "and I have no assurance it will pass on the other side. The question is whether you and Gary Sasse will affirm it if we go forward."

I assured him I would. I knew Sasse was in the building and went to find him.

During the next break, Revens pitched the compromise to the Senate Committee on Special Legislation. "It's not what we passed back in March," he said, "but it's genuine reform. I have assurances that RIPEC and Common Cause and RIght Now! will urge voters to approve it." He paused. "Who knows if historians will cite this amendment as a major accomplishment of the 1994 session?"

The committee approved, and the full Senate quickly followed for the second time. The compromise resolution went back to the House with an armload of other legislation. Caruolo was on his feet, telling representatives to have a good Fourth of July weekend and come back ready to finish up. "I know some of you have vacation plans, but there's one matter left of great interest to certain members of this chamber and the public, and that's a compromise version of the bill we passed four weeks ago about downsizing and raising legislative compensation."[42]

Groans rose around the chamber. Despite Caruolo's bluster, he and Harwood had compromised on merit selection of judges, they had backed downsizing recommended by the Blue Ribbon Commission, and they had supported passage of the Common Cause bill to put legislative data online. Now the gruff majority leader gave his exhausted rank-and-file a positive signal about what could still become Ballot Question 2.

After the long holiday weekend, lawmakers returned to finish up. Final versions of the Langevin and Revens amendments had been printed, their numbers listed in long calendars of other bills. As I watched from the gallery Harwood allowed disgruntled representatives to sound off about the ways legislative downsizing would increase the cost of campaigns or weaken the bond between lawmakers and their constituents. After their complaints wound down, representatives reluctantly approved the Senate compromise.

Formal business ended, and farewells began. The first class of Rhode Island legislators elected in the wake of RISDIC reminisced about their work together, wished each other well in fall campaigns, and said goodbye to those who were not seeking re-election.

I had known for a month that merit selection of all Rhode Island judges would be Question 1 on the November ballot. Now our proposal for downsizing the House to 75 and the Senate to 38 — compromised but worthy — would appear as Question 2. Reporters in the rotunda asked me what difference this amendment on legislative size and pay might make. I replied that it would provide "a leaner, fairly paid, and hopefully better informed legislative body that will be more accountable to the people." Even if voters approved, the downsizing would take effect eight years in the future, in 2002. "We need to recognize that reform doesn't happen overnight," I said. "It's a long, slow process of generations rather than weeks or legislative sessions."[43]

Outside, rain had left the marble balustrades glistening. Century-old cobblestones felt smooth and slippery under foot. All had been new when the State House was built between 1896 and 1901.[44] Since then, through more than ninety years, voters had kept rejecting pay raises for their senators and representatives. Would voters again refuse to raise legislative salaries? Would they balk at health care for part-time legislators? Would union leaders campaign against downsizing? What if bitter voters simply rejected Question 2?

Historic Votes
1994

EARLY IN 1993, after the upset over my candidacy,[1] the Ethics Commission hired Sara Quinn as executive director for a second time. She quickly launched a flurry of bold ventures: pushing to investigate pre-1987 conflicts, suing to collect unpaid ethics fines, shaping rules for the commission to file its own complaints, and proposing mandatory ethics education for public officials. She also lodged an ethics complaint against John Harwood and tangled with other powerful legislators.[2]

Quinn made enemies and revealed a hard edge that irritated even her allies. Commissioner John J. O'Brien, who had worked with her over a decade, told reporter Thomas Frank he wished she would "learn to temper justice with mercy." And Quinn was irked when members questioned her legal dictates. In what proved a final straw, she publicly accused the panel's chairperson, Richard Morsilli, of "coercing" her to seek legal advice from a judge.

Guy Dufault, the state Democratic Party chair, ended the impasse by offering her a slot on the party's 1994 statewide ticket. Over breakfast he suggested that she run for attorney general. A few days later, she resigned from the Ethics Commission for the second time and announced her candidacy.[3]

My heart sank. Quinn had no chance against the formidable Republican incumbent Jeff Pine. Once Democrats got her out of the Ethics Commission they would invest little in her campaign, nor would they dream of rewarding her unsuccessful race with a judgeship, as they had compensated others who ran against powerful Republican incumbents.

No matter how people voted, Rhode Island's 1994 election would be historic. For the first time in the state's history voters would elect a governor for a four-year term. In another first, they could pick women for four of five statewide executive offices: governor, secretary of state, attorney general, and general treasurer. For the first time in American history, they might elect a quadriplegic secretary of state.

Voters might also decide to end a 247-year tradition under which the General Assembly named justices to the Supreme Court, and they might break the bitter impasse over legislative pay and pensions.

1994 would also provide an acid test of the 1992 Comprehensive Campaign Finance Law. Candidates for the five statewide executive offices could decide whether to draw down public matching funds. Any who opted into the process must swear to comply with limits on contributions and expenditures.[4]

All of the 1994 candidates for governor signed into the program, and among contenders for the five statewide general offices, only Jim Langevin chose not to participate. He had told me beforehand that he would not take matching funds in his campaign for secretary of state. Because he faced a primary in his own party and a Republican incumbent, Barbara Leonard, in the general election, Langevin thought he had to spend more than the half-million dollars the program would allow. "I won't be in debt to any special interest," he assured me. "Whatever I can't raise from individual donors, I'll take from my trust fund."

Langevin had been a teenager dreaming of a career in law enforcement when a bullet fired accidentally inside the Warwick police headquarters shattered his neck. The near-death experience and resulting quadriplegia had galvanized his sense of purpose. In our 1992 Common Cause scorecard, he tied at the top of our House rankings, and from his motorized chair, he led the move to impeach Chief Justice Fay. He had eagerly pledged not to participate in the Grand Committee election of a new chief justice, co-sponsored merit selection, and he became lead sponsor of the constitutional amendment to modernize the legislature. He accomplished all this without any air of superiority or provocation. Though I could not endorse him or any candidate for office, I trusted Jim Langevin.

Our RIght Now! campaign for Question 1 — merit selection of all Rhode Island judges — garnered priceless publicity at little cost when Gov. Bruce Sundlun appointed the members of the Judicial Nominating Commission — now established by law for all lower court vacancies. Of the nine, he appointed three women and one Latino; as envisioned in the law, no more than five of the appointees were attorneys.[5] In the summer of 1994 they began meeting in a windowless conference room at the Department of Administration, across Smith Street from the State House, where they faced a backlog of judicial vacancies.

Never before had Rhode Island witnessed an open casting call for would-be judges.[6] In response to newspaper ads inviting applicants for seven judicial vacancies in the Superior, Family, District, and Workers' Compensation Courts, nearly 190 applicants submitted their reams of required paperwork. The new law required the panel to name between three and five "highly qualified" nominees for each judicial vacancy.[7]

Michael J. Yelnosky, who now chaired the Common Cause judicial reform committee, monitored every meeting.[8] With his abundant brown hair and large eyes, Yelnosky looked too young to be a professor at the Roger Williams University School of Law. As commissioners considered procedural rules, he argued that the names of all judicial applicants should be made public.[9]

"Why?" demanded Peter J. McGinn, a crusty corporate lawyer and lobbyist on the panel. "I don't see any great public interest in revealing those who didn't get an initial review."

Michael A. Kelly, an attorney Sundlun appointed to chair the panel, agreed. "I wouldn't want someone's professional reputation tainted or damaged because he or she didn't make the interview list."

Yelnosky answered that the entire exercise was intended to bring backroom deals into the sunlight. "To be credible, this process has to be accessible to the public. It can't look like you're quietly ditching applicants."

Commissioners persisted in their plan to release the names only of those they chose to interview. They also voted to conduct interviews behind closed doors unless a candidate opted to answer questions in public.

Yelnosky argued that it would be absurd to exclude citizen observers from interviews with prospective judges. "How can members of the public comment on the nominees if they haven't been allowed to observe the interviews?" he asked.

The pressure of public opinion quickly prompted open interviews.[10]

During the past year, deaths and retirements had created seven lower court vacancies, which forced the new commission to schedule nearly a hundred individual interviews, typically fifteen to twenty minutes each. As each candidate entered the bland conference room, commissioners around the table asked about their legal practice, specialties, and court cases. Reporters and ordinary citizens surrounded the panel, listening and taking notes. The fact that lawyers and current judges were submitting themselves to public scrutiny became newsworthy. Newspapers, radio, and even television covered the process.

On August 4, the fledgling commission invited public comments on the nominees. Commissioners listened to hours of mostly supportive testimony from judges, lawyers, litigants, activists, and friends, then voted publicly on candidates, winnowing names. In a single evening they prepared four lists for Superior Court vacancies, three lists for Family Court, and a single list for District Court. The *Providence Journal* published photos of four Superior Court nominees on its front page. Of the thirty-nine candidates presented to the governor, only four had ever served in the General Assembly — former representatives Elaine T. Bucci and Gilbert V. Indeglia, and former senators Marilyn Shannon McConaghy and Gilbert T. Rocha.

Sundlun quickly began interviewing all the candidates, and on August 12 he appointed Netti C. Vogel, Michael A. Silverstein, Stephen J. Fortunato Jr., and Edward C. Clifton as Superior Court judges, announcing that he would send their names to the Senate for confirmation. A day later, he appointed Pawtucket Municipal Court Judge John A. Mutter, District Court Judge Gilbert T. Rocha, and Workers' Compensation Court Judge John Rotondi Jr. to vacancies on the Family Court. He also named Frank J. Cenerini, a lawyer and former social worker, to District Court.[11]

Even an ensuing glitch with one of the candidates showed that merit selection marked a quantum leap beyond the secrecy of previous centuries. Despite a bitter divorce, Workers' Compensation Court Judge John Rotondi Jr. had applied for a seat on the Family Court. His ex-wife complained of spousal abuse in a letter to the nominating commission. Commissioners questioned Rotondi in executive session about her charges and kept the dispute confidential. They put Rotondi on the short list for Family Court and passed his entire file to Sundlun. The governor, who had been through three divorces, discounted the letter, kept it to himself, and nominated Rotondi. He sent Rotondi's file to the Senate Judiciary Committee, where the dispute exploded.

Three women senators announced that they had received copies of a letter that made them question Rotondi's suitability to decide matters of divorce and custody. M. Teresa Paiva Weed, vice chair of the Judiciary Committee, said she had spoken to thirty lawyers but most were afraid to testify against Rotondi because they might later have to appear before him in court. While Paiva Weed did not question Rotondi's competence in the Workers' Compensation Court, she suggested he might be "an inappropriate selection for the Family Court."[12] Maryellen Goodwin added that attorneys in her district were raising concerns about Rotondi, and that in her eight years as a senator she had never received such calls about a judicial nominee.

In a dramatic public hearing of the Judiciary Committee Rotondi's former wife, Susan A. Epstein, testified against his nomination. She reiterated charges from her letter that he "emotionally battered" her and their daughter, and declared it "totally inappropriate" for him to judge "the intimate affairs of women and their children who would come before him." After wrenching deliberations, the committee voted 10–7 to reject Rotondi's appointment, and Sundlun wisely withdrew the nomination before its likely defeat on the Senate floor.[13]

Whatever the truth of Rotondi's life, his volatile confirmation showed that merit selection — with three venues for evaluating each nomination — created valuable space for issues to surface.

THE COMMON CAUSE STATE GOVERNING BOARD decided which votes to count in our 1994 legislative scorecard. At the top of the list were merit selection of judges, modernizing the legislature, and online access to legislative computers. We would also tally votes on ethics, campaign finance, voter registration, state purchasing, and pension reform — nineteen votes each in the Senate and House of Representatives.

One board member asked if we would include those pledges that had successfully blocked the Grand Committee from electing a new chief justice. "They showed a lot of chutzpah," she said. "Their moratorium turned the tide." So in the scorecard published ten days later, we included a special column marked "Moratorium" at the top and a letter "M" by the scores of senators and representatives whose courage forced the General Assembly to change a practice that stretched back to 1747. We gave bonus credit to senators and representatives who forced the constitutional showdown.

Rhode Island's September primaries brought fierce gubernatorial campaigns in both major parties. In the Republican contest, U.S. Attorney Lincoln C. Almond gained support by promising to root out corruption. "It's been one conflict of interest after another," Almond declared in one radio debate against 1st District Congressman Ronald K. Machtley. "We've never been so weighted down by a state government that is so arrogant, so corrupt, so inefficient and so dominated by political insiders."[14] Almond garnered 59.7 percent of the vote against the higher spending Machtley.[15]

In the Democratic race, Sen. Myrth York crushed incumbent Gov. Bruce Sundlun with 57.2 percent in a four-way contest.[16]

Three Republican incumbents running statewide — Jeffrey B. Pine, Nancy J. Mayer, and Barbara M. Leonard — had no primary opponents. Four Democrats campaigned for their party's nomination to run against Leonard for secretary of state, and Jim Langevin outspent three rivals to win 49.1 percent of the vote.[17] Sara Quinn had no challenger in her campaign for attorney general.

Our hardest job in the spring of 1994 had been to convince House leaders to give up the Grand Committee. A tougher sell in the fall would be to convince voters to raise legislative pay for the first time since 1900. Merit selection of judges, which was Question 1, rode a wave of public support, but Question 2 on modernizing the General Assembly felt like a lost cause.

The summer passed without visible statewide opposition. The AFL-CIO Executive Council had opposed plans to downsize the General Assembly, but a labor lobbyist let slip that beyond a few mailings to union members, they were not planning to spend money to defeat Question 2. "It may not be quite dead on arrival," he scoffed, "but we know Hassenfeld won't bankroll any TV ads this time. It'll go down as decisively as the pay raise did in 1986."

RIght Now! shaped a strategy of promoting judicial reform and legislative modernization as dovetailed responses to problems that had corrupted Rhode Island for generations. Our coalition's network of organizations — business, religious, civic, environmental, and reform — would distribute campaign flyers to hundreds of thousands of voters across the state. Wherever possible, we would make the case face to face.

On one side of a flyer, we explained Question 1. On the back, we gave reasons to approve Question 2. On both sides, a thumbs-up hand approved the numbers 1 and 2 with exclamations: "Yes! Yes!"

Whether voters received flyers in a place of worship, outside the supermarket, at a community meeting, at a bus stop, or from volunteers at their front door, our first words would remind them of recent scandals:

> If you're sick of insider games in our state government, vote YES on Questions 1 & 2.

A Q&A format showed readers how this pair of constitutional amendments would address root causes. We presented essential facts with simple but memorable tag lines:

> YES on #1 to choose judges for qualifications, not connections.
> YES on #2 to create a modern legislature for the 21st Century.

The flyer highlighted the RIght Now! logo and listed the array of organizations that were supporting both amendments: the state AARP Legislative Committee, the Greater Providence and Northern Rhode Island Chambers of Commerce, Common Cause, the Diocese of Providence, the Jewish Federation, the League of Women Voters, the NAACP, the NCCJ (National Conference of Christians and Jews), the Rhode Island State Council of Churches, RIPEC, and Save the Bay.[18] These groups would distribute flyers to their members and in communities they served.

As with four-year terms in 1992, we aimed to convince local newspapers to publish editorials in support of both questions. Gary Sasse and I scheduled days of going in person to editorial offices. "I like this," he said as we drove away from the *Newport Daily News* building on a hill overlooking the harbor. "With the *Providence Journal* on your desk, it's easy to forget that these smaller dailies and weeklies reach significant numbers of people."

Publishers in tiny backroom offices understood the issues before we arrived. Like the devil's advocates they had to be, editors asked the important questions that skeptical readers would raise. Their reporters covered the substance of Questions 1 and 2, and most published editorials in support. The *Narragansett Times* rehearsed the state's history of voters rejecting legislative pay raises — followed by legislators creating and fattening their pensions. "At long last," the editors wrote, "there is a genuine proposal to reduce the size of the House and Senate chambers and to rectify the compensation system that, in the minds of many taxpayers, has been subverted over the years with pension ploys."[19]

With their gearwheel logos, omnipresent banners, and nonstop "happy bucks," Rotary Clubs exuded a spirit of civic duty. Over the clinking of coffee cups at one meeting, members listened politely to my stump speech.

"So tell us about why they let union hacks buy their way into the state pension system," one man asked. "Did they ever stop and think what those special pensions would cost the taxpayers?"

I answered that General Treasurer Nancy Mayer's bill to evict those union officials from the retirement system had finally become law in 1994.

"When voters rejected legislative pay raises," another Rotarian said, "the General Assembly turned around and increased their pensions. Why on earth should we reward them with a raise to $10,000 a year?"

I agreed with his premise. Voters had rejected a 1986 legislative pay increase by nearly two to one,[20] only to have legislators double their pensions and the Supreme Court rule that pensions were not "compensation."[21] Since then, recriminations between the people and their elected representatives had become ever more bitter. I explained that Question 2 would amend the Constitution to state explicitly that no lawmaker elected after passage could ever receive pension credits for time in the legislature. The amendment would also establish a process for periodic pay raises linked to inflation. Under Question 2, Rhode Island lawmakers would still receive less than half what legislators received in Connecticut, Delaware, and Maryland, three states with comparable part-time legislatures. "Legislative pay has been a problem since before most of us were born," I said. "Let's solve it once and for all."

I drove back toward Providence doubting that facts and figures made any difference. Rhode Islanders harbored a deep suspicion of people they elected in a system that seemed rigged against them. Could these constitutional amendments make any lasting difference?

In the 1994 elections, Rhode Island Rep. Patrick J. Kennedy won the 1st Congressional District and Congressman Jack Reed was re-elected in the 2nd. In the state's first campaign for a four-year gubernatorial term Lincoln C. Almond narrowly defeated Myrth York.[22] Although York had won their primary, leaders of Rhode Island's dominant Democratic Party had done little to help her campaign.

For the first time, every candidate for governor had accepted matching public funds and campaigned within tight contribution and spending limits. Almond and York spent roughly equal amounts — their combined total spending fell $1.2 million below the $4.26 million Bruce Sundlun spent to beat DiPrete in 1990. Ironically, Almond's campaign to win the first four-year gubernatorial term cost only slightly more than a third of what Sundlun had spent in 1990 for a two-year term. The governor-elect told reporters he could not have run statewide without public matching funds.

Jim Langevin, newly elected secretary of state, promised voters that he would transform the office from that of a repository of documents to an open government service for the people. His campaign touted the fact that the 1993–94 Common Cause scorecard credited him with 100 percent support for reform, noted his early commitment to merit selection of judges, and headlined his leadership in modernizing the General Assembly for the twenty-first century. But from his trust fund Langevin spent three times what the Republican incumbent, Barbara Leonard, could muster, and he crushed her at the polls.

In the race for attorney general, incumbent Jeffrey Pine won every city and town, trouncing Sara Quinn with 76 percent of the statewide vote. Both candidates had participated in the matching-funds program, but Pine qualified for nearly five times as much in matching public funds.[23] Whatever support Guy Dufault originally promised Quinn from the Democratic Party, he produced virtually nothing.

Seventy percent of state voters approved Question 1 on merit selection of all Rhode Island judges. Their votes ended the election of Supreme Court justices by the legislature, which had begun before the American Revolution. Question 2 on modernizing the General Assembly garnered 51.8 percent of the vote. Voters agreed to downsize the General Assembly, end its outsized pensions, and provide a fair salary with health insurance.[24]

Right Now! had helped to bring historic changes. We could celebrate constitutional reforms that were reshaping all three branches of state government. New laws had lessened the cost of running for statewide office and built a bulwark against corporate cash. The Rhode Island Ethics Commission now operated with its constitutional authority reinforced by two unanimous Supreme Court opinions.

But it all seemed too good to continue. Legislative leaders would soon learn that Common Cause had committed itself — with or without support from the RIght Now! coalition — to fixing the deepest defect in Rhode Island's Constitution. Would they continue on the path toward constitutional reform? Or would we face backlash and retrenchment?

3
Separation of Powers | 1

27

Deep Root
1994

UNDER THE RADAR and without public announcement, a study group in Common Cause had been digging toward the deep root of Rhode Island's corruption. Our research began two years earlier.

In April 1992, I had gone to see Sheldon Whitehouse, Gov. Sundlun's policy chief, to negotiate for RIght Now! on the revolving door bill. Spring sunshine poured into the conference room along with cheering from a co-ed volleyball game outside on the lawn. Whitehouse burst through the door, a shock of dark hair mostly swept to one side. He had a prominent cleft chin and broad smile. "Sorry," he said, "it's hard to get off the phone when Bruce calls."

He settled at the head of the table with a yellow pad and flipped through a folder of bills to our proposed ban on revolving door jobs. Whitehouse wanted to define carefully which officials would be covered: "Without clarity here, you'll gum up all kinds of transfers within and between departments." He explained language from several U.S. Supreme Court decisions relating to people who held "senior policy-making, discretionary, or confidential" positions. That terminology became part of the revolving door bill that passed and Sundlun signed — before he challenged its constitutionality.[1]

Whitehouse and I agreed to take the revisions to our higher authorities — he to Sundlun and I to the RIght Now! steering committee. I folded photocopies of his marked-up bills into my notebook.

"Five more minutes?" He asked, and then plunged in. "All this work you've been doing on ethics and campaign finance reform is good, but you'll never cut the deep root of Rhode Island's corruption until you get to separation of powers."

I nodded but barely understood what he meant. I knew the term "separation of powers" only vaguely, like "separation of church and state." I asked how he connected separation of powers with corruption.

Whitehouse unwrapped his discovery with a grin. "I never saw this as a problem until I became Bruce's legal counsel. Here I was approving legal payments for boards and commissions that were set up as exclusive franchises, quasi-public bodies that do everything from supplying clean water to processing sewage for discharge into the bay. Every one of them — or so it seemed — was populated with legislators."

I tried not to look as ignorant as I felt.

"Plain and simple," he went on, "It's about dispensing jobs — from economic development to the landfill. Pots of public money, heaps of patronage, conflicts up the kazoo."

I nodded. "Help me with the part about legal payments."

"Tipping contracts at the landfill. We had a beef over legal bills and put a hold on payments. We got static over that. Not where you'd expect from the Solid Waste Management Corporation. Somebody high up in the speaker's office phoned. 'Why the hell is Whitehouse not letting these lawyers get paid?'" He paused as if that made everything clear.

"You mean the legislature was really running these quasi-public operations?"

He nodded. "That flipped a switch from my law school days. The U.S. Supreme Court and courts in other states have always made a sharp distinction: legislatures write laws and executive branch officials enforce those laws. Legislatures legislate, executives execute. In the federal system and in other states, that's bedrock. The chief executive appoints the bureaucrats who run agencies."

"Everywhere but here?"

"Everywhere but here."

From the hallway came the sound of the bell summoning the House into session.

"The Supreme Court even imposed separation of powers on the Philippines Provisional Government. The Philippines, of all places! It wasn't even part of the United States, but they deemed it a core principle. My point is that you can't have American-style democracy without honest-to-God separation of powers. But there's no such thing in Rhode Island. Never has been. The legislature runs the show."

It had the ring of truth, but I felt like an imposter, conversing about constitutional theory when I had never gone to law school.

"Under proper separation of powers," Whitehouse explained, "not even the whole legislature gets to make appointments. But in Rhode Island, the speaker of the House appoints the lion's share of members to powerful boards and commissions that execute laws. For all practical purposes, the speaker and Senate majority leader administer our state's laws."

"So you're saying the 'deep root of Rhode Island's corruption' is the General Assembly's power to hire and fire people who carry out the laws they've written."

"Precisely." He leaned back in his chair until I caught up taking notes.

"How did you figure this out?"

"When we came in, Bruce asked me to make a list of reforms that were most urgent — a kind of intellectual ranking. Day in and day out, I tried to figure out which we should push first, second, third. That process kept bringing me back to separation of powers. It's the bedrock principle of American government everywhere but in Rhode Island."

Outside, the session bell kept clanging. "So where's your legislation? Have I missed it?"

"We couldn't get to it right away. We were in the throes of trying to solve the banking crisis and the workers' comp mess. We were all working impossible hours."

I asked what happened.

"My research showed Rhode Island completely out of line with the rest of the country," he said. "I drafted a legal brief on separation of powers. Gave it to Bruce."

"And?"

"'I like that!'" Whitehouse growled in imitation of his mentor and boss. "'Go ahead! We'll file it.'"

"But you didn't?"

The young lawyer smiled. "Bruce has an absolute fetish about what he calls 'touching base.' He gave each of us a little sign for our desk: 'Always Touch Base Before Taking Action.' So, he decided to touch base with the legislative leadership. My brief went up to the third floor."

He hesitated, as if trying to decide whether to finish his story. "They were furious. I wasn't with Bruce when he met with them, but what came back to me was like a hand grenade with the pin pulled: 'You file that, and we're done with any kind of cooperation. File that brief, and it's a fucking declaration of war!'"

The bell was still clanging as I left the policy office. I checked my notes of what he had said. A key phrase stood out: "Your work on ethics and campaign reform is good, but you'll never cut the deep root of Rhode Island's corruption until you get to separation of powers."

The executive committee at Common Cause wanted to do our own research on separation of powers, and over the next two years our study confirmed Whitehouse's conclusions. A trove of historic documents showed that the General Assembly had ruled Rhode Island for three centuries. In critical disputes, lawmakers trumped judges and governors. Practically speaking, the necessary checks and balances were nonexistent. Without separation of powers, corruption rooted itself and took hold like poison ivy.

A fireproof safe outside the Senate chamber displayed the Royal Charter of 1663, sealed behind glass. King Charles II of England had granted the charter, and his stern visage adorned its sepia parchment. Archaic English script established the General Assembly as Rhode Island's government. Generations of legislators had guarded their vast, unchecked powers — through the American Revolution, Rhode Island's Dorr Rebellion of the 1840s, and the Bloodless Revolution of 1935. The names of these upheavals marked convulsive changes, but nothing had brought separation of powers to Rhode Island. In 1842, the "law and order" forces of Governor Samuel Ward King crushed the populist movement led by Thomas Wilson Dorr. The victors adopted Rhode Island's first Constitution, which allowed the General Assembly to exercise all the powers it had possessed under the Royal Charter unless explicitly prohibited in the Constitution.[2] The legislature could do whatever it pleased.

By the 1990s, the General Assembly controlled the state through scores of boards that oversaw coastal development, funded water projects, awarded scholarships, floated bonds, operated video slot machines, disposed of trash, processed sewage, and carried out dozens of other administrative functions. The legislature had created these bodies and then appointed its own members to run them. Our research confirmed what Whitehouse had explained to me two years earlier.

On an August afternoon in 1994, Common Cause devoted a special meeting to separation of powers. We asked two lawyers to guide us. The first, Robert D. Kilmarx, was a member of our advisory council and had taken a pivotal case to the state Supreme Court in 1986. "Our case," he began, "involved the Coastal Resources Management Council, which we call by its initials, the CRMC. The controversy centered on a proposal to build a sixty-room time-share hotel on Easton's Beach. Many of you know that lovely beach between Newport and Middletown." Kilmarx explained that he and another lawyer represented a neighborhood group, the Easton's Point Association, which opposed the project.

"The developers did better," Kilmarx said. "They hired Joe DeAngelis, the House majority leader." He paused to let that fact sink in. "The statute establishing the CRMC requires that legislative leaders appoint a majority of its members. On the day of the key vote, all eight legislative appointees showed up, and they all voted for the DeAngelis-supported hotel. We lost by two votes."[3]

Around the Common Cause board table, we all groaned.

"We appealed to the Superior Court, where Judge Ronald Lagueux asked for briefs on a crucial issue: whether the law requiring legislative appointments to the CRMC was constitutional.[4] We found a 1982 case from North Carolina, *Wallace* v. *Bone*, where the state Supreme Court ruled that a coastal body partially appointed by the legislature was unconstitutional. We argued that legislative appointments also made the CRMC unconstitutional."[5]

Heads nodded.

"In a truly eloquent decision, Judge Lagueux declared that the CRMC appointment scheme violated separation of powers. He wrote that the law requiring that legislative leaders appoint eight members of a seventeen-member board — two representatives, two senators, and four public members — usurped the governor's power to appoint officials who execute state laws."[6]

Kilmarx opened a manila folder. "Listen to what Judge Lagueux wrote: 'The position that the appointment power rests with the General Assembly, carried to its logical conclusion, would allow the legislature a free hand to appoint all administrative personnel in government. If the legislature can control all appointments to the executive branch, save the governor, then in essence the governor is nothing more than a ceremonial head of state.'"[7]

Kilmarx savored Lagueux's words and continued: "DeAngelis, of course, appealed to the Rhode Island Supreme Court. You remember that all five justices were former legislators — all chosen in Grand Committee. They were all keenly aware that the Grand Committee could dismiss them, exactly as it sacked their predecessors in the Bloodless Revolution."

The Supreme Court had issued its ruling in March of 1987, with Chief Justice Thomas F. Fay writing a unanimous opinion. "Curiously," Kilmarx observed, "They didn't overrule Lagueux on the merits of the case, but on a technicality. They said it was improper for Lagueux to raise separation of powers on his own, since both parties had submitted themselves to the jurisdiction of CRMC. The court said our neighborhood and environmental groups could not turn around and challenge CRMC's constitutional legitimacy."[8]

Disbelief rippled through the room, and Kilmarx closed with a curious footnote. The community group had run out of judicial options, and the developers got their permit to build. "But then a recession hit and the developer ran out of money," he said. "The time-share never went up. We lost the battle but won the war. Unfortunately, the Supreme Court never ruled on the merits of our separation of powers case."

"How could we get them to do that?" asked Bill Colleran.

"We would need a contested case," Kilmarx said. "Some litigant who lost before CRMC or one of the other administrative bodies and was ready to appeal on separation of powers grounds."

Sheldon Whitehouse, recently appointed U.S. Attorney for Rhode Island, had arrived during Kilmarx's presentation. I reminded the board how he had introduced me to separation of powers.

"You could be at the beach today," Whitehouse began with a smile, "or maybe out on the water. But I'm glad you're here." He slid his chair closer to the table.

"Our problem in Rhode Island is that the legislature exercises broad appointing power of a kind forbidden to Congress by the Supreme Court. By naming people to boards that execute state laws, the speaker and Senate majority leader control most of state government."

Still not forty, Whitehouse had survived his baptism of fire on Sundlun's staff during the winter and spring of RISDIC. It was plain why Sundlun and U.S. Senator Claiborne Pell had taken him under their wings. He loved legal ideas and seemed to gain both competence and confidence in each new post.

Whitehouse affirmed Bob Kilmarx's presentation of the Easton's Beach case. "Members of the legislature profit handsomely from their ability to make appointments and also represent clients before agencies. That should never happen, but it happens frequently. And that's why the impetus for change has to come from outside government."

"What about the governor?" asked Greta Abbott. "Your former boss, Sundlun? He's had four years to take this on. If it's so crucial, why hasn't he uttered a peep about this?"

"Because the immediate pressures of governing prevented him from doing so," Whitehouse replied. "We raised the question with House leaders, but they let us know in no uncertain terms that to proceed with separation of powers would be a 'declaration of war.' Everything else would stop.

"When something goes south in Rhode Island government, we blame some corrupt politician. In fact, Ed DiPrete may be a crook, or Bob Bianchini may have had countless conflicts. But they got away with corrupt practices because the system failed to deter them. In my experience, trouble starts when some governmental mechanism fails. I start from the assumption that government is an engine that can be fixed.

"Montesquieu and Locke had theorized about separation of powers," he continued, "but our founders put it into practice. They designed American government with inherent rivalries. Congress could make laws, the president and cabinet could execute them, and the courts could resolve disputes. Separate functions gave the branches turf interests that each would defend. Madison wrote that each branch of government must have the means and the motives to 'resist the encroachments of the others. Ambition must be made to counteract ambition.'"

Whitehouse brought his argument forward to a series of U.S. Supreme Court rulings. "The bedrock is that Congress can create a position but cannot appoint the officer who fills it. One case arose when the Philippines were under American control. Legislators had set up coal, banking, and other companies and put themselves on the boards. Because the islands were under American jurisdiction, a lawsuit went all the way to the Supreme Court, which ruled that legislative appointments were unconstitutional on separation of powers grounds.

"After Watergate, Congress passed a law that created the Federal Elections

Commission and directed congressional leaders to appoint some of the FEC's members. Again, the Supreme Court declared those legislative appointments unconstitutional because they violated separation of powers. That ruling, *Buckley* v. *Valeo,* required the president to make those appointments with the advice and consent of the Senate."

Like a law professor, Whitehouse traced other cases.

"The problem in Rhode Island," he explained, "is that the General Assembly has few effective checks on its power. Some of our most significant public functions take place in administrative agencies where lawmakers sit as voting members: CRMC, Solid Waste Management, and lots of others. Legislators constitute a majority on the Unclassified Pay Plan Board, and you know how Matty Smith manipulated that. Our legislature bestows insider opportunities on favored people, and they repay the favor. If you'll excuse a coarse phrase: 'You don't kick your own ass.'"

After Whitehouse and Kilmarx answered questions, the board voted unanimously to establish separation of powers as its highest priority. Our board president, Cathy Speer, asked for a second motion to create a task force on separation of powers. She said it would develop strategy, draft legislation, engage other groups, and educate the public.

"So moved," said several people at once, and our task force was born.

For two centuries, Rhode Island's industrial wastes and raw sewage had flushed directly into the Narragansett Bay. In 1980, to end this fetid discharge and comply with the Federal Clean Water Act of 1972, Gov. J. Joseph Garrahy proposed to create the Narragansett Bay Commission (NBC). The NBC would treat sewage from metropolitan Providence and the Blackstone Valley, including North Providence, Johnston, Pawtucket, Central Falls, Cumberland, Lincoln, the northern portion of East Providence, and small sections of Cranston and Smithfield. It would issue bonds and collect funds directly from sewage ratepayers in its catchment area. Garrahy envisioned a small board that would be appointed by the governor and confirmed by the Senate. During legislative deliberations, Garrahy's proposed nine-member commission more than doubled in size to twenty-three members and included two representatives appointed by the speaker and two senators named by the majority leader.[9]

North Providence Rep. Vincent J. Mesolella Jr. got a seat on the NBC board in 1980 and ten years later became its chairman. In 1993, when John B. Harwood was elected speaker of the House, Mesolella became deputy House majority whip. With dual roles in the House leadership and the sprawling sewage treatment authority, he hosted lavish parties for politicians and lobbyists, who toasted him as "Mr. Chairman."[10]

Proof of Mesolella's clout came in his campaign cash. Beverly Clay, a leader in the recently renamed Operation Clean Government (formerly Operation

Clean Sweep), analyzed contributions to top legislative leaders for 1993–94. Her figures showed that Mesolella had amassed $101,840, more than any other member of the General Assembly except John Harwood. Clay noted that only seven percent of Mesolella's campaign contributions came from residents of his North Providence district; NBC employees gave $5,249 during the two-year election cycle, and NBC bidders or vendors contributed $21,775. During the two years after officers of New England Treatment Co. (NETCO) donated $2,125 to Mesolella, the commission paid their company $417,995.[11]

Mesolella earned his living as a developer and was never fastidious about conflicts of interest. He was half owner of Cogenics Inc., a start-up company that sought to build an incinerator capable of turning waste into electricity and heat. Under his leadership, Cogenics scored a coup. A Baltimore company, Enviro-Gro, was negotiating with the Narragansett Bay Commission to convert sewage sludge into fertilizer pellets; it shelved plans to fire its plant with natural gas and signed a deal with Cogenics instead. The two companies submitted a joint proposal to the NBC.[12]

Besides chairing the NBC's board, Mesolella also headed its Committee on Construction, Engineering, and Operations. During a meeting where the joint venture from Enviro-Gro and Cogenics was discussed, Mesolella stepped away from his chair and sat in the audience, apparently to comply with an advisory from the Ethics Commission that he not personally participate in the conversation.[13] He insisted afterward that he had not said a word. When reporter Thomas Frank pointed to his name and comments in minutes of the meeting, Mesolella acknowledged that he had spoken only "to clarify a point." Then, after eight months of controversy over the Enviro-Gro and Cogenics proposal, the NBC restarted the bidding process.

Mesolella next promoted a new deal with NETCO, which was already burning trash and sewage sludge at its Woonsocket plant. Late in 1993, the Bay Commission picked NETCO to build and operate a $17.9 million incinerator at the edge of Washington Park, a South Providence neighborhood.

Community groups protested that the plant would spew toxic gasses and ash into the city's poorest neighborhoods. The non-profit organization Save the Bay criticized the NBC in particular for failing to consider composting, an approach that might save money without harming the environment.[14]

Sen. Myrth York sponsored a 1994 bill to block the incinerator, pending scientific evidence that it would not pose health risks. York's legislation passed the Senate but died in the House Corporations Committee. She blamed Mesolella, citing his role as deputy House majority whip, and called for his resignation. "Frankly," she told reporters, "I see little chance that this vital legislation can pass when, for members of the House, a vote in favor of the bill constitutes a slap in the face of one of their most powerful colleagues."[15]

No one seemed able to block the incinerator. The Public Utilities Commission, the attorney general, and the governor all challenged its legality and sought to delay the signing of a contract until the issue could be resolved in court. But nothing deterred Mesolella. Environmental reporter Robert Frederiksen wrote that, after an hour-long, closed-door session, NBC board members authorized Mesolella to sign the contract with NETCO.[16]

I met Frederiksen for the first time on a slow elevator going up to a meeting of the NBC board. A seasoned journalist whose hair had gone gray, he wore a rumpled gray tweed jacket. With a knowing grin, he asked what brought me there.

"Your stories," I said, and we both laughed.

We stepped into a lobby where huge windows framed a view down to Promenade Street and westward along the tree-lined Woonasquatucket River. Frederiksen drew me to a quiet spot. "I hear you're going after separation of powers," he began.

I told him Common Cause had made the issue our highest priority.

"You'd be taking away their bread and butter," he replied. "I think you're in for a hell of a fight."

We entered the hearing room together. Members of the NBC board sat around a large table. Staff and environmental advocates filled seats along the walls as Mesolella held forth at the head of the table.

"Uh-oh," he exclaimed. "The *Providence Journal* and Common Cause have just arrived. From here on, nothing improper, please."

Laughter filled the room.

Mesolella had the neck, shoulders, and arms of a body-builder. While exuding power, he ran his agenda graciously, and the meeting purred like a luxury car. At the end, he adjourned with thanks to all who attended. Lobbyists and board members thronged around him.

No wonder Rhode Island was in trouble. State law placed Mesolella in a position to wield vast executive powers with virtually no checks or balances. The Narragansett Bay Commission employed a staff of 250 and collected nearly $30 million each year from ratepayers. Ensconced in his quasi-public fortress with powerful allies at the State House, Mesolella could withstand a protracted political siege.

Back at our office, I immersed myself in drafting the separation of powers bills we would propose in 1995. Each would remove legislators from boards that exercised executive powers and would end legislative appointments. One prime target was the Narragansett Bay Commission.

The RIght Now! Coalition had surprised both skeptics and cynics. Our landmark ethics and campaign finance reforms had all become law in 1992, and voters approved our four-year terms constitutional amendment. We built on that base in 1994 with further amendments that established merit selection for all Rhode Island judges and modernized the General Assembly.

Alan Hassenfeld invited the steering committee to celebrate over a December dinner at Hasbro headquarters in Pawtucket. We gathered for cocktails and hors d'oeuvres in a glassed-in garden room: religious leaders, executives from chambers of commerce, environmental advocates, heads of civil rights and reform groups.

"I'm thrilled you're all here," Hassenfeld said, his sleeves rolled up and rubber bands around both wrists. "We've accomplished things together that are truly historic. Load up your plates and enjoy yourselves. We have only one item of business tonight. Over dessert, Phil will regale you with a new challenge."

Feeding on flame-grilled meats and vegetables, members of the steering committee marveled at victories racked up in less than four years since we first joined forces. Leaders who barely trusted each other at the beginning had become fast friends.

"This is an astonishing assembly," the toymaker said with mock seriousness. "I hope you all remember that there are only thirteen shopping days left until Christmas."

Hassenfeld waited for the laughter to subside. "Seriously, we've proved again what can happen when people of diverse backgrounds and interests commit themselves — if you'll excuse my pun — in a common cause."

He smiled mischievously. "Did I really say that? Well it's true, and we've depended on Common Cause for many proposals that have made a real difference. And we'll hear one more tonight. I'm going to ask my vice chairperson to lay it on you."

I thanked him for the fine meal and for his leadership. I catalogued our accomplishments and focused on the impact of our 1992 Campaign Finance Law. "The data show that Linc Almond and Myrth York spent almost equal amounts. They both got their message out, and the winner's spending dropped 65 percent from what Bruce Sundlun spent in 1990. Linc Almond will take office next month without being in anybody's pocket."

Gary Sasse started the clapping. He and Marcel Valois — who first suggested that Alan Hassenfeld lead the coalition — had begun work as co-chairs of the governor-elect's transition team. I thanked Sasse for proposing the Blue Ribbon Commission and shepherding its members through the study.

"Here! Here!" someone called, and applause spread again.

"Thanks to Gary," I said, "we've laid the groundwork for a more responsive, more professional, and less corrupt General Assembly."

I rehearsed the struggle for merit selection of judges and our 70 percent statewide victory. "Governor Almond will exercise that power when he appoints a new chief justice."

Cheers and clapping filled the room.

"Looking ahead, I want to enlist your support for separation of powers." I moved between the round tables, describing the 1992 meeting when Sheldon Whitehouse raised the issue. "One comment struck me then and has stayed with me ever since. He said the work we were doing on ethics and campaign finance reform was good. 'But,' he said, 'you'll never cut the deep root of Rhode Island's corruption until you get to separation of powers.'"

Around the tables, no one stirred.

I sketched Rhode Island's unbroken legislative supremacy since colonial times. "It was only as we looked at the scores of boards where lawmakers execute the very laws they've written that I began to understand." I distributed lists of the seven boards where Common Cause proposed to start. "I won't pretend that changing these boards will be easy," I said. "Ultimately, we'll have to amend the Constitution again. But with broad support from RIght Now! we can do this."

"Good you said it won't be easy," Jim Hagan interrupted. He headed the Greater Providence Chamber of Commerce and had served in the state Senate. "This 'legislative supremacy,' as you called it, is their bedrock and has been since the Royal Charter of 1663. They will not give it up. Pushing separation of powers to Rhode Island will bring all-out trench warfare."

"So what are you saying?" Jim Miller asked. "That we shouldn't take this on because it's deeply engrained?"

Hagan smiled. "I'm saying that what Phil has told us is true. But as the head of the Chamber, I can't recommend separation of powers to my board at this time. The business community has priorities that would go down in flames if we took this on."

Amid the glow of tiny white holiday lights, a heavy silence filled the room.

"I agree with Jim," said John Gregory, recently hired as president of the Northern Rhode Island Chamber of Commerce. "I don't claim to know the issue as well as Jim does, but I can't take us on a kamikaze mission."

Near a glass wall with darkness behind him, Curt Spalding stood to speak. "I can't say what Save the Bay might decide," he said, "but I'll tell you from firsthand experience that legislative appointments on these quasi-public boards are hugely problematic. I've been frustrated with three of the seven boards on this list. They were set up for good purposes, but legislative appointees have repeatedly skewed their decisions for political reasons. Like the chambers of commerce, we have practical reasons to shy away from separation of powers, but this is a core issue. It won't go away. There are so few checks on legislative power. The leadership gets whatever they want, and they're infiltrating more legislators every year."

"What will you recommend to your board?" Alan Hassenfeld asked.

"I'm not sure," Spalding said. "We have environmental priorities to consider."

Jim Miller rose at his seat. "I can't say what our interfaith community will decide, and I need to learn more about this. If this really is the root of Rhode Island's corruption, and if it's getting worse every year, I don't know how we can simply stand aside. I acknowledge that the Council of Churches has fewer legislative priorities than the business community, so I'm going to ask our people to look at this issue."

"Is there any consensus?" Hassenfeld asked.

For a long moment no one spoke. Then Gary Sasse raised a hand. "I don't think the RIPEC board would go beyond what the chambers will do. At the same time, this separation of powers issue goes to the heart of what's wrong with our state. If we're not ready to fight, maybe we should put RIght Now! into hibernation again. At least until there's more clarity."

"I'm for that," said Jim Hagan from his seat. "Alan can always call us together."

No one else spoke.

"'Hibernation again'?" Hassenfeld asked. "Is that where we are?"

Heads nodded.

Hassenfeld tamped his pipe but did not light it. "So we're not saying no. We're just not saying yes yet?"

"Maybe not yes for a long time," Hagan corrected. "Maybe never."

"But individual groups are welcome to work with Common Cause," Jim Miller suggested. "Only not under the RIght Now! banner?"

Alan Hassenfeld confirmed: "So our consensus is not to dissolve RIght Now! but to hibernate again."

Steering committee members were subdued as they left Hasbro's garden room. Alan Hassenfeld walked me to the main entrance. "You heard legitimate caution tonight," he said gently. "The chambers of commerce really would suffer worse than any of our other groups." We stood talking inside large glass doors. "Let's stay in touch," he said. "If this becomes war, I intend to support Common Cause. Let me know when you need funds for legal briefs or whatever."

Our handshake became a hug. Outside, the December night was bitterly cold. I walked across the nearly empty parking lot to my car. Why had I thought they would take this on? Could we wage this war without a powerful coalition?

At least Hassenfeld understood and said he would help.

28

Declaration of War
1994–95

THE RHODE ISLAND LOTTERY COMMISSION created scandals like scratch tickets rolling from a spool. A former Senate majority leader, John P. Hawkins, had designed the gambling operation and driven its creation in 1974. He named himself and two other senators to the board; the speaker of the House added three representatives; the governor got three public members. Hawkins ran "The Lot," as it was called, in various guises — board chair, legal counsel, and executive director — all while brushing aside every suggestion of impropriety. During his tenure as majority leader he served as vice chair of the State Properties Committee, which awarded him a $21,000 per year lease on a house that he owned.[1]

In the fall of 1993, shortly after Hawkins became executive director of "The Lot," he converted video poker consoles at Lincoln Greyhound Park and Newport Jai Alai into video slot machines. Anti-gambling groups blasted the video slots as highly addictive, but Hawkins dismissed their complaints as the product of "warped minds."[2]

Pawtucket Sen. Harold Miller, chaired the lottery when it hired Hawkins as director. Miller and two other commissioners flew to Florida for a conference, where they rented a Lincoln Town Car with state funds. Miller also took his wife with him to Paris, where they stayed at the Hotel Meurice, whose décor copied Versailles. *Providence Journal* reporter Christopher Rowland tallied the price of Miller's 1994 junkets: $9,160.31. Miller's tab had first claim on proceeds from scratch tickets and video slots, since only net profits made their way to state coffers.[3]

Embarrassed by negative publicity, Miller did not run for re-election in 1994. When Pawtucket Sen. John McBurney succeeded him, the gambling board promptly raised Hawkins's salary by nearly 23 percent. McBurney told reporters that high salaries were needed to get and keep "qualified people." With this raise the former Senate majority leader would make $11,000 more than the director of the far larger lottery in neighboring Massachusetts.[4]

This news sparked a firestorm. Governor-elect Lincoln Almond blasted the raise and called for legislation to abolish the Lottery Commission, proposing to absorb it into the Department of Administration. Senate Majority Leader Paul Kelly agreed to consider Almond's idea. Removing McBurney from the lottery, he appointed his Senate Judiciary Committee chair, Domenic DiSandro, to one of the three Senate seats.

While Kelly only replaced one senator with another, I wondered if he would consider separation of powers. The next day I hand-delivered a letter at his third-floor office. In it I thanked him for removing McBurney from the Lottery Commission and reminded him that the Senate under his leadership had played a crucial role in passing the constitutional proposals for judicial merit selection and modernizing the General Assembly. "Your actions," I wrote, "refute the argument that the legislature is unwilling or unable to pass reforms that limit its reach."

I urged Kelly to take the lottery crisis as the occasion for resolving a bedrock constitutional question: "Should the General Assembly be exercising the broad appointive powers that are traditional in Rhode Island but are barred in most other states under the separation of powers doctrine and are forbidden to Congress by the U.S. Supreme Court?" I asked for a meeting to discuss how the Senate could resolve these issues.[5]

In their 1992 battle against John Bevilacqua's faction, Kelly's stalwarts had demanded the most stringent versions of RIght Now! proposals. In 1993, they blocked the Grand Committee from replacing the disgraced chief justice. In our 1994 scorecard, they scored well on reform. I stepped out of the State House into a warm December breeze that felt like spring. What would Kelly do with the letter? Would he discuss it with his Senate leadership team? Or would he crumple and lob it into the trash?

The 1995 legislative session began festively with the inauguration of Lincoln Almond as Rhode Island's first four-year term governor. After the Senate session, I waited to greet Paul Kelly and asked if I could bring Common Cause leaders to meet with him.

"About?" he asked.

"About separation of powers. I sent you a letter before the holidays."

"Phil," Kelly said with abundant cheer that masked his message from those around us, "raising that issue this year is like pulling the pin on a hand grenade and rolling it into a tent."

I pushed back. "Would next year be any better?"

Kelly fidgeted with his tie, and Peanuts characters writhed beneath his fingers. "Truthfully, probably not."

"May we sit down with you and your leadership team?" I asked again. Half a dozen other lobbyists stood at a respectful distance, waiting their turn.

Kelly shook my hand, signaling an end. "Honestly, Phil, I don't think it would make any difference."

East Providence Sen. James P. McStay, a funeral director, had a self-effacing and gentle manner that demonstrated why his profession enjoys more respect than many politicians. He had scored 97.5 per cent on our 1994 Senate report card. McStay was close to Kelly, but I knew he would do what he believed right. We leaned against a broad marble railing on the third floor. Far above us stretched the dome, with its fresco of Roger Williams greeting the Narragansett chief Canonicus. I showed McStay the list of seven boards we hoped to challenge in 1995.

"I've thought about this mess," he said. "Often. But there are so many of these boards and so many legislative appointments. I never know where to start." Looking up from my list of boards, he continued, "All of these are good. You know, of course, that none will pass?"

"We've assumed this will take several years," I said. "We need to educate the public and soften things up."

He laughed. "'Soften up' may be the wrong expression. I guarantee you that these bills will only harden Harwood and Caruolo." He nodded toward the speaker's office at the far end of a hallway where afternoon sunshine gleamed on a polished stone floor. "Those guys don't care about policy or principle. All that matters to them is power."

"Are we making a mistake to try this?"

McStay shrugged. "We may all be dead before it's done, but heaven knows it's overdue."

"So will you sponsor one or two of these bills?"

He scanned the list again. "The Lottery Commission and the Unclassified Pay Plan Board are the two worst. Shall I take those?"

"They're yours," I said. "If you can get some Republican co-sponsors, that would be great."

Above us, four Roman arches bore the weight of the majestic dome. Gold letters in a dark band circled its base: RARA TEMPORUM FELICITAS UBI SENTIRE QUAE VELIS ET QUAE SENTIAS DICERE LICET. The Latin I had learned decades earlier deserted me, but I scribbled the words and later found the epigram from Tacitus: "It is the rare fortune of these days to think what one likes and speak what one thinks."

A few days later, snow fell steadily and covered a marble balcony outside the

House lounge. I sat at a round oak table near lofty windows with Rep. Charlene Lima, a math teacher who made eye contact and held it. My folder full of lists and bills lay open before us. I showed her the list. "We'd like to start with these seven. We're not under any illusions that they'll pass this year."

"Good thing," she said mischievously. "You're really going after the family jewels."

I waited while she skimmed several drafts. I told her we would welcome her suggestions.

"Won't this take a constitutional amendment?" she asked. "You're making an assault on three centuries of tradition."

"We'll need an amendment," I agreed. "But at the start, we want to call attention to specific abuses of these seven boards. I assume they'll go to different committees. That'll give us plenty to talk about."

Lima drew a deep breath. "I would do the Coastal Resources Management Council. And the Narragansett Bay Commission."

"You're not afraid of Mesolella?"

"No!" She scowled. "Vinny doesn't like me, and I don't particularly like him."

At the end of February we held a press conference and unveiled our separation of powers bills in the Senate Lounge, a magnificent space with green walls and plush velvet curtains. A massive mirror above the fireplace framed the podium. Despite his reservations about the topic, Paul Kelly had granted permission for us to use the space.

I welcomed reporters, sponsors, and leaders of groups that backed the campaign: Save the Bay, Operation Clean Government, and the League of Women Voters. "We're here today," I said, "to talk about the separation of legislative, executive, and judicial powers."

I explained that two centuries had passed since Rhode Island ratified the U.S. Constitution. While all the other states had established separation of powers as the bedrock of sound governance, Rhode Island had veered off in the opposite direction. We would try to rebuild seven boards, all created in the last fifty years, where legislators actually executed state laws: the Lottery Commission, the Coastal Resources Management Council, the Commission on Judicial Tenure and Discipline, the Narragansett Bay Commission, the Port Authority, the Solid Waste Management Corporation, and the Unclassified Pay Plan Board. Then I introduced the senators and representatives who sponsored these bills.[6]

Sen. Jim McStay described the Lottery Commission's headlong rush into video slot machines. "With virtually no public discussion," McStay said, "the Lottery board took giant steps toward full-fledged casinos in Lincoln and Newport. I think they conducted one public hearing before making a huge change in state policy that would never have passed the entire General Assembly."

He looked out over the microphones. "I'm not saying what they did was illegal. That's just the problem. It was perfectly legal under Rhode Island law where six legislators on a nine-member panel can vote to install video poker terminals, then turn around and convert them into video slot machines. That was perfectly legal and completely wrong."

"My other bill," he continued, "would remove legislative members from the Unclassified Pay Plan Board." He said decisions about how much to pay department directors and utility regulators had long been made entirely within the Department of Administration. But in the 1970s, the General Assembly changed the law to add the heads of the House and Senate Finance committees, then two more legislators. "Before you could say 'Whoopee,' the General Assembly had four members on a seven-person board. The legislature gained control of top salaries in the other two branches of government. Again, all perfectly legal and completely wrong."

Rep. Charlene Lima outlined her bills to end legislative appointments on the Narragansett Bay Commission and the Coastal Resources Management Council. "The people of my district are fed up with sweet-smelling toxic fumes that mysteriously vent from chemical plants in the dark of the night. The people of my district don't want to live downwind from a sewage sludge incinerator that spews poisons from its smokestack. Maybe they could be convinced by a good environmental study, but we don't have one because the House scuttled Myrth York's legislation last year."

Lima made eye contact around the room. "I'm not blaming my colleagues who sit on all these boards. I am saying we have a broken system, and it's up to us to fix it. It's time we as elected officials put aside our egos."

Myrth York, the recently defeated Democratic candidate for governor, strode to the podium. Speculation persisted that her call for Vincent Mesolella to step down as head of the Narragansett Bay Commission had cost her the party's support in her race. Rumors abounded that John Harwood preferred a Republican governor above any Democrat who might push for separation of powers.

"I no longer serve in the Senate," York declared in a resonant voice, "but I strongly support these bills. More often than we would like to remember, our state has been embarrassed by the blatant conflict of interest that is inevitable when the same individuals write and also execute state laws." She described her bill that would have required an environmental impact analysis before the Bay Commission could proceed with a sewage sludge incinerator. The Senate had passed her bill, but the House Corporations Committee buried it. "I remain convinced," York declared, "that Rep. Mesolella — who continues to serve simultaneously as chairperson of the NBC and as deputy majority whip in the House — ordered the hit.

"I called on Rep. Mesolella to step down from his role on the Bay Commission. It was clear that his dual roles created conflicts of interest and prevented the General Assembly from exercising legislative oversight in this crucial area. This must end."

Each of our sponsors came across as smart, passionate, and on-message.

Afterward M. Charles Bakst, the *Providence Journal*'s political columnist, retrieved his microcassette recorder from the podium. Over nearly two decades Bakst had produced a wealth of columns that backed strong ethics, campaign reform, open government, and judicial selection. He had not liked four-year terms for general officers or downsizing the General Assembly.

Bakst thrust his tiny recorder toward my face. "So how do you keep people from falling asleep on this?"

I laughed. "By getting you to write about it."

After our press conference, Bakst prowled the House and Senate chambers with his recorder. In his column, he quoted Paul Kelly as defending the current system for providing checks and balances. He also got John Harwood on the record declaring that the legislators' service on boards was a way of "overseeing and interacting." Harwood added that the current system "gives the legislature, which controls the money, a better feel for what's going on."[7]

Bakst also tracked down Mesolella, who acknowledged testifying against York's bill to delay and study the incinerator. "That bill died of its own weight," Mesolella insisted, dismissing his critics as "hypocrites" or as wielding "special-interest axes." In his column, Bakst summarized Mesolella's campaign contributions from Bay Commission employees and from contractors who wanted business. "Mesolella," Bakst wrote, "waves the question off. Fundraising activities have been part of the political scene for centuries, he says."

In response to this unveiling of our bills, Vincent Mesolella promptly launched a counterattack. He filed a bill that would require nonprofit organizations "to report any donation in excess of membership fees" as part of their lobbying reports if they sent "any representatives to testify before legislative committees or governmental agencies." Failure to comply would subject the group to a thousand-dollar fine.[8]

Was his bill a joke or a warning? Would he really try to force nonprofits to name their contributors if they spoke at the State House? Did he believe he could make religious leaders disclose their donor base or else keep silent in our most Catholic state? I knew that timing mattered. Mesolella filed his bill on the day of our separation of powers press conference. Had word of our legislation reached him? Had he rushed his idea into print? Why was he the bill's only sponsor? Was the whole thing just a ruse?

Our separation of powers bills were scattered widely among House and Senate committees. Covering multiple hearings before the days of affordable cell phones required running from room to room, upstairs and down. Members of the separation of powers task force testified as often as they could, but some afternoons I found myself alone. I signed witness sheets wherever our bills were scheduled. Whenever my name was called, I had to be present and ready to speak. One tradition helped: as a courtesy to sponsors who might be in other hearings when their bills were called, committee chairpersons routinely sent for them. When a sponsor arrived, a Common Cause volunteer or intern came for me, and I raced to that hearing.

Our testimony rose from talking points for each of the seven boards. I carried a dog-eared paperback of the *Federalist Papers* full of intricate constitutional lessons that I was learning on the fly. I often found myself jousting with lawmakers who had read these broadsides in college but forgotten their message. Some protested that such lessons did not apply because the Rhode Island Constitution was fundamentally different from the United States Constitution.

Shortly after his appointment as U.S. Attorney for Rhode Island in 1994, Sheldon Whitehouse had begun publishing articles on separation of powers, first in the *Providence Journal*. With calm and formal language he declared: "Encroachment by the Rhode Island General Assembly outside its legislative sphere, through appointments to positions in state agencies, boards, commissions and corporations, violates the separation of powers doctrine as expounded by the U.S. Supreme Court for more than 100 years."[9] For a column in the *Rhode Island Bar Journal* he drew from Federalist Paper 48 where James Madison warned that the legislative branch "is everywhere extending the sphere of its activity, and drawing all power into its impetuous vortex." The General Assembly, Whitehouse argued, routinely demonstrated what Madison feared. He wrote that the Rhode Island Supreme Court — in its first comment on the state's new Constitution — had declared in 1854: "The union of all the powers of government in the same hands is but the definition of despotism. To guard against such a government was one great object of the Constitution. This was to be done by the distribution of powers. This is the great principle of American liberty." In one legislative committee after another, I distributed copies of his articles.[10]

Bill Colleran, our NASA engineer, turned his number-crunching skills to laws passed since the 1870s. He produced a chart that showed how the General Assembly added legislators or legislative appointees to existing boards, and to the new boards it established. The pace of such enactments had accelerated in the 1950s and swelled through each succeeding decade into the 1990s. His chart looked like a city where low structures gave way to skyscrapers.

Colleran wrote with droll humor in opinion pieces with titles like "Our Unclassified Pay Plan Follies." He had discovered that many Rhode Island directors took home higher pay than their counterparts in neighboring Connecticut or Massachusetts. He attributed that anomaly to the Unclassified Pay Plan Board, the powerful seven-member body that set salaries for department directors, regulators, and judges. Until 1973, a director of personnel proposed pay plans for employees in the state's "classified" or merit system and for "unclassified personnel," mostly administrators in the three branches of state government. The director of administration, the budget officer, and the general treasurer presented recommendations to the governor.

A 1973 law created the Unclassified Pay Plan Board (UPPB) and added the chairs of the Senate and House Finance committees. Colleran wrote, "The executive branch still had the majority, but the camel's nose was in the tent." In 1978, a new law added two more legislators to the board, along with the Superior Court administrator, and it gave them each a vote. As a consequence lawmakers gained a majority on the seven-person board that set top salaries across state government. General Assembly leaders claimed this was a model of cooperative consultation, but in practice it became a den of deal-making. In 1988, House Speaker Matthew J. Smith chaired the Unclassified Pay Plan Board while at the same time administering the state court system. Smith's deals had laid tinder for the fire that burned him and Chief Justice Thomas Fay in 1993.

"It is high time," Colleran wrote, "for the Assembly to be extricated from their executive role. Perhaps then, they might devote their attention to the task of making laws."[11]

James Madison's warning about the legislature drawing "all government powers into its impetuous vortex" proved prescient when House leaders tried to hijack the Department of State Library Services (DSLS), an executive agency with a staff of two dozen and a budget of $5.5 million.

The new governor, Lincoln Almond, had unwittingly created a take-over target when he presented his first budget. He sought to save money by cutting library services by $162,000 and downgrading State Library Services from a cabinet department to an office within the Department of Elementary and Secondary Education. Librarians were stunned, and the Library Board of Rhode Island began searching for a rescuer.[12]

Like scores of other administrative bodies, the library board included members of the House and Senate Finance committees — Rep. David Panciera, a librarian himself, occupied the House seat. Besides his job as the director of the Ashaway Free Library, he sat on the House Finance Committee, which typically spent its spring in endless televised budget hearings. Most committee members walked onto its blue-draped set in dark suits and conservative ties, but Panciera typically wore a pullover sweater and open-necked shirt. He listened attentively and often brought a voice of reason to the discussions.

In April, Rep. Frank Montanaro introduced a bill with Panciera and two other members of House Finance as co-sponsors.[13] Although sounding innocuous, it would sweep the entire Department of State Library Services into the legislature's embrace. Common Cause board member Mike Cerullo learned of it and warned me that this was "the greatest piece of empire building that most of us will ever see."[14] Soon afterward, I bumped into the department's deputy director, Beth Perry, at a reception. She whispered that the library board had approved criteria for moving their department "under the legislature's umbrella." The board wanted assurances that funding, staffing, and independent decision-making would continue, and it wanted to keep library services free from political pressure.

I stifled a laugh. "Excuse my cynicism."

"There's more," said Perry. "On April 3, the board reviewed this legislation and agreed to go along with it." Clearly, Panciera had taken copies to the library board's meeting and made the legislation sound harmless. I approached Montanaro, the lead sponsor, before a House session with his bill in hand and asked why he had done this.

"Why not? It would be like the Library of Congress."

"No," I argued. The Department of State Library Services did not own any books, but managed inter-library loans and services for the blind. I reminded him these were executive functions. "Your bill creates one more situation where legislators would be executing state law."

In his mid-thirties and brawny, Montanaro shrugged. "How many boards are there now where that happens?"

"We're counting," I answered. "A lot."

"So?"

"So it's time to stop and not make more."

Montanaro shook my hand with a muscular grip. "Phil, I like you. We've always gotten along. But take it from me, you will never get separation of powers — not in your lifetime or in mine."

Then a secret document leaked. Richard Kearns, a former representative who worked as a top House lawyer, had written a confidential memo to the speaker. Its text was rife with jargon but also revealing. "Legislative control of this apparatus," Kearns wrote of the department takeover, "could prove seminal in its impact, and would undoubtedly provide an increasing largess of both political and operational opportunities, some of which are obvious now, others becoming apparent in the future."[15]

But even Kearns's embarrassing memo did not slow the rush toward passage. Members of the House Finance Committee settled themselves under television lights to hear Montanaro argue that it was appropriate to move library services "under the legislative umbrella." Again, he made the comparison to the Library of Congress.

Joan Ress Reeves, who chaired the Library Board, testified that her organization supported Montanaro's bill. She said the library community did not believe that moving the Department of State Library Services into the General Assembly would make it more vulnerable to politics. In answer to a question, Reeves said she was not put off by Richard Kearns's leaked memo.

I made my way to the witness table. "We are here," I began, "because the

Department of State Library Services faces a crisis. Like most crises, this one occurred when a number of competent, well-meaning people did what they thought were their jobs without seeing the whole picture. We also face this crisis because Rhode Island government has traditionally ignored our nation's revered doctrine of separated powers."

I outlined misunderstandings that left library services at risk. "Part of the problem," I said with a glance at Panciera, "may be that Westerly has a good librarian, who is also a member of the General Assembly, who is also a member of the Library Board, who is also a member of this committee, and who is also a co-sponsor of this bill. Last Monday morning he explained to his fellow members of the Library Board why this legislation is appropriate. And then, out of an abundance of caution, he recused himself from the actual vote."

At this Panciera smiled. Was he a good soldier following orders? Had he conceived and drafted this legislation? By criticizing his role I forfeited any chance of ever hearing his side of the story. In any case, despite the Kearns memo and our public warning that the legislature's takeover would further weaken separation of powers in our state, the Montanaro-Panciera bill flew through the House. In the Senate, it was referred to Senate Finance whose chairperson was Sen. J. Michael Lenihan.

A sturdy former Brown University football player, Lenihan earned his living as a high school history teacher. He taught students about separation of powers, and his desk at the State House displayed a motto from Thomas Jefferson: "In matters of style, swim with the current; in matters of principle, stand like a rock." The senator did not have the leverage to impose separation of powers on countless other Rhode Island boards where lawmakers already executed state law, but within his committee he could block this hijacking of the Department of State Library Services.

I asked what he planned to do.

He shrugged. "I hadn't decided before, but they've got my Irish up. So what am I going to do with this bill? Nothing. Precisely nothing."

The Montanaro-Panciera bill died in his committee. Lenihan protected Rhode Island from the creation of yet another patronage mill. But how would House leaders retaliate against him?

When it became obvious that House leaders would bury all seven of our separation of powers bills in various committees, Common Cause decided to test the issue in other ways. The Rhode Island Constitution required the Supreme Court to issue an advisory opinion "upon any question of law whenever requested by the governor or by either house of the general assembly."[16] We would ask Gov. Almond and legislative leaders to seek a separation of powers advisory from the high court.

Our draft resolution summed up the duty of legislative leaders under many sections of Rhode Island law to appoint senators or representatives as members of quasi-public boards and commissions. We noted that the Supreme Court had never ruled whether these legislative appointments were constitutional. I delivered our requests to Gov. Lincoln Almond, Speaker John Harwood, and Senate Majority Leader Paul Kelly.[17]

Joseph Larisa, Almond's executive counsel, phoned to endorse our position. "We think you're spot on," Larisa told me. "The current situation is absurd, and we want to work with Common Cause on this. But we can't just pop the question."

"Why not?"

"Because everything else would go down the tubes," he said. "We're confident that we'll get a contested case before long. This situation can't endure."

"It's endured for three centuries, hasn't it?" I asked.

"But it won't continue," Larisa insisted. "This governor is absolutely committed on this issue. With us pushing from inside and you working from outside, we'll force some movement. I guarantee you."

Winter's frozen ground thawed, but our bills to end legislative appointments on the seven troublesome boards were entombed in ice. House and Senate leaders hardened in their shared determination not to seek an advisory opinion.

We decided to try the last resort for stranded bills, a study commission. In an April memo, we proposed a new panel like the Blue Ribbon Commission on the Future of the General Assembly. As that previous panel had broken Rhode Island's log jam over legislative size, pay, and pensions, a successor could ask whether legislative participation on quasi-public boards was "consistent with the separation of powers doctrine" and what it might cost to create "a more professional legislative oversight process for the Rhode Island General Assembly."[18] I hand-delivered our proposal to the House and Senate leaders. Kelly promised to look at it.

Only days later, Sen. Jim McStay told me on the Senate floor that the issue had come up in a meeting with the governor. "A few of us think a study could be the way to go," McStay said.

"A few, but not a majority?"

"Probably not a majority," he agreed. "The real resistance is in the House."

I began staking out the speaker's office before each day's legislative session. Without a private stairwell or elevator, Harwood and his entourage took public stairs from the majority offices on the third floor to the House chamber on the second. Typically, the speaker burst into the hallway amid a coterie of top staff and deputies; they moved in a pack down the switchback stairs while I trailed behind like a palace courtier.

One rainy spring day, Harwood started down with House Majority Leader George Caruolo and Deputy Majority Whip Vinny Mesolella in tow.

"Mr. Speaker," I asked, "if I could have just a word with you?"

Harwood hesitated. Caruolo and Mesolella continued down the stairs. We paused on a landing beside tall windows.

"I left our proposal at your office for a new blue ribbon commission," I said, "to address some basic questions about separation of powers."

"I don't think I've seen it," he said cheerfully. "I've always had a sense that legislative appointees bring back good information. Besides, I thought you were trying to get your answer from the Supreme Court."

"We are," I said, "but that could take years. It might be better to address these questions in a non-adversarial way."

"You haven't exactly started with that approach," he said and continued down without shaking hands.

Caruolo was waiting for me at the bottom of the stairs. "You've been way out of line," he grumbled. "We've given you a lot in the last couple of years. Instead of resting on your laurels, you start attacking reps' roles on boards. Who the fuck do you think you are?" He spun away and strode into the chamber.

The only visible result from months of effort on separation of powers was retaliation against our sponsors. Rep. Charlene Lima had filed legislation to require labels on milk if the cows received bovine somatotropin (BST),[19] a hormone believed to increase milk production from cows and the risk of breast cancer in humans. The House Health, Education and Welfare Committee deleted the mandatory labeling provision, allowing the dairy industry to use labels voluntarily, precisely as its lobbyists asked. Mesolella, a member of the committee, had not attended all year, but arrived to join in a 15–0 vote to gut Lima's bill.[20]

Lima told me that Mesolella had literally bumped into her — not once, but twice — she thought to intimidate her. She laughed it off. "He doesn't scare me," she said. "I've never liked bullies."

I nodded. "It's almost as if he wants to make himself into a poster-child for separation of powers."

Several times, I noticed Mesolella watching me from a distance. Our eyes locked briefly, never close enough to speak. I avoided him in the hallways or on the House floor, but one day we came face to face in a doorway. I backed out of his way but felt his fury. "So you're making me your 'poster-child,' you self-righteous. . . ." He stopped himself.

"You're making yourself the poster-child," I said. "All we've done is publicize your record."

"Our record at the Bay Commission is one of the best in the country," he said. "We've stopped the dumping of raw sewage. We've won national awards. Why don't you put that in your press releases?"

"That's not the issue."

"So no good deed goes unpunished?" he jeered. Lobbyists and lawmakers were watching.

I forced a smile. "Maybe not, Rep." I excused myself and stepped by him into the hearing.

Both Rep. Charlene Lima's bill to end legislative appointments on the Narragansett Bay Commission and Rep. Vincent Mesolella's legislation to force nonprofits to disclose their donors landed in the House Corporations Committee.[21] Mesolella's bill had seemed a bluff. After he introduced it in February, it lay dormant until the April deadline for committees to vote the bills in their files up or down. Hundreds appeared on lists outside hearing rooms. House Corporations killed Lima's NBC bill but — to my astonishment — voted unanimously to send Mesolella's nonprofit disclosure bill to the full House. It became deadly serious.

I faxed warnings to scores of nonprofit organizations across the state. Several had opposed Mesolella's plan for a sewage sludge incinerator but were not interested in separation of powers. I hoped they would resist his move to silence them or expose their donors. I also faxed the editors of daily and weekly newspapers, asking for editorials on Mesollela's abuse of his dual positions as head of the Narragansett Bay Commission and deputy House majority whip. I suggested that he was pushing his nonprofit disclosure bill to rebuke Common Cause and Save the Bay for challenging his conflicts of interest.

Editors and reporters phoned for more information, and the nonprofit community reacted swiftly. From the Council of Churches, Jim Miller notified denominational leaders and hundreds of member congregations. Thirty-two nonprofit organizations — from the ACLU and Boy Scouts to the NAACP, Save the Bay, and United Way — fired off letters urging representatives to reject Mesolella's proposal. Most wrote that it would infringe on the privacy of contributors, multiply their administrative burdens, and stifle their advocacy at the State House.

The House took up Mesolella's nonprofit disclosure bill on April 27. During a 45-minute floor debate, Mesolella claimed he had introduced his bill only in the interest of good government. In a wild reach, he used the recent Oklahoma City bombing to justify his legislation, claiming the public needed to know about groups that support individuals like Timothy McVeigh.

Charlene Lima called this "ludicrous" and blasted Mesolella's bill as "bad legislation" that would have a chilling effect on nonprofits. Rep. David Cicilline, a Providence attorney and separation of powers sponsor, cited a 1958 decision in which the U.S. Supreme Court struck down an Alabama law that required the NAACP to identify its members. "This is a very dangerous bill," he said. "There's no need for it, and it would be burdensome."

Next Mesolella offered an amendment to exempt charitable groups, but to no avail. Rather than lose on the House floor, he moved to recommit his bill to the House Corporations Committee. His colleagues approved almost unanimously.[22]

Lisa Prevost, news editor for the *Providence Phoenix,* breached Mesolella's defenses and got him to say things on the record that he kept from other reporters. She profiled him under a bold tabloid headline: "V.I.P. Vin," asking, "Is Representative Mesolella's role as Bay Commission chairman in the public interest, or in his?" An illustration by David Opie showed Mesolella with two heads rising from a muscular torso. One face looked toward a door marked "Narragansett Bay Commission," the other toward a sign that read "QUIET. House in session."

Prevost wrote about the NBC Christmas parties that Mesolella hosted each year, where funds from his campaign account provided a lavish spread for hundreds of lobbyists, engineers, and public officials. She described the flow of campaign funds from NBC employees and vendors to "the Chairman's" campaign fund. She reprised the $18 million NETCO deal to build a sewage sludge incinerator at the edge of an impoverished neighborhood; protests by civil rights and environmental groups; the way Mesolella thwarted Myrth York's call for a moratorium and study; and York's demand that he resign from the NBC because of the conflict between his legislative and executive roles. Prevost described the ways Mesolella bullied other lawmakers and tried to intimidate nonprofits, citing the Common Cause message on separation of powers: "What contributors are interested in is not his legislative power. It is blended legislative and executive power. And that ought to scare people."[23]

During the spring of 1995, news of rabid animals frightened many. A Hopkinton family needed shots after contact with a raccoon carcass that tested positive for the virus. Tests confirmed that nine cats on a Coventry farm were infected and must be euthanized. In Tiverton, calves had to be destroyed. Even in Providence, a rabid raccoon leaped from a fence and attacked a walker.

I never noticed a little bill that altered the Rabies Control Board, a tiny executive entity previously comprised of farmers, veterinarians, and citizens who opposed cruelty to animals. Senate Majority Whip Bill Enos, who represented a rural district, filed legislation that clarified definitions and procedures for rabies control; it also thrust two legislators — a senator and representative — onto the Rabies Control Board.[24] I noticed Enos's bill on the last night of the session, too late to sound an alarm. I blamed myself as it slipped through the Senate and House without a protest.

A few days after the session ended, I stopped at the first floor office of Gov. Almond's executive counsel, Joe Larisa. Hundreds of bills had passed in the final hours and were piled on his credenza; unless the governor vetoed them, all would become law without his signature in ten days.

I mentioned the rabies control bill. "Sorry, Joe," I said. "I missed it entirely."

"We didn't." Triumphantly, Larisa lifted the original bill from his desk. Its face sheet bore cursory stamp-marks and signatures from its travel through committee hearings and floor votes in both chambers. "Their imagination and arrogance have no limits."

"So why would they put legislators on the Rabies Control Board?" I asked.

"Beats me," said Larisa. "It's utterly worthless in terms of patronage. Maybe they just wanted to see if we would notice."

"And the governor will veto it?"

"Absolutely!" Larisa exclaimed. "This will be our first veto. They have the votes to override, but our veto will send a message."

I mentioned my frustration that both chambers had buried Almond's bill to fold the lottery into the Department of Administration, as well as our bills to remove legislative appointments from seven executive boards.

Larisa smiled. "Relax. This was only the first inning. Separation of powers is a battle worth fighting. People will get this."

On June 14, Almond vetoed the Rabies Control Board legislation. His veto message lauded separation of powers as the cornerstone of American government everywhere but in Rhode Island. I rushed out a letter to lawmakers affirming the veto and sent copies to reporters and editors, reminding them that the General Assembly rejected a range of opportunities to address "commingled powers in state government."

A week later the *Providence Journal* published an editorial entitled "Rabid conflicts of interest."[25] The editors asked why legislators should be in charge of rabies control, given that it is a function of the executive branch and not the legislature. They went on to lament the fact that every bill backed by Common Cause to remove legislators from powerful boards had died in committee, even a compromise plan to study other ways of achieving proper legislative oversight of executive bodies. The editorial endorsed our call for an advisory opinion from the Supreme Court. In what would clearly be a rancorous campaign for separation of powers, the *Providence Journal's* editorial support could prove crucial. Nonetheless, on a searing Friday in August, three-quarters of the General Assembly members trooped back from vacation and voted in overwhelming numbers to override Almond's vetoes of several bills, including rabies control.[26]

Since the Royal Charter of 1663, the General Assembly had governed Rhode Island. Three centuries later, lawmakers swatted away every move toward separation of powers, flatly refusing to study the question or request an advisory opinion from the Supreme Court. How could we break through their bulwark of legislative supremacy?

A Question of Ethics
1995–98

THE RHODE ISLAND SUPREME COURT had twice affirmed the Ethics Commission's authority to write ethics rules for all public officials, but the old order had not changed. During 1994, legislative assaults had morphed into a bureaucratic siege against the commission's budgets, personnel, and office. Although his agency was under attack, Martin F. Healey, its new executive director, never cringed. He had the look of an altar boy and spoke in a clear tenor. After stints as assistant U.S. Attorney in San Francisco and Boston, he had worked for the Massachusetts attorney general. Healey had come to the Rhode Island Ethics Commission while Sara Quinn was in charge, and when she resigned to run for attorney general he became acting director. In August 1994, he negotiated the settlement of an ethics complaint Quinn had filed against John Harwood, who paid $5,000 in fines but did not confess wrongdoing. The settlement was paltry but was the closest any speaker had ever come to being held accountable for conflicts of interest.[1]

Three months later, the commission hired Healey as executive director, but a new barrier loomed: the Supreme Court's Committee on Character and Fitness stalled his application to practice law in Rhode Island. Lawyers on the committee blocked him for more than a year, and the chief clerk acknowledged that few attorneys from other states had to wait more than six weeks.[2]

Meanwhile, the State Properties Committee, which had been the venue for corrupt leases during the DiPrete and RISDIC scandals, still obstructed a new office lease. Two legislators on the panel — Rep. Vincent Mesolella and Sen. John McBurney — quibbled endlessly over technicalities, insisting they only wanted to get it right. Other lawmakers used the Unclassified Pay Plan Board to block new hires and delay routine pay raises. Though the Ethics Commission had no moat or castle walls, the bureaucratic siege threatened everything it tried to do.

Early in 1995, though Healey lacked staff and had no permanent office space, he urged the nine-member commission to begin a systematic review of state ethics rules. Two Supreme Court advisory opinions had acknowledged the commission's constitutional authority to adopt ethics rules for all government officials. In fact, no ethics agency in the United States possessed such broad powers to legislate, investigate, and prosecute public officials.[3] Healey began researching remedies that had already been enacted in other states, typically in the wake of scandal, and he told the commission, "Lessons they learned the hard way we can apply as prophylactic measures."

When Lincoln Almond became governor in January 1995, he issued an executive order requiring subordinates to pledge that they would never use public service for private gain or misuse confidential information. He suggested that the Ethics Commission launch its public hearings at the State House and, after barely a month in office, he testified before the panel: "The people and our Constitution have assigned to you the role of making the law, interpreting the law, and enforcing the law."[4]

With the General Assembly refusing to budge on separation of powers bills, the Common Cause state board decided to ask the Ethics Commission about the inherent conflicts of legislators on quasi-public boards. In May 1995, I delivered a fateful proposal to Marty Healey's desk with a cover memo that read: "Nothing in the current code prohibits individuals from dual office-holding, even where that creates impropriety or a severe appearance of impropriety."[5] I attached packets of correspondence, court decisions, columns, newspaper articles, and bills.

A few days later Rae Condon, who had rotated off the Common Cause board, phoned me. "I'm not sure this is a good idea," she said. "The Ethics Commission is politically vulnerable. You're piling on an enormous burden."

I told her we assumed the question would wind up before the state Supreme Court, just as the previous questions of the commission's authority had.

"But what if the court rules against you? Or worse, what if you hand the General Assembly their chance to crush the commission?"

The next morning our board president, Cathy Speer, told me Condon had phoned her. "She thinks we've made a mistake that could harm the commission," Speer said. A military wife for forty years, she had lived on bases in many states. "I think in their heart of hearts, legislative leaders know that the separation of powers is right. They say separation of powers functions differently in Rhode Island, but they're just clinging to power. If the legislature won't create a forum where Rhode Island can discuss abuses of power, maybe the Ethics Commission will."

Over several months Marty Healey and his staff culled strong provisions from ethics laws enacted after scandals in Hawaii, Illinois, Louisiana, Maine, South Carolina, and Texas. Other possible new rules came from states as diverse as Alaska, Florida, and New Hampshire. Commission members lugged around loose-leaf binders thick with photocopied laws and draft regulations.

One new regulation proposed to eliminate the *quid pro quo* requirement that the Supreme Court had used to absolve DiPrete of the Tutela violation and its related $15,000 fines, while another would bar public officials from soliciting subordinates for their charities. In a pending case, for example, Workers' Compensation Court Chief Judge Robert Arrigan had solicited lawyers representing clients in his courtroom for contributions to his wife's favorite charity.

A new gift rule aimed to prevent public officials — from the governor down to a cop on the beat — from accepting "anything of value," including political contributions, "in exchange for being influenced in the performance of any official act." Healey explained that this "zero-tolerance" gift rule would be one of the most stringent in the nation. A related section proposed to stop public officials from accepting honoraria for speeches related to their official duties. Other prohibitions outlawed personal use of government equipment, vehicles, telephones, and frequent flyer miles. Still others would broaden existing anti-nepotism rules to include "household members," even those not related by birth, adoption, or marriage in order to stop public officials from shoehorning their live-in partners onto the public payroll.

Our memo about the inherent conflicts of lawmakers who served on executive and quasi-public boards also made the cut. Healey and his staff developed two options. The first recognized tacitly that the commission might lack constitutional authority to oust legislators from public and quasi-public boards. It presumed lawmakers would continue as members but would prohibit them from accepting campaign contributions or "anything of economic value" from vendors who did business with their boards. It also proposed to bar them from voting on legislation involving the agencies where they served. The second and more stringent alternative declared that legislators could not serve on executive or quasi-public boards at all.

On October 10, 1995, as required by state law, commissioners voted to publish these draft ethics rules for public comment. Their 49-page package was both historic and controversial, and the cumulative effect left me giddy. At one fell swoop, the commission's new rules would outlaw practices that had spread like crabgrass. Persuading the General Assembly to adopt such rules would have taken decades; by packaging them, the Ethics Commission seized the high ground. I guessed that the new ethics rules would win broad support from citizens fed up with sleaze.

Not surprisingly, legislators blasted the Ethics Commission for questioning their role on executive boards. When a *Providence Journal* reporter asked House

Judiciary chair Charles Knowles about it, the lawyer fired back: "Who the hell do they think they are?"[6]

Vincent Mesolella also bristled. "I think they're exceeding — really exceeding — their authority," he declared. "I don't see myself resigning simply because the Ethics Commission says I can't serve. Unless the Rhode Island Constitution forbids me from doing that, I'm going to serve."

On a mild November afternoon, Bob Kilmarx and I testified in the Department of Health auditorium that the Ethics Commission — still without its own space — had borrowed. Kilmarx rehearsed the Easton's Beach case he had litigated a decade earlier: a developer applying to build a time-share hotel on the beach between Newport and Middletown hired House Majority Leader Joe DeAngelis as attorney for the project. Kilmarx described warnings of professional biologists and DeAngelis's conflict of interest. "Legislative leaders appointed half of the Coastal Council's members. On the day of the key vote, they all showed up and supported the hotel that DeAngelis represented. Needless to say, it passed."

"Mr. Kilmarx?" Richard Morsilli, the commission's chair, interrupted. "Was that legal?"

"Not only legal," Kilmarx replied. "The law establishing the Coastal Council required those legislative appointments."

Morsilli's eyebrows shot up. "Let me be clear about this. The majority leader of the House was representing the developer? Isn't that a conflict of interest?"

"We thought so," Kilmarx replied. "One newly elected representative had never before attended a meeting of the CRMC, but he showed up and voted for the project."

"And the courts agreed to that?" Morsilli made no effort to hide his astonishment.

"We appealed to the Superior Court," Kilmarx replied. "Judge Ronald Lagueux asked the parties to brief the question of whether legislative appointments to the Coastal Council were constitutional. We found a case where the North Carolina Supreme Court had ruled that the Environmental Management Commission was unconstitutional because it had four legislative appointees. We argued that eight legislative appointments made our Coastal Resources Management Council unconstitutional." Kilmarx clearly relished the retelling. "Judge Lagueux issued an eloquent decision that legislative appointments violated the separation of powers doctrine."[7]

"Predictably," Kilmarx continued, "DeAngelis appealed to the Rhode Island Supreme Court, where all the justices were former legislators chosen by the General Assembly in Grand Committee. Not surprisingly, Chief Justice Thomas Fay wrote for a unanimous court that it was improper for Lagueux to raise separation of powers *sua sponte,* meaning 'on his own motion.' With that technicality, our Supreme Court ducked the underlying constitutional question. It ruled that once the parties submitted themselves to the CRMC's jurisdiction, they could not challenge its authority."

Morsilli asked if Common Cause favored the stricter regulation that would prohibit legislators from even serving on boards with executive duties.

Kilmarx chose his words carefully. "Gov. Almond has made it clear that he favors the second version, the absolute ban. That's the question he wishes the Supreme Court to resolve on the merits."

"So you think the Rhode Island Supreme Court will ultimately have to decide this matter?"

"We do," Kilmarx answered. "The current situation is rife with similar conflicts of interest, and the Supreme Court ruled in 1992 that the Ethics Commission possesses constitutional authority to address such conflicts."

"What about the argument that senators and representatives on boards provide legislative oversight?"

"Members of the General Assembly can get all the information they need by attending meetings or having staff attend. These boards comply with the Open Meetings Law, but having legislators and legislative appointees as voting members creates unresolvable conflicts."

"One last question," Morsilli said. "Will this regulation banning legislators from these quasi-public boards solve the problem?"

"If the Supreme Court agrees," Kilmarx said, "it will. I learned early in my legal career not to predict what the court will say."

Doug Riggs, a reporter for the *Providence Journal,* attended the Ethics Commission hearing and went back to our office for a story on the twenty-fifth anniversary of Common Cause. He asked how confident I felt that our approach on separation of powers would work.

"I believe we're right on the issue," I said. "Most other states and the federal government don't allow legislators to sit on quasi-public boards or administrative agencies. In Rhode Island, it's routine to have legislators on the Lottery Commission, the Board of Bank Incorporation, the Narragansett Bay Commission — the list goes on and on. It's been a source of great corruption, and in our view is a factor in the fact that we have the third-highest per capita indebtedness in the nation."

"People at the State House say you'll never win this fight," Riggs countered. "How sure are you that you can prevail?"

Many thought we could never win. In my darker moments, so did I. "We haven't gotten a lot of attention on this," I said. "The problem is that people don't see how it connects to their pocketbooks."

I told the reporter that public agencies were operating in casual ways, ignoring sound management practices, and tolerating conflicts of interest. "Sooner or later, we're going to have another explosive scandal that will rattle the foundations."

Sunday dawned gray and spitting sleet. I heard the paper thump onto our porch. A front-page story stretched across three columns with the headline: "A milestone for Common Cause." Above a photo of me at the Ethics Commission hearing was a priceless subhead: "Can the godfather of political reform in Rhode Island maintain his reformist zeal?"

In his article Riggs pictured the Ethics Commission meeting in a borrowed auditorium, hurrying through part of its agenda because women in maroon leotards were filtering in for an aerobics class. He described my relief that the commission was going forward with "an ongoing, preventive process" and pictured a firm foundation laid for continuing reform in the nation's strongest ethics agency, which could adopt its own code and enforce it "untouched by legislative hands."

Listing the reforms that Common Cause had helped lobby into law or into the state's Constitution over the years, the piece portrayed us — now without support of the RIght Now! Coalition — taking on a foe that had grown vastly more resistant over separation of powers. He sketched our case, quoting my critique of several boards where lawmakers routinely executed laws they had written.

The Senate majority leader had spoken to Riggs on the record. "I totally disagree with Phil on that," Paul Kelly said. "The only checks and balances the public has on boards and commissions, especially quasi-boards, are legislators who are directly accountable to the taxpayers. Remove them from the boards and you wouldn't even know there are problems coming down."

Riggs left his readers with a question: "Do Rhode Islanders really want to change? Can a people raised in a state that has behaved more like a dysfunctional family since colonial times, when it was known as 'Rogues' Island,' find their true political comfort zone anywhere but in the cynicism that is their birthright?"[8]

The pace quickened when Gov. Lincoln Almond testified for a second time before the Ethics Commission. "I am here today to reaffirm my support for this process," he declared, "which will result in a new code of ethics to help maintain the highest standards of ethical behavior for all levels of public service." As he had during his February appearance, Almond emphasized the commission's bedrock authority. "The people of Rhode Island, by constitutional amendment, created a powerful ethics commission to respond to what they viewed as rampant unethical behavior in all three branches of government."

Almond affirmed the proposed rule that would bar lawmakers from service on public and quasi-public boards.

"Governor," asked Chair Richard Morsilli, "would you seek an advisory opinion from the Supreme Court to confirm that?"

"If this commission were to formally ask me," Almond replied, "I would."[9]

Almond rose from the witness table, taller than anyone in the room. Few thought this contest would end during his first four-year term or even a second.

An immediate dilemma remained: *which* separation of powers rule? Almost from the spring day when I first delivered the Common Cause memorandum and supporting documents, the commission had recognized two distinct paths. One assumed the commission lacked constitutional authority to bar lawmakers from boards that executed state laws. Instead it proposed to prohibit their "asking, demanding, soliciting, accepting, receiving, or agreeing to receive . . . anything of economic value" from vendors or others who wanted special treatment from their agencies. The second, that Gov. Almond favored, aimed to ban legislators from any boards that exercised executive powers. Almond's executive counsel, Joe Larisa, made clear that the governor would present the outright ban to the Supreme Court but would not advance the more cautious first version.

Uncertain about their constitutional power to enact the outright ban that Almond sought, the Ethics Commission hired a national expert in state constitutions to advise them. Geoffrey C. Hazard Jr., a professor from the University of Pennsylvania's American Law Institute, analyzed the issues and replied cautiously. He acknowledged the Rhode Island General Assembly's "long history" on boards, "some of it unsavory or worse," and he recognized the value of "a prophylactic prohibition of the scope proposed." But he concluded that the proposed ban "exceeds the authority conferred on the Ethics Commission" by the state's Constitution.

But then he hedged, writing that "in light of the severity and long duration of the problems involved," the Supreme Court might "permit the Ethics Commission to impose a strong preventive measure."[10]

Less than two weeks after the Ethics Commission's hearing, a *Providence Journal* investigative reporter revealed flagrant corruption involving a powerful state senator who used his dual executive and legislative positions to enrich himself. Reporter Thomas Frank had followed a paper trail left by former Sen. John Orabona until he retired. The headline read: "Ex-senator seeks $106,000 in pensions."

Though only fifty-two, Orabona had claimed 79 years' worth of employment credits and a $106,057 annual pension — nearly $33,000 more than he had earned during any year in his life. Orabona's claim combined three pensions: $10,000 a year for his time in the legislature, $53,042 a year for work in the Providence school system, and $43,015 per year for various political jobs in Providence. Orabona cited summer pool jobs while he was in high school and a stint as an aide to the mayor, and he expected to collect for service on several nonprofit boards.[11]

How had this happened? With his $300 per year legislative salary as a base, Orabona had purchased credits for sixteen years of part-time city jobs. He paid only $768. Had he bought those same credits based on his pay as a teacher, he would have had to pay $74,611. The senator had then transferred credits between the city and state retirement systems, which allowed him to retire at the age of fifty-two after years of padding his pension. Orabona purchased or transferred credits at discrete intervals that would not alert the clerks who processed his requests. His scheme had been systematic, clever, hard to trace, and lucrative. He relied on special pension bills that routinely appeared on a "consent calendar," which was supposed to include only noncontroversial items that were not subject to debate. The end-of-session consent calendar often reminded me of cattle being herded through a gate in a cloud of dust; no one could tell one from another. I often suspected that many of these bills were rewards for lawmakers who had done the leadership's bidding, but I had no way of finding out who benefitted or how. After the dust settled, special pension bills faded into bureaucratic oblivion, forgotten except by their beneficiaries.

Only rarely did investigative reporters pore through them in often-fruitless attempts to identify recipients and compute their likely rewards. A 1987 special pension bill that passed in the last-minute rush had allowed full-time officers of public employee unions to buy their way into the state pension system at fire-sale prices. The following year *Providence Journal* reporter Katherine Gregg put them on the front page, and taxpayer fury forced a repeal, but the damage had been done. Twenty-four union leaders had already bought into the system, all but two of them employees of teachers' unions, which sued to protect these fraudulent buy-ins. Together the labor leaders would reap an estimated $12 million in pensions. For generations, such pension gimmicks had multiplied under a shroud of official secrecy because a section of the state's public records law had kept personnel information "identifiable to an individual applicant for benefits" confidential. Under that rubric, pension files were sealed until Kathy Gregg unraveled the web of pension abuses, broke the code, and exploded the lies.[12]

In 1991, once again because of Katherine Gregg's reporting on pension corruption, Rhode Island's Access to Public Records Law was amended to make retirement files public records. But Orabona had secured his pension during the 1980s, while secrecy and exploitation still prevailed. Even against a sordid backdrop of rigged pensions, he set the record with a pension claim of $106,057.

On the day of the Orabona exposé, Peter Hufstader strode into our office. A retired teacher and veteran of the Navy's Cold War search for Soviet submarines, he offered to help Common Cause. "This man is robbing taxpayers," he said of Orabona. "If I can help track him down, I'm at your service."

He went directly to the State House Library and began poring through volumes of old public laws. Ten days later, he came back and slid a memo across the table detailing a 1983 bill that allowed legislators to combine their legislative service with "service to a municipality" for retirement credit. A separate bill allowed any active legislator to receive credit for service on a municipal board or commission. These changes were tiny and technical; they passed without objection. The documents suggested that Orabona had drafted both.

Hufstader pointed further down in his memo. "Until 1984," he said, "nobody employed by the state could retire with full benefits until fifty-five but Orabona cosponsored a bill that eliminated the age requirement. His legislation allowed him to retire at fifty-two. Now look at who was supposed to be minding the store!" He handed me photocopied lists of those who served on the legislature's Joint Committee on Retirement over the span of the decade from 1983 to 1992. Orabona's name appeared every year, several times as secretary, once as chairperson.

Nor was Orabona alone. Sen. Donald R. Hickey had chaired the Senate Finance Committee while he served on the Retirement Board. Like Orabona, Hickey had sat on the Joint Committee on Retirement during the 1980s but left the Senate in 1985 to accept a full-time job as executive director of the State Retirement System. He retired in 1990 with a state pension of $55,455.[13]

"What makes my blood boil," Hufstader said, "is that these guys should have been watching out for the people's interest. They were elected members of the General Assembly. They'd sworn to uphold the Constitution, but they exploited its flaws."

John Orabona's achievement sprang from a State House tolerance for self-dealing compounded by two underlying flaws in government: sealed personnel records and laws that empowered legislators to execute the very laws they wrote. On the legislature's Joint Committee on Retirement, Orabona wrote pension legislation; as a member of the Retirement Board, he administered pensions. Those two information-rich roles enabled him to learn and exploit the system's arcane secrets. Instead of using his positions to provide oversight and protect taxpayers, he finessed incremental changes in state pension law. He gamed the system to his own advantage.

We prepared summaries of Orabona's machinations for the Ethics Commission and for General Treasurer Nancy Mayer, who chaired the Retirement Board. "The problem," we wrote in a press statement, "is that lawmakers were in position to both write and execute retirement statutes. By switching hats, these legislators could play both ends against the middle. They always won, and taxpayers always lost."

No one at the Ethics Commission underestimated the challenge of taking on separation of powers. Commissioners and staff wrestled with the implications.

Marilyn A. Hines, the commission's education coordinator, identified 147 state agencies, boards, and commissions where legislators served or made appointments. She calculated that legislative members or appointees constituted a majority in thirty agencies and half of the membership in four. Functions of those agencies, she wrote, "cover the full spectrum from legislative to executive to judicial."[14]

Meanwhile Peter Hufstader appeared several days a week — always in a tie, beneath mostly white hair and with a neatly trimmed beard. He became an unpaid research director for Common Cause. He pored over laws, gleaning the powers lawmakers exercised. His color-coded chart illustrated the vast array of executive functions in legislative hands: purchasing, managing, and selling property; employing architects, engineers, and managers; issuing bonds; receiving taxes and fees; lending and investing state money; enforcing laws; investigating and prosecuting complaints; adopting rules and regulations; suing and being sued on behalf of the state; making assessments and imposing user fees.[15] In August 1996, we argued before the commission that legislators should be prohibited from all these tasks that properly belonged to the executive branch.

From the day I delivered the Common Cause request until a final vote, the panel's painstaking deliberation took nearly three years. On June 2, 1998, after many public hearings, the Ethics Commission voted unanimously to bar legislators from serving on public and quasi-public boards.[16] To leave time for the state Supreme Court's decision, they set the new rule to take effect on July 1, 1999, more than a year away. Its members knew they were swimming in dangerous currents and that the constitutional struggle would be fierce. Questions remained: Would Gov. Almond present the advisory opinion request? And how would the Rhode Island Supreme Court respond?

30

Retaliation
1996–97

IN JANUARY 1996, Thomas E. Wright, executive director of the Solid Waste Management Corporation, was afraid. I had never met him before he came to my office at dusk with haunted eyes. "They've given me a choice," he said. "Resign or be fired."

I knew that three legislators sat on the trash agency's nine-member board. Wright described the pressure he had been under to hire specific people, qualified or not. "For a long time I gave in to them," he said wistfully, "probably too long." He said he had been coerced into hiring a young man named Joseph Rotella for a community relations position and then into promoting him to property manager. "In both cases," Wright said, "I had to select him over qualified female applicants."

"And the women were better qualified?"

"I thought they were. For the second position — managing houses we owned around the landfill's perimeter — our job description required both a college degree and real estate license. Rotella didn't have either. The promotion raised his pay about eight thousand a year."

"And you felt pressure?"

Wright nodded.

"From Vincent Ragosta?"

"Yes. That's when I learned that Joseph Rotella was the nephew of Andrew Rotella, the vice chair of the Narragansett Bay Commission. I assume he's close to Vinny Mesolella."

"Vincent Ragosta is Mesolella's cousin," I added.

Wright nodded that he knew. "Family is family. Ragosta made it clear what he wanted."

Outside my window, the winter sky had gone dark. My office was growing cold. I asked if he had felt pressure from General Assembly members on the board.

"From Rep. McCauley."

"Who represents this district," I said. Although I seldom saw him there, Rep. John J. McCauley Jr. had a storefront office just across Smith Street.

Wright said he hoped McCauley had not seen him come and wondered if he were paranoid. "McCauley wanted me to hire one of his constituents, a guy named Kenneth Lyons, as a laborer. I told him we'd had a job freeze on laborer positions for five years. I thought that was the end of it, but McCauley kept calling, kept asking me to give Lyons an interview. And Ragosta started prodding me."

"And you hired him?"

"In the end, I didn't. It turned out that Lyons had a felony record that disqualified him for a license to operate bulldozers. I told him it was a Superfund site, and he would have to take a drug test. At that point, he bailed out."[1]

Years earlier, I toured the state-of-the-art recycling facility that Tom Wright built. Machines and workers separated metals and glass of different colors. Environmental advocates thought highly of him. I asked what reason they would give for firing him.

He shrugged. "They can always concoct something. I serve at the board's pleasure."

I walked Tom Wright down our back stairs to the parking lot and wished him well, then plodded back up and wrote a verbatim. Wright had not asked me to do anything, but his experience illustrated the evils of legislative patronage in administrative agencies.

His firing came a few days later. The Solid Waste Management Corporation board made its decision in closed session and would not let Wright defend himself in the public portion of the meeting. The trash agency's lawyer, Robert G. Flanders Jr., said Wright was fired because Chairman Vincent Ragosta preferred "a more hands-on, proactive administration."

Afterward, Wright told reporters his side of the story, saying staff morale suffered when Ragosta insisted on the hiring of "at least five unqualified people" in the last year. Media attention zoomed in on Rep. John McCauley's attempts to get a landfill job for Kenneth Lyons. *Providence Journal* reporter Bob Wyss discovered that Lyons had convictions in the last five years for assault, domestic assault, passing bad checks, resisting arrest, and possession of heroin.[2] Telephone records showed that McCauley had made at least seven calls to Wright on Lyons's behalf. "People call looking for help from me," McCauley told Wyss. "If I can't help, then what use am I?"

I wrote to House Speaker John Harwood and Senate Majority Leader Paul Kelly, asking for a legislative investigation of improper hiring pressures at the

Solid Waste Management Corporation, noting that Wright's charges were "only the latest controversy in the SWMC's history of hiring practices that appear dubious, improper, or illegal." I added that it lay "within the oversight authority of the General Assembly to investigate." But neither Harwood nor Kelly responded, and I restated those concerns in a second letter, which they also ignored.

W. Edward Wood, who had served both as director of two state departments and as Gov. Bruce Sundlun's chief of staff, blasted Wright's firing. "In many ways," Wood wrote in an opinion piece, "Tom Wright is an engineer's engineer." He added that Wright "absorbed the new programs without a hitch, never complained, made few mistakes, and took responsibility rather than running from it." Wood praised Wright for his managerial virtues, including "absolute incorruptibility."[3]

The sacking of Tom Wright laid bare the reality of legislative patronage on quasi-public boards. Family connections often trumped conscientious service. By their silence, Harwood and Kelly signaled that they would not embarrass their appointees.

Less than two months after his firing, Tom Wright landed a top job in the Connecticut Resource Recovery Authority.

James J. Malachowski held one of the riskiest posts in state government: he chaired the Public Utilities Commission (PUC). Bald, tall, and tough, he dared to thwart two leaders in the House, Vincent Mesolella and George Caruolo. Malachowski had also saved homeowners and businesses more money than they would ever know. Between 1984 and 1994, the Narragansett Bay Commission had proposed sewer rate increases of $33.3 million from its customers, but the PUC had blocked $10.2 million.[4]

I knew Malachowski but was stunned when he phoned confidentially for help.[5] "I'm in an awkward situation," he said. "I'm a utility regulator, and I'm about to block an incinerator contract the NBC really wants at Fields Point."

I asked how he could stop what sounded like a steamroller.

He said the commission needed a rate increase of $2.325 million to go forward with the multi-year, multi-million-dollar contract. "They haven't done due diligence," he said. "Their process is flawed. If we block the rate increase they've requested, they won't be able to build."

I barely understood.

"The awkward part," he continued, "is that if I deny Mesolella his rate increase, he'll go to House leaders, and they'll slash my budget. I'm getting not-so-subtle signals that the House Finance Committee will cut our staff in half. We'll block the rate increase, but it's like inviting a punch in the nose."

Malachowski also had reason to fear George Caruolo, who convened a press conference early in 1996 to unveil his legislation aimed at deregulating electric utilities. From a podium in the House lounge, Caruolo announced that Rhode

Island would be the first state to let consumers choose their energy suppliers the way they already picked long-distance phone companies. "The word 'historic' has been repeatedly used here to describe what we are trying to do," he told the crowd of lobbyists, officials, and reporters.[6]

Caruolo's bill was thick and studded with esoteric legalese that made dense reading: "the nonbypassable transition charge" and "net unrecovered commitments."[7] Its obtuse text contained a plan to compensate the Narragansett Electric Company and several small regional producers for surrendering their monopoly status. Electric utility companies would sell off their power plants and buy electricity from companies their customers chose.

But what were these massive generating stations worth? After secret negotiations with executives of Narragansett Electric, by far the largest producer of electricity, Caruolo priced the power plants at $930 million. With charts and graphs, he called for consumers to cover up to three additional cents per kilowatt-hour over the next 25 years to pay the power companies for their "stranded costs." He claimed that competition would more than offset that amount, allowing consumers to shave between 13 and 17 per cent from their electric bills.[8]

Few people knew enough to question Caruolo's numbers, but a study group of utilities and consumers' groups convened by the PUC a year earlier cried foul. Under the leadership of former Barrington Rep. Mary N. Kilmarx, the Rhode Island Electric Industry Restructuring Collaborative had been analyzing the data for months. Her group's forty-six-page report challenged Caruolo's estimate of $930 million in stranded costs as too much for the million people in Rhode Island to pay off, and she presented those data to the Public Utilities Commission.[9]

Brown University Economics Professor George Borts declared in an opinion piece that Caruolo's bill would "transfer at least $1 billion of Rhode Island wealth to the electric power companies" and "effectively emasculate the Public Utilities Commission, replacing the existing commissioners with legislative appointees." Moreover, he wrote, other deregulated industries — particularly airlines and trucking — had received no such payments. Borts disputed Caruolo's analogy to telephone deregulation: "AT&T was not compensated when it wrote billions of dollars of assets off its books."[10]

Within Caruolo's Utility Restructuring Act of 1996 lurked a brazen assault on the Public Utilities Commission. Caruolo would oust three experienced commissioners appointed by several governors for staggered terms and bring in five novices, three appointed by legislative leaders. Instead of the current six-year terms, the new commissioners would serve only three-year terms, a change that would make them doubly vulnerable to political pressure. Other provisions would end the PUC's authority over the Narragansett Bay Commission and exempt the quasi-public sewage agency from revolving door and other ethics requirements.

Weekend television throbbed with college basketball playoffs, the start of March Madness. I found myself drafting an opinion piece that compared public utility commissioners to referees who have the thankless task of making tough calls. Caruolo's bill, I wrote, would destroy their independence. I asked how would referees call a hotly contested game, "if they were subject to instant dismissal by power brokers in the box seats?"[11]

Throughout the spring, Jim Malachowski decoded the majority leader's calculations on stranded costs. His testimony before legislative committees amazed me. Contrary to Caruolo's promises, Malachowski predicted that the legislation would raise most electric bills, stall competition, and allow local utilities to reap windfall profits.

On June 20, the Public Utilities Commission shattered tradition with a report to the General Assembly. Malachowski and his fellow commissioners declared Caruolo's bill rife with "sweetheart items" that would help utilities and harm consumers. The PUC report deplored the fact that customers must compensate Narragansett Electric and other providers for existing power plants. Contending that the transition costs were excessive and had "no relation to stranded investments," they dismissed the bill's central formula as "fatally flawed."

Caruolo fired back: "This report is long on criticism and devoid of anything constructive. Is it possible that after all of this time they can't say anything positive about this bill?" Meanwhile, Sen. William V. Irons, chair of the Senate Corporations Committee that would conduct hearings on the bill, welcomed the report. He told reporter Bob Wyss: "They are the most knowledgeable group on this subject in the state."[12]

I never found out how Caruolo's bill took its final form in the Senate Corporations Committee, which Irons chaired. The substitute left the three PUC commissioners in place but stripped them of their power to regulate public utilities, which their predecessors had held since 1969. The latest version created a new agency called the Retail Electric Licensing Commission to administer electric utilities. Three of its nine members would be appointed by the governor, three by the speaker of the House, and three by the Senate majority leader — the same as the Lottery Commission. Irons's compromise allowed Malachowski and his fellow commissioners to retain broad regulatory authority over gas, electric, telephone, water, and pipelines.

Caruolo's Utility Restructuring Act of 1996 came before the Senate on a cool, showery August day. To assure passage, House leaders held hostage a high priority Senate bill to outlaw tobacco sales to children. Senators expressed their doubts. "What we are doing today," declared Sen. John Roney, "is passing a bill that is opposed by all the people we hired to know and to represent us against the utility."

Sen. Michael Lenihan read a list of reasons why the bill would be bad for the state. He insisted that the technical language of the legislation would protect the Narragansett Electric Company and subvert "the principles of an open and competitive market."[13]

In the end, only Roney, Lenihan, and two other senators voted against Caruolo's utility legislation. Clerks stamped it as passed by the Senate. Irons carried it across to the House and handed it to Caruolo in exchange for the Senate's hostage tobacco bill.

Speaker John Harwood opened the 1997 legislative session by warning his colleagues from the rostrum that they would soon become the "punching bag for a chorus of reformers." Framed by burgundy velvet drapes, he glanced up from his text and glared at me in the gallery. "Brace yourself for that experience," Harwood urged. "We must all be prepared to explain that it is the legislature which is the heart and soul of government. We must remind our fellow citizens that the General Assembly has filled its central governing role during more than three centuries of Rhode Island constitutional history and tradition. We must be prepared, unfortunately, to have these truths ignored and twisted by naysayers and would-be reformers."[14]

I stared back and absorbed the Speaker's rage. The day before, Caruolo had attacked us with a letter to the editor. "The zealots at Common Cause," he wrote, "have excelled at slandering the collective reputation of the General Assembly while they crusade to ban legislators from boards and commissions." He added that he could not think of "a single instance in which a legislator was ever charged in any judicial or ethical forum, much less convicted, for malfeasance while serving on a state board or commission."[15]

As much as they despised the campaign for separation of powers, Caruolo and Harwood had little leverage against Common Cause, but they used the Unclassified Pay Plan Board to retaliate against Jim Malachowski. The pay board's transformation from an executive office for setting salaries to a hybrid dominated by legislators empowered legislative majority leaders to control top officials across state government. The buck no longer stopped on the governor's desk. Accountability vanished. No one had greater power than those who set salaries for department directors, judges, and top regulators. The Unclassified Pay Plan Board was a perfect venue for high-stakes political deals.

The pay board's January 1997 agenda comprised a half-inch packet of obscure documents. Buried amid routine motions were raises of up to 13.9 percent for traffic court judges. Leo Skenyon, the tribunal's administrator, would get an 8.7 percent mid-year increase, while Director of Transportation William Ankner would walk out with an 11 percent annual boost. The most shocking item on their agenda was a new job title and pay cut for Malachowski in a Public Utilities Commission that had been restructured under Caruolo's Utility Restructuring Law. In place of Malachowski's $94,123 salary, his proposed new position carried a pay range of $53,295 to $63,045.[16] No one could miss the public humiliation of a thirty-three percent pay cut. This shot at the PUC chief who had dared to challenge Caruolo would send shockwaves through state offices. The message was clear: *Never cross legislative leaders.*

Months earlier, Gov. Almond had backed Malachowski's critique of the Caruolo utility legislation, but now the governor's director of administration announced that Malachowski's job was "being restructured." It baffled me that Almond had been bold in June but seemed ready in January to support slashing Malachowski's pay. Why had Almond gone along with House leaders on what seemed a matter of principle?

Despite overwhelming odds, Jim Malachowski refused to go quietly. "I set profit levels of companies that are traded on the stock exchange," he told reporter Kathy Gregg. "I make decisions that affect every home and business in Rhode Island." No changes in his duties, Malachowski added, could justify cutting an official's salary during his term of office. That was against the law.

The assault on Malachowski seemed to prove our point that the Unclassified Pay Plan Board had gone rogue. During my rounds at the State House, I spoke to as many of its members as I could. The four lawmakers on the board mouthed the leadership's line that their hands were tied because Malachowski would be in a new position. "I hear you," said Sen. John Roney. "I'm going to offer an amendment that will lessen Malachowski's loss."

Only General Treasurer Nancy Mayer opposed the cut, and she was furious. "The fix is in," she fumed. "The House leadership will make an example of Malachowski. People across state government will get the message." She, Almond, and Malachowski were all Republicans. I asked her why the governor would go along with this charade.

Mayer shook her head. "Beats me. I called his top people, but they won't talk to me about it."

Beyond criticizing the "stranded costs" calculations in Caruolo's electricity restructuring bill, Malachowski had committed a worse sin: publicly contradicting House leaders on a bill they really wanted.

Malachowski mentioned several other moments when top figures in the House had pressured him. "There's a case in litigation," he told me. "Obviously, the details are confidential. All I can tell you is that House Policy Director Frank Pontarelli called to demand that we change our position on a lawsuit." And Woonsocket Rep. Gerry Martineau — chairman of the powerful House Corporations Committee — had walked into the Public Utilities Commission with a trucking executive who had a case pending. "He was very clever," Malachowski said. "Just sat in my office while the trucking guy made his case. No threats. 'Only a courtesy to a constituent.' The mere presence of somebody from the leadership was intimidating enough." Martineau was the speaker's appointee on the Unclassified Pay Plan Board.[17]

Malachowski had already written to Gov. Almond about Martineau's intimidation. "Of all people," said the beleaguered regulator, "the governor should push for an investigation."

I offered to challenge Martineau's conflict of interest, and Malachowski agreed. I faxed a letter to all seven members of the pay board, urging them to address Martineau's apparent conflict of interest and not to cast the second and final vote to cut Malachowski's salary. "These are serious matters," I wrote. "Rep. Martineau is a member of the Unclassified Pay Plan Board."

I also defended the fact that Malachowski had testified against Caruolo's 1996 Utility Restructuring bill. "Responsibility to raise such public questions lay clearly within Mr. Malachowski's role as head of a regulatory agency," I wrote. "Few others in the state have the expertise or access to the technical data." I added that the pending cut in Malachowski's pay would violate the ban on lowering the salaries of directors and judges during their term of office.[18]

Finally, I asked what message the Unclassified Pay Plan Board would send by publicly punishing Malachowski.

I barely knew Margaret "Meg" Curran when Gov. Lincoln Almond nominated her on January 2, 1997, for a vacant seat on the Rhode Island Supreme Court. Curran had been editor-in-chief of the law review at the University of Connecticut Law School and graduated second in her class. When Almond served as U.S. Attorney for Rhode Island, he hired Curran as a federal prosecutor, and she became his chief appellate lawyer. He picked her from a list submitted by the Judicial Nominating Commission.[19] Under the judicial selection compromise that RIght Now! accepted in 1994, the House and Senate would vote separately on her confirmation. In preparation for what most thought would be a routine confirmation, she went to meet top legislative leaders.

The House Judiciary Committee took up her nomination on a gusty, rainy day. I found an empty seat in the audience behind Curran, her husband, and their 8-year-old daughter, Margy. Committee members had received Curran's file, including cover sheets from 152 briefs she had filed in federal cases. U.S. Supreme Court Justice Stephen Breyer sent an enthusiastic letter about her appearances before the First Circuit Court of Appeals while he served as chief judge, and a clerk read it into the record. I had never heard of a U.S. Supreme Court Justice supporting a judicial candidate in Rhode Island.

U.S. Circuit Judge Bruce M. Selya came to testify about Curran's extraordinary work as his law clerk. "She has an ideal temperament to be a judge," Selya said. "She is fair-minded and has an abiding intellectual curiosity. And among my colleagues on the Court of Appeals, she is regarded as one of the two or three best attorneys who regularly appear before us." Sheldon Whitehouse, who had followed Almond as U.S. Attorney, also spoke enthusiastically of her work on appeals for the office, declaring that she would bring "a keen intelligence, a wealth of scholarship, and a strong record of appellate experience."

A host of others added to the chorus of praise. John "Terry" MacFayden had been on the list of five highly qualified candidates with Curran, but affirmed her enthusiastically. Asked if he had any misgivings about Curran's lack of state court experience, MacFayden said he did not.

Curran finally stepped to the witness seat, her unruly reddish hair gathered in a bun. In a low contralto voice, she promised to serve without any political agenda. "I would try to bring intelligence, respect, and compassion," she said. "I recognize the awesome power of the law to affect people's decisions and their very lives." Then, in a scene that would reverberate through the state, eleven Democrats on the House Judiciary Committee began pummeling her with a single charge: she did not know enough about Rhode Island courts.

Curran answered that appellate law worked the same way in state and federal courts. A constitution and the laws enacted under it were comprised of carefully chosen words. Findings of fact were contained in transcripts. Precedents were precedents. Lawyers on opposite sides presented their best arguments. Appellate judges sort through, listen, interpret, and finally decide. She sat stoically as her assailants railed against her. Her husband cupped his face in his hands. Curran's mother picked up their daughter and carried her out of the hearing room.

Rep. William J. Murphy, a trial lawyer from West Warwick, dissented. "I've worked with her," Murphy said. "She is very qualified, and I can say she is excellent." Two other Democrats, Mabel M. Anderson of Pawtucket and Mark B. Heffner of Barrington, also broke ranks to defend Curran, but her attackers overwhelmed them. Three Democrats and all three Republicans on the committee voted for Curran's confirmation. Eleven Democrats voted against.

"It's a shame what happened," declared Rep. Susan B. Iannitelli, of Smithfield. "Nobody testified against her. She was very strong in her interview with us. I was surprised at the vote."[20]

In a newspaper story, John Harwood flatly denied orchestrating the public humiliation of Meg Curran. "My attitude," he insisted to reporters, "is let the committee decide what they think is right. As a matter of fact, go ask any member you wish. Go up and down. Call them tonight and ask them if I talked to them. I never talked to them."

Two days after the vote, a constituent of Johnston Rep. Alfred Russo Jr. phoned me at the office. She described calling Russo and quoted his response: "They made us vote like that."

She asked Russo who "They" were.

"The House leadership," he told her. "When I want something for the Town of Johnston, I have to go to them."

The House Judiciary spectacle galvanized public attention. In the *Providence Journal,* cartoonist Jim Bush showed a bunch of burly men in suits marching triumphantly away from the bludgeoned nominee. Another cartoonist, Don Bousquet, pictured a masked executioner labeled "House Judiciary" with a huge

axe called "Curran Rejection" over a cowering voter. "This ain't about qualifications," the executioner roars. "Everybody needs to be reminded just who is
running this state!!!"

Columnist M. Charles Bakst followed up with a call to John Ryan, dean of
the new law school at Roger Williams University, who told him that Curran
had been "brutalized. If there's such a thing as legislative rape, I would put it
in that category. And for no reason whatsoever." The dean declared that the
House leaders and the committee had "done a gross disservice" to the people
of Rhode Island.[21]

Before the House floor vote I sent a letter to each representative. "From close
observation," I wrote, "we are convinced that all five candidates presented by
the Judicial Nominating Commission are highly qualified to serve as associate
justice of the Supreme Court, and the House Judiciary Committee provided no
contrary evidence." Another volley of letters went from Rev. Jim Miller at the
Rhode Island Council of Churches.

On January 28, the day of the House debate, Providence Rep. David N.
Cicilline, a Democrat, moved to confirm Curran, "notwithstanding the recommendation of the Judiciary Committee."

"Our rules," retorted Majority Leader George Caruolo from his desk, "do not
provide for debate on committee reports. A report has been given. The rules are
that the committee chair speaks, the majority leader speaks, and the minority
leader speaks. Then we vote."

Cicilline insisted: "There is no word in the House rules concerning the confirmation process. The public deserves a full debate."

Pawtucket Rep. Mabel Anderson, who voted for Curran in the Judiciary
Committee, backed Cicilline. "The House has an obligation to vote on the candidate," she declared. In her seventies, Anderson spoke her mind and loved
to show her independence. "Accepting the recommendation of the Judiciary
Committee is not the same as voting on the nominee."

From desks in rows that curved across red carpet, other representatives signaled that they wanted to speak, not merely vote the Judiciary Committee's
written report up or down. House leaders agreed to suspend the rules. Rep.
Charlene Lima blasted the committee by alluding to Harwood's persona as a
hard-driving hockey player. "It was a cheap shot. If this were a hockey game,
they would be in the penalty box." She continued: "I looked at Margaret Curran's
papers, and she is superbly qualified. There wasn't a word of negative testimony
about her. The only negatives came from members of our committee. If we have
a problem with the new judicial nominating process, let's debate that issue in
public but not take it out on this nominee."

Portsmouth Rep. Charles Levesque rose with microphone in hand. "I've been
deeply troubled," he began. "She has never appeared before any of our courts.
She has never held the hand of any litigant in any of our courts." Levesque

scanned the room. "Many have spoken to me on behalf of Margaret Curran, but there are thousands of practicing attorneys who ask if she even knows where the Supreme Court is. How much does she know about practice of law in this state?"

Rep. Scott P. Rabideau rose in the tiny block of Republican seats. He represented rural Burrillville and had cast one of six Judiciary Committee votes for Curran. "I was initially skeptical about this nominee," he began. "When I got the committee package with her letters of reference, I called the people who wrote them. I called the state police to find how they did their report." He said the answers swept away his doubts.

"During the hearing," Rabideau continued, "I asked Mr. MacFayden, who had also been in the running. He said Ms. Curran is highly qualified. Now that his name was out of running, he had no reservations whatever about her confirmation." A wetlands biologist, Rabideau was rail-thin with a mischievous smile. "Then I asked Sheldon Whitehouse, who has worked closely with the nominee: 'Does her lack of state trial experience in any way reflect on her ability?' Whitehouse, who is a Democrat, said it did not. Then I asked Judge Bruce Selya, and he answered: 'You may think she doesn't have experience before Rhode Island courts, but don't let that sway you. She has all the tools to be an excellent justice.'"

From the gallery above, I watched casual conversations around the chamber. Few were listening to Rabideau; they knew how they would vote.

"The issue for me," declared Harold Metts of South Providence, "is the lack of minority representation on the Supreme Court. A highly qualified candidate of color, Superior Court Judge Rogeriee Thompson, was on the list from the nominating commission, but friends still appoint friends, and that's what the governor has done." He paused until a hubbub of private conversations subsided, and then continued, "In the hearing last week, I asked Mrs. Curran if she had attended functions in the minority community, and she answered honestly that she had not. Until a qualified minority person is appointed to the Supreme Court, I will continue to vote against Governor Almond's friends."

Cranston Rep. Frank Montanaro, part of Harwood's leadership team, served on the Judiciary Committee and had voted against Curran. "Let's be clear," he said, "only a small professional club came to speak on behalf of Curran, and the governor's office really did nothing to advance her candidacy. Those who want this candidate haven't done their homework. Nothing in the judicial selection statute made the Judiciary Committee into a rubber stamp."

"Let's also be clear," countered Mark Heffner, who had voted for Curran, "that we're talking about an appellate court of last resort. The only real question should be: Who is the best appellate lawyer?" In his late forties, Heffner was balding and intense. "I'm a trial lawyer," he added, "but there's a certain temperament you need for appellate work, which is an isolated pursuit. Every witness thought Curran would be an ideal candidate, and I became convinced of the same thing."

West Warwick Democrat Timothy Williamson, vice chair of the Judiciary Committee, said he took offense at Don Bousquet's cartoon in the *Providence Journal.* "I was offended to be portrayed as the executioner. Was Meg Curran a sacrificial lamb? Yes, she was, but that's politics. Politics is always involved."

I listened from the gallery, almost embarrassed for Williamson. Why did he seem to delight in playing the buffoon?

David Cicilline countered that voters had fundamentally changed the role of the legislature in choosing judges. "The question is not whether Meg Curran is my first choice. I'm not the governor, so it's not my choice. The system has changed. She is highly qualified. I will vote to confirm her, and I hope many of you will, too."

Sixty-one Democrats voted to accept the Judiciary Committee's recommendation not to confirm Curran. Among the thirty-six who voted against the committee's report were fifteen Republicans and eighteen women. After the vote, Caruolo told reporters, "This woman is probably a delightful woman, and she'll probably make a fine judge some day, but she's not qualified at this time to go on the Supreme Court."[22]

Only two days after the House rejected Curran, Gov. Almond was to deliver his State of the State address. The House chamber filled for the occasion: the entire General Assembly, judges in black robes, department heads, dignitaries, reporters, and crews to broadcast live on three commercial channels. Galleries above filled with lobbyists, friends, family, and ordinary citizens.

Unlike his previous major addresses in the chamber, Almond did not release advance copies of his text. He marched into the House chamber behind a receiving committee and up onto the rostrum. With his mane of white hair, he towered over legislative leaders on either side. In fierce opening remarks he told of meeting with Harwood and Caruolo a week earlier and warning them that if the House rejected Curran for political reasons, he would not present his annual address in this chamber. With measured cadence Almond said he had changed his mind. He had decided to speak "from the village green and directly to the people."

He glared down at Caruolo behind his desk in the second row and branded Curran's rejection "the Tuesday night massacre, or, as described in this chamber, 'the sacrifice of a lamb.'"

With his audience stunned into silence, Almond demanded of them: "What does the rejection of a qualified person say to the young people in our schools, particularly young girls, who are taught: 'Work hard and you will succeed in any endeavor you choose?'"[23]

Spink Davis whispered to me on the phone that the real story behind Curran's

rejection by the House was the separation of powers. A retired lawyer who had
served on the Common Cause board, he often had good information from reliable sources. "This is not public," he told me, "and I only have it second-hand.
House leaders asked her to pledge that she would 'be safe on separation of
powers,' but she refused." He said the story had come indirectly from Sheldon
Whitehouse.

I phoned Whitehouse about the rumor attributed to him. Had Harwood
and Caruolo asked Curran whether she would "be safe" if separation of powers
came to the high court?

He was silent, then said: "I can't say anything for publication."

"Not for publication," I agreed.

"Absolutely not for publication?"

"Absolutely not for publication, at least, not until you agree."

"I think you heard pretty well," Whitehouse said.[24]

I phoned Joe Larisa, Governor Almond's brainy executive counsel. "It's worse
than outrageous," he groused. "We're not choosing candidates for their positions
on separation of powers or anything else."

"Do you think Harwood and Caruolo are asking nominees?"

"Absolutely. Meg wouldn't agree to 'be safe' on the subject."

"Are you going public with that?"

Larisa hesitated. "We can't. It would make a bad situation immeasurably
worse. It wouldn't move us forward."

I asked if the governor would still seek an advisory opinion on separation
of powers.

"We're committed to completing that process," Larisa said, "but we can't ask
for the advisory until we have the fifth justice in place. Obviously, we hoped
that would have been Meg."

David Cicilline and Charlene Lima, both Democrats, filed our first constitutional amendment to establish separation of powers on February 4, 1997. Its
wording came directly from the People's Constitution of 1841, which began with
the single separation of powers clause that comprised Article V: "The powers
of the government shall be distributed into three departments: the legislative,
executive and judicial."

Now we proposed to add three sentences from the People's Constitution that
the victorious Whigs had rejected in 1842:

> The legislative, executive, and judicial departments and powers of
> government shall be separate and distinct from each other.
>
> No member of the General Assembly shall, during the term for
> which elected, hold or accept any appointive position or office
> in the judicial or executive department of state government, nor

appoint another person thereto. No person holding any office in
the judicial or executive department of state government shall be
a member of the General Assembly while serving in such office.[25]

"It'll never pass in this form," Cicilline told me in a husky voice, "but I like
its historical roots. I hope it reminds people what happened here in 1842."

I asked what House leaders would do to him and Lima for introducing the
resolution. He laughed. "I can barely imagine, and maybe I'm a glutton for
punishment. But this is both right and long overdue."

That same afternoon, a bipartisan group of four senators filed an identical
amendment with their signatures at the Senate's mahogany rostrum. Democrats
J. Michael Lenihan and Rhoda E. Perry risked alienating their leadership, while
Republicans John A. Patterson and Mary A. Parella had the full backing of Gov.
Lincoln Almond. No one expected passage of this amendment soon, and all
knew it would cost them.[26]

I wondered if people across Rhode Island had any idea how high the stakes
were. Despite what seemed to be blatant abuses of power, few people outside
the State House seemed aware of our campaign for separation of powers. Two
years of public effort had provoked backlash and retaliation, but no positive
change.

On Valentine's Day, the Unclassified Pay Plan Board met in a colorless room
in the new administration building, across Smith Street from the State House.
No one on the board showed concern over my entreaty for them not to cut Jim
Malachowski's pay. Just as Sen. John Roney had assured me, a revised agenda
specified a less drastic pay cut for Malachowski.

In what seemed like theatre of the absurd, Robert L. Carl Jr., Almond's director of administration whom everyone called "Dr. Carl," led the charge against the
state's top utility regulator. Carl announced that the old law made Malachowski
responsible for regulatory and administrative duties of the Public Utilities Commission, but the revised law split those duties. "This is not an attack upon Jim
Malachowski," Carl said unctuously. "Frankly, many people were concerned
that the PUC was a double-headed hybrid: at one time an advocate, at one time
a regulator. The legislature redefined the Public Utilities Commission so that
there would be a difference between administration and advocacy."

With his career on the line, Jim Malachowski sat alone, facing six stone-faced
men who could destroy him and one peppery woman who had no power to
protect him. "This is not about my pay," he declared. "It's not about my job.
Utility regulation is a highly specialized field that requires technical knowledge
and moral backbone. The law recognizes the need for independence by giving
each commissioner a six-year term."

Somehow, he managed to control his indignation. "I know from many hearings during the years that people want and need strong regulatory agencies. The governor has a duty to support administrative agencies against pressure from regulated industries. That's not politics, it's principle."

If the men of the pay board were embarrassed, none let it show.

"Every one of you," Malachowski contended, "knows that my duties increased under last year's Utility Restructuring Act. I ask you to consider the ramifications of the vote you're about to take. Your action today will send a signal throughout state government. I ask you not to send the wrong message."

Nancy Mayer interrupted him. "Mr. Malachowski," she began, "you're aware that Senator Roney has proposed an amendment that would lower your salary considerably less than the original recommendation. What do you make of that?"

"With all due respect," Malachowski replied, "the law explicitly prohibits the Unclassified Pay Plan Board from lowering salaries of department directors and judges during their term of office. Inquiring whether I would accept having my pay cut by twelve thousand dollars instead of twenty is like asking: 'Do you want both of your legs cut off or one of your arms?'"

Joe Larisa, Almond's executive counsel pounced. "I respectfully disagree with Mr. Malachowski," he said. "I conclude, as the governor does, that the action proposed would not violate the statute. This board is not reducing pay of the Public Utilities Commission Chairman. The law enacted last year created two distinct positions. Mr. Malachowski will continue to fill only one of them."

Mayer, tiny by comparison with men around the table, challenged the governor's lawyer directly. "Mr. Larisa, if you had the CEO of a firm under contract for six years and changed the contract, wouldn't you have to buy out the contract? It seems to me a six-year appointment at set salary is an implied contract."

"The legislature," Larisa replied dryly, "is entitled to tear up the contract and create different positions. The law protects department directors and judges from having their salary cut during their term of office. The chairman of the Public Utilities Commission is neither a department director nor a judge."

"People want to make this nefarious," Carl added. "It is not. The General Assembly makes the law. Our job is to administer the law as it is written, not to make up new rules as we go along."

Mayer ridiculed the votes that these six male politicians were about to cast. "I have not heard one thing today to lead me to believe the responsibilities are diminished or that the salary should be lowered. Excuse me for trying to think logically, but why should traffic court judges make $80,000 a year when the salary for the person who oversees the state's vast and complex utility industry is cut to $71,790?"

The final vote was six to one. Only Mayer's vote signaled the absurdity of the pay board's action.

Malachowski did not go quietly. "I think it's obvious what went on," he told reporters after the meeting. "We have a history in this state where regulatory agencies have not been strong enough. The banking crisis was partly due to regulators not standing up and speaking out. I think that's the core issue here today: whether or not you want strong, independent regulatory agencies. I am disappointed that the governor has turned his back on that and ignored these issues."[27]

As I walked the half-mile back to our office, a street vendor selling balloons and red roses reminded me that it was Valentine's Day, the anniversary of a famous Mob massacre. I remembered vaguely that Al Capone's underlings had donned Chicago police uniforms and executed rival mobsters while their boss basked in Florida sunshine. Our Valentine's Day massacre had no machine guns or blood-spattered walls, but bore its own grim finality. Jim Malachowski could still breathe and talk, but the assault left him no way to lead the Public Utilities Commission. Why had Almond excoriated House leaders for trashing Meg Curran but allowed his subordinates to assault Malachowski with bureaucratic doublespeak? Had Robert Carl negotiated some Faustian bargain between the governor and speaker?

Opening Government

1995–98

Jim Langevin had won election as secretary of state in 1994 on a promise of government transparency, campaigning to transform the office "from that of record keeper and filing clerk to the people's partner in government." Langevin vowed to provide information citizens needed: calendars of public meetings, lobbyist reports, and hard-to-get legislative data. He also pledged to make government data available through personal computers and at a new public information center in the State House.[1]

Within days of his inauguration, Langevin's staff began scanning, compiling, and posting General Assembly documents on an electronic bulletin board. Legislative staff trying to provide the data electronically as required by our 1994 law got off to a slower start. Both offices were testing new technologies and competing to show results. In February 1995, both offices began offering legislative data through telephone hookups, and Langevin provided public computers at the State House. Many of us who had trekked to the State House each morning to scribble data from posted agendas gained chunks of valuable time.

Langevin quickly launched a new "online office" in order to level the playing field, since corporations had paid lobbyists to track legislation for them while ordinary citizens had to fend for themselves. Reporter Timothy Barmann wrote that even the Royal Charter of 1663 had been digitized and made available on the Internet, along with "a plethora of reports chronicling today's happenings in Rhode Island state government."[2]

The rivalry intensified in April 1996, when the legislature mounted its website. George Caruolo invited reporters to test a new legislative system that featured many functions prescribed in the 1994 law. "This is real open government," he declared. "This isn't talk. It is action."[3]

Langevin relished the race and recognized that his efforts to post legislative data on a website could end when the General Assembly came fully online. "We've changed the environment," Langevin said, "from being one of competition to keep secrets to one that opens up state government and provides easy access to public information."

Both systems provided email, biographical information, and photos of all 150 state legislators. Langevin made double use of those data, replacing the state's hardcover *Rhode Island Manual* with a far less expensive paperback called *Rhode Island Government Owner's Manual.* Lowering the costs of publishing allowed him to install networked personal computers in place of an obsolete Wang system.

During the summer of 1996, Langevin closed the musty basement room where copies of bills had long been stacked haphazardly on gray steel shelves. Workers covered glass panes in the oak doors with butcher paper, blocking sight but not sounds of construction. Word leaked that the new secretary of state was spending $115,000 for renovations to what he proudly called the Public Information Center. Before its official opening, John Harwood and George Caruolo asked for a preview, and Langevin gave them a tour. A few days later Harwood sent identical letters to Langevin, Almond, and Nancy Mayer: "We must find a way to provide our members with the basic tools, including office space, that they need to be effective representatives of the people." He noted that this would require "dislocation of current occupants of the building." He demanded that Langevin and Mayer move to available quarters across Smith Street in order to make room for a part-time legislature.

Both stood their ground. "This is not about office space," Langevin told reporters. "It's about getting the secretary of state out of the public information business. It's a dangerous abuse of power."[4]

As lawmakers returned for the 1997 legislative session, Langevin opened his new public information center, which was a stunning transformation of the musty storeroom. Contractors had exposed century-old ironwork and brick ceiling vaults. Surfaces were now smoothed and brightened in pastel peach. Brass lighting fixtures illumined rows of counters that held hundreds of shallow drawers where bills became available by number. A side room contained computer terminals, where visitors could find schedules or search for key words in bills. Framed letters and historic drawings lined the walls. Television monitors showed proceedings in the Senate and House chambers. During one reception, Langevin whirred his motorized wheelchair into a side aisle and opened up drawers of bills, praising the new information tools as essential to open government. "We can't wait for another banking crisis," he said, "to highlight the need for the free and truthful flow of information, from government to its people."

The young secretary of state also did television and radio interviews. "I just find it too ironic," he told reporters, "that on the eve of us opening up this public information center, all of a sudden we're getting an eviction notice."

Nancy Mayer fired off a letter to Harwood. "It defies common sense and logic," she wrote, "to replace a full-time constitutional officer's year-round presence in the Capitol building with offices for our part-time citizen's legislature."

The refusal of Langevin and Mayer to move out of the State House brought a groundswell of public support. John Hazen White, the 82-year-old president of TACO, Inc., bought radio ads urging citizens to call their representatives and the speaker's office. "Keep your friend Jim Langevin in the State House," White urged listeners. White also published a broadside that filled four full pages in the *Providence Sunday Journal*. "Open Government a Necessity," the first page proclaimed with a statement from Langevin about the public information center. Following pages included photos of computer terminals, bill drawers, and a conference room. On the fourth page, White included Harwood's opening-day statement mocking "naysayers and would-be reformers."[5]

One day after White's "Red Alert" appeared, Harwood and Senate Majority Leader Paul Kelly scuttled the move to oust Mayer and Langevin. The speaker told reporters that the secretary of state had threatened to spin the confrontation as an issue of open government. "That's unfortunate," Harwood said, "because the issue is space."[6] No one dared to disagree with him publicly, but out of his sight many rolled their eyes.

After organizing quietly, a new open government coalition began its public campaign in January 1997. Three years earlier Robert Utter, publisher of the *Westerly Sun* and president of the Rhode Island Press Association, had suggested that we have lunch. At Little Chop Sticks on Smith Street, he rehearsed the trade group's work with a paid lobbyist: they pushed for improvements in the state's open meetings and open records laws but passed nothing. "As journalists," Utter said, "we face peculiar constraints. We need to change the law, but it's awkward when we also report on the General Assembly." The publishers wanted to build a broad coalition like RIght Now!

I reminded him that RIght Now! had come together after RISDIC imploded and when depositors had felt betrayed by their government. Without scandal it would be harder to organize an open government coalition.

Utter agreed. "But we have to start somewhere," he said, "and we're in for the long haul."

Over the next two years, ACCESS/RI took shape, its name an acronym contrived from first letters: All Citizens Concerned about Ending Secrecy in our State. Leaders of Rhode Island groups that shared a commitment to open government quickly joined: the American Civil Liberties Union, the League of Women Voters, Common Cause, Operation Clean Government, the Library Association, and the Rhode Island Press Association. But unlike the RIght Now!

Coalition, which had been formed with organizational members, individuals incorporated ACCESS/RI in 1996. Tom Heslin, a managing editor at the *Providence Journal*, agreed to head the new coalition, and I served as vice president. Editors of two smaller papers — Mary Harrington at the *Newport Daily News* and Rudi Hempe at the North Kingstown *Standard-Times* — also joined the board.[7]

We began drafting legislation to update the state's Watergate-era open meetings and open records laws. Rhode Island's Access to Public Records Law listed twenty-three kinds of records that were "not deemed public" under any circumstances, including most personnel records, law enforcement records, technological secrets, adoption records, exam questions, and tax returns. By contrast, the federal Freedom of Information Act (FOIA) allowed judges to decide on a case by case basis whether government records could be forced into the open — thus balancing privacy or security interests against the public's right to know. We decided to push for a similar "balancing test" in the Rhode Island law.

Other sections of our bill proposed to speed the release of government documents, to make computerized records as accessible as paper documents, and to raise the fines from $1,000 to $5,000 for any public official or body that blocked public access.

The new coalition for open government held its first press conference on New Year's Day of 1997, the bone-chilling sixth anniversary of RISDIC's collapse. On the broad marble steps where new exterior lights had first illumined the Capitol the night before, I announced the new coalition's mission to shine new lights inside the State House.

"Our goal," ACCESS/RI President Tom Heslin announced, "is to end government secrecy that may advance special interests, promote personal advantage, hide corruption, conceal official mistakes, avoid embarrassment in high places, intimidate activists or otherwise inhibit public participation in or knowledge about public activities."[8] Not surprisingly, our modest kick-off landed on front pages across the state.

ACLU director Steve Brown and I set out to find sponsors, and Rep. Mark Heffner agreed to introduce both ACCESS/RI bills in the House. "However good and needed our legislation is," he reminded me, "it won't pass the first year anyway. With the press on our side, we can take a long view. I predict we'll win in the end."

Heffner, an attorney, proved a tenacious advocate. As winter gave way to spring he kept pressing for a vote in the House Judiciary Committee, where he sat as a member. Warwick Rep. Robert E. Flaherty, a close ally of Harwood, chaired the powerful committee, and he stalled until an April deadline when bills must either pass or die. As time ran out, members of the committee were beginning to leave. Heffner raised a hand and asked Flaherty yet again for a vote on his open records bill.[9]

Almost instantly Frank Montanaro, another Harwood loyalist, stood up and walked out, depriving the committee of a quorum. Heffner bolted into the hallway behind Montanaro and tried to talk him back, their voices loud enough to hear inside the room, but Montanaro stormed away. Without a quorum there could be no more voting. Our bill and dozens of others died quiet deaths. Without a vote who could be blamed?

The Senate Judiciary Committee, by contrast, unanimously approved the open records and open meetings bills sponsored by J. Michael Lenihan and Rhoda Perry.[10] Newport Sen. M. Teresa Paiva Weed, newly chosen to chair the powerful committee, presented the open government bills on the Senate floor. She advocated for a balancing test based on the federal Freedom of Information Act.

Lenihan, as prime sponsor, got the last word. "We're saying to our citizens, 'You do have the right to information. You do have the right to know.'"[11]

Senators voted in overwhelming numbers — 45–0 and 40–5 — for the two open government bills proposed by ACCESS/RI. But would the House ever follow?

During the fall of 1997, teams of college students fanned out across Rhode Island on what their faculty advisors jokingly called a scavenger hunt. Professors Ross Cheit at Brown and Linda Lotridge Levin at the University of Rhode Island both served on the ACCESS/RI board. Their political science and journalism classes would test how well municipal officials were complying with the state's current Open Meetings and Access to Public Records Laws.

To prepare, students rehearsed introducing themselves to public officials. They played roles, practiced unflappable patience, and answered hostile questions about why they wanted the records. Student teams drove to police stations, town halls, and school offices in each of Rhode Island's thirty-nine cities and towns. They requested specific documents that were explicitly public under current law. Where they encountered resistance, they repeated their walk-in visits. At each office, they noted what records were provided or denied. On a scale from "courteous" to "discourteous" they charted how officials treated citizens' requests. Above all, they aimed to be scrupulously fair.[12]

At local police departments, they asked for daily logs, recent arrest reports, and any complaints of brutality — all public under the current law. But few local police departments obeyed the law. When URI student Matthew Cotnoir visited the Smithfield Police Department to ask for records, he wound up speaking with four officers in succession. The fourth marched him into a back room, demanded his driver's license, and photocopied it. "He interrogated me," Cotnoir wrote afterward, "asking questions such as if I had reason to think the Smithfield police were watching me or if I had done anything wrong in the town that day and wanted to see if the police knew about it." After questions and insinuations,

Smithfield police refused to release the arrest reports or let Cotnoir see their police log.

Neighboring Burrillville police also photocopied a student researcher's license and demanded to know why he wanted the reports. Commanding officers claimed they were "not obligated to give out that information." In Cumberland police turned students away three times — first because the record keeper was out sick, then because she was on vacation, and finally because she had left for the day. Eight weeks after a written request, Cumberland police provided three arrest reports.

From their visits students concluded that police departments obeyed the open records law only about a third of the time. They described a "culture of police secrecy."

City and town clerks fared better, furnishing all the public documents requested, while school committees provided ninety-four percent of the materials.

The students unveiled their 77-page report, *Access to Public Records; An Audit of Rhode Island's Cities and Towns*, on March 16, 1998. It made headline news on television and radio, and in newspapers across the state.

Police departments tried to deflect an avalanche of negative publicity. Chiefs around the state attacked the students' methodology and conclusions. "You are asking kids to make judgments on government," said Bristol Chief Russell Serpa. "I don't think that's right." But defensive reactions like these only increased public pressure. Police departments began acknowledging their failures, and several promised to comply fully with the state's open records law.[13]

The controversy also nudged lawmakers toward approving open government legislation in the 1998 legislative session. The Senate passed the open government bills by J. Michael Lenihan and Rhoda Perry, which included the balancing test modeled on the federal Freedom of Information Act (FOIA).[14]

In the House, Mark Heffner had filed both open records and open meetings bills like those that had died without a vote a year earlier.[15] On a bright day late in March, the House Judiciary Committee prepared for the annual deadline when House bills had to be voted up or down. Dozens signed in to testify in support of Heffner's open government legislation.

Students from Brown and the University of Rhode Island passed out copies of their report to committee members, and several told how intimidated they had felt when requesting public documents from the police. Leaders from the League of Women Voters, the ACLU, and the Rhode Island Press Association explained fine points of the legislation and urged passage. Gerry Billings, chair of the Common Cause freedom of information committee, urged the Judiciary Committee to act. "It's really time," he closed, "to show some resolve."

Nisha Purushotham testified for the Rhode Island Organizing Project, which represented churches and community groups. Her group had requested records for dilapidated and abandoned buildings in Providence, but was refused until forty people staged a sit-in at City Hall and finally got the documents.

To my delight, the House Judiciary Committee approved several technical amendments and then voted to send Heffner's bills to the full House.[16] On May 6, I watched from the gallery as the House finally took up Heffner's Open Meetings legislation. The speaker was nowhere to be seen, but Majority Leader Caruolo signaled where the leadership stood on a slew of amendments. The question of penalties was crucial, and Heffner's legislation proposed to raise the maximum fine for state or municipal bodies that violated the Open Meetings Law from $1,000 to $5,000. But Rep. Charles Levesque proposed an amendment that would roll the limit back down to $1,000, claiming that the higher fine would be unfair and calling the whole process "a trap for the unwary."

Heffner pushed back that the higher maximum penalty could be imposed only for a knowing and willful violation. "This is not about a clerk who's sloppy or had a bad day," he said. "There must be a deterrent for severe violations."[17] But with Caruolo in the lead, Levesque's amendment passed 64–20[18] and the higher fines vanished. The weakened Open Meetings bill passed almost unanimously.

The next day, representatives returned to deliberate on Heffner's Access to Public Records bill. Several pounced on the "balancing test" that would allow judges to weigh public interests against personal privacy in government records. Rep. Peter Kilmartin warned that it might make personal privacy "subject to a bureaucrat" empowered to decide. Rep. Barbara C. Burlingame argued that the bill would let the press "publish anything they wanted" regardless of personal privacy. Caruolo loyalists removed it by a vote of 57–30.[19]

Further floor amendments amputated one provision after another, which left the bill a bloodied corpus that the House finally passed and sent to the Senate. The Harwood majority Democrats sent a clear message: critics and reformers would get nothing until we showed respect. But by passing the weakened bill, Harwood loyalists could still campaign for re-election claiming they had voted for open government. Many seemed to believe the public would not understand the legislative fine points.

But newspaper reporters — long stymied as the students had been — reported the bloodletting in detail. The *Providence Journal's* Bruce Landis contacted national experts who refuted representatives' claims that the balancing test would jeopardize personal privacy, and ACLU director Steve Brown — widely recognized as Rhode Island's leading privacy advocate — demolished the specious arguments that had carried the House debate.[20]

SEVERAL DAYS after the House passage of the weakened bill, the ACCESS/RI board met Rep. Mark Heffner at the Common Cause office. Heffner distributed a list of negotiating options, but the mood was gloomy. ACLU director Steve

Brown scoffed at his suggestion that the bill could be revived. "What they did was pure mayhem," Brown said. "They took out the balancing test, higher fines, and the requirement that people who file lawsuits can cover their legal costs. Support from us would only give them cover."

"So you're ready to drop the whole thing?" Heffner asked.

"What's worth keeping?" Brown demanded.

"It's a long shot," Heffner said, "but hear me out. The Senate bills — which we all like — are now in the House Judiciary Committee. I'd like to make one last effort to reach a productive compromise — not everything we want, but better than nothing. There's time to modify the Senate bills, bring them to the House floor, and get them back to the Senate."

Brown shrugged it off. "What makes you think the House will suddenly become amenable?"

"They've made their point," Heffner said. "And they've been pounded in the press for trashing our bills. If we come back respectfully, it'll be in their political interest to compromise. I think it's worth trying to bring them around."

Brown asked what made him think so.

Heffner mentioned rumors that Caruolo was leaving the House and that Gerry Martineau would become majority leader. "I think that'll happen, and they'll let Gerry play the healer."

"What about Kilmartin?" asked Brown.

Kilmartin, a Pawtucket police officer, had been furious about the students' report after Pawtucket had been rated poorly for withholding police and school documents. His department's scores were among the worst in the state. "Kilmartin's proud of his fellow cops and his city," Heffner said. "You ruffled his feathers."

People chuckled.

"You can laugh," Heffner said, "but Peter Kilmartin could help us achieve some constructive compromises."

"The House will never agree to a balancing test," Brown said.

"You may be right," said Heffner. "But what if we can reach agreement on other parts of the bill? Wouldn't that be a step forward? You've generated tremendous pressure with the reports of students being treated badly and turned away."

"So why didn't they go ahead and pass basic corrective measures?" asked journalism professor Linda Lotridge Levin, who had supervised the University of Rhode Island students. "What further proof do they need that the system's broken?"

"It's not about proof," Heffner said. "It's about pride." Nearly bald but with a neat mustache, he instructed us on the fundamentals of lawmaking: "Your report got their backs up, and they weren't your fans to begin with. But I think they know they went too far. Now that they've made their point and cooled down, I'd like to give it one last try. But there won't be any compromises unless you around this table want them."

No one spoke, and Heffner continued. "Look, here's my bottom line. Suppose we can get half a loaf — not everything you want, but more than we have now. If we reach agreement and you blast it as insufficient, that would make this a useless exercise."

Someone asked if the ACCESS/RI board could have final say on any further compromises.

"There may not be time for that," said Heffner. "Things happen so fast in the final hours of the session. I hope you would authorize a couple of people from this body to speak on your behalf."

From the chair, Tom Heslin suggested that Steve Brown and I consult on possible compromises and speak for the board. "So moved," said several people, and it was done.

One blindingly bright June afternoon, Heffner whispered to me that George Caruolo was resigning as House majority leader and Gerry Martineau would take over. "I think that's good," Heffner said. "While Martineau negotiates with the Senate, he's making Peter Kilmartin his point-man on my bills."

"Kilmartin?" I shuddered. The Pawtucket police lieutenant, who was commuting to law school, had sponsored a House leadership bill to create the Rhode Island Cancer Council, a monster modeled on the Lottery Commission. Of its nine members, the speaker would appoint three, the Senate majority leader would appoint three, and the governor three. It would control all federal cancer research funds flowing into Rhode Island and defy separation of powers.[21] I told Heffner I had testified vigorously against it.

Heffner said softly that he hoped we could keep the separation of powers question away from negotiations over his open government bills.

Against all odds, we would try to persuade Kilmartin about fine points of legislation that he resented and might not fully understand. Over several days Heffner, either alone or with Steve Brown or me at his side, reasoned with Kilmartin. Far from negotiating behind closed doors, our talks took place in the rotunda, hallways, House chamber, and lounge. Arguments were mostly civil though occasionally loud. To my surprise, our list of disagreements dwindled.

A sticking point remained over how a judge could fine public officials or bodies that wrongly withheld public records. Current law allowed a judge to impose a civil fine up to $1,000. ACCESS/RI had proposed raising the top penalty to $5,000 and adding language that would allow judges to award court costs and attorney's fees for citizens who had to sue for access. But the House had stripped out both the higher fines and possible pay for lawyers. Without lawyers' fees the ACLU would find it hard to attract volunteer attorneys.

The dispute boiled down to two words: "may" and "shall." Kilmartin insisted that language approved by the House on May 7 was fair to both parties: the judge *may impose* a fine of $1,000 on the public body or official, *may award* attorney fees to the complaining plaintiff, *may order* the public body to provide the records at no cost, and *may award* attorney's fees and court costs to the official if the complaint proves groundless. "If it's fair to fine police departments," Kilmartin said, "it's also fair to fine students who file frivolous complaints and lose in court."

Steve Brown, in shirtsleeves, shook his head. "You forget that ACCESS/RI called for tougher penalties for violators. Now we'd be stuck with the old $1,000 penalty, and on top of that you've added the possibility that citizens might be forced to pay court costs and attorneys' fees."

"Fair is fair," Kilmartin insisted. "Make it mandatory or permissive — whichever you like — but impose the same risk on both sides."

Heffner condensed the dispute over a 124-word section of proposed law into legal shorthand: *may/may/may/may* versus *"shall/shall/shall/may.*

"It's gotta be *shall/shall/shall/may,*" Brown said. "Mandatory fines and obligations for public bodies that break the law, but only optional fines for citizen plaintiffs who lose in court."

"What?" Kilmartin demanded incredulously. He stalked away.

Heffner chased Kilmartin and talked him back. Negotiations hung on a wisp of hope. "One more time, Peter," Heffner asked. "Your bottom line?"

"Fair is fair," Kilmartin said. "Make it 'may/may/may' or 'shall/shall/shall.' You decide, but either way, all parties assume the same risk and let the judge decide."

"But the citizens seeking government records have nothing," Brown parried. "Government officials have budgets, lawyers, and bureaucracies at their disposal."

"Nonsense!" Kilmartin waved him off. "They're equal before the law. You can pick whichever you want — 'shall/shall/shall' or 'may/may/may.' But I won't agree to half and half."

Brown shook his head. "This will stop the bravest people on earth from seeking public records." Over this one detail the entire package might go down. We agreed to talk again at suppertime.

Mark Heffner and I went to see Sen. Mike Lenihan in his high-ceilinged Senate office. Heffner guided Lenihan through the grid of compromises already agreed upon and ended with the remaining deal-breaker.

Lenihan rolled his eyes. "I wish I could help," he said wistfully. "All I can do is have these items drafted as amendments and be ready to amend your bills that are over here."

"Including *shall/shall/shall/may*?" Heffner asked.

Lenihan nodded. "Assuming you can get agreement from Kilmartin. Our leadership team would rather pass my bill as we passed it in May, but we'll settle for less." He asked if we thought Kilmartin would agree.

"Half an hour ago, he wouldn't," Heffner said. "Steve Brown is off looking for precedents that could help us."

Brown found a 1978 U.S. Supreme Court decision that involved federal anti-discrimination laws. The prevailing plaintiff — such as students denied access to public records — was to be awarded attorney's fees, but the defendant — like an official who wrongly denied access — would be awarded such fees only when a federal judge "found that the plaintiff's action was frivolous, unreasonable, or without foundation."[22]

"So that's a similar case," Brown explained to Kilmartin. "And the case law clearly follows *shall/shall/shall/may.*"

Kilmartin stood between fluted marble columns as he silently read and re-read a highlighted section of the federal court ruling. "I see your point," he finally said. "But I'm not sure the federal precedent applies."

Gently, Heffner offered to go with him to a lawyer they both respected.

"I'll check it on my own," Kilmartin said.

Meanwhile, unknown to any of us, the carefully choreographed dance between House and Senate that normally ended each legislative session was breaking down. Ironically, one flashpoint was Kilmartin's bill to create a cancer council. I had provoked members of the House a few days earlier with testimony against a new public corporation under direct legislative control, but the bill flew out of committee and passed easily on the House floor, 65– 17.[23]

In the Senate Judiciary Committee, however, it hit a wall. Professional lobbyists from the American Cancer Society, Rhode Island Medical Society, Brown University Medical School, Hospital Association of Rhode Island, and Lifespan — a network of leading hospitals — all testified against the proposed cancer council. A lobbyist from Brown objected to giving the new public corporation "exclusive responsibility" for gathering data and making research grants.[24]

I testified again that the proposed council would create another egregious separation of powers violation. In an accompanying letter to the Judiciary Committee I warned against entrusting "these vast executive powers" to a board "directly controlled by leaders of the General Assembly through six of nine direct appointments."

The next day, July 1, Senate Majority Leader Paul Kelly interrupted his chamber's session and sent the senators home, blaming the impasse on Caruolo's departure and Martineau's sudden rise. Roughly twenty-five "must-pass" Senate bills were held hostage in the House Judiciary Committee, while at the same time House leaders were demanding the passage of more than seventy bills stranded in Senate committees, including Kilmartin's cancer council.

During the impasse, *Providence Journal* reporter Bruce Landis asked about the prospects for our open government bills. I said the House had weakened the legislation, making it "simply not a step forward." Steven Brown was more blunt: "My guess is, it's dead."

"I'm going to keep pushing," Heffner told Landis. "I'd give it one in five chances of passing." In his story Landis quoted an anonymous representative saying that some House leaders hated me and were angry enough to run me over in their cars. Senators, by contrast, had approved the open government bills in May, and Sen. Teresa Paiva Weed told Landis: "One certain way to improve public confidence and trust in what we're doing is to let them see the records."[25]

Negotiations between House and Senate leaders finally cleared the way for lawmakers to reconvene on July 14, 1998, weeks after the session normally ended. Piles of legislation hung in the balance, and Kilmartin had still not told us which version he could accept. Heffner and I were on the House floor when Kilmartin entered the chamber, and Heffner darted over to ask. Moments later, he returned. "He may not like it," Heffner said, "but he's learned enough law to appreciate a Supreme Court precedent."

With only hours to go we would need to amend bills in both the House and Senate Judiciary committees, get floor votes in both the House and Senate, and then deliver the amended bills back to their chambers of origin in time for final floor votes. I asked Heffner if he was sure Kilmartin's word would get us through.

"I'm not sure of anything," Heffner said. "But it's all we've got."

While Heffner went in search of House Judiciary Chairman Robert Flaherty, I went to find Mike Lenihan and Teresa Paiva Weed.

In the final days of each legislative session, the House and Senate typically suspended rules for posting bills before floor votes. Leaders in each chamber wanted their priority bills passed and carried back to them or transmitted to the governor before they allowed final votes on bills they held hostage. Tensions soared; tempers flared.

I sat on a couch that curved along the back of the Senate chamber while senators plodded through committee reports and hundreds of votes. Forty-second on the calendar was Kilmartin's bill to create the Rhode Island Cancer Council. Paiva Weed, as chair of the Judiciary Committee, presented a floor amendment and announced that her committee recommended it. Although I had no way of reading the actual text, I inferred that the bill still included the six House and Senate appointments.

Paiva Weed offered a floor amendment urging the appointment of cancer survivors to the board, and the senators approved. The amendment seemed futile, since cancer survivors could not deter systemic patronage and passage would give lawmakers control over many millions of research dollars. In the dull routine of parliamentary procedure, this new monster was becoming law before my eyes. I wanted to protest, but sat silently. Only four senators dared to vote against it.[26] A clerk stamped the amended bill, and a routine motion sent a messenger carrying it back to the House chamber for final passage.

Late in the evening, Paiva Weed announced the substitute version of Mark Heffner's open records bill. With sheaves of paper in his arms, Lenihan described details of the compromise, more than two-dozen specific changes, which most members of the Senate were hearing for the first time. He explained that the revised legislation would prevent public officials from demanding to know why a document was being sought, would limit what agencies could charge for copies, would require agencies to provide computerized records, and would make it clear that arrest reports must be open to the public. "It would require a judge to award reasonable attorneys' fees to the prevailing plaintiff," Lenihan added. "As some of you will remember, this is the first comprehensive open records reform since our current law was enacted in 1979."

While Lenihan spoke, I noticed Heffner hovering at the far end of the Senate's mahogany rostrum. By custom lawmakers moved freely in both chambers, but I had not expected to see him there. He had told me earlier that the new House majority leader, Gerry Martineau, had warned him to get the Senate version of his bill back quickly because representatives would not delay adjournment for it.

"This is far from perfect," Lenihan was saying, "and I much prefer the version we approved back in May, but this compromise is a substantial step in the right direction."

After cursory debate, the lieutenant governor ordered the electronic vote. Thirty-nine green lights came on, overwhelming five red ones. The gavel came down and a clerk in the well stamped and signed the face sheet to authenticate its passage. A page would normally carry a box of bills across to the House, but I saw Heffner whispering to Senate officers. A clerk handed the bill to him, and he bolted toward a side door. I slipped out into the rotunda just in time to see Heffner racing down the hallway. He sprinted toward the House chamber, skidded around a turn and toward the main entrance. I dashed up a stairway to the House gallery.

On his feet near the front of the House, Gerry Martineau, the chamber's new majority leader, was asking his colleagues for unanimous consent to consider Heffner's legislation, which had just arrived from the Senate. "For those of you who may have forgotten," he said, "we passed a version of this legislation in May. Rep. Kilmartin had major objections at that time, and he's been talking with proponents since then. He's been our point-man on this, and he's satisfied with a series of compromises in the bills."

There were no copies of the final text for representatives to read. The Senate versions had not escaped from House Judiciary. Everyone was exhausted. There was no more time.

Heffner's bills were the last two approved in the House in the 1998 legislative session. Compromised though they were, they contained the first comprehensive reforms of Rhode Island's Open Meetings Law and Access to Public Records Law since the original enactments two decades earlier. These bills enshrined in law a laundry list of significant reforms.[27]

Six days later, on July 20, Gov. Lincoln Almond signed both bills into law and handed the pen to Heffner. I applauded enthusiastically. For all the work by ACCESS/RI and all the students' struggles to get records, three lawmakers had delivered these two bills. Peter Kilmartin had agreed to essential compromises, Mike Lenihan had shepherded them through the Senate under great pressure, and Mark Heffner deserved historic credit for literally dragging these bills into being.

As I left the governor's elegant State Room, Almond's executive counsel, Joe Larisa, held a sealed envelope. "I'll give you this if you promise not to open it until you're back in your office."

I agreed and shook his hand. With his mysterious envelope in my briefcase, I walked the half-mile west along Smith Street. While I waited for my lunch order at the Mandarin Garden, I read the longest veto message I had ever seen: four pages of single-spaced text. Almond vetoed Kilmartin's cancer council bill. The governor wrote that he "wholeheartedly" supported the goals of "providing cancer care, research, prevention, detection, and education" but that he must veto the legislation "because its legislative appointment provisions violate the constitutionally-mandated separation of powers."[28]

Anticipating the struggle yet to play out before the state Supreme Court, Almond added: "Soon after the adoption of our Constitution in 1843, the Rhode Island Supreme Court held that separation of the powers of the three branches of Rhode Island government was 'the great principle of American liberty.'"

Earlier chief executives, no matter how bold, had shied away from what legislative leaders had warned would be a declaration of war. Almond — the state's first governor with a four-year term — had vetoed previous bills that violated separation of powers with polite, even deferential, language. But now, with full-throated eloquence and ample citations, the towering former prosecutor was throwing down his gauntlet. He clearly believed separation of powers was necessary for Rhode Island and would help him win a second term.

As the summer of 1998 slipped away, I wondered why Democrats who held overwhelming majorities in the House and Senate never tried to override the Republican governor's veto. Since the Senate had passed the cancer council bill under duress, had Senate leaders signaled Harwood that they would not return to override? Were Democrats only offended by the cancer council boondoggle? Or could they be pondering separation of powers?

32

Heavy Hands
1998

By 1998, Vincent J. Mesolella Jr. had become an icon of legislative over-reach, yet nothing prepared Rhode Island for what he did that spring with the Pascoag Reservoir. Mesolella managed the historic Sayles Mill complex, which consisted of ten stone mill buildings, an earthen dam constructed in 1860 to provide hydropower, and Pascoag Reservoir — also called Echo Lake — that stretched for miles through rural Burrillville and Glocester.[1]

Sayles Mill Associates, a partnership that included Mesolella's father, had purchased the properties in 1980 and authorized the son to represent them. The next year, fires on three successive nights burned out the stone structures and tower whose 500-pound bell had marked the changing of shifts for sixty-six years. During demolition of the ruined bell tower, a slab of granite crushed a crane operator in his cab. Two 17-year-olds pleaded guilty to arson and the tragic death. An insurance settlement put Mesolella and the Sayles Mill partners ahead of their investment with picturesque real estate to sell.

In 1982, Mesolella offered the dam and land under the reservoir to owners of cottages along the lakeshore for $300,000 — far higher than its assessed value of $14,550. Homeowners refused his offer, and one accused him of intimidation.

In 1997, Mesolella tried to sell the dam and reservoir to the Department of Environmental Management (DEM) for $400,000, but the state agency turned him down. In 1998, he tried again, asking $425,000, but was again refused. Ironically, if DEM had agreed to buy his lake, Mesolella might have had to switch sides at the table, since he also served as John Harwood's designee on the powerful State Properties Committee that controlled the acquisition of real estate.[2] By 1998, the insurance settlement, land sales, and rents had grossed more than $1.2 million dollars.

Mesolella resented having to pay taxes on property he could not sell, and he blamed DEM for stalling. He ratcheted up the pressure by posting a No Trespassing sign at the only public ramp for launching boats onto the reservoir. "We own the lake," he told a reporter. "We pay the taxes on the lake, and we pay the insurance. The DEM put a dock in our lake."[3]

DEM quickly countered that it had built the ramp, could document thirty years of continuous public use, and had a deed that guaranteed public access. The environmental agency posted a sign allowing boaters.

Not to be bested, Mesolella cranked open heavy gates in the dam and locked the gatehouse. Water gushed out through a submerged drain. Owners of cottages that dotted ten miles of shoreline watched their lake vanish. From their docks, they peered out at boats stranded on mud flats. Local volunteer fire departments wondered how to stretch hoses from shore to the distant shallows. Angry letters poured in to the *Providence Journal*'s editorial pages, including one that blasted Mesolella for his Mob-like extortion. "It's a shame that he is dragging the Italian culture to a new low with this act," wrote John A. Fazzino.[4]

DEM quickly charged the powerful state representative with violating the Freshwater Wetlands Act and sought an injunction. A Superior Court judge ordered Mesolella to close the sluice gates within three hours. He complied but again locked the gatehouse. Over the weekend nearly two inches of rain fell on Rhode Island. As watercourses swelled with run-off, Pascoag Reservoir filled to its normal level and kept rising to a record depth, encroaching on lawns and threatening cottages. A whitewater torrent surged through its granite spillway.

Reporters tried without success to reach Mesolella while pundits had a field day. Editors at the *Providence Journal* summarized Mesolella's dual roles as a powerful legislator and member of the House leadership who executed laws as chairman of the Narragansett Bay Commission and a member of the State Properties Committee.[5]

What the *Journal* did not mention, however, was that the representative also controlled a fund that dispensed gasoline taxes to replace leaky underground fuel tanks. In 1996, the DEM had reported fuel leaking from 107 underground tanks scattered around the state. Leaking gasoline glistened on the surface or migrated into aquifers that fed thousands of wells. DEM estimated that it would cost $18.8 million to dig up leaky tanks and stop the seepage.

To pay for the cleanup the legislature levied a penny-per-gallon tax on gasoline. Instead of directing the funds to DEM, which legislative leaders loathed, the General Assembly created the Underground Storage Tank Financial Responsibility Fund Review Board. Lawmakers got seats on the new board, and Rep. Mesolella became its chair.[6] While House leaders subsequently wrestled with Gov. Almond over control of the fund, the likely costs to fix leaking gas station tanks soared from an estimated $18.8 million to $40 million.[7]

In June of 1997, as the General Assembly rushed toward adjournment, Mesolella shoehorned a special article into the state budget, raising the allocation for his Underground Storage Tank Fund from $125,000 to $550,000.[8] He had not cleared his request with the fuel board, and the House Finance Committee had never held a public hearing on the unprecedented four-fold increase. When they heard that the extra $425,000 would not go for cleanup work but for administrative costs, environmental groups were incensed. The process reeked of insider influence.[9]

In response to a reporter's question, I pointed out that Mesolella was exercising both legislative and executive powers in ways that would be unconstitutional for members of Congress and legislators in other states. As the deputy House majority whip, Mesolella had enormous influence on enacting budgets and laws. Meanwhile, as chairperson of two quasi-public bodies — the Narragansett Bay Commission and the Underground Storage Tank Fund Board — he directly administered public funds. And if that were not enough, he sat on two other executive entities — the State Properties Committee, which controlled state leases and purchases, and the Rhode Island Telecommunications Authority, which operated WSBE-TV, the state's only public television station. Mesolella's political leverage had grown to legendary proportions.

Mesolella announced that he would step down from the fuel board. "I don't want Phil West or the *Journal* to think they chased me out," he told reporter Peter Lord. "It was always my intention — as soon as the program was up and running — that I would resign as chairman, and maybe as a member of the board."[10]

Months passed by and Mesolella continued to run the board, hiring staff and spending tax dollars, repeating his promise to resign the following May. In June 1998, he announced that he would not seek an eleventh term in the House of Representatives. During farewells on his last night in the House, I heard genuine affection in the stories his colleagues told. Mesolella basked in several standing ovations. "Without me around next year," he quipped, "I hear the *Journal* is going to have to lay off two reporters and a columnist."[11]

But even after he left his seat in the House, leaders juggled appointments to keep Mesolella in charge of both the fuel board and the bay commission. Still close to House leaders, he visited the State House frequently.[12]

One afternoon, as I entered through a legislators' parking lot nestled against the building's broad marble base, Mesolella drove toward me in a forest-green BMW. In an instant, we recognized each other. He touched the gas and pretended to swerve toward me. Never in danger, I dodged between the parked cars and laughed, wondering if under other circumstances I could have placated him. Instead, I had goaded him and drawn out the worst. When his father died that fall,[13] I read the obituary and felt sympathy for my muscular antagonist. How had the father shaped his son?

UNLIKE MESOLELLA, House leaders used a carrot-and-stick approach with those who became too visible or vocal in the campaign for separation of powers.

Save the Bay, Rhode Island's largest environmental group, filled the entire main floor of a former bank building on Smith Street, where Common Cause rented a second-floor office. A convenient flight of central stairs touched down near a massive vault that stood perpetually open. Environmentalists filled the space: educators, receptionists, a bookkeeper, development staff, and the savvy executive director, Curt Spalding. Besides being our landlord, Save the Bay had been a strong partner in the RIght Now! Coalition.

Christopher Hamblett, known as "Topher," worked as Save the Bay's lobbyist, and we often exchanged tips at the State House. Sturdy and cheerful, he had served in the Peace Corps, digging wells in Sierra Leone. He welcomed an invitation to serve on the Common Cause state governing board. Over several years he helped me understand Mesolella's conflicted roles as a legislative leader and key player in four public or quasi-public boards.

Topher Hamblett came into my office one spring day in 1998. I knew he had been struggling with House leaders over funds to restore salt marshes and eelgrass beds along the margins of Narragansett Bay,[14] but he had not come to talk about that. Frank Pontarelli, director of policy of the House Policy Office, had drawn him into a room, closed the door, and offered him a job. I knew Pontarelli as a shrewd operative who always acted on behalf of George Caruolo.

"What job did he offer you?"

"Environmental policy analyst for the House majority," Hamblett said. The job would pay much more than he was making at Save the Bay. I had often seen him driving an old Subaru, dropping off his two daughters at a home day care center behind our building, or picking them up at the end of the day. Though his father was Stephen Hamblett, publisher of the *Providence Journal,* Topher Hamblett's modest manner made it clear he had higher values than wealth or power. Still, he had a young family and might easily rationalize his ability to influence environmental policy at the State House.

I asked if Pontarelli had mentioned separation of powers. He shook his head. "But I'm sure they would expect me to follow their lead."

A few days later, he told me he had turned down the offer.

On the last day of the 1998 session, I found Topher Hamblett in a State House alcove, dazed and dejected. Save the Bay had spent $200,000 for aerial surveys and other scientific documentation that Narragansett Bay eelgrass was in crisis. Hamblett said their bills to strengthen wetlands protection and to replenish eelgrass had passed the Senate but lay like beached whales in House committees. A few hours later the session ended, and the environmental legislation was dead.

Karina Lutz, the Sierra Club's state director, was outraged. Curt Spalding, Save the Bay's normally soft-spoken executive director, blasted the House for

not having "any desire to improve the Bay, the air, or the water." He told reporters: "We took everybody at their word that if we did this right, the bill would
be passed. We feel like we've been betrayed by the process."[15]

Had House leaders killed those bills to send a message? What if Topher
Hamblett had accepted their offer? Or if Save the Bay had steered clear of the
controversy over separation of powers?

Another warning came with blunt force. A vocal member of the Common
Cause board, Kevin Grau, worked for the Rhode Island Historical Society. A
graduate student at Brown University, he sported round glasses, shoulder-length
hair, and bow ties. After one separation of powers task force meeting, he lingered to tell me his boss had gotten a call from the speaker's office with a blunt
warning: unless Grau backed off from his advocacy for separation of powers,
the Historical Society might lose its legislative grant, worth many thousands
of dollars.

"They're not even subtle," Grau said.

I asked if the message from House leaders meant he had to leave the Common Cause board.

"They weren't entirely specific. It sounded like they just wanted me gagged."

We agreed that he would tell the Historical Society's executive director he
would cease public advocacy for separation of powers.

Then Richard Morsilli phoned and asked me to his office. Under his leadership
the Ethics Commission had completed a two-year process of revising rules for
public officials. One new rule prohibited public officials from accepting gifts
from lobbyists and other "interested persons,"[16] which had sparked indignant
responses from lawmakers and the governor. Another rule was advancing the
question of legislators on public and quasi-public boards — separation of powers — to the Supreme Court.[17] Legislative leaders had taken umbrage at the rule
designed to end their participation in such boards.[18]

I drove to Morsilli's office in the Citizens' Bank Tower, recently completed
on a narrow point where the Moshassuck and the Woonasquatucket Rivers
converged. Round turreted towers at its three corners made it look ready to blast
off, and his window offered a panoramic view of downtown Providence. On a
pair of computer screens brightly colored numbers danced, showing transactions on the New York Stock Exchange in real time.

Although the State House was not visible from his window, Morsilli pointed
in that direction. "Those sons of bitches," he seethed. "They've been sending
Providence Journal clippings anonymously to my superiors on Wall Street. Can
you imagine?"[19]

On his desk lay familiar headline stories whose common thread seemed to
be that the Ethics Commission under the leadership of Richard W. Morsilli was
cracking down on public officials. I asked what was wrong with that.

"Nothing's wrong with the stories," he said. "It's the goddamned way that they're being used against me. All of a sudden Smith Barney can't get the bonding business we always used to get."

Pieces of a jigsaw puzzle snapped into place. The legislative press office photocopied newspaper stories and distributed them each day to State House offices. Those familiar layouts now lay on Morsilli's desk, faxed from Salomon Smith Barney headquarters on Wall Street. Someone had been mailing these copies anonymously as a warning.

I said I thought his bosses favored ethical government.

"When I first went onto the commission," he said, "they did. Good visibility for me as their branch manager. But after these articles they've lost business and gotten cold feet." He had felt the change coming. When people from Wall Street came to Providence, they normally came to his office before other business. But that had stopped, and he wondered why. Morsilli stood by his window and peered down at the river. "I think those conniving bastards are going to fire me."

"On what grounds?"

He shook his head. "Whatever it may be, they're not saying. They've just gone silent on me. You know the line: 'Just because you're paranoid doesn't mean they're not out to get you.'"

"But you've left the commission."

"My term was up, and I thought that would satisfy them." He drew a deep breath. "I don't think it did."

Morsilli's premonition proved right. A few weeks later Salomon Smith Barney dismissed him on the pretext that he favored male brokers over female in the Providence office and gave them the most promising leads.

Word spread quickly. The firing of Richard Morsilli — like the salary cut for Jim Malachowski — became a warning to anyone tempted to stand up. Even Wall Street would cave in. With loyal lawmakers on the State Investment Commission and Retirement Board, legislative leaders could turn the state's bonding business on or off like a spigot.

When Salomon Smith Barney replaced him with a 34-year-old manager, Morsilli sued the company for defamation, wrongful termination, and age discrimination. The case went eventually to a three-member arbitration panel, and Morsilli refuted charges that he had shown bias against women employees. Many of his female former subordinates in the Providence office testified to his fairness and professionalism.

Ironically, neither side brought up what Richard Morsilli had called me to his office to discuss: anonymous faxes that implied Salomon Smith Barney's bonding business would dry up if the company kept Morsilli at the helm of its Rhode Island office. Because his leadership at the Ethics Commission lay out of bounds, the lawyers battled over sham issues. In September 1999, arbitrators ruled unanimously in Morsilli's favor, awarding him $1.9 million plus legal fees — the largest arbitration award on record in an age-discrimination case.[20]

Slow Motion Battle
1997–99

SEPARATION OF POWERS inched its way toward the Rhode Island Supreme Court. Just before Thanksgiving in 1997, Lincoln Almond had formally presented three questions to the high court for an advisory opinion. First, he inquired whether the 1986 constitutional amendment that authorized the Ethics Commission to "adopt a code of ethics" also empowered it to bar lawmakers from serving on public boards.[1]

Next he asked the court to compare separation of powers in the United States and Rhode Island constitutions. Did Rhode Island's existing clause bar members of the General Assembly and their appointees from executive and quasi-public boards? Were Rhode Island lawmakers excluded as members of the U.S. Congress were?[2]

Third, Almond asked whether Rhode Island's separation of powers clause imposed "any limits whatsoever" on legislative appointments to boards that executed state laws. Did the Rhode Island Constitution prohibit sitting legislators from serving on public boards? Did it bar them from "constituting a majority of the membership of a public board or body?"[3]

Only six days after the governor's request, the high court invited supporters and opponents of the Ethics Commission's rule to present their arguments. The question would prompt an avalanche of legal briefs. I knew that filing a brief with the Supreme Court is no small project. Twice before, Common Cause had filed "friend of the court" briefs, both times benefiting from the work of appellate attorney Lauren Jones. The pony-tailed lawyer had done his legal research and writing at no charge to us beyond photocopying and printing copies of his briefs. I phoned Jones to seek his help on the separation of powers question.

"Sorry," Jones told me, "the speaker's office called last week. I agreed to represent the House."

My heart sank. I asked if he thought the General Assembly had a strong argument.

"Strong?" he replied. "Rhode Island's entire history is on their side."

Common Cause had no budget for legal briefs, but Natalie Joslin, our chapter's original founder, was back as president of the board. Over a brown bag lunch of the advisory council — mostly retired executives and lawyers — Bob Kilmarx and I explained the process.[4]

"So," Joslin said as she passed a plate of cookies, "who will pledge to start a fund to make our case for separation of powers?"

"What will it cost?" John Sapinsley asked.

Kilmarx estimated $25,000.

By the time they went home, advisory council members had pledged $16,000.[5]

Later, I walked Kilmarx down the back stairs to his car. During the years since he and Sheldon Whitehouse had made the case at that same table, he had led our separation of powers task force. Now he seemed energized by the battle ahead. I told him Lauren Jones thought the court would rule against us.

"Lauren could be right," he agreed. "Courts make reactionary decisions more often than we lawyers like to acknowledge. In the Easton's Beach case, they completely ducked the issue." He squinted in the afternoon sun. "I thought they were afraid they'd be sacked, just as their predecessors were in the Bloodless Revolution." On January 1, 1935, Democrats staged a political coup that ended nine decades of increasingly corrupt Republican rule. To preserve their victory, the General Assembly ousted all five Republican Supreme Court justices and replaced them. The new justices affirmed the legislature's power "to remove any judge from office at any time at its pleasure."[6]

"You may not have thought about this," Kilmarx added, "but the General Assembly's power to sack the entire Supreme Court continued until 1994. Your constitutional amendment establishing the Judicial Nominating Commission and authorizing the governor to appoint justices finally ended that threat."[7]

"Would that make the justices any more amenable on separation of powers?"

"I wish," Kilmarx said. "I'd like to believe they would affirm separation of powers because it's right. Our problem is that they have centuries' worth of precedents and a culture of legislative domination. Do I believe they'll break with all that?" He seemed perplexed by his own question. "I'd like to believe at least three of the five will support separation of powers, but I've learned not to speculate. Better to make sure our brief is legally sound."

A few days later Kilmarx and I met with appellate lawyer Karen Pelczarski in her sunny office overlooking Kennedy Plaza. She agreed that separation of powers was probably the most important question facing Rhode Island. "They've built an entire system of government that would be unconstitutional anywhere else in the country," she said. "Our challenge will be to convince the court that what's always been must not continue. I worry that if they say no on Almond's question about the Ethics Commission's authority, they may duck the other two questions."

Over the next month, we loaded Pelczarski down with all the research that Peter Hufstader and others had been collecting over several years. While she drafted and redrafted our brief, I reached out to organizations and leaders who might join the legal contest. First I went to Alan Hassenfeld, who needed no convincing. "Count me in," he said. "The victories we've won so far — ethics, campaign finance, four-year terms, judicial selection, legislative pay — are stones in an arch that's not complete. Separation of powers puts the keystone in place."

The Rhode Island State Council of Churches' Committee on Advocacy and Justice asked how separation of powers related to their mission of providing justice for the poor, and I described the unfair effects of patronage and corruption. A week later, the full council voted to sign onto the Common Cause *amicus* brief, and the League of Women Voters did the same.

John Hazen White sat at a massive antique desk in a square brick tower at TACO, Inc. The wily manufacturer of heating and cooling pumps was a libertarian who saw the General Assembly's intrusion into executive functions as hopelessly corrupt. "We've gotta give 'em hell," he said. "Move aggressively. Separation of powers could be our most crucial triumph of all." The feisty octogenarian had paid for dozens of full-page ads in the *Providence Journal*. His self-funded organization, RedAlert, Inc., could mobilize hundreds on short notice. As he wrote a check toward our legal brief I wondered if he would live to see separation of powers or, for that matter, if any of us would.

Operation Clean Government needed no invitation. From a band of rowdy RISDIC depositors OCG had matured into a vigorous grassroots movement, whose cadre of volunteers had begun producing a tabloid-sized newsletter and a monthly television program. They had no office or staff, but Sara Quinn, the former director of the Ethics Commission, had guided them in drafting ethics complaints that made them a force to reckon with. Beverly Clay, the vice chair, had participated in the separation of powers task force, and Robert Senville, a volunteer attorney, had already begun work on their brief.

The Environment Council also had a running start. Its forty-two member organizations ranged from the American Lung Association and Appalachian Mountain Club to the Sierra Club and Woonasquatucket River Watershed Council. Their leaders gathered each month around a large square of tables at the Audubon headquarters in Smithfield. Chairperson Paul A. Beaudette introduced me to attorney James P. Marusak, who had already begun work on their brief. "Separation of powers is a no-brainer for environmentalists," Beaudette said. "We want decisions made on the basis of science. It does no good to enact wetlands regulations when lawmakers on boards subvert the process for political gain."

Marusak pulled a thick bill out of his briefcase. "I don't know how closely you've looked at this, but it provides a textbook example of how legislative tinkering can ruin environmental policy-making and enforcement."

I had seen what people at the State House called "the Kennedy bill"[8] but had not analyzed it. Beaudette and Marusak skipped from page to page, pointing out places where the legislation by Hopkinton Rep. Brian P. Kennedy took planning and enforcement duties away from the Department of Environmental Management (DEM) and assigned them to other bodies controlled by the General Assembly, including the Coastal Resources Management Council (CRMC) and the Resource Recovery Corporation. In one fell swoop, this legislation would fragment the work of enforcement.

Beaudette pointed to a section about hearing officers. "If you read this closely," he said, "you'll see how it guts DEM's power to prosecute wetlands violators."

I asked where those enforcement powers would go.

"They're also creating a new Joint Legislative Oversight Committee," he said. "How do you think its eleven members would be appointed?"

"By the speaker and Senate majority leader?" I speculated.

He raised his palms in mock surrender. "Nine lawmakers and two legislative staff! Kennedy's bill says they 'shall also resolve any questions regarding an overlap in or conflict in the authority of any state department, agency, commission, or any public corporation of the state or any similar entity.'[9] How's that for consolidating power in legislative hands?"

"Yet another legislative committee," Marusak chimed in, "with vast executive and judicial powers. The point of our brief is that neither legislators nor their appointees have any valid roles as administrators or judges. Regardless of whether the Ethics Commission had ever raised this question, the Rhode Island Constitution itself prohibits such appointments."[10]

Karen Pelczarski welcomed research compiled by Peter Hufstader and Bill Colleran about the soaring number of legislative appointments since the 1950s. "I knew there were a lot," she said, "but these lists — seventy-five public boards with over two hundred seats for legislators and another hundred for legislative appointees — are truly staggering. And if that weren't enough, a whole bunch of gubernatorial appointments need to be confirmed by the Senate. That means that lawmakers can block the governor's appointments, but the 'chief executive' gets no say on appointments by the speaker and Senate majority leader."

She unclipped a pile of 1998 bills. "They're not even content to lay low with what they've already got," she said. "They keep proposing new ones all the time: this Cancer Council, Film Commission, even a new Board of Locksmiths. Everywhere you look, legislators and legislative appointees pop up on executive bodies."

Peter Hufstader had been checking minutes of meetings for various boards. He could not see how part-time representatives and senators had enough hours in the day for all these administrative bodies. Pelczarski laughed. "They probably miss more meetings than they make. I assume they show up when agenda items involve contracts or patronage."

She slid several pages of draft language across to me. She had written that legislative appointees responsible for executing state laws "seriously weaken the power of the executive branch to faithfully execute the laws and impermissibly shift the executive power to the legislature." The results, she noted, were "serious conflicts of interest, failures of oversight, and opportunities for corruption."[11]

Pelczarski paraphrased a 1984 ruling in which the Rhode Island Supreme Court had declared that the ability to appoint was "essential and central to the executive power to faithfully execute the laws." Her text reduced it to absurdity: "If legislators placed themselves and their appointees on all the seats of all executive agencies, the governor would lose every shred of power to faithfully execute the laws. In effect, the governor would be a mere figurehead. It would be absurd to argue that the framers of the Rhode Island Constitution intended that result."

I told her that Lincoln Steffens had visited Rhode Island's gleaming new State House in 1905 and interviewed Gov. Lucius F.C. Garvin. Steffens wrote that he found Garvin sitting "helpless, neglected, alone in his office, with plenty of time to tell me all about the conditions which distressed him and his utter lack of power."[12] Calling the state's governors "administrative mummies," Steffens wrote in his autobiography: "General Charles R. Brayton, the political boss, was the actual, permanent gov ernor or dictator of Rhode Island." He ridiculed the state's chronic corruption as "the best established, most accepted, most shameless system" he had seen anywhere. He called Rhode Island a "State for sale, and cheap."[13] Pelczarski quickly noted the irony: Democrats had hated the Republican Boss Brayton and the law named for him that consolidated his power. When they seized power in 1935, they repealed the Brayton Act and modernized the executive branch, but they quickly reverted to Brayton's practices.

She flew us through a matrix of dates, events, issues, and precedents, calling our attention to a highlighted section. "Here," she read. "In the *Annals of Congress, 1789*, James Madison defined our issue: 'I conceive that if any power whatsoever is in the nature of the executive, it is the power of appointing, overseeing and controlling those who execute the laws.'"

I asked how she would answer House leaders' claim that the Rhode Island Constitution was fundamentally different from that of the United States.

"They can argue that all they like," Pelczarski said, "but they can't rewrite the dictionary on a whim. The definitions of executive and legislative don't change when you cross the border into Rhode Island."

On another page of the draft she quoted an 1854 decision of the Rhode Island Supreme Court that warned against the uniting of all government powers "in the same act of hands."[14] The Justices continued: "To guard against such a government was one great object of the Constitution. This was to be done by this distribution of powers. This is the great principle of American liberty." The case had involved Thomas Wilson Dorr.

"That's a pivotal Rhode Island decision," she said, "but most lawyers — and I'll bet most General Assembly members — have never read it. We'll make sure they do."

Hufstader tabulated national data that Pelczarski wove into our brief. Forty-one states permitted lotteries or gambling, and thirty-three had lottery agencies. But no other state allowed lawmakers or their appointees to serve as voting members of a board that regulated lotteries. By contrast, lawmakers held six of nine seats on Rhode Island's Lottery Commission, an agency plagued by scandal. All fifty states had environmental authorities like Rhode Island's Underground Storage Tank Review Board to oversee the cleanup of leaky gasoline tanks, but only six allowed legislative participation, and only Rhode Island allowed a legislator to run the operation.[15]

I found Pelczarski's argument compelling, but I left her office with nagging doubts. I knew that House leaders had killed Meg Curran's nomination to the high court because she would not commit "to be safe on separation of powers." As for the other justices, Joseph R. Weisberger had been a Republican senator and an early mentor to George Caruolo. Catapulted to the high court by Grand Committee in 1978, Weisberger had announced his retirement several months before scandal engulfed Thomas Fay. When Fay resigned, Weisberger became acting chief, and in 1995 he became the first chief justice chosen through Merit Selection. His years in the state Senate and his special relationship with Caruolo seemed likely to work against us now. Victoria Lederberg had been the last justice chosen by the Grand Committee. She had served fourteen years in the General Assembly and had helped swing crucial votes that made John Harwood Speaker of the House. Gov. Almond had named Maureen McKenna Goldberg to the high court in 1997. Her husband, a former Senate minority leader, was now a high-powered lobbyist. If Weisberger, Lederberg, and Goldberg went against separation of powers, we would lose.

By any ordinary logic, our case for separation of powers was solid. But what if Lauren Jones was right? What if Rhode Island's constitutional history came down on the other side?

WITH NO TIME TO SPARE before briefs were due, Gov. Almond's executive counsel, Joe Larisa, invited the lawyers who were writing in support of the Ethics Commission's rule to a series of meetings in his corner office. Tall windows offered splendid views of College Hill and downtown Providence. Attorneys on our side settled into Larisa's long black leather couch and deep armchairs around an oriental rug.

Larisa began without ceremony. He would not suggest what anyone should write, but wanted each to know what the others were writing to avoid inconsistencies the other side could then use against separation of powers. One by one, the lawyers rehearsed their premises, arguments, and conclusions. They agreed to exchange drafts and meet again. As we left, Jim Marusak handed me a copy of his draft on behalf of the Environment Council.[16]

I read it eagerly. Marusak used historic examples in which Rhode Island's colonial lawmakers acknowledged the authority of British kings, writing that "the General Assembly's legislative power in colonial times was often dominated, and once entirely trumped by executive edicts issued by the King and his Royal Commissioners." For this reason, Marusak wrote, the General Assembly and its apologists had misread history — colonial governors had been weak chiefly because the king imposed his authority through royal commissioners. Only two years after the Royal Charter of 1663, emissaries from Charles II demanded loyalty oaths and the repeal of "all laws and expressions in laws derogatory to his Majesty." The General Assembly acquiesced, pledging "cheerful obedience" to the British Crown.

In a pointed critique of current General Assembly practices, Marusak argued that the Coastal Resources Management Council (CRMC) and other environmental quasi-publics were executive agencies. Proof, he wrote, lay in the state's Administrative Procedures Act (APA),[17] which defined administrative agencies and allowed them to make rules for enforcing laws and resolving contested cases. Marusak emphasized that the law applied to all boards, commissions, departments, and officers apart from the legislature or the courts. He insisted that what these entities did — their core functions — branded them as indisputably executive. Whether they were legally established as part of the executive branch or created as separate commissions made no difference. Executive functions made them subject to appointment by the state's chief executive, and no amount of sophistry could justify lawmakers or their surrogates exercising executive powers.

In particular, Marusak targeted environmental agencies where legislators sat as voting members, including the Coastal Resources Management Council, the Narragansett Bay Commission, the Resource Recovery Corporation,[18] the Underground Storage Tank Fund Review Board, and the Water Resources Board. The Supreme Court, he noted, had explicitly recognized several of these operations as lying within the executive sphere. His draft ended with a plea for the high court to agree that separation of powers principles had played a vital part in Rhode Island's history, and to exert the doctrine's "cleansing effect" on environmental boards.

In his brief for Operation Clean Government, Robert Senville analyzed practical problems that flowed from lawmakers' participation on executive boards. Without the benefit of evidence from a contested case, the Supreme Court should ponder the facts and testimony that had convinced the Ethics Commission to address this glaring problem in the first place.[19] Senville focused on the flood of campaign contributions flowing from contractors, vendors, and law firms to the coffers of Vincent Mesolella as chair of the Narragansett Bay Commission, all of which prevented the General Assembly from exercising proper legislative oversight. Consequently the Bay Commission was given more autonomy, with the freedom to raise rates and take on debt, all to the detriment of its customers.

This was no mere academic theory, Senville wrote. Mesolella had funneled money he received from NBC vendors to other lawmakers who then voted to remove controls the Public Utilities Commission had historically exercised over the NBC. In effect, the move "gave the Narragansett Bay Commission vast autonomy to raise rates and incur debt," a consequence that NBC and its vendors sought. Such machinations, Senville argued, destroyed public confidence in government.

He noted that although other state laws barred officials who could award public contracts and jobs from receiving campaign contributions, legislators with dual roles as lawmakers and administrators were exempt. Corruption could arise whenever such lawmakers received donations from individuals who hoped to benefit from their influence over contracts and jobs. Five years earlier, he added, the justices had affirmed the Revolving Door Law and its precursor ethics rule. They declared in a unanimous opinion: "A democracy is effective only if the people have faith in those who govern, and that faith is bound to be shattered when high officials and their appointees engage in activities that arouse suspicion."[20]

In his brief, Joe Larisa wrote that the framers of the U.S. Constitution saw separation of powers as "the first principle of good government and essential to the preservation of liberty." He showed that the Rhode Island Supreme Court had "consistently applied federal precedent" to separation of powers cases within the state, adding: "The doctrine of separation of powers absolutely forbids the extension of legislative power into the core duties of the judicial branch and the executive branch." He cited a litany of Rhode Island Supreme Court cases that explicitly affirmed the doctrine and linked it to federal practice.[21]

Generations of Rhode Island justices had relied on James Madison as their authority, Larisa wrote. His summary of their rulings provided a way for the justices to uphold the separation of powers clause in Rhode Island's Constitution

even if they decided that the Ethics Commission lacked authority to bar lawmakers from boards. All the briefs on our side reconfirmed what Sheldon
Whitehouse and Bob Kilmarx had taught: separation of powers was the bedrock of American constitutional practice, and it was woven through Rhode
Island jurisprudence.

I knew the other side would argue that the General Assembly was entitled
to create executive bodies and appoint its members to run them. Lauren Jones's
confidence in their case weakened my faith in ours. Would the justices rise
above personal ties and promises they might have made? What if the separation
of powers question we had delivered to the Ethics Commission in 1995 brought
unintended consequences? What if our strategy swept Rhode Island backwards
into a political ice age?

Protocol of the Rhode Island Supreme Court required that lawyers on our side
send copies of their briefs to attorneys for the other side, who would then frame
their answers. In July 1998, defenders of the status quo filed seven briefs, which
represented the views of top Democrats in the General Assembly, Republican
Atty. Gen. Jeffrey B. Pine, historian Patrick T. Conley, political science professor
Jay S. Goodman, who was also a State House lobbyist, and a property rights
group called Rhode Island Wise Use.[22]

Lauren Jones, representing John Harwood, laid out the House leadership's
case in seven spare sentences that covered history, legal interpretation, and
constitutional analysis.[23] He held that policy arguments against the General
Assembly's appointment power were critically flawed. "Under the guise of ethics
reform," he wrote, "the Governor asks this Court . . . to redistribute government
power by stripping the appointment power from the General Assembly and
assigning it to the Governor." He added that the governor based "his transparent power grab on an overbroad, unconstitutional regulation adopted by the
Ethics Commission."

Jones then distilled and dismissed our case: "In an attempt to usurp the state's
constitutional prerogative, they argue that after 300 years of its own republican form of government, Rhode Island has no choice but to follow the federal
model." While our briefs had emphasized comments in which the Rhode Island
Supreme Court had affirmed separation of powers, Jones stressed a single clause
that gave lawmakers the broad powers they possessed under the Royal Charter
of 1663: "The general assembly shall continue to exercise the powers they have
heretofore exercised, unless prohibited in this Constitution."

I had read that clause — Article VI, Section 10 — hundreds of times. Each
time my mind recoiled from its meaning: unless voters had outlawed a specific
legislative practice in the very text of the state's Constitution, the General Assembly remained free to "exercise" that power.

Jones wrote that the legislature possessed all powers but periodically delegated specific appointing powers to Rhode Island's governors. He buttressed his argument with a 1908 Supreme Court advisory opinion that validated the infamous Brayton Act of 1901. Under Brayton, if the Senate did not confirm a gubernatorial appointment in three days, it could appoint whomever it chose. "This Court," Jones insisted, "made it plain that the appointment power is not an inherent executive power; it is a power which could have been given to any branch of government and which was given to the legislative branch." He pointed out that the Supreme Court had upheld Brayton in 1908 and that ninety years later its opinion still stood. "Contrary to the Governor's and Common Cause's depiction," Jones wrote in a footnote, "all five justices firmly believed that the General Assembly possessed, if it so chose, the constitutional power to appoint."

Patrick T. Conley, the leading authority on Rhode Island history, also filed a massive 168-page brief on the legislature's behalf.[24] Conley argued that throughout its history Rhode Island's General Assembly had created commissions and appointed their members. He dismissed Jim Marusak's brief on behalf of the Environment Council for using "history as a drunk uses a lamppost — more for support than light."

Referring to the supremacy of the legislature as an essential feature of colonial government, Conley listed twenty-five legislative committees formed before the Revolutionary War. In every way imaginable, they functioned as administrative agencies, settling boundary disputes, managing real estate, repairing forts, setting tax rates, paying soldiers, and running lotteries. In 1775, moreover, after the battles of Lexington and Concord, the General Assembly appointed Nathanael Greene to command the colony's militia. In this and countless other executive appointments, Conley wrote, Rhode Island's General Assembly "exercises more power than any other in the American system."[25] His brief also noted that the People's Constitution of 1841 provided for a clear separation of powers; its Article III would have separated the legislative, judicial, and executive branches, and it would have banned dual office-holding. Conley argued that if forces loyal to Thomas Wilson Dorr had won, their strong separation of powers clause would have shaped the state's Constitution during the intervening century and a half.

But, in fact, Dorr's forces were routed, and a convention of victorious Whigs, "who, like their namesakes in England, exalted the legislature and feared the executive," drafted what became Rhode Island's "Law and Order Constitution." That document, approved by voters in 1843, gave Rhode Island governors "no veto, no appointive power, and no budgetary power. By contrast, it granted the General Assembly broad and virtually limitless power.[26] Conley traced the General Assembly's continuing dominance through the nineteenth century to its climax under Charles "Boss" Brayton.

Although we at Common Cause understood that history as an unfolding demonstration of legislative abuses, Conley interpreted it as constitutionally valid practice. Where Karen Pelczarski wrote that the Brayton Act of 1901 had usurped the governor's appointive power, Conley averred that governors had few powers except by the legislature's leave.[27]

Ironically, Conley had written the authoritative history of Rhode Island between the American Revolution and the Dorr Rebellion, years when the Royal Charter of 1663 was its *de facto* constitution. In 1977 he had published *Democracy in Decline: Rhode Island's Constitutional Development, 1776–1841*, in which he declared: "Most of the constitutional crises which convulsed Rhode Island during the century and a quarter following adoption of the 1843 Constitution would have been avoided had the People's Constitution prevailed."[28]

But now his brief for the General Assembly downplayed any connection between ethics reform and separation of powers, stating that "the structure of government is morally neutral" and attacking our separation of powers campaign as "moralism run rampant." The lawyer-historian closed his brief with a declaration that the "strict separationists" would need to make their case, not through an Ethics Commission rule, but through a constitutional convention and an amendment that could be approved or rejected by state voters.[29]

In November 1998, Lincoln Almond again defeated Democrat Myrth York to secure his second four-year term. Both Almond and York were strong advocates for separation of powers. After the botched prosecution of Ed DiPrete, Jeffrey Pine had not run for another term. U.S. Attorney Sheldon Whitehouse and General Treasurer Nancy J. Mayer had battled to replaced Pine. It made no financial sense for Whitehouse to move from being the top federal prosecutor to chief state prosecutor, a post with less power and far lower pay. But Whitehouse won, and his decision proved politically wise: victory carried him over the crucial divide from appointive positions to statewide elective office.[30]

As attorney general-elect, Whitehouse announced that his first act in the office would be to withdraw the brief Pine had filed with the Supreme Court on separation of powers.

Pine's top appellate attorney, Thomas M. Dickinson, had written that while the U.S. Constitution explicitly authorized the president to appoint judges and "officers of the United States" and prohibited persons who held any federal appointed office from serving in Congress, Rhode Island's Constitution contained no such provisions. Dickinson named three recent governors — Frank Licht, Philip Noel, and J. Joseph Garrahy — who had signed legislation that established executive boards with members appointed by the General Assembly.[31]

On November 10, one week after the election, Dickinson rose before the Rhode Island Supreme Court to argue on Pine's behalf. He declared that members of Congress did, in fact, make executive appointments. With a pointed glance toward Whitehouse in the audience, he reminded the robed justices of a television commercial in which Whitehouse told viewers he had been appointed U.S. Attorney by Rhode Island's revered U.S. Senator Claiborne Pell. Even though everyone knew that Pell, as senior senator of the president's party, had only recommended Whitehouse to President Clinton, Dickinson scored his point.

Edward M. Fogarty, the bearded Senate counsel, argued that the Rhode Island Constitution allowed the General Assembly to make all of its current appointments and to enlarge its list whenever it wished. Justice Robert G. Flanders Jr. interrupted to ask if there were any limits on the General Assembly's power. And if so, what were those limits? Fogarty replied there were few: according to the Constitution, the legislature could confer upon itself authority to enforce the laws it might enact or delegate enforcement authority to others, including the governor.[32]

In that case, Flanders asked, what authority did the state's Constitution grant the governor when it used the terms "executive" or "chief executive"?

"The governor has very little executive power," Fogarty answered. Rhode Island's Constitution described the veto power and the governor's role as commander in chief of military and navy.

In his turn at the central lectern, Patrick Conley reprised state history from his brief and asked rhetorically how the Ethics Commission could presume to change "335 years of Rhode Island constitutional history?"

Next Joe Larisa cited the Rhode Island Supreme Court's 1854 rebuke to the General Assembly. The justices had called separation of powers "the great principle" of democracy for both the United States and Rhode Island.

The court had scheduled an entire morning of oral arguments. As the five justices listened and asked questions, nothing in their demeanor telegraphed their decision. Soon they would retire behind the deep green velvet curtain that separated the courtroom from their conference room. I imagined them peering over piles of briefs, sorting through the thrust and parry of arguments. I hoped they had not already decided. The proscenium above their polished mahogany bench featured vines carved in dark wood with a gold-lettered Latin inscription: NON SUB HOMINE SED SUB DEO ET LEGE. It meant: "Not under man but under God and Law." Would at least three of these five subscribe to a higher authority than the Whigs' military victory of 1842? Would they recognize any check on the General Assembly's power, or would Rhode Island's government and people be forever subject to legislative extortion?

One day after his inauguration as attorney general, Sheldon Whitehouse filed a legal memo with the Supreme Court on separation of powers, which stated that his office "now withdraws and disavows the arguments and conclusions" his predecessor had made.[33] Whitehouse argued that four articles of the state's Constitution made reference to separation of powers, while only one suggested that the legislature could exercise any powers not explicitly prohibited. He wrote that "generations of Americans who lived in slavery, or under Jim Crow laws, for instance, knew the promise in the American Constitution of equal protection of the laws as a promise unfulfilled. In short, prior political practice is a particularly poor principle in constitutional argument." Furthermore, political power yielded "only reluctantly" to change: "The very reason we have a constitution is to restrain the exercise of political power and to prevent the exercise of absolute power by any agency of government."

Pine blasted Whitehouse for coming in "at the eleventh hour and fifty-ninth minute" to argue that the brief of the previous attorney general should be ignored.

Larisa told reporters that Almond was pleased with the new bipartisan consensus: "We now have the chief legal officer of the state agreeing with both the governor and Common Cause and the other good-government groups that separation of powers properly prohibits legislators from serving on executive boards and commissions of the state."

I hoped our 1994 constitutional amendment that had ended the Grand Committee's power to pick Supreme Court justices would embolden the current justices to support separation of powers. Few justices or lawmakers had forgotten the General Assembly had sacked the entire high court on January 1, 1935, in a political coup that ended nine decades of increasingly corrupt Republican rule. Their chief strategist was a Harvard-trained lawyer and reformer named Theodore Francis Green.

In 1932, Green ran for governor and campaigned to put his longtime friend, Franklin Delano Roosevelt, in the White House. Both Democrats won. As the Depression deepened, Roosevelt steered recovery funds to Rhode Island, but Republicans controlled the General Assembly and tried to block New Deal projects. Republicans used the Brayton Law of 1901 to obstruct Green and Roosevelt. But their tactics backfired. In 1934, Green won re-election, and Democrats achieved a virtual tie in the all-important state Senate.[34]

On New Year's Day 1935, Lt. Gov. Robert E. Quinn — Green's fiercely partisan ally — presided at the Senate's long mahogany rostrum. Vote counts remained in dispute for South Kingstown and Portsmouth. "Fighting Bob" Quinn refused to let senators from those towns take the oath of office. Both were Republicans, and Quinn's move left the Senate with twenty Republicans, twenty Democrats, and himself as lieutenant governor able to break any tie. Senate Democrats quickly certified both contested seats to the Democrats.

Republicans shouted in protest and tried to bolt from the chamber only to find police and sheriffs blocking all three exits. With no means of escape, they had no way of denying the quorum Democrats needed to complete Green's carefully executed State House coup.[35]

Victorious Democrats faced one final obstacle. Since the 1850s, most of the justices of the state Supreme Court had been Republicans, and the court would surely invalidate the Democrats' coup. Green's forces convened the Grand Committee and swiftly fired all five high court justices, a move that was legal under the "broad powers clause" in the 1843 Constitution — the General Assembly could exercise any powers it had under the Royal Charter of 1663 unless explicitly prohibited. Replacing these justices was dramatic but did not differ functionally from the General Assembly's annual election of Supreme Court justices during the colonial era.

Green and Quinn had picked five respected jurists — two were native Yankees, two were Irish, and one was Italian. The Grand Committee "elected" these five, a move that left the Republicans seething but without legal recourse. The new Supreme Court had three Democrats and two Republicans, a ratio that would endure for generations.

Gov. Green went on the radio to explain what his forces had done, citing the ideals of Roger Williams and the courage of Thomas Wilson Dorr. He told listeners that Democrats would establish majority rule.[36]

Nine decades after a coalition of urban Whigs and rural Democrats formed the Law and Order Party to crush the Dorr Rebellion, Dorr's political heirs had toppled Rhode Island's Republican power structure. Historians quickly called this "the Bloodless Revolution."

Democrats in the legislature quickly merged eighty commissions and boards into eleven modern executive departments under Green's control. They also repealed the Brayton Act, which had allowed the Senate to ignore gubernatorial appointments in favor of appointing its own.

But the 1950s brought a relapse, as the General Assembly reverted to the old practice of creating boards with legislative members or surrogates. Democrats seemed to have no qualms about doing what Brayton had done in 1901 — using executive appointments to hold power.

At the start of 1999, the question remained: how would the justices rule now that the General Assembly could no longer sack them?

34

Quintessential
1999

No ONE KNEW how long it might take for the high court to rule. After oral arguments on November 10, I mounted a chart on the wall by my desk. On Day 57 Whitehouse withdrew and disavowed Pine's brief. Week after week, I marked off one day at a time on my wall chart. Ash Wednesday fell on Day 99. At the State House, scores of lawmakers and lobbyists wore black smudges on their foreheads as a symbol of spiritual mortification. On March 17, the Irish and Italians feted their patrons — shamrocks and green carnations for St. Patrick, zeppole with powdered sugar and Maraschino cherries for St. Joseph. It was Day 127.

Yellow daffodils and forsythia dappled April days, and May brought a pale dusting of pollen. My chart needed more pages and ran down the wall. Day 200 was Memorial Day. Why was the Supreme Court taking so long?

Bob Kilmarx told us at a separation of powers task force meeting that he saw two possible reasons for the delay. Either the justices were still struggling to refine the language of an opinion they hoped would stand the test of time, or they were deeply divided and trying to address a dissenting opinion.

Nancy Rhodes, now president of Common Cause Rhode Island, asked what would happen if the court failed to announce an opinion by July 1, 1999, the date on which the Ethics Commission's ban would take effect.

Kilmarx said it would mean that a whole raft of state boards would lose their ability to obtain a quorum. No one could be sure how contracts signed after July 1 would be affected. Roger Williams University law professor Carl Bogus wondered aloud how rational judges could even think about an American state without separation of powers. "If these justices declare themselves against our nation's core principle," Bogus said flatly, "they would become a laughingstock among their colleagues in other states."

On June 9, Day 211, Superior Court Judge Michael A. Silverstein issued an injunction that boded well for separation of powers. A bare majority of the Lottery Commission had voted to install 850 new video slot machines at Lincoln Greyhound Park and Newport Jai Alai. Five legislators appointed by the speaker and Senate majority leader had backed the new machines, while three public members appointed by the governor and one Republican senator voted against their installation. Almond's court challenge to the video slots vote melded two causes he cherished: his desire to force a Supreme Court ruling — rather than an advisory opinion — on separation of powers and his abhorrence of video slots, which he called "the crack cocaine of gambling."

On the pro-slots side, attorney Daniel V. McKinnon also approached the dispute with a double motive. McKinnon served as counsel for Lincoln Park and was both cousin and law partner of John Harwood. McKinnon had told reporters he respected the governor, but thought Almond's lottery challenge might be more "imaginary than substantive." Robert M. Silva, a prominent Middletown attorney who represented the Lottery Commission, had insisted that the quasi-public gambling authority was merely operating as required under Rhode Island law. Finally, Patrick Conley testified as an expert witness that the General Assembly had exercised absolute control over state lotteries "from their inception in 1744 for financing public improvement projects" until a ban in the Constitution of 1843.[1]

Almond's counsel, Joe Larisa, had argued two constitutional doctrines: bicameralism and presentment. Under the constitutional requirement of bicameralism, Larisa said, all bills must travel through both chambers and receive up-or-down votes by all elected legislators, not a select few. Presentment was the constitutional requirement that legislation be presented to the governor for signature or veto. Larisa argued that the expansion of video slots defied both requirements.

On June 9, Silverstein issued a preliminary injunction against additional machines, stating that the General Assembly's legal requirement that two-thirds of the Lottery Commission members be legislators infringed on the governor's constitutional obligations. Silverstein also affirmed that the General Assembly could not delegate its responsibility for regulating games of chance to a handful of its members.

Larisa applauded Silverstein and told reporter M. Charles Bakst that he could not imagine a better test case than the Lottery Commission, where sitting legislators dominated the commission against the wishes of the governor's few appointees.[2] Lawyers for the Lottery Commission and the state's two gambling venues appealed to the Rhode Island Supreme Court.

As the 1999 legislative session spun into its final weeks, I sensed a buzz in the House lounge. Between portraits of former speakers on the deep red walls, I found historian Patrick Conley autographing copies of a book for legislators and lobbyists. Entitled *Neither Separate nor Equal: Legislature and Executive in Rhode Island Constitutional History,* it was a bound version of the history Conley had filed as a brief with the Supreme Court.

"Take one," Conley urged me. "No hard feelings. I'll even autograph it if you like." He did, and I slipped it into my briefcase. Later, in a gallery above the House floor, I perused it. Conley noted in the acknowledgments that House Speaker John Harwood had contributed "both moral and monetary" support toward publication. Hundreds of copies in the House lounge had all been free — their cost covered through a legislative grant paid for by Rhode Island taxpayers.[3]

Conley's dedication page assigned Harwood a heady place in history: "To Roger Williams, Dr. John Clarke, Stephen Hopkins, Thomas Wilson Dorr, Samuel Ames, William E. Powers, and John B. Harwood — none of whom saw a conflict between their simultaneous roles as legislators and commissioners."

Perhaps the others saw no conflict, but I believed Thomas Wilson Dorr had recognized and tried to address the problem. Otherwise the People's Constitution would not have included a strong separation of powers clause and a ban on dual office holding. What if that ban had made it into the Constitution of 1843? Would the people have been spared a century and a half of secrets and scandals involving lawmakers who presumed to execute the very laws they had written? How would Rhode Island's history have changed if the victors had accepted Dorr's ban on dual office holding?

On the morning of June 29, Day 231 since the oral arguments on separation of powers, Tom Mooney called from the *Providence Journal* to tell me the Supreme Court clerk was handing out copies of the advisory opinion. I rushed to the courthouse and found a scrum of reporters and lawyers. The document looked impossibly thick, over a hundred pages, and I settled into a secluded nook to devour it. Four signatures stacked up on page 33: Joseph R. Weisberger, Victoria Lederberg, John P. Bourcier, and Maureen McKenna Goldberg. Robert G. Flanders had signed a dissent on page 101.

The first four justices began by analyzing the extraordinary power that voters had granted the Ethics Commission in 1986.[4] They acknowledged that a unanimous court had confirmed it in 1992, but added that the commission's authority "does not include unbounded power, without limitation." The majority opined that government agencies deserve close scrutiny when interpreting their own authority because they "are likely to have an expansive view of their mission." The Royal Charter of 1663 delegated "virtually unlimited power to govern" upon the General Assembly. That authority allowed the legislature "to appoint persons, including from its own membership" to various administrative bodies.[5] The Constitution of 1843 contained a broad powers clause that allowed the legislature "to continue to exercise the powers it has heretofore exercised, unless prohibited in this Constitution."[6] In 1986, the justices noted, Rhode Island voters reaffirmed the broad powers clause as part of the revised Constitution.

The four added that drafters of the state's first Constitution intentionally rejected a ban on dual office holding. "Moreover," they added, "legislative appointment of executive-type boards has been a long-standing practice in this state even under the first Constitution as early as 1844." They rolled on with a sentence that took my breath away: "Thus, Rhode Island's history is that of a quintessential system of parliamentary supremacy."[7]

I read that sentence several times. Their astonishing phrase had rhythm that demanded repetition: "a quintessential system of parliamentary supremacy."

For Supreme Court justices to advance such a phrase was mind-boggling. The four argued in favor of parliamentary systems like those "in Europe and in over fifty countries throughout the world." They insisted that parliamentary systems were "completely different from the structure adopted by the framers of our federal Constitution," but that parliamentary systems were not "structurally unethical. The question of the structure of the government is not an ethical question, but a constitutional one."

Their tone struck me as defensive and bizarre. The majority opinion insinuated that the Ethics Commission's rule prejudged lawmakers as guilty; they flatly rejected the Ethics Commission's conclusion that "legislative appointments to executive agencies create an inherent conflict of interest." In their opinion, "any system may be operated in an unethical manner, depending upon the officials who may from time to time be placed in charge of the government."[8]

The four justices concluded that the 1986 Constitution never intended to allow the Ethics Commission to change centuries of tradition, nor had the voters empowered it to prohibit legislators and legislative appointees from serving on boards that executed state laws.

In answer to Almond's first question about whether the Ethics Commission had authority to address separation of powers, the four declared an emphatic "No." Then they declined abruptly — they claimed "respectfully" — to answer his second and third questions about separation of powers in Rhode Island.

The result of their opinion practically leapt off the page: "We suggest that the sole and proper procedure for restricting legislators from serving on or appointing 'any other person' to executive boards and commissions is through an amendment to the Constitution approved by the electorate, not by an ethics regulation."[9]

Surely these justices understood the virtual impossibility of getting a separation of powers amendment through the General Assembly. They also knew that the next conceivable date for a constitutional convention lay seven years in the future. They offered no hint that separation of powers might be a worthy goal for Rhode Island.

Throughout the majority opinion, references to "our colleague" burned on page after page — virtual scorch marks of their verbal struggles with Associate Justice Robert Flanders, whom the majority never honored as our "esteemed" or "learned colleague," referring to him only as "our colleague." And there lay the reason behind the delay, as the four justices struggled to win Flanders over to their position. For months, they had tried to blunt his argument.[10]

On the page after their signatures, Flanders launched a 53-page dissent.[11] He leaned on the high court's 1993 advisory opinion supporting the Ethics Commission's 1991 Revolving Door rule.[12] That decision, he reminded the four, "flatly barred any member of the General Assembly from seeking or accepting state employment" while in the legislature and for one year after leaving. That unanimous opinion had affirmed that "a ban on multiple-government-position holding by legislators and other public officials was 'an effective device by which the public trust may be enhanced.'" The core of that opinion recognized the inevitable link between revolving door jobs and conflicts of interest. "Obviously," Flanders continued, "this same prophylactic reasoning that the justices wholeheartedly embraced in 1993 to uphold the revolving-door ban applies with equal force to the commission's ban on legislators participating in appointments to executive entities." He challenged his colleagues to uphold the commission's ban on "plural-government-office holding by legislators and their designees."[13]

He also reminded the majority that a previous decision had prohibited municipal employees from holding elective office in the towns where they were employed, precisely because "a public employee's right to hold such an elective office 'is outweighed by the government's interest in preventing a potential conflict of interest.'"[14] The 1986 Ethics Amendment, Flanders wrote, demanded that public officials and employees "adhere to the highest standards of ethical conduct" and "avoid the appearance of impropriety." This constitutional mandate justified the Ethics Commission's conclusion that it must bar lawmakers from conduct "that might subject them to conflicts of interest or expose them to potentially conflicting demands on their time, their loyalties, or their responsibilities as legislators."[15]

I marked margins and turned pages, amazed that the majority had rejected Flanders's logic. Their effort to separate ethical behavior from government structure felt trifling beside his analysis. He noted that what were called the "ineligibility and incompatibility clauses" of the U.S. Constitution had been dubbed "America's constitutional ethics rule."[16] Its precise language barred members of Congress from appointment to federal positions and prohibited federal office-holders from simultaneously serving in Congress. Flanders also reviewed the interplay of separation of powers and bans on dual office holding in forty state constitutions. Such bans were "the paradigmatic type of ethical restraint," which framers of constitutions used to establish "what conduct is and is not ethically permissible for public officials."[17]

ESTABLISHING ETHICS

The Rhode Island Conflict of Interest Commission was created in 1976 with broad authority to prosecute conflicts of interest involving state and local officials. The 1986 Constitutional Convention saw it as a model for a new Ethics Commission with constitutional authority to "adopt a code of ethics." Members in 1984 (seated, left-right) Robert. C. Newbold, Miriam R. Plitt, Juanita M. Handy, Edward L. Casey, Angelo R. Iannitelli Jr.; (standing, left-right) Michael A. Morry, Marie M. D'Amico, William F. Shields, Peter J. Davis, Rae B. Condon, Executive Director. (*Photo courtesy of Rae Condon*)

The Rhode Island Ethics Commission was created in 1987 as the strongest such body in the United States, but it struggled against legislative resistance and bureaucratic siege. Insider appointments led to a 2001 meltdown and required years to rebuild. Members in 2005 (left-right) James V. Murray, Ross E. Cheit, Barbara K. Binder, Patricia M. Moran, James Lynch Sr., chairperson, Kathleen Managhan, counsel, Richard E. Kirby, Frederick K. Butler, James C. Segovis, George E. Weavill Jr.

Photos not otherwise credited are by H. Philip West Jr.

COMBATTING CORRUPTION

Sen. Sean Coffey (left) and Rep. Ray Rickman (right), who worked for open government, met with Common Cause Rhode Island founder Natalie C. Joslin and President Cathleen S. Speer. Ethics, campaign finance, and open government reforms developed by Common Cause were buried, year after year, in the House and Senate Judiciary Committees.

On Dec. 27, 1988, Common Cause board members signed an ethics complaint against Gov. Edward D. DiPrete for steering state contracts to cronies and large campaign contributors. On Dec. 20, 1991, the Ethics Commission ruled that DiPrete had violated the law and levied a record fine of $30,000. Part of that fine was overturned in 1994 by the Rhode Island Supreme Court on grounds that there was no explicit understanding between the governor and donor.

Only weeks later, Gov. DiPrete and his son Dennis were indicted on charges that they had extorted $294,000 in bribes and kick-backs and had committed perjury before the Ethics Commission.

On Dec. 11, 1998, after a botched prosecution, the former governor pled guilty to eighteen felony charges, was sentenced to a year in prison, and lost his state pension. Dennis DiPrete confessed to a single misdemeanor charge. (*Associated Press photo by Matt York*)

ADDRESSING THE RISDIC SCANDAL

Newly inaugurated Gov. Bruce G. Sundlun announced on Jan. 1, 1991, that he was closing credit unions and banks insured by the Rhode Island Share and Deposit Indemnity Corporation (RISDIC).

House Judiciary Chair Jeffrey J. Teitz (right) led the RISDIC Investigating Commission that showed how systemic conflicts and a failure of oversight contributed to the collapse. In 1986, he had led the impeachment investigation of Chief Justice Joseph A. Bevilacqua's continuing Mob connections. Teitz drafted the Comprehensive Campaign Finance Law of 1992.

Sundlun's executive counsel, Sheldon Whitehouse (above left) managed the governor's efforts to repay depositors and reopen financial institutions. In 1992, Whitehouse raised the issue of separation of powers with Common Cause when he said: "You'll never cut the deep root of Rhode Island's corruption until you get to separation of powers." (*Providence Journal photos by Andy Dickerman*)

WIELDING POWER

House leaders (left-right) Thomas Lamb, Christopher Boyle, and Speaker Joseph DeAngelis, with Senate Majority Leader John Bevilacqua, approve as Gov. Bruce Sundlun signs the budget near the end of the 1991 legislative session, which had been dominated by the RISDIC collapse. No significant ethics reforms were enacted in 1991. (*Providence Journal photo by Ruben W. Perez*)

On Jan. 31, 2003, House Speaker William J. Murphy and Senate President William V. Irons answered reporters' questions. Murphy had just gained control of the powerful Joint Committee on Legislative Services (JCLS), which administers business of the entire legislative branch. With a 3–2 majority on the JCLS, the speaker had always been the most powerful official in the dominant branch of government. Before Murphy and Irons, the JCLS usually met in secret.

REINFORCING PARLIAMENTARY SUPREMACY

For seven years House Speaker John B. Harwood resisted separation of powers. On his watch the General Assembly multiplied executive boards and appointed its members to serve on them. Meanwhile, his wife won a lifetime appointment as magistrate, and he represented private law clients before state agencies. Scandal toppled him in 2002.
(*Providence Journal photo by Connie Grosch*)

In June 1999 four justices of the Rhode Island Supreme Court rejected separation of powers. Chief Justice Joseph R. Weisberger (seated), Justices Victoria S. Lederberg, John P. Bourcier, and Maureen McKenna Goldberg declared that Rhode Island's government was a "quintessential system of parliamentary supremacy."

Justice Robert G. Flanders Jr. (left) dissented: "In the end, the people of Rhode Island ultimately will decide how best to divide the power pot that lies at the center of our state government."
(*Supreme Court photo*)

DEMANDING SEPARATION OF POWERS

Lincoln Almond, Rhode Island's first governor with a four-year term, challenged the General Assembly over the separation of powers. In 1995, he vetoed the appointment of legislators to the Rabies Control Board; in 1997, he backed the Ethics Commission's rule against legislators on boards that executed state laws; in 1998, he vetoed legislation that would have created a Cancer Council; in 1999, he challenged the constitutionality of the Lottery Commission; in 2000 and 2002, he put advisory questions on the statewide ballot.

Almond also packed the Ethics Commission with politically connected lawyers who overturned the 1998 gift rule and nearly destroyed the panel.

In the wake of the Supreme Court's 1999 "quintessential parliamentary supremacy" ruling, reform groups welcomed Almond's 2000 Question 6, which asked if voters wished to convene a constitutional convention to consider separation of powers. Without much money, the campaign depended on lawn signs and flyers. Ready to make the case were (left-right) Alan Flink, Nancy Rhodes, Donna Cameron Gricus, Paul Boghossian, Sid Green, and Greta Abbott.

Two-thirds of state voters said yes on Question 6. In 2002, Almond posted Question 5, a second advisory referendum on separation of powers, and 76.2 per cent demanded the change.

TRYING TO BLOCK REFORM

On the last night of the 2001 session, after his separation of powers resolution was buried in the House Judiciary Committee, Rep. Nicholas Gorham (left) used a procedural rule to force the first House vote on the issue. Speaker John Harwood (right) and House Judiciary Chair Robert Flaherty met Minority Leader Robert Watson (jacket). A 57–25 vote recommitted Gorham's bill to Flaherty's committee, a crucial vote against the first principle of American government.

A year later, Rep. Betsy Dennigan declared that the speaker had withheld a legislative grant for handicapped residents of her district because she had supported separation of powers and ethics reforms. Behind her (dark suit) Rep. Tony Pires, a long time Harwood ally, deplored the practice of steering public funds to punish reformers.

TURNING THE TIDE

In June 2002, members of the Separation of Powers Task force celebrate two overwhelming Senate votes to put separation of powers on the ballot. Seated are former chairperson Bob Kilmarx and board president Nancy Rhodes. Standing (left-right) Jim Davey, Bob Cox, Don Koehn, Peter Hufstader, Burt Hoffman, Carl Bogus (chairperson), Bill Aldrich, Greta Abbott, Topher Hamblett, Bob Sumner-Mack. Only weeks before scandal would topple Speaker John Harwood, the Senate, governor, reform community, and most citizens of Rhode Island were united in demanding constitutional separation of powers.

During final negotiations on the separation of powers, Robert Arruda, chair of Operation Clean Government, argued against allowing House leaders to weaken the text that the coalition had been promoting throughout the spring of 2003.

Lawmakers finally approved on June 30, 2003, with only one word change, the bipartisan Gorham-Lenihan language filed in January. Instead of "separate and co-equal," the three branches of government would be "separate and distinct," an older word used in many state constitutions. The amendment would also (1) end legislative appointments to boards that execute state laws, (2) empower the governor to appoint state administrators, commissioners, and regulators, (3) bar officials from holding office in two branches of government, and (4) delete the "broad powers clause" that had allowed the General Assembly to exercise any powers not explicitly prohibited in the Rhode Island Constitution.

FIGHTING GERRYMANDERS

In the redistricting of 2002, Senators Charles D. Walton and Mary A. Parella became targets but fought to fix their gerrymandered districts. Each offered amendments that would restore their communities. Although both lost on the Senate floor and in the fall election, they forced a series of votes that laid the groundwork for federal and state lawsuits involving Providence and East Bay districts.

With the support of national civil rights organizations African-American and Latino plaintiffs filed federal lawsuits. Nellie Gorbea, chair of the Rhode Island Latino Political Action Committee, charged that the Senate plan violated the rights of Latinos. With Gorbea at the press conference were (left-right) Sylvia Bernal, Edwin Cancel, Anthony Affigne, Pablo Rodriguez, and Tomás Ávila.

CREATING ROOM FOR A SETTLEMENT

Sen. William V. Irons often proclaimed himself a reformer and charged that other senators were corrupt. After orchestrating a factional coup that made him majority leader, Irons used the redistricting process to give former Majority Leader Paul S. Kelly and senators who had stood with him districts they could never win. Kelly supporter Sen. Charles Walton had to run against Juan M. Pichardo in a blatantly gerrymandered district on the South Side of Providence.

In 2003, while federal lawsuits moved toward trial, Irons and his ally, Sen. John A. Celona, became embroiled in scandals for failing to disclose funds they had received from CVS and Blue Cross/Blue Shield while they killed pharmacy freedom-of-choice bills that the companies opposed.

Under the shadow of scandal, Irons and Celona resigned from the Senate, and the new Senate President Joseph A. Montalbano began negotiations with African-American and Latino plaintiffs in the lawsuit. The districts that Irons and Celona vacated were in East Providence and North Providence, which allowed surrounding districts to slip and slide into a configuration similar to one proposed two years earlier by the Fair Redistricting Coalition.

On May 21, 2004, Senate leaders announced the settlements and unveiled the new districts. Tomás Ávila and Gertrude F. Blakey, both members of the Common Cause state board, point to the districts that elected Senators Juan M. Pichardo and Harold M. Metts the following November.

CAMPAIGNING FOR SEPARATION OF POWERS

Sheldon Whitehouse addresses a kick-off rally for the 2004 Question 1, the Separation of Powers Amendment. Recognizable in the crowd (from left) are Speaker William Murphy, Majority Leader Gordon Fox, Separation of Powers Committee Chair Elaine Coderre, Lt. Gov. Elizabeth Roberts, Gov. Don Carcieri; (front row) Reps. Mary Cerra, Eileen Naughton, Sen. Michael Lenihan, Rep. Carol Mumford; Common Cause President Jim Miller (dark jacket), and AAUW President Judy Terry (lower right). The amendment won overwhelming (78.3 percent) approval on Nov. 2, 2004. (*Photo by Jake Paris*)

Sen. J. Michael Lenihan (right) and Phil West (left) spoke outside the State House. During two decades at the State House, Sen. Lenihan established a unique legacy. Among reforms he led in enacting were: State Vendor Disclosure (1992), Online Legislative Information (1994), Public Corporation Financial Accountability (1995), Open Meetings and Open Records

amendments (1998), Lobbyist Disclosure, often called "the Celona Law" (2004), the Public Accountability and Reform Act (2006), and amendments to the Access to Public Records Law (2008). Over several years, he pushed the Senate to adopt separation of powers, and he played a key role in passage of the bipartisan Separation of Powers Amendment (2003). After passage, he led the Senate effort to reconstruct boards and commissions to comply with the amendment (2005–06). If Senate leaders had adopted his Fair Redistricting legislation (2001), the state might have been spared years of litigation and millions of dollars in legal fees. (*Photo by Diana M. Kelly*)

RECONSTRUCTING BOARDS AND COMMISSIONS

House Separation of Powers Committee Chairperson Elaine Coderre (above center) and Vice Chairperson Paul Crowley (left) with their attorney, Michael Egan, negotiated with Gov. Carcieri's executive counsel, Andrew Hodgkin (center right), over countless details in scores of bills needed to abolish boards or change their composition to comply with the 2004 Separation of Powers Amendment. After a rocky start and several gubernatorial vetoes, the working relationship became pragmatic, even cordial.

Lobbyist Robert Goldberg (right) testified at a Senate hearing in March 2006 that the General Assembly could still appoint members of the Coastal Resources Management Council. A former senator and husband of Supreme Court Justice Maureen McKenna Goldberg, he led the legal battle that ousted a special prosecutor who was investigating his brother and law partner, Ethics Commissioner Thomas Goldberg.

RESTORING THE VOTE

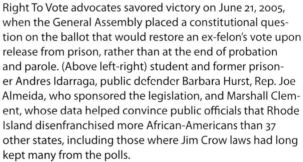

Right To Vote advocates savored victory on June 21, 2005, when the General Assembly placed a constitutional question on the ballot that would restore an ex-felon's vote upon release from prison, rather than at the end of probation and parole. (Above left-right) student and former prisoner Andres Idarraga, public defender Barbara Hurst, Rep. Joe Almeida, who sponsored the legislation, and Marshall Clement, whose data helped convince public officials that Rhode Island disenfranchised more African-Americans than 37 other states, including those where Jim Crow laws had long kept many from the polls.

Sol Rodriguez (inset above) led a program now called Open Doors that helps former prisoners reintegrate into their communities. She envisioned a broad coalition of religious, civil rights, and good government groups that could help change the state constitution.

Koren Carbuccia appealed to a wide audience by sharing her incarceration and her longing to vote in school board elections that would affect her son's education. The day after she spoke at a State House rally, the *Providence Journal* and the *Pawtucket Times* began their front-page stories with her name.

Many groups from the State Department's International Visitors Leadership Program came to study ethics, open government, and separation of powers in Rhode Island. (from left) Phil West; Nuru Seid, Federal Judge from Ethiopia; Neneh Dabo, Director of the Anti-Corruption Commission, Sierra Leone; Kamoleh S. Kamoleh, Member of Parliament, Kenya; Jacqueline Costa-Horsey, State Dept.; Kibru Woubshet, Federal High Court, Kenya: Musikari Kombo, Member of Parliament, Kenya; Lydia Effimba, Chair, Liberal Democrat Alliance, Cameroon. (*Photo by Gilbert Raiford*)

PURSUING REFORM

In 2005, Alan Hassenfeld, Natalie Joslin, and Henry Sharpe Jr. were honored by Common Cause as John Gardner Fellows for their enduring commitment to reform. Hassenfeld led the Right Now! Coalition from 1991–1994 during the successful campaign for ethics, campaign finance reform, four-year terms for General Officers, merit selection of all Rhode Island judges, and modernizing the legislature. He also led in the final push for separation of powers. Natalie Joslin was a founder of Common Cause Rhode Island in 1970 and returned in 1990 to build membership and financial support. She founded the Advisory Council and served as president from 1995–98. Henry Sharpe served on the advisory council, led fund-raising campaigns, and worked diligently to enact separation of powers. All three contributed toward the publication of this book.

◄ facing page

Troubled by the influence of special interest money in American elections, several generations of students in the Brown University chapter of Democracy Matters worked diligently to win passage of Clean Elections legislation to provide public financing for campaigns. In 2006, these students testified before committees and lobbied legislators about the need to provide alternate funding for candidates of modest means: (front left-right) Elizabeth Kimzey, Christina Ma; (standing left-right) Dorothy Tegeler, Benjamin Logan, Aden Van Noppen, Phoebe Sloane, John Rozehnal, Jonathan Bogard, Sebastian Benthall, Josh Drago, Kristin Jordan.

BREAKING STORIES

Reporters spend countless hours listening to witnesses and sorting documents before they write stories. At a budget hearing in 2006, (seated, left-right) were Scott Mayerowitz (*Providence Journal*), Martha Bebinger (RI Public Radio), Jim Baron (*Pawtucket Times*), and Linda Pratt DiCecco (Associated Press).

Providence Journal State House Bureau Chief Katherine Gregg (right) pressed House Fiscal Advisor Michael O'Keefe for details. Gregg often unearthed insider pension deals and hidden conflicts of interest. In the fall of 2003, she revealed secret payments from CVS and Blue Cross/Blue Shield to Senators John Celona and William Irons. She also exposed conflicts that forced then-House Majority Leader that led then-House Majority Leader Gordon Fox (right) to settle an ethics complaint by paying a $10,000 fine and leaving the law firm where he had worked. As Fox (right) left the hearing, reporters Jack White (WPRI/12) (left), and Dan Yorke (WPRO-AM) (second from left) questioned him, while his lawyer, Lawrence O'Brien listened. Fox became speaker of the House in 2010 but was forced to resign amid scandal in March 2014.

In response to Almond's separation of powers questions, Flanders observed that the Rhode Island Constitution vested the "chief executive power" in the governor and required him or her to take care "that the laws be faithfully executed."[18] If the governor's duty to execute laws faithfully had any meaning, Flanders declared, it "must be deemed to include, at a minimum, the right to superintend how the laws of this state will be executed." With the chief executive power, he wrote, came the related duty to appoint executive officers. Without that power, Flanders argued, the governor would be "the functional equivalent of a show captain, propped up on the ship of state's main deck in full-dress regalia for all the passengers to ogle, while the real legislative bosses steered the ship, barked orders, hired, fired, and supervised the crew and all those who toiled away in the boiler rooms below."[19]

Flanders reminded the other justices that delegates at the 1986 Constitutional Convention had considered and rejected a proposal to place the legislature's power of appointment in the text of the Constitution. He urged them to draw a lesson: "The mere repetition of a constitutional wrong — no matter how frequent — cannot ripen into a lawful constitutional amendment." He concluded with this question: "Shall the powers of our state government be checked and balanced? Or shall they be unchecked and imbalanced?" He expressed the hope that these advisory opinions would be only "the opening salvos in the greater and the potentially more dispositive crossfire that will now ensue. Let the people be heard. *Vox populi, vox Dei* (The voice of the people is the voice of God.)"[20]

Flanders's signature stood alone on the final page. He had been outnumbered but not overwhelmed. Whatever politicians might make of the stark contrast between these two opinions, Flanders had established the legitimacy of our case.

The next day a three-column *Providence Journal* headline declared, "Top court keeps power with Assembly — for now." The legislature claimed victory. Under the photo of a smiling John Harwood stood a bold quote: "It's clear to me that legislators can clearly sit on boards and commissions." Paul Kelly looked pensive, but affirmed, "We feel the issue has been clearly put to bed." A photo showed Almond reading the thick opinion. "They punted on the two big questions," the governor declared. Reporter Tom Mooney also interpreted the majority's advisory to mean this might not be the final word on "the tug-of-war between the executive and legislative branches."

Sheldon Whitehouse, now Rhode Island's top law enforcement officer, voiced his disappointment. "Regrettably," he told reporters, "today's decision again postpones the day when Rhode Island will finally enjoy a government that adheres to all the basic principles of American democracy." In his article Tom Mooney gave me the last word. The Lottery Commission case, I told him, would soon land on the Supreme Court's docket and was "the kind of case where there is a clear abuse of power, where there is no other commission like this in the whole United States, and where the absurdity of the Rhode Island practice is obvious for all to see."[21]

The winners moved quickly to exploit their triumph. The day after the Supreme Court's advisory, lawyers for the Lottery Commission and Lincoln Greyhound Park urged the high court to lift the injunction against the additional 850 video slot machines. Justices Weisberger and Bourcier bounced that question back to Judge Silverstein, who had imposed the earlier injunction. Two weeks later, lawyers representing the Lottery Commission, the House, the Senate, Lincoln Greyhound Park, and Newport Grand Jai Alai crowded the front bench of Silverstein's narrow courtroom. I sat directly behind Daniel McKinnon, John Harwood's cousin and law partner, who represented Lincoln Park, a seedy dog track now filling up each night with people hunched over video slot machines.

McKinnon strode forward with a posse of pro-slots lawyers. I wanted to stand up and shout that all three representatives Harwood appointed to the Lottery Commission had voted for the additional machines. Now the law firm Harwood and McKinnon would profit handsomely from this latest expansion of gambling.

"Today," declared Robert Silva, a lawyer representing the Lottery Commission, "the landscape is markedly different than it was when this court last entertained this issue. There is no question the legislature has the power to have its members sit on commissions." Silva suggested that if the judge had known a month earlier what he now knew, he would not have blocked the installation of new machines. He asked Silverstein to lift his injunction and allow the 850 new slot machines, and the judge had no choice but to comply.[22]

Carl Bogus was an intellectual sparkplug. He sent a column to the *Providence Journal* blasting the majority opinion as "one of the most radical decisions ever rendered by the highest court of an American state." He hammered the notion of a "quintessential system of parliamentary supremacy," noting that although parliamentary systems lack co-equal branches of government, they establish checks and balances through other means, including "the ability to bring an administration to an end at any time through a vote of no confidence." In parliamentary systems the prime minister serves as chief executive and appoints government ministers. In Rhode Island, by contrast, the governor is theoretically the chief executive, but the speaker controls lawmaking, budget, and administrative appointments.[23]

He wrote that the majority should have looked to the historic moment in 1841 when a decisive majority of citizens approved the People's Constitution. The Law and Order Constitution of 1843 won approval with only half as many votes. "In looking to history," he wrote, "the court should have taken into account the fact that the people of Rhode Island voted overwhelmingly for the People's

Constitution, with its unequivocal adoption of the separation-of-powers principle." With the state's "ambiguous constitution and history," he concluded, "the
Rhode Island Supreme Court could have given the people of Rhode Island the
benefit of a government of separated powers." The four justices in the majority,
he wrote, had deluded themselves, but few Rhode Islanders would join them
in this delusion.

The Common Cause Rhode Island state board met twice in July to decide
what next. "It doesn't get more basic than this," said Nancy Rhodes, our new
president. "It's time to redouble our efforts and let them know we're not the
least bit cowed."

Vice President Daniel Siegel proposed that Common Cause raise $20,000
for legal work and publications.[24] "We may not have the money now," Siegel
said, "but we can raise it. People are starting to understand that Rhode Island
is floating half way between the American and British systems of government,
and either would be better than what we've got."

The board's determination buoyed me up, but I could not imagine how to
raise that much after such a defeat. Even if the money came through, legislative
leaders would outspend us many times over. After all, over five legislative sessions our separation of powers bills had never received even a committee vote.
Five years of effort had taught me that legislative leaders would never abandon
their long tradition of running state government through executive boards.
Instead of backing off in the face of criticism, they would thrust legislators onto
more boards. They could also create new versions of the Lottery Commission
where legislators could steer state contracts and dispense legislative patronage.
And any who dared to confront their juggernaut would face retaliation.

On the cusp of a new century Rhode Island's highest court had affirmed the
legislature's colonial authority to execute laws. Four justices had tangled the
ropes on the ship of state and scuttled our quest for separation of powers.

Legislative leaders spent taxpayers' money to publish a triumphal 86-page
annotated edition of the Supreme Court's advisory opinion, featuring portraits
of the robed justices in living color.[25]

Our quest suddenly felt like a fool's errand. I shuddered to think how we
could sustain a separation of powers campaign until 2004, when voters might
decide about a constitutional convention. If we kept advocating for the principle, nothing else would pass; if we backed off, our cause would fade, and we
would have trouble reviving it.

As summer settled in, I felt myself moving in slow motion or not at all.
I lay awake through the dark of night, watching red numbers on the alarm
clock change. Defeat left me wondering if I could continue at Common Cause.
Could I ever go back to the State House? Could I face the sneering of John Harwood's cronies? Could I find another job in Rhode Island beyond the speaker's
reach?

4
Separation of Powers | 2

35

Gifts
1997–2000

THE MELTDOWN OF THE ETHICS COMMISSION may have begun at Fenway Park on Patriots' Day in 1996.[1] Terrence Murray, chairman of Fleet Bank, hosted lunch in his corporate box for Gov. Lincoln Almond, his wife, son, and three top staff members. They chatted about the ball game and plans for the bank's expansion in Rhode Island. Almond agreed that the state would buy a building for lease to Fleet; Murray promised that Fleet would hire 350 people over the next two years.

Providence Journal reporter Bob Wyss later wrote that the tickets and lunches at Fenway had been worth $74 per person. His story ran on the front page just as the Ethics Commission began mulling ways to stop public officials from taking such gratuities. Readers knew Almond had little taste for luxury, but some took offense at his hobnobbing high above the ball field. Wyss listed other gifts that Almond had accepted: an academic robe and hood, framed lithographs and paintings, a rocking chair, medals, luggage, and items of clothing. The reporter also described trade missions to Asia, Latin America, and Portugal. Marilyn Almond had traveled with her husband, her expenses covered by corporate donors who funneled their payments through the Rhode Island Economic Development Corporation.[2]

Almond insisted that trade missions were vital to the state's economy and were not intended as gifts to him. He promised to refuse any gift he felt was inappropriate, saying he would always err on the side of caution. When Wyss asked me about this, I mentioned that the Ethics Commission had warned against free travel for family members. I said I wished he had sought an advisory opinion first. The story reflected poorly on his judgment about gifts.

Nor was Almond the only recipient. The *Journal* reported that Johnston Town

Council President Joseph R. Ballirano had accepted a flight to New Orleans and a ticket to watch the New England Patriots in Super Bowl XXXI. Louis Vinagro Jr., a notorious pig farmer and trash hauler, had paid Ballirano's way while his $37,000 per month trash hauling and recycling contract was up for renewal. Ballirano claimed he had reimbursed Vinagro $1,800 in cash but quickly became the target of ethics complaints. When subpoenaed, he could not document the expenses or his repayment. In the civil equivalent of a plea bargain, Ballirano negotiated a settlement, admitted violating the law, and paid a $4,000 fine.[3]

When the Ethics Commission began public hearings on a proposed gift ban, Almond sent executive counsel Joe Larisa to testify that the rule would disrupt state business. Larisa claimed that the governor's meetings with officials of the New England Patriots over their possible move to Providence would have been hampered if they had to split the cost of sandwiches. Almond could support disclosure of food or gifts worth more than $50, but opposed a complete ban.[4]

Legislative gratuities also raised eyebrows. Reporter Christopher Rowland calculated that Speaker John Harwood and Majority Leader George Caruolo had spent $50,000 wining and dining guests in pricey Providence restaurants. Lobbyists had contributed most of the money as campaign contributions. Caruolo described his and Harwood's philosophy as, "If you can't drink the lobbyists' drinks and eat their food and then vote against them, you don't belong at the State House."[5]

Others were less credulous. Providence firefighters filed an ethics complaint against their union leader, Stephen T. Day, who had accepted lavish gifts and entertainment from two money managers while he served on the city's Retirement Board. In December 1997, the Ethics Commission found probable cause that Day had accepted gifts on at least nineteen occasions between 1991 and 1995. While the money managers plied him with $3,393 worth of cocktails, lunches, dinners, and a hotel room, he steered more than $15 million to the funds they managed. Day had not reported these gratuities on his ethics disclosure forms.

The imbroglio made headlines through the spring of 1998, just as the Ethics Commission pondered a new gift rule that would outlaw the common practice of accepting gifts from "interested persons." The commission's executive director, Martin Healey, explained that the federal government and ten other states had adopted similar rules.[6] At its first meeting in June 1998, after months of the public testimony and debate required under state law, commissioners brushed aside dire predictions and adopted a carefully crafted rule, a gift ban that many began calling "zero tolerance."[7]

The second-guessing began instantly. Lobbyists and legislators mocked the proposed rule as nitpicking. William A. Farrell, who lobbied for associations of lawyers, bankers, insurance brokers, hospitals, and trash-haulers, told reporter Scott MacKay, "You're not going to stop guys from Johnston from taking trips to the Super Bowl by passing some rules at the Ethics Commission."[8] Critics ridiculed zero tolerance for banning cups of coffee, bologna sandwiches, or sticks of gum.

Without announcing a plan, Governor Almond and General Assembly leaders began replacing members of the Ethics Commission — not suddenly, but one appointment at a time. During deliberations on the gift rule, Almond appointed Melvin L. Zurier, a Harvard-educated lawyer and respected community elder, who had largely retired from Tillinghast, Licht & Semonoff. Zurier's colleagues at the firm included former House Speaker Joseph DeAngelis, former Lt. Gov. Richard A. Licht, and top lobbyist Joseph W. Walsh. Zurier argued against the policy of zero tolerance and voted against its passage.

The gift ban took effect in July 1998. Commissioner John O'Brien, a staunch supporter, reached the end of his term in September. In his eighties, O'Brien was grouchy, diligent, and incorruptible. He had served for decades as Providence district director of the Internal Revenue Service and chaired the old Conflict of Interest Commission during the ten years Rae Condon was its executive director. "If he hadn't been at the helm," Condon told reporter Maria Miro Johnson, the commission "probably would not have survived." In 1987, when the old Conflict of Interest Commission gave way to the new Ethics Commission, O'Brien was appointed to the new panel and became vice chair. A fierce advocate for zero tolerance, O'Brien called it absurd for public officials to quibble about the size of gifts. "It makes no common sense," he growled, "when you take a public service job, that you're also entitled to take gifts."[9]

Commissioners routinely served many months beyond their terms, but Almond had O'Brien's replacement waiting in the wings even before his term expired. House Majority Leader Gerard M. Martineau had nominated James V. Murray, a staff attorney for Amica Insurance, whose two top lawyers were State House lobbyists.[10] Almond appointed Murray in record time and later sent O'Brien a two-sentence form letter thanking him and wishing him well.

During the next year, the governor and the legislature dismantled the panel of ethically alert individuals who had adopted the gift ban, including a school administrator, an urban pastor, an accountant, a financial services manager, and a criminal defense lawyer.[11] Within the next two years, politically connected lawyers were appointed to the commission: Richard E. Kirby, Thomas D. Goldberg, and Robin L. Main.[12] Zurier, Murray, Kirby, Goldberg, Main, and Newport attorney Francis J. Flanagan all later recused themselves from a complaint against Harwood.[13] While no strategy was ever announced, these appointments clearly signaled that Harwood and Almond meant to block new lobbying rules and overturn the gift ban.

In the spring of 1999, the Ethics Commission began exploring the ethics rules of other states that limited lobbyist contributions or banned campaign fundraising during the legislative session. Executive director Martin Healey asked that commissioners who were business associates of registered lobbyists disclose their relationships and recuse themselves.[14] Commissioner Thomas D. Goldberg was the law partner and brother of a former Senate minority leader and one of the state's top lobbyists, but rather than step aside, he requested an advisory opinion.

Staff attorneys recommended that Goldberg not discuss or vote on rules involving lobbyists and legislators since his relationship — both as brother and law partner of a lobbyist — could affect his judgment. The draft advisory hinged on differences between lobbyists: some were paid well by commercial clients, but many others worked at low salaries for nonprofit groups or volunteered their time. The advisory cited sections of law and twenty-two previous advisory opinions. It declared that Goldberg should not "participate in the consideration of proposed regulations affecting the relationship between lobbyists and members of the General Assembly."[15]

Goldberg disagreed and brought an attorney to represent him.[16] Kathleen Managhan argued that Commissioner Goldberg's brother and law partner would not benefit any more than the other five hundred or more State House lobbyists. She insisted that his participation was protected under the "class exception" section of the law, under which lobbyists were a "significant and definable class."

Healey disagreed, arguing that the draft advice to Thomas Goldberg matched opinions the commission had approved for other officials. He described the differences between classes of lobbyists.

Commissioner David McCahan, a retired insurance executive, argued that the Ethics Commission's credibility depended on public perception that commissioners would always "avoid the appearance of impropriety." With tears welling in his eyes, the 70-year-old McCahan reminded his fellow commissioners of their constitutional duty to rise above the bare legal minimum and exemplify the highest standard of ethics.

Richard Kirby disagreed, arguing that lobbyists were a significant and definable class. "When the law provides a class exception," he declared, "it is neither unethical nor inappropriate for Commissioner Goldberg to invoke it."

Amelia E. Edwards, the commission's new legal counsel,[17] asked a rhetorical question whose answer seemed obvious: "How can a brother represent his brother without a conflict of interest?"[18]

No one answered.

Four commissioners, none of them lawyers, approved the advisory opinion that warned Goldberg not to participate, while three voted against it. Since under the law a valid advisory opinion required five affirmative votes, this split left Thomas Goldberg without an advisory and without legal protection against any ethics complaint that might be filed against him.

Beyond the wide windows of the commission's eighth floor hearing room, clouds mushroomed into a spring squall. More ominous by far, pressure mounting within the Ethics Commission felt like the tension of tectonic plates that might produce an earthquake.

On June 1, Thomas Goldberg filed suit against the Ethics Commission on which he served.[19] His petition stated that — despite the fact that his brother and law partner was a lobbyist — he sought clearance to make rules that would affect lobbyists. Although Goldberg conceded that staff lawyers and four of his fellow commissioners thought he had a conflict of interest and must recuse himself, three members did not agree. Without five votes he lacked a legally binding advisory opinion that would protect him against a complaint. He petitioned for a judicial ruling and wanted an injunction to delay proceedings until he received the court's clearance to vote.

Tom and Bob Goldberg both sported neat mustaches. Both had broad fore-heads and were going bald. Although they were roughly the same height, I guessed that Bob outweighed Tom by eighty pounds. Bob was extroverted, Tom shy. I suspected this was not the first time Tom Goldberg had been sent to fight his big brother's battles.

I finally got to speak privately with him during a break. "Commissioner," I said quietly, "you don't need this. You can't participate. It's an obvious conflict."

"That's your opinion," he shot back. "I disagree."

That summer I assigned two college interns to comb through lobbyist reports. Far from finding a "significant and definable class," as Tom Goldberg's lawyer claimed, the data revealed real differences among the 774 registered lobbyists, depending on whether they served commercial interests, nonprofits, quasi-publics, or government agencies. Commercial lobbyists were typically well com-pensated attorneys, and only twenty-four of them reported lobbying for three or more profit-making clients, trade associations, or unions. Rhode Island's ten top-grossing lobbyists represented eighty-two clients, and their median income from lobbying in the 1999 legislative session appeared to be $125,250.

By contrast, a different class of lobbyists served as staff for nonprofit groups. Most worked for only one organization and attributed percentages of their salaries for lobbying. I reported $11,740 as lobbying income, a figure just below the median for the top ten nonprofit lobbyists.

The third group included government employees deployed by their agencies or quasi-public corporations to track and promote their legislation. Many were lawyers with other duties in their agencies. The law treated agency lobbyists differently and did not require them to report compensation.

Campaign contributions dramatically distinguished commercial lobbyists from all the rest. Our interns found only one nonprofit lobbyist who had made a campaign contribution: $200 to John Harwood in the spring of 1999. Com-mercial lobbyists received huge sums and spread their largesse, mostly at spring fundraisers where ticket prices ranged from $75 to $150. The dates rose and fell along a bell curve that peaked between March and June, precisely when most bills passed or died. My mail typically brought two or three invitations each week — fundraising requests apparently sent to all registered lobbyists. I never donated to these groups and often sent personal notes explaining that Common Cause policy prohibited me from attending.

Far from being "no different from five hundred other lobbyists who are registered to work the State House hallways," as Tom Goldberg's lawyer had claimed, commercial lobbyists were in a class by themselves, and they contributed vastly more than their nonprofit counterparts.[20] For example, at a single event — on the day before the House deadline for action on most bills — corporate and union lobbyists gave $102,550 to John Harwood.[21] They also spent lavishly on dinners, sports tickets, and gifts to lawmakers. Entertainment expenses were costs of doing business; they could be itemized on tax returns but rarely appeared on lobbyist reports. Few doubted that such gratuities greased the skids.

In September 1999, our Common Cause newsletter listed the top ten commercial lobbyists, their clients, and their total compensation. We also named the top ten nonprofit lobbyists.

Within days of our publication, Dennis J. Roberts II, a former attorney general listed among the top grossing lobbyists, left a phone message that our figures were too high. "Tell Mr. West that if he can negotiate the fees reported in your newsletter, I'll go halves with him."[22]

Sixth in our ranking of commercial lobbyists was Robert Goldberg, whose clients included companies that were fending off lawsuits over asbestos and lead paint, the gambling giant GTECH, the Smokeless Tobacco Council, and — ironically — United Healthcare. We reported his income from lobbying as $120,500. Bob Goldberg phoned. "What the fuck is this?" he demanded. "Who says I made a hundred and twenty thousand dollars from lobbying?"

"Your lobbyist reports," I said.

"You got it wrong!" he shouted.

"So what's your figure?" I asked. "How much did you really make?"

"Figure it out yourself!" He slammed down the phone.

The confrontation troubled me, and I wished I had double-checked the data before we published. The lobbyist disclosure forms I completed each month were confusing, with spaces to report expenses, retainers, contractual fees, and agreed fees, but no line for salaries. I computed my lobbyist compensation as sixty percent of my salary during the legislative session.

Our interns had gone back to school, but Peter Hufstader pored through the documents they had photocopied. He noted ambiguities in the forms and different ways that lobbyists interpreted the questions. Lobbyist reports did not distinguish between amounts billed to clients and payments actually received. Confusion arose over contract fees that some lobbyists billed month after month as opposed to payments received only once. Hufstader compiled new estimates of what these lobbyists had received during the 1999 legislative session. As we first reported, Democratic Party chair Guy Dufault earned $130,000, and Robert Goldberg remained one of the highest-paid lobbyists. To set the record straight, I wrote to each lobbyist on our top ten list. I apologized for our error, promised a public correction, and asked each to confirm our revised estimate. Several called or wrote to agree with Hufstader's revised numbers. Goldberg did not reply, but we reported his income from lobbying as $100,500.

Hufstader and I met with Secretary of State Jim Langevin and several of his staff to share problems our study revealed in the lobbyist reporting forms. Langevin explained that his staff registered lobbyists, received their forms, time-stamped the documents, and made them available for public inspection, but no one compiled the data. He promised to revise the forms. Our October 1999 newsletter reported Langevin's promise. We apologized for our errors and published Hufstader's corrected numbers.[23]

By the fall of 1999, most of the commissioners who had approved the gift ban in June 1998 were gone. Newly appointed lawyers now dominated the panel. They elected Melvin Zurier as chair and Richard Kirby, a protégé of John Harwood, as vice chair.

Former commissioner Mel Topf warned that the concentration of lawyers and politically connected commissioners had weakened the panel. What would happen, he asked, if six lawyers had to recuse themselves from a complaint against a judge? I told reporters that the commission was being packed with politically connected lawyers who shared a commitment to overturn the 1998 zero-tolerance gift rule.[24] I believed that the fix was in and the game was being rigged in front of our eyes.

The formal process for administrative agencies like the Ethics Commission to amend rules was designed to be slow and transparent, with public notice required at least thirty days before a hearing. Efforts to rescind the gift ban were fully under way by October 26, when I shared a slow elevator up to the eighth floor with House Parliamentarian and Brown University Political Science Professor Elmer E. Cornwell Jr. I knew Cornwell was paid over forty thousand dollars a year to stand on the rostrum at the speaker's elbow and interpret House rules. He and I had clashed publicly over separation of powers and the gift rule, and our small talk in the elevator did not diminish the distance between us.

On a table inside the Ethics Commission's hearing room lay alternate drafts of proposed gift rule revisions. Both versions would open the door for any public official to accept gratuities from any "interested person." Commissioners were to choose among bracketed gift amounts to legalize: [$10 – $15 – $25 – $50 – $100 or less] [but in no case having an aggregate value of $50 – $100 – $200 – $500 in any calendar year]. One draft applied to meals, the other to gifts.

One at a time, witnesses walked to a small table that faced commissioners.

My heart sank as John Roney attacked the zero-tolerance gift rule. Roney had prosecuted our ethics complaint against Gov. Edward DiPrete in 1991 and won a Providence Senate seat in 1994. Now he claimed that the gift ban rested on an assumption that "people in public life are either so venal or so stupid that they need to be protected from those who would try to influence them by buying them a cup of coffee." He argued that the rule was "demeaning to public servants," that officeholders were subject to "tremendous burdens," and that the rule made it difficult "to get good people to run for office." Then Elmer Cornwell took the tack that the gift rule was absurd, unfair, and unenforceable. He insisted that a state representative would violate the rule by accepting a stick of gum from a lobbyist; he warned that the commission could prosecute only a few selective cases.[25]

John Gregory lumbered toward the witness table. Only five years earlier, he had been an ally on the RIght Now! steering committee. Now president at the Northern Rhode Island Chamber of Commerce, he testified that the gift rule kept lawmakers away from chamber dinners they had previously attended. Asked what limits he thought appropriate, Gregory glanced at the bracketed amounts. He said the chamber wanted to entertain General Assembly members every year with a reception, a dinner, some lunches, and a golf tournament. He suggested an annual cap of $150 to $250 for each legislator in a calendar year.

The notion of legalizing a gift of $250 from each "interested person" left my brain spinning. If the Northern Rhode Island Chamber of Commerce was free to host 150 lawmakers at a dinner, what could stop every corporation that hired a lobbyist from treating legislators to dinners at the Capital Grille? Our top ten lobbyists represented eighty-two commercial clients. Would Bob Goldberg get a green light to take key lawmakers to separate dinners for each of his commercial clients?

In my turn to testify, I reminded the commission that companies and trade associations had routinely plied lawmakers with meals and gifts before the 1998 zero-tolerance rule. I described a cozy dinner in 1986: only days before a key vote on federal credit union insurance, RISDIC officers bought drinks and dinner at the Aurora Club for the House Finance Committee.[26] The committee had proceeded to ignore Robert Stitt's confidential report of looming dangers that RISDIC would collapse. The legislation they buried might have prevented the worst financial crisis in Rhode Island's history.

In December, I wrote to Zurier on behalf of Common Cause with copies to each member of the commission, asking that they not amend the gift rule until conflicts of interest within the commission could be resolved. The gift rule, I said, aimed "to protect public servants and the public alike from the corrosive cynicism that permeates a culture steeped in periodic scandals."[27] For the first time in its history, a majority of Ethics Commission members were attorneys, and several worked at firms that deployed lobbyists. We were not questioning their character or integrity, but it was clear that by voting on the gift rule, several would face conflicts of interest. Only the most distorted reading of the law's class exemption clause could conclude otherwise.

John Gudavich, an Operation Clean Government board member and a federal fraud investigator, testified the following February and urged the commissioners not to roll back the gift rule. Zero tolerance was easy to understand and to manage, but relaxing the rule would tarnish the reputation of government officials in the eyes of the taxpayers. Gudavich argued that Rhode Island's reputation for government corruption was one reason the state lagged behind the rest of New England in business expansion and job creation.[28]

Sen. John Roney disagreed with Gudavich, charging that proponents of this rule wrongly equated "human commerce with corruption." He favored revising the rule to allow $100 per occasion and a $200 limit per calendar year.

Joe Larisa appeared again on Almond's behalf, testifying, "We didn't think the gift ban was necessary, appropriate, or prudent in 1998, and we don't think it is today." He argued that most people saw no problem with a working lunch. "Business is discussed, and at the end of the day someone who may or may not be an interested party picks up the tab. And if public officials are swayed by that, we have a lot bigger problem in Rhode Island than the gift ban."

In March, the commissioners began an internal debate that stretched through several public meetings. Commissioner James V. Murray proposed a new rule limiting gratuities to $150 on one occasion up to an aggregate $750 per year from any interested party. "I'm in favor of officials like the governor having access to people," he said.[29]

Commissioner Francis Flanagan, a former Navy JAG officer, said he favored $200 per event but with "an overall aggregate" limit of $1,000 per year from any one donor. "I'm a product of the restaurant industry," he explained.

Robin Main agreed, suggesting that the commission not impose any "other type of cap, because I think we're only creating an administrative nightmare." She mused about a hypothetical case in which several Blue Cross employees might give a legislator gifts that added up to $40,000 from the same corporation.

Richard Kirby said he would favor $150 per event. "I reference a golf outing as a touchstone," he said, "the cost with dinner and greens fees being approximately $150." Kirby added that he would favor a reporting requirement so that constituents could "see what their representatives might be doing on state business."

Thomas Goldberg also favored a limit of $150 to $200. "I don't need a bright line as to what's reasonable," he said. "I hope I have enough common sense and enough decency to do the right thing, and I think most of the public officials in the state do." He wanted no overall cap on what officials could accept.

Commissioner James Lynch was incredulous. "I was waiting to have somebody convince me that what I previously thought was wrong," he said. "I waited to hear any person tell me that they could not perform their job because the gift regulation prevented it. I didn't hear that." Seated behind the table in a business suit, Lynch retained his military bearing. "I have lived under gift regulations of this type for over forty years, and I had no problem with it. Did I like it? No. But it worked." He urged his fellow commissioners to keep the gift rule intact. "I think that we're going to open Pandora's box by altering it in any of the fashions that have been mentioned."

After remaining silent while younger and newer members spoke, David McCahan said he believed any change would be a major step backwards. "This commission came into being because of a perception and a reality of graft in government and the loss of confidence among people in their government." Bald and pale, he spoke so softly that several of us in the audience cupped hands to our ears. He played off Kirby's proposed touchstone of a golf outing. "What's wrong with a legislator saying, 'You know, Joe, I'd love to come play as your guest, but I want to be fair to everybody. I don't want this to look bad. I just want to pay my own way. If you'll let me come and let me know what my cost is to play in that golf tournament, I'd love to play with you.'"

Then the hearing bogged down over whether a change in the text would require more hearings.

Flanagan suggested new numbers for a gift rule: $150 per event with an annual limit of $750 per donor to any public official. He suggested that the rule require officials to report what they received, but not set an aggregate limit on what any official could accept. The newly appointed lawyers agreed.

Seats in the room filled quickly on May 23, the date scheduled for the final vote. Witnesses stood along the back and side walls as TV crews positioned cameras and placed microphones on the red-topped table. Commissioners entered and took their seats. Behind them, wide windows afforded a view over city rooftops toward Narragansett Bay. Chairman Melvin Zurier explained the process and called witnesses from a list.[30]

Kevin McAllister introduced himself as a lawyer and president of Cranston City Council. He said that such an office made him subject to the commission's regulations. "The regulations as they exist today make my job as a public official easier," McAllister said. "They remove all the awkwardness and make it easier for me to maintain my neutrality. If I'm out at a public function or someone invites me for a drink, I can simply pay my own way. I say, 'No, thank you, the Ethics Commission rule prohibits me from accepting a gratuity.' Nobody's feelings are hurt. It's very easy, very simple."

McAllister reminisced about working at the bar his parents owned. One patron would buy a drink for another, which created an obligation "to even things off" by buying in return. Without mentioning Cranston's former mayor, Edward

DiPrete, McAllister described the struggle to clean up Cranston's image. "Many of us have been doing our best to raise public perception of elected officials as honorable. The current regulation that prohibits accepting gifts makes our job easier — if we're not encumbered by feelings that I owe this person."

Nondas Voll described twenty-six grassroots groups that were members of the Fund for Community Progress, where she was executive director. She said those agencies struggled for environmental, economic, and social justice. To change the gift rule would hurt them because nonprofits could never compete in providing meals and gifts. She noted that members of Congress were limited to accepting $100 in meals for an entire year. "Why do we need $750 in Rhode Island?"

Richard J. Frechette, the chief financial officer from the Department of Corrections, said the zero-tolerance rule was an inconvenience, but also urged the commission to keep it. "We public officials haven't had a good track record with common sense rules. I believe we are at a point in history right now where we have to follow absolute rules."

Witness after witness — students, teachers, parents, religious leaders, business owners, retired public officials — all opposed the permissive new rule. Only one witness gave credence to the proposed rule, attorney Michael A. Kelly, who served as counsel and lobbyist for Cumberland Farms convenience stores. He declared the zero-tolerance policy restrictive and unnecessary, using as an example the luncheon his clients hosted for local legislators, adding that they preferred not to wait around the State House and "chase their legislators down." The lunch, Kelly said was "not anything elaborate. I think they served chicken wings and roast beef sandwiches." He said the whole notion of zero tolerance was "flawed and should be changed."

A girl with long dark hair and glasses rose from where she had been sitting on the floor. She went to the witness table and introduced herself as Catherine Karner. "I'm in the sixth grade and twelve years old," she said. "I came in fourth in the state geography bee." She spoke of hard questions, like the capital of Burkina Faso, and easy questions, like which state had the highest ethical standards on gifts to public officials. "Today," she said, "the answer is Rhode Island. How students answer that question tomorrow rests squarely on your shoulders."

After the last witness, Zurier invited the commissioners to declare themselves. They followed judicial protocol, with the least senior member speaking first. Robin Main said she thought the gift rule was too extreme, but did not support the $750 top limit currently under consideration. She favored amending the draft rule to "achieve some balance."

A second lawyer, Francis Flanagan, lambasted a comment I had made that the new gift rule would legalize bribery. He called this "mean-spiritedness" and suggested they drop the $750 annual cap to $450 from any "interested person."

James Murray, the third recently appointed lawyer, said if he had been on the commission when it approved the gift rule he would have voted against it. He told the crowd he appreciated their comments: "They have not fallen on deaf ears. I'm in favor of changing this regulation, but not at the amounts that have been proposed."

Speaking from notes, Thomas Goldberg said zero tolerance "reflects a belief that we can never have any faith in our public officials to carry out their duties responsibly and ethically. I think we can have some faith in our public officials." He went on to defend himself against media stories criticizing his role in the debate. "During my tenure on this commission, I've had one hundred percent attendance at all commission meetings. That included advisory opinions, promulgation of rules, and adjudication of complaints. I have not hesitated to withdraw from my participation in matters I felt were appropriate for my disqualification. I do not believe that this amendment falls within that category. Believe me, the easiest thing for me would be to disqualify myself and walk away from this controversy. That would make my life a lot easier."

His eyes found me in the crowd. "Finally," he said, "I believe that many of the individuals who object to my participation would not object were I to be persuaded to vote against any amendment. I am convinced this criticism is intended simply to alter the result today, and it amounts to an attempt to improperly influence the deliberative process of a duly appointed Ethics Commission."

Richard Kirby, the fourth recently appointed lawyer to speak, mentioned that he had phoned me twice to discuss the amounts specified in the proposed rule. He spoke without notes and made eye contact with people in the audience. "I want to thank you all for your really passionate argument and discussion about this," he said. "I heard the comments about $750 being very, very high — a number that was shocking to a lot of people. I would be inclined to a lower number."

David McCahan, the retired insurance supervisor, had taken close notes. He said he agreed with forty-seven of the forty-eight people who had testified, adding that several witnesses who held public positions had affirmed zero tolerance. "'It makes my job easier,' they said. 'Makes it easier to attract people into those kinds of jobs because they're not beholden to some special interest.'" From his seat near the center McCahan spoke gently, focusing on the lawyers on the L-shaped ends of the table. "I urge you to think in terms of what zero tolerance really means. I would urge you also in voting for anything other than zero tolerance to think about what the message sends to your children and your grandchildren."

Paul Verrecchia reminded his colleagues that he was chief of police at Brown University. He had served twenty-two years on the Providence Police and retired as a major. He declared himself against the proposed new gift rule. "I think the limits are unreasonable," he said. "Another reason that I'm adamantly opposed to it is — even if the limits were reasonable — it does not put a limit on the total number of gifts that a public official can accept. So a public official under this regulation could accept a $750 limit per year from 100, 200, 300, or 5,000 donors."

Verrecchia let his numbers sink in before pushing on. "Two years ago I voted against the zero gifts regulation. I felt that back then that it was not practical. I felt that it would hinder the operation of government to worry about whether or not a public official in a business meeting has to worry about paying for his or her sandwich."

He asked whether a single rule could cover all public officials. "Do we want police officers accepting gifts? Do we want fire safety inspectors accepting gifts? Do we want building inspectors accepting gifts? Do we want health inspectors accepting gifts? Do we want people in enforcement and regulatory agencies accepting gifts from interested parties? I know I don't, and those are more than rhetorical questions. I teach police officers that there is no such thing as a free cup of coffee."[31] He asked the commission to draft a rule that would go "beyond the legislature, well beyond the legislature."

James Lynch, the retired army colonel, sat beside Zurier. Still sturdy in his late sixties, Lynch was unfailingly gracious. He said he had supported zero tolerance three years earlier. "Since then, I've listened to everybody who complained, and there were many. I read the newspapers, I listened to the talk shows, and I attended every hearing on the gift regulation. I wanted to hear one person — just one person — tell me that they could not perform the function for which we are paying them because they cannot accept gifts. Five hearings, and I have yet to hear one individual tell me that they could not perform because they could not accept gifts."

From his seat at the center Mel Zurier spoke last. "Unlike some of our critics," he said, "I still believe after almost fifty years of being a lawyer that the legal profession is still honorable. That we lack some diversity on the commission by having six of our nine members who are lawyers may be a valid criticism, but it is not a valid criticism to question the motives or integrity of our members, whether lawyers or non-lawyers."

Zurier explained why he had voted against zero tolerance in 1998 and why he still opposed it. He spoke in the unhurried way of one who had dictated many letters, proposing a $50 cap on a working lunch or dinner and a $500 limit on the total any government official could accept from all sources in a year. "In sum," he suggested, "I say let's not move precipitously. Now that we've had the benefit of public input, we ought to have our staff and our legal counsel give us some new alternative draft embodying the matters that I've mentioned."

He urged his colleagues to delay action because the rule as they had amended it now contained "very important deficiencies." He noted that the version now before them implied that a public official "could demand or accept gifts of less than $150. And I'm sure that's not the intention of any of you." He said corrections were needed and asked for a motion to "take no further action on this proposal at this time."

"Mr. Chairman," Flanagan broke in, "with all due respect, I move that we accept the proposed regulation as modified with $150/$450."

Kirby seconded instantly and added: "But, Mr. Chairman, if we're going to amend this regulation, I would insist that it remove the words 'shall ask, demand, or solicit.'"

Flanagan instantly accepted Kirby's amendment.

Zurier and the commission's legal counsel, Amelia Edwards, tried to parse the parliamentary tangle and requirements of the state's Administrative Procedures Act. Edwards said any substantial change required that the amended rule be advertised again and considered after public testimony at a new hearing. Kirby was prepared for this and cited a federal case in which the nation's highest court had opined that "procedural rules were meant to ensure meaningful public participation, not to be a strait jacket for agencies."

Executive Director Martin Healey responded that Flanagan's motion changed the rule substantially and triggered the requirement for another public hearing. Zurier asked for a vote to postpone, and the three most senior members — Lynch, McCahan, and Verrecchia — joined him in raising their hands. The five recently appointed lawyers — Flanagan, Kirby, Murray, Main, and Goldberg — voted to push forward.

"Have we not been hearing?" Verrecchia demanded. "I'm at loss as to why we're even considering $150, let alone $450. I think $450 is just as irrational as $750. There's not even a total cap on the amount of gifts that any public official could accept. I'm not talking about the individual aggregate from each donor. I'm talking about total. The cap isn't there." He seemed perplexed, indignant, and vulnerable all at once. "I don't see the logic. I think it's totally ludicrous, and it's not practical. And now taking the testimony we heard into consideration, voting for this regulation is a direct slap in the face to the people who came and testified."

David McCahan asked how the commission could enforce the proposed new rule. "We're just opening up Pandora's box to do whatever you want, and that's not right." Lynch also urged those who favored the higher limits to reconsider. "Give the chairman and the rest of us an opportunity to revisit this and perhaps come back with something more workable."

At the center of the table, Zurier seemed forlorn. "Whom will this cover?" he cried. "Will it cover the policemen? Will cases of wine or gift certificates be permissible under this? Can the aggregate number of gifts received in the course of a year be thousands of dollars or more?" He looked for some sign of compromise from the five lawyers at opposite ends of their table, who sat stone-faced.

Zurier hung his head. "I want to note my profound sorrow over the action that's being taken," he said plaintively. "I really regret this. I think that — years from now when we talk of the Ethics Commission — we'll realize this was sort of like the Dred Scott decision. It's a self-inflicted wound." His reference to that 1857 U.S. Supreme Court decision deepened the sense of foreboding. The justices had ruled that Dred Scott and other slaves were not citizens "within the meaning of the Constitution of the United States." Their decision propelled the nation toward the Civil War.

But Zurier's warning was to no avail. Just before noon, the panel voted. Flanagan, Goldberg, Kirby, Main, and Murray carried the day. With their vote Rhode Island veered from zero tolerance to the most permissive gift rule in the United States.

The crowd sat stunned but did not go quietly. As the panelists rose, someone in the audience shouted: "Shame! Shame on you!"

Richard Kirby tried to make his way through the crowd to a coatroom, but a white-haired woman blocked his way. "Shame on you, Mr. Kirby!" she declared to his face. "Shame on you!"

David McCahan, his eyes wet with tears, shook the hands of many who flocked to thank him. Ever the teacher, Peter Hufstader made his way to young Catherine Karner and her sister. Both had testified against gutting the gift rule. "Some civics lesson," Hufstader said softly to them and their mother.

Tom Goldberg's tie-breaking vote came as no surprise. In anticipation, I had drafted an ethics complaint against him, listing a series of tie-breaking votes he had cast. By coincidence the Common Cause state board had long been scheduled to meet that very evening, and I had emailed a draft complaint the night before. It listed essential facts: Thomas D. Goldberg was the brother and law partner of lobbyist Robert D. Goldberg; Robert Goldberg had collected over $100,000 from eight commercial clients in 1999;[32] by a 4 to 3 vote the Ethics Commission had warned Thomas Goldberg not to participate in gift rule changes;[33] the law required five votes for a binding advisory; without the protection of an advisory, Thomas Goldberg knew he was vulnerable to a complaint; during a year of public discussion, he had "persistently rejected" private and public requests that he recuse himself.

"As a member of the constitutionally-mandated authority on ethics for public officials," I wrote, "Thomas D. Goldberg bears an extraordinary responsibility to comply with 'the highest standards of ethical conduct, to avoid even the appearance of impropriety and not to use his position for private gain or advantage.'"

I listed seven motions where he provided the crucial tie-breaking fifth vote and continued: "By participating in these discussions and votes, Thomas D. Goldberg used his public office to modify the conditions under which commercial lobbyists, including his brother and law partner Robert D. Goldberg, could provide entertainment and other gratuities to public officials."

The Common Cause board met just after five o'clock and went into closed session for only the second time I could remember. I passed out photocopies of the complaint. The board voted unanimously to file it and fifteen of us signed the document.[34] In sharp contrast to our complaint against Gov. DiPrete, this would be open. The next morning, I delivered copies to the Ethics Commission and reporters.

Several days later, after a State House event, Gov. Almond drew me into his office. "I'm troubled," he said, "that the sides have hardened on this gift ban question. I always thought zero tolerance was unworkable, but these new numbers are far too high." He asked if I thought we could undo the damage, and I explained to him why we could not. I had tried to reason with Tom Goldberg, first privately and then publicly. Four members of the commission had approved an advisory opinion warning Goldberg not to participate. Those four, including Mel Zurier, had pleaded for compromise, but the five most recent appointees — all lawyers — had forced the decisive vote. As a result Rhode Island had the most permissive gift rule in the United States, and once Tom Goldberg cast his series of tie-breaking votes, Common Cause had no choice but to file an ethics complaint against him.

Towering over me, Almond was baffled. "So, have we passed a point of no return?"

"I think so, Governor."

I explained that Goldberg's majority on the Ethics Commission would circle the wagons around him. Even Almond, as governor, had no power to overrule them. The battle lines were drawn. No one knew how this would end.

36

Referendum
1999–2000

ROGER WILLIAMS UNIVERSITY LAW SCHOOL PROFESSOR CARL BOGUS was
ready for a cosmic struggle. Once the Supreme Court declared Rhode Island's
government "a quintessential system of parliamentary supremacy," he called
for a full frontal attack on the General Assembly's fortress. He compared our
quest to *Saving Private Ryan*, a film about the Normandy landing in World War
II that had won five Academy Awards.

With painful irony, the law school professor declared our courtroom defeat.
"The legal battle is over," he wrote to me in an email after the high court rejected
separation of powers. "Supreme Court briefs are beside the point. The court's
opinion is unequivocal and gratuitous. The four justices not only leave absolutely no doubt where they stand. They went out of their way to do it. I can't
imagine them changing their minds now. Even if they wanted to, how could
they go about disowning what they have just written? This is now a political
battle."[1]

Now the head of our separation of powers task force, Bogus began contact-
ing professors of law, history, and political science at colleges and universities
across the state. He wrote to them and followed up with phone calls proposing
that faculty members publish an open letter, a full-page ad proclaiming separation of powers as fundamental in American democracy. He asked each signer
for $35 toward the cost. Because faculty at the three publicly funded colleges
might face retaliation, he concentrated on the seven private institutions: Brown,
Bryant, Johnson & Wales, Providence College, Rhode Island School of Design,
Roger Williams, and Salve Regina. He promised that if he got fewer than forty
signers the ad would not run and no one would pay.[2]

Among Bogus's colleagues at Roger Williams, sixteen professors quickly signed on. Over the next six weeks he phoned faculty at the other schools but found many reluctant. Why were historians and political scientists at private colleges unwilling to endorse the core principle of American government?

Edward Achorn arrived at the *Providence Journal* as deputy editorial pages editor that summer of 1999. His inaugural column catalogued characters he had covered in Washington, D.C., and Massachusetts: swindlers, power brokers, bullies, and corrupt pols.[3] "I thought I was a jaundiced newsman," he wrote, "my sense of outrage and astonishment forever blunted." But his first week at the *Journal* left him dazzled. He called Rhode Island "a veritable Mardi Gras of scandal."

I wrote to Achorn about reforms enacted in response to recent scandals and sketched the separation of powers challenge. Peter Hufstader and I met him for lunch at Trinity Brewhouse, near the *Journal*'s headquarters in downtown Providence. We gave him folders full of research on ethics and separation of powers. "He has a gift with words," Hufstader said as we drove back to the office. "He could blow a bugle for the battles ahead."

The state's Economic Development Corporation (EDC) was one of seven boards Common Cause originally targeted in 1995 for violating separation of powers.[4] Four lawmakers sat on its thirteen-member board, two from the House and two from the Senate. With a freewheeling agenda to lure new businesses to Rhode Island, the quasi-public agency burned through budgets with little oversight.

In November 1999, Christopher Rowland reported in the *Providence Journal* that top staff at the EDC had used official credit cards to charge meals at upscale restaurants: 229 credit card bills covered hospitality for only twenty-eight clients.[5] Most of the rest went for entertaining the four General Assembly members who served on the EDC's board, along with John Harwood, Providence Mayor Vincent "Buddy" Cianci, and top staff in Gov. Almond's office. Rowland listed the expensive Providence restaurants where EDC director John Swen routinely picked up the tab: The Capital Grille, The Boathouse, The Gatehouse, Capriccio's, Raphael's, J. Goff's, and the Westin Hotel's International Yacht & Athletic Club. Swen violated state credit card rules by buying alcoholic beverages, and he could not provide receipts for seventy restaurant outings that totaled $4,408. The EDC paid $325 for staff parking tickets and covered Swen's nearly $5,000 annual membership at the elegant University Club. Records also revealed that the agency's legal counsel, Richard Stang, had taken his son to Disney World and charged his $135 American Bar Association membership on an EDC credit card. Other dubious expenditures included tuxedo rentals, picture framing, flower purchases, a personal stereo system, pet supplies, and car repairs, most never reimbursed.[6]

The burgeoning scandal reminded many of the Supreme Court slush fund and patronage that toppled Chief Justice Thomas Fay and Court Administrator Matthew Smith in 1993.[7] Public rage quickly forced Swen and Stang to resign, and the quasi-public agency closed its credit card accounts. Gov. Almond, who by law chaired the EDC board, ordered a full audit. He demanded strict accounting procedures and banned all personal use of credit cards.[8]

As explosive as these developments were, many were astonished when Senate Majority Leader Paul Kelly announced that the Senate would investigate credit card abuses at the EDC.[9] Over the holidays, Kelly appointed a high-profile Senate select commission to study quasi-public corporations. Kelly's written charge spelled out an unprecedented mission: to examine the quasi-publics' managerial systems and ensure public accountability. "Our intent," he said, "is not to go on a witch hunt. It's to look at the whole quasi-public agency situation. We want to prevent this kind of thing from happening again."[10]

Kelly's announcement struck like lightning in December. Never before had the General Assembly probed wrongdoing in quasi-public bodies where its own members sat and might be embarrassed.

Kelly appointed Senate Finance Committee Chair J. Michael Lenihan to lead the panel, and Judiciary Chair M. Teresa Paiva Weed to serve as vice chair.[11] Lenihan announced hearings on seven Wednesday nights in January and February of 2000 and summoned twenty-nine public and quasi-public bodies.[12] In advance of their testimony, executives were to provide their annual reports and answer six pages of questions about their internal accounting, administrative control, auditing, purchasing, public debt, personnel, ethics, travel, motor vehicles, entertainment, and credit cards. Lenihan also asked about agencies' compliance with the state's Open Meetings, Public Records, and Administrative Procedures laws. Cable television would allow people across the state to watch the proceedings.

On a snowy January night, Lenihan and Paiva Weed took center seats against a gleaming mahogany backdrop with American and Rhode Island flags behind them. Five other senators and the commission's counsel flanked them in the top row while fiscal and policy advisers sat below. Lenihan announced in a somber voice that Swen and Stang, the former director and lawyer of the EDC, had refused to appear. Never one to vent, he summarized unsuccessful efforts to contact them.

The Airport Corporation, an EDC subsidiary, was present and ready to respond. Executive Director Elaine Roberts, unpretentious with close-cropped hair and wearing a dark suit, delivered thick tabbed binders full of answers and supporting documents. Roberts described the airport's evolution. She inspired confidence as she presented details of labor relations, budgeting, accounting software, audit procedures, and internal controls.

"What is your policy with regard to credit cards?" Lenihan asked.

"There is no formal policy," Roberts answered, "but there is no allowance for personal use in any way. All of our credit cards have receipts documenting every purchase."

"Do you think it would be wise, where you have no formal policy, to establish one?"

"Absolutely," Roberts said with no trace of defensiveness. "We'll get caught up with that."

Without highlighting the fact that no lawmakers or legislative appointees served on the Airport Corporation board, Lenihan showed how policies, routines, and scrutiny discouraged fraud. As Paiva Weed and other senators asked questions, the panel demonstrated a new standard of oversight at the State House.

On January 26, Sherry Giarrusso-Mulhearn testified before the Lenihan Commission. Tall and self-confident, she had replaced Thomas Wright as executive director of the state's Solid Waste Management Corporation. Under her leadership, the quasi-public had been renamed the Rhode Island Resource Recovery Corporation.

Giarrusso-Mulhearn had gotten credit cards for herself and three other top staff at the trash agency. Like the EDC executives, she had charged questionable items, such as lunches at expensive Providence restaurants, flowers for secretaries, Christmas gift certificates for staff, a candelabra for an employee who married, and bar association dues for the corporation's counsel. She hoped these "employee incentives" would head off efforts to form a union, and testified that they were "reasonable, appropriate, and not excessive."[13] When Paiva Weed asked whether the state should enact uniform standards for business expenses at agencies like hers, Giarrusso-Mulhearn answered that she would welcome a clear rule.

Vincent Mesolella seemed uncharacteristically meek when he arrived to testify about the Underground Storage Tank Review Board (USTRB), the lesser of two quasi-publics he had controlled during his time in the House and since his departure. Since 1996, the USTRB had been collecting a penny-per-gallon surcharge on gasoline and diesel fuel to pay for the cleanup of leaky underground tanks. Four factors made this fund a prize: decisions were made in utter secrecy, contractors were paid huge amounts of money, the work was quickly covered over, and Mesolella was accountable to no one but Harwood.

Mesolella and Lenihan had twice locked horns over funds. The first time Mesolella had managed to shoehorn an article into the budget that raised his agency's annual allocation for "administrative costs" from $150,000 to $550,000. With Harwood's support, Mesolella's appropriation became a steamroller that Lenihan could not stop. A year later, again without public hearing or Senate consent, the House inserted $550,000 into the budget for the same purpose. This time Lenihan told Senate Majority Leader Paul Kelly that if the Senate allowed this boondoggle, he would resign as chair of the Senate Finance Committee.

In the session-ending struggle, the USTRB administrative budget was cut back to $350,000.[14]

Now Mesolella — no longer a representative but still close to Harwood and still running the USTRB fund — came before Lenihan's commission without his usual bravado. Michaela Brockmann, the fund's executive director, took the seat beside him. Like a model playing down her glamour, she wore a pin-striped navy blue suit with a white shirt and patterned tie, her sandy blond hair pulled back in a bun. Mesolella fidgeted like a student summoned to the principal's office, taking his glasses off and putting them on over and over.

"A memo from your legal counsel," Lenihan said with elaborate respect, "says that you are an 'autonomous entity.' I would like to explore your perception of where that puts the agency."

Mesolella nodded. "I think we are neither a quasi-public nor a department of state government. We were created by an act of the General Assembly, but we have no provision to incur debt, none whatsoever. Unlike other quasi-publics that have already appeared before you, we have no user fees. Our revenue is strictly based on a one cent per gallon gas tax, a restricted receipt account administered through the Clean Water Finance Agency. We have no cash, no cars, no credit cards, no checking account."

Lenihan asked if the underground storage board complied with the state's Open Meetings and Open Records laws.

"Yes, Mr. Chairman, we do."

"What about the Public Corporation Financial Integrity and Accountability Act?"[15]

Mesolella had heard that question asked of other quasi-public leaders, and he answered with exaggerated politeness. "Not unlike those who have come before you, we were unaware of that particular act. We are now aware of it, and we will make every effort to comply with any provisions that we can."

Lenihan read from a letter by the state's auditor general about two disbursements, totaling $120,590, that had been misclassified as an administrative expenditure.

Brockmann took responsibility for the mistake. "I prepared the invoices myself," she said. "It was strictly a human error."

Lenihan asked why disbursements for leaky tanks could not be done by the Clean Water Finance Agency.

Mesolella replied that it would cost four times as much. "To answer your question directly, there's no reason why the state government can't take over this operation or any other quasi-public agency, but it would be better to leave us as an independent body." He pursed his lips and nodded his head, as if to reinforce his point, adding, "We're very proud of our work."

Without theatrics, Lenihan had prompted Mesolella to acknowledge publicly that there was no need for his board to exist outside state government.

Mesolella had good reason to avoid a confrontation. He was again drawing

fire as head of the Narragansett Bay Commission (NBC), the quasi-public empire that processed sewage for the northern half of the state. When ratepayers
fell behind on sewage bills, the bay commission routinely sold liens on their
homes. To regain title, homeowners had to pay fees and charges many times
their original obligation. At one NBC meeting early in 2000, a woman waved
her mother's bill for $174.75 at Mesolella. "Where do you get off selling some-
one's property out from under them?" she yelled. "I don't know how you sleep
at night."[16] Quasi-publics chaired by lawmakers or legislative appointees often
rode roughshod over ordinary people. Victims complained, but few Rhode
Islanders recognized the underlying pattern.

During his hearings, Lenihan routinely asked public agency leaders about
the Public Corporation Financial Integrity and Accountability Act, legislation
he had led in enacting. Its central premise was that weak accounting systems
multiplied opportunities for fraud. That law made the leaders and executives
of agencies responsible for establishing and maintaining effective systems of
internal control.[17] Of twenty-three agencies that came before the Lenihan Commission, a dozen had failed to conduct regular audits. The hearings showed
how many quasi-public executives were ignorant of laws that governed their
operations; their agencies exercised vast government powers in a netherworld
without adequate accountability. Inexorably, the Senate probe showed that
Rhode Island's peculiar paradigm — where legislative appointees sat as voting
members and presumably reported back to House and Senate leaders — provided no effective oversight.

The Lenihan Commission's final report questioned the very existence of the
Underground Storage Tank Board and the Housing Resource Commission. It
asked why these quasi-public agencies "should not be folded into another department or agency of state government." The report noted that Rhode Island
law lacked any legal definition of "quasi-public corporation," but these bodies
exercised the same executive functions that the Common Cause separation
of powers task force had identified five years earlier. The credit-card scandal
involving the Economic Development Corporation and Resource Recovery
Corporation and other agencies was only the tip of an iceberg.[18]

Questions remained. Would other senators bother studying the report?
Would Senate leaders recognize that having legislators on executive boards
invited abuses? Would they stop appointing lawmakers to perform executive
functions?

My mother had turned ninety in January. I was with her in Florida on July 27,
when the Rhode Island Supreme Court slammed the door for a second time
on separation of powers. I arrived home from the airport to absorb the news: A
three-justice majority had ruled that General Assembly leaders could legally appoint lawmakers to six of nine seats on the state's Lottery Commission.[19] Adding

insult to injury, they reinforced the principle that the General Assembly could exercise any governmental authority it wished unless the state's Constitution expressly forbade it. Again Justice Robert Flanders filed a stinging, eloquent, futile dissent.

Our phone rang informing me that my mother had suffered a serious fall. I booked the first available flight back to Jacksonville and arrived at her bedside just before she died. During a crucial time in Rhode Island my attention was far away, arranging her memorial service, closing her accounts, disposing of her possessions.

Meanwhile, Gov. Almond seized on an arcane provision in state law that allowed him to place an advisory question on the ballot. He asked voters if the state should convene a constitutional convention to address separation of powers.

When I returned and read its text, I saw that he had overstated our case. "Should a Constitutional Convention be called," he asked, "to expressly establish that Rhode Island government consists of separate and co-equal legislative, executive, and judicial branches similar to the governments established by the United States Constitution and by the Constitutions of all 49 other states?" That final claim that the constitutions of "all 49 other states" established separation of powers went too far. State constitutional texts and practices differed: some, like the U.S. Constitution, separated powers without an explicit clause, while several others with constitutional clauses still lacked a robust separation of powers. But only Rhode Island had a "broad powers" clause that allowed the legislature to do whatever it liked unless specifically prohibited in the Constitution.

Regardless of what I thought, Almond's question had gone to the secretary of state before a printing deadline. Separation of powers would be Question 6 on the November ballot, solely as an expression of public opinion. What backlash would it provoke from defenders of the status quo? And could we use the Supreme Court's decisions to mobilize public support?

In the middle of August, and with no money, we began organizing support for Almond's ballot question. Without a convincing majority in November, the push for separation of powers would lose all credibility. As it turned out, John Hazen White, the industrialist who had spent lavishly on RedAlert! ads in the *Providence Journal,* agreed to help. On a sweltering August afternoon, leaders of the six groups that had been working for separation of powers found our way into the cool, brightly lit training room at Taco, Inc., White's factory in Cranston. We needed a clear message, a credible coalition, and money to produce lawn signs and hundreds of thousands of flyers.[20]

As we sipped iced tea, I reported that leaders of several chambers of commerce and other groups had said they would participate but were on vacation.

"Did you invite organized labor?" Greta Abbott asked. Still a member of the Common Cause board, she was a part-time lobbyist for the League of Women Voters.

I said I had not tried: organized labor clearly preferred a safely Democratic General Assembly over the process that might emerge under separation of powers. Labor would not support Question 6 any more than they had backed downsizing the legislature.

"You were right," declared Bob Arruda, who now led Operation Clean Government (OCG). "Since when have labor leaders in this state ever cared about real reform?"

Arruda was quick and fierce. Under his leadership, the cadre of OCG volunteers had launched a nonpartisan candidate training school, begun producing a monthly public access program on cable television, and filed dozens of ethics complaints against public officials. On top of that, Arruda ran a business called Quality Behavioral Health. His stamina amazed me.

"Separation of powers is the crucial reform," Arruda declared. "OCG intends to rally our members and throw our full energy into winning a huge majority for Question 6."

With less than three months before the November election, we planned a campaign that would require few meetings and fewer subsequent decisions. Our goal was to educate the electorate statewide. Organizations in the Question 6 coalition would mobilize their own members to distribute flyers and lawn signs. OCG would organize an October rally, while Common Cause coordinated press coverage and outreach to other groups. With data from Peter Hufstader's research, I had drafted a flyer that followed the Q&A format of our previous campaigns.

"I like this," Arruda said, "particularly this chart that shows 5,549 jobs in quasi-public agencies where legislators serve on boards. They've created endless golden opportunities for patronage!"

Since he walked through the door five years earlier, Peter Hufstader had been translating headline stories into policy questions and linking scandals to abuses of power. He contrasted the Senate's scrutiny of quasi-public bodies with the work of a House panel that had earlier investigated the Department of Environmental Management through a process that environmentalists blasted as a witch hunt. Many believed Hopkinton Rep. Brian P. Kennedy's goal was to transfer powers from the Department of Environmental Management, an executive agency, to the Coastal Resources Management Council, which was controlled by the legislature.

Hufstader drafted a report — *Democracy Betrayed: Conflicts of Interest and Failures of Oversight in Rhode Island State Government* — that summarized the recurring scandals in quasi-public bodies that lawmakers had created and run but failed to oversee. Separate chapters analyzed abuses in the state retirement system and in five quasi-public boards. Rampant conflicts of interest and pervasive secrecy multiplied the costs paid by taxpayers and ratepayers.

In his final chapter, Hufstader focused on the Lottery Commission ruling.

"The state Supreme Court," he wrote, "has now declared that it is constitutionally permissible for the state legislature to delegate its legislative authority to a board controlled entirely by its own members." Only two boards — the Unclassified Pay Plan Board and the Lottery Commission — currently had legislative majorities, but the Supreme Court had changed the rules. "The Lottery Commission ruling," Hufstader wrote, "has become an invitation for the General Assembly to seize additional opportunities for letting contracts and hiring staff. Rhode Island's General Assembly and Supreme Court have now joined forces to embrace a practice that has been repeatedly struck down by federal courts and by other state courts, the delegation of legislative authority to a small group of legislators."[21]

Common Cause published *Democracy Betrayed* in September for release during a clambake at the Bristol estate of Stanley and Martie Livingston celebrating the thirtieth anniversary of Common Cause. Now in their seventies, the Livingstons were life-long Rhode Islanders and embraced separation of powers as the most crucial reform. Stan Livingston waved us into a parking space on their lawn. "Don't let this lottery decision get you down," he said as we pulled boxes brimming with copies of *Democracy Betrayed* out of the back seat and trunk.

A huge white tent and clambake pit stood at the top of a lawn that sloped westward down to Narragansett Bay. The crowd swelled to more than three hundred. Atty. Gen. Sheldon Whitehouse, the most visible official advocate of our cause, embraced me. Rep. David Cicilline, the lead sponsor of separation of powers resolutions over several years in the House, worked his way through the crowd.

Topher Hamblett brought his father Stephen Hamblett, publisher of the *Providence Journal*, whose vision of good government shaped the editorial pages.

The sun sank slowly behind a dark shoreline across Narragansett Bay. After dinner, toasts, and speeches, I held up a copy of *Democracy Betrayed* and introduced Peter Hufstader as our unpaid research director. "We have these for each of you." Applause and cheers swept the crowd.

I thanked several dozen public officials, calling them out in the crowd. I praised Sheldon Whitehouse and David Cicilline for their leadership on the issue. "Separation of powers should be the cornerstone of our government," I said, "but these leaders have paid a high price for supporting it. The General Assembly may never forgive them, but history will prove them right."

Beneath my public optimism lurked a gnawing sense that we had already been crushed on the issue that had now been our highest priority for six years. As if to confirm our defeat, I noticed Chief Justice Weisberger, the author of two majority opinions denying separation of powers, seated in the crowd, his deeply lined face fixed in a public smile.

"I apologize," I said with a wave toward him. "I need to make one more introduction. Chief Justice Joseph Weisberger is here." I did not mention his majority opinions against separation of powers, but when Weisberger waved to the crowd, people responded with tepid applause. They knew.

On a bright October Sunday afternoon, Operation Clean Government hosted a rally for Question 6. Groups in the coalition gathered at the Community College of Rhode Island's modernistic Warwick campus, where hundreds found seats in a circular, raw concrete theater. Speeches were short and focused on convincing neighbors, friends, and family to vote yes on Question 6. "They may think the election's only about picking a president," yelled Bruce Lang, a founder of OCG. "Convince them that separation of powers matters just as much!"

Though the Rhode Island Supreme Court had already issued two adverse rulings, this crowd was fired up. People streamed past tables, picking up lawn signs and boxes of flyers destined for windshields in supermarket parking lots, church bulletins, and high school football games. We had no money for television, but these old-fashioned election tools would make our campaign visible across the state.

That November Question 6 won a nearly 2-to-1 victory — 218,139 approved, while 111,292 voted no.[23] In every city and town overwhelming majorities declared their support for a constitutional convention to address separation of powers. Our win would not launch a convention, but we hoped it would pressure the General Assembly to place the question of a convention on the 2002 ballot.

37

Downsizing Revisited
1999–2000

FIVE YEARS HAD PASSED since voters amended Rhode Island's Constitution to create a new General Assembly for the twenty-first century. Nirvana had not yet arrived at the State House, but at least the bitter impasse over legislative pay and pensions had faded from memory. Special pension bills no longer clogged the consent calendars and lawmakers were pleased with their new laptop computers, email, and voicemail.

The 1994 constitutional amendment had scheduled the cut in legislative districts to coincide with redistricting that would follow the 2000 U.S. Census. Mapmakers would use new population data to carve a hundred House districts down to seventy-five, and fifty Senate districts to thirty-eight. Incumbents worried about campaigning against friendly colleagues. Tales of downsizing in neighboring states — Vermont, Connecticut, and Massachusetts — began to circulate.[1] As if a hurricane were barreling toward us, anxiety spread.

A bill filed in January 1999 signaled the struggle. Lincoln Rep. John D. Barr II, a deputy majority leader, proposed a ballot question that would ask voters to retain the current number of representatives and senators.[2] Yet Barr's text did not touch those parts of the 1994 constitutional amendment that raised legislative pay and ended the old legislative pensions. Uncertain whether Barr's bill was a joke, a trial balloon, or a shot across the bow, I asked him.

"Of course it's serious, Phil," Barr exclaimed in a high-pitched laugh. "Would I jerk you around?"

I smiled but did not answer. "Even if you put that on the ballot," I said, "the voters will never agree."

"I think they'll go along," Barr grinned. "Downsizing would make a terrible mess."

"What about the pay raise and health insurance you've been taking for four years?"

"What about them?"

"The pay raise and downsizing were a package deal. Everybody knew that."

"Did they?" Barr laughed.

I sounded the alarm with emails to the reform community.

Barr's bill was never posted for a hearing and died with the 1999 session, but it was revived in September with new frills.

During deliberations in 1993 of the Blue Ribbon Commission on the Future of the General Assembly, a teachers' union leader had vehemently opposed legislative downsizing.[3] The reasons seemed obvious. For decades, public employee unions had dominated the reliably Democratic General Assembly. Legislative stability and continuity were in labor's interest; the chaos and conflict of downsizing were not.

It became clear in September 1999 that organized labor would try to rescind the downsizing. Robert A. Walsh Jr., a leader in one of two powerful state teachers' unions, told the *Providence Journal* that voters had not had "a fair opportunity to speak solely and exclusively about what they felt the size of the legislature should be."[4] Tall and balding, Walsh conveyed labor's resistance to downsizing in a gentle voice. Leaders of Ocean State Action, a labor-funded coalition, surrounded him in a *Providence Journal* photo.[5] The new anti-downsizing coalition called itself "Democracy Counts," and their hand-out claimed that larger legislative bodies "tend to be better organized so that they are able to get their work done efficiently."

"Now that we have found the door of the State House," said Victor Capellán, the executive director of CHisPA, the Center for Hispanic Policy and Action, "they are shutting the doors in our face."

A week later, I sat with Capellán in his headquarters on Elmwood Avenue, only a few blocks from our home. With Capellán was Tomás A. Ávila, the agency's director of policy. Both had arrived in Rhode Island since the 1992 round of redistricting. This elegant mansion that embodied Elmwood's past now belonged to CHisPA; Capellán and Ávila represented the neighborhood's future.

"The issue isn't the number of House and Senate seats," I told them. "It's who draws the district lines and how they draw them."

"So who does draw the lines?" Ávila asked.

I explained that legislative leaders would appoint a redistricting commission to analyze demographic shifts and take testimony. Unrolling maps from the previous redistricting process, I showed them how legislative leaders created safe districts for their political allies. First drafts of 1992 Senate maps had protected white incumbents in our neighborhood by reaching south across the Providence city line and pulling in largely white blocks in Cranston. After Common Cause and the Urban League testified at public hearings against those racial gerrymanders, the incumbent senator, a Bevilacqua ally, had seemed embarrassed and quietly told Senate leaders to bring the district border back to the city line.

"That was Bob Kells," Capellán recalled. "Juan Pichardo never got a fair shot against him."

"Senate leaders were trying to protect Kells," I said. "They used redistricting to split the heaviest concentration of Latinos in half."

I showed them a district Sen. Charles Walton and I had drawn in 1992, when the influx of Latinos barely warranted a single seat in the House. Our creation looked like a loose bow tie, but Anastasia Williams, a young Latina, had won that seat and had served there ever since. "I hope," I said, "that we can work together this time around for districts that serve communities rather than incumbents."

"I like that," Ávila said. "Can you leave these maps with us?"

"Absolutely," I agreed.

In February, Rep. Marsha E. Carpenter — an African-American whose district included our home on the South Side — sponsored a House leadership bill to rescind the downsizing. Hers began with John Barr's proposed constitutional amendment and piled a series of dubious "whereas" clauses on top. One of Carpenter's "whereas" clauses declared, as if it were a proven fact: "Any reduction in the size of the membership of the house of representatives and senate will inevitably render it more difficult for minority and/or women candidates to successfully run for and gain election to the general assembly."[6]

Nothing I knew supported such a sweeping claim. In fact our research suggested the opposite, at least for women. In 1978, Massachusetts had cut the size of its House from 240 to 160, and four years later, Illinois reduced its lower chamber from 177 seats to 118. Newspaper stories from both states were rife with fears that women and minorities would lose out. Neither Massachusetts nor Illinois kept statistics on race or ethnicity, but we counted the names of women before and after downsizing. In 1975, only 5.0 and 5.1 percent of representatives in the two states were female, while women comprised 8.1 percent of state legislators across the United States. Both began behind the curve, but after downsizing the numbers of women lawmakers in the two states soared. Illinois surpassed the 1985 national average of 14.8 percent first and reached 16.5 percent. Massachusetts caught up and went ahead to 16.9 percent.

Women in Massachusetts and Illinois Houses of Representatives After Downsizing							
	1975	1977	1979	1981	1983	1985	% increase
Massachusetts	5.0%	5.7%	7.5%	9.5%	13.0%	16.5%	11.5%
Illinois	5.1%	7.6%	1.0%	13.6%	15.3%	16.9%	11.8%
United States	8.1%	9.2%	10.3%	12.1%	13.3%	14.8%	6.7%

The House Judiciary Committee scheduled testimony on Carpenter's bill before television cameras in Room 313, a handsome setting with banked seats for lawmakers amid dark mahogany panels. Carpenter made her way down from her place in the committee to the witness chair. Less than four years earlier her son had been gunned down on a street in our neighborhood, but she turned tragedy into anti-gang legislation.[7] As brave as Carpenter was, however, she faced formidable odds in the September Democratic primary because preliminary census figures showed that the Hispanic population in the district had surged since the last round of redistricting.

Now she began softly. "My bill would put the question of downsizing the General Assembly back on the ballot in November. My reason for wanting this back on the ballot is that the question, as it appeared on the ballot in 1994, was very misleading. There were three questions within one question. Each of those questions should have stood alone on the ballot, but they did not." She said that the chief problem was that voters had to approve or reject three questions as a total package.

"I believe the voters in my district wanted to increase legislative salaries. I believe they wanted to abolish legislative pensions, but I do not believe they wanted to reduce the size of the General Assembly. Since the question was so misleading and confusing, I think it's only fair that it go back on the ballot and give the voters another chance to vote on it."

Carpenter testified that only eight out of seventeen state representatives from Providence were people of color. "Minorities stand to lose two to three. It took so long to get here, and now to get rid of two or three? If the downsizing goes through, we'll all be taking two steps back when we should be going forward."

Rep. Scott Rabideau, a Republican from the rural northwest corner of the state, asked if she would prefer to have downsizing, the legislative pay raise, and pension reform back on the ballot as separate questions. "If it's so confusing, shouldn't we put all three?"

"If that's a fair way," Carpenter replied, "then we should do that. I don't believe it was fair the first time."

Rep. Joe Almeida represented the South Providence neighborhood adjacent to Carpenter's. Retired from the Providence police, he ran a nightclub and headed the Black Caucus of State Legislators. "With this downsizing," he said, "I feel as though our community will not be represented, and we will be set back again. The black, Hispanic, and Southeast Asian communities will no longer be represented in the General Assembly, and our voice will die." Almeida usually spoke at length and with fierce intensity, but this testimony against downsizing felt devoid of passion.

Rep. Paul Moura, a senior deputy majority leader, settled at the microphone. "I'm a proud co-sponsor of this bill," he began. "Most of the proponents of downsizing never served a day in public office in their lives." Movie star handsome with abundant black hair, supple eyebrows, and expressive eyes, Moura was one of three full-time union employees — along with Sens. Dominick Ruggiero and John Tassoni — serving in the General Assembly.

He praised the small-town familiarity of the current districts, where his constituents "like the fact that they can pull into a gas station and say, 'Oh, Representative, have you got a minute? Can I talk with you?'"

Behind him, Larry Purtill, president of NEARI, the largest block of teachers' unions, nodded. In the bluest of blue states, organized labor rarely lost a vote.

Moura looked up at the Judiciary Committee. "I strongly support putting this question before the people. Let them answer the question clear cut and all alone: 'Do you feel that the legislature should be downsized, or should we overturn the downsizing?'"

George Nee, tall and bulky in a gray suit, came to the microphone. Although only in his forties, his hair was white. "On behalf of the AFL-CIO," Nee said, "I wholeheartedly support this bill. In a smaller General Assembly, there would be a danger of moneyed interests influencing legislation."

I stifled a laugh. In the wake of RISDIC's collapse, we had tried to persuade the AFL-CIO Executive Council to support campaign finance reform legislation that ultimately outlawed direct contributions from the treasuries of corporations and unions. Nee and the cadre of labor lobbyists had never supported campaign finance reform, nor had they spoken out against districts gerrymandered in 1992 to protect white incumbents against black and Latino challengers.[8]

"We deserve to have this issue get a clean vote," Nee continued. "The issue was cloudy in 1994. Our organization thought downsizing the General Assembly was a bad idea then, and we think it is today."

Marty Rosenberg followed Nee, her short hair swept back. She ran Ocean State Action, a nonprofit organization based in a teachers' union headquarters. "The problems pointed out by the Blue Ribbon Commission were apt," she began in a resonant voice, "but we think that downsizing is not the answer. Perhaps we should talk about campaign finance, but I'll leave that for another hearing."

I had to smile. I liked Rosenberg and had worked with her on a half dozen bills. I had spoken to the Ocean State Action steering committee about campaign finance reforms, but like the larger labor establishment they neither supported campaign finance proposals nor offered alternatives.

"Downsizing passed with 51.8 percent of the vote," Rosenberg continued, "not an overwhelming majority in any sense. We know people were riled up about the pensions, but since they were upset over the pensions, you'd think the question would have passed with a 75 percent margin." She paused. "I think people were torn because they couldn't decide which side to vote for."

The parade of labor and minority witnesses kept coming. Victor Capellán came to the microphone in a dark, open-necked shirt. "We're asking you to put this question back on the ballot," he said passionately. "We have a citizens' legislature. We're being included. We believe that the legislature is working, and this is not the time to change it. What downsizing would do is push us out. My agency would not be able to come up here."

Capellán's voice rose as he spoke. He said America was about recognizing and fixing mistakes: eradicating slavery, undoing Jim Crow. He insisted it was not wrong to go back and make things right.

Larry Purtill wrapped up the opposition to downsizing. As president of Rhode Island's National Education Association, he represented more than eleven thousand teachers across the state. "I don't have to reiterate the concerns others have laid out," he began. In a double-breasted suit, he communicated power. "We think downsizing of the legislature will do exactly the opposite of what the proponents want it to do. We think it will limit access to legislators and make committees smaller. We think that the grassroots lobbying that makes Rhode Island special will be limited."

Gary Sasse, executive director of the Rhode Island Public Expenditure Council, a business-backed think tank, and former head of the Blue Ribbon Commission, came forward. He spoke of the disillusionment from the RISDIC scandal that led to the appointment of the commission and described its work: soliciting recommendations from all current and former members of the General Assembly, conducting public meetings and five televised public hearings, releasing a draft report, and seeking public comment. The process stretched over a year and a half.

Then Sasse outlined our recommendations: maintain a part-time citizens' legislature, but make the General Assembly more effective with modern information technology; enlarge the opportunity and power of individual legislators; persuade voters to provide reasonable legislative pay; increase competition; and modestly enlarge the districts.

"If we had recommended that the size of districts be doubled," Sasse said, "I would agree with some of the testimony you have heard tonight. What we were trying to achieve was a balance among competing concerns. An increase in population of a House district from ten thousand to thirteen thousand would not have drastic results." Sasse made the case without sounding argumentative. "While there's no magic number of state representatives and senators, our House districts would have roughly one third the population of representative districts across the country. Our Senate districts would have roughly a quarter of the national average population."

He added that the commission did not believe the downsizing would harm minority representation and noted, "This was thoroughly debated before the General Assembly voted to place the question on the ballot."

Rep. David Cicilline challenged Sasse. "You said this Blue Ribbon Commission made those recommendations. I don't know who was on it, and surely it didn't hear from the Center for Hispanic Policy and Progreso Latino and the Urban League and women's organizations and labor organizations. Don't you think we have some obligation to hear from them?"

"I'll give you a list of the commission members," Sasse replied dispassionately, "and we did hear from different groups. Labor was represented on the commission and had a minority position with regard to downsizing. We had hearings that lasted late into the night. We heard from a broad cross-section of Rhode Islanders."

As he moved to the question of whether downsizing would hurt minorities, his gestures punctuated each point. "The commission told the legislature in 1994: 'Don't put the question before the people if you felt this would hurt minority or gender equity representation.' That was highlighted in the commission's report," he said, "and the General Assembly voted to go forward."

Sasse concluded softly: "There have been a lot of statements tonight that downsizing passed because voters wanted to get rid of legislative pensions. I think you could argue that the relatively narrow margin was because the people didn't want to increase legislators' pay."

Common Cause president Nancy Rhodes and I moved to the witness table. I handed the clerk documents to distribute. One chart showed how few constituents each Rhode Island legislator represented by contrast with lawmakers in other states. On a fifty-state list of constituents per lawmaker, downsizing would move Rhode Island from sixth fewest to eighth fewest. The packet included newspaper stories that showed how thoroughly the commission's deliberations were reported and pages from the *House Journal* that traced the lengthy debate on June 2, 1994.

I reminded the committee that voters were still seething over the roles key lawmakers had played in RISDIC's collapse. "There was a sense that the legislature uniquely had let down the citizens," I said. "The question for our commission was: How could we strengthen this legislature to provide effective representation? We quickly saw that legislators were not being adequately paid. State voters — in misplaced cynicism and resentment of the legislature — had refused to raise legislative pay on several occasions."

I explained how the General Assembly had created its legislative pension system and then doubled it, and why so many opposed raising legislative pay. But we believed it was only fair to provide a $10,000 salary and family health coverage. "We knew that would be a tough sell," I said, "but we knew it was right." The voters' resistance to the pay increase was the main reason for the narrow majority when the amendment passed.

Committee Chairman Bob Flaherty interrupted: "We have other witnesses and other bills to hear tonight."

In closing, I pointed out that Common Cause believed that the issue was not the size of districts but how the lines were drawn.

Rep. David Cicilline launched an attack on one of the commision's central premises. "The commission," he read from the report, "believes that the recommended reduction in size should not cause any reduction in the proportion of minority representation in the General Assembly."

"That's nice," he said, "but there's no data, no empirical evidence from which the commission can decide that it shouldn't, in fact, cause a reduction. We know for sure it's going to cause a reduction."

I kept silent, and Cicilline kept going. "What particularly concerns me, as I look at the groups that have come forward in opposition to this. . . . "

Then he switched gears in mid-sentence. "I'm a member of Common Cause. I introduce a lot of legislation for Common Cause. I'm beginning to question whether I should be involved with Common Cause because this is an organization that I'm sensing doesn't have a great representation in the minority community, and is displaying a real arrogance and insensitivity to the plight of minorities and disenfranchised people in this state. I'm embarrassed right now to say that I'm associated with Common Cause because I'm hearing from a broad cross-section of this community that they will be hurt by their inability to be involved in the political process if we downsize. I think the empirical data shows that this is unequivocally true."

"What empirical data?" I interrupted.

"That there will be fewer members of the minority community who will be elected. And fewer women. And I'm not hearing from Common Cause or RIPEC that we need to reexamine this issue, because good government isn't just lean government. It's inclusive government. It's representative democracy. I'm hearing: 'We committed ourselves to this plan. It's part of a reform package. Therefore we're going to support it.' That really disturbs me."

"May I answer?" I asked.

"Certainly."

I said there was no way — with or without downsizing — to say that the number of Providence representatives would remain the same. The real issue was how new districts would be drawn to protect minority rights, a concern Common Cause had fought for in the 1992 round of redistricting.

Chairman Robert Flaherty interrupted that he would not allow what he called "private debate about legislation that's not before this committee."

Cicilline's attack felt like grandstanding, and Flaherty would not let me address the question of fair redistricting.

Several other members of the committee asked questions, and I managed to close by warning that voters would react strongly against any effort to put the downsizing question back on the ballot by itself. "There was a deal," I said, "to end a corrupt legislative pension system and downsize a huge legislature by one quarter. That was the deal. Voters understood."

The Judiciary Committee adjourned without voting on Carpenter's bill. The

Providence Journal's State House chief, Kathy Gregg, reported the hearing in a front-page story. Her summary of the debate juxtaposed Carpenter's assertion that voters in 1994 did not understand the downsizing against my insistence that they knew. Gregg quoted my closing prediction: "Some voters will say General Assembly members were ready to take the pay increase. They were ready to take the health insurance. They don't seem to be ready to accept the competition. Voters will say that."[9]

Editorial writers at the *Providence Journal* pounded the committee, calling its behavior "a pathetic ruse to derail this reform: They are saying the voters did not really mean it." The editorial accused the committee of "trying to stop reform by whipping up racial animosity and division, charging — without a smidgen of sense — that a smaller legislature is automatically bad for blacks, other minorities, and women. What an insult to the public's intelligence!"[10]

The editorial also blasted Cicilline for having "the gall to insinuate that Common Cause, which is open to all and champions minority representation, is a racist organization."

The Judiciary Committee eventually voted, 12–1, to send Carpenter's bill to the full House.

Dueling opinion columns kept the question boiling until the House finally took up Carpenter's legislation on May 31. Rep. Mark Heffner argued on the floor, as he had in committee, that it was wrong to ask voters to reconsider the 1994 downsizing question without giving it a chance to be tested. Rep. Mabel M. Anderson of Pawtucket made a speech so memorable that House leaders took the extraordinary step of publishing its full text in the *House Journal*. "There is a saying," the 76-year-old began, "that if you're going to tell a lie, tell it often, and the bigger the better. I have listened to the proponents of downsizing the legislature, and it appears that they have learned that lesson well."[11]

Anderson, wearing her trademark baseball cap, recited names of polling places in her Pawtucket district where voters rejected the 1994 ballot question that included downsizing. "Indeed, at every polling place in my district, people voted it down." Her oratory caught the attention of other representatives around the chamber. "Now I know," Anderson continued in high dudgeon, "what the good folks at Common Cause have said about me: 'The voters of District 77 are not very bright, after all, they keep re-electing Mabel Anderson.'" She named Pawtucket voting places outside her district. "Now I know what my dear friends at Common Cause are now saying: 'Well, what can you expect from Pawtucket?'" On her feet by her desk near the back of the chamber, she had her colleagues' attention. Many swiveled their chairs to watch.

"So who voted for it?" Anderson mocked. "Rumstick Point in Barrington, Poppasquash Point in Bristol, the Dunes Club in Narragansett, Carriage Heights in Lincoln, the East Side of Providence. Well la-de-da!" She chortled, and other representatives hooted along with her. "Well, ladies and gentlemen, that looks like the membership of Common Cause. And that's all downsizing is — a power grab by the people behind Common Cause. You know it, and I know it."

On a roll, she plunged ahead. "Having sat here for almost twenty years, I know exactly what's going to happen if redistricting and downsizing take place together: the same old communities are going to be protected, and the same old communities are going to be screwed. Is the East Side of Providence going to be downsized? Of course not! They'll just chop up Pawtucket like they did ten years ago. Downsize Rumstick Point? Never, when they can rip Warren to shreds."

I watched from the gallery. Who did she believe controlled the mapmaking — Common Cause or the speaker of the House?

The House cheered Anderson and approved Carpenter's anti-downsizing resolution by a vote of 84–15.

Senate leaders recognized the folly of another ballot question on downsizing. They sent Carpenter's proposed amendment to the Committee on Special Legislation, where it died without a hearing or vote.

House leaders may have regretted their reckless anti-downsizing campaign, particularly after the Senate buried their amendment. Several Harwood backers claimed that the Senate majority leader had hung them out to dry, but it was more likely that the Senate leaders saw the public reactions to the House's anti-downsizing spectacle and decided not to subject their members to more of the same. The question remained: Would General Assembly leaders protect communities from being chopped up, as Mabel Anderson had warned? Or would they use downsizing and redistricting — as their predecessors had — to purge mavericks from their ranks?

I liked Marsha Carpenter and voted for her in the September primary. But Latinos had flooded into the district where we lived, and Leon F. Tejada defeated her in the all-important Democratic contest by fewer than one hundred votes. Her career in Rhode Island politics was over and within a year, she and her husband moved to Georgia.

Mabel Anderson won re-election that November, but retired in 2002. Only months after she left the General Assembly a man backing up in a parking lot ran over her. She was rushed to Rhode Island Hospital but died. Among the many tributes to the feisty legislator who wore quirky caps throughout her twenty years in the State House, Rep. Elaine A. Coderre told a reporter that Anderson had talked her into running: "She believed in me before I believed in myself."

38

Kingly Power
1999–2001

THE CALLER BARELY WHISPERED, "I hope you'll understand why I can't tell you my name." I pressed the phone to my ear. She said it was important for Common Cause to review a folder at the Department of Environmental Management (DEM). I scribbled the case number and went that day.

A clerk brought me the folder. DEM had charged Peter K. Wiechers with illegally draining a pond on his farm and clearing marshland along its shore. For bulldozing the centuries-old refuge of migrating birds, Wiechers could face a $3,000 fine and the more costly obligation of restoring the wetlands. Wiechers had hired an environmental lawyer, Sean O. Coffey, who tried to negotiate a settlement.

I knew Coffey as a former senator and skilled attorney who had served as counsel for DEM, but as I paged through the legal documents it became clear that Wiechers had fired Coffey and hired new lawyers. A familiar signature jumped out at me: John B. Harwood. I had never met Wiechers or seen his farm, but I understood why he had fired one of the best environmental lawyers in Rhode Island and hired an attorney with no wetlands experience. Harwood's patronage on behalf of his clients and friends was legendary: he delivered public jobs with excellent benefits and was repaid with reliable tips and eager cooperation across state government. I knew state offices where employees played video solitaire, immune to discipline or firing, more loyal to their patron than their agency. No wonder the person who phoned me had barely spoken above a whisper.

An ethics rule barred public officials like Harwood from advocating for private clients before state agencies where they exercised "fiscal or jurisdictional control."[1] To my mind the speaker exercised fiscal control over DEM through shaping the agency's budget and using his surrogates on the Unclassified Pay Plan Board to set salaries. The only exception to the ethics prohibition allowed lawyer-legislators to practice law in state courts of public record. But DEM was an administrative agency, and Harwood surely knew that its wetlands hearings were out of bounds.

I assumed that the whistleblower who whispered this file number to me had also contacted Operation Clean Government and leaked it to reporters. The secret would come out, but Harwood had beaten ethics complaints before. After six years as speaker his power seemed unassailable, even regal.

Two days after Christmas of 2000, when few were paying attention to political stories, John Harwood's wife received a lifetime appointment as a magistrate in the Superior Court. Patricia Lynch Harwood would start at $100,157, a large step up from the $20,484 annual salary she got for one morning and one evening each week in the Pawtucket Municipal Court. Chief Justice Weisberger announced the appointment of his former law clerk. "I have a very high opinion of her abilities," he told reporter Jonathan Rockoff. Joseph Rodgers, Chief Judge of Superior Court, confirmed the wisdom of this choice. "I don't think," Rodgers said, "she should be disqualified because she is married to the speaker of the House of Representatives."[2]

Harwood swatted away any suggestion that he had influenced his wife's appointment or salary, insisting it made no difference that the House controlled the state budget or that he appointed two members to the Unclassified Pay Plan Board that set salaries for department directors, judges, and magistrates. But her appointment brought a flood of unanswered questions. Who else had applied for this magistrate position? And why, in recent years, had magistrates multiplied like rabbits?

By becoming a magistrate, rather than a judge, Patricia Harwood avoided the judicial selection process that voters established in the 1994 constitutional amendment. Deprived of their historic patronage through judgeships, the General Assembly had fought back by creating magistrates and allowing chief judges to appoint them with no public scrutiny.

Both Bob Arruda of Operation Clean Government and I blasted Patricia Harwood's appointment. "The question arises of the appearance of patronage and nepotism," Arruda told the *Journal*. "In a court system that is seeking to build public confidence, they cannot afford those questions."

Alan Flink, former president of the Bar Association and a member of the Common Cause board fired off a letter to the editor declaring it "unimaginable" that an appointed judge could appoint a magistrate to a life term without review. Flink reminded readers that House leaders had trashed the nomination of Margaret Curran: "It is quite ironic that a superb appointment to the Supreme

Court was struck down by the House and an appointment of the spouse of the House speaker to a judicial office sails through without public scrutiny of any kind. It's just plain wrong."[3]

Operation Clean Government filed a public records request for the names of the thirty applicants the chief justice claimed to have considered. Court officials and the state personnel administrator refused, but could not cite a section of law that backed their position. "The public should know," announced Bob Arruda, and public pressure mounted.

A *Providence Journal* editorial denounced the way Patricia Lynch Harwood landed a "plum job" through a covert process. "The public cannot help harboring suspicions that this was an inside deal for the speaker — especially since court officials refuse to release the names of the thirty applicants to the public. The Judicial Nominating Commission, by contrast, releases the names, résumés, and applications of those who seek judgeships."[4]

After nearly a month of saying that other applicants did not want their names released, Chief Justice Joseph Weisberger released the names of nine.

John Castellucci, a *Providence Journal* reporter, reached me on my cell phone at the State House. Did I know that Daniel V. McKinnon, Harwood's cousin and law partner, was the top contender to replace Patricia Lynch Harwood in the Pawtucket Municipal Court?

I laughed. "Let me get this straight — Patty Harwood got this municipal judgeship while she was at McKinnon and Harwood. Now that she moves up to Superior Court, McKinnon will follow her in the Pawtucket court?"

"You got it."

"Who made the nomination?"

"Chip Hoyas, a member of the city council," Castellucci replied. I knew Hoyas as a highly political insider on the Senate staff.[5] A childhood game came to mind, and I saw McKinnon sliding into a vacant seat. "I suddenly have this picture of a game of musical chairs," I told the reporter. "The ironies are so rich, so troubling. But after a while, nothing surprises."[6]

After two days of public criticism and talk show fire, McKinnon withdrew his name, blaming what he called "self-appointed guardians of what is righteous and holy." He complained: "They are driving good people out of government. I could make more money spending the same amount of hours in my office."[7]

M. Charles Bakst, the *Journal's* political columnist, approached me with a stunning question: Had the mere fact that Patricia Harwood's husband was speaker of the House made her a magistrate, even without his intervention? I answered that no one could tell. "I wonder if there's a sweeping effect when you're in the speaker's family or law firm. The speaker may not even need to ask for the favor. His reach becomes almost kingly."[8]

HARWOOD'S UNBOUNDED POWER brought him legal clients but also began prompting tips and leaks to the press. In February, the *Providence Journal* headlined his advocacy in a liquor license dispute. Harwood's role in the Wiechers wetlands case was hardly unique. The Fox Point Citizens Association had complained that Big Daddy's, a huge nightclub near the Providence waterfront, was filling neighborhood streets with traffic, noise, and crime. The city's board of licenses conducted hearings on the club, and voted unanimously to reject the owner's request to renew her liquor license.

She appealed to the state's liquor control officer and bolstered her legal team by hiring John Harwood. At the hearing, Harwood grilled neighborhood leaders, including Providence Rep. Paul E. Moura of Providence, who had backed the neighbors' case against Big Daddy's. Harwood and Moura were friends and political allies, and Moura — caught between his constituents and his speaker — treated Harwood with elaborate respect. Over and over Moura called Harwood "Mr. Speaker."

The president of the Fox Point Citizens Association told reporter Ariel Sabar what that meant: "We all kind of said, 'Oh my God!' We knew he was the speaker of the House, an enormously powerful and influential guy."[9]

The Big Daddy's dispute landed on the docket of State Liquor Control Administrator Jeffrey J. Greer, a lawyer I had known for ten years in several government posts. He came across as modest, consistent, and professional, and we had lunch occasionally. He struck me as virtually impervious to intimidation. He lived by a motto he took from Ben Franklin: "Glass, china, and reputation are easily cracked, and never well mended."

Despite intense pressure from Big Daddy's attorney John Harwood, Greer declared the club "a continual festering sore on the neighborhood." He found the club owners responsible for "a chronic pattern of disorderly activity" and upheld the license revocation. Big Daddy's closed for good.[10]

As the third longest-ruling speaker in Rhode Island history, Harwood relished his reputation as a hard-checking hockey player; he denied that his legal work for private clients before state agencies was improper. "I have to feed my family," he told reporter Ariel Sabar. But as each new revelation prompted a rehash of prior stories, an aura of sleaze surrounded him. With the prospect of another damaging story slated for the *Providence Sunday Journal's* front page, Harwood did something unexpected and unprecedented — he sent out a press release announcing that he would refrain from representing private clients before state agencies. "As speaker of the house," his statement read, "I must not only refrain from unethical conduct, but I must adhere to ethical standards that assure my legislator colleagues and most importantly the people of Rhode Island that my conduct, both at the State House and in my private law practice, is acceptable."[11]

But only days after Harwood's public announcement, a new House bill proposed to legalize his lucrative practice. Harwood's protégé, Rep. William J. Murphy, filed legislation that would bar rules or regulations of the Ethics Commission from "in any way prohibiting or restricting the practice of law by any individual duly admitted" to the practice of law in Rhode Island.[12] Like a slap shot in hockey, Murphy's bill was a frontal assault on the state's Code of Ethics. It would exempt lawyer-legislators from key ethics rules.

Murphy also filed a companion resolution: the House would ask the Supreme Court whether his first bill would violate the 1986 Ethics Amendment to the Rhode Island Constitution.[13] He requested immediate consideration of his advisory opinion request. No one outside the House leadership had seen the text of Murphy's resolution, nor had any committee heard testimony or voted to recommend going to the Supreme Court. No one publicly discussed the wisdom of scrapping the Ethics Commission's jurisdiction over lawyer-legislators. The request for an advisory opinion passed on a voice vote usually reserved for inconsequential matters.[14]

Harwood wielded the gavel, and like a magician performing a trick, he did his sleight of hand on the record and in plain sight. An ingenious ploy, Murphy's legislation would appeal to judges who thought the Ethics Commission was trying to usurp power from the other three and become a fourth branch of government.

The House Judiciary Committee scheduled a hearing on Murphy's bill exempting lawyer-legislators from the ethics panel's jurisdiction. I emailed an alert to reform groups and concerned citizens statewide. A week later, as members of the House Judiciary Committee arrived to hear the bill, a crowd surrounded the doorway. Inside, except for committee seats at the table, protesters packed the room.

The committee clerk answered a phone call and announced that the hearing had been cancelled. She said the speaker's office had decided to wait for the Supreme Court's advisory. Harwood assured reporter Katherine Gregg that the delay was news to him; Murphy told her he had requested the postponement, although not to "short-circuit" opposition to his bill. "I'm willing to sit down with them at any time," he said.[15]

The entire exercise made Harwood's team look foolish and conniving. The next morning, leaders of Operation Clean Government filed an ethics complaint against the speaker. Sara Quinn had bundled Harwood's intervention on the wetlands case and liquor license hearings. Bob Arruda and Beverly Clay had co-signed the complaint. Within days of the House request for an advisory, the Supreme Court invited briefs from the Ethics Commission, attorney general, Bar Association, and "all other interested persons or organizations." Those of us who opposed the House move on lawyer-legislators had two months to file.

Common Cause had no budget for litigation, but the executive committee set out to raise extra funds. Karen Pelczarski researched and wrote a brief for Common Cause. She argued from the 1986 constitutional amendment on ethics and the Supreme Court's 1992 and 1993 advisory opinions that affirmed the Ethics Commission's constitutional authority to write ethics laws "subject only to judicial review." Her brief noted that federal elected officials were barred from "receiving compensation in connection with any proceeding before any federal government agency." She listed similar prohibitions in twenty-five other states that banned legislators from the private practice of law before government agencies. In eight additional states such appearances were permitted but circumscribed through strict disclosure requirements.[16]

"Lawyer-legislators," Pelczarski wrote, "occupy positions of trust from the public as well as their private clients, and should therefore be required to adhere to ethics codes as well as codes of professional responsibility. If a lawyer-legislator undertakes private representation of a client against his or her governmental unit, either the client or the public must necessarily suffer."[17]

She described the range of potential abuses by lawyer-legislators: "Legislators have the ability to retaliate against agencies that give unfavorable rulings to their private clients, including taking action to cut agency budgets, weaken their powers, and challenge their regulations. Agency officials are aware that legislators possess the power to retaliate, and consequently may feel pressured to take actions in favor of legislators' clients and thereby lose their impartiality. Although lawyer-legislators may not actually retaliate, the appearance of undue influence alone can be damaging."

Twelve days after Pelczarski filed the *amicus* brief for Common Cause, House leaders abruptly withdrew their request for an advisory opinion. As they had filed the request with minimum publicity, they also withdrew it without notice. From the gallery, I saw Murphy drop a folded resolution at a counter below the rostrum. An instant later the clerk announced its number and asked for immediate consent. Members of the House barely heard what it was about before they approved the withdrawal by "unanimous consent" with a voice vote.[18]

Rep. Nicholas Gorham was a legislative bulldog. Short and sturdy, with tousled hair, he seemed eternally cheerful in the face of overwhelming odds. A classic New England Republican, he practiced law with his father, a former House minority leader and state senator. Gorham believed passionately in separation of powers and gladly led the charge even when doing so guaranteed retaliation.

With several other Republicans, he filed a resolution to hold a constitutional convention — specifically to address separation of powers. His resolution incorporated Almond's Question 6:

> WHEREAS, The voters of the state of Rhode Island resoundingly approved, by sixty-six percent (66%), in the general elections

of 2000, the following question: "Should a Constitutional
Convention be called to expressly establish that the Rhode
Island government consists of separate and co-equal legislative,
executive, and judicial branches similar to the governments
established by the United States Constitution and by the
Constitutions of all 49 other states?"[19]

I stood with him in the tiny GOP corner of the House chamber, reviewing its
text. "Let's see," he said with a grin, "if they dare to vote down what two-thirds
of the voters approved last November."

His bill finally got a hearing on March 29 in the House Judiciary Committee,
when only a handful of committee members remained. Gorham acknowledged
that the state Supreme Court had rejected separation of powers. "The justices
left the question squarely before us," he said, "and sixty-six per cent of the people
voted for a chance to resolve it. Once the voters have spoken plainly, it's our
duty to answer on the record."

He reprised the state's historic year when Democrats seized control of the
General Assembly and sacked the entire Supreme Court. "My party, the Republicans," he admitted, "had controlled the General Assembly non-stop for more
than eighty years. But they got greedy. They created boards and commissions
to serve the needs of their friends and business associates. My party abused
power.

"But in the Great Depression," he continued, "the people elected Democrats
under Theodore Francis Green, Robert Quinn, Thomas McCoy, and others. The
people did the right thing for Rhode Island."

His candor about the history captivated the handful of us who remained in
the room. He described how the newly-empowered Democrats had reformed
state government: "They abolished the Republicans' self-serving commissions,
and Lt. Gov. Quinn called for amending the Constitution to bar senators and
representatives from holding any other state office during their terms." Gorham
relished the authority of Quinn's words from the grave.

"Quinn's prescription in 1935 was a constitutional amendment," Gorham said,
"but the newly empowered Democrats never let the voters decide. And here
we are — sixty-six years later — back in the same mess. Only now Democrats
are driving the gravy train."

Gorham had baited his rhetorical hook. He eyed the remaining committee
members around the table. Several avoided his eyes, staring down at their thick
binders of bills. Only Rep. David Cicilline spoke in support of Gorham's resolution. For four years, Cicilline had been sponsoring amendments to establish
separation of powers; all had died in this committee.

Carl Bogus followed Gorham. He introduced himself as a law professor at
Roger Williams University School of Law, and then launched with a question:

"If I were to ask you what the most basic principle of American democracy is, what would you say?" He let the question hang. When no one spoke, he offered two answers. "The first is that 'We the people' get to vote. The second is that all power is not placed in one set of hands. That was the genius of the founders: they separated power among three branches and established checks and balances between those branches."

Without notes Bogus described challenges the U.S. Supreme Court and Congress had faced as administrative agencies developed in the twentieth century. "How could they create bureaucracies and make sure checks and balances continued?" He looked eager for an answer, but again no one spoke, and he continued: "What they did was to carefully divide power over administrative agencies. Congress decides what the agency is, what its powers are, what its funding may be. But that's where the authority of Congress ends. Congress cannot operate the agency or appoint those who execute the law. Congress oversees the agencies with an elaborate structure of review."

No one disputed his point.

"Less than two years ago," Bogus continued, "the Rhode Island Supreme Court said this second most important principle does not exist in Rhode Island. Four justices wrote that plenary power rests in one set of hands: yours." He had led methodically and logically to that absurd conclusion.

"So what happens now?" he asked. "The citizens of Rhode Island are asking you to do an extremely difficult thing: give up power. No less than the most basic principles of American democracy are at stake here. Americans have fought and died for these principles." He asked the Judiciary Committee to send Gorham's resolution for a constitutional convention to the full House. "For an up-or-down vote," he said. "It's that simple."

Rep. Raymond E. Gallison, a Democrat from Bristol and Warren, picked up Bogus' observation that Congress creates federal agencies but the president appoints the officers that run them. "You say that the Rhode Island legislature makes these appointments. So what are the agencies here that the General Assembly has taken over?"

"A long list," said Bogus. "Among them are the Coastal Resources Management Council, the Lottery Commission, and the Unclassified Pay Plan Board. I can rattle off thirty others if you'd like."

Gallison shook his head. "They may appoint a few individuals, but I don't see how the legislature has complete control of those agencies."

Bogus raised his eyebrows. "The appointees are the servants of those who appointed them. We are not children. In the political realm, people are appointed and do what the appointing authority asks. Otherwise they're not reappointed. That's why the United States Constitution and most other state constitutions are explicit in prohibiting legislative appointments to administrative agencies."

By my time to speak only four representatives remained in the room, and the speaker's protégé, Rep. Bill Murphy from West Warwick, was presiding. Looking far younger than his mid-thirties, Murphy wore an impish grin.

I passed out the lists of votes to approve or reject Question 6 in each of the state's thirty-nine communities. Eleven towns, I explained, had approved the measure by seventy percent or higher. "The lowest percentage of approval votes," I noted from the chart, "was recorded in West Warwick — 59.4 percent."

"West Warwick?" Murphy quipped. "My town?"

I told him no other city or town fell below sixty percent. "Even so, Rep. Murphy, a lopsided majority of your constituents want you to address separation of powers."

"Thank you," Murphy said, cheerily. "We'll take it under advisement."

The House Judiciary Committee would not vote that night, but met again to vote on dozens of bills. At one point, I walked behind the seat of Chairman Robert E. Flaherty on my way to the door and noticed his list of bills with the usual codes — a smiley face or frown — beside bill numbers, indicating whether House leaders wanted them passed or held for further study. The committee never voted on Gorham's bill, effectively killing it.

Seven weeks after the House Judiciary Committee buried his call for a constitutional convention, Gorham emailed me to meet him in the House Minority Office, where he came right to the point: "So what do you know about Rules 32(e) and 32(g)?"

Triumphantly, he handed me photocopied pages with sections 32(e) and 32(g) highlighted. The first stated that if the principal sponsor of a bill asked in writing for a vote, the committee must vote within eight days unless the sponsor agreed to a later date. The second permitted a sponsor who had not been granted a vote to write a letter to the speaker, who then became responsible to have the bill discharged from the committee for a vote by the entire House. Harwood's leadership team had established these rules in 1993 to gain Republican support and burnish their reform credentials.

"Try it," I laughed. "The worst they can do is stiff you again."

On May 22, Gorham delivered a letter to the speaker's office. It summarized the committee's failure to vote and formally requested that Harwood "order the immediate discharge of 2001-H 6022 from the Judiciary Committee to the House floor."[20]

During the next month, nothing happened.

On June 28, the final night of the 2001 legislative session, Gorham rose at his desk and publicly invoked Rule 32(g) to place his resolution on the House calendar. He read aloud from his letter.

For a shocked instant, everything stopped. Harwood waved Judiciary Chair Robert Flaherty and House Minority Leader Bob Watson to the rostrum.

Watson — the only one of the four still wearing a suit jacket — brought Gorham. Harwood peered down from the rostrum for a brief private conference. They finished and returned to their places.

"Bottom of the calendar," Harwood intoned from the rostrum and banged his gavel. This was uncharted territory. I watched from the gallery above and behind the weary representatives. I knew that during the hour or two before Gorham's bill came up Harwood's lieutenants would find a parliamentary way to win. I saw whispered exchanges — hands shielding mouths — as indecipherable as football coaches on distant sidelines.

At a microphone below the rostrum, the clerk called a campaign finance reform bill we had wrestled over all spring.[21] Like Murphy's bill to gut ethics enforcement involving lawyer-legislators, this campaign finance legislation originated in scandal. The *Providence Journal* had reported that Woonsocket Mayor Susan D. Menard had spent thousands of dollars from her campaign account at luxury clothing shops.[22] Our 1992 Comprehensive Campaign Finance Law prohibited the personal use of campaign funds; it cited an IRS definition and limited legal expenses to "gaining and holding public office."[23]

Legislative leaders routinely stretched that definition to bizarre lengths, often treating lobbyists to dinner at country clubs and pricey restaurants. They paid with credit cards that they covered from campaign war chests, which were replenished by lobbyist contributions. Lawmakers and lobbyists had used that cozy arrangement to evade the zero-tolerance gift ban — until their backers on the Ethics Commission demolished the rule.[24]

In the 2000 election John Harwood had faced no opponent in his Pawtucket district. Kathy Gregg reported that Harwood raised $180,290 during the year, mostly from lobbyists; he spent $165,970, much of it on expensive meals, sports tickets, gifts, and eighteen out-of-state trips. Gregg noted the speaker's campaign finance reports did not explain where he went on most of those jaunts or how they related to his "gaining or holding public office," a requirement of the 1992 Campaign Finance Law.[25]

Harwood's majority leader, Gerard M. Martineau, had raised $84,145 and spent roughly $73,325 on fancy meals and golf outings. Senate Majority Leader Paul S. Kelly and Sen. William V. Irons, who ousted Kelly late in 2000, had done the same on a smaller scale. In a legislature where Democrats outnumbered Republicans by 5 to 1, the latter had little ability to shape legislation and raised mere pittances. Outspent by a ratio of 10 to 1, House Minority Leader Robert Watson told the *Providence Journal*: "The Republican caucus is Chelo's and Appleby's, not Capital Grille and Raphael's."[26]

Over several years, Common Cause had been pressing the Board of Elections to audit campaign accounts for improper expenditures, but the board claimed it had no authority for such probes. Year after year, efforts to strengthen the law had failed. But headlines in this spring of 2001 evoked the quasi-public abuses of credit cards and lobbyists' gratuities. Under the pressure of public disgust, legislative leaders finally formed a Joint Ad Hoc Committee on Campaign Finance Reform. They directed the panel to resolve "ambiguities" in the law over what constituted "personal use" of campaign funds.

Reform advocates seized the opportunity to push proposals that had been routinely buried in previous years: an auditing and compliance program within the Board of Elections and Rep. Edith Ajello's bill for online filing and disclosure of campaign finance reports. Electronic reporting would allow reporters and citizen researchers to examine contributions and expenditures without copying reams of data. Neither idea was new; together they would make the campaign finance system more accountable and transparent. Both were incorporated verbatim in the *ad hoc* committee's legislation, which Sen. Maryellen Goodwin introduced on June 21.[27]

Goodwin's bill split the difference on what seemed to be legitimate expenses for the "seeking, holding, or maintaining a position within the legislature or other publicly elected body." It outlawed country club dues, most sports tickets, and sundries, but explicitly permitted trips and meals related to the duties of a particular office. It also obligated campaigns to document expenditures, so that legislators could no longer take their families to the Virgin Islands for Christmas and write it off as a campaign expense as Harwood had done.

Goodwin's legislation passed the Senate on June 27 and advanced to the House, which took it up on what would clearly be the last night of the 2001 legislative session. The campaign finance drama played out between skirmishes over separation of powers.

Chaos often reigned on the last night of the session. With House rules suspended, bills backed by the leadership routinely flew over obstacles — sometimes without committee hearings or time for representatives to read their text. Rep. Elaine Coderre, a trusted leader who had served as co-chair of the *ad hoc* committee, presented Goodwin's Senate bill and explained it briefly. Everyone in the red-carpeted chamber knew that Coderre spoke for the House leadership.

I was alarmed when Portsmouth Rep. Charles J. Levesque moved to raise the threshold for mandatory electronic filing of campaign finance reports from $5,000 to $10,000. From the gallery, I could not see the text of his amendment, but I understood instantly that it would have excused many legislators from filing their reports electronically. Whether Levesque meant to create a two-tiered reporting system, his amendment would have done so. I felt relieved when Rep. Gordon D. Fox, who had served on the *ad hoc* panel, urged his colleagues to reject Levesque's amendment, and they did, 66–9. After minor technical amendments, final House passage came on a vote of 89–0. Campaign finance reform — compromised and imperfect but still a long step forward — went back to the Senate for a final vote.

Then, without warning, the clerk droned the number of Gorham's separation of powers resolution. Before the sound faded, Judiciary Chair Bob Flaherty was on his feet. He moved to recommit the resolution to his committee. Rep. Timothy Williamson, the committee's vice chair, shouted a second. From the rostrum, Harwood declared that a motion to recommit was not debatable. This was a classic parliamentary power play.

Fifty-seven House Democrats quickly sided with Harwood to prevent public debate, while twenty-five voted to address the issue. The move to recommit preempted the need for a vote against separation of powers, but aborting the debate had the same result. The public call for a constitutional convention to address separation of powers was dead — at least for 2001.

I met Nick Gorham in an empty hallway outside the chamber. "Harwood won tonight," he said, "but it'll be a Pyrrhic victory for him." He handed me a printout of the vote, which included thirteen Republicans and twelve Democrats who voted for a full debate on separation of powers. I liked the balance and promised a Common Cause honor roll.[28]

"Gotta go back in," he said energetically. We shook hands and then hugged.

The young lawyer reminded me of Thomas Wilson Dorr, the lawyer-legislator who drafted the People's Constitution 160 years earlier and led the People's Convention of 1841. With chunky torsos and round faces, both Gorham and Dorr ran fearlessly at their foes; both understood the need to study history and shape it; and both worked toward government structures that would empower ordinary people to participate.

Dorr lost the rebellion that historians later named for him. The victors convicted him of treason against the state and sentenced him in 1844 to life in prison. Months in a frigid jail cell broke Dorr's health. Released by an act of the General Assembly, the iconic advocate died of pneumonia in 1854 believing he had failed.[29] I hoped Gorham would fare better. But would he or any of us live to see separation of powers in these marble halls? Or would legislative leaders continue to rule Rhode Island as they and their predecessors had for three centuries?

39

Ethics Meltdown
2000–02

THE MELTDOWN OF THE ETHICS COMMISSION became inevitable on May 23, 2000, when five recently appointed commissioners — all attorneys — voted to rescind the zero-tolerance gift rule and replace it with the most permissive gratuities rule in the United States. Any public official could accept gifts worth up to $450 in a year from any "interested person." Four members of the Ethics Commission — one lawyer and three non-lawyers — had pleaded for delay, arguing that the new rule was so poorly crafted that it would legalize virtually unlimited gifts to legislators, town council members, zoning board members, health inspectors, and police officers. But in a series of 5–4 votes, the new attorneys approved the rule.[1]

That night Common Cause board members and I signed an ethics complaint against Thomas Goldberg. Our complaint charged: "Thomas D. Goldberg used his public office to modify the conditions under which commercial lobbyists, including his brother and law partner Robert D. Goldberg, could provide entertainment and other gratuities to public officials." The new gift rule, we argued, would financially benefit a small class of commercial lobbyists, particularly Bob Goldberg and the Goldberg brothers' law firm."[2] Further, we charged, Goldberg had rejected private and public requests that he recuse himself.

One important fact did not appear in the complaint: Maureen McKenna Goldberg, the wife of Robert Goldberg and sister-in-law of Thomas Goldberg, sat as a justice on the Rhode Island Supreme Court.

On June 20, the Ethics Commission authorized its executive director, Martin Healey, to hire an independent prosecutor for the case.[3] Healey searched for a Rhode Island lawyer who had experience with white-collar crime and would dare to face the Goldbergs. He found a former state prosecutor who was about to sign a contract[4] when — seven weeks after the Common Cause complaint against Tom Goldberg — Operation Clean Government filed three complaints: one each against Commissioners Goldberg, Melvin Zurier, and Robin Main.[5]

The OCG complaints complicated the case — legally, politically, and emotionally. Zurier and Main worked in large firms and had only peripheral connections to lobbyists; by contrast, Bob Goldberg's lobbying looked like the family firm's core business.

A serious legal issue emerged when the special prosecutor announced a conflict involving Zurier or Main and had to withdraw.[6] Healey had to restart the search for an independent prosecutor. After several weeks, he phoned to tell me he was hiring Daniel I. Small, a former deputy U.S. attorney from Massachusetts. He said Small probed corruption in the office of former Boston Mayor Kevin White, and he had defended former Louisiana governor Edwin Edwards. "He teaches at Harvard," Healey added. "It may be better that he comes from Massachusetts."

That made sense. Even with thousands of lawyers in Rhode Island, the top guns all knew each other. Small would not be intimidated by the fact that Goldberg's sister-in-law sat on the state Supreme Court.

Small wasted no time in coming to meet with the Common Cause board members who had signed our complaint. He warned that no matter how clear the facts might seem, it would be tough to convince five commissioners that Goldberg had committed knowing and willful violations. "If I were picking a jury," he said dryly, "this would be a non-starter."

"We understand that," said Burt Hoffman, who had been a newspaper editor in Washington and a top staff member for Democrats in Congress, "but they've left us no choice. Those hacks opened the door for corporate lobbyists to make out like bandits. Unless this gets prosecuted there'll be no ethics left in the Ethics Commission."

At the time I never imagined that Dan Small would come under fire over an obscure principle called *pro hac vice,* which roughly translated means "for this turn" or "for this particular occasion." Out-of-state attorneys with special expertise routinely practiced in Rhode Island courts, so I paid little attention to the concept before Healey drew me into his office in September. "Nothing may come of this," he said confidentially, "but I want to mention *pro hac vice.*"

Healey said he had been playing phone tag with Superior Court Judge Frank J. Williams who was then presiding over motions for out-of-state attorneys to practice in Rhode Island courts.[7] "When we finally connected," Healey told me, "Williams said he'd been calling for me to cover a class for him at Roger Williams Law School. When I asked him whether we needed to seek *pro hac vice* for a Massachusetts attorney to investigate a matter of probable cause before the commission, he said it wasn't necessary at this stage."

Healey described for me the technicalities of *pro hac vice* in Rhode Island, where thousands of lawyers competed for a small market and did not welcome outsiders. It had been used to stall Healey's own application to practice law in Rhode Island until the state Supreme Court granted permission.[8] He had not mentioned Small's name to the judge or the fact that this investigation involved members of the commission. "Williams told me to come back later if the case went up to Superior Court. He said, 'Don't worry for now. It's just chickenshit.'"

I laughed. "He actually said it was 'just chickenshit'?"[9]

"He did. Would I put those words in his mouth?"

We both laughed. It was September, and neither of us had any idea how crucial Williams's unforgettable phrase would become.

The Goldbergs waged a scorched earth campaign, and a Supreme Court interpretation of a law enacted in 1991 — ironically at the urging of Common Cause — helped them. The ethics complaint Common Cause filed against Edward DiPrete in January 1989 had languished for more than two years. DiPrete served a term as governor, lost the 1990 election, and left office. In June 1991, twenty-nine months after we filed the complaint, commissioners finally agreed there was probable cause — the civil equivalent of an indictment — to prosecute the former governor.[10]

To speed this process for future complaints Rae Condon drafted legislation that would require the Ethics Commission to complete its preliminary investigation within 180 days. To accommodate legal stalling and procedural delays, our bill allowed two additional sixty-day extensions "for good cause shown." Our proposal became law in 1991[11] and seemed to keep investigations moving. In 1994, a Superior Court judge interpreted the law as allowing investigators 300 days to complete their report.

Problems emerged in 1998 when the Rhode Island Supreme Court ruled on a case in which investigators submitted their report before the 300-day deadline, but the commission voted on probable cause at its next meeting, just beyond the 300th day. The high court overturned an obscure case but wiped out several high-profile cases in which probable cause hearings occurred after the three hundredth day. The Ethics Commission was forced to dismiss cases against former House Speaker Matthew Smith, former Secretary of State Barbara Leonard, a former lottery commissioner, two town administrators, and former Providence Retirement Board Chair Stephen T. Day.[12] In that case members of Fire Fighters' Local 799 had filed a complaint against Day for steering Providence pension funds to money managers who plied him with expensive meals, sports tickets, trips, and hotel stays.[13] Under law, the Ethics Commission might have levied a $25,000 fine for each of forty-three specific charges.

Let off by the scheduling technicality, Day crowed to reporters: "Say goodbye to the Sham Squad!"[14]

The 300-day rule became a target for the Goldbergs. Thomas Goldberg refused to answer Dan Small's questions, while his brother Robert sued to quash subpoenas for information about their firm.[15] With a rhetorical flourish, Bob Goldberg complained to the attorney general that Small had "knowingly and flagrantly violated the rules and regulations of the Commission to the detriment of my client. He has done so in a deceitful manner."[16] He fired off similar complaints to disciplinary groups responsible for attorneys in Rhode Island and Massachusetts.[17]

In a memo defending the need to subpoena documents Small wrote bluntly that the Goldberg brothers were deliberately delaying the investigation. But when Small gave the *Providence Journal* a copy of his legal memo on the need for a subpoena, Robert Goldberg blasted him for releasing confidential material related to a complaint.[18]

The Goldberg brothers clearly meant to run out the 300-day clock. Between December 2000 and February 2001, the Ethics Commission spent countless hours in executive session — not dealing with the substance of the complaints against Thomas Goldberg, but with barrages of litigation Robert Goldberg launched. Reporters and the public left outside closed doors could only wonder what was being debated about complaints filed against Goldberg by Common Cause and Operation Clean Government.[19]

Documents on the question of whether Daniel Small could investigate the complaints against Thomas Goldberg became public when the case went to Superior Court. At the end of January 2001, Judge Michael A. Silverstein ruled that other available sources should have been subpoenaed first. "Based upon the papers before this court," Silverstein wrote, "the information can be obtained from a non-party in this matter, specifically the respondent's brother, Robert Goldberg."

Bob Goldberg reveled in Silverstein's ruling. "From the outset," he told a reporter, "we have said there were other ways to do this without subpoenaing Tom. Now, how many state dollars later, the judge told them the same thing."[20]

Goldberg's charge that Small was practicing law illegally went up to the Supreme Court, and Martin Healey traced the events in an affidavit. The Ethics Commission had authorized him to hire an outside prosecutor, and he had chosen Small "because of his qualifications and experience in investigations of this type." Healey noted that he had contacted Judge Williams, who had been in charge of the formal and special cause calendar in Superior Court, about *pro hac vice* for Small. "Without providing specific information about the cases at issue," Healey wrote, "I advised Judge Williams that the issue involved an attorney whose office, practice, and admission to the bar were outside the State of Rhode Island, but who would appear before the commission on a complaint matter."

Healey added: "Judge Williams advised me that since there was no matter pending before the courts he did not see a basis for bringing such a motion. He further advised me it was his recommendation that the attorney's status be disclosed to the commission — which I told him had been done — and that if an objection were lodged at some future date, it might be appropriate for his court to deal with the matter." Healey noted that he also communicated Williams' comments to the vice chair of the Ethics Commission, Richard E. Kirby.[21]

In February 2001, five months after his "chickenshit" conversation with Marty Healey, Superior Court Judge Frank Williams became Chief Justice of the Rhode Island Supreme Court. When the question of *pro hac vice* for Daniel Small came to the high court, he and Associate Justice Maureen McKenna Goldberg recused themselves.

On March 1, two justices — Victoria S. Lederberg and John P. Bourcier — issued a one-page order denying *pro hac vice* for Daniel Small to continue work on the ethics complaints. They gave no explanation and provided no written opinion, even though critics correctly noted that the Supreme Court had routinely granted permission in similar cases. One legal article later blamed the two for failing to give adequate reasons for denying *pro hac vice* in an important case.[22]

Justice Robert Flanders dissented and later wrote that he did not remember the high court ever withholding *pro hac vice* "merely because the attorneys involved may have rendered legal services to the clients in question before they sought or obtained court approval to represent them in connection with pending or contemplated judicial proceedings." He noted that parties "should not be allowed to use 'kill the messenger' litigation tactics as a transparent ploy" and observed that by denying a reasonable request the court had fanned "a small brush fire into a raging conflagration."[23]

Robert Goldberg's charge that Healey had engaged in "criminal acts" by paying Small roughly $40,000 landed in the lap of the high court's Unauthorized Practice of Law Committee. The panel's chairperson told the *Providence Journal*: "It is an awful waste of court resources, our time, the attorney general's time and the time and resources of public officials to get involved in these things, when the only real practical result is that one party to a controversy may get some advantage over another."[24]

Wasteful or not, the strategy served its purpose — stalling the investigation to death. The Common Cause complaint against Tom Goldberg hit its 300-day limit and died, but the Ethics Commission held an emergency meeting to extend the OCG investigation for another sixty days.

On March 13, the Ethics Commission fired Daniel Small and voted not to pay his outstanding bill. Healey recommended that J. Richard Ratcliffe, the former assistant attorney general whose sleuthing brought indictments against key operatives in the DiPrete administration, be hired to salvage the case. The commissioners voted instead to hire William C. Maaia, a decent lawyer who had little experience investigating conflicts of interest or white-collar crime. I told reporters I was troubled by the commission's choice of Maaia over Ratcliffe.[25]

Robert Goldberg responded with a sarcastic question about Healey: "He did such a good job with the first one, he wants to hire another?"

Providence Journal columnist Bob Kerr wrote: "A majority of the commission members did what they could to further the impression that the investigation was being sent to a place the sun doesn't reach." A *Journal* editorial noted that the clock was ticking on the ethics complaints and asked: "What is one to make of all this? Simple: The powerful do not want an aggressive Ethics Commission holding officials accountable."[26]

Dan Small ended his investigation with a dramatic public act. After being accused, denigrated, and denied payment, he appeared at the commission's open session on March 20 to demand $60,000 on his contract. He declared that out-of-state lawyers had often done special work for Rhode Island commissions without seeking or obtaining *pro hac vice* permission. Then, without warning, Small drew a thick printed document from his briefcase and plopped it at the center of the commission's table, declaring there was ample probable cause that Commissioner Thomas Goldberg had violated the law.[27]

Tom Goldberg leaped to his feet, shouting that Small was violating his rights and the commission's rules against public disclosure of an investigative report. Small waited for quiet. He then announced that he did not think there was probable cause against Zurier and that that his investigation on Main was not complete.[28]

After months of maneuvers and rhetoric from lawyers on the Ethics Commission, Dan Small had laid a case on the table. Whether his findings would ever become public, his dramatic act exposed the sham. Predictably, Bob Goldberg phoned reporters to accuse Small of "plain bad-faith conduct."[29]

Justices Bourcier and Lederberg had not explained why they denied Small permission to prosecute the case, but when controversy boiled over they rushed to justify themselves. Bourcier told reporter Jonathan Rockoff that Small had wrongly practiced law for the Ethics Commission without obtaining proper permission. "Had he come here before engaging in criminal activity in this state, I would have approved it," Bourcier said in an interview. "Had this guy come here with clean hands, we would have permitted it."[30]

Martin Healey reported his conversation with Judge Frank Williams about *pro hac vice* many months earlier, who had told him it was not necessary at the investigative phase. Healey told Rockoff he had rechecked his own notes and that he had discussed his call with Judge Williams with several people at the time they spoke about *pro hac vice.*

Small confirmed to Rockoff that they would have sought written permission if they had any "inkling" that it was necessary before he investigated allegations in the pending complaints. Then the reporter went to Williams, who fudged: "Even if I had said 'no problem,'" the chief justice said, "my opinion is worthless in comparison with the statutes and regulations of the Supreme Court."

Sara Quinn, now a lawyer for Operation Clean Government, related the history of outside lawyers brought in for special investigations by state commissions without first seeking or obtaining *pro hac vice* permission. Even Alan I. Baron, one of the "Baltimore Bullets" who investigated the RISDIC collapse, said, "I don't think I ever appeared in court, which is normally when you file for permission."

Justice Victoria S. Lederberg weighed in with an extraordinary opinion piece in the *Providence Journal*.[31] "Almost all *pro hac vice* motions are unopposed and are granted by this court," she wrote. "In Small's case, however, the motion was vigorously opposed by allegations that Small violated rules of practice and criminal statutes of the state." Lederberg quoted the decision of Superior Court Judge Silverstein, which ruled that without a written order from Williams, "I am not prepared to deal with Mr. Small's request for *pro hac* status." She condemned any suggestion that she and Bourcier had denied Small permission because of their relationship with Justice Maureen McKenna Goldberg.

The *coup de grâce* came when Chief Justice Frank J. Williams wrote personally to each member of the Ethics Commission and enclosed an op-ed piece he was submitting to the *Providence Journal* entitled: "Ethics flap is Mr. Healey's fault." He wrote that while he presided over the Superior Court's Formal and Special Cause Calendar, he had spoken twice with Healey about hiring an out-of-state counsel to practice before the commission. He added that since the Ethics Commission was not a court, and since there was no action filed in the Superior Court, "I could not consider any application to permit this Massachusetts lawyer to practice in Rhode Island — particularly if it were only before the commission." In an interesting twist, Williams argued that Healey's own experience trying to obtain *pro hac vice* in 1995 should have alerted him to the problem. Without acknowledging the rule's ambiguity about outside lawyers who never appear in court, Williams laid all the blame on Healey: "The failure by Mr. Healey to follow proper protocol for admission for Mr. Small is the sole reason for this unfortunate imbroglio."[32]

The chief justice could not have issued a clearer invitation to fire Healey, and three lawyers on the ethics panel set out to do it. On April 3, vice chair Richard Kirby spoke of Williams' newspaper piece as grounds for firing the executive director. As if it were planned, Francis Flanagan moved to terminate Healey and James Murray seconded the motion.

James Lynch, the retired Army colonel, said he could not support Flanagan's motion. "If we have a problem with our executive director, we should tell him what the problem is and give him a chance to correct it." He reminded commissioners that they had been talking about opinion pieces in newspapers. "The only specific that's changed is this letter from Chief Justice Williams, and it's clear to me that he may have contributed to the misunderstanding at the heart of this crisis."

Healey sat at a small square table near the commissioners, his face drained of color. He listened as commission counsel William J. Conley said the director was an "at-will" employee, that he had a right to know the basis of his termination, and that he must have an opportunity to respond.

Although not in any official role as prosecutor, Commissioner Frank Flanagan was in effect prosecuting Healey. Asserting that Williams' version of the *pro hac vice* phone calls was true and Healey's false, he accused Healey of not telling the commission that his own 1995 *pro hac vice* case was a roadmap and charged that he had not followed through on getting the special counsel admitted. Finally, he blamed Healey for not detailing Small's bills for the investigation, adding that the commission needed to have more confidence in its executive director. "To use a navy phrase," the former JAG declared, "this ship has run aground, and it's time to right the course."

Healey responded without visible anger as he described the challenge of investigating complaints against three members of the commission. "I perceived it as my responsibility to act as a buffer between the commission and the investigation." He insisted that the amount of Small's contract was a public record and that he had said so on at least one occasion when commissioners asked. He rattled off numbers he had given in December and said the minutes showed that commissioners had not asked for more information. Case by case Healey summarized the problems that contributed to the overturning of several commission decisions, not least among them the lack of a hearing room in the mid-1990s.

Then he described his two phone conversations with Frank Williams, a man he had considered his friend. "I've searched my mind," he said, "and I stand on my recollections of those conversations. I took notes, a staff member was present for part of one conversation, and within ten minutes I related what he said to people in the office."[33]

From the center chair, Richard Kirby declared his personal affection for Healey. "What this comes down to is that Marty Healey is a fine lawyer, but there are philosophical differences between him and members of this commission. Passion, conviction, and zeal have clouded his judgment."

Commissioner Paul Verrecchia, the chief of security at Brown, said he could not remember one instance when Healey had not leveled with them. He said complaints against members of the commission created a dilemma: "We felt awkward about micromanaging. Maybe he should have hit us in the head, but that's not the way he works."

I listened, took notes, counted votes. Zurier, Main, and Goldberg had recused themselves, and only six commissioners remained. Less than a year earlier,

Flanagan, Murray, and Kirby had voted with Goldberg to get rid of the gift ban. Now their measured words, like a drum roll, presaged a firing.

Mel Zurier sat behind me in the audience. He had undergone his own shock of recognition when he compared their vote on the hastily amended $150/$450 gift rule to the Dred Scott decision. Their vote for a recklessly permissive gift rule had begun the meltdown of the Ethics Commission.

Lynch and Verrecchia had voted no on the gift rule. Their comments indicated that both would vote against firing Marty Healey. The one unknown was a newly appointed dentist, the first non-lawyer appointed in years, Diane T. Monti-Markowski. If she voted no, there would be a 3 to 3 tie, and the motion to fire Healey would fail. I held my breath.

When her turn came, Monti-Markowski explained that she was new to the commission and did not want to make a mistake. She abstained.

Still seated at his table, Healey sucked in air. It was over.

Afterward, in comments to reporters, he dismissed the reasons given for his firing as pretext. The author of the original zero-tolerance gift rule said sadly that he had been fired for doing his job too well. "Nobody likes a watchdog."[34]

Providence Journal political commentator M. Charles Bakst, who sat through the Healey firing, wrote that it had been years since he "felt such alarm about ethics in Rhode Island." He added: "It was obvious that the commissioners who wanted to fire Healey were not interested in such small details as, um, facts. For example, they did not question Williams over discrepancies between his version and Healey's version of their conversations."[35]

I told reporters I blamed the chief justice: "It's clear that Marty has been made a scapegoat and that Judge Williams's op-ed piece was as close as you could come to a directive to fire him."

Williams tried to deflect blame by again slamming Healey for failing to obtain *pro hac vice* at the start. "The problem was not what the court did, but what the Ethics Commission did not do," the chief justice told the *Providence Journal*. Williams insisted that he spoke out because watchdog groups were attacking the court's integrity: "Just because you get an adverse ruling doesn't mean there is a vast conspiracy. They ought to look at the source: the commission and its staff."[36]

Besides his opinion piece blaming the meltdown on Healey, the chief justice did interviews on talk radio shows, defending himself and his fellow justices.

Law professor Carl Bogus, a member of the Common Cause board, took Williams to task in a *Providence Journal* commentary. The justices had been stung, he wrote, by a firestorm of criticism. But they had failed to issue a written opinion when they disqualified Small. "They may routinely grant *pro hac vice* applications without opinions, but here they were taking the more unusual step of denying an application — and doing so in a case of great public interest."

Bogus also noted that the justices had other ways "to vindicate the principle that out-of-state lawyers may not practice before Rhode Island commissions without prior permission. Small could have been sanctioned, fined, or perhaps been made to forfeit fees for prior work, for example." He concluded that the justices' media efforts were bound to fail: "By leaving the bench and thrusting themselves into the hurly burly of political debate, the justices made themselves appear even more politically interested and opened themselves up to further questions and criticisms, fair or unfair."[37]

The *Providence Journal* also printed my comments on Healey's ouster. I wrote that after commissioners enacted the zero-tolerance gift ban, Gov. Almond and legislative leaders packed the panel with well-connected lawyers who rescinded the gift ban and opened the floodgates to gifts from lobbyists. Watchdog groups filed complaints against commissioners, and Healey had needed to find independent counsel. He hired Small, but the Goldbergs stonewalled and filed false charges. Worst of all, Williams hid his own role in the controversy and scapegoated Healey.[38]

I proposed a series of reforms aimed at restoring the Ethics Commission, but the damage had already been done. Many Rhode Islanders, even Common Cause board members, said the time had come to scrap the Ethics Commission and start over. I wrote that reconstruction — particularly the hiring of a new executive director — would be hard. Who would take the job after what happened to Healey?

A few members of the General Assembly recognized the urgency of rebuilding the commission. Over several years, Rep. David Cicilline had introduced bills to strengthen it, and now he filed new legislation that would open the process and set standards for appointments. "There's been a real loss of confidence in the way the Ethics Commission is operating," he told reporters. "The public has grown very frustrated with watching this process." Cicilline pushed without success to get his legislation onto the House floor for a vote.[39]

Common Cause honored Martin Healey at our annual meeting that November, when we brought together the likely candidates for governor in the election still one year away. Five prospective candidates sat near the front, ready for our town hall meeting — Republicans James S. Bennett, Donald L. Carcieri, and Bernard A. Jackvony, with Democrats Antonio J. Pires and Sheldon Whitehouse — when Healey's award was announced.

Resembling a slim, grown-up Harry Potter, Healey made his way through a ballroom filled with round tables. People began clapping, then rose to their feet and cheered him. I read a framed citation that praised "his professionalism in office, his personal integrity, and his courage in the face of relentless attack." As I handed it to him, applause washed over him again.

"Thank you," he called out, his boyish tenor full of emotion. "I don't think I can tell you how much that meant to me."

He outlined the problems he had faced in investigating complaints against members of the commission and his decision to hire Dan Small. He sketched stalling tactics that ran out the clock and ended with the opinion piece by Frank Williams. Making light of the ugly drama, Healey told us how he tried to answer his 8-year-old daughter's question about why he was coming back to Providence for our event. "I said, 'Your Daddy is going to get an award,' and she said, 'Is that like a trophy?'

"I said, 'Well, sort of,' and she said, 'What for?'

"And I said, 'There were some people who are supposed to make sure other people obey the law, whom a lot of people thought broke the law themselves, and they didn't want that to be investigated. And I told them that they had to play by the same rules as everybody else, and they didn't like that, but I insisted on it.'

" 'Then somebody else who was supposed to enforce the law didn't tell the truth about some conversations he had with me, and people tried to make me change my story about that, and I wouldn't. And people didn't like that.'

" 'Then the people I worked for wanted the investigator I had hired to go away. They wanted me to fire him, and I wouldn't do that. I insisted they play by the same rules as everybody else.' So, I said, 'That is why I am getting an award.'

"At that point, my son, who is six, piped up and asked, 'Why are you getting an award again?'

"My daughter, without missing a beat, said: 'Daddy's getting a trophy because he's stubborn.' "[40]

Our audience burst into laughter and thunderous applause.

Healey turned his attention to the likely gubernatorial candidates who were about to come on stage for a town hall conversation. "Whoever becomes the next governor hopefully will take more seriously than Gov. Almond did the people he puts on what is a very important agency."

40

Redistricting Revenge
2000–02

REDISTRICTING may be the deadliest political weapon — and the one that voters understand least. State constitutions require the redrawing of legislative and congressional districts every decade, and most establish minimal standards.[1] But state legislative leaders often manipulate the mapping process to cull mavericks or for partisan advantage. Redistricting rewards allies, demolishes enemies, and drives American politics.

The practice of gerrymandering legislative and congressional districts began with America's founders. Elbridge Gerry, who signed the Declaration of Independence and the Articles of Confederation, became governor of Massachusetts in 1810. In 1812, Gerry oversaw the redrawing of state senate districts that packed Federalist voters into a contorted district that allowed his Democratic-Republicans to win in the surrounding districts. Though Gerry despised partisanship, he signed the new districts into law.

The Federalists felt cheated, and the editor of their newspaper, the *Boston Gazette*, likened the bizarre district to a salamander. A cartoonist added wings to create the dragon that merged Gerry's name into a new word that functioned as either a noun or verb: "gerrymander."[2]

Exactly 170 years later, Rhode Island Senate Majority Leader Rocco A. Quattrocchi and his backers, nicknamed "Rocco's Robots," thrust Minority Leader Lila M. Sapinsley and maverick Democrat Richard A. Licht into a single district on the East Side of Providence. No matter which one lost, Quattrocchi expected to eliminate one troublemaker, but his gerrymandering ravaged neighborhoods and provoked lawsuits in both state and federal courts.

On June 3, 1982, Superior Court Judge James Bulman struck down Quattrocchi's Senate maps for violating constitutional standards of compactness and diluting the African-American vote.[3]

Too late to redraw districts before the 1982 election, the General Assembly revived the decade-old Senate districts, and Republicans promptly sued in U.S. District Court.

In February 1983, Senior U.S. District Judge Raymond J. Pettine ruled that blatant political gerrymanders violated the one-person, one-vote principle established by the U.S. Supreme Court. Pettine ordered new districts and a special Senate election to be held that June.[4]

Quattrocchi's botched gerrymandering wasted $1.5 million in tax dollars and left a lame duck Senate operating through the 1983 legislative session. Payback came in the June special election, when voters tripled the number of Republican senators to twenty-one. The surviving Democrats ousted Quattrocchi from his post.

In a defensive interview, he told the *Providence Journal*: "I didn't rob a bank, I didn't kill anyone. If I did, it would be justified. But I treated all those people fairly."[5] Ironically, Quattrocchi's heavy-handed redistricting empowered the very mavericks he meant to harm. Public support prompted both Sapinsley and Licht to run for lieutenant governor, ironically against each other. In the 1984 statewide election, Licht won by less than one percent.

Since the Bloodless Revolution of 1935, factions of Democrats had often battled for control of the General Assembly. Leadership contests resembled family feuds more than policy debates. After the 1988 election, two Democrats — David R. Carlin Jr. and John J. Bevilacqua, son of the former chief justice — had battled to lead the state Senate. Carlin won a narrow majority among Democrats and became majority leader, but Bevilacqua forged an alliance with Minority Leader Robert D. Goldberg that gave him *de facto* control. Goldberg reaped his reward when his wife, Maureen McKenna Goldberg, vaulted from serving as the Westerly town solicitor to a Superior Court judgeship.[6]

In 1990, after a majority of Democrats chose John Bevilacqua as their leader, some Carlin supporters — particularly East Providence Sen. William V. Irons — kept railing against him. In November 1992, Bevilacqua allies lost to Republican challengers in four key races,[7] which shifted the balance again, and Senate Democrats elected North Smithfield Sen. Paul S. Kelly as majority leader.[8] Bevilacqua loyalists lost their committee leadership positions, offices, and prime parking places.

Although Bevilacqua chose not to seek re-election in 1994, survivors from his faction remained at odds with Kelly's troops through several election cycles. As the 2000 legislative session ended, the Senate seethed with caustic comments, hostile glances, and clenched jaws. One afternoon, I bounded up a zigzagging back stairway and crashed a furtive huddle of senators who had been Bevilacqua stalwarts. Too late to turn away, I made a joke. "Sorry," I said, "is this your office now?"

Sen. Stephen Alves shifted position to let me pass. "It's all we've got," he quipped, "at least for now."

Barely two weeks after the session ended, smoke cleared from the battlefield. One of Majority Leader Paul S. Kelly's long-time supporters, East Providence Sen. William V. Irons, launched a hostile take-over.[9] Though he had long been Bevilacqua's implacable foe, Irons now formed an alliance with Bevilacqua survivors and made no secret of his ambition. "This is not about Paul Kelly," he told reporter Christopher Rowland. "It's about me wanting my opportunity."[10]

In a legislature where the pivotal battles involved factions of Democrats, Irons and Kelly targeted the all-important September 12 primary election. Each recruited surrogates, helping them with money and expertise. On primary night, four of Irons' candidates defeated Kelly backers. "With tonight's elections," Irons declared, "the tide has turned. The momentum is now in our camp."[11]

One contest had racial overtones. Irons backed incumbent Robert T. Kells, a Providence police lieutenant and former Bevilacqua ally who was white, against Juan M. Pichardo, a Latino challenger supported by Kelly. Kells won by 94 out of 2,466 votes cast.[12] Late in September, Irons snagged Kelly's Deputy Majority Whip Thomas R. Coderre, and the contest ended. Other senators fell into line. "I almost felt like I had swallowed a bowling ball when I had to make the decision," Woonsocket Sen. Marc A. Cote told a reporter. "That's the way the dynamics of leadership politics takes place."[13]

Well before the November 2000 election it became obvious that Irons would lead the Senate. The question remained: in the redistricting soon to begin, how would Irons treat Kelly and the fifteen senators who stuck with him?[14]

Since the 1980s, Common Cause had promoted rules that would make redistricting independent, fair, and open, but we achieved little. For the 2001–02 remapping, we set out to build a coalition that could expose gerrymanders and discourage the manipulation of racial minorities. We began meeting with civil rights leaders, community organizers, lawyers, and clergy. Most were amazed at the maps from 1991–92, where — like fossils in layers of shale — the gerrymandered districts were obvious.

Leaders of the Urban League and the NAACP had challenged racial gerry-manders in the 1982 Senate plan and eventually prevailed in federal court. From that victory came new Senate districts and the special 1983 election in which Charles D. Walton became Rhode Island's first African-American state senator.

At the Urban League's squat, fortress-like headquarters on Prairie Avenue, I unrolled maps for executive director Dennis B. Langley and several staff members. "Our community knows both the pitfalls and the promise of redistricting," Langley said with a soft Caribbean inflection. "The influx of Latinos creates a new dynamic that we need to handle with great care." He asked who might lead a coalition to fight for fair redistricting.

I suggested Angel Taveras, a young Latino lawyer who had gone from public schools in South Providence to Harvard University and Georgetown Law School. At twenty-nine, Taveras had run a credible campaign for Congress in the 2nd District, winning hundreds of votes in white suburbs and villages across South County. In Providence, he ran a close second behind incumbent Congressman Jim Langevin.

A week later, Angel Taveras sat with his back to a glass wall in a conference room at Brown Rudnick, the Providence law firm.[15] Behind and below him lay a patchwork quilt of historic houses. "Why me?" he asked with a smile. "You're not even letting me catch my breath."

I talked about his personal biography and influence in the Latino community. I said the coalition would need his intellect and skills.

Slim and geeky behind rimless glasses, he was not eager. "Why not Juan Pichardo?" he asked.

I said Pichardo had been aligned with Paul Kelly in 2000 and planned to run again in 2002. "Part of our job will be to prevent the drawing of districts that pit blacks against Latinos on the South Side."

"What would you want me to do?"

"Lead the coalition," I said. "I'd be glad to serve as secretary and do a lot of the legwork. We can run it out of the Common Cause office, but you would be the coalition's face and voice."

"Let me read these materials," he said. "It's a highly specialized area of the law. I've never done this work or read the Supreme Court cases."

On a bitter December night, I made my way along the side of a huge church, up steep stairs into a former convent that was now home to Progreso Latino, the leading social services agency in Central Falls. Tomás Ávila, its executive director, invited the dozen visitors around a square of tables to introduce ourselves.[16]

Patrick Tengwall described the Urban League's work in previous rounds of redistricting. "We've seen huge changes in technology," he said, "but redistricting remains the ultimate insiders' game. It will take strong voices to protect our communities."

Nancy Rhodes introduced herself as president of Common Cause. "I don't know the technicalities, but I know the only way we can get this right is by working together."

Next to her was Joe Buchanan, a burly community activist from South Providence. "I represent the black community and the Green Party," he began. "I don't know about this computer stuff, but I know the way they've messed with black people's lives, and I don't like it." He brought down a massive fist next to Rhodes' elbow, but she did not flinch.

"I know my community," he rumbled on. "Black people have been here a long time. When people see new minorities coming in, it pits minority against minority. I'm mad about our always getting the crumbs, and I'm ready to do anything it takes. Anything."

Next in line was Joseph T. Fowlkes, a former professional football player who now headed the Providence NAACP and an umbrella group called the Civil Rights Roundtable. Fowlkes laid a large hand on Buchanan's arm. "I understand Joe Buchanan's anger," he said gently, "and I want to make sure we address these most basic issues of community representation."

Tony Affigne, a professor at Providence College and a leader in the Green Party, worried aloud about the danger of conflict between the African-American and Latino communities. "We need solutions that both communities perceive as fair. The problem is that there is no preprinted definition of fair. Fair is what we negotiate."

Angel Taveras arrived as the introductions ended. "Angel Taveras," he said simply and sat down.

I projected acetate transparencies of gerrymanders that legislative leaders had pushed in ten years earlier. Under public pressure, they had retreated from the most egregious, but improvements in computers and software had vastly increased their ability to protect incumbents. Shapes of districts could be shifted with the click of a mouse. Their database held income levels, race, and voting patterns. Any change in the lines instantly produced new data calculations. Within months the General Assembly would pass enabling legislation, create a redistricting commission, and appoint its members.

We appointed working groups and scheduled a larger coalition meeting in January. One group would propose ways to lessen tensions between blacks and Latinos in Rhode Island's cities; another would reach out to organizations we hoped would join; a third would draft legislation to introduce in the General Assembly. Angel Taveras agreed to serve as temporary chairperson. He closed with a warning that the districts drawn in 2001 would shape political life for the next decade. "Even with the holidays," he said, "we have a lot of work to do before our next meeting. If we don't set the agenda, others will set it for us."

Our next meeting took place on a January night with sleet splattering in windy gusts against the windows at the Urban League. Taveras congratulated coalition leaders who made it through the storm. "If this is the worst we face, we'll be in great shape," he said cheerfully. I thought everyone understood English, but he paused to translate into Spanish.

"When you study our legislation tonight," he went on, "its elements may look technical but you can summarize them in three words. Every time you boot your computer, three letters pop up on your screen: DOS. Let DOS remind you what we demand: Diversity, Openness, Standards."

Joseph M. Fernandez passed out photocopies of the draft legislation. A son of Philippine immigrants and now in his mid-thirties, Fernandez had graduated from Harvard Law School. "Everything we want is fair and reasonable," he began with a smile. "We may not get all we ask for, but this legislation gives us the high ground to plant our flag." Fernandez proposed standards for mapmakers: districts must, wherever possible, conform to existing municipal boundaries; and no district should dilute the representation of communities that were identifiable by race or national origin.

"I think," said ACLU director Steve Brown, "that we need to add an explicit requirement that would say something like: 'In compliance with the Voting Rights Act of 1965, no district shall dilute the representation of communities that are identifiable by race or national origin.'"

"Absolutely," Fernandez agreed, then moved on. "Here's the standard they're most likely to resist: 'The places of residence of incumbents or candidates shall not be identified or considered.'"

"No kidding!" Joe Fowlkes peered over his text at Fernandez. "They are not going to like this one bit."

"It's the key," Fernandez replied. "Without it, they win."

The most radical section spelled out appointments to the redistricting commission. "In the past," Fernandez said, "House and Senate leaders appointed all members of redistricting commissions. Our drafting committee proposes to divide and spread that appointing power. We would argue that a broad range of appointing authorities produces a more responsible body." The legislation listed elected officials who would choose commissioners. General Assembly leaders would appoint eight of thirteen members, but the governor and the four members of Rhode Island's congressional delegation would appoint five others. On that rainy winter night no one believed we could wrestle even five of thirteen appointments away from General Assembly leaders, but we agreed to try.

Within a few weeks twenty-six grassroots groups joined what we began calling the Fair Redistricting Coalition.[17]

Finding sponsors was a struggle. Senators and representatives skimmed the text of our bill and raised their eyebrows. A few who had supported William

V. Irons over Paul Kelly for majority leader took copies to review, and I knew they would show him. In the days that followed, several said they had decided to co-sign Irons's redistricting bill instead of ours.

Senators who had stood with Paul Kelly in the leadership fight clearly understood what they risked with the Fair Redistricting Coalition's bill. "No offense," said Sen. Charles D. Walton, the state's only African-American senator. "If you can find someone else to lead, that would be better." The Providence waterfront limited how far east his South Providence district could go, and preliminary census figures showed a huge influx of Latinos across Broad Street to the west. "If you can't find someone else," he offered, "come back to me."

Sen. Mike Lenihan welcomed me to the tiny office he got after Irons ousted him from chairing the Senate Finance Committee. In the previous redistricting, Bevilacqua's commissioners gave him a district that wrapped around another they chose to protect. Lenihan looked up from our redistricting bill and drew a long breath. "Do you know what you're asking?"

"Probably not as well as you," I said. "What will this cost you?"

"With Billy Irons running the Senate, I'm never quite sure."

"So is that a yes or no?"

"If you can't find anyone else, it's an extremely reluctant maybe."

On the House side, Rep. Joseph S. Almeida, who headed the Black Caucus of State Legislators, was less anxious. "Understand I'm not saying this will pass," Almeida said. "But we might get some provisions into the final bill."

Word from the tiny House Republican Caucus was that several would sign as co-sponsors and that they would speak at a press conference where we would unveil the bill.

But unpleasant surprises came quickly. First was a furtive word from one of the thirteen House Republicans that House Minority Leader Robert A. Watson had changed his mind. "That's my prerogative," Watson declared as I sat in his first floor office. "We're filing our own bill tomorrow."

"You know it'll never pass," I said.

"Neither will yours," he shot back. A bust of Abraham Lincoln sat on the bookcase behind him. Outside his window, heavy snow fell, blotting out sounds of traffic on Smith Street.

"We were hoping for a bipartisan counterforce to Harwood's juggernaut," I said.

"I don't think you'll have any House Republicans on your bill."

The second shock came when Joe Almeida failed to appear for a 3 o'clock press conference called to announce the Fair Redistricting Coalition's bills. We waited fifteen minutes and finally began without him.

Sen. Mike Lenihan walked reporters through his Senate bill.[18] A broad range of elected officials would appoint the commission; redistricting commissioners must stay at arms' length from the General Assembly; numerous public hearings would inform communities; and clear legal standards would make it difficult to "pack or crack" communities into weirdly shaped districts. Lenihan coined a phrase for the difficulty and danger of this effort. He said, "I liken it to carrying a handful of balloons through a roomful of cacti."

Later that afternoon, I entered the Senate chamber and saw senators, staff, and lobbyists clustered at the left side, studiously ignoring a scene that instantly made my face burn. With his back toward me, Irons excoriated Lenihan, who sat in his high-backed seat facing the diatribe. Lenihan said nothing, maintained eye contact, and let the smaller man's petulance run its course.

Our press conference landed on the front page of papers across the state: "Forget about the shape of the state's new political districts," wrote Ariel Sabar in the *Providence Journal.* He described the opening skirmish as a "quarrel over whether the bargaining table should be octagonal or oval." Our bill brought "a first whiff of gun smoke in a battle where no detail is too small to fight over and no one has delusions of an easy victory."[19]

I knew from talking with Almeida several times in January that he supported the Fair Redistricting Coalition's principles. When I asked why he missed the press conference, he mumbled excuses. There was no need to tell me that Harwood had pressured him. I had badly underestimated the heat that he and Lenihan would take for putting our proposals in play.

The U.S. Supreme Court and many state courts viewed legislative redistricting as an inherently political process, and only a handful of state legislatures had ever relinquished control. In 1980, Iowa established a nonpartisan process for redrawing its congressional and state legislative districts in accord with strict criteria.[20] The law declared that those drawing the maps could not consider the addresses of incumbents or candidates, and previous election results were also out of bounds. Redistricting plans went to public hearings and then a vote in the legislature, where lawmakers could not change the panel's plan, only vote it up or down. If they rejected a plan, they would get a second plan that they could approve or reject but not amend. In contrast to Iowa, Rhode Island seemed paternal, petty, and profligate.

In a Machiavellian move, legislative leaders asked individual representatives to draw the districts they preferred. For loyalists they chose to protect, that would be easy. But how should those at odds with their leaders respond? Should they reveal their ideal districts or offer a ruse?

Three weeks after he upbraided Mike Lenihan for sponsoring the Fair Redistricting Coalition's proposal, Senate Majority Leader Bill Irons filed his own bill.[21] A quick reading made me think Irons had studied our bill and deliberately tacked in the opposite direction. He followed previous redistricting laws in having legislative leaders appoint the entire commission. There were no restrictions as to whom could be appointed: lobbyists and political hacks would be welcome, along with community people House and Senate leaders felt they could control.

Furthermore, Irons' bill would not allow Rhode Island's Republican governor or four Democratic members of Congress to make any appointments.

Where the Fair Redistricting Coalition's bill called for districts to stay within municipal boundaries and geographic barriers wherever possible, Irons declared that districts should "reflect natural, historical, geographical and municipal and other political lines, as well as the right of all Rhode Islanders to fair representation and equal access to the political process." His laundry list of vague standards would legitimize oddly-drawn or distorted maps.

The Irons bill also ignored the coalition's requirement that mapmakers not identify or consider the residences of incumbents and candidates. Without that restriction, mapmakers could slip incumbents or challengers into districts they were bound to lose; maps could exclude incumbents from districts they had served or challengers from districts where they planned to run. During the 1991–92 round of redistricting, Irons had protested vehemently when Bevilacqua's forces tabled a Common Cause amendment to create a nonpartisan redistricting commission. He raged when the Bevilacqua panel gerrymandered his East Providence district.[22] Now he copied those rules he had once condemned, so that his bill would empower him to control the commission and bend boundaries to suit his strategic interests.

The census bureau reported in March 2001 that Rhode Island's Hispanic population had doubled since the 1990 count and produced a net growth in the state's population. The capital city — now thirty percent Latino — showed more population growth in the 1990s than in any other decade since European immigrants swelled the count in 1910. The census confirmed what people on the city's South Side already knew: Broad Street had filled with bodegas, jewelry shops, and car repair businesses that flew Dominican flags. Pawtucket, Central Falls, and Woonsocket experienced similar surges, mostly from the Dominican Republic, Colombia, and Guatemala.[23]

A notable rise in non-Hispanic populations had occurred west of Narragansett Bay, where Washington County grew 12.3 percent. In Kent County, rural West Greenwich almost doubled in population as developers carved new neighborhoods out of forest and farmland — most with quaint names like Arcadia Farms, West Country Farms, and Wickaboxet Hills. Meanwhile seven cities or towns had lost population. Newport and Middletown, where Navy cuts had taken a toll, lost most. These changes would shift the shapes of East Bay districts.[24]

Angel Taveras phoned me at Common Cause, speaking so softly that traffic noise almost blotted him out. House Majority Leader Gerry Martineau had called him. "Martineau says he's handling redistricting for the speaker. He said they haven't picked all the members of the commission, but they want me to serve."

"That sounds positive."

"That's what I thought," Taveras replied. "I told him that after the legislation passes, I would consider an appointment. Until then I would continue with the coalition. That didn't seem to bother him."

"Any compromise on elements of our bill?"

"They're reluctant about specific reference to the Voting Rights Act of 1965. His argument is that including it could throw a challenge into federal court."

"A challenge could throw it into federal court even without that reference."

"I said that but got nowhere," Taveras replied. "Martineau also insists that — as in past redistricting — all the commission appointments be by legislative leaders. He doesn't want criteria for public members."

"So all they're offering is to put you on the commission?"

"Martineau said they would actually hold more public hearings than the fourteen we called for." Taveras hesitated. "I also talked with Bill Irons, who said he wants me on the commission. He told me people will be happily surprised with the way they do this."

"Excuse my skepticism," I said. "Irons always says stuff like that. What else did he say?"

"Only that his bill will be the vehicle. And that it will go from the Senate to the House."

"Angel, there's an advantage to having you on this commission, even if you're only one. But I think they're trying to peel you away from the coalition."

"I agree," he said. "But I'm staying with the coalition, and I hope these calls show that they're taking us seriously."

The *Providence Journal*'s political columnist M. Charles Bakst wrote in May that Taveras had landed a seat on the redistricting commission. His profile opened: "It's a good time to be Angel Taveras." Bakst speculated about future races, such as mayor of Providence or lieutenant governor. Taveras replied modestly that he was young and learning. "I have an opportunity to help people. I'm developing as a lawyer. I'm developing in politics."

Taveras told Bakst about a moment of truth in the parking garage below his law firm. A driver had rolled in and asked if he worked there. When Taveras said yes, the driver started to get out, assuming he was a parking attendant.

"No, no," the young lawyer laughed. "I work upstairs."

Instead of grumbling about being stereotyped, Taveras told Bakst: "It keeps you humble."[25]

The Senate Judiciary Committee finally took up redistricting legislation on June 5, 2001. From his seat at the center of the top row, Chair Joseph A. Montalbano explained and defended Irons' bill, which he had co-sponsored. He described lawsuits over the 1982 Senate plan that had cost the state $1.6 million, and contrasted that with the 1991–92 round of redistricting when he served on the panel:

"We traveled across the state, and the end product was not challenged. Senator Irons' bill sets forth standards that we considered important ten years ago."

Next, Lenihan presented his redistricting bill. "At the time I introduced this legislation on behalf of the Fair Redistricting Coalition," he began, "there was no other bill. Subsequently, Majority Leader Irons also filed a bill. If elements of my bill could be incorporated in his, I would be happy."

Lenihan looked up over half-frame glasses. "Nine years ago, my experience was horrific. My district slithered southward and wrapped around the district of another senator who was in better standing with the leadership at that time." Protests from Lenihan's constituents and the reform community were fruitless, and the gerrymander became law. Since then, Lenihan had tried to keep up with town councils in East Greenwich, Exeter, and North Kingstown. Ironically, the Bevilacqua stalwart who should have benefitted from his compact district in North Kingstown had lost to a Republican in 1992.[26]

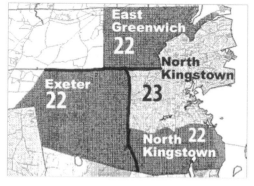

Angel Taveras led an array of witnesses for the Fair Redistricting Coalition. "This time is historic," he announced. "What we do, people will remember. The public needs to feel confidence in this process. Everyone needs to see how the maps are drawn. We don't want this to end up in litigation."

He outlined the coalition's aims. "One of the standards in this legislation needs to keep communities together. If you follow municipal boundaries wherever possible, most senators will have to deal with only one city council. When you go into multiple cities and towns, that makes it harder for those reps and senators. We think it's hard to justify two senators crossing the same border and covering parts of the same two towns.

"We also need to take race into consideration," Taveras continued. "We've proposed that Senator Irons's bill, which we assume will finally pass, be amended to include reference to the Voting Rights Act of 1965. We believe that law is crucial, and if you require the commission to comply, you will almost surely avoid the kind of legal challenge that overturned the Senate's 1982 plan. We think that's just practical."

Joe Fernandez, the lawyer who drafted our bill, explained its details. He said that any state redistricting that violated the Voting Rights Act of 1965 could be overturned. "So," he suggested, "why not incorporate those requirements in the text of the redistricting law you pass for Rhode Island?"

A dozen witnesses — all representing groups in the Fair Redistricting Coalition — testified to the need for stronger anti-gerrymandering standards, as in Lenihan's legislation.

Nellie M. Gorbea, the head of the Rhode Island Latino Political Action Committee (RILPAC), urged the Judiciary Committee to take elements from both bills. She rejected the notion that downsizing necessarily hurt minorities: "What matters is how you structure redistricting. If you establish clear standards, you'll have room to say, 'Those were the rules of the game, and we followed them.'" Without threatening in words or tone, she eyed each member of the committee.

"Finally," she said, "I think that members of the General Assembly have a conflict of interest on this issue. It would be a positive step if you would put this process in the hands of people who don't have a vested interest in the outcome."

Predictably, members of the Judiciary Committee praised Irons's legislation, rejected all amendments, and recommended passage to the full Senate. No one from outside the General Assembly spoke in support of Irons's bill.

The Irons bill became law during the rush toward adjournment in early July.[27] It specified that the speaker and Senate majority leader each appoint six commissioners, half of them lawmakers and half public members; the minority leaders in the House and Senate would each name two legislators. A 12 to 4 majority of Democrats ensured no surprises.

The Fair Redistricting Coalition offered House and Senate leaders a diverse list of community leaders who would be willing to serve as public members. All were intelligent, pragmatic, and rooted in their communities.[28] We still expected that Angel Taveras and at least one other community advocate might serve on the sixteen-member commission

The lists announced by legislative leaders felt like a backhand slap. Although House leaders appointed two people of color — Rep. Joe Almeida and Luisa Murillo — no one from the coalition's list was named, and Majority Leader Gerry Martineau reneged on his public promise to appoint Taveras. When *Providence Journal* reporter Kathy Gregg phoned for comment, I asked why House leaders had changed their mind. "What would be so dangerous about having Angel Taveras on the commission that they would risk publicly breaking their word?"[29]

Taveras was characteristically diplomatic. "We have a lot of talented people in the state," he told Gregg. "It is a tremendously difficult job, and I wish them the best."

At the end of July, Irons appointed three powerful senators and a trio of public members that included two Latinas: housing developer Alma Felix Green and banker Yahaira Placencia.

Joe Fowlkes objected that Irons had failed to appoint even one African-American. "The group that has bled more, cried more and tried to ensure voting rights for everybody is a group that should be at the table," he told reporters. "To say the least, I was not only disappointed but felt insulted."

Irons replied that he thought Yahaira Placencia was black because of her "non-Caucasian" skin color and the fact that a black constituent had recommended her.[30]

Republicans, with four seats on the sixteen-member panel, might protest partisan abuses but lacked the votes to change any outcomes. The five women and four people of color gave an impression of diversity, but they had little experience with redistricting, and seasoned legislative loyalists would surround them on the panel. Would legislative leaders try to entice them with legislative grants for nonprofits several ran? Would they risk retaliation by challenging gerrymanders? Without strong standards or independent commissioners was the game rigged?

During a brief meeting at the end of August, the Redistricting Commission announced its schedule—the first hearing on September 11, 2001.

The shock of hijacked jetliners crashing into the Twin Towers, Pentagon, and a Pennsylvania field overwhelmed all else. While Rhode Islanders watched nonstop live coverage, the Redistricting Commission postponed its first public hearing.

The second went ahead on September 13 at South Kingstown High School, but the shadow of 9/11 made it seem surreal. In a nearly empty auditorium, spectators clumped together among hundreds of vacant seats. Commissioners appeared quietly from the wings and took seats behind individual microphones on white-draped tables. Chairperson Rep. Denise C. Aiken welcomed the audience and television viewers. She introduced Vice Chairperson Sen. Joseph A. Montalbano and her fellow commissioners. They would begin with six information-gathering sessions around the state; then, during five public workshops at the State House, they would work on the plans. Finally, they would travel around the state again to solicit feedback.

"You're going to like our new software," Kimball W. Brace told me on my first visit to the mapping room at the State House. The president and CEO of Election Data Services, was back. He still wore aviator glasses, but gray had lightened his hair and beard since his Virginia-based redistricting firm remapped the General Assembly in 1991–92. "This software's more powerful and more user friendly than what we had ten years ago," he said as if we were friends.

A dozen jet-black PCs with flat-screen monitors stood on tables along the walls behind him. "Each of these can create alternative statewide maps quickly and precisely," Brace said. "You get access to all of our data and maps. You can schedule appointments, and my staff will help you learn the software."

I asked if he would share the software and data so neighborhood groups could create maps and bring them to the public hearings.

"Sorry," he smiled. "Software's proprietary. But if you're suspicious of anyone looking at your files, bring a zip-drive to save your maps and data. Better than that I can't do."

As news media reported on the commission's hearings around the state, attendance grew.[31] Brace projected vividly colored maps on a huge screen and handed out packets that contained three separate sets of maps: Senate and House versions were separately labeled Plans A, B, and C, for the three plans being considered. With the maps came population data tables for hundreds of possible districts. Brace told audiences that they knew their neighborhoods better than his technicians or members of the redistricting commission. "Compare these various plans," he suggested, "and come to the workshop sessions ready to make specific recommendations."

The alternate maps sparked questions of geography, populations, neighborhoods, and political power. The process looked and felt transparent. Members of the Fair Redistricting Coalition attended all the hearings and provided testimony in their home counties. Angel Taveras and Kevin McAllister had battled a year earlier in the Democratic primary for the 2nd District Congressional seat. Now they pushed the coalition's principles with a single voice: follow municipal boundaries wherever possible; never crack a community into multiple Senate or House districts if it can be kept whole; keep districts compact and contiguous; pay special attention to representation of ethnic minority communities, particularly groups that have suffered historic discrimination; and avoid creating "voting pockets" of fewer than 200 voters, which are costly and confusing.

After the audience left one hearing, I stood virtually alone with Sen. Joe Montalbano in a vast auditorium. I reminded him that the population of Providence warranted 6.29 Senate seats, and minorities now constituted sixty-five percent of the capital city. I argued that those numbers obliged the commission to create at least two senate districts where African-Americans and Latinos could choose senators who would represent them authentically. I told him resentment was brewing in the black community as Dominicans filled Broad Street with new businesses, and I warned against Senate maps that might force an ethnic showdown. If new districts were to pit the state's only black senator against a Latino — especially if those maps enabled white incumbents to keep four or five other Senate seats in Providence — ethnic tensions might boil over.

"I hear you, Phil," Montalbano said in a soothing voice. "Watch and see what we produce."

My cautious hopes for reasonable redistricting crashed on November 8. During a State House hearing, Kim Brace distributed two new pairs of alternative plans — Senate plans D and E, and House plans D and E.[32] As I sat in the audience comparing maps, suspicious shapes emerged. Blatant gerrymanders appeared like boulders in a stream, forcing other districts to bend around them.

Both Senate plans protected the turf of Federal Hill Sen. Frank T. Caprio, an Irons ally who now chaired the Senate Finance Committee. Caprio's district maps reminded me of a castle with sturdy battlements. Both seized predominantly black blocks that were part of Sen. Charles Walton's district. Both alternatives would force Walton into the heavily Hispanic neighborhood where Leon Tejada had crushed Marsha Carpenter, an African-American, only a year before. If either plan were enacted into law, the only African-American ever to serve in the Rhode Island Senate would lose.

In the East Bay, both Senate plans created a district that straddled the wide Sakonnet River, joining bucolic Little Compton and parts of southern Tiverton on the mainland with densely populated Middletown and Newport on Aquidneck Island. In either configuration, Middletown's popular Republican incumbent June N. Gibbs would trounce Tiverton Democrat William Enos, a stalwart of former Majority Leader Paul Kelly. But the two communities had little in common, and serving towns on opposite shores of the Sakonnet River made no sense. A one-way trip from Gibb's home in Middletown to Town Hall in Little Compton would take her north on Aquidneck Island, across a bridge to the mainland, and then south to Little Compton — four miles by helicopter but more than twenty by car. This bizarre configuration would force her to drive through two other Senate districts to cover her own. Gibbs blasted the maps as "pure gerrymander" and told reporter Edward Fitzpatrick about her family tree, which traced directly to Elbridge Gerry.[33]

During a brief chance for public testimony, several of us deplored what looked like blatant gerrymandering in both proposed Senate plans. On my way out, I reached to shake Bill Irons's hand, but he pulled away. "You talk like that," he roared, "and then want to shake my hand? You are utterly disingenuous! I will never shake your hand again in this building."

A few days later, the *Providence Journal* published my critique of the new Senate maps. I called the Federal Hill district that would protect Irons's ally "Caprio's Castle," and the East Bay plan that would oust Sen. William Enos "the Sakonnet Swim." I noted that earlier Senate maps had offered more neighborhood-friendly districts but those had now been "swept into the trash."

I wrote that both Senate plans contained variants of a Coventry district that looked like a land-locked riverboat. It lay stranded across the backyards of four communities — its waterline stretched along the boundary between Coventry and West Greenwich, its smokestack rose toward Cranston, and its prow plunged through East Greenwich and West Warwick into Warwick. I dubbed it "the Coventry Steamboat." What could possibly justify it?[34]

The map made no sense until I checked on representatives who might run for the Senate seat. An aggressive and ambitious Warwick Republican, Rep. Joseph A. Trillo, lived in the prow, at 19 Gilbert Stuart Drive in Warwick. The "steamboat" presented Trillo with unpalatable choices: run in a Coventry Sen-

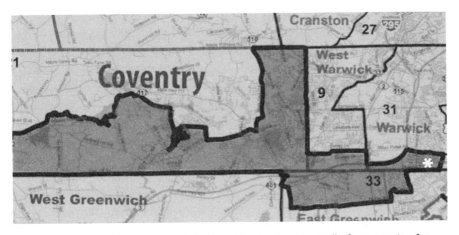

The "Coventry Steamboat" seemed designed to stop Rep. Joe Trillo from running for either Senate District 31 or 33. * Rep. Trillo's home

ate district he could never win, move elsewhere in Warwick, or stay put in the House of Representatives.

House leaders also produced cartoon-like maps. I called one the "West Warwick Warbler." It sat squarely at the southern end of West Warwick with its neck stretched east into Warwick, as if it were pecking at Interstate 95. Its tail feathers spread westward into Coventry, where it seemed to be laying an egg — Tiogue Lake. The new district would fracture representation for West Warwick, one of Rhode Island's poorest cities. Two of the three House districts in the city would reach needlessly both east into Warwick and west into Coventry, mocking the principle of keeping districts within municipalities wherever possible.

As Irons had done in the Senate, Harwood thrust his antagonists into districts they would find hard to win. Rep. Charlene M. Lima, an early separation of powers sponsor who often challenged House leaders, would have to battle two incumbent female Democrats: Beatrice A. Lanzi and Mary Cerra.[35] Elizabeth M. "Betsy" Dennigan, who also pushed separation of powers, found her East Providence district flipped north into Pawtucket with little more than her own block on familiar turf.[36] The bulk of the proposed new district had belonged for twenty years to Mabel Anderson, who was retiring but had bestowed her political mantle on her son.

The *Providence Journal* analyzed the redistricting maps and found that sixty-seven percent of women in the House would have to campaign against other incumbents, while only forty-one percent of their male colleagues would. On the Senate side, seven of the ten female senators were pitted against other incumbents, but fewer than half the men were.

Sen. Rhoda E. Perry declared the Senate still "a boys' club." Like Lima, she had sponsored separation of powers bills since 1995 and had remained loyal to ousted Majority Leader Paul Kelly; now she found herself among the women forced to square off against other incumbents. "I think it will reduce the number of effective women legislators," Perry told reporters, "and we are a minority group within the General Assembly."[37]

The Senate plans also overwhelmed people of color. White incumbents held three Senate districts with large minority populations, while the sole African-American senator would probably lose to a Latino. I warned publicly that if that were to happen, "Senator Irons will rue this day, and there will be lawsuits." Irons fired back that I was being "disingenuous" and blamed me for pushing to downsize the legislature. He declared that I had created the dilemma being visited upon minorities and accused me of jeopardizing their future.[38]

As the Redistricting Commission finished its final public hearings, the real drama played out in private meetings as Irons and Montalbano summoned senators individually to Irons's office and unrolled their final maps. With no hope of change, the Fair Redistricting Coalition notified the press that it would make an announcement half an hour before the commission's next-to-last public hearing.

Dozens of clergy and community leaders arrived at the hearing room but found its door closed. Bishop Robert E. Farrow, an imposing presence and long-time pastor of the Holy Cross Church of God in Christ on Broad Street, pushed it open and looked inside. There, at the long witness table, Irons and Montalbano sat with Charles Walton. Maps lay between them as they humiliated Walton and prevented others from entering the room.[39]

"Out here in the hall," Farrow declared in a booming voice and slammed the door. "We shall not be put to shame!" His King-like cadences filled the hallway. "We shall not be defeated! All of us together, we shall not be moved! Let us join hands and pray!" Farrow began calling down fire on the Senate's gerrymandering. Shouts of "Amen!" drove his message through the thick oak door.

From the hallway protesters raised their voices. Dr. Pablo Rodriguez, a respected obstetrician and president of the Rhode Island Latino Political Action Committee, blasted the Senate maps. "We will not allow African-Americans to be pitted against Latinos in a struggle for political crumbs," he declared. "We are here today together, we will protest together, and we will go to court together, if that is the path we are forced into."

Former Rep. Harold Metts, now head of the Minority Reapportionment Committee, bellowed that the issue was racial packing: "One super majority-minority district of eighty-one per cent that pits blacks against Hispanics is not the answer. Two districts could easily be created to protect the interests of both communities, but they have not done that."

Irons later spoke with reporters. He insisted that the commission had "done its best to empower the minority community." He accused his critics of simply trying to elect both Walton and Pichardo. "That's not about empowering minorities for the future," he insisted. "That's about anointing a few minority candidates."[40]

Irons also criticized Paul Kelly. "We have no split, no faction," Irons insisted. "Right now there is a great degree of collegiality, and we went for eight years with tremendous discord and rancor under Kelly."

For the first time, Kelly fired back at the gerrymandering that would eliminate him and his supporters. The proposed Senate map would leave Kelly with less than nine percent of his old Smithfield and North Smithfield district. He found himself in a district that looked like water sloshing over the top of an aquarium that was Glocester and Burrillville — with his house in the splash. To continue in the Senate, Kelly would have to run against his ally, Sen. Paul W. Fogarty, on Fogarty's home turf, a move he would never attempt.

"It seems to me a blatant abuse of redistricting," Kelly told reporter Edward Fitzpatrick, "to come from Glocester through Burrillville to my house on Victory Highway in North Smithfield. I wonder what their position would be if I moved over two streets. Would they reconfigure the maps again?"[41]

Neighborhoods and entire towns were being dismembered so that Irons and his faction could oust Kelly loyalists. Irons seemed to be multiplying the very mistake Rocco Quattrocchi had made twenty years earlier, and the consequences could again be ugly.

On December 11, all sixteen members of the Redistricting Commission approved the Senate leadership's plan.[42] The closest thing to a protest came from Rep. Joe Almeida, who chaired the Black Caucus of State Legislators. He asked to vote separately on the House and Senate plans. He said he could not vote against the House maps, which were fair for his district, but neither could he approve the Senate maps, which were not. In an extraordinary ruling, Chair Denise Aiken rejected Almeida's request to vote on the legislation by sections. Almeida expressed his disappointment: "I know that the new census figures show more than half of Providence's population is now nonwhite. We are not going to wait ten years or five years or even three years."

"It didn't have to be this way," declared Pablo Rodriguez, head of the Rhode Island Latino PAC. "We could have had two districts where minorities could have been elected." Rodriguez blamed the three Latinas — Alma Felix Green, Yahaira Placencia, and Luisa Murillo — who sat virtually silent on the commission throughout the process.[43] All three voted for the plan; none raised the challenges that an array of community groups sought. Had the women been naïve participants in this performance? Would their nonprofits receive legislative grants or other favors?[44]

One January afternoon at the State House I stepped into a men's room. From the back, Bill Irons's familiar shoulders and neatly trimmed gray hair were unmistakable at the next urinal. For an instant, we stood shoulder to shoulder in silence.

"How are you?" I asked.

"Fine," he said, trapped. "How are you?"

"Fine."

"Good." He stepped away to the marble sinks.

We dried our hands in awkward silence, both aware of his pledge never to shake my hand again in the State House. Our eyes met for the first time. I offered my hand.

He shook it. "Take care," he said and left.

With final floor votes only days away, leaders of the Fair Redistricting Coalition met at the Urban League with Sen. Charles Walton. "I've talked with a lawyer in Washington," he said. "She thinks we've got a strong case that this is racial gerrymandering. She suggests that we file in U.S. District Court. We've laid a good foundation. We pushed to incorporate the Voting Rights Act of 1965, and they refused. That's unmistakable legislative history. Irons knew I was establishing a record but took that as a sign of me not trusting him, or not being loyal. At one point, he stormed by me and said: 'I will never forget this.'"

"He thinks he's righteous on race," said Kevin McAllister. "He's protecting incumbents who are loyal to him, and the U.S. Supreme Court has said they can consider incumbency. They'll argue that they carved your district up because they had no choice."

Walton nodded. "My answer is that you can't come in legally and destroy the largest cohesive minority district in the state. They carved the only predominantly black district into three pieces."

McAllister agreed that Walton's point was strong. The question remained whether protecting minority communities of interest would trump protecting incumbents.

Walton focused his indignation. "I would argue that — downsizing aside — Juan Pichardo ran hard against Bob Kells in District 10. We got so close that it was a photo finish. Now they've split that district, too, and they force me to run against Pichardo on his turf. For two decades we've had steadily increasing minorities on the South Side, and every time we get close, they redraw lines to favor Caucasian incumbents, in this case Caprio and Igliozzi."

Irons's redistricting bill landed on the Senate calendar for February 7, 2002. Its street-by-street description of boundaries filled ninety-two pages.[45]

Only a handful of senators dared to attack the Irons-Montalbano maps. None expected to win, but their strategy was to force public votes on two sets of amendments. The first set aimed to make the East Bay Senate districts "compact and contiguous" under the requirements of the Rhode Island Constitution. The second set would establish Providence districts that would pass muster under the Voting Rights Act of 1965.

Newport Sen. Clement Cicilline offered an amendment that would restore an early alternative plan in place of what I dubbed "the Sakonnet Swim." In one stroke, Cicilline's motion harmonized the entire map of East Bay Senate districts so that no senator would need to cross through any other senators' districts to reach distant constituents. The amendment went down to defeat, 39–8.

Then Mary Parella of Bristol offered a similar amendment. The Senate leadership's plan fractured her historic town into three pieces, each joined with parts of neighboring towns. With Parella's replacement plan, as with Cicilline's, the scrambled districts could become whole and compact, despite the area's picturesque peninsulas and islands.

Sen. Bill Enos — the majority whip under Kelly — spoke for Parella's amendment and blamed Senate leaders for fracturing the entire East Bay to knock him out. "Gerrymandering is bad," he roared at Irons, "but 'Billy-mandering' makes Gerry's plan look good."[46] I had never heard Enos attack in such a personal way. "Hear me, Senator Irons. You're a proud man. I know you are, Billy. Don't leave your legacy this way — that you decimated Newport County."

Murmurs spread against Enos as Irons sought recognition from the lieutenant governor and asserted, "I wish Senator Enos would stop haranguing other senators," Irons growled. "It is totally out of the decorum of this chamber."

When Parella's amendment failed, 34–11, Enos presented his own amendment and reargued his case for keeping Tiverton and Little Compton — both on the Massachusetts side of the Sakonnet River — as a single district. His amendment went down in a blaze of red lights on the electronic tote boards: 36–9.[47]

Finally, Charles Walton rose to present the first of four amendments. He asked his colleagues to take parts of Upper South Providence away from Frank Caprio's district and create two majority-minority districts on the South Side. Even in the supercharged heat, he spoke with the quiet modesty of his North Carolina childhood: "After all this time, to have only one minority district — shame on us for not having the vision to be more inclusive."

Montalbano defended the commission's plan against Walton's amendments but seemed to be only going through the motions. "To suggest that we either ignored or disrespected minority voting rights," he insisted, "is disingenuous, at best." He claimed Providence would have five majority-minority districts in spite of the downsizing. "In two, four, ten years from now," he insisted, "if the population trends continue, these districts will be very good targets for minority voting strength."

As if he had been waiting for that, Walton reached for a book. "I've been here twenty years, ever since a civil rights lawsuit proved racial gerrymandering in 1982. I keep hearing the same refrain: 'Wait a little longer. Your time will come.'" He raised Dr. Martin Luther King's book *Why We Can't Wait* so all could see its title. "This is a real chance to enfranchise the community. How long do we have to wait for the representation we deserve in Rhode Island?"

Predictably, each of Walton's four maps went down to defeat under columns of mostly red lights. In a few months he would lose in the Democratic primary to his friend, Juan Pichardo. The stage was set for lawsuits.

Black plaintiffs from the South Side of Providence were first through the federal courthouse door. Their suit claimed the final Senate plan "unnecessarily diluted the voting strength of black voters" while it was possible to draw a map that did not. "We are not alleging discriminatory intent," said Anita Hodgkiss, director of voting rights for the Lawyers' Committee for Civil Rights under Law. "We are just saying the impact of the districts — for whatever reason they put them there — has the effect of denying black voters an equal opportunity."

Hodgkiss spoke with a quiet certainty born of experience. She embodied a long record in federal courts and knowledge of stratagems used in various states. We were relative novices, but she was more than a match for Kim Brace and his redistricting software.

"The effect is simple," she told reporters. "It undermines African-American voting strength and participation. This is not an isolated case. We are seeing this in a variety of places throughout the country as state elected officials engage in redistricting efforts."[48] The suit asked the U.S. District Court to block Senate elections until the map could be completely redrawn. New districts, she declared, must be drawn for primary elections in September and the general election in November.

Latinos filed their suit with a late afternoon news conference in Kennedy Plaza, across from the massive federal courthouse. Speakers contended with the roar of busses arriving and leaving the open-air hub. "Redistricting is designed to take into account changes in population," Nellie Gorbea shouted over the din. Gorbea was president of the Rhode Island Latino Political Action Committee (RILPAC), one of six predominantly Hispanic groups that filed the suit. "By not drawing a Senate District in South Providence that has Latinos as a majority of its voting-age population," she said, "the state has violated the voting rights of Latinos in Providence."[49]

Pablo Rodriguez, also from RILPAC, followed her. "We are being told to yet again wait our turn. If we need to wait for ten years, then what is the point of redistricting?" He argued that political power for one minority group must not come at the expense of another. "In this case, given the current maps, it comes at the expense of both African-Americans and Latinos."

Predictably, Senate Majority Leader Bill Irons, whose redistricting maps were the target of both lawsuits, defended his plan. He predicted that as more Hispanics reached voting age there would be "significant potential" to elect five Hispanic senators. "I have great respect for the Latino community, but I disagree with their position on this issue. The problem Latinos have is that they are a young population."

Plaintiffs from the East Bay faced different challenges in Rhode Island Superior Court. Senate leaders had chopped Bristol into three parts. Little Compton and Tiverton, on the mainland east of the Sakonnet River, suffered a less grievous split but joined in Bristol's suit. Karen Pelczarski filed suit in Superior Court on behalf of the three towns. She argued that the Senate plan was unconstitutional because the districts were neither "contiguous" nor "compact." Like the lawsuits against the 1982 Senate redistricting, these new challenges to the 2002 maps cited alternatives submitted by community groups that would have fulfilled all the legal requirements without packing, cracking, or fracturing communities. But would these lawsuits make any difference?

After the legislative session ended, most lobbyists vanished from the marble hallways and brass elevators; the hubbub of voices fell silent. I climbed the majestic central stairway alone. Sunlight streamed through windows beneath the dome far above, its glow diffused in columns and balustrades.

The whine of a power sander drew me toward the Senate chamber, where carpenters had removed desks and torn up the green carpet, revealing broad floorboards. I saw for the first time how desks had been held in place by tabs that went down through the carpet and century-old wood. Workers on their knees were filling and sealing inch-wide slots, sanding the boards smooth, marking places where they must cut new slots for the thirty-eight desks that would be reinstalled.

From the Senate's massive central doorway I savored the moment: downsizing was irreversible. The number of districts would finally drop, but Kim Brace had thwarted us. Like a street magician slipping cards, Brace had drawn districts that looked legitimate and almost hid the trickery. Even if challenges on the South Side and East Bay were to prevail, incumbents favored by Irons and Harwood would enjoy huge home turf advantages. Most voters would be none the wiser, barely noticing the maps drawn around them. Only insiders understood. Instead of voters choosing their senators and representatives, computer technicians let lawmakers pick their voters.

When the carpenters took a break, I walked across the bare boards. Would anything change once the carpet and desks were back? Would all our efforts for downsizing and fair redistricting create a fairer and more representative system? Would Irons and Harwood ever be held accountable?

41

Plunder Dome
2000–02

Vincent A. "Buddy" Cianci Jr. had won widespread respect for prosecuting Mob figures, including New England crime boss Raymond L.S. Patriarca. In 1974, Cianci campaigned for mayor of Providence as "the anti-corruption candidate." At thirty-four, he became the first Italian-American chief executive in the capital city's history. But fraud, extortion, scams, kickbacks, and conspiracies flourished in his administration. Thirty subordinates were indicted, twenty-two convicted, and sixteen sentenced to prison for state and federal crimes.[1]

Cianci's abusive behavior caused his downfall. In March 1983, he suspected his estranged wife, Sheila, was having an affair with Raymond DeLeo. With help from a uniformed Providence policeman, Cianci took DeLeo captive. For hours, he drank heavily while taunting, humiliating, and torturing his rival. Cianci eventually pled guilty to assault with a dangerous weapon, received a five-year suspended sentence, and was forced to resign.[2]

In 1990, despite the welter of corruption in his first administration, Cianci embarked on a comeback. "Yes, I have sinned," he apologized. "But let he who is without sin cast the first stone. That's what the Bible says." In a three-way contest, he slipped between two lackluster opponents, his victory margin a mere 317 votes.[3]

During Cianci's second tenure as mayor, I witnessed his magic in person. I had become president of the board of Greater Elmwood Neighborhood Services (GENS), a nonprofit community development corporation where we live on the South Side of Providence. Executive Director Irwin Becker had watched children suffer the devastating effects of lead paint in old, poorly maintained buildings. He helped the state Health Department design a demonstration project to abate lead, obtained $3.7 million from two federal agencies for a demonstration project, and hired Joan M. Carbone to manage the work.[4]

In 1997, the three of us went to Mayor Cianci's office in hopes of expanding the project. Becker and I said little. Carbone explained how lead paint in old wood-framed triple-deckers was causing permanent harm to children. A Health Department study showed that a third of the city's children under six had dangerous levels of lead in their blood. Carbone described the comprehensive approach we were using: homeowner education, block-by-block renewal, job training in lead-abatement, and police cracking down on drug hot spots.[5]

In his ornate office, Cianci disputed the idea that lead paint could be removed in any cost-effective way from dilapidated triple-deckers.

Carbone took him on. She joked, jousted with him, and deluged him with data. "We're making apartments lead-safe for a third less than in previous efforts. We're stopping the damage lead does to children's brains. Mr. Mayor, even if you didn't care that lead-poisoning causes irreversible harm, a simple cost-benefit analysis more than justifies abatement."

Noncommittal behind his huge desk, Cianci scribbled notes in the margin of her spreadsheet.

"Kids with lead poisoning," Carbone continued, "require extra staff in schools. Every child in special education increases your school costs by more than $6,000 a year." She multiplied the one-year increase for one child by years of school. In two years, extra school costs surpassed the $10,000 cost of abating the lead in an ordinary apartment. "Often," she said, "lead-poisoning harms several children in the same apartment. Abatement is way cheaper than special education. You do the numbers."

Three weeks later, Cianci led a parade through our neighborhood. The march ended on the wide lawn of Algonquin House for hot dogs, beans and rice, speeches, and music. Before an audience of dignitaries and neighborhood people Cianci joked and strutted, then got serious. "On the way here," he announced, "we marched through a block where the apartments have been made lead-safe. I want to enlarge this effort for children who deserve a brighter future. I want to abate lead for the taxpayers, too. When we prevent lead poisoning, we save huge amounts on health care and special education. I'm proud to announce that we're going to abate lead all across the City of Providence."[6]

Cianci had absorbed our data about the health hazard, its causes in dilapidated housing, the cost of special education, and the need for comprehensive abatement. He trumpeted our facts and figures as if they were his own and amplified Joan Carbone's central point: even those who cared nothing about children or thought making apartments lead-safe was not government's job must recognize the substantial savings for taxpayers.

True to his word, Cianci appointed a citywide lead task force that included Joan Carbone, and the state soon received a $7.67 million federal block grant to follow our approach in 935 apartments.

But Cianci's memory for slights was legendary, and he never gave credit to our agency or to Irwin Becker, against whom he held an old grudge. When Cianci launched his comeback in 1990, Becker had answered a reporter's question bluntly: "This is an embarrassment. He's a criminal, and people should be afraid of him."[7] In 1997, when the City of Providence invited proposals for funds from the federal grant, Becker submitted a request to do more of what he and Carbone had pioneered. Despite vast massive unmet needs on the South Side and our proven success, Greater Elmwood Neighborhood Services got nothing.

Many were punished for failing to support Buddy Cianci. As I left a funeral at St. Michael's Church, half way down a long flight of brown stone steps smoothed by the feet of generations of immigrant parishioners, a police officer asked to speak with me.

"Can I ask you a question?" He introduced himself as Lt. Richard Tarlaian. Despite his placid public face, I heard consternation in his voice. Tarlaian described recent police promotions. "Five of us made lieutenant at the same time," he said. "When we took the captain's exam, I got the highest score. The other four made captain, and I didn't. Why do you think that was?"

He answered his own question: "Because they each coughed up for Cianci's campaigns, and I didn't. Does anyone think it's wrong for him to shake down city employees and rig police promotions?"[8]

On April 28, 1999, fifty FBI agents swooped into offices at Providence City Hall as well as the homes and businesses of Cianci's confidants. They seized records from the tax assessor, tax collector, building inspector, Planning Department, and School Department. The head of the FBI's Providence office, W. Dennis Aiken, announced: "A number of Providence public officials accepted bribes. All were recorded on audiotape, videotape, or both." Aiken had dubbed the previously secret investigation "Operation Plunder Dome," alluding to the dome of City Hall and the routine plundering of taxpayer funds that went on beneath it.[9]

The probe had begun early in 1998. Providence air-conditioning and sheet metal contractor Antonio R. Freitas believed he had submitted the lowest bid to provide office space to the city. When he failed to get the lease, Freitas concluded that he needed to pay a bribe. He went to the office of U.S. Attorney Margaret E. Curran and offered to help root out corruption. FBI agents put him to work investigating rigged contracts, leases, and tax levies. Initially identified only as a "cooperating witness," Freitas caught Cianci subordinates on videotape as they took bribes.[10]

A month after FBI agents raided City Hall, prosecutors from Curran's office indicted three tax officials: Deputy Tax Assessor Rosemary H. Glancy and the top two officers of the Providence Board of Tax Assessment Review, Joseph A. Pannone and David C. Ead.

Probing Cianci's role in the scandal proved vastly more complicated than the investigation of Pawtucket Mayor Brian Sarault in 1991. An abundance of suspicious behavior did not prove that Cianci had committed any crime, and Cianci declared his innocence. "I can tell the people of the City of Providence that it absolutely will not lead to me," he said. He then alluded to President Bill Clinton's incriminating semen stain on Monica Lewinsky's dress, uttering the unforgettable phrase he would often repeat: "You're not going to find any stains on this jacket."[11] For the next two years, through hundreds of Plunder Dome media reports, the main question remained — would the evidence finally ensnare Cianci?

The FBI agents and prosecutors went by the book. They arrested minor players, tried to turn them, indicted them, and put them on trial, always seeking a chain of proof to Cianci. One Cianci defense lawyer blasted this bottom-up approach: "They teach their witnesses not only to sing, but to compose."[12]

Cianci had learned his trade by prosecuting mobsters. Since his return to the mayor's office in 1991, he had either willfully ignored his subordinates' corrupt practices or skillfully insulated himself from them. On one videotape, tax board chairman Joseph Pannone told Freitas how Cianci had instructed him: "Never talk on the phone, never get a check, but get cash when you're one on one." These were classic Mob tactics.

"Understand," Pannone told Freitas, "there's nothing for nothing. There's no free lunches. It's money that counts."[13]

With Plunder Dome investigators on the hunt, Cianci swaggered, announcing that he would establish a special office to investigate any city department and refer officials suspected of fraud or corruption to prosecutors. "In a city with a work force of more than 7,000 employees," he told reporters with a straight face, "there is a need to be more proactive in ensuring that all employees are aware of the parameters as they apply to ethics."[14] He never followed through, and when months passed without an indictment against him, Cianci began taunting the FBI. "It's been seven or eight months and people keep waiting for things to happen," he told reporter Mike Stanton. "If what they have is substantial, then they ought to produce it."[15]

A week later, Pannone pleaded guilty to fourteen charges of extortion conspiracy, attempted extortion, and mail fraud. The plea bargain required him to testify about other schemes. In turn, other corrupt officials began to plead out. In January 2000, lawyer Angelo A. "Jerry" Mosca Jr. admitted facilitating a bribe to cut the tax bill for a client from $581,000 to $100,000. In February, David C. Ead, who had been vice chair of the Board of Tax Assessment Review, pleaded guilty on six charges that included orchestrating bribes to a "high-ranking City of Providence executive." In exchange for Ead's testimony, prosecutors agreed to drop eleven previous felony charges. Assistant U.S. Attorney Richard W. Rose announced that the payments "were euphemistically referred to as 'campaign contributions.'"[16]

In March, Anthony E. Annarino Jr., the retired city tax collector, pleaded guilty to taking payoffs from taxpayers to wipe out late fees for delinquent property tax payments. Cianci had appointed Annarino deputy tax collector and later promoted him to director. Annarino had contributed $5,545 to Cianci's campaign war chest.[17]

Since 1992, state law had required that campaign funds be spent only for necessary costs of "gaining or holding public office,"[18] but Cianci had spent lavishly from his campaign war chest for family events. Journalists Mike Stanton and Tracy Breton investigated expenditures Cianci had reported as "political." They described a Christmas Day party at his home for more than forty relatives and close friends. The event featured champagne and a catered six-course dinner; its printed menu was embossed with the mayor's seal. A jazz ensemble and professional clown provided entertainment. Cianci had covered his Christmas gift list from campaign funds, but he reported the expenses as political. His "Friends of Cianci" account also funded birthday parties for his grandchildren, complete with balloons, a clown, and Barney the Dinosaur. Political columnist M. Charles Bakst reminded readers that Cianci ran "a round-the-clock fundraising machine, constantly dunning municipal workers and those who look to City Hall for contracts."[19]

In response to stories like these, both the FBI and the state Board of Elections began reviewing Cianci's campaign finance reports. The FBI focused on expenditures that should have been reported on Cianci's income taxes, and the elections board subpoenaed documents that might reveal cash contributions or personal use — both illegal under the law. The board concluded that the Cianci campaign had violated the law and ordered him to repay his campaign more than $42,000 spent improperly on family gifts and travel. But Cianci claimed there was "nothing sinister or illegal or criminal" in the findings. "If they want to pick on me and this campaign, maybe they ought to look at everyone else."[20]

Indictments landed ever closer to the mayor's door. In June 2000, the federal grand jury indicted Frank E. Corrente, formerly Cianci's campaign treasurer and director of administration, for nine felonies that included extortion, bribery, mail fraud, and conspiracy.[21]

Cianci was finally indicted on April 2, 2001 — thirty felony counts that included racketeering, conspiracy, extortion, mail fraud, and witness tampering. The charge sheet alleged that Cianci and his associates took more than $1.5 million during the 1990s in the form of cash and campaign contributions. It also charged that Cianci and his cronies had extorted money for towing lists, jobs, promotions, contracts, leases, building permits, and tax breaks. Indicted with Cianci, several for the second time, were five subordinates: Richard E. Autiello, Joseph A. Pannone, Edward E. Voccola, Artin H. Coloian, and Frank E. Corrente. Closest to Cianci and with direct lines of authority to him were Coloian, the mayor's chief of staff, and Corrente, his director of administration.[22]

The major players appeared to have operated franchises. Though Cianci's allies managed separate shakedowns, all reported through Corrente. It was classic Mob strategy.

Only one count departed from that pattern. During his first stint as mayor, Cianci had applied for membership in the elite University Club. Despite the backing of influential friends, he was turned down. When he returned triumphantly in 1991, he was spurned again, and his rejection became a joke at the exclusive club.

Cianci got even. When the University Club needed variances for costly renovations, he intervened with the Building Board of Review to block permits. Club officers went to court, but when Cianci promised to carry an appeal to the state Supreme Court, they changed tactics. Two top club officials delivered a written apology and showed obeisance. When they walked into Cianci's office, one wore a Cianci bumper sticker plastered on the back of his suit jacket. Cianci harangued them, ending with a taunt that won knowing guffaws when it was repeated: "Be careful how you act. The toe you stepped on yesterday may be connected to the ass you have to kiss today."[23]

A month later, emissaries from the University Club offered him a free lifetime membership. Cianci demanded to know whether the membership was for the office of mayor or for him personally. Assured that it was for him, Cianci allowed renovations to go forward. Ironically, in this case he had revealed his machinations and reveled in them. Prosecutors could compel witnesses from the University Club and his own staff to testify about how he had bullied his way to a lifetime membership in the exclusive enclave.

Despite being indicted, Cianci kept proclaiming his innocence. "I assure you that I'm not guilty of these charges," he declared at a City Hall press conference. "I'm not afraid of this. Ninety-seven times zero is zero." He also reprised his "no stains on this jacket" refrain, adding: "I'll defend myself against these charges until the day I die."

Cianci's defense lawyer, Richard M. Egbert, added: "There are hundreds of thousands of indictments where people are acquitted every year." He reminded reporters that the last Rhode Island mayor indicted in federal court — North Providence Mayor Salvatore Mancini — had also been his client and had been cleared.[24]

Calls rolled in for Cianci to step aside, but since the City Charter had no provision to suspend or remove a mayor, he carried on with scheduled speeches and appearances.

His life grew more complicated when Chief U.S. District Judge Ernest C. Torres granted a restraining order that froze bank and brokerage accounts belonging to Friends of Cianci. For the first time, the mayor could not tap those funds.

Reporter Scott MacKay noted that Cianci had become the longest-serving mayor of Providence and described the character everyone knew: "The gap-toothed smile; the basset-hound eyes; the fancy wig; the rapier wit . . . running from one event to another, encircled by the scent of cologne and a nimbus of cigarette smoke." MacKay also reminded readers of Cianci's Clintonesque mantra: "I assure you that I'm not guilty of these charges. I said before there are no stains on this jacket, and there are still no stains on this jacket."[25]

Missing from Cianci's public protestations about stains was the legendary rage he unleashed against any who fell short of his expectations. In the late 1990s, City Planning Director John F. Palmieri hosted community meetings to repave Broad Street and upgrade its businesses. With fine technical skills and a gentle manner, Palmieri smoothed our way through complex decisions. But several times neighborhood people assembled at the planning office and waited while Cianci hijacked Palmieri's schedule. Once, we began without the planning director, only to have him rush in, visibly shaken and pale. Later, he told me privately that Cianci had badgered him.

What did it mean when a diligent department director like Palmieri performed well for the city, and Cianci bullied him? Where was Cianci's volcanic temper when his chief of staff, his director of administration, and several trusted lieutenants were indicted? Why did a mayor famous for his outbursts sound barely perturbed when his cronies behaved like the mobsters he had prosecuted?

Cianci continued as mayor and took the drumbeat of Plunder Dome stories in stride. A performer since childhood, he was quick with one-liners, often gallows humor. Under a tent for a ribbon cutting, Cianci set up a self-deprecating joke. "Good mayors are risk takers," he vamped. "Well, maybe not all the risks that I've taken." Later, while posing with former transportation directors, he quipped: "Which one of you guys did I grab the most money from?"[26]

From April to June of 2002, the gray Federal Courthouse across Kennedy Plaza from the Providence City Hall drew national attention. On trial with Cianci were Frank E. Corrente, Richard E. Autiello, and Edward E. Voccola. Corrente had been Cianci's director of administration and chief fundraiser. Autiello ran a body shop and towing business while hustling campaign contributions from other tow-truck operators. Voccola, charged with paying bribes for a $1 million

School Department lease, had Mob connections and felony convictions for insurance fraud, stolen vehicles, and assault.

In those closing weeks of a pivotal legislative session, I had no time to attend the trial, but I watched nightly summaries on TV and devoured details in the morning paper. From the start of the trial, journalists relied heavily on commentary by Daniel Small, the former federal prosecutor hired two years earlier to investigate ethics complaints against members of the Ethics Commission but denied *pro hac vice* permission to practice law in Rhode Island. Lawyers on the panel had fired Small and refused to pay his bill.[27] Now he returned to Providence as a nationally acclaimed expert on white-collar crime.

On April 23, lead prosecutor Richard W. Rose finally pointed his finger at Vincent "Buddy" Cianci and accused him of running what he called "the Cianci criminal enterprise."[28] During his opening statement, Rose called Cianci "the head of the criminal enterprise" and derided Corrente as "the bagman." The evidence, he said, would show that the action went through Corrente to Cianci. This enterprise "collected illegal contributions and cash in exchange for hundreds of thousands of dollars in tax breaks, jobs, leases and city contracts. Indeed, when defendant Cianci wanted a private club membership and the club said 'no,' he used his criminal enterprise to take one."

Cianci's defense lawyer Richard M. Egbert, in his opening, pounded back. He declared that the government's witnesses were "liars, cheats, and thieves." He told the jury: "These are people who have been committing crimes since the day they could breathe. They would con anyone. They would lie to their friends, their family. They would lie to the government, and they are people who will lie to you."[29]

After six weeks of testimony by prosecution witnesses, lawyers representing Cianci, Corrente, Autiello, and Voccola launched their defense on June 3.[30] They asked Judge Torres to acquit their clients because the prosecutors failed to prove knowing participation in a criminal conspiracy. Egbert rejected the claim that Cianci had any *quid pro quo* arrangement with tow companies that contributed to his campaigns. "You simply have an allegation without a scintilla of proof," he insisted.

Torres mulled their motions overnight. The next day he ruled that prosecutors had failed to prove Voccola was part of a conspiracy and removed him from the case. Charges against Cianci, Corrente, and Autiello went forward. It was clear that Torres' instructions to the jury would be crucial. Unless the judge drew the case in precise terms, he might give defense lawyers grounds for an appeal. The concepts were complicated. Conspiracy, racketeering, and extortion all had distinct legal meanings that jurors would have to apply to the impressions they gleaned from many weeks of testimony.[31]

On June 11, Richard Rose summarized the prosecution's case, stating that the evidence proved "beyond a reasonable doubt, that the city, the so-called Renaissance City, was a city for sale." He came up with a refrain that drew on a common number across Cianci's franchises. "The evidence shows that the price of admission was often $5,000," Rose chanted. "Want a job? Five thousand. Want to be on the tow list? Five thousand. Want to grease the chairman of the tax board? Five thousand. It was a city for sale, where anything could be had for a price."[32]

Rose also argued that Cianci was not in the position of "a coach who gets a team and inherits the players." On the contrary, Cianci had picked his people and placed them in positions of authority. "He picked 'em and he reappointed them," Rose declared. "Why? Because they were standup guys."

In his summation, Richard M. Egbert took a cool and calm approach. He told of strolling around downtown Providence at dawn. "I walked around, looking at some of the things — the Westin, Providence Place, the convention center, the rivers moved." Providence really was "a Renaissance City," whose mayor "was the leader, the backbone, the visionary."

Then he went on to vilify the men who testified against Cianci, imagining Providence as it had been in simpler times when people knew their neighbors personally. Egbert argued that Pannone and Ead had run their own bribery for tax break scams. They were tax officials who made corrupt deals, presented them to the mayor as sensible, and rather than paying off Cianci, kept the money for themselves. They were convicted tax officials who were not to be trusted. He called them "bums, thieves, and liars."

Corrente's attorney, C. Leonard O'Brien, took a sharply different tack, conceding his client took a bribe. "I'm not about to tell you that it was in any way acceptable. It was wrong and it shouldn't have happened. He's sorry and he's ashamed." Then O'Brien pivoted, reminding jurors that the tape showed Corrente taking a single bribe, not "managing a racketeering enterprise going back ten years."

Attorney Richard C. Bicki, portrayed his client, Richard Autiello, as a mere lobbyist who used his influence to get Joseph Maggiacomo III into the Police Department. Bicki acknowledged but minimized the fact that Autiello took the cash. "Though you may be bothered by the fact that he requested and received $5,000," the lawyer argued, "being bothered doesn't constitute a criminal offense."

The highly charged day ended with rebuttal from the top prosecutor. Richard Rose urged jurors to use their "collective wisdom." He asked them, in their verdict, to say whether Providence was "the Renaissance City" or a "city for sale."

On June 12, Judge Torres guided the jury through the law on racketeering, conspiracy, bribery, mail fraud, and extortion. He described precisely what would be necessary for a guilty verdict on each of the charges. In a supreme understatement, Torres said, "The law is complicated and the case is lengthy." He added, "It is not your prerogative to decide what the law is or should be, but to follow the law as I give it to you."[33]

The jury of public opinion seemed skewed by Cianci's roguish charm. For three years, Brown University surveys had showed him defying the drumbeat of Plunder Dome stories. Five months after the scandal exploded into public view, three-quarters of those polled statewide rated his performance "excellent or good."[34] By June 2001, eighty-one percent thought corruption was a serious problem in Providence city government, forty-one percent thought the mayor was guilty of crimes, and half of them thought he was not "an honest person." Yet, incongruously, sixty-four percent still answered that he was doing a "good" or "excellent" job.[35]

On the day jurors began deliberations on Plunder Dome, Brown released data from its latest poll of 482 Rhode Island voters. Fifty-two percent thought Cianci guilty, but fifty-six percent thought jurors would acquit him and fifty-nine percent still thought he was doing a good or excellent job. "Half the people think he is dishonest," political science professor Darrell M. West told the *Providence Journal.* "But the leadership number is very impressive, because leadership is a quality people really respect."[36]

With or without Plunder Dome, Cianci would have been up for re-election in 2002. Already the longest-serving big-city mayor in America, he remained wildly popular in segments of the population. City Council President John Lombardi told the *Providence Journal,* "I think if this guy gets acquitted, he will be a very difficult candidate to beat."[37]

Cianci's fate seemed inextricably bound up with that of the city he professed to love above all else. In February, state Rep. David N. Cicilline had declared that regardless of how Cianci's trial ended, he would campaign to become mayor. In eight years at the State House, Cicilline had sponsored separation of powers and ethics legislation that infuriated House Speaker John Harwood. In his announcement, Cicilline promised that he would not seek or accept campaign contributions from city workers and that he would make sure all projects and permits were evaluated on their merits. Without naming Cianci, he alluded to a culture of corruption. "Recently I spoke to a police officer who explained to me how demoralized he felt," Cicilline said. "Despite the fact that he was qualified, worked hard, and played by the rules, he knew he would not be promoted because of his lack of political influence. This must end. And when I am mayor, it will end."[38]

In April, former Rep. Keven McKenna, who had chaired the 1986 Constitutional Convention, jumped into the mayoral race.[39] In early ads both candidates emphasized the need to stop corruption in the capitol city. In a radio commercial, McKenna asked: "Have you had enough of Plunder Dome?"

Cianci had countered them both with irony. "I'm on television every day," he told reporter Scott MacKay. "These other people need to get some name recognition because nobody knows them. Everybody knows who I am."

A week into their deliberations, the Plunder Dome jurors appeared unable to decide; they asked Judge Torres for further information about the meaning of legal definitions. Deliberations extended into a second week with no verdict. Speculation spread about a hung jury.

Finally, on June 24, the jury notified Judge Torres that they had decided most counts but were deadlocked on racketeering, extortion, and mail fraud counts involving the University Club. Torres called the jury to his courtroom and asked for the verdicts on which jurors agreed.

Forewoman Mary Dole handed the verdict sheet to Torres's clerk, who read the results: "Count 1, racketeering conspiracy, as to Vincent A. Cianci Jr., Guilty." Corrente and Autiello were guilty on the same charge. Reporter Bill Malinowski noted that Cianci checked off the charges on a blank verdict sheet but did not look up, his face briefly ashen. Corrente shook his head in disbelief, and Autiello showed no emotion.[40]

After his guilt on racketeering conspiracy, Cianci was acquitted of all the other criminal charges. Corrente was guilty of five felonies: racketeering conspiracy, racketeering, bribery conspiracy, extortion conspiracy, and two counts of attempted extortion. Autiello was convicted for racketeering conspiracy and two counts of bribery conspiracy.

The immediate question arose whether Cianci's conspiracy conviction could stand without guilty verdicts on any of the underlying crimes. Torres told jurors that he would study the law further and decide whether that single count against Cianci could stand. "Whatever I decide," he said, "will be subject to further review by the Court of Appeals."

After further deliberation, the jury declared all three defendants not guilty on the remaining counts, including extortion of a lifetime membership at the University Club.

Juror Ann Duchesne told reporter Tom Mooney her votes that Cianci was "not guilty" on many charges did not mean she believed him innocent, only that there "wasn't enough evidence" to find him guilty. Other jurors had managed not to be dazzled by Cianci's flamboyant persona. "You had to take the person out of it," said one. "It didn't make any difference to me at all. It wouldn't matter if he was the president of the United States." Another said: "After the first day, he was just another guy."[41]

In comments to the *Washington Post*, Operation Clean Government chair Bob Arruda scoffed at Cianci's "no stains on this jacket" refrain. He declared the racketeering conviction "one big stain." And lest anyone doubt the depth of criminality Cianci had tolerated or orchestrated, lawyers in the office of

U.S. Attorney Margaret E. Curran released a list of kickbacks and bribes worth hundreds of thousands of dollars that Cianci was alleged to have taken during his previous terms in office.[42]

While Cianci ignored calls for him to resign, he did not file candidacy papers to run again.

On September 5, Judge Torres peered down from the bench and spoke of "two very different Buddy Ciancis. The first is a skilled, charismatic political figure, one of the most talented Rhode Island has ever seen. Then there's the Buddy Cianci who's been portrayed here. That's the Buddy Cianci who was mayor of an administration that was corrupt at all levels." Cianci had operated the city he was supposed to serve "as a criminal enterprise to line his own pockets."[43]

Torres said his job was to sentence the second Buddy Cianci. He gave the rogue mayor five years and four months in federal prison for racketeering conspiracy. He sentenced Corrente to one month less than Cianci. He gave Autiello three years and ten months.

Cianci bowed to the law and resigned as mayor. On December 6, 2002, he reported to the federal prison at Fort Dix, New Jersey and on August 4, 2004, the U.S. Circuit Court of Appeals unanimously affirmed Torres's judgment. The three appellate judges agreed that "there existed an organized structure with Cianci at the top, Corrente as a middle man facilitating and often initiating transactions, and others, including Autiello, Ead, and Pannone, that fed deals into the organization."[44]

It struck me as a story full of sad irony. The mayor who came to power by prosecuting mobsters had practiced their values. The performer who charmed and dazzled found himself hustled from the stage. The bully finally became guilty under the law he flaunted. In the end, he was not above the law, and he could not fool all the people all the time.

42

Perfect Storm?
2001–02

WEATHER FORECASTERS WARNED that March 2001 would come in like a lion. A low-pressure system roiling with winter thunderstorms lumbered up the east coast, while a blizzard pushed eastward from the Great Lakes. The National Weather Service predicted that the storms would converge over New England with hurricane-force winds and heavy precipitation — sleet and wet snow along the coast, up to twenty inches of wet snow inland — a perfect storm. Hundreds of events were cancelled. Barometric pressure plummeted as the two merged.

Over several days the predicted superstorm dumped inches of rain and slush but little snow. But despite the weather forecasters' embarrassment, the metaphor of a perfect storm — still fresh from Sebastian Junger's novel and blockbuster movie about the loss of Gloucester fishermen — remained potent. For the Common Cause spring financial appeal we used a satellite photo of the vast storm swirling over New England and warned of three powerful disturbances converging — a perfect storm at the State House.

The first storm was John Harwood's almost regal power, his wife's lifetime post as magistrate at $100,157 per year, his illegal representation of private clients before state agencies, and his chamber's rush to strip the Ethics Commission of authority over lawyer-legislators.

Redistricting and downsizing would form the second storm: Harwood's tacit support for the anti-downsizing crusade, his refusal to implement a fair redistricting process and standards, gerrymandering that protected loyal incumbents but fractured communities, and the prospect of taxpayers having to pay for costly lawsuits.

We suggested that separation of powers would become the third storm. Rhode Island's Supreme Court had declared twice that the General Assembly could do whatever it pleased because the state government was a "quintessential system of parliamentary supremacy." Harwood loyalists were creating new boards dominated by legislative members who scorned the two-to-one vote for a constitutional convention to address the issue.

Our appeal declared, "Nothing like the convergence of three such powerful political storms has occurred since Rhode Island's Bloodless Revolution of 1935 — an event that blew away eighty years of one-party rule and cleared the way for historic reforms. No one knows what will happen as these storms converge within the corridors of power."[1]

The question remained: would Rhode Island get a political perfect storm or a washout?

Nearly fifty, John Harwood was at the top of his game. After nine years as speaker, he seemed unassailable. He had consolidated his power through patronage. His network was vast, supple, and resilient. Physique and disposition enhanced his power. He handled stress well, stayed cheerful, played hard, rarely committed errors, and took occasional defeats in stride. He listened carefully, remembered well, valued performance. His team seemed unbeatable. Had we made a mistake in predicting that a perfect storm might topple him?

In February 2001, Operation Clean Government (OCG) charged in an ethics complaint that the speaker represented private clients before state agencies whose budgets he controlled, charges that involved wetlands permits and liquor licenses.[2] Under public pressure, the speaker announced that he would stop taking such clients,[3] but his network of relationships still shielded him. Seven of nine members of the Ethics Commission recused themselves, citing conflicts of interest.[4] Even William J. Conley Jr., the commission's counsel, said he might recuse himself because his law partner was George Caruolo, who had long been Harwood's political alter ego.

It came as no surprise when the lawyer-dominated panel punted. Chairman Mel Zurier announced that they would wait for the appointment of commissioners without such conflicts of interest. Lauren Jones, who had represented Harwood in settling earlier ethics charges,[5] agreed to extend the legal deadline until new commissioners could be appointed. But that never happened, and after several months, commissioners quietly dropped OCG's complaint. Donald L. Carcieri, a Republican businessman campaigning for governor, denounced the dismissal, decrying an appointment system that left the Ethics Commission "toothless." He demanded that voters be allowed to decide on separation of powers.[6]

Whatever mistakes Gov. Almond made in packing the Ethics Commission with politically connected attorneys, he committed himself to separation of powers and fought to end legislative encroachment into executive functions.[7] Though Almond saw most of his vetoes overridden, both of his court challenges crushed, and the results of his advisory referendum stonewalled, he rarely backed off. As Rhode Island's first governor with a four-year term, he used his two terms boldly. As he entered his last year in office, many wondered if any successor, whether Republican or Democrat, would dare to continue the fight.

At the Common Cause annual meeting in November, all of the likely candidates for governor pledged to make separation of powers a priority. But Sheldon Whitehouse, who had raised the issue a decade earlier, suggested that Common Cause might accomplish more with a gentler approach. This suggestion bothered many in the audience, and the separation of powers task force invited him to explain his thinking. A week later the attorney general arrived, out of breath, at our office. The room was full. I gave him my seat and sat in a doorway, taking notes.[8]

"I asked for a couple of minutes on your agenda," Whitehouse began, "to raise some questions about strategy." He rehearsed his long cooperation with Common Cause on separation of powers and argued against confronting the General Assembly with "a posse of gubernatorial candidates." He warned: "Some of them are recent converts to the cause. They have no track record on this issue and may let you down if one of them were elected. Forgive a whiff of skepticism."

He proposed that we leave the legislature "some wiggle room" on a constitutional amendment, possibly agreeing to legislative appointments on a few boards in exchange for ending their wholesale encroachment.

From the head of the table, Carl Bogus replied, more softly than he usually spoke: "What makes you think it's a mistake to confront the General Assembly in an election year?"

"John Chafee," Whitehouse replied, referring to the former governor and U.S. senator who had died two years earlier, "had an aphorism that I always thought was sound, 'Do not tease the crocodile until you've crossed the stream.'"

"Meaning that we should not push too hard until after the election in November?" Bogus asked.

"That's my advice," Whitehouse said. "The leadership, particularly on the House side, is already furious with you. We'll need their cooperation to get a question on the ballot." He said legislative leaders knew they had a problem and that, off-camera, a lot of legislators would acknowledge separation of powers as right.

Bogus asked what made him think this approach would work.

"Because in politics," Whitehouse replied, "you can't lose face. If they were to back down after years of strife and two wins at the Supreme Court, that would be a huge loss of face." He noted that all our efforts to educate the public had not made separation of powers a burning issue.

"That may be," said Bogus, "but they've shown no interest whatsoever in compromise. What makes you believe we would gain by offering concessions?"

"You wouldn't offer concessions. We'd take a back channel approach."

"Explain exactly what's wrong with our current approach," Bogus pressed.

"Phil has become radioactive," Whitehouse said. "There's more sympathy for separation of powers than you see, but the General Assembly still has its pride." Negotiations might become possible, he predicted, if Common Cause took a conciliatory approach.

My face burned. He had conferred with House leaders and wanted a truce.

Members of the task force peppered him with questions until he rose to leave. Whitehouse made a final request — that we not invite Rep. Tony Pires to sponsor separation of powers legislation. Pires had chaired the House Finance Committee until he and Harwood split in 1999. Now Whitehouse expected to face Pires and former Sen. Myrth York in a three-way Democratic primary.

The attorney general left, and task force members refilled their coffee mugs. When they settled down again Carl Bogus asked what they had heard.

"That Phil is 'radioactive,'" said Bob Cox from the State Council of Churches. "Frankly, I found that offensive."

"That Sheldon wants us to lay low until he becomes governor," said Nancy Rhodes, now president of the Common Cause state board.

"And what if he doesn't become governor?" asked Donald Koehn, who represented Operation Clean Government. "We'd lose the leverage of an election year and gain nothing."

"Or what if he becomes governor and can't deliver?" Burt Hoffman growled. Decades in Washington had left him a perpetual cynic. "Sheldon wants Harwood's support in the primary. He wants us to shut up so this doesn't catch fire during his campaign. Fire is just what we need."

Topher Hamblett, the lobbyist for Save the Bay, spoke last. "We can understand Sheldon's concerns without submitting to them. House leaders are already overextended. I think we can push them into making mistakes."

"Let me be clear," said Bogus. "We've just heard the attorney general — a leading candidate for governor and one of the most articulate advocates for our cause — ask us to lighten up. And we're saying no. Are we sure?"

"I'm very fond of Sheldon," said Bob Cox. "He's come several times to talk with us about separation of powers, and he's taught us a lot that I didn't know. But he's wrong about this. Dead wrong."

No one favored Whitehouse's proposed strategy. Bogus summarized what he had heard in our conversation after the attorney general left: go forth and build our separation of powers coalition, increase grassroots organizing, continue educating the public, push for legislative oversight, and "let everyone know we're not burying our swords." The task force agreed unanimously, and the meeting adjourned. No one was assigned to tell Whitehouse about our decision. I knew that I should phone him but kept putting it off. Night after night, his rebuke that I was "radioactive" woke me up.

In my pique I did not phone Whitehouse to let him know. Nor did he call me to ask what we decided.

With Almond and his staff, we began planning an event that could lock all the candidates for governor into fighting for separation of powers. We would also rally legislators to the cause. We set out to pack the State Room on January 29, 2002.

On the morning of the event, Ed Achorn published a call to arms in his weekly *Providence Journal* column. "Through a remarkable convergence of forces," Achorn wrote, citizens actually have a fighting chance in 2002 to make a profound change. If fixing Rhode Island's inherently corrupt form of government becomes the central issue of this campaign — if citizens *demand* that politicians commit themselves to a balance of powers — the legislature could finally move to honor the public's will."[9]

Our January day felt like spring, and the temperature in Providence soared to nearly seventy degrees. Across the ceiling of the State Room stretched a perfectly painted blue sky with wispy white clouds. Hundreds of activists squeezed into the resplendent space, packing it to the walls and windows, while scores more stood in the open double-doors or pressed close in the hallway. Above the crowd, massive portraits of revolutionary war heroes occupied the walls as television crews positioned cameras and clamped microphones onto the podium. Over the carved white marble fireplace, Gilbert Stuart's portrait of George Washington evoked Rhode Island's place in American history.

All the chairs for dignitaries, reporters, and spectators were taken. From a bank of microphones I welcomed the crowd and praised Almond for hosting this event, for taking separation of powers to the Supreme Court, and for putting Question 6 before voters. I thanked the scores of grassroots groups that had helped win a two-to-one victory for the issue, and I asked members of the legislature who were sponsoring separation of powers legislation to stand. The audience gave them a thunderous standing ovation.[10]

We were not the first to fight for separation of powers in Rhode Island. Common Cause Vice President Dan Siegel, a rare book dealer, had given me a copy of *Might and Right,* a book by Frances Whipple McDougall Green, published shortly after the Dorr Rebellion, and I held it up, open to its frontispiece etching of Thomas Wilson Dorr. *Might and Right* included a full text of the "People's Constitution," which contained a ban on dual office holding: "No person or persons connected with one of these departments shall exercise any of the powers belonging to either of the others, except in cases herein directed or permitted."[11] That clause would have ended legislative appointments to executive boards, but those who crushed Dorr kept it out of the new Constitution. Without Dorr's ban, members of the General Assembly kept writing and executing state laws.

Amid enthusiastic applause, Almond stepped to the podium, towering over me beneath a shock of white hair. He thanked the citizens groups that had worked to move separation of powers front and center on the Rhode Island agenda. "This is long overdue," he said. "This is what Rhode Islanders want, and they've made that point crystal clear." He summarized his frustrations through the seven years when the General Assembly kept thrusting additional legislative appointments onto quasi-public bodies and executive boards. "Can you imagine?" he asked indignantly. "What possible good government rationale could there be?"

In alphabetical order, the candidates to replace Almond took the podium. Republican Jim Bennett, former head of the Convention Center Authority, spoke of the General Assembly's ability to interfere with businesses as one reason that large corporations stayed out of Rhode Island. Don Carcieri, also a Republican, used an image that became the media's hook for the event. In a reference to Jules Verne's *Twenty Thousand Leagues under the Sea,* Carcieri compared the General Assembly to the giant squid whose tentacles almost crushed the submarine *Nautilus.* Laughing at the absurdity, he added, "The speaker of the House is the *de facto* governor!"

Next Tony Pires cited what he had seen while he chaired the House Finance Committee: "Great opportunities for abuse in such areas as patronage, consulting contracts, construction projects, pension benefit enrichment, and excessive salary increases." Finally Myrth York explained why separation of powers was not a partisan issue. "It's the heart of what's wrong with Rhode Island government," she declared. "The U.S. Supreme Court isn't going to come in and help us. We have to do this ourselves, and we can, if all of us, Republicans and Democrats, work together."

The candidates spoke from prepared statements, and we distributed copies of a letter from Atty. Gen. Sheldon Whitehouse. "I want to reiterate my strong support for separation of powers," he wrote. "I have pressed this issue continuously for more than ten years. I have argued personally before the Rhode Island Supreme Court for a proper separation of the legislative, executive, and judicial powers."

Enthusiasm was high as the crowd filtered out of the State Room. Joe Larisa, Almond's executive counsel pulled me aside. "Couldn't have been better," he said. "The governor loved it. We need to keep their feet to the fire, and we will."

Larisa made sure no one was listening. "What's with Sheldon?" he asked. "I was amazed he didn't show."

"He didn't like this approach," I said.

Larisa laughed. "Sounds like he didn't want the others to have equal footing on this issue."

The next day Whitehouse wrote me a letter on elegant vellum with a fountain pen — mailed from his home to mine. "We have worked together too long on this for me not to express to you my disappointment at your latest tactics. I met with you and members of your board to offer my opinion as to how we should best proceed. I never even received the favor of a reply."[12]

He had learned that Tony Pires would sponsor a separation of powers amendment. "If it was your considered purpose to provoke and annoy the leg-islature, you could not have chosen better." In fact, I had not asked Pires; he had decided to file a clone of Gorham's.[13]

"I am no stickler for ceremony," Whitehouse continued, "but I do 'stickle' a bit here personally. After all we have been through, after all the real work and real risk I have undertaken, to be subjected to the manipulative stunt of invitation into this line-up of arrivistes and into a strategy you know I think is self-defeating, or be absent on an issue that I have put more into than the rest of them together — I think it's beneath you."

I crumpled his letter and hurled it into a wastebasket. Why had I not called him after the task force decided to go forward with the event? I knew the an-swer. Although I took it as a badge of honor that House leaders were furious with me, his reproach that I was "radioactive" had stung. In my annoyance I had delayed calling him and never followed up. I retrieved his letter, smoothed it, read it again.

Common Cause had an apt motto: "No permanent friends, no permanent enemies." Beneath my anger, I admired Whitehouse, a New England blueblood who typically put principle above personal advantage. No matter how political calculations had clouded his judgment, Whitehouse had been a leader on sepa-ration of powers. And just as leading Democrats had not helped Myrth York in her 1994 campaign against Almond, he understood an aggressive attack could sink his campaign for governor.

I assumed he had reported the meeting at our office to House leaders. By not telling him we had decided to go ahead with the candidates' event, I had left him looking inept. Whatever his reasons, Whitehouse stayed away, and Don Carcieri's metaphor — giant squid tentacles crushing the life out of Rhode Island government — had led the news and filled front pages across the state.

Carcieri made separation of powers his rallying cry. When all six guber-natorial candidates took the stage before business leaders at the Rhode Island Convention Center, he opened by urging the audience to lobby for a separation of powers amendment. "There is nothing more important that the business community can do today," the former Cookson America CEO declared. "This General Assembly is much too heavily involved with the day-to-day operations of the state. We are trying to run a modern state with a $2.6-billion budget with a group of part-timers who think it's their business to run the state."[14]

Another Republican candidate, former Lt. Gov. Bernard Jackvony, made the same point with a provocative play on Mesolella's role at the Narragansett Bay Commission: "When we flush our toilets, the legislature is involved. They run the largest sewer system in the state."

"The stall" is a classic tactic for discouraging citizen-activists. It never appears in House or Senate rules but nestles in the authority of committee chairs to rearrange agendas. On March 26, a rainy Tuesday, House Judiciary Committee Chairman Robert E. Flaherty convened his members to hear testimony on guns and separation of powers. Until recently, Flaherty had chaired the Rhode Island Lottery Commission. Because six of its nine members were legislators, "The Lot" had been an inviting target for seven years. Flaherty's committee agenda listed bills in numerical order, but he took the gun bills first. "We have some police officers signed in to testify tonight," he announced. "I'm going to give them the courtesy of speaking first on each bill, so they can go home to their families." Flaherty stalled separation of powers until after 9 p.m., when newspaper reporters ducked out to write their stories. The next day's headlines would be about weapons.

Our witnesses still packed the room, standing along walls, holding signs:

> **We, the People, Demand a Vote**
> **for Separate and Co-Equal Branches.**
>
> **We, the people, by 66% to 33% on Question 6,**
> **asked you to let us amend the Constitution.**
>
> **When will you respond to our request?**

In their mute solemnity, they reminded me of the "Silent Sentinels" of 1917, who picketed the White House for women to vote. Even when seats opened up, several continued to stand.

Flaherty finally announced what he called "Rep. Gorham's latest so-called separation of powers bill." He then excused himself stiffly and retreated to his office. Several committee members followed him or disappeared into the hallway. The committee's long oak table was nearly empty. I hoped our witnesses would not feel deflated.

As prime sponsor, Gorham testified first: "Last year, I brought you legislation that included the precise text of Governor Almond's advisory Question 6, which called for a constitutional convention to consider separation of powers. As the signs that these patient people are holding remind us, voters approved Question 6 by a two-to-one margin. And as you remember, in spite of overwhelming public support, the House recommitted my bill to this committee on the last night of the 2001 legislative session. I suppose that means you could bring it out of your files, if you chose."

He suggested instead that they save a step: the General Assembly should place a constitutional amendment before voters without a convention. "It's number 7050 in your binders," he said, "and I'd like to walk you through it. I hasten to add that this isn't a partisan bill in any way. Rep. Pires introduced 7113, which is identical, word for word."[15]

Gorham paused. "The current text of Article V already says that 'The powers of the government shall be distributed into three departments: the legislative, executive and judicial.' We propose to add a single sentence that will be clear to anyone who reads it: 'These departments shall be separate and co-equal, as under the Constitution of the United States.'"

"If I may, Rep. Gorham?" Bristol Rep. Fausto Anguilla interrupted. Short and stocky, he was cordial in the role of acting chairperson: "Does this word 'co-equal' appear in other state constitutions?"

"Excellent question, Rep. Anguilla," Gorham replied. "In fact, it does not. Many other states use the older phrase: 'separate and distinct.' But the word 'co-equal' appears in many modern decisions by the U.S. Supreme Court. We think 'co-equal' is more current and more intelligible, but we could live with 'distinct.'"

"Who do you mean by 'we,' Rep Gorham?"

"I worked with Common Cause on this text, but we're not rigid if this committee is willing to really work on an amendment."

"And you could live with 'separate and distinct'?"

"Of course," Gorham said brightly. "It certainly has a noble pedigree."

Gorham segued to proposed changes in Article IX. "We propose to follow the federal model, where the president appoints executive officials with the 'advice and consent of the senate.'" He led the handful of committee members still at the table through the text.

"Finally," Gorham said, "we come to 'Article VI: Of the Legislative Power.'" He glanced along the table. "I know this will be the most controversial part. We propose to delete Article VI/Section 10, often called 'the broad powers clause.'"

"You're not serious." Anguilla was incredulous. "This is the foundation of legislative power."

"We are dead serious, Rep. Anguilla. Legitimate legislative power will continue uninterrupted. What will end is the General Assembly's power to do anything its leaders want unless it's explicitly prohibited by the Constitution."

A dozen witnesses from environmental, business, reform, and religious groups followed Gorham to the witness chair. In my turn, I reminded committee members that overwhelming numbers of voters in all of their cities or towns had voted for separation of powers. "It's not our view that legislators are bound to do what their districts ask, but neither are you free to ignore constitutional questions your voters ask you to consider."

All evening, a man with a bowtie had stood with his back to one of the huge windows, holding a "We the people" sign. When there seemed to be no more witnesses, he raised a hand, and Anguilla called on him.

"My name is Harvey Perry," he said. "This is my first time testifying here. I'll be brief." He had no notes and stood against the table. "I drove up from

Westerly in the rain because I consider it my duty as a citizen of Rhode Island. I don't want to be harsh with those of you who have stayed until the end, but I hope you'll pass my warning on to those who walked out just when the committee got to separation of powers. They may not want to hear, but they will not escape this issue."

Perry swept a hand through a thick wave of chestnut hair. "From my work in a bank I know that numbers have a way of catching up with people who ignore them. I think everyone here needs to take seriously the numbers of people from their home communities who voted for separation of powers. 'We the people' have trusted you to represent us. 'We the people' have asked you to correct a defect in our state government. 'We the people' are asking you to let the voters fix a flaw that has crippled our state for hundreds of years. You didn't cause this problem, but you can address it by placing Rep. Gorham's constitutional amendment on the November ballot. 'We the people' are urging you, our representatives, to let voters establish genuine legislative oversight. 'We the people' are asking you to seal a door that stands open to patronage and corruption." Perry hesitated, then finished: "Mark my word, if you ignore these numbers, 'We the people' will throw you out of this lovely building."

He stepped back from the table, and Anguilla affirmed him: "For your first testimony, Mr. Perry, that was powerful. Thank you."

After the hearing, I asked Anguilla if I could ride down with him in the elevator. Years earlier, a mentor in New York[16] taught me about lobbying: "Don't leave the building until the last legislator leaves for home. Walk him to his car. In those moments when the pressure's off, you may get some crucial information. At the very least, you'll build a relationship."

Anguilla and I rode an elevator from the second floor to the sub-basement, where we stepped into a passageway through the foundation. Brick footings that bore the weight of upper floors and the dome spread like pyramids enameled white; black iron pipes ran overhead. We walked beneath them toward the legislators' exit. A year ago, Anguilla had stood solidly with House leaders to kill Gorham's bill. I said I thought he had sounded more sympathetic in this hearing.

"I've never been unsympathetic," he said as we walked. "You've put your finger on a weakness that's been at the core of our state government for hundreds of years. But we need to be extremely careful with a constitutional amendment. We have to avoid the trap of good intentions that produce unintended consequences."

We passed the guard station and stepped out into rain from rapidly moving clouds. "On the political front," Anguilla said as we walked toward his car, "you've done your job. I've been getting a lot of calls from my district."

"Does that mean you'll support Gorham's bill in the vote next week?"

"Whoa!" he laughed. "Let's not get ahead of ourselves here."

"Just counting noses," I said. "That's my job."

"Count me leaning your way. But don't mention my name." He opened his car door. "There's a lot of pressure not to let Gorham's bill see the light of day."

We shook hands, and he drove off into the night. I walked through the rain to my car. None of tomorrow's papers would tell of witnesses holding signs or of Harvey Perry's impromptu "We the people" speech, but this had been a productive night.

A week later, members of the House Judiciary Committee gathered for crucial votes before their deadline. I approached Rep. Gene Garvey, who represented a picturesque south coastal district that included Charlestown, South Kingstown, and Block Island. Warm and white-haired, Garvey was a retired insurance broker whose smile was etched in place. A deputy majority leader on Harwood's leadership team, he was under pressure to keep others in line. He shrank from my approach. "So, Gene," I asked, "are you with us on Gorham's separation of powers amendment?"

"I don't think tonight," Garvey said grimly.

"Gene," I persisted, "more than seventy-two percent of your constituents approved Question 6."

"The way it was phrased, I'm not sure they understood."

"They understood, Gene, and we'll inform them about tonight's vote."

"Do what you have to do, Phil. I'll do what I have to do."

Moments later, *Pawtucket Times* reporter Jim Baron squeezed into a seat next to me. "So what's your count?" he whispered.

I held up a hand with my thumb and index finger almost touching. "More than last year. Too close to call."

The Judiciary Committee members slid their chairs against the table. House leaders would weigh votes here as they decided how committee members' priority bills would fare, the size of legislative grants for their districts, and how much support House leadership political action committees would provide for their fall campaigns.

Flaherty gaveled for order. He held a multi-page agenda marked with codes to show what House leaders wanted done with each bill. The hearing droned on for an hour with occasional questions. Most bills passed unanimously or with dissenting votes from the tiny contingent of Republicans. I had long ago ceased being amazed that lawmakers followed their leaders despite missing testimony on bills.

"On Rep. Gorham's resolution 7050," Flaherty announced, "I move non-passage. Quite frankly, I see no need to consider an amendment now. The question of a constitutional convention will be on the 2004 ballot. Let's let a convention consider this properly."

That seemed an ironic point for Flaherty to make, since Gorham's 2001 resolution sought to start the convention process until Flaherty moved to bury it. Harwood's team had clearly calculated they could delay separation of powers to death. They expected that voters would lose interest.

As the clerk called the roll, I tallied votes on my chart. The final count was 10–8 for "non-passage," killing Gorham's bill. Rep. Gene Garvey backed Flaherty's motion for "non-passage." Among the eight who voted to send separation of powers to the floor for a full debate were Fausto Anguilla and three other Democrats who had voted the previous year to recommit the bill.

I followed Jim Baron to the hallway to comment. "This is impressive," I told him. "The leadership wanted to kill this."

"Didn't they just kill it?" He held his recorder for my answer.

"With a 10–8 vote, it's not dead. Tony Pires's version is still alive, and there are two similar bills in the Senate. We're closer to passage than we were before."

Baron's *Pawtucket Times* story on the committee's 10–8 vote[17] scooped the *Providence Journal*. The statewide paper's Ed Fitzpatrick caught up with committee members the next day. "Because it's an election year," Republican Nick Gorham said, "you are going to see more people from the other side of the aisle who are going to put what the people want over what the leadership wants." Rep. Robert D. Sullivan, a Democrat, explained to Fitzpatrick that he had switched to support separation of powers in 2002 because "a lot of people" from his East Providence district said they wanted to vote on it.

I said separation of powers was not "a flaky esoteric new idea. It is the core principle of American democracy. It has been tested in our federal government and in other state governments over a period of two hundred years. Our message to members of the House and Senate is to remember your district."[18]

After this close vote in the House Judiciary Committee, our challenge was to ramp up outside pressure and force a floor vote in the House. We dispatched email updates to broadcast and print reporters, organizations, and activists.[19] Our memo included town-by-town tallies on Question 6 and a list of House Judiciary Committee votes for and against Gorham's amendment. We hoped weekly papers would highlight how local representatives had voted.

Columns and editorials favoring separation of powers burst forth like daffodils. Edward Achorn's weekly alarum went to homes across the state. "Politicians have long been propping up a rotten edifice in Rhode Island," he wrote, "a more than 300-year-old system that gives the General Assembly too much power, breeding corruption. But this week, citizens may finally have an opportunity to knock it down — if they can rise above their apathy and act." He described the likely House vote and hammered Harwood for treating "the vast majority of the public with contempt." He urged readers to call their representatives and demand a November vote on a separation of powers amendment.[20]

To force debate on separation of powers Rep. Nick Gorham invoked a different section of the obscure rule he used on the last night of the 2001 session. Rule 32 allowed the minority to bring legislation to the floor after its defeat in committee. The showdown came on April 10. As representatives entered the House chamber, activists stationed outside each of three entrances handed them detailed explanations of Gorham's separation of powers amendment.

From the west gallery, I watched TV reporters and radio talk show hosts prowling the red-carpeted chamber. Commercial stations had cameras mounted on tripods near the rostrum that would record the debate. Below me on the dais, in what sounded like a routine question, Harwood asked Robert Watson, the blustery minority leader, if he would like to place Gorham's bill on the regular House calendar.

"Would that allow a full debate on the merits?" Watson asked.

"It could," Harwood replied.

Watson missed the procedural trap and agreed.

When Gorham's bill came up on the calendar, Flaherty moved instantly to recommit it to House Judiciary.

Watson jumped to his feet to challenge the motion.

"Any rep can move to recommit any item on the calendar," Harwood ruled from the rostrum.

"If we're playing a clever game," Watson roared, "congratulations. You just scammed the people of the state of Rhode Island. What you are about to do is an offense and an outrage to the people."

Harwood's agreement to place the separation of powers amendment on the calendar rather than to process it under Rule 32 changed the rules of debate. A move to recommit was not debatable. In an instant the speaker ordered a vote and Flaherty's motion to recommit passed 49–38. Harwood's heavy-handed parliamentary maneuver blocked debate on separation of powers a second time, but the good news was that the number of representatives supporting debate climbed from twenty-five the previous June to thirty-eight only ten months later.

"We got sandbagged, plain and simple," Gorham told reporters. "What this tells me is that they are afraid to debate this issue, because they know they can't win."

House Majority Leader Gerry Martineau dismissed the move as an election-year ploy. "I consider it one of the defining issues for Republicans," he said. "The debate would have been an opportunity for them to grandstand on the issue."

I suggested to reporters that it was risky for House leaders to put 49 representatives on the record opposing separation of powers. "If you're afraid of a debate on the substance, you use a procedural maneuver to prevent debate. In the long run, they will not prevail. It's a volcano that, sooner or later, will erupt."[21]

News articles, opinion pieces, editorials, columns, and letters to the editor flayed Harwood and the representatives who backed his stonewalling,[22] but throughout the spring, House leaders feigned indifference to negative press. Finally, in May, Rep. Paul Crowley sent an opinion piece to newspapers, arguing that fifteen other states allowed legislative appointments to boards and commissions. "Louisiana may be the champion," Crowley wrote, "with almost 500 boards and commissions. In that state, legislators sit on the Compensation Review Commission, the Educational Assessment Testing Commission, the Judicial Compensation Commission, the Board of Trustees for Municipal Teachers, and the State Employees' Retirement Systems."[23]

"Louisiana is our toughest case," Peter Hufstader told me, "but most of those bodies are either parish-level or study commissions."

We quickly sent a response that showed state by state how rarely lawmakers served on executive bodies: "In a review of the 500 boards Rep. Crowley cites for Louisiana, the supposed 'champion' of state boards and commissions, only thirty-one are marginally executive. Contrast that to Rhode Island's fifty-four." I noted that Louisiana and Rhode Island had long been famous among the nation's most corrupt states. But I asked: even if Louisiana really were the champion of legislative infiltration, would that be the standard we sought?[24]

Throughout the spring of 2002, House leaders had been flexing their political muscles with bills we branded "power grabs" because they conferred executive powers on sitting members of the General Assembly. Crowley, for example, long considered the dean of education in the House, filed legislation to give House and Senate leaders hands-on control of the Board of Regents for Elementary and Secondary Education.[25] House Finance Committee Chair Gordon D. Fox proposed to put the Veterans' Memorial Auditorium under direct General Assembly control.[26] His new board would have nine members: five appointed by the speaker and four by the Senate majority leader. Seven of the nine would be members of the legislature. The concert hall would become a patronage mill.

Another leadership bill would convert Vincent Mesolella's Underground Storage Tank Fund into a quasi-public corporation — freed from fiscal control of the Clean Water Finance Agency and oversight by the general treasurer.[27] Five members of the thirteen-member board would be legislative appointees. Mesolella had chaired the board since its creation in 1994; the conversion would vastly expand his authority over funds and contracts. Mesolella, a Harwood crony and developer, also appeared to be the likely beneficiary of a controversial $33.5 million subsidy for a new luxury hotel in Providence. The hotel proposal popped up late in the session and sped through both chambers.[28]

The most lucrative power grab of all involved land. Under a cover of platitudes, the bill proposed a I-195 Redevelopment Board to sell off land that would become available when a dangerous section of the interstate highway was re-located out of the Jewelry District in Providence. Rep. William J. Murphy and Sen. Domenic J. Ruggerio proposed identical bills for a nine-member board with three members appointed by the speaker, three by the Senate majority lead-er, and three by the governor — the same appointment scheme as the Lottery Commission. Both bills idled in committee for five months, then revved their engines for a screeching run through the House and Senate during the last days of May.[29]

Piling insult upon injury, a budget article created a corporation with compre-hensive executive powers to borrow against Rhode Island's share of a $2.8 billion national settlement with tobacco companies. The governor, speaker, and Senate majority leader would comprise its three-person board. Atty. Gen. Sheldon Whitehouse wrote to legislative leaders that this would be "utterly impermissible under our Constitution . . . because it is legislatively controlled."[30]

The $2.64-billion state budget put forward a second blatant power grab. Un-precedented new language would require that the governor, speaker, and Sen-ate majority leader all approve "any single item or contract expected to exceed $100,000 other than those within the Office of the Governor and Legislature." It would strip Almond's authority to hire personnel or spend money during his final months in office.[31] Many state constitutions gave governors line-item vetoes to block wasteful spending, but this new proposal would empower Rhode Island's legislative leaders to veto expenditures under budgets they already ap-proved. It would let Harwood and Irons veto contracts or new hires anywhere in state government.

As the session ended, House leaders threw up a procedural hurdle to thwart separation of powers. Rep. Mabel Anderson filed a bill that would outlaw any constitutional amendment or statewide referendum that contained "more than one question" within its text. Her bill would prevent separation of powers amendments, since they would amend several articles of the Constitution at once. I testified against it but was met with stony resistance. Democrats on the House Committee on Special Legislation approved it on May 29 and sent it to the House floor. That night, I fired off emails to every member of the House. Their in-boxes would be clogged with hundreds of messages, but I kept trying to warn them. To my astonishment, Anderson's "single-question" bill appeared on the House Calendar the very next day.[32]

I started along the rows of House desks, leaving a letter at each, but the doorkeepers stopped me, confiscated the letters I had already distributed, and trashed them. I warned representatives as they entered the chamber. Most said they knew nothing about Anderson's "single-question" bill; several who were aware of it admitted they were under pressure to vote for passage. By a vote of 56–3, representatives approved it, and its journey from the House Special Leg-islation Committee to Senate Judiciary took less than twenty-four hours. Amid scores of other bills in the closing hours of the session, it was getting priority treatment and no press coverage.

Harwood's team exuded confidence and enjoyed leverage. Many senators had labored through the session on bills that still awaited action in House committees. Each would feel the squeeze to pass Anderson's "single-question" legislation and bills we called "power grabs." What would the Senate do?

Throughout the spring, Senate Majority Leader William V. Irons had been watching Harwood's heavy-handed tactics from a safe distance. In April, he had told reporters Rhode Island was "not like all the rest of the states," and he insisted that the issue was "not as simple as referendum proponents make it sound." But as public reaction against House leaders mounted, Irons suggested that there might be "a middle ground between the absolute change that the proponents of the referendum seek and the status quo that the House wants." He quietly designated Sen. Mike Lenihan and the Senate policy chief Ken Payne as emissaries to Common Cause. Lenihan had risked punishment to sponsor separation of powers amendments, and Payne was a seasoned political operative who would report verbatim to Irons.[33]

Carl Bogus, Nancy Rhodes, and I squeezed into Lenihan's tiny office. With Payne at his side, Lenihan began cautiously: "We think we can deal with a portion of this by creating a well-staffed study commission." He mentioned the study commission he had led in 2000 that probed the credit card scandals in quasi-public boards. "We could do something like that again," he said. "Our report might include a separation of powers amendment that the General Assembly could consider for the 2004 ballot."

But Senate leaders wanted something in return. The House held a 3–2 edge in the all-important Joint Committee on Legislative Services, and senators were determined to "balance power" between the two chambers.[34] Payne reminded us that the speaker controlled the number of Senate staff and their levels of pay. Lenihan gave an example of how petty House leaders could be: his laptop was a hand-me-down from a representative who had gotten a new one.

"With this commission idea," Rhodes said, "what if you identify all the problems, but the House still has all the power?"

"I'm not sure," Lenihan replied. "At least, we would expose the public to the relevant information."

We agreed to get back to them, and the three of us debriefed over coffee. "I'm reluctant," Carl Bogus said. "We've always known that the balance of powers between the Senate and House is an issue, but it complicates the primary question of separating legislative and executive power." He thought that a study commission would delay the process, break our momentum, and make it harder to revive public support.

We decided to push for an up-or-down vote in the Senate. A Senate vote would mark a watershed. After that, a formal study could work out details. I phoned Lenihan at home, and he seemed relieved that we would not back off. We ramped up our campaign of emails and phone calls.

As pressure mounted, cracks appeared in Irons's base. Sen. Frank T. Caprio and his younger brother, Rep. David A. Caprio, were partners in the family law firm founded by their father, chief judge of the Providence Municipal Court. Still in their thirties, the youthful Caprio brothers were bright, ambitious, and photogenic with black hair, intense eyes, and height that made them stand out in crowds.

Frank Caprio had aided Irons's coup against Paul Kelly, and Irons rewarded him by appointing him chair of the Senate Finance Committee, awarding him the spacious office that had been Lenihan's, and granting him his preferred district on Federal Hill, which I had dubbed "Caprio's Castle."

In April, David Caprio had played an aggressive role in the House scuffle over separation of powers. I had watched him scurry around the House chamber, holding a soft drink to prevent anyone from reading his lips, as he rallied support for Gorham's resolution. I wondered whether he was fighting for the principle or against Harwood — or both.

In May, Frank Caprio groused to reporters that Irons had cut him out of budget negotiations with House leaders. He accused Irons and Harwood of conspiring to keep separation of powers off the November ballot.[35]

Word of the brouhaha over separation of powers drew curious journalists from beyond Rhode Island's borders. Don Aucoin, a writer from the *Boston Globe,* asked to shadow me around the State House. Wherever I introduced him, jaws dropped, and I stepped away while he talked with supporters or opponents of the amendment. Aucoin's feature ran in the *Globe* the very day a Senate committee was scheduled to take testimony on separation of powers. Aucoin summarized what he called "the cozy folkways of 'Rogue Island.'" He sketched the seven-year struggle for separation of powers and profiled me as fighting historic corruption, which he called "a task to make Sisyphus grateful for the comparatively light duty of rolling a rock uphill for all eternity."[36] A few lawmakers congratulated me on the *Globe* profile, and others glanced my way with what struck me as grudging respect. No one could buy that kind of publicity.

Two separation of powers resolutions were posted for an extraordinary noontime hearing of the Senate Committee on Special Legislation. Ironically, Sen. Maryellen Goodwin was the first female chair both of this committee and of the Rhode Island Lottery Commission. Senate Minority Leader Dennis Algiere had introduced a Senate clone of Nick Gorham's House bill. It would make the branches of state government "separate and co-equal, as under the Constitution of the United States," grant the governor power to make all executive appointments, and delete the "broad powers" clause that allowed the General

Assembly to do whatever it liked unless the action was explicitly prohibited in the text of the Constitution.[37]

Lenihan had filed a resolution with similar features,[38] but he phoned confidentially about a substitute that Irons wanted. "You'll like one section," he said discreetly. "You'll also notice a deletion you won't like. You understand that this isn't for me to decide."

Our witnesses filled the sign-in sheets with signatures. Nearly every seat in the mahogany-paneled Room 313 was occupied when Goodwin gaveled her committee to order. "I have a SubA for Senator Lenihan's bill," she announced. "Our clerk is distributing copies to the committee, and I hope we'll have enough for all members of the public."

The substitute version made my heart sink. The clause "separate and co-equal, as under the Constitution of the United States" had vanished. Gone also was the crucial deletion of the "broad powers clause." If that clause stayed, the General Assembly would continue exercising the same unchecked powers as it always had.

The substitute contained one redeeming feature: a robust ban on dual office holding. Like the spurned People's Constitution of 1841, it would bar representatives and senators from serving on any board or quasi-public entity that exercised "executive power under the laws of this state."[39] A reciprocal clause would bar members of such boards from running for the General Assembly as long as they served on such boards.

I felt some relief that the substitute version of Lenihan's bill did not contain Irons's demand that administrative parity between the House and Senate be included in a constitutional amendment.

Senate rules allowed the majority and minority leaders to participate in committee hearings, but they rarely did. On this day, Irons strode in and took a seat. With gruff indignation, he attacked what he called "false and misleading statements" by separation of powers supporters. "The governor's question in 2000 misled voters when it asked whether they wanted 'separate and co-equal branches of government similar to those established by the U.S. Constitution and by the Constitutions of all forty-nine other states.'" Irons declared correctly that many state constitutions were silent on the subject.

He waved a campaign postcard that Republican gubernatorial candidate Jim Bennett had mailed to thousands of voters and read it out in a mocking tone: "'Right now, the Assembly dominates nearly every board and commission in the state, and it has to stop.' If not a lie," Irons thundered, "that's an absolute misstatement of the truth. The fact is that legislators constitute a majority on precisely two boards: the Lottery Commission and the Unclassified Pay Plan Board." But for all his bluster, Irons did not try to amend Lenihan's proposed constitutional amendment to balance power between the Senate and House.

After nearly four hours of testimony, Goodwin asked the committee's pleasure on both Algiere's original legislation and the substitute version of Lenihan's bill. By votes of 14–2 and 13–3, they sent both to the Senate floor. Never before had a committee in either the House or Senate backed separation of powers.

"I look at this as establishing a beachhead," Lenihan told reporters after the vote. "I hope passage of this bill will lead to a victory on the issue."

I said with less restraint, "The people have said it, the candidates for governor have said it, and now a Senate committee is saying Rhode Island needs to have an authentic American-style separation of powers. After a while, if the House leadership persists unreasonably, they will break themselves on this rock."[40]

On May 30, the Rhode Island Senate made history when both Lenihan's and Algiere's separation of powers amendments appeared on the calendar. The oratory did not soar, but awareness of a sea change permeated the chamber.

John Roney — who had prosecuted our complaint against former Gov. DiPrete eleven years earlier — railed against passage. He declared that a change of such historic import should come from a constitutional convention. "This is just what we should not be doing in the closing hours," he declared. "Constitutional amendments, like diamonds, are forever." Domenic Ruggerio also opposed passage, telling his colleagues that only six people had contacted him about separation of powers. "And five of them," he said, "had no idea what separation of powers was. They said they heard it on the talk show."[41]

Quietly, Lenihan defended the principle: "Separation of powers, as manifested in these bills, is not a cure-all for all our governmental ills. Simply vesting powers in a governor is by itself no assurance against abuse. We don't have to go back too far in our memories to note that." He reminded his colleagues that the legislature had historically dominated state government. "Rhode Island," he said, "would benefit from a healthy tension between the three branches of government."

Paul Kelly, who had blocked separation of powers for years, reiterated an argument he used often — legislators on boards and commissions brought back vital information about crucial issues. Nonetheless, Kelly announced, it was "the inherent right of the people to determine how their state government is going to be run." He said he would vote to put separation of powers on the ballot.

Uncharacteristically low-key, Bill Irons warned that Algiere's version would sever the legislature's "broad powers" from the Constitution. "I'm not sure what powers are being taken away," he said.

Despite Irons's urging, senators approved both the Algiere and Lenihan resolutions by identical votes of 40–6. The two Senate separation of powers resolutions went to the House Judiciary Committee, where they would surely die.

Gorham tried another procedural rule: if he could get 40 signatures on a discharge petition, that would require House leaders to bring his resolution to the floor. Against the massed power of Harwood's leadership team he got 38: 23 Democrats and 15 Republicans.[42]

The 2002 legislative session ended with new laws that violated separation of powers. Instead of adhering to the principle it had endorsed, the Senate succumbed to pressure from House leaders and consented to four new power grabs.[43] Gov. Almond vetoed these bills and the state budget, but the General Assembly returned on June 12 and overwhelmed his vetoes. Huge Democratic majorities in both chambers made the overrides seem like child's play.[44]

On a quiet Friday after lawmakers went home, two Democrats who had helped Gorham round up signatures on his discharge petition came back to the State House with some of their neediest constituents. Reps. Betsy Dennigan and Tom Palangio convened a press conference between massive marble columns outside the House chamber. Flanked by constituents with physical disabilities, they announced that House leaders had withheld funding for vulnerable groups and the nonprofits that served them. The punishment, Dennigan announced, came because of her votes for separation of powers amendments in 2001 and 2002 and because she had supported regular audits of the Assembly's finances. "I have stood strong on my beliefs that there should be separation of powers," she declared. "Unfortunately, House leaders do not share these views, and the members of the Summit Association — who are innocent bystanders — are being punished for my beliefs. It's tremendously unfair."

Palangio, a Providence Democrat, said he had sought funds for a baseball team of children with handicaps. "Using grants as a political club is the wrong thing to do," he said and restated his support for separation of powers: "It's the right thing to do. We need to take power away from the speaker's office — this speaker in particular because he uses power as a billy club."

Gubernatorial candidate Tony Pires stood with them, listening somberly. He told reporters about sixteen years as a representative, eight as chair of the House Finance Committee. "I understand the politics of the grant system," he said. But it was inappropriate to use this "for leverage against Rep. Dennigan for her willingness to be independent on separation of powers."

Harwood's chief of staff, former Rep. Frank J. Anzeveno Jr., watched from nearby and dismissed Dennigan's complaint. "Shame on her," he told reporter Edward Fitzpatrick, "I think it's unfair, and she's being political. The bottom line is that this has nothing to do with the separation of powers vote."[45]

In addition to being deprived of legislative grants, Dennigan was fighting for her political life in a district gerrymandered to contain only a tiny fraction of her old turf. "They think they're going to get rid of me by sticking me into a district where hardly anybody knows me," she said. "Could I be paranoid for thinking they're out to get me?"

A decade earlier, she had served on the Common Cause board and shaped proposals that finally won passage in the 1992 Campaign Finance Law. An emergency room nurse and mother of four energetic daughters, she had completed law school. But she faced a fierce uphill fight to hold her seat in the House.

Harwood seemed unassailable. With his wife ensconced in a lifetime magistrate appointment, he deflected ethics complaints, breezed through downsizing, gerrymandered districts, hijacked boards, crushed separation of powers, swatted away vetoes, and overpowered the Senate. I understood why even Sheldon Whitehouse needed his support. Had I been naïve to imagine that a perfect storm would engulf John Harwood?

43

Scandal

2002

Every election year since 1992, Common Cause had issued a legislative score-card. With the last gavel, we turned from pleading with the General Assembly to unveiling the mysteries of how bills became law — what Otto von Bismarck may have meant when he compared legislating to sausage making.[1] We never endorsed candidates, but incumbents often featured high Common Cause scorecard rankings in their campaign brochures. Those with poor scores took pains to explain.

Peter Hufstader arrived at the office with bundles of House and Senate jour-nals. On our long table he opened a binder full of recommendations. He pro-posed to tally votes in six areas: separation of powers; oversight and account-ability; campaign finance reform; ethics; election reform; and redistricting. We built lists of significant votes for the state governing board. Like engineers test-ing aerodynamic designs in a wind tunnel, they looked for weaknesses. They needed to know that we had informed lawmakers of our concerns and that the scorecard matched our priorities. For the 2001–02 scorecard the board settled on twenty-four votes in the Senate and nineteen in the House. Then began days of tedium as we entered yeas and nays one vote at a time, checked totals, and verified the count.

A centerfold in our newsletter listed a hundred representatives and fifty senators — the last time before the 2002 election would reduce the number to seventy-five and thirty-eight. For each lawmaker, we tallied votes for or against reform, absences on key votes, and a final average. On a separate honor roll we named the thirty-eight representatives who had dared to sign Nick Gorham's discharge petition.

Our front page emphasized a fundamental contrast. "House defiant as Senate advances powers question for people's vote," our headline proclaimed. "A hundred years from now," the story began, "historians may identify 2002 as the year voters connected the dots."

"House leaders punish reform effort," declared a second front-page headline. Our photo showed Rep. Betsy Dennigan charging that House leaders had cut off funds for a program that served blind and disabled people in her district. She charged that they were punishing constituents because she supported separation of powers.

The contrast between the two chambers was stark. Senate Majority Leader Bill Irons voted for what we considered reforms 79.2 percent of the time, and his chamber averaged 79.5 percent. Representatives averaged only 60.7 percent, and House Speaker John Harwood scored 25.8 percent, third from the bottom. When reporter Edward Fitzpatrick asked me to interpret Harwood's poor showing, I said, "He may have been elected as a reformer, and that's clearly how he portrayed himself. But in practice as speaker, he has done little in recent years to advance any reforms. In fact, the contrary appears to be true."[2] Under Harwood's leadership, representatives' scores had dropped sharply as the House weakened or buried major reforms passed by the Senate.

The *Providence Journal* featured our scorecard on its front page, with color photos of what it called "the Best" and "the Worst." Sen. Bill Enos (100.0%) and Rep. Susan Story (95.0%) stood in contrast to Sen. John Roney (50.0%) and Rep. Bambilyn Breece Cambio (17.4%), at the bottom. In a large box, the *Journal* listed the fifty senators and one hundred representatives in descending order of their scores. Fitzpatrick included a retort from Harwood's chief of staff, Frank Anzeveno: "One's political career is not measured in a very small snapshot. The ultimate report card will rest with the people in November, as it should."

Carl Bogus and Burt Hoffman, both members of the Common Cause state board, believed separation of powers advocates needed sharper teeth. Hoffman came from years in journalism and as a senior aide to Tip O'Neill, speaker of the House in Washington for a decade. They linked up with Bruce R. Lang, a founder of Operation Clean Government, and established a political action committee that they called the Rhode Island Separation of Powers Committee (RISOP). The new entity could raise money and endorse candidates; without apology it would try to influence the fall election. They recruited Alan Hassenfeld and Ron Machtley, president of Bryant University, to serve as co-chairs, while former General Treasurer Nancy Mayer became its treasurer. Under the new committee's banner they invited both incumbents and challengers in all General Assembly races to sign pledges of support for a separation of powers amendment and the procedural steps needed to bring it to a floor vote.[3]

ON JULY 24, Carl Bogus and I went to the governor's office to work on a second separation of powers advisory question for the November ballot. Almond's top lawyers, Joe Larisa and Tom Dickinson, met us there. To my surprise, Almond sat in and presided.

We quickly agreed not to wait for a constitutional convention. We would ask voters to demand a constitutional amendment that would repeal the "broad powers" clause that allowed the General Assembly to do anything not prohibited in the text of the Constitution. Our ballot question tied the clause to Rhode Island's history:

> Should the Rhode Island Constitution be changed to eliminate article VI section 10, which preserves to the General Assembly today broad powers granted to it by King Charles II of England in 1663, and also be changed to expressly provide that the legislative, executive, and judicial branches of Rhode Island government are to be separate and co-equal consistent with the American system of government?

The text rang like a bell. In sixty-four words, it unwrapped the historic issue and named the problem. It would leave no room for debate about whether voters meant to eliminate the "broad powers" clause.

"They'll object that it's a loaded question," Bogus said.

Larisa laughed. "The law says explicitly, 'The governor shall have the power to order the secretary of state to submit any question or questions that he shall deem necessary to the electors at any election.'[4] Where does it say we can't present a pointed question?"

Our question became Question 5 on the 2002 statewide ballot. Approval would not amend the state's Constitution, but would multiply pressure on lawmakers to present a constitutional amendment. Almond's lawyers would prepare a one-page explanation for the voter information booklet, which would emphasize the Supreme Court's declaration that Rhode Island government was "a quintessential system of parliamentary supremacy," not "the traditional American system of separate and coequal branches of government."[5]

Carl Bogus and I stepped into the marble hallway. Eight summers after the Common Cause state governing board had made separation of powers our highest priority, our meeting in a small conference room adjacent to the governor's formal office left us feeling hopeful. But would another public referendum change anything in the House?

Months had passed since the Ethics Commission dismissed Operation Clean Government's complaint against Harwood. Gerrymandering had brought lawsuits against Senate maps, but only scattered protests against new House districts. Harwood's kingly power grew with each new board while his heavy-handed maneuvers blocked separation of powers. Would the perfect storm we predicted ever come?

WHJJ-AM radio talk show host John DePetro proclaimed himself "the Independent Man," a reference to the bronze statue atop the State House dome. The gleaming figure balanced a ship's anchor against his heel and held a long spear pointed toward the sky. DePetro referred to himself in third-person — "the Independent Man has learned" — and typically skewered Democrats while lauding Republicans. Above all, he cultivated sources.

During the summer doldrums — on August 15, 2002 — DePetro perked up his audience when he unleashed a scandal involving a woman named Wendy Collins. In a recorded interview, Collins told DePetro that she would have been "very successful" if she had filed a sexual harassment suit against the speaker. Instead, she accepted a secret settlement with the words "sexual harassment and retaliation" blacked out.[6]

Speaker John Harwood had been forty-seven when he met the 29-year-old Collins at Family Court in 1999 and hired her, with few qualifications, ostensibly to conduct legislative research. She held the job for two years and left in August of 2001. DePetro had obtained documents from the Department of Labor showing that Collins had received a secret $75,000 workers' compensation settlement and a newly created job at Rhode Island College.

Within hours of DePetro's blockbuster, Rep. Tony Pires, Harwood's political ally until eighteen months earlier and now a candidate for governor, convened a press conference on the State House steps. He called on Atty. Gen. Sheldon Whitehouse, who was also running for governor, to investigate. "At the very least," Pires declared, "one has to question how someone who received a $75,000 workers' comp claim at the end of their service at one state job could then be rehired by Rhode Island College." Not to be outdone, Myrth York, now running strong in her third gubernatorial campaign, publicly urged Whitehouse to appoint an independent prosecutor.

Documents soon showed that Harwood's top lawyer and administrator, former Rep. Richard P. Kearns, had signed off on the secret settlement, advising the Department of Administration that he believed the pact was "in the best interest of the State of Rhode Island."[7]

Day after day, steamy details made the news. Then Rhode Island College President John Nazarian acknowledged that the position created for Collins was the first added in twenty-five years — and came only weeks before the House Finance Committee slashed $12 million from the budget for state colleges. Nazarian told the *Providence Journal* that he had been asking for a dozen additional positions but not the job that Collins got.

Television and talk radio gave endless play to the lurid particulars of what many quickly called "Wendygate." Cameras panned a State House hallway to a windowless committee room, where unnamed sources said trysts took place. After a week of salacious revelations, the *Providence Journal* editorialized: "The public must wonder whether Mr. Harwood's power lets him make secret deals, use patronage for personal advantage, and shield himself from scrutiny or responsibility. . . . That kind of unchecked power is unhealthy and breeds corruption."[8]

Inexplicably, Harwood left it to his chief of staff, former Rep. Frank Anzeveno, to deal with the press, but as the media clamored for details, Harwood finally convened a news conference to complain about the "innuendos and rumors surrounding this settlement." Without naming Collins, he insisted he had no role in creating the Rhode Island College job. "To be perfectly honest with you," he said, "I am rather angry. I've been in this building for twenty-two years. I feel I've been personally wronged. My reputation has been tarnished and most of all, my family."

Echoing President Bill Clinton four years earlier, Harwood flatly denied any sexual relationship with Collins. "I had no relationship at all," he said with lawyerly precision. "She, in fact, came up to me and asked if, in fact, there was any work at the State House. She, in fact, was recommended to me like everyone else. I said, fill out an application, bring a résumé, get your qualifications." As reporter Katherine Gregg kept pushing, Harwood's anger boiled over and he stormed out of his own press event.[9]

Several hours later Harwood accused Collins of demanding compensation above the $75,000 she had already received. "I have requested a complete investigation of this matter by the State Police," he announced.[10] That defense collapsed when State Police Superintendent Steven M. Pare acknowledged that he had met with Harwood and explained to the speaker that the allegations did not rise to the level of extortion. The State Police had declined to investigate.[11]

Columnist M. Charles Bakst wrote that the speaker reminded him of "a tin-horn dictator . . . whiny, often dodging questions. . . . And records stayed under wraps." He also noted that Harwood's wife, a Superior Court magistrate, had yet to make any public statement in support of her husband.[12]

More details popped up like mushrooms after summer rain. Tony Pires led a group of representatives and candidates in demanding that Harwood resign as speaker. Rep. Betsy Dennigan rehearsed how Harwood surrogates chastised her for challenging increases in legislative spending. "I get a pat on the back," Dennigan said, "and they tell me, 'Don't worry Betsy, we are doing good things with that money.'"[13]

The 2002 primaries fell less than a month after the scandal broke, and Myrth York edged out Sheldon Whitehouse by less than one percent of the votes cast.[14] Pires came in a distant third. On the GOP side, Don Carcieri crushed Jim Bennett, a Harwood friend and fellow hockey player. Meanwhile community activist Matthew A. Brown trounced Harwood's hand-picked incumbent, Secretary of State Edward S. Inman III.[15]

Primary results for House races showed incumbents supported by Harwood had won or lost by narrow margins. In his campaign against Harwood loyalist Rep. Eugene F. Garvey, challenger Matthew J. McHugh raised the Collins scandal and pounded Garvey for supporting Harwood in the 10–8 Judiciary Committee vote to kill separation of powers. Garvey had represented his South County district for a decade and was well liked, but McHugh ousted him.

In an adjacent district, Harwood had backed Narragansett Councilman George F. Lenihan against Rep. David A. Caprio, who had rallied support for separation of powers and featured the issue in his campaign. Charging that Harwood had recruited Lenihan to run against him and had stacked the district committee, Caprio crushed Lenihan by more than two-to-one.[16]

All summer Betsy Dennigan had campaigned in the gerrymandered district that barely included her home. She outpolled two well-known Democrats, one backed by Harwood, and won 51.2 percent of the primary vote.[17]

Harwood loyalists read the writing on the wall. A TV crew caught Deputy Majority Leaders Paul Moura and John McCauley leaving Harwood's State House office. The pair told reporters they had spent two hours with the speaker and asked him to resign. "The members," Moura added, "have lost confidence in his ability to initiate the fundamental reforms we need and to lead us to the next level." Moura added that he and other representatives were committing themselves to enact separation of powers.[18]

As the scandal heated up, pledges came flooding back to RISOP, the political action committee founded by Carl Bogus and Bruce Lang. Nearly all challengers pledged yes on separation of powers. Thirty sitting senators signed the RISOP pledge; only three refused. Thirty-eight incumbent representatives said yes, while Harwood and twenty-five die-hard loyalists said no. Full-page ads in newspapers listed lawmakers, and asterisks beside each name indicated previous votes on separation of powers.

With the tide running our way, the separation of powers task force, now augmented by leaders of religious, environmental and reform groups, set a goal of winning voter approval of seventy percent or more on Almond's second separation of powers advisory question, Question 5. But our message needed to thread a needle. We had to remind voters of John Harwood's abuses without hyperbolic language that would antagonize lawmakers who genuinely liked Harwood, were likely to win re-election, and would cast votes on a separation of powers amendment. We also needed to prevent separation of powers from becoming a partisan issue. Already some Republicans were mocking Democrats for jumping on what they claimed was their bandwagon.

Our approach would rely on earned media: stories and editorials in

newspapers; radio and television interviews. Groups that supported separation of powers would post information to their websites. Volunteers would
distribute flyers within their organizations, at houses of worship, door-to-door
in neighborhoods, and under the windshield wipers of cars in parking lots.

"Yes on Q5," our flyers declared in huge type. In smaller text, we explained:
"Question 5 for Separation of Powers." Bold caps across the cover urged voters
to "TAKE BACK DEMOCRACY." Our text summarized the General Assembly's
historic dominance, which left the executive and judicial branches powerless
to block legislative abuses. We wrote that our state needed separation of powers
as a bulwark against corruption.

> Two years ago, a 2 to 1 statewide majority passed Question 6, call-
> ing for a constitutional convention on the subject. Every town and
> city in the state voted yes. The question passed in all House and
> Senate districts as well.

> Q: So what happened?

> A: In 2001 and again in 2002, a majority of the state representa-
> tives killed separation of powers bills — first the call for a consti-
> tutional convention, then for a direct amendment. People were
> furious but had no power to force their representatives to pass
> the legislation.

As if John Harwood needed more trouble, the unthinkable happened: a challenger rose up on his home turf. On October 9, less than a month before the
election, Bruce Bayuk announced that he would run a write-in campaign against
the most powerful politician in Rhode Island. A Hewlett-Packard sales executive, Bayuk had a way with words and exceptional people skills. In his announcement, he reminded a gathering of politicians, candidates, reporters, and
voters that Harwood had received 606 votes in the previous month's primary,
but 855 voters had left that part of the ballot blank. "John Harwood," Bayuk
summarized, "essentially lost to 'none of the above.'"[19]

In neighboring Lincoln, William J. McManus took on Harwood protégé
John Douglas Barr II, who had always voted to bury separation of powers but
now pledged to support passage. McManus worked at CVS headquarters in
Woonsocket and delighted in telling voters that a Harwood loyalist had phoned
CVS's top lobbyist in hopes he would talk McManus out of the race. McManus
kept reminding voters that the absence of checks and balances had empowered
Harwood to cover up the Wendy Collins scandal.[20]

The final weeks of the campaign brought an October surprise: a grand jury
investigation bubbled into the headlines. As reporters camped outside, witnesses

spilled their stories. A worker's compensation administrator had testified that a sexual harassment claim filed by Collins had bypassed normal investigative procedures. The official said he and his supervisor had been warned not to talk about the case if they wanted to keep their state jobs and pensions. Collins's psychiatrist had described her as distressed over Harwood's sexual demands, claims which he disputed. Her lawyer, Stephen J. Dennis, insisted to reporters that she stood by her claim that she was fired for refusing. "She stood by it then," Dennis told reporters. "She stands by it now."[21]

Bruce Bayuk pounced on the grand jury information and on a report that the Joint Committee on Legislative Services (JCLS), which Harwood chaired, was paying lawyer-lobbyist Robert Goldberg to defend the speaker. Bayuk mocked the relationship. "It's ridiculous for attorney Goldberg to suggest the Wendy Collins settlement was a JCLS matter," Bayuk charged, "since there is no evidence any member of the JCLS other than Speaker Harwood knew about the case."[22] The challenger charged that the taxpayers should not have to pay for Harwood's "political survival team."

Harwood put on a game face. After dodging the press, he did several radio talk show interviews, insisting that he was the target of a shakedown by Collins for $750,000. The state had settled for $75,000, which he thought reasonable. He claimed he had yet to receive a bill from Goldberg and insisted he had more than enough votes to continue as speaker. In a town meeting of his constituents at Pawtucket's City Hall, one man asked the embattled speaker for a plain answer. Were the Wendy Collins allegations true or false?

"False," Harwood answered.

When a female attorney in the crowd asked why he allowed a worker's compensation settlement if the charges were false, Harwood replied that once the sexual-harassment allegations were removed he had no problem with Collins receiving a settlement for other "legitimate claims." When asked about separation of powers, Harwood offered his standard answer: removing lawmakers from boards would make state government less responsive to the people. "I think you need legislators, from my point of view, because they're accountable."[23]

In a private interview Harwood told *Providence Journal* columnist Mark Patinkin that his newspaper had overlooked contradictions in Collins's story. He asserted that despite defections from his leadership team, he would continue as speaker.[24]

In the November 5 election, Rhode Island voters approved Governor Almond's advisory Question 5 on separation of powers by a landslide. The statewide vote, 223,151 to 69,748, swept every city and town: 76.2 percent, a dramatic increase from 66.2 percent for Question 6 in 2000. Except for Tiverton, at 69.6 percent, no city or town approved by less than seventy percent.[25] The advisory question had no force of law but delivered a huge mandate for the 2003 session of the General Assembly.

Punished by Harwood and his allies in the Democratic Party for her early support of separation of powers, former senator Myrth York lost the gubernatorial race to Republican businessman Don Carcieri by nine percentage points. Their race became the most expensive in state history. Carcieri spent $2.76 million, mostly his own money, and York poured out $4.82 million, largely from family funds. Neither participated in the matching-funds program.

Carcieri's election continued a pattern of GOP victories in statewide elections. Republicans had occupied the governor's office for fourteen of the past twenty-two years, apparently reflecting voters' will to counterbalance the overwhelming and unshakable dominance of Democrats in the General Assembly.

Republican incumbents clung to six seats in the downsized Senate but lost three in the House. Minority Leader Bob Watson blamed the Rhode Island Separation of Powers Committee because its ads "obscured" the voting records of representatives who voted in April to send separation of powers back to committee but eventually pledged support. Faulting RISOP for causing "probably half-a-dozen races to go south on us," Watson also took a shot at Almond and his own party. "It has hurt that for the last eight years, nothing was done to build the grassroots of the party. Clearly, leadership starts from the top and works its way down."[26]

In Pawtucket, amid evidence of problems at the polls and charges of voting fraud, John Harwood barely survived the write-in challenge of Bruce Bayuk. The election turned on a jammed machine but finally ended with a narrow Harwood victory. After investigations and recounts by the Board of Elections, the speaker barely won his own district. University of Rhode Island political science professor Marc A. Genest thought the close result undid Harwood as speaker: "He may be the only candidate elected who actually loses. He's a dead man walking."[27]

Adjacent to Harwood's district, Betsy Dennigan garnered more than eighty-five percent of the vote in the district gerrymandered against her.

In Lincoln, Independent William J. McManus took just under sixty percent of the votes against Harwood protégé John Douglas Barr II.

A 19-year-old Republican novice, Anthony G. Spiratos, nearly defeated Paul Crowley of Newport, the only member of Harwood's team to make a public case against a separation of powers amendment. Crowley had been in the House for twenty-one years but won re-election by a scant 134 votes out of 4,008 cast. Humbled by his close call, Crowley told reporters he would seek a better way of bringing separation of powers to Rhode Island.[28]

In Providence, Rep. David Cicilline, who had sponsored separation of powers and ethics bills since 1995, easily won the mayor's office over two opponents.

At first glance, it looked like those who predicted that downsizing would hurt women were right. As the House dropped from one hundred to seventy-five members, the number of female representatives fell from twenty-four to thirteen, which translated into a seven percent loss. In fact, women represen-tatives interviewed by the *Providence Journal* blamed redistricting decisions made by men. Rep. Charlene Lima complained that women had been pitted against other incumbent women. "But women worked extremely hard to beat the odds," Lima said.

A computer analysis by the *Providence Journal* confirmed Lima's observation. In the House 62.5 percent of women faced other incumbents, while only 45 per-cent of men did. The number of women senators slipped from ten to nine, but the percentage of women in the downsized Senate rose from 20 to 24 percent.

"I hate to lose even one woman," said Sen. Teresa Paiva Weed. "But overall, women did extremely well in the Senate. They all invested a lot of time and energy in getting re-elected. They never blinked."[29]

On the South Side of Providence, Sen. Juan Pichardo took 74.3 percent against two independents and a Republican. No one was surprised at his bit-tersweet victory in what remained of the district long served by his friend Sen. Charles Walton. As the legislative leaders had done with women, they had also pitted minorities against each other.

Three days after the election, House Democrats caucused at the Providence Biltmore Hotel to pick their leadership team for 2003–04. Officially the entire House would choose the speaker in January, but Democrats commanded an overwhelming majority and seemed desperate for a new leadership team.

John Harwood put on his game face, claiming that both the grand jury and Pawtucket voters had "exonerated" him. Nonetheless, he said, "I feel it is time to step back and let others lead. I feel very, very comfortable with the team that's left behind." Still proud, he gave the impression that he had chosen his successor and that he might return to the top post once the dust cleared. William J. Murphy from West Warwick and Gordon D. Fox from the East Side of Providence had been contenders, but united their forces. Members quickly elected them speaker and majority leader.

At thirty-nine, Murphy was boyish, smooth-shaven, and charming. "I am here tonight," he told his colleagues, "to tell all within the sound of my voice that substantive change — for the better, for the good — is the number one priority of the Democratic majority in the Rhode Island House of Representatives."

"We are Democrats who are not threatened by change," Fox added. "We ac-cept the people's mandate to bring about change as reform, change as rejection of the politics of favoritism and self-enrichment, change as the adoption of a new political system that is open, responsive, honorable and fair." Descended from a Cape Verdean mother and an Irish-American father, Fox became the first person of color to serve as a majority leader in either chamber. He and Murphy said they were committed to separation of powers, reform of legislative hiring, and criteria for the award of legislative grants.[30]

Nine days after the election, a bipartisan team met at the office of outgoing Atty. Gen. Sheldon Whitehouse to draft a separation of powers amendment that all would support in the 2003 legislative session.[31] Eight of us sat at one end of an immense conference table between photographs of former attorneys general; at the head of the table Whitehouse took charge. "I think we're all aware that this could become a divisive session," he said. "I have little doubt that we'll see efforts to pass an amendment riddled with loopholes or that will lead to endless litigation."

Rep. Nick Gorham suggested that the essential elements seemed clear. "We have a decent House bill that hasn't passed," he said, "and two Senate bills that have."

We slid copies of the 2002 separation of powers resolutions to everyone around the table.[32] The elements included a ban on dual office holding, a section on gubernatorial appointments, a more explicit separation of powers clause, and strike-outs that indicated that the "broad powers" clause must be entirely deleted.

"If I may?" Mike Lenihan launched the discussion. "In my bill, it may seem redundant to have both a ban on dual office-holding and a detailed gubernatorial appointments clause. But I think of it as wearing both a belt and suspenders. Redundancy doesn't hurt, and it may help."

"Makes perfect sense," said Whitehouse, "and it's good language. Am I right that you modeled this on the presidential appointments clause of the U.S. Constitution?"

"You are," Lenihan said. "Notice that we've included the quasi-publics both in the ban on dual office-holding and in the gubernatorial appointments clause."

"Good to be explicit," Whitehouse agreed, "even redundant." He passed out copies of the relevant clause from the U.S. Constitution.[33] "The nice thing about following the federal model is that it's been so thoroughly litigated."

"I think," said Carl Bogus, "that by forbidding legislative appointments to any and every entity that 'exercises executive powers under the laws of this state,' we've captured all the important positions."

Everyone agreed that we had to delete the "broad powers clause" that had allowed the General Assembly to do whatever it pleased unless a particular action was specifically prohibited in the text of the Constitution.

"That'll be the toughest part," Whitehouse said. "They'll fight tooth and nail to keep it, but if we let it remain, we'll have accomplished very little."

Within an hour, the group reached consensus on details of an amendment that would be clearer, leaner, and stronger than any of its antecedents. We agreed that we must have both Democratic and Republican sponsors on the bills filed in each chamber. Lenihan and Gorham, long-term sponsors in the Senate and House, would sign up co-sponsors and file the new drafts in their respective chambers.

ON A DECEMBER EVENING, leaders from more than a dozen groups gathered
in the warm, glassed-in atrium at First Unitarian Church in Providence for an
update on the amendment and our strategy for winning approval. Flanked by
Sheldon Whitehouse and Mike Lenihan, Jim Miller, now president of Common
Cause Rhode Island, welcomed the crowd. "I'm a Baptist preacher," he said. "I'm
not going to talk much tonight, except to lay out a warning that our greatest
danger would be to take final passage by the General Assembly for granted. The
fact that seventy-six percent of the voters said they want separation of powers
means very little in the State House."

Whitehouse, now in his final month as attorney general, traced his commitment on the issue. Most people in the brightly lit space knew that he had paid
dearly among Democrats for his leadership on the issue over ten years. "A lot of
people have paid a price to bring us this far," Whitehouse said. "Everyone should
understand that we stand in the shoes of Thomas Wilson Dorr, who was tried
for treason and thrown into a dank cell on the site of what is now the Providence
Place Mall. Dorr got pneumonia and died without seeing any positive results.
We have reason to hope for more if we keep our eyes on the prize."

Whitehouse laid out the amendment we had drafted and answered
questions.

A somber Mike Lenihan spoke from his seat. "We got the votes in the Senate last May in part because everyone in the chamber knew that the House
would never pass separation of powers. Reluctance is the name of the game.
Enthusiasm is not."

Always the happy warrior, Rep. Nick Gorham thanked his colleague, Betsy
Dennigan, for coming. "She's a Democrat," he said. "And her party hammered
her for standing tall on separation of powers. I want to thank her publicly for
signing her name — time after time — when she knew they would punish her.
I expect some of their overt opposition will lessen this spring. Instead, we'll
see lots of righteous proclamations for an amendment. But all of that will be
little more than window-dressing. Watch them try to change a few words here
and a phrase there to weaken it. The watchword for us has to be vigilance until
this is done."

Jeff Grybowski, a lawyer for Governor-elect Don Carcieri, spoke about Carcieri's commitment to establish separation of powers as the foundation of state
government.

Carl Bogus spoke last. "American democracy," he said, "rests on two pillars:
the vote for all citizens and separation of powers between branches of government. A very large battle over this is coming. We will need every tool of political
action during coming months: letters, editorials, calls to talk show radio, calls
to friends, as well as more money to keep the public informed. We must hold
fast to the basic principle of separation of powers without compromise. There
is no compromise on that principle. Either you have it or you don't."

A warm rain fell as I drove home. Despite our predictions that three powerful disturbances would converge into a perfect storm, I never imagined that a sex scandal would tip the balance toward separation of powers. Harwood loyalists had concealed their settlement with Wendy Collins and the new job created for her. But the secret leaked and the maelstrom engulfed John Harwood.

Even our repeated defeats on separation of powers, both at the Supreme Court and in the General Assembly, had proved ultimately beneficial. Each new iteration of our constitutional amendment grew stronger than the one before, and we would enter the 2003 legislative session with the most watertight text yet. But could we get it through the General Assembly in 2003? Or would new legislative leaders cling to parliamentary supremacy as their predecessors had since 1663?

Four-Letter Word
2003

IN HIS INAUGURAL ADDRESS from the gleaming State House steps, Don Carcieri called for "a constitutional amendment that clearly separates the power between the executive and legislative branches." Diplomatically, the new governor said he was criticizing a defective system of government, not members of the General Assembly.[1] He invited everyone back in two days for the public unveiling of bipartisan separation of powers legislation that would be the centerpiece of his agenda.

On January 9, the State Room was packed. Leaders of the House and Senate sat in front as the new governor recognized Rep. Nicholas Gorham, Sen. J. Michael Lenihan, Sheldon Whitehouse, and me. He declared the bipartisan constitutional amendment "one of the most important things, if not the most important thing, we can get done."

The new House majority leader, Gordon Fox, promised to pass "meaningful" separation of powers legislation. He called the moment a "wonderful opportunity to redefine the working relationship between the legislative and executive branches."

Carcieri welcomed RISOP Chairperson Alan Hassenfeld and Common Cause President Jim Miller to the podium for final comments.[2]

An hour later, I stood on the new emerald green carpet and watched senators signing as co-sponsors of Mike Lenihan's separation of powers amendment. District numbers that followed their illegible signatures would allow clerks to decipher the list. Freshly elected to the new constitutional office of Senate president,[3] Sen. William V. Irons signed second, a powerful signal that the Senate would pass our bipartisan bill.[4] Of the thirty-eight senators in the downsized chamber, thirty-five became co-sponsors.

Rep. Nick Gorham faced slower going in the House.[5] At his desk on the wine-red carpet, he showed me his list of thirty-eight co-sponsors, a majority of the seventy-five members. "Much easier than last year," he said with a grin. "What a difference an election makes!"

But ominously missing from his list were the new speaker, majority leader, majority whip, and chairs of House committees.[6]

Nor had Bristol Rep. Fausto Anguilla signed Gorham's bipartisan resolution. In December, under strict secrecy, Anguilla had asked my reactions to a draft amendment he was preparing on behalf of Murphy's leadership team. I marked up sections that would cause problems, and the version he introduced in January showed minor improvements.

Our bipartisan version proposed to add only three words to Article V: "The powers of the government shall be distributed into three (3) separate and co-equal departments: the Legislative, the Executive and the Judicial."

Instead of three new words, Anguilla proposed to add almost two hundred to Article V: "Except as expressly provided in this Constitution," Anguilla's bill read, "all legislative powers are vested in the general assembly and no department of government but the general assembly shall exercise legislative power."[7]

I had warned him privately that this language might cripple the Ethics Commission's authority to "adopt a code of ethics" and prompt law suits against scores of administrative agencies that promulgated rules. It troubled me even more that Anguilla proposed to keep the "broad powers" clause which the state Supreme Court had cited twice since 1999 as the source of unfettered legislative supremacy.

Forty-three representatives, all Democrats — including the leadership and many who had thwarted separation of powers in 2001 and 2002 — signed on as co-sponsors of Anguilla's bill. Were they feigning action on separation of powers to force a compromise that would preserve legislative supremacy?

On a frigid January night, more than three hundred people leaned through a biting wind from the ocean to attend a separation of powers forum at the Atlantic Beach Club in Newport. The stylish restaurant stood where the creamy sands of Easton's Beach gave way to a rock-ribbed peninsula, the very spot where a developer had proposed his time-share hotel. Approval by the Coastal Resources Management Council in 1984 had launched the modern controversy over separation of powers.[8]

Now, the new governor and key legislative leaders took seats with their backs to huge windows overlooking a dark sea. Gov. Carcieri ad libbed themes from his inaugural address: the General Assembly's domination of state government was dangerous, and it was time to pass the bipartisan separation of powers amendment. The audience cheered.

Newport Rep. Paul Crowley, a ten-term incumbent who had barely won re-election over a 19-year-old Republican challenger, countered the governor's demand for haste. "This is a serious debate," Crowley insisted. "For Rhode

Island to adopt this bill without discussing this issue is not doing justice to the question."[9]

Crowley's hometown crowd booed him, and from her seat next to mine, Sen. Teresa Paiva Weed whispered that the audience was not being fair to Crowley. In her turn at the microphone, Paiva Weed urged patience with the legislative process. "This is an exciting time," she said with a wide smile. "We're going to be restructuring government, and we need to talk, debate, and discuss how we do that."

Another night, despite a rapid fall of heavy, wet snow, people filed into the historic nave at St. Michael's Episcopal Church in Bristol for a debate between Rep. Fausto Anguilla and Roger Williams University Law Professor Carl Bogus. The combatants took turns behind the lectern, a polished brass eagle that gleamed in a beam of light from darkness far above. "We can't rush this," Anguilla declared. "We have to get it right, because this is probably the most important issue the legislature will take up for generations."[10]

Bogus and Anguilla differed sharply over how to treat the "broad powers clause," which allowed lawmakers to exercise powers rooted in the Royal Charter of 1663. Bogus pointed out that the state Supreme Court had ruled twice in two years that the clause allowed the General Assembly to create and also operate boards like the Lottery Commission. "The voters," he said, "by an overwhelming majority, favored removing that clause."

Anguilla parried that most voters had not understood the issue. "My legislation makes it clear that no branch of government can exercise 'any of the powers properly belonging to either of the others, except as expressly provided in this Constitution.'"

Audience members listened politely, then lined up at a microphone to ask questions. Several urged Anguilla to remove his name from the leadership bill. "We elected you," said one woman, "and we want you to support real separation of powers. We've come too far for a bill full of gobbledygook."

Anguilla tried to mollify her: "At the end of the day, I think you're going to be pleased. We'll produce a separation of powers amendment that everyone can live with."

"Respectfully, Representative," the questioner pushed back, "we can't live with any continuation of the 'broad powers clause.'"

In February, two fiery tragedies overwhelmed all else. NASA's space shuttle Columbia broke up as it re-entered the earth's atmosphere. Fragments streaked across the Texas sky. Seven astronauts died. Then a Warwick roadhouse called "The Station" went up in flames, leaving a hundred people dead and scores more in burn units.

Both tragedies involved reckless indifference on the part of officials who might have averted the disasters.

While medical examiners worked to identify charred corpses, Rhode Island's new governor and his wife set up a refuge at a nearby hotel where families could wait for news. Don and Sue Carcieri comforted families and visited horribly burned survivors in hospitals. Carcieri spoke tenderly at memorial services,[11] and while the issues were not linked, his presence and compassion enhanced his call for separation of powers.

In March, with legislative hearings about to begin, editors at the *Providence Journal* declared their unequivocal support for our amendment. "Rather than signing on to a bipartisan bill that would quickly get the job done," the editors wrote, "House leaders have chosen to back a bill that, it appears, would leave them in charge and reform little." The editorial pummeled Fausto Anguilla for trying to preserve the broad powers clause and for vastly complicating separation of powers language.[12]

A few days after the editorial, I spoke with Rep. Elaine Coderre on the House floor. In her fifties, she had represented her working-class Pawtucket district for nineteen years. A veteran of countless battles, she now had the thankless duty of chairing the new House Committee on Separation of Powers, which included Nick Gorham, Fausto Anguilla, and Paul Crowley.

Peter Hufstader, our research director, had analyzed separation of powers provisions from state constitutions across the country. I handed Coderre a copy of his thick binder, *Separation of Powers Provisions Reference Manual,*[13] and paged through its tabbed sections with her.

"This should save us time," Coderre said. "How many boards do you think legislators serve on?"

I flipped to a tab that listed seventy-three boards where legislators and legislative appointees executed state laws. She skimmed the list, which included a precise enumeration of legislative appointments. Printouts of the enabling statutes listed executive functions in bold type. Coderre slid her finger down a page. "I can't argue with that one," she mused. "Or that." She asked how we defined executive functions.

I said the Rhode Island General Laws had no definition and showed her a list we had culled from enabling statutes for particular boards: managing property, executing contracts, receiving taxes, investing funds, enforcing rules, issuing permits, collecting fees for licenses, and scores of variants.[14]

"I may not agree with every detail," Coderre said, "but this research helps. If you could present copies of this to our entire committee at our first hearing, I'll put you on right after the governor." Her face seemed to sag with the burden. "There's one fact I hope you'll remember," Coderre continued wearily. "No matter what the *Journal*'s editors think, we are not devious. We want to get this right."

Two days later, she gaveled her new committee to order for the first of what she explained would a series of hearings. In contrast to John Harwood's resistance, William Murphy had arranged for Room 313, one of two rooms equipped for live television. In another dramatic departure, Murphy and Majority Leader Gordon Fox sat together in the audience.

"As we start," Coderre said, "I want to be clear that better distinguishing between the three branches of Rhode Island government is an issue whose time has definitely come. I know feelings are strong, but we are going to do this fairly."

Rhode Island's new chief executive testified for nearly an hour from a prepared text, urging the committee to pass the bipartisan bill promptly.

"Respectfully, Governor," asked Rep. Paul Crowley, vice chair of the committee, "under separation of powers, should a truly independent court system submit its budget directly to the General Assembly rather than to the governor first?" Crowley's question set a trap for the novice governor.

"Frankly," Carcieri answered agreeably, "I don't have a problem with that."[15]

I winced. The Constitution required the governor to present a consolidated budget that included court expenses each year.[16] His answer invited tampering with the bipartisan amendment.

Rep. Peter Kilmartin, a Pawtucket police detective who was now studying law, tested Carcieri with the argument that legislators who served on boards were providing needed oversight. He rehashed the traditional trope that lawmakers on boards became effective advocates for funding.

Carcieri tried to turn the argument. "The governor should be making the appointments," he declared, "and if the people I appoint don't do the job, I hope you'll hold my feet to the fire."

When Carcieri left, Coderre called on Peter Hufstader and me. We handed boxes full of tabbed binders to the clerk and took seats at the witness table. I introduced Hufstader, and he walked committee members through the reference manual.

Sen. Mike Lenihan's steady focus and unflappable demeanor had won back the favor of Senate President Bill Irons. Irons put Lenihan in charge of the Senate Committee on Government Oversight, which had jurisdiction over separation of powers. With Irons as co-sponsor of Lenihan's bipartisan amendment, no one expected fireworks when Lenihan posted it along with a rival bill by Sen. Daniel Connors for public hearing.[17]

Both Gov. Don Carcieri and former Atty. Gen. Sheldon Whitehouse were waiting to testify when Irons took his seat in the committee and upstaged them. "While we're considering separation of powers," Irons announced, "the balance of powers between the House and Senate should not be left unattended." His target was the Joint Committee on Legislative Services (JCLS), where the House had three votes and the Senate only two. For generations, speakers of the House had held hostage Senate personnel, offices, computers, and pride. Irons hurled his grudge like a grenade into the separation of powers debate. "What sense does it make," he demanded, "to have a half-hearted reform?"

Amid stunned silence, Irons pushed on: "I know it confuses some, but the issue here is building a government our citizens can trust."

As long as I had known him, Irons had reveled in political theater. Was he bluffing? Would he jeopardize separation of powers to force parity between the chambers? Once he took such a strong public stand, could he back off without losing face?

"I have every appreciation of the Senate president's position," Lenihan told reporters after the hearing, "but I have reservations based purely on pragmatism about pairing these issues. I don't want the issue of separation of powers to fall over an issue that is related but not identical."

When the reporters asked me, I told them Common Cause agreed with Irons about the need to balance powers between the House and Senate in managing the legislature. But I said a simple change in the law could resolve the problem without incorporating that change in a separation of powers amendment.

Speaker William Murphy soon heard what Irons had said and issued a statement. "Management of the legislature," Murphy said "has absolutely nothing to do with separation of powers." He lambasted the comment as "an eleventh hour power grab."[18]

Many were sporting green for Saint Patrick's Day when Lenihan convened his committee again. Every witness urged the committee to pass his bipartisan amendment. Topher Hamblett argued that it was impractical for lawmakers to hold day jobs, deliberate in the General Assembly, and serve on quasi-public boards.

Lenihan announced that the Senate would not tie the question of balancing power between the House and Senate to the constitutional separation of legislative and executive powers. He explained that he was not sure how the bipartisan amendment might be reconciled with a House version, which might differ in significant detail. "I've been around here long enough to know there are many ways to wordsmith a bill," he said. "But the policy I'm going to follow is: 'On matters of principle, stand like a rock.'" His committee voted unanimously to send his bipartisan resolution to the Senate floor.[19]

The Senate took up separation of powers on March 26. Without pride in his voice, Lenihan hoped his bill would "restore that vital but eroded faith" in state government. All thirty-six senators in the chamber voted for Lenihan's bipartisan amendment.[20]

Debate over separation of powers in Rhode Island took place against the surreal backdrop of war in Iraq. Television showed spectacular nighttime bombing attacks on the palaces of Saddam Hussein. On the day Baghdad fell to American forces, the House Separation of Powers Committee held a crucial public hearing. Patrick T. Conley, a former history and constitutional law professor at Providence College, spoke at the committee's request. "In my testimony," he announced, "I want to look at American history rather than hysterics." He dismissed the drive for separation of powers as "a partisan plea for power."

Conley praised the Royal Charter of 1663 as the most liberal government document of its time, and said the theory of separation of powers was not expounded until the middle of the seventeenth century. "And because Rhode Island was already the most democratic colony," he said, "the General Assembly saw no reason to draft a constitution." Conley summarized increasing pressure for a Constitution that led to the Dorr Rebellion and the Constitution of 1843. "In that constitution," he said, "the legislature was dominant, and few express powers were granted to the governor."

He catalogued constitutional amendments that had enlarged the powers of the state's traditionally weak chief executive: establishing the gubernatorial veto; directing the governor to prepare an annual budget; extending the governor's term from one to two years, and then from two years to four; ending the Grand Committee election of Supreme Court justices; and letting the governor appoint judges from a list. All of those advances, Conley said, had been granted by the General Assembly and approved by voters.

Conley criticized Gov. Almond's two non-binding referenda on separation of powers, which he said were "framed as leading questions. The voters were provided with misleading information. The wording was reminiscent of P.T. Barnum. There is no overwhelming popular mandate for the radical change that's being proposed here."[21]

Members of the audience waiting to testify became restive as the historian's testimony stretched into a second hour. "Madam chair," called former Rep. Rod Driver, "is there a time limit for testimony?"

"I haven't imposed time limits on other witnesses," Coderre replied.

"Well, you should!" came a shout from the back of the room. "We've heard enough!" John Carothers, a Warwick activist, was on his feet, yelling.

"Please," Coderre shouted. "We must have order."

Carothers carried on loudly until Capitol Police hustled him out. With order restored, Conley argued that the broad powers clause should not be deleted but amended by adding a single word. He proposed that the General Assembly "continue to exercise the *legislative* powers it has heretofore exercised, unless prohibited in this Constitution."

"Professor," Nick Gorham asked, "can you tell us another state that has a similar phrase?"

Conley thought several might and said he would get back with an answer.

"To your knowledge," Gorham persisted, "has any other state supreme court said their system of government is one of 'quintessential parliamentary supremacy'?"

"Not to my knowledge," Conley replied. "I regarded that part of the 1999 advisory opinion as hyperbolic. I don't believe we have such a system."

Many others were waiting to testify. Henry Sharpe, the retired president of Brown and Sharpe, took his turn. "I'll be very brief," he began. "I've published no books, and I'm not a lawyer. I did have the experience for fifty years of running a major corporation in Rhode Island. At our peak, we had over eleven thousand employees in the state. Today, we have only about two hundred left."

The retired executive said he had always been both a promoter and a critic of Rhode Island. He told of driving IBM's president Thomas J. Watson from an event at Brown University to the airport. "Since I had him as a captive audience, I put my Rhode Island promoter hat on. 'Tom,' I said, 'IBM should build a plant in Rhode Island.'"

Watson shouted that he would never do that. "We were on Interstate 95, just going into the Thurbers Avenue curve," Sharpe recounted. "I almost wrecked the car." The IBM executive had said he could never build where people were so jaded about government corruption.

"I knew Watson was right," Sharpe said. "I'd always known it. It's too cozy, and not just because we're small. It's because the legislative leaders have their fingers in everything. It's because we lack separation of powers to keep the General Assembly in check."

He spoke of the two overwhelming votes of the people for separation of powers. "Seventy-five per cent of the electorate know there's trouble here that shouldn't be. They sense that unless this gets straightened out, we'll be in even worse trouble."

"And which bill do you support?" Gorham asked.

"Yours," Sharpe replied. "The citizens have made their recommendations clear. The governor has joined. The Senate has voted its support. Now it's up to you in the House." Sharpe closed by observing that separation of powers would not solve all problems but would be what he called "a great start."

Providence Journal reporter Liz Anderson broke the story that House leaders had paid two academics, Robert F. Williams and G. Alan Tarr, to defend their legislative turf.[22] A third, Alan Rosenthal, came from Rutgers without pay at the request of his former student, political science professor Maureen Moakley. Rosenthal's specialty was state legislatures, and he suggested that Rhode Island's problems might stem more from single-party control of the General Assembly than from weak separation of powers. If too many Democrats was the problem, he joked, the state could import Republicans from Ohio or take steps to increase Republicans' birth rate.

Rosenthal said he favored separation of powers but wondered what problem the amendments under consideration aimed to address. Had legislators on boards done dreadful things? Were the boards not functioning well? What was the infirmity?

"You've got the solution," he said, speaking confidently without notes. "Prohibit legislators from serving on boards and add language that separates the powers. But couldn't the problems be solved by statute rather than constitutional amendment?"

Wondering aloud whether the Rhode Island governor's office was really too weak, Rosenthal noted that governors typically had an upper hand over legislatures via the bully pulpit through which they could command the media with a single voice. The General Assembly had given Rhode Island's governor unique power to place a referendum on the ballot. No other governor — as far as he knew — had such a powerful tool for mobilizing public opinion. Legislators had made mistakes, the Rutgers professor suggested, but why "punish the whole legislature because a few may have screwed up?"

Rosenthal made it sound as if separation of powers advocates were obsessing over superficial problems. In a masterful performance, he advised the committee to take a minimalist approach when amending the Constitution — lest they "open a can of worms and not be able to get the worms back into the can."

University of Rhode Island political science professor Maureen Moakley cast the issue in historical terms. "Given the historical hostility toward the British monarchy," she testified, "Massachusetts in 1780, Vermont in 1793, New Hampshire in 1784, Maine in 1819 and, of course, Rhode Island in 1842 all approved constitutions that granted broad powers to the legislative branch and severely limited the power of the executive."[23] She omitted the fact that since the nineteenth century the other New England states had established robust separation of powers, but Rhode Island had not.

Curiously, Moakley acknowledged that Superior Court Judge Michael Silverstein's ruling on the Lottery Commission "got it exactly right" because power in the hands of lawmakers "was in fact too separate — in that just a few people on that commission were essentially making laws, bypassing the entire representative system." She noted correctly that the commission "was creating regulations and policy relating to lotteries without the consent of the entire House and Senate and without the ability of the governor to weigh in with a veto."

Moakley did not mention that the Supreme Court had overruled Silverstein and reaffirmed the Lottery Commission's board with a lopsided majority of legislators.

The citizens of Bristol took pride in American history. Since 1785 they had been mounting Fourth of July parades, the longest continuous series in the United States. In 1993, the town celebrated the opening of Rhode Island's only law school, an event that transformed what began as a junior college into Roger Williams University. Perched on a breathtaking peninsula that stretched into Mount Hope Bay, the school was a source of jobs and pride. Two members of the House Separation of Powers Committee — Raymond E. Gallison Jr. and Fausto Anguilla — represented parts of historic Bristol.

Carl Bogus's cachet as a member of the law school faculty enhanced his credibility in the historic town. In an interview with the *Bristol Phoenix* he dissected Anguilla's legislation and stressed the need for both of the town's representatives to work for authentic separation of powers.

His advocacy produced results. On two successive Thursdays, the *Phoenix* ran forceful editorials. The first, entitled "Lords of the manor still blocking the gates," ripped Bristol's hometown representatives. "As the debate comes to a head," declared editor Scott Pickering, "the future of Rhode Island government will be determined." Pickering urged his readers to demand that Anguilla and Gallison switch their support to the bipartisan bill. He also listed their home phone numbers with email addresses. "Tell them it's time to give up the castle," the broadside ended. "The old ways are changing."

A second editorial hit even harder. "With the aid of Rep. Fausto Anguilla, the House of Representatives leadership has attempted to stonewall real reform," Pickering wrote. "Rep. Anguilla and his cohorts in the House now stand alone in support of a watered down bill that will not get the job done."[24]

Predictably, Bristol's representatives defended themselves in letters the *Phoenix* published in full. Gallison wrote that "the voters want our legislature reined in but not totally eviscerated," and Anguilla complained of bullying in the House.[25]

Not long after that, the law school's interim dean, Bruce I. Kogan, dropped by Bogus' office to deliver a message: whenever Bogus spoke about separation of powers, he must make clear that he was expressing his own opinion and not that of the university.

Stunned, Bogus demanded to know more, and Kogan told him that the university's president, Roy J. Nirschel, had raised the concern after a conversation with two legislators. Bogus marched to the president's office for an explanation. Nirschel acknowledged that two legislators whom he refused to name had spoken with him about separation of powers and the university's tax-exempt status. Rather than let the matter simmer in silence, Bogus contacted reporters, who phoned the president's office.[26]

Gallison and Nirschel admitted separately to Brian Comfort, a reporter at the *Bristol Phoenix*, that they had discussed the issues, but Nirschel insisted: "Nobody ever held the university hostage. There were no threats, implicit or explicit."

"With respect to someone threatening the tax exempt status of Roger Williams University," Gallison said, "I certainly did not do that."[27]

Spring came in fits and starts across southern New England. Outside the State House, skateboarders sped along Smith Street, oblivious to traffic. Near the end of April, Bill Irons fired a shot across the bow of House leaders. In comments first to *Providence Journal* reporter Liz Anderson and then in an unprecedented conversation with the Common Cause board, Irons urged separation of powers advocates to hold out for the Gorham-Lenihan version and not accept any compromise from the House. "There is no reason for these groups to negotiate," he declared. "Why would you accept something other than what you think is right?"

Irons's stand with a Republican governor and community activists in defiance of House Democrats surprised many. "This is one of the few times in my twenty years," Irons said, "that the voters of this state have clearly, with good representation, said they want a specific piece of legislation. I'm standing up for what the people of this state have said."[28]

The tide was running with us, but weeks slipped away without a final text, and no one knew what compromises might become necessary. My hackles went up when leaders of several groups in the coalition told me they had been invited to the speaker's office to discuss what their organizations wanted in an amendment. Was the new speaker of the House testing the coalition's resolve, or trying to divide and conquer?

Murphy avoided me. Each day I cruised the red-carpeted aisles of the House chamber to check with members of the Separation of Powers Committee. Occasionally, I posted myself at the top of the marble stairs that the speaker and his entourage had to take down to the floor. When I asked to walk him down, he grinned playfully. "I know what you want, Phil. We still don't have consensus on a text."

"When do you expect to, Mr. Speaker?"

"Wish I could tell you," Murphy said cheerily. "We're just not there yet." Our conversation over, he swept onto the House floor and bounded up to the rostrum.

Finally, in the fourth week of April, he promised me the text. "On Monday," he said. "Call my office, and we'll have a copy for you."

I shook his hand and thanked him. With his handshake promise we scheduled back-to-back meetings for Monday, April 28. The bipartisan drafting committee would analyze the House text and then report its recommendations to our growing coalition.

I should have known better. I kept calling the speaker's office, hoping for a copy. "It's not ready," said Larry Berman, Murphy's spokesperson. "I've told him you called. What else can I tell you?"

Time ran out without their text. The drafting committee met in a conference room at the First Baptist Church on College Hill where Jim Miller was now senior pastor. Sheldon Whitehouse, Nick Gorham, Mike Lenihan, and Carl Bogus were waiting when I arrived. I apologized for not having the promised text from Murphy.

"No surprise," Gorham grumbled. "I thought he was just stringing you along."

Always hopeful, Miller suggested that we review the versions we had. All agreed that Anguilla's bill was unacceptable, and we saw no clear path toward a reasonable compromise or victory.

The movement had grown and evolved. About thirty leaders of eleven groups showed up for the full coalition meeting.[29] From behind an antique brass music stand Miller welcomed them. "As you know," he said, "we expected to have the House version, but we don't." He asked members of the drafting committee to share their thoughts.

"I think they're in flux," Carl Bogus began. "We've upset their applecart. They've been reaching out to groups in our coalition, probably testing to see if they can split us apart. I hope we'll all hold together and not let that happen." He stepped from behind the brass lectern. "I want to say as forcefully as I can that Anguilla's bill will not produce separation of powers in any recognizable form. It may be well-meant, but it's fraught with problems."

"I'm with Carl on that," declared Gorham. "They paid witnesses to come in, and we went through the formalities of hearings. Even their hired guns had problems with Anguilla's version, but none of that mattered. Committee hearings really don't mean a thing. When they figure out what they can accept, the word will come down from Murphy's office on the third floor. They didn't provide a text today because they haven't got their ducks lined up. They're still desperate for some way to cling to their power and convince everybody that they've given us authentic separation of powers."

Sheldon Whitehouse stood up. Not yet fifty, his abundant hair had gone gray on top, but he seemed more comfortable in his skin than he had a year earlier when he was campaigning for governor. "This is a critical moment," he began. "We wrote the Gorham-Lenihan language, and we all want closure on it. But I think the House and Senate and governor have to work out the final details."

"Sheldon's right about that," said Jeff Grybowski, a young lawyer who had represented Carcieri in the original drafting process. With close-cut hair and muscular shoulders, he looked more like a football player than an attorney. "We're talking frequently with Murphy and Irons. Obviously, I can't tell you the details, but it will help if you give us space to get this done."

"Why didn't Murphy provide a text today?" Burt Hoffman demanded. "It's serious to promise with a handshake and not deliver."

"I can't speak for the speaker," Grybowski said. "I can tell you that they know how much is riding on every word."

"My concern," Whitehouse added, "is that we not let the perfect become the enemy of the good. We may be at the point where outside pressure stops being helpful. I think our pressure must now be on the triumvirate — Carcieri, Murphy, and Irons — to work it out."

"I have to disagree," said Bogus. "Public pressure and fear of the voters have brought us this far. We can't be nasty, but we have to be specific about what language we can accept, and we have to keep the pressure on."

Jim Miller looked to Mike Lenihan, who had still not spoken, and asked if he had anything to add.

"To tell this coalition what to do," Lenihan began with a smile, "is above my pay grade. But I hope you'll stand solid behind the bill we drafted last fall and now seems to have my name and Rep. Gorham's stamped on it. After hearings in my committee, the Senate passed it unanimously." He peered over half-frame glasses. "The challenge now will be for all of us to speak with a consistent and collective voice. We'll probably have to accept some final trade-offs, if only to let the House finish this process without losing face."

"What kind of trade-offs?" Hoffman called.

"Always hard to tell," Lenihan answered. "I assume we could let go of 'separate and co-equal' and accept 'separate and distinct' instead, which they clearly like. Since so many other states use that language, it would make little or no difference. I remain seriously troubled about keeping the broad powers clause in any way, shape, or form. If the House leadership gets to keep it, the rest may be for naught. But if they give it up, they'll need some face-saving device."

"And what might that be?" Hoffman asked.

"Hard to tell," Lenihan answered again. "Perhaps some kind of preamble."

"To go into the Constitution?"

"Probably not. Just to express legislative intent to the voters and for the record." Lenihan sat down.

Bob Arruda, the president of Operation Clean Government, stood up at one side of the crowd. "This has been helpful," he said. "I agree that we can't accept continuation of the broad powers clause in any form. I'm fine with substituting 'separate and distinct' for 'separate and co-equal.'" Arruda clasped his hands. "I think we need to agree among ourselves that no one from our coalition will go in to negotiate with Murphy. They've proven extremely skillful at divide and conquer."

"Second," someone said, and Miller called for a vote that was unanimous.

A second vote declared "a strong consensus in support of the bipartisan Lenihan-Gorham resolution."

A third expressed "disappointment that the House leadership has not yet provided any substitute text for public discussion."

"I would move," Whitehouse said, "that the coalition also tell the speaker that this historic moment demands political agreement among the House, the Senate, and the governor."

"Second," several shouted, and the motion passed. They assigned me to write about these four points of agreement to all the State House players and members of the coalition.

Two weeks later Rep. Nick Gorham called me into the House Minority office before the afternoon's session. "We have agreement on my bill," he said. "I think you'll be pleased."

"Show me."

"I can't," he said. "The speaker made us promise. They're keeping it extremely close until a press announcement on Thursday."

"Who agreed?"

"Murphy, Fox, and Coderre for the House majority, Bob Watson and I for the House minority, and Jeff Grybowski for the governor's office."

"Has the Senate agreed to it?"

"Not that I know of."

"Has Sheldon seen it?"

"I don't think so."

"So can you tell me anything that's in it?"

"You'll be happy," Gorham said, barely above a whisper, "that they've agreed to delete the broad powers clause."

"Entirely?"

"Entirely. They've tweaked a section about legislative power in Article VI, Section 2. Aside from that, it's pretty much our whole bill."

"And you're satisfied?"

"I think I am. And once they pass it, there'll be no going back."

Few substitute bills rate the exposure of a televised press conference, but word went out that House leaders would unveil a revised version of Gorham's separation of powers legislation on May 15 in the House Lounge. As we gathered, portraits of former speakers stared down from gilded frames on crimson walls: Harry Curvin, John Wrenn, Joseph Bevilacqua, Matty Smith, Joe DeAngelis. Each, during his time on the dais, had been the most powerful politician in Rhode Island. I assumed that all would have been horrified at whatever these new leaders of the House were about to offer as a compromise constitutional amendment on separation of powers.

As representatives filled the seats, few seemed pleased that I was there. Every chair was taken, and scores of people stood along the walls when House leaders, both Republicans and Democrats, marched in together. In his opening remarks, Murphy thanked Anguilla for agreeing to withdraw his bill in deference to a revised version of Gorham's bill. This legislation, Murphy said, would fulfill the promise his leadership team had made in January: the House would pass a separation of powers bill during this session.

"This exercise has proven that the deliberative legislative process works," Murphy added. "I'm proud that we were able to bring all the parties together — after much debate — and reach an agreement on what we believe will be the best bill for the people of Rhode Island."

Majority Leader Gordon Fox followed Murphy at the podium. "Over the course of many years," he said, "the issue of separation of powers has been discussed in Rhode Island, perhaps more frequently than any other. Yet it has never been debated by this chamber. This bill," he added, "is one of many reforms that represent the dawning of a new era here."[30]

Was this real or merely spin? Either way, public pressure had moved him and Murphy in our direction.

Staff members passed copies of the proposed substitute version of Gorham's bill down the rows of chairs. It used "separate and distinct" in place of "separate and co-equal." We could live with that.

Much more important, it would delete the broad powers clause entirely. But it would amend another section on legislative power by striking one word and adding four:

> Article VI Section 2. Power vested in general assembly — Concurrence of houses required to enact laws – style of laws. ~~The~~ <u>Full</u> legislative power, under this Constitution, shall be vested in <u>and exercised by</u> two houses, the one to be called the senate, the other the house of representatives; and both together the general assembly. The concurrence of the two houses shall be necessary to the enactment of laws.[31]

I wondered why they wanted to add the underlined words in a section of the Constitution we had not proposed to change.

"From the start of this discussion," Fox was saying, "our leadership made clear that we were committed to passing true separation of powers legislation. Today you are witness to this historic first step."

The self-congratulation and accolades continued. Sheldon Whitehouse had slipped into the room, and several speakers praised him as "the Father of Rhode Island's modern separation of powers movement." Now in private practice with a major downtown law firm, Whitehouse beamed and waved.

At the podium, Nick Gorham savored his triumph. "This just shows," he declared, "that if you really believe in something, and you stick to it, you can actually get something done up here. Even against tremendous odds."[32]

"We're not there yet," Sheldon Whitehouse told me the next morning on the phone. "The Senate and House might still refuse to accept each other's bills. The House clearly wants 'separate and distinct' instead of 'separate and co-equal.'"

I reminded him Common Cause had no problem with "distinct," which had been in amendments we had been pushing since 1997. "But 'full legislative power' is a problem. No other state constitution has language like that."

"Could be a problem," Whitehouse agreed. "Without court rulings on that specific language, it could spawn litigation. But it's amazing how far they've come. Too bad Murphy didn't recognize the contribution Common Cause and the coalition have made."

"Thank you," I said. "I think they see us as the enemy for pushing so hard."

Whitehouse laughed. "As you remember, I argued against a frontal assault, but your approach clearly worked."

"That was more than two years ago," I said. "I was glad — after all this has cost you — that they're calling you 'the Father of separation of powers in Rhode Island.'" I reminded him of his comment that "we would never cut the deep root of Rhode Island's corruption until we got to separation of powers."

"That sounds pretty good," Whitehouse said, "but I don't remember saying it."

"I wrote it down the moment I left your office," I said. "I'd love to take credit for it, but you're the one who said it."

With the House leadership's bill finally available, the separation of powers coalition and Common Cause board again held back-to-back meetings at the First Baptist Church in America. Members of the drafting committee again sat across the front of the room.

Liz Anderson, the *Providence Journal* reporter who had been covering the issue all spring, had asked to come. She sat unobtrusively at one side.

"We've had a few days to look at the revised bill," Jim Miller began. "I hope we can reach consensus this afternoon, so that all of our organizations speak with one voice at the hearing tomorrow."

Nick Gorham spoke first, arguing that the addition of "full legislative power exercised by" the House and Senate was not a trap, but an affirmation of the General Assembly's role.

Sheldon Whitehouse expressed concern that the new House language might prompt some future judge to interfere with the duty of administrative agencies to promulgate regulations. Kevin McAllister, a lawyer on the Common Cause board, agreed. "I'm queasy about this assertion that 'full legislative power' is to be exercised exclusively by the General Assembly. I think those words, when read together, distill the broad powers clause and move it to a different section."

"Forgive me," Gorham said. "I just don't see that. I wouldn't have signed on if I didn't believe it would work. The General Assembly can already change any rule adopted by any executive agency. All we have to do is change the law."[33]

"For the life of me," said Bob Arruda, "I can't understand why we're debating Nick's amended bill when we have the Lenihan bill, which is much better. We should stand strong for the original."

Kendra Beaver, a lawyer for Save the Bay, rose with the text in hand. She affirmed "separate and distinct" as acceptable because judges would find precedent from other states, but she thought the phrase "full legislative power exercised by the Senate and House" would cause problems precisely because it was unique. "Judges will look to other states but find no precedent," she said. "That alone should make us cautious about accepting the revised House text."

One lawyer after another expressed concern about the "full legislative power" clause. Despite Gorham's reluctance, a clear consensus formed: we would applaud how far the House had come, and we would agree to "separate and distinct." For all the rest, we would push for the original bipartisan Gorham-Lenihan amendment.

In his weekly *Providence Journal* column, Ed Achorn asked: "Why did the House leaders take six months to join the reformers? Clearly, these leaders adopted a waiting game, praying that the firestorm for separation of powers would subside. They hoped to slip in deceptive language that would protect their vast power." He went on to say that the ploy had failed because ordinary Rhode Islanders "kept calling lawmakers, urging action . . . kept packing hearings at the State House . . . kept arguing that they wanted less corrupt and more accountable government." He warned that House leaders were now proposing language found in no other state constitution.[34]

At the start of her committee's hearing on May 20, Elaine Coderre had her clerk pass out a written report stating that "full legislative power" had not been added to allow tampering with administrative rule-making. Comprised of three sentences, the report seemed barely a footnote:

> The committee wishes to make clear that the amendments to the Gorham bill are not intended to change and should not be construed as changing the ability of the General Assembly to delegate legislative powers to the Executive branch in accordance with existing law. . . . The purpose is to assure reviewing courts that the legislature retains all legislative powers.[35]

Paul Crowley added that the legislature could give up the broad powers clause but must refuse to "let another branch strip us clean in the future."

Advocates for the original bipartisan bill tore into the amended version. "The new language makes me queasy," Kevin McAllister told the committee. "As a lawyer, I know that courts interpret 'the plain language' of a constitutional provision, and I'm not at all sure this committee report would carry any weight."[36]

"Changes are made for a purpose," Carl Bogus told the committee. "What the heck is the purpose here? In writing a constitution, every word is deemed to have meaning. Every change has meaning. As sure as I am sitting here," he continued, "those added words are going to be the focal point of some future court action. We don't know when, we don't know what the particular cause will be, and we don't know who the advocates will be. But it will happen."

I testified that the existing language on legislative power was virtually identical to comparable sections of forty-four other state constitutions. Adding "full" and "exercised by" would make that section of Rhode Island's Constitution unique. "Why are you doing this?" I asked. "Is it necessary? What does it add?"

None of us believed our testimony would persuade the committee to restore the original text of Gorham's bill. Only the speaker's office could do that, but we had to lay down markers.

The committee voted unanimously to recommend Gorham's revised bill, with their explanatory report, to the full House. This was the first time a House committee had recommended a separation of powers amendment for passage. "It feels great," Gorham told reporters after the vote. "It's a good day for all Rhode Island."[37]

Two days later, I sat in the House gallery above the dais for the debate. In a rare convergence, Majority Leader Gordon Fox and Minority Leader Bob Watson moved jointly to suspend the rules so that Gorham's amended bill could be moved forward from the next day's calendar. Then, in a step that would have been unthinkable a year earlier, Elaine Coderre recommended Gorham's amended bill for passage. "The system worked," Coderre said. "It didn't work fast. It worked deliberately and with a lot of research. We were asked to fix something, and we came up with language to fix it."[38]

Fausto Anguilla, who had withdrawn his competing bill, opened the debate. "We did not kowtow to anyone," he declared. "We were not bullied into this. We did not rush the process to please anyone who was criticizing us. What we did was the people's work, and we did it well."[39]

Several representatives groused about the votes everyone knew they must cast. Thomas Slater of Providence said he had been intimidated and bullied over the issue, and would cast a "very reluctant" yes.

Nick Gorham, buoyant after having his separation of powers bill crushed in each of the two previous years, told his colleagues that Thomas Wilson Dorr had fought unsuccessfully for genuine separation of powers in a state constitution. "In voting for this now," Gorham exulted, "we are fulfilling the last piece of what Dorr wanted in the People's Constitution."

Even Providence Rep. Paul Moura, a long-time foe of separation of powers, urged passage of Gorham's amended bill.

Gordon Fox spoke last. "This does include an element of stepping into the unknown," Fox declared emotionally. "I'd be lying to you if I didn't say that. As an institution, we will change. But I have no hesitation to believe that this institution will adapt."

From the gallery above the rostrum, I watched John Harwood rise from his seat near the back and walk toward the rear exit. He wore a tailored tan suit that emphasized his muscular shoulders. He had not spoken during the debate and hid his feelings behind a practiced smile. He paused briefly as Rep. John McCauley rose to shake his hand and whisper in his ear. Then the man who had for ten years been the most powerful political figure in Rhode Island walked alone between the massive oak doors and out into the rotunda. Without looking back, he descended the broad marble stairs.

"Shall 5081 as amended pass?" Murphy called Gorham's bill number from the rostrum. "All those in favor, press the green button. Those opposed, press red."

The vote for passage was 71–1. Rep. Joseph Faria of Central Falls cast the only negative vote.

After the House broke for the day, *Providence Journal* reporter Liz Anderson quizzed Faria about his reasons. Avoiding any mention of patronage, he said, "We just gave up a lot of say for our constituents that we are no longer going to have on those boards." He added: "Half the people in this room voted for this bill so they could get re-elected. They're not concerned about doing any good. It's ridiculous the way they voted."

I often gave Edward Achorn details that landed in his Tuesday columns or *Providence Journal* editorials, which he wrote in deft strokes. The newspaper quickly called for "the obvious compromise," the Senate trading "separate and co-equal" for "separate and distinct," which the House preferred. "In return," he suggested, "take out the House's redundant (and possibly mischievous) words 'full' and 'exercised by' in delineating the legislature's functions."[40]

Witnesses crammed the Senate Lounge when Sen. Mike Lenihan convened his Committee on Government Oversight for the first of two hearings. In an extraordinary move, Rep. Nick Gorham crossed over to testify before the Senate committee. He insisted the words "full" and "exercised by," had been added to ensure that no court would interpret the amendment as stripping away legislative power over quasi-publics and agencies that promulgated rules. The changes, Gorham said, were "inconsequential, of almost vanishing significance."

Carl Bogus disputed Gorham's word "inconsequential" to describe the House's new phrasing. "Courts," he declared, "do not construe any words in a constitution as 'inconsequential.' It would be an Alice-in-Wonderland argument to tell a court that we made changes to something so it would remain unchanged."

Sheldon Whitehouse called the new House language "potentially treacherous." He added: "The public would be well served if that were taken out."

Nancy Rhodes, the former president of Common Cause, offered a new metaphor, a jetliner without radar trying to land in dense fog. "All of us want to bring this plane in, but we have to circle the field until we're assured of a safe landing," Rhodes said.[41]

Pawtucket Times reporter Jim Baron told Lenihan he had heard talk of time running out for agreement on separation of powers. "That's a lot of hogwash," said Lenihan. "Let me say emphatically, there is more than enough time to get this issue resolved." Without criticizing House leaders, he added: "I've said all along that there are different ways to wordsmith a bill, but on matters of principle you stand like a rock. There are principles involved here, and I'm certainly not going to abandon them."[42]

Several days later Mike Lenihan phoned to say that House and Senate leaders were deadlocked on a final text, and he was ready — in classic football language — to blitz the House. He would introduce a new version — identical to the original, except that it would include "separate and distinct" in place of "separate and co-equal." He would also amend Gorham's bill to get rid of "full legislative power" and make it exactly the same as his new bill. The Senate would push both bills back over to the House.

"What will matter," he added, "is how much pressure you can generate over on the other side."

On June 11, Lenihan called his Government Oversight Committee to order. In an extraordinary display of support, both Irons and Majority Leader Joe Montalbano took seats in the committee. Lenihan opened with a carefully crafted statement. He explained for those in the room and watching on television that negotiations with House leaders over the controversial four words had been fruitless. The House agreed to drop the phrase "exercised by" but still insisted on "full legislative power."

"I want to make clear," he explained, "that our action on the Senate side is not a 'take it or leave it' position, but neither are we angling for further adjustments in this legislation."

The clerk passed out copies of his new resolution and a substitute version of the Gorham amendment — now a clone of his new bill.[43] The committee approved both.

Irons told reporters that the ball would now be squarely in the House's court and leaders there needed to rethink their position. "I would hope we do not see this measure again. It is now time to put separation of powers behind us."[44]

On June 12, the full Senate unanimously passed both Lenihan's new separation of powers amendment and their revision of the Gorham bill. A page carried both across to the House of Representatives.

Spring temperatures lingered into June, leaving the State House relatively comfortable. Graduations ended and beach weather began without any sign that House leaders would accept Lenihan's compromise.

In the hope that people would make more phone calls, I sent an opinion piece entitled "Four-letter word threatens reform" to newspapers across the state. The four-letter word was "full." I noted that no other state used the phrase "full legislative power" in its constitution.

"Throughout this spring's hearings," I wrote, "many on the House Separation of Powers Committee have argued against 'separate and co-equal' because they said this is untested constitutional language. They insisted that because 'co-equal' would be unique in the nation, its use in our Constitution would invite costly litigation. Now many of the same representatives argue that 'full' legislative power needs to be added to the Constitution, even though no other state constitution incorporates this untested new term." With "full legislative power" in the Constitution, developers might argue that the Department of Environmental Management could not adopt wetlands regulations. Or brokers might claim that rules promulgated by the Department of Business Regulation were unconstitutional. I encouraged readers to urge their state representatives to pass the versions of Gorham-Lenihan passed by the Senate. "No need for 'full,' " I concluded. "No more changes."[45]

A few days later Lenihan phoned to say he thought the House leadership was agreeing to drop "full" but attach a series of "whereas" clauses.

" 'Whereas' clauses saying what?" I asked.

"I haven't seen them yet. They say it's a preamble that would go to the voters but not become part of the Constitution." He expected to get the written text that afternoon. And so, late that Friday, in his tiny office, Mike Lenihan handed me a copy of the five "whereas" clauses that House leaders were proposing as a preamble to the amendment.

I skimmed the four-page document. Each of the "whereas" clauses summarized an element of the amendment, and all looked like face-savers for the House. The amendment's text was exactly as we had drafted it seven months earlier, except that the three branches of government would be "separate and distinct" instead of "separate and co-equal." The much abused "broad powers" clause would be deleted from the Constitution. The words "full" and "exercised by" had vanished.

"I want to check with our counsel," Lenihan said. "I assume you'll do the same."

Over the last weekend in June a flurry of emails confirmed that groups in the coalition were comfortable with the face-saving "whereas" clauses. Leaders were ecstatic that only one word of the original bipartisan text would change. Instead of three "separate and co-equal" branches of government, Article V would declare them "separate and distinct."

On Monday, June 30, Nancy Rhodes and several other Common Cause board members joined me in the east gallery of the House to watch the historic vote. Speaker Bill Murphy called the House to order at 4:26 p.m.

Rep. Fausto Anguilla proposed a floor amendment that would insert his five "whereas" clauses above the amendment's text. He explained that they would be preamble to the bill but not part of the actual separation of powers amendment.

Gordon Fox praised Anguilla. "Last summer," Fox said, "he took it upon himself to read the *Federalist Papers*. Since then, he has worked constantly on the issues and worked within the Separation of Powers Committee to reach a compromise. Today, we see his efforts bearing fruit." He called the resolution historic, stronger than the original proposals filed in January. "It relies on the work of Democrats and Republicans, with the help of many advocacy groups. This is what good government should be about, and we have kept our promise."

Nick Gorham congratulated the speaker for delivering on his promise, Anguilla for his diligence in the process, and those of us in the gallery for keeping the pressure on. "We're going to let the people of Rhode Island decide the future of our state," Gorham declared. "We're going to fulfill what many generations throughout Rhode Island history have only talked about. Let's get on with it."[46]

When Murphy called for the vote, green lights quickly lined the electronic board: sixty-six in favor. No red lights appeared. Eight representatives were either absent or chose not to vote.[47] Lenihan's version, now introduced by the "whereas" clauses, quickly passed by the same unanimous vote. Our group rejoiced quietly and then climbed the carpeted stairs. Only *pro forma* Senate votes remained, and we watched from that gallery.

"This day was a long time coming," Sen. Mike Lenihan said to his colleagues. "I reported to you that we had an impasse with the House. They insisted on additional words in the text of the amendment. I told them that went beyond the obvious compromise. I suggested that we expand the committee note. At first, the House rejected that idea, but they have now accepted that and drafted a preamble to the resolution."

Lenihan explained the new "whereas" clauses, avoiding the temptation to dismiss them as face-saving for the House after months of delay. Modestly, he offered thanks around the room and special praise for Gorham and Anguilla. "Today marks the seventh and eighth times that we in the Senate are passing separation of powers," he said.

"Lastly," Lenihan added, "I want to thank the citizens of Rhode Island. You have provided enormous support for this legislation. Often government gets bashed around, sometimes justifiably, but this time we have produced something for the ages. And so I say to all who have worked on this: congratulations."

Amid cascading congratulations, Sen. James C. Sheehan, a history teacher, compared this watershed moment in Rhode Island to the Velvet Revolution in Czechoslovakia. "The most noble thing any legislature can do," Sheehan said, "is give up power. We have had to tolerate a lot of negativity in the press. We've had constituents at our throat. Now, we are making history by giving up the power we have been accused of misusing."

Senators voted unanimously for the two bills.

After the votes, reporters asked for reaction from our contingent.

"Can you believe it?" Nancy Rhodes exclaimed. "It's absolutely stunning that this has finally happened. Now," she continued, "on to the next event, which is doing legislative oversight."[48]

The day had been hot and humid. As we left the State House a little after six, rain had spread puddles across the plaza. Though the air felt steamy, sunlight broke in shafts through clouds.

5
Reconstruction

WAITING FOR THE OTHER QUESTIONABLE ETHICS SHOE TO DROP...
...AND THE OTHER .... AND THE OTHER ...

45

Minimalist Principles
2003–04

"WE'VE WON A FABULOUS VICTORY!" Carl Bogus poured champagne into paper cups and lifted a toast. "Now to a landslide from the voters!"

Cheers filled the Common Cause office on a bittersweet July afternoon. Nine days earlier the General Assembly had placed separation of powers on the ballot. Shortly before the climactic vote, Bogus had announced that he would leave the separation of powers task force. He needed to refocus on his academic duties, an article about our long struggle,[1] and a book he had postponed.

"Regardless of their unanimous votes ten days ago," Bogus continued, "if they'd had secret ballots in the House and Senate, we'd have lost in both chambers. Deep resistance remains. Legislative supremacists have not disappeared. From here on, they'll just pursue their agenda in more subtle ways. The challenge will be to defend what we've won and make it work."

Will Barbeau, a leader of Operation Clean Government, wondered when we could start recruiting qualified people to take seats on those boards.

"We should eliminate a lot of boards entirely," Bogus replied.

"And do what with them?" asked John Holt, who had followed Jim Miller as executive minister of the Rhode Island State Council of Churches.[2]

"Fold them into executive agencies," Bogus said. "Move Coastal Resources into the Department of Environmental Management. Merge the Lottery Commission into the Department of Administration. They could operate just as well under a director appointed by the governor."

"Whoa! Whoa!" Holt interrupted. "I have to go back to my board before we morph this into a new issue. We have to agree on an approach."

"We've won a huge battle," agreed Bob Kilmarx, who had led the task force for its first five years, "but we haven't won the war. Our top priority has to be keeping our coalition energized through the 2004 election. That means all of us staying on message for the next sixteen months. We can't open ourselves to the charge of harboring hidden agendas or risk splitting groups off."

From a corner of the table former board president Nancy Rhodes spoke: "I hear three crucial things. First, we can't take anything for granted. As Carl says, we need a vigorous campaign to overcome lingering resistance."

"Nancy," growled Burt Hoffman, "they held their noses, but they voted for it. How can they campaign against it now?"

"Sensible, Burt, as always," she affirmed. "They could create a front group to fund negative ads that sow doubt. Second, we need to work on reconstructing all those boards before the mischief starts. And third — with all due respect to you, Carl — we absolutely can't say a word about folding boards into executive branch agencies. Lots of those boards, like the Rivers Council and the Resource Recovery Corporation, have constituents who will be furious if we propose absorbing them into any bureaucracy. We could be goring people's oxen left and right, which could turn key constituencies against separation of powers itself."

"I'm with Nancy," said Bob Cox. "Right now, our brand is strong, but we can't squander our advantage."

Kevin McAllister agreed that the General Assembly would come back full of tricks. "They'll hire some high-priced consultant to help them take back in new laws for quasi-publics what they gave up in the amendment. They'll make it technical and confusing to non-lawyers. We can develop principles to make that harder. Peter Hufstader's research gives us a head start, but we still have to watch them like hawks."

Common Cause planned a gala event for September 2003: "Celebrating Separation of Powers 160 years after the Dorr Rebellion." We would create the Thomas Wilson Dorr Fund for research and advocacy, aimed at making separation of powers fully effective in Rhode Island.

Brian Heller, a board member, handed me a wooden box the size of a paperback book with a brass knob and hinges. Inside I found the etched portrait of Thomas Wilson Dorr and a laminated text of our Separation of Powers Amendment as it would appear on the 2004 statewide ballot.

"What do you think?" Heller asked.

"It's exquisite," I said. "What will you do with it?"

He shrugged. "I'll make several hundred as table favors for the celebration. Finishing Dorr's work is a really big deal."

Our celebration filled a huge white tent at Newport's Castle Hill Inn. Below lay rocky shoals and a lighthouse marking the entrance to Narragansett Bay. After dinner, we presented awards. One certificate praised Nick Gorham, saying that "no one had entered a more hostile arena or engaged fiercer foes" than he had in the House of Representatives. The citation for Mike Lenihan read. "He labored over the text and persuaded many reluctant senators that the time had come to repair Rhode Island's flawed Constitution." A third framed certificate went to Gov. Carcieri "for his effective leadership in the struggle for constitutional Separation of Powers."[3]

With the sun setting, lights came up inside the tent, and Brian Heller presented the boxes he had made as table favors. He opened a tiny door that revealed the historic etching of Thomas Wilson Dorr and the Separation of Powers Amendment. "These are your awards," he said, "for helping to open 'the Dorr to Rhode Island's Future.'"

Then Heller lifted a framed poster above his head for the crowd to see. Over the image of Dorr he had superimposed my head as I typed, smiling, on my laptop.

The crowd burst into laughter.

Any of us who made the mistake of thinking that quasi-public boards were boring and off the public radar were wrong. People started phoning Common Cause to ask how they could claim seats on these boards that were now held by legislators. Almas Kalafian, a legally blind woman, wanted to get people with handicapping conditions onto the Rhode Island Public Transportation Authority (RIPTA). She explained that RIPTA had long ignored their concerns. Similarly, members of the Kay Coalition had fought against casinos and demanded counseling for compulsive gamblers. Now they would demand places on the Lottery Commission. Property owners in the Jewelry District wanted seats on the I-195 Redevelopment Board. Neighbors of the state landfill, sickened by garbage smells long after the Solid Waste Management Corporation was renamed Resource Recovery, demanded representation on that board.

Though mission, structure, and appointment scheme differed widely from one quasi-public to the next, separation of powers would require the restructuring of every board where legislative appointees exercised executive powers. Peter Hufstader had identified seventy-three that had been created and codified over generations. Most carried the imprint of special interests, lobbyists, and lawmakers. No two were identical, and no single design would repair more than a few. Hufstader and I brought these lists to a Common Cause board meeting and began unpacking the data.

"Wait a minute," Doree Goodman objected. "Wait just a minute! Smart people may get this, but I'm totally lost. You're giving us way too much detail. What principles are you proposing?"

I knew she was right. We needed ground rules for reconstructing boards that people could understand and lawmakers could apply.

Over several weeks Hufstader led the separation of powers task force in analyzing the data and extracting what we called "minimalist principles" for reconfiguring boards. Laws establishing those boards listed 153 seats reserved for lawmakers and sixty-six for public members appointed by legislative leaders.

We suggested that the General Assembly launch public hearings at the start of the 2004 legislative session — months before voters would approve the amendment. Rather than introduce separate bills for all seventy-three boards, we recommended omnibus legislation to reconfigure groups of related boards. We hoped legislative committees would consider the mission, composition, and operation of each board in public hearings. We suggested reducing the size of boards wherever practical and creating a standard process for appointing all members and chairpersons.[4]

After the confusion of trying to deal with boards we barely knew, our minimalist principles provided a functional way to approach every board, no matter how obscure. Clauses that required legislative leaders to appoint senators or representatives must be repealed, and most boards could shrink but still remain functional. Wherever current law empowered legislative leaders to appoint public members, this appointing authority would shift to the governor with a boilerplate clause for Senate confirmation. We recommended that each revised law require the governor to ensure diverse public participation, particularly with respect to gender, race, and areas of social concern or professional expertise, and we urged that professional licensing boards include public members.

On December 9, we convened an information meeting on separation of powers and the restructuring of boards at the First Unitarian Church. As public officials and coalition leaders arrived, Peter Hufstader and I passed out the latest draft of our principles. Then former Atty. Gen. Sheldon Whitehouse, now in private law practice, outlined the history of our struggle. He reminded public officials and advocates in a large semi-circle how our new amendment would change scores of state laws.

From the back row Mike Lenihan rose to speak. Large but no longer as sturdy as when he played college football, he had a gift for metaphors. "When we passed separation of powers," he said gently, "we recognized that it would be complicated. I think of this as digging a canal. Last year we did the blasting. Now we have a lot of shoveling to do."

He described a meeting the previous week when Senate leaders and senior staff discussed our minimalist principles, and confirmed that the leadership found this approach reasonable. "With some boards," Lenihan added, "I would prefer to do more than just take legislators off. Some boards might be put out of existence. Some might be put under an executive department."

He invited public testimony before his Committee on Government Oversight as to what other principles should be considered. "Everyone has a right to speak. We'll create the opportunity for many people to put their oars in the water." Since Senate leaders wanted to start with fifteen boards whose operations were crucial, he would package those boards in an omnibus bill and then move on to less urgent ones. Finally, Lenihan said, he favored downsizing some boards, particularly those like the Coastal Resources Management Council with sixteen members. Such boards relied on huge amounts of highly specialized work and not many volunteers were waiting in the wings.

His canal-digging metaphor was an apt description — last year the blasting, this year the shoveling. Reconstructing boards to comply with separation of powers would take a lot of muddy toil.

Triple Scandal
2003–04

SCANDALS CREATE FLEETING CHANCES FOR CHANGE. In the fall of 2003, Kathy Gregg, the *Providence Journal's* State House bureau chief, broke headline stories that engulfed three powerful lawmakers. On October 1, she reported that House Majority Leader Gordon Fox had backed a deal to relocate GTECH's world headquarters to a new $65 million building in downtown Providence.[1] The gambling company would get $8.3 million in property-tax breaks and an exclusive twenty-year "master contract" to provide scratch ticket and video slot machines for the Rhode Island Lottery Commission. Three weeks after the contract cleared the General Assembly, GTECH hired Ferrucci-Russo P.C., the law firm where Fox worked. The firm later billed GTECH for twenty-seven hours of legal work done before the House vote, including hours attributed to Fox.

These front page stories prompted ethics complaints against Fox from state Republican chair Patricia Morgan and Operation Clean Government.[2] The Ethics Commission quickly reached an "initial determination," the first step toward a full probe.[3] The evidence seemed straightforward: the law firm billed GTECH for Fox's work on legislation that he later voted for, a clear conflict of interest. W. Mark Russo, a partner in the firm, had billed GTECH retroactively in an effort to "recapture" payment for preliminary work.

Rather than face adjudicative hearings before the Ethics Commission, Fox and his lawyers negotiated a settlement — the equivalent of a plea bargain. On January 20, 2004, the commission voted to accept a fifteen-page informal agreement stipulating that the majority leader did not know about the hours billed in his name, but that he "knew or should have known of the existence of this legal and business relationship." It acknowledged that Fox had a substantial conflict of interest when he voted for the GTECH deal and that it was reasonable to expect that his law firm would profit from his vote. In signing, Fox accepted unequivocal responsibility, paid a fine of $10,000, and left the firm of Ferrucci-Russo.[4]

In December, Gregg revealed secret business deals involving two top state senators. She first named Sen. John A. Celona of North Providence, who chaired the Senate Committee on Commerce, Housing, and Municipal Government. CVS, the Woonsocket-based pharmaceutical giant, was paying Celona as a consultant, while Blue Cross/Blue Shield of Rhode Island, the state's largest health insurer, funded a cable TV program that gave him priceless free publicity. Celona's ties to the two health care giants appeared to clash with his committee's jurisdiction over legislation of interest to them.

Gregg reported that Celona had approached Thomas A. Lynch, a former senator who had become a lobbyist for Blue Cross, about the television program that he would host. Lynch and the other executives conferred with Celona in his corner office at the State House. Michael A. Sisti, a Blue Cross vice president of marketing, told Gregg that he had argued against the TV program because the insurer already had one, and Celona's proposal — then estimated at $75,000 — was too expensive. Gregg quoted Sisti saying it had become "a political necessity to do this show."[5] Eventually, a single media company produced both the Blue Cross program and Celona's public access cable show, *The Celona State House Report*.

Celona's CVS connection proved doubly damaging. A public relations officer for the pharmaceutical company admitted that CVS had hired Celona as a "community outreach specialist" and paid him a monthly retainer for three and a half years.[6] A pair of CVS government-relations employees had supervised him. Their other duties included blocking passage of the pharmacy freedom of choice legislation — assigned to Celona's committee — that might have weakened the drugstore chain's dominance in Rhode Island. CVS spokesperson Todd Andrews refused to reveal the amount of Celona's compensation but admitted that it exceeded $1,000 each year — the threshold at which public officials were required to disclose income under Rhode Island's ethics law. Celona had not listed any earnings from CVS on his financial disclosure forms.[7]

Walgreens and Stop & Shop — CVS's competitors in the lucrative prescription drug market — protested vehemently. Year after year, they had promoted pharmacy freedom of choice bills that would have allowed insured employees to fill prescriptions at pharmacies other than CVS and Brooks. CVS and Blue Cross had lobbied aggressively to kill the legislation. In 2003, two such bills had passed the House but died in Celona's Senate committee. Ironically, the senator had co-sponsored similar legislation before he took over the committee and began taking payments from CVS.[8]

Celona tried to stamp out the fires burning around him with an apology. "If there's an appearance of impropriety," he told reporter Bill Malinowski, "I apologize. If there is a perception that I voted a certain way on pharmacy issues because of my relationship with the charitable endeavors of CVS, then I should have recused myself from those matters."[9] He claimed to have phoned the Ethics Commission and been assured that his work for the pharmacy "was proper," but staff at the commission had no authority to offer advice by phone. By the time Celona sought an advisory opinion and went to plead his case, his efforts at damage control were pointless. Operation Clean Government filed an ethics complaint against him, based on the *Providence Journal* stories.[10]

On December 11, under pressure from Senate leaders, Celona announced that he would relinquish his committee chairmanship temporarily.

The burgeoning scandal quickly entangled Senate President William Irons as well. *Providence Journal* reporter Liz Anderson asked Irons about his insurance business. "I will never divulge who my clients are," he growled.[11] He cited a 1999 advisory from the Ethics Commission.[12]

Anderson soon reported that between 1995 and 1998 — while Irons chaired the Senate Corporations Committee — a number of pharmacy freedom of choice bills had died there. Early in 1999, then-Majority Leader Paul S. Kelly had queried Irons about his financial ties to CVS and Blue Cross. Irons indignantly denied any conflict of interest. He refused to name his insurance clients but agreed to seek advice from the Ethics Commission. In his letter to the commission, he described himself as "an independent insurance broker representing many companies in the area of life, health and disability insurance." He said his committee was considering a bill "that a corporate insurance client of mine has an interest in along with a number of other parties."[13]

No one on the ethics panel had pushed him for details about his client, and the advisory authorized him to vote on "broad-based legislation involving general health care issues of public interest." The opinion hinged on his declaration that his "corporate insurance client" would not benefit more than "any other similarly situated members of a significant and definable group." That claim had clearly been false.[14]

I imagined Irons in his private meeting with Kelly and Enos, pushing back hard and going resentfully to the commission. He quickly began forging alliances with survivors of Bevilacqua's faction. Once he toppled Kelly, Irons gerrymandered his former allies — Paul Kelly, Bill Enos, Charles Walton, and Donna Walsh — into districts they could never win. He drove them out of the Senate.

Hindsight revealed the timing. In December 2003, when Irons forced Celona from his post as committee chair, Enos revealed to the *Providence Journal* what Irons had hidden from the Ethics Commission in 1999. Like Celona, Irons had been earning commissions from CVS and Blue Cross while killing freedom of choice bills that would open the market to their competitors .

When reporter Liz Anderson asked Irons about his insurance business, he snapped that he would not divulge his clients, cited his 1999 advisory opinion, and insisted that he would recuse himself whenever he had a conflict of interest.

With these stories swirling, Irons phoned me. Would I meet him at 3 o'clock that afternoon? Windows on College Hill gleamed gold in late sunshine as I settled into a leather chair in his corner office. Irons thanked me for coming on short notice. He wore a crisp white shirt and perfectly knotted tie, but looked as if he had not slept in days. He wanted to tell me in person that he would step down as Senate president and asked me to keep his decision confidential until he made an official announcement after Christmas.

I wondered whether he would really resign or was only testing the idea. During the fifteen years we had been allies and antagonists, he had blustered about quitting. Now, in the December twilight, his eyes were hollow as he defended himself. Hounded by reporters, he had boxed himself in by making Celona step down. Now he must do the same.

After spending twenty-one years — more than a third of his life — in the Senate, he wanted me to remind people of the good he had done. When depositors staggered through the rubble of RISDIC, he had risked an epic battle against John Bevilacqua. When Rhode Island's campaign finance system invited corruption, he fought for Jeff Teitz's legislation to fix it. When insiders were trading votes for permanent state jobs, he backed our revolving door bill. When governors had too little time to build competent teams, he worked with RIght Now! to place a Four-year Term Amendment on the ballot. When scandal engulfed the Supreme Court, he pushed the Senate toward merit selection. He had supported ending legislative pensions, setting reasonable pay, and downsizing the General Assembly. When John Harwood tried to crush our campaign for separation of powers, he led the Senate in approving Mike Lenihan's breakthrough amendment a full year before it finally passed. "You and I haven't always agreed," the beleaguered Senate president said, "but you know I've taken positions of principle."

I kept listening as Irons vented about attacks on his integrity and insults to him, his clients, and his business. He insisted that he had always done what he believed was right.[15]

When I left his office, the State House was empty and silent. I jotted down what I could remember of his lament. His defensiveness made me wonder whether he would actually step down.

Through the holidays, pressure mounted. Sen. Leonidas Raptakis, who had sided with Irons in the leadership struggle, published an opinion piece in the *Providence Journal*. Raptakis was getting even. He had sponsored the pharmacy legislation. "The fix was in," he wrote, and "good people were hoodwinked." He accused Irons of "submitting a cleverly worded question" to the Ethics Commission, which was "designed to hide the truth and let him operate with the appearance of propriety."[16]

Two days before Christmas, the attorney general's office and state police confirmed that a criminal investigation had begun.[17]

On New Year's Eve, Rhode Island's first Senate president announced his resignation from the Senate. Irons's office faxed out a five-page statement that touted his "reform efforts," his "spirit of service," and his career in the insurance industry. "I have been blessed to be a person who has achieved success in both the private and public realm," he wrote. "I have always known that strong leaders create strong enemies. . . . Despite my painstaking efforts to follow the law and the rules as I understand them, some political opponents have begun an attack." He blamed his resignation on "the time-old process of backroom destabilization to bring down my position as President of the Senate."[18]

With Irons gone, the thirty-seven remaining senators elected Senate Majority Leader Joseph A. Montalbano, who had led the redistricting panel, as Senate president.[19] Democrats chose Sen. M. Teresa Paiva Weed as majority leader, the first woman to rise so high. "She's a little waif of a thing," a friend told one reporter, "but she's got a metabolism that can run a nuclear power plant. She runs on Diet Coke."[20]

Former Senate Majority Leader Paul Kelly confirmed that two detectives from the state police had interviewed him about Irons' CVS and Blue Cross connections. Kelly admitted that he had told the officers he should have pressed harder for answers. State police also asked Raptakis about Irons's ties to the drugstore chain and health insurer.[21]

From documents filed with the federal government reporter Mike Stanton learned that CVS had paid Irons $70,315 in commissions during a two-year period that ended the previous May. Though the drugstore chain reported twenty-three health-insurance programs for its employees across the country, it listed only a single broker's commission — the one paid to Irons for its Rhode Island personnel. Officers declined to explain when, why, or how Irons had become CVS's only broker of record.[22]

Operation Clean Government packaged newspaper stories about Irons's secret payments from CVS and Blue Cross in an ethics complaint, which its leaders filed on January 20.[23] Ominously for Irons, the Ethics Commission immediately reviewed his 1999 request for an advisory. Commissioners wondered aloud whether he had concealed information. They revoked the advisory opinion and the immunity it conferred.[24]

An idea woke me up at 4 a.m. No law could force attorneys or physicians to name their clients, and the General Assembly would never compel other professions to disclose their customers. But what if we could turn the problem inside out?

Income tax forms covered my desk at home. Common Cause reported my salary to the Internal Revenue Service on a W-2 form and mailed identical copies that I filed with our federal and state tax returns. Our bank sent a 1099 listing interest it paid on our savings, and it transmitted our data directly to the IRS. The law made these payers report both to the taxpayer who received a benefit and to the enforcing agency. Such identical copies were simple, efficient, and widespread. Current Rhode Island law already required companies with lobbyists — including CVS and Blue Cross — to report what they spent on lobbying. Why not require lobbyists and those who hired them to report non-lobbying payments to legislators? Serving in the General Assembly brought business to lawmakers who owned insurance brokerages, law offices, farms, restaurants, and liquor stores. Unions had public officials on their payrolls and paid them well, but who knew how much?

What if we required any corporation that deployed a lobbyist to report payments it made to public officials? Why not require identical reports each January to the Secretary of State, who regulated lobbyists; to the Ethics Commission, which monitored financial disclosure by public officials; and to public officials who received any payments? I sketched a new reporting requirement: businesses or unions that paid lobbyists would have to divulge "money or anything of value" worth more than $250 which they paid to any "major state decision-maker" in a calendar year.[25]

I shared my draft with leaders at Common Cause, and they relished the idea of forcing CVS and Blue Cross to disclose such payments or lose their license to lobby. Nancy Rhodes suggested calling our proposal "The Celona Law." With their approval, I explained the concept to Mike Lenihan and to Gordon Fox, who had been fined $10,000 because of his undisclosed tie to GTECH. Fox pondered the text for several days and agreed to file it in the House. We shook hands, both of us understanding what rode on its passage.

Lenihan quickly introduced a Senate version, but weeks passed without any sign of Fox's bill in the House. The normal deadline for bill introductions came and went, and I began to worry that House leaders were resisting. I prompted Fox several times, and his bill finally appeared on March 18.[26]

John Celona made headlines again in February for a second set of undisclosed "consultant payments." He had been receiving monthly fees of $1,200 for two years from the New England Ambulance Company, a total of $14,400 each year, but never disclosed those payments on financial disclosure forms he filed with the Ethics Commission. John Vernancio, the company's owner, explained to reporter Mike Stanton that he had hired Celona out of pity after his lawnmower shop closed.

In a curious twist, Celona had used his position as chair of the Corporations Committee to lobby lobbyists for Rhode Island Hospital and St. Joseph Health Service — Mark Montella and Frank McMahon — to steer their hospitals' business to New England Ambulance. Both had bills before the Corporations Committee and needed the chairman's good will, but neither knew that New England Ambulance was paying Celona.

"We must be doing something right," the ambulance company's owner crowed to Stanton, "because we keep growing. As long as we keep growing, I'm not going to change what I'm doing."[27]

Celona had also promoted New England Ambulance with Sen. Jack Reed and Congressman Patrick Kennedy for runs to the Veterans Administration Hospital in Providence.

As the Celona and Irons scandals kept erupting, television news and radio talk shows amplified public awareness of the senators' split loyalties. In response to a Brown University poll conducted during the second week of February, eighty-seven percent of those questioned believed that corruption in Rhode Island government was either "very common" or "somewhat common."[28]

With Irons absent from the State House his name almost vanished from the news, but Celona arrived awkwardly each day. Unlike Congress, the General Assembly had no internal ethics committees or rules for expelling members, but Celona was shunned. Sen. Susan Sosnowski managed to move her seat, leaving Celona — formerly one of the most powerful members of the Senate — with empty desks on both sides of his. Sosnowski and five other senators called for him to resign. "This is nothing personal," she told reporters. "I just think it is hurting the Senate. People look at government with a jaundiced eye because of this."

Sen. Maryellen Goodwin told reporters the scandal had "virtually paralyzed the Senate," and eighteen senators signed a call for Celona's resignation.[29]

Lt. Gov. Charles J. Fogarty and Secretary of State Matthew A. Brown joined the clamor. "When credibility for an elected official ceases to exist," Fogarty told reporters, "we have a responsibility to say that it's time to put the public interest ahead of our personal interest, no matter how difficult."

On March 8, state police swarmed through Celona's North Providence home, emerging with computer equipment and cartons of papers. Atty. Gen. Patrick C. Lynch told reporters it might take two months to analyze the haul. "I use the analogy of an iceberg. We've all seen the tip and we're wondering how deep and how wide it runs beneath the water."[30]

The next day, Celona resigned from the Senate. President Joseph A. Montalbano read Celona's letter aloud to a packed press conference. "I take no personal pleasure in the difficulties that Senator Celona is going through," Montalbano said. "A majority of the Senate had really felt that it was time to move beyond the distraction of what was going on in his personal life."[31]

Answering for Common Cause, I tried to shift the focus to loopholes that had tempted Celona and Irons to seek secret income from lobbying interests. I urged passage of "an airtight lobbying law, better ethics disclosure, and better ethics enforcement."

Our case became stronger as more discrepancies started to appear between the gifts reported by public officials and the payments disclosed by lobbyists. Four years earlier, when the Ethics Commission passed a controversial rule raising the limit on gifts to $150 per occasion and a maximum $450 per calendar year from any "interested person," it also required public officials to file annual reports each January. Lawmakers began listing receptions, breakfasts, lunches, dinners, Christmas ornaments, books, baseball caps, sports jerseys, and children's clothes. Others reported Newport Harbor cruises, rounds of golf, and tickets to the theater, circus, or sporting events. Curiously, many tickets topped out at $150.

"My Palm Pilot is my life," Sen. Leo R. Blais explained to a reporter. "I had my assistant print out my calendar for the year and I went through everything to think of what could be reportable. I gave it a lot of thought." Speaker William J. Murphy was less conscientious, listing only "various breakfasts, lunches, and dinners," on "various dates," costing "various amounts."[32]

Secretary of State Matthew Brown directed his staff to crosscheck gift reports filed by legislators against lobbying reports submitted by lobbying groups. When Brown's subordinates queried lobbyists about discrepancies, some amended their lobbying reports and others said the legislators must have been mistaken about who provided the gifts. Some lobbyists told reporter Scott Mayerowitz that differences occurred because they were required to report only expenses "for the specific purpose of promoting or opposing legislation." AFL-CIO Secretary-Treasurer George H. Nee acknowledged that he and union president Frank Montanaro had played golf with William Irons the previous May, but he denied any lobbying.

CVS admitted paying $120 for Irons to play in its Charity Golf Classic and $150 for House Speaker William J. Murphy and his wife to attend a CVS charity dinner. But the company wrote to Brown: "There was no intention on the part of CVS to use the tickets to the events as a means of promoting or opposing any legislation before the General Assembly, and CVS did not do so."[33]

When the reporter asked for my reaction, I asked where companies "got the gall to write this sort of thing."

True to his simile about digging a canal — last year blasting, this year shoveling — Sen. Mike Lenihan filed three bills to remove lawmakers and legislative appointments from boards that executed state laws.[34] He followed the Common Cause "minimalist principles" by packaging boards in three large omnibus bills. Each bill ended with a proviso that the new law would take effect sixty days after voters ratified the Separation of Powers Amendment.

Senate leaders referred Lenihan's monumental bills to his recently created Senate Committee on Government Oversight. I testified at a first hearing that reconstructing boards would not be the committee's most exciting mission but might be among its most important. "Few people will understand what you do here, yet your work this spring may well shape state government for the next forty or fifty years."[35]

Separate from his three omnibus bills and on a faster track, Lenihan introduced legislation to abolish the Unclassified Pay Plan Board. This board had always been vulnerable to political manipulation and was among our first seven separation of powers bills in 1995, but in nine years we had made no headway. Lenihan now proposed the approach Carl Bogus had urged: fold the pay board's salary-setting duties into the Department of Administration. The director of administration would recommend raises for unclassified staff; the governor would make the decision and be accountable for the decision. If enacted, this would mark a monumental shift from the abuse-prone process in current law.[36]

No matter how positive the dynamics of a legislative session, dangerous bills could cause real harm. Sen. Frank A. Ciccone III filed one in 2004 to prevent gubernatorial nominees from assuming their duties before Senate confirmation, specifically banning "acting" or "interim" appointments.[37] Current law gave the Senate thirty legislative days to confirm or reject gubernatorial appointments, but if it failed to act, the nominee would take office as if confirmed.

The Judiciary Committee produced a substitute that completely reversed that dynamic: removing the Senate's obligation to act within thirty legislative days and declaring that if the Senate did not approve, the nominee was "rejected." In that case the governor would have to appoint "a different person as director and so on in like manner until the senate shall vote to approve the governor's appointment."[38] Five days before the scheduled floor debate, I emailed every senator to warn that Ciccone's bill evoked the infamous Brayton Act of 1901, which had allowed the Senate to reject a governor's nomination simply by ignoring it for three days. I suggested a plain English translation of Ciccone's new language: "Governor, we'll ignore your appointments until you nominate someone we like." I said Ciccone's legislation would make a sham of the Separation of Powers Amendment.

I sent a copy of my email to Edward Achorn at the *Providence Journal*, and that Sunday, the paper ran a blistering editorial that accused Senate leaders of undercutting separation of powers. "Rhode Island must not go back," the editors declared. "Passage of this bill would signal that the new Senate leaders do not truly care about the public's will."[39] It urged readers to phone the Senate president's office and gave the number.

A few days later, Majority Leader M. Teresa Paiva Weed offered a floor amendment that doubled the time for Senate confirmation to sixty days and restored the automatic confirmation if the Senate failed to act. Senators approved Paiva Weed's amendment unanimously, and the amended confirmation process later passed the House.[40]

Lawsuits over the Senate districts that had been gerrymandered two years earlier made their way fitfully through state and federal courts. Karen Pelczarski argued in Superior Court on behalf of Barrington, Bristol, Little Compton,

Tiverton, and Warren that the Senate map failed the constitutional requirement that districts be "as compact in territory as possible." When Superior Court Judge Susan McGuirl ruled that the towns had "failed to establish, beyond a reasonable doubt, that the redistricting statute is irrational and has abandoned the principle of compactness," they appealed her decision to the Rhode Island Supreme Court.[41] Meanwhile, the federal suits on behalf of African-American and Latino plaintiffs from South Providence worked their way toward trial in U.S. District Court.

Suddenly, on May 21, rumors raced through the State House that the federal case would end with a settlement. Senate leaders were to speak at a press conference in the Senate lounge, where a tripod held what were obviously maps to be unveiled.

Joseph Montalbano and Teresa Paiva Weed, strode to the lectern, both smiling broadly. Montalbano seemed uncharacteristically theatrical as he reviewed the complications caused by the 2002 redistricting. Downsizing had caused extraordinary problems, but the Senate had been sensitive to minorities and he believed the courts would have upheld the 2002 redistricting plan. He wished to "make it very clear that the Senate was not admitting fault."

Then, with a shy smile, Montalbano brightened and described himself as "someone who knows how to build a consensus." He explained that the resignations of Senators Irons and Celona from districts adjacent to the City of Providence had allowed all sides to take a fresh look at the map. Paiva Weed added that ten senators had "put the principle of inclusiveness ahead of themselves."

Their new map superimposed the 2002 district lines over brightly colored new Senate districts. No fewer than twelve had been squeezed and stretched into new shapes. What I had called "Caprio's Castle" on Federal Hill gave many blocks back to what had been Charles Walton's heavily black district on the South Side of Providence, and the redrawn district added a largely black neighborhood around Hope High School.

The district where Sen. Juan Pichardo overwhelmed Walton in the 2002 primary now reabsorbed heavily Latino blocks in Elmwood. Whether Walton would run again or not, the redrawn "majority minority" districts made it possible to elect both an African-American and a Latino to the Senate.

Charles Walton, the only African-American ever to serve in the state Senate, had stood stoically in the face of humiliation, introducing maps that would restore minority representation and forcing floor votes on them. The Senate had followed Irons's lead in rejecting all of Walton's amendments, and Walton accepted his 2002 primary loss to Pichardo with characteristic grace, leaving the Senate without rancor. Irons had won but seeded resentments that sprang up to haunt him. By forcing Celona to step down, Irons virtually invited Kelly stalwarts who knew about his lucrative CVS business to blow the whistle, and they did. Now, with Irons and Celona gone, a dozen districts slid and bent to undo several — but not all — of Irons's gerrymanders. Vivid colors on the new Senate map restored a measure of justice.

At the microphone, former Rep. Harold Metts, lead plaintiff in the federal suit,[42] looked as happy as I had ever seen him. "We believe the plan the Senate is now proposing, by uniting upper and lower South Providence in one Senate district, is fair to black voters," Metts said. "The plan is also fair to Latino voters because it allows them to elect the candidate of their choice to the Senate in a separate district."[43]

Beside me in the crowd, Tomás Ávila represented both the Rhode Island Latino Political Action Committee and the Common Cause board. He had hosted the first meeting of what became the Fair Redistricting Coalition at Progreso Latino five years earlier. "What do you think?" I whispered.

"Absolutely terrific," Ávila enthused. "But why didn't they just do right the first time? Think what the lawyers cost!"

Gerrymandering had cost the state millions, but Montalbano's redistricting settlement quickly became law.[44]

The 2004 legislative session rushed toward its close. Under the pressure of scandal, lawmakers passed and sent to the governor Common Cause's new lobbying bill, now informally called "the Celona Law."[45] Other ethics reforms also moved forward. For five years, Sen. Teresa Paiva Weed had been trying to reduce the number of officials required to file annual ethics disclosure forms. The paperwork annoyed community leaders who volunteered for unpaid posts that carried little power, and it forced Ethics Commission employees to request, receive, file, and monitor disclosure reports from thousands of officials who had no contracting or hiring authority. Meanwhile, a quirk of law allowed some school superintendents, public works administrators, and chiefs of staff to escape the filing requirement.

Paiva Weed's legislation sought to resolve this by defining "major decision-making positions" and requiring financial disclosure from state officials who held them. It would require financial disclosure by municipal decision-makers authorized to spend over $50,000 and by all building inspectors, fire and police chiefs, and directors of public works. Members of boards with authority over education, zoning, and local taxation would also be required to disclose. Meanwhile, this new framework would excuse more than a thousand local officials from the annual filings.[46]

In four previous years, unions representing unclassified employees had blocked passage, but Paiva Weed's new clout as Senate majority leader enabled her to push her common-sense reform into law.[47]

Another Paiva Weed bill required people who sought to influence decisions by executive departments or public corporations to register as lobbyists and report their activities.[48] With separation of powers looming, House leaders were glad to pass Paiva Weed's bill and a companion by Rep. Fausto Anguilla. Equally important in a year of scandal, Gordon Fox helped secure additional funding for the Ethics Commission that had fined him. Its budget increased by twenty-four percent.

But leadership had its limits. The Ethics Commission's move in 2000 that permitted gifts of up to $150 on any occasion — or $450 per year from any "interested person" to any public official — had opened the floodgates. In 2004 Joe Montalbano sponsored legislation to restore a limit on gifts to public officials. He proposed to bar public officials from accepting gifts worth more than $25 from any "person or business that has a direct financial interest" in a decision that official might make.[49] The legislation passed the Senate early in May but died without a vote in the House Judiciary Committee.

To his credit, Mike Lenihan had assumed this would happen, and he filed a bill requiring public officials to report any gift worth more than $100 on an annual financial disclosure form. Late in the spring, House Majority Leader Gordon Fox introduced an identical bill, which passed the House in June.[50]

Lenihan was also busy with separation of powers. In April, his Committee on Government Oversight unanimously approved his bill to abolish the Unclassified Pay Plan Board, and the full Senate did the same.[51] On June 9, his committee recommended the three monumental omnibus bills to restructure or eliminate ninety one boards. The full Senate took them up a week later. I watched from the gallery as Lenihan, in his civics teacher mode, explained a series of technical amendments. Around him in the semi-circular chamber senators absorbed the details without any sign of astonishment that these bills, once finally enacted, would end more than three centuries of what the state Supreme Court had called "quintessential parliamentary supremacy."[52]

Two years earlier, the Senate had led the way in passing constitutional amendments by Lenihan and Senate Minority Leader Dennis L. Algiere. One year ago, senators had approved the bipartisan Separation of Powers Amendment co-sponsored by Lenihan and Algiere. Now the Senate unanimously passed all three of Lenihan's bills aimed at reconstructing boards to comply with separation of powers. Few expected the House to pass these bills, but they set a standard and established a process that House leaders could not ignore.[53]

During supper break on what seemed to be the last night of the 2004 legislative session, I felt a hand on my shoulder. Sen. Joseph M. Polisena, who had co-sponsored Mike Lenihan's ethics and lobbying bills, stood behind me. "Hey, Phil, how'd you like to climb the dome with us?"

Rhode Island's State House boasts the fourth largest unsupported dome in the world, after St. Peter's in Rome, the Minnesota State Capitol in St. Paul, and the Taj Mahal. I had described its features to international visitors and dreamed of going up there someday. "Climb the dome?" I asked. "When?"

"Now."

On the third floor, just beneath the dome, Polisena drew together seven legislators and me.[54] As the lone lobbyist I wondered why, but did not ask.

At the base of one massive pillar, a uniformed officer worked his key in a cranky lock. I had always assumed the four mammoth uprights that held the dome were solid stone, but when the door finally opened, musty air flowed out around us. A light switch revealed a zigzag iron stairway. Like mischievous schoolboys, we stepped into a hidden shaft and started climbing the steep, narrow metal stairs. Each followed the calves and heels of the one ahead. From a landing, we stepped out onto a roof at the base of tourelles that stood on four sides of the dome.

Beneath an overcast sky, the state flag fluttered on a stubby pole that rose from the Senate's arched skylight, looming large below us. We paused for photos, reentered the columned drum, and clambered up a steep spiral staircase. As we entered the dome, our stairway then bent along its curve. Out of breath, we reached a circular inner balcony where a heavy gilded chain stretched hundreds of feet down to the central chandelier. Just below us, larger than life on the dome's inner surface, the mural showed Roger Williams purchasing land from the Narragansett sachems.

Finally, we climbed a few more steep steps up into the cupola and stepped out onto a tiny circular walkway. Only a metal railing protected us from a dizzying drop to the brick and marble plaza hundreds of feet below.

"Notice, Phil," Polisena joked behind me, "it's a long way down."

I had enjoyed moments of triumph in the State House, but none like this. With jackets and legislative lapel pins far below, we were all on a first name basis. I felt giddy with the height and camaraderie. I knew we would make our way back down into familiar spaces and roles, but none of us would forget this adventure.

47

Restoring Ethics
2003–06

CATASTROPHIC MELTDOWNS occur in nuclear power plants, financial markets, and public institutions. The Rhode Island Ethics Commission had survived bureaucratic sieges and challenges to its constitutional authority, only to melt down in 2001. Commissioners fired their executive director and dismissed ethics complaints against three of their colleagues. This disaster stunned many, and it left the nation's most powerful ethics commission in ruins.[1]

Common Cause proposed to fix the Ethics Commission by establishing qualifications for commissioners, mandating diversity on the commission, and barring the appointment of the business associates of registered lobbyists. To avoid mistakes of the past, we urged the governor to seek public comment on nominees before actually making the irrevocable appointment. In 2001, as in several previous years, Rep. David Cicilline sponsored this legislation to require greater independence and higher standards for appointments.[2]

At the State House, several lawmakers who asked me about the Ethics Commission barely disguised their delight at its downfall, and it came as no surprise when Cicilline's bill died without a vote in the House Judiciary Committee.[3]

Yet deep in the ruins, almost unseen, change had begun. I warned in a newspaper column that the ethics disaster might prevent any competent director from taking the post,[4] but Mel Zurier proved me wrong. The commission's beleaguered chairperson recruited Kent Willever, a retired Navy judge, to assist Katherine D'Arezzo, a young staff attorney, who had become acting executive director.[5]

I had met Willever in 1995, when the Judicial Nominating Commission interviewed him for chief justice of the Supreme Court. A career Navy officer, he had served as chief judge of the Navy-Marine Corps Court of Criminal Appeals in Washington and was teaching at the Naval War College in Newport. Willever had no visible pretensions and displayed a deep devotion to the rule of law. He made a vivid impression as he answered questions from the nominating commission, but it came as no surprise when Almond appointed acting Chief Justice Weisberger, who won quick confirmation. The same thing happened when Willever later made the short-list for several Superior Court vacancies. As much as we had tried to squeeze politics out of the judicial selection process, connections still counted.

Those rejections became the Ethics Commission's gain. Amid the turmoil of Healey's dismissal, Zurier hired Willever on a part-time basis to help restore order. At fifty-seven, he proved professional and nonpolitical. When the commission advertised for a permanent director, Willever and acting executive director Katherine D'Arezzo became finalists. Two months after they fired Healey, commissioners chose Willever.

Before speaking, he honored D'Arezzo with a hug. "I have not had an agenda other than to be fair and follow the law," he said modestly, "and that is what I will do here. I'd much rather educate people than prosecute them, but if I have to prosecute them, I will. I have been a prosecutor."[6]

M. Charles Bakst, political columnist for the *Providence Journal*, wrote that he had "never seen a state agency so messed up." He said the panel needed "a steady hand." He quoted Willever's wife, Nina, saying he had a strong sense of duty, brought out the best in people, and liked to "organize situations that may be chaotic."[7] Kent Willever was mellow, but when asked about his life, his smile faded. His first wife had died several years earlier of brain cancer. "She was smart and she was pretty and she was the mother of my daughters," he said. "She didn't smoke, she didn't drink, she exercised." Her decline and death had been the toughest time in his life.

He had grown up in a church-going family seared by the death of his parents' first-born child. His father, a New Jersey paper mill worker, told him never to whine; his mother, a school secretary, taught him to write thank-you notes. He learned cooperation on his high school football team, joking that his coach made him quarterback because he could remember the plays. He led his team to a state championship and went to Yale on a Navy ROTC scholarship. During the Vietnam War, he served on an aircraft carrier and ocean-going minesweeper. Taking leave to attend law school, he returned to active duty and then rose through the ranks to become the Navy's highest judge.[8]

Willever empowered the staff in his chain of command. He believed in teamwork, delegated duties, and expected results. He mounted a print of the Picasso drawing, "Don Quixote," on his wall because he refused to believe that ethics in Rhode Island was an impossible dream.

DEPARTURES AND NEW APPOINTMENTS reshaped the Ethics Commission. The day after Diane Monti-Markowski voted to hire Willever, she resigned. Melvin Zurier also asked to be replaced. He resented Operation Clean Government for tarnishing his reputation with an ethics complaint and condemned what he called their "abuse of the process." He insisted that no one in public service should have to go through what had happened to him.[9]

Despite the General Assembly's resistance to establishing criteria in the law, Gov. Almond changed his approach to ethics appointments. In 1997, before controversy over Red Sox tickets and other gifts soured him, Almond had appointed retired Army Lt. Colonel James Lynch to the Ethics Commission. A decorated Vietnam War veteran, Lynch was the first African-American Almond had named. He embodied discipline, practiced diplomacy, and stood up to lawyers on the commission. At the end of August 2001, Almond reappointed him. In an interview with the *Providence Journal*, Lynch said, "I'll be able to assist the new members and the old members to carry out what we think is necessary to make the Ethics Commission what it used to be."[10]

That fall Almond strengthened the panel by appointing two commissioners who openly shared Lynch's hope for restoration. George E. Weavill Jr. had chaired the planning board in Lincoln, the governor's hometown, run a Sears store, and been business manager for the statewide conference of the United Church of Christ. I had appreciated Weavill's leadership at meetings of the Rhode Island State Council of Churches, where he presided over discussions of policy on ethics and separation of powers. "Hopefully," he told the *Providence Journal*, "I can make a contribution to what has been a real difficulty for the state."[11]

Almond also appointed James C. Segovis, who taught business ethics at Bryant College,[12] to fill the seat Zurier left. Segovis had worked in the U.S. Treasury Department and was director of the John H. Chafee Center for International Business at Bryant. He had published papers on workplace stress and assigned his students ethics readings that ranged from Niccolò Machiavelli to Martin Luther King Jr. Finally, when Paul Verrecchia's term ended, Almond picked Patricia M. Moran from a list supplied by Senate Majority Leader William Irons.[13] Moran held finance and business degrees from Bryant College. She had served as administrator of the state Health and Educational Building Corporation but seemed to have little political experience. At the table with other commissioners, she listened carefully but said little.

During the first week of October 2001, Thomas Goldberg resigned. When a reporter asked my reaction, I answered with one word: "Good."[14]

Donald Carcieri became governor in January 2003 with a promise of ethical government but little practical knowledge beyond pledging during his campaign to work for separation of powers. After a slow start on ethics, he made three impressive appointments to the Ethics Commission. Frederick K. Butler replaced Thomas Goldberg. Tall and gracious, Butler had risen through the ranks at Textron, a Providence-based conglomerate, to become vice president of business ethics and corporate secretary. Now, for the first time, two African-Americans served simultaneously on the Ethics Commission.

Carcieri then appointed Barbara R. Binder and Ross E. Cheit. Either would have been formidable; together they consolidated the hopes of reform-minded Rhode Islanders.[15] Binder, a public interest lawyer, had served as deputy counsel at the Department of Business Regulation under Nancy Mayer, and then as chief of staff when Mayer became general treasurer. She shared Mayer's passion for open and accountable government.

Cheit, also trained as an attorney, now taught ethics and public policy at Brown University. In 1991, he had played a central role in drafting *Carved in Sand,* the Gregorian report on RISDIC. We had worked together in forming ACCESS/RI, and he won my respect by guiding students to request public records at town halls, school boards, and police departments.[16] Cheit's concern for justice sprang from personal pain — in the mid-1990s, flashbacks had disrupted his life as memories broke through of being sexually molested at a summer camp. He struggled to understand and eventually shared his story. He filed suit against the San Francisco Boys Chorus, which had covered up rampant sexual abuse by its staff.[17]

These seven appointments — Lynch, Weavill, Segovis, Moran, Butler, Binder, and Cheit — restored the personal and professional diversity that had undergirded the commission's authority in the 1990s. These commissioners were politically independent and embodied a wealth of ethics experience. With the exception of James V. Murray at Amica, no member of the Ethics Commission shared offices or financial interests with lobbyists.

Over several years, with new commissioners and Kent Willever's steady hand, the Ethics Commission rebuilt from within. After Zurier left the panel, Richard Kirby served briefly as chairperson until the remaining commissioners elected James Lynch to head the panel. Under Lynch's unflappable leadership commissioners studied the law they were charged with enforcing, listened to public officials who came for advisory opinions, and adjudicated complaints in open session. Despite differences of perspective and style, they developed an impressive *esprit de corps.* Individual differences faded as they took pride in their constitutional mandate.

Gift reports filed in January 2004 roused the Ethics Commission to reconsider its $150/$450 rule. Under a commission requirement that they disclose all gifts worth $100 or more, public officials listed eye-popping gifts.[18] Building inspectors got gift certificates from builders. State House staff took tickets from lobbyists to watch the Celtics, Red Sox, Patriots, and Barnum and Bailey Circus.[19]

William Irons acknowledged over three thousand dollars worth of free meals, golf, games, and other entertainment. He conspicuously failed to report flights on a CVS corporate jet to a World Series game in Yankee Stadium and a golf outing at the Augusta National Golf Club.[20] Shortly before lawmakers approved a twenty-year no-bid lottery contract for GTECH, the gambling firm's executives took Irons to dinner once at the Capital Grille and twice at Capriccio's. GTECH's highly paid lobbyist Robert Goldberg did not disclose these expenses on his lobbying reports.[21] Former Sen. John Celona had golfed as often as five times a month, courtesy of lobbyists who had legislation before his committee.

Richard Licht, a former state senator and lieutenant governor turned lobbyist, tried to dismiss reporter Katherine Gregg's question about lunch and golf with Joseph Montalbano, Irons's successor, at the Ledgemont Country Club. Licht insisted that the event was merely social: "Joe Montalbano has been a friend of mine for twenty years," he said. "It was after the legislative session was over."[22]

AFL-CIO Secretary Treasurer George H. Nee said he had not reported a late-session golf outing with Irons because it had not been "for the specific purpose of promoting or opposing" legislation.[23]

In response to a question from reporter Scott Mayerowitz, I replied: "Here we have highly paid lobbyists who have set up situations where they were closeted with top legislators at the peak of the legislative session and try to say afterwards that this was not lobbying. Do they really expect anybody to believe that?"[24]

In October 2004, the Ethics Commission quietly began the months-long process required to rescind the $150/$450 gift rule. James Lynch, George Weavill, and James Segovis spoke in open session about the need to restore credibility. Then in February, commissioners voted to publicize and schedule a final vote that would slash the allowable gift limit from $150 per occasion to $25. The annual limit any public official could accept from any "interested person" would plunge from $450 to $75. Chairperson James Lynch made no pretense of neutrality on the question. "There's no reason for any elected or appointed official receiving anything — other than their salary — for performing their jobs," Lynch declared.[25]

Former chair Richard Kirby, one of the five lawyers who had pushed the $150/$450 rule, voted to post the lower limit for public hearing.[26]

Commissioner James Segovis announced his vote against the proposal because he wanted to ban gifts entirely. He warned that any dollar amount above zero tolerance could become a "slippery slope" back to the $150/$450 figures: "There will be pressure to go back."

On March 22, in contrast to the packed hearing room five years earlier when the commission narrowly voted to rescind the zero-tolerance gift rule, a smaller group signed up to speak. Robert Sumner-Mack, a retired public health physician, told of canvassing his neighborhood when he ran for a seat in the General

Assembly. "Ninety-seven out of a hundred people favored a tighter gift rule," he said.[27] "We, the people of this state, are not corrupt people."

Attorney and Common Cause board member Kevin McAllister testified that while he was president of the Cranston City Council people approached him frequently on behalf of developers and others who wanted favors from the city. Requests usually came with invitations to dinners or Red Sox games, he said. "It was always very helpful to me to be able to say, 'No, I am not allowed under the gift regulations to accept that. Thank you very much.' No one was snubbed and no one's feelings were hurt. It was a real easy thing."[28]

Tory McCagg, chair of the Common Cause ethics committee, spoke in favor of the proposed new $25/$75 rule as a reasonable compromise. "We don't see a problem with a glass of wine and hors d'oeuvres at an event," she said, "but that's vastly different from what's been going on for the last few years."

Harry Staley, president of the Rhode Island Shoreline Coalition, also testified in favor of the new gift limit.

Commissioners paused to review a packet of emails from citizens. All supported the lower gift limit or a return to zero tolerance. The formal vote for a new $25/$75 gift rule had little drama. Eight commissioners voted yes; one was absent.[29] "It's only right," Richard Kirby told me as we shook hands afterward. "This puts us all in a better place."

Following the Plunder Dome trials, Rep. David Cicilline, now mayor-elect of Providence, set out to establish ethical government in the capital city. No one knew how widely corruption had spread during nearly twelve years of Vincent "Buddy" Cianci's second act. Operation Plunder Dome had shown how police promotions, towing lists, building permits, and tax breaks were sold and traded. Many offenses could never be prosecuted, however, and Cianci loyalists were entrenched in city departments. A residue of corrupt conduct still coated the city like slime from a toxic flood.[30]

I had not attended Cianci's inaugurals in 1991, 1995, or 1999, but I could not miss David Cicilline's swearing-in on a snowy January day in 2003. Like his hero, New York's legendary Mayor Fiorello LaGuardia, Cicilline was short and drew from the compatible strengths of his Jewish mother and Italian father. He was also Providence's first openly gay mayor. Like LaGuardia, Cicilline needed to restore public faith in a city government permeated by cynicism and corruption.[31] In response to a press question, Cicilline cited LaGuardia's comment when he became mayor of New York: "To the victor belongs the responsibility of good government."[32]

Wind whipped falling snow through a crowd that stretched from the steps of City Hall deep into Kennedy Plaza. Bareheaded and without an overcoat, Cicilline addressed an exultant crowd. "Over the past three decades," he called out hoarsely, "a culture of self-service, insider dealing, and arrogance established at the very top has made us cynical about the capacity of city government to behave ethically, let alone respond to our concerns." He explained how corruption corroded democracy. "Cynicism may make for shrewd politics, but it makes for ineffective government and a disengaged citizenry."[33]

Rejecting the notion that large numbers of city employees were corrupt, Cicilline promised to create an ethics ordinance tailored to the city. He said it would not "solve the problem, but it will make it clear what is proper conduct and what isn't. Particularly with what we have just been through, we want to set high ethical standards." With a flourish he added: "Today we turn our backs on the practices and customs of the recent past. Today I declare a new approach to city government, grounded in ethics and strong values, and in fact, guided by those old-fashioned principles of right and wrong."

Barely a month later, at a press conference in his City Hall office of dark woodwork and ornate wallpaper that still reeked of Cianci's cigarettes, Cicilline announced formation of a task force that would draft the ethics code. He introduced its eight members: former U.S. Attorney Margaret E. Curran, Ethics Commission Director Kent A. Willever, former Rep. Joseph E. Newsome, City Councilwoman Rita M. Williams, newly appointed City Solicitor Joseph M. Fernandez, former RI Bar Association President Alan S. Flink, URI Ethics Professor Alfred G. Killilea, and me. Deputy Solicitor Adrienne G. Southgate would staff the task force.[34]

Pamela Ferdinand, a reporter from the *Washington Post,* popped the question whether any of us would have accepted a similar assignment from Cianci. When no one else answered, I said I would have rejoiced if Cianci had asked in good faith. I reminded the audience of reporters, union leaders, and public officials how often Cianci claimed there were no stains on his jacket, but never expressed dismay at his subordinates' misdeeds. "Why didn't he demand, 'Did they really do that in my city?' Why was there no indignation or anger at what they had done?"[35]

The Mayor's Ethics Task Force met in an industrial building that Joe Newsome had renovated for the South Providence Development Corporation. Large thermal windows filled the conference room with light. Cast-iron pillars supported massive timber beams, and ducts for air-conditioning hung exposed beside mechanical systems painted in pale hues.

When Meg Curran was diagnosed with multiple sclerosis and had to stop chairing our meetings, Kent Willever took over. Our goal was a code that would foster fair and impartial public service. We aimed to create a culture where all city officials and employees would "strive to meet the highest standards of ethics consistent with this code and state law, regardless of personal considerations, recognizing that maintaining the respect of the people must be their foremost concern."[36] As Al Killilea said, the culture could change when employees were trained to avoid conflicts of interest and inspire public trust.

To achieve those goals, we proposed that the mayor appoint a cabinet-level municipal integrity officer who would educate, advise, and only occasionally prosecute employees. A hotline would allow ordinary citizens or city workers to report wrongdoing. The municipal integrity officer would investigate allegations and decide next steps — whether to prosecute serious offenses or to discipline minor misconduct with a written warning.

But we aimed first for voluntary compliance. Because the ordinance would contain exhaustive legal language, we designed a "plain English" handbook to help employees understand ethics rules. The municipal integrity officer would work closely with integrity officers who would be appointed to promote compliance in each city department. At the same time, we had to avoid confusion over differences between the state and city ethics codes.[37] During our deliberations, the state rule still allowed gifts up to $150 per occasion. Since no one knew if or when the state Ethics Commission might lower that limit, we proposed a $25 gift limit for all city officials.[38]

The state's revolving door rule affected state but not local elected officials, and Buddy Cianci had routinely co-opted his opponents on the City Council with permanent city jobs. We proposed specific language to lock that revolving door.[39]

The task force also wrestled with the question of lobbyists who swarmed City Hall without badges or reporting of any kind. State law split the problem: lobbyists disclosed their activities to the secretary of state, while public officials reported their financial obligations to the Ethics Commission. By contrast, Los Angeles led the nation in empowering its ethics commission to police both government officials and the lobbyists who tried to influence them.[40] Several cities followed that model and I urged the same for Providence, but the task force decided to leave lobbyist regulation for a later phase.[41]

On December 12, 2003, the task force delivered our report to Mayor David Cicilline. "An Ethics Code," we declared, "will restore confidence only as the people perceive that all who are elected or appointed or employed in public service guard against both impropriety and the appearance of impropriety in their everyday behavior." We urged Cicilline to begin its implementation with an executive order and present the draft ordinance to the City Council. Only the mayor and council together could create the necessary legal framework.[42]

Over the next six months, the administration reviewed our draft code internally and with the union that represented most city employees. Donald S. Iannazzi, president of Laborers International Union Local 1033, stood at Cicilline's side during a press conference to support the draft in principle. He said previous city leaders had talked about an ethics code but never produced one. "We are public servants," Iannazzi said, "and we take ethics as an obligation."[43]

Our proposed ban on revolving door jobs touched off explosions at City Hall, just as similar provisions had at the State House in the early 1990s. Ten City Council members had recently swung through the revolving door to permanent city jobs, most with good pay and pensions.[44] Several had been critics of Buddy Cianci, but as the 1998 election loomed they moved into full-time jobs — most newly created, well paid, and never advertised. With those appointments Cianci captured his enemies, silenced dissent, and built a pliant City Council.[45]

Frank Corrente, Cianci's felonious director of administration, had routinely rationalized the practice. "Certain conditions arise," he had told reporter Ken Mingis, "certain jobs become available." Corrente had claimed he asked himself only two questions before any hiring: "Does he know city government? Is he best qualified for the job?"[46]

Without giving reasons, the Providence City Council stalled the ethics code for more than a year — despite the fact that Councilwoman Rita M. Williams had served on the task force that drafted it. She had held office during Cianci's rule, resisted his badgering, and suffered his retaliation when Cianci purged her husband from a city-funded job. Williams now chaired the council's Ordinance Committee. In April 2005, she convened a public hearing on the proposed ethics ordinance, but only one other council member attended. As she explained to a *Providence Journal* reporter, the need for an independent specialist in ethics who would serve as an honest broker was great. "It's very, very important," she said, "especially in light of what we've been through."[47]

Members of the council refused to budge. Although the draft ordinance was clear, several council members complained publicly that they did not know who would appoint the ethics officer or how investigations would be conducted.[48] One councilman warned that a mayor might use the integrity officer to strong-arm council members or bring charges against political opponents. Several wanted assurances that the city ethics commission would offer protection against an aggressive mayor who tried to abuse the ethics process.[49]

Nearly two years after the task force delivered its draft, the mayor and council president jousted with a series of extraordinary public letters. Cicilline expressed "surprise and disappointment that members of the Providence City Council are only now becoming familiar with the content of the proposed ethics ordinance." He added: "The reputation of City Hall was badly tarnished from the lax ethical atmosphere that was allowed to prevail here."

Council President John J. Lombardi fired back: "Surely, three years into your term, you must feel it is time to stop 'running' against the previous administration." He blamed Cicilline for what he called "lapses in 'ethical' conduct" within his administration.[50]

The dispute prompted Lombardi to fly Florida ethics officials to Providence. Carla Miller had successfully prosecuted corrupt officials and led the Jacksonville Ethics Commission. In May 2006, she spoke to the Providence City Council about delays and difficulties in getting an ethics code right. She suggested that Providence copy Jacksonville's code. Lombardi hired lawyers R. Kelly Sheridan, who had earlier drafted the RIght Now! Coalition merit selection legislation, and James A. Musgrave to draft a new code of ethics for Providence.[51]

In July 2006, the attorneys submitted a draft that adapted specific prohibitions from the Jacksonville ethics ordinance. Although it had no revolving door prohibition, it did outlaw funneling business to particular vendors, using the city seal or public property for private gain, manipulating jobs or promotions, and misusing government positions for private gain. Sheridan worked from the Jacksonville template to propose additional bans on "No Show Jobs" and "Outside Work During Business Hours," both chronic problems in Providence.[52]

The standoff between Cicilline and Lombardi seemed bound for stalemate until both agreed to seek common ground. The mayor assigned deputy solicitor Adrienne Southgate, and the council president asked Kelly Sheridan to draft a compromise ordinance. Together they produced a draft that struck me as more robust than either of the original proposals. From our task force proposal they kept the revolving door prohibition and rules against city employees representing private clients. From the Jacksonville Ethics Code they added prohibitions against various kinds of employee fraud and abuse. The compromise ordinance retained our task force's proposal for a municipal integrity officer appointed by the mayor and confirmed by the council. From the Jacksonville code, they proposed a Providence Ethics Commission: seven independent community leaders would oversee education, advisory opinions, and enforcement as unpaid volunteers. The mayor and council would each appoint three members, and those six would choose a seventh, who would serve as chairperson.

The City Council's Ordinance Committee, still chaired by Rita Williams, met twice during the last two weeks of July 2006. Despite sweltering nights, the entire committee filled seats around a long table to ponder the compromise draft. The narrow, high-ceilinged room pulsed with energy. Williams assured her members that the ordinance was better for the time and work they had invested in it.[53]

A looming primary election on September 12 also raised the stakes. Cicilline had recruited candidates to run against six Lombardi backers in wards across Providence.[54] By passing a credible ethics ordinance, the incumbents could deflect charges that they were soft on corruption. Then, on August 3, a day when temperatures soared to 98° in Providence, the full City Council voted unanimously to enact the ethics ordinance and send it for the mayor's signature.[55]

RESTORING ETHICS required far more than the Ethics Commission's new gift rule and a new ethics ordinance in Providence. It took years of work by key public officials. Kent Willever, James Lynch, and David Cicilline each strode into the dismal aftermath of scandals, when many Rhode Islanders felt government integrity was a lost cause. They staked their reputations on rebuilding public trust.

Nor were they alone. Mel Zurier, who chaired the Rhode Island Ethics Commission, had found himself overrun by his allies and targeted in an ethics complaint. Despite deep disappointment, he stayed to recruit Kent Willever as executive director.

Two governors — Linc Almond and Don Carcieri — took seriously their duty to appoint independent individuals with ethics expertise to the commission. And the commissioners they named — Frederick Butler, George Weavill, James Segovis, Patricia Moran, Barbara Binder, and Ross Cheit — put in hundreds of hours with their veteran chair James Lynch to rebuild. Attorney Richard Kirby, whose votes had contributed to the Ethics Commission's meltdown, stayed to repair the damage. Kirby never said publicly that he and his cohorts had gone too far, but he worked to enact the new \$25/\$75 rule.[56]

In a similar vein, the effort to cleanse Providence after Cianci's corrupt regime required patience and pragmatism. Mayor David Cicilline's Ethics Task Force had no idea what we could accomplish as we drafted an ethics ordinance. City Council President John Lombardi, meanwhile, tried to adapt Jacksonville's ordinance as an alternative. To their credit, Cicilline and Lombardi directed Adrienne Southgate and Kelly Sheridan to mesh the rival ordinances. The final version proved stronger than either draft.

Councilwoman Rita Williams had tried to bridge the chasm between two administrations, Cianci's and Cicilline's. She supported David Cicilline for mayor and worked diligently on his Ethics Task Force, where her painstaking work helped Providence finally establish one of the best municipal ethics codes in the United States. But she found herself targeted in a primary by a Cicilline ally and ultimately defeated. She left public life with little thanks for her integrity, courage, and diligence.

Presumption Prize
2004

IN 2002, Alan G. Palazzo had marched into the Common Cause office unannounced. With military bearing, shaved head, and a binder full of documents, he came armed for battle but needed help. A retired lieutenant commander in the Navy who now taught public school, Palazzo described the controversy in West Warwick over the costs of a new elementary school. He told me that state Sen. Stephen D. Alves, who served on the town's school building committee, had conflicts of interest involving the contractor and the location.

Palazzo had criticized Alves at public meetings and in letters to the *Kent County Daily Times,*[1] charging that costs for the new school would balloon from $10.5 to $12 million and that taxpayers in the cash-strapped town would be stuck for the difference. Alves struck back in November 2001 with a lawsuit, alleging that Palazzo had slandered and libeled him. He also accused Palazzo, who had lost to him in a 2000 Senate race, of conducting a political vendetta.[2]

I knew Stephen Alves as vice chair of the Senate Finance Committee and a wily survivor, but I believed Palazzo had the law on his side because of Rhode Island's anti-SLAPP suit law, enacted in 1993, refined in 1995,[3] and upheld by the Rhode Island Supreme Court in 1996.[4] SLAPP was an acronym for Strategic Litigation Against Public Participation.

I photocopied the law for Palazzo and explained its essentials: any citizen who petitioned a government agency was "conditionally immune" against being sued for slander or libel as long as the request was genuine. Under the law, anyone "SLAPPed" for seeking government action could move to have the SLAPP suit thrown out of court. A SLAPP suit could go forward only if the judge decided the citizen's speech was both wrong on the facts and motivated by malice.[5] An important provision of the law required a judge who dismissed a SLAPP suit to award attorney's fees to the prevailing party. Nancy Hsu Fleming, the environmental advocate who protested toxins seeping into neighborhood wells, had won a $400,000 judgment against the former congressional candidate, Charles Gifford, who had SLAPPed her.[6]

Since the ACLU had volunteer lawyers ready to defend citizens against SLAPP suits, I also encouraged Palazzo to talk to Steve Brown. He quickly got a lawyer who moved to dismiss the SLAPP suit, and on September 12, 2002, Superior Court Judge Netti C. Vogel threw out most of Alves's slander and libel charges. She wrote that the high court had affirmed the two-pronged test and affirmed that complaints published in newspapers could constitute legitimate petitioning activity. She ordered Alves to pay Palazzo's court costs and attorney's fees, which came to $17,471.99.[7]

Alves appealed to the Rhode Island Supreme Court, which ruled unanimously for Palazzo on August 4, 2004. "Are litigants in Rhode Island SLAPP-happy?" the justices asked. "This is the second case in as many months that calls upon us to determine whether judgment was granted properly in favor of the defendants . . ." who sought protection under the anti-SLAPP law.[8]

Stephen Alves had his eyes on a prize much bigger and more lucrative than a school building. Throughout the 2004 legislative session, he pushed for a Narragansett Indian casino at the southern end of West Warwick. Harrah's Entertainment, which would actually own the "destination casino," produced plans for a thousand-room hotel with its own I-95 entrance and exit ramps. Proponents hoped to lure gamblers driving toward Foxwoods and the Mohegan Sun, two huge tribal casinos that lay in Connecticut more than an hour farther south on the interstate. Senate legislation that Alves sponsored would authorize the project and promise one quarter of the proposed casino's profits to state coffers — far less than the sixty percent from video slot machines at Lincoln Park and Newport Grand.[9]

The stakes were high. Between New Year's Day and mid-May, supporters and opponents poured more than $750,000 into advertising alone — on radio, billboards, and bus shelters. Television ads would not begin until the General Assembly approved a statewide ballot question. Former Common Cause board member and state Sen. Robin Porter, who chaired the Kay Coalition Against Gambling, predicted far more spending if the referendum went forward. "They will spend a fortune to persuade us against our will," he told the *Providence Journal*.[10]

Alves claimed that West Warwick had done its due diligence and had entered into a preliminary agreement, but when reporters pressed to see documents, Harrah's attorney and two top West Warwick officials admitted there was none. House Speaker William J. Murphy, whose district included part of West Warwick, met behind closed doors with Harrah's CEO. "We are attempting to get the best deal possible for the people of Rhode Island," Murphy told reporters afterward.[11]

As negotiations stretched deep into June, Gov. Carcieri pounced on Harrah's disclosure that it and not the Narragansett Tribe would own the proposed casino. He accused Harrah's promoters of "using the Narragansetts as a foil here and calling it a Narragansett Indian casino. It is not."[12]

On June 22, still without a written agreement from Harrah's, the Senate Committee on Constitutional and Gaming Issues approved Alves's resolution. The bill finally appeared two days later, only minutes before the full Senate was scheduled to vote. Sen. Leonidas Raptakis blasted it on the floor: "This legislation reminds me of the state going to a pawn shop and selling its future for whatever the pawnbroker offers us."[13]

Senators voted 23–11 to put the casino question on the November ballot. The House followed, approving it by 52–18.[14]

From the beginning, Alves's Senate bill and a companion House version had contained a question for the November statewide ballot: "Shall there be a casino in the Town of West Warwick operated by an Affiliate of Harrah's Entertainment in association with the Narragansett Indian Tribe?"[15] Alves and the Harrah's lawyers who drafted his bill rightly recognized that they could not build the casino without the approval of voters.[16] But in an astonishing error they overlooked an equally important requirement: the Rhode Island Constitution appeared to require that all gambling be "operated by the state."[17]

Lawyers for the governor saw this defect, but kept quiet until the General Assembly passed final versions of the casino bill and went home. On July 1, Carcieri vetoed the legislation. His veto message gave a raft of reasons: casino gambling was wrong for Rhode Island on principle; the Harrah's deal had been consummated without competitive bidding; the Narragansett Tribe would gain no equity ownership or economic independence; no one knew how West Warwick would be compensated; the proposed financing would undercut state revenue from Lincoln Park and Newport Grand; this new gambling venue would "lead to more addictions, more crime, and more Rhode Islanders whose lives will be turned upside down by the false promises of the casino interests." Carcieri's strongest point came at the end: "Absent an amendment to the Rhode Island Constitution, the General Assembly does not have the authority to permit the operation of a casino by a non-state entity."[18]

Lawmakers expected a veto and had corralled enough votes to override, but they had no easy fix for the fatal flaw: if Harrah's operated the casino, it could not also be operated by the state, which was an explicit requirement in the Constitution. As the General Assembly prepared to override his veto, Carcieri asked the Supreme Court for an advisory opinion on the constitutional question.

West Warwick Rep. Timothy A. Williamson, who had sponsored the House version, groused to reporters, "If it is unconstitutional now, why wasn't it unconstitutional in February when the bill was first put in? Why did Governor Carcieri wait until July 2004 to seek an advisory opinion?"[19]

Alves, West Warwick's senator, incorrectly claimed that Lincoln Park and Newport Grand were not state-operated. He told the *Providence Journal*: "I think he pretty much knows that we are going to override his veto. So he's trying what he can, and that's certainly his prerogative. But according to all the legal counsel we've had look at it, we don't believe he has any standing in his arguments."

Rumors spread that casino backers were revising the proposed constitutional amendment and would seek its approval when the General Assembly came back to override vetoes.

Nick Gorham, a sponsor of the Separation of Powers Amendment that would be Question 1 on the November ballot, was incredulous. "Why not amend the Constitution to say that Harrah's can take over the town of West Warwick, with an option on the state of Rhode Island?" he demanded. "I really don't think we need to start fooling around with the Constitution just to accommodate some huge corporate behemoth from Las Vegas."[20]

On July 21, 2004, Sen. Alves filed two new casino bills. One was a modified version of his casino legislation that had been amended several times during the session.[21] The second was an entirely new section to the Constitution:

> Article VI Section 23 — Casino Gambling. — A casino is
> authorized to be owned and operated in the town of West
> Warwick by an entity consisting of the Narragansett Indian Tribe
> and any other parties licensed as authorized by statute, subject to
> taxes and/or revenue sharing and other conditions as enacted in
> the Rhode Island General Laws and notwithstanding Article 6,
> Section 15 or any other provision of this constitution.[22]

The proposed "notwithstanding" clause would make an end run around the article that all lotteries within Rhode Island be operated by the state. Alves's amendment dropped all mention of Harrah's Entertainment, which would own and operate the casino.

I scanned the "resolved" clauses that described how this constitutional amendment would be presented. A final clause exploded off the page. It ordered the secretary of state to place this casino amendment on the ballot "for the statewide election in November 2004 as QUESTION #1."

Tradition held that constitutional questions appear on the ballot in order of their passage, and the Separation of Powers Amendment had passed both the House and Senate more than a year earlier. We had already ordered lawn signs, bumper stickers, and a huge banner that called for people to "Vote Yes on #1. Separation of Powers."

It would do no good to get angry at Alves. Instead, I made a round of press calls and fired off an email to our coalition. "Only a deluge of calls can stop this outrage," I wrote. "The idea of proposing and passing a constitutional amendment in 48 hours is absurd. There have been no hearings, virtually no legal research, no public debate."

Editors at the *Providence Journal* amplified this concern, urging readers to phone their legislators to oppose hasty consideration of a constitutional question "at the eleventh hour of a special session on a Friday night in late July."[23]

On July 22, the day before the Senate override vote, State House visitors and reporters got an eyeful. In the rotunda, where marble staircases met at a central landing beneath the dome, an actor bronzed from head to toe — wearing a bronze loincloth and wielding a bronze spear — struck a pose like the Independent Man statue high above. He had no hair on his chest and hardly seemed to breathe. Executives from Lincoln Park and Newport Grand mugged for TV cameras as they presented him an oversized check for $217 million. They warned lawmakers not to put that money at risk by approving a Harrah's casino that would take more from gamblers and pay far less to the state.

The following day, as its first order of new business, the full Senate referred both Alves's revised bill and his proposed constitutional amendment to the Committee on Constitutional and Gaming Issues.[24] A dozen witnesses signed in to testify against the last-minute amendment. When Sen. Maryellen Goodwin gaveled her committee to order, I thought we had the votes to kill the bill, and Alves apparently knew we did. When she called him to present his legislation, he forced a smile and said that after consultation with Senate leaders and members of the committee he thought it better to hold both bills "until a later date."

In a matter of seconds the committee moved, seconded, and approved a motion to hold for further study. For all practical purposes, Alves's latest legislation and proposed casino amendment were dead. As the committee recessed, reporters asked my reaction. I told them the proposed amendment was dishonest, and the committee's vote was "a good sign of sanity in the building."

Back in the Senate chamber, pages passed out copies of Carcieri's veto message of the casino bill they had already passed. Minority Leader Dennis L. Algiere, who rarely gave speeches on the floor, stood at his seat. Tall and lean, with a strong chin and graying hair, he argued quietly for the Senate to uphold the governor's veto. He pressed Carcieri's point that it would be illegal and unconstitutional for Harrah's to own a casino in Rhode Island. In turn, Stephen Alves — shorter than Algiere but handsome with large eyes and black hair — acknowledged that his bill might be "the most controversial piece of legislation in modern history," but urged the Senate to approve it and let the people decide.[25]

Green and red lights flickered on. Senators overrode Carcieri's veto by a vote of 21–13,[26] only one vote above the sixty percent needed. From snippets of conversation, I sensed that senators were embarrassed to approve what they must have suspected was an unconstitutional ballot question. A week later, after perfunctory debate, the House also overrode the governor's veto: 47–19.[27] The West Warwick casino to be owned and operated by Harrah's was on its way to the November ballot.

Harrah's claimed its legislative victory and promised a $2 million campaign to persuade voters. Lincoln Park, one of the state's video slot parlors, said it would top that with $3 million against the casino, but groups that feared more gambling addictions, bankruptcies, and broken families had little money to broadcast their message.[28]

On August 6, a three-justice panel of the Rhode Island Supreme Court took up Gov. Carcieri's request for an advisory opinion on the constitutionality of Alves's original question that was still slated for the November ballot: "Shall there be a casino in the town of West Warwick operated by an affiliate of Harrah's Entertainment in association with the Narragansett Indian tribe?" Chief Justice Frank Williams, retired Chief Justice Joseph Weisberger, and Associate Justice Paul Suttell questioned lawyers on both sides but did not reveal their views.

Their ruling six days later was unanimous and could not have been more emphatic. The justices noted that the governor and attorney general both found the Casino Act "constitutionally infirm." They wrote: "If, as we believe, the question and legislation are void and unconstitutional, then members of the public will waste much money, time, effort, and energy to familiarize themselves with the controversial issues that the proposed casino has raised." They added: "If we were to sit idly by while an unconstitutional question was submitted to the voters, only to later issue a binding decision declaring the Casino Act and the referendum question void, chaos might well ensue."

The justices noted that the ballot question laid out in the legislation "asks whether there shall be a casino 'operated by an Affiliate of Harrah's Entertainment in association with the Narragansett Indian Tribe?'" Asserting there could be no "clearer identification of the casino operator," they held that "on its face, the referendum question is contrary to art. 6, sec. 15 and, thus, is fundamentally flawed."

Emphasizing the functional differences between operating and regulating a casino, the three justices called the arrangement "an unconstitutional divestiture of operational control" to a private corporation. They noted that although the legislation contained a severability clause, "To parse out the constitutionally repugnant portions of the Casino Act would leave the legislation in tatters." They declared it "invalid in its entirety." This was only an advisory opinion, but the principles they set forth would probably stand in any litigated case that might follow. Nothing could have been more direct.[29]

On Friday, August 13, Superior Court Judge Daniel A. Procaccini ordered the casino question off the ballot. "As precious as the right to vote is," Procaccini wrote, "to permit it to be exercised in a way that violates the Rhode Island Constitution would render this important act of the citizenry meaningless and futile."

If there had been a prize for political presumption, Alves might have won it. In his comments to reporters — as in his treatment of Alan Palazzo — the West Warwick senator ignored the Supreme Court justices' dismissive opinion on his legislation. Without acknowledging the failures of research that he and Harrah's highly paid lawyers had made, Alves expressed frustration on behalf of West Warwick and the Narragansett Tribe. "Every time they reach the threshold," he said of the tribe, "they encounter a new roadblock."[30]

Defeat of yet another casino proposal was bitter fruit for the Narragansetts. In all the years I had known him, Chief Sachem Matthew Thomas had towered — physically and morally — above lobbyists and legislators at the State House, often rehearsing injustices the Narragansetts had suffered over centuries at the hands of Rhode Island officials. Robbed of their ancestral lands, the Narragansetts were systematically "detribalized" in the 1880s but struggled to retain their identity. After legal incorporation in 1934, the tribe had reclaimed its lands. They won federal recognition in 1983 but lacked an economic base. After being blocked from building a casino on tribal lands in Charlestown, they worked with Boyd's Gaming and then Harrah's to build a casino anywhere else in the state.

Now, Thomas voiced their resentment. "I have to give it to the state," he told the *Providence Journal*. "They find new ways to shaft us."[31]

George and Grace Wilcox, neighbors across our street on the South Side of Providence, were Narragansetts who felt the sting of yet another defeat for their tribe. Though we held contrary views on the casino, they always treated me with respect. Long after the 2004 campaign for a Narragansett casino in West Warwick ended, a lawn sign still stood near their front porch, a reminder that government often proved unfair for those whose ancestors had lived here long before Europeans arrived.

49

Finally?

2004–05

THE 2004 COMMON CAUSE SCORECARD cited both breakthroughs and throwbacks. "The session stretched into August of the election year," we wrote, "producing a blizzard of bills that delighted and dismayed reform advocates." As the dust settled, it became clear that more major reforms passed in 2004 than in any other year since the post-RISDIC crop of 1992.[1] But lawmakers who voted for an unconstitutional casino amendment harmed their credibility.

During the summer, our separation of powers task force had morphed into a Separation of Powers Coalition with Alan Hassenfeld and Sheldon Whitehouse as co-chairs. In 1992, Whitehouse had raised the issue with his unforgettable comment — "You will not cut the deep root of Rhode Island's corruption until you get to separation of powers" — and Hassenfeld had backed the effort even when other business leaders bowed out. Now, with his encouragement, the RIght Now! Coalition came out of hibernation.

Nearly every member of the General Assembly had voted to put separation of powers on the ballot, but we believed that many resented the loss of legislative supremacy and might seek other ways to preserve their prerogatives. To lock lawmakers in, we mailed pledge cards to every member of the House and Senate: "I hereby declare my public support for Separation of Powers, Ballot Question One. I pledge that if elected I will consider smooth transition and effective implementation priorities." Piles of the yellow pledge cards came back to the Common Cause office, and we invited the entire General Assembly to a kick-off event on September 20, 2004.

In the State House rotunda, bright shafts of sunlight fell from narrow windows far above and moved like slow spotlights across a crowd festooned with signs and banners. People from thirty-nine groups in the coalition held a long banner in RIght Now! colors: "Vote Yes on #1. Separation of Powers."[2] Others on the converging stairways held lawn signs with the same message.

From a podium on the central landing, Gov. Don Carcieri reminded the crowd that he had made the Separation of Powers Amendment a top priority of his administration. "This is an issue that the future of our state rests on," Carcieri declared, "and I don't think I'm underestimating that one bit."[3] Since his speech two years earlier about giant tentacles crushing the ship of state, separation of powers had become his mantra.

Speaker Bill Murphy and Majority Leader Gordon Fox clapped politely, as did most of the thirty-five or so legislators behind Carcieri on the marble staircase. I expressed appreciation to Murphy and Fox for coming. Under the proposed amendment the youthful speaker would sacrifice more power than any other public official had done in all of Rhode Island's history. He would surrender his legal authority to appoint surrogates to an array of public and quasi-public boards that controlled thousands of jobs and millions of dollars.[4]

In his turn at the microphone, Murphy shared none of Carcieri's triumphant tone, saying merely that the House Separation of Powers Committee would meet several times that fall to prepare for the coming transition. He credited chair Elaine Coderre, who stood near him on the stairway, for taking time from her campaign to do the necessary research. "It's something of utmost importance," Murphy said. "We have to proceed with great caution. We'll hopefully have most of the framework done by, I'd say, mid-January and we'll go from there."

The crowd applauded. Less than two years had passed since Murphy had become speaker, but on his watch the House had approved the Separation of Powers Amendment, something unthinkable under John Harwood.

Sheldon Whitehouse called it ironic that Rhode Island — a leader in fighting for independence from Great Britain and in pushing for a Bill of Rights in the U.S. Constitution — should only now "be bringing itself into alignment with one of the most basic principles of the American system of government: the separation of the executive, legislative, and judicial powers. I expect those brave Rhode Islanders of history will look down on us from the heavens this November, and I hope they will be proud. Thomas Wilson Dorr, I hope you in particular are watching."[5]

Whitehouse also suggested a new argument. "Consider a family that owns an old house and decides to bring the electrical system up to code. That family will never know what tragedy it spared itself. Would a child someday have been shocked or even electrocuted? Would a short circuit have sparked a fire? You'll never know. You do it anyway. You do it because it's the right thing to do. Like that family, we will never know what scandal or disaster this referendum will spare us." He ended by declaring that Rhode Island was finally coming into alignment "with the principles of that first miraculous Constitutional Convention in Philadelphia in 1787. At long, long last, may it be so."

Alan Hassenfeld warned against complacency. "Unless we are willing to work harder than ever to get out the vote and ensure separation of powers becomes a reality, it won't happen," he said, announcing the RIght Now! Coalition was coming out of its ten-year hibernation for one last hurrah. "People forget," he said tenderly, "but I don't want them to forget, because we've come so far."

A few hours after the rally, Kenneth McKay, phoned me at the office. McKay had run Donald Carcieri's 2002 campaign and become the governor's chief of staff. I could count the times we had spoken on one hand.

"To what do I owe the honor?" I asked.

"No honor," McKay yelled. "We did this Separation of Powers Amendment, and you gave Whitehouse top billing."

"Ken," I managed to say in soft voice, "Gov. Carcieri has done a lot, and he got a top slot, as he deserved. What's wrong with that?"

"Whitehouse is already running against us for 2006," McKay complained, "and you gave him top billing."

When he finished venting, I said Whitehouse had raised separation of powers with me when he worked for Gov. Sundlun. "That was in 1992," I said. "Democrats in both chambers took his support as an act of war. They punished him for taking the lead on this issue." I reminded McKay that his boss had done nothing for separation of powers before he started campaigning in 2001.

Question 2 asked voters whether to convene a constitutional convention. A 1973 amendment required that at least once every ten years voters be asked the question: "Shall there be a convention to amend or revise the Constitution?"[6] Wisely, the amendment also called for appointment of a bipartisan commission to "assemble information on constitutional questions for the electors."

In 1994, the General Assembly and Gov. Sundlun failed to create the required panel, but legislative leaders had done the job in 2004: four state representatives, four senators, and four knowledgeable citizens.[7] In August, the panel reported a list of possible convention topics. They did not recommend for or against a convention, but did raise the question of cost. The Constitutional Convention of 1986 had cost $891,000, and they projected over $2 million for 2006.

While all of the reform groups strongly supported Question 1 for Separation of Powers, we clashed over the need for another convention. Speaking for Operation Clean Government, former Rep. Rod Driver told the *Providence Journal*, "We just see all kinds of changes that are needed. We've had a very frustrating experience with the legislature."[8]

I explained our board's more cautious position: "We think the legislature can do some things well if it takes time and works on them." I mentioned the ten-year battle for the Separation of Powers Amendment in which the final text had been refined and strengthened in the struggle.

Bob Arruda, chair of Operation Clean Government argued that ten years was too long and that it took a series of high-profile scandals to get separation of powers onto the ballot. "If we have to wait that long and wait for the right scandal to get such things as line-item veto for the governor and some of the other reforms we think are necessary to bring this Constitution into the twenty-first century, we all are going to grow old waiting," he argued. "It's just not going to happen."

Gov. Carcieri also urged people to approve a convention. "If it's done well, with a balanced representation and lots of input from the public," he said, "I think there are significant issues here that I'd like to see addressed." He cited the need for a line-item veto amendment, term limits for legislators, and voter initiative.[9]

A coalition of twenty-three groups came together in haste to urge voters against a convention. We announced our opposition in the Old State House on Benefit Street.[10] Lila M. Sapinsley, a founder of Common Cause Rhode Island and former Senate minority leader, told what happened when she served in the 1986 Constitutional Convention. Still elegant in her eighties, Sapinsley said she began with high hopes that delegates would create a line-item veto and approve "a nonpartisan way" to choose judges.

"Of course, I was extremely naive," Sapinsley said dryly. "I want to say to the people of Rhode Island: please do not repeat my mistake and that of others." She argued that Democrats in the General Assembly had dominated the election of delegates and controlled the convention.

ACLU Director Steve Brown said the 1986 gathering had been preoccupied with an anti-abortion amendment. He warned that with a rising tide of anti-gay amendments on the ballots in many states, definitions of marriage would inevitably become the flashpoint of any new convention. He insisted the Constitution was "not some student's tenth-grade essay that every few years we get together and edit it to try to make it look a little better."[11]

Will Barbeau of Operation Clean Government answered us in a *Providence Journal* opinion piece. "Convention opponents try to scare citizens with undocumented stories of hot-button social issues related to marriage, guns, birth control, etc. Yet every decision reached in a convention must pass the muster of your ballot vote months later."[12]

The *Journal's* editorial board urged readers to vote yes on Question 2, noting that opponents "worry about a runaway train discarding worthy parts of the constitution and going off the tracks by bickering over such social issues as same-sex marriage and abortion rights." The editorial concluded: "We should not let fears conquer the hope of creating a government that better serves the public."[13]

A decade earlier, RIPEC director Gary Sasse had chaired the Blue Ribbon Commission on the Future of the General Assembly and had served on the bipartisan panel that reported on possible convention issues. Sasse and I co-wrote an opinion piece against the convention. We reminded readers that during the last twelve years, public pressure had forced four major amendments onto the ballot: four-year terms for statewide general officers; merit selection of all state judges; a smaller legislature without pensions and with reasonable pay; and the separation of powers.

We added that it would take time to fully implement the Separation of Powers Amendment, which would "restructure state government in ways that need to be absorbed and understood before we rush into further changes." By way of example, we explained how the restructuring of public and quasi-public boards would affect the wording of any line-item veto.

Our final point stressed accountability. "The convention delegates are chosen in off-year elections, when voter turnout is low," we wrote. "There are no limits on the amount of campaign contributions that the delegates may accept, and because they do not have to stand for re-election, the delegates can focus on single interests."[14]

Election day brought a warm light rain. I voted, went to the Common Cause office, and tried to concentrate on backlogged work. The office was empty and silent. Gail Walker, our reliable office manager for twelve years, had just retired and was moving to New Hampshire. Diana Kelly, a recent Phi Beta Kappa graduate of William and Mary College, would start the next day.

Under the shadow of wars in Afghanistan and Iraq, experts predicted a higher turnout in Rhode Island for the 2004 presidential election than the gubernatorial contest had drawn in 2002.[15] Though John Kerry was almost certain to carry "deep blue" Rhode Island, presidential contests always drew more voters than other elections. Radio stations reported long lines at polling places. There was no way to gauge how this surge of voters would rate the Separation of Powers Amendment or the question of calling a constitutional convention.

Polls closed at 9:00 p.m., and the first returns on Question 1 appeared within minutes. Separation of Powers jumped off to a solid lead and never faltered. By contrast, numbers fluctuated as Question 2 hovered between victory and defeat.

The amendment prevailed with 78.3 percent of the votes cast. In the town by town tallies, Speaker Bill Murphy's hometown, West Warwick, had the lowest level of approval: 72.2 percent. By contrast, voters rejected Question 2 — the proposed constitutional convention — by a statewide margin of 175,596 to 162,293, just under four percent.[16]

Defeat of Question 2 enraged its backers. In a letter to the editor, one couple from Cranston wrote: "Government reform has been set back years because of the fear and narrow-minded, sludge-brained thinking of a few special-interest

groups that oppose open discussion of issues and prefer to shut down debate."
They added: "One of the most disheartening revelations in all of this is that
Common Cause was an integral participant in this coalition."[17]

Operation Clean Government vice chair Beverly Clay wrote to the *Providence
Journal:* "The unions stayed in the background as Phil West, from Common
Cause, and Steve Brown, from the American Civil Liberties Union, gave their
message. Union money paid for radio ads, cable-TV ads, automated phone
calls and several 3-by-6-foot signs that were hung illegally over Route 95."[18] The
organization also filed formal complaints with the Board of Elections charging
that two coalitions had violated election spending requirements: Citizens for
Representative Government that opposed Question 2 and the RIght Now! Coalition that supported Question 1. In another press release Bob Arruda denounced
both coalitions for "behaving as if they were above the law."[19]

In fact, the renewed RIght Now! Coalition had gone to great lengths to comply with Rhode Island's muddled ballot advocacy law. Sheldon Whitehouse had
distributed a legal memorandum in September that explained the law and how
groups in the coalition must comply with its financial reporting requirements.[20]
By contrast, Citizens for Representative Government, a loose and hastily organized coalition, had met only for a single press conference. I made sure Common Cause reported our expenditures and hoped all the other groups would
do the same. I found out later that several unions had formed a political action
committee to cover the costs of printing and advertising.[21]

In his Tuesday column, Ed Achorn, a supporter of Question 2, announced
that he had tried to track down Edward O'Brien, whose signature appeared
on a campaign finance report as treasurer for the Citizens for Representative
Government. Achorn discovered that Guy Dufault, a former chairperson of
the Democratic Party, had worked with public employee unions to broadcast
commercials against the constitutional convention. Dufault had said O'Brien
was a member of Common Cause and lived in Narragansett.

When Achorn phoned me, I found no Edward O'Brien in our database of
current or lapsed members. Achorn exposed other deceptions and concluded
that Dufault had concealed his own role and organized labor's financial contribution. Achorn stopped short of asserting that Question 2 would have passed if
voters had fully understood that labor unions were working to defeat it.[22]

Labor had not influenced the Common Cause decision to oppose convening
another constitutional convention, but I wished I had asked more questions
before I participated in the hasty press conference against Question 2.

But the charge that those who opposed Question 2 were shills for organized
labor was false.[23] Lila Sapinsley, Steve Brown, and I had articulated clear, distinct
messages. Most of the groups in the coalition opposed a constitutional convention out of practical or policy concerns. Planned Parenthood and the Coalition to Preserve Choice were dismayed by the anti-abortion referendum that

the 1986 Constitutional Convention had placed on the ballot. The Civil Rights Roundtable, Latino PAC, Urban League, Ministers' Alliance, Poverty Institute, and Commission for Human Rights were all troubled by the avalanche of ballot questions in other states that restricted powers to tax, banned affirmative action, or outlawed same-sex marriage.

Eight months passed without any word of an investigation of the OCG complaints. Finally, I phoned Robert Kando, a new executive director at the Board of Elections, and said we had not heard from investigators.

"No, you haven't heard from us," Kando said. "The law makes us keep complaints confidential, even if the complainant makes them public. As you know, the ballot advocacy law's a mess. We can't enforce it. I don't think it's enforceable."

"So what happens to the OCG complaints?"

"Exactly what's happened so far."

"Which is nothing," I said.

"Exactly."

"So can we fix the law?" I asked.

"Not easily," Kando said. "I would hardly know where to start."[24]

Within weeks of its landslide approval, Rhode Island's new Separation of Powers Amendment began to raise practical questions. For several years people on Block Island had been fighting a $1.89 million expansion of Champlin's Marina in their Great Salt Pond.[25] At a December 2004 hearing of a Coastal Resources Management Council (CRMC) review committee, attorney R. Daniel Prentiss, representing the Committee for the Great Salt Pond, argued that the Rhode Island Constitution now barred Sen. V. Susan Sosnowski and two other legislative appointees from further participation.

Committee chair Paul Lemont shot back: "Your conclusion would lead to an absurdity. All the state's commissions would be disemboweled and the government would grind to a halt."[26]

Sosnowski understood Lemont's point. As a member of the committee reviewing Champlin's expansion, she had studied hundreds of pages of documents and listened to endless hours of testimony. But the previous spring, on the Senate Committee on Government Oversight, she had supported Mike Lenihan's three omnibus bills to end legislative appointments on public boards, including her seat on the CRMC.[27] Each of Lenihan's three bills ended with an implementation clause: sixty days after voters ratified the Separation of Powers Amendment, legislative appointments to CRMC and other executive boards would end.

Sosnowski had joined in three unanimous Senate votes that approved Lenihan's bills and sent them to the House, where they died. Nonetheless, she knew that passage of the Separation of Powers Amendment had rendered her appointment to CRMC unconstitutional. Sosnowski weighed her vote on Champlin's marina against her duty to uphold the Constitution. She stopped voting and announced that she would resign from the CRMC on New Year's Day, when the Separation of Powers Amendment would take effect.

Other lawmakers followed Sosnowski's lead. Just before Thanksgiving, House Deputy Whip Paul E. Moura told reporter Liz Anderson that House leaders were recommending that their members abstain from votes on the affected boards or resign altogether. Moura gave up his seat on the powerful Capital Center Commission. Rep. Peter T. Ginaitt still sat on the controversial Narragansett Bay Commission (NBC), but he abstained from voting because he wanted to "err on the side of caution." Two senators on the sewage agency's board — Michael J. McCaffrey and Daniel DaPonte — followed his lead.[28]

No one knew what would happen with other boards, but I hoped the House would move quickly to make them comply with the new amendment.

On a gray December morning, Pulitzer-Prize-winning investigative reporter Jack White phoned me from Channel 12, the CBS Network affiliate.[29] "I've just come off the set from interviewing Bill Murphy and Joe Montalbano for *Newsmakers*," White said. "They claim the Lottery and Coastal Council are not included in separation of powers, and we have him on tape saying they intend to 'carve them out.' I wonder if I could come by for your reaction." Twenty minutes later, White arrived with a camera operator.

On their tiny monitor, Murphy smiled through a question about whether the Lottery Commission was covered by the amendment. His reply dropped a bombshell: "I think the Constitution itself is pretty clear that the General Assembly controls lotteries in the State of Rhode Island." Murphy said the Lottery Commission should have "representations from both the House and Senate. The language of the Constitution is unambiguous."[30]

"That will come as news to a lot of people," White countered. He said the lottery had been mentioned repeatedly before the vote.

Murphy stood firm: "It's clear in the Constitution that lotteries are regulated by the General Assembly." Moments later he and Montalbano agreed that the Coastal Resources Management Council (CRMC) could also include legislators, citing Article I, Section 17 of the Constitution, which held that the General Assembly had a duty "to regulate the shoreline."

"The speaker is wrong," I told White on camera. "The people of the state will not tolerate that kind of reading. Voters understood that the Lottery Commission is one of the first that has to change under the amendment they approved. A 'carve-out' is unthinkable."

News of Murphy's claim spread to other news outlets. When *Journal* reporter Liz Anderson asked me, I said the Constitution distinguished between the "prescribing and regulating" roles assigned to the General Assembly and the "operating" duty of the Lottery Commission, an executive function that the Separation of Powers Amendment assigned decisively to the executive branch. I suggested that Murphy was slipping into "a turn-back-the-clock mode," departing from public pledges he and many of his members had made that they would ensure "smooth and effective implementation" of the amendment.[31]

When my comments landed on the front page, Murphy phoned me, sounding less angry than either of his predecessors would have been. I told him he had played a positive role in placing the Separation of Powers Amendment on the ballot, but his recent statements were wrong. I reminded him that the Lottery Commission and Coastal Resources Management Council had been central to the separation of powers debate for ten years and throughout the fall campaign. Each had executive functions, and both were on the minds of the 78.2 percent of voters who had approved Question 1. "Mr. Speaker," I said, "no one can just 'carve them out.'"

Murphy told me the Lottery Commission had hired John Tarantino, a top Providence lawyer, to analyze its constitutional status under the amendment, and Tarantino's preliminary conclusions supported keeping legislators on those two boards.

I reminded Murphy no other states had sitting legislators or legislative appointees holding a majority of seats on executive boards. I also told him his comments on *Newsmakers* had floored me: "You said — and you repeated — that you intended to carve the lottery out for special treatment. I hope you understand that since you brought this up, I need to make our case."

"I hear you, Phil," he said. "I'm just acting on the legal advice we're getting. I think we need to clarify it at the Supreme Court."

"With an advisory opinion?"

"With an advisory opinion."

"Mr. Speaker," I said, "briefs and oral arguments before the Supreme Court could take many months."

"Our legal advice is strong," Murphy said.

Holiday festivities had already begun. I asked him to hold off on his advisory opinion request until I could bring leaders from Common Cause to meet with him early in January. He agreed, and we wished each other Merry Christmas.

I spent the weekend drafting a letter to Murphy on behalf of Common Cause, reminding him of the written pledge that he and forty-four of his supporters in the House had signed as well as the historic statewide vote. I urged him "not to drag this disagreement out with a court test" and pressed him to lead the House in fulfilling its constitutional duty by passing the three omnibus bills the Senate had approved the previous June. More than six months had passed since those bills went to the House Committee on Separation of Powers, which had met four times in September and October without even looking at the Senate bills. Both the lottery and CRMC, I said, "carry vast fiscal and administrative responsibilities. Until their membership conforms to the constitutional amendments passed by the voters in November, their actions after January 1, 2005, in which legislative members and appointees participate will be of questionable legality."[32]

In his column on December 21, M. Charles Bakst noted that the Senate had approved legislation in 2004 that ended legislative appointments to scores of boards. "It is bizarre but typical," Bakst wrote, "that this debate is being carried into the 2005 Assembly." He added: "If Murphy thinks he really needs guidance on the lottery issue, my guess is that the court could provide it to him after deliberating for oh, maybe an hour. But it will take much longer than that for Murphy to recover from a public perception that he is trying to cling to an enclave of Assembly dominance long after the voters have made plain they want a change."[33]

Ed Achorn also weighed in, accusing Murphy and Montalbano of "a bait-and-switch" that he called "worse than disgraceful: It appears to be an attempt to usurp the voters' basic right to self-government."[34]

Four days before Christmas, Gov. Carcieri sent Murphy a blistering public letter. "Your reversal is a breach of trust with the people of Rhode Island that has no basis in law," Carcieri wrote. He vowed to "do everything in my power as the chief executive of this state to stop your attempt to derail separation of powers."[35]

Andrew M. Hodgkin, Carcieri's executive counsel, struck me as the least pretentious lawyer in the State House. In his fifties — slim, with graying hair and wire-rimmed glasses — he moved through crowds of lobbyists and legislators without attracting attention. He wrote about complex subjects with precise clarity, and he avoided Carcieri's provocative putdowns of those who disagreed with him. Hodgkin's careful use of language gave the governor's letters and veto messages quiet credibility, while his self-effacing service stood in stark contrast to Carcieri's showmanship.

Hodgkin's strategic use of the law appeared in a letter Carcieri sent to Senate President Joe Montalbano on January 5, 2005. The envelope conveyed résumés of eight Carcieri appointees to the Coastal Resources Management Council and six to the Lottery Commission.[36] "Both boards serve critical state executive functions," Carcieri wrote, and they might be unable to perform those functions without these new appointments. He asked Montalbano for prompt Senate confirmation, since both boards were scheduled to meet in less than three weeks.

Carcieri's letter laid out his reasons. Newly approved sections of the Constitution disqualified legislators from exercising the kinds of executive powers inherent in the work of these two boards. Furthermore, as governor he was now responsible for appointing members of all boards that exercised executive powers, subject to advice and consent of the Senate.[37]

While Carcieri began making appointments, representatives on Murphy's leadership team began resigning from many boards where they served. Among the thirty-six Democrats who resigned were Paul Crowley from the Board of Regents for Elementary and Secondary Education, and Steven Costantino and Kenneth Carter from the Board of Governors for Higher Education. The speaker resigned from the Rhode Island Water Resources Board.[38] By contrast, his allies on the Lottery Commission — House Judiciary Chairman Robert E. Flaherty and Rep. William San Bento — sent carefully conditional letters. "Although I do not believe that I am currently a member of any board, commission, or other entity which exercises executive function, I hereby resign, effective immediately" from any that do. What did that mean?

Senate President Joseph Montalbano told reporter Liz Anderson that his members presumed they were off many boards, including the Lottery Commission.

Sheldon Whitehouse published a commentary entitled "Don't trifle with separation of powers," which insisted there were no exceptions to the new amendment. He reminded readers that the lottery board had been central to the debate for years, and not "some odd constitutional cousin off in the attic that no one was paying attention to while we fought — and voted — for separation of powers."[39] He also dismantled arguments that the CRMC was an exception because of the General Assembly's constitutional duty to protect the environment.

I spent much of that winter weekend phoning the representatives, including Murphy, who had signed pledges to implement separation of powers. Many of the Democrats on the list supported Murphy for speaker of the House. Few answered their phones, but I left messages on answering machines. I thanked them for putting the amendment onto the ballot and for their pledges to uphold it. I urged them to speak with Murphy about finishing what they had begun.

On January 10, two members of the Common Cause executive committee and I were to meet Murphy in his office. Daniel G. Siegel and Kevin J. McAllister were both skilled negotiators who understood the pressures that might be weakening Murphy's spine.

We waited for an hour without word from the speaker, and McAllister finally had to leave. Siegel and I later entered the speaker's office together and sat across from him at his vast desk. I watched Murphy at closer range than at any other time since he won the post two years earlier. His soft cheeks had aged, and his eyes looked as if he had not slept well. While we had been pressuring him to implement separation of powers, Murphy had been fighting for his political life. The Harrah's casino proposal designed for his hometown had imploded, stirring doubts about his ability to manage. Since the summer, Rep. John J. DeSimone and maverick Democrats David A. Caprio and Rene R. Menard had been openly wooing members of Murphy's faction. The tiny contingent of House Republicans had pledged to support DeSimone.[40]

Murphy had been fighting his way out from under John Harwood's mantle. A pair of boxing gloves autographed by Rhode Island's world lightweight champion Vinny Pazienza hung near his door. "To my friend, the Speaker of the House," Paz had written, "Stay strong!" Murphy had won re-election as speaker with a comfortable margin, but his eyes showed the price he had paid.

Dan Siegel pressed the case for prompt action on Mike Lenihan's three omnibus Senate bills. "This isn't rocket science," he said dryly. "You could package these bills any way you like to get the job done. Our concern is time. You see the quorum problems already with the CRMC trying to rule on Champlin's Marina."

"Those bills are dead now," Murphy said. "This is a new session."

"Of course," I agreed. "But you could have your own versions introduced and instruct the committee to begin hearings." I knew that might be hard for Murphy. Rep. Rene Menard, a leader of the insurrection against him, had introduced a virtual clone of one 2004 Lenihan restructuring bill,[41] and I assumed the other two were in the pipeline.

Siegel moved to our second concern: we thought seeking an advisory opinion from the Supreme Court would only delay and distract. "The text of the amendment is unequivocal," Siegel said. "Legislators cannot serve on boards that execute state laws. The Lottery Commission administers $1.48 billion each year, a clearly executive function. There's no other state that puts legislators in charge of gambling operations. We've given you our research."

"Have you?" Murphy asked. "I'd like to see that." I pulled out a copy of Peter Hufstader's chart comparing authority for lotteries and gambling state by state — from Alabama to Wyoming — and slid it across his desk. Thirteen had no state lotteries, and seven operated lotteries under various departments of state government without a commission. Thirty states empowered an appointed board to operate their lotteries. "Of those," I reiterated, "not one has even one legislator on the board that operates lotteries or casinos. On our Lottery Commission, six of nine members are sitting legislators."[42]

Only one other state allowed legislative appointees. The chart showed Connecticut's thirteen-member Lottery Corporation with six,[43] and Murphy spotted it. "What about Connecticut?" he asked. "They're almost like us. So what's wrong with our doing that?"

"Our voters approved a more robust appointments clause than Connecticut's," I said. "Our Article IX, Section 5 now says the governor 'shall appoint all members of any board that exercises executive power under the laws of this state.'"[44]

Murphy replied that Article VI, Section 15 specified that lotteries had to be "operated by the state," and all were "subject to the prescription and regulation of the General Assembly."[45] He was convinced the earlier section on lotteries trumped the new appointments clause.

Three days later Paul Crowley introduced legislation that would abolish the Lottery Commission and transfer its duties to a "Division of State Lottery within the Department of Administration."[46] His co-sponsors included top lieutenants in Murphy's leadership team. The bill authorized the governor to appoint a director with the advice and consent of the Senate. It listed specific duties for the director and proposed to create a new "Permanent Joint Committee on State Lottery," which would provide oversight and recommend legislation regarding its operation."

Many months earlier, Carl Bogus had proposed folding boards into executive departments, but some of us had thought that approach too radical. Now, as I studied the legislation, I thought we could not have designed anything better than Crowley's bill. The governor would control the executive duties, and the General Assembly would provide oversight. The legislature could still make major changes by passing laws that would go to the governor's desk for signature or veto.

But Bob Arruda blasted Crowley's compromise. "I find the whole proposal outrageous," he told reporters. "When it becomes imminent the legislature is going to lose control over the Lottery Commission, they now see fit to abolish it." He dismissed Crowley's proposal as "a violation of the intent and the spirit of the separation-of-powers amendment."[47]

January 18 felt like the coldest day of the winter. After a meeting in a downtown law office I walked through Waterplace Park toward the State House, alone on the cobblestone walkway where thousands flocked on summer nights for Water-Fire. Ice from the receding tide coated uprights that held the empty braziers. My cell phone buzzed.

Kathy Gregg, calling from the State House, said Murphy had just issued an extraordinary written statement: the House would not seek an advisory from the Supreme Court. As I walked, she read me his comments: "While I still believe there are merits to the legal questions involved in this issue, I have reached this decision to expedite the implementation of separation of powers and to honor the will of the people."

"Your reaction?" Gregg asked.

I said Murphy's decision did not settle everything but opened the door for us to move forward with hearings on new legislation, including Crowley's lottery bill. I said Murphy was taking a wise step that would let us start.

She asked why I thought Murphy had made this decision.

"I don't want to speculate about his motives," I said. "I think the constitutional case was clear in terms of what the amendment says. There's no way and maybe no political will to carve out exceptions."[48]

Through bare branches the State House gleamed in January sunshine. Instead of a sidewalk along Francis Street, I chose the central brick pathway toward the broad marble steps. Far above were the windows of Murphy's office where we had made our case a few days earlier. One floor down on the Senate side, I picked out the single window of Mike Lenihan's tiny office, thankful for his quiet courage. His simile came back to me. Separation of powers was like digging a canal — first the blasting, then the shoveling. Had we finished with the dynamite? Could we finally begin building anew?

50

Unfinished Business

2005

WITH THE DECADE-LONG CAMPAIGN for separation of powers nearing its end, Common Cause mulled its next priorities. Board member Kevin McAllister, who had worked on ethics, redistricting, and separation of powers, agreed to chair a "next phase agenda committee."[1]

In the mid-1980s Common Cause had embraced voter initiative — a Progressive Era petitioning process that enabled reformers to get around stubborn legislatures — but the issue stalled. In 1993 other reform groups proposed forming the Voter Initiative Alliance, and we agreed to join if the proposed amendment included robust standards to protect civil liberties.[2] Ever since, the proposed legislation had outlawed any initiative that could "abridge the civil rights or liberties, including those guaranteed by" Rhode Island's Bill of Rights "of any individual or group of individuals . . . ."[3] With that and several procedural protections, Common Cause supported voter initiative throughout the 1990s.

But tensions flared. Leaders of traditional civil rights groups, particularly the NAACP and the Urban League, were wary that Rhode Island would spawn clones of California's Proposition 209. That deceptively named Civil Rights Initiative, a 1996 ballot question, barred government agencies from preferential treatment in the areas of public employment, public education or public contracting based on race, color, ethnicity or national origin. Rhode Island's Alliance for Gay and Lesbian Civil Rights was equally disturbed by the 1992 Colorado amendment that barred municipalities and the state from granting any legal protection to gays and lesbians.

Year after year, these groups testified against voter initiative, declaring that our proposal to prevent any abridging of civil rights would not work. Rep. Marsha Carpenter, who represented the district where I lived, observed that most of the people who supported voter initiative were white and had no worries about their civil rights. "I find it kind of offensive," she testified.[4]

While civil rights groups attacked Common Cause for supporting voter initiative, other groups in the Voter Initiative Alliance dropped out. At one House Judiciary hearing, I was the only person who testified in favor of the initiative process. When I told the Common Cause board, members suggested that we "go silent" on the issue: not formally rejecting our previous position but no longer expending political capital for a process we had come to doubt.

When the next phase agenda committee began ranking priorities, few favored voter initiative. That raised questions about breaching a familiar Common Cause motto: "We don't take on issues lightly, but once we take an issue on, we never let go until we win." Because the state organization had never reversed itself on legislation, the committee recommended that we simply remain silent on the issue.

McAllister's group suggested instead that we give priority to "clean elections," a system that aimed to level the campaign playing field through full public financing for legislative and statewide campaigns. Arizona and Maine had adopted variations of the model, and Connecticut was on the verge of doing the same. Over several years, our campaign finance committee had worked with a group of Brown University students to develop similar legislation for Rhode Island.[5]

Clean elections laws required candidates to demonstrate that voters trusted them by collecting signatures and $5 contributions from registered voters in their districts. Candidates for state representative would be required to raise fifty qualifying donations with signatures, and Senate candidates one hundred $5 contributions and signatures, because Senate districts were twice as large. Once certified, candidates for state representative could receive $8,000 in public funds, while Senate candidates could get $16,000. Gubernatorial candidates were expected to gather 2,500 signatures and $5 contributions but could qualify for $1,500,000, while the four lower general officers could get $600,000 each.

Our committee also recommended a constitutional amendment written by former justice Robert Flanders, who now served on the Common Cause state governing board. He told us about his dissent in a 1998 case in which a driver with blood alcohol twice the legal limit had grievously injured a motorcycle rider, Robert J. Bandoni. Under state law and a section of the Constitution, police and prosecutors were required to keep the victim informed of his case and enable him to address the court before sentencing.[6] But Coventry police failed to notify Bandoni, and he never got to speak in court. The drunk driver pled to lesser charges, was required to pay $250 into the Victims' Indemnity Fund, and was sentenced to a year of unsupervised probation. He never lost his license to drive.

Bandoni sued the drunk driver, the Town of Coventry, and state prosecutors who had failed to notify him of court proceedings. But the Supreme Court majority ruled that since the legislature had not created "specific provisions or mechanisms" that allowed crime victims to sue, Bandoni could not do so. In legal terms, the victims' rights section of the Constitution was not "self-executing."[7]

Flanders dissented sharply: "What vexes me is the majority's remarkable refusal to enforce the plain language of the victims' rights amendment to our State Constitution." He wrote that the framers of the amendment "did not intend for the amendment to be unenforceable until and unless the General Assembly enacted legislation providing for an express private right of action."

Since the Supreme Court had essentially declared the Constitution's promise void, Flanders drafted specific constitutional language to close that loophole. His amendment would make constitutional guarantees "self-executing" with or without enabling legislation.[8]

A third issue for the next phase agenda committee was close to my heart. A few blocks from our home on the South Side, the Family Life Center helped inmates being released from prison to reconnect with society, assisting them with job searches and education. The nonprofit's executive director was Solangel Rodriguez, a visionary social worker. She wore no make-up and swept her graying hair back as if she had no time for superficialities.

"We need your help," Rodriguez told me. "People come back to their families, but because they're on probation or parole they can't vote." One member of her board had earned a graduate degree but stayed on parole for a crime he committed decades earlier. She was organizing a campaign to restore the vote the moment an inmate walked out of prison — rather than at the end of probation and parole, as specified in the Rhode Island Constitution. "Becoming responsible in the community," she said, "means voting. Studies show that former prisoners who vote are fifty percent less likely to commit new crimes. Voting makes people less prone to slip into old patterns." She handed me a research paper and the draft of a constitutional amendment.[9]

Within a long section on "Persons entitled to vote," the proposed text would strike out and replace words in two sentences:

EXISTING language in Article II, Section 1:
No ~~felon~~ shall be permitted to vote until ~~completion of~~ such ~~felon's sentence, served or suspended, and of parole or probation regardless of a nolo contendere plea~~. Upon ~~such completion,~~ such person's right to vote shall be restored.

PROPOSED Article II, Section 1:
No person who is incarcerated in a correctional facility upon a

> felony conviction shall be permitted to vote until such <u>person is
> discharged from the facility</u>. Upon <u>discharge</u>, such person's right
> to vote shall be restored.[10]

The text replaced the pejorative word "felon" with the more neutral "person" and dropped the current requirement of completing "parole or probation" after prison. Disenfranchisement would end "upon discharge."[11]

Drug crimes had exploded prison populations across the country, but the local figures stunned me. Since 1986, Rhode Island's rate of felon disenfranchisement had grown almost seventy percent. Our tiny state now boasted the nation's second highest percentage of former prisoners ineligible to vote. In raw numbers, most of those barred from voting were Caucasians, but minorities were shut out in far higher percentages: Latinos were four times more likely than whites to be disenfranchised, African-Americans nine times more likely. As a result Rhode Island excluded more minorities than thirty-seven other states, including many where Jim Crow laws and racial violence had blocked the franchise of the descendants of slaves until the Voting Rights Act of 1965. Racial bias ran deep in Rhode Island, and I told Rodriguez that restoring the vote would be a tough sell.

"We know," she said. "That's why we're building a broad coalition of civil rights groups, community organizations, and congregations. We need credible advocacy groups like the ACLU and Common Cause."

I said it might take years to get voting rights onto the ballot. "We understand that," she replied. "I've been hoping you could take some of the energy you put into separation of powers and apply it to voting rights."

That would depend on the Common Cause board, I said: "I can't act without their support."

"I assume most of your board members are white."

I nodded. Of twenty, we had only one African-American and one Latino, but I promised her Common Cause would take this challenge seriously.

I outlined her request at the next meeting of McAllister's committee and proposed that we help form a Right To Vote Coalition with two goals: to put the voting rights amendment on the ballot and to pass enabling legislation that would authorize the Adult Correctional Institution (ACI) to register inmates as they were discharged.[12] The committee recommended that Common Cause begin this work.

The full board met for a potluck dinner at Jane Austin's home on a bluff above Narragansett Bay. Moonlight glinted across dark water. With the historic Separation of Powers Amendment now part of the Rhode Island Constitution, spirits were high.

The committee's proposed next phase agenda had gone out by email, and Kevin McAllister presented his committee's proposals.[13] "I don't want to overstate," he said, "but our leadership on the Separation of Powers Amendment has strengthened our credibility. That makes what we do next particularly important."

Board members affirmed that reconstructing boards to comply with the Separation of Powers Amendment would be our top priority. They voted unanimously to adopt the next phase agenda committee's recommendations. Bob Flanders argued that it was a mistake for Common Cause to remain silent on voter initiative, but McAllister rehearsed his committee's reasoning, and the board agreed. No one imagined that we would need to battle a counterattack against one high-profile success from the previous year.[14]

The 2004 "Celona Law" required lobbyists and the firms that deployed them to disclose all cash and anything of value over $250 that they gave to any "major state decision-makers" in the previous calendar year. Payments might include fees, salaries, commissions, rents, royalties, gifts, gratuities, or other payment that would be reportable as income under the IRS Code. The new law also doubled the penalties for violations of the lobbying statute.[15]

In compliance with the new law, many lobbyists filed reports in January 2005. Similar to the multiple filing of a W-2 or 1099 in tax reporting, they sent identical copies to the Secretary of State, whose office regulated lobbyists; to the Ethics Commission, which received financial disclosure forms from public officials; and to the officials who were required to disclose sources of income.

In January 2005, Kathy Gregg caught public attention with the headline: "New law shows public the money." Her numbers almost burst off the page. After he resigned as Senate president, Bill Irons had continued in office for three months, during which Blue Cross paid him $77,048 in broker commissions. The insurer's highest previously reported payment to him had been $42,189 for an entire year.[16]

Blue Cross also reported providing $21,500 in insurance benefits to Superior Court Judge Edward C. Clifton for serving on its board. It paid $19,363 in fees and health insurance benefits for Sheldon S. Sollosy, chairman of the quasi-public Rhode Island Public Telecommunications Authority. Neither payment had been public, and both prompted questions.

Gregg wrote that CVS paid lobbyists but had not filed a report. A spokesperson told her the pharmaceutical company had not provided "any gifts or payments that would trigger the reporting requirement." Knowing that was false, she contacted Rep. William J. McManus, who readily acknowledged working for CVS at a salary of roughly $125,000, which he reported annually on ethics disclosure forms.

Two entities whose lobbyists prowled the State House hallways reported paying full-time salaries to Rep. Peter T. Ginaitt. The City of Warwick had paid Ginaitt $69,271 for his work as an emergency rescue captain, while Rhode Island

Hospital paid him $82,992 as its "emergency preparedness coordination officer." Both jobs were legal, but the story left many wondering how Ginaitt could juggle those jobs along with his obligations as a state representative.

For the first time ever, unions reported salaries and benefits they paid to legislators. Council 94 of the American Federation of State, County and Municipal Employees (AFSCME) paid its business agent Sen. John J. Tassoni Jr. a salary of $79,060. In her article Gregg calculated the salaries and benefits other union entities had provided: New England Laborers' Labor-Management Cooperation Trust paid Senate Majority Whip Domenic J. Ruggerio $163,717; Local 808, Rhode Island Judicial, Professional and Technical Employees paid $135,177 to Sen. Frank A. Ciccone; and the New England Laborers' Health and Safety Fund paid Deputy House Majority Whip Paul Moura $91,663. Ruggerio, Ciccone, Tassoni, and Moura were priceless agents who defended labor's interests tenaciously in leadership meetings, on committees, and in floor debates. Generous salaries and benefits paid to "major state decision-makers" were legal, and organized labor gained immense value from having legislators on their payrolls.

Lobbying groups had also paid impressive amounts to public officials as commissions, salaries, health benefits, and other perks. The amounts paid came as a shock even for regulars at the State House.

Pushback against the Celona Law came without announcement or fanfare. On February 10, a seemingly innocuous bill sponsored by Gordon Fox proposed to add two lines to the lobbyist disclosure legislation he had sponsored a year earlier at the request of Common Cause. Where the 2004 original law required those who deployed lobbyists to disclose anything over $250 they paid to any "major state decision-maker," Fox's new bill proposed to eliminate the reporting requirement if money paid to a public official was for "the purchase or sale of goods or services or anything else of value in the ordinary course of business and for fair market value."[17]

I reminded Fox that his 2004 bill had marked a major step forward in lobbyist disclosure, but this proposed new language would gut it. "I hear you, Phil," he said with a smile. "Let's not make too much of this. We haven't even had a hearing yet."

Fox assigned his chief legal counsel to negotiate. William R. Guglietta had a full head of curly black hair in contrast to my bald dome and graying fringe. He seemed offended that Common Cause would oppose what he considered a mere technical correction. House leaders thought business was business, and no law should require reporting of goods or services that changed hands "in the ordinary course of business and for fair market values."

I replied we were not trying to stop lobbyists from taking their business to the restaurants, liquor stores, law offices, insurance agencies, or other enterprises owned by members of the General Assembly, but we wanted those payments disclosed. Now, for the first time, the January reports made them visible, but Fox's proposed amendment would hide them again.

Guglietta countered that the reports were intrusive and demeaning to legislators who needed to make a living. He complained, for example, that it was wrong to require Cox Communications to report on the broadband and entertainment packages legislators bought.

I replied that nothing in the law required the communications company to report any of its sales to public officials. The only reportable number would be its purchases from major decision-makers or its payments to them.

In the course of several meetings I also offered language on behalf of Common Cause that would explicitly exclude a menu of goods and services that decision-makers might purchase from lobbying entities — food, clothing, utilities, health care, financial services, and vehicles. There would be no reports of what legislators bought.[18]

But Guglietta rejected our list, seemingly determined to gut the law Fox had sponsored. For months the stalemate continued. Who was pushing the repeal? Was the pressure coming from lobbyists or legislators?

Nor was it clear what House leaders would finally do about separation of powers. On January 18, Murphy had announced his decision "to expedite the implementation of separation of powers and to honor the will of the people."[19] That same day, attorney John A. Tarantino delivered a "Privileged and Confidential Memorandum" to Rep. Robert Flaherty, who chaired the Lottery Commission. Flaherty and his board had hired Tarantino to analyze what the separation of powers meant for the gambling operation where senators and representatives constituted two-thirds of the board. Tarantino wrote that only the Supreme Court could decide: "This would be a case of first impression concerning the meaning and scope of the Separation of Powers amendments and in particular their effect, if any, on the Lottery Commission."[20]

Flaherty was self-effacing but wielded real power. Besides his top post at the Lottery Commission, he chaired the House Judiciary Committee and had considered challenging Murphy for speaker. His older brother was Supreme Court Justice Francis X. Flaherty.

Despite Murphy's public commitment not to seek an advisory opinion on the lottery and CRMC, he told reporter Peter Lord he remained uncertain about the coastal council. "Everything's on the table," the speaker said. "I can't tell you right this minute exactly how we're going to proceed, but when we look at the Constitution, it says natural resources come under the charge of the legislature."[21] Murphy seemed to be dancing to Tarantino's tune.

Members of Murphy's leadership team moved toward fixing other boards. House Majority Whip Peter F. Kilmartin filed legislation to abolish the

Unclassified Pay Plan Board and fold its work into the Department of Administration.[22] On January 20, I testified in favor of Kilmartin's bill before the House Finance Committee. To my astonishment the committee — after years of protecting legislative control over salaries of department directors and judges — voted to send Kilmartin's bill to the full House.

In February, the House Separation of Powers Committee[23] began meeting regularly, and chair Elaine A. Coderre submitted an omnibus bill to abolish nine obsolete boards.[24] Several had not been on our lists because they had either no legislative appointees or no executive powers. It looked like Coderre meant to clean out the legislative attic. On March 10, she filed a bill to end legislative appointments on six boards that did exercise executive powers: the State Crime Laboratory Commission, State Medical Examiners Commission, Health Professional Loan Repayment Board, State Building Code Standards Committee, State Traffic Commission, and State Properties Committee.[25]

Going beyond the Senate's 2004 legislation, Coderre added provisions that would improve oversight. She would require every restructured board to submit an annual report on its fiscal activities. Her new language would require operating statements, lists of regulations promulgated, plans developed or modified, and financial statements for all funds. She also demanded performance audits, with "accomplishments, shortcomings, and remedies" and "a synopsis of hearings, complaints, suspensions, or other legal matters." Five years earlier, Mike Lenihan's commission on quasi-public agencies had sought similar data board by board, but now Coderre was proposing a way to enable systematic legislative oversight.

Coderre also tackled the Underground Storage Tank Fund with a bill that would remove legislative appointees, authorize gubernatorial appointments, and establish Senate confirmation.[26] Then she went after the infamous Solid Waste Management Corporation, which had been renamed the Resource Recovery Corporation. This was the third of seven boards Common Cause had originally targeted in 1995.[27] Coderre introduced so many bills that tracking which boards were in various bills became a constant chase.

In all of her bills, Coderre removed legislators, transferred appointments to the governor, and added Senate confirmation. Her bills required that within six months of their appointment, all board members were to be trained in the Code of Ethics, Open Meetings Law, and Access to Public Records Law.

Throughout the spring, sparks flew between Murphy's victorious House leadership and the DeSimone faction they had defeated. Allies of Rep. John J. DeSimone introduced clones of Sen. Mike Lenihan's 2004 Senate bills that reconstructed more than ninety boards.[28] Those bills had passed the Senate but died without a hearing in the House Separation of Powers Committee. Factional sniping slowed deliberations.[29]

At a hearing on March 9, Gov. Carcieri's executive counsel Andrew Hodgkin testified that Coderre's bills went too far in specifying qualifications for appointments to several boards. Seated with Hodgkin, deputy chief of staff Jeffrey Grybowski warned that requiring the governor to appoint members of specific community or professional organizations was unconstitutional.[30]

I cringed. Criteria for board appointments were written into most quasi-public board statutes. Through years of the separation of powers campaign, no one had talked about dropping such requirements. Carcieri's move would make the task of reconstructing boards immeasurably more complicated.

Beneath Coderre in the banked committee box, Cranston Rep. James F. Davey turned and raised a hand. He had retired from a career administering federal courts and served on the Common Cause board until he decided to run for a seat in the House. The previous November, he narrowly defeated nine-term incumbent Rep. Frank Montanaro. "Madam chair," Davey said respectfully, "I believe that at the federal level they address this problem with a few well-chosen words. Federal laws say the president 'shall give due consideration' to recommendations from whatever the professional group may be. What would happen if we tried some language like that?"

Davey's suggestion surprised everyone, and Coderre asked for more information. Six days later Hodgkin wrote to her on Carcieri's behalf, acknowledging that federal law did contain principles to guide the president in making some appointments. For example, as Davey had said, one statute directed the president "to give due consideration" to nominations presented by various national academies of sciences and engineering, or by associations of land grant colleges and state universities. Hodgkin affirmed this precedent for Rhode Island and suggested a boilerplate phrase: "the Governor shall give due consideration to the appointee's background and experience" in a particular area.[31]

Jim Davey pointed the way forward, and Andy Hodgkin's precise prose provided the roadmap. Coderre grasped the constitutional principle and directed her staff lawyer, Michael R. Egan, to start weaving the "due consideration" language into the separation of powers bills that had piled up in her committee. One of her next bills before the committee used a simple boilerplate to restructure the Clean Water Finance Agency:

> The governor in making these appointments shall give due
> consideration to persons skilled and experienced in law, finance,
> and public administration and give further due consideration
> to a recommendation by the general treasurer for one of those
> appointments.[32]

With consensus on that formula, Coderre's committee began churning out bills. Senate leaders consented to the approach, and Mike Lenihan filed identical versions that his Committee on Government Oversight quickly approved. Both committees labored through May and June to move as many bills as they could. Meanwhile bills to restructure six powerful boards — the Clean Water Finance Agency,[33] Economic Development Corporation,[34] Lottery Commission,[35] Resource Recovery Corporation,[36] Unclassified Pay Plan Board,[37] and Underground Storage Tank Fund Board[38] — advanced separately.

Other bills traveled in packs. The Scenic Highways Board, Historical Preservation and Heritage Commission, and Historic District Commission became a natural package.[39] A less obvious collection — the Budget and Review Commission, Housing and Conservation Board, Information Resources Management Board, New Shoreham Tourism Council, Student Loan Authority, Tobacco Settlement Financing Corporation, and Commission on Uniform State Laws — passed together after Coderre tossed aside several boards that had problems.[40]

Several bills that packaged groups of boards passed both chambers but provoked Carcieri's veto on technical grounds. The governor invited lawmakers to resubmit the legislation "with the minor changes that I believe would correct the problems."[41]

Meanwhile the Right To Vote Coalition decided that former inmates could be the most effective lobbyists for legislation to restore their vote.[42] By meeting legislators, shaking their hands, looking in their eyes, answering questions, and telling personal stories, they could begin to dispel negative stereotypes.

Marshall Clement, policy researcher at the Family Life Center, prepared a list of hostile questions our volunteer lobbyists could expect:

> *Shouldn't they have to prove themselves before they get to vote?*
> *What about rapists and murderers? Should they get to vote, too?*
> *Won't criminals vote to legalize crime?*[43]

Former prisoners brought street savvy to their role-playing. At the State House, their muscled shoulders under casual shirts contrasted with the suave suits of professional lobbyists. For those who shadowed me, I compared lobbying to fishing — some lobbyists picked their spots and waited for legislators to drift by, but I did better by cruising like a shark. We moved through the House chamber as members arrived for the session.

Providence Rep. Edie Ajello, in her fifties with a shock of white hair, rose at her desk and welcomed us like old friends, nodding as they spoke. She encouraged them to keep telling their stories and promised to work on her colleagues in the House Judiciary Committee. Next we eased our way through the House lounge, with its imposing portraits of former speakers, and into the House Judiciary room, which was empty except for a clerk at her desk. The long table was bare. Tall windows reflected on polished oak. I explained the hearing process, where committee members would sit, and how witnesses would speak from the end of the table.

Andres Idarraga stepped behind the witness chair and stroked its curved back. "Not bad," he said softly. "I expected more like a courtroom." We crossed to the Senate side, slipped between lobbyists and senators outside a committee room toward stairs silhouetted against clear eastern windows. "This is beautiful," Idarraga said as we climbed. "All this glass and marble."

As we reached the third floor, senators emerged from the Senate Judiciary Committee's office. Among them was Harold Metts, who had led black plaintiffs in the redistricting lawsuit and participated in the negotiated settlement. He had won election in the new district and sponsored the right to vote legislation. "Senator Metts," I called out, "may I introduce you?"

Metts turned toward us and smiled broadly. "You don't have to introduce this gentleman," Metts beamed at one former prisoner. "He played football for me." They hugged each other.

April sunshine warmed the crowd at our voting rights rally on the brick and marble State House plaza. After speeches and songs, dozens of advocates filed into the House Judiciary's hearing room, quickly occupying every chair and standing in spaces between the chairs. Scores more crowded the hallway. Committee members with huge three-ring binders full of bills sat around the table.

Rep. Joe Almeida explained the need for prompt passage of the proposed constitutional amendment and enabling statute he had introduced. "In South Providence we understand that when people go to prison they lose all their rights. But once they come back out, they carry jobs and care for families. Most are working somewhere — part time jobs or whatever — but they're working and putting taxes back into the society. Our country began with the idea that there should be no taxation without representation. That's what this legislation is about, my friends. Let's let their voices be heard."

During legislative sessions, senators and reps often crossed the rotunda to lobby for passage of their priority bills, but they rarely testified at hearings. On this occasion, Sen. Harold Metts testified before the House Judiciary Committee, where he had served as a member in the 1990s. Instead of sitting in the witness chair, Metts stood behind it. He told of leaving public office to devote more time to his duties as a deacon, particularly his prison ministry at the Adult Correctional Institutions (ACI). "I've seen people turn their lives around," he said, "but struggle on the outside. I'd been up here so long they thought I was still in office. They'd say: 'Harold, I need a job. I did my time. I got a wife or I got a girlfriend. I need a job. I want to support my family.'"[44]

Metts spoke in biblical cadences, his body balanced, hands moving with his voice. He gave statistics that showed lower recidivism among ex-inmates who voted. "We're talking about giving people hope," he finished. "Without that hope we have high recidivism. We're spending $161 million every year on the ACI. That's why we have to restore the vote and restore the dignity that goes with voting."

Barbara Hurst, the state's Deputy Public Defender, said she had served on the Preparatory Commission for the Constitutional Convention. "I don't take amending the constitution lightly," she said, "but we must put this amendment onto the ballot." She said that, until 1986, felons lost their right to vote permanently unless they could get a special act of the legislature. The 1986 Constitutional Convention recommended an amendment to end that lifetime disenfranchisement. Voters approved, and ex-felons who completed parole and probation could register to vote.

Hurst had a no-nonsense manner, her voice roughened by countless cigarettes and courtroom appearances. She described the lengthening of probations, sometimes for life, that had undercut the 1986 reform. "What clearly began as a progressive attempt to expand voter rights," she said, "has resulted in a seventy-percent increase in disenfranchised voters since 1987." The desired reform now prevented one of every thirty adults in Rhode Island from voting. Now our state ranked second in the United States for disenfranchising former felons, and Hurst urged the committee to let voters undo this unintended damage.

Marshall Clement told of analyzing raw data from the Department of Corrections: "Nearly sixteen thousand people are disenfranchised in Rhode Island. Of those, eighty-six percent — about 13,500 — are out of prison. They're in the community, living on probation or parole." He said men were six times more likely than women to be barred from voting. Blacks were disenfranchised at ten times the rate of whites, and Hispanics at four times the rate.

"Every town is impacted," Clement said softly, "and not just the individuals involved. Entire communities are weakened. Crime affects these communities, but so does the loss of voting rights for substantial numbers of their citizens."

From the far end of the table, Rep. Fausto Anguilla asked if there were discernable effects on children who grew up in households where parents could not vote.

Clement replied that the highest percentage of disenfranchisement was among young black men between eighteen and thirty-five. "Forty percent can't vote," he said, "and when they're barred from voting, their children will be less likely to vote."

I testified that forty years had passed since Alabama police officers at the Edmund Pettus Bridge in Selma attacked voting rights marchers with dogs, clubs, and firehoses. Television had carried their brutality nationwide, and "Bloody Sunday" prompted President Lyndon B. Johnson to seek the Voting Rights Act of 1965. "In 1965," I told the committee, "only nineteen percent of

African-Americans in Alabama could vote, compared with sixty-nine percent of whites. Today, seventy-four percent of blacks in Alabama are registered to vote, compared with seventy-seven percent of whites." By contrast, the unintended consequence of Rhode Island's constitutional exclusion gave our state a higher percentage of disenfranchised minority voters than Alabama.

Andres Idarraga took his turn in the witness chair. He told of making easy money by selling drugs. Two years after high school he was arrested with drugs and an illegal gun. He spent six and a half years in prison and now faced four years of parole plus twenty-seven years of probation. "That means not until my fifty-eighth birthday will I be able to vote."

Without notes, and making eye contact, he segued to his current full-time job and studies at the University of Rhode Island. "I'm proud to say that I'm a straight A student, but my name will always carry the scarlet brand of being an ex-felon. God has decided to give me a second chance. But the Constitution of Rhode Island says no matter what I accomplish, I will be relegated to second-class status."

Next called was Koren Carbuccia. She entered from the hallway overflow, leading her four-year-old son, who planted himself by her elbow and peered over the table's edge. Mother and child had large, expressive eyes.

"This bill directly affects me," she began. "Growing up, I didn't have the role models in my life to show what was important. I realized that when I was incarcerated at the ACI. I've been back in society for over a year, but I have twelve years left on probation. I attend the Community College of Rhode Island so I can better myself. I want to set the right example for my son in every way I can. It's hard being a felon and a single mother. I want to show him the right way of living and not have him do what I did."

ACLU director Steve Brown blamed racial profiling for high rates of minority imprisonment. "If you look at the racial profiling statistics, you'll see that police stop and search blacks and Hispanics much more than whites. If you stop minorities more often, you'll make more arrests. So there's this element of race in the way that our laws are enforced that only exacerbates the problem of these individuals — once they get out of prison — not being able to vote. This bill is not asking you to do something extreme or radical. It's asking you to put Rhode Island in the mainstream of the country, while addressing this serious problem of racial inequality in the right to vote."

No one testified against Almeida's legislation, but the Judiciary Committee held the amendment and enabling legislation for further study.

Former prisoners had already shared their stories with members of the Senate Committee on Constitutional and Gaming Issues, and Metts pushed Senate leaders who, only a year earlier, had settled the federal redistricting lawsuit with him and other plaintiffs. Groups in the Right To Vote Coalition bombarded the committee with emails and phone calls.

On April 27, a crowd waited in the hearing room for senators to arrive. Our witnesses were primed to testify again, and I sat in their midst, amazed at how quickly our voting rights legislation was gaining traction. Metts came in and whispered that the leadership would allow a vote; he thought the committee would approve both of his bills.

The Committee on Constitutional and Gaming Issues filed in, and Chairperson Maryellen Goodwin welcomed the crowd. She said her committee understood the issue and would not need extensive testimony. In short order the committee recommended both the constitutional amendment and the enabling statute for passage. Our audience stood and cheered.

Two weeks later, the full Senate had both on its calendar. Metts rose at his seat and recited the statistics on Rhode Island's burgeoning numbers of long-term probationers who could not vote. "We must move beyond our knowledge of the crime," he preached on the floor. "Is it not our goal to help people become productive members of society?"

Sen. Leonidas Raptakis, who represented most of rural Coventry, raised the question we dreaded. "Are we encompassing every single crime?" he asked.

From across the pale green chamber, Harold Metts answered: "If you have served your time for the crime, and you are released, your vote would be restored. That's only fair."

"What about restoring the vote for a murderer?" Raptakis demanded. "Those they killed can't come back and vote ever again."

Sen. Joseph Polisena described the recent, brutal murder of Detective James Allen at the Providence Police Headquarters. A deranged man had grabbed Allen's gun, blasted him at point-blank range, shot out a window, and leapt from the third floor to the ground below. Officers quickly captured him, but his shocking crime struck fear in the hearts of the public.[45] Polisena expressed concern that such a "cop killer" might be allowed to vote. "Quite frankly, as I read it, it kind of scares the hell out of me," Polisena said.

Metts stood his ground: "Senator, I think someone that kills a police officer is going to get life without parole, so you don't have anything to worry about."[46]

Despite Polisena's emotional appeal, only he and Raptakis voted against the proposed constitutional amendment, and only four senators voted "No" on Metts' enabling legislation. Both bills went to the House, where Rep. Jim Davey, a Republican, rose to say that he had been swayed by advocates' testimonies. "What's the harm in letting someone vote?" he asked. "What's the social good that's achieved by denying them that right?"[47]

Representatives approved, and advocates celebrated in a sun-drenched hallway outside the chamber. Our constitutional amendment for voting rights would be Question 1 on the 2006 statewide ballot.

But huge questions remained: Would emotional appeals about cop killers sway ordinary Rhode Islanders to reject it?

Throughout the spring I had engaged in sporadic negotiations with the House leadership's lawyer, Bill Guglietta, over Gordon Fox's legislation that would have gutted significant reforms in the Celona Law. Guglietta rejected every compromise. But there had been no hearings, and I hoped the bill might die quietly. I was wrong. Fox's legislation appeared on the House Finance Committee's agenda for June 7. I saw the latest substitute version for the first time only moments before I was called to the witness table. The exception Fox proposed in February had tripled in size with additional exemptions.[49]

Many members of the House Finance Committee had chafed under the 2004 disclosure law — I believed because they feared it would hurt their businesses. The family of Chairman Steven M. Costantino owned Venda Ravioli, a popular Italian grocery and eatery on Federal Hill, while Jan P. Malik owned Malik's Fine Wine & Spirits in Warren. Paul W. Crowley owned La Forge Casino Restaurant at the Tennis Hall of Fame in Newport, and one Republican on the committee, Carol A. Mumford, was part-owner of the Mumford Christmas Tree Farm in Scituate. Arthur J. Corvese practiced optometry in North Providence, and several others were attorneys.

I testified that CVS, Blue Cross, and other businesses had never reported their payments to John Celona or Bill Irons. None of the state's laws that regulated lobbying, financial disclosure, or campaign finance had previously required businesses to disclose until the Celona Law. I said the new law had not restricted payments to legislators or other major state decision-makers, but it did require disclosure by lobbying entities. Similar to multiple tax reporting on W-2 or 1099 forms, payers provided identical copies to the secretary of state, the Ethics Commission, and the public official who received the benefit.

Costantino interrupted. "If CVS wanted to buy a hundred Christmas trees or five Christmas trees for their office buildings, or if someone happens to drop in at Venda and have dinner or lunch or buy a sandwich to go, or if someone going home stops by Malik's Liquors, what would be required?"[50]

I explained that lobbyist payments above the $250 threshold to any of those businesses would trigger the reporting requirement.

Jan Malik expressed shock: "Are you saying that if somebody comes into my store and purchases something for private use, he has to claim that? I think that law is asinine." I told Malik the public had a right to see the rainmaking effect for legislators' businesses — for example, concert promoters had been coerced into renting portable sound stages from a company owned by the previous speaker and House majority leader.[51]

Paul Crowley insisted that the law needed to take account of the fact that legislators might face the choice of leaving office or losing loyal customers who might not want to track such spending. "I think somebody's got to empathize with myself and Jan Malik," he said.[52]

The hearing ran nearly forty minutes. Guglietta promised further efforts to resolve differences, and the Finance Committee approved the substitute version. Clearly, House leaders intended to reject any finite threshold for lobbyists to disclose their purchases from state decision-makers.

I described the stalemate in a column for newspapers across the state, and the *Providence Journal* published it only days before the final debate. "Whether or not payments are technically for lobbying," I wrote, "lobbyists and those who hire them must file annual public reports. Nothing in the law limits or bans such payments. It simply requires disclosure."

I warned that House leaders were seeking a broad exemption that would restore "secrecy around the financial transactions between special interests, lobbyists, and major decision-makers in Rhode Island government." With negotiations stalled, I predicted that the amended bill would surface on the House floor in the final hours of the legislative session. "Its passage would nullify the lobbyist-disclosure requirements that Mr. Fox sponsored only last year."[53]

Former Sen. John Celona came to the rescue. On June 27, U.S. Attorney Robert C. Corrente announced that Celona would plead guilty in three separate schemes he had executed in exchange for $318,565 and a free golf outing in San Diego. The institutions that paid Celona were not named, but unmistakably they were CVS, Blue Cross/Blue Shield of Rhode Island, and the Roger Williams Medical Center. Mike Stanton's front-page *Providence Journal* story reprised the Celona scandal.[54]

I sent letters to all members of the House, reminding them that they had approved the Celona Law only one year earlier. "Since then there has been no argument before the House Finance Committee that the 2004 lobbyist disclosure law has actually harmed any business owned by any state decision-maker. Nor has any lobbyist testified against the reporting requirement." I urged representatives to approve an amendment Rep. John Savage would offer on the floor to restore the $250 threshold, adding that Common Cause would even accept a higher amount. But without a number that would trigger disclosure, I wrote, "passage of this legislation would slam the door on public access to vital information about money that flows from deep pockets to powerful public officials."[55]

Savage was one of four Republicans on the nineteen-member Finance Committee. As debate began on July 1, he offered an amendment to restore the $250 threshold. He emphasized that the disclosure covered payments from lobbyists and those who hired them to major decision-makers, not officials' purchases from vendors. Savage said any lobbyist could buy furniture from the business owned by East Providence Rep. Henry Rose. Whether the lobbyist purchased furniture for his own home or 300 rooms of furniture for a new hotel, Savage said, "there's nothing wrong with either of those transactions, but we know what perceptions are, and where there is smoke, people seem to believe there is fire — even if there's not."[56]

A retired high school principal, Savage urged his colleagues toward transparency. "No smoke, no mirrors, no cloud. It's simply a matter of reporting. It's not up to the representative to report it. It's up to the lobbyist. It's up front. It's out there. If people have questions, they can ask."

Steven Costantino rebutted Savage's argument, mentioning others in the committee who owned or worked for businesses that might be affected. He implied that responsibility for reporting fell on the representative who owned the business. "How difficult it is even to know who's coming into your business and whether they're lobbyists. This raises a lot of questions about the balance between being an elected official and having a business. That's why the $250 reporting issue doesn't seem practical, particularly the fact that we're a part-time legislature where we all have businesses."

From my seat in the gallery I wondered if Costantino was deliberately creating the false impression that the law required legislative business owners to keep track of everyone entering an establishment. "If somebody comes into a restaurant, and they have a birthday party — nothing to do with legislative business — it's personal. It puts all of us in a very difficult position when we don't even know that's happening."

Al Gemma countered that argument. When serving on the Warwick City Council, he received a plastic Showcase Cinemas card with his name embossed on it. He said everyone on the council got movie passes, and the multiplex got approval to expand. "I knew my neighbor could not get that, and that's why it bothered me. That was wrong. It looks bad. It detracts from what we try to do."[57] Both Gemma and Jim Davey, who followed him, pointed out that the onus to report rested on the lobbyist, not the legislator.

Betsy Dennigan also supported the Savage amendment. She asked what reporting limit would be reasonable, noting that she was an attorney. "What if a lobbying firm hired me to be 'of counsel' to their firm for $75,000 fee? Kind of unclear what my duties are, but in the back of their mind, I'm 'a major decision-maker.' Without this amendment, the sky's the limit. It could be $75,000. It could be a million."

Jan Malik rose in a blue knit shirt. He reminded his colleagues that the Fourth of July was coming, gave his liquor store's address, and got a laugh. "What do they have to put on this form?" he demanded. "People come in and ask for bags because they don't want their neighbors to know what they're drinking. And I don't think we should have to put anybody through that."

Savage rebutted by portraying himself as a hypothetical lobbyist who hired Rep. Peter Lewiss, an attorney, to draw up an estate trust for his cat. He said he would have to report paying Lewiss $850, but not what the legal issues were.

Carol Mumford, another Republican on the Finance Committee, opposed Savage's $250 threshold. She argued that lobbyists might not know that her family operated a Christmas tree farm in Scituate. "Do they have to troll through all the Ethics Commission statements to find out that I am part owner in a small farm? There are nonprofits that don't know that I'm a state legislator, and I would bet the Boy Scouts don't know that they have a lobbyist up here. When they purchase more than $250, they will now be in violation for not having information that is not accessible at the moment." She warned that until all the ethics forms were online, Savage's $250 language "would just be a gotcha amendment."

Half an hour into the debate Gordon Fox rose to speak. The problem, he said, lay with a strict interpretation of the law by Secretary of State Matthew Brown. Fox asserted that utility companies would have to report the amount that legislators bought from them. "We said those purchases that you make 'in the ordinary course' of your life are not reportable if they're offered to the general public 'at fair market value.'" He announced that several companies had planned a class action lawsuit to block enforcement. Fox insisted that he wanted disclosure but not for "personal, ordinary type of business."

Paul Crowley also declared himself against the Savage amendment. "It's about competition," he claimed. A lobbyist might go out for a meal in Newport and think, "'Well, if I go to Paul Crowley's restaurant, I'm going to have to put that on my report. So you know what? It's just as easy to go somewhere else and not do that.' Or he might think, 'It's Christmas, and I always used to get my family's fruit baskets at Venda. But then I have to put down on my report that I spent a couple of thousand dollars buying fruit baskets, even though I've been buying them for years.'"

From the gallery I felt the indignation in Crowley's voice. He worried that reporting would cost him lobbyists' business.

"Then you have the next issue," Crowley said on the floor. He acknowledged that "crooks" would conceal what they were doing "until they finally get indicted by the feds — which recently happened — and they plead guilty. This law is not going to stop that behavior."

He turned to his third point. An opponent running against him might look up amounts reported by lobbyists and then claim, "'In the last two years, Rep. Crowley did ten thousand dollars worth of business with lobbyists.' Now you say, 'That's a lot of money. It should be reported.' Somebody comes in and has an anniversary dinner, a holiday party, a rehearsal dinner, a wedding. That's nothing. But rest assured that the press will write the story: 'How did the lobbyist influence the legislature?' And those of us who did any business will show up on the list. And the perception then will be that every one has these shady exchanges with the lobbyist. And that's what disturbs me the most."

Crowley's voice brimmed over with emotion. "I've served here a long time, and when I leave, it will be after years of honorable service. You know what? You're creating so many tripwires that somebody's not going to file the report, and the perception is that you didn't serve honorably."

He was winding down. "There's one final problem," he said. "We all know what it is. Common Cause came in and said a thousand or five hundred. And you know it's going to wind up in the Common Cause newsletter. It's going to say 'Crowley voted wrong on this, and he gets a bad Common Cause rating.' And my opponent will take that and say, 'See, he got a low ranking.'"

As he and I had agreed before the debate, Savage offered an oral amendment to raise the reporting threshold in his amendment from $250 to $1,000, which was quickly approved.

Fox, as sponsor, closed the debate. Even in the steamy chamber he wore a dark jacket and tie. He insisted that his office had spent six months trying to work out a solution with Common Cause. "What if you're in the business of selling guppies?" he asked rhetorically. "What if you're selling trees? That's where the traps come in." He did not want lobbyists to "purchase us in our roles as legislative members. But there has to be a balance. Five hundred? Two-fifty? A thousand? Fifteen hundred? I don't know what's reasonable."

In an instant, he switched back to legislators making purchases. "What happens," Fox demanded, "if somebody in here is late on your telephone bill? Do they put on that report that it includes late fees? Now they figure out that rep so-and-so is a deadbeat. Is that fair? Is that fair? When the intent is to make sure they're not trying to buy you or you're not trying to sell yourself. That's the balance I've spent six months trying to reach."

In the gallery, I was astonished. Throughout the spring, we had negotiated with his executive counsel, Guglietta. Our proposed change would have exempted from reporting all purchases by "major state decision-makers at a price and upon terms generally available to the public" in seven broad categories, including telephone bills. Fox had either deliberately misunderstood or misrepresented the language we had given to Guglietta.[58]

Still with his microphone in hand, Fox insisted: "A thousand dollars is an artificial safety net. You're going to get trapped." The further he ran with misinformation, the worse it sounded. He mentioned the Cookie Place, which was managed by people with disabilities. "They were fighting for their funding. They're lobbyists. Is someone that's manning the cash register supposed to report that every morning Rep. Fox comes in and gets a cookie and coffee? And at some point — Bingo! It triggers the aggregate amount. And therefore, we've got to report him. And if they don't report, Communities with Disabilities is in violation. Rep. Fox is now a violator. It doesn't make sense to put an amount. If I go in there, and I'm not looking for something special, and they're not offering something special, that's the test! That's the test!"

Fox seemed not to understand his own bill as he urged his members to vote the Savage amendment down and pass his legislation.

Speaker William Murphy ordered the clerk to unlock the machine for a vote on the Savage amendment to set a $1,000 threshold at which lobbyists must report purchases from decision-makers.

Lights flickered on the electronic board: 31 green to approve the $1,000 threshold, 31 red to reject it. Murphy declared that the amendment had failed. Without it Fox's substitute bill passed 41–20.[59]

The bill went to the Senate, where Mike Lenihan moved to insert the $1,000 threshold at which lobbyists would need to report their purchases from decision-makers.[60] Senators rejected Lenihan's amendment by a vote of 22–10 and then approved the bill by a vote of 24–7.[61]

After one o'clock in the morning on July 2, senators agreed to transmit boxes of bills to the governor. It would be several weeks before the final *Senate Journal* was printed, noting unanimous consent for transmitting "most matters on the secretary's desk" to the governor.

A *Providence Journal* story began: "Legislation carving out a swath of new exemptions to the one-year-old state law requiring lobbyists to report anything of value they give to a lawmaker in Rhode Island is headed for a veto by Governor Carcieri."[62]

Like everyone else, I assumed that Fox's bill had gone to the governor's office. Secretary of State Matt Brown called publicly for the governor to veto Fox's bill, and Carcieri's press secretary announced that he probably would.

But as Andy Hodgkin worked his way through hundreds of bills to be signed or vetoed, he discovered that Fox's lobbyist disclosure bill was nowhere among them. Senate leaders had never transmitted the controversial bill. Whether they paused because they recognized the harm this bill would cause or because they feared negative publicity, we learned many weeks later that the Senate "held it on the desk."

During a routine exam in August my doctor found a lump. "What's this?" he asked.

I told him I had never noticed it.

Hidden beneath my collarbone was a lump the size of a golf ball. Surgery confirmed that it was cancerous. An oncologist at Miriam Hospital diagnosed non-Hodgkin's lymphoma, a cancer of the lymphatic system. He started me on a regimen of oral chemotherapy. I asked about the prognosis. "If this works," he said, "you could do well for a time and then need stronger chemo. That could be several years from now."[63]

Anne and these physicians sustained me through this first medical crisis of my life. I decided to retire after the 2006 election when I would turn sixty-five. For years I had been taking notes, recording public events, and debriefing over supper with Anne on a series of cassette and digital recorders. Now I needed time to write but was not sure how much time I might have.

When I told the Common Cause Rhode Island executive committee that I planned to retire, they convened a retreat to plan succession. On a sparkling October Saturday, the full board and advisory council met at Save the Bay's new headquarters overlooking Narragansett Bay. A panoramic view of water in three directions lent a perspective of enduring beauty and constant change.

Gordon Fox's bill gutting the Celona Law lay in limbo. It had passed both the House and Senate on the last day of the session but had never been sent to the governor's office. On behalf of Common Cause, I wrote to Senate President Joseph Montalbano, reminding him that we had opposed wiping out lobbyist disclosure requirements enacted only the previous year in response to influence peddling. "Nevertheless," I wrote, failure to transmit any bill approved by the House and Senate "deprives the Governor of his constitutional duty to sign, veto, or allow the legislation to become law without his signature."[64] I asked Montalbano to confer with leaders of Common Cause about this.

On a blustery October afternoon, Daniel Siegel, Tory McCagg, Kevin McAllister, and I met with Senate President Joe Montalbano, Majority Leader M. Teresa Paiva Weed, and several of their staff. On deep leather couches in the Senate president's office, we reviewed the Irons and Celona scandals that had prompted passage of the Celona Law in 2004. We expressed Common Cause's disappointment that the House and Senate had voted — only a year later — to gut that law.

Montalbano listened patiently. Neither he nor Paiva Weed defended Fox's controversial 2005 bill. Nor did they explain why they had passed it or why they held it on the Senate desk. "I hear you," Montalbano said gently. "Now that things have cooled down, give us a chance to take another look at this."

Rather than formally adjourn in July, the Senate had voted only "to recess." In January, Senators would formally adjourn their 2005 legislative session and then begin their 2006 proceedings.

On January 3, 2006, Fox's bill again lay on the desk. A nonchalant motion suggested recommitting the 2005 House bill numbered 5477 to the Finance Committee. There was no hint of the controversy around this legislation. Montalbano asked if there was objection and heard none. There was no debate or recorded vote. He declared the motion approved and banged his gavel. The entire process — roll call, recommittal, and adjournment of the 2005 session — took less than eight minutes.[65]

Reconstruction
2005–06

AFTER THEIR 2004 CASINO PROPOSAL crashed and burned, promoters tried again in 2006. West Warwick Rep. Timothy A. Williamson began quietly circulating a draft that would permit a Narragansett Tribe casino to be "privately owned." He made no mention of Harrah's Entertainment, which had bankrolled the 2004 effort. "Tax proceeds" would be "dedicated to property tax relief for Rhode Island citizens," and the tax rate would be written into the Constitution: twenty-five percent of net gambling revenues would flow to the state, far short of the sixty percent Lincoln Park and Newport Grand were paying.[1]

Williamson also proposed to "carve out" an exception from the Separation of Powers Amendment for a new seven-member gaming commission that would be controlled by legislative appointees. The speaker, Senate president, and governor would each appoint two; the attorney general would name one. The three executive branch appointees would require Senate confirmation.

Providence Journal State House bureau chief Katherine Gregg got a secret draft of Williamson's legislation and asked several people for reactions.

Joe Larisa, who had served as executive counsel to Lincoln Almond, blasted Williamson's plan: "Before the ink is even dry on the Separation of Powers Amendment, which was a decade-long battle to introduce good government into our three-branch system, this constitutional amendment is proposing to gut it."

I hammered both Williamson's attack on separation of powers and his attempt to set a tax rate in the Constitution. I pointed to the near impossibility of ever raising a tax rate once it was written into the Constitution. "I can bet you that Harrah's will raise and spend enormous amounts of money to prevent any higher tax rate."

Reactions were so negative that Williamson backed off and reconsidered. Two months later, he finally filed legislation that would grant exclusive constitutional status to "the Narragansett Indian Tribe and its chosen partner." This time he specified a tax rate that would start at twenty-five percent of net gaming income and rise to forty percent — still significantly less than the sixty percent Lincoln Park and Newport Grand paid. I saw only one improvement: his plan for a gambling control board with four legislative appointees had vanished.[2]

A danger faced Rhode Island that few understood. No one knew what rules — if any — would govern campaigns for or against a casino. Two years earlier the ACLU had sued to block the Board of Elections from enforcing Rhode Island's current ballot advocacy law, which restricted the ability of organizations to advocate on ballot questions.[3] U.S. District Judge Ernest C. Torres invited all interested parties to file *amicus curiae,* or "friend of the court," briefs.[4]

Common Cause board member Thomas R. Bender drafted a *pro bono* brief. He wrote that the current ban on groups "acting in concert" had been intended to prevent corruption in candidate elections, but the Board of Elections had improperly expanded the rule to outlaw such cooperation in ballot question campaigns. Bender emphasized that political action committees with clever names — far from revealing sources of support — actually confused voters.

Former Supreme Court Justice Robert Flanders prepared a brief for the Rhode Island Foundation and United Way, attacking the state's current ballot advocacy law as "fundamentally unfair." He urged Judge Torres to declare a 1995 advisory opinion the Board of Elections had issued "unconstitutionally overbroad."[5]

The elections board had proposed new legislation in 2005 to replace its unenforceable ballot advocacy rules with a new reporting process for "ballot question advocates,"[6] but House and Senate committees buried the bills.

To most people ballot advocacy rules were mumbo jumbo, but few favored a high-spending casino campaign without any disclosure rules. Rhode Island hurtled toward its 2006 election without a credible disclosure process for ballot advocacy. With the clock running, the Rhode Island Foundation's director of strategy, Ari A. Matusiak, invited several nonprofits that were planning ballot advocacy campaigns to address the problem. Representatives of the Rhode Island Foundation, the United Way, Rhode Island Housing, the Right To Vote Coalition, the ACLU, and Common Cause met for lunch and formed a working group.[7] "This is tough," Matusiak said over sandwiches and coffee. "We need to untangle a real Gordian knot."

Attorney Howard A. Merten, who had filed the ACLU lawsuit, outlined a fundamental dispute: the ACLU sought to protect donors' privacy and abhorred mandatory disclosure of donors to ballot campaigns, while Common Cause feared that streams of anonymous money would influence votes on constitutional amendments or bond issues. Steve Brown and I both believed the current ballot advocacy law was unconstitutional, but our national organizations differed sharply about how to fix it.

Our impasse lasted several weeks, until Michael V. Milito, an attorney for Rhode Island Housing, came to a meeting with a list of possible compromises. He used memos prepared by the ACLU and Common Cause to chart alternative ways to amend the unsuccessful 2005 ballot advocacy legislation. The most difficult issue involved thresholds for donor disclosure. Where current law required that campaigns disclose contributors who gave over $100 in a calendar year to any candidate, Milito suggested $1,000-per-year for ballot question donors.

Brown and I struggled over the details but tested Milito's compromises with our organizations. National ACLU and Common Cause leaders fired back withering criticism,[8] but our state boards recognized the necessity of a middle path. The working group welcomed the proposed compromises, as did the Board of Elections. House and Senate sponsors introduced the new ballot advocacy legislation in mid-February 2006.[9]

Maureen Maigret ushered me into her office, a windowless room crammed with papers and books. It had a high ceiling but only three walls: one sidewall followed the curve of the Senate chamber wall above. As policy director for Lt. Gov. Charles J. Fogarty — whose only official duty was to step in if the governor were incapacitated — Maigret had no official power. In the last year of his second four-year term, Fogarty had nowhere to go but up or out. Pundits saw him as the Democrat most likely to oust first-term Republican Gov. Don Carcieri, but most predicted a tough slog.

Maigret was a savvy political operator who had served as a state representative from Warwick in the 1970s and 1980s, as Gov. Bruce Sundlun's Director of Elderly Affairs in the early 1990s, and since 1998 as Lt. Gov. Fogarty's director of communications and then his policy chief. "We've been drafting some reform legislation," she said in a clipped Rhode Island accent. "We'd like your suggestions to make it the best it can be." She slid a draft across her desk. "Charlie's committed. He'll do all he can to make this become law."

Its title held promise: "The Public Accountability and Reform Act of 2006." Maigret worked at her computer while I paged through her draft, which included proposals to close loopholes in campaign finance, ethics, and lobbying laws. Several concepts were drawn from Common Cause bills that had died many times in House and Senate committees. One particularly pleased me: since the Ethics Commission's meltdown in 2001,[10] we lobbied without success for a law that would bar business associates of registered lobbyists from serving on the commission. I told her I liked it.

"We thought you would."

Other sections would improve ethics education, strengthen financial disclosure, and increase possible criminal penalties for ethics violations. Fogarty's legislation created an extraordinary opportunity to enact genuine ethics reforms. Democrats who ran the General Assembly despised Carcieri and might swallow this bitter medicine to help Fogarty win. Common Cause could not support Fogarty's bid for governor, but we could play the role of honest broker on this legislation.

Nearly everyone liked Fogarty and called him "Charlie." The scion of a revered Irish-American political dynasty, his father had been in the state Senate before him, and his brother Paul currently served three northwest corner towns. His uncle John E. Fogarty had spent twenty-six years in the U.S. Congress, where he championed medical research and led in creating the National Institutes of Health.[11]

In several subsequent meetings, Maigret and I polished the bill and identified sponsors. House Majority Whip Peter Kilmartin and Sen. Mike Lenihan introduced identical versions of the legislation during the third week of February.[12] At a press conference in the House Lounge, Fogarty described the cynicism many people felt toward public officials and declared it urgent that we "restore confidence in government."[13]

Maigret had asked me to stand with Fogarty, Lenihan, and Kilmartin, as the lieutenant governor outlined his proposals for increasing transparency and accountability. The bill would broaden disclosure requirements under the State Vendor Disclosure program, which had been enacted after the RISDIC collapse. That law required contractors and vendors to file a list of their campaign contributions to statewide general officers with their bids. Fogarty's bill would require them to list contributions to members of the General Assembly. Another section would require lobbyists to report their campaign contributions as lobbying expenses. The legislation would require secretaries of state to monitor lobbyist reports and to publish annual reports on their expenses, gifts, and campaign contributions. These reporting requirements would bring to light details that often fell through the cracks.

No more relatives or law partners of lobbyists could serve on the Ethics Commission, and anyone with an ownership interest or job in a lobbying business would be barred from appointment. One section would require every "major state decision-maker" to participate in ethics training within six months of being sworn in, appointed, or hired.[14] That requirement would take away the excuse of not knowing.

Finally, Fogarty's legislation would require state general officers to disclose more details of their income. Categories of disclosure would follow those for members of Congress:

Less than $1,000
greater than $1,000 but no more than $10,000
greater than $10,000 but no more than $25,000

greater than $25,000 but no more than $50,000
greater than $50,000 but no more than $100,000
greater than $100,000 but no more than $200,000
greater than $200,000 but no more than $500,000
greater than $500,000 but no more than $1,000,000

During the press conference, a reporter asked whether my standing beside Fogarty constituted an endorsement. I answered that it did not: "We don't endorse candidates for office. If this were a political stunt, I wouldn't be here." I said this important legislation deserved universal support.

The prime sponsor in the House, Majority Whip Peter Kilmartin, would work to deliver the necessary votes. His sponsorship alone would help move the bill, and he clearly intended to burnish Fogarty's reform credentials.

I was disappointed when Kilmartin also filed a one-page bill to revoke the power of Carcieri or any future governor to place an advisory question on the ballot.[15]

On the House floor, before the gavel, I asked him why.

"Fool me once," Kilmartin said, "shame on you. Fool me twice, shame on me. Fool me three times?" He rolled his eyes.

Almond had put separation of powers advisory questions on the ballot in 2000 and 2002, and huge majorities of voters approved. House leaders had clearly decided to take a political hit to prevent any future gubernatorial advisory questions.[16]

For five years, Common Cause had remained silent on voter initiative, but backers of the process were not happy. Bob Flanders, who now served on our board, had become chairperson of the Voter Initiative Alliance. He and Operation Clean Government vice-chair Beverly Clay asked to address the board and seek its renewed support.

Kevin McAllister had led the next phase agenda committee that studied our history and recommended silence on the issue. Now McAllister's committee offered a formal resolution opposing voter initiative. Board members listened to both sides and discussed the arguments. Over several hours, four of the committee's "whereas" clauses gained traction:

> WHEREAS experience has shown there is no practical or effective way to limit, control or otherwise regulate expenditures either for or against initiative campaigns;

> WHEREAS voter initiative has been used to undermine the rights and aspirations of minorities, and we believe no proposal for voter initiative can be crafted to protect against this possibility;

> WHEREAS voter initiatives tend to offer short-term, simplistic solutions to complex problems;

> WHEREAS no matter how carefully drafted and how sincere the motivations of its adherents, the various forms of voter initiative nevertheless contradict the fundamental American political system that was designed to temper the excesses of popular majorities. . . .

These and other WHEREAS clauses gave rise to a resolution:

> THEREFORE, BE IT RESOLVED that although voter initiative can provide a mechanism for reform and bring about change in the status quo, the Common Cause Rhode Island State Governing Board believes that on balance, the pitfalls of voter initiative outweigh the benefits, and Common Cause Rhode Island opposes changes to the Rhode Island Constitution that would authorize a form of voter initiative.

After years of supporting what political scientists called direct democracy, the state board — for the first time — reversed its previous position on an issue.

On March 28, 2006, the House Judiciary Committee took up four pieces of voter initiative legislation, which Gov. Carcieri and House Republicans were making their *cause célèbre*. Rep. Nick Gorham, a stalwart ally in the campaign for separation of powers, sponsored the constitutional resolution and testified passionately.[17]

I had signed in to oppose voter initiative for the first time. Committee Chair Donald J. Lally called me immediately after Gorham. I passed out copies of the board's resolution. "As some of you know," I reminded the committee, "I helped write this legislation. For years, I came before you on behalf of Common Cause to testify in support of the very bills that we oppose today." I explained why we were reversing our policy on a major issue: "In a whole series of states where voter initiative exists, majorities of voters have crushed affirmative action and gay rights. We in Common Cause have reached the painful conclusion that nothing we can draft will prevent similar abuses from happening here."[18]

Bob Flanders testified after me that the clause we had drafted to prevent initiatives from abridging civil rights was clear and would be upheld in court. Witnesses who followed him differed sharply on the Common Cause reversal. Former critics praised us, while old allies in the Voter Initiative Alliance heaped blame. My face burned. I kept reminding myself of our motto: "No permanent friends, no permanent enemies."

Testimony continued until after 11:30 that night. As the tumult ended I had little doubt that voter initiative would die again in 2006.[19] I left the hearing room feeling older, wiser, and humbled. I had carried out the will of the Common Cause state board, and years of experience had convinced me that this well-intentioned Progressive-era reform had outlived its usefulness.[20]

Democrats had more than enough votes to pass Peter Kilmartin's bill revoking the governor's power to place advisory questions on the ballot. Kilmartin assured his colleagues on the House Separation of Powers Committee that the current law was "a clear-cut issue of the executive branch exercising legislative powers in violation of separation of powers."[21]

The governor's deputy chief of staff, Jeffrey Grybowski, disagreed. "The placement of a question on the ballot is not a legislative power," he insisted. "The governor's placing of a nonbinding question on a ballot is not making law."

When my turn came, I testified that the public interest required some way to pose questions in areas where the legislature stonewalled challenges to its power. State voters had approved Almond's 2000 separation of powers question by a 2 to 1 majority, and his 2002 question by more than 3 to 1. I said measurable expressions of the public will had prompted legislative action. Without voter initiative, Rhode Island should keep the governor's advisory question process.

Kilmartin swatted that argument away with an email from the National Conference of State Legislatures. A researcher wrote that she did not know any other state that allowed the governor to place questions on the ballot. The committee quickly recommended passage.

On the very day the House was to debate Kilmartin's bill, Carcieri upstaged legislators and raised the stakes by announcing that he had ordered two advisory questions onto the November ballot. The first would ask whether voters wanted a constitutional amendment to establish voter initiative; the second would ask about limiting increases in state spending and property taxes.

From the House floor Kilmartin fired a salvo at Carcieri. "It's very clever of him to propose two sexy political questions for the ballot," Kilmartin declared. "He's trying to legislate on the ballot." By a vote of 50–17 the House rescinded the governor's power. A week later the Senate followed suit, 23–7.[22]

Carcieri vetoed Kilmartin's bill and refuted the charge that an advisory question intruded on the legislative process. "That claim is false," Carcieri wrote. "Non-binding questions do not enact laws; they merely permit the governor to ask about matters of public concern" and allow voters to respond.[23]

Although both chambers easily overrode Carcieri's veto, the drama continued. Kilmartin's revocation bill included a standard clause that made it effective "upon passage," but six weeks had elapsed since Carcieri formally directed Secretary of State Matthew Brown to place his two nonbinding advisory questions on the November ballot. Brown petitioned the Superior Court for a declaratory judgment: should he follow Carcieri's order to place those two questions on the November ballot? Or did the veto override block him from following the order?

Lawyers for the legislature and governor filed briefs in Superior Court. Carcieri noted that nothing in the act suggested that it could be applied retro-actively. The General Assembly argued that because the ballot had not been certified, the power had not yet been exercised. Where would the courts come down?

As spring brightened Rhode Island, Rep. Elaine Coderre led her committee in systematically restructuring boards and commissions to comply with the Separation of Powers Amendment. With counsel Michael R. Egan at her elbow, Coderre applied its requirements to thirty-six boards, ranging from the Agri-cultural Lands Preservation Commission to the Retirement Board and State Traffic Commission.[24] Employees, lobbyists, and activists trooped to the State House to seek special treatment. Coderre and her committee listened patiently, addressed technical issues, and coordinated their drafts with Senate leaders. Consistent with the amendment, they added Senate confirmation for members of three administrative bodies where legislators had never served.[25]

But House leaders resisted reconfiguring three major boards — the Coastal Resources Management Council (CRMC), the Narragansett Bay Commission, (NBC), and the I-195 Redevelopment Commission.

Since 1995 Common Cause had targeted legislators and legislative appointees on the CRMC and NBC.[26] The I-195 board, created in 2002, had been House Speaker John Harwood's last such achievement before scandal toppled him.[27] Its structure followed the traditional template: public members appointed by the speaker, Senate majority leader, and governor. The mayor of Providence would also name two, and the Providence Foundation, a business group, would get one. The question remained whether House leaders would finally agree to end legislative appointments on these three powerful public boards.

On March 27, two Senate committees gathered in the Senate Lounge for a joint hearing on the CRMC.[28] Sen. Susan Sosnowski chaired the Environ-ment and Agriculture Committee, and Sen. Mike Lenihan led the Government Oversight Committee. Since CRMC's creation in 1971, legislative leaders had appointed eight of the board's seventeen members. When voters approved the amendment, Sosnowski resigned from her seat, and the other legislators fol-lowed. But four public members appointed by legislative leaders continued to serve. Early in 2005, Gov. Carcieri had named new members to fill the eight seats held by legislators and legislative appointees, but the Senate never held confirmation hearings.[29]

Witnesses before the joint Senate hearing described the CRMC's history and mission. But conflict flared over its duties. Were its powers legislative or executive?[30]

Lawyer-lobbyist Robert D. Goldberg offered explosive testimony. He announced that the state Supreme Court had ruled in *Westerly* v. *Bradley* the previous summer — seven months after voters approved the amendment — that control of the coastline still belonged to the legislature. He read a key sentence from the decision: "Under the public trust doctrine, the General Assembly is vested with the authority and responsibility for regulating and preserving tidal lands and may determine appropriate uses for tidal land, grant tidal land to another, or delegate the authority to regulate that land on the state's behalf."[31]

Goldberg looked triumphantly at the senators around a circular glass-topped table. "That is as clear as it gets in the law," he declaimed. "This is a clear definition from the Supreme Court — after all those amendments became law. The courts still recognized and declared that this is a legislative function."[32]

I assumed that Goldberg's wife, Justice Maureen McKenna Goldberg, had debriefed her role in this unanimous decision with him.

Later, when I looked up the decision, I saw that Westerly had prosecuted a man for swimming in the Weekapaug Breachway, a channel where swift tidal currents raced between the Atlantic Ocean and Winnapaug Pond. The swimmer challenged the town's jurisdiction, but the high court supported Westerly's authority with a rhetorical flourish: "This ordinance is related directly to preserving the public peace, safety, comfort and welfare and is authorized by the town charter. Accordingly, the defendant's contention that Westerly has no authority to prohibit swimming in the breachway is waterlogged."

Bob Goldberg's testimony was waterlogged, too. The Supreme Court's decision had focused on a Westerly ordinance. The swimmer had appeared *pro se,* without a lawyer. No one argued about or even mentioned the 2004 Separation of Powers Amendment.

Earlier in the joint committee hearing, I had reminded the two committees that Rhode Island's new appointments clause was adapted directly from Article II, Section 2 of the U.S. Constitution, which empowered the president to name all federal officials who execute federal laws. That became the template for Rhode Island's Article IX, Section 5.[33] "The test here," I told the senators, "is not whether a board or commission may exercise legislative or even judicial power. The test is whether a public or quasi-public board 'exercises executive power under the laws of the state.' If it does, then the governor needs to appoint the members, subject to the advice and consent of the Senate."[34]

Andrew Hodgkin, Carcieri's executive counsel, followed me. He testified that the Coastal Council exercised executive powers whenever it issued permits, enforced laws, conducted hearings, promulgated regulations, or managed programs. Then he explained that its authority had rested on the "broad powers" clause, which had given the General Assembly unique powers until voters repealed it. "I think," Hodgkin said, "residual powers stood for the proposition that the executive only had those powers the General Assembly saw fit to designate to the executive. That's no longer the law in Rhode Island."[35]

The next morning, *Providence Journal* reporter Peter Lord framed the CRMC question in the context of Goldberg's tenacious drive to win approval for Champlin's Marina to occupy much of Block Island's Great Salt Pond. Lord reminded readers that political, economic and environmental interests were intense along Rhode Island's priceless coastline. "But now," he wrote, "political control of the one small state agency that regulates almost every waterfront activity has become extremely uncertain." He described "a growing sense in the General Assembly that maybe it should retain control of the CRMC and not turn it over to the governor."[36]

Robert Goldberg had gotten the last word with his comments about the Weekapaug Breachway case. So how widely had he peddled his line that—even after the Separation of Powers Amendment—the Supreme Court had reaffirmed legislative control of the coastline? How many who heard his spiel had bothered to read the decision?

Construction crews had begun building a new intersection between I-95 and I-195. Called the "Iway," the project featured a 400-foot bridge with three graceful parallel arches. Vehicles still rumbled along the old roadway, over crumbling bridges buttressed with timber and iron, but bulldozers would soon start to clear the original right-of-way and open up more than thirty-five acres of prime land.

House leaders were in no hurry to relinquish their control over platting and leasing the new land. Already, Johnson & Wales University officials had made a formal presentation to the powerful I-195 Redevelopment Board. The school's senior vice president and its architect — ironically, accompanied by lobbyist Robert Goldberg — had made the presentation. They described "a campus-like group of buildings" with amenities including retail space.[37]

In February 2006, the leadership team of Speaker William Murphy filed I-195 legislation that purported to address separation of powers problems.[38] The bill would transfer "state-owned property" to the I-195 board "for sale, lease or utilization pursuant to a public-private partnership, when the highway use shall be discontinued." Yet despite authorizing major executive duties, the legislation made no change in the membership of the nine-member board. Legislative leaders would still control four of nine members, and they would provide meeting space. Furthermore, instead of sending their new I-195 bill to the Separation of Powers Committee, House leaders referred it to the Finance Committee, which scheduled a hearing for April 24.

In response to an email alert, separation of powers advocates barraged members of the Finance Committee with emails and phone calls. I arrived at the committee's basement hearing room prepared to argue that they must reconfigure the I-195 Redevelopment Board to comply with the 2004 Separation of Powers Amendment. Without explanation, the committee crossed the I-195 legislation off its agenda.

I later saw Providence Mayor David Cicilline entering an elevator and slipped in behind him. I knew he was unhappy about our declaration that the governor must appoint all members of the I-195 Redevelopment Board. We stepped out of the elevator in the sub-basement, both aware that we needed to talk privately.

Lobbyists and legislators flowed out of the elevators and down a low passageway toward an exit. Cicilline and I hung back in an alcove between enameled white brick pyramids that spread the weight of the dome. Both of us understood that without agreement on mayoral appointments, the I-195 legislation might be shelved. The mayor said he was troubled that Common Cause was opposing his appointments to the I-195 board.

"Why exclude mayors?" Cicilline demanded. "I agree that there should be no legislative appointments. I supported separation of powers when very few others in this building would. I was one of your earliest sponsors."

"You were courageous," I agreed, "and they punished you for that."

"I'm in an executive position now," Cicilline insisted. "I should be able to make appointments that affect my city."

"I'm sorry," I said. "No one meant to exclude you. The bipartisan drafting team overlooked the question of mayoral appointments. The best we can do now is to write into law that the governor must 'give due consideration' to your recommendations."

Cicilline shook it off. "We need to fix the appointments clause."

"Too late," I said. "I told you that we missed it. But you missed it, too. All through the spring of 2003 you were mayor, and there were lots of hearings, but no one from your office testified that the amendment should be revised to allow mayors to make appointments to boards like this."

Cicilline and I walked in silence toward the exit. Outside, in April sunshine, his official car and driver were waiting. He climbed in. We had not resolved the impasse or even agreed what came next.

As his black car with the license plate "City 1" rolled out of the legislators' parking lot I pondered his political rise during twelve years since he told me he intended to run for a seat in the House. He had worked hard on ethics legislation and introduced the first resolution to put a separation of powers amendment on the ballot. Through all the defeats and setbacks, the amendment had only grown stronger. Now that it was implanted in the Constitution, he felt whipsawed by an unintended consequence, while I felt great urgency to implement the amendment, not change it.

House leaders seemed equally determined to keep the Narragansett Bay Commission beyond the governor's grasp and under local control. Elaine Coderre had introduced legislation to recast the state's sewage treatment agency as a "regional commission" rather than a state agency.[39] She proposed to cut the board from twenty-three members to nine. No longer would the speaker and Senate president name two members each, nor would the governor appoint ten public members. Instead, the mayor of Providence would pick two members of the board and the chief executives of Central Falls, Cumberland, East Providence, Johnston, North Providence, and Pawtucket would each choose one.

Throughout the spring, Save the Bay, the Conservation Law Foundation, the Environment Council, and Common Cause all lobbied Coderre and her committee against this plan "to regionalize" the commission. Since 1970, Save the Bay had been fighting pollution in Narragansett Bay and its watershed, attacking the flood of industrial wastes and raw sewage that poured into the estuary and its tributary rivers. Bumper stickers on countless cars carried the organization's three-word name and message in white letters against a bold red background — **SAVE THE BAY**. Save the Bay delivered data to policy-makers, conducted education programs for children, backed bond issues for sewage treatment facilities, managed annual swims across the bay, and filed a lawsuit that prompted creation of the Narragansett Bay Commission in 1980.[40]

Save the Bay lobbyist Jane Kenny Austin pressed the case that the NBC had a statewide mission. She wrote to policy-makers that the NBC board, "should continue to reflect a cross section of Rhode Island citizens," not merely sewage-producing cities. Downstate communities also had a large stake in the health of Narragansett Bay. Furthermore, the Bay Commission's plants in Providence and East Providence treated thirty-two billion gallons of wastewater each year. She wrote: "As the largest discharger into the Bay, the performance of NBC is of critical interest to all of Rhode Island." Furthermore, its Combined Sewer Overflow project — a system of tanks and tunnels being blasted out hundreds of feet below ground — was the largest public works project in Rhode Island's history and was funded with state bonds. Austin argued that the commission affected the entire state, and its integrity depended on a broadly representative statewide board.[41]

The House Separation of Powers Committee listened to unanimous testimony from environmental and reform organizations against regionalizing the Narragansett Bay Commission, but on June 14, it recommended Coderre's bill to the full House.

A week later Gov. Carcieri trumpeted the alarm at a State Room press conference, where Cynthia Giles, director of the Conservation Law Foundation in Rhode Island, stressed the absurdity of regionalizing. "The sewage pipes of the Narragansett Bay Commission may not cover the entire state, but its decisions certainly do," Giles declared in a voice that would have filled the room without a microphone. "If the health of Narragansett Bay isn't a matter of statewide interest, it's hard to imagine what is."[42]

Carcieri emphasized the sewage agency's statewide financing. Rhode Island was still paying off $33 million in outstanding bonds, and debt service alone for the fiscal year beginning July 1 would be $1.5 million. I argued that the bill relied on "sheer revisionist fantasy," as if twenty-five years of the commission's history as a state board could be compressed into a regional project. "Leaders of the House," I said, "seem determined to try an end-run around the Separation of Powers Amendment."

Rep. Jim Davey announced that he would propose an amendment on the House floor to reconstitute the Bay Commission with twelve members. Nine would come from the communities whose residents paid sewage bills, and three at-large from the rest of the state. Mayors of rate-paying communities would present lists; the governor would give "due consideration" and make the appointments; the Senate would confirm members of the new board.

On April 25, U.S. District Court Judge Ernest Torres cited three U.S. Supreme Court decisions — which he labeled *Buckley, Bellotti,* and *Berkeley* — as he struck down key elements of Rhode Island's Ballot Advocacy Law. He overturned the law's ban on corporate contributions to ballot question campaigns, its limit on the amounts individuals or corporations could contribute to ballot campaigns, and its prohibition against groups "acting in concert" or coordinating expenditures on ballot campaigns. Torres barred the Board of Elections from enforcing those sections of the law. But he also affirmed the state's interest in requiring disclosure of contributions:

> "Unlike expenditures, which pass directly from the party making them to the vendor of the goods or services being purchased, a contribution may pass through many hands before being expended for its ultimate purpose. Consequently, unless contributions are reported at each step along the way, the true source of the funds may be concealed from public view."[43]

Two days after the Torres decision, I bumped into Christopher Boyle at the State House's main security checkpoint. The son of a federal judge, Boyle had been House majority whip when I first met him. After he decided not to run for re-election in 1992, we served together on the Blue Ribbon Commission on the Future of the General Assembly. Like numerous other legislators from the 1980s, he had caught the wave of generous legislative pensions and returned to the State House as a lobbyist representing Newport Grand, one of two vast video slot parlors in Rhode Island.[44] Both were fighting to block casino bills that would open their market to Harrah's Entertainment or Trump Casinos.

Although the courts had knocked the 2004 Harrah's casino amendment off the ballot, the enabling statute remained in state law.[45] Its special rules for gambling referenda were fraught with problems but remained in full force.[46]

As often happened at the State House, all sides referred to the section simply by its number in the Rhode Island General Laws: 17-25.1. Newport Grand and Lincoln Park needed to rescind the statute, and Boyle said they wanted the repeal inserted into our ballot advocacy legislation.

Civil War cannons on either side of the high marble vestibule pointed toward the center where Boyle and I stood. I feared that our delicately balanced ballot advocacy legislation would get shredded in the crossfire between the gambling behemoths. Although the House Judiciary Committee had already approved our legislation,[47] Boyle had been lobbying the House and Senate sponsors to add the repeal of 17-25.1 as a floor amendment. During two weeks when our bill should have been debated and passed, it had been postponed a half-dozen times to the next day's House calendar. I asked Boyle if he had anything to do with the delays.

He shrugged in a knowing way. "Don't you think any rewrite of the ballot advocacy section also needs to repeal the section on gambling referenda?"

"It's a separate section of law, Chris. We think any repeal should go forward as a separate bill."

"Why not as part of your legislation?" Boyle demanded.

"Because some of the organizations in our working group can't take positions on gambling referenda." I explained that the ballot advocacy coalition—which now included the Rhode Island Foundation, Rhode Island Housing, United Way, University of Rhode Island, Family Life Center, ACLU, and Common Cause—had resolved difficult issues in our legislation, which was poised to become 17-25.2. Most of our nonprofit institutions had no reason or authority to take positions on gambling referenda in a separate section of state law.

"You mean Common Cause doesn't care about the rules for gambling referenda?"

"Of course, Common Cause cares," I said. "But we're part of a coalition that can't jump into your fight over casino gambling." I suggested that he call Ari Matusiak at the Rhode Island Foundation or leaders of the other groups I had mentioned.

As we parted, he leaned close and whispered that the only way 17-25.1 could be repealed was with passage of 17-25.2. "And, without the repeal of 17-25.1 your bill won't become law."

I emailed the ballot advocacy coalition about the impromptu conversation, including Boyle's threat. Reminding them that he had served as majority whip and knew the game, I warned them to expect his call.

Two weeks later, Boyle distributed a five-page memo to the entire General Assembly. "Common Cause and the Rhode Island ACLU," he wrote, "have turned a blind eye to the implications of not addressing gambling referenda and have, therefore, served up legislation that contains cherry-picked reform."[48] With bold caps and multiple exclamation points, he wrote:

> **PENALTIES** — The penalty for failure to register with the govern-
> ment? A person who fails to comply with Chapter 25.1 is guilty of
> a **FELONY**!!! (17-25.1-2).

His final section began with a rhetorical question in bold type: Why had
Common Cause and the ACLU "fought full ballot question reform?" Boyle
added that his organization, the Rhode Island Hospitality and Tourism Association, was "deeply disappointed in the 'ostrich-like' approach of Common
Cause and the ACLU."[49] He made no mention of the charities, foundation, housing agency, and university that he knew also comprised the working group.

Boyle's attack on the ACLU and Common Cause also ignored the fact that
he and his clients had not bothered to file a brief in response to Judge Torres's
request for *amicus* briefs. Nor had he testified on the ballot advocacy legislation
during a Senate Judiciary Committee hearing the day after Torres ruled. Nonetheless, in the weeks that followed it became clear that Boyle and his backers
had enough clout to sabotage our bill.

Meanwhile, Harrah's lobbyist Terrence M. Fracassa — although at odds with
Boyle on casino questions — also pushed to insert the repeal of 17-25.1 into the
ballot advocacy bill. Boyle and Fracassa forced a new round of negotiations, this
time over whether Boyle's Rhode Island clients could agree with Fracassa's Las
Vegas employers on rules to govern campaigns for or against a Rhode Island
casino. As chair of the Senate Judiciary Committee and prime sponsor of ballot
advocacy legislation, Sen. Michael J. McCaffrey brought all the parties into his
corner office on the third floor to thrash out our differences. As was his style,
McCaffrey directed us to find a solution we could all live with and come back
to him.

On the House side, leaders had placed all the responsibility for sponsoring
the election agency's legislation on freshman Rep. Edwin R. Pacheco. Pacheco
was smart and eager to resolve problems. Though he had neither portfolio nor
office, he had met with the working group to probe our disagreements and
press for solutions.

Several weeks of tense negotiations produced a new "gambling referenda"
section that required disclosure by contributors of who gave $1,800 or more
to advocate on gambling in any two-year election cycle.[50] Reports were to reveal whether the contributor had "any direct or indirect affiliation" with any
promoter of gambling "in any jurisdiction and, if so, the name of such facility
or entity." The new text deleted the dysfunctional portion of 17-25.1 and piggy-
backed the revised section onto our newly drafted 17-25.2, entitled the "Ballot
Question Advocacy and Reporting Act."

The final substitute versions of 17-25.2 accomplished what our working group
intended. It removed sections of the current law that Judge Torres had ruled
unconstitutional, defined "ballot question advocate" as anyone who spends

$1,000 or more in a calendar year to advocate on a particular ballot question, and created rigorous disclosure requirements for ballot advocates, whether individuals, nonprofit groups or corporations. It also outlawed contributions under false names "or in any manner for the purpose of disguising the true origin of the contribution." Further, the substitute bill prohibited the formation or use of legal entities to advocate for or against a ballot question that would disguise the "true origin of the funds" or evade the reporting requirements. Finally, it empowered the Board of Elections to enforce the new law and established penalties for violators up to triple the dollar amount of contributions or expenditures made in violation of the law or not reported.

With these compromises, those who had been working for many months hoped for smooth passage through the Senate and House. The Senate passed McCaffrey's substitute version at the end of May with a unanimous vote, but House debate turned raucous. I watched from a gallery above, as Minority Leader Robert A. Watson moved to recommit Pacheco's bill to committee and thereby kill it. His Republican caucus and dissident Democrats had apparently decided to defy the leadership over this bill. The House rejected Watson's move to recommit, 33–17.[51]

Rep. Rene R. Menard then offered an amendment that would have affected candidate elections but not ballot advocacy. Like Watson's motion to recommit the entire package, Menard seemed intent on scoring political points. Pacheco debated, and a majority crushed both of Menard's amendments in successive votes. Pacheco's bill passed with a final vote of 63–1 and flew to the Senate, where it won unanimous approval and went to Gov. Carcieri, who signed both Pacheco's House version and McCaffrey's Senate twin into law on July 3.[52]

Rhode Island's new Ballot Advocacy Law provided no dramatic advance, but it did create enforceable rules for the fall's ballot questions. Nonprofits could campaign without fear of breaking the law, and voters would at least know who paid for the casino ads.

Broad-shouldered, tall, and tenacious, Narragansett Chief Sachem Matthew Thomas had spent the spring of 2006 promoting the casino. He reminded lawmakers that governments — federal, state, and local — had often betrayed his people. A 1996 amendment to the federal Indian Gaming Regulatory Act had thwarted the tribe's plan to build a casino on its 1,800-acre reservation in Charlestown. It left the Narragansetts as the only federally-recognized tribe barred by U.S. law from operating a casino on their tribal land.[53] In 2003, frustrated tribal leaders had begun selling cigarettes at a tax-free shop on tribal land. Their business grew until Gov. Carcieri ordered the operation closed down. State troopers came in force, and members of the tribe fought back. The raid brought injuries, arrests, and humiliation that evoked bitter memories from Rhode Island's history.[54] Those disappointments propelled the Narragansetts

toward their partnership with Harrah's Entertainment and the 2004 West Warwick casino proposal, which the General Assembly approved but the Rhode
Island Supreme Court disqualified.

Again in May 2006, Matthew Thomas and top Harrah's officials made the
tribe's case before the House Finance Committee. The constitutional amendment under consideration, a newly revised version of Timothy Williamson's legislation, stated that the casino would be privately owned and operated by a new
corporation established under Rhode Island law by "the Narragansett Indian
Tribe and its chosen partner."[55] The revised amendment no longer mandated
a gaming commission with legislative appointees or specified a tax rate. The
resolution required it to appear on the ballot as the first referendum question
and as a result, would bump our Voting Rights Amendment to second place.

The Finance Committee recommended Williamson's legislation to the full
House, but Thomas told reporters it was only "round one." He added that the
years had taught him "never to count any chickens before they hatch in Rhode
Island." The governor blasted Finance Committee members for casting "a momentous vote on a bill they had seen only moments before." He added: "Voting
to approve this amendment without that critical information was breathtakingly
irresponsible and could put the state at great financial risk."[56]

During House debate two days later, Nick Gorham pushed an amendment
to bar legislators and general officers from receiving "any remuneration" from
business interests related to the casino during their terms in public office and
for five years afterward. Although this might have kept lawmakers out of commercial gambling, red lights swamped green on the board, defeating Gorham's
amendment 44–25.[57]

Steven R. Ucci of Johnston then moved to delete specific references to West
Warwick and the Narragansett Tribe. He proposed new constitutional language
to permit a single resort casino whose operator would be "selected by a competitive process" and "subject to regulation and taxation by the State of Rhode
Island." Ucci's motion forced the House to vote up or down on competitive
bidding, which a House study panel had recommended three years earlier, but
that motion was crushed.

Rep. James F. Davey then proposed to change the requirement that the casino
amendment become "the first referendum question," ahead of the Voting Rights
Amendment. Davey's proposal went down by a vote of 46–23. The vote counts
established a pattern, and the final vote for passage tallied 44–28.

During Senate debate on June 1, Sen. Joseph M. Polisena of Johnston offered
the same competitive bidding amendment, which was narrowly rejected, and
final passage in the Senate came by a vote of 23–13.

Consequently Williamson's strange casino package would go to the ballot
as Question 1. How much would Harrah's spend to win? Would a promise of

constitutionally mandated property-tax relief sway voters, or would the empa-
thy many felt for the Narragansetts translate into pro-casino votes?

Though the Right To Vote Amendment was on the November ballot — now as
Question 2 — the campaign still needed action on Joe Almeida's Restoration of
Voting Rights Act, which would enable the Department of Corrections, secre-
tary of state, and other agencies to begin registering former prisoners after state
voters approved the constitutional amendment. Despite continuous lobbying,
Almeida's legislation seemed stuck in the House Judiciary Committee. Our
Right To Vote Coalition, now comprising more than fifty groups, again deluged
lawmakers with calls to pass the legislation.[58]

Almeida's bill finally popped up on the House Judiciary Committee's agenda
for June 20, and the committee approved it with little discussion. Two days later,
the full House passed it, 64–6.[59] Senators had approved identical legislation a
year earlier and quickly did so now. Gov. Carcieri, who had never supported
the idea of restoring the vote for prisoners, allowed it to become law without
his signature.

Now that we had run our legislative gauntlet — getting the amendment onto
the ballot, enacting a workable ballot advocacy law, and finally passing the enabling statute — a huge question remained. Could we persuade Rhode Island
voters to restore the vote for ex-convicts that many feared and shunned?

Diana Kelly had been associate director at Common Cause for more than two
years. But administrative duties consumed her time. On June 23, probably the
last day of the 2006 session, she went with me to the State House for the first
time.

We found the broad brick and marble plaza outside the main entrance
mobbed. Hundreds of staff members, lobbyists, legislators, and reporters spilled
quickly into broiling sunshine. The brick sidewalks on both sides of Smith Street
filled up with clusters of people. Police cars blocked the cobblestone drive, and
sirens wailed.

A bomb threat had been phoned in. It might be a hoax or real, and the entire
State House was being evacuated. Senate Majority Leader Teresa Paiva Weed
stood on the north side of Smith Street in a blazing salmon-colored dress. Near
her, a senator in a bright red shirt with white suspenders had left his jacket inside. Stan Israel, the lightly bearded head of SEIU Local 1199, sported a ponytail,
sunglasses, and a Panama hat. As cell phones and cigarettes sprouted in the
crowd, a black-suited SWAT team raced toward the entrance with automatic
weapons. K-9 units appeared, and handlers rushed their dogs toward the huge
oak doors.

As the bomb search stretched to a half-hour, black SUVs loaded up and left for Patrick's Pub, a political watering hole a few blocks west of I-95. Those of us who stayed found shade under trees outside the Department of Administration. I used the time to lobby senators for a piece of crucial legislation that was not scheduled for a vote: Lt. Gov. Charlie Fogarty's Public Accountability and Reform Act of 2006. The House had passed Kilmartin's slightly amended version a week earlier and sent it to the Senate. Now it was stuck in the Senate Judiciary Committee with Mike Lenihan's companion bill, which had been held for further study two months earlier. Had I been wrong in thinking Democrats would pass it to boost Fogarty's chances of becoming governor?

"I'll bring it up with leadership," Lenihan told me. He had been out sick but returned on this chaotic last day. Several other senators were not aware that Fogarty's legislation had disappeared and promised to ask Judiciary Chairman Mike McCaffrey.

When police declared the State House safe, a tide of agitated people flowed back in, slowed by a bottleneck through security.

"So you're retiring?" A legislative staff member appeared at my side. "Have they got a replacement?"

"Not yet," I said. "The search committee was reviewing résumés this morning."

"So what's the pay?" he asked, openly interested.

I brushed off the question.

"Above fifty thousand?" he persisted.

"Yes," I said, "but that would depend on skills and experience."

After he left, Kelly said she would not have given him any figure.

I asked what she would have told him.

She chuckled. "I would have said: 'If that's your first question, this is not the job for you.'"

I was relieved when Senate Judiciary met in haste and recommended Fogarty's bill for passage.[60] The final version would allow citizens to see more clearly than ever before the flow of funds from special interests to public officials. It would require general officers and candidates for the five statewide offices to start disclosing their outside income in nine brackets — less than $1,000, between $1,000 and $10,000, between $10,000 and $25,000, and so on, as members of Congress were required to do. The legislation would also bar appointment to the Ethics Commission of anyone who worked for or had any ownership interest in businesses that derived income from lobbying.

Both the House and Senate versions went to the Senate floor and passed with unanimous 35–0 votes. When the Senate version flew back to the House for final passage, representatives approved it 59–6.[61] I reminded myself to congratulate Fogarty and his policy director, Maureen Maigret, for delivering a package of substantial reforms.

THE 2006 SESSION ended with a bang and a whimper over separation of powers. For reasons only they knew, House leaders moved to recommit Coderre's bill for a regional Narragansett Bay Commission to her committee.[62] The House Finance Committee never recommended any action on the I-195 Relocation Commission. Without action, those two powerful boards and the Coastal Resources Management Council would still not comply with the Separation of Powers Amendment.

House leaders waited until the maelstrom of the last hours to launch a stealth attack. On May 31, Coderre had quietly filed a bill that proposed to delete the entire existing law on the CRMC and then reenact it, word for word, under a slightly changed chapter number in the Rhode Island General Laws.[63] Instead of appearing as 46-23, it would become 46-23.3. Coderre's committee never conducted a hearing on her reenactment, and I thought it had died. Then, on the final day of the session, she filed a resolution asking the Rhode Island Supreme Court for a written advisory opinion, citing her strange CRMC repeal and replacement bill. Her committee met without notice and sent the advisory opinion request to the floor "with a recommendation of passage."[64]

Coderre's resolution asked the justices to answer four distinct questions: Would the proposed reenactment with legislators listed for appointment to the CRMC violate the "so-called Separation of Powers Amendment?" Could the speaker of the House appoint members of the CRMC? Was the "so called Separation of Powers Amendment" self-executing or did it require legislative implementation? And was the CRMC "by its nature, purpose, and operation" a legislative body?

These questions were disturbing — as if there had been no decade-long debate, and as if a huge percentage of state voters had not already approved the amendment. After three years of claiming they supported separation of powers, House leaders brought the reactionary resolution to the floor after midnight on the last day of the session. Although exhausted and dazed, representatives engaged in a perfunctory debate and then approved Coderre's request for an advisory.

The night air smelled of rain when I left the State House for the last time as lobbyist for Common Cause. I had hoped to retire with the separation of powers struggle settled, but fierce resistance remained. Instead of obeying the plain language of the amendment, House leaders were clearly launching a new battle. Had they believed John Tarantino's memo? Bob Goldberg's testimony? Would the Supreme Court trample our carefully crafted amendment? How much would this new legal battle cost? Could it be resolved in only five months before my retirement?

52

Déjà Vu

2006

DON CARCIERI AND HIS STAFF expected a gubernatorial challenge from the blueblood Yankee Democrat Sheldon Whitehouse. But Whitehouse set his sights on the U.S. Senate, where Lincoln Chafee's ties to the Republican Party of President George W. Bush made him vulnerable.[1] Instead of Whitehouse, Carcieri found himself facing Charles J. Fogarty, a cheery populist whose political roots reached Rhode Island's bedrock. Although Democrats outnumbered them on voting rolls, Republicans had occupied the governor's office for all but four of the last twenty years.[2] Pundits suggested that independents — and even many registered Democrats — routinely chose Republican governors to counter perpetual Democratic majorities in the General Assembly.

Carcieri launched his 2006 reelection campaign by decrying "long-entrenched lobbyists, public union bosses, special interests and career politicians." He declared that they were "trying once again to make state government their private playpen. They will fight me with everything they have, because I will never do their bidding. Never."[3]

But Fogarty also promised reform. "The main reason I'm running for governor is to fundamentally change the way Rhode Island does business," he told reporter Mark Arsenault. "We have a great state but we've been held back by this cloud of corruption, individuals as well as institutions that have zapped the confidence of Rhode Islanders. We need to turn that around."[4]

On the last night of the legislative session, both the Senate and House passed Fogarty's loophole-closing Public Accountability and Reform Act of 2006. When Carcieri allowed this legislation to become law without his signature, Fogarty tweaked him for not signing. "What's your problem with the bill?" the challenger asked. "What about it don't you like?"

Jeffrey Neal, Carcieri's press secretary, fired back that Fogarty's legislation failed because "self-employed lawmakers — such as lawyers and insurance brokers — are not required to disclose who their clients are or from whom their income is derived." Neal dismissed the new law as "a recipe for continued conflicts of interest."[5]

Neither Neal nor the governor grasped a central issue in passage of the 2004 Celona Law, which Carcieri had signed. The rules of lawyer-client confidentiality barred attorneys from naming their clients — a fact that was too technical for a sound bite. The *Providence Journal* explained this technicality in a single story, but most media ignored it entirely.

Meanwhile, throughout the 2006 campaign season, the corrupt practices of John Celona kept making headlines. From stories in the *Providence Journal*, Operation Clean Government had distilled three complaints involving the former senator's work for CVS, Blue Cross/Blue Shield of Rhode Island, and Roger Williams Medical Center.[6] On July 25, Celona stood with clasped hands and smelling of sweet cologne before the Rhode Island Ethics Commission.

Chairman James Lynch read a list of ten specific "knowing and willful violations" from a negotiated settlement. With attorney Lauren Jones at his shoulder, Celona admitted to each count and then read a prepared statement: "I'm sorry that I let my personal financial needs overwhelm my duty to act ethically and be a good senator. While I might not have started out intending to violate the code of ethics, at some point I knew I had stepped over the line and I failed to correct my conduct. I do not blame anyone but myself." He closed with, "I hope that by trying to do the right thing now, I can salvage whatever honor I may have left."[7]

The Ethics Commission could have levied a fine of $25,000 for each of the ten violations, but prosecutor Jason Gramitt recommended lower fines for eight charges, and commissioners agreed. Even so, the final tally of $130,000 became the highest ethics fine in Rhode Island history. I guessed that Celona would never pay. He had burned through everything he earned.

Celona also agreed to plead guilty to three federal felonies. His plea bargain required his testimony against those who had bought his services.[8]

Federal prosecutors made him a star witness at the September trial of Roger Williams Medical Center and three top executives accused of stealing his "honest services." At the gray U.S. District Courthouse on Kennedy Plaza, the three faced charges of paying Celona more than $260,000 over six years "to cause him to use his influence, power and authority as a state senator to benefit the political and financial interests" of the hospital.[9]

I had never met the hospital's vice president, Frances P. Driscoll, or Peter J. Sangermano Jr., who managed its assisted living complex called the Village at Elmhurst, but I remembered the institution's president, Robert A. Urciuoli, from our work on the Blue Ribbon Commission. Urciuoli and I had not seen each other or spoken since December 1993, when the panel issued its final report.

The prosecution and defense agreed that Celona had approached Urciuoli in the summer of 1997 for a job. When Urciuoli hired him as a recruiter for the Village at Elmhurst, Celona's pay flowed from the hospital through its subsidiary.

In his opening statement, Assistant U.S. Attorney Luis M. Matos told jurors that Urciuoli and his subordinates secretly paid Celona to raise reimbursement rates from insurers, increase ambulance runs to their hospital, and promote the hospital's position on key legislation. "A corrupt politician doesn't act on his own," Matos declared. "He needs someone to pay him and tell him what matters to work on. And he needs someone to help him hide his actions." The prosecutor pointed to Urciuoli as the one "who bought, and agreed to buy, John Celona's corrupt services."[10]

Boston defense lawyer Richard M. Egbert countered that Celona had used a "sob story" about his failed lawnmower business to plead for sympathy. Urciuoli hired him for legitimate work with senior citizens. At the time Celona was hired, Egbert told jurors, he "was without influence, power, or authority. He could open no doors."

Whatever the truth was when John Celona began work in 1997, he became immensely more valuable to Roger Williams Medical Center in 2000, after he helped William Irons seize control of the Senate. At that point Celona succeeded Irons as chair of the powerful Senate Corporations Committee — later renamed the Commerce, Housing, and Municipal Government Committee — that handled hospital and health care legislation.

The prosecutor elicited damning testimony from his prime witness. Celona told of using his leverage as committee chair to push higher reimbursements from insurers to the hospital. In cross-examination Egbert reminded jurors that Celona's work for the Village at Elmhurst had been no secret. In fact, it was listed in his profile in the *Rhode Island Government Owner's Manual.*[11]

The hospital's attorney, James R. McGuirk, testified that Urciuoli had approached him in 1997 about hiring Celona and he had warned against it, in part because of potential conflicts of interest. At Urciuoli's request, McGuirk prepared a consulting contract and a letter requesting an advisory from the Ethics Commission.[12] Significantly, both documents named the Village at Elmhurst but not Roger Williams Medical Center. McGuirk testified that Urciuoli never told him Celona was legislating for the hospital.[13]

The Roger Williams Medical Center trial also exposed the banality of backstage legislative discourse. Celona testified that Senate leaders designated bills they intended to bury as "NGN — Not Going Nowhere."[14] Stories from the trial stoked newspaper headlines, television news, and talk radio. The scandal hung over Rhode Island like smoke from burning oil.

I NEVER CARED FOR FASHION SHOWS or knew why a nonprofit called RISE asked me to be in one. RISE stood for Rhode Islanders Sponsoring Education. Its motto was "Empowering children of incarcerated parents." Founded by Brown University physicians, RISE aimed to break cycles of addiction, poverty, and violence.[15] An incongruously expensive boutique fitted me with tapered shirt and paisley tie. The clerk handed me a velvet jacket he estimated was worth a thousand dollars.

"What about pants?" I asked.

He asked if I had old jeans that were ripped and splattered with paint. I said I did. "Wear those," he said. He promised to have my outfits waiting in the men's dressing area.

The event fell on a September Saturday across Kennedy Plaza from the federal courthouse. A vast white tent covered the skating rink, filling at dusk with a well-heeled audience. As daylight faded, campy models pranced to the end of a spot lit runway and pirouetted. Two candidates for lieutenant governor — Democratic Sen. Elizabeth H. Roberts and Republican Reginald A. Centracchio, the retired adjutant general of the state's National Guard — wowed the crowd in bipartisan splendor.

Organizers paired me with Mark S. Weiner, who had famously raised phenomenal amounts of money for Democrats, most recently as finance chair for John Kerry's 2004 presidential campaign. We sashayed to the turnaround, where he ripped off his jacket and flung it to the audience. We shook hands, high-fived, and bowed to the crowd.

I spoke briefly backstage with Dr. Pablo Rodriguez, a leader in the 2002 Latino redistricting lawsuit and the medical director of Planned Parenthood. Nineteen months earlier, he and family members had been riding an airport van on a Texas highway when a drunk driver slammed into them. Rodriguez and his son landed in intensive care with life-threatening injuries, and his niece died.

I slipped out of the tent and watched from the darkness as a bent figure in a bathrobe, wearing a gray wig and oversized medical sunglasses, pushed a walker haltingly onto the runway. The audience hushed. The invalid struggled to the end where, with perfect comic timing, he shoved his walker aside, cast off the wig, dark glasses, and robe. In a bright blazer and faded jeans, Pablo Rodriguez waved in triumph and boogied to music. The audience leapt up, cheering and dancing with him.

Mark Weiner and I had both come through bouts with non-Hodgkin's lymphoma. His had been in the newspaper.[16] Mine had not. We shared our experiences and a survivors' hug.

I had never spoken with Fred Butler — a diligent member of the Ethics Commission — outside the commission's office. Now, at this light-hearted fundraiser, we were joined in a cast of goofy characters, as the visionary nonprofit turned our shenanigans into $100,000 worth of scholarships for the children of prisoners.

As the event ended, people lingered to talk. I was turning to leave when Bob Urciuoli stepped out of the shadows. We had not shaken hands in years, and his voice cracked with stress. He explained that his wife chaired the RISE organizing committee, and he had come to support her.[17]

Testimony in his trial had just ended. Urciuoli had not taken the stand in his own defense but wanted to talk. He told me of meeting John Celona at church in the late 1970s. In 1997, when Celona's lawnmower business went under, the new senator asked for work. Urciuoli said he had felt Celona's desperation and looked for some legitimate way to help. One obvious answer lay in marketing the Village at Elmhurst to seniors, a population Celona had courted successfully in his campaigns for the North Providence City Council and state Senate.

Urciuoli explained that from our work on the Blue Ribbon Commission he knew the ethical dilemmas of a part-time legislature. Aware that unions and businesses employed many legislators, he directed the hospital's attorney to seek an advisory opinion from the Ethics Commission. To avert potential conflicts Urciuoli had distributed copies of the advisory to senior staff at the hospital and its extended care affiliate. He assured me that Celona had recused himself from scores of Senate votes that involved the medical center. He insisted that Celona had delivered many times in patient fees what he had been paid.

The former hospital president and I stood alone in a shadowed corner among hundreds of empty chairs. Jury selection had dismayed him. Prosecutors had dismissed business owners who might have understood his plight. "We got a jury of people who have never been to the legislature, don't know how a bill gets introduced, don't understand how people lobby for and against bills." He complained that prosecutors had presented an email from Celona about working to defeat the cancer council as if that proved criminal conspiracy.[18] He shook his head at the absurdity. "Phil, you remember that boondoggle. The Hospital Association, Brown University, and Common Cause all opposed it." He sagged under an ominous awareness that these jurors seemed credulous of evidence as weak as Celona's cancer council email.[19]

I walked home along Saturday night streets, past bars and parties, pondering Urciuoli's plight. I imagined how hard it would have been to turn Celona away when both men were communicants at the same church. Ethics laws were never intended to prevent institutions from hiring legislators. Rather, the law mandated financial disclosure and penalized conflicts of interest. Urciuoli had required that Celona disclose his work. CVS and Blue Cross executives had not. Had Urciuoli used the ethics process as cover? Was I gullible to take him seriously?

Two weeks later, on Friday October 13, the jury declared Bob Urciuoli guilty on one charge of conspiracy and thirty-five counts of "honest services mail fraud."[20] Each paycheck mailed to Celona became a mail fraud felony. Jurors found Frances Driscoll, the hospital's vice president, guilty on a single count of mail fraud. They acquitted Peter Sangermano, of the Village at Elmhurst, on all counts.

"The verdict sends a loud message," declared U.S. Attorney Robert Clark Corrente. "The people of Rhode Island are sick and tired of corruption and inside deals. To those who would accept these inside deals as 'typical Rhode Island,' today's verdict says 'not anymore.'"

Judge Ernest Torres scheduled sentencing for the spring.[21] Meanwhile, the daily drumbeat of corruption stories permeated election debates as Don Carcieri and Charlie Fogarty each claimed the mantle of corruption fighter.

During the summer of 2006, Rhode Island courts had hurried to address the General Assembly's repeal of gubernatorial authority to place advisory questions on the ballot. In July, Superior Court Judge Stephen J. Fortunato Jr. had upheld Carcieri's proposed questions on voter initiative and property tax limits. In a broad ruling, Fortunato went beyond what Carcieri's lawyers had argued, affirming his two questions and opening the door for future governors to do the same. "It is the declaration of this court," Fortunato wrote, "that the governor has the prerogative to submit questions for inclusion on the ballot, with or without any legislative action."[22]

Supreme Court justices came back from summer vacations to hear emergency arguments. They ruled that Secretary of State Matthew Brown no longer had any "authority to comply with the governor's letter" because the veto override had "extinguished the governor's authority well before the secretary could prepare the ballot."[23] The justices added that Fortunato had overreached in declaring that Rhode Island governors possessed a constitutional power that neither side had argued.[24]

Gov. Carcieri's advisory questions would not go before state voters, but the Narragansett Indian Casino question remained. On August 8, U.S. District Court Judge William E. Smith dismissed a lawsuit that aimed to knock it off the ballot. "Courts should not wade into constitutionally torrid waters unless doing so is unavoidable," Smith wrote. "That is not the case here."[25]

The Rhode Island Supreme Court also appeared wary of "torrid waters." I took it for granted that House leaders had dispatched their request for an advisory opinion about legislators serving on CRMC to the high court. No one expected the justices to schedule briefs before a calendar conference early in September, but when that date passed without an announcement, I wondered what their silence meant. The mystery thickened when the high court's October scheduling conference came and went without word.

On October 12, I went to the RIPEC annual meeting and dinner at the

Marriott Hotel. Businesses hosted tables for executives, managers, legislators, judges, general officers, and a few public interest advocates. Across my assigned table sat Chief Justice Frank Williams. We had not spoken since the Ethics Commission's meltdown five years earlier when he blamed "the ethics flap" on former director Martin Healey.[26] I believed that Williams had hidden his own role and made Healey a scapegoat.

Throughout the dinner the chief justice and I sat too far apart in a talkative throng to communicate except for when our eyes locked. After the speeches and awards, I made my way to Williams in the crowd. Startled, he accepted my handshake. I asked him why the September and October scheduling conferences had both passed without any announcement about briefs and arguments on the House request for an advisory opinion on the CRMC.

"We didn't get to it," he said abruptly and ducked away.[27]

As people streamed toward the exits, I caught up with Bob Flanders and told him about my terse exchange with Williams. "Why would he say 'they didn't get to it?'" I asked.

Flanders burst into laughter. "They're scared to death of it," he said. "Imagine the reaction of their colleagues across the country if they were to rule — even after voters approved such a clear amendment — that Rhode Island still had no separation of powers. They would make themselves a laughing stock."

Campaign spending wars dominated fall TV. Incumbent U.S. Senator Lincoln Chafee fought for his political life against Sheldon Whitehouse, while Gov. Carcieri battled Lt. Gov. Charlie Fogarty. Both contests drew national attention and money.

Pro-and-anti casino forces also squared off with vast amounts of money. Former Gov. Lincoln Almond led an anti-casino coalition called Save Our State (SOS). When the *Providence Journal* reported that between June 1 and August 31 Harrah's had spent $5.2 million, Almond mocked the Nevada firm for "trying to buy our Constitution." Save Our State, by contrast, had raised just over $1 million, half from Lincoln Park and half from Newport Grand. Chambers of commerce, hotels, and restaurants chipped in another $40,000. "It's $5,000 here and $2,000 here," Almond told reporter Scott Mayerowitz. "I expect we'll have enough money to do our job."[28]

Common Cause joined Lincoln Almond's coalition. Vice President Brian Heller explained to reporters that our organization had never taken a position either for or against gambling, but we were outraged that Harrah's casino would be "planted permanently in the Rhode Island Constitution." He cited a 2003 House gambling study: "Their own report called for a competitive process and creation of an independent regulatory body before the naming of a casino developer or host community. They produced a solid report and then trashed it."[29]

The Casino Amendment had bumped our Right To Vote Amendment from Question 1 to Question 2 on the November ballot. Our steering committee had no money for advertising or polling but developed a two-pronged strategy.[30] We would organize in the state's urban core — Providence, East Providence, Pawtucket, Central Falls, Woonsocket, and Newport — where eighty percent of disenfranchised ex-convicts lived. Our paid staff — mostly street-wise former prisoners — would lead teams of volunteers, mostly college students. They would canvass block by block, educate potential voters, and connect with prisoners' families who could motivate their neighbors. We hoped this get-out-the-vote campaign could deliver enough urban support to overcome likely negative votes in small towns and suburbs.

Our second prong would rely on traditional reform allies to build support in outlying areas. Barbara Hurst, a public defender and member of the steering committee, recruited officials who had prosecuted crimes. Our list of supporters soon included retired judges, former attorneys general, U.S. attorneys, police, and parole board members.[31] Many shared our belief that voting would lessen recidivism. At the steering committee's request, Providence Police Chief Dean Esserman and I published an opinion piece in several papers, and several of us began meeting with publishers and editors to secure their support.[32]

Mayors, city council members, state legislators, and members of Congress agreed to be listed as publicly endorsing Question 2. Gov. Donald Carcieri and Atty. Gen. Patrick C. Lynch refused to back the effort.[33]

Professional organizations and reform groups — particularly the ACLU, Common Cause, and the League of Women Voters — had volunteers distributing flyers. The AFL-CIO, teachers' unions, AFSCME, and SEIU promised to encourage their members to support Question 2.[34] The only statewide organization that publicly opposed restoring the vote was the Rhode Island Police Chiefs Association.[35]

Right To Vote Coalition partners with religious roots — ranging from the American Friends Service Committee to the Unitarian Universalists for Social Justice — pulled together in support. The Rhode Island State Council of Churches scheduled a "Day for Justice" on October 22, when congregations would distribute information and urge "Yes" on Question 2. Urban churches with large minority congregations participated enthusiastically, while predominantly white suburban and rural churches were less supportive. Former prisoners recruited priests, pastors, and imams who had helped them behind bars. We hosted an interfaith clergy breakfast where we distributed flyers and a sample sermon. In churches where I spoke, I asked worshippers to call out words at the heart of their faith. Their responses came like drops of rain: "Love . . . Compassion . . . Mercy . . . Forgiveness." I preached from the question posed by the prophet Micah: "What does the Lord require of you? Only to do justice, love mercy, and walk humbly with your God."[36]

Though Koren Carbuccia would never claim to be a preacher, she had testified and lobbied courageously to get the amendment onto the ballot. On a Monday night in the reception room at the Family Life Center she practiced her most crucial speech. In the morning she would face reporters, speaking for more than fifteen thousand former prisoners. Nervous, she kept interrupting herself. Nancy Kirsch, hired by the campaign to focus our public message, reassured her. "Relax, Koren," Kirsch coached, "you're a natural, and you have a really important story to tell. Relax and take your time."

Carbuccia started for the fourth time. "Good morning. My name is Koren Carbuccia. I'm a student at Community College of Rhode Island working toward a degree in substance abuse counseling." Her eyes showed the stress she felt.

"Today I am a mother of four-year-old Vaskan, and we live together in Pawtucket. Today I took Vaskan to pre-kindergarten for the very first time. It was a proud moment. My life wasn't always this good." She told of life behind bars during the first two and a half years of Vaskan's life. She had nursed him in the visiting area and decided, for his sake, to break with her past.

"I take care of my son. I read to him. I play with him. I'm a responsible parent now. I'm a responsible citizen." Without bitterness, she went on to say that the state would not allow her to be the best parent she could be because it would not let her vote. "Voting is important to me," she said, "especially in the school board election. Why? Because Vaskan has special needs that must be addressed. If I can't vote in school board elections and local elections, I can't speak for him. Under our current law, Vaskan will be fifteen before I can vote."

Hers was a gentle song in a minor key, its emotion beneath the surface. Her voice steadied like a cello. As she finished, I felt the sting of tears. "I'm crying," I said. "You'll touch their hearts in the morning." If she could hold her composure, she would make unseen people visible to those who would rather not see them.

Next day, in the State House rotunda, reporters clipped their microphones onto a podium at one corner of the central landing. Carbuccia stood on the stairs in a black pants suit, waiting her turn while political leaders, civil rights organizers, and a preacher improvised. Finally, beneath a gleaming bronze lamp stand, she spoke. With tight curls closely cropped, large eyes, and scarcely any makeup, she conveyed quiet authority.

Afterward, reporters for the *Providence Journal* and *Pawtucket Times* wanted exclusive interviews with her. I held my breath as each, in turn, held their tiny recorders near her lips and asked tough questions. She spoke candidly about her drug crimes, experiences in prison, Vaskan's special needs, and her hopes.

The next morning lead stories in both newspapers began with the same two words: "Koren Carbuccia." Jim Baron of the *Times* told her story in tight paragraphs for readers in the city where she lived and longed to vote. Karen Lee Ziner at the *Journal* led with a crisp summary — "Koren Carbuccia is working hard to change her life after spending more than two years in prison for drug offenses" — that turned one ex-inmate's story into a lens that focused on facts of felony disenfranchisement.[37]

The *New York Times* ran a front-page story that made Rhode Island's effort emblematic of a national need to help former prisoners reconnect. "What we're witnessing," state prison director A.T. Wall told reporter Erik Eckholm, "is a great turning of the wheel in corrections policy." The story described more than 600,000 inmates emerging from the nation's prisons each year and the dismal fact that more than half of those would return. Even with help from programs like the Family Life Center, the story continued, "odds against staying straight are formidable."[38]

The *Westerly Sun* ran a profile of Peter A. Slom, a sensitive former prisoner who had been convicted of selling cocaine fifteen years earlier, served twenty-six months in the Adult Correctional Institutions, been released, stayed straight, and earned a degree in social work. Reporter Chris Keegan described Slom's efforts as a youth soccer coach, chair of a school building committee, and chair of the Right To Vote Steering Committee. But Slom could not vote and would not become eligible to vote for two more years.[39]

Despite their reporter's article and a campaign visit to their office, publishers of the *Sun* warned readers about another ex-convict who, while still on parole, blasted a Westerly woman with a shotgun. "Had his release shown he had turned his life around?" the editors asked.[40]

Coventry Sen. Leonidas Raptakis sounded a similar refrain in an opinion piece that appeared in several papers. "While the advocates of Question 2 are careful to offer up heart-warming stories of felons who have turned their lives around," he wrote, "the fact of the matter is that approval would restore voting rights to violent felons who may have little or no interest in contributing to the quality of life in our community. We are talking about giving voting rights back to offenders who may have killed, crippled, maimed or viciously attacked their fellow citizens."[41]

But the usually conservative editors at the *Providence Journal* turned Raptakis's question around, suggesting that voters ask instead: "What policy would serve to promote the safety and other interests of most citizens?" As if the answer were self-evident, the editors answered: "It is in society's interest to encourage felons to reconnect lawfully with their community." The editorial closed by reminding readers that current Rhode Island law barred "blacks and Latinos from voting at rates higher than 37 other states. The Ocean State can join the American mainstream, removing this obstacle to minorities' participation in civic life, by voting yes on Question 2."[42]

The *New York Times* chimed in as well: "Allowing former convicts to vote strengthens democracy, and helps them to integrate into society and move beyond a life of crime." Its editorial encapsulated our entire campaign: "Felon disenfranchisement is a relic of another America. It was often done to keep blacks from voting, or to stigmatize ex-offenders. Rhode Island, which was founded by religious dissenters, can strike an important blow for inclusion by allowing people who have paid their debt to society to participate in democracy."[43]

From the start of the gubernatorial race, Don Carcieri and Charlie Fogarty had jousted over who would be tougher on corruption. At the Common Cause annual meeting in September they answered questions in a town hall format.[44] Despite public civility and a smiling handclasp with board president Dan Siegel, their mutual contempt was obvious in body language as each listened to the other. But our audience got no advance notice of what lay ahead.

During the last week of October, a national Republican group mounted an attack ad aimed at the reform legislation Fogarty had coaxed to passage during the spring.[45] "In Charlie Fogarty's world," an authoritative voice began, "life is good, *if* you're an insider." Video showed silhouettes of men in suits shaking hands and passing a satchel, while Fogarty's smiling face appeared with the caption: "Fogarty's Ethics Bill: 'Lawmakers still aren't required to name clients.' "

Four shadowy men marched into a police line-up beneath a caption: "Charlie Fogarty's Supporters." The ominous voice-over continued: "Fogarty wrote the law that allows bureaucrats like him to hide who's paying them, opening the door to special interests, inviting backroom deals. Little wonder Fogarty's big money political supporters look like a line-up."

With faces obscured but still labeled "Charlie Fogarty's Supporters," the camera zoomed in on the caption "Mayor Buddy Cianci donated $1,000" in 1999. A red stamp declared in bold capital letters: "CONVICTED OF CORRUPTION."

The next dark figure was a man tagged "Frances Driscoll donated $2,250," as the red stamp appeared: "CONVICTED OF MAIL FRAUD." Ironically, Frances Driscoll was female.

"Convictions! Bribery! Indictments!" the voice warned over two more silhouetted men in the lineup. The last was captioned: "House Speaker John Harwood donated $1,000 in 1998." The bold red stamp read: "DRIVEN FROM OFFICE."

The four shadowy men in the lineup swaggered as the announcement ended with, "Fogarty claims he wants to clean up Rhode Island. Why does he want to keep all of us in the dark?"

The screen went black, and a headline dropped to its center: "We Need Solutions."

Another line knocked it away: "Charlie Fogarty is part of the problem."

Red letters squeezed in: "Charlie Fogarty is **STILL** part of the problem."

At the bottom came disclosure in tiny block caps: "PAID FOR BY THE REPUBLICAN GOVERNORS ASSOCIATION."[46]

It looked as if the Republican Governors Association had taken a page from the playbook of the Swift Boat Veterans for Truth, who had turned John Kerry's respected Vietnam record against him. This commercial misrepresented new transparency requirements, implying dishonestly that Fogarty actually added layers of secrecy. Beyond its devious content, the commercial used illicit funds. This was the second time national Republican cash had funded an attack ad that helped Carcieri and violated Rhode Island's campaign finance law.

Since 1992, Rhode Island's Campaign Finance Law had outlawed aggregate contributions above $25,000 to any candidate or political party.[47] But in October 2002, the Rhode Island Republican Party took $250,000 — ten times the legal limit — from the Republican National Committee for a commercial that cited "insider deals, scandal, corruption," and "state spending out of control." The ad promoted Carcieri as a "fresh start for Rhode Island" and directed viewers to his campaign website.[48] At a Board of Elections hearing on October 21, 2002, a lawyer for the Rhode Island GOP claimed its commercial was only an "issue ad," since it did not contain the words "Vote for Don Carcieri." Carcieri's campaign disavowed the ad, insisting it had been produced independently, although Ken McKay, Carcieri's campaign manager, acknowledged that Carcieri welcomed national support.[49]

The bipartisan Board of Elections had ruled unanimously that the Rhode Island Republican Party had violated state campaign finance laws and ordered the ad taken down, and the state Supreme Court refused to hear an appeal. The case dragged on for years with volleys of motions until Superior Court Judge Stephen J. Fortunato condemned the board for bungling the probe and barred further investigation.[50]

Carcieri had won in 2002, and the 2006 commercial "In Charlie Fogarty's World" followed an eerily similar path. But who had fed crucial intelligence to a production company paid by the National Republican Governors Association? Had Carcieri's campaign broken the law? Though neither question would be answered before November 7, the commercial "In Charlie Fogarty's World" was grotesquely false.

With support of the Common Cause Rhode Island executive committee I sent a press release to media across the state to set the record straight. I summarized what I called "six new and significant reforms" in the law Fogarty had pushed. "What I find disturbing about this attack ad," I wrote, "is that it disparages the lieutenant governor for conceiving this bill, and it blames the lawmakers who worked diligently to pass it. This new law constitutes real progress toward open, accountable government, but no one would know that by watching this commercial."

I added details that had never been publicized: "Neither Governor Donald Carcieri nor his staff testified on this legislation. A huge and bipartisan majority in the House of Representatives approved the bill. Only one Republican and one Democrat voted against passage." The governor had allowed the legislation to become law without his signature.[51] And if Fogarty's bill was as bad as this commercial claimed, why had Carcieri not vetoed it?

I wrote that Common Cause Rhode Island had never weighed in on any campaign commercial. "But this attack ad cries out for fact-checking. Besides dishonoring both Governor Carcieri and Lieutenant Governor Fogarty, it misleads Rhode Island voters."[52]

Print reporters phoned for further comment, and newspapers across Rhode Island ran stories on the deceptive ad. Joe Baker wrote in the *Newport Daily News* that I had never — even in off-the-record conversations — engaged in partisan politics. "In the countless times I've spoken with West, I have never heard him give any hint of endorsement for or against a state official." That history, he wrote, gave my statement about the anti-Fogarty ad its "jaw-dropping impact."[53]

For several days, I wondered why television stations ignored such a blatant lie about Fogarty's signature reform. The mystery ended when the Republican Governors Association filed a required report with the Board of Elections. Their report — ironically filed while trick-or-treaters were donning costumes for Halloween — revealed two payments only days earlier. One check for $25,000 went to Stevens & Schriefer Group for "media production" and a second of $595,000 to Stevens & Schriefer Group Media Inc. for "media buy."[54] Virtually all of that money would have gone to the network affiliate stations — ABC, CBS, NBC, and Fox — to mesmerize voters with "In Charlie Fogarty's World."

Rhode Island law required anyone who made independent expenditures for or against a candidate to certify that they were "not acting in concert with any other person or group."[55] From a Washington office less than a block from the White House, Melinda Anderson had signed on behalf of the GOP governors that they were "not acting in concert" with Carcieri's campaign, but no reasonable person could believe that. The ad's message fit hand-in-glove with Carcieri's criticism of Fogarty's bill.[56] It distilled and amplified the governor's naïve demand that the legislation should have required lawyers to name their clients — even though such disclosure would have violated lawyer-client confidentiality.

As Rhode Island rushed toward the election, it appeared that Fogarty and Carcieri were neck and neck, each spending about $2 million. Republican governors had poured another $620,000 into Carcieri's race — nearly twenty-five times what they could have legally contributed. Would they tip the race to Carcieri?

With polls running against its proposed "Narragansett Indian Casino," Harrah's gambled that it could win voters over with a barrage of commercials. The Las Vegas giant spent $3.2 million in September — roughly $106,000 per day.[57] Still behind in the polls, Harrah's quadrupled its spending in October, shattering all previous Rhode Island campaign records. Save Our State, the anti-casino coalition, spent far less but clung to a lead in state polls.

By comparison, our Right To Vote Campaign drew $350,000 from progressive foundations for our entire campaign.[58] We remained all but invisible, which our young field director preferred. Scrawny, unkempt, and brilliant, Dan Schleifer dodged reporters. His get-out-the-vote operation was a secret weapon that he kept hidden until after the election.

During two years since his graduation from Brown University, Schleifer had lived on a subsistence wage from the Family Life Center. As field director for the Right To Vote Campaign, he deployed former prisoners who were now students — Andres Idarraga at Brown and Bruce Reilly at Rhode Island College — to sign up their classmates as volunteers. Recruiters appealed to the students' desire to make a difference. They promised that the work would be grueling but would end on November 7, leaving plenty of time to complete the fall term's academic work. By mid-October, nearly two hundred student volunteers had joined. Fifteen paid canvassers — most disenfranchised former prisoners or their relatives — led the teams.[59] Schleifer deployed his teams to gritty neighborhoods and monitored them by cell phone. He became a guerilla general, sitting on a curbstone, clipboard in hand, exhausted but calm.

I settled beside Schleifer to look at one sector map. During the final weekend, his teams would canvass their blocks three more times. "Our teams know people by name in every house on this block," he said proudly. "We know who supports Question 2 and why. If they have a phone, we know the number." On November 7, his teams would monitor each urban polling place. They would track who had voted and who had not. "We'll cover our blocks in every city. We'll call people, go to their doors, keep after them until they actually vote."

When a last-minute grant enabled us to buy several newspaper ads and blitz the state with computer-generated phone calls, the steering committee asked me to record our message. And so the calls went out: "Hello, this is Phil West at Common Cause asking you to vote YES on Ballot Question 2 on November 7. Question 2 will restore voting rights to thousands of Rhode Islanders — U.S. citizens who have paid their debt to society and who now live, work, raise families, and pay taxes here in Rhode Island. Please vote YES on Question 2."[60]

On Saturday morning before the election, I ran my favorite path along the eastern shore of connected lakes in Roger Williams Park. From across the water came sounds of a political rally at the Temple to Music, so I rounded the spillway to see for myself. An audience of hundreds surrounded the marble stage. Classic columns framed Sheldon Whitehouse and a slim man I recognized from television as U.S. Senator Barack Obama.

The Senate race between Whitehouse and Lincoln Chafee had broken the mold. Chafee had beaten Cranston Mayor Steven Laffey, a far-right rival, in a bitter GOP primary, but he then pivoted to battle Whitehouse in the general election.[61] While many in blue-state Rhode Island appreciated Chafee's votes against the Iraq War, against President George W. Bush's tax cuts, against drilling in the Arctic, and against cuts in Medicaid and Medicare, Whitehouse argued none of that would matter if Chafee's first vote in a new term kept the U.S. Senate in Republican hands.[62]

Whitehouse and the young presidential contender from Illinois embellished these themes to a crowd that filled the marble plaza, grassy half-circle, and slopes around the Temple to Music. Wearing my grungy sweatpants, I skirted the margins of the rally, careful not to compromise my nonpartisan role by clapping. On the southern fringe of the crowd I found six Palestinian officials I had escorted around the State House the previous afternoon. All were from the West Bank, and I stood with them on the grassy slope until the rally ended.

"Who will win?" asked the only woman in the group.

"Probably Whitehouse," I said. The day before I had described the campaign for separation of powers and shared with them the comment Sheldon Whitehouse had made in 1992 that without separation of powers Rhode Island would never "cut the deep root of corruption."

"And if Whitehouse wins," she asked, "will he block the policies of Bush?"

"I know he'll try," I said. Separation of powers was crisp as a concept but often messy in its application.

Election Day finally faded into night. Weary Right To Vote volunteers finished their phone calls, drove late voters home from the polls, and straggled to an upstairs reception room at Ada's Creations on Broad Street in Providence. With finger foods, beer, and wine, weary campaign workers came to life again in the camaraderie of a shared cause.

Across Rhode Island the polls closed at 9:00 p.m. From that moment on, people chatted with eyes checking TV screens as the count came in. While Whitehouse built a growing edge over Chafee, many races remained in doubt. Numbers on the screen showed Don Carcieri and Charlie Fogarty hovering within a few hundred votes of one another.

"Casino," someone yelled, and our crowd flocked to watch the wall-mounted flat-screens. From the first, it became obvious that in spite of Harrah's extravagant spending, Question 1, the Casino Amendment, was being crushed. "They had no ground game," one student said of Harrah's operatives. "They had paid people trying to convince voters going into the polls. Way too late."

A hush fell as numbers for Question 2 appeared. In Coventry, Sen. Lou Raptakis's town, just over 55 percent rejected our amendment. In Westerly — despite the *Westerly Sun*'s negative editorial — 54.2 percent approved. The televised numbers cycled to other contests. People nervously switched channels and switched back, watching.

As we expected, several small towns went against us — Exeter, Foster, Glocester — but we lost those three by only 610 total votes. In Johnston, where

Sen. Joe Polisena had railed against restoring the vote and was winning his race for mayor, voters rejected Question 2 by a relatively small 626-vote margin. Then tiny New Shoreham — Block Island — appeared on screen with its single polling place. Of 904 voters, 563 or 62.3 percent had approved restoring the vote. A cheer went up. As North Kingstown and North Providence reported with incomplete counts, we were losing both. We lost East Greenwich by 1,006 votes but won Barrington by 628.

Although I had not seen Koren Carbuccia in several weeks, I loved seeing a color photo of her and her son on a billboard poster and the sides of busses with a checklist:

☑ I am a U.S. citizen.

☑ I live and work in Rhode Island.

☑ I raise a family in Rhode Island.

☑ I pay taxes in Rhode Island.

☐ I vote in Rhode Island.

She had spent the day at a polling place in Pawtucket and was startled by how many people recognized her. Several had sneered at her. "But I put on my game face," she told me, "even to those who were negative. And other people started telling me: 'Oh, I didn't know you were a felon.' And I'm like, oh . . ." Her voice dropped. "I didn't realize how many people didn't know. But people who really knew me said it didn't matter to them."

She said Vaskan was thrilled to see his picture on busses. "He doesn't understand it all now, but he keeps saying, 'Mommy, that's me and you. Mommy, that's me and you.' I saved every article, so one day I'll explain it all to him that we made history."

I asked how she felt about the State House press conference. She laughed. "My self-esteem just soared. That was the right key to my car. It got my engine going and made it positive for me."

As results began flowing from Rhode Island's core cities, the tally shifted in our favor. Newport came through with a nearly fifteen percent victory margin, more than 1,100 votes. Tiny Central Falls showed 63.2 percent approving, a surplus of 611 votes. East Providence produced a cushion of more than a thousand. Returns from Pawtucket added two thousand. Each round of urban numbers brought a cheer. Even before the final districts reported, Providence delivered a landslide, better than 2-to-1, a surplus of more than thirteen thousand votes. The cities were providing a narrow statewide victory.

Trumpets blared from a doorway. Cymbals crashed. A commotion of drums burst into the room. A sousaphone player bent his unwieldy instrument forward to fit through the door and straightened up with an elephantine blast — Dan Schleifer flushed with triumph. Trombones and saxophones wailed — a wild mélange of John Philip Sousa, Bollywood, and hip-hop. Their sound could fill a football stadium. A second sousaphone bobbed through the door with the greeting "What Cheer?" painted brightly on its bell. Legend held that the Narragansetts welcomed Roger Williams with a greeting that combined the Elizabethan phrase with their word for friend: "What cheer, natop?" We had won. At Ada's Creations on Broad Street, the roof lifted.

Later I asked Schleifer about their What Cheer? Brigade. What was that irrepressible music they played? He laughed. "Luddite hardcore," he said. "No amplifiers, but very loud and danceable."

In the six cities where Schleifer's teams had canvassed block-by-block, Question 2 built up a margin of 18,719 votes. In the thirty-three cities and towns where we depended on reform groups, churches, and newspapers, we lost by 7,192. Our final count showed the Right To Vote Amendment had prevailed with a statewide margin of 11,527 — 3.1 percent.[63] This was no small victory. With passage, Rhode Island voters became the first in the United States to approve a state constitutional amendment that authorized the restoration of voting rights to convicted felons the moment they walked out of prison.

In the highest spending contest ever recorded in Rhode Island, voters solidly rejected the Harrah's-Narragansett Indian Casino. Question 1 lost by 100,199 votes, 26.1 percent of the votes cast.

Sheldon Whitehouse swept 53.5 percent of the vote and ousted Lincoln Chafee, largely by stirring fears of a Republican majority in the Senate. In two years leading up to the Senate election, Whitehouse had raised and spent $6.42 million, compared with Chafee's $3.53 million.[64]

Gov. Carcieri won with 51.01 percent: a margin of 7,804 votes out of 386,928 cast statewide. This was the first gubernatorial race in which one candidate, Charlie Fogarty, participated in the matching-funds program while the other did not.[65] Fogarty raised roughly $863,000 in private contributions — enough to qualify for $981,000 in public matching funds. He also had the advantage of getting a 2-to-1 match for contributions below $500.[66] Carcieri raised $1.57 million in private funds.

Although Fogarty had signed into the program while Carcieri opted out, they had traded leads in several polls, mostly within the margin of error, until the Republican Governors Association put its heavy hand with $620,000 on the scale. "In Charlie Fogarty's World," their devious ad broadcast nonstop for the last week, narrowly returned Don Carcieri to office for a second term.

On a frigid November night leaders of Common Cause threw a party at the Convention Center for my retirement. Anne, our sons, and daughters-in-law surrounded me at dinner in the main ballroom. More than five hundred people bought tickets with proceeds going to a quarter-million-dollar endowment to continue this work. Hasbro provided table favors with my face as a jigsaw puzzle while Anne presented a PowerPoint of photos and stories.[67] Comedian Charlie Hall and his Ocean State Follies made light of scandals and attempts at reform. I called out thanks to activists and public officials who had put their careers at risk to promote reforms.

After the last handshakes and hugs, we hauled mementos to the street beneath the warm glow of a neon art installation and loaded our car. Looming across Sabin Street was the sedate brick headquarters of the *Providence Journal* where I had trained as a copy editor in the summer of 1988. I had failed at that because I kept trying to rewrite the news. My failure at the *Journal* had kept me searching the want ads until Common Cause posted its tiny announcement that changed my life. Now I could begin writing about scores of people who had worked together in our microcosm of a state to bend the moral arc of the universe toward justice.[68]

6
Afterword

Afterword
Making Government Good
2006–2014

HISTORY NEVER PAUSES. During the years I have looked back to write this book, events have rushed forward. In this afterword, I want to sketch recent developments in ethics, election reform, open government, and separation of powers. How are the reforms enacted between 1986 and 2006 working? Have these efforts made any difference?

LEGISLATORS IN TROUBLE

As *Secrets & Scandals* went into galleys, federal agents with search warrants raided the home and State House office of Speaker Gordon D. Fox.[1] Fox had already paid two ethics fines — $10,000 in 2004 to settle for his conflicted vote for a GTECH contract, and $1,500 in 2014 for failing to report nearly $43,000 in fees from the Providence Economic Development Partnership.[2] Only hours after the March 2014 raid, he resigned as speaker. As this book goes to print no charges have been filed. Even in a state inured to scandal, Fox's fall stunned and saddened many.

The greatest irony in this narrative may involve former Senate President William V. Irons, who often claimed to be a champion of ethics. Scandal over secret insurance commissions had engulfed Irons in 2003 and prompted his resignation in December of that year.[3] Leaders of Operation Clean Government filed an ethics complaint against him, charging that he had taken $70,000 in insurance commissions from CVS while using his power as a committee chair to kill pharmacy freedom of choice legislation that his clients, CVS and Blue Cross/Blue Shield, opposed.[4] The Ethics Commission found probable cause that Irons had violated the law.[5]

The next step would have been a full adjudicative hearing, but Irons and his lawyers sought a settlement — the civil equivalent of a guilty plea — with the Ethics Commission.[6] Hidden from public view, settlement talks continued for three years. When negotiations failed, Irons's attorneys filed two motions. The first sought to dismiss the charges on grounds that the state Constitution's speech in debate clause made him immune to prosecution for legislative acts; the second demanded a jury trial rather than an adjudicative hearing before the Ethics Commission. The commission voted unanimously to deny both motions.[7]

Irons appealed to Superior Court, where Judge Francis J. Darigan ruled in October 2008 that the speech in debate clause trumped the Ethics Amendment. Darigan blocked the prosecution.[8]

The Rhode Island Supreme Court heard Irons's case in May 2009. In June a three-justice majority affirmed Darigan's ruling that speech in debate shielded the former Senate president. Chief Justice Frank J. Williams, joined by Justices Francis X. Flaherty and William P. Robinson III, traced legislators' speech in debate immunity from the English Parliament in 1455 to the U.S. Constitution in 1787 and the Rhode Island Constitution of 1843. They emphasized that speech in debate immunity extended to "core legislative acts," namely "proposing, passing, or voting upon" specific legislation.[9] Their central premise was that state voters in 1986 had "adopted a neutral rewrite" of the speech in debate clause on the same day they approved the Ethics Amendment. The three gave both clauses equal weight, and they nullified the Ethics Commission's authority to prosecute members of the General Assembly for their "core legislative acts."[10]

Justice Paul A. Suttell dissented. He agreed that the speech in debate clause and Ethics Amendment were incompatible, but he urged "a different approach to this vexing constitutional dilemma." Suttell quoted a recent precedent where the justices had written: "In construing provisions of the Rhode Island Constitution, our 'chief purpose is to give effect to the intent of the framers.'" He then noted that delegates to the 1986 Constitutional Convention declared their determination to take "the fox away from the chickens,"[11] a phrase that signified protecting the public against corrupt legislators. Suttell wrote that state voters had approved the framers' "plain and unequivocal" language: "All elected and appointed officials . . . shall be subject to the code of ethics."[12]

Suttell stressed the seamless consensus from delegates at the 1986 Constitutional Convention to voters who approved the Ethics Amendment in 1986[13] and Supreme Court justices who affirmed the Ethics Commission's authority in a unanimous 1992 opinion.[14] His dissent ended cogently:

> I would hold that in matters concerning the ethical conduct of
> legislators the ethics amendment creates a narrow exception to the
> immunity historically adhering to legislators in the performance

of their legislative activities. Such a construction of our constitution, I believe, gives greater effect to the intent of the convention
delegates and electorate in 1986 than an interpretation that places
legislators beyond the reach of the ethics commission for violations of the code of ethics with respect to their performance of
legislative activities. It would also preserve the full measure of
protections accorded legislators by the speech in debate clause as
to questioning from any person or entity *except* the ethics commission. (Suttell's emphasis)[15]

His emphasis on the will of the people is sound.

The majority wrote: "The electorate of this state reaffirmed the speech in
debate clause" as part of "a neutral rewrite of the then-existing provisions of
the Rhode Island Constitution." They cited a handbook produced by the Constitutional Convention that said the neutral rewrite did not "change the intent
of any section."[16]

That was literally true, but I believe they wrongly presumed that voters who
approved a gender-neutral rewriting of the Rhode Island Constitution in 1986
were even remotely aware of the speech in debate clause. The three justices
glossed over the fact that neither the handbook nor a booklet on statewide
referendums published by Secretary of State Susan L. Farmer alluded anywhere to speech in debate.[17] The *Providence Journal* published more than six
hundred stories about the convention, ballot questions, and campaigns. Not
one mentioned the speech in debate clause. Only a constitutional scholar who
read through the entire text of the revised Constitution might have wondered
whether a defense lawyer would someday use that obscure clause to attack the
Ethics Commission's authority.

In contrast, the 1986 Ethics in Government question was widely discussed.[18]
It declared explicitly that "all elected and appointed officials" were to be subject
to the Code of Ethics and jurisdiction of the Ethics Commission.[19]

Justices Williams, Flaherty, and Robinson built their 2009 decision in *Irons* v.
Rhode Island Ethics Commission on a false premise. They overturned a quarter-
century of jurisprudence. They destroyed the Ethics Commission's authority to
advise legislators about conflicts of interest or investigate any complaint involving what the majority called legislators' "core legislative acts."[20]

Common Cause then drafted and began promoting a constitutional amendment that would explicitly authorize the Ethics Commission "to investigate and
adjudicate all alleged violations of the code of ethics, including acts otherwise
protected by Article IV, Section 5," the speech in debate clause.[21] Then-House
Majority Leader Gordon D. Fox introduced this resolution on February 5,
2010, less than a week before he was elected speaker.[22] The House passed Fox's
resolution and sent it to the Senate,[23] where Senate President M. Teresa Paiva

Weed, who had sponsored sound ethics legislation earlier in her political career, blocked consideration.

Five legislative sessions have passed since the Supreme Court exempted senators and representatives from prosecution by the Ethics Commission. John Marion, who became director of Common Cause Rhode Island in 2008, contrasts the number of recusals — written announcements members make when not voting because of a conflict — from the four years before the Irons ruling to the four years after it. The number of recusals dropped 62.4 percent in the House of Representatives and 43.1 percent in the Senate. During the four legislative sessions after the Irons decision the count of representatives who bothered to recuse themselves even once dropped by half.[24]

In June 2014, the Senate passed legislation that purported to address the speech in debate problem but was immediately denounced by Common Cause, Operation Clean Government, the League of Women Voters, and the Rhode Island Taxpayers Association as "hopelessly compromised." Instead of a narrowly crafted amendment to address speech in debate issues involving legislators, the proposed constitutional amendment would open the door for any public official found to have violated ethics laws while serving on school committees, zoning boards, town councils, or quasi-public corporations to get a new trial rather than the current appeal to Superior Court.[25]

At one 2010 hearing on the proposed amendment to restore the commission's authority, Rep. Scott M. Pollard declared: "I've been here a year and a half now. There aren't any corrupt people in the building. And if you do know them to be corrupt, then I suggest that you call the attorney general's office and seek to have them prosecuted."[26]

Pollard had become a representative shortly after former House Majority Leader Gerard M. Martineau pled guilty on federal charges that he had sold his "honest services" to CVS and Blue Cross. Martineau — like Irons and Celona — had killed pharmacy freedom of choice bills over four legislative sessions. He admitted taking $911,435 from Blue Cross and invoicing the insurer for ten million printed bags but delivering only two million.[27] In February 2008, he was fined $100,000 and sentenced to three years and one month in federal prison.[28]

Other legislators went to jail for felonies unrelated to their roles as members of the General Assembly. In June 2010, Johnston Sen. Christopher B. Maselli was indicted for submitting fraudulent documents to get loans worth $1.525 million. Maselli pled guilty to eight felonies and was sentenced to two years and three months in prison.[29] Former Rep. John J. McCauley Jr. and his business partner pled guilty in 2012 after their companies underreported their income by nearly $1.8 million and underpaid their taxes by about $500,000. Like Maselli, McCauley was sentenced to 27 months in federal prison.[30]

Providence Rep. Leo Medina ran afoul of numerous authorities during the single term, 2011–12, that he served in the House. Charges against him included failure to file campaign finance reports, practicing law without a license, and felony misappropriation of $28,000 entrusted to him by a friend. Medina has demanded a jury trial.[31] Voters who gave him a 26-vote victory in the 2010 Democratic primary rejected him by a nearly two-to-one margin two years later.

The fallout continues from other scandals involving legislators. In 2005, the Ethics Commission fined former Sen. Patrick Timothy McDonald $4,000 for failing to file financial disclosure forms over several years.[32] A state jury found McDonald guilty of conspiring to embezzle over $160,000 from his law clients. In May 2014 he was sentenced to twenty years in prison, with four-and-a-half to serve.[33]

In 2007 Bristol Rep. Raymond Gallison was charged with failing to report income from the College Readiness Program on his financial disclosure forms, a total of $102,020 over three years. Legislative grants flowed from House leaders to the program and back to Gallison. Rather than contest the facts, Gallison paid a $6,000 settlement.[34] Nevertheless, when Speaker Gordon Fox resigned, Gallison advanced to chair the powerful House Finance Committee, a post Fox had held for several years.

Municipal corruption leads to a code of ethics

Municipal corruption also made headlines. In 2009, North Providence Town Council Member Paul F. Caranci bravely wore a wire for the FBI to gather evidence against three fellow council members: Raymond L. Douglas III and John A. Zambarano, as well as Council President Joseph S. Burchfield, who was constituent services director for the state Senate.[35] The trio eventually pled guilty to taking a $25,000 bribe to arrange supermarket zoning for developer Richard P. Baccari Sr., who later became the target of a federal indictment. A jury found Robert S. Ciresi, the city's solicitor, guilty of delivering the bribe.[36] Ciresi was sentenced to sixty-three months in federal prison. The three council members got sentences ranging from sixty-four to seventy-eight months,[37] and several were tagged for additional crimes. Nor were these major players alone in North Providence corruption: another former town council president, former zoning board chair, acting finance director, an unlicensed insurance adjuster, radio personality, and strip club manager all made headlines, pled guilty, paid fines, and received sentences.[38] Baccari is awaiting trial.

Early in 2010, independent investigative reporter Jim Hummel broke the news that Central Falls Mayor Charles D. Moreau had steered lucrative no-bid contracts for boarding up abandoned buildings to his friend and campaign contributor Michael G. Bouthillette, who had a new furnace installed in Moreau's house.[39] For his work, Bouthillette charged ten times the average for similar board-ups by contractors in neighboring cities. These costs became liens on at least 167 dilapidated structures, making it prohibitively expensive to sell or rehabilitate them. While Rhode Island's smallest and poorest city had struggled with deficits before Moreau became mayor in 2004, his corrupt practices tipped it into receivership in 2010 and bankruptcy in May 2011.

Bouthillette's furnace prompted an ethics complaint against Moreau for accepting a "gift" from "an interested person." The mayor eventually acknowledged "knowingly and willfully" violating the $25 gift rule; he agreed to pay a fine of $7,000.[40] Moreau also pled guilty on federal charges that carried a sentence of two years in prison and a $25,000 fine. Bouthillette pled to a single felony. He got three years of probation, a $5,000 fine, and an obligation to work two thousand hours for the City of Central Falls. He was also required to establish a $160,000 endowment at the Rhode Island Foundation to help provide housing for the poor in Central Falls.[41]

The scandal marked a new beginning for the tiny city. James A. Diossa, the son of Colombian immigrant parents, had returned after college and challenged the corrupt Moreau machine. In 2009, while the city spiraled into state receivership and then bankruptcy, Diossa won a seat on the Central Falls City Council but found himself locked out of meetings. When Moreau pleaded guilty, Diossa ran for mayor, promising an ethics ordinance that would make the corrupt practices of recent years illegal. He won and was inaugurated on the high school stage where he graduated ten years earlier.

Diossa quickly proposed an ordinance adapted from the Providence Code of Ethics, and the state-appointed receiver John F. McJennett III, acting in place of the council, approved it.[42] One section allowed the city to revoke the pension of any official or employee who commits a felony in office. That provision proved necessary when Joyce Tager, a city collections officer, was arrested for embezzling from the cash-strapped city. Tager resigned, pled guilty, paid full restitution of $17,000, and agreed to have her pension revoked.[43]

Pensioners had suffered grievous losses in the city's bankruptcy, but the receivership cleared a road to recovery, and a new generation of Central Falls leaders began the journey. In 2013, Diossa won a full term, and a new city council was elected with a female majority of citizen reformers. During Diossa's first full fiscal year, Central Falls built up an operating surplus of $1.3 million.[44] Although the struggle was far from over, Central Falls had new leadership and was bouncing back.

U.S. SUPREME COURT RAVAGES REFORMS

During the years since I retired from Common Cause, the U.S. Supreme Court has ravaged reforms begun more than a century ago under President Theodore Roosevelt. Tutored by muckraking journalists, Roosevelt pushed for the Tillman

Act of 1907 that banned corporate contributions in federal campaigns. Later laws — some born of famous scandals — limited campaign contributions, required the disclosure of contributions, and regulated the use of campaign funds.

During the 1972 campaign to re-elect President Richard M. Nixon, investigative reporters exposed massive campaign finance abuses. Watergate wrenched the nation, forced Nixon's resignation, and prompted passage of the Federal Election Campaign Act Amendments of 1974. That legislation tightened limits on contributions to campaigns for federal offices and required full disclosure of campaign contributions. It also provided public funds for presidential campaigns and established the Federal Elections Commission to enforce campaign finance laws.[45] Rhode Island and many other states adapted these approaches for use in state elections.[46]

In 2002, Congress passed the Bipartisan Campaign Reform Act (BCRA), often called McCain-Feingold for its Senate sponsors. BCRA raised the limits on contributions to candidates and political party committees and banned the use of soft money — funds raised and spent outside campaign finance laws to influence federal elections. It also restricted so-called "issue ads" that were funded by corporations or unions to influence federal elections. The bipartisan law also required candidates to appear in each ad and approve its content.[47]

For nearly a century, U.S. Supreme Court decisions upheld the ban on corporate contributions, limits on individual contributions, and disclosure requirements as constitutional mechanisms for discouraging corruption. In 2003, the high court upheld McCain-Feingold in *McConnell* v. *Federal Election Commission.*[48]

During their confirmation hearings, both Chief Justice John G. Roberts Jr. and Associate Justice Samuel A. Alito Jr. promised *stare decisis* — that they would stand by legal precedents. Yet once they took their seats in 2005 and 2006, they joined with Justices Antonin Scalia, Clarence Thomas, and Anthony M. Kennedy to dismantle long-established campaign finance reforms.[49]

In seven years, these five justices — by the narrowest of majorities — obliterated nearly a century of precedents. Among their targets were a section of law that prohibited sham issue ads (2007), the Millionaires' Amendment that allowed candidates facing wealthy self-funded opponents to raise additional private contributions (2008), long-standing restrictions on union and corporate spending in candidate elections (2010 and 2012), state programs that provide matching public funds to candidates who abide by expenditure limits (2011), and limits on the total amounts contributors can give in federal elections to all candidates (2014).[50] The Roberts group seems not to recognize any corruption short of *quid pro quo* bribery for specific government actions. They shut their eyes to the obligations that million-dollar contributions hang around the necks of elected officials. Taken together, these precedent-shattering decisions have opened American elections to massive influence peddling.

Though the Supreme Court signaled that Congress could mandate disclosure without suppressing speech, Congress has refused to pass such legislation. In July 2010, U.S. Senate Republicans used a filibuster to bury legislation that would have forced full disclosure by groups or corporations that fund independent ads. The bill would have banned contributions from foreign-controlled corporations, government contractors, and firms that received federal TARP (Troubled Asset Relief Program) bailout funds.[51]

While the Rhode Island General Assembly could not restore contribution curbs shattered by the Roberts Court, it did enact significant disclosure requirements in 2012. Rep. Christopher R. Blazejewski in the House and Sen. Juan M. Pichardo in the Senate cited the *Citizens United* v. *FEC* decision as cause for alarm. Their legislation defined "independent expenditures" that seek to influence candidate elections or ballot questions. Among tightly woven strictures, the new law required disclosure by the donor or chief officer of the group that pays for a campaign commercial and a list of the top five donors to the organization paying for the ad.[52]

In another hopeful Rhode Island sign, three candidates running for governor in 2014 — Gina Raimondo, Angel Taveras, and Clay Pell — joined in a Peoples' Pledge on April 28, 2014. The signing followed conversations hosted by John Marion at Common Cause. The agreement creates incentives for candidates to discourage independent spending by outside groups, whether SuperPACs, 527 groups, or various 501(c) organizations. The candidates pledged not to allow any coordination with such groups. Raimondo and Taveras quickly sent email blasts to let people know they had signed. A Common Cause press release called solutions like the People's Pledge "our best hope of restoring elections that are about candidates speaking to voters and not being drowned out by outside special interests."[53]

The Roberts-Alito-Scalia-Kennedy-Thomas block has also pounded minority voters. Its June 2013 ruling in *Shelby County* v. *Holder*, the five struck down a key protection from the Voting Rights Act of 1965. States with histories of racial discrimination had been required to clear changes in their election procedures before implementing them. The five activist judges swept away that reform.

In a fierce dissent, Justice Ruth Bader Ginsburg noted that, although the preclearance process had dismantled traditional obstacles to black voting, jurisdictions had evolved many "second-generation barriers" to circumvent the law.[54] As if to prove Ginsburg's point, within months of *Shelby County* v. *Holder,* Republican legislatures in nine states passed laws that made voting more difficult or less available for minorities.[55]

In 2006, after passage of Rhode Island's Right to Vote Amendment, staff members at the Adult Corrections Institution began notifying inmates that they could register to vote upon their release. Program records show that of 3,196 ex-felons released by 2013, 44.8 per cent actually registered, 12.9 per cent took forms to complete later, and 42 percent refused.[56] During a voter registration drive conducted by the Family Life Center — renamed Open Doors Rhode Island — 6,330 former prisoners registered in time to vote in the 2008 election.[57]

For any who doubt the wisdom of restoring the franchise upon release, rather than at the end of probation and parole, Koren Carbuccia posed a vital question: "Isn't the point of the criminal justice system to return responsible, law-abiding citizens back into their communities?"[58]

SEPARATION OF POWERS PROMPTS OVERSIGHT

While I was writing this book the Rhode Island Department of Transportation completed a new interchange between I-95 and I-195 in Providence. Between November 2007 and October 2011, DOT opened graceful ramps that let traffic flow smoothly across the iconic Iway bridge onto I-95 north and south or to the cluster of hospitals beyond the highway. This new infrastructure ended drivers' desperate dashes across lanes of traffic to reach exits. Although the reconnection of surrounding streets and neighborhoods has only begun, the new order is unquestionably faster, smoother, and safer.

Separation of powers — although less visible than a relocated highway interchange — is transforming Rhode Island government. Pressures that invited risky behavior when legislators served on executive boards have diminished, along with chances for corrupt insider deals. Routine decisions have become more orderly. The insight of our nation's founders about separating legislative, executive, and judicial functions is clearly affecting political decisions in positive ways.

Contrary to what I believed when I retired, House leaders had not sent their 2006 request for an advisory opinion on the CRMC to the high court, but they did so in 2007.[59] Four justices of the Rhode Island Supreme Court heard oral arguments in October 2008 and issued a unanimous advisory opinion in December.[60] The justices concluded that two new sections of the Rhode Island Constitution — the ban on dual office holding and the clause empowering the governor to appoint members of executive boards — were effective without further enabling legislation. Each was "self-executing."

The justices declared the CRMC's powers "manifestly executive in nature," adding that to call these functions "legislative" would require willful blindness to the separation of powers clause, "which expressly requires the three departments of government to be 'separate and distinct.'" Their unanimous advisory emphasized that separation of powers did not diminish the General Assembly's "constitutional duty to protect the natural environment of the state through the vigorous and proactive exercise of its legislative powers."[61]

From the start of the drive for separation of powers, advocates had aimed to provide effective legislative oversight for executive departments, boards, and commissions. As far back as 2000, the Senate Select Commission on Quasi-Public Agencies led by J. Michael Lenihan and M. Teresa Paiva Weed had conducted rigorous oversight hearings.[62] In 2003, the Senate established a standing Committee on Government Oversight with Lenihan as chairperson. Over several years, he refined oversight practices as alternatives to the old model that presumed lawmakers on boards were somehow "providing oversight."

Sen. James C. Sheehan, who now chairs Senate Government Oversight, says that before separation of powers, legislators sometimes developed cozy relationships with the boards on which they served. Some may have feared that "problems or wrongdoing could reflect on them if brought to light." Sheehan plans "regular performance audits of quasi-public agencies." He notes that Senate rules now permit other standing committees to conduct oversight over parts of the executive branch "within the committee's purview."[63]

In the House, too, old claims that legislators on boards and commissions provided oversight became passé. Early in 2009, only two months after the Supreme Court disqualified state legislators and legislative appointees from serving on the CRMC, the House renamed its Committee on Separation of Powers, adding "and Oversight" to reflect its additional duties.[64] In 2011, new House rules rebranded the committee again as simply "House Oversight."[65] In both chambers, oversight committees now follow the playbook of Sen. Mike Lenihan's 2000 hearings on quasi-publics.[66] The House Oversight Committee meets in a room refurbished for digital video.

These changes are not merely matters of nomenclature or style. After years of resistance to separation of powers, legislative practices shifted decisively toward a congressional model in which lawmakers question executive decision-makers in public sessions.

Under the leadership of Chairperson Karen L. MacBeth, the House Oversight Committee has begun preparing subpoenas for a range of officials involved in the ill-fated $75-million loan guarantee for 38 Studios.[67] In May 2014, after barely a month at the helm of the oversight committee, MacBeth demanded a forensic audit of the defunct gaming company, including building permits and contractors' bills. As they began digging, MacBeth and committee secretary Michael W. Chippendale got unsigned threats against them and their families. "We're moving in the right direction," Chippendale told a reporter. "We've kicked the hornets' nest."[68]

"Threats or not," MacBeth said, "I'm going to continue what I'm doing. I was raised by a marine. I don't know how to back down." MacBeth had tried initially to keep the threats confidential. "We're beginning to see that some light restores faith in government," she observed. "I think we're supposed to shed light."[69]

Moving toward pension reform

Together, the 2004 Separation of Powers Amendment and the 1992 Four-Year Terms Amendment gave Gov. Lincoln D. Chafee and General Treasurer Gina M. Raimondo a firm foothold for a crucial fight.

In 2010, Raimondo ran for general treasurer on a promise of pension reform. For decades Rhode Island's pension fund had been underfunded and subject to insider abuse.[70] Invested funds had taken a hit in the deepest crash since the Great Depression. Retirees were living longer and collecting compounded annual cost-of-living increases. Estimates of the unfunded liability ranged from $7 billion to $13.7 billion. Raimondo pledged to make the system reliable for retirees and affordable for taxpayers.

Raimondo's warnings resonated with voters, who gave her the largest majority in any of the five statewide races, a genuine mandate for reform.[71] Early in her tenure, Raimondo issued a report entitled TRUTH IN NUMBERS: *The Security and Sustainability of Rhode Island's Retirement System*. Her data showed dire consequences for state employees and teachers, threats to vital public services, unsustainable taxes, and the inevitability of pension default.[72] She warned that inaction would bring devastating consequences. "This will not go away," she said. "It will get harder to fix every day that we ignore it."[73]

She persuaded Gov. Chafee and legislative leaders — House Speaker Gordon Fox and Senate President Teresa Paiva Weed — to tackle pension reform in a special fall session of the General Assembly. Raimondo said her legislation would provide retirement security for employees, reduce the state's unfunded liability by $3 billion, save taxpayers $4 billion and municipalities another $1 billion over twenty years.[74] During a special session in October and November 2011, legislators approved her 113-page package, which Chafee signed into law on November 18.[75] The new law protected existing benefit levels but reduced some future pay-outs. It temporarily suspended retirees' annual cost-of-living allowances (COLAs), raised minimum retirement ages, and launched a new 401(k)-style defined contribution retirement plan for current employees.[76]

Bond rating agencies praised the new law. Fitch Ratings declared: "The reform is unusually expansive. Specifically, it changes the benefits available to currently vested employees as well as current retirees going forward. The sweeping nature of the reform may inspire similar efforts in other states grappling with large unfunded pension obligations."[77]

Time magazine featured Raimondo in a story titled "The Little State That Could." It declared that this was not a "fix" like previous pension reforms "with nods, winks, phony accounting and fingers crossed. But fix as in repair, cure, or mend." *Time* said the new law showed "that difficult, self-sacrificing decisions are still possible . . . . Change hurts, but it can be done. Ask Raimondo."[78]

Public employee unions, which had sometimes defended perpetrators of past pension abuses, were less sanguine. J. Michael Downey, president of AFSCME Council 94, complained: "Our elected officials have unwisely chosen to steal the retirement security of Rhode Island's public employees." Philip M. Keefe, president of the State Employees International Union Local 580, said his members were bitterly disappointed that they had been "targeted again, again, and again." He warned: "This injustice leveled against the hard-working members of Council 94 and all public employees in our state will not be forgiven or forgotten."[79]

When six union groups sued the state, Superior Court Judge Sarah Taft-Carter ordered the parties into confidential negotiations. A year of tightly guarded talks produced a tentative settlement that went to a vote of active members and retirees. While five union groups approved the deal, local police officers rejected it. The pension dispute is scheduled for trial in September 2014,[80] and no one knows what the outcome will be.

But Raimondo says separation of powers helped in launching pension reform. She notes that despite actuarial warnings as early as 1974 the boards responsible had made things worse. "Prior to 2004 and the Separation of Powers Amendment," she writes, "key decisions were made by various government boards and commissions against the advice of actuarial experts. Each time these actuarial techniques caused a reduction in taxpayer and employer contributions to the pension plan and increased its unfunded liability."

In 2006, during his last year as general treasurer, Paul J. Tavares helped reconfigure five financial boards to comply with the Separation of Powers Amendment. All were moved into the office of the general treasurer.[81] Five years later, the Retirement Board and the State Investment Commission played crucial roles in effectively shaping overdue pension reforms. "Separation of powers," Raimondo says, "allowed the executive and legislative branches of government to work as contemplated by our founding fathers toward a common solution that made the retirement system stronger for public employees, retirees and taxpayers."[82]

Transparency matters

Citizens need clear signage to navigate the new infrastructure set up under separation of powers. For signs along the way, they need public access to government meetings, documents, regulations, and laws. Rhode Island took a giant step toward transparency in 2012. The General Assembly enacted historic amendments to the state's Access to Public Records Law.[83] In a departure from his practice as a captain in the Pawtucket police department and House majority whip in 1998,[84] Atty. Gen. Peter Kilmartin supported legislation that speeds the release of government records, including detailed arrest logs.[85] New sections improved the process for educating public officials and doubled penalties for public officials who violate the law.

Possibly most important, the new law contained a "balancing test" that open-government advocates had sought since 1997.[86] Under the state's Watergate-era Access to Public Records Law, documents that were "identifiable to an individual" could not be disclosed. The new law followed the federal Freedom of Information Act in "balancing" the public's right to know against a "clearly unwarranted invasion of personal privacy." Backers included the ACLU, the League of Women Voters, the Rhode Island Press Association, the New England First Amendment Coalition, and Common Cause, whose executive director John Marion called the balancing test "a huge leap forward."[87]

Lobbyist reporting has also improved significantly in recent years. Secretary of State A. Ralph Mollis publishes an online annual report that runs nearly three thousand pages and contains printouts from lobbyist reports filed during the previous year. It also holds the annual reports of lobbying firms that report paying "anything of value" over $250 to state decision-makers. The *Providence Journal* reports these payments each January.

While lobbyists still find ways to ingratiate themselves with decision-makers, more stringent reporting and the Ethics Commission's renewed gift rule may have curbed influence-peddling. Lobbyist Robert Goldberg quipped to a reporter: "The public perception or the myth is that we're always all out drinking every night. I wish it were true. In my dreams," he said. "They've changed the rules such that the socializing is all but over. If anybody's buying a round of drinks, it's the legislators. We can't."[88]

GOVERNORS, LEGISLATORS, AND JUDGES UNDERCUT MERIT SELECTION

Voters approved the 1994 Judicial Selection Amendment — merit selection of all Rhode Island judges — by a margin of 211,394 to 91,294, just under seventy per cent. But from the beginning, governors and legislative leaders sought to disable the new process. In a fuller analysis than I can provide here, John Marion explained how the political branches have undermined the merit selection "both by neglect and deliberate attempts to circumvent the system."[89]

Tracy Breton, a member of the *Providence Journal* team that won a Pulitzer Prize for the 1993 series "The Making of an Empire," recently confirmed that view. "I don't see that there's really any less political influence that goes into selecting the judges," she told Rhode Island Public Radio reporter Ian Donnis. "So while there's this merit selection thing and the public is allowed to come in and ask questions and see this in this very sort of transparent way, I don't think the system has changed at all."[90]

Governors and legislative leaders have routinely appointed lobbyists and trusted associates to the Judicial Nominating Commission. Gov. Bruce Sundlun appointed top-earning State House lobbyist Peter J. McGinn in 1994. Other lobbyists with large stakes in legislative outcomes followed: former Sen. David P. Kerins,[91] Richard M. McAuliffe Jr., and D. Faye Sanders.[92] Speaker John Harwood put his neighbor Sharon Burgess on the panel in 1994, and she served nearly four years beyond her four-year term limit.[93] Speaker William J. Murphy named his law partner, Norman L. Landroche Jr., and Gov. Donald Carcieri appointed his former chief of staff, Jeffrey Grybowski.[94] These appointments were legal but gave an unmistakeable impression of insider influence. Lobbyist Rick McAuliffe assured me that although he makes a substantial income from lobbying, he had never been contacted by anyone in the General Assembly regarding any candidate for judicial nomination.[95]

A key element of merit selection required the governor to appoint each judicial nominee within twenty-one days of receiving the list.[96] That time limit aimed to prevent governors from waiting until the end of a legislative session when judgeships became high-value chits to trade with legislative leaders. Gov. Lincoln Almond occasionally missed his deadlines, but *Providence Journal* judicial reporter Katie Mulvaney noted that Gov. Donald Carcieri "was notoriously late in nominating judges, sometimes leaving openings lingering for a year."[97] Roger Williams Law Professor Michael Yelnosky, a close observer of the process through fifteen years since he chaired the Common Cause judicial reform committee, added: "This is not an ambiguous statute. The more unfilled positions he has, the more deals the governor can cut."

The model developed by the American Judicature Society was widely discussed during passage of the bill and constitutional amendment in 1994. The law required that the Judicial Nominating Commission present to the governor "not less than three and not more than five highly qualified persons for each vacancy."[98] Governors Almond and Carcieri understood this "short list" as essential to the merit selection model, but both chafed under it.

In 2007, Carcieri proposed legislation that would let a governor consider all nominees for vacancies on the same court during the previous three years.[99] Legislators of both parties rushed to oblige him and raised the three-year "lookback window" to five years. Democrats and Republicans together demolished the cornerstone of judicial merit selection: short lists of three to five "highly qualified" nominees for each judicial vacancy. By multiplying the number of candidates for each vacancy, Carcieri and legislative leaders restored the kinds of backstage candidate swapping that had been routine before the Supreme Court patronage scandal of 1993.[100] The change became law in 2007 and has been reenacted each year since then.[101]

This multi-pronged attack on merit selection also sabotaged prohibitions against revolving door jobs. The bans, imposed by the Ethics Commission in

1991 and the General Assembly in 1992, were upheld by the Supreme Court in 1993.[102] With the revolving door locked, legislative leaders could no longer move their favored supporters, attorneys, and family members directly into judgeships. So the General Assembly began creating "magistrates," who wore judicial robes, exercised judicial powers, and took home judicial salaries. But magistrates were appointed by the chief judges of the various courts and were not vetted by the Judicial Nominating Commission. In 1994, when voters approved merit selection for all state judges, there were five "masters" in the entire judicial branch. Renamed "magistrates," their number swelled to twenty-one by 2012.

Although hard to prove, it appears that trading magistrates for judicial budget items has become commonplace. Among the newly minted magistrates were: Patricia Lynch Harwood, named while her husband, John B. Harwood, was speaker of the House;[103] Mary E. McCaffrey, chosen as magistrate and later elevated to a District Court judgeship while her brother chaired the Senate Judiciary Committee;[104] Christine S. Jabour, named while her husband chaired the Judicial Nominating Commission,[105] Colleen M. Hastings, assistant legal counsel to Sen. Majority Leader M. Teresa Paiva Weed;[106] William R. Guglietta, chief legal counsel to House Majority Leader Gordon D. Fox,[107] John J. Flynn, legal counsel to Speaker Gordon Fox;[108] Patrick T. Burke, deputy assistant to Speaker William J. Murphy;[109] former Senators R. David Cruise,[110] John F. McBurney III,[111] and Charles J. Levesque.[112] Former Senate President Joseph A. Montalbano also became a magistrate and then a Superior Court judge.[113] Once safely parked in ten-year magistrate terms, insiders could wait out the Revolving Door Law, establish judicial résumés, and apply for permanent judgeships.

Christine Lopes, who followed me as director of Common Cause Rhode Island, criticized the appointment of William Guglietta as chief magistrate of the Traffic Tribunal — with authority to appoint other magistrates — saying it perpetuated "a perception by the public that things are fixed."[114] John Marion, who succeeded Lopes in 2008, compares the process to a "secret bazaar" where leaders barter behind closed doors over the budget, magistrates, judges, and other delights.[115]

Keven A. McKenna, who chaired the 1986 Constitutional Convention, frequently blasts what he calls "unholy alliances between the judicial branch and the General Assembly" that violate separation of powers. "The power of appointing judges belongs only to the president or the governor," McKenna writes. "Both the state and federal constitutions prohibit the judiciary and the legislature from making appointments to executive branch offices or to appoint judges."[116]

In 2001 and 2002, Charlestown Sen. Donna M. Walsh proposed legislation that would have required all magistrates to "be appointed in the same manner" as judges were appointed: through the Judicial Nominating Commission.[117] In

2002, Walsh found herself gerrymandered out of her Senate seat.[118] In 2006, she ran for a House seat and won. She again began promoting an open process for public scrutiny and comment before the appointment of magistrates. Year after year, Walsh's bills were buried in committee but served as a reminder that people of conscience were troubled by the continuing use of magistrate positions as rewards for loyal service.[119] In 2014, she also introduced a related bill that would require members of the Judicial Nominating Commission to be insulated from politics and lobbying, as members of the Ethics Commission are.[120] Both bills were "held for further study" by the House Judiciary Committee.

REDISTRICTING REQUIRES A NEW MODEL

Of all the struggles citizens waged to make Rhode Island's government open and accountable to the people, redistricting delivered the least tangible results. Through four successive rounds of redistricting in 1982, 1992, 2002, and 2012, reformers advocated an independent process that would serve communities rather than incumbent legislators. Neither constitutional amendments nor genuine reforms were enacted, and legislative abuses carried the day.[121] New computer technology makes it exponentially easier each decade for legislative leaders to draw districts that protect their allies and eliminate their enemies.

Federal lawsuits filed in 2002 ended in a negotiated settlement and the redrawing of Senate districts around Providence.[122] But five East Bay towns that sued in Superior Court over blatant factional gerrymandering were rebuffed. Ironically, Sen. President William Irons prevailed in Superior Court[123] only weeks before scandal engulfed him. The Rhode Island Supreme Court later upheld gerrymanders that shaped the East Bay district maps for a generation after Irons left the Senate in disgrace.[124]

Gerrymandering has become the rule rather than the exception in many states. Before state elections in 2010, the Republican State Leadership Committee — a 527 group that took corporate money from the U.S. Chamber of Commerce, American Crossroads, Blue Cross/Blue Shield, AstraZenica, Verizon, AT&T, Wal-Mart, and other familiar brands[125] — invested $30 million in state legislative races "to erect a Republican firewall through the redistricting process."[126] The venture paid off with new GOP majorities in seven key state legislatures. In 2012, those majorities gerrymandered both state legislative and Congressional districts.

Cleverly drawn maps produced wildly disproportionate partisan gains. Analyst Sam Wang noted that in those seven states where new Republican majorities redrew congressional districts, the GOP won 16.7 million votes to the Democrats' 16.4 million. But because Republicans had packed supermajorities of Democrats into a small number of districts, the gerrymandered districts sent more than twice as many Republicans to Congress: 73 to 34. In congressional races nationwide, Democrats won 1.4 million votes more than their Republican opponents, but partisan gerrymandering allowed the GOP to control the U.S. House of Representatives by a margin of 234 to 201. Wang notes that this is only the second such reversal since World War II.[127] These GOP gerrymanders could shape American politics and policy until the next redistricting in 2022.

In 2008, Common Cause California sponsored the successful Proposition 11, which established an independent Citizens Redistricting Commission. Voters submit their résumés, which state auditors screen for skills, impartiality, and diversity. Random selections produce a pool of sixty potential commissioners. Auditors then randomly pick a balanced panel of Democrats, Republicans, and Independents. The fourteen-member panel is required by law to follow eight criteria in ranked order. The process must be "incumbent-blind," taking no notice of where officeholders or candidates live.[128] Two years later, 61.3 percent of California voters approved Proposition 20, which expanded the commission's remapping authority to Congressional districts.[129] The California model offers an obvious improvement after Rhode Island's long history of gerrymandering for factional or partisan advantage. Past experience suggests that nothing short of a new constitutional convention will be able to place such an amendment on the ballot.

Making government good

In 1988, when I failed as a copy editor at the *Providence Journal,* the newspaper routinely sent teams of investigative reporters to dig into public contracts, departmental budgets, and campaign contribution reports. The paper won its fourth Pulitzer Prize for its 1993 exposé of patronage at the Rhode Island Supreme Court.[130] With the backing of publisher Steve Hamblett, the *Journal* revealed secrets that aroused public rage and sparked reform.

But the *Journal*'s 1996 sale to the Texas-based Belo Corporation coincided with a relentless rise in Internet competition for classified and display advertising — a digital force that hollowed out newspapers everywhere. The *Journal's* Sunday circulation plummeted from a high of 262,000 to 104,000 at the end of 2013. Financial pressure forced the closing of regional bureaus and cutbacks in coverage. The paper laid off or bought out many veteran journalists and is up for sale again.[131]

A colonial publisher understood the integral connection between information and citizenship. Benjamin Franklin was eighty-one when he and other delegates at the Constitutional Convention of 1787 drafted the U.S. Constitution. One delegate told how, as he and Franklin left Independence Hall, a woman asked: "Well, Doctor, what have we got — a republic or a monarchy?"

"A republic," Franklin answered, "if you can keep it."[132]

From Franklin's printing press to the Internet that speeds complex data to laptops, our challenge remains essentially the same. How can we protect and defend a government that empowers us to govern ourselves? How can we make government good for us all, not just the privileged few?

I hope this narrative from Rhode Island's latest "era of reform" demystifies the workings of government for ordinary people who sometimes feel so disgusted that they leave politics to the mercenaries. People who care about public policy and civic order must join forces in a dedicated effort to make government good. This is a doable and worthy goal, but it requires constant vigilance and perseverance — like maintaining the homes and infrastructures that make our lives secure.

One day a group of us met at the governor's office in a little inner room with no gold letters on the door, only plain frosted glass. Gov. Don Carcieri, two of his top lawyers, and a couple of us from Common Cause huddled around a small table.

Suddenly, from the hallway, came strumming on a twelve-string guitar. Gentle voices began to sing, "This land is your land, this land is my land. . . ." They sang Woody Guthrie's Depression-era tune with new verses about our state budget. From inside, we could hear every word. I had trouble concentrating, and I knew others did, too.

Like ocean waves, the singing surged and subsided until our meeting ended. We left through the governor's formal office, through the receptionist's office, and through the magnificent State Room. Once in the marble hallway, I circled back toward the singers.

Outside the governor's unmarked door were Nancy Gewirtz, who had founded the Poverty Institute at Rhode Island College, and Rick Harris, who led the state chapter of the National Association of Social Workers. With them were families who would be harmed by severe cuts in the state budget. Nancy Gewirtz's face was gaunt as she neared the end of a long struggle with cancer, but she sang her heart out. Together, they gave voice to thousands who have no high-paid lobbyists.[133]

"We were with the governor right inside that door," I said softly. "It may feel like nobody's listening. But I want you to know we could hear every word."

Our republic needs constant repair to keep government from morphing into a gilded court. We all need to make ourselves at home in the People's House, to understand its workings and learn its ways. Singing together will sustain our hope far better than grumbling alone.

Abbreviations

ACLU	American Civil Liberties Union
AFL-CIO	Labor Council, often as Executive Council
AFSCME	American Federation of State, County and Municipal Employees
AFT	American Federation of Teachers
AP	Associated Press
CCRI	Common Cause Rhode Island
	(commonly Community College RI)
CHisPA	Center for Hispanic Policy and Advocacy
CRMC	Coastal Resources Management Council
DEM	Department of Environmental Management
DBR	Department of Business Regulation
DOA	Department of Administration
DOC	Department of Corrections
DOT	Department of Transportation
ECRI	Environment Council of Rhode Island
FOIA	Freedom of Information Act
FRC	Fair Redistricting Coalition
HJrnl	House Journal. See SJrnl
HPW	H. Philip West Jr.
JNC	Judicial Nominating Commission
LWV	League of Women Voters
NBC	Narragansett Bay Commission
NCSL	National Conference of State Legislatures
NDN	Newport Daily News
NEA	National Education Association
NYT	New York Times
OCG	Operation Clean Government
OCS	Operation Clean Sweep (predecessor of Operation Clean Government)
PETF	Providence Ethics Task Force
PJ	Providence Journal
PL	Public Law (with year of enactment)
PT	Pawtucket Times
RIBOE	Board of Elections
RIEC	Rhode Island Ethics Commission
RIGL	Rhode Island General Laws
RIPEC	Rhode Island Public Expenditure Council
RIPS	Rhode Island Publications Society
RN!	RIght Now! Coalition
RWU	Roger Williams University
SJrnl	Senate Journal. See HJrnl.
URI	University of Rhode Island
USTF	Underground Storage Tank Fund

Notes

AUTHOR'S NOTES · pages ix–xiii

1   W. Zachary Malinowski, "State of the MOB," *PJ*, 28 Jan. 2007: A-01.
2   http://webserver.rilin.state.ri.us/RhodeIslandHistory/chapt9.html.
3   Patrick T. Conley, "Constitution Day Lecture," 16 Sep. 2011, and email 12 Nov. 2013.
4   The BGA is a citizens' watchdog organization with a 90-year history of fighting cor-
    ruption in Chicago. http://www.bettergov.org/about/history.aspx#2009_to_present.
5   The 2002, 2008, and 2013 BGA Alper Integrity Index reports are online:
    http://www.bettergov.org/2008_bga-alper_integrity_index_/
    http://www.bettergov.org/action_policy/bgaalper_services_integrity_index_2013.
    aspx.
6   U.S. Department of State, Bureau of Educational and Cultural Affairs, International
    Visitor Program, 27 Jul. 2001.

1 | BREAKING GROUND (1986) · pages 1–11

1   A rigid process for amending the Rhode Island Constitution had long stifled reform.
    During a limited convention in 1973, Patrick T. Conley proposed and delegates
    recommended a new Article XIV on "Constitutional Amendments and Revisions."
    Section 1 greatly simplified the process of amending the constitution: instead of
    requiring passage by two sessions of the General Assembly with an intervening
    election plus a ⅗ vote of the electors, the new process required passage by majori-
    ties in the House and Senate, followed by a simple majority of the voters. Section 2
    simplified the process of convening a constitutional convention. At least once every
    decade voters would answer a statewide ballot question: "Shall there be a conven-
    tion to amend or revise the constitution?" Voters approved the new Article XIV. In
    November 1984, voters approved a convention; in 1985, they elected delegates to a
    convention that met in the spring of 1986 and recommended questions for the 1986
    statewide ballot.
2   Robert Kramer, "Bevilacqua frequented motel linked to mob crime," *Providence
    Journal*, 12 Apr. 1985: A-01. (Hereafter cited as *PJ*.) The women later named as
    meeting Bevilacqua in the motel denied any involvement with Bevilacqua. See
    M. Charles Bakst, "Civiletti cites alleged adultery of Bevilacqua and court aide," *PJ*,
    5 Mar. 1986: A-01. Brian C. Jones, "Bevilacqua notified of formal charges," *PJ*, 19 Apr.
    1985: A-01 (Story contains timeline).
3   Board members include the Director of Administration, the General Treasurer, the
    Director of Business Regulation, and four public members appointed by the gover-
    nor with the advice and consent of the Senate.
4   Thomas S. Mulligan, Katherine Gregg, and Elliot G. Jaspin, "Police say Pari took
    woman, 2 girls to Fla, and RIHMFC paid bills," *PJ*, 18 May 1985: A-01 (Story contains
    timeline). Thomas S. Mulligan, "RIHMFC cached $2.9 million for mortgage favors,"
    PJ, 3 Jul. 1985: A-01.
5   "565 qualify to run for convention delegates," Candidate lists in regional editions of
    PJ, 2 Oct. 1985: C-10.
6   State constitutions have various thresholds for approving amendments, and some
    require a second vote after an intervening election. RI simplified that process in

1973. See fn1. The state has only two paths for placing amendments on the ballot: (1) resolutions passed by both the House of Representatives and the Senate; (2) resolutions approved by a majority of delegates to a duly convened constitutional convention. Article XIV, Sections 1 and 2. See Patrick T. Conley, *Rhode Island in Rhetoric and Reflection: Public Addresses and Essays* (East Providence: RIPS, 2002), 196–203.

7   M. Charles Bakst, "Licht to ask Constitutional Convention for policy on public financing of campaigns," *PJ*, 13 Nov. 1985: A-03.

8   John Kiffney, "DiPrete recommends Sapinsley elected chairman of Constitutional Convention," *PJ*, 21 Nov. 1985: C-03; John Kiffney, "Convention delegates get acquainted at State House party," *PJ*, 22 Nov. 1985: A-12.

9   John Kiffney, "Delegates elect McKenna to chair as Constitutional Convention opens," *PJ*, 7 Jan. 1986: A-01; John Kiffney, "McKenna: a maverick long on experience," *PJ*, 8 Jan. 1986: A-13.

10   "McKenna names heads of convention panels," *PJ*, 29 Jan. 1986: A-18.

11   M. Charles Bakst and Thomas E. Walsh, "House gets resolution to impeach Bevilacqua," *PJ*, 9 Jan. 1986. House Majority Whip Thomas A. Lamb and House Minority Leader Bradford Gorham filed the resolution.

12   M. Charles Bakst and Scott MacKay, "Witness testifies Bevilacqua vowed to keep up his ties with crime figures," *PJ*, 16 May 1986: A-01.

13   M. Charles Bakst and Thomas E. Walsh, "Contractor for court tells of free work at Bevilacqua homes," *PJ*, 21 May 1986: A-01; Thomas E. Walsh and M. Charles Bakst, "Official says electrical contractor that did Bevilacqua favors has gotten all courts' work," *PJ*, 22 May 1986: A-01.

14   M. Charles Bakst and Thomas E. Walsh, "House panel told of moves to veil Bevilacqua's use of motel rooms," *PJ*, 28 May 1986: A-01.

15   Personal interview, Jeffrey J. Teitz, 27 Dec. 2006.

16   M. Charles Bakst and Thomas E. Walsh, "Day of Bevilacqua's resignation was a day filled with high drama," *PJ*, 29 May 1986: A-19.

17   John Kiffney, "Convention approves new plan for nominating state judges," *PJ*, 5 Jun. 1986: A-14.

18   John Kiffney, "Convention panel, by 1 vote, backs proposal to let voters enact own laws — with limits," *PJ*, 9 Apr. 1986: A-03.

19   Hawaii Constitution, Article XIV, Code of Ethics, 1978.

20   The final text changed only a few words from the draft of May 22, 1986. Question 6 proposed to add the following to the Rhode Island Constitution: Article III.7. Ethical Conduct. The people of the State of Rhode Island believe that public officials and employees must adhere to the highest standards of ethical conduct, respect the public trust and the rights of all persons, be open, accountable and responsive, avoid the appearance of impropriety, and not use their position for private gain or advantage. Such persons shall hold their positions during good behavior.
Article III.8. Ethics Commission. Code of ethics. The general assembly shall establish an independent non-partisan ethics commission which shall adopt a code of ethics including, but not limited to, provisions on conflicts of interest, confidential information, use of position, contracts with government agencies and financial disclosure. All elected and appointed officials and employees of state and local government, of boards, commissions and agencies shall be subject to the code of ethics. The ethics commission shall have the authority to investigate violations of the code of ethics and to impose penalties, as provided by law; and the commission shall have the power to remove from office officials who are not subject to impeachment.

21   1986 Rhode Island Constitutional Convention, Question 6 proposed to amend the

Rhode Island Constitution by adding the following: Article IV.10. Limitations on campaign contributions — Public financing of campaign expenditures of general officers. The general assembly shall adopt limitations on all contributions to candidates for election to state and local office in any primary, general or special election and shall provide for the adoption of a plan of voluntary public financing and limitations on total campaign expenditures of campaigns for governor and such other general officers as the general assembly shall specify.

22   Question 4 and Question 3, respectively.

23   Questions 10, 8, and 9, respectively.

24   In addition to drafting the proposed constitutional amendments, the Constitutional Convention grouped three separate questions under Question 6: (1) Shall more specific impeachment standards be established? (2) Shall an ethics commission be established with authority to adopt a code of ethics and to discipline or remove public officials and employees in violation of that code? (3) Shall the General Assembly adopt limits on campaign contributions and shall the General Assembly enact a voluntary system of public campaign financing coupled with limitations on total campaign spending by participating candidates?

25   Richard C. Dujardin, "Debate over proposed abortion amendment," *PJ*, 18 Sep. 1986: A-01. 1986 Constitutional Convention Question 14: To the extent permitted by the U.S. Constitution, shall all persons, including their unborn offspring, without regard to age, health, function, or condition of dependency, be endowed with an inalienable and paramount right to life; and to the extent permitted by the U.S. Constitution, shall abortion be prohibited, except that justified medical procedures to prevent the death of a pregnant woman be permitted: Shall the use of government to fund abortions be prohibited by the Constitution?

26   John Kiffney, "Doctors: Groups mobilizing opposition," *PJ*, 18 Sep. 1986: A-01.

27   John Kiffney, "Stay away from abortion issue, Chafee tells convention delegates," *PJ*, 11 Feb. 1986: A-13; M. Charles Bakst, "DiPrete advises convention to avoid fight over abortion issue," *PJ*, 15 Feb. 1986: A-01.

28   John Kiffney, "Drive to publicize amendments begins," *PJ*, 6 Sep. 1986: A-12.

29   Peter Lacouture, "A vote for a standard of ethics," *PJ*, 26 Oct. 1986: A-19.

30   "Chafee urges rejection of Constitutional Amendments," *PJ*, 15 Sep. 1986: A-03. Historian Patrick T. Conley notes that Chafee used similar arguments in urging voters to reject recommendations of the Constitutional Convention that stretched from 1964–69.

31   John Kiffney, "DiPrete announces his support for eight amendments on the ballot," *PJ*, 25 Oct. 1986: A-04.

32   Editorial, "Flawed ethics amendment: Vote 'No' on 6," *PJ*, 28 Oct. 1986: A-20.

33   Delegate Robert Milette, 1986 Rhode Island Constitutional Convention, Transcript of the Constitutional Convention Committee on Ethics, 22 May 1986, 60.

34   87-S 1108, "An Act Relating to Ethics in Government," by Sen. Victoria Lederberg. M. Charles Bakst, "Bill would give conflict panel broader powers to enforce laws," *PJ*, 6 Mar. 1987.

35   87-H 6714, "An Act Relating to the Rhode Island Code of Ethics in Government," by Reps. Lamb, Teitz, Gorham, and others.

36   Katherine Gregg, "House panel OKs revised 'ethics' legislation," *PJ*, 11 Apr. 1987: A-13.

37   Rae B. Condon, "Crippling the state ethics commission," *PJ*, 24 Apr. 1987: A-22.

38   Katherine Gregg, "House approves new commission to oversee ethics," *PJ*, 7 May 1987: A-03. Five years later, the RISDIC investigation revealed that Casinelli had (1)

helped kill legislation that would have required federal insurance for Rhode Island's troubled credit unions, (2) received a loan of $250,000 from the Rhode Island Central Credit Union to buy a towing company, and (3) failed to repay $230,000 of that loan when the state closed RI Central. The *Journal* reported that Casinelli had argued against reporting loans only a week before he argued that disclosing loans only satisfied "prurient interest." See John Sullivan, "The political rise of Joseph Casinelli: A Rhode Island story," *PJ*, 10 Jan. 1993: A-01.

39   The amended text of 87-H 6714 exempted public officials from disclosing the names of "any person, business entity or other organization" owed any amount "in excess of one thousand dollars ($1,000) other than family members "within the third degree of consanguinity" or "any financial institution licensed and regulated by the state of Rhode Island or by the United States of America."

40   M. Charles Bakst, "Senate panel OKs ethics commission," *PJ*, 18 Jun. 1987: A-01.

41   Bakst.

42   Ward Pimley, "Senate sends ethics bill without debate to DiPrete," *PJ*, 20 Jun. 1987: A-11.

43   M. Charles Bakst, "DiPrete abolishes conflict commission for new ethics commission," *PJ*, 27 Jun. 1987: A-10.

44   86-H 7867, "An Act Requiring RICUL Corporate Credit Union to comply with certain requirements under General Laws 19-21-36, 44-15-2, and 19-9-11," by Rep. Francis A. Gaschen; 86-S 2506, "An Act Requiring RI Credit Union League to comply with reserving requirements, deposit tax requirements, and deposit insurance requirements," by Sen. John C. D'Amico.

45   These facts were well established in investigations that followed the RISDIC collapse on January 1, 1991. See Chapter 5, "Collapse of Credit."

46   Katherine Gregg, "Lack of vote leads conflict panel to clear assemblyman," *PJ*, 22 Jul. 1987: A-01.

2 | Governor Pay-to-Play (1988) · pages 12–24

1   Ken Mingis and Peter Lord, "A land deal in Cranston," *PJ*, 31 Jul. 1988: A-01.

2   Vincent Charles Teresa with Thomas C. Renner, *My Life in the Mafia* (Garden City, NY: Doubleday, 1973), 85, 79.

3   Dan Barry, "To the Mafia born: Young Ray Patriarca inherited empire of crime," *PJ*, 28 Jun. 1992: A-01.

4   John W. Gardner, *In Common Cause,* rev. ed. (New York: Norton, 1973), 117.

5   Rhode Island Constitution, Article III.8. The general assembly shall establish an independent non-partisan ethics commission which shall adopt a code of ethics including, but not limited to, provisions on conflicts of interest, confidential information, use of position, contracts with government agencies and financial disclosure. All elected and appointed officials and employees of state and local government, of boards, commissions and agencies shall be subject to the code of ethics. The ethics commission shall have the authority to investigate violations of the code of ethics and to impose penalties, as provided by law; and the commission shall have the power to remove from office officials who are not subject to impeachment.

6   RIGL 36-14-2 (3) "Business associate" means a person joined together with another person to achieve a common financial objective.

7   Ken Mingis, "DiPrete land deal has citizens grumbling," *PJ*, 10 Aug. 1988: A-01; Ken Mingis, "DiPrete severs tie with family-run firm," *PJ*, 12 Aug. 1988: A-01.

8   Elizabeth Abbott, "Texas Builder Moseys North," *New York Times*, 3 May 1987.

9   Ken Mingis, "DEM prodded on project involving DiPrete's son," *PJ*, 1 Sep. 1988:
     A-01.
10   Peter Lord, "Usual channels bypassed as state gives contracts to DiPrete friend's
     firm," *PJ*, 16 Oct. 1988: A-01.
11   Ann Macari Healey, "DiPrete calls story 'outrageous distortion,'" *PJ*, 17 Oct. 1988:
     A-01.
12   Editorial: "Edward D. DiPrete for governor," *PJ*, 6 Nov. 1988: B-14.
13   RIBOE, 1988 Election Results, Vote for Governor.
14   Memorandum in support of Respondent's motion to dismiss complaint 89–1, signed
     by attorneys John J. Partridge and Normand G. Benoit, 28 Jan. 1989.
15   Tracy Breton, "Judge blocks enforcement of ethics gag rule," *PJ*, 8 Mar. 1989: A-03.
16   Ethics Rhode Island, "How much should we know and when should we know it?"
     produced by CCRI and the LWVRI Education Fund with a grant from the Rhode
     Island Foundation, video from broadcast 4, 29 Nov. 1989.

3 | LOBBYING 101 (1989) · pages 25–31

1   This bill was finally enacted in 1992 as RIGL 36-14-5(m).
2   The law, as finally enacted in 1992, included a new and broader definition of family
     in RIGL 36-14-2 (1).
3   M. Charles Bakst, "Smith situation accents failure to pay lawmakers," *PJ*, 10 May
     1987: C-02.
4   Scott MacKay, "Kennedy spent $63 per vote for seat," *PJ*, 13 Oct. 1988: D-01. In
     the final primary vote count, Kennedy got 1,324 votes to 1,009 for the incumbent
     Democrat, Rep. John M. Skeffington, in House District 9, which included the cam-
     pus of Providence College, where Kennedy was a student.
5   Russell Garland, "A tangled tale of campaign finances," *PJ*, 5 Feb. 1989: B-01.
6   Garland.
7   89-H 7178, "An Act Relating to State Agencies — Registration of Voters," by Rep.
     Patrick J. Kennedy.
8   "Voting drive demonstrators meet DiPrete on his way out," 2 Jun. 1989: A-14.
9   Patrick T. Conley, "No Landless Irish Need Apply: Rhode Island's Role in the
     Framing and Fate of the Fifteenth Amendment," *Constitution Day: Reflections by
     Respected Scholars* (East Providence: RIPS, 2010), 211–33. Alexander Keyssar, *The
     Right to Vote: The Contested History of Democracy in the United States* (New York:
     Basic Books, 2000), 29.
10   Keyssar: 100-102.
11   PL 89-346, "An Act Relating to State Agencies — Registration of Voters," added the
     state agency registration in RIGL 42-6-14.

4 | A COSTLY ELECTION (1990) · pages 32–39

1   RIBOE campaign finance reports showed that in four gubernatorial races (1976,
     1978, 1980, and 1982), Joseph Garrahy and his Republican opponents spent a total
     of $3,027,184. In the next three races (1984, 1986, and 1988), Edward DiPrete and his
     Democratic opponents spent $9,702,858, an increase far greater than the rate of in-
     flation. Garrahy's expenditures for four races totaled $1,967,040. DiPrete's spending
     in three contests totaled $5,093,514, nearly 2.6 times what Garrahy had spent in four
     elections.
2   Question 6 proposed to amend the Rhode Island Constitution by adding the

following: Article IV.10. Limitations on campaign contributions. — Public financing of campaign expenditures of general officers. — The general assembly shall adopt limitations on all contributions to candidates for election to state and local office in any primary, general or special election and shall provide for the adoption of a plan of voluntary public financing and limitations on total campaign expenditures of campaigns for governor and such other general officers as the general assembly shall specify.

3   PL 87–420.

4   Russell Garland, "Common Cause urges DiPrete, Paolino to limit campaign funds," *PJ*, 8 Feb. 1990: B-05.

5   Russell Garland, "It looks like the sky's the limit in the race for governor," *PJ*, 13 Jun. 1990: A-01.

6   Scott MacKay, "Flaherty attacks rivals on campaign spending," *PJ*, 24 Jul. 1990: B-05.

7   Russell Garland, "Paolino's spending breaks R.I. record," *PJ*, 16 Aug. 1990: A-01.

8   Scott MacKay, "Would-be governors spent over $10 million on election," *PJ*, 9 Dec. 1990: A-01.

9   Russell Garland, "Call for campaign laws opens DiPrete's drive," *PJ*, 14 Sep. 1990.

10 M. Charles Bakst, "After years of controversy, DiPrete running as 'Mr. Reform,'" *PJ*, 23 Sep. 1990: D-01.

11 Sundlun: 264,411; DiPrete: 92,177. http://www.elections.ri.gov/elections/results/1990/ governor.php

12 MacKay, "Would-be governors."

13 Mike Stanton, Tracy Breton, David Herzog, and W. Zachary Malinowski, "Rhode Island on Trial, Chapter 1: Fugitive banker's dealings with state draw investigators to DiPrete's inner circle," *PJ*, 9 Aug. 1998: S-01.

14 Dean Starkman, "Joe Mollicone: A Rhode Island Life," *PJ*, 29 Dec. 1991: A-01. See also Vincent Teresa, *My Life in the Mafia*, with Thomas C. Renner (Garden City, NY: Doubleday & Company, 1973), 206.

15 Dean Starkman, "The banker is missing and the paper trail's a financial maze," *PJ*, 18 Nov. 1990: A-01.

16 Starkman, "Joe Mollicone: A Rhode Island Life."

17 "Rhode Island on Trial, Chapter 8: Easy come, easy go: Brusini's accounts of cash, and trash, bolster his hope to escape prosecution," 9 Aug. 1998: S-15.

18 John Kostrzewa, "Grand jury begins probe of Heritage; $1.2 million in deposits withdrawn," *PJ*, 14 Nov. 1990: C-01.

19 John Kostrzewa, "DiPrete closes Heritage; Examiners to sort out 'terrible mess,'" *PJ*, 19 Nov. 1990: A-01.

5 | Collapse of Credit (1991) · pages 40–54

1   Bruce Sundlun, "World War II gave me an indelible lesson in separation of church and state," *PJ*, 3 Dec. 2009.

2   Russell Garland, "Sundlun sworn in as state plunges into banking crisis," *PJ*, 2 Jan. 1991: A-01.

3   Russell Garland, "Sundlun signs broad ethics edict," *PJ*, 2 Jan. 1991: B-03.

4   Gregory Smith, "R.I. closes 45 credit unions, banks. Sundlun order freezes $1.7 billion in institutions insured by RISDIC," *PJ*, 2 Jan. 1991: A-01.

5   Dan Barry, Neil Downing and John Sullivan, "How the RISDIC time bomb was left ticking for 5 years," *PJ*, 6 Jan. 1991: A-01.

6   John Sullivan, "Dec. 13, 1985: 'The existing R.I. situation should be tolerated no lon-

ger.' A report to the attorney general predicted today's crisis 5 years ago," *PJ*, 4 Jan.
1991: A-01.

7   Robert S. Stitt and Charles O. Black, memo to Attorney General Violet: "Financial
Crisis Regarding Credit Unions and Related Financial Institutions Not Covered By
Federal Depositors' Insurance," 13 Dec. 1985.

8   Normand G. Benoit, "Memorandum: Credit Unions and Related Financial
Institutions Not Covered by Federal Depositors' Insurance," 20 Feb. 1986: 21–23. See
also Ira Chinoy, "2nd warning to DiPrete failed to curb RISDIC," *PJ*, February 10,
1991: A-01.

9   RIGL 19-1-2. In 1985, the Board of Bank Incorporation included the Director of
Business Regulation, Clifton Moore; General Treasurer Roger Begin; Attorney
General Arlene Violet; Rep. Joseph Casinelli, appointed by the Speaker; and Sen.
Albert Russo, appointed by the Senate Majority Leader. After the 2004 Separation of
Powers Amendment, the board's legislative members were replaced by members of
the public appointed by the governor with the advice and consent of the Senate.

10   Edward D. DiPrete, "Inter-Office Memo: RISDIC/Attorney General Violet," 17 Feb.
1986 (Supplement and Supplemental Appendix to *Carved in Sand: A Report on the
Collapse of the Rhode Island Share and Deposit Indemnity Corporation*, 18 Apr. 1991.)

11   Brian Dickinson, "A financial disaster that was waiting to happen," *PJ*, Jan. 4, 1991:
A-13.

12   86-H 7867, "An Act Requiring RICUL Corporate Credit Union to comply with
certain requirements under General Laws 19-21-36, 44-15-2, and 19-9-11," by Rep.
Francis A. Gaschen; 86-S 2506, "An Act Requiring RI Credit Union League to comply with reserving requirements, deposit tax requirements, and deposit insurance
requirements," by Sen. John C. D'Amico.

13   Transcript of House Finance Committee meeting held on 12 May 1986: 75–77.

14   Jan Brogan, "Bianchini denies conflict of interest in hearing," *PJ*, 31 May 1986:
A-05. See also testimony of former Rep. Elizabeth Morancy before the RISDIC
Investigating Commission, 24 Jun. 1992.

15   Katherine Gregg, "Lack of vote leads conflict panel to clear assemblyman," *PJ*, 22 Jul.
1987: A-01.

16   Katherine Gregg, "DiPrete names new ethics unit," *PJ*, 25 Jul. 1987: A-01.

17   Associated Press, "Ethics Commission member was credit union president;
Common Cause demands resignation," *Westerly Sun*, 16 Jan. 1991: A-1.

18   Scott MacKay, "House deputy whip resigns for opposing RISDIC extinction," *PJ*,
8 Jan. 1991: A-07.

19   Christopher Beall, "3,000 seek answers from E. Providence Credit Union board," *PJ*,
8 Jan. 1991: A-01.

20   Christopher Beall, "Sen. fought RISDIC bill while in post at credit union," *PJ*, 29 Jan.
1991: A-01.

21   Thomas E. Pulkkinen and Eric S. Rosengren, "Lessons from the Rhode Island Banking Crisis," *New England Economic Review*, May/June 1993. "From its very creation,
RISDIC was susceptible to failure caused by exposure at its insured institutions.
While the insurer appeared stable for almost two decades, several of its members
were sufficiently large and weak to have caused its failure during that period. That
RISDIC did not fail earlier was attributable to its political clout and its ability to
mask severe financial difficulties within its underlying membership."

22   Dan Barry and John Sullivan, "RISDIC probes lack clear goal; Critics wonder who's
in charge," *PJ*, 13 Jan. 1991: A-01.

23   H. Philip West (hereafter HPW), CCRI letter to Gov. Bruce G. Sundlun, 11 Jan. 1991.

24   Gregory Smith, "Heavyweight prosecutors, panel to probe RISDIC crisis," *PJ*, Feb. 15, 1991.

25   Vartan Gregorian, et al., *Carved in Sand: A Report on the Collapse of the Rhode Island Share and Deposit Indemnity Corporation*, 14 Mar. 1991.

26   Mike Stanton and Gregory Smith, "RISDIC 'Carved in Sand;' Politicians share blame in credit union report," *PJ*, 14 Mar. 1991: A-1.

27   Gregory Smith, "Gregorian report spreads blame for bank crisis across government," *PJ*, 15 Mar. 1991: A-01.

28   Ira Chinoy, "RISDIC became steady donor to DiPrete campaigns," 17 Mar. 1991: A-01.

29   Dan Barry and John Sullivan, "Rare hero of the RISDIC fiasco fought the good fight to the end," *PJ*, April 19, 1991: A-01.

30   Christopher Beall, "Credit union on verge of rescue; Loan swap a key to East Providence plan," *PJ*, June 1, 1991.

31   Neil Downing, "Individual payouts from closed institutions: Amounts fixed through three-step process," *PJ*, June 2, 1991.

32   John Kostrzewa and Jeffrey L. Hiday, "Sundlun offers payback plan; New agency would take over ailing banks, credit unions," *PJ*, 7 Jan. 1991: A-01; Neil Downing, "Proposed measure gives DEPCO wide powers, much independence," *PJ*, 11 Jan. 1991: A-11.

33   Jeffrey L. Hiday and Scott MacKay, "1,000 noisy depositors rally against DEPCO," *PJ*, 27 Apr. 1991: A-01.

34   Dan Barry and John Sullivan, "The sound and fury of depositors made protests pay off; As crowds became more volatile, Sundlun had to act," *PJ*, 15 Sep. 1991: A-01.

35   Steven Krasner and Deborah Barfield, "Credit union protesters halt traffic; 7 arrested," *PJ*, 27 Aug. 1991: A-01.

6 | Dashed Hopes (1991) · pages 55–66

1   91-H 6750, "An Act Relating to Campaign Finance Reform," by Rep. Jeffrey Teitz.

2   91-H 6206, "An Act Relating to the Rhode Island Ethics Commission — Finding of Probable Cause," by Rep. Francis Gaschen; 91-S 0506 (same title), by Sen. John Lyle.

3   Judy Rakowsky, "Pettine scraps ethics gag rule," *PJ*, 15 Jul. 1989: D-08.

4   91-H 6318, "An Act Relating to the Rhode Island Ethics Commission — Adjudicative Hearings," by Rep. Mark Heffner; 91-S 0422 (same title), by Sen. David Carlin.

5   91-S 0375, "An Act Relating to Code of Ethics — Members of the General Assembly," by Sens. York, McStay, Gray, Perry, and Lenihan. Rep. Nancy Benoit filed an identical House bill: 91-H 5935. The text proposed to add a single sentence in the Prohibited Activities section of the Ethics Code. The new 36-14-5 (o) would read: "No member of the general assembly shall seek or accept other state employment, not held at the time of the member's election, while serving in the general assembly and for a period of one (1) year after leaving legislative office."

6   Scott MacKay, "Common Cause airs ethics plan for state," *PJ*, 7 Feb. 1991.

7   Doane Hulick and Katherine Gregg, "Court won't let Sundlun disclose pension payments," *PJ*, 6 Mar. 1991: A-01.

8   Katherine Gregg, "Pensions: Double-dipping, retirees as 'consultants," *PJ*, 30 May 1991: A-01. Gregg and Landis provided additional details in emails, 13 and 14 Jan. 2013.

9   Katherine Gregg, "Set for Life — Special Deals; How the state took care of its own," *PJ*, 31 Mar. 1991: A-01.

10   Katherine Gregg, "Set for Life — Paying the Tab 1985: Ex-URI athletes win credit for part-time campus jobs," *PJ*, 1 Apr. 1991: A-06.

11   Katherine Gregg, "Set for Life — The Secrecy — Master of the system's windfalls; Former Senate adviser, 50, retired last year with 3 pensions," *PJ*, 2 Apr. 1991: A-04.

12   Katherine Gregg, "Set for Life — Paying the tab; Pensions may be the state's next financial time bomb," *PJ*, 1 Apr. 1991: A-01.

13   91-H 6052 "An Act Relating to Access to Public Records," Rep. Jeffrey Teitz and 91-S 1079, (same title), by Sen. John Bevilacqua, with similar provisions, became the primary vehicles. With minor amendments, Bevilacqua's bill passed both chambers and became Public Law (hereafter PL) 91-208, 17 Jun. 1991.

14   *Rhode Island Federation of Teachers, et al. v. Bruce Sundlun and Intervenors Company and Katherine Gregg*, 91-1697, 24 Apr. 1991: 19.

15   Scott Freeman, "Sarault kicks off campaign for 3rd term; Motto: 'Progress, not politics,'" *PJ*, 4 Jun. 1991: B-01.

16   Judy Rakowsky, "Pawtucket's Sarault faces extortion, mail fraud charges; Mayor arrested in his office by FBI agents," *PJ*, 13 Jun. 1991: A-01.

17   Interview with James P. McStay, 2 Oct. 2009; interview of Weygand by URI students Karena Ruggiero, Robert Rock, Michael Duarte, and Matthew Chudy, Nov. 2012.

18   Rakowsky, "Pawtucket's Sarault faces extortion."

19   Scott Freeman and W. Zachary Malinowski, "Sarault admits he was head of extortion ring from City Hall," *PJ*, 15 Nov. 1991: A-01; Lynn Arditi, "The spreading stain of corruption in Pawtucket," *PJ*, 1 Dec. 1991: A-01; Russell Garland, "Judge rejects union's bid to bar pension data release," *PJ*, 24 Apr. 1991: A-01; Doane Hulick, "High court rejects plea to seal pension records," *PJ*, 18 May 1991: A-01.

20   Garland, "Judge rejects union's bid;" Hulick, "High court rejects plea."

21   Katherine Gregg, "Sundlun OKs disclosing all pension data," *PJ*, 28 May 1991: A-01.

22   Katherine Gregg, "Bills to open some pension records advance," *PJ*, 4 May 1991: A-03.

23   PL 91-208, 91-S 1079 Sub B, "An Act Relating to Access to Public Records," 17 Jun. 1991.

24   PL 91-177, 91-H 6206 Sub A, "An Act Relating to the Ethics Commission — Finding of Probable Cause," by Rep. Francis Gaschen; 91-S 0506, (same title), by Sen. John Lyle; and 91-S 645 Sub A, (same title), by Sen. Thomas Lynch, 17 Jun. 1991. With enactment, RIGL 36-14-12 (c) established a time limit for its preliminary investigations. The commission must find probable cause or dismiss a complaint within 180 days after the filing, but it allows two 60-day extensions "for good cause shown." up to another 120 days. The Supreme Court would later interpret this section in a way that required the dismissal of significant cases. See 98-10 M.P., *Clarke v. Morsilli*, 14 Jul. 1998.

25   91-H 6750 by Rep. Jeffrey Teitz, as passed by the House, would have prohibited personal use of campaign funds and testimonial proceeds, required that all loans be reported on campaign finance reports as contributions until they were repaid, lowered the threshold for reporting campaign contributions from $200 to $100, closed a loophole that allowed who contributed to their campaigns to escape reporting, barred wealthy contributors from evading the annual contribution limit by giving in the names of their spouse and minor children, ended the laundering of contributions above the legal limit ($2,000) through political parties, prevented contributors from giving more than $25,000 annually to candidates, provided free cable television time for candidates who agree to limit spending under the matching-funds program.

26   Russell Garland, "House panel OKs stricter campaign finance limits," *PJ*, 31 May
     1991: B-3.

27   91-H 6206 SubA, "An Act Pertaining to the Rhode Island Ethics Commission," by
     Rep. Francis Gaschen and 91-S 645 SubB by Sen. Thomas A. Lynch. The Senate
     amended Lynch's version to make it identical to Gaschen's bill. Gov. Sundlun signed
     both the House and Senate versions into law on 17 Jun. 1991. Both required the
     Rhode Island Ethics Commission to complete its preliminary investigation within
     180 days of the filing of a complaint, allowing up to two 60-day extensions for "good
     cause shown," which made the time allowable 300 days. See RIGL 36-14-12 (c) Upon
     receipt of a written complaint alleging a violation of this chapter, the Commission
     shall within one hundred eighty (180) days of receipt of the written complaint com-
     plete its investigation; provided, that the Commission may, for good cause shown,
     grant no more than two (2) extensions of sixty (60) days each.

28   91-S 519, "An Act Pertaining to the Code of Ethics," by Sen. Myrth York and 91-H
     6331 by Rep. Sandra Campbell were signed into law on 17 Jun. 1991. These identical
     bills strengthened conflict-of-interest provisions by prohibiting self-representa-
     tion except in case of hardship, and only then after consultation with the Ethics
     Commission to avoid any appearance of impropriety. See RIGL 36-14-5 (e) No
     person subject to this Code of Ethics shall:
        (1) Represent him or herself before any state or municipal agency of which he
        or she is a member or by which he or she is employed. In cases of hardship the
        Ethics Commission may permit such representation upon application by the
        official and provided that he or she shall first:
           (i) Advise the state or municipal agency in writing of the existence and the
           nature of his or her interest in the matter at issue, and
           (ii) Recuse him or herself from voting on or otherwise participating in the
           agency's consideration and disposition of the matter at issue, and
           (iii) Follow any other recommendations the Ethics Commission may make to
           avoid any appearance of impropriety in the matter.

29   91-S 590, "An Act Relating to Public Officers and Employees — Code of Ethics," by
     Sen. Walter Gray.

30   91-H 5708, "An Act Relating to Political Contributions by State Vendors," by Rep.
     Jeffrey Teitz. The legislation passed in 1992 and now stands as RIGL 17-27, Reporting
     of Political Contributions by State Vendors.

31   91-S 375, "An Act Relating to the Code of Ethics — Members of the General
     Assembly," by Sen. Myrth York and 91-H 5935 by Rep. Nancy Benoit.

32   91-H 5708, "An Act Relating to Political Contributions by State Vendors, by Rep.
     Jeffrey J. Teitz. *SJrnl*, 11 Jun. 1991: 75–80.

7 | New Beginnings (1991) · pages 67–77

1   Mike Stanton, "Key figure in RISDIC takes Fifth," *PJ*, 10 May 1991: A-01.

2   Dan Barry, "The RISDIC hearings, Ground Rules: 'Nobody gets in without a pass,'"
    PJ, 10 Jul. 1991: A-01.

3   Mike Stanton, "Correia defends his financial motives; First witness explains
    $210,000 'transaction,'" *PJ*, 10 Jul. 1991: A-01.

4   "Excerpts of Baron questioning Correia," *PJ*, 10 Jul. 1991: A-11.

5   Jeffrey L Hiday and Mike Stanton, "RISDIC lawyer calls withdrawals 'prudence,'" *PJ*,
    11 Jul. 1991: A-09.

6   Mike Stanton, "Lanfredi silent on withdrawal; Friend says he took $280,000," *PJ*, 11 Jul 1991: A-01.

7   Peter Phipps, "These are men whose business was taking care of themselves," *PJ*, 14 Jul. 1991: F-01.

8   "Excerpts on Bianchini's $85,000 loan," *PJ*, 18 Jul. 1991: A-04.

9   Dean Starkman, "Bianchini cool under withering committee exam," *PJ*, 18 Jul. 1991: A-04.

10   Twenty years later, Robert Bianchini still blames Sundlun. I interviewed him twice (22 Jul. 2010 and 27 Sep. 2012). Video of the second interview is online: http://www.youtube.com/watch?v=x6nEllC20aE&feature=youtube_gdata_player; http://www.youtube.com/watch?v=AFTZe4mKDhM&feature=youtube_gdata_player; http://www.youtube.com/watch?v=CXWEuCYTnjQ&feature=youtube_gdata_player.

11   Mike Stanton, "RISDIC's first family moved to protect its money in collapse; They refuse to answer commission 27 times," *PJ*, 12 Jul. 1991: A-01.

12   Neil Downing, "Final tab for crisis remains elusive," *PJ*, 30 Jun. 1991: F-01.

13   Ira Chinoy, "Diocese demonstrated little faith in RISDIC," *PJ*, 5 Aug. 1999: A-01.

14   Stephen Heffner, "Bishop reviles corrupt politicians," *PJ*, 3 Nov. 1991: A-01.

15   Scott MacKay, "New Ethics Task Force gets pep talk from Gov. Sundlun," *PJ*, 28 Mar. 1991: B-03. Members included William T. O'Hara (retired president of Bryant University), Perry Ashley (associate dean at Brown University), Frank Montanaro (executive director of the Rhode Island Association of Firefighters), Robert L. McCabe (president of Narragansett Electric Co.), Wayne Franklin (senior rabbi at Temple Emanu-El), Edmund Beck (former president of the National Federation for the Blind), Sandra Mack, Karen Lucas, and David J. Wawer (members of major law firms), Nicholas Long and John Farley (assistant attorneys general), Casby Harrison (Sundlun's deputy legal counsel), and Sara Quinn (former director of the Conflict-of-Interest Commission).

16   Scott MacKay, "DeAngelis says he'll back four failed ethics measures," *PJ*, 4 Sep. 1991: A-09.

17   Scott MacKay, "Sweeping ethics reforms urged," *PJ*, 8 Oct. 1991: A-01.

18   Brian C. Jones, "Government ethics is the only news that matters here," *PJ*, 8 Oct. 1991: E-01.

8 | Hope for Ethics (1991) · pages 78–90

1   On 9 Feb. 1989, the six-member investigating committee had dismissed all allegations that related to events before June 25, 1987, the date when DiPrete signed PL 87-194, which established the Rhode Island Ethics Commission. Commissioners concluded that these were not "within the jurisdiction of the Ethics Commission." As volunteer counsel for Common Cause Rhode Island, Rae Condon later filed several motions on this subject. In a motion dated October 15, 1991, she argued that a six-member investigating committee was not authorized to set policy on such a matter for the entire fifteen-member commission. "Allegations of official misconduct occurring prior to June 25, 1987 should not be automatically dismissed without investigation." She argued from the 1987 law that "there should be no interruption of official accountability," adding that the investigating panel had gratuitously granted "general amnesty to all officials whose misconduct predates the enactment of the current Ethics Law." Boxed in and acting more than two years later, the nine-member adjudicative panel had little choice but to stand by the investigative panel's vote.

2 John M. Roney, "Attorney Designee's Report: Part I, Tutela-Olney Pond," 29 May 1991: 7–8.

3 Personal interview with Nancy C. Rhodes, former DiPrete policy director for education, later president of the CCRI state governing board, 8 Feb. 2010.

4 Atwood Associates Realty Trust was formed on September 18, 1987 to buy the land for an apartment complex. James L. Taft Jr., provided $8,000 of $40,000 to capitalize the partnership. Attorney Designee's Report by John M. Roney: Part III, DiMuro-CRMC: 6.

5 Roney noted that Dennis DiPrete and Edward DiPrete each claimed that they had never discussed the St. James Estates project. Attorney Designee's Report by John M. Roney: Part IV: 2–7.

6 Russell Garland, "Land deal complaints dropped," *PJ*, 22 Jun. 1991: A-01.

7 Martin Finucane, "DiPrete says he has been cleared," Associated Press, *Westerly Sun*, 23 Jun. 1991: 11.

8 91-H 6318, "Relating to the Code of Ethics — Open Hearings," by Rep. Mark Heffner; 91-S 0422, (same title), by Sen. David Carlin.

9 Minutes of Open Session of the Rhode Island Ethics Commission, 13 Jun. 1991: 11.

10 Scott MacKay and Russell Garland, "Assembly adjourns; ethics bills fail to pass," *PJ*, 13 Jun. 1991: A-01.

11 Mark Eckstein, "New Regulations as Additions to the Code of Ethics," Memorandum to the members of the RIEC, 1 Jul. 1991.

12 91-H 5894, "An Act Relating to the Code of Ethics—Prohibited Activities," by Rep. Nicholas Tsiongas; and 91-S 590, (same title), by Sen. Walter Gray.

13 91-H 5935, "An Act Relating to the Code of Ethics—Members of the General Assembly," by Rep. Nancy Benoit; 91-S 375, (same title), by Sen. Myrth York. Both bills would have barred members of the General Assembly from "seeking or accepting other state employment, not held at the time of the member's election, while serving in the general assembly and for a period of one (1) year after leaving legislative office."

14 Gary Yesser, "Memorandum in connection with the question of the ability of the Ethics Commission to adopt a code of ethics with provisions beyond those provided for in the current code as adopted by the Rhode Island Legislature," RIEC, 11 Jul. 1991.

15 RI Constitution, Article III.8; Article VI.1-2.

16 Gary Yesser, "Memorandum in connection with the question of the ability of the Ethics Commission to adopt a code of ethics with provisions beyond those provided for in the current code as adopted by the Rhode Island Legislature," RIEC, 11 Jul. 1991.

17 Melvyn A. Topf, "Commission's authority to amend the code of ethics," Memo to commissioners of the RIEC, 22 Jul. 1991: 2,4,5.

18 Katherine Gregg, "DiPrete names new ethics unit," *PJ*, 25 Jul. 1987: A-01.

19 Minutes of Open Session of the RIEC, 22 Aug. 1991: 2.

20 Scott MacKay, "Ethics board says it can update law alone," *PJ*, 24 Aug. 1991: A-3.

21 Letter from Joseph DeAngelis, Speaker; John J. Bevilacqua, Senate Majority Leader; Thomas A. Lamb, House Majority Leader; to William H. Rizzini, Chairperson, RIEC, 11 Sep. 1991.

22 Gary Yesser, "Confidential Memorandum: Supplemental Information Regarding Status of Commission's Ability to Promulgate Additions or Modifications to the Code of Ethics, and Report after Meeting with Governor's Counsel and Legislative Counsel," 27 Sep. 1991.

23   McAllister's term ended on 25 Jul. 1991, but he continued to serve until Sundlun
      appointed Morsilli on 29 Aug. 1991.
24   Minutes of Open Session of the RIEC, 3 Oct. 1991: 5–6. Any documents related to
      the complaint, except the commission's investigatory materials would be open to the
      public. Equally important was an amended regulation regarding hearings before the
      adjudicative panel, 36-14-13 (d)(5), which would read: "The hearings shall be open to
      the public, except for the deliberations of the panel."
25   Minutes of 3 Oct. 1991: RIEC Reg. 36-14-5005.
26   Minutes of 3 Oct. 1991: RIEC Reg. 36-14-5006: "No elected or appointed official may
      accept any appointment or election by the body of which he or she is or was a mem-
      ber, to any position which carries with it any financial benefit or remuneration, until
      the expiration of one (1) year after termination of his or her membership in such
      body, unless the Rhode Island Ethics Commission shall give its approval for such
      appointment or election."
27   Minutes of 3 Oct. 1991: RIEC Regulation 36-14-5007, which read: "No member of
      the General Assembly shall seek or accept full time state employment, not held at
      the time of the member's election, while serving in the General Assembly and for a
      period of one (1) year after leaving legislative office, unless the Rhode Island Ethics
      Commission shall give its approval for such employment." Voting aye on each mo-
      tion were Ernest G. Ashton, Richard A. Blaine, Peter J. Davis, Cheryl M. Fisher-
      Allen, Roger M. Freeman, Paul L. Gaines, Joan M. Giampietro, Richard W. Morsilli,
      John J. O'Brien, Francis P. Pellegrino, William H. Rizzini, and Mel A. Topf. Michael
      A. Morry voted no on each proposed new regulation, and Roger R. Hall abstained.
28   Scott Mackay, "Tougher rules on ethics kindle political fire storm," *PJ*, 5 Oct. 1991:
      A-01.
29   Scott MacKay, "Sundlun asks high court for ruling on ethics dispute; Legislative
      leaders, commission claim right to revise code," *PJ*, 5 Nov. 1991: E-03.
30   The following material is drawn from RIEC transcript: *Proceedings at Hearing in Re:
      Proposed Actions on Regulations to Expand the Code of Ethics*, 6 Nov. 1991: 6, 18-22,
      23, 51-54, 55-62, 39-40, 43-51.

9 | Olney Pond (1991) · pages 91–113

1   See Ch. 2, "Governor Pay-to-Play."
2   "John J. Tuohy dies of accident injuries; headed ethics unit," *PJ*, 16 Dec. 1987: C-03.
3   The following material is drawn from *Vol. I, Proceedings at Hearing in Re: Complaint
      89-1*, RIEC, 43 Jefferson Blvd., Warwick, RI, 17 Oct. 1991, Vol. 1: 5 ff.
4   Motion by Common Cause Rhode Island to Reinstate Complaint Allegations
      Dismissed by the Investigating Committee, filed by its attorney, Rae B. Condon,
      15 Oct. 1991.
5   Doug Cullen, "Memo to Judith Benedict, the DEM's chief of Planning and
      Development," 23 Mar. 1988.
6   Minutes of the Architectural/Engineering Services Selection Committee dated
      8 Apr. 1988, list the four participants in the Olney Pond review: Dennis M. Lynch,
      State Purchasing Agent; Mathies J. Santos, Executive Assistant to the Director of the
      Department of Administration; Gilbert R. Parrillo, Public Member; Judith Benedict,
      Director of Planning and Development, DEM. Other attendees were present for
      other projects, but only those four voted on the Olney Pond proposals.
7   Frederick Lippitt, Letter from Director of Administration to Dennis Lynch, chair-
      man of the Architectural/Engineering Services Selection Committee, 25 Apr. 1988.

8 Memo from Robert L. Bendick, Director of the DEM, to Frederick Lippitt, Director of Administration, 3 May 1988: Selection of Engineering Consultant for EPA-funded Olney Pond Diagnostic/Feasibility study.

9 The following material is from *Vol. II, Proceedings at Hearing in Re: Complaint 89-1,* RIEC, 43 Jefferson Blvd., Warwick, RI, 31 Oct. 1991: 23. (Note: The transcript index incorrectly identifies Dennis Lynch as William.)

10 Peter Lord, "Usual channels bypassed as state gives contracts to DiPrete friend's firm," *PJ,* 16 Oct. 1988: A-01.

11 The following material is drawn from *Vol. III, Proceedings at Hearing in Re: Complaint 89-1,* RIEC, 43 Jefferson Blvd., Warwick, RI, November 26, 1991.

12 Executive Order 85-23 was issued on 4 Nov. 1985 and modified slightly under 86-13 on 19 May 1986.

13 The following material is drawn from *Vol. IV, Proceedings at Hearing in Re: Complaint 89-1,* RIEC, 43 Jefferson Blvd., Warwick, RI, 4 Dec. 1991.

14 Memo from Doug Cullen, Project Administrator for the Olney Pond Project, to Judith Benedict, Chief of Planning and Development for the DEM, 23 Mar. 1988. Transcript of 4 Dec. 1991: 99.

15 The following material is drawn from *Vol. V, Proceedings at Hearing in Re: Complaint 89-1,* RIEC, 43 Jefferson Blvd., Warwick, RI, 10 Dec. 1991.

16 Peter Lord, "Usual channels bypassed as state gives contracts to DiPrete friend's firm," *PJ,* 16 Oct. 1988: A-01.

10 | Jamestown Bridge (1991) · pages 114–128

1 G. Wayne Miller, "State balks at paying extra $30 million for pilings for new bridge," *PJ,* 16 Sep. 1987: A-01; G. Wayne Miller, "DiPrete seeks ouster of bridge contractor," *PJ,* 13 Feb. 1988; Gregg Krupa, "Contractors sued over Jamestown bridge problems," *PJ,* 23 Apr. 1988: C-08; Russell Garland and Dean Starkman, "Bay Bridge firm renews charges against state," *PJ,* 8 Jun. 1989: A-03.

2 The following material is drawn from *Vol. II, Proceedings at Hearing in Re: Complaint 89-1,* RIEC, 43 Jefferson Blvd., Warwick, RI, 12 Nov. 1991: 4 ff.

3 DiPrete had appointed Matthew J. Gill Jr. as director of the Dept. of Transportation in March 1986. See Editorial, "Sensible choice for the DOT challenge," *PJ,* 30 Mar. 1986: B-14.

4 Material drawn from *Vol. III, Proceedings at Hearing in Re: Complaint 89-1,* RIEC, 43 Jefferson Blvd., Warwick, RI, 19 Nov. 1991: 13 ff.

5 Material drawn from *Vol. I, Proceedings at Hearing in Re: Complaint 89-1,* RIEC, 43 Jefferson Blvd., Warwick, RI, 7 Nov. 1991: 21-89.

6 89-1 Decision and Order, *In Re: Edward D. DiPrete,* 20 Dec. 1991: 15.

7 The following material is drawn from *Vol. VI, Proceedings at Hearing in Re: Complaint 89-1,* RIEC, 43 Jefferson Blvd., Warwick, RI, 17 Dec. 1991: 5 ff. Preliminaries included consideration of Rae B. Condon's motions for Common Cause. After brief argument, the panel (1) dismissed the motion to reinstate allegations for conduct before July 25, 1987, (2) referred the motion about the role of complainant's counsel in adjudicative hearings to the full commission for consideration, and (3) denied the motion for Common Cause to address the question of fines.

8 RIGL 36-14-5; 36-14-7.

9 RIGL 36-14-6.

10 RIGL 36-14-5.

11 89-1 Decision and Order, *In Re: Edward D. DiPrete,* 20 Dec. 1991: 17 ff.

12   Editorial, "The $30,000 message," *PJ*, 28 Dec. 1991: A-12.
13   Scott McKay, "Sundlun fires Taft's law firm from bridge suit," *PJ*, 1 Jan. 1992: A-01.
14   Costs of the 7,350-foot span increased from an estimated $69 million in 1985 to more than $160 million. Unforeseen construction costs added $30 million. See Stephen Heffner, "Everyone's invited to celebrate opening of Jamestown span," *PJ*, 30 Sep. 1992: A-03.

11 | RIght Now! (1991–92) · pages 129–140

1   M. Charles Bakst, "Coalition wants ethics reform RIght Now!" *PJ*, 15 Dec. 1991: D-1. Bakst listed significant paid jobs that four of the former speakers whose portraits hung in the House Lounge had taken: Matthew Smith became State Court Administrator; Harry Curvin went to the Board of Elections; Joseph Bevilacqua became Chief Justice of the Supreme Court; and Edward Manning became legal counsel for the Lottery Commission.
2   The founding members of the RIght Now! Coalition comprised its steering committee: Common Cause Rhode Island (Phil West), the Environmental Council and Save the Bay (Curt Spalding), the Rhode Island Chamber of Commerce Federation (Frank Holbrook), the Jewish Federation of Rhode Island (Norman Orodenker), the Greater Providence Chamber of Commerce (Jim Hagan), the Northern Rhode Island Chamber of Commerce (Herb Hansen), the League of Women Voters (Suzette Gephard), Hasbro (Al Verrecchia), the Legal Community (Alan Flink), the United Way of Southeastern New England (Doug Ashby), the Rhode Island State Council of Churches (Jim Miller), the Urban League of Rhode Island (B. Jae Clanton), Rhode Island Public Expenditure Council (Gary Sasse).
3   Alan G. Hassenfeld, "Press Conference Statement," 11 Dec. 1991; HPW, "Press Conference Statement," 11 Dec. 1991.
4   Russell Garland, "Battle looms over state's plum posts," *PJ*, 8 Dec. 1991: A-01.
5   G. Wayne Miller, "Good-government coalition is born," *PJ*, 12 Dec. 1991: A-01.
6   By the end of January, 1,804 people signed pledges not to contribute until the General Assembly acted on reforms proposed by RIght Now! See G. Wayne Miller, "RIght Now! stands firm on campaign donations," *PJ*, 30 Jan. 1992: B-06.
7   G. Wayne Miller, "Catholic Diocese joins coalition, but the AFL-CIO says it will stay out," *PJ*, 14 Dec. 1991: A-01, A-06.
8   Mark Micheli, "Not now, say some RIght Now! skeptics, " *Providence Business News*, 23 Dec. 1991: 1.
9   Russell Garland, "'Clean Sweep' eyes elected officials," *PJ*, 10 Aug. 1991: A-03; "Civic-minded reformers invite disgruntled to Bristol meeting," *PJ*, 17 Oct. 1991: B-01.
10   During the fall of 1991, Charles Silverman came to the Common Cause office to work on reform issues and was eager to have Operation Clean Sweep join the RIght Now! Coalition. An illustrator, he had drawn a broom sweeping the State House, which became the Operation Clean Sweep (OCS) logo. Beverly and William Clay, leaders in the Government Accountability Project (GAP), were always more concerned about getting reform done than in taking credit. GAP later merged with OCS to form Operation Clean Government (OCG), which kept the dynamic broom as its symbol, often giving "Golden Broom Awards" to public officials.
11   Louis E. Gelineau, "Bishop Gelineau's Pastoral Letter on Ethics," *The Providence Visitor*, 2 Jan. 1991: 12-13.
12   G. Wayne Miller, "Thousands pray for reform," *PJ*, 6 Jan. 1992: A-01.

13 G. Wayne Miller, "Group links social justice to the debate over ethics," *PJ*, 22 Jan. 1992: A-9.

14 91-H 5894, "An Act Relating to Public Officers and Employees — Code of Ethics," by Representative K. Nicholas Tsiongas. 1992 versions of the bill were 92-H 7297 and 92-S 1377.

15 G. Wayne Miller, "Religious, community leaders urge Senate to back ethics bills," *PJ*, 4 Mar. 1992: A-01.

16 Ira Chinoy, "Public Interest Alliance slams campaign finance reform bill backed by House leadership," *PJ*, 4 Feb. 1992: E-3.

17 Scott MacKay, "Chamber calling for halt to political contributions solicits for candidates," *PJ*, 11 Feb. 1992: B-03.

12 | STRUGGLES (1992) · pages 141–154

1 G. Wayne Miller, "High court hears arguments on powers of ethics panel," *PJ*, 5 Mar. 1992: A-3.

2 The following material is from Lauren E. Jones, "*In Re: Governor's Request for an Advisory Opinion (Ethics Commission Code of Ethics)*, Brief and Appendix of Amicus Curiae, Common Cause of Rhode Island," 22 Jan. 1992: 1; 9-11, 13, 22, 24.

3 Rae B. Condon, "Argument Outline," 3 Mar. 1992. See also, "*In Re: Governor's Request for an Advisory Opinion (Ethics Commission Code of Ethics)*, Reply Brief of Amicus Curiae in Support of the Rhode Island Ethics Commission," 13 Jan. 1992.

4 Rae B. Condon, "Reply Brief of Amicus Curiae, a Member of the Rhode Island Bar, in Support of the Rhode Island Ethics Commission," 13 Jan. 1992: 10.

5 Condon, Brief and Appendix: 10.

6 Condon, Reply Brief: 16, quoting *R.I. Bar Assoc. v. Automobile Service Assoc.*, 55 R.I. at 140.

7 Ira Chinoy, "Favored 10 held purse strings," *PJ*, 3 Mar. 1992: A-01.

8 Peter Phipps, "But who put all that money in RISDIC?" *PJ*, 7 Jul. 1991: F-03.

9 Dean Starkman, "Panel steps closer to details of mob involvement," *PJ*, 13 Mar. 1992: A-08; Mike Stanton, "Barbatos' $2 million windfall financed Sox tickets, Rolls," *PJ*, 13 Mar. 1992: A-01.

10 Dan Barry, "Brothers give hearings air of the underworld," *PJ*, 13 Mar. 1992: A-01.

11 Transcript, "Bevilacqua denounces panel as 'self-serving,'" *PJ*, 13 Mar. 1992: A-09.

12 Stanton, "Barbatos' $2 million."

13 Ira Chinoy, "Favored 10 held purse strings," *PJ*, 3 Mar. 1992: A-01.

14 Dean Starkman, "Cambio's campaign funds link crisis to DiPrete," *PJ*, 2 Apr. 1992: A-01.

15 Mike Stanton, "Borrower played market with loans; Cambio funneled funds to DiPrete campaign," *PJ*, 2 Apr. 1992: A-01.

16 Dan Barry and Ira Chinoy, "Feds arrest developer Cambio; Brother, partner also nabbed on RISDIC loan fraud charges," *PJ*, 14 May 1992: A-01.

17 G. Wayne Miller, "Senate passes campaign reform bill," *PJ*, 15 Apr. 1992: A-01. See also Ch. 6, "Dashed Hopes."

18 Christopher Beall, "Angry Sen. Irons says he'll step down," *PJ*, 17 Apr. 1992: A-01

19 *HJrnl*, 28 Apr. 1992: 4.

20 *HJrnl*, 28 Apr. 1992: 8; G. Wayne Miller, "House OKs campaign finance reform bill," *PJ*, 29 Apr. 1992: A-01.; *HJrnl*, 28 Apr. 1992: 8.

21 G. Wayne Miller, "Sundlun signs reform legislation; Law limits campaign contributions, broadens public financing," *PJ*, 29 Apr. 1992: A-01.

22   RIght Now! press release, "RIght Now! Coalition lifts moratorium on campaign contributions," 29 Apr. 1992.

23   Indeglia and Suttell would eventually advance to the RI Supreme Court.

24   Russell Garland, "Feud mars opening-day ceremonies in Senate," *PJ*, 4 Jan. 1989: A-03.

25   Kevin Sullivan and Russell Garland, "Carlin accuses DiPrete of 'unholy alliance' to avert probe," *PJ*, 6 Jan. 1989: A-01.

26   James M. O'Neill, "4 nominated for state court seats," 26 May 1990: A-01. Maureen McKenna Goldberg would advance in 1997 to the Supreme Court.

27   Scott Mackay, "Tougher rules on ethics kindle political fire storm," *PJ*, 5 Oct. 1991: A-01.

28   G. Wayne Miller, "500 rally in support of ethics reform," *PJ*, 28 Apr. 1992: A-01.

29   G. Wayne Miller "Legislators rated on ethics bills, but the foundation of Clean Sweep's analysis is criticized," *PJ*, 4 Jun. 1992: B-07.

13 | RISDIC TV (1992) · pages 155–164

1   Mike Stanton, "RISDIC spotlight on government; State House the focus of final round of TV hearings," *PJ*, 19 May 1992: A-01.

2   Mike Stanton, "Violet faults top officials; Targets many in RISDIC testimony," *PJ*, 4 Jun. 1992: A-01; "The RISDIC Hearings: 'We're sitting here discussing this because of The Network,'" *PJ*, 4 Jun. 1992: A-10. See also "Institutional response was 'don't worry,'" *PJ*, 30 May 1992: A-07. Former General Treasurer Roger Begin also noted that Auditor General Anthony Piccirilli produced a report on RISDIC's risks but that Calderone publicly "slammed" him "for releasing state banking information."

3   Dean Starkman, "Powerful attacker becomes the accused," *PJ*, 9 Jun. 1992: A-01.

4   Excerpt, "Bianchini: '. . . I was overly aggressive . . . I was angry,'" *PJ*, 9 Jun. 1992: A-08. Twenty years later, Bianchini blames Violet and the Department of Business Regulation: "The Attorney General refused to respond to our request to work with her to address her concerns. If RISDIC or the DBR had information indicating that there were serious problems involving any of our member credit unions, it was not shared with the league." Email to HPW, 21 Nov. 2013.

5   Katherine Gregg, "Lack of vote leads conflict panel to clear assemblyman," *PJ*, 22 Jul. 1987: A-01. See Ch. 1, "Breaking Ground."

6   Jeffrey L. Hiday, "They didn't tell Violet," *PJ*, 10 Jun. 1992: A-09.

7   Jeffrey L. Hiday, "Gaschen paid dearly for trying to avert the banking crisis," *PJ*, 12 Jun. 1992: A-10.

8   Through an intermediary, I asked to interview Smith for this book. He declined.

9   "The RISDIC Hearings Excerpts: Smith testifies he didn't kill 1986 bill," *PJ*, 16 Jun. 1992: A-09; Mike Stanton, "Bevilacqua's mother cashed in CDs late in '90; Senator says he didn't tell her, aide of crisis," *PJ*, 16 Jun. 1992: A-01.

10   Dean Starkman, "Contradictory testimony prompts rare public dispute; DeAngelis: Both leaders knew of crisis," *PJ*, 16 Jun. 1992: A-08.

11   Mike Stanton, Ira Chinoy, Christopher Rowland, "DiPrete got 5 warnings about RISDIC," *PJ*, 7 Jun. 1992: A-01. See Ch. 5, "Collapse of Credit."

12   Mike Stanton, "RISDIC told in 1986 to shape up in 1 year," *PJ*, 12 Jun. 1992: A-01.

13   Russell Garland, "A tangled tale of campaign finances," *PJ*, 5 Feb. 1989: B-01.

14   Excerpt, "DiPrete: 'I did not close the credit unions,'" *PJ*, 19 Jun. 1992: A-09.

15   Stanton, Chinoy, Rowland, "DiPrete got 5 warnings."

14 | Triumphs (1992) · pages 165–180

1   *In Re: Advisory Opinion to the Governor (Ethics Commission)*, 91–577 M.P., 612 A. 2nd (R.I. 1992), was signed by Chief Justice Thomas F. Fay and Associate Justices Thomas F. Kelleher, Joseph R. Weisberger, Florence K. Murray, and Donald F. Shea. The following quoted material is drawn from this document.

2   Tracy Breton and G. Wayne Miller, "High court says ethics panel can govern conduct of state officials," *PJ*, 11 Jun. 1992: A-01.

3   92-H 9314, "An Act Relating to the Rhode Island Ethics Commission," by Rep. Francis Gaschen.

4   92-H 9002, "An Act Relating to the Rhode Island Ethics Commission," by Rep. Thomas Lamb.

5   HPW, "To the Honorable Jeffrey J. Teitz, Chairperson, House Judiciary Committee, Re: 92-H 9002 Substitute A," 29 Jun. 1992.

6   G. Wayne Miller, "Turf war on ethics control not over," *PJ*, 2 Jul. 1992: B-03.

7   This conversation compresses events over several days that would be confusing if they were interspersed in their chronological sequence.

8   Russell Garland, "Sundlun names 4 new judges," *PJ*, 19 Jun. 1992: A-01.

9   92-H 8542 Substitute B, "An Act Relating to the General Assembly," by Rep. Nancy Benoit. SubA versions of bills have been amended in the chamber of origin; SubB versions in the opposite chamber.

10 G. Wayne Miller, "Senate panel OKs revolving-door bill some say goes too far," *PJ*, 24 Jun. 1992: B-03.

11 G. Wayne Miller, "Senate approves tough ethics bill; House may resist," *PJ*, 26 Jun. 1992: A-01.

12 G. Wayne Miller, "Senate sends 4 revolving-door bills to House," *PJ*, 27 Jun. 1992: A-01.

13 92-S 2759 would bar state candidates from permanent state jobs for one year after their elected term; 92-S 2760 would bar municipal candidates from permanent municipal jobs for one year; 92-S 2761 would bar municipal elected officials and top staff from permanent municipal jobs for one year; 92-S 2762 would bar state elected officials and senior appointed officials from permanent state jobs, including judgeships, for one year.

14 Judy Rakowsky, "Sundlun Counsel nominated for judgeship wasn't on panel's list," *PJ*, 7 Jul. 1992: A-03.

15 G. Wayne Miller and Tom Mooney, "Angry rally at State House; Weary over delays on ethics bills, 300 demand action," *PJ*, 8 Jul. 1992: A-01.

16 RIGL 36-14-5 (n)(4) and (o)(5): Nothing contained herein shall prohibit the Rhode Island Ethics Commission from authorizing exceptions to this subsection where such exemption would not create an appearance of impropriety.

17 G. Wayne Miller, "House OKs revolving door ban," *PJ*, 10 Jul. 1992: A-08.

18 92-H 9002 Substitute A, "An Act Relating to the Rhode Island Ethics Commission," by Rep. Thomas Lamb.

19 Russell Garland and Scott MacKay, "In the end, Assembly did its work," *PJ*, 15 Jul. 1992: A-01.

20 1992 PL 131, 132, 396, and 436.

21 G. Wayne Miller, "With ethics reform, R.I. tries to put shameful past behind it," *PJ*, 19 Jul 1992: A-13.

15 | Keeping Score (1992) · pages 181–191

1   *HJrnl*, 28 Apr. 1992: 3-8. In floor debate on 92-H 7293, "An Act relating to elections—campaign contributions," by Rep. Jeffrey Teitz and others, floor amendments were proposed by Reps. Ray Rickman, Wayne L. Salisbury, William H. Greene II, Lawrence J. Ferguson, Rodney D. Driver, and Bruce J. Long. None had been presented during hearings of the House Judiciary Committee in 1991 or 1992. RN! and CCRI supported Teitz's successful effort to table all of these amendments. The final vote on the bill was 94 in favor, 5 opposed.

2   HPW, "Rating the State House at cleaning up politics in Rhode Island," *PJ*, 15 Sep. 1992: A-11.

3   "Common Cause rankings," *PJ*, 11 Sep. 1992: C-01; Karen Lee Ziner, "Grass-roots groups rate lawmakers," *PJ*, 12 Sep. 1992: A-05.

4   Christopher Beall, "Common Cause issues report card on reform movement," *PJ*, 4 Sep. 1992: B-01.

5   Editorial, "The ratings game," *PJ*, 13 Sep. 1992: B-12.

6   RI Constitution, Article IV.1 includes recall provisions.

7   Paul Edward Parker, "Wild Kingdom: Gus Hebb opens his gates for a rare glimpse of a well-kept secret," *PJ*, 30 Aug. 1992: C-01.

8   Stephen Heffner, "Business executives go to bat for measure on four-year terms at unusual fund-raiser," *PJ*, 19 Oct. 1992: A-03.

16 | A Pivotal Election (1992) · pages 192–197

1   Judy Rakowsky, "Pawtucket's Sarault faces extortion, mail fraud charges," *PJ*, 13 Jun. 1991: A-01; Scott MacKay and W. Zachary Malinowski, "Rep. Weygand: Issues-oriented and outspoken," *PJ*, 13 Jun. 1991: A-01.

2   Scott MacKay and Russell Garland, "Begin eschews bid for reelection as obstacles rise," *PJ*, 3 Jun. 1992: A-01.

3   "Campaign briefs: Sundlun, Clinton top poll," *PJ*, 30 Oct. 1992: B-05.

4   Katherine Gregg, "A hard-hitting race for attorney general; O'Neil running on his record," *PJ*, 18 Oct. 1992: A-01.

5   Tracy Breton and John Sullivan, "Failed bank escapes state scrutiny; Jefferson's stockholders included friends of attorney general," *PJ*, 17 May 1992: A-01.

6   Katherine Gregg, "Pine attacks O'Neil on RISDIC testimony; GOP challenger says his statements were contradictory, evasive," *PJ*, 18 Sep. 1992: A-01.

7   Former Attorney General Arlene Violet had founded the Government Accountability Project (GAP) as a nonpartisan research organization. Under the leadership of Thomas McHugh, GAP rented an office at 206 Smith Street, Providence, where the new coalition met. Violet and business leader Bruce Lang had organized US-PAC. Joseph Devine, who ran for governor as an independent, organized Reform '92, which held a political convention and endorsed candidates. David Bibeault led the Rhode Island Taxpayers' Association.

8   Press Advisory, "Groups back 18 Procedural Reforms," 30 Nov. 1992.

9   Editorial, "Vote for Proposition 1," *PJ*, 25 Oct. 1992: I-06; editorial, "4-year terms: The crucial reform," *PJ*, 1 Nov. 1992: A-01.

10   Dan Barry, "Rally puts spotlight on reform," *PJ*, 2 Nov. 1992: A-01.

11   Brian C. Jones, "Voters give in, top officers to win 4-year terms in '94," *PJ*, 4 Nov. 1992: A-01.

12   RIBOE results showed 215,040 (60.2%) to approve Question 1 and 142,130 (39.8%) to reject it. http://www.elections.ri.gov/elections/results/1992/referenda.php.

13 RIBOE results showed Democrat Bruce Sundlun with 261,484 (61.6%), Republican Elizabeth A. Leonard with 145,590 (34.3%), and Reform '92 Joseph F. Devine with 14,511 (3.4%). http://www.elections.ri.gov/elections/results/1992/governorcounty.php.

14 RIBOE results showed Democrat Robert A Weygand with 256,331 (66.8%), Republican Ronald F. Iacobbo with 86,174 (22.5%), and Independent Michael C. Campbell with 41,177 (10.7%). http://www.elections.ri.gov/elections/results/1992/ltgovcounty.php.

15 RIBOE results showed Republican Nancy J. Mayer with 227,290 (58.0%) and Democrat Marlene Marcello McKenna with 164,787 (42.0%). http://www.elections.ri.gov/elections/results/1992/treasurercounty.php.

16 RIBOE results showed Republican Jeffrey B. Pine with 206,326 (49.5%) and Democrat James E. O'Neil with 196,994 (47.3%). http://www.elections.ri.gov/elections/results/1992/agcounty.php.

17 "Connell took donations from vendor, foe says," *PJ*, 29 Sep. 1992: D-03.

18 Sens. John Correia, James D'Ambra, James Donelan, and John Sabatini.

19 Four Bevilacqua loyalists lost to Republican challengers on 3 Nov. 1992. In Senate District 19 (West Warwick), Republican John Feroce defeated Stephen D. Alves; in Dist. 21 (Coventry and Scituate), Leo R. Blais defeated Raymond J. Monahan; in Dist. 23 (North Kingstown), Robin Porter defeated Paul Pederzani III; in Dist. 45 (Bristol and Warren), Mary A. Parella defeated Richard M. Alegria.

20 Parella received 4,623 votes (53.7%) to Alegria's 3,991 (46.3%). http://www.elections.ri.gov/elections/results/1992/risenate.php.

21 CCRI published its first two-year Legislative Scorecard in 1992. Although there is no way to measure the report card's impact, the 28 highest-ranking state Senators were all re-elected, as were 40 of the top 50 Representatives. Among the bottom 50 House members, 26 retired or were defeated. Of the bottom 22 Senators, eleven stepped down or were voted out.

22 Christopher Beall, "Irons focuses on Assembly leadership; Says Alegria's defeat is boost to Kelly," *PJ*, 5 Nov. 1992: B-01.

23 Scott MacKay, "Bevilacqua won't lead Senate," *PJ*, 5 Nov. 1992: A-01.

24 Carlin won 48,092 votes, Machtley 135,982. Minor party candidates took 10,015. http://www.elections.ri.gov/elections/results/1992/congresscounty.php.

17 | Loose Ends (1992–93) · pages 198–209

1 PL 92-396, 92-H 8542 Substitute C as amended. See Ch. 14, "Triumphs."

2 Russell Garland, "Sundlun move allows 4 bench nominees to serve; He withdraws names, then gives them all interim appointments," *PJ*, 22 Jul. 1992: A-03.

3 Russell Garland, "Senate panel OKs Sundlun's 4 judicial appointments," *PJ*, 23 Jan. 1993: A-03.

4 Thomas Frank, "Sundlun asks R.I. high court if job-curbs law is legal," *PJ*, 2 Mar. 1993: D-06.

5 Mike Stanton, "RISDIC panel faults DiPrete, urges massive state overhaul," *PJ*, 9 Dec. 1992: A-01.

6 Phase IV: 36-37. Select Commission to Investigate the Failure of RISDIC-Insured Financial Institutions, Phase IV: *The Failure of Governmental Oversight* (Providence: Select Commission, 1992) 36–37.

7 Phase IV: 58.

8 Phase IV: 81 ff.

9 See Ch. 19, "Paying the Piper," note 1.

10   Ira Chinoy, "Commission recommendations will be heeded; 2 point to recent reform efforts," *PJ*, 9 Dec. 1992: A-12.

11   Stanton, "RISDIC panel faults DiPrete."

12   Rae B. Condon, "Individual rights were slighted by the RISDIC Commission," *PJ*, 13 Jan. 1993: A-13.

13   Tracy Breton, "Judge upholds $30,000 fine of DiPrete," *PJ*, 18 Aug. 1992: A-01.

14   PL 92-436, which Sundlun signed on 21 Jul. 1992, required him to appoint five members from lists provided by the speaker of the house, house majority leader, house minority leader, senate majority leader, and senate minority leader and four individuals without regard to those lists (RIGL 36-14-8 (a)). No member of the commission could (1) hold or campaign for public office, (2) hold office in any political party or political committee, (3) participate in or contribute to any political campaign; or (4) directly or indirectly attempt to influence any decision by any governmental body, except as the authorized representative of the commission on a matter within the commission's jurisdiction, or (5) have held or been a candidate for elective public office for one year prior to appointment.

15   See Ch. 8, "Hope for Ethics."

16   Elizabeth Abbott, "Sundlun, Nields hail Jean Hicks for her 'vision,'" *PJ*, 11 Dec. 1992: B-01.

17   RIEC, "Minutes of Open Session," 22 Dec. 1992.

18   RIEC, *Decision and Order, In Re: Edward D. DiPrete (89-1)*. On March 3, 1989, the six-member Investigating Committee ordered a full investigation of allegations in the Common Cause complaint against former Gov. Edward DiPrete that related to actions after July 25, 1987, but it dismissed allegations relating to events before July 25, 1987, "on grounds that said actions were not within the jurisdiction of the Ethics Commission . . ."

19   Thomas Frank, "Common Cause's West a finalist to direct ethics unit," *PJ*, 23 Dec. 1992: A-03.

20   Thomas Frank, "Changes in ad for ethics post spark complaint; Amendments apparently allow West to meet job qualifications for director," *PJ*, 30 Dec. 1992: A-03.

21   HPW, "A Response to Recent Reports," 2 Jan. 1993; John Castellucci, "Ethics panel candidate rebuts critics," *PJ*, 3 Jan. 1993: D-04.

22   HPW, Letter to Amanda Clark, Personnel Committee Chairperson, RIEC, 6 Jan. 1993.

23   Thomas Frank, "West withdraws as candidate to direct state ethics panel," *PJ*, 7 Jan. 1993: A-01.

24   RIEC, "Minutes of Open Session," 11 Jan. 1993: 1–2.

25   Brian C. Jones, "Phil West showed us what ethics is all about," *PJ*, 10 Jan. 1993: C-01.

18 | WHEN PROSECUTORS FAIL · pages 210–219

1   *Edward D. DiPrete v. Richard Morsilli, et al.*, PC 91-8642: 17 Aug. 1992: 9–11, 25, 34.

2   Tracy Breton, "Judge upholds $30,000 fine of DiPrete," *PJ*, 18 Aug. 1992: A-01.

3   Tracy Breton, "DiPrete lawyers hit ethics panel," *PJ*, 8 Oct. 1993: A-01.

4   *DiPrete v. Morsilli*, 92-433-M.P., 635 A. 2nd (R.I. 1994) 11 Jan. 1994: 1155, 1166.

5   Thomas Frank, "Justices set aside DiPrete fine," *PJ*, 12 Jan. 1994: A-01.

6   "The Charges," Text of the indictments, *PJ*, 30 Mar. 1994: A-06.

7   Katherine Gregg, "DiPrete, son indicted for extorting kickbacks," *PJ*, 30 Mar. 1994: A-01.

8   J. Richard Ratcliffe, Personal interview, 8 Feb. 2010; Robert P. Mattos, Personal interview, 26 Mar. 2012.

9   Mike Stanton, Tracy Breton, David Herzog, and W. Zachary Malinowski, "Rhode Island on Trial, Chapter 1: Fugitive banker's dealings with state draw investigators to DiPrete's circle," *PJ*, 9 Aug. 1998: 1-2.

10 Unindicted co-conspirators included Rodney M. Brusini, Frank N. Zaino, and Michael Piccoli. Also named in the 24-count indictment as being extorted and/ or giving bribes: Joseph M. Cerilli, Donald Conlon, Pen Fang, Richard Johnson, Armando F. Lusi, A. Robert Lusi, Carl Marcello, Joseph Mollicone Jr., David Presbrey, and Norton E. Salk. See "The Charges," Text of the indictments, *PJ*, 30 Mar. 1994: A-6.

11 "Rhode Island on Trial, Chapter 10: New AG Pine puts tough crime fighter on state's case against the DiPretes," 5, 7.

12 "Rhode Island on Trial, Chapter 2: Architects and engineers swear they paid to get state contracts," 4–5.

13 Ira Chinoy, "RISDIC straw donations," *PJ*, 5 May 1992: A-01.

14 Presbrey declined to be interviewed for this book. "The memories are painful," he wrote on 26 Jul. 2011. "I still try to put them behind me."

15 "Rhode Island on Trial, Chapter 12: DiPretes' defense lawyers suspect prosecutors may be holding back evidence," *PJ*, 16 Aug. 1998: 7, 9, 11.

16 "Rhode Island on Trial, Chapter 14: DiPretes' defense lawyers suspect prosecutors may be holding back evidence," *PJ*, 16 Aug. 1998: 11, 13.

17 "Rhode Island on Trial, Chapter 15: Through turmoil and tragedy, the state's case moves ahead," *PJ*, 16 Aug. 1998: 13–14. Two sitting justices recused themselves from *State* v. *DiPrete*. Retired Justices Florence K. Murray and Donald F. Shea returned to hear arguments with Chief Justice Joseph R. Weisberger, Victoria S. Lederberg, and John P. Bourcier.

18 Following quotes are taken from *State of Rhode Island* v. *Edward D. DiPrete and Dennis L. DiPrete*, 710 A2d 1266, 1 May 1998.

19 Tracy Breton, "Justices explain DiPrete decision," *PJ*, 2 May 1998: A-01.

20 "Rhode Island on Trial, Chapter 15," *PJ*, 16 Aug. 1998: 15.

21 "Rhode Island on Trial: The story of the Case against Edward DiPrete, Prologue," 9 Aug. 1998: 1.

22 Mike Stanton, "Surprise deal includes a year to serve at the ACI," *PJ*, 12 Dec. 1998: A-01. See also Edward D. DiPrete, "Edward DiPrete's Statement," *PJ*, 12 Dec. 1998: A-15.

23 Edward DiPrete made essentially the same arguments with me during a two-hour interview at his home on 24 Apr. 2014. I came away with a sense that he genuinely believed he was not guilty of the charges.

24 Francis J. Darigan Jr., "Judge Darigan's Statement," *PJ*, 12 Dec. 1998: A-15.

25 Tracy Breton, "DiPrete agreed to plea for family's sake, son says," *PJ*, 12 Dec. 1998: A-01.

26 Mike Stanton, "Surprise deal includes a year to serve at the ACI," *PJ*, 12 Dec. 1998: A-01.

19 | Paying the Piper · pages 223–232

1   Members of the Blue Ribbon Commission on the Future of the General Assembly included four legislators who had decided not to seek re-election: House Majority Whip Christopher Boyle, D-Newport; Rep. David W. Dumas, R-East Greenwich; Sen. Edward Marrone, D-Westerly; Senate Minority Leader Albert Russo, R-Hopkinton. Public members were: Chairperson Gary Sasse, executive director of the Rhode Island Public Expenditure Council; Vice Chairperson Charles H. Goss, CEO

of Valley Resources; Thomas J. Anton, director of the Alfred Taubman Center for Public Policy at Brown University; lawyer Raymond Dettore Jr., chairman and secretary of the Providence Bureau of Licenses; Patricia Houlihan of the AFL-CIO; Mary S. Lima, community relations liaison officer for the state Department of Human Services; Wilma E. Lopez-Round, a former member of the Reapportionment Commission; James V. Rosati, chairman of Old Stone Bank; Robert A. Urciuoli, president of Roger Williams Hospital; and H. Philip West Jr., executive director of Common Cause Rhode Island.

2   The retreat was and all of the commission's meetings were posted under the Open Meetings Law: RIGL 42-46-6(b).

3   NCSL, "Full and Part-Time Legislatures," http://www.ncsl.org/research/about-state-legislatures/full-and-part-time-legislatures.aspx).

4   RI Constitution, Article VI. 3. In the Board of Elections totals 64.4% (178,775) rejected Question 3 (Legislative Compensation), and 35.6% (98,845) approved it.

5   The 1990 Census showed that New Hampshire, with 400 in its House of Representatives, had the smallest number of persons per legislator among the 50 states. (Square miles includes water. Without water, RI is only 1,214 sq. miles.)

	State	1990 Population	Senators	Reps	Persons/ Legislator	Sq. Miles/ Legislator	Square Miles
1	New Hampshire	1,113,915	24	400	2,627.16	22.1	9,350
2	Vermont	564,964	30	150	3,138.69	53.4	9,615
3	North Dakota	641,364	53	98	4,247.44	468.2	70,700
4	Wyoming	455,975	30	64	4,850.80	1,040.6	97,813
5	Montana	803,655	50	100	5,357.70	980.3	147,042
6	South Dakota	699,999	35	70	6,666.66	736.7	77,353
7	Maine	1,233,223	33	151	6,702.30	192.3	35,385
8	Rhode Island	1,005,984	50	100	6,706.56	10.3	1,545
9	Alaska	551,947	20	40	9,199.12	11,054.5	663,267
10	Idaho	1,011,986	35	70	9,637.96	795.9	83,570

6   The 1990 Census showed that only New Jersey had a higher population density than that of Rhode Island.

	State	1990 Population	Senators	Reps	Persons/ Legislator	Sq. Miles/ Legislator	Square Miles
49	Rhode Island	1,005,984	50	100	6,706.56	651.1	1,545
50	New Jersey	7,748,634	40	80	64,571.95	888.4	8,722

7   *PRIMER: Reducing the Size of the Rhode Island General Assembly* (Common Cause Rhode Island, 1987).

8   James Madison, "Federalist No. 58," Clinton Rossiter, ed., *The Federalist Papers* (New York: Penguin, 1961), 360.

9   *PRIMER: Reforming Legislative Compensation* (Common Cause Rhode Island, 1987), revised 1992: 1. Charles Mahtesian, "Legislative Pay when the Voters Freeze Your Pay," *Governing Magazine*, Dec. 1993: 18.

10   RIBOE totals: 64.4% (178,775) rejected Question 3 (Legislative Compensation), and 35.6% (98,845) approved it.

11   M. Charles Bakst, "Assembly considers pension increases," *PJ*, 14 May 1987: A-03. Orabona's legislation proposed to raise the minimum annual pension after eight years of service from $2,400 to $4,800, and after twenty, from $6,000 to $12,000; M. Charles Bakst, "Assembly may double its pension benefits," *PJ*, 25 Jun. 1987: A-01.

12   Katherine Gregg, "Bill allows union staffs R.I. or other pensions," *PJ*, 3 Sep. 1987: A-03. Attempts to rescind the law and revoke the illicit pensions would take years. See Ch. 25, "Hard Choices."

13   Katherine Gregg, "Radio host asks funds to fight pension hike," *PJ*, 1 Sep. 1987: A-03.

14   Katherine Gregg, "Kass to sue Assembly on pensions," *PJ*, 14 Nov. 1987: A-01.

15   Article VI.3 of Rhode Island's revamped 1986 Constitution set legislative compensation at $5 per day up to a maximum 60 days of actual attendance. The 1986 Constitutional Convention Question 3 proposed to raise legislative compensation to $76.55 per day without changing legislative pensions.

16   Jim Hummel, "Arguments heard on pension for legislators," *PJ*, 13 Apr. 1988: A-16.

17   Kevin Sullivan, "High court: R.I. legislators can increase own pensions," *PJ*, 15 Dec. 1989: A-01. See *Kass* v. *Retirement Board*, 88-348-A, 567 A.2d 358 (1989).

18   Tracy Breton, "Former judge charged with accepting bribe," *PJ*, 22 Jul. 1991: A-01.

19   Editorial, "Remaking the legislature," *PJ*, 14 Jan. 1993: A-10.

20   Following summaries are from HPW notes of the Blue Ribbon Commission hearings on 25 Jan., 8 and 22 Feb., 1 and 8 Mar. 1993.

21   *Licht* v. *Quattrocchi*, 82-259-Appeal, 449 A.2d 887 (1982), and *Farnum* v. *Burns*, 82-0500P, 561 F. Supp. 83 (1983). See also Thomas E. Walsh, "Rocco Quattrocchi, after the fall," *PJ*, 22 Jan. 1984: C-01. For more on the 1982 gerrymandering, see Ch. 40, "Redistricting Revenge."

22   Maria Miro Johnson, "The Life and Climb of John Revens," *PJ*, 18 Jan. 1987: M-06.

23   Blue Ribbon Commission, *Draft Report: The General Assembly in Rhode Island, A Blueprint for the 21st Century*, 1 Aug. 1993. See Thomas Frank, "Special panel urges better-paid, smaller Assembly," *PJ*, 1 Aug. 1993: A-01.

24   In 1990, term-limit referenda were approved in California, Colorado, and Oklahoma. In 1992, voters passed similar referenda in Arizona, Arkansas, Florida, Michigan, Missouri, Montana, Ohio, South Dakota, and Wyoming. Maine voters would establish term limits in 1993. http://www.termlimits.org/content. asp?pl=18&sl=19&contentid=19. 13 Jul. 2011.

25   RI Constitution, Article VI.3: "Commencing in 1996, the rate of compensation shall be adjusted annually to reflect changes in the cost of living, as determined by the United States Government during a twelve (12) month period ending in the immediately preceding year."

26   Blue Ribbon Commission, *The General Assembly in Rhode Island: A Blueprint for the 21st Century*, Dec. 1993. *Library Archive*. Paper 25. http://helindigitalcommons.org/lawarchive/25.

27   Russell Garland, "Proposals aimed at modernizing R.I. legislature are unveiled," *PJ*, 14 Dec. 1993: A-01.

20 | Under New Management · pages 233–245

1   Katherine Gregg, "House leaders defend their tenure; DeAngelis, Lamb irked at efforts to oust them," *PJ*, 1 Jan. 1988: A-01; Gregg, "DeAngelis likely to be new speaker," *PJ*, 6 Jan. 1988: A-01; Gregg, "Democrats nominate DeAngelis to post on 61-18 vote," *PJ*, 13 Jan. 1988: A-14; "DeAngelis is elected speaker of the House by vote of 77-19 over GOP's Gorham," *PJ*, 14 Jan. 1988: A-16.

2   Scott MacKay, "Democrats split over Bramley, Harwood for House speaker; 43–42 vote could leave decision in hands of Republican minority," 11 Nov. 1992: A-03.

3   Russell Garland, "3 Democratic defectors bolster Harwood in race for House speakership," 9 Dec. 1992: B-03.

4   Editorial, "Politics and the law," *PJ*, 2 Dec. 1992: A-12.

5   Katherine Gregg, "Harwood bill in 1984 paved way for lawsuit by his firm," *PJ*, 11 Jan. 1993: A-01.

6   Katherine Gregg, "The leading candidate for House speaker flies tattered ethics banner," *PJ*, 27 Dec. 1992: A-01.

7   Special Reprint, *Final Reports of the Select Commission to Investigate the Failure of RISDIC-Insured Financial Institutions*, Vol. IV. The General Assembly: A. Historic Treatment of RISDIC and Its Insured Institutions, *PJ*, 9 Dec. 1992: R-01.

8   Katherine Gregg and Scott MacKay, "Bramley calls for ethics probe of Harwood's legislative moves; Asks reform groups to back him in race for House speaker's post," *PJ*, 29 Dec. 1992: A-03.

9   Scott MacKay, "Harwood to gather Democrats to claim House speaker's post," *PJ*, 31 Dec. 1992: D-03.

10   Katherine Gregg and Scott MacKay, "Bramley calls for ethics probe of Harwood's legislative moves; Asks reform groups to back him in race for House speaker's post," *PJ*, 29 Dec. 1992: A-03.

11   Scott MacKay, "Harwood chosen as speaker," *PJ*, 6 Jan. 1993: A-01.

12   Scott MacKay, "Compromise results in truce among House Democrats," *PJ*, 13 Jan. 1993: B-03.

13   MacKay, "Harwood chosen."

14   Scott MacKay, "Bevilacqua won't lead Senate," *PJ*, 5 Nov. 1992: A-01.

15   PL 78-205, Budget Article XII, expanded the UPPB to seven members, by removing the state budget officer and adding an additional representative and senator, appointed by the speaker and Senate majority leader. It also gave the judicial branch a seat, originally designated for the clerk of Superior Court, later for the State Court Administrator.

16   Peter Hufstader, *Democracy Betrayed: Conflicts of Interest and Failures of Oversight in Rhode Island State Government* (Providence: CCRI, 2000), 47–48.

17   Katherine Gregg, "Speaker giving up the power and glory," *PJ*, 8 Jan. 1988: A-08.

18   Jonathan Saltzman and Christopher Rowland, "Cost of ticket snafu will never be known," *PJ*, 13 Dec. 1997: A-03; Christopher Rowland and Jonathan Saltzman, "Disorder in the Court," *PJ*, 10 Feb. 1998: A-01; Christopher Rowland, "Weisberger: Tough task to reform traffic court," *PJ*, 1 Jul. 1998: A-01; Jonathan Saltzman, "Governor signs law to dismantle traffic court," *PJ*, 4 Jul. 1998: A-03.

19   Katherine Gregg, "Harwood calls raises 'outrageous,'" *PJ*, 22 Jan. 1993: A-01; Katherine Gregg, "Pay raises vetoed by Sundlun may make comeback," *PJ*, 28 Jan. 1993: A-03.

20   Katherine Gregg, "Matthew Smith's son got job created by board led by father," *PJ*, 10 Feb. 1993: A-03.

21   John Sullivan and Dean Starkman, "Administrator concealed theft of court funds," *PJ*, 14 Mar. 1993: A-01.

22   Scott MacKay, "Sundlun leaving action on Smith to chief justice," *PJ*, 17 Mar. 1993: A-01

23   Katherine Gregg, "Sampling of details on pensions shows $3.9 million tab," *PJ*, 17 Mar. 1993: A-01. The cost to taxpayers would be another $3,989,506.

24   Jonathan Saltzman, "Court move may benefit judge, official," *PJ*, 3 Dec. 1989: C-01.

25   John Sullivan, "Fay to get Smith's report on cover-up," *PJ*, 22 Mar. 1993: A-01.

26   Scott MacKay and Tracy Breton, "Assembly delays choosing new judge; Divided Senate votes to decide on justice, but House wants to wait," *PJ*, 18 Sep. 1992: A-01.

27   Laura Denvir Stith, "Judge Stith's remarks concerning Missouri's nonpartisan merit selection plan for judges," 11 Sep. 2007 (http://www.courts.mo.gov/pressrel.nsf.

28   At the request of CCRI, lawmakers introduced a constitutional amendment and a proposed statute. The amendment would end Grand Committee election of Supreme Court justices and establish a judicial nominating commission as a constitutional body to recommend "no more than five nor fewer than three" highly qualified persons for each vacancy. The governor would choose from that list and submit the name for advice and consent of the Senate. The statute would create the judicial nominating commission and spell out its procedures for filling vacancies in all lower courts. The constitutional resolutions were: 93-H 6633 by Rep. Nancy Benoit, 93-H 6610 by Rep. Mark Heffner, and 93-S 0792 by Sen. Rhoda Perry. The bills were: 93-H 5858 by Rep. Charles Knowles, 93-H 6609 by Rep. Nancy Benoit, and 93-S 0721 by Sen. Rhoda Perry. During the 1993 session, Sen. Myrth York and Sen. Walter Gray introduced duplicate versions.

29   The American Judicature Society (AJS) was founded in 1913 as an independent, national, nonpartisan organization of judges, lawyers, and other members of the public who seek to improve the justice system. Based in Chicago during the 1990s, the AJS promoted nonpartisan judicial nominating commissions. Its executive director, Kate Sampson, provided guidance and technical support in the design of merit selection proposals. See https://www.ajs.org/about/.

30   Scott MacKay, "Lederberg leads nominees to state Supreme Court," *PJ*, 6 Mar. 1993: A-01.

31   Tracy Breton, "Judge blasts high court candidate," *PJ*, 13 Mar. 1993: A-03.

32   Tracy Breton, "Rodgers criticizes candidate for bench," *PJ*, 20 Mar. 1993: A-03.

33   Tracy Breton, "Lederberg supporters out in force at hearing," *PJ*, 23 Mar. 1993: A-01.

34   Tracy Breton, "R.I. lawyers prefer Bourcier for high court," *PJ*, 26 Mar. 1993: B-05.

35   Editorial, "There's a better way," *PJ*, 1 May 1993: A-14; "Supreme Court selection process needs overhaul," *Woonsocket Call*, 2 May 1993: editorial page.

36   Editorial, "Politics dirties the system for picking judges," *Newport Daily News* (hereafter *NDN*), 5 May 1993: D-16.

37   Steven Stycos, "Courting Reform: Common Cause, Sundlun at odds on judge selection," *Providence Phoenix*, 6 May 1993: 1-01. Sundlun's informal screening panel included Judge Robert D. Krause, seven lawyers (Leonard Decof, Peter A. DiBiase, Louise Durfee, Robin E. Feder, Mark S. Mandell, Ralph P. Semonoff, and Walter F. Stone), and two lay people (Sister Claire Dugan and B. Jae Clanton).

38   HPW, Notes of conversation with Sheldon Whitehouse, 19 Apr. 1993. During an interview on 17 Jul. 2006, Whitehouse confirmed his comments and gave permission for me to acknowledge him as the source. He reveled in literary allusions. Valhalla appears in Norse sagas as the mythic hall for warriors killed in battle.

21 | PETITIONING GOVERNMENT · pages 246–256

1   Doane Hulick, "Judge limits enforcement of campaign finance law," *PJ*, 28 Aug. 1992: A-03. Scott MacKay, "Agreement allows political contributions from business," *PJ*, 6 Oct. 1992: A-07. Senior Judge Raymond J. Pettine overturned the ban on corporate contributions to referenda campaigns and a provision that gave publicly funded candidates free access to RI Public Broadcasting Channel 36 and some cable networks.

Russell Garland, "Section of R.I. Campaign law voided," *PJ*, 13 Jan. 1993: A-07. Pettine overturned the requirement for Political Action Committees (PACs) to report the source of all campaign contributions.

2   Michael L. Baker and Edward B. Mancini were partners in Hometown Properties Inc., but they kept a low profile, leaving Gifford as spokesperson.

3   Paul Edward Parker, "Gifford, partners in dump sue for libel," *PJ*, 19 Feb. 1991: B-01; Paul Edward Parker, "Gifford suit accuses woman of slander," *PJ*, 26 Mar. 1991: D-01; Paul Edward Parker, "Dump owners sue woman who wrote letter to DEM," *PJ*, 3 Dec. 1992: B-01.

4   Peter Lord, "Jeanne Foster never thought fighting development of housing at Warwick Pond might jeopardize her own home in a SLAPP suit," *PJ*, 23 Dec. 1990: A-01.

5   Peter Lord, "SLAPP: One man's concern is another's malice," *PJ*, 23 Dec. 1990: A-10.

6   93-S 829, "An Act Limiting Strategic Litigation Against Public Participation," by Sen. Myrth York. An identical anti-SLAPP bill, 93-S 853 was introduced by Sen. Robin Porter.

7   HPW, "SLAPP suit bill bolstered by activist's boldness," CCRI Newsletter, Sep. 1993: 6.

8   Minutes of the CCRI State Governing Board, 23 Feb. 1993.

9   Marilyn A. Hines and Mollie Gibbons, *Initiative and Referendum: A Report on its History and Use in the United States and a Model Constitutional Amendment* (CCRI: Providence, 1986). Voter initiative and referendum involves three distinct procedures. "Direct initiative" petitions to place a constitutional amendment or a statute directly on the ballot. "Indirect initiative" requires lawmakers to consider a proposal or have it go directly onto the ballot. "Direct referendum" would allow voters to approve or veto a law enacted by the legislature.

10   David D. Schmidt, *Citizen Lawmakers: The Ballot Initiative Revolution* (Philadelphia: Temple University Press, 1989), 7.

11   South Dakota (1898), Utah (1900), Oregon (1902), Montana (1904), Nevada (1904), Missouri (1906), Oklahoma (1907), Maine (1908), Michigan (1908), Arkansas (1909), Colorado (1910), Arizona (1910), California (1911), Washington (1912), Nebraska (1912), Ohio (1912), Idaho (1912), North Dakota (1914), and Massachusetts (1918).

12   John Kiffney, "Expenditure Council opposes state voter initiative process," *PJ*, 14 Mar. 1986: A-06; John Kiffney, "Controversial issue of voter initiative comes before delegates Thursday night," *PJ*, 29 Apr. 1986: A-03.

13   "Constitutional Convention committees to meet this week on a variety of issues," *PJ*, 4 May 1986: C-03. By a vote of 51–43, delegates approved the restrictive version that would prohibit measures like California's Prop 13 or Massachusetts's Prop 2½.

14   "ACLU is against half of proposed amendments," *PJ*, 30 Sep. 1986: A-14.

15   Dirk Johnson, "A Ban on Gay-Rights Laws Is Put on Hold in Colorado," NYT, 16 Jan 1993: 1.6. See Dirk Johnson, "Colorado Judge Overturns Initiative Banning Gay Rights," NYT, 15 Dec. 1993: 22.

16   *First National Bank* v. *Bellotti*, 435 U.S. 765 (1978). An excellent plain-language summary appears in *Democracy by Initiative: Shaping California's Fourth Branch of Government*, 2nd Edition, 2008: 303.

17   Scott MacKay, "Agreement allows political contributions from business," *PJ*, 6 Oct. 1992: A-07.

18   The proposed constitutional amendment included explicit guarantees: "No initiative shall be permitted which affects or concerns the political, personal or civil rights or liberties, including those guaranteed by Article I of the Rhode Island Constitution,

of any individual or group of individuals. The superior court shall have original jurisdiction to hear complaints arising under this section. Any individual shall have standing to bring an action at any time to enforce this section." Over several years, the language about affecting civil rights further evolved to read: "No initiative shall be permitted which shall abridge the civil rights or liberties. . ."

19   Greta Abbott, "Policy Recommendation on Initiative and Referendum," CCRI, 28 Oct. 1993.

20   "N. Kingstown lawmaker seeks to protect those who speak out on issues before government," *PJ*, 30 Jan. 1993: A-10.

21   Ron Cassinelli, "Pine: Suit tries to inhibit freedom," *PJ*, 5 Mar. 1993: C-10.

22   Cassinelli.

23   Scott MacKay, "House approves measure that discourages builders from suing vocal critics," *PJ*, 15 May 1992: B-03.

24   RI Constitution Article VI.22, "Restriction of gambling."

25   PL 93-249, "An Act Relating to Political Contributions by State Vendors," 27 Jul. 1993, added a new section, § 17-27, to the Rhode Island General Laws.

26   PL 93-354 and 93-448, "An Act Limiting Strategic Litigation against Public Participation," 27 Jul. 1993, added a new section § 9-33 to the Rhode Island General Laws.

22 | EMPIRE OF CRONIES · pages 257–264

1   Tracy Breton, Dean Starkman, and John Sullivan, "The Making of an Empire: Chief judge, top clerk preside over network of high-priced patronage," *PJ*, 25 Jul. 1993: A-01.

2   Breton, Starkman, Sullivan, list Fay at $128,500 per year in 1992.

3   "A written Q&A with Chief Judge Fay," *PJ*, 25 Jul. 1993: A-06. Question 2 asked if political influence had played a part in the hiring of 15 new employees: Charles A. Aube, John H. Barrette, Richard B. Bessette, Laura Boyle, Anthony J. Carnevale Jr., Louis Cioci, John D'Amico, Gail H. Fogarty, Edward M. Gorman, William J. McAtee, Robert J. Melucci, Anthony Piccirilli Jr., Ralph Pinto, Andrew Smith, and Austin O. Tague.

4   Dean Starkman and John Sullivan, "Secret court fund paid for liquor and limousines despite state bans," *PJ*, 7 Aug. 1993: A-01; "Fay, Smith maintain secret account at court," *PJ*, 6 Aug. 1993: A-01; "Court fund paid for Fay oil portrait," *PJ*, 8 Aug. 1993: A-01; $175,000 spent since 1988 from secret account," *PJ*, 9 Aug. 1993: A-01.

5   Dean Starkman and John Sullivan, "Inquiry sought into Fay's role in account," *PJ*, 12 Aug. 1993: A-01; "Justices lay blame with Smith for secret fund," *PJ*, 14 Aug. 1993: A-01.

6   John Sullivan, "Fay disclaims role in secret fund," *PJ*, 18 Aug. 1993: A-01.

7   Dan Barry and John Sullivan, "23 senators seek probe, ask Fay to step aside," *PJ*, 19 Aug. 1993: A-01; "House speaker urges Fay to quit high court," *PJ*, 20 Aug. 1993: A-01.

8   Ira Chinoy and Mike Stanton, "Probe faults $170,000 paid from accounts under Fay," *PJ*, 21 Aug. 1993: A-01. See also Dan Barry, "Repay $92,000, high court told," *PJ*, 3 Sep. 1993:A-01. The three accounts were (1) The Rhode Island Bar Examiners account, which administered bar exams, (2) The Character and Fitness account, which covered costs of background checks, and (3) the Special Account, which received money from the other two. Auditors determined that $61,497 from the Special Account was improper.

9   Dan Barry, Ira Chinoy, Dean Starkman, and John Sullivan, "Fay gives arbitration work to friends, allies," *PJ*, 24 Aug. 1993: A-01. The five attorneys listed in the article were Everett A. Petronio, Christopher Boyle, Paul Foster, Mark S. Krieger, and Jonathan F. Oster.

10 Dan Barry, Ira Chinoy, Mike Stanton, Dean Starkman, and John Sullivan, "Fay leaves high court until charges are resolved," *PJ*, 26 Aug. 1993: A-01; Dan Barry and Mike Stanton, "Chief Justice Fay pleads not guilty to ethics counts," *PJ*, 27 Aug. 1993: A-01. Under authority granted in RIGL 36-14.1-4 (b), Attorney General Jeffrey B. Pine charged Fay with using his office to benefit a business associate, a violation under RIGL 36-14-5 (d).

11 Mike Stanton, "House to Fay: It's time to leave," *PJ*, 1 Sep. 1993: A-01.

12 Dean Starkman and John Sullivan, "Fay rejects call to leave high court," *PJ*, 2 Sep. 1993: A-01. In addition to the article, the newspaper published the text of Fay's letter.

13 M. Charles Bakst, "Fay's words on propriety come back to haunt him," *PJ*, 29 Aug. 1993: I-01.

14 Mike Stanton, "Harwood sets impeachment against Fay in motion," *PJ*, 14 Sep. 1993: A-01.

15 Russell Garland, "Impeachment first step toward removal," *PJ*, 28 Sep. 1993: A-11.

16 Scott MacKay, "Poll says Fay should resign or be removed," *PJ*, 28 Sep. 1993: A-10.

17 Dan Barry, Mike Stanton, Dean Starkman, and John Sullivan, "Fay intervened on tickets," *PJ*, 1 Oct. 1993: A-01.

18 Thomas F. Fay, Letter to His Excellency Bruce G. Sundlun, Governor of the State of Rhode Island and Providence Plantations, 8 Oct. 1993. Facsimile printed in the *PJ*, 9 Oct. 1993: A-04.

19 RI Constitution, Article IV.7 reads, in part: "A quorum of the grand committee shall consist of a majority of all the members of the senate and a majority of all the members of the house of representatives duly assembled pursuant to an invitation from one of said bodies which has been accepted by the other . . ."

20 G. Wayne Miller, "RIght Now! urges reform in choosing judges," *PJ*, 27 Aug. 1993: A-08.

21 Scott MacKay, "Most lawmakers want moratorium on selecting judges," *PJ*, 14 Sep. 1993: A-09. On September 13, Silverman sent letters to Senate Majority Leader Paul S. Kelly and House Speaker John B. Harwood listing 26 senators and 53 representatives who had signed the pledge. Eighteen of the Senate signers were Democrats (Roger Badeau, William Enos, William P. Fitzpatrick, Maryellen Goodwin, Walter J. Gray, Catherine E. Graziano, William V. Irons, Thomas Izzo, J. Michael Lenihan, James P. McStay, John R. O'Leary, M. Teresa Paiva Weed, Rhoda E. Perry, Joseph M. Polisena, Dominick J. Ruggerio, Eleanor C. Sasso, Paul J. Tavares, Myrth York), and eight were Republicans (Dennis L. Algiere, David E. Bates, John Feroce, June N. Gibbs, John W. Lyle Jr., Mary A. Parella, Robin Porter, W. Michael Sullivan). Forty-four of the Representatives who signed were Democrats (Edith H. Ajello, Stephen Anderson, Sandra M. Barone, John D. Barr II, Nancy L. Benoit, Melvoid J. Benson, Russell Bramley, Robert Brousseau, Barbara Burlingame, Bambilyn B. Cambio, Kenneth Carter, Elaine Coderre, Raymond C. Coelho, Paul W. Crowley, Rodney D. Driver, Joseph Faria, Eugene F. Garvey, Francis A. Gaschen, Peter Ginaitt, James J. Ginolfi, Ellen A. Kellner, Linda J. Kushner, James Langevin, Beatrice A. Lanzi, Donald D. Large, Mark C. Lauzon, Charles J. Levesque, Mary Levesque, Charlene Lima, Hubert E. Little, Maria Lopes, Robert B. Lowe, Jennifer A. Martelli, William C. McGowan, Rene R. Menard, Frank A. Montanaro, Paul E. Moura, Thomas A. Palangio, Leonidas P. Raptakis, Clinton O. Remington III, Henry C. Rose, Paul

V. Sherlock, Steven Smith, Anastasia P. Williams), and nine were Republicans (Christine Callahan, Sandra J. Campbell, Richard E. Fleury, Leona Kelley, Bruce J. Long, Charles E. Millard Jr., Mary C. Ross, Wayne L. Salisbury, Mary Lou Walter).

22 "Senate panel named to study judicial reform," *PJ*, 8 Sep. 1993: A-05. Senate Judiciary chairperson Domenic A. DiSandro III was to chair the select committee. Members were Democrats Sandra K. Hanaway, Joseph J. McGair, James P. McStay, M. Teresa Paiva Weed, and Walter J. Gray; and Republicans Dennis L. Algiere, David E. Bates, and Robin Porter.

23 | REVOLVING DOOR · pages 265–267

1 See Ch. 17, "Loose Ends."
2 Katherine Gregg, "High court hears arguments; Ethics law attacked," *PJ*, 22 Sep. 1993: A-01.
3 Lauren Jones, "Brief and Appendix of Amicus Curiae, Common Cause of Rhode Island *In re Governor's Request for an Advisory Opinion*," 93-120-M.P., 7 Sep. 1993: 1. The years preceding the 1986 constitutional convention were marked by scandal and corruption at all levels of government. Indeed, widespread breaches of trust, cronyism, impropriety, and other violations of ethical standards decimated the public's trust in government. *In Re: Advisory Opinion to Governor (Ethics Commission)*, 91-577 M.P., 612 A.2d 1 (RI 1992).
4 Jones: 26.
5 *In Re: Advisory from the Governor*, 93–120 M.P., 633 A.2d 664, (RI 1993), 15 Nov. 1993: 16.
6 The justices paraphrased the RI Constitution, Article III. 7. The actual text reads: "The people of the state of Rhode Island believe that public officials and employees must adhere to the highest standards of ethical conduct, respect the public trust and the rights of all persons, be open, accountable and responsive, avoid the appearance of impropriety and not use their position for private gain or advantage. Such persons shall hold their positions during good behavior."
7 *In Re: Advisory from the Governor*, 93–120 M.P., 633 A.2d 664, (RI 1993), 15 Nov. 1993: 10.
8 Scott MacKay, "High court upholds revolving-door law," *PJ*, 16 Nov. 1993: A-01.
9 RI Constitution, Article IX.5: Authority to fill vacancies. The governor may fill vacancies in office not otherwise provided for by this Constitution or by law, until the same shall be filled by the general assembly, or by the people.
10 Jones: 32.

24 | ELECTRONIC ACCESS · pages 268–274

1 "Change the World Contest Winners," *Apple Catalog*, Spring 1993: 2, 18.
2 Kevin T. Grau and Michael C. Cerullo, "Q&A on public access to legislative process data," Common Cause Rhode Island, 5 Apr. 1994.
3 Blue Ribbon Commission on the General Assembly, *The General Assembly in Rhode Island: A Blueprint for the 21st Century* (Providence, Dec. 1993), 40.
4 94-H 9065, "An Act Relating To The Joint Committee On Legislative Services — Public Access To General Assembly Proceedings And Legislative Information," by Rep. Antonio J. Pires; 94-S 2389, (same title), by Sen. J. Michael Lenihan.

5   West Publishing compiled laws enacted each year and linked them to judicial decisions in *West's General Laws of Rhode Island Annotated* (Eagan, MN).

6   94-S 2389 Substitute A/3, "Relating to the Joint Committee on Legislative Services — Public Access to General Assembly Proceedings and Legislative Information," by Sens. Lenihan, Porter, Gray, Sullivan, and Paiva Weed. The Lenihan version became PL 94-377. Its text appears in RIGL 22-11-3.1(b).

7   Mike Stanton, "Secrecy in Rhode Island: At the doors of democracy, fighting for the right to know," *PJ*, 24 Jul. 1994: A-01.

8   Years later Melissa Menard Goldberger contacted me through Facebook. She assured me she had not been a spy, that her uncle had nothing to do with her being assigned to Common Cause but that he was curious about what she did for us. Email 25 Mar. 2014.

25 | Hard Choices · pages 275–293

1   Scott MacKay, "Most lawmakers want moratorium on selecting judges," *PJ*, 14 Sep. 1993: A-09. See Ch. 22, "Empire of Cronies," fn21, for the list of 26 senators and 53 representatives who signed the pledge.

2   "Senate panel named to study judicial reform," *PJ*, 8 Sep. 1993: C-05; Scott MacKay, "Senate panel considers judicial selection," *PJ*, 28 Oct. 1993: D-16.

3   Scott MacKay, "Agreement near on process for picking judges," *PJ*, 11 Dec. 1993: A-01.

4   Russell Garland, "RIght Now! offers plan for picking judges," *PJ*, 17 Dec. 1993: A-08.

5   Russell Garland, "Proposals aimed at modernizing R.I. legislature are unveiled," *PJ*, 14 Dec. 1993: A-01.

6   John Kiffney, "Constitutional Convention Delegate candidates from District 2," *PJ*, 21 Oct. 1985: C-03.

7   "2 women senators picked to head committees," *PJ*, 7 Jan. 1993: B-06. Majority Leader Paul S. Kelly appointed York to head the Committee on Health, Education, and Welfare; he appointed Goodwin to head Special Legislation.

8   93-S 1047, "An Act Providing for Judges to be Selected by Judicial Nominating Committee," by Sen. Myrth York.

9   Katherine Gregg, "Myrth York to take on Sundlun in a primary," *PJ*, 24 Feb. 1994: A-01.

10 94-H 8490, "Joint Resolution to Approve and Publish And Submit to the Electors a Proposition of Amendment to the Constitution of the State (Regarding the Composition of the House of Representatives and the Senate)" by Rep. James Langevin.

11 Scott MacKay, "Kelly, Harwood split on court post," *PJ*, 8 Jan. 1994: A-03.

12 Russell Garland, "Judicial selection report due in 2 weeks," *PJ*, 21 Jan. 1994: B-04.

13 93-H 7657, "Joint Resolution to Approve and Publish and Submit to the Electors a Proposition of Amendment to the Constitution of the State (Judicial Selection)," by Rep. Nancy Benoit; 94-H 8081, (same title).

14 94-H 8082, "An Act Relating to Judicial Selection," by Rep. Barbara Burlingame.

15 Associated Press, "Legislators support judicial reform bill," *The Westerly Sun*, 27 Jan. 1994: 2.

16 94-S 2194, "Joint Resolution to Approve and Publish and Submit to the Electors a Proposition of Amendment to the Constitution of the State (Judicial Selection)," by Sen. Myrth York; and 94-S 2190, "An Act Relating to Judicial Selection—Create Eleven-Member Commission on Judicial Nominations," by Sen. Rhoda Perry.

17 94-S 2348, "Joint Resolution to Approve and Publish and Submit to the Electors a

Proposition of Amendment to the Constitution of the State (Judicial Selection)," by Sens. Paul Kelly and Domenic DiSandro; and 94-S 2346, "An Act Relating to Judicial Selection," by Sens. Paul Kelly and Domenic DiSandro.

18 In the 1994 legislative session, 22 bills were introduced to address judicial selection, 3 to establish judicial review.

19 HPW, "Q&A: Choose Judges for Merit, Not Politics," CCRI, 4 Mar. 1994.

20 In January 1994, the RIght Now! Steering Committee included Rhode Island presidents, chairpersons, or executive directors from: AARP (American Association of Retired Persons, State Legislative Committee), AAUW (American Association of University Women), AIA (American Institute of Architects), Chambers of Commerce (Greater Providence and Northern Rhode Island), Common Cause, Community Relations Council of the Jewish Federation, Diocese of Providence, League of Women Voters, NAACP (National Association for the Advancement of Colored People), NCCJ (National Conference of Christians and Jews), Rhode Island Bar Association, RIPEC (RI Public Expenditure Council), State Council of Churches, Save the Bay and the United Way of Southeastern New England.

21 HPW "Letter to Senate Select Panel on Judicial Selection," 23 Sep. 1993. RIght Now! urged the panel to establish a nine-member judicial nominating commission under a formula that would direct the governor to choose attorneys and non-attorneys: one attorney from a pool of four submitted by majority leaders of the House and Senate; one attorney from a pool of four submitted by minority leaders of the House and Senate; two attorneys from a list of eight submitted by the Rhode Island Bar Association; one professor of law from a list of four nominees submitted by the Bar Association; one non-attorney from a pool of four submitted by majority leaders of the House and Senate; one non-attorney from a pool of four submitted by minority leaders of the House and Senate; two non-attorney public members without regard to lists.

22 Exodus 18: 21-22.

23 Dean Starkman, "The making of a cover-up," *PJ*, 13 Feb. 1994: A-01; Dan Barry and Mike Stanton, "Smith cars left a $2,000 trail of tickets on Providence streets," *PJ*, 13 Feb. 1994: A-08.

24 Katherine Gregg, "Mayer seeking pension repeal for union leaders," *PJ*, 18 Feb. 1994: A-01. An affidavit of James M. Reilly, assistant director of the State Retirement System, 12 Sep. 1994, in Superior Court CA 94-0389L, listed the ages and pension history of 24 union officials: John Callaci, Diana Casey, Edward Casey Jr., Robert Casey, Bernard Connerton, Ronald DiOrio, Denise Felice, Joseph Grande, Gloria Heisler, Karen Comiskey Jenkins, Robert Joy, Janice Lanik, Charlene Lee, Cornelius McAuliffe, Edward McElroy, Harvey Press, Vincent Santianiello, Joan Silva, Bernard Singleton, Diane Thurber, Jeanette Wooley, Jennie Blanchet, Richard DeOrsey, and Frank Montanaro.

25 Katherine Gregg, "Credit for union time paid off for DiOrio," *PJ*, 31 Mar. 1991: A-11.

26 94-S 2921, "An Act Relating to Public Officers and Employees — Evicting Non-Employee and Non-Teacher Members from the Retirement System," by Sen. Michael J. Flynn.

27 94-S 2194, "Joint Resolution to Approve and Publish and Submit to the Electors a Proposition of Amendment to the Constitution of the State (Judicial Selection)," by Sen. Myrth York; 94-S 2190, "An Act Relating to Judicial Selection," by Sen. Rhoda Perry.

28 94-S 2346 Substitute A, "An Act Relating to Judicial Selection," by Sen. Domenic DiSandro.

29   Russell Garland, "Senate approves changes in way R.I. judges would be selected," *PJ*,
      16 Mar. 1994: D-05.

30   94-H 9173, "Joint Resolution to Approve and Publish and Submit to the Electors a
      Proposition of Amendment to the Constitution of the State (Judicial Selection)," by
      Rep. Charles Knowles.

31   Russell Garland, "Judge-selection bill is approved," *PJ*, 9 Apr. 1994: A-06. The bills
      were 94-H 9174 SubA/3, "Joint Resolution to Amend the Rhode Island Constitution
      – Judicial Selection," and 94-H 9173 SubA/2, "Judicial Reform Act of 1994 – Create
      Commission on Judicial Nominations," both by Reps. Charles Knowles and George
      Caruolo.

32   94-S [2426/2672], "Amendment to the RI Constitution Regarding Compensation of
      the House of Representatives and the Senate," by Sen. John Revens.

33   94-S 2427, "Amendment to the RI Constitution Regarding Composition of the
      House of Representatives and the Senate," by Sen. John Revens.

34   Russell Garland, "Senate approves smaller Assembly," *PJ*, 14 Apr. 1994: D-16.

35   Senators approved the legislative pay amendment by a vote of 42–2 and the downsiz-
      ing vote by 42–4. *SJrnl*, 22 Mar. 1994: 6; 13 Apr. 1994: 10.

36   94-H 8490, "Joint Resolution to Approve and Publish and Submit to the Electors a
      Proposition of Amendment to the Constitution of the State (General Assembly)," by
      Reps. Langevin, Knowles, Williamson, Flaherty, and Crowley.

37   *HJrnl.*, 2 Jun. 1994: 8.

38   Russell Garland, "Key issues still face Assembly," *PJ*, 16 May 1994: A-01; Garland,
      "R.I. changes the method of selecting its judges," *PJ*, 3 Jun. 1994: A-01.

39   94-S 2921, "An Act Relating to Public Officers and Employees — Evicting Non-
      Employee and Non-Teacher Members from the Retirement System," by Sen. Michael
      J. Flynn.

40   "Mayer seeking pension repeal for union leaders," *PJ*, 18 Feb. 1994: A-01.

41   "ACLU against pension revocation," *PJ*, 27 Apr. 1994: B-10; "Bill to kill unionists'
      pensions goes to governor," *PJ*, 17 Jun. 1994: A-01; PL 94-413, "An Act Relating
      to Public Officers and Employees — Evicting Non-Employee and Non-Teacher
      Members from the Retirement System."

42   Katherine Gregg and Scott MacKay, "Adjournment plans may waylay initiative to
      shrink legislature," *PJ*, 1 Jul. 1994: C-06.

43   "Assembly sends cut in size, pay hike to voters," *PJ*, 8 Jul. 1994: A-01; Elinor Mills,
      "Debate on assembly's record centers on quality of reform," Associated Press/
      Newport Daily News, 9 Jul. 1994: A-1.

44   Janet Hayden Jagger, *Most Admirable: The Rhode Island State House*, (Providence: RI
      State House Restoration Society: 2002), 21.

26 | HISTORIC VOTES · pages 294–301

1   Thomas Frank, "West withdraws as candidate to direct state ethics panel," *PJ*, 7 Jan.
      1993: A-01. See Ch. 17, "Loose Ends."

2   Thomas Frank, "Ethics panel to probe pre-'87 matters," *PJ*, 10 Mar. 1993: C-07;
      Thomas Frank, "$69,150 in ethics fines goes unpaid," *PJ*, 28 Feb. 1994: A-01; Thomas
      Frank, "Ethics panel ends policy of acting only in response to complaints," *PJ*, 11
      Aug. 1993: B-05; Lynn Arditi, "Ethics Commission agrees to consider mandat-
      ing ethics courses for officials," *PJ*, 29 Sep. 1993: C-06; Thomas Frank, "Harwood
      accused of ethics violations," *PJ*, 15 Oct. 1993: A-01; Thomas Frank, "Turf hostility
      between Assembly, ethics panel evident at House hearing," *PJ*, 3 Mar. 1994: D-10.

3   Thomas Frank, "Quinn's power alienated Ethics Commission," *PJ*, 12 Jun. 1994: A-01; "Ethics Commission in dilemma involving — that's right, ethics," *PJ*, 21 Apr. 1994: D-15; Thomas Frank, "Quinn ends a stormy tenure to run for attorney general against Pine," *PJ*, 8 Jun. 1994: A-01.

4   The matching-funds program appears in RIGL 17-25-18, 19, and 20; RIGL 17-25-21 allowed candidates with a primary to raise and spend 1/3 more than the limit. Participating candidates for governor could spend no more than $2 million if they faced a primary opponent or $1.5 million if they did not; candidates for the other four statewide offices could spend $500,000 if they had a primary or $375,000 if they did not.

5   Russell Garland, "Commissioners to screen judges are sworn in," *PJ*, 16 Jun. 1994: D-20. The first lawyers on the panel were: Michael A. Kelly, chair, partner at Adler Pollock & Sheehan; William Devereux, a partner at McGovern Noel & Benik; Lise J. Gescheidt, a former public defender in private defense practice; Peter J. McGinn, a partner in Tillinghast Collins & Graham; and Girard R. Visconti, a partner in Visconti & Petrocelli. The four non-lawyers were: Sharon Burgess, a Blood Bank technician; Barbara Colvin, a former director of surgical nursing at Rhode Island Hospital; George C. Hartmann, a professor emeritus of biology from Rhode Island College; and Dr. Pablo Rodriguez, the medical director of Planned Parenthood.

6   Russell Garland, "Panel to submit nominees to fill seven judge posts in three state courts," *PJ*, 24 Jul. 1994: B-05.

7   RIGL 8-16.1. This section has been modified many times since 1994. For the latest version, check http://www.rilin.state.ri.us/Statutes/TITLE8/8-16.1/8-16.1-6.htm. See Afterword, "Making Government Good."

8   Brown Mathematics Prof. Thomas Banchoff had left the state on sabbatical, and Roger Williams Law School Asst. Prof. Michael J. Yelnosky took over. See Michael J. Yelnosky, "Rhode Island's Judicial Nominating Commission: Can 'Reform' Become Reality?" *RWU Law Review*, Spring 1996: Vol. 1, Num. 1: 87 ff.

9   Russell Garland, "Panel to nominate state judges seeks opinions on candidates," *PJ*, 19 Jul. 1994: C-07.

10   For analysis of how interviews became public, see Yelnosky: 91–94.

11   Thomas J. Morgan, "Judicial nominees selected," *PJ*, 13 Aug. 1994: A-01; Michael Maynard, "Sundlun nominates 4 more people for Family, District Court seats," *PJ*, 14 Aug. 1994: B-02.

12   Russell Garland, "Judicial nominee put in position of defending fitness to serve on court," *PJ*, 3 Sep. 1994: A-03.

13   Russell Garland, "Letters imperil Rotondi approval as judge," *PJ*, 15 Sep. 1994: D-13; Scott MacKay, "Judgeship nomination withdrawn," *PJ*, 16 Sep. 1994: A-01.

14   Katherine Gregg, "Machtley, Almond slug it out," *PJ*, 8 Sep. 1994: A-01.

15   Vote counts in the 1994 Republican primary for governor were: Almond (26,873) and Machtley (18,150). http://www.elections.ri.gov/elections/results/1994/repprimary.php.

16   Vote counts in the 1994 Democratic primary for governor were: York (56,719), Sundlun (27,432), Louise Durfee (11,914), and Donald Gill (3,067). http://www.elections.ri.gov/elections/results/1994/demprimary.php state.

17   In the race for secretary of state: Langevin (43,076), Ray Rickman (22,990), Julia P. Califano (14,432), and John M. Carval012 (5,283). RIBOE, http://www.elections.ri.gov/elections/results/1994/demprimary.php.

18   In the spring of 1994, Operation Clean Sweep merged with US-PAC, the Government Accountability Project (GAP), Reform '92, and the Rhode Island

Taxpayers Association (RITA) to form Operation Clean Government (OCG). OCG played a strong role in passage of the judicial reform amendment but did not participate in the campaign for modernizing the General Assembly.

19   Editorial, "Assembly needs trimming," *Narragansett Times*, 26 Oct. 1994: 15.

20   RIBOE totals: 64.4% (178,775) rejected Question 3 (Legislative Compensation), and 35.6% (98,845) approved it.

21   See Ch. 19, "Paying the Piper." See also *Kass* v. *Retirement Board*, 88-348-A, 567 A.2d 358 (1989).

22   RIBOE, http://www.elections.ri.gov/elections/results/1994/governor.php, Almond received 171,194 (47.4%) votes statewide to 157,361 (43.5%) for York and 32,822 (9.1%) for Cool Moose Party candidate Robert J. Healey Jr.

23   Katherine Gregg, "Spending limit for campaigns leveled the field in governor's race," *PJ*, 8 Dec. 1994: D-15. Pine qualified for $163,029 in public money, while Quinn could match only $33,422.

24   RIBOE, http://www.elections.ri.gov/elections/results/1994/referenda.php.

27 | Deep Root · pages 305–316

1   See Ch. 14, "Triumphs." Whitehouse's "senior policy-making, discretionary, or confidential position" became a lynchpin of the General Assembly's final Revolving Door Law, where it appeared ten times in RIGL 36-14-5 (n) and (o). The precise language would become contentious in 2013 when a department director sought permission to apply for a judgeship. Katherine Gregg, "Licht looking at Superior Court seat," *PJ*, 4 Oct. 2013: 1, and Philip Marcelo, Katherine Gregg, Randal Edgar, "Licht gets through the door," *PJ*, 14 Oct. 2013: 2.

2   RI Constitution, Article VI.10: Continuation of previous powers. — The general assembly shall continue to exercise the powers it has heretofore exercised, unless prohibited in this Constitution.

3   Ken Mingis, "Group appeals decision to build hotel on beach," *PJ*, 2 Oct. 1984: C-01.

4   M. Charles Bakst, "Ripples from beach project may touch state panel members," *PJ*, 20 Oct. 1985: C-12.

5   *State of North Carolina, James C. Wallace and David Howells* v. *Roger W. Bone and Robie L. Nash*, 286 S.E.2d 79 (1982).

6   Robert C. Frederiksen, "Coastal Council membership law is ruled illegal grab for power," *PJ*, 22 Apr. 1986: A-01.

7   *Easton's Point Association, Inc.* v. *Coastal Resources Management Council*, 84–3737, (RI Superior Court, 21 Apr. 1986): 13.

8   Tracy Breton, "High court takes hands-off approach, preserving makeup of suspect agencies," *PJ*, 10 Mar. 1987: A-01. See *Easton's Point Association, Inc.* v. *Coastal Resources Management Council*, 522 A.2d 199 (RI 1987).

9   PL 80-342 established the NBC: RIGL 46-25. See Peter Hufstader, *Democracy Betrayed: Conflicts of Interest and Failures of Oversight in Rhode Island State Government*, (Providence: Common Cause, 2000), 25–26. The four charter legislative members were all Democrats: Reps. Vincent J. Mesolella (North Providence) and Donald J. Ferry (Johnston); Sens. William Castro (East Providence) and Donald Hickey (Providence).

10   Lisa Prevost, "V.I.P. Vin," *Providence Phoenix*, 23 Jun. 1995: 10.

11   Beverly M. Clay, "1994 Campaign Finance — Rep. Mesolella," *Focus RI*, OCG, May 1996: 5; Beverly M. Clay, "August 28 Ethics Commission Testimony," *Focus RI*, OCG, Sep. 1996: 2. Clay analyzed public documents at the RI Board of Elections. She listed

contributions to Rep. Vincent Mesolella during the election cycle 1993–94 and NBC payments to vendors in 1994–1995.

12   Thomas Frank, "Enviro-Gro finds a winning business situation, but officials deny politics influenced panel's decision on sludge disposal contract," *PJ*, 17 Nov. 1991: A-03.

13   The commission ruled that as long as Mesolella did not "personally participate in the presentation," the existing law "does not prohibit the interests of his company from appearing before the Bay Commission." RIEC Adv. Op. 89–108: 5 Jan. 1990.

14   Robert C. Frederiksen, "Incinerator firm seeks out-of-state sludge," *PJ*, 8 Jun. 1994.

15   Robert C. Frederiksen, "Conflict over sludge incinerator at Fields Point heats up in House," *PJ*, 19 Jun. 1994: A-05; "York asks head of Bay panel to resign," *PJ*, 15 Jun. 1994: D-06.

16   Robert C. Frederiksen, "Bay panel set to sign sludge contract," *PJ*, 13 Sep. 1994: D-08.

28 | DECLARATION OF WAR · pages 317–331

1   Scott MacKay, "Naming of Hawkins unleashes political storm," *PJ*, 27 Oct. 1993: A-04.

2   Christopher Beall, "Video poker change sparks confrontations at Lot hearing," *PJ*, 2 Dec. 1993: A-01; Christopher Rowland, "Vendors paid bill for Lottery hearing," *PJ*, 17 Dec. 1993: A-01.

3   Christopher Rowland, "Lottery chairman's Paris convention trip cost state $5,890," *PJ*, 30 Jul. 1994: A-01.

4   Russell Garland, "Lottery chairman McBurney given the boot," *PJ*, 1 Dec. 1994: A-01; Robert Kramer, "Sundlun: 23 percent raise for lottery chief 'excessive,'" *PJ*, 1 Dec. 1994: D-13.

5   HPW, "Letter to Senate Majority Leader Paul S. Kelly," 2 Dec. 1994.

6   Coastal Resources Management Council (Created in 1971): Sen. Rhoda Perry (95-S 1200) and Rep. Charlene Lima (95-H 6211); Commission On Judicial Tenure And Discipline (Created in 1974): Sen. David Bates (95-S 0538) and Rep. David Cicilline (95-H 6455); Lottery Commission (Created in 1956): Sen. James McStay (95-S 0708) and Rep. Ellen Kellner (95-H 6247); Narragansett Bay Commission (Created in 1980): Sen. Will Fitzpatrick (95-S 0864) and Rep. Charlene Lima (95-H 6670); Port Authority (Created in 1956, renamed Economic Development Corporation): Rep. Bruce Long (95-H 6482) and Sen. Robin Porter (95-S 1107); Solid Waste Management Corporation (Created in 1976): Rep. Francis Gaschen (95-H 6252) and Sen. Rhoda Perry (95-S 1177); Unclassified Pay Plan Board (Created in 1952 but expanded with legislators in 1973 and a legislative majority in 1978): Rep. Nancy Benoit (95-H 5852) and Sen. James McStay (95-S 0707).

7   M. Charles Bakst, "At State House, there's theory - and reality," *PJ*, 28 Feb. 1995: D-01.

8   95-H 6447, "An Act Relating to the General Assembly — Disclosure by Non-profit Organizations," by Rep. Vincent Mesolella.

9   Sheldon Whitehouse, "Assembly's appointments should end," *PJ*, 19 Jan. 1995: A-13.

10   Sheldon Whitehouse, "The Impetuous Vortex," *Rhode Island Bar Journal*, Apr. 1995: 7. Whitehouse expanded that article in "Appointments by the Legislature Under the Rhode Island Separation of Powers Doctrine: The Hazards of the Road Less Traveled," *Roger Williams University Law Review*, Vol. 1, No. 1: Spring 1996.

11   William E. Colleran, "Our unclassified pay follies," 24 Feb. 1995: A-15. Other pieces include: "A short history of the Revolving Door," *PJ*, 24 Apr. 1992; "Waiting for doors to revolve open," *PJ*, 20 Sep. 1992; "The RISDIC Class of '86," *PJ*, 8 Jan. 1993; "Our

crowded Hall of Shame," *PJ*, 4 Apr. 1993; "A jarring jaunt through the budget," *PJ*,
2 Aug. 1993; "For 100 years in R.I., the judicial cart was upright," *PJ*, 29 Sep. 1993;
"Don't let them go along to get along," *PJ*, 20 Feb. 1994; "R.I.'s pensioners: Well,
shiver your timbers!" *PJ*, 4 May 1994; "We could get rolled by those 'good times,' " *PJ*,
1 Jul. 1994; "More R.I. budget porkers," *PJ*, 27 Jul. 1994.

12   Russell Garland, "Library Board likes move to Assembly over Almond's plan," *PJ*,
9 May 1995: D-06.

13   95-H 6907, "An Act Relating to State Library Services," by Reps Montanaro, Panciera,
Pires, Carter, and Menard.

14   Michael Cerullo, email to HPW, 8 Apr. 1995.

15   Russell Garland, "Library Board."

16   RI Constitution, Article X.3.

17   HPW, "Draft Senate Resolution Requesting that the Rhode Island Supreme Court
Advise the Senate Regarding Separation of Powers," 8 Feb. 1995. On the same day, we
presented similar resolutions to House Speaker John B. Harwood and Gov. Lincoln
C. Almond.

18   HPW, "To the Honorable John B. Harwood, Speaker of the House, and the
Honorable Paul S. Kelly, Majority Leader of the Senate," CCRI, 5 Apr. 1995.

19   95-H 5683, "An Act Relating to Food and Drugs — Milk Content," by Reps. Lima,
Palumbo, Bramley, Montanaro, and S. Anderson.

20   95-H 5683.

21   95-H 6670, "An Act Relating to Narragansett Bay Water Quality Management District
Commission," by Reps Charlene Lima and Bruce Long; 95-H 6447, "An Act Relating
to the General Assembly," by Rep. Vincent Mesolella. The House legislative counsel
summarized: "This act requires nonprofit organizations to report any donation in
excess of membership fees to the Secretary of State's office if the organization has any
representatives testify before legislative committees or governmental agencies."

22   "Mesolella withdraws bill requiring lobbying nonprofit groups to identify their
donors," *PJ*, 28 Apr. 1995: B-05.

23   Lisa Prevost, "V.I.P. Vin," *Providence Phoenix*, 23 Jun. 1995: 10.

24   95-S 867, "An Act Relating to Rabies Control," by Sen. William Enos.

25   Editorial, "Rabid conflicts of interest," *PJ*, 22 Jun. 1995: B-08.

26   PL 95-388 "An Act Relating to Rabies Control," Passed in Concurrence,
Notwithstanding the Veto of the Governor, 4 Aug. 1995.

29 | A QUESTION OF ETHICS · pages 332–341

1   RIEC, *In Re: John Harwood*, Settlement of Complaint 93–66, 31 Aug. 1994. See
Thomas Frank and Thomas J. Morgan, "Speaker Harwood pays $5,000 to settle eth-
ics matter, denies he erred," *PJ*, 3 Sep. 1994: A-01.

2   "Healey named permanent director of ethics panel," *PJ*, 8 Nov. 1994: D-04.

3   See Ch. 14, "Triumphs," and 23, "Revolving Door."

4   Lee Dykas, "Ethics Commission starts public hearings leading up to revising ethics
code," *PJ*, 3 Feb. 1995: A-05.

5   HPW, "Memorandum to Martin F. Healey," 18 May 1995.

6   Thomas Frank, "Ethics panel drafts a 'drastic' code," *PJ*, 30 Oct. 1995: A-01.

7   North Carolina Supreme Court, *Wallace v. Bone*, 286 S.E.2d 79 (N. C. 1982); *Easton's
Point Association, Inc. v. Coastal Resources Management Council*, C.A. No. 84-3737
(21 Apr. 1986)

8   Doug Riggs, "A milestone for Common Cause," *PJ*, 5 Nov. 1995: A-01.

9   Robert Kramer, "Court to weigh revision in code of ethics. The question, to be referred to the high court by the governor, is whether the Ethics Commission can bar legislators from sitting on independent boards and commissions," *PJ*, 17 Nov. 1995: A-01.

10 Geoffrey C. Hazard Jr., "Re: Authority of Rhode Island Ethics Commission to Promulgate Code of Ethics Proposed Section 5013A," 9 Aug. 1998.

11 Thomas Frank, "Ex-senator seeks $106,000 in pensions," *PJ*, 15 Nov. 1995: A-01.

12 See Ch. 6, "Dashed Hopes," for the dramatic story of how Gregg got crucial pension documents.

13 M. Charles Bakst, "Sen. Hickey seeks post of retirement director despite possible conflict," *PJ*, 3 May 1985: A-08; Katherine Gregg, "How some state retirees made '$50,000 Club,'" *PJ*, 14 Oct. 1991: A-01. Hickey was a teacher and later principal at Bishop Hendricken High School.

14 Marilyn A. Hines, "Memorandum: Quasi-Public Agencies and Draft Proposals 5013 & 5013A," 26 Jul. 1996: 2–3. Hines had been executive director of CCRI during the 1986 Constitutional Convention.

15 HPW, "Testimony before the Rhode Island Ethics Commission," 28 Aug. 1996. We argued that legislators should be prohibited from executive functions they had taken into their hands by enacting laws: (1) Purchase, take, receive, lease, mortgage, or otherwise acquire, own, hold, improve, use real or personal property; (2) Sell, convey, mortgage, pledge, lease, exchange, transfer, and otherwise dispose of real or personal property belonging directly or indirectly to the state; (3) Employ architects, engineers, attorneys, accountants, advisors, consultants, and agents for the administration of properties controlled directly or indirectly by the state; (4) Establish agencies, implement programs, administer or supervise projects, execute contracts pursuant to law; (5) Borrow money, pay debt service on general obligation bonds or on notes issued pursuant to law; (6) Receive or administer taxes, fees, gifts, contributions, bequests, or other funds received by the state from public and private sources pursuant to law; (7) Lend money, invest or reinvest its funds, take or hold real or personal property as security for the payment of funds so loaned or invested pursuant to law; (8) Enforce laws, investigate or prosecute complaints, issue subpoenas related to alleged violations, conduct adjudicative hearings, issue reprimands as required by law; (9) Issue permits, grant licenses, conduct regulatory hearings, examinations, investigations as required by law; (10) Formulate plans, adopt rules, issue regulations, set standards as required by law; (11) Sue and be sued on behalf of the state or any public or quasi-public agency established by law; (12) Make assessments, set rates, impose user charges pursuant to law.

16 Draft regulation 5013A had been renumbered 36-14-5014 (Regulation 5014) and refined: "Prohibited Activities — Members of the General Assembly— Restrictions on activities relating to Public Boards.
(1) No member of the General Assembly shall serve as a member of a Public Board. No member of the General Assembly shall participate in the appointment, except through advice and consent as provided by law, of any other person to serve as a member of a Public Board.
(2) For purposes of this regulation, 'Public Board' means all public bodies within the executive branch of state government, and all state executive, public and quasi-public boards, authorities, corporations, commissions, councils or agencies; provided, however, that the foregoing definition shall not apply to any such entity which (i) functions solely in an advisory capacity, or (ii) exercises solely legislative functions.
(3) The effective date of this regulation is July 1, 1999."

30 | Retaliation · pages 342–357

1   Many of the details Wright shared with me before his firing later appeared in print. See Bob Wyss, "Favoritism alleged at solid waste agency," *PJ*, 28 Jan. 1996: A-01.

2   Bob Wyss, "5 convictions since '90 for state job hopeful," *PJ*, 19 Jan. 1996: A-01.

3   W. Edward Wood, "Tom Wright's distinguished service," *PJ*, 7 Feb. 1996: B-06.

4   Peter Hufstader, *Democracy Betrayed: Conflicts of Interest and Failures of Oversight in Rhode Island State Government* (Providence: Common Cause, 2000), 31.

5   Jim Malachowski and I had been classmates in the Leadership Rhode Island Class of 1991. We had no other political or personal contact before this phone call.

6   Bob Wyss, "You may shop for your electricity," *PJ*, 8 Feb. 1996: A-01.

7   96-H 8124, "The Utility Restructuring Act of 1996," by Reps. Caruolo, Faria, Benson, Kelley, and SanBento, 7 Feb. 1996, became PL 96–316, 7 Aug. 1996.

8   Bob Wyss, "'Transition charge' by competing electric utilities questioned," *PJ*, 29 Feb. 1996: A-01; "The PUC to decide utilities structure," *PJ*, 6 Mar. 1996: B-01.

9   Bob Wyss, "Power deregulation bill won't cut rates enough, says collaborative chief," *PJ*, 14 Feb. 1996: A-01. Wyss listed members of the collaborative: Narragansett Electric, Blackstone Valley Electric, Newport Electric Corp., the Pascoag Fire District, the Conservation Law Foundation, the Smaller Business Association of New England, the New England Cogeneration Association, Energy Council of Rhode Island, Governor Almond's Policy Office, Atty. Gen. Jeffrey B. Pine, and the state Division of Public Utilities and Carriers. Mary Kilmarx had been married to Robert Kilmarx for 45 years. She had been elected to the 1973 Constitutional Convention and then to the House, where she represented Barrington for three terms.

10   George H. Borts, "Should the public subsidize a sweetheart deal for NEES?" *PJ*, 18 Feb. 1996: E-08.

11   HPW, "Don't let them throw out the refs!" *PJ*, 14 Mar. 1996: B-07.

12   Bob Wyss, "PUC assails electricity restructuring," *PJ*, 21 Jun. 1996: A-01.

13   Elliot Krieger, Christopher Rowland and Russell Garland, "Assembly ends session by passing electricity bill," *PJ*, 2 Aug. 1996: A-01. 96-H 8124SubB, PL 96–316, 7 Aug. 1996. RIGL 39-1-27.2

14   Russell Garland and Christopher Rowland, "Assembly opens on belligerent note," *PJ*, 8 Jan. 1997: A-01.

15   George Caruolo, "A response to Common Cause," *PJ*, 6 Jan. 1997: B-11.

16   Katherine Gregg, "Board to take up proposed pay raises," *PJ*, 28 Jan. 1997: B-01.

17   Martineau became House Majority Leader in 1998 and pled guilty in 2007 after taking bribes. Mike Stanton, "Former R.I. House majority leader admits selling office to CVS, Blue Cross," *PJ*, 3 Nov. 2007: A-01.

18   HPW fax memo to members of the Unclassified Pay Plan Board, 12 Feb. 1997.

19   Russell Garland, "Almond picks Curran for top court," *PJ*, 3 Jan. 1997: A-01.

20   Jonathan D. Rockoff, "Cool wind, cold reception for nomination," *PJ*, 26 Jan. 1997: A-15.

21   M. Charles Bakst, "Return to evil: Handling of Curran recalls the dark days," *PJ*, 28 Jan. 1997: B-01.

22   Russell Garland and Scott MacKay, "House rejects Curran," *PJ*, 29 Jan. 1997: A-01; "How the House Voted," *PJ*, 29 Jan. 1997: A-06.

23   Russell Garland, "Almond chastises Assembly," *PJ*, 31 Jan. 1997: A-01.

24   Nine years later, during an interview on 17 Jul. 2006, Sheldon Whitehouse gave me permission to disclose this. On the evening she received a CCRI public service award, 6 Nov. 2003, Margaret Curran confirmed to me that she had refused to "be

safe on separation of powers." During the furor, Whitehouse defended Curran in an op-ed but said he was not writing to assign blame. See Sheldon Whitehouse, "My colleague, Meg Curran," *PJ*, 31 Jan. 1997: B-05.

25 97-H 5852, "Joint Resolution: To Approve and Publish and Submit to the Electors a Proposition of Amendment to the Constitution of the State (Separation of Powers)," by Reps. Cicilline and Lima, 4 Feb. 1997.

26 97-S 0459, "Joint Resolution: To Approve and Publish and Submit to the Electors a Proposition of Amendment to the Constitution of the State (Separation of Powers)," by Sens. Patterson, Parella, Perry and Lenihan, 4 Feb. 1997.

27 Katherine Gregg, "Board slashes PUC chief's pay, hikes traffic judges," *PJ*, 15 Feb. 1997: A-01. In 2005, the Rhode Island Supreme Court agreed that Malachowski was entitled to the same protection as department directors and judges. See *James J. Malachowski v. State of Rhode Island et al.*, 2003-268-M.P., 2003-339-Appeal, 8 Jul. 2005: 11. The Supreme Court ruled that Malachowski has "statutory immunity from a salary reduction during his term as chairperson of the PUC" under RIGL 36-4-16.4(c). Malachowski, long out of government service, was able to collect more than $30,000 that the UPPB cut improperly from his salary. See Timothy C. Barmann, "State Supreme Court rules ex-PUC chief is due back pay," *PJ*, 6 Aug. 2005: B-01. "It feels very good," Malachowski said. "It took quite a while. It's clearly a victory."

31 | OPENING GOVERNMENT · pages 358–371

1 Russell Garland, "Langevin computer plan will put Assembly at public's fingertips," *PJ*, 21 Dec. 1994: D-08.

2 Timothy Barmann, "Web site delivers access to government," *PJ*, 1 Oct. 1995: E-01.

3 Russell Garland, "Web site puts Assembly at your fingertips," *PJ*, 26 Apr. 1996: B-01.

4 John Mulligan and Katherine Gregg, "General Assembly covets State House office space," *PJ*, 23 Dec. 1996: B-01.

5 Robert Mayoh, *Wind on the Sail: The Life and Times of John Hazen White* (Providence: John and Happy White Foundation, 2003), 84; John Hazen White, RED ALERT! Ad, "Open Government a Necessity," *PJ*, 12 Jan. 1997: A-11.

6 Christopher Rowland and M. Charles Bakst, "Assembly leaders drop bid to move Langevin out," *PJ*, 14 Jan. 1997: A-01.

7 Minutes of ACCESS/RI, 19 Sep. 1996. Founders voted to form ACCESS/RI, 501(c)(3) nonprofit corporation. Officers were Thomas E. Heslin, president; HPW, vice president; Linda Lotridge Levin, secretary; Staci L. Sawyer, treasurer. Members included Mary E. Harrington, Rudolph Hempe, Barbara J. Meagher, Joyce H. Morgenthaler. Other founding members include: Steven Brown, Joseph V. Cavanagh, Ross E. Cheit, Beverly Clay, David H. Leach, and Kathleen Odean.

8 Laura Meade Kirk, "ACCESS/RI vows to turn new light on government," *PJ*, 2 Jan. 1997: A-01.

9 97-H 6022, "An Act Relating to Public Records," by Reps. Heffner and Dennigan, was an omnibus bill that included extensive revisions of both the state's Access to Public Records Act (RIGL 38-2) and Open Meetings Law (RIGL 42-46).

10 97-S 0395 SubA, "An Act Relating to Access to Public Records," by Sens. Lenihan, Raptakis, Connors, and Patterson, 5 Feb. 1997; 97-S 0544 SubA, "An Act Relating to Open Meetings," by Sens. Perry, Walaska, Nygaard, and Gibbs, 11 Feb. 1997.

11 Christopher Rowland, "Senate backs two bills for open access," *PJ*, 10 May 1997: A-01.

12 Students under supervision of Professors Ross E. Cheit and Linda Levin, *Access*

to Public Records: An Audit of Rhode Island's Cities and Towns (ACCESS/RI: Providence, 1998).

13   Michael Corkery, "Police chief calls criticism by researchers too subjective," *PJ*, 19 Mar. 1998: C-01; Marion Davis, "Police move quickly on records law compliance," *PJ*, 26 Mar. 1998: D-01.

14   98-S 2246 SubA, "An Act Relating to Open Meetings," by Sens. Perry, Patterson, Nygaard, Gibbs, and Sosnowski; 98-S 2393SubA, "An Act Relating to Public Records," by Sens. Lenihan, Paiva Weed, Perry, O'Leary, and Kelly. The balancing test based on FOIA would allow a judge to decide whether the release of otherwise confidential records "would constitute a clearly unwarranted invasion of privacy or the records are otherwise exempted from disclosure by statute." RIGL 38-2-2 (A)(I).

15   98-H 7888, "An Act Relating to Access to Public Records," by Reps Heffner, Dennigan, and Barone, 3 Feb. 1998; 98-H 7911, "An Act Relating to State Affairs and Government — Open Meetings," by Reps Heffner, Dennigan, Benoit, and Barone, 3 Feb. 1998.

16   Bruce Landis, "Bills to toughen access laws get boost in House," *PJ*, 10 Apr. 1998: A-01.

17   Bruce Landis, "Open meetings bills approved," *PJ*, 7 May 1998: A-01.

18   Landis lists a vote of 62–18 in favor of the Levesque amendment, based on a printout on the floor. The official House Journal listed the vote as 64–20.

19   *HJrnl*, 7 May 1998: 12.

20   Bruce Landis, "Lawyer: Privacy issue is moot," *PJ*, 14 May 1998: B-01; "ACLU finds proposal poses no privacy threat," *PJ*, 14 May 1994: B-04.

21   98-H 7647, "An Act Relating to Health and Safety — The State of Rhode Island Cancer Council, Inc.," by Reps Kilmartin, Moura, Lally, and Henseler, 29 Jan. 1998.

22   *U.S. Supreme Court, Christiansburg Garment Co. v. EEOC,* 434 U.S. 412.

23   *HJrnl*, 25 Jun. 1998. http://www.rilin.state.ri.us/journals98/housejournals/hjour-nal6-25.htm.

24   Scott MacKay and Katherine Gregg, "Still plenty of unfinished business," *PJ*, 30 Jun. 1998: A-01.

25   Bruce Landis, "Stronger records law unlikely this year," *PJ*, 11 Jul. 1998: A-01.

26   *SJrnl*, 14 Jul. 1998. Sens Stephen D. Alves, Catherine E. Graziano, John Patterson, and Eleanor Sasso voted against the Cancer Council.

27   Provisions of PL 98-378, "Access to Public Records," 98-H 7888SubB as amended: (1) Remove statement that public has access to those records that "pertain to the policy making function of public bodies and/or are relevant to public health, safety and welfare," a heavy burden of proof on those who seek access to government records; (2) Ensure citizen access to records stored only on computers by including electronic data and other computer records in definition of public records; (3) Require agencies to supply information in computerized versions as well as printed hard copies, as requested; (4) Prevent public bodies from requiring written requests for public information in existing documents or that is otherwise readily available; (5) Prohibit the practice of withholding records "based on the purpose for which the records are sought;" (6) Stop public bodies from charging more than the "reasonable actual cost" for public records and require the public body to itemize the costs for search and retrieval; (7) Allow a court to waive the costs for search and retrieval if it determines that the information requested is in the public interest and is not primarily in the requester's commercial interest; (8) Require that documents submitted at a public meeting become public upon submission; (9) Make clear that all police records or reports reflecting the initial arrest of an adult be open to the public; (10) End the

practice of withholding public documents that contain confidential information and require confidential information be segregated or deleted; (11) Establish a definition of "prevailing plaintiff" linked to Federal case law; (12) Require a court to "award reasonable attorney fees and costs to the prevailing plaintiff" and require that a public body that "wrongfully denied access to public records" provide the records at no cost; (13) Allow a court to award attorney's fees and costs to the prevailing defendant only if the judge finds that "the plaintiff's case lacked a grounding in fact or in existing law or in good faith argument."

Provisions of PL 98-379, "Open Meetings," 98-H 7911SubA as amended: (1) Require that minutes of public meetings be provided to citizens upon request; (2) Require public bodies to provide written advance notice to subjects of disciplinary proceedings that they may have the matter discussed in open hearing; (3) Require that any votes of a public body taken in closed session be reported when the session is reopened and require any vote closed to protect strategy, negotiation or investigation must be reported once that process is completed; (4) Strengthen posting requirements for public meetings; (5) Prohibit action on last-minute additions to a public body's agenda unless it was "necessary to address an unexpected occurrence that requires immediate action to protect the public;" (6) Allow public bodies to schedule meetings but not conduct other business over the phone; (7) Extend time allowable for filing an Open Meetings complaint from 90 to 180 days; (8) Require a public body to prove a meeting was justifiably closed if a complaint was made; (9) Allow the attorney general to initiate an Open Meetings complaint in the public interest; (10) Consider Open Meetings complaints also filed under applicable sections of the Access to Public Records Law; (11) Place the burden of proof on a public body to demonstrate that the meeting in question was properly closed or exempt from the Open Meetings Law; (12) Provide for an increase in the maximum penalties for willful violations of the law from $1,000 to $5,000; (13) Provide also for attorney's fees, under the discretion of the court, if a plaintiff is successful in bringing a complaint.

28   Lincoln Almond, "To the Honorable House of Representatives, Veto of 98-H 7647, Substitute A as amended, The State of Rhode Island Cancer Council, Inc." 20 Jul. 1998.

32 | HEAVY HANDS · pages 372–377

1   Gerald M. Carbone and Peter B. Lord, "Unnatural resource: The story of Pascoag Reservoir," *PJ*, 14 Jun. 1998: A-01. The Pascoag Reservoir and Dam Limited Liability Corp. owned 342 acres that were submerged after the dam's construction in 1860. The partners in Sayles Mill Associates were Vincent Mesolella Sr., Thomas Mesumuci, and developer Richard Ahlborg.

2   RIGL 37-6, entitled "Acquisition of Land," lays out the powers of the State Properties Committee. In 1998, § 37-6-1 specified its composition: the state's chief purchasing officer; the attorney general; a representative of the department of administration to be designated by the director; one member representing the public; one member of the house of representatives appointed by the speaker; and one member from the senate appointed by the senate majority leader. See Ch. 29, "A Question of Ethics."

3   Drake Witham, "Echo Lake landowners, DEM wage water fight," *PJ*, 4 Aug. 1997: C-01.

4   John A. Fazzino, "The Mesolellas of Echo Lake," *PJ*, 6 Apr. 1998: B-06.

5   Drake Witham, "And now . . . The reservoir's too full," *PJ*, 12 May 1998: A-01; editorial, "A private servant," *PJ*, 26 Mar 1998: B-06.

6   Robert C. Frederiksen, "Fuel-cleanup board slow to get started," *PJ*, 27 Mar. 1996:
     B-01. Frederiksen listed members of the USTB: Rep. Vincent J. Mesolella Jr.; Sen.
     William V. Irons; Rep. Robert A. Watson; Charles H. DeBlois, DB Companies;
     Dennis Hebert, Oil Heat Institute; Paul Hicks, Rhode Island Petroleum Association;
     John Gilsta, Gilsta's Automotive Service, Charlestown; Albert Conti, Rhode Island
     Marine Trades Association; Eugenia Marks, Environment Council of Rhode
     Island; G. Cameron Matheson, Middletown; Ernest Almonte, state auditor general;
     Florian R. Boulay, Department of Business Regulation; and James W. Fester, DEM.
     Technically, the board elected Mesolella as its chairman.

7   Bob Wyss, "Fund for leaking fuel tanks swirls down budget drain," *PJ*, 30 Apr. 1997:
     A-01.

8   PL 97-30, "An Act Making Appropriations for The Support of the State for the Fiscal
     Year Ending June 30, 1998, Article 39." Instead of raising the USTF allocation from
     $125,000 to $150,000, as recommended, Art. 39 raised it to $550,000.

9   Peter B. Lord, "Environmentalists decry tank bill," *PJ*, 21 Jun. 1997: A-01.

10   Peter B. Lord, "Mesolella says he'll leave fuel board," *PJ*, 28 Oct. 1997: B-01.

11   Scott MacKay and Christopher Rowland, "No arms were twisted in this fond fare-
     well," *PJ*, 06 Jul. 1998: B-01.

12   Christopher Rowland and Katherine Gregg, "He's back: Mesolella reappears as head
     of commission," *PJ*, 25 Jan. 1999: B-01.

13   Obit. "Vincent J. Mesolella Sr.," *PJ*, 21 Oct. 1998: C-06. A decade later, Meso-
     lella's college-age daughter was killed in a Long Island car crash. See W. Zachary
     Malinowski, "Former official's daughter is killed," *PJ*, 24 Jun. 2008: B-01.

14   Two related bills had passed the Senate: 98-S 2401 Substitute A as amended, "An Act
     Relating to Waters and Navigation — Oil Spill Response Fund," by Sens. Fogarty,
     McDonald, Paiva Weed, Algiere, Connors, et al.., proposed that the expenditure of
     funds from a settlement after the North Cape oil spill to restore eelgrass and other
     habitat; 98-S 2730 Substitute A as amended, "An Act Relating to Freshwater Wet-
     lands," by Sens. Irons and Bates, proposed to increase DEM's powers, including fines
     up to $10,000 and other revisions of environmental rules.

15   Christopher Rowland, "Environmental groups blast Assembly for killing key legisla-
     tion," *PJ*, 16 Jul. 1998: A-11.

16   RIEC Regulation 36-14-5009 prohibited public officials from accepting "any gift or
     other thing of economic value to the recipient" from any "interested parties," defined
     as persons or businesses that had a "direct financial interest" in any decision that the
     public official "is authorized to make, or to participate in the making of, as part of
     his or her official duties."

17   See Ch. 29, "A Question of Ethics."

18   RIEC Regulation 36-14-5014 prohibited members of the General Assembly from
     serving on boards that exercised executive powers. The effective date, July 1, 1999,
     was intended to allow the Rhode Island Supreme Court to consider questions of
     constitutionality.

19   HPW notes of 6 Apr. 1998, reconfirmed by Richard W. Morsilli, interview 26 Aug.
     2006.

20   Russell Garland, "Firm must pay broker $1.9 million for age bias," *PJ*, 10 Sep. 1999:
     A-01

33 | Slow Motion Battle · pages 378–391

1   Lincoln Almond, "Request for Advisory Opinion from the Rhode Island Supreme Court," 20 Nov. 1997. Question 1: Does Article III, section 8 of the Rhode Island Constitution, which empowers the Rhode Island Ethics Commission to "adopt a code of ethics, including but not limited to provisions on conflicts of interest . . . (and) use of position" provide the Ethics Commission with the power to adopt Regulation 36-14-5014? (This is the regulation that would bar lawmakers and their appointees from serving on any public board.)

2   Almond Question 2: Is the principle of separation of powers contained in the Rhode Island Constitution properly interpreted in the same fashion as it has been interpreted in the United States Constitution with respect to appointments, such that neither legislators, nor their appointees, may serve on any public body within the executive branch of state government, or state executive, public and quasi-public boards, authorities, corporations, commissions, councils or agencies except those which: (i) function solely in an advisory capacity; or (ii) exercise solely legislative functions?

3   Almond Question 3: Does the separation of powers principle contained in the Rhode Island Constitution impose any limits whatsoever on legislative appointments to a public board or body (as defined above)? In particular, does the Constitution prohibit legislators and/or their appointees from constituting a majority of the membership of a public board or body? Does the Constitution prohibit appointment of sitting legislators to a public board or body?"

4   Joslin had founded the CCRI Advisory Council in 1990-91 to strengthen fundraising and membership development. It became and remains a vital part of the organization's success. See Ch. 4, "A Costly Election."

5   Initial pledges for the CCRI brief came from Adelaide Armbrust, Robert Spink Davis, Warren Galkin, Natalie Joslin, Herbert Kaplan, Robert Kilmarx, John and Lila Sapinsley, and Henry Sharpe.

6   *Gorham v. Robinson*, 186 A. 832, 836 (R.I. 1936).

7   RI Constitution, Article X.4, as amended in 1994.

8   98-H 7861, "An Act Relating to State Affairs and Government — Department of the Environment," by Reps Kennedy, Henseler, Naughton, Carter, and Quick, 3 Feb. 1998.

9   Section 23 of 98-H 7861 proposed to amend RIGL 22-14-1, 22-14-3, and 22-14-4. The proposed changes were not enacted.

10 James P. Marusak, "Brief of Amicus Curiae, Environment Council of Rhode Island, Inc.," 97-572 M.P., 2 Mar. 1998: 3–4.

11 Karen A. Pelczarski, "Brief of the Amici Curiae Common Cause of Rhode Island, the Rhode Island State Council of Churches, the League of Women Voters of Rhode Island, and Red Alert, Inc," 97-572 M.P., 16 Mar. 1998. 4 ff.

12 Lincoln Steffens, *The Struggle for Self-Government* (New York: McClure, Phillips & Co., 1906), 160.

13 Lincoln Steffens, *The Autobiography of Lincoln Steffens* (New York: Harcourt, Brace & Co., 1931), 465–468.

14 Pelczarski: 10, quoting *In Re: Thomas W. Dorr*, 3 R.I. 301: (RI 1854).

15 Pelczarski: 47, quoting results from Peter Hufstader, "Authority for Lotteries," CCRI, 30 Dec. 1997: 1–7; also reporting statutes Hufstader compiled in "Legislative Oversight: a Rhode Island Fairy Tale," 14 Aug. 1996: 63.

16 James P. Marusak, "Brief of Amicus Curiae, Environment Council of Rhode Island, Inc.," 97-572 M.P., 2 Mar. 1998.

17   RIGL 42-35, the Administrative Procedures Act, lays out the procedures for rule-
      making by agencies that execute state laws.
18   PL 96-300, "An Act Relating to the Solid Waste Management Corporation," had
      changed the name to "Resource Recovery Corporation," 6 Aug. 1996.
19   Robert Senville, "Brief of Amicus Curiae, Operation Clean Government," 97-572
      M.P., 27 Feb. 1998.: 4 (fn. 1). Leaders of OCG had testified in support of the Ethics
      Commission's proposed regulation 36-14-5014 on five occasions between 25 Apr.
      1996 and 22 Jan. 1997.
20   *In Re: Advisory from the Governor,* 633 A.2d 664 (RI 1993)
21   Joseph S. Larisa Jr., "Brief of Governor Lincoln Almond," 97-572 M.P., 16 Mar. 1998.
22   Briefs opposing the Ethics Commission's authority were filed by Lauren E. Jones,
      representing House Speaker John B. Harwood, Edward M. Fogarty for Senate
      Majority Leader Paul S. Kelly, Thomas M. Dickinson for Attorney General Jeffrey
      B. Pine, Brian Bishop for Rhode Island Wise Use, historian and attorney Patrick T.
      Conley, Wheaton College professor and State House lobbyist Jay S. Goodman, and
      Daniel A. Curran.
23   Lauren E. Jones, "Brief and Appendix of the Rhode Island House of Representatives,
      through its Speaker, John B. Harwood, *In Re: Advisory Opinion from the Governor
      to the Justices (Rhode Island Ethics Commission-Separation of Powers),* 97-572 M.P.,
      13 Jul. 1998.
24   Patrick T. Conley later published his brief as a book, *Neither Separate Nor Equal:
      Legislature and Executive in Rhode Island Constitutional History* (Providence: RIPS,
      1999). For simplicity, I refer to the book rather than the original brief. Conley later
      told me he had accepted Harwood's request to defend legislative supremacy primari-
      ly because Marusak had disputed his historical conclusions in *Democracy in Decline:
      Rhode Island's Constitutional Development, 1776–1841* (Providence: RI Historical
      Society, 1977). Conley said: "I had to defend the accuracy of my historical analysis."
      Despite their differences, Conley and Marusak have since become close friends.
25   Conley 5, 9, 16–18, 32, 47.
26   Conley 69–70, 74.
27   Conley 89–101, 102–112.
28   Patrick T. Conley, *Democracy in Decline: Rhode Island's Constitutional Development,
      1776–1841* (Providence: Rhode Island Historical Society, 1977), 375.
29   Patrick T. Conley, *Neither Separate nor Equal,* 134–35, 142.
30   Whitehouse outspent Mayer $697,924 to $341,168 after loaning his campaign
      $250,000. He won with 67.2% of the statewide vote to Mayer's 32.8%.
      http://www.elections.ri.gov/elections/results/1998/agcomm.php.
31   Based on the summary prepared by Thomas W. Lyons, "The Supreme Court Decides
      the Balance of Power," *Rhode Island Bar Journal,* 47 (Nov. 1998): 3–7, 23–39.
32   Christopher Rowland, "Lawyers argue of balance of power in R.I. government," *PJ,*
      11 Nov. 1998: A-01.
33   Maria Miro Johnson, "Whitehouse 'disavows' court filing by Pine," *PJ,* 8 Jan. 1999:
      A-01.
34   William G. McLoughlin, *Rhode Island; A History* (New York: W.W. Norton, 1986),
      201.
35   Patrick T. Conley and Robert G. Flanders Jr., *The Rhode Island Constitution:
      A Reference Guide* (Westport, CT: Greenwood Publishing, 2007), 29.
36   McLoughlin 202–203.

34 | Quintessential · pages 392–402

1   Patrick T. Conley and Robert G. Flanders Jr., *The Rhode Island State Constitution: A Reference Guide* (Westport, CT: Praeger Publishers, 2007), 38.

2   M. Charles Bakst, "Judge gives Almond a dramatic victory on video-slot issue," *PJ*, 10 Jun. 1999: B-01.

3   I have tried without success to obtain records showing how much taxpayer money Harwood provided as legislative grants to cover the cost of the many briefs proclaiming legislative supremacy; the State Library has no record of who received the controversial grants during the years Harwood was speaker.

4   *In Re Advisory Opinion to the Governor (Rhode Island Ethics Commission-Separation of Powers)*, 732 A.2d 1, 60 (R.I. 1999). Note: Since copies of the original decision are not widely available, I cite sections and page numbers from West's *Atlantic Reporter*, 2nd Series, 6 Aug. 1999.

5   Advisory Opinion 62.

6   RI Constitution, Article VI.10: Continuation of previous powers. — The general assembly shall continue to exercise the powers it has heretofore exercised, unless prohibited in this Constitution.

7   Advisory Opinion 64.

8   Advisory Opinion 69.

9   Advisory Opinion 71–72.

10 In an interview on 30 Dec. 2008, Flanders confirmed that sharp disagreements over his dissent had caused the exceptionally long delay from the previous November to the end of June.

11 Advisory Opinion 74.

12 See Ch. 23, "Revolving Door."

13 Advisory Opinion 83–6. Without naming Justices Weisberger or Lederberg, Flanders noted that two of his colleagues who joined in that unanimous opinion now rejected the Ethics Commission's ban on dual-office-holding.

14 Advisory Opinion 82. See *Cranston Teachers Alliance Local No. 1704 AFT v. Miele*, 495 A.2d 235-7 (R.I. 1985).

15 Advisory Opinion 80.

16 Advisory Opinion 92. Flanders is quoting Steven G. Calabresi and Joan L. Larson, "One Person, One Office: Separation of Powers or Separation of Persons?" 79 *Cornell Law Review* 1045, 1119 (1994). United States Constitution, Article I.6: "No senator or representative shall, during the time for which he was elected, be appointed to any civil office under the authority of the United States, which shall have been created, or the emoluments whereof shall have been increased during such time; and no person holding any office under the United States, shall be a member of either house during his continuance in office."

17 Advisory Opinion 94.

18 RI Constitution, Article IX.1 and 2:1.

19 Advisory Opinion 99–100.

20 Advisory Opinion 107, 11.

21 Tom Mooney, "Top court keeps power with Assembly – for now," *PJ*, 30 Jun. 1999: A-01.

22 Tom Mooney, "Video slot proponents ask judge to rethink ban," *PJ*, 14 Jul. 1999: B-01; Marion Davis, "Court lifts temporary ban on video slots," *PJ*, 28 Jul. 1999: A-01.

23 Carl T. Bogus, "Rhode Island's radical difference," *PJ*, 10 Aug. 1999: B-07.

24   Minutes of the State Governing Board, CCRI, 27 Jul. 1999.
25   RI Supreme Court, *Advisory Opinion to the Governor (Rhode Island Ethics Commission — Separation of Powers)*, 97-572-M.P. (Providence: JCLS, 1999).

35 | GIFTS · pages 403–418

1   Patriots' Day commemorates the battles of Lexington and Concord on April 19, 1775. The observance takes place on the 3rd Monday of April. In 1996, the holiday fell on April 15.
2   Bob Wyss, "Ethics experts voice concerns on gifts to Almond," *PJ*, 14 Dec. 1997: A-01.
3   Mark Johnson, "Councilman took trip to Super Bowl with Vinagro," *PJ*, 28 Mar. 1997: A-01; RIEC, Informal Resolution and Settlement of Complaint 97–16 against Joseph R. Ballirano, 21 Apr. 1998.
4   Jody McPhillips, "Officials fight to save freebies from ethics rules," *PJ*, 7 Jan. 1998: A-01.
5   Christopher Rowland, "Donations buy legislators power — and dinner," *PJ*, 9 Feb. 1997: A-01.
6   Scott MacKay, "No more freebies for public officials, panel says," *PJ*, 4 Jun. 1998: A-01.
7   RIEC Minutes of Open Session, 2 Jun. 1998. Six commissioners (Chadwick, Connor, Lynch, Mason, McCahan, and O'Brien) voted for the rule, while three (DeRobbio, Verrecchia, and Zurier) voted against Regulation 36-14-5009 Prohibited Activities — Gifts.
8   Scott MacKay, "No more freebies for public officials, panel says," *PJ*, 4 Jun. 1998: A-01.
9   Maria Miro Johnson, "Parting shots from John J. O'Brien," *PJ*, 29 Nov. 1998: A-01.
10   Amica's Senior Vice President and General Counsel, Kenneth H. Nails, and its Assistant General Counsel, Robert P. Suglia, both registered as lobbyists for the insurance company. They were "business associates" of James V. Murray.
11   Replaced were Robert DeRobbio (chairperson), John J. O'Brien (vice chairperson), Rev. Henry A. Belin III, Kathie Chadwick, Richard Connor, Stephen Famiglietti, and Lori J. Mason.
12   Between 1997 and 1999, Gov. Lincoln Almond named six lawyers who pushed the Ethics Commission to reverse the zero-tolerance gift rule: Melvin L. Zurier in 1997 appointed without a list shortly before passage of the gift rule; James V. Murray in 1998 from a list by House Majority Leader Gerard M. Martineau; Thomas D. Goldberg in 1998 from a list provided by House Minority Leader Wayne D. Salisbury; Richard E. Kirby in 1998 from a list by House Speaker John B. Harwood; Francis J. Flanagan in 1999 from a list by Senate Minority Leader Dennis Algiere; Robin L. Main in 1999 without a list. Almond also appointed three non-lawyers: James Lynch Sr. in 1997 without a list; Paul V. Verrecchia in 1997 from a list by Senate Majority Leader Paul S. Kelly; David McCahan in 1998 without a list.
13   Jonathan D. Rockoff, "Conflicts complicate probe of Harwood," *PJ*, 19 Apr. 2001: A-01.
14   The Ethics Commission had no authority over lobbyists, who registered with the secretary of state. Like the rule barring public officials from seeking or accepting gifts, any rules the commission might adopt would approach the problem by restricting legislators' ability to raise campaign contributions during the legislative session.

15 RIEC draft advisory to Thomas D. Goldberg, Esq., 1 Apr. 1999.

16 RIEC Minutes of Open Session, 18 May 1999: "Commissioner [Thomas D.] Goldberg and his attorney, Kathleen Managhan, were present before the Commission. Commissioner Goldberg stated that he disagreed with the opinion and that he was represented by counsel. Ms. Managhan argued that Commissioner Goldberg should be allowed to participate and vote on any regulations that relate to lobbyists because lobbyists should be considered a significant and definable class. She further argued that any regulations that affect lobbyists would affect all lobbyists the same and different types of lobbyists as denominated in the advisory opinion are a meaningless distinction. In addition, she stated that there would be no financial consequence for the Goldbergs and requested that the Commission reverse the advisory opinion."

17 Gary Yesser, who had served as legal counsel to the RIEC and its predecessor Conflict of Interest Commission, had died of cancer on 14 Jan. 1998.

18 Bruce Landis, "Ethics panel member says he won't abide by vote," *PJ*, 24 May 1999: B-01.

19 Superior Court Complaint PC 99-2736, *Thomas D. Goldberg v. Rhode Island Ethics Commission*, 1 Jun. 1999.

20 The 1992 Campaign Finance Law had banned cash contributions and required contributors to write checks that listed both their home addresses and places of employment, which made it possible to follow some of the money.

21 Katherine Gregg, "End of campaign trail for lobbyists? The bucks may stop here," *PJ*, 23 Jan. 1999: A-01.

22 Verbatim from recorded phone message, 21 Sep. 1999.

23 Peter Hufstader and HPW, "Common Cause corrects lobbyist figures; Langevin will revamp reporting process," CCRI Report, Oct. 1999: 2.

24 Bruce Landis, "Shift on ethics board worries reformers," *PJ*, 13 Dec. 1999: A-01.

25 Bruce Landis, "Ethics panel reconsiders 'no gift' rule," *PJ*, 27 Oct. 1999: B-01.

26 See Ch. 5, "Collapse of Credit," and 13, "RISDIC TV."

27 HPW to Melvin Zurier, Chairperson of the RI Ethics Commission, 20 Dec. 1999.

28 RIEC, Transcript of hearing on proposed changes to regulation 36-14-5009, 15 Feb. 2000.

29 RIEC, Transcript of hearing on proposed changes to regulation 36-14-5009, 21 Mar. 2000.

30 RIEC, Transcript, *Public Hearing In Re: Regulation* 36-14-5009, 23 May 2000. Commissioners present were Chairman Melvin L. Zurier, Francis J. Flanagan, Thomas D. Goldberg, Richard E. Kirby, James Lynch Sr., Robin Main, David McCahan, James V. Murray, and Paul Verrecchia.

31 Scott MacKay, "Ethics panel lifts ban on gifts," *PJ*, 24 May 2000: A-01.

32 Glidden Co., GTECH Corp., Millennium Inorganic Chemicals, NL Industries, RI Roofing Contractors Association, Sherwin-Williams Co., Smokeless Tobacco Council, United Health Plans of New England.

33 RIEC, Draft advisory 2001-70, *In Re: Thomas D. Goldberg, Esq.*

34 CCRI, Governing Board Minutes, 23 May 2000: 1-3. Fourteen board members signed the complaint: Greta L. Abbott, Warren G. Billings, Michael C. Cerullo, Joan Countryman, Joan I. Gray, Donna Welk Cameron Gricus, Christopher S. Hamblett, Burton Hoffman, Elizabeth W. Newberry, Nancy C. Rhodes, Helen Sebesta, Daniel G. Siegel, Rebecca L. Spencer, Jeffrey D. Taber. As executive director, I also signed.

36 | Referendum · pages 419–428

1   Carl T. Bogus, email to HPW, 28 Jul. 1999. See Ch. 34, "Quintessential."
2   Carl T. Bogus, "The Battle for Separation of Powers in Rhode Island,"
    56 *Administrative Law Review* 77 (2004): 84–5.
3   Edward Achorn, "'Like the monthly cable bill' — An expensive entertainment tax,"
    PJ, 13 Jul. 1999: B-05.
4   PL-95 370 merged the Port Authority and Economic Development Department into
    a new quasi-public corporation. RIGL 42-64-8 established the 13-member board
    with 2 representatives appointed by the speaker, one from the minority party, and
    2 senators, one each appointed by the Senate Majority and Minority Leaders.
5   Christopher Rowland, "Questions raised over agency's use of credit cards," *PJ*, 4 Nov.
    1999: A-01; "A different standard for agency's expenses?" *PJ*, 5 Nov. 1999: A-01;
    "Audits failed to detect credit card irregularities," *PJ*, 6 Nov. 1999: A-03; "Few agency
    expenses used to win clients," *PJ*, 9 Dec. 1999: A-01.
6   Christopher Rowland, "EDC chief resigns — Swen felled by credit card controversy,"
    PJ, 17 Dec. 1999: A-01.
7   See Ch. 22, "Empire of Cronies."
8   Christopher Rowland, "Questions raised over agency's use of credit cards," *PJ*, 4 Nov.
    1999: A-01.
9   Jonathan Saltzman, "Senate to probe EDC spending; criticism grows," *PJ*, 16 Dec.
    1999: A-01.
10 Ariel Sabar, "Senate leader names panel to look into EDC," *PJ*, December 30, 1999:
    A-01.
11 Senate Select Commission on Quasi-Public Agencies: Sens. J. Michael Lenihan,
    Chair, M. Teresa Paiva Weed, Vice Chair; Members: Marc A. Cote, Daniel DaPonte,
    John Patterson, Mary A. Parella, Leonidas P. Raptakis. 29 Dec. 1999.
12 *Senate Select Commission on Quasi-public Agencies Report to the Rhode Island*
    Senate, 20 Dec. 2000: 28. The quasi-public agencies were: Board of Governors for
    Higher Education, Board of Regents for Elementary & Secondary Education, Capital
    Center Commission, Channel 36 Foundation, Convention Center Authority, Hous-
    ing Resources Commission, Narragansett Bay Water Quality Management District
    Commission, Quonset/Davisville Management Corporation, RI Airport Corpora-
    tion, RI Clean Water Finance Agency, RI Children's Crusade for Higher Educa-
    tion, RI Depositors Economic Protection Corporation, RI Economic Development
    Corporation, RI Health & Educational Building Corporation, RI Higher Education
    Assistance Authority, RI Housing & Mortgage Finance Corporation, RI Industrial
    Facilities Corporation, RI Industrial Recreation Building Authority, RI Lottery,
    RI Partnerships for Science & Technology, RI Public Building Authority, RI Public
    Telecommunications Authority/Channel 36 WSBE-TV, RI Public Transit Authority,
    RI Refunding Bond Authority, RI Resource Recovery Corporation, RI Student Loan
    Authority, RI Turnpike and Bridge Authority, RI Underground Storage Tank Board,
    RI Water Resources Board Corporate.
13 Jonathan Saltzman, "Agency queried on credit cards," *PJ*, 25 Jan. 2000: B-01; "Agency
    defends spending practices," *PJ*, 27 Jan. 2000: B-01.
14 PL-98 031, 98-H 8478aa. Article 23 SubA contained the amendment reducing the al-
    lowable administrative costs for the next fiscal year from $550,000 to $350,000. See
    Ch. 32, "Heavy Hands."
15 RIGL 35-20, "Public Corporation Financial Integrity and Accountability," enacted in
    1995 with Lenihan as sponsor: PL 95-86 (95-S 0125 as amended), 21 Jun. 1995.

16 Jonathan Saltzman, "Ratepayers lose homes over unpaid sewer bills," *PJ*, 9 Feb. 2000: A-01.

17 RIGL 35-20-1ff.

18 J. Michael Lenihan, et al.., Senate Select Commission on Quasi-public Agencies Report to the Rhode Island Senate, 20 Dec. 2000: 6–7, 9–10.

19 *Lincoln C. Almond* v. *Rhode Island Lottery Commission*, 99-525-Appeal, 27 Jul. 2000. Justices Joseph R. Weisberger, Victoria Lederberg, and John P. Bourcier were the majority; Justice Robert G. Flanders Jr. filed the dissent. Justice Maureen McKenna Goldberg recused herself.

20 Groups represented at the first meeting of the Yes on Question 6 Coalition included Common Cause, the Environment Council of RI, the League of Women Voters, Operation Clean Government, the RI State Council of Churches, and Save the Bay, 17 Aug. 2000.

21 Peter Hufstader, *Democracy Betrayed: Conflicts of Interest and Failures of Oversight in Rhode Island State Government* (Common Cause Rhode Island: Providence, RI, 2000), 65.

22 See Ch. 32, "Heavy Hands."

23 RIBOE: http://www.elections.ri.gov/elections/results/2000/generalelection/.

37 | Downsizing Revisited · pages 429–438

1 Edward Fitzpatrick, "The Incredible Shrinking Legislature," *State Legislatures Magazine,* NCSL, July-Aug. 2002: 51 ff. Three neighboring New England states had downsized their Houses of Representatives in the 1960s and 1970s: Connecticut from 294 to 151, Massachusetts from 240 to 160, and Vermont from 246 to 150.

2 99-H 5047, "Joint Resolution To Approve And Publish And Submit To The Electors A Proposition Of Amendment To The Constitution Of The State (General Assembly)," by Reps Barr, Menard and Reilly, 12 Jan. 1999.

3 See Ch. 19, "Paying the Piper."

4 Katherine Gregg, "Groups buck downsized Assembly," *PJ*, 24 Sep. 1999: B-01.

5 Union members of Ocean State Action included: National Education Association; Hotel & Restaurant Employees Union Local 217; the RI chapter of the National Association of Social Workers; District 1199 of the New England Health Care Employees Union; United Nurses & Allied Health Professionals; Service Employees International Union, Local 134; and the United Auto Workers. Non-union members were: 2 to 1: The Coalition to Preserve Choice; Progreso Latino; and Quisqueya en Accion.

6 00-H 7688, "Joint Resolution to Approve and Publish, and Submit to the Electors A Proposition of Amendment to the Constitution of the State (Composition of the General Assembly)," by Reps. Carpenter, M. Anderson, Moura, Fox, and Shavers, 3 Feb. 2000.

7 Lee Dykas, "State representative's son gunned down after car chase," *PJ*, 19 Dec. 1995: A-01; Thomas Frank, "Carpenter seeks to stem violence, with bill backing anti-gang efforts," 5 Jan. 1996: A-01.

8 See Ch. 40, "Redistricting Revenge," which includes the 1992 controversy.

9 Katherine Gregg, "A smaller General Assembly, Having second thoughts," *PJ*, 23 Mar. 2000: A-01.

10 Editorial, "Solons vs. legislative reform," *PJ*, 26 Mar. 2000: K-06.

11 Mabel M. Anderson, "House Address," *HJrnl.* 31 May 2000: Appendix.

38 | Kingly Power · pages 439–450

1   RIEC Regulation 36-14-5008.
2   Jonathan D. Rockoff, "Speaker's wife lands court position," *PJ*, 28 Dec. 2000: A-01.
3   Alan S. Flink, "Injudicious choice," *PJ*, 4 Jan. 2001: B-07.
4   Editorial, "A little sunshine, please," *PJ*, 10 Jan. 2001.
5   Raymond "Chip" Hoyas would later plead guilty to 52 counts of forgery for obtaining $71,168 by fraudulently cashing Senate paychecks while he was deputy chief of staff to then Senate President Joseph A. Montalbano. Hoyas was sentenced to home confinement, required to pay restitution, and lost his state pension. See Tatiana Pina, "Former Senate aide accused of check scheme," *PJ*, 6 Jan. 2010: A-01; Katie Mulvaney, "Ex-Senate aide Hoyas admits forgery, larceny," *PJ*, 26 Oct. 2012: A-12.
6   John Castellucci, "Harwood ally tapped for municipal court," *PJ*, 10 Jan. 2001: A-01.
7   Joanne Marciano, "Harwood's law partner turns down nomination," *PJ*, 12 Jan. 2001: A-01.
8   M. Charles Bakst, "State House doings: Inman ascendant, Harwood Triumphant," *PJ*, 11 Jan. 2001: B-01. In a personal interview on 25 Mar. 2014, Harwood repeated his claim that the choice was entirely Weisberger's. He said she had served a record three terms as Weisberger's law clerk and that he was her mentor.
9   Ariel Sabar, "Harwood handled four cases for clients before state agencies," *PJ*, 10 Feb. 2001: A-01.
10 Richard C. Dujardin, "Nightclub's doors shut for good," *PJ*, 27 Jul. 2001: C-01. Ten years after these events, Jeff Greer died of a massive heart attack at 54, a great loss to his family and Rhode Island.
11 Ariel Sabar, "Harwood handled four cases for clients before state agencies," *PJ*, 10 Feb. 2001: A-01.
12 01-H 5485, "An Act Relating to Public Officers and Employees — Code of Ethics," by Rep. William J. Murphy, 6 Feb. 2001. Murphy's bill proposed a new section of the Prohibited Activities section of the Code of Ethics: 36-14-5 (p) Nothing contained in this section or in the rules and regulations promulgated by the ethics commission, shall prohibit or, in any way, restrict the practice of law by any individual duly admitted to practice in this state pursuant to the power vested in the supreme court.
13 01-H 5486, "House Resolution Respectfully Requesting the Justices of the Supreme Court to Give a Written Opinion upon a Question of Law," by Rep. William J. Murphy, 6 Feb. 2001.
14 *HJrnl*, 6 Feb. 2001.
15 Katherine Gregg, "Ethics exclusion for lawyer-politicians delayed in face of heavy opposition," *PJ*, 14 Feb. 2001: A-01.
16 Karen A. Pelczarski, "Brief of the Amicus Curiae Common Cause of Rhode Island as a Proponent of the Proposition that the Proposed Bill No. 2001-H 5485 is Unconstitutional," 12 Apr. 2001: 24. See *In Re: Advisory Opinion to the Governor (Ethics Commission)*, 612 A. 2d 1, 9–12 (R.I. 1992).
17 Pelczarski: 25–26.
18 01-H 6347, "The Rhode Island House of Representatives requests of the Rhode Island Supreme Court that the Advisory Opinion sought regarding House Bill 2001-H 5485 be withdrawn," by Rep. W.J. Murphy, 24 Apr. 2001. See *HJrnl* under "New Business," 24 Apr. 2001.
19 01-H 6022, "Joint Resolution Providing for a Bi-Partisan Preparatory Commission to Assemble Information on Constitutional Questions in Preparation for a Vote by the Qualified Electors on the Holding of a Constitutional Convention in Accordance

with Article XIV Section 2 of the Rhode Island Constitution and Making an Appropriation Therefor," by Reps. Gorham, Fleury, Mumford, Trillo, and W.H. Murphy, 8 Feb. 2001.

20 Nicholas Gorham, "Letter to Speaker John Harwood," 22 May 2001.

21 01-S 1027 SubA as amended, "An Act Relating to Campaign Finance," by Sens. Goodwin, Lenihan, Bates, and Irons, http://www.rilin.state.ri.us/PublicLaws/law01/law01176.htm.

22 Michael Smith, "Mayor's purchases highlight vague campaign spending," *PJ*, 11 Feb. 2001: C-01.

23 RIGL 17-25-7.2. "Personal use of campaign funds prohibited — (a) The personal use by any elected public office holder or by any candidate for public office as defined in section 17-25-3 of campaign funds contributed after April 29, 1992 shall be prohibited. For the purposes of this section "personal use" is defined as any use other than expenditures related to gaining or holding public office and for which the candidate for public office or elected public official would be required to treat the amount of the expenditure as gross income under § 61 of the Internal Revenue Code of 1986, 26 U.S.C. § 61, or any subsequent corresponding Internal Revenue Code of the United States, as from time to time amended."

24 See Ch. 35, "Gifts."

25 Katherine Gregg, "Harwood charged 18 trips to his campaign war chest," *PJ*, 4 Mar. 2001: A-19.

26 Katherine Gregg, "Lawmakers tap campaign funds to cover meals, golf, gifts," 4 Mar. 2001: A-01. House Minority Leader Robert Watson raised $7,751 and spent $6,080 in 2000. Senate Minority Leader Dennis Algiere raised only $450 and spent $396.10.

27 Over five years Rep. Edith H. Ajello had researched, developed, and refined legislation for electronic filing of campaign finance reports. Her 01-H 5550, "An Act Relating to State Board of Elections," was incorporated verbatim in 01-S 1027, "An Act Relating to Campaign Finance," by Sens. Goodwin, Lenihan, Bates, and Irons.

28 Twelve Democrats and 13 Republicans voted against recommitting 01-H 6022: Democrats: Edith H. Ajello, Mabel Anderson, David N. Cicilline, Elizabeth M. Dennigan, John J DeSimone, Charles J. Levesque, Charlene Lima, Frank A. Montanaro, Roger Picard, Michael S. Pisaturo, Steven Smith, Peter N. Wasylyk; Republicans: Joseph N. Amaral, Brock D. Bierman, Richard E. Fleury, Nicholas Gorham, Bruce J. Long, Carol A. Mumford, William H. Murphy, Scott T. Rabideau, John A. Savage, Joseph H. Scott, Susan Story, Joseph A. Trillo, Robert A. Watson.

29 Conley, *Democracy in Decline*, 366–79. See also Patrick Conley, "The Constitution of 1843: A Sesquicentennial Obituary," in *Rhode Island in Rhetoric and Reflection: Public Addresses and Essays* (East Providence: Rhode Island Publications Society: 2002), 173–81.

39 | ETHICS MELTDOWN · pages 451–461

1 See Ch. 35, "Gifts."

2 Complaint 2000-2, *In Re: Thomas D. Goldberg* , 24 May 2000: 10.

3 RIEC Minutes of Open Session, 20 Jun. 2000.

4 I never asked, and Healey never told me the name of this lawyer. See RIEC Response Memorandum to Objection of Thomas Goldberg, *In Re: RIEC Case No. 2001-79*, 28 Feb. 2001: 4.

5 Complaints 2000-6, *In Re: Melvin L. Zurier*; 2000-7, *In Re: Thomas D. Goldberg*; 2000-8, *In Re: Robin L. Main*, all filed 10 Jul. 2000. See Christopher Rowland,

"Citizens group files suit over ethics panel's gift hearing," *PJ*, 15 Jul. 2000: A-03. OCG also filed suit in Superior Court charging that the RIEC had violated the APA by amending the new rule without a separate hearing.

6   The RIEC authorized Healey to hire an outside prosecutor to handle the 3 OCG complaints, 1 Aug. 2000. See Affidavit of Martin F. Healey, 25 Jan. 2001; RIEC Response Memorandum to Objection of Thomas Goldberg, *In Re: RIEC Case No. 2001-79*, 28 Feb. 2001.

7   RI Superior Court Formal and Special Cause Calendar. Article II, Rule 9 of the Supreme Court Rules sets conditions for participation of out-of-state attorneys in RI courts.

8   A committee of lawyers had stalled Healey's application to practice law in RI. The Supreme Court finally authorized his work at the Ethics Commission, *In Re: Healey*, 654 A.2d 705 (R.I. 1995). See Ch. 29, "A Question of Ethics."

9   During a personal interview on 17 Dec. 2013 retired Chief Justice Frank J. Williams confirmed that he had used this phrase. He expressed regret that he had not been more candid during the controversy but said he believes that the composition of the Ethics Commission made Healey's firing inevitable.

10   See Ch. 8, "Hope for Ethics."

11   PL 91-177. The final version stands as RIGL 36-14-12 (c) Upon receipt of a written complaint alleging a violation of this chapter, the Commission shall within one hundred eighty (180) days of receipt of the written complaint complete its investigation; provided, that the Commission may, for good cause shown, grant no more than two (2) extensions of sixty (60) days each.

12   *Clarke* v. *Morsilli*, 723 A.2d 785 (R.I. 1998). Elliot Krieger, "Decision puts 15 ethics cases in jeopardy," *PJ*, 22 Jul. 1998: A-01; Katherine Gregg, "State court ruling prompts dismissal of 11 ethics cases," *PJ*, 11 Dec. 1998: A-01.

13   RIEC, Order and Finding of Probable Cause, *In Re: Stephen Day*, Complaint 97–9, 22 Dec. 1997.

14   C.J. Chivers, "Time ruling in ethics case bolsters former fire union chief," *PJ*, 22 Jul. 1998: C-01.

15   *Thomas D. Goldberg* v. *Martin Healey, et al.*, Superior Court No. 01-0089.

16   Robert D. Goldberg, "To Rhode Island Department of the Attorney General," 31 Jan. 2001.

17   Robert D. Goldberg letters, "To David D. Curtin, Disciplinary Counsel," 15 Feb. 2001; "To Daniel C. Crane, Bar Counsel, Massachusetts Board of Bar Overseers," 15 Feb. 2001.

18   Jonathan D. Rockoff, "Ethics dispute headed to court," *PJ*, 4 Jan. 2001: B-01.

19   RIEC Minutes of Open Session, 12 Dec. 2000, 3 Jan. 2001, 23 Jan. 2001, 29 Jan. 2001. Open session minutes noted that the executive session dealt with the investigation of complaints 2000-2 and 2000-7 against Thomas Goldberg.

20   Karen Lee Ziner, "Court rejects effort by Ethics Commission to subpoena member," *PJ*, 31 Jan. 2001.

21   Superior Court Civil Action No. 01-0089, "Affidavit of Martin F. Healey," 25 Jan. 2001.

22   See Peter S. Margulies, "Protecting the Public without Protectionism: Access, Competence, and *Pro Hac Vice* Admission to the Practice of Law," *RWU Law Review* (Spring 2002, Vol. 7), refers to 3 flaws in the decision: "First, the court's retroactive application of the comprehensive model has disrupted settled expectations, disallowing compensation to attorneys for work done competently and in good faith. Second, the court has been inconsistent in its outcomes. For example, the court denied *pro hac vice* admission to attorney Small, who was conducting a high-profile

ethics investigation, while it granted admission to other lawyers on similar facts. Third, the court has failed to provide adequate reasons for its decisions, exemplified by its issuance of a stark unpublished order in place of an opinion in Small. While justices of the court subsequently published op-ed pieces that offered valuable insights on their ruling, judges' use of the media cannot substitute for a well-reasoned judicial opinion." Margulies notes that the justices denied Small's application "despite the fact that the Ethics Commission's retention of Small clearly fulfilled one of the criteria set out in the court's own rules."

23   Supreme Court Dissenting opinion, *In Re: Rhode Island Ethics Commission,* 01-79-M.P., 15 Jun. 2001: 2–4.

24   Katherine Gregg, "AG opts out of ethics dispute," *PJ*, 13 Mar. 2001: B-01.

25   Jonathan D. Rockoff, "Commission fires lawyer, rejects his $60,000 bill," *PJ*, 14 Mar. 2001: A-01.

26   Bob Kerr, "The ethics of this move are a mystery," *PJ*, 16 Mar. 2001: B-01; editorial, "All in the extended family," *PJ*, 18 Mar. 2001: B-06.

27   Daniel I. Small, *In Re: Thomas Goldberg,* Special Counsel's Investigative Report, 27 Apr. 2001. Even a heavily redacted copy I obtained under an APRA request showed that Small found likely violations of numerous sections of the law.

28   Daniel I. Small, *In Re: Melvin L. Zurier,* Special Counsel's Investigative Report, 27 Apr. 2001. Small concluded that Zurier's law practice was "largely independent of" Tillinghast, Licht, Perkins, Smith & Cohen, a firm that deployed lobbyists, and that Zurier relied on the firm only "for his office space and support staff needs, and these are matters of convenience." Small concluded that the RIEC should dismiss the complaint because it fell short of "its threshold allegation" that Zurier was a "business associate." (p. 15)

29   Jonathan D. Rockoff, "Barbs fly in Ethics Commission dispute," *PJ*, 21 Mar. 2001: A-01.

30   Jonathan D. Rockoff, "Ethics panel lawyer practiced illegally, justice contends," *PJ*, 23 Mar. 2001: A-01.

31   Victoria Lederberg, "We're victims of erroneous innuendoes," *PJ*, 23 Mar. 2001: B-06.

32   Frank J. Williams, "Protocol is important; Ethics flap is Mr. Healey's fault," *PJ*, 25 Mar. 2001: B-07. In his 17 Dec. 2013 interview with me, Williams acknowledged that he also bore responsibility for the meltdown and that he had made a mistake in blaming the confusion entirely on Healey. He acknowledged telling Healey the issue was mere "chickenshit."

33   RIEC Minutes of the Open Session, 3 Apr. 2001: 8.

34   Jonathan D. Rockoff, "Ethics panel fires its director," *PJ*, 4 Apr. 2001: A-01.

35   M. Charles Bakst, "Darkness descends again on R.I.," *PJ*, 8 Apr. 2001: B-01.

36   Rockoff.

37   Carl T. Bogus, "Exactly why judicial silence is golden," *PJ*, 12 Apr. 2001: B-06.

38   HPW, "How to fix the Ethics Commission," *PJ*, 16 Apr. 2001: A-08.

39   Ariel Sabar, "Bill seeks to tighten control of appointees to state ethics panel," *PJ*, 11 May 2001: B-01.

40   Katherine Gregg, "Political Scene: York moves closer to run," 12 Nov. 2001: A-05.

40 | REDISTRICTING REVENGE · pages 462–483

1   *Redistricting Law 2010* (Denver: NCSL, 2009) contains an excellent summary of current constitutional sections, statutory provisions, and court rulings. http://www.ncsl.org/legislatures-elections/elections/redistricting-law-2010742.aspx.

2   Mark Monmonier, *Bushmanders & Bullwinkles: How Politicians Manipulate Electronic Maps and Census Data to Win Elections* (Chicago: Univ. of Chicago Press, 2001), 1–2. Cartoon by Elkanah Tisdale for the *Boston Gazette*, 26 Mar. 1812, from James Parton, *Caricature and other Comic Art* (New York: Harper, 1877), 316.

3   *Licht* v. *Quattrocchi*, 82-1494 (R.I.Sup.Ct. June 3, 1982). The Rhode Island Supreme Court later affirmed the Superior Court ruling. *Licht* v. *Quattrocchi*, 449 A.2d 887 (R.I., 1982).

4   *Farnum* v. *Burns*, 548 F.Supp. 769 (DRI 1982). Pettine concluded: "The Court is convinced that a political gerrymander did in fact occur in this case. There is no legitimate, nondiscriminatory explanation for the way in which the Select Senate Redistricting Committee redrew the Providence district lines. Placing sections of the East Side into four separate senatorial districts simply cannot be justified in view of that areas' distinct boundaries and stable population. In fact, the only plausible explanation of the defendants' proposed Providence district lines and the particular configuration of the southern boundary of district 2 is that they were drawn for a specific political purpose. As the testimony of Sens. Licht and Sapinsley indicates, that purpose was to preserve the senatorial seats of incumbents favorable to the democratic leadership and punish incumbents critical of that leadership." See also *Reynolds* v. *Sims*, 377 U.S. 533, (1964).

5   Thomas E. Walsh, "Rocco Quattrocchi, after the fall," *PJ*, 22 Jan. 1984: A-01.

6   James M. O'Neill, "4 nominated for state court seats," *PJ*, 26 May 1990: A-01. As noted in Ch.30, "Retaliation." Maureen McKenna Goldberg advanced to the state Supreme Court in 1997 after House leaders killed the nomination of Margaret Curran.

7   On 3 Nov. 1992, Republicans defeated four Bevilacqua loyalists: In Sen. Dist. 19 (West Warwick), John Feroce defeated Stephen D. Alves; in Dist. 21 (Coventry and Scituate), Leo R. Blais defeated Raymond J. Monahan; in Dist. 23 (North Kingstown), Robin Porter defeated Paul Pederzani III; in Dist. 45 (Bristol and Warren) Mary A. Parella defeated Richard M. Alegria. See Ch. 15, "Keeping Score," and Ch. 16, "A Pivotal Election."

8   Scott MacKay, "Kelly named majority leader in state Senate," *PJ*, 13 Nov. 1992: A-03.

9   Christopher Rowland and Katherine Gregg, "Kelly's grip on Senate no longer iron-clad," *PJ*, 17 Jul. 2000: B-01.

10   Christopher Rowland, "Irons claims he has the votes to lead Senate," *PJ*, 28 Sep. 2000: A-01.

11   Jonathan Saltzman, "Irons supporters victors in four key Senate races," *PJ*, 13 Sep. 2000: A-16. Warwick Sen. James M. Donelan defeated Barbara K. Gautieri and Warwick Rep. Aram G. Garabedian crushed newcomer John J. Casey; Providence Sen. Robert T. Kells beat Juan M. Pichardo; former Johnston Sen. Joseph M. Polisena ousted Sen. William P. Tocco Jr.

12   RIBOE http://www.elections.ri.gov/elections/results/2000/statewideprimary/dem-dissum.php.

13   Christopher Rowland and Scott MacKay, "Defections tipping scales in Sen. Irons's favor," *PJ*, 10 Oct. 2000: B-01.

14   Senators from Providence: Maryellen Goodwin, Rhoda E. Perry, John M. Roney, and Charles D. Walton; Cranston: Hannah M. Gallo, Thomas J. Izzo, and Elizabeth H. Roberts; Newport: M. Teresa Paiva Weed and J. Clement Cicilline; Charlestown: Donna M. Walsh; East Greenwich: J. Michael Lenihan; Glocester: Paul W. Fogarty; South Kingstown: V. Susan Sosnowski; Tiverton: William Enos; and Warren: Walter S. Felag Jr.

15   BrownRudnick later moved from its offices at 121 South Main St., Providence.

16   Ariel Sabar, "Looking for their fair share," *PJ*, 13 Dec. 2000: A-01. For simplicity, this
      section condenses the meetings of 12 and 19 Dec. 2000 as if they were a single event.

17   Rhode Island affiliates included: American Association of University Women
      (AAUW), American Civil Liberties Union (ACLU), Common Cause, Green Party,
      League of Women Voters (LWV), National Association for the Advancement of
      Colored People (NAACP), National Conference for Community & Justice (NCCJ),
      Sierra Club, State Council of Churches, and Urban League. Local organizations
      included: Civil Rights Round Table, Coalition for Consumer Justice (CCJ), Fund for
      Community Progress, Greater Camp Concerned Citizens, John Hope Settlement,
      Liberian Community Association, Mathewson Street United Methodist Church,
      Mothers Against Drunk Driving (MADD), Nigerian Institute of Policy and Advo-
      cacy, Operation Clean Government (OCG), People to End Homelessness, Progreso
      Latino, Project BASIC, Rhode Island Latino Political Action Committee (RILPAC),
      Silver-Haired Legislature, and Socio-Economic Development Center (SEDC).

18   01-S 0621, "An Act Relating to Redistricting," *PJ*, Sens. Lenihan, Walton, Raptakis,
      Parella, and Perry, 14 Feb. 2001.

19   Jim Baron, "Drawing the lines," *Pawtucket Times*, 7 Feb. 2001: 1; Ariel Sabar, "No
      detail too small as redistricting interests line up," *PJ*, 7 Feb. 2001: A-01.

20   Monmonier: 101. See Ed Cook, *Legislative Guide to Redistricting in Iowa* (Iowa
      Legislative Services Agency: 2007). https://www.legis.iowa.gov/Resources/Redist/
      about.aspx.

21   01-S 0778, "An Act Establishing a Reapportionment Commission," by Sens. Irons,
      Caprio, Montalbano, Celona, and Goodwin, 27 Feb. 2001.

22   Scott MacKay, "Plan would eliminate districts of Kennedy, other mavericks," *PJ*,
      11 Dec. 1991: A-14.

23   Marion Davis, "Up and down Broad St., Latino community thrives," *PJ*, 30 Mar.
      2001: A-01; and Ariel Sabar and David Herzog, "Influx of Hispanics, South County
      boom highlight changes," *PJ*, 30 Mar. 2001: A-01; "Some fast facts from Census
      2000," *PJ*, 30 Mar. 2001: A-01.

24   "Figures show what many already know: West Bay's growing," *PJ*, 20 Mar. 2001:
      C-01; "Some fast facts from Census 2000," *PJ*, 30 Mar. 2001: A-01; Ariel Sabar and
      David Herzog, "Influx of Hispanics, South County boom highlight changes," *PJ*,
      30 Mar. 2001: A-01.

25   M. Charles Bakst, "The challenge of being Angel Taveras," *PJ*, 13 May 2001: C-01.

26   Sen. Paul Pederzani III, a Democrat and son of a Superior Court judge, was blamed
      for early attempts to draw a district that excluded rival Warren R. Pizik. He lost to
      Republican Robin Porter in 1992. http://www.elections.ri.gov/elections/results/1992/
      risenate.php.

27   PL 01-315, "An Act Establishing a Reapportionment Commission," by Sens. Irons,
      Caprio, Montalbano, Goodwin, et al.. 13 Jul. 2001.

28   Angel Taveras, Letter to Senate Majority Leader William V. Irons, 2 Apr. 2001.
      Taveras listed commissioners recommended by the Fair Redistricting Coalition:
      Tomás Ávila (Progreso Latino), Belinda Bermingham (Urban League), Joseph
      Fernandez (FRC pro bono attorney), Patricia Martinez (Prov. School Dept.),
      Faynese Miller (Brown University), Charles Newton (Minority Business Enterprise),
      Cathleen Speer (Common Cause), Rev. Theodore Wilson (Congdon St. Baptist
      Church), James Vincent (RIHMFC, Urban League).

29   Katherine Gregg, "House picks 8 to realign districts," *PJ*, 20 Jul. 2001: B-01.

30 Edward Fitzpatrick and Ariel Sabar, "Makeup of redistricting panel assailed," *PJ*, 29 Aug. 2001: B-01.

31 Public hearings to gather information were held at South Kingstown High School (13 Sep. 2001), State House (18 Sep.), Warwick City Hall (20 Sep.), Barrington High School (24 Sep., rescheduled from 11 Sep.), Newport City Hall (25 Sep.), Woonsocket City Hall (27 Sep.). A second round of hearings provided opportunity for public comment on alternative maps prepared by Election Data Services: South Kingstown High School (13 Nov.), Woonsocket City Hall (14 Nov.), Warwick City Hall (15 Nov.), State House (20 Nov.), Barrington High School (27 Nov.), Newport City Hall (29 Nov.).

32 In September, EDS distributed three House plans (marked House A, B, and C) and 3 Senate plans (Senate A, B, and C). On November 8, Brace released two new House plans (D and E) and two new Senate plans (also D and E).

33 Edward Fitzpatrick and David Herzog, "Female lawmakers lose in proposed remapping," *PJ*, 18 Nov. 2001: A-01.

34 HPW, "Going swimmingly in Sakonnet — Gerrymandering the R.I. legislature," *PJ*, 17 Nov. 2001: B-06. The Little Compton Town Council and Tiverton Town Council later declared their support for earlier Senate plans that would have kept Little Compton and all of Tiverton in a single district. See Alisha A. Pina, "Town Council endorses redistricting plan," *PJ*, 21 Nov. 2001: C-01; Bryan Rourke, "There's little to like in county redistricting plans," *PJ*, 30 Nov. 2001: C-01.

35 Fitzpatrick. The final House plan put the three women in separate districts, but Lima had to campaign against a male colleague in Cranston: http://riredistricting.com/ images/existing-district-maps/house_14.pdf.

36 House Dist. 62: http://riredistricting.com/images/existing-district-maps/house_62. pdf.

37 Edward Fitzpatrick and David Herzog, "Female lawmakers lose in proposed remapping," *PJ*, 18 Nov. 2001: A-01.

38 Edward Fitzpatrick, "Cianci criticizes new Senate maps," *PJ*, 21 Nov. 2001: B-01.

39 Steven Stycos, "Man in the middle," *Providence Phoenix*, 5 Mar. 2004: 1.

40 Edward Fitzpatrick, "Minorities blast plan for districts," *PJ*, 8 Dec. 2001: A-01.

41 Edward Fitzpatrick, "Some see political payback in maps," *PJ*, 9 Dec. 2001: A-01.

42 Edward Fitzpatrick, "Commission serves up its plan for redistricting," *PJ*, 12 Dec. 2001: A-01.

43 Alma Felix Green and Yahaira Placencia were appointed by Senate Majority Leader William V. Irons; Luisa Murillo was appointed by House Speaker John Harwood.

44 The State Library has lists of legislative grants awarded before John Harwood became speaker and since he left office but none for the years when he was arguably the most powerful political figure in Rhode Island.

45 02-S 2258, "An Act Relating to Redistricting of the General Assembly" by Sens. Montalbano, Irons, Graziano, Bates, and Blais.

46 Edward Fitzpatrick, "Senate approves historic redrawing of Assembly districts," *PJ*, 8 Feb. 2002: A-01.

47 *SJrnl*, 7 Feb. 2002, floor amendments to 02-S 2258.

48 Edward Fitzpatrick, "Suit seeks to nullify Senate districts," *PJ*, 3 May 2002: A-01.

49 Edward Fitzpatrick, "Lawsuit challenges new map," *PJ*, 3 Jul. 2002: A-01.

41 | PLUNDER DOME · pages 484–495

1   Mike Stanton, the Pulitzer Prize-winning *Providence Journal* reporter, tells Cianci's story in his superb book, *Prince of Providence: The True Story of Buddy Cianci, America's Most Notorious Mayor, Some Wiseguys, and the Feds* (New York: Random House, 2003). Cherry Arnold created an Emmy Award-winning documentary, *Buddy: The Rise and Fall of America's Most Notorious Mayor* (Laurel Hill Films, 2005). Cianci wrote an autobiography: *Politics and Pasta: How I Prosecuted Mobsters, Rebuilt a Dying City, Dined with Sinatra, Spent Five Years in a Federally Funded Gated Community, and Lived to Tell the Tale* (New York: St. Martin's Press, 2011). By contrast with the work of Stanton and Arnold, Cianci's tale is poorly documented and largely self-serving.

2   Stanton, 166–88.

3   Stanton, 203–07.

4   Richard Dujardin, "Homes begin to shed the lead," *PJ*, 7 Oct. 1996, C-01. The U.S. Centers for Disease Control and Prevention and the U.S. Department of Housing and Urban Development jointly funded the GENS lead abatement pilot project, one of two in the country. Becker gives particular credit to Dr. Peter Simon, Medical Director of the state's Childhood Lead Poisoning Control Program since 1977.

5   Karen Lee Ziner, "Crackdown on lead — Landlords served notice," *PJ*, 3 Aug. 1996: A-01.

6   Gina Macris, "Neighborhood gathers to parade, celebrate," *PJ*, 18 May 1997: B-01.

7   Kevin Sullivan, "City leaders pleased, baffled by ex-mayor," *PJ*, 29 Jun. 1990: A-10.

8   Laura Meade, "Cianci ally promoted despite low exam score," *PJ*, 10 Jul. 1991: A-01.

9   Mike Stanton, "FBI arrests 2 city officials for money laundering," *PJ*, 29 Apr. 1999: A-01. For the name, see Stanton, *Prince of Providence*, 292–3.

10 Stanton, *Prince*, 260–72. CCRI awarded its Public Service Achievement Award to Freitas on 18 Nov. 1999. The award's text described early stages of the investigation: "At the eye of this legal hurricane stands a solitary citizen whose indignation and sense of civic responsibility drove him to risk his home, his business and his life itself to become what the FBI called its 'cooperating witness' in Plunder Dome."

11 Mike Stanton and C.J. Chivers, "Corruption probe widens," *PJ*, 28 May 1999: A-01.

12 C. J. Chivers, "'Plunder Dome' case follows FBI script," *PJ*, 23 May 1999: A-01.

13 Stanton, *Prince*, 297, 263.

14 W. Zachary Malinowski and Jonathan D. Rockoff, "Cianci, council propose special ethics unit," *PJ*, 8 Nov. 1999: B-01.

15 Mike Stanton, "Lawyer says he delivered client's bribe to tax official," *PJ*, 25 Nov. 1999: A-01.

16 David Herzog and Tracy Breton, "Ead admits to extortion," *PJ*, 15 Feb. 2000: A-01.

17 W. Zachary Malinowski, "Collector pleads guilty to payoffs," *PJ*, 30 Mar. 2000: A-01.

18 RIGL 17-25-7.2 Personal use of campaign funds prohibited. (a) The personal use by any elected public office holder or by any candidate for public office, as defined in § 17-25-3, of campaign funds contributed after April 29, 1992, is prohibited. For the purposes of this section, "personal use" is defined as any use other than expenditures related to gaining or holding public office and for which the candidate for public office or elected public official would be required to treat the amount of the expenditure as gross income under § 61 of the Internal Revenue Code of 1986, 26 U.S.C. § 61, or any subsequent corresponding Internal Revenue Code of the United States, as from time to time amended.

19 Tracy Breton and Mike Stanton, "Cianci spent campaign money for family gifts, par-

ties," *PJ*, 28 May 2000: A-01; M. Charles Bakst, "Mr. Entitlement: Cianci fund story a comment on ego," *PJ*, 1 Jun. 2000: A-01.

20   Mike Stanton, "Cianci faces state probe of campaign financing," *PJ*, 21 Jul. 2000: A-01.

21   David Herzog, "Former top aide to Cianci indicted on bribery charges," *PJ*, 30 Jun. 2000: A-01.

22   Mike Stanton, "Cianci indicted — Grand jury indicts Cianci, 5 others on 30 counts of racketeering, conspiracy," *PJ*, 3 Apr. 2001: A-01; W. Zachary Malinowski, "The elements of the grand jury's indictment," *PJ*, 3 Apr. 2001: A-06.

23   Stanton, *Prince*, 289–91.

24   Karen Lee Ziner, "Cianci indicted — Cianci friends offer kisses, condolences," *PJ*, 3 Apr. 2001: A-09. See Michael Corkery, "Almond calls upon Cianci to resign," *PJ*, 4 Apr. 2001: A-01.

25   Scott MacKay, "Special report–Our Rascal King," *PJ*, 8 Apr. 2001: B-01.

26   Mike Stanton, "'Good mayors are risk takers,'" *PJ*, 7 Apr. 2002: A-01.

27   See Ch. 39, "Ethics Meltdown."

28   Mike Stanton, "Plunder Dome prosecutor's life shaped by childhood trials," *PJ*, 15 Apr. 2001: A-01. Rose had grown up with his mother and four siblings on Public Street in South Providence. He dropped out of school to become a Marine, eventually returned for college, then law school. He mentored neighborhood youth and worked to end street violence. Personal experience had shown him how corruption siphoned money away from poor communities and increased cynicism. Leading the Cianci prosecution proved both triumph and challenge. When he made the mistake of showing an FBI tape to three people he trusted, he was suspended for thirty days and fined $500.

29   Mike Stanton and Tracy Breton, "Prosecutor points to Cianci as head of criminal enterprise," *PJ*, 24 Apr. 2002: A-01.

30   Judge Ernest C. Torres also presided over the trial of Artin H. Coloian on bribery and conspiracy charges during the last week of June. See Tracy Breton, "Aide's trial opens with Cianci still awaiting a verdict," *PJ*, 24 Jun. 2002: A-01; Gerald M. Carbone and W. Zachary Malinowski, "Cianci aide's trial opens with opposing portraits," *PJ*, 25 Jun. 2002: A-07; W. Zachary Malinowski, "Coloian acquitted," *PJ*, 28 Jun. 2002: A-01.

31   Tracy Breton, "Instructions to jury a critical element in case," *PJ*, 11 Jun. 2002: A-17.

32   Mike Stanton, "Lawyers make last pitch," *PJ*, 12 Jun. 2002: A-01.

33   Tracy Breton and Mike Stanton, "City Hall corruption case goes to jury," *PJ*, 13 Jun. 2002: A-01.

34   Brown University Survey, 29 Sep. 1999, http://www.brown.edu/academics/ taubman-center/research-and-initiatives/public-opinion-polls/providence-city-survey-september-1999.

35   Brown University Survey, "81 percent believe corruption is problem in Providence City Government," 13 Jun. 2001, http://www.brown.edu/academics/taubman-center/ research-and-initiatives/public-opinion-polls/rhode-island-state-survey-june-2001.

36   Scott MacKay, "Brown University poll shows Cianci still has strong following," *PJ*, 12 Jun. 2002: A-12.

37   Scott MacKay, "Mayoral politics on hold as candidates wait on verdict," *PJ*, 9 Jun. 2002: A-16.

38   Gregory Smith, "Cicilline tosses hat into mayor's contest," *PJ*, 12 Feb. 2002: C-01.

39   Richard C. Dujardin, "McKenna enters mayoral race," *PJ*, 15 Apr. 2002: B-01.

40   W. Zachary Malinowski, "Cianci guilty of racketeering charge," *PJ*, 25 Jun. 2002: A-01.

41 Tom Mooney, "Jurors comfortable with their verdicts," *PJ*, 25 Jun. 2002: A-04.
42 Pamela Ferdinand, "Providence Mayor Is Found Guilty," Washington Post, 25 Jun. 2002: A-02; Tracy Breton, "Feds were ready with Cianci's past — Earlier allegations unveiled," *PJ*, 3 Jul. 2002: A-01.
43 Stanton, *Prince*, 387.
44 *United States* v. *Cianci*, 378 F.3d 71 (1st Cir.) 10 Aug. 2004.

42 | Perfect Storm? · pages 496–516

1 CCRI spring financial appeal, "Three Storms Converge in Rhode Island," 9 Mar. 2001. The "Perfect Storm" appeal brought in a record $124,087 from 451 donors; 274 donors increased their contributions by more than ten per cent over what they had given in 2000. Many were new contributors or former givers who had not given in 1999 or 2000.
2 Complaint 2001-5, *In Re: John B. Harwood*. See Michael Corkery, "Ethics complaint filed against House speaker," *PJ*, 15 Feb. 2001: B-01. See also Ch. 38, "Kingly Power."
3 Ariel Sabar, "Harwood steps away from cases before state," *PJ*, 4 Feb. 2001: A-01.
4 Jonathan D. Rockoff, "Conflicts complicate probe of Harwood," *PJ*, 19 Apr. 2001: A-01. Recusing were Commissioners Richard E. Kirby, Robin L. Main, Diane T. Monti-Markowski, James V. Murray, and Melvin L. Zurier; announcing that they expected to recuse were Thomas D. Goldberg and Francis J. Flanagan.
5 RIEC Informal Resolution and Settlement, *In Re: John Harwood,* Complaint No. 93-66. Harwood had paid $5,000 but did not admit wrongdoing. See Ch. 29, "A Question of Ethics."
6 Bruce Landis, "Ethics panel assailed over Harwood ruling," *PJ*, 28 Nov. 2001: B-04.
7 In 1995, Almond vetoed the appointment of two legislators to the Rabies Control Board; in 1997, he supported the Ethics Commission's rule against legislators on boards that executed state laws; in 1998, he vetoed legislation that would have created a Cancer Council; in 1999, he challenged the constitutionality of the Lottery Commission; in 2000, he asked state voters to demand a constitutional convention to establish separation of powers.
8 Notes by Peter Hufstader and HPW, 15 Nov. 2001.
9 Edward Achorn, "A fighting chance this year," *PJ*, 29 Jan. 2002: B-06.
10 Katherine Gregg, "Rally targets R.I. Assembly's grip on power," *PJ*, 30 Jan. 2002: A-01.
11 *The People's Constitution,* Article III.2: Dec. 1841.
12 Personal letter from Sheldon Whitehouse, 30 Jan. 2002.
13 02-H 7113, "Joint Resolution to Approve and Publish, and Submit to the Electors a Proposition of Amendment to the Constitution of the State (Separation of Powers), by Reps. Pires, Montanaro, Ajello, Long, and Picard, 31 Jan. 2002; 02-H 7050, "Joint Resolution to Approve and Publish, and Submit to the Electors a Proposition of Amendment to the Constitution of the State (Separation of Powers)," by Reps Gorham, Fleury, W.H. Murphy, Savage, and Story, 29 Jan. 2002; (same title), by Reps Pires, Montanaro, Ajello, Long, and Picard, 31 Jan. 2002.
14 Edward Fitzpatrick, "Candidates keen on separation of powers," *PJ*, 10 Apr. 2002: A-04.
15 See n13. Except for a minor clerical error, 02-H7050 and 02-H7113 were identical.
16 Rev. F. Herbert Skeete and I met on a United Methodist Church urban ministries task force when he served in Queens and I in Brooklyn. Eleven years older, he taught and encouraged me. He later became pastor of Salem Church in Harlem. Elected bishop in 1980, he served in Philadelphia and Boston before retiring in 1996.

17 Jim Baron, "Separation of powers bill defeated," *PT*, 3 Apr. 2002: 1.

18 Edward Fitzpatrick, "Separation of powers bill gets new push," *PJ*, 4 Apr. 2002: B-01.

19 CCRI, Urgent Legislative Alert, 8 Apr. 2002.

20 Edward Achorn, "Time to fight for R.I.," *PJ*, 9 Apr. 2002: B-05.

21 Edward Fitzpatrick, "House leaders block 'powers' bill," *PJ*, 11 Apr. 2002: B-01. See also Jim Baron, "Procedural gambit sandbags balance of powers bill," *PT*, 11 Apr. 2002: 1; Joe Baker, "Balance of power won't be seen soon," *NDN*, 12 Apr. 2002: 1.

22 Edward Fitzpatrick, "Minds were changed on powers vote," *PJ*, 12 Apr. 2002: A-01; editorial, "Legislature defies will of the people," *NDN*, 12 Apr. 2002; Editorial, "RI lawmakers can't bypass voters on separation issue," *Westerly Sun*, 14 Apr. 2002; Harvey Perry, "Residents must step up and demand action for separation of powers," *Westerly Sun*, April 14, 2002; Jim Baron, "General Assembly displays power at its most arrogant," *PT*, 15 Apr. 2002; Katie Haughey, "A question of separation of powers," *Westerly Sun*, 16 Apr. 2002; Edward Achorn, "Don't give up yet, R.I.," *PJ*, 16 Apr. 2002: B-05; Neal Jones, "State lawmakers defend votes on balance of power," *Narragansett Times*, 17 Apr. 2002: 1; Peter Hufstader letter, "Rep. Knickle misleads on balance of power," *PJ*, 18 Apr. 2002; Burt Hoffman letter, "Four local Assembly members don't represent the will of the people," *NDN*, 19 Apr. 2002; editorial, "Don't let self-interest rule in Statehouse," *NDN*, 19 Apr. 2002. Judith Terry letter, "Tell lawmakers balance of power must be changed," *NDN*, 20 Apr. 2002.

23 Rep. Paul W. Crowley, "Base separation of powers issue on facts," *PJ*, 11 May 2002: B-06.

24 HPW, "Rhode Island is different; Separation around the nation," *PJ*, 3 Jun. 2002: A-09.

25 02-H 7548 "Relating to Education," by Rep. Paul W. Crowley.

26 02-H 7794, "An Act Relating to Public Property and Works — State Auditorium," by Reps Fox, Jacquard, Giannini, Moura, and Costantino, 28 Feb. 2002.

27 02-H 8068 Relating to the Rhode Island Underground Storage Tank Review Board, by Reps Malik, Winfield, Menard, Munschy, and Anguilla, 30 Apr. 2002.

28 02-H 8179 SubA, "An Act Relating to the Convention Center Authority," by Reps. Moura and Williams, which Gov. Almond vetoed on June 10, but which was enacted over his veto: PL 02-426, 12 Jun. 2002

29 02-H 7701 "I-195 Redevelopment Act of 2002," by Reps. Murphy, Montanaro, Moura, Naughton, and Long, 12 Feb. 2002: 02-S 2740, (same title), by Sens. Ruggerio, Celona, and Bates, 7 Feb. 2002.

30 02-H 7732 Article 8, SubAaa, "An Act Making Appropriations for the Support of the State for the Fiscal Year Ending 30 Jun. 2003: Tobacco Settlement Financing Corporation Act," by Reps. Watson and Quick. Powers appear in RIGL 42-133-5, corporation membership in 42-133-6. Katherine Gregg, "Whitehouse, Almond blast legislature's 'power grab,'" 4 Jun. 2002: A-01; Edward Fitzpatrick, "Whitehouse says legislators must not control tobacco panel," 6 Jun. 2002: B-01.

31 Katherine Gregg, "'Power grab' puts Almond administration on defensive," *PJ*, 31 May 2002: A-01.

32 02-H 8149, "An Act Relating to Elections — Statewide Referenda Elections," by Rep. Mabel Anderson, 21 May 2002.

33 Edward Fitzpatrick, "Separation of powers bill gets new push," *PJ*, 4 Apr. 2002: B-01; "Powers bill up in the air," *PJ*, 14 Apr. 2002: B-01.

34 RIGL 22-11-1. The Joint Committee on Legislative Services (JCLS) includes the House Speaker, House Majority Leader, House Minority Leader, Senate Majority

Leader, and Senate Minority Leader. Sen. J. Michael Lenihan had raised the need for administrative parity between the Senate and House in a speech to Common Cause, 27 Feb. 2002.

35 Katherine Gregg, "Tempers flare as senators voice frustration over budget process," *PJ*, 22 May 2002: A-01.

36 Don Aucoin, "Will work for change; In Rhode Island, West is fighting the good fight," *Boston Globe*, 29 May 2002: D-01.

37 02-S 2440, "Joint Resolution to Approve and Publish, and Submit to the Electors a Proposition of Amendment to the Constitution of the State (Separation of Powers)," by Sens. Algiere, Gibbs, Breene, Bates, and Parella, 30 Jan. 2002.

38 02-S 2288, (same title), by Sens. Lenihan, Cote, Raptakis, Parella, and Enos, 29 Jan. 2002.

39 Proposed new Article III, Section 6 (current language struck through, proposed new language underlined): ~~Holding of offices under other governments.~~ Holding of offices under other governments – Senators and representatives not to hold other appointed offices under state government. — No person holding any office under the government of the United States, or of any other state or country, shall act as a general officer or as a member of the general assembly, unless at the time of taking such engagement that person shall have resigned the office under such government, and if any general officer, senator, representative, or judge shall, after election and engagement, accept any appointment under any other government, the office under this shall be immediately vacated; but this restriction shall not apply to any person appointed to take depositions or acknowledgment of deeds, or other legal instruments, by the authority of any other state or country. No senator or representative shall, during the time for which he or she was elected, be appointed to any office, board, commission or other state or quasi-public entity exercising executive power under the laws of this state, and no person holding any executive office or serving as a member of any board, commission or other state or quasi-public entity exercising executive power under the laws of this state shall be a member of the senate or the house of representatives during his or her continuance in such office.

40 Edward Fitzpatrick, "Separation-of-powers referendum a step closer to November ballot," *PJ*, 30 May 2002: B-01.

41 Edward Fitzpatrick, "Senate OKs power separation," *PJ*, 31 May 2002: B-01.

42 Signatures on the discharge petition of Rep. Nicholas Gorham to bring 02-H 7050 to the floor for debate: 23 Democrats: Aisha W. Abdullah-Odiase, Edith H. Ajello, Joseph S. Almeida, Melvoid J. Benson, Stella G. Brien, David A. Caprio, Mary Ann F. Carroll, David N. Cicilline, Elizabeth M. Dennigan, John J. DeSimone, Nancy C. Hetherington, Beatrice A. Lanzi, Charles J. Levesque, Charlene Lima, Frank A. Montanaro, Thomas A. Palangio, Antonio J. Pires, Michael S. Pisaturo, Donald O. Reilly Jr., Maxine B. Shavers, Steven F. Smith, Peter N. Wasylyk. 15 Republicans: Joseph N. Amaral, Brock D. Bierman, Christine H. Callahan, Richard E. Fleury, Nicholas Gorham, Bruce J. Long, Carol A. Mumford, William H. Murphy, Joan B. Quick, Scott T. Rabideau, John A. Savage, Joseph H. Scott, Susan Story, Joseph A. Trillo, Robert A. Watson. (Note that two representatives were named William Murphy: Jamestown Republican William H. Murphy and West Warwick Democrat William J. Murphy, Harwood's protégé.)

43 PL 02-065, "An Act Making Appropriations for the Support of the State for the Fiscal Year ending June 30, 2003" (including both the requirement that the governor, speaker, and Senate majority leader authorize expenditures $100,000 and

the Tobacco Settlement Financing Corporation); PL 02-111 and 427, "Route I-195 Redevelopment Act of 2002;" PL 02-297, "Rhode Island Underground Storage Tank Financial Responsibility Act;" and PL 02-426, "Convention Center Authority Act."

44   Liz Anderson, "Almond vetoes 3 more bills as Assembly reconvenes today," 12 Jun. 2002: B-05; Katherine Gregg, "Legislature overrides veto of state budget," *PJ*, 13 Jun. 2002: A-01.

45   Edward Fitzpatrick, "Legislators say they're being punished," *PJ*, 8 Jun. 2002: A-01. After his retirement, Frank Anzeveno confirmed what the reform community had long suspected: during this era only the total amount of legislative grants was approved by the entire General Assembly; legislative leaders doled out grants at various times during the year. Anzeveno insisted that the grants did "a lot of good in the community." Private conversation on 30 May 2014.

43 | Scandal · pages 517–529

1   Many credit German Chancellor Otto von Bismark, 1815–1898, with the unforgettable comment: "There are two things you don't want to see being made — sausage and legislation." Rutgers Prof. Alan Rosenthal challenges this metaphor in "The Legislature as Sausage Factory," *State Legislatures Magazine*, NCSL, Sep. 2001: 12 ff.

2   Edward Fitzpatrick, "R.I. lawmakers graded," *PJ*, 25 Jul. 2002: A-01.

3   Carl T. Bogus, "The Battle for Separation of Powers in Rhode Island," 56 *Administrative Law Review* 77 (2004): 128. The pledge read: "If I am elected to public office in Rhode Island this year, I will support a constitutional amendment to incorporate the principle of Separation of Powers among the three branches of government, and if I am elected to the General Assembly, I will vote for a Separation of Powers amendment and support procedural measures designed to bring it to the floor for a vote."

4   RIGL 17-5-2, as it existed in 2002. Four years later, lawmakers passed 06-H 6874, "An Act Relating to Elections," by Reps. Kilmartin, Crowley, Anguilla, E. Coderre, and Lima, which became PL 06-080. It revoked the governor's power to place an advisory question on the ballot. See Ch. 51, "Reconstruction."

5   *2002 Voter Information Handbook; A Guide to State Referenda and Voting Procedures*, Sep. 2002: 12-13.

6   For an extensive summary of the scandal, see Edward Fitzpatrick and W. Zachary Malinowski, "*Harwood* v. *Collins*: 'I did nothing wrong,' " *PJ*, 13 Oct. 2002: A-01.

7   Katherine Gregg, Edward Fitzpatrick, and Bruce Landis, "Pires questions settlement payments," *PJ*, 16 Aug. 2002: A-01; W. Zachary Malinowski, "State politicians demanding disclosure in Collins case," *PJ*, 28 Aug. 2002: A-08.

8   Editorial, "Harwood's secrets," *PJ*, 22 Aug. 2002: B-04.

9   Katherine Gregg, "Harwood: 'Rather angry,' " *PJ*, 23 Aug. 2002: A-01.

10   Katherine Gregg, "Harwood asks police probe of 'demands' by ex-worker," *PJ*, 28 Aug. 2002: A-01.

11   Katherine Gregg, "Pare: Police declined to probe Collins case," *PJ*, 29 Aud. 2002: A-01.

12   M. Charles Bakst, "Today's special: three columns for the price of one," *PJ*, 27 Aug. 2002: B-01.

13   Michael Corkery, "Pires initiates campaign to push Harwood aside," *PJ*, 31 Aug. 2002: A-06.

14   York received 46,806 to 45,880 for Whitehouse; Pires got 26,838. RIBOE, http://www.elections.ri.gov/elections/results/2002/statewideprimary/summary.php.

15   Incumbent Inman got 43,236 to 60,193 for Brown.

16   Adam C. Holland, "Wills outraged by selection of House Dist. 34 committee," *PJ*,
      27 Jun. 2002: D-01; Paul Davis, "Caprio overwhelms Lenihan," *PJ*, 11 Sep. 2002: C-01.

17   RIBOE, http://www.elections.ri.gov/elections/results/2002/statewideprimary/
      staterepdem.php.

18   Edward Fitzpatrick, Katherine Gregg and Liz Anderson, "Party support crumbling
      for Harwood," *PJ*, 18 Sep. 2002: A-01.

19   Mark Arsenault, "Independent steps forward as write-in foe to Harwood," *PJ*,
      10 Oct. 2002: A-12.

20   Elizabeth Gudrais, "Challenger counting on mood for change," *PJ*, 10 Oct. 2002: C-01.

21   Tracy Breton, "Collins claim fast-tracked, official tells grand jury," *PJ*, 12 Oct. 2002:
      A-01; Katherine Gregg and Tracy Breton, "Collins lawyer: Harwood's story 'fiction,'"
      PJ, 19 Oct. 2002: A-01.

22   "Opponent: Harwood should pay lawyers out of his pocket," *PJ*, 12 Oct. 2002: A-06.

23   John Castellucci, "Harwood faces the public," *PJ*, 18 Oct. 2002: A-01.

24   Mark Patinkin, "Upbeat Harwood speaks his piece," 13 Oct. 2002: A-02.

25   RIBOE, *2002 Primary & Election Count Book,* 65.

26   Scott MacKay and Edward Fitzpatrick, "Democrats still rule RI after inept effort by
      GOP," *PJ*, 10 Nov. 2002: A-01.

27   Edward Fitzpatrick, "Harwood seen holding on to seat with tenuous lead," *PJ*, 6 Nov.
      2002: A-01.

28   RIBOE, *2002 Primary & Election Count Book,* 62–3.

29   Edward Fitzpatrick, "Women lose ground in new, downsized General Assembly," *PJ*,
      13 Nov. 2002: A-01.

30   Katherine Gregg and Edward Fitzpatrick, "Harwood won't run for speaker," *PJ*,
      8 Nov. 2002: A-01.

31   On 14 Nov. 2002, at the invitation of CCRI, a bipartisan drafting group met in the
      conference room of outgoing Atty. Gen. Sheldon Whitehouse. Participants in-
      cluded: Whitehouse, Rep. Nicholas Gorham (R-Coventry), Sen. J. Michael Lenihan
      (D-East Greenwich), Jeffrey Lanphear (representing Senate Minority Leader Dennis
      Algiere), Jeffrey Grybowski and Alan Gelfuso (representing Gov.-elect Donald
      Carcieri), RWU Law School Prof. Carl T. Bogus, and CCRI director HPW. Sen.
      Mary A. Parella (R-Bristol) was not able to attend because of a scheduling conflict.

32   02-H 7050 by Reps Gorham, Fleury, W.H. Murphy, Savage, and Story; 02-S 2288
      SubAaa by Sens Lenihan, Cote, Raptakis, Parella, and Enos; 02-S 2440 by Sens
      Algiere, Gibbs, Breene, Bates, and Parella.

33   U.S. Constitution, Article II.2.2.

44 | Four-Letter Word · pages 530–552

1   Donald L. Carcieri, "Inaugural Address," 7 Jan. 2003.

2   Liz Anderson, "Carcieri, House and Senate leaders praise bill to realign government
      power," *PJ*, 10 Jan. 2003: B-01.

3   In addition to ending legislative pensions prospectively, raising legislative pay, and
      downsizing the General Assembly, the 1994 Question 2 created a new constitutional
      office: president of the Senate, equivalent to the speaker of the House.

4   03-S 0180, "Joint Resolution to Approve and Publish and Submit to the Electors A
      Proposition of Amendment to the Constitution of the State (Separation of Powers),"
      by Sens. Lenihan, Irons, Algiere, Montalbano, and Parella, 29 Jan. 2003. See Articles
      VI.3 and VIII.2.

5   03-H 5081, (Same title), by Reps. Gorham, Story, Savage, Almeida, and Dennigan, 15 Jan. 2003.

6   Liz Anderson, "Legislators quick to back separation of powers bill," *PJ*, 17 Jan. 2001: A-01.

7   03-H 5360, (Same title), by Reps. Anguilla, Enos, Malik, Lewiss, and Crowley, 30 Jan. 2003.

8   See Ch. 27, "Deep Root." Ken Mingis, "Group appeals decision to build hotel on beach," *PJ*, 2 Oct. 1984: C-01; Robert C. Frederiksen, "Law creating coastal panel ruled unconstitutional over membership requirements," *PJ*, 22 Apr. 1986: D-04; Tracy Breton, "High court takes hands-off approach, preserving makeup of suspect agencies," *PJ*, 10 Mar. 1986: A-01.

9   Joe Baker, "Forum explores separation of powers issue," *NDN*, 27 Jan. 2003: 1.

10   Alex Kuffner, "The Seat of Power — Forum explores where it will lie in R.I.," *PJ*, 14 Mar. 2003: C-01.

11   Andrew C. Helman, "Vigils embrace mourners," *PJ*, 25 Feb. 2003: A-01.

12   Editorial, "The superior SOP plan," *PJ*, 6 Mar. 2003: B-06.

13   Peter Hufstader, *Separation of Powers Provisions Reference Manual*, Common Cause Education Fund, 12 Mar. 2003.

14   Hufstader: 20. The RIGL had no definitions of executive and/or administrative functions. CCRI compiled a list of 12 executive functions from the lists of duties and powers of various boards, commissions, and quasi-public bodies: (1) Purchase, take, receive, lease, mortgage, or otherwise acquire, own, hold, improve, or use real or personal property; (2) Sell, convey, mortgage, pledge, lease, exchange, transfer, and otherwise dispose of real or personal property belonging directly or indirectly to the state; (3) Employ architects, engineers, attorneys, accountants, advisors, consultants, and agents for the administration of properties controlled directly or indirectly by the state; (4) Establish agencies, administer or supervise programs, or execute contracts pursuant to law; (5) Pay debt service on general obligation bonds or on notes issued pursuant to law; (6) Receive or administer taxes, fees, gifts, contributions, bequests, or other funds received by the state from public and private sources, including the federal government; (7) Lend money, invest or reinvest funds, take or hold real or personal property as security for the payment of funds so loaned or reinvested pursuant to law; (8) Formulate plans, adopt rules, issue regulations, set standards; (9) Enforce laws, enforce rules and regulations, investigate or prosecute complaints, issue subpoenas related to alleged violations, conduct adjudicative hearings, or issue reprimands as required by law; (10) Issue permits, grant licenses, or conduct regulatory hearings, examinations, and investigations as required by law; (11) Make assessments, set rates, impose user charges as required by law, charge and collect fees for licenses and permits; (12) Sue and be sued on behalf of the state or any public or quasi-public agency established by law.

15   Liz Anderson, "House panel starts debate on separation of powers," *PJ*, 13 Mar. 2003: B-01.

16   Article IX.15. State budget. — The governor shall prepare and present to the general assembly an annual, consolidated operating and capital improvement state budget.

17   03-S 0206, "Joint Resolution to Approve and Publish and Submit to the Electors A Proposition of Amendment to the Constitution of the State (Separation of Powers)" by Sen. Daniel P. Connors, 30 Jan. 2003.

18   Liz Anderson, "Debate begins on separation of powers," *PJ*, 11 Mar. 2003: A-01.

19   Liz Anderson, "Separation-of-powers bill gets Senate panel ok," *PJ*, 21 Mar. 2003:

B-01. Lenihan kept an inscription of Thomas Jefferson's pithy comment on his desk: "On matters of style, swim with the current, on matters of principle, stand like a rock."

20 Liz Anderson, "State Senate passes separation of powers," *PJ*, 27 Mar. 2003. See also Jim Baron, "Senate OKs separation of powers," *PT*, 27 Mar. 2003: 1.

21 Joe Baker, "History lesson riles hearing participants," *NDN*, 10 Apr. 2003: 1.

22 Liz Anderson, "House pays witnesses for powers bill," *PJ*, 4 Apr. 2003: B-03.

23 See also Maureen Moakley, "Take care in how we fix balance of powers," *PJ*, 15 Mar. 2003: B-07.

24 Editorial, "Lords of the manor still blocking the gates," *Bristol Phoenix*, 3 Apr. 2003; editorial, "Still fighting to the bitter end," *Bristol Phoenix*, 10 Apr. 2003.

25 Raymond E. Gallison Jr., "Here's my position on separation of powers," *Bristol Phoenix*, 10 Apr. 2003; Fausto C. Anguilla, "Separation of powers editorial was off base," *Bristol Phoenix*, 10 Apr. 2003.

26 Liz Anderson, Katherine Gregg, Edward Fitzpatrick, "Degrees of separation," *PJ*, 21 Apr. 2003: B-01.

27 Brian Comfort, "Professor says he was asked to keep quiet," *Bristol Phoenix*, 12 Jun. 2003: 1.

28 Liz Anderson, "Irons rejects new House draft of separation-of-powers bill," *PJ*, 26 Apr. 2003.

29 By the end of April, thirty-one groups formally endorsed the bipartisan Gorham-Lenihan separation of powers text: American Association of University Women RI; Citizens Concerned About Casino Gambling; Coalition for Consumer Justice; Common Cause RI; Conservation Law Foundation; Chambers of Commerce (Cranston, East Greenwich, Central RI, Greater Providence, Hispanic-American, Newport County, and Northern RI); Energy Council of RI; Environmental Council of RI; Environmental Committee of the Diocese of RI; Jamestown Town Council; Kay Coalition Against Casino Gambling; League of Women Voters RI; Manufacturing Summit; Newport City Council; Operation Clean Government; Portsmouth Concerned Citizens; Priests for Justice (Diocese of Providence); RI Public Interest Research Group; RI Separation of Powers Committee; RI State Council of Churches; RI United Methodist Association; Save the Bay; Sierra Club of RI; Unitarian-Universalist Churches; and the Urban League of RI.

30 Gordon D. Fox, "Remarks for Separation of Powers Press Conference," 15 May 2003.

31 03-H 5081A, as proposed for amendment, 14 May 2003.

32 Liz Anderson, "House in accord on 'powers' plan," *PJ*, 16 May 2003: A-01.

33 Liz Anderson, "'Separation' bill draws skepticism," *PJ*, 20 May 2003: B-01.

34 Edward Achorn, "The roar that R.I. leaders heard," *PJ*, 20 May 2003.

35 Committee Report: House Separation of Powers, *HJrnl*, May 21, 2003.

36 Liz Anderson, "House panel OKs fundamental change in balance of power," *PJ*, 21 May 2003: A-01.

37 Jim Baron, "Separation of Powers bill clears committee," *PT*, 21 May 2003: 1.

38 Jim Baron, "Reps make history," *PT*, 22 May 2003: 1.

39 Liz Anderson, "House OKs separation of powers, 71–1," *PJ*, 22 May 2003: A-01.

40 Editorial, "Closing in on SOP," *PJ*, 26 May 2003: A-10.

41 Liz Anderson, "Compromise needed in powers bill," *PJ*, 5 Jun. 2003: B-01.

42 Jim Baron, "House, Senate work on separation of powers compromise," *PT*, 5 Jun. 2003: 1.

43 03-S 1140, "To Approve and Publish and Submit to the Electors a Proposition of

Amendment to the Constitution of the State (Separation of Powers)," Sen. J. Michael Lenihan, 11 Jun. 2003; 03-H 5081aa, (same title), Reps. Gorham, Story, Savage, Almeida, and Dennigan, 15 Jan. 2003.

44 Liz Anderson, "Language delays powers bill," *PJ*, 12 Jun. 2003: B-01.

45 HPW, "Separation of Powers — Four-letter word threatens reform," *PJ*, 26 Jun. 2003: B-06.

46 Liz Anderson, "General Assembly unanimously approves separation of powers," *PJ*, 1 Jul. 2003: A-01.

47 *HJrnl*, 30 Jun. 2003. Absent or not voting were Reps. Brian G. Coogan, Joseph L. Faria, Peter T. Ginaitt, John B. Harwood, David E. Laroche, Joseph H. Scott, Thomas C. Slater, and Joseph J. Voccola.

48 Liz Anderson, "General Assembly unanimously approves separation of powers," *PJ*, 1 Jul. 2003: A-01.

45 | Minimalist Principles · pages 555–559

1 Carl T. Bogus, "The Battle for Separation of Powers in Rhode Island," 56 *Administrative Law Review*, 77 (2004).

2 Rev. James C. Miller had become senior pastor at the First Baptist Church in America on 1 Dec. 2000, and Rev. John E. Holt became executive minister of the RI State Council of Churches.

3 From texts of Public Service Achievement Awards presented to Rep. Nicholas Gorham, Sen. J. Michael Lenihan, and Gov. Donald L. Carcieri for their leadership in the struggle for constitutional Separation of Powers, 14 Sep. 2003.

4 Peter Hufstader and HPW, "Principles recommended by Common Cause for reconfiguring Rhode Island Boards with executive-administrative functions/draft," Common Cause, 11 Nov. 2003.

46 | Triple Scandal · pages 560–572

1 Katherine Gregg and Andrea Stape, "Fox dismisses any impropriety in work for GTECH," *PJ*, 1 Oct. 2003: A-01; Katherine Gregg, "House speaker backs Fox in GTECH deals," *PJ*, 2 Oct. 2003: A-01.

2 RIEC, Complaint 2003-6 by Patricia Morgan, 10 Oct. 2003; Complaint 2003-7 by Robert P. Arruda and Beverly M. Clay, 20 Oct. 2003. OCG also demanded that Fox be expelled from the House for violating Article VI.4 of the RI Constitution. See also Patrick T. Conley, "Article VI.4: A Case Study in Constitutional Obsolescence," *People, Places, Laws, and Lore of the Ocean State* (East Providence: RIPS, 2012), 417–426.

3 Bruce Landis, "Panel to pursue ethics complaint against Rep. Fox," *PJ*, 15 Nov. 2003: A-03.

4 RIEC, *In Re: Gordon D. Fox*, Complaint Nos. 2003-6, 2003-7, Informal Resolution and Settlement, 20 Jan. 2004.

5 Katherine Gregg, "CVS confirms paying key senator as consultant," *PJ*, 5 Dec. 2003: A-01; "Senator's cable program raises conflict questions," *PJ*, 4 Dec. 2003: A-01.

6 Mike Stanton, "CVS: Retaining Celona 'an error in judgment,'" *PJ*, 16 Jan. 2004: A-01.

7 Katherine Gregg, "CVS confirms paying key senator as consultant," *PJ*, 5 Dec. 2003: A-01. On his financial disclosure form Celona had listed his work for the Village at Elmhurst, an assisted living facility affiliated with Roger Williams Hospital.

8 The House had approved two such bills in 2003 that died in Celona's Senate committee: 03-H 5215 and 03-H 5828, both proposing a new chapter 5-19.3 and entitled "Pharmacies — Freedom of Choice"; 99-S 0110, "An Act Relating to Business and Professions, Pharmacies — Freedom of Choice," by Sens. Raptakis, Montalbano, Celona, Igliozzi, and Graziano, 12 Jan. 1999.

9 W. Zachary Malinowski, "Celona offers apology for ethics lapse," *PJ*, 6 Dec. 2003: A-01.

10 RIEC Complaint 2003-9, 9 Dec. 2003.

11 Liz Anderson, "Celona steps aside pending ethics ruling," *PJ*, 12 Dec. 2003: A-01.

12 RIEC AO 99-63, *In Re: Honorable William v. Irons*.

13 Liz Anderson, "Senate chief's insurance ties draw questions," *PJ*, 21 Dec. 2003: A-01.

14 See Irons' request, 11 Mar. 1999, and RIEC AO 99-63, *In Re: Honorable William v. Irons*, which relied on RIGL 36-14-7(b), often called "the class exception." Thomas D. Goldberg also used the controversial section to justify his voting on ethics rules that would affect lobbyists.

15 Nine years after this conversation, I emailed Irons to ask for an interview for this book. He replied: "I consider my contributions to be part of the public record and really have no interest in an interview." 2 Aug. 2012.

16 Leonidas Raptakis, "Sen. Irons must disclose dealings," *PJ*, 25 Dec. 2003: A-18.

17 Katherine Gregg, "R.I. to probe legislators who work as consultants," *PJ*, 24 Dec. 2003: A-01.

18 William V. Irons, "Thank you, Rhode Island: President of the Senate William V. Irons' Departure Communication," 31 Dec. 2003.

19 Scott MacKay, "Montalbano poised to succeed Irons as Senate president," *PJ*, 3 Jan. 2004: A-01.

20 Richard Salit, "Self-made Paiva Weed stays close to home," *PJ*, 18 Jan. 2004: E-01.

21 Mike Stanton, "Police question Irons' colleagues over Blue Cross, CVS connections," *PJ*, 6 Jan. 2004: A-01.

22 Mike Stanton, "Irons paid as broker for CVS workers' health plan," *PJ*, 14 Jan. 2004: A-01. It later became clear that Irons had grossed over $100,000 from his unique relationship with CVS. See Mike Stanton, "Drugstore industry paid conference tab for R.I. legislators," *PJ*, 22 Nov. 2004: A-01.

23 RIEC Complaint 2004-1, *In Re: William v. Irons*, 20 Jan. 2004.

24 Bruce Landis, "Senator Irons faces a new complaint, ethics board review," *PJ*, 21 Jan. 2004: A-09.

25 For several years, Common Cause had worked with Sen. Teresa Paiva Weed to reduce the number of low-level public officials required to file ethics disclosure forms. Her bill defined "major state decision-making position" for the first time. See 04-S 2667 below.

26 04-S 2420, "Relating to Lobbying," by Sens. Lenihan, Sosnowski, Sheehan, Polisena, and Cote, 11 Feb. 2004; 04-H 8309, "Relating to the General Assembly — Lobbying," Reps. Fox, Anguilla, Carter, Crowley, and Lewiss, 18 Mar. 2004.

27 Mike Stanton, "Celona failed to report pay as ambulance consultant," *PJ*, 24 Feb. 2004: A-01.

28 Katherine Gregg, "Most say state government is corrupt," *PJ*, 11 Feb. 2004: B-01.

29 Scott Mayerowitz, "No word from Celona; calls for ouster mount," *PJ*, 25 Feb. 2004: A-01.

30 Mike Stanton and W. Zachary Malinowski, "Troopers search Celona's residence," *PJ*, 9 Mar. 2004: A-01.

31 Katherine Gregg, "Celona quits Senate," *PJ*, 10 Mar. 2004: A-01.

32   Meaghan Wims, Zachary R. Mider, Daniel Barbarisi, Alice Gomstyn, Tony De Paul, "Legislators, others report '03 gifts," *PJ*, 3 Mar. 2004: C-01.

33   Scott Mayerowitz, "Companies question lobbying laws," *PJ*, 9 Mar. 2004: B-01.

34   Each bill was titled "An Act Relating to Separation of Powers," and all three were introduced on 21 Apr. 2004. 04-S 3048 by Sens. Lenihan, Perry, Goodwin, Gallo, and Parella; 04-S 3049 by Sens. Lenihan, Cote, Tassoni, Fogarty, and Ciccone; 04-S 3051, by Sens. Lenihan, Montalbano, Paiva Weed, Connors, and Blais.

35   HPW, Testimony before Senate Committee on Government Oversight, 20 Jan. 2004.

36   04-S 2396, "An Act Relating to Public Officers and Employees — Merit System," Sens. Lenihan, Sosnowski, Sheehan, Polisena, and Cote, 11 Feb. 2004. See also Ch. 30, "Retaliation."

37   04-S 2193, "An Act Relating to Public Officers — Appointments," by Sens. Ciccone, Connors, DaPonte, Lanzi, and Lenihan, 29 Jan. 2004.

38   04-S 2193 Substitute A, same title.

39   Editorial, "Sneak attack on SOP," *PJ*, 18 Apr. 2004: I-08.

40   *SJrnl*, 21 Apr. 2004: 14; PL 04-590, 30 Jul. 2004.

41   *Joseph F. Parella, et al. v. William Irons*, 02-4578, 8 Dec. 2003: 48. Two more years would pass before the RI Supreme Court ruled against them.

42   Metts had been the lead plaintiff in *Metts* v. *Almond*, 217 F. Supp. 2d 252 (D.R.I. 2002), which had been dismissed in U.S. District Court in Sept. 2002 but was reinstated for trial in Mar. 2004 by the U.S. Court of Appeals, 1st Cir. as *Metts* v. *Murphy*, 02-2204, 30 Mar. 2004. The prospect of a full trial motivated both sides to seek a settlement.

43   Edward Fitzpatrick, "New Senate map settles lawsuit over redistricting," *PJ*, 22 May 2004: A-01.

44   04-S 3137, "An Act Relating to the General Assembly — Composition of the Senate," by Sen. Montalbano, 20 May 2004, PL 04-024, 4 Jun. 2004.

45   04-H 8309 SubBam, "An Act Relating to the General Assembly — Lobbying," by Reps. Fox, Anguilla, Carter, Crowley, and Lewiss, 18 Mar. 2004, became PL 04-207, 29 Jun. 2004; 04-S 2420 SubBam, "An Act Relating to Lobbying," by Sens. Lenihan, Sosnowski, Sheehan, Polisena, and Cote, 11 Feb. 2004, became PL 04-413, 5 Jul. 2004.

46   RIGL 36-14-2 (14) "Major decision-making position" means the executive or administrative head or heads of a state agency, whether elected or appointed or serving as an employee and all members of the judiciary, both state and municipal. For state agencies, a "major decision-making position" shall include the positions of deputy director, executive director, assistant director and chief of staff.

47   04-S 2667 SubAam. See also Ch. 46, "Triple Scandal," fn25. For reasons he never made clear, Gov. Don Carcieri refused to sign the bill, and it became law without his signature: PL 04-389, 5 Jul. 2004.

48   04-S 2478, "An Act Relating to State Affairs and Government — Lobbying of State Employees," by Sens. Paiva Weed, Goodwin, Montalbano, McCaffrey, and Gallo, 11. Jan. 2004; 04-H 7150, (same title), by Reps. Anguilla, Crowley, Lima, Ginaitt, and Lewiss, 13 Jan. 2004. Both became law as PL 04-375 and PL 04-297, respectively, 3 Jul. 2004.

49   04-S 2173, "An Act Relating to Public Officers and Employees — Code of Ethics," by Sens. Montalbano, Lenihan, Paiva Weed, Revens, and Sheehan, 27 Jan. 2004.

50   04-S 2421, "An Act Relating to the Code of Ethics," by Sens. Lenihan, Sosnowski, Sheehan, Polisena, and Cote, 11 Feb. 2004, became PL 04-181, 26 Jun. 2004; 04-H 8443, "An Act Relating to the Code of Ethics," by Reps. Fox, Costantino, Lewiss, Lima, and Crowley, 22 Apr. 2004, became PL 04-248, 1 Jul. 2004.

51 04-S 2396, *SJrnl*, 21 Apr. 2004: 13.

52 04-S 3048 SubA, 3049 SubA, and 3051 SubA, each entitled "An Act Relating to Separation of Powers," by Sen. Lenihan, et al.

53 03-S 0180, "Joint Resolution to Approve and Publish and Submit to the Electors a
Proposition of Amendment to the Constitution of the State (Separation of Powers)"
by Sens. Lenihan, Irons, Algiere, Montalbano, and Parella, 29 Jan. 2003; *SJrnl*, 16 Jun.
2004: 15-75.

54 Sens. Leo R. Blais, Kevin A. Breene, Michael J. Damiani, Walter S. Felag Jr., Michael
J. McCaffrey, Joseph M. Polisena, and Rep. Peter T. Ginaitt. Damiani climbed only to
the roof.

47 | Restoring Ethics · pages 573–583

1 See Ch. 35, "Gifts," and 39, "Ethics Meltdown."

2 Ariel Sabar, "Bill seeks to tighten control of appointees to state ethics panel," *PJ*,
11 May 2001; 01-H 6060, "An Act Relating to the Code of Ethics," by Rep. Cicilline,
13 Feb. 2001. Cicilline had pushed these reforms for several years: 98-H 7584,
"An Act Relating to the Code of Ethics," by Reps. Cicilline, Ajello, Hetherington,
Coderre, and Lima, 28 Jan. 1998; 99-H 5378, (same title), by Rep. Cicilline, 27 Jan.
1999; 00-H 6915, (same title), by Rep. Cicilline, 19 Jan. 2000. He and others continued for several more years: 02-H 7944, "An Act Relating to Public Officers and
Employees—Code of Ethics," by Rep. Cicilline, 27 Mar. 2002; 03-H 5372, (same title),
by Reps. Montanaro, Anderson, Smith, and Kilmartin, 4 Feb. 2003; 04-H 04-S 2422,
(same title), by Sens. Roberts, Lenihan, and Paiva Weed, 11 Feb. 2004; 04-H 8088,
(same title), by Reps. Reilly and Coogan, 24 Feb. 2004.

3 Legislative repair of the Ethics Commission finally came in several sections of
the "Public Accountability and Reform Act of 2006" (06-S 2799 by Sen. Michael
Lenihan and 06-H 7455 by Rep. Peter Kilmartin), which became PL-06 428 and 429.
See Ch. 51, "Reconstruction."

4 HPW, "How to fix the Ethics Commission," *PJ*, 16 Apr. 2001: A-08.

5 Tom Mooney, "Ex-Navy lawyer hired to assist ethics panel," *PJ*, 21 Apr. 2001: A-03.

6 Jonathan D. Rockoff, "Willever to head Ethics Commission," *PJ*, 20 Jun. 2001: A-01.

7 M. Charles Bakst, "New ethics director takes on a tough job," 2 Sep. 2001: D-01.

8 Personal interview, 4 Apr. 2012.

9 Jonathan D. Rockoff, "Ethics panel loses two," *PJ*, 28 Jun. 2001: B-01. The commission later voted to pay Zurier's $3,750 in legal costs for defending himself against the
OCG complaint. Jonathan D. Rockoff, "Ethics panel approves paying Zurier legal
bills," *PJ*, 26 Sep. 2001: B-01.

10 Jonathan D. Rockoff, "Reappointment of member to Ethics Commission lauded," *PJ*,
31 Aug. 2001: B-01.

11 Jonathan D. Rockoff, "Lincoln man selected to fill seat on ethics panel," *PJ*, 13 Oct.
2001: A-03.

12 Bryant College became Bryant University in 2004.

13 RIEC Member Appointments, 6 Jun. 2008: 1. Sen. Maj. Leader William V. Irons
nominated Patricia M. Moran, and Gov. Almond appointed her on 2 Nov. 2001.

14 Bruce Landis, "Goldberg resigns from Ethics Commission," *PJ*, 4 Oct. 2001: B-01.

15 Cathleen F. Crowley, "Textron executive named to ethics panel," *PJ*, 8 Jan. 2004:
B-03.Carcieri appointed Cheit from a list supplied by Sen. Minority Leader Dennis
Algiere. The fact that his policy director Jeffrey Grybowski had studied under Cheit
at Brown and worked with Binder in the office of Gen. Treas. Nancy Mayer made me

think he had played a role in both appointments.

16   See Ch. 31, "Opening Government."

17   Mike Stanton, "Bearing Witness: A Man's Recovery of his Sexual Abuse as a Child," a series in 3 parts *PJ*, 7-9 May 1995: A-01. See Ross Cheit, *The Witch-Hunt Narrative: Politics, Psychology, and the Sexual Abuse of Children* (Oxford University Press, February 2014).

18   Scott Mayerowitz, "From toy trucks to trees, officials report their gifts," *PJ*, 2 Feb. 2004: B-01.

19   Katherine Gregg, "Disclosure forms show free meals, golf are routine," *PJ*, 3 Feb. 2004: A-01; Paul Davis, "Lawmakers were 'entertained' by few big ticket items," *PJ*, 13 Feb. 2004: C-01; "Legislator, others report '03 gifts," *PJ*, 3 Mar. 2004: C-01.

20   Katherine Gregg, "Irons discloses gifts worth thousands," *PJ*, 4 Feb. 2004: B-01.

21   Katherine Gregg, "Disclosure forms show free meals, golf are routine," *PJ*, 3 Feb. 2004: A-01; Paul Davis, "Lawmakers were 'entertained' by few big ticket items," *PJ*, 13 Feb. 2004: C-01; "Legislator, others report '03 gifts," *PJ*, 3 Mar. 2004: C-01; Katherine Gregg, "Irons discloses gifts worth thousands," *PJ*, 4 Feb. 2004: B 01.

22   Katherine Gregg, "Lawmakers file reports of gifts received," *PJ*, 31 Jan. 2004: A-01.

23   Gregg.

24   Scott Mayerowitz, "Companies question lobbying laws," *PJ*, 9 Mar. 2004: B-01.

25   Katherine Gregg, "Lower gift limits sought," *PJ*, 8 Feb. 2005: B-01.

26   RIEC Open Session Minutes, 7 Feb. 2005: 4. Kirby came to believe the $150/$450 gift rule was excessive. HPW interview with Richard E. Kirby, 10 Apr. 2012.

27   RIEC Minutes of Open Session, 22 Mar. 2005: 1-3.

28   Katherine Gregg, "Ethics panel sets $25 lid on gifts to officials," *PJ*, 23 Mar. 2005: A-01.

29   Commissioner James V. Murray was absent. He and Richard Kirby had voted for the $150/$450 gift rule on 23 May 2000.

30   See Ch. 41, "Plunder Dome."

31   Scott MacKay, "Little big man—David N. Cicilline takes oath of office tomorrow," *PJ*, 5 Jan. 2003: A-01. Cicilline was also the city's first openly gay mayor.

32   M. Charles Bakst, "A new tone in Providence," *PJ*, 13 Feb. 2003: B-01.

33   Scott MacKay, "Spirited Cicilline sworn in as mayor," *PJ*, 7 Jan. 2003: A-01.

34   Gregory Smith, "Mayor names panel to write ethics code," *PJ*, 7 Feb. 2003: C-01.

35   Pamela Ferdinand, "Cicilline Sets Providence on Road to Recovery," *Washington Post*, 29 Mar. 2003: A-03.

36   Providence Municipal Code, Sec. 17-33(a). References in this chapter are to sections as later enacted by the City Council: Ord. 2006-28, § 1, 20 Apr. 2006; Ord. 2006-42, 9 Aug. 2006.

37   The task force was determined to avoid the confusion of overlapping legal codes and the legal issue of pre-emption, the notion that a municipality may not adopt rules that conflict with a state statute on the same subject. Several decisions of the RI Supreme Court make clear that any city or town ordinance that infringes on state law may be categorically preempted. See *Town of East Greenwich* v. *O'Neil*, 617 A.2d 104, 109 (R.I. 1992), *Town of East Greenwich* v. *Narragansett Electric Co.*, 651 A.2d 725, 729 (R.I. 1994), and *Town of Warren* v. *Thornton-Whitehouse*, 740 A.2d 1255, 1261 (R.I. 1999).

38   Draft Code, 9 Dec. 2003. Sec. 17-33(c)(9). This section on gifts became redundant when the RIEC adopted a statewide ban on 22 Mar. 2005 and was deleted from the final version of Providence Code of Ethics.

39   Sec. 17-33 (e)(5) closely tracked the RIEC revolving door provision, RIGL 36-14-5

(n)-(o). The RIEC later enacted a regulation banning municipal revolving door employment 36-14-5014.

40 HPW memo to Providence Ethics Task Force, "Gifts, Lobbyists, and Whistleblowers," 11 Aug. 2003. See Charlene Wear Simmons, et al., *Local Government Ethics Ordinances in California* (Sacramento: CA Research Bureau, 1998).

41 PETF minutes, 12 Aug. 2003. A decade later, Providence finally adopted Chapt. 2013-3, No. 84, *An Ordinance Amending 2011-16, No. 336, Relative to Lobbyist Registration,* 28 Feb. 2013. The online system went live 12 Jun. 2013. See Richard C. Dujardin, "Lobbyists will have to register to work in city," *PJ,* 19 Mar. 2011: A-03.

42 Mayor Cicilline's Ethics Task Force, "Executive Summary," 9 Dec. 2003.

43 Karen Davis, "Cicilline unveils city ethics code," *PJ,* 11 Jun. 2004: C-01.

44 Ken Mingis, "Glavin quits council to take city planning job," *PJ,* 14 May 1997: A-01; Ken Mingis, "Council Alumni find door's open to city jobs," *PJ,* 17 Sep. 1997: C-01. Cianci hired ten council members during the 1990s: Phillip "Sharkey" Almagno became Sealer of Weights and Measures; Carolyn F. Brassil, City Collector; Nicholas Easton, Assoc. Dir. for Special Projects in the Planning Department; Lawrence K. Flynn, Executive Director of the Board of Canvassers; Thomas M. Glavin, Assoc. Dir. for Special Projects, Planning Department; Charles R. Mansolillo, City Solicitor; John H. Rollins, Minority Business Enterprises/Women Business Enterprises Coordinator; Robert Salvatore, Collections Supervisor at the Providence Water Supply Board; Edward Xavier, Public Information Officer at Office of Civil Preparedness.

45 Historian and attorney Patrick T. Conley, who had served briefly as Cianci's chief of staff, notes that a favorite political tactic was co-opting opponents. Cianci's motto was: "Keep your friends close and your enemies closer."

46 Ken Mingis, "Council alumni find door's open to city jobs," *PJ,* 17 Sep. 1997: C-01.

47 Cathleen F. Crowley, "Council takes up tougher policy on ethics," *PJ,* 17 Nov. 2005: D-01.

48 Cathleen F. Crowley, "Ethics ordinance returned to committee," *PJ,* 18 Nov. 2005: D-01.

49 Richard Dujardin, "Council, mayor seek to end impasse on city ethics code," *PJ,* 21 Jul. 2006: D-01.

50 Cathleen F. Crowley, "Mayor, Lombardi squabble over ethics," *PJ,* 25 Nov. 2005: C-01.

51 Cathleen F. Crowley, "Creating ethics code takes time, expert says," *PJ,* 19 May 2006: D-01.

52 Sheridan's draft code included a section entitled "Prohibited Conduct Relating to Employment," derived directly from § 602 Jacksonville Ethics Code. Among its prohibitions were: Coercion for trading with a particular business (Jax 602.301), Use of Public Property (602.302), City Seal (602.308), Activities Relating to Promotion or Appointment (602.309), Misuse of Position (602.310), etc.

53 Richard C. Dujardin, "City Council panel approves ethics ordinance," *PJ,* 28 Jul. 2006: D-01.

54 Cicilline supporters did unseat incumbents Rita M. Williams, Carol A. Romano, and Patrick K. Butler. See Gregory Smith, "Providence City Council—Three incumbents fall in battle of Democrats," 13 Sep. 2006: D-01.

55 *Providence City Council Journal of Proceedings,* Special Meeting, 3 Aug. 2006: 489. Voting aye were Councilpersons John J. Lombardi, Luis A. Aponte, Patrick K. Butler, Joseph DeLuca, Josephine DiRuzzo, Terrence M. Hassett, John J. Igliozzi, Kevin E. Jackson, Miguel C. Luna, Peter S. Mancini, Carol A. Romano, and Rita M. Williams; no nayes. See Richard C. Dujardin, "City OKs ethics code," *PJ,* 4 Aug. 2006: D-01.

56   HPW interview with Richard E. Kirby, 10 Apr. 2012. Kirby later became city solicitor
     in Central Falls. In that role, he helped craft a tough new ethics ordinance for the
     bankrupt city. Attorney James V. Murray also stayed with the Ethics Commission for
     more than a decade but did not attend the meeting that established the $25/$75 rule.
     He was unwilling to be interviewed for this book.

48 | Presumption Prize · pages 584–590

1   Alan G. Palazzo, "Natick school building methodology is flawed," *Kent County Daily
     Times*, 21 Aug. 2001; "Senator Alves is pushing the envelope again," 5 Sep. 2001;
     "Building committee finally schedules meetings," 13 Sep. 2001; "Cost of project may
     rise to $12 million-plus," 1 Oct. 2001; "Cost of Natick school will probably be higher,"
     5 Oct. 2001; "It's soon time to get out your checkbooks," 26 Oct. 2001.
2   Verified Complaint, *Stephen Alves v. Hometown Newspapers, Inc., The Kent County
     Daily Times, Alan G. Palazzo, and William Palazzo*, Superior Court, 21 Nov. 2001.
3   PL 93-354 created and PL 95-386 amended RIGL 9-33, "Limits on Strategic Litigation
     against Public Participation." See Ch. 21, "Petitioning Government."
4   94-606-M.P. *Hometown Properties, Inc. v. Nancy Hsu Fleming*, 680 A.2d 56 (R.I.
     1996) 25 Jun. 1996.
5   RIGL 9-33-2 (a) confers "conditional immunity" on the petitioner.
6   Erin Emlock, "Woman gets $400,000 in anti-SLAPP lawsuit," *PJ*, 13 Dec. 2001: A-01;
     Elizabeth Abbott, "After a long ordeal, free speech pays off," *PJ*, 23 Dec. 2001: C-01.
7   01-1030, *Stephen Alves v. Hometown Newspapers, Inc.*, 12 Sep. 2002. See Zachary
     R. Mider, "Legislator must pay in SLAPP suit case," *PJ*, 19 Sep. 2002: A-01. Palazzo
     estimates that actual legal expenses for him and his brother William B. Palazzo were
     $109,000 and they ultimately received $34,000.
8   03-181-Appeal, *Stephen Alves v. Hometown Newspapers, Inc.*, et al., 857 A.2d 743 (R.I.
     2004) 4 Aug. 2004.
9   04-S 2338, "An Act Relating to Sports, Racing and Athletics — And Extension of
     Gambling Activities and Other Facilities," by Sens. Alves and Ruggerio, 11 Feb. 2004;
     Zachary R. Mider, "Tribe unveils latest plan to build a casino," *PJ*, 5 Feb. 2004: A-01.
10   Scott Mayerowitz, "$750,000 spent this year on casino ads," *PJ*, 19 May 2004: B-03.
11   Katherine Gregg and Scott Mayerowitz, "Grilling of Harrah's shifts to Senate," *PJ*,
     25 May 2004: A-01; "Assembly asks Harrah's for more," *PJ*, 4 Jun. 2004: A-01.
12   Katherine Gregg, "Casino talks set for public airing," *PJ*, 19 Jun. 2004: A-10.
13   Katherine Gregg, "Casino deal held close to the vest," *PJ*, 22 Jun. 2004: A-01;
     Katherine Gregg and Scott Mayerowitz, "Senate votes to put casino on Nov. ballot,"
     PJ, 25 Jun. 2004: A-01.
14   *SJrnl*, 24 Jun. 2004: 53; *HJrnl*, 25 Jun. 2004: 45.
15   04-S 2388, "Relating to Sports, Racing and Athletics — And Extension of Gambling
     Activities and other Facilities," by Sens. Alves and Ruggerio, 11 Feb. 2004; 04-H 7844,
     (same title), by Reps. Williamson, Williams, Voccola, Flaherty, and Rose, 12 Feb.
     2004. Both bills placed the question in a new section 41-9.1-9.
16   RI Constitution, Article. VI.22, amended in 1994, prohibited any expansion of "the
     types of gambling" in the state without approval both in a statewide referendum and
     by a majority in the municipality where the gambling would occur.
17   RI Constitution, Article VI.15, amended in 1973. "Lotteries. — All lotteries shall be
     prohibited in the state except lotteries operated by the state and except those previ-
     ously permitted by the general assembly prior to the adoption of this section, and all
     shall be subject to the prescription and regulation of the general assembly." Historian

Patrick Conley pointed out in 2005 that the Supreme Court had misinterpreted this section in a 1981 decision, *Roberts* v. *Communications Investment Club*, which wrongly lumped all forms of gambling under the term "lotteries." Casinos were not lotteries, he wrote in 2005, noting that 39 states and the District of Columbia had state-run lotteries, but none operated casinos. See Conley, "A Lot of Confusion: Is the Casino a Lottery?" in *People Places, Laws and Lore of the Ocean State* (East Providence: RIPS, 2012) 445–52.

18   Gov. Donald L. Carcieri, Veto of 04-S 2338 SubA as amended, 1 Jul. 2004: 2–3.

19   Katherine Gregg and Scott Mayerowitz, "Carcieri seeks court opinion on casino question," *PJ*, 10 Jul. 2004: A-01.

20   Katherine Gregg, "Casino foes fear effort to amend the Constitution," *PJ*, 20 Jul. 2004: A-01.

21   04-S 3238, "An Act Relating to Sports, Racing and Athletics — and Extension of Gambling Activities and other Facilities," by Sen. Stephen D. Alves, 21 Jul. 2004.

22   04-S 3237, "Joint Resolution to Approve and Publish and Submit to the Electors a Proposition of Amendment to the Constitution of the State (Allowing Casino Gambling)," by Sen. Stephen D. Alves, 21 Jul. 2004.

23   Scott Mayerowitz, "Casino amendment not on House agenda," *PJ*, 23 Jul. 2004: A-01; editorial, "Legislators' bad gamble," *PJ*, 23 Jul. 2004: B-04.

24   *SJrnl.* 23 Jul. 2004: 2.

25   Scott Mayerowitz, "Casino vote still on track," *PJ*, 24 Jul. 2004: A-01.

26   *SJrnl.* 23 Jul. 2004: 4.

27   *HJrnl.* 30 Jul. 2004: 11.

28   Zachary R. Mider, "Battle for R.I. casino now moves to the voters," *PJ*, 1 Aug. 2004: B-01.

29   04-210-M.P., *In Re: Advisory Opinion to the Governor (Casino)*, 12 Aug. 2004: 5–6, 13, 17, 19.

30   Liz Anderson, "Casino vote is off Nov. ballot," *PJ*, 14 Aug. 2004: A-01; "Justices advise casino bill illegal," *PJ*, 13 Aug. 2004: A-01.

31   Anderson.

49 | FINALLY? · pages 591–604

1   HPW, "Breakthroughs, throwbacks stand side-by-side in Common Cause report on session," CCRI Report, 3 Aug. 2004: 1. See Bruce Landis, "Common Cause applauds state's major reforms," 2 Aug. 2004: B-01.

2   AARP-RI, Alliance to Preserve Tiverton's Quality, American Association of University Women, Aquidneck Island Clergy Association, Central RI Chamber of Commerce, Citizens Concerned about Casino Gambling, Coalition for Consumer Justice, Common Cause RI, Conservation Law Foundation, Cranston Chamber of Commerce, Democracy Matters, East Greenwich Chamber of Commerce, Energy Council of RI, Environment Council of RI, Environmental Committee of the Diocese of Providence, Greater Providence Chamber of Commerce, Hispanic-American Chamber of Commerce, Jamestown Town Council, Jewish Federation of RI, Kay Coalition Against Casino Gambling, League of Women Voters, Little Compton Taxpayers Association, Manufacturing Summit, Newport City Council, Newport County Chamber of Commerce, Northern RI Chamber of Commerce, Operation Clean Government, Portsmouth Concerned Citizens, Priests for Justice (Diocese of Providence), RI Latino Political Action Committee, RI Public Interest Research Group, RI Shoreline Coalition, RI Separation of Powers Committee, RI State Coun-

cil of Churches, RI Unitarian Universalists for Social Justice, RI United Methodist Association, Save the Bay, Sierra Club RI, and Urban League of RI.

3   Liz Anderson, "They're united on separation of powers," *PJ*, 21 Sep. 2004: B-01.

4   Boards to be reconfigured were: Administrative Committee of the State Register, Agricultural Lands Preservation Commission, Board of Bank Incorporation, Board of Curators, Board of Governors for Higher Education, Board of Regents for Elementary and Secondary Education, Budget and Review Commission, Capital Center Commission, Coastal Resources Management Council, Commission on Judicial Tenure and Discipline, Committee to Establish and Administer a Comprehensive Automated Civil Information System, Committee to Establish and Administer a Comprehensive Criminal/Juvenile Justice Information System, Fort Adams Foundation, Historic District Commission (Providence), Housing Appeals Board, Judicial Nominating Commission, Library Board of RI, Mosquito Abatement Board, Motor Vehicle Inspection Commission, Narragansett Bay Commission, Narragansett Indian Land Management Board, Newport County Convention and Visitors' Bureau, New Shoreham Tourism Council Bureau Inc, Persian Gulf War Information Relief Commission, Prepurchase Firearm Safety Training Review Board, Public Finance Management Board, Rabies Control Board, RI Clean Water Protection Finance Agency, RI Economic Development Corporation, RI Ethics Commission, RI Higher Education Assistance Authority, RI Historical Preservation and Heritage Commission, RI Housing and Conservation Board, RI Human Resource Investment Council, RI Lottery Commission, RI Public Telecommunications Authority, RI Public Transit Authority, RI Refunding Bond Authority, RI Resource Recovery Corporation, RI Student Loan Authority, RI Underground Storage Tank Financial Responsibility Fund Review Board, RI Vehicle Value Commission, RI Water Resources Board Corporate, Scenic Roadways Board, Sinking Fund Commission, State Building Code Standards Committee, State Comprehensive Plan Appeals Board, State Conservation Committee, State Crime Laboratory Commission, State Investment Commission, State Properties Committee, State Retirement Board, State Traffic Commission, Unclassified Pay Plan Board.

5   Sheldon Whitehouse, "Remarks for SOP Rally," 20 Sep. 2004.

6   RI Constitution, Article XIV.2.

7   "Comments sought on convention," *PJ*, 10 Aug. 2004: C-01. Co-Chairpersons of the bipartisan commission were Rep. Fausto Anguilla and Sen. Maryellen Goodwin. Members were Reps. Peter F. Kilmartin, William J. McManus, and Anastasia P. Williams; Sens. Leo R. Blais, Marc A. Cote, and Daniel DaPonte; Barbara Hurst, Gary Sasse, Harry Staley, and Christopher Stanley.

8   Liz Anderson, "Panel reports pros and cons of convention," *PJ*, 26 Aug. 2004: B-01.

9   Liz Anderson, "R.I. voters to decide if change is in the air," *PJ*, 18 Oct. 2004: A-01.

10   Am. Assoc. of University Women RI, Common Cause RI, National Assoc. of Social Workers, RI Chapter, NEA/RI, Ocean State Action, Planned Parenthood of RI, Poverty Institute at RIC, RI ACORN, RI ACLU, RI Affirmative Action Coalition, RI AFL-CIO, RI Alliance for Lesbian and Gay Civil Rights, RI Civil Rights Roundtable, RI Commission for Human Rights, RI Federation of Teachers and Health Professionals, RI Jobs with Justice, RI Ministers Alliance, RI Latino PAC, 2 to 1: The Coalition to Preserve Choice, Urban League of RI, Women's Health and Education Fund, and Working RI.

11   Liz Anderson, "Coalition urges voters to oppose a Convention," *PJ*, 19 Oct. 2004: B-01.

12   Will Barbeau, "Reform activism booming in R.I.," *PJ*, 20 Oct. 2004: B-05.

13   Editorial, "Vote yes on Question 2," 25 Oct. 2004: A-08.

14 Gary Sasse and HPW, "No need now for a constitutional convention," *PJ*, 28 Oct. 2004: B-05.

15 Bruce Landis, "High turnout expected at local polls," *PJ*, 2 Nov. 2004: A-09. In 2002, 332,056 voters cast ballots for governor; in 2004, 436,289 voted in the presidential contest.

16 Qstn 1 approved: 257,302 (78.32%) to 71,234 (21.68%), Qstn 2 rejected: 175,596 (51.97%) to 162,293 (48.03%). RIBOE, http://www.elections.ri.gov/elections/results/2004/generalelection/ref.php.

17 Beverly and Sam Parente, "Rhode Islanders cheated out of convention," 17 Nov. 2004: B-05.

18 Beverly Clay, "Constitutional convention killed by unions," *PJ*, 15 Dec. 2004: B-05.

19 Robert P. Arruda, "Press Advisory: Citizen activists file complaints with Board of Elections while calling for board's overhaul," OCG, 5 Jan. 2005.

20 Sheldon Whitehouse, "Re: Referendum Advocacy," 15 Sep. 2004. Whitehouse had reviewed his analysis with Raymond A. Marcaccio, legal counsel to the RIBOE. On the basis of that RIght Now! instructed its member organizations to report their independent spending and payments to the public relations firm Duffy & Shanley: "(1) We properly recognize the ambiguity for 'preexisting entities' that appear to 'act in concert' but go forward with separate payments to Duffy & Shanley for campaign materials, (2) We take the position that our groups that raised money from within our memberships can separately pay Duffy & Shanley for the printing and production of materials, and (3) Each organization needs to report separately to the Board of Elections on a separate Form CF-8 (attached as PDF)."

21 Liz Anderson, "Election spending reports probed," *PJ*, 18 Nov. 2004: B-01.

22 Edward Achorn, "Hiding behind Mr. O'Brien," *PJ*, 25 Jan. 2005: B-05.

23 Liz Anderson, "R.I. voters to decide if change is in the air," *PJ*, 18 Oct. 2004: A-01.

24 A year later, OCG's complaint failed when Chief Judge Ernest C. Torres ruled that (1) RIGL 17-25-10(b), which prohibited groups from "acting in concert" without forming a PAC was unconstitutional, (2) RIGL 17-25-10.1(h) and (j) which barred corporations from using their own funds for or against ballot questions violated the First Amendment, and (3) the dollar limits in RIGL 17-25-10.1(a) could not be applied to ballot advocacy. See *ACLU* v. *Begin*, 04-487-T, 25 Apr. 2006. See Ch. 51, "Reconstruction."

25 Peter B. Lord, "$1.89-million project pits marina owners, Block Island residents," *PJ*, 6 May 2004: B-03.

26 Peter B. Lord, "Coastal panel continues to hear Block Island marina proposal," *PJ*, 8 Dec. 2004: B-01.

27 04-S 3048 SubAam, "An Act Relating to Separation of Powers," by Sens. Lenihan, Perry, Goodwin, Gallo, and Parella, 21 Apr. 2004; 04-S 3049A, (same title and date), by Sens. Lenihan, Cote, Tassoni, Fogarty, and Ciccone; 04-S 3051A, (same title and date, by Sens. Lenihan, Montalbano, Paiva Weed, and Blais.

28 Liz Anderson, "When does separation of powers kick in?" *PJ*, 23 Nov. 2004: A-01.

29 Jack White, while an investigative reporter for the *Journal*, won a Pulitzer in 1974 for disclosing President Richard M. Nixon's underpayment of income taxes.

30 *Newsmakers*, 12WPRI, 17 Dec. 2004. Murphy later made similar comments to other reporters.

31 Liz Anderson, "Murphy says legislators may stay on Lottery Commission," *PJ*, 17 Dec. 2004: A-01.

32 HPW "Letter to the Honorable William J. Murphy, Speaker of the House," 18 Dec. 2004.

33 M. Charles Bakst, "Speaker Murphy, the lottery, and the people," *PJ*, 21 Dec. 2004: B-01.

34 Edward Achorn, "Your vote means nothing to Murphy and Montalbano," *PJ*, 21 Dec. 2004: B-05.

35 Liz Anderson, "Separate views on separate powers," *PJ*, 22 Dec. 2004: B-01.

36 CRMC appointees: Paul Hansen, Anna F. Prager, Cynthia Fuller, Carol Hueston, William Meyer, Janice Williams Oliver, Leslie M. Gray III, and Cristina T. Harsch; Lottery Commission appointees: Julie G. Duffy, Patricia W. Farley, Sherry E. Ferdinandi, Barry G. Hittner, Peri Ann Aptaker, Richard L. Pastore.

37 Donald L. Carcieri, "Letter to Joseph A. Montalbano, President of the Senate," 5 Jan. 2005.

38 Liz Anderson, "Separation of powers spurs resignations," *PJ*, 5 Jan. 2005: A-09

39 Sheldon Whitehouse, "Don't trifle with separation of powers," *PJ*, 5 Jan. 2005: B-04.

40 Ian Donnis, "Murphy's moment," Providence Phoenix, 17 Sep. 2004: 1; Liz Anderson, "Candidate for speaker picks up support," *PJ*, 3 Dec. 2004: B-01; Katherine Gregg, "DeSimone has quietly worked way up ranks," *PJ*, 13 Dec. 2004: A 01; Scott MacKay and Liz Anderson, "Murphy in for a fight after 2 years at top," *PJ*, 14 Dec. 2004: A-01.

41 05-H 5003, "An Act Relating to Separation of Powers," by Reps. Menard, Ucci, McHugh, Winfield, and Petrarca, 5 Jan. 2005; 04-S 3051 SubA, (same title), by Sens. Lenihan, Montalbano, Paiva Weed, and Blais, 21 Apr. 2004.

42 Peter H. Hufstader, "50 States Project: Authority for Lotteries," CCRI, revised 22 May 2003. See Gen. Statutes of CT, Sec. 12-802.

43 Hufstader: 1. CT Lottery Corporation has 13 directors: The governor appoints 5 members with the advice and consent of the Senate. The State Treasurer and the Secretary of the Office of Policy and Management are *ex officio* members. Six members are appointed respectively by the president pro tem of the Senate, majority leader of the Senate, minority leader of the Senate, speaker of the House, House majority leader, and House minority leader.

44 RI Constitution, Article IX.5. Powers of appointment. — The governor shall, by and with the advice and consent of the senate, appoint all officers of the state whose appointment is not herein otherwise provided for and all members of any board, commission or other state or quasi-public entity which exercises executive power under the laws of this state; but the general assembly may by law vest the appointment of such inferior officers, as they deem proper, in the governor, or within their respective departments in the other general officers, the judiciary or in the heads of departments.

45 RI Constitution, Article VI.15. Lotteries. — All lotteries shall be prohibited in the state except lotteries operated by the state and except those previously permitted by the general assembly prior to the adoption of this section, and all shall be subject to the prescription and regulation of the general assembly.

46 05-H 5074, "An Act Relating to State Affairs and Government — State Lottery," by Reps. Crowley, Flaherty, Anguilla, Fox, and Costantino, 13 Jan. 2005. See Liz Anderson, "Lawmaker pitches compromise on lottery panel," *PJ*, 12 Jan. 2005: B-01.

47 Liz Anderson, "Plan to end Lottery panel criticized," *PJ*, 13 Jan. 2005: A-01.

48 Katherine Gregg, "Murphy withdraws challenge to powers," *PJ*, 19 Jan. 2005: B-01.

50 | Unfinished Business · pages 605–625

1   Next Phase Agenda Committee: Kevin McAllister, Greta Abbott, Jane Austin, Doree Goodman, Burt Hoffman, Diana Kelly, Tory McCagg, Daniel Siegel, Charles Sturtevant, HPW.

2   See Ch. 21, "Petitioning Government."

3   05-S 0124, "Joint Resolution to Approve and Publish and Submit to the Electors a Proposition of Amendment to the Constitution of the State (Initiative and Referendum)," by Sens. Code, Badeau, Bates, Raptakis, and Lenihan, 25 Jan. 2005.

4   Katherine Gregg, "Barbed criticism greets new voter-initiative bill," *PJ*, 17 Mar. 1999, B-04.

5   05-H 6080, "Relating to Elections — Rhode Island Clean Elections Act," by Reps. Ajello, Dennigan, Davey, Rice, and Naughton, 1 Mar. 2005; 05-S 0714, (same title), by Sens. Perry, Sosnowski, and Roberts, 17 Feb. 2005. See Ian Donnis, "Is Rhode Island ready for Clean Elections?" *Providence Phoenix*, 25 Feb. 2005: 1. See photo pages.

6   RIGL 12-28-9 and RI Constitution, Article I.23.

7   *Bandoni v. State*, 715 A.2d 580 (RI 1998).

8   05-H 5195 "To Approve and Publish and Submit to the Electors A Proposition of Amendments to the Constitution of the State (Enforcement)," by Reps. Anguilla, Davey, Gemma, Rice, and Dennigan, 27 Jan. 2005; 05-S 0762, (same title), by Sen. J. Michael Lenihan, 17 Feb. 2005.

9   Christopher Uggen and Jeff Manza, "Voting and Subsequent Crime and Arrest: Evidence from a Community Sample," 24 June 2004.

10 05-S 0458, "To Approve and Publish and Submit to the Electors A Proposition of Amendments to the Constitution of the State (Elections)," by Sens. Metts, Pichardo, Levesque, and Perry, 10 Feb. 2005; 05-H 6579, (same title), by Rep. Joseph Almeida, 9 Jun.2005.

11 Steve Brown told me later that the lawyers at Brennan Center for Justice had worked with the ACLU to draft the text.

12 05-S 0575, "An Act Relating to Elections," by Sens. Metts, Pichardo, Levesque, and Caprio, 10 Feb. 2005; 05-H 6069, (same title), by Reps. Almeida, Williams, Slater, and Diaz, 1 Mar. 2005.

13 Kevin McAllister, "Report of Ad Hoc Committee on the Next Phase Agenda," CCRI, 9 Dec. 2004.

14 CCRI, Minutes of Special Board Meeting, 14 Dec. 2004.

15 04-PL 207, enacted 29 Jun. 2004, and PL 04-413, enacted 5 Jul. 2004, both amended RIGL 22-10-9 to require that every lobbyist and firm that deployed lobbyists must report by 15 Jan. of every calendar year: anything worth more than $250 that they had paid to any "major state decision-maker" in the previous year. The law specified that "anything of value" included "fee, salary, commission, expense allowance, forbearance, forgiveness, royalty, rent, capital gain, gift, loan, reward, favors or services, gratuities or special discounts, or any other form of recompense that constitutes income under the Federal Internal Revenue Code." See Ch. 46, "Triple Scandal."

16 Katherine Gregg, "New law shows public the money," *PJ*, 23 Jan. 2005: A-01.

17 05-H 5477, "An Act Relating to the General Assembly Lobbying," by Reps. Fox, Anguilla, Kilmartin, Jackson, Sullivan, 10 Feb. 2005.

18 Common Cause proposed: "Nothing in this section shall require the reporting of the sale to a major state decision-maker at a price and upon terms generally available to the public of the following: (1) food or beverage; (2) clothing, merchandise, consumer goods; (3) utility services, including but not limited to gas, electric, telephone,

cable or satellite services; (4) health care products or services; (5) insurance or financial services; (6) vehicles; (7) legal, medical or accounting services."

19   Katherine Gregg, "Murphy withdraws challenge to powers," *PJ*, 19 Jan. 2005: B-01.
20   John A. Tarantino, "Privileged and Confidential Memorandum to Robert E. Flaherty and Gerald S. Aubin," 18 Jan. 2005: 14. Tarantino argued that lawmakers could continue on the Lottery because several Supreme Court decisions (*Almond* v. *RI Lottery*, 756 A.2d 186, 190-92 (RI 2000) and *In Re: Advisory to the Governor (Casino)*, 856 A.2d 320, 322 (RI 2004) "appear to place the Lottery Commission outside the scope of the Separation of Powers amendments . . . . because unless the definition of 'executive power' or the functions of the Lottery Commission have changed as a direct result of the amendments, then the Lottery Commission is not performing executive powers, but exercising legislative powers." Several days passed before I got a copy of this memo.
21   Peter B. Lord, "Rhode Island coastal regulator braces for change," *PJ*, 23 Jan. 2005: C-01.
22   05-H 5104, "Relating to Public Officers and Employees — Merit System," by Reps. Kilmartin, Moura, Crowley, Anguilla, and Jackson, 18 Jan. 2005.
23   House Separation of Powers Committee: Elaine A. Coderre, chair; Paul W. Crowley, vice chair; Joseph S. Almeida, secretary; Reps. Fausto C. Anguilla, James F. Davey, John J. DeSimone, Raymond E. Gallison Jr., Al Gemma, Joanne M. Giannini, Nicholas Gorham, J. Russell Jackson, Peter F. Kilmartin, Charlene M. Lima, Joseph J. Voccola, Timothy A. Williamson.
24   Central Falls Review Commission, Jamestown Ferry Commission, RI Board for the Classification of Motion Pictures, Committee to Establish and Administer a Comprehensive Automated Civil Justice Information System, Socially Responsible Corporations Commission, Commission on the Port of Galilee, Administrative Committee of the State Register, Board of Curators, and Drivers' Training School Licensing Board. 05-H 5817, "An Act Relating to Separation of Powers," by Reps. Coderre, Ginaitt, Kilmartin, Crowley, and Lima, 17 Feb. 2005.
25   05-H 6217, "An Act Relating to Separation of Powers," by Reps. Coderre, Lima, Kilmartin, Jackson, and Crowley, 10 Mar. 2005.
26   05-H 6323, "An Act Relating to Waters and Navigation — RI Underground Storage Tank Fund Responsibility Act," by Reps. Coderre, Kilmartin, Ginaitt, Lima, and Williamson, 5 Apr. 2005.
27   05-H 6378, "An Act Relating to Health and Safety — RI Resource Recovery Corporation," by Reps. Coderre, Gemma, Almeida, Crowley, and Gallison, 13 Apr. 2005.
28   05-H 5003, "An Act Relating to Separation of Powers," by Reps. Menard, Ucci, McHugh, Winfield, and Petrarca, 5 Jan. 2005; 05-H 5044, (same title), by Reps. McHugh, Brien, Giannini, Menard, and Petrarca, 12 Jan. 2005. See 04-S 3048 SubAam, "An Act Relating to Separation of Powers," by Sens. Lenihan, Perry, Goodwin, Gallo, and Parella, 21 Apr. 2004; 04-S 3049A, (same title and date), by Sens. Lenihan, Cote, Tassoni, Fogarty, and Ciccone; 04-S 3051A, (same title and date), by Sens. Lenihan, Montalbano, Paiva Weed, and Blais.
29   Liz Anderson, "Separation anxiety," *PJ*, 3 Mar. 2005: B-01.
30   Liz Anderson, "Carcieri aides warn of veto to powers bills," *PJ*, 10 Mar. 2005: B-03.
31   Andrew M. Hodgkin and Jeffrey M. Grybowski, Letter to Elaine A. Coderre, Chair, House Separation of Powers Committee, 15 Mar. 2005: 1.
32   05-H 6477 SubAam, "An Act Relating to Separation of Powers," by Reps. Coderre, Ginaitt, Naughton, Crowley, and Almeida, 10 May 2005; PL-05 320, 15 Jul. 2005.

33   05-H 6477 SubA and 05-S 1175, signed by the governor, became PL-05 320 and 316.

34   05-H 6539am and 05-S 1178, signed by the governor, became PL-05 321 and 318.

35   05-H 5074 SubAam and 05-S 0551am, became effective without the governor's signature, PL-05 234 and 236.

36   05-H 6378 SubAam and 05-S 1176, passed both chambers but were recommitted to committees.

37   05-H 5104 SubBam and 05-S 0117 SubAam, signed by the governor, became PL 05-051 and 052.

38   05-S 1177am, signed by the governor, became PL-05 317; 05-H 6323 SubAam, became effective without signature, PL-05 239.

39   05-S 1090am, signed by the governor, became PL 05-315; 05-H 6163 SubBam became effective without signature, PL-05 228.

40   05-S 1179 SubAam, signed by the governor, became PL05-319; 05-H 6170 SubAam, became effective without signature, PL-05 241. Without agreement on the details, the Capital Center Commission, East Providence Special Development District, I-195 Redevelopment Board, and Vehicle Value Commission were dropped from this package.

41   Donald L. Carcieri, "Veto Message to the Honorable Speaker," 23 Jun. 2005. Together, the vetoed bills, 05-H 6171 Sub B as amended, 05-H 6217 Sub B as amended, 05-H 5816 Sub B as amended, 05-H 5817 Sub B as amended, would have restructured 31 separate boards.

42   05-S 0458, "Joint Resolution to Approve and Publish and to Submit to The Electors a Proposition of Amendment to the Constitution (Elections)," by Sens. Metts, Pichardo, Levesque, and Perry, 10 Feb. 2005, and 05-H 6280, (same title), by Reps. Almeida, Williams, Diaz, and Anguilla; 05-S 0575, "An Act Relating to Elections," by Sens. Metts, Pichardo, Levesque, and Caprio, 10 Feb. 2005, and 05-H 6069, (same title), by Reps. Almeida, Williams, Slater, and Diaz, 1 Mar. 2005. For technical reasons Almeida reintroduced the constitutional amendment, 05-H 6579, 9 Jun. 2005, and it passed the House on 23 Jun. 2005.

43   Marshall Clement, "Effective Arguments & Frequently Asked Questions," FLC, Feb. 2005.

44   See Tom Mooney, "Advocates push for probationers to vote," *PJ*, 14 Apr. 2005: B-03.

45   Mark Arsenault, Amanda Milkovits, Cathleen Crowley, "Providence police officer killed at headquarters with own gun," *PJ*, 18 Apr. 2005: A-01; Cathleen F. Crowley, "Accused's family says he was having 'nervous breakdown,'" *PJ*, 19 Apr. 2005: A-01; Elizabeth Gudrais, "NAACP asks FBI to probe police treatment of suspect," *PJ*, 22 Apr. 2005: A-12.

46   Katherine Gregg, "Allow some felons to vote?" *PJ*, 12 May 2005: B-01.

47   Amanda Milkovits, "Voting rights for felons approved," *PJ*, 22 Jun. 2005: B-01; Liz Anderson, Scott MacKay, Scott Mayerowitz, "Restoring felons' right to vote tops legislative proposals," *PJ*, 24 Jun. 2005: A-14.

48   *HJrnl*, 23 Jun. 2005: 12–13 and 15–16. For technical reasons, Almeida reintroduced his constitutional resolution 05-H 6579am on 9 Jun. 2005. On 23 Jun., the House approved it, 59 to 6, and 05-S 0458am, 58–5.

49   05-H 5477 SubA now proposed three additional exemptions: (e) Nothing in this section shall be deemed to require the reporting of the sale of goods or services or anything else of value to a major state decision-maker in the ordinary course of business and for fair market value.
      (f) Nothing in this section shall be deemed to require the reporting of the purchase of goods or services or anything else of value from a major state decision-maker in

the ordinary course of business and for fair market value, except for employment
and consulting contracts which shall be fully reportable hereunder.

(g) The fact that a major state decision-maker or the employer of a major state
decision-maker is a member of a trade association or of a professional association
that has engaged a lobbyist shall not give rise to the reporting requirements of this
section.

50   Video of House Finance Com., 7 Jun. 2005.

51   Dan Barry and John Sullivan, "Lolla-politics: Concert gets help from House leaders,"
     PJ, 19 Feb. 1995: A-01; M. Charles Bakst, "Lollapalooza saga calls for change in politi-
     cal script," *PJ*, 21 Feb. 1995: D-01.

52   Liz Anderson, "Legislators struggling with lobby reporting bill," *PJ*, 14 Jun. 2005:
     B-01.

53   HPW, "Beware R.I. solons' last-minute moves," *PJ*, 28 Jun. 2008: B-07.

54   Mike Stanton, "Celona admits selling office for own gain," *PJ*, 28 Jun. 2005: A-01.

55   HPW, Letter: "Dear Friends in the House," 1 Jul. 2005.

56   Video of floor debate on 05-H 5477 SubA as amended, 1 Jul. 2005.

57   Gemma spoke twice in the debate. I condense his two speeches into one here.

58   Fox spoke as if Common Cause had proposed exempting categories of purchases
     from major state decision-makers. The language we had given to Guglietta which
     would have exempted from reporting any purchases *by* "major state decision-makers
     at a price and upon terms generally available to the public" seven categories: (1) food
     or beverage; (2) clothing, merchandise, consumer goods; (3) utility services, includ-
     ing but not limited to gas, electric, telephone, cable or satellite services; (4) health
     care products or services; (5) insurance or financial services; (6) vehicles; (7) legal,
     medical or accounting services.

59   *HJrnl*, 1 Jul. 2005: 27–29. See Scott Mayerowitz, Liz Anderson, Katherine Gregg, and
     Bruce Landis, "Backlog of bills tests Assembly's efforts to adjourn," *PJ*, 2 Jul. 2005:
     A-01.

60   Identical to the Savage amendment in the House, Lenihan's proposed amendment
     read: "Nothing in this section shall be deemed to require the reporting of purchases
     from a major state decision maker of goods or services or anything else of value that
     does not exceed one thousand dollars ($1,000); provided, however, that employment
     and consulting contracts
     and fees of any amount shall be fully reportable hereunder."

61   *SJrnl*, 1 Jul. 2005: 39–40.

62   Katherine Gregg, "Veto expected of less severe disclosure bill," *PJ*, 7 Jul. 2005: B-01.

63   This account condenses consultations with four fine physicians, two with identical
     names: my urologist, Steven I. Cohen, and surgeon Steven I. Cohen. My general
     practitioner, Michael C. Rosenberg and oncologist Edward G. Wittels guided the
     process, saving my life and extending it by years.

64   HPW, "To the Honorable Joseph A. Montalbano," 29 Sep. 2005.

65   *SJrnl*. Last day of the 2005 session, 3 Jan. 2006: 1. Recommittal of 05-H 5477 SubA.
     Nine years later, in 2014, the original Celona Law, RIGL 22-10-9, still stood: c) Not
     later than January 15 of each year, every lobbyist and every individual, firm, business,
     corporation, association, partnership, or other group which employed a lobbyist
     or engaged any person to act as a lobbyist or who was required to register with the
     office of secretary of state during the preceding year pursuant to § 22-10-6 shall file
     with the secretary of state a complete and detailed report of all money or anything
     of value which in the aggregate exceeds two hundred fifty dollars ($250) provided
     or promised to any major state decision-maker within the preceding calendar year.

"Money" and "anything of value" in this subsection and in subsection (d) of this section shall mean any fee, salary, commission, expense allowance, forbearance, forgiveness, royalty, rent, capital gain, gift, loan, reward, favors or services, gratuities or special discounts, or any other form of recompense that constitutes income under the Federal Internal Revenue Code.

(d) Not later than January 15 of each year, every individual, firm, business, corporation, association, partnership or other group specified in subsection (c) of this section shall provide an exact copy of the report required in subsection (c) of this section to the Rhode Island ethics commission and to any major state decision-maker to whom it provided or promised money or anything of value which in the aggregate exceeds two hundred fifty dollars ($250) within the preceding calendar year.

51 | RECONSTRUCTION · pages 626–645

1   Katherine Gregg, "Amendment would allow privately run casino," PJ, 19 Jan. 2006: A-01.

2   06-H 7935, "Joint Resolution to Approve and Publish and Submit to the Electors a Proposition of Amendment to the Constitution of the State to Permit a Resort Casino in West Warwick, Rhode Island, to be Privately Owned and Operated in Association with the Narragansett Indian Tribe," by Reps. Williamson, Moura, Williams, Malik, Palumbo, 3 Mar. 2006.

3   Bruce Landis, "ACLU challenges spending rules," PJ, 19 Nov. 2004: B-01. Howard A. Merton, a volunteer lawyer for the ACLU, filed suit 18 Nov. 2004.

4   Edward Fitzpatrick, "Federal court seeks briefs in Board of Elections case," PJ, 9 Jan. 2006: C-03.

5   Thomas R. Bender, "Brief of Amicus Curiae Common Cause of Rhode Island," in *RI ACLU* v. *Begin*, 04-487-T, 15 Feb. 2006: 5–9, 24–25; Robert G. Flanders, Jr. and Mitchell R. Edwards, "Brief of Amicus Curiae the Rhode Island Foundation and the United Way of Rhode Island," in *RI ACLU* v. *Begin*, 04-487-T, 15 Feb. 2006: 4–6.

6   05-S 0708, "An Act Relating to Elections — Ballot Advocacy and Reporting," by Sen. Michael McCaffrey, 17 Feb. 2005; 05-S 0950, "An Act Relating to Elections," by Sen. Roger Badeau, 10 Mar. 2005, and 05-H 5978, (same title), by Rep. Charlene Lima, 1 Mar. 2005.

7   The University of Rhode Island was concerned about voter approval of bonds for new construction and soon joined the working group.

8   Martha M. Tierney, "Confidential response to litigation request," 22 Feb. 2006. Tierney argued: "At Common Cause we have consistently taken the position that requiring groups to organize as PACs and disclose donors is the goal of open and accountable government and a cornerstone of our campaign finance reform platform." She cited a Colorado law that required disclosure of all donors over $20. By contrast, Maine law allowed groups to spend up to $1,500 without reporting; once spending crossed that threshold, expenditures over $100 had to be reported.

9   06-H 7529 SubA, "An Act Relating to Elections — Campaign Expenditures (separate reporting requirements for expenditures on ballot questions from political campaigns)," by Reps. Pacheco, Lewiss, San Bento, Corvese, and Gallison, 16 Feb. 2006; 06-S 2797 SubA, (same title), by Sen. McCaffrey, 14 Feb. 2006.

10   See Ch. 39, "Ethics Meltdown."

11   Patrick T. Conley, "Principal Address, John E. Fogarty Centennial Celebration," 10 Jan. 2013.

12   06-H 7455, "An Act Relating to Public Offices and Employees — Public

Accountability and Reform," by Reps. Kilmartin, Moura, Sullivan, Jackson, and Church, 16 Feb. 2006; 06-S 2799, (same title), by Sen. Lenihan, 14 Feb. 2006.

13   Katherine Gregg, "Fogarty advocates greater disclosure," *PJ*, 4 Apr. 2006: B-01.

14   See RIGL 22-10-10 (9); RIGL 36-14-8 (f)(6); RIGL 36-14-10.1. Major state decision-makers are defined in RIGL 36-14-2(14).

15   06-H 6874, "An Act Relating to Elections," by Reps. Kilmartin, Crowley, Anguilla, Coderre, and Lima, 19 Jan. 2006. Kilmartin's bill would repeal RIGL 17-5-2, "Questions ordered by governor. The governor shall have the power to order the secretary of state to submit any question or questions that he or she shall deem necessary to the electors at any election."

16   Years later, I learned that historian Patrick T. Conley had advised legislative leaders to revoke this section of the law. For his reasons, See "The Distribution of Governmental Power in Rhode Island," particularly pp. 383–89 in *People, Places, Laws, and Lore of the Ocean State* (East Providence: RIPS, 2012).

17   06-H 7827, "An Act to Approve and Publish and Submit to the Electors A Proposition of Amendment to the Constitution of the State (Initiative and Referendum)," by Reps. Gorham, Picard, Mumford, Trillo, and Singleton, 1 Mar. 2006; 06-H 7828, "Joint Resolution, (same title)," by Reps. Erhardt, Long, and Watson, 1 Mar. 2006; 06-H 7829, "An Act Relating to Initiative and Referendum," by Reps. Gorham, Picard, Rose, McManus, and Erhardt, 1 Mar. 2006; 06-H 7830, (same title), by Reps. Erhardt, Long, and Watson, 1 Mar. 2006.

18   HPW, "Testimony before House Judiciary against Voter Initiative: 7827 & 7829," 28 Mar. 2006.

19   On 10 Apr. 2006, the House Judiciary Committee voted "no passage" of the House voter initiative bills. On 5 Apr. 2006 the Senate Committee on Constitutional and Gaming Issues "defeated in committee" the Senate voter initiative bills: 06-S 2478, "Joint Resolution to Approve and Publish and Submit to the Electors A Proposition of Amendment to the Constitution of the State (Initiative and Referendum)," by Sens. Cote, Lenihan, Bates, Breene, and Raptakis, 9 Feb. 2006, and 06-S 2488, "An Act Relating to Initiative and Referendum, by Sens. Cote, Lenihan, Bates, Breene, and Raptakis.

20   Useful resources are available online: *Veiled Political Actors* (http://paccenter.usc.edu/centers/cslp/assets/docs/cslp-wp-013.pdf), *A Buyer's Guide to Ballot Measures* (http://bisc.3cdn.net/52b42d131e618ea434_brm6iyuyt.pdf); Initiative and Referendum Institute (http://www.iandrinstitute.org/ballotwatch.htm); National Conference of State Legislatures (http://www.ncsl.org/legislatures-elections/elections/task-force-report.aspx).

21   Elizabeth Gudrais, "It's a separation-of-powers face-off," *PJ*, 10 Feb. 2006: B-02.

22   Kate Bramson, "Carcieri to place nonbinding questions on November ballot," *PJ*, 4 May 2006: B-02; *HJrnl*, 18 May 2006: 7–8. Elizabeth Gudrais, "Will lawmakers revoke power governor holds?" *PJ*, 19 May 2006: B-01; *SJrnl*, 25 May 2006: 24–25. Elizabeth Gudrais, "Gubernatorial ballot-question wins approval in Senate," *PJ*, 26 May 2006: B-01.

23   Donald L. Carcieri, "Veto of 06-H 6874, 'An Act Relating to Elections,' " 30 May 2006.

24   Reconfigured in 2006 House and Senate bills: Agricultural Lands Preservation Commission, Board of Bank Incorporation, Board of Examiners of Interpreters for the Deaf, Board of Governors for Higher Education, Board of Regents for Elementary-Secondary Education, Building Code Standards Committee, Child Advocate Appointing Committee, East Bay Economic Initiative Steering Committee, Fire Education and Training Coordinating Board, Fort Adams Foundation, Health Pro-

fessional Loan Repayment Board, Library Board of Rhode Island, Mosquito Abate-ment Board, Motor Vehicle Inspection Commission, Permanent Committee on Medal of Honor Recipients, Public Finance Management Board, Rabies Control Board, RI Farm, Forest, and Open Land Value Subcommittee, RI Higher Education Assistance Authority, RI Public Telecommunications Authority, RI Public Tran-sit Authority, RI Refunding Bond Authority, RI Resource Recovery Corporation, RI Rivers Council, RI Water Resources Board, RI Water Resources Board Corpo-rate, Sinking Fund Commission, State Building Code Standards Committee, State Comprehensive Plan Appeals Board, State Conservation Committee, State Crime Laboratory Commission, State Investment Commission, State Medical Examin-ers' Commission, State Properties Committee, State Retirement Board, State Traffic Commission. See Public Laws listed at http://webserver.rilin.state.ri.us/Lawrevision/plshort/pl2006sub.htm

25 Among those repaired were the Pilotage Commission, Greenways Council, and Industrial-Recreational Building Authority. See PL 06-21, 22, 23, 24, 27, and 33.

26 See Ch. 28, "Declaration of War."

27 See Ch. 32, "Heavy Hands." 02-H 7701, "I-195 Redevelopment Act of 2002," by Reps. Murphy, Montanaro, Moura, Naughton, and Long, February 12, 2002: 02-S 2740, (same title), by Sens. Ruggerio, Celona, and Bates. The scheme finally enacted in PL 02-427 and PL 02-111 handed off two appointments on the 9-member board to the mayor of Providence and the Providence Foundation.

28 06-S 3051, "An Act Relating to the General Assembly — Coastal Resources Management Council," by Sens. Sosnowski, Lenihan, Paiva Weed, McCaffrey, and Walaska, 27 Apr. 2006.

29 See Liz Anderson, "Carcieri picks replacements for Lottery, coastal panel," *PJ*, 6 Jan. 2005: A-01.

30 RI Senate Policy Office, "A summary of the Joint Hearing of the Senate Committee on Environment and Agriculture and the Senate Committee on Government Oversight," 8 May 2006.

31 *Westerly v. Bradley,* 877 Λ.2d 601, 21 Jun. 2005.

32 RI Senate Policy Office: 34.

33 RI Constitution, Article IX.5: "The governor shall, by and with the advice and con-sent of the senate, appoint all officers of the state whose appointment is not herein provided for and all members of any board, commission or other state or quasi-public entity which exercises executive power under the laws of this state; but the general assembly may by law vest the appointment of such inferior officers, as they deem proper, in the governor, or within their respective departments in the other general officers, the judiciary or in the heads of departments."

34 RI Senate Policy Office: 28–29.

35 RI Senate Policy Office: 32.

36 Peter B. Lord, "Senate committees consider CRMC'S fate," *PJ*, 28 Mar. 2006: B-01.

37 Bruce Landis, "J&W seeks I-195 land," *PJ*, 14 Dec. 2004: B-01.

38 06-H 7296, "An Act Relating to Public Property and Works — The I-195 Redevelopment Act of 2002," by Reps. Slater, Williams, Dennigan, Diaz, and Lima, 15 Feb. 2006.

39 06-H 6949, "An Act Relating to Separation of Powers," by Reps. Coderre and Kilmartin, 31 Jan. 2006: 4–5.

40 RIGL 46-25, PL 80-342.

41 Jane Austin, "Memo to Gary Bliss: Narragansett Bay Commission and Separation of Powers," 4 May 2006.

42   Elizabeth Gudrais, "Bill to reconfigure Bay Commission runs into opposition,"
     22 Jun. 2006: B-02. Cynthia Giles was married to Carl Bogus and would later be-
     come an EPA administrator in Washington, DC.

43   *RI ACLU* v. *Begin*, 04-487, 431 F. Supp. 2d 227, 25 Apr. 2006.

44   Boyle presented himself as lobbying for the Rhode Island Hospitality and Tourism
     Association (RIHTA), but his representation of Newport Grand was well known and
     a matter of public record.

45   PL 04-594, "Casino gambling — Rhode Island gaming control and revenue act —
     state referendum," enacted over veto, 30 Jul. 2004. See 04-S 2338 SubAam, "An Act
     Relating to Sports, Racing, and Athletics — And Extension of Gambling Activities
     and Other Facilities," by Sens. Alves and Ruggerio, 11 Feb. 2004.

46   RIGL 17-25.1-3 contained rules for registering ballot advocates; 17-25.1-4 set up a
     reporting process; 17-25.1-5 required disclosure of advertising activities. These were
     repealed.

47   06-H 7529 SubA, "An Act Relating to Elections — Campaign Expenditures," by Reps
     Pacheco, Lewiss, San Bento, Corvese, and Gallison, 16 Feb. 2006, amended and ap-
     proved by House Judiciary on 12 Apr. 2006.

48   Christopher Boyle, "Memorandum, Rhode Island Hospitality and Tourism
     Association, Re: Rhode Island Ballot Question Advocacy and Reporting Act," 15 May
     2006.

49   Scott Mayerowitz, "Bill on ballot questions is facing its own detractors," *PJ*, 17 May
     2006: B-01.

50   RIGL 17-25.1-1.1 "Gambling referenda — Ballot question advocates."

51   *HJrnl*, 15 Jun. 2006: 55–6.

52   06-S 2797 SubA as amended during Senate debate on 30 May 2006 became PL 06-
     174 27 Jun. 2006; 06-H 7529 SubA as amended during House debate on 15 Jun. 2006
     became PL 06-292 on 3 Jul. 2006. Gov. Carcieri signed both into law.

53   The Indian Gaming Regulatory Act of 1988 (IGRA) appeared to permit a casino on
     the Narragansetts' settlement lands, and Gov. Bruce Sundlun had entered a compact
     with tribal leaders, but in 1996 then U.S. Sen. John Chafee pushed through an
     amendment to IGRA (PL 104-208) which stated that the Tribe's "settlement lands
     shall not be treated as Indian lands" for the purposes of IGRA, effectively barring
     construction of a Charlestown casino. See Letter from the National Indian Gaming
     Commission to Randy Noka, First Councilman, Narragansett Indian Tribe, 17 Jan.
     1997.

54   Katie Mulvaney and Paul Davis, "Clash over smoke shop," *PJ*, 15 Jul. 2003: A-01; Scott
     MacKay, "R.I. police, Narragansetts clash," *PJ*, 15 Jul. 2003: A-01; M. Charles Bakst,
     "Indian melee puts Carcieri in tough spot," *PJ*, 15 Jul. 2003: B-01.

55   06-H 7935 Sub A.

56   Katherine Gregg and Scott Mayerowitz, "Panel OKs casino vote," *PJ*, 23 May 2006:
     A-01.

57   For more on the following votes, see *HJrnl*, 25 May 2006: 7–20.

58   06-H 7938, "An Act Relating to Elections," by Reps. Almeida, Williams, Ajello, Diaz,
     and Slater, 28 Mar. 2006. With final passage of 05-H 6579am and 05-S 0458am on
     23 Jun. 2005, the Right to Vote Amendment went to the 2006 statewide ballot.

59   06-H 7938, *HJrnl*, 22 Jun. 2006: 46–7. See PL 06-476: 7 Jul. 2006.

60   06-S 2799 Sub A and 06-H 7455 Sub Aam.

61   *SJrnl*, 23 Jun. 2006: 52, 54; *HJrnl*, 23 Jun. 2006: 134.

62   *HJrnl*, 23 Jun. 2006: 19.

63   06-H 8170, "An Act Relating to Waters and Navigation — Coastal Resources

Management Council," by Reps. Coderre, Lima, Gallison, Crowley, and Kilmartin, 31 May 2006.

64   *HJrnl*. 23 Jun. 2006: 12.

52 | DÉJÀ VU · pages 646–663

1   Chafee had voted against the Iraq War and battled the efforts of Vice President Dick Cheney and others on the far right. See Lincoln Chafee, *Against The Tide: How a Compliant Congress Empowered a Reckless President* (New York: Thomas Dunne, 2008).

2   Republican governors were elected in 1984, 1986, and 1988 (Edward D. DiPrete); 1994 and 1998 (Lincoln C. Almond); and 2002 (Donald L. Carcieri). Democrat Bruce G. Sundlun won in 1990 and 1992.

3   Elizabeth Gudrais, "Saying state's in better shape, Carcieri launches reelection bid," *PJ*, 8 Jun. 2006: A-01.

4   Mark Arsenault, "Fogarty says it will be an uphill battle against Carcieri," *PJ*, 30 Apr. 2006: A-01.

5   Katherine Gregg, "Fogarty raps governor for not signing ethics law," *PJ*, 10 Jul. 2006: C-01.

6   RIEC Decision and Order, *In Re: John A. Celona*, Complaints 2003-9, 2004-4, and 2004-8, 25 Jul. 2006. OCG Chair Robert P. Arruda and Vice Chair Beverly M. Clay had filed complaints on 9 Dec. 2003 and 3 Mar. 2004. Commission investigator Peter J. Mancini filed the supplemental complaint on 29 Jun. 2004.

7   Jim Baron, "Celona smacked with fine," *PT*, 26 Jul. 2006: 1.

8   Mike Stanton, "Celona admits selling office for own gain," *PJ*, 28 Jun. 2005: A-01. See Ch. 46, "Triple Scandal."

9   Mike Stanton, "Roger Williams Medical Center indicted in corruption case," *PJ*, 6 Jan. 2006: A-01.

10   Mike Stanton, "Urciuoli trial: Good deed or illegal deal?" *PJ*, 12 Sep. 2006: A-01.

11   Mike Stanton, "Celona grilled on secrecy," *PJ*, 16 Sep. 2006: A-01.

12   RIEC Advisory Opinion 98-59, *In Re: John A. Celona*.

13   Edward Fitzpatrick and W. Zachary Malinowski, "Celona's activities worried lawyer," *PJ*, 22 Sep. 2006: A-01.

14   Stanton.

15   Another nonprofit with the same acronym is Rhode Islanders Saving Energy.

16   Katherine Gregg, "Political scene," *PJ*, 12 Jun. 2006: C-01.

17   Donna Paolino Urciuoli was the sister of former Providence Mayor Joseph Paolino.

18   See Ch. 31, "Opening Government." 98-H 7647 by Rep. Peter Kilmartin attempted to create a Cancer Council modeled on the Lottery Commission.

19   Notes from 30 Sep. 2006 and personal interview, 23 Jan. 2009.

20   Mike Stanton, "Roger Williams corruption verdict," *PJ*, 14 Oct. 2006: A-01.

21   On 31 Jan. 2007, Torres sentenced Celona to 2 years in prison, Urciuoli to 3 years, and Driscoll to 8 months in prison and 8 months of home confinement; Mike Stanton, "Trio sentenced to jail," *PJ*, 1 Feb. 2007: A-01.

22   Elizabeth Gudrais, "Ballot ruling backs Carcieri," *PJ*, 4 Jul. 2006: A-01.

23   2006-199-Appeal. *In Re: Matthew A. Brown*, in his capacity as secretary of state, 8 Aug. 2006: 5.

24   2006-199: 6–7.

25   Scott Mayerowitz, "U.S. court keeps casino question on Nov. ballot," *PJ*, 9 Aug. 2006: A-01.

26   See Ch. 39, "Ethics Meltdown."

27   During a personal interview on 17 Dec. 2013, I asked retired Chief Justice Frank
      Williams about this. He barely remembered our exchange at the RIPEC dinner and
      insisted that the high court never put off cases for political reasons. He surmised
      that the advisory opinion request did not, in fact, reach the high court in 2006. He
      phoned a clerk for the docket sheet, which confirmed proceedings from 10 Dec.
      2007 to 18 Dec. 2008, when the court issued *In Re: Request for Advisory Opinion
      from the House of Representatives (CRMC)* 07-370-M.P. See *Supreme Court Docket
      Event Listing, Case ID No: SU-07-370.* Williams's surmise is supported in the advi-
      sory opinion, which cites the House request as 07-H 6266. The mystery remains why
      House leaders passed the advisory opinion request in 2006 but delayed their formal
      request to the Supreme Court for an entire year.

28   Scott Mayerowitz, "Harrah's 3-month casino promotion costs $5.2 million," *PJ*, 9 Sep.
      2006: A-03.

29   "'Outraged' Common Cause joins anti-casino campaign," *PJ*, 31 Aug. 2006: B-02.

30   Right To Vote Steering Committee: Peter Slom, Chair; Andres Idarraga, Vice Chair;
      Barbara Hurst, Treasurer; HPW, Secretary; Joe Benton, Steve Brown, Julian Dash,
      Dennis Langley, Peter Wells, Jeffrey Williams, and Myrth York, Members. Staff of the
      Family Life Center regularly participated in meetings: Solangel Rodriguez, Executive
      Director; Ronald Fortes, Finance Director; Daniel Schleifer, Field Director; Nancy
      Kirsch, Communications Director.

31   Dean Esserman and George Stamatakos of the Providence police; attorneys
      Margaret Curran, Julius Michaelson, James E. O'Neil, Dennis Roberts, and Sheldon
      Whitehouse; Superior Court judges Stephen J. Fortunato Jr. and Richard J. Israel;
      Parole Board officers Lisa Holley and Kenneth Walker.

32   Dean Esserman and HPW, "Without a vote, citizens have no voice," *PJ*, 25 Sep. 2006:
      C-04.

33   Endorsers included U.S. Sen. Lincoln Chafee; U.S. Reps. Patrick Kennedy and Jim
      Langevin; Lt. Gov. Charles Fogarty, Secy. of State Matt Brown; State Sens. Joseph
      Montalbano, Teresa Paiva Weed, Dennis Algiere, Frank Caprio, Daniel DaPonte,
      June Gibbs, Charles Levesque, Harold Metts, Elizabeth Roberts, Rhoda Perry, Juan
      Pichardo; State Reps. William Murphy, Gordon Fox, Joseph Almeida, Edith Ajello,
      Elaine Coderre, James Davey, Grace Diaz, Arthur Handy, Helio Melo, Amy Rice,
      Thomas Slater, Anastasia Williams; Mayors David Cicilline, James Doyle, Scott
      Avedisian; Providence Councilpersons John Lombardi, Luis Aponte, Kevin Jackson,
      Miguel Luna, David Segal, and Balbina Young.

34   AFSCME is the American Federation of State, County, and Municipal Employees,
      Council 94; SEIU is the Service Employees International Union, District 1199.

35   Michael Leo Owens and Marion Orr, "Changing Policy Designs for 'Deviants': Po-
      litical Lessons from the Rhode Island 'Right to Vote' Campaign," American Political
      Science Association 2011 Annual Meeting Paper, 4 Sep. 2011: 15.

36   Micah 6:8 in various translations. KJV: "What doth the LORD require of thee, but to
      do justly, and to love mercy, and to walk humbly with thy God?"

37   Jim Baron, "Rally for felons' vote," *PT*, 19 Sep. 2006: 1; Karen Lee Ziner, "Supporters
      rally to urge passage of Question 2," *PJ*, 20 Sep. 2006: B-01.

38   Erik Eckholm, "Help for the Hardest Part of Prison: Staying Out," NYT, 12 Aug. 2005.

39   Chris Keegan, "Should felons still on probation have the Right To Vote?" *Westerly
      Sun*, 27 Sep. 2006: 5.

40   Editorial, "Felons deserve a vote — but only after full sentence 'debt' is paid," *Westerly
      Sun*, 1 Oct. 2006.

41 Leonidas Raptakis, "No to Question 2," *PJ*, 13 Oct. 2006: B-04.

42 Editorial, "Yes on Question 2," *PJ*, 21 Oct. 2006: F-04.

43 Editorial, "Building Better Citizens," NYT, 28 Oct. 2006: A-14.

44 CCRI annual meeting, 25 Sep. 2006. See Elizabeth Gudrais, "Gubernatorial candidates debate tonight," *PJ*, 25 Sep. 2006: C-01.

45 See Ch. 51, "Reconstruction." PL 06-428 and PL 06-429, "Public Accountability and Reform Act of 2006," 7 Jul. 2006.

46 Republican Governors Association, "In Charlie's world," 30-second ad produced by Stevens & Schriefer Group (SSG), who advertised: "We are the most experienced and seasoned Republican campaign strategy, message and media consultants in the business. From multi-candidate primaries in the reddest of states to come-from-behind general election victories in blue states, we have consistently helped our clients win the toughest races." In 2013, the firm merged with another to become Strategic Partners & Media with Stuart Stevens and Russ Schriefer as partners. http://strategicpartnersmedia.com/news/schriefer-and-partners-launch-firm-expand-services/.

47 RIGL 17-25-10.1 (a) and (e).

48 See 07-220-Appeal, *RIGOP* v. *Daluz,* 18 Dec. 2008. Note 3 describes the ad in detail.

49 Scott MacKay, "Elections Board rules state GOP broke campaign law," *PJ*, 22 Oct. 2002: A-10.

50 Edward Fitzpatrick, "High Court rebuffs GOP in appeal of ad ruling," *PJ*, 25 Jun. 2003: B-01; Bruce Landis, "GOP to Elections Board: Halt probe," *PJ*, 1 Dec. 2005: B-03; Scott Mayerowitz, "Elections Board to Begin: Resign," *PJ*, 14 Dec. 2005: B-01; Bruce Landis, "Complaint over Carcieri's 2002 ad stalled," *PJ*, 16 Aug. 2006: B-01. The RI Supreme Court eventually reviewed the long-running dispute but declined to take further action. See 07-220-Appeal, *RIGOP* v. *Daluz,* 18 Dec. 2008.

51 PL 06-428 and PL 06-429, "Public Accountability and Reform Act of 2006," 7 Jul. 2006.

52 HPW, "Common Cause criticizes National Republican Governors Association commercial as inaccurate and misleading," CCRI, 26 Oct. 2006.

53 Ray Henry, "Government watchdog group blasts GOP ad," AP wire story; Joe Baker, "Common Cause Draws the Line with Attack Ad," *NDN*, 30 Oct. 2006: B-1.

54 Republican Governors Association, CF-8 report to the Board of Elections, 31 Oct. 2006.

55 RIGL 17-25-10 (b), 17-25-23.

56 Katherine Gregg, "Fogarty raps governor for not signing ethics law," *PJ*, 10 Jul. 2006: C-01.

57 Scott Mayerowitz, "Harrah's spends millions in Question 1 campaign," *PJ*, 11 Oct. 2006: A-01.

58 The Rhode Island Foundation and individual donors provided contributions from within Rhode Island that leveraged funds from other states: Haymarket People's Fund, Hull Family Foundation, JEHT Foundation, RockIt Fund, and Tides Foundation.

59 Daniel Schleifer, "Unlocking the Vote: Activists and disenfranchised former felons restore voting rights in Rhode Island," *The Nation,* 18 Dec. 2006.

60 The RockIt Fund, 350 Fifth Ave., New York, NY. 10118 sent $31,000 on 19 Oct. 2006. We paid $3,000 to Stones' Phones for automated calls. See Family Life Advocacy Center, Summary of Ballot Question Advocacy (BQA-1) 30 Nov. 2006.

61 See Scott MacKay, Mark Arsenault, and Katherine Gregg, "Chafee staves off challenger — Laffey concedes GOP primary; Democrats tap Whitehouse," *PJ*, 13 Sep. 2006: A-01.

62 Scott MacKay, "Bush is the issue in R.I. Senate race," *PJ*, 10 Oct. 2006: A-01.
63 RIBOE State Board of Elections, *2006 Primary & Election Count Book:* 52. http://
    www.elections.ri.gov/publications/Election_Publications/Countbooks/RI_Election_
    Countbook_2006.
64 http://www.fec.gov/finance/disclosure/candcmte_info.shtml.
65 Mark Arsenault, "Governor's race a test of matching-fund program," *PJ*, 2 Aug. 2006:
    B-03.
66 RIGL 17-25-20 (2)(ii) empowered the Board of Elections to revise the amounts of
    matching funds from the 1994 limit of $1.5 million to keep pace with the Consumer
    Price Index. RIGL 17-25-19 (b). In addition, as a participant in the program, Fogarty
    could accept contributions up to $2,000 — twice the legal limit for nonparticipating
    candidates — from any individual. This incentive was repealed in 2011 (PL 11-229 and
    230).
67 http://annegrant.blogspot.com/2007/01/blog-post.html.
68 With thanks to the abolitionist Theodore Parker and Martin Luther King Jr., who
    paraphrased him: "The arc of the Moral Universe is long, but it bends toward Justice."

AFTERWORD: MAKING GOVERNMENT GOOD · pages 667–684

1   Katherine Gregg, Tom Mooney, Randal Edgar, "Agents raid Fox's office, home," *PJ*,
    22 Mar. 2014: A-01; Paul Edward Parker, "Fox broke barriers, has faced scrutiny," *PJ*,
    22 Mar. 2014: A-06.
2   See Ch. 46, "Triple Scandal." RIEC, "Investigative Report, Complaint 2013-5," 10 Jan.
    2014. See Tom Mooney, "Fox to pay ethics fine of $1,500," *PJ*, 29 Jan. 2014.
3   See Ch. 46, "Triple Scandal."
4   RIEC Complaint 2004-1, *In Re: William v. Irons,* 20 Jan. 2004.
5   RIEC Order and Finding of Probable Cause 2004-1, *In Re: William V. Irons,* 15 Nov.
    2004.
6   I have not seen these negotiations publicly reported, but several individuals involved
    have confirmed the unsuccessful attempt to reach a settlement.
7   RIEC Minutes of Open Session, 20 Nov. 2007: 3–4.
8   The final clause of RI Constitution, Article VI.5 reads: "For any speech in debate in
    either house, no member shall be questioned in any other place." Francis J. Darigan,
    Irons v. RIEC, PC 07-6666, 29 Oct. 2008: 28.
9   Justices Francis X. Flaherty, William P. Robinson III, and retired Chief Justice Frank
    J. Williams signed the majority opinion, 08-335-M.P., *William v. Irons v. RIEC,* 973
    A2d 1124, 29 Jun. 2009: 15 in PDF.
10 The majority rightly noted that two booklets mailed to voters, the *Convention
    Alert: Constitution Rewrite and Resolutions Approved by the 1986 Rhode Island
    Constitutional Convention* and the *Voter's Guide to Fourteen Ballot Questions for
    Constitutional Revision,* both emphasized that the "neutral rewrite of the constitu-
    tion" would not "change the intent of any section."
11 Suttell dissent: 22.
12 RI Constitution, Article III.8. See Paul A. Suttell, Dissent in *Irons v. RIEC,* 08-335: 20.
13 See Ch. 1, "Breaking Ground."
14 *In Re: Advisory Opinion to the Governor (Ethics Commission),* 91-577 M. P., 612 A.
    2nd (R.I. 1992). See Ch. 14, "Triumphs."
15 Suttell dissent: 27–28.
16 Majority opinion: 9.
17 Keven A. McKenna, *Convention Alert: Constitution Rewrite and Resolutions*

Approved by the 1986 Rhode Island Constitutional Convention, Sep. 1986; Susan L. Farmer, *Voter Information #9 Referendums: What's on the Ballot*, Office of the Secretary of State, Oct. 2006.

18   See Ch. 1, "Breaking Ground."

19   RI Constitution, Article III.8.

20   Majority opinion: 9, 11–12, 16.

21   CCRI Board Member and attorney Thomas R. Bender drafted the amendment which became 10-H 7357, "Joint Resolution To Approve and Publish and Submit to the Electors A Proposition of Amendment to the Constitution of the State (Ethics Commission)," by Reps. Fox, Fierro, Hearn, Marcello, and Walsh, 4 Feb. 2010; 10-S 2391, (similar title), by Sens. Lenihan, Sheehan, O'Neill, Algiere, and Bates, 11 Feb. 2010. Identical resolutions have been filed every year since 2010 but never approved.

22   Randall Edgar, "Fox solidifies backing to become speaker of House," *PJ*, 10 Feb. 2010: A-06; Katherine Gregg and Steve Peoples, "Fox is House speaker," 12 Feb. 2010: A-01.

23   *HJrnl*, 2 Jun. 2010: 15.

24   John Marion, "Assembly must adopt strong ethics rule," *PJ*, 27 Mar. 2014: A-14. See also Marion, "General Assembly recusals: 2006–13."

25   14-S 2824 SubAam, "Joint Resolution to Publish and Submit to the Electors a Proposition of Amendment to the Constitution of the State (Ethics Commission), by Sens. Sheehan, Conley, McCaffrey, O'Neill, and Cote, 25 Mar. 2014. See Michael P. McKinney, "Senate passes bill on ethics jurisdiction," *PJ*, 13 Jun. 2014: A-06.

26   Katherine Gregg, "Placing ethics panel issue on ballot advances," *PJ*, 27 May 2010: A-01.

27   Gerard B. Sullivan and Stephen G. Dambruch, "Information," and "Plea Agreement," in *United States* v. *Gerard M. Martineau,* 4 Oct. 2007.

28   W. Zachary Malinowski, "Ex-House leader sentenced to 3 years," *PJ*, 23 Feb. 2008: A-01.

29   U.S. Attorney's Office, District of Rhode Island, "Rhode Island Real Estate Attorney Indicted in Schemes Netting $1.5 Million in Mortgages," 18 Jun. 2010. See Mark Reynolds, "Ex-senator going to prison for fraud," *PJ*, 11 Feb. 2011: A-04.

30   W. Zachary Malinowski, "Politician gets 27 months," *PJ*, 22 Dec. 2012: A-01. See McCauley's behavior as a member of the Solid Waste Management Corporation in Ch. 30, "Retaliation."

31   Karen Lee Ziner, "Medina may be facing prosecution," *PJ*, 8 Jul. 2011: A-01; "R.I. Rep. Leo Medina is charged with a felony," *PJ*, 2 Sep. 2011: A-01; Ziner, "Medina charged with illegal law practice," *PJ*, 15 Aug. 2012: A-01.

32   RIEC Decision and Order, *In Re: Patrick McDonald* Complaints 2001-41 and NF 2002–13, 25 Jan. 2005.

33   Katie Mulvaney, "Ex-R.I. senator McDonald to serve 4½ years for embezzling law clients," *PJ*, 1 May 2014: A-01.

34   RIEC, Informal Resolution and Settlement, Complaint 2007-1, *In Re: Raymond E. Gallison Jr.,* 18 Dec. 2007.

35   Mike Stanton, "FBI arrests 3 councilors on charges of extortion," *PJ*, 7 May 2010: A-01; Mark Reynolds, "3 plead not guilty to extortion, bribery," *PJ*, 8 Jun. 2010; W. Zachary Malinowski, "Bribery scandal widens with new indictments," *PJ*, 20 Aug. 2010; W. Zachary Malinowski, "Three admit guilt," *PJ*, 24 Feb. 2011: A-01; Mark Reynolds, "Ex-council members plead guilty to extortion," *PJ*, 1 Mar. 2011: A-01; Mark Reynolds, "Jailed for extortion," *PJ*, 7 May 2011: A-01.

36   Mark Reynolds, "Developer Baccari indicted," *PJ*, 24 Oct. 2013: A-01; Reynolds, "Ciresi guilty on all counts," *PJ*, 27 Apr. 2011: A-01.

37   Mike Stanton, "FBI arrests 3 councilors on charges of extortion," *PJ*, 7 May 2010:
      A-01; W. Zachary Malinowski, "Three admit guilt," *PJ*, 24 Feb. 2011: A-01; Mark
      Reynolds, "Ex-council members plead guilty to extortion," *PJ*, 1 Mar. 2011: A-01;
      Mark Reynolds, "Jailed for extortion," *PJ*, 17 May 2011: A-01.

38   W. Zachary Malinowski, "Bribery scandal widens with new indictments," *PJ*, 20 Aug.
      2010; Mark Reynolds, "Developer says fear motivated him to pay bribe," *PJ*, 16 Apr.
      2011: A-03; Michael P. McKinney, "Sergiacomi, Ricci sentenced for defrauding insur-
      ance company," *PJ*, 26 Aug. 2011: A-01.

39   Hummel Report video: http://www.youtube.com/watch?v=T-VCrL9yPtQ; Mike
      Stanton and W. Zachary Malinowski, "Boarding up Central Falls," *PJ*, 25 Apr. 2010:
      A-01.

40   RIEC, *In Re: Charles D. Moreau,* 2010-2, Informal Resolution and Settlement, 28 Jan.
      2013. For more on the restored gift rule, see Ch. 47, "Restoring Ethics."

41   W. Zachary Malinowski, "Moreau given 2-year jail term; codefendant avoids prison,"
      PJ, 13 Feb 2013: A-01.

42   W. Zachary Malinowski, "Diossa proposes ethics measures," *PJ*, 24 Jan. 2013: A-04,
      Ian Donnis, "Central Falls Moves Forward on Ethics," RIPR.org, 21 Feb. 2013; Jim
      Baron, *PT*, "Mayor Diossa aims to 'set a new standard,'" 24 Feb. 2013: 1. See *Central
      Falls Municipal Code of Ethics,* http://centralfallsri.us/.

43   W. Zachary Malinowski, "City Hall worker arrested," *PJ*, 7 Feb. 2013: A-01;
      Malinowski, "Ex-clerk is sentenced for stealing from city," *PJ*, 9 Apr. 2014.

44   W. Zachary Malinowski, "In new political landscape, mayor has a clear path," *PJ*,
      9 Sep. 2013: A-01; Malinowski, "For once-bankrupt city, a financial turnaround," *PJ*,
      21 Mar. 2014: A-01.

45   Federal Election Campaign Act Amendments of 1974 (FECA) PL 92-225. http://
      www.fec.gov/info/appfour.htm.

46   Rhode Island's 1973 Constitutional Convention recommended an amendment, now
      RI Constitution, Article IV.9, that directed the General Assembly to enact a law re-
      quiring all candidates for general office to report all contributions and expenditures
      in their campaigns. See Ch. 1, "Breaking Ground;" 4, "A Costly Election;" 6, "Dashed
      Hopes;" 11, "RIght Now!;" 14, "Triumphs;" 38, "Kingly Power;" and 41, "Plunder
      Dome."

47   Federal Election Commission, http://www.fec.gov/pages/bcra/major_resources_
      bcra.shtml.

48   *Buckley* v. *Valeo*, 424 U.S. 1 (1976) upheld campaign finance limits and laid the
      groundwork for matching-funds programs; *Austin* v. *Michigan Chamber of Com-
      merce*, 494 U.S. 652 (1990) barred unions and corporations from contributing di-
      rectly to campaigns; *Nixon* v. *Shrink Missouri Government PAC*, 528 U.S. 377 (2000)
      upheld the ability of states to limit campaign contributions; and *McConnell* v. *Federal
      Election Commission,* 540 U.S. 93 (2003) upheld the McCain-Feingold bans on "soft
      money" and on corporate and union contributions for campaign ads.

49   Geoffrey R. Stone, "Roberts, Alito and the Rule of Law," *Huffington Post*, 28 Jun.
      2007.

50   *Federal Election Commission* v. *Wisconsin Right to Life, Inc.* (2007); *Davis* v. *FEC*
      (2008), *Citizens United* v. *FEC* (2010), *Arizona Free Enterprise Club* v. *Bennett* (2011),
      American Tradition Partnership v. *Bullock* (2012), and *McCutcheon* v. *FEC* (2014).

51   James Oliphant, "Republicans block campaign finance measure," *Los Angeles Times,*
      28 Jul. 2010: A-01. David Welna, "Senate Republicans Block Campaign Finance Bill,"
      NPR, 27 Jul. 2010: http://www.npr.org/templates/story/story.php?storyId=128804239.
      TARP was an acronym for Troubled Asset Relief Program.

52 PL 12-446, "An Act Relating to Elections — Disclosure of Political Contributions and Expenditures," by Reps. Blazejewski, Fox, Ajello, Marcello, and Edwards, 28 Feb. 2012, enacted 26 Jun. 2012. Pichardo filed a Senate bill, identical to Blazejewski's, but it did not pass.

53 CCRI, "Rhode Island People's Pledge," 28 Apr. 2014.

54 Ruth Bader Ginsburg, dissent, *Shelby County* v. *Eric Holder*, 12-96, 25 Jun. 2013: 35–6.

55 Steven Yaccino and Lizette Alvarez, "New G.O.P. Bid to Limit Voting in Swing States," *NYT*, 30 Mar. 2014: A-01.

56 Figures from forms provided by Teresa Foley and Mary Louise Joseph, Department of Corrections, 19 Oct. 2013.

57 Daniel Schleifer, "Over 6,000 on probation or parole register to vote in 2008 elections," *Inside/Out* (Newsletter of Open Doors, 2010) 2. http://www.opendoorsri.org/sites/default/files/InsideOutv5FINAL2.pdf.

58 Koren Carbuccia, *My First Vote*, ed. by Garima Malhotra (New York: Brennan Center, 2009), 10.

59 07-H 6556, "House Resolution Respectfully Requesting the Justices of the Supreme Court to Give a Written Opinion upon Certain Questions of Law," by Rep. John J. DeSimone, 20 Jun. 2007.

60 07-370, *In Re: Request for advisory opinion (CRMC)*, 961 A2d 930, 18 Dec. 2008. Chief Justice Frank J. Williams joined with Justices Francis X. Flaherty, Paul A. Suttell, and William P. Robinson III. Justice Maureen McKenna Goldberg recused herself.

61 07-370, *CRMC*, 961 A2d 930: 9–10, 15–16, 19.

62 See Ch. 36, "Referendum."

63 Sen. James A. Sheehan, e-mail to HPW, 18 Apr. 2014.

64 09-H 5529 SubAam, "House Resolution Adopting Rules of the House of Representatives for the Years 2009–2010," by Rep. Eileen S. Naughton, 24 Feb. 2009.

65 11-H 5316 SubAam, "House Resolution Adopting Rules of the House of Representatives for the Years 2011–2012," by Rep. Peter G. Palumbo, 9 Feb. 2011.

66 See Ch. 36, "Referendum."

67 Katherine Gregg, "Opponent of repaying 38 Studios bonds will chair R.I. House Oversight Committee," *PJ*, 2 Apr. 2014: A-01. House Com. on Oversight, http://ricaptv.discovervideo.com/embedviews/vod.

68 Katherine Gregg, "Investigation into loan is expanding," *PJ*, 7 May 2014: A-01; Kate Nagle, "38 Studios Contractor Ordered to Install Equipment in Fox's Crony's Bar," GoLocal.com, 7 May 2014.

69 Rep. Karen L. MacBeth, telephone interview, 6 May 2014.

70 See Ch. 19, "Paying the Piper," and 20, "Under New Management."

71 Raimondo won with 62.1 per cent. See RIBOE http://www.ri.gov/election/results/2010/general_election/.

72 Gina Raimondo, *TRUTH IN NUMBERS: The Security and Sustainability of Rhode Island's Retirement System*, Office of the General Treasurer, May 2011.

73 Paul Edward Parker, "Amid scalding report, financial leaders call for action," *PJ*, 26 Apr. 2011: A-05; Mike Stanton, "RI Courts may have last say on public-sector pensions," *PJ*, 19 Jun. 2011: A-01.

74 Gina M. Raimondo, Remarks before the General Assembly: "The Rhode Island Retirement Security Act of 2011," 18 Oct. 2011.

75 PL 11-408 and 409, "Rhode Island Retirement Security Act of 2011," 18 Nov. 2011.

76 Tom Mooney and Paul Edward Parker, "Landmark overhaul becomes law," *PJ*, 19 Nov. 2011: A-01.

77   Fitch Ratings press release: "Effect of Sweeping Rhode Island Pension Reform May Be Felt Nationwide," http://www.reuters.com/article/2011/11/18/.

78   David Von Drehle, "The Little State That Could," *TIME Magazine*, 5 Dec. 2011. http://content.time.com/time/magazine/article/0,9171,2100110,00.html.

79   Mooney and Parker, *PJ*, 19 Nov. 2011: A-01.

80   Katherine Gregg, "Police 'no' votes send combatants back to table," *PJ*, 8 Apr. 2014: A-01; Randal Edgar, "State, unions declare impasse," *PJ*, 12 Apr. 2014: A-01; Katherine Gregg, "As case heads for trial, 'gag order' remains," *PJ*, 15 Apr. 2014: A-03.

81   PL 06-319 and PL 06-444, enacted on 4 and 7 Jul. 2006, changed the composition of all four boards.

82   Gina M. Raimondo, e-mail to HPW, 1 May 2014.

83   PL 12-448 and PL 12-454 were signed into law on 26 Jun. 2012.

84   See Ch. 31, "Opening Government."

85   RIGL 38-2-3.2.

86   RIGL 38-2-2 (A)(I)(b).

87   Tracy Breton, "Bills address access to public records," *PJ*, 16 Mar. 2012: A-05; Bruce Landis, "Open-records bills stall because of 'balancing test,' " *PJ*, 9 Jun. 2012: A-06; Katherine Gregg, "Law's rewrite seen improving public's access to records," *PJ*, 27 Jun. 2012: A-01.

88   Steve Peoples, "Under the radar, State House lobbyists are key dealmakers," *PJ*, 10 Jun. 2007: D-01.

89   John Marion, "Judging How We Pick Judges: Fifteen Years of Merit Selection in Rhode Island," 15 *Roger Williams U. L. Rev.* 735, Fall 2010.

90   Ian Donnis, "Tracy Breton on the ProJo and 40 Years of Covering RI Courts," RIPR. org, 16 Oct. 2013.

91   Peter Hufstader, "Commercial lobbyists: 1999 payments reported from clients," CCRI Newsletter, Oct. 1999: 2. McGinn and Kerins ranked in the top ten commercial lobbyists at the RI State House.

92   A. Ralph Mollis, *2006 Annual Lobbying Report, et seq,* Secretary of State. Lt. Gov. Charles Fogarty's Public Accountability and Reform Act of 2006 added RIGL 22-10-10 (9) that required the secretary of state to prepare and publish by March 1st each year a report on lobbying the previous year. Copies are online: http://sos.ri.gov/ltpublic/?page=reports_view.

93   Jonathan D. Rockoff, "Burgess to remain on judicial panel," 18 Nov. 2000: A-06.

94   Edward Fitzpatrick, "Independence, merit key to success of JNC," *PJ*, 1 Dec. 2009: A-04.

95   McAuliffe had worked in the offices of U.S. Sen. Jack Reed, Cong. Patrick J. Kennedy, and Lt. Gov. Charles J. Fogarty before he started his own lobbying firm, the Mayforth Group. In a personal interview on 17 Feb. 2014, McAuliffe insisted no one in the General Assembly had contacted him regarding any candidate for judicial nomination.

96   RIGL 8-16.1-6 (b) The governor shall fill any vacancy within twenty-one (21) days of the public submission by the commission.

97   Katie Mulvaney, "The governor's legacy," *PJ*, 14 Nov. 2010: A-01.

98   RIGL 8-16.1-6. See Ch. 25, "Hard Choices," and 26, "Historic Votes."

99   Edward Fitzpatrick, "Governor asking for more flexibility in picking state judges," *PJ*, 21 Feb. 2007: B-02. See 07-S 0892, "An Act Relating to Courts and Civil Procedure — Courts — Judicial Selection," by Sens. Blais, Breen, Algiere, and Gibbs, 22 Mar. 2007; 07-H 6324, (same title), by Rep. Watson, 26 Apr. 2007.

100   See Ch. 22, "Empire of Cronies."

101 PL 07-120, 27 Jun. 2007 and PL 07-220, 2 Jul. 2007.

102 See Ch. 7, "New Beginnings;" 8, "Hope for Ethics;" 11, "RIght Now!;" 12, "Struggles;" 14, "Triumphs;" and 23, "Revolving Door."

103 See Ch. 38, "Kingly Power." During a personal interview on 25 Mar. 2014, Harwood insisted that Chief Justice Joseph Weisberger had phoned his wife, Patricia Lynch Harwood, who had served as his law clerk. "She was so gifted that he brought her back three times as clerk, an all-time record."

104 Cynthia Needham, "Senate confirms District Court judge, traffic magistrates," *PJ*, 27 Jun. 2008: B-02.

105 Scott MacKay, "Senate panel OKs Jabour nomination," *PJ*, 23 Apr. 2003: B-01. In further irony, this was the second time Visconti served, despite the law's explicit requirement that no member should be reappointed.

106 Edward Fitzpatrick, "Court appointee is counsel to majority leader," *PJ*, 26 Jul. 2008: A-03.

107 Edward Fitzpatrick, "Legislative lawyer chosen as traffic judge," *PJ*, 12 Oct. 2007: B-01. See Guglietta's role in efforts to gut the "Celona Law" in 2005, as described in Ch. 50, "Unfinished Business."

108 Katherine Gregg, "Magistrate nominees need Senate approval," *PJ*, 8 Jun. 2012: A-05.

109 Katherine Gregg, "Senate unanimously approves Murphy aide for court post," *PJ*, 6 Mar. 2009: B-03.

110 Needham, "Senate confirms judge." Jun. 2008: B-02.

111 John Hill, "McBurney is selected for magistrate's post," *PJ*, 17 Mar. 2012: A-03.

112 Katherine Gregg, "Magistrate nominees need Senate approval," *PJ*, 8 Jun. 2012: A-05.

113 Michael P. McKinney, "Montalbano is tapped as magistrate," *PJ*, 5 Mar. 2011: A-01; Katherine Gregg, "Senate confirms Montalbano as magistrate," *PJ*, 4 Apr. 2011: A-05; Katie Mulvaney, "Montalbano gets Senate OK as judge," *PJ*, 31 May 2013: 6.

114 Fitzpatrick, "Legislative lawyer chosen."

115 Mike Stanton, "Paiva Weed signs on," *PJ*, 13 Nov. 2011: A-01.

116 Keven A. McKenna, "R.I. Assembly flouts constitution daily," *PJ*, 28 Mar. 2014: A-15; McKenna, "Justice Williams's patronage grab," *PJ*, 5 Jul. 2007: B-05; Steve Peoples, "House passes magistrates bill," *PJ*, 4 Jan. 2008: B-02.

117 01-S 0206, "An Act Relating to Courts — Judicial Selection," by Sens. Walsh, Gibbs, Graziano, Sosnowski, and Lenihan, 31 Jan. 2001; 02-S 2629, (same title), by Sens. Walsh, Paiva Weed, Parella, and Lenihan, 6 Feb, 2002.

118 Adam C. Holland, "Sen. Donna Walsh to run for reelection in redrawn district," *PJ*, 7 Jun. 2002: C-01. Walsh had remained loyal to Sen. Majority Leader Paul S. Kelly and received a district designed to defeat her. See Ch. 40, "Redistricting Revenge."

119 08-H 7129, "An Act Relating to Courts," by Reps. Walsh, Long, Lima, Ajello, and Menard, 15 Jan. 2008; 09-H 5433, "An Act Relating to Courts and Civil Procedure," by Reps. Walsh, Ajello, Driver, and Segal, 11 Feb. 2009. Walsh continued to introduce the legislation in each subsequent year, most recently 14-H 7071.

120 14-H 7864, "An Act Relating to Courts and Civil Procedure — Courts — Judicial Selection," by Reps. Walsh, Valencia, Marcello, Chippendale, and Ferri, 4 Mar. 2014.

121 See Ch. 40, "Redistricting Revenge," which describes problems with the 1982 and 2002 rounds of redistricting. With the rush of events in 1991–92, this narrative makes only fleeting references to gerrymanders in the 1992 maps.

122 Edward Fitzpatrick, "New Senate map settles lawsuit over redistricting," *PJ*, 22 May 2004: A-01. See *Metts* v. *Almond*, 217 F. Supp. 2d 252 (D.R.I. 2002), which was moving to trial in Mar. 2004 before the U.S. Court of Appeals, 1st Cir. as *Metts* v. *Murphy*, 02-2204, 30 Mar. 2004, when the settlement came.

123 02-4578, *Parella* v. *Irons,* 8 Oct. 2003.

124 *Parella* v. *Montalbano,* 899 A.2d 1226, 9 Jun. 2006. See Ch. 40, "Redistricting Revenge." See also http://www.elections.ri.gov/publications/Election_Publications/ Voter_Info/2012_RI_Senate_Districts.pdf.

125 2010 contributions listed by OpenSecrets. http://www.opensecrets. org/527s/527cmtedetail_contribs.php?cycle=2010&ein=050532524.

126 "How a Strategy of Targeting State Legislative Races in 2010 Led to A Republican U.S. House Majority in 2013," www.redistrictingmajorityproject.com, 4 Jan. 2013.

127 Sam Wang, "The Great Gerrymander of 2012," NYT, 2 Feb. 2013: SR-01; For a rebuttal, see John Sides and Eric McGhee, "Redistricting didn't win Republicans the House," *Washington Post,* 17 Feb. 2014. See also: Nate Silver, "As Swing Districts Dwindle, Can a Divided House Stand?" http://fivethirtyeight.blogs.nytimes.com/2012/12/27/as-swing-districts-dwindle-can-a-divided-house-stand/.

128 Common Cause, "What is Redistricting Reform?" http://www.commoncause.org/ states/california/ issues/voting-and-elections/redistricting/what-is-redistricting-reform.html http://www.commoncause.org/site/p.sp?b=3537383&c=dkLNK1MQIwG.

129 California Citizens Redistricting Commission, http://wedrawthelines.ca.gov/maps-final-drafts.html.

130 See Ch. 22, "Empire of Cronies." See Tracy Breton, Dean Starkman, and John Hill, "The Making of an Empire," *PJ,* 25 Jul. 1993, and follow-up stories.

131 Scott MacKay, "Providence Journal, We Knew Ye Well," RIPR, 6 Dec. 2013.

132 James McHenry's notes were included in *The Records of the Federal Convention of 1787,* ed. Max Farrand, Vol. 3, Appendix A: 85. http://www.bartleby.com/73/1593. html.

133 Nancy Gewirtz, dubbed "A Voice for the Voiceless" by the Fund for Community Progress, founded the Poverty Institute in 1999 as a nonpartisan research and policy group. She died in 2004, and the institute changed its name in 2012 to the Economic Progress Institute. See Richard C. Lewis, AP/*Boston Globe,* 16 Nov. 2004.

Index

About the Author

H. PHILIP WEST JR. served from 1988 to 2006 as executive director of Common Cause Rhode Island. *Secrets and Scandals* chronicles major government reforms during those years.

West often hosted delegations from the U.S. State Department's International Visitor Leadership Program. In 2000 he addressed a conference on government ethics laws in Tver, Russia. After retiring from Common Cause, he taught Ethics in Public Administration to graduate students at the University of Rhode Island.

Before Common Cause, West served as pastor of United Methodist churches and ran a settlement house on the Bowery in New York City. In 1985, he delivered medicines to victims of the South African-sponsored civil war in Mozambique and later assisted people displaced by Liberia's civil war.

He has been involved in developing affordable housing, day care centers, and other community services in New York, Connecticut, and Rhode Island.

West graduated, Phi Beta Kappa, from Hamilton College in Clinton, N.Y., received his masters degree from Union Theological Seminary in New York City, and published biblical research he completed at Cambridge University in England. In 2007, he received an honorary Doctor of Laws degree from Rhode Island College.

He is married to writer Anne Grant, and they have two grown sons.

"Corruption in City Hall destroyed any trust that Central Falls residents had left in local leadership. During transition to Mayor James Diossa, Phil West helped us write and pass a tough new ethics ordinance that addressed the injustice in pay-to-play politics, nepotism, and cronyism."

Stephanie Gonzalez, President Pro Tem, Central Falls
City Council, Chair of Charter Review Commission

Special thanks to

Leticia and John Carter
Warren and Joyce Galkin
Jocelin Hamblett
Alan Hassenfeld
Natalie Joslin
Henry and Peggy Boyd Sharpe
Daniel Siegel
John Hazen White Jr.